Theory of Macroeconomic Policy

Theory of Macroeconomic Policy

CHRISTOPHER TSOUKIS

OXFORD

UNIVERSITY PRESS

OXFORD

UNIVERSITY PRESS

Great Clarendon Street, Oxford, OX2 6DP,
United Kingdom

Oxford University Press is a department of the University of Oxford.
It furthers the University's objective of excellence in research, scholarship,
and education by publishing worldwide. Oxford is a registered trade mark of
Oxford University Press in the UK and in certain other countries

First Edition published in 2020

Impression: 1

Published in the United States of America by Oxford University Press
198 Madison Avenue, New York, NY 10016, United States of America

British Library Cataloguing in Publication Data

Data available

Library of Congress Control Number: 2020942140

ISBN 978–0–19–882537–1 (hbk.)
978–0–19–882538–8 (pbk.)

DOI: 10.1093/oso/9780198825371.001.0001

Printed and bound by
CPI Group (UK) Ltd, Croydon, CR0 4YY

To Chryssa and Vasiliki

Preface

This book reviews the theoretical foundations of macroeconomic, fiscal, and monetary policy. It is aimed at the crossroads between graduate and undergraduate levels. While the field of graduate macro texts is becoming increasingly populated, there is a large gap between that level and the already rich collection of available intermediate undergraduate texts. The overall motivation and objective of this textbook is to bridge this gap; to provide material that is more rigorous in method and detailed than the undergraduate texts, while being more intuitive than the graduate ones. It is also fair to say that it is wider in scope than most, covering topics and themes that are not usually found all in one place. This stems from the belief that, while we have a well-developed body of macroeconomic theory, reality keeps furnishing us with surprises; e.g. the financial crisis of 2007–9 and its aftermath has thrown open a wide array of fresh questions (while some old ones have also resurfaced). Thus, we cannot be narrowly focused or complacent; we must cast our eye far and wide and keep 'fishing for insights' from wherever we can derive them. This is the organizing principle of this book.

In terms of selection of topics, the aim is to strike a balance between the old and timeless, the new and exciting (with references right up to July 2019); the more accessible and the slightly advanced; between analytics, intuition, empirical evidence (extensively discussed), and narratives; theoretical and policy perspectives; the mainstream and the slightly more heterodox or 'exotic' (but no less interesting or relevant); the standard and the more exploratory; macroeconomics and elements of history, psychology, or economic sociology. A variety of topics not usually dealt with in macroeconomics textbooks is reviewed here; a brief list would start from inequality and include bounded rationality, 'six policy ineffectiveness propositions', the credit channel of monetary policy transmission, macro-prudential regulation, the financial crisis of 2007–9, austerity, a 'toolkit of fiscal multipliers', Goodwin cycles, Japan, technology and job polarization, secular stagnation, oil and the macroeconomy, the housing market, and much more. At the end of it is a rather panoramic view of macroeconomics, informed by my own ideas and preferences (and abilities and limitations) but eventually, hopefully, representative of the field. Once again, the book is an affirmation that there is a well-developed body of theory that is invaluable for an in-depth understanding of the macroeconomy and policy; equally, there is much scope for critical discussion and debate. Therefore, another objective of the book is to be a conduit between academic macroeconomics and public discourse and debates.

The chapters are largely self-contained (at the cost of a small amount of repetition) so that different courses, instructors, and students can select and 'zoom in' at different places without having to read everything cover-to-cover. UG macroeconomics courses can draw on the more discursive or diagrammatic expositions, while MA/MSc courses can draw on the more analytical ones. The extensive literature reviews and Guidance for Further Study sections at the end of each chapter are portals into the literature and should provide plenty of ideas for independent study at all levels, from UG Projects to M.Sc. dissertations to Ph.D. theses. As such, the book should appeal to a variety of instructors and students of macroeconomics at various levels, advanced undergraduate or graduate, as well as those in related fields such as political economy. Ultimately, of course, the reader is the arbiter as to whether the objectives have been met.

Finishing a book is a time of celebration (providing one can find some time to think about it). It is also a time to look back and remember that scholarly work is team work. I have immensely benefited over the years from the inspiration, encouragement, advice, collaboration, friendship, and good laughter of many people. With apologies in advance to those I surely forget, thanks and gratitude go to John Addison, George Aghiomirgianakis, Yunus Aksoy, Ali Al-Nowaihi, Ahmed Alyoushaa, Parantap Basu, Keshab Bhattarai, the late Tapan Biswas, Robin Bladen-Hovell, Spyros Bougheas, George Bratsiotis, Guglielmo Maria Caporale, Jagjit Chadha, Georgios Chortareas, Tony Conibear, William Dixon, Stelios Fountas, Max Gilman, Richard Green, Barry Harper, George Hadjimatheou, Junichi Itaya, Mike Jenkins, Menelaos Karanassos, Panayiotis Koutroumpis, Daniel Levy, Yorgos Makedonis, Gerry Makepeace, Chris Martin, Xavier Mateos-Planas, Charles Nolan, Joe Pearlman, Gianluigi Pelloni, George Perendia, Manolis Pikoulakis, Keith Pilbeam, Thomas Renstrom, Nicholas Sarantis, Avichai Snir, Soterios Soteri, Jim Steeley, Chris Stewart, Andromachi Tseloni, Simon Vicary, Guglielmo Volpe, Amos Witztum, and Athina Zervoyianni. Above all, my deepest gratitude goes to my life-long friends, Ioannis Bournakis, George Kapetanios, Claudio Piga, Nikitas Pittis, Anna Soci, and Frederic Tournemaine.

Many years ago, David Currie, John Driffill, Neil Rankin, and Christopher Gilbert provided invaluable help and guidance in my formative years; I am always indebted to them. Everyone at Oxford University Press, particularly Katie Bishop, Samantha Downes, and Jane Robson, have been very helpful and efficient; without their help and support this project would not have materialized. Finally, the book is dedicated with love to my wife Chryssa and daughter Vasiliki for their encouragement, stimulating criticism, and unwavering support.

Post-Script: The book was finished when, in early Spring 2020, COVID-19 struck; as a result, it does not even mention the (still unfolding) pandemic. An analysis of its economic effects will have to wait for another day.

Contents

Detailed Contents

List of Figures

List of Tables

1

From AD-AS to Advanced Macroeconomics

A Review

1.1 Building Blocks: The Production Function, Labour Demand, and Labour Supply

The purpose of this chapter is to review basic models, concepts, and tools that are the cornerstones of macroeconomic theory, and show how they may be linked to more advanced models and approaches. These will be familiar from a traditional undergraduate macroeconomics course, so this all serves as a reminder and further discussion. A traditional undergraduate course starts from building an IS-LM model, then proceeds to show how this leads to the Aggregate Demand part of the AD-AS model. Subsequently, the labour market is analysed, leading on to the Aggregate Supply part of the same model. Here, we follow essentially the same structure, but we begin with review of the basics of supply: the production function, labour demand and supply; then we work our way towards the AD-AS model and the Phillips Curve.[1]

1.1.1 The Production Function

Every macroeconomic model hypothesizes an aggregate production function, i.e. a simple way of relating inputs of an economy (mainly aggregate labour and aggregate capital) to aggregate output.[2] This captures the available technological possibilities: the same level of output can be produced by different combinations of capital and labour because of the availability of different techniques.[3] Though it appears intuitive, the very assumption that such a well-defined relation exists at all in the aggregate economy, and the form it takes, involves considerable leaps of faith (it is more readily obvious for individual firms). But let us leave controversial points to one side and assume that such a relation exists. (We review the role and form of technology and productivity growth in the next section.) So, let a relation between productivity, T (on which more below),

---

[1] Elementary notions, such as the distinction between nominal and real variables, stock versus flows, and endogenous versus exogenous variables, are taken as known here.

[2] There are two main factors of production, capital and labour. We ignore here land and energy. By 'capital' we mean physical capital (machinery, equipment, buildings, vehicles) throughout this book—as is standard in macroeconomics. Financial capital (equity and shares, bonds, deposits) are the form of ownership over physical capital and will not concern us (except in relation to particular topics). We are interested only in the resources that the economy has available for production, not in who owns them or how. 'Labour' refers to the total amount of hours of work put into production.

[3] The essentials of the production function as a concept have been analysed by Samuelson (1962).

Theory of Macroeconomic Policy. Christopher Tsoukis, Oxford University Press (2020). © Christopher Tsoukis.
DOI: 10.1093/oso/9780198825371.003.0001

aggregate physical capital, K, and labour (total hours worked), L, and aggregate output, Y, be captured by the equation:[4]

$$Y = F(K, L, T) \qquad (1.1)$$

This equation is called an aggregate production function if it has the following properties:

- $F(0, L) = F(K, 0) = 0$: Both factors of production are indispensable—if any of them is missing, there is no production at all.
- For either of the factors $(x = K, L) : F_x > 0, F_{xx} < 0$: Positive but diminishing marginal products—the marginal product of each one (the contribution of an additional employed unit, keeping the other factor constant) should be positive but diminishing. In other words, as we use more of one factor, with the other fixed, its marginal contribution remains positive but it declines. Figure 1.1 plots output as a function of labour, given a certain level of capital (with overbar). The Marginal Product of Labour (MPL) is the slope of this line. A symmetrical graph can be drawn for capital, given labour.

The following 'Inada conditions' show the 'diminishing marginal products' property at the limits—again, refer to Figure 1.1:

- $F_x(K, L)|_{x \to 0} = \infty$: The marginal product of any factor that is extremely scarce tends to infinity (i.e. the output line at the origin is near-vertical).
- $F_x(K, L)|_{x \to \infty} = 0$: The marginal product of any factor that is in abundant supply tends to zero (i.e. the output line asymptotically tends to become horizontal).
- $F_{KL} > 0$: Complementarity—the factors help one another, in the sense that if you increase capital, MPL increases (and vice versa).
- $F(ZK, ZL) = ZY$: Constant returns to scale—if you multiply each input by Z, you get Z times the output.[5] The reasoning behind this is a 'replication argument'. If you were

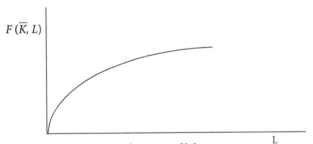

Figure 1.1. Output as a function of labour

[4] Throughout the book, upper-case Y, C, K, refer to GDP, consumption, and capital ALL in real terms (i.e. at constant prices). W, P, M are the wage, price level, and money in nominal terms. Lower-case r is the real interest rate and w(= W/P) the real wage. 'Local' changes in conventions will be clearly explained.
[5] A clear distinction needs to be made between the diminishing marginal products and constant returns—the former involves only one factor changing at a time, while the latter involves both (by the same proportion Z).

to build a replica of the economy in question (another economy exactly identical), you would get double the output. This argument is not entirely convincing, however. If you build two factories, you may economize on such services that do not depend on the size of Y (or not proportionately), such as management, administration, or marketing. If this is the case, you may economize on resources to be used more productively elsewhere, so that output may rise more than Z. Also, if Z is a fraction (Z per cent), then again the replication argument is not applicable. These caveats would suggest that there may be occasions in which increasing returns to scale appear. This issue is linked to the idea of 'scale effects' that is sometimes built into growth models, so we defer discussion until Chapter 9. Having said all this, the assumption of constant returns is received wisdom, and routinely built into models.

1.1.2 The CES Functional Form

A convenient form for a production function that embodies these properties is the 'Constant Elasticity of Substitution' (CES) function originally due to Arrow et al. (1961); this functional form seems now to be experiencing a 'comeback', see Klump and Preissler (2000), and Klump et al. (2012):[6]

$$Y = (\alpha K^b + (1 - \alpha)L^b)^{1/b}, \qquad 0 < \alpha < 1, \quad b < 1. \tag{1.2}$$

It is easy to see that the previous properties are maintained, especially diminishing returns and constant returns to scale. A key property of this function is a constant 'elasticity of substitution' between factors, defined as,

$$\varepsilon \equiv -\frac{d \log(K/L)}{d \log(r/w)} \tag{1.3}$$

This is the percentage change in the K-L ratio generated as a response to a 1 per cent change in the ratio of their remunerations, (real) interest rate (r) to real wage (w).[7] In other words, this elasticity measures the ability of firms to alter the mix of factors (by adopting more capital- or more labour-intensive methods) as the ratio of their costs to the firm changes. The negative sign turns it into a positive quantity (why?). This elasticity is related to parameter b by $\varepsilon = 1/(1 - b)$.

Among the CES class of production functions, special and convenient cases include:

- $Y = \min(AK, BL)$: The 'Leontieff' function, where no substitutability exists at all ($\varepsilon = 0, b \to -\infty$). In this case, the factors need to be employed at the given ratio $K/L = B/A$. Any unit, of any factor, that is surplus to that rule is redundant—employed and paid for without effect, so they will be eliminated. This rule may sound intuitive in

---

[6] Productivity, T, is suppressed in this sub-section. It will be reintroduced below.

[7] These factor payments are notional and do not coincide exactly with real-world variables. The real interest rate (r) encompasses all payments to capital such as dividends on shares, interest on bonds and deposits. In the case of a self-employed person with some equipment (e.g. a shop owner), part of their pay should be properly classed as wage and part as interest (payment to the capital they employ). See Chapter 11 for more details.

some cases (e.g. one driver, one lorry), but on second thought, it may be too restrictive (e.g. the size of the lorry may vary, so that K can vary, although L = 1).

- $Y = K^\alpha L^{1-\alpha}$: The 'Cobb-Douglas' function with a unitary elasticity of substitution ($\varepsilon = 1, b = 0$). This functional form underlies much theoretical and empirical work, therefore it is worth analysing its key properties in some detail. These properties are:
  - Simplicity and tractability while allowing for some generality;
  - Proportionality between marginal and average products:
    $MPL = \partial Y/\partial L = (1 - \alpha)K^\alpha L^{-\alpha} = (1 - \alpha)Y/L$ and likewise
    $MPK = \alpha Y/K$. This property is useful in various contexts, particular in growth theory.
  - If the factors are remunerated by their marginal products, i.e. w = MPL and r = MPK, then the factor shares in total GDP are constant: $wL/Y = MPLxL/Y = 1 - \alpha$ and $rK/Y = \alpha$. This yields a very simple theory of distribution of the final product across these factors.

But there are also serious criticisms to be levelled against Cobb-Douglas. For instance, there is growing empirical evidence that casts serious doubt on the unitary elasticity of substitution. Chirinko et al. (2004) with US data and Barnes et al. (2006) with UK data estimate the elasticity of substitution between capital and labour to be about 0.4. Naturally, this number masks considerable heterogeneity (e.g. substitutability between labour and buildings maybe different (less) than between labour and equipment), but such an estimate is no doubt a rejection of the Cobb-Douglas form. Chirinko's (2008) survey suggests that the bulk of estimates lie in the 0.4–0.6 range for the US; the studies reviewed by Klump et al. (2012) overwhelmingly suggest estimates less than unity both with US and international data; see also Antras (2004) and Leon-Ledesma et al. (2010). Notable exceptions are Duffy and Papageorgiou (2000) and Karabarbounis and Neiman (2014) who find an elasticity greater than unity. Overall, the balance of the evidence seems in favour of a less-than-unity hypothesis at this stage.

A second criticism against Cobb-Douglas is that the distribution of the final product between factors ('factor shares') is determined by a single parameter (α) that is technical in nature and difficult to measure. There is no role for 'institutions' like trade unions, the welfare state, nature of markets, technology, etc. It is also restrictive because there is evidence that the proportion between factors shares has been changing in recent decades; a distributional theory that depends on a fixed technical parameter will be uninformative about such developments. As we shall explore in Chapter 10, the CES gives us a much richer framework where the issue can be analysed; we defer a discussion of factor shares until then.

1.1.3 Augmenting, Biased, or Saving? A Digression on Technical Progress

Productivity, which in the context of (1.2) we have labelled T, is a multi-faceted concept. By definition, any rise of it means that a given stock of capital and labour will be translated into a higher level of output. There are three main sets of factors that productivity subsumes. First, technology and technical sophistication of the production process and all that it involves. Second, the quality of the labour force: the level of education, training, skills, and health of workers; in one word, 'human capital'. Lastly, the institutional organization of firms, society, government, and markets: the structure of businesses, the rules and regulations, structure and quality of government, the form of product and labour markets, even culture, are all included here. Of the three, technology has the greatest scope for rapid evolution, followed by human capital, and lastly by organization and institutions which change quite sluggishly. As a result, most of the time, the emphasis is on technology as the main factor underpinning productivity.

Technical progress has been a process closely connected with the modern epoch, in particular its phase since the industrial revolution at the end of the eighteenth century. Associated with the introduction and widespread use of the steam engine of that time, later with electricity and the internal combustion engine, some would say with information technology more recently, and countless other lesser advances around these break-throughs, technical progress has been at the heart of the inexorable rise of living standards in industrialized economies in the last two centuries or so. Moreover, there are arguments that in the last forty years, technical progress has been associated with labour market inequality and unemployment. Therefore, it features prominently in any aggregate pro-duction function like (1.1). But there is a question mark over its precise form; in this area, there is a bewildering array of concepts. We present a few here, drawing on chapter 3 of Burmeister and Dobell (1970) among others.

Technical progress is said to be 'factor augmenting' if a general production function $Y = F(K, L, T)$ can be written as $Y = F(K, TL)$ or $Y = F(TK, L)$ or $Y = F(TK, TL)$. In the first case, it is 'labour-augmenting'; in the second and third, 'capital' and 'equally augmenting', respectively. It is of course possible that the function $Y = F(K, L, T)$ that describes production in reality takes a functional form that does not admit any of the above cases; in that case, technology is not augmenting of any kind.

Another relevant concept is that of 'factor saving'; technical progress is said to be labour or capital saving if it decreases the labour or capital share, respectively. The notions of 'augmenting' and 'saving' technical progress are linked.

- Labour-augmenting progress is neutral (neither saving nor using more intensively any factor) if it is such that, all considered, the economy remains on a path that maintains a fixed capital-output (K/Y) ratio.
- Equally augmenting progress is neutral if it is such that, all considered, the economy remains on a path that maintains a fixed capital-labour (K/L) ratio.
- Capital-augmenting progress is neutral if it is such that, all considered, the economy remains on path that maintains a fixed labour-output (L/Y) ratio.[8]

These concepts may be used to shed light on various broad macroeconomic facts. First, over the past 150 years or so, we have had continuous 'capital deepening', i.e. a rise in the K/L ratio. In parallel, the real wage has been rising steadily, giving rise to quite impressive rises in living standards for the big majority of society in all western indus-trialized countries over the last 100 years. In contrast, a number of other ratios or

---

[8] These types of neutrality are called, respectively, Harrod-, Hicks-, and Solow-neutrality.

variables appear to be roughly constant: the real interest rate (r), the output-capital ratio (Y/K), and the relative factor shares. These stylized facts have become known as the 'Kaldor facts' related to very long-run growth and development and will be reviewed in Chapter 9 on growth. These stylized facts suggest that technical progress is labour-augmenting (hence the real wage rises following a rising marginal product of labour), and at the same time Harrod-neutral (implying constant factor shares along a constant Y/K path). Hence, labour-augmenting technical progress is the default hypothesis in growth theory and more general macroeconomic models. It is as yet unclear how the standard view of technical progress will be altered by the emerging evidence on shifting factors shares reviewed in Chapter 10 on inequality.

Recent debates have focused on another concept, that of biasedness. This refers to how the ratio of marginal products changes with technology (T), i.e. to the sign of:

$$d\left(\frac{\partial Y/\partial K}{\partial Y/\partial L}\right)/dT$$

- Technical progress is capital-biased if the above is positive;
- Technical progress is labour-biased if the above is negative;
- Technical progress is unbiased if the above is zero.

In other words, technical progress is capital-biased if it raises the marginal product of capital more than that of labour; analogously for labour-biasedness. Biasedness has been used more with reference to skilled and unskilled labour (sub-categories of labour that we have not introduced explicitly); recent technical progress is said to be 'skills-biased' and as such has widened the pay gap between skilled and unskilled labour. We review such developments in Chapter 4 on unemployment. Additionally, some more specialized notions of technical progress (directed, embodied, general-purpose, etc.) will be reviewed in Chapter 9 on growth and its 'stylized facts'.

1.1.4 Labour Demand

We now review labour demand. The typical firm -i- is assumed to be monopolistic in the goods market (its product is somewhat differentiated from that of its competitors), but competitive in the labour market (it needs exactly the same type of labour or skills as other firms).[9] This practically means that the firm has some price-setting power regarding its own price P_i, but it only takes the market nominal wage (W) as given without having any

---

[9] Traditionally, we distinguish the following types of market: Perfect competition (where a multitude of sellers sell a homogeneous good, so that they have no market power), monopoly (one firm and good without substitutes; a lot of market power), monopolistic competition (an intermediate situation whereby a number of firms sell somewhat differentiated goods, so that each has some market power, but cannot unilaterally affect the market), and oligopoly (a handful of big sellers). Perfect competition and monopoly may be thought of as the limiting situations either end of monopolistic competition; oligopoly, on the other hand, is set apart as it assumes interactions between the firms which require game theory to be analysed, so it is rarely invoked in macroeconomics. See section 3.2.1 for more.

influence on it. The market demand for its own product (in real terms) is given by $Y_i^D = Y(P_i)$, which is assumed to have constant elasticity, e:

$$e \equiv -\frac{dY(P_i)}{dP_i}\frac{P_i}{Y_i} \tag{1.4}$$

This elasticity tends to infinity in the case of a near-perfectly competitive firm, while it falls as the monopoly power of the firm increases. On the supply side, the firm produces by varying labour only (capital is assumed to be fixed). Otherwise, standard Inada conditions apply, in particular a diminishing marginal product to labour.

The firm chooses the labour input L in order to:

$$\max \quad \Pi_i = P_i Y_i - W L_i,$$

subject to (1.4)

Π_i: Nominal profit (of the representative firm i);
P_i: The price it sets for its good;
Y_i: Firm i's real output;
W: The nominal wage (given by the market, exogenous to the firm);
L_i: Firm i's (real) labour input.

First Order Conditions (FOC): Totally differentiating the above with respect to L_i (taking care to let both Y_i and P_i to vary with it), we obtain:

$$\frac{dP_i}{dY_i}\frac{dY_i}{dL_i}Y_i + \frac{dY_i}{dL_i}P_i - W = 0 \tag{1.5}$$

The second-order condition of $\frac{d^2\Pi_i}{(dL_i)^2} < 0$ guarantees a maximum (as opposed to a minimum), but this is rarely checked in macroeconomics. Rearranging, using the definition of elasticity (1.4):

$$\frac{dY_i}{dL_i}\left[1 + \frac{dP_i}{dY_i}\frac{Y_i}{P_i}\right] = \frac{dY_i}{dL_i}\left[1 - \frac{1}{e}\right] = \frac{W}{P_i}$$

Using the intuitive relation between elasticity of demand and the monopoly power of the firm (elasticity falls as monopoly power rises), we can define more precisely the latter (μ) as:

$$1 + \mu \equiv \frac{e-1}{e} \geq 1$$

Perfect competition is the limiting case of $\mu = 0$, $e \to \infty$. Using this notion, (1.5) can be rewritten as:

$$MPL = \frac{W}{P_i}(1 + \mu) \tag{1.6}$$

The marginal product of labour equals the real wage adjusted (upwards) by a quantity $\mu \geq 0$: This increases with the degree of monopoly power in the product market from a benchmark value of $\mu = 0$ for a perfectly competitive firm. Practically speaking, the higher the monopoly power, given the real wage the firm faces, the higher is the marginal product of labour and (because of diminishing marginal product) the lower the demand for labour. In other words, for a given real wage, a firm with greater monopoly power demands less labour. In the traditional labour demand-supply diagram, shown in Figure 1.2, this means that that the labour demand curve shifts left as monopoly power increases.

Another informative way of expressing (1.6) is as:

$$P_i/P = (1 + \mu)\frac{W/P}{MPL} \tag{1.6'}$$

In this formulation, the real price should be set as a markup over real marginal cost (MC), the latter being $MC = (W/P)/MPL$ (roughly, the wage divided by how many units of the good are produced per unit of time). This formula would also apply in a more general setup where the firm uses both labour and capital (and not only labour as here).

In the two-input case, instead of $(W/P)/MPL$, we get an MC that combines marginal products and factor costs in an optimal manner. E.g. in the case of the CES production function (1.2), the MC is given by (details are left as an exercise for the reader):

$$P_i/P = (1 + \mu)MC = (1 + \mu)\left(\frac{r}{\alpha}\right)^{\alpha}\left(\frac{W/P}{1 - \alpha}\right)^{1-\alpha}$$

This is a very intuitive formula. The parameter α essentially tells us how 'heavily' production depends on capital. The marginal cost is essentially a weighted average of the two factor prices, the real interest rate r and the real wage, W/P. (The average is a geometric, not arithmetic one.) Thus, the cost of capital services, r, should take a weight equal to α; with a similar reasoning, the weight of $w(= W/P)$ should be $1 - \alpha$.

Going back to (1.6'), we can take the average over all individual prices, which is the price level itself: $E(P_i) = P$. Assuming MPL to be common across firms, taking averages of both sides, we then have:

$$MPL = (1 + \mu)(W/P) \tag{1.6''}$$

The marginal product of labour is a multiple of the real wage, with equality only under perfect competition. (1.6'') is essentially the labour demand curve (L^D) in an implicit form. To see that, let us recall that MPL depends on L negatively (diminishing MPL) and on K positively (because of the complementarity between the factors). It also rises with an exogenous rise in productivity (due say to technical progress, or better organization, etc.),

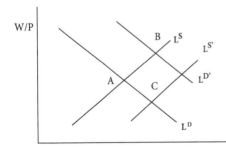

Figure 1.2. The labour market

given the level of employment. From these, we may derive the following properties ('comparative statics') of the labour demand curve (L^D in Figure 1.2):

- Demand for employment falls ($dL < 0$) with the real wage W/P (movement up along the L^D curve)—practically, the labour demand curve is downward-sloping.
- Employment demand increases ($dL > 0$) with the capital stock K (shift up of the L^D curve itself).
- Employment demand falls ($dL < 0$) with the degree of market power as exemplified by the markup μ (shift down of the L^D curve).

1.1.5 Labour Supply

Labour supply is built up from the first principles underlying the individual's utility maximization. The representative individual's utility is assumed to depend on 'the' consumption good (C) and leisure (l). Both these are individual-specific but there is no distinction here between the 'representative individual' and society as a whole, so superscripts are not needed:

$$U(C, l) \tag{1.7a}$$

The utility function in (1.7a) is assumed to have similar properties as the production function; for each good separately, utility depends on the quantity but at a diminishing marginal rate:

$$U_C(C, l) > 0, \quad U_{CC}(C, l) < 0, \quad U_l(C, l) > 0, \quad U_{ll}(C, l) < 0$$

(where subscripts indicate first and second derivatives). This is because we are never satiated by consumption, whether it is of food, clothing, or gadgets, but the utility we obtain from each additional unit falls with the consumption we already enjoy. Likewise with leisure, it gives us utility, because it also means that we enjoy family, interests, or hobbies, but at a decreasing rate. The sign of the cross-derivative, $U_{Cl}(C,l)$, determining whether consumption and leisure are complements or substitutes, is a more moot question.

There is an equivalent way of presenting the above utility function. If our total time endowment is normalized to 1 (say, one day, or one year), then if L is labour, $l = 1 - L$ (i.e., both labour and leisure are percentages of our total time). We can then re-express utility as:

$$U(C, L) \tag{1.7a'}$$

With the partial derivatives with respect to consumption as above and $U_L(C, L) < 0$ and $U_{LL}(C, L) < 0$. In this equivalent formulation, which is followed often, the interpretation is that labour gives us disutility at an increasing rate, as work is hard and progressively more exhausting.

The representative individual faces the constraint:

$$PC = WL \tag{1.7b}$$

C: Real consumption, assumed to be of a single homogeneous good;
L: Labour;

P: The price level;

W: The nominal wage.

The constraint (1.7b) ('consume as much as you earn') assumes that labour income is the only source of revenue; there are no assets (those will be introduced in the analysis of Chapter 5).

We can equivalently postulate that the individual maximizes either (1.7a) or (1.7a') subject to the constraint (1.7b), by choosing the level of either leisure or labour supply, as appropriate. Following the first case, by rearranging (1.7b) and using it to substitute C out of (1.7a), we can express utility as: $U((1 - l)W/P, l)$. The First Order Condition of this with respect to l is:

$$-\frac{W}{P}U_C + U_l = 0 \qquad (1.8)$$

(1.8) presents a (marginal) cost-benefit analysis of the work-leisure dilemma. If you work one hour less, you lose the real wage times the marginal utility valuation of that wage, the marginal utility of consumption; but you also get more leisure (the second term). In other words, (1.8) presents the balance between the marginal opportunity cost of leisure (the foregone wage times the marginal utility of consumption) and the marginal benefit of leisure, both in utility terms. This cost and benefit should be equated at the margin, otherwise there is an opportunity for the individual to increase his/her total utility by shifting hours between the two uses appropriately.

Rearranging (1.8), we can state:

$$\frac{U_l}{U_C} = \frac{W}{P} \qquad (1.8')$$

The same relation can now be interpreted slightly more formally: The marginal rate of substitution between the consumption and leisure (ratio of marginal utilities) equals the marginal rate of transformation between the two—the real wage. In practice, the two ratios in (1.8') will often not equalize; the discrepancy between them is called the 'labour wedge'; see the 'Guidance for Further Study' section for more information. Finally, if we are using (1.7a'), the equivalent condition takes the form:

$$-\frac{U_L}{U_C} = \frac{W}{P} \qquad (1.8'')$$

A rise in the real wage elicits the standard two effects on labour supply. As it represents the opportunity cost (effectively: price) of leisure, a substitution effect leads the individual to 'consume' less leisure (offer more work) and turn more towards the consumption good. On the other hand, an income effect allows the individual to consume both of each. The net effect is in principle uncertain, but usually presumed to imply that the substitution effect dominates: with a higher real wage, the individual offers more hours of work. The elasticity of labour supply to the real wage is very relevant for theory and policy in various contexts, including business cycles, taxation, and the effect of government spending on economic activity (the 'fiscal multiplier' considered in Chapter 8). We review this elasticity in the next sub-section in some detail.

1.1.6 The Elasticity of Labour Supply in the Long and Short Runs: Discussion

There is a problem with the presumption that a rise in the real wage elicits more work. In a typical industrialized economy, the real wage has increased manifold over the last 100 years (or over long periods generally), yet overall labour supply has been unaffected. (In fact, it has decreased—but let us take a zero change as an approximation.) As a result, over the long run, the elasticity of labour supply to the real wage appears to be quite low, perhaps indistinguishable from zero. This should be a property embedded into any long-run model such as those used to study growth (see Chapter 9). In contrast, in the short run, a worker may inter-temporally shift hours around (e.g. one can work harder during a period of peak demand such as Christmas when wages may be higher and take leisure or concentrate on studies later on), so that the response of labour supply to the real wage may be higher. We shall see in Chapter 6 on business cycles that this elasticity of labour supply with respect to the (expected) real wage is a point of contention between theories. Next, we consider the restrictions on the utility function that guarantee the distinction between short- and long-run elasticities.

There is no agreement on specifics but a sensible functional form of (1.7a') that obeys the restrictions discussed above is the one proposed by Kimball and Shapiro (2008—see also King et al., 1988):

$$U(C,L) \equiv \frac{\left(C \exp\left\{-\frac{L^{1+\eta}}{1+\eta}\right\}\right)^{1-b}}{1-b}, \quad \text{when } b \neq 1, \quad \eta > 0 \tag{1.9}$$

$$U(C,L) \equiv \log C - \frac{L^{1+\eta}}{1+\eta}, \quad \text{when } b = 1. \quad \eta > 0 \tag{1.9'}$$

We shall see in the introduction to dynamic macroeconomics in Chapter 5 that parameter b has an important economic interpretation (being the 'intertemporal elasticity of substitution'). It can easily be checked that $U_L(C, L) < 0$ and $U_{LL}(C, L) < 0$. In actual analytical work, simpler utility functions are used, with similar properties as those of (1.9).

With the above functional form, we have:

$$-\frac{U_L}{U_C} = CL^{\eta} = W/P, \quad \text{for all b.}$$

In the long run, C and W/P increase equiproportionately, and L stays constant. This guarantees a zero long-run elasticity of labour supply to the real wage, which is consistent with the historical experience discussed above. In the short run, with a constant level of consumption (i.e. unaffected by the real wage), we have the elasticity:

$$\frac{\partial L}{\partial (W/P)} \frac{W/P}{L} = \frac{1}{\eta}$$

$1/\eta$ equals the so-called 'Frisch elasticity' of labour supply: the elasticity given by the substitution effect only, when the income effect is assumed away. Practically, this represents the temporary sensitivity of labour supply to a temporary increase in the real wage, while keeping lifetime resources constant. The detailed study by Kimball and Shapiro (2008), which is quite informative about all the related concepts, estimates the Frisch elasticity to be mostly in the range 0 to 1, sometimes quite close to 0 (see their tables 7, 10, and 11); their partial review of the literature suggests the same.

A further issue concerns the distinction between the so-called 'internal' and 'external' margins. So far, we have assumed that all variations in employment come from the behaviour of the typical individual, as they rationally vary their labour supply in response to changes in the real wage. We have implicitly assumed that all workers provide the same amount of work and that none is entirely unemployed. This assumption is obviously at odds with everyday reality, where some individuals are not able to find any employment at all, even though they are willing to work at the going wage (involuntary unemployment), and some even choose not to offer any work. In other words, variations in the total amount of hours of work do not arise only as a result of an individual changing their equilibrium hours but also (and significantly more) by individuals alternating between employment and unemployment. According to some estimates, between recessions and booms, about two-thirds of total employment (total labour hours supplied) is done at the 'extensive margin' of workers getting in and out of unemployment, and only one-third at the 'intensive margin' of the workers already employed varying their hours (King and Rebelo, 1999; Gordon, 2010). With Swedish data, Christiano et al. (2010) find this proportion to be four-fifths and one-fifth, respectively. Against that, see Ohanian and Raffo (2012), who find that a large fraction of labour adjustment is along the 'intensive margin'. In a micro-to-macro study, Fiorito and Zanella (2012) estimate the intensive margin elasticity to be in the range 0.3–0.4, and the extensive margin elasticity in the range 0.8–1.4. These findings suggest a macro labour supply elasticity that ranges from 1.1 to 1.7. A good summary of the state of play is in Rogerson and Keane (2012). While the consensus view among labour economists seems to be that labour supply elasticities are small, macroeconomic models generally assume an elasticity that is quite large, often in the range of 1 to 2. A large part of the explanation seems to lie in the external margin that is more obvious at the macro level and which is missing in the micro estimates made by labour economists (see also Chetty et al., 2011). In all, the recent findings of Erosa et al. (2016) seem to summarize well the available evidence; they find that 'the aggregate labour supply elasticity to a transitory wage shock is 1.75, with the extensive margin accounting for 62% of the response. Furthermore, . . . the aggregate labour supply elasticity to a permanent-compensated wage change [NB: due to the substitution effect only] is 0.44.'

This leads us to examine briefly the evolution of labour supply. In a careful study, Blundell et al. (2013; see also 2011) document the changes in labour supply along the two margins and along various other dimensions (men-women, young-old, etc.) in three countries, US, UK, and France, over the forty-year period 1968–2008. The patterns are too complicated to summarize fully in a paragraph (and to be explained by just one model), but a couple of features stand out: the key observation is that total hours over this period increased in the US, remained largely constant in the UK, and strongly declined in France; thus, this pattern invites the question why the US works harder than Europe (Prescott, 2004). Prime-aged men's employment rate has declined in all three countries, in Britain and France more. But the female employment rate has almost doubled over the period; and the women's mean hours of work *conditional on them being employed* (i.e. along their intensive margin) have also increased. Youth (16–19 years) non-employment is strikingly higher in France than in the other two countries.

We may summarize by saying that there is an important distinction to be made between individual labour supply and total employment (or total labour hours). In Chapter 4 on unemployment, we shall see that recent literature has cast aside the traditional labour supply–labour demand framework (that of Figure 1.2) and has instead relied on a 'wage-setting' and 'price-setting' framework. One big reason is that the wage/price-setting framework can incorporate the extensive as well as the intensive margin, whereas the labour demand/supply framework is based only on the latter. For the rest of this chapter, though, we continue with labour demand/supply; we indicate by L the hours worked per person (where all individuals in the economy work).

1.1.7 The Labour Demand-and-Supply Framework

The workings of the labour market as a whole are shown in Figure 1.2, which has the real wage (W/P) and employment (L) on the axes. It brings together the labour demand (L^D) implicit in (1.6"), and the labour supply (L^S) underlying the analysis of the previous sub-section. The presumption behind the labour supply is that its response to a change in the real wage is positive ($\partial L^S / \partial(W/P) > 0$); the slope of L^S can vary to accommodate any views one might hold about the elasticity, in whatever horizon (e.g. if one thinks that the elasticity is zero in the long run, L^S should be vertical over that horizon). The endogenous variables are employment (hours per person—L) and the real wage (W/P).

Shifts in L^D arise for the reasons explained in sub-section 1.1.4. The following effects shift labour demand out to $L^{D'}$:

- a rise in productivity;
- a rise in the installed capital stock;
- a decrease in market power of firms or of the markup (a move towards more competition in the goods market);
- a decrease in oil prices and raw materials (though not explicitly modelled, this works in the same way as a markup—it changes prices relative to the wage).[10]

The result of an outward shift of L^D for whatever reason, moves the equilibrium from A to B and induces a rise in both employment and the real wage.

One issue meriting more discussion is the effect of a rise in capital (or productivity) on employment. As either increases, so does labour demand, essentially because of the greater marginal product of labour. This contrasts sometimes with casual observation, which suggests that when firms install more capital, or when there is productivity growth due to technical progress, firms are in a position to produce their usual amount with less labour and therefore their employment falls. This however may be more likely at an individual firm level than at the aggregate level. The reason is that an individual firm takes the amount of sales it is likely to be able to make as given, whereas for the aggregate economy there is

---

[10] The effect of oil price rises on employment, growth, and the wider macroeconomy is quite possibly very important, but also hotly debated. An overview of the debate is given in Chapter 6 on Business Cycles.

no compelling reason why the aggregate demand for goods and sales should not itself expand when firms increase their size, the profits they generate, etc. At the end of the day, therefore, how hours worked responds to an improvement in productivity and/or technology is an empirical matter. The framework unambiguously predicts a rise of hours worked (and of the real wage) when capital increases or productivity/technology improves. The nature of technological change has already been briefly discussed; its effects on structural unemployment will be discussed in Chapter 4; while its effects on the cyclical employment variations will be discussed in Chapter 6 on business cycles.

Shifts in L^S arise from the general willingness to work, captured by the marginal rate of substitution: $-U_L/U_C$. This may be affected by various considerations in the background such as unemployment benefits, family support, or the costs of childcare (in principle, all these factors reduce the willingness to work and shift L^S left). But these effects are more fruitfully analysed in the alternative 'wage/price-setting' framework, to be considered in Chapter 4 on unemployment, so we defer these discussions until then. For our purposes here, an alternative origin of shifts in L^S is more important, namely discrepancies between the actual and the expected price level (P and P^e, respectively). It has been traditionally argued that workers may not know exactly the price level at the moment they decide their optimal amount of work, or when their wage is decided. This is because the price level is relevant for the period (e.g. year) ahead, and not clearly known; it is also estimated with a delay by statistical offices and the initial estimates are frequently revised thereafter. This contrasts with the experience of firms which set the prices, and therefore may have a clearer idea of what the price level actually is. Now, the way to introduce these considerations is to write the supply schedule as $L = L^S(W/P^e) = L^S((W/P)(P/P^e))$; the former is the expected real wage that actually influences workers' decisions, whereas the latter trivially decomposes that into the real wage times the actual-expected ratio. We therefore need to consider the (exogenously given) actual-to-expected price ratio when we position L^S on the graph—for any given W/P, an increase in P/P^e (individuals are more mistaken) results in an increase in labour supply, as individuals in effect think that the real wage is higher than it actually is—L^S shifts out to $L^{S'}$. The result (from A to C) is an increase in employment and a fall in the equilibrium real wage. Such effects will be important in the analyses of aggregate supply.

Before we leave this sub-section, one note about the nature of unemployment in this framework: if we assume that the total amount of hours available to each individual (net of sleep) is 1, then the distance between equilibrium employment and 1 represents unemployment. Unemployment in this framework is entirely voluntary, as it is based on the (voluntary) choices of labour supply underlying the L^S curve. In other words, unemployment here results from the interplay between the responses of the individual and the various changes in their environment. For example, employment at A may be too low and the individual may be better off at B or even at C (in comparison to A), but given the condition of the economy (productivity, installed capital) as shown by L^D, A is the individual's preferred point as dictated by their L^S curve. Hence, at A, individuals choose (says the model) to work fewer hours (higher unemployment) as the real wage is low enough not to make more work worthwhile. The wage/price framework reviewed in Chapter 4 on unemployment will be more compatible with the existence of involuntary unemployment.

1.1.8 The 'Natural' or 'Structural' Rate of Unemployment, Cyclical Unemployment, the Output Gap, and Okun's Law

The resulting unemployment in Figure 1.2 (whether voluntary or involuntary) can be broken down conceptually into cyclical and more permanent components. We can decompose (the per cent rate of) unemployment into two parts, as follows,

$$u_t = u_t^N + u_t^C \tag{1.10}$$

where superscripts N and C stand for 'natural' and 'cyclical' (rates of) unemployment. In a long-winded but remarkably clear sentence, Friedman (1968) gave this definition of the 'natural rate of unemployment':

> The 'natural rate of unemployment,' in other words, is the level that would be ground out by the Walrasian system of general equilibrium equations, provided there is imbedded in them the actual structural characteristics of the labor and commodity markets, including market imperfections. stochastic variability in demands and supplies, the cost of gathering information about job vacancies and labor availabilities, the costs of mobility, and so on.
>
> (Friedman, 1968, p. 8)

Thus, 'natural' unemployment is a by-word for the rather permanent part of unemployment due to the various structural characteristics of the economy—understanding the determinants of this part of unemployment will be the focus of Chapter 4 on unemployment. In analytical terms, and with reference to Figure 1.2, we say that the 'natural rate' unemployment is $u = 1 - L^n$, where L^n is the employment level resulting from an L^S curve which assumes $P^e = P$, i.e. that level of expectations that holds in the long run. Many analysts, including this author, would tend to think that there is nothing 'natural' in a rate of unemployment, which is a product of human societies. Therefore, we tend to favour the term 'structural' instead, but this term does not seem to have caught on in the literature; so, we shall use the two interchangeably in this book.

The other part of unemployment is 'cyclical' unemployment, due to the temporary fluctuations in economic activity, schematically captured by fluctuations of P/P^e around the average value of 1. This part of unemployment averages zero over the long term. It is closely linked to fluctuations in economic activity itself, therefore it will be dealt with in Chapter 6 on business cycles. While conceptually clear, though, the 'structural' vs. 'cyclical' distinction of unemployment is not so clear-cut in practice. What complicates things is that the natural rate also changes over time, as the structural characteristics mentioned in Friedman's definition also change over time (one of them, not emphasized by Friedman but very relevant today, is the nature of new technology). Thus, disentangling u_t into its two components is, in statistical practice, a rather tricky problem. These issues will be considered further in Chapter 6.

Corresponding to the 'natural rate of unemployment' we have a definition for the 'natural level of output'. Thus, the 'natural' level of output is what an economy produces under normal conditions dictated by its structural characteristics. If, however, the macro-economy happens to work in a more lax manner, there is excess capacity or slackness—we say that we have an 'output gap', defined as percentage excess capacity. In logs, we may write it as

$$ygap_t \equiv \hat{y}_t - y_t, \qquad (1.11)$$

where $\hat{y}_t$ is log-natural output and y_t is log-actual output. If the economy is in a boom and working more intensively than normal, then the output gap (defined in the same way) is negative. Thus, the output gap includes the cyclical variations of output. How is the 'natural' output statistically disentangled from actual output? Again, wait till Chapter 6!

As may have been surmised, cyclical unemployment and the output gap are closely linked. This relationship is termed 'Okun's law' (Okun, 1965): as more production requires more hours of the labour input, a smaller (larger) output gap will be accompanied by a smaller (larger) rate of cyclical unemployment; the proportion being perhaps two-to-one. But this figure is only suggestive, and is bound to change as the structure of the economy, including technology, changes. Okun's (1965) original estimates with US data suggested that for each three points of extra real GDP growth there would be a 1 per cent reduction in the unemployment rate. Today, 'Okun's law' is considered as an intuitive relation, but lacking theoretical foundations (Blinder, 1997) and with only weak empirical grounding. Some modern estimates suggest that that output grows by about 2 per cent for each percentage point drop in unemployment (Freeman, 2001); but others are more sceptical, pointing towards lack of robustness (i.e. sensitivity of the estimates to sample period, selection of countries, estimation methods, etc., see Lee, 2000), structural breaks over time (Lee, 2000; Gordon, 2010), and asymmetry in the relationship between downturns and upturns (Lee, 2000; Cuaresma, 2003). It is also suggested that the true change in unemployment is much lower than usually thought, and that much of the change in output is due to changes in labour hours per employee and capacity utilization (Prachowny, 1993; see also Gordon, 2010).

The concepts of natural (rate of) unemployment and natural (level of) output, and of the output gap, play a prominent role in macroeconomics. In particular, it is thought that inflation is linked to cyclical unemployment and the output gap. This will be evident in the discussion of the Phillips Curve in this chapter, and in the New-Keynesian model of inflation and the Phillips Curve reviewed in Chapter 3.

1.2 Aggregate Demand and Aggregate Supply (AD-AS)

Armed with more detailed knowledge of the production function and labour markets, we can now review briefly the structure of the traditional AD-AS model.

1.2.1 From the Labour Market to Aggregate Supply

The equilibrium level of employment (L^*) determined in the labour market (Figure 1.2) depends on a number of exogenous factors; in particular, the ratio of actual-to-expected price level. We have that $L = L(P/P^e)$, with the derivative of this function being positive, i.e. that a rise of actual prices relative to what is expected or estimated increases the labour supply and unemployment, as analysed. The aggregate production function (1.1) then translates this equilibrium employment to output. We thus obtain the Aggregate Supply function (AS):

$$Y^S = F(K, L(P/P^e)) \equiv Y^S(P/P^e), \text{ with } dY^S/d(P/P^e) > 0 \text{ and } Y^S(1) = \bar{Y} \qquad (1.12)$$

Given expectations P^e, this relation is depicted as the upward-sloping AS in Figure 1.3 which has P and Y on its axes—it is marked short-run AS. A benchmark point of particular significance is the one (say, A) which arises when actual and expected prices are equal ($P = P^e$)—the corresponding level of output is $\bar{Y}$ and has a particular significance to be discussed below. The Y^S curve shifts right with all the factors that shift the L^D and L^S curves right, as analysed in previous sub-sections. Among those, productivity and installed capital (K) work in a dual way: they help increase both equilibrium unemployment (refer to Figure 1.2), and also raise the output produced by each hour of work. Conversely, any adverse supply-side development (a left shift in $Y^S(P/P^e)$) results in higher prices and lower output. An additional factor is price expectations, P^e: because a rise in those affects labour supply adversely (workers think that the real wage has declined), a rise in P^e (given P) shifts $Y^S(P)$ to the *left*. This is a key point in much of what follows and indeed in much of modern macroeconomics.

1.2.2 Aggregate Demand

Aggregate Demand is summarized by the following system of equations:

$$Y^D = C + I + G \qquad (1.13)$$

From National Income Accounting, planned demand (Y^D) is made up of three components, namely consumption, investment, and government spending (a closed economy is assumed).

$$C = C_0 + c(Y - T) \qquad (1.14)$$

This simple consumption function assumes an 'autonomous' consumption that does not depend on current income ($C_0 > 0$) and a constant marginal propensity to consume ($0 < c < 1$) out of disposable income ($Y - T$). T is taxes, assumed lump-sum (fixed) here.

$$I = I(r),$$
$$I' < 0 \qquad (1.15)$$

Investment (I) is a negative function of the interest rate (r) as is standard; we make no distinction between nominal and real rate here. Combining, we have the IS curve:

$$Y^D = \frac{C_0 - cT + I(r) + G}{1 - c} \qquad (1.16)$$

The effect of the interest rate on aggregate demand has been the subject of some contention. The AD equation (1.16) tells us that it arises because of the negative effect of the interest rate on investment, which has been the focus of the traditional 'transmission mechanism' of monetary policy. However, this appears to be rather weak (Chirinko, 1993). More sizeable may be the wealth effects of interest rates on consumption, either from stock markets or housing (Poterba, 2000; Case et al., 2005). We discuss all these issues in more detail in Chapter 11.

Furthermore, the interest rate is an inverse function of the real monetary stance, determined by the real money supply (M/P). (Think of the analysis underlying the LM curve with monetary authority exogenously setting money.)

$$r = r(Y; M/P)$$
$$\partial r/\partial Y > 0$$
$$\partial r/\partial(M/P) < 0 \tag{1.17}$$

(1.17) and the underlying LM curve is standard fare in textbook macroeconomics. It is built on the key assumption that the nominal money supply (M) is exogenous and is the monetary policy instrument. This does not quite reflect how monetary policy is done these days, as will be explored in Chapter 7. As the standard practice in most monetary authorities internationally is to set the (policy) interest rate directly, rather than indirectly via the money supply, an alternative to equation (17) is closer to reality:

$$r = r(Y^{cyclical}; P)$$
$$\partial r/\partial Y^{cyclical} > 0$$
$$\partial r/\partial(P) > 0 \tag{1.17'}$$

In (1.17), the interest is directly set by the monetary policy-maker and rate responds positively to both output and the price level; in these ways, it is not different than the textbook relation (1.17). The differences are that the money supply (M) does not appear as it endogenously follows after the interest rate is set (the monetary authority must provide just about enough monetary base as the market demands, otherwise the set interest A is not supported); and the cyclical output ($Y^{cyclical}$) is the relevant one, not just actual output. A relation such as (1.17') is called a 'Taylor rule' and will be analysed further in Chapter 7. But, as will be argued there, as a first approach we may continue to use the traditional LM curve (1.17), and we do so in this chapter.[11]

Given the exogenous nominal money supply, the last three equations boil down to the Aggregate Demand (AD) equation:

$$Y = \frac{C_0 - cT + G + I(r(Y; M/P))}{1 - c} \equiv Y^{AD}(G, T; M/P) \tag{1.18}$$

This is depicted as the downward-sloping AD curve in Figure 1.3 in (P,Y) space. As is well known from undergraduate macro, this is downward-sloping. (Can you explain why?). Also, this shifts right with:

- Expansionary fiscal policy (a rise in government spending, a *decrease* in taxes);
- Expansionary monetary policy (a rise in the money supply);

[11] Romer (2000) and Woodford (2010) suggest replacing the traditional LM curve by the Taylor rule (1.17'). We adopt this approach together with the IS curve (1.16) and a version of the Phillips Curve such as (1.20') below to form the 'three-equation New Keynesian model' in Chapter 3.

- Non-policy exogenous changes such as an improvement in consumer sentiment (consumers feel more optimistic, all else equal, and spend more—an effect captured by 'autonomous consumption', C_0);
- A rise in world trade and net exports (which are not modelled here but they can be easily incorporated).

From Figure 1.3, the effects of these changes are obvious; they result in higher equilibrium output and/or prices, the exact mix depending on the slope of the AS curve.

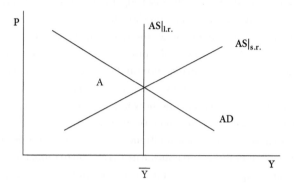

Figure 1.3. The Aggregate Demand—Aggregate Supply system

As mentioned, the upward-sloping AS is labelled short-run, as it accommodates any P/P^e ratio. Such actual-expected deviations exist only in the short run, however; surely, in the long run agents will learn to 'get it right' ($P/P^e = 1$) (according to the Rational Expectations Hypothesis reviewed in the next chapter, they should get it right much sooner than the long run). When $P/P^e = 1$, according to (1.12), output supply (Y^S) becomes a constant, corresponding to the 'natural' or 'structural' level of output (indicated $\bar{Y}$). In particular, it is independent of the price level, hence $AS|_{l.r.}$ is shown as a vertical line.

1.2.3 Three 'Million-Dollar' Questions in Macroeconomics

Time now to consider where this is leading; what it is all about. We do so by asking three fundamental questions and inspecting the range of possible answers.

Question 1: Effects of changes in aggregate demand
If we trivially write $NAD = Y \times P$, nominal aggregate demand (NAD) is decomposed as the product of real output (quantities of new goods and services) times the price level. Then the question arises: if NAD changes, how much of the change will manifest itself into a change in quantities and how much into a change in prices? The change in NAD may come about by some policy measure, or by exogenous developments like a change in consumer sentiment or world incomes; we are interested about policy the most. This question is one of the overarching and most important ones in macroeconomics; indeed, it runs through its entire body. To gain a bit more insight, time-differentiating the above and dividing by itself, we obtain:

$$dNAD/NAD = dY/Y + dP/P$$

The growth rate of NAD is the sum of growth rates of real output and prices—the latter is known as the inflation rate. So, the question can be rephrased: how much of the growth rate of NAD will feed into growth of quantity of output, and how much into inflation?

The framework above can give us a way of thinking. If the change in NAD is engineered by fiscal policy (or by an exogenous rise in net exports due e.g. to a change in the world economy; or a change in 'consumer sentiment' captured by C_0), the IS records these exogenous changes by shifting. A lot then depends on the slope of the LM curve, essentially on how interest rates respond to the initial rise in output demand. As the interest rate is likely to rise, this will then have a 'crowding out' effect, partially offsetting the rise in NAD. (As an exercise, draw an IS-LM graph and show these effects. Can you show the 'crowding out' effect on this graph?) Eventually, NAD will record a net change; the question is how much this will feed into a change in quantities and how much into prices. This information will be provided by the AD-AS diagram (Figure 1.3). A lot depends on the slope of AS, which in turn depends on the actual-expected price ratio and how quickly this changes, but also more generally on the nature of supply (to what extent and how fast employment can change to accommodate the rise in demand), the particular state of the economy (above or below the 'normal' level $\bar{Y}$), etc. The analyses on the fiscal multiplier of Chapter 8 consider in detail many of these issues. Similar considerations and issues arise in relation to monetary policy. Eventually, all of these issues are empirical matters and, because empirical evidence does not speak with one voice, are subject to the viewpoints and ideologies of various schools of thought.

Question 2: What are the main lines of thinking by the various schools of thought?

There is a range of views that the various schools of thought have proposed. One possible view is monetary (or nominal aggregate demand) neutrality: the rise in NAD, particularly if engineered by monetary policy and an increase in the money supply, will lead to an equiproportional rise in all nominal values, including prices and nominal wages, and no increase in real output. There is a long lineage of economic thinking along these lines; the 'Classics' and the 'Monetarist' schools, on which more below, held such views, although with varying details and sophistication. The later school of 'New Classicals' gives a subtler answer, which begins by decomposing the change in NAD as:

$$dNAD = E_{-1}(dNAD) + (dNAD - E_{-1}dNAD)$$

The change in NAD is broken down into that portion that was anticipated (introduced by the 'expectations operator' E) one period ago (subscript –1), and that part which was not anticipated, i.e. that part that came as a surprise (or 'expectational error'). The New Classical School argues that monetary neutrality applies to the anticipated portion of the NAD change, while the unanticipated portion will likely have some real effects. But in an important twist, invocation of the 'Rational Expectations Hypothesis' implies that the expectational error will, under certain conditions, be entirely random and quite unrelated to the overall stance of policy. Therefore, the end effect on real output will be random, and far from the intended one: NAD policy is unable to influence real output meaningfully (a result known as the 'Policy Ineffectiveness Proposition').

New Keynesians, along with the mainstream of the academic economics profession, argue that there is no monetary policy neutrality in the short to medium run, a horizon during which real output can meaningfully be affected by monetary policy. At the same time, prices will also be affected in the same direction, so that the x per cent initial increase in NAD will be broken down into y per cent change in real output and $(x - y)$ per cent change in the price level, both in the same direction (i.e. $0 < y < x$). The exact mix of effects on output and prices (i.e. the exact relation of y to $x - y$) depends on a number of factors, including the specifics of the policy that is being implemented, the nature of the supply constraints (roughly, whether we are in a boom or recession), wage and price flexibility or rigidity (frequency of revising wage contracts, costs of raising output vs. cost of raising prices), etc.

So, the majority of academic economists, vaguely influenced by New Keynesian ideas, would argue that AD policies matter in the short-to-medium run. Some, perhaps not many, influenced by the New Classicals, would deny any role for AD policy at all. More consensus perhaps exists about the long run, to which we turn next.

Question 3: Appropriate policies for the long run

Despite the potency of monetary policy in the short to medium run (accepted by most, if not all professional and academic economists), it is commonly accepted that increases in economic welfare sustainable in the long run require other types of policy than those related to aggregate demand. For sustainable rises in living standards over the long run (i.e, thinking over decades and generations as opposed to years), appropriate supply-side policies are required; such that raise productivity/technology, physical capital, human capital/education/skills, improve the institutional setup so as to encourage entrepreneurship. Such issues have an important bearing on unemployment, as will be discussed in Chapter 4; they will be further discussed in Chapter 9 on growth.

There is more to be said about fiscal policy. It is widely accepted that this type of policy is more complicated in its analysis than monetary policy (and that may be the reason why monetary policy has been more thoroughly analysed), because fiscal policy involves supply-side as well as demand-side effects. For example, taxation may have important supply-side effects related to labour supply, demand, investment, and general business activity. Some of these will be discussed in Chapter 7 on fiscal policy. Additionally, there is a view that fiscal policy helps the supply side if it is directed towards education, health, infrastructure, and a more efficient administration. If so, fiscal policy also affects long-run growth. We review such issues in Chapter 9.

But not everyone would agree that AD policies are completely irrelevant in the long run. Older Keynesians and some others would argue that restrictive AD policies ('austerity'), in particular, may have long-lasting effects as they can destroy productive capacity which is difficult to rebuild. In this way, AD reductions and 'consolidations' may influence structural unemployment, not only the cyclical one (i.e. will have more permanent effects). We review such views in Chapter 4; but it is fair to say that such views are in the minority.

1.2.4 The 'Real-Monetary Dichotomy' and Monetary Neutrality

In the long-run AS curve (i.e. based on $P^e = P$), the resulting output level ($\bar{Y}$) does not depend on money or nominal values (the real wage W/P is involved in its determination, but it is very different than either W or P). To understand that, we can use the parable of 'real-monetary dichotomy' (note that it is only a parable, fiction, an analytical device that helps us to understand). The macroeconomic system can be split (in jargon: it 'dichotomizes') into a real 'sphere' (where real variables like real output or employment are determined) and the 'nominal sphere' determining the nominal values.[12] The real sphere works like in microeconomics textbook, where prices are always relative, therefore real (i.e. always P_i/P or P/W, never P_i or P in levels). It is entirely supply side: it underpins point $\bar{Y}$ in Figure 1.3. Quantities and relative prices are determined by relative demands and supplies, and all those analyses that underpin these (expenditure decisions of all types, labour demands and supplies, productivity, etc.). After real variables have been determined in the real sphere, nominal variables are determined in the nominal sphere by both aggregate demand (including monetary policy) and supply. The key feature of this dichotomy is that the real sphere is exogenous to the nominal one: the factors in the real sphere affect the working of the nominal one, but not the other way around.

It follows from this logical structure (if true) that aggregate demand cannot affect quantities (real output) but only nominal values. With reference to monetary policy, the monetary-real dichotomy implies 'monetary neutrality'. An x per cent rise in nominal money will raise everything nominal (P_i of all goods i. P. W, nominal output, etc.) by x per cent, leaving everything real (W/P, relative individual prices P_i/P, real output) unchanged. The real interest rate is determined in the 'real sphere' by such fundamentals of the economy as productivity, profitability, and willingness to save (see Chapter 9); therefore it will be unaffected by monetary policy. The nominal interest equals the real interest rate plus inflation, which equals the rate of growth of the money supply under monetary neutrality. The dichotomy implies (as a logical consequence) monetary neutrality; but the opposite is not true: monetary neutrality may obtain for reasons other than the complete separation of real and monetary 'spheres'.

Apart from the (rather fictitious) real-nominal dichotomy, what other conditions may give rise to monetary neutrality? The precondition for it to hold is that all wages and prices are fully flexible, and expectations have had the time to catch up with actual variables. In this case, the macroeconomy is fully determined by supply-side factors. As already mentioned, most academic economists would think that price/wage flexibility and the resulting monetary neutrality are a good approximation of how the macroeconomy works in the long run. To emphasize the point, the major policy proposition that follows from this is that if one cares to improve the economy's fortunes over decades and generations, one should be thinking of appropriate supply-side policies. Most mainstream academic economists would subscribe to this position.

The point of contention is the short run. Here, most but not all academic economists would think that the dichotomy and monetary neutrality break down, that demand plays a role in affecting (real) quantities and not only prices, and that important scope exists for appropriate demand-oriented policies to stabilize the economy in the short run. A minority would argue that monetary neutrality is how the world works all the time. The point of contention of the two camps is the 'distortions' that hold in the short run and impede the macroeconomy's full adjustment. These merit some more discussion, which is done in the next sub-section.

---

[12] These spheres or 'sectors' are entirely notional and should not be confused with real-world sectors such as agriculture, manufacturing, services, etc.

1.2.5 The Short Run

When we admit the possibility of errors in expectations, output supply increases with the actual-expected price discrepancy, so that $AS|_{s.r}$ is not vertical, as stated. There are various arguments why this may be so, nicely summarized by Mankiw (1990) on which we draw here. First, we have the 'workers' misperception' argument, given above, that labour supply may move around simply because workers are not sure of the price level for the period ahead; in that case, the labour supply may be formalized as:

$$L^S = L^S \left(\frac{W^+}{P} x \frac{P^+}{Pe} \right) \tag{1.19}$$

Given the real wage W/P, a higher actual-to-expected price ratio implies more labour supply: workers think that their real wage is more attractive than it actually is, and offer more labour (labour supply shifts to $L^{S'}$ in Figure 1.2). The resulting higher labour supply (than if the price were correctly calculated) leads to greater output; hence, a higher P/P^e places us on a higher point on $AS|_{s.r}$. But this view is open to the criticism that it is only workers that miscalculate (why not the firms, too), and they do so when information on a wide range of economic statistics is compiled reasonably soon and disseminated almost instantly.

A related second view would argue that workers get it wrong not because of miscalculation of P but because of fixed nominal wages for a while; i.e. they may know how W/P has evolved since they signed their contracts, but cannot do much until they sign new ones—an argument first advanced by Keynes. The effects on L^S and $AS|_{s.r}$ are pretty much the same. A problem with the stories centred on erroneous expectations by workers or fixed nominal wages is that they predict a countercyclical real wage: a movement along L^D in Figure 1.2 between points A and C, a movement of the real wage and labour (therefore also real output) in opposite directions, whereas evidence shows that the real wage is (mostly) mildly procyclical—see Chapter 6 on business cycles.

To overcome these difficulties, further theories have focused on misperceptions on behalf of firms or stickiness in prices—thus making up a sort of symmetric matrix of theories. The 'Lucas island model' reviewed in the next chapter is one in which the firm is trying to gauge the general price level, and in doing so, it varies output and its price at the same time and in the same direction—resulting in an upward-sloping short-run AS curve; but the story now arises from the firm side. The 'menu cost' model of sticky prices reviewed in Chapter 3 on the New Keynesians, on the other hand, begins with the observation that it may take some time for some prices to adjust in the face of an aggregate demand shock because of the costs of frequent reprinting of price catalogues and menus ('menu costs'). Those businesses that do not change their prices will be happy to serve the higher demand, for a while. Hence, some prices will be rising at the same time as the output of some other firms (and therefore, aggregate GDP) is also rising—again giving rise to an upward-sloping short-run AS. The firm-centred theories complement really the ones focusing on worker behaviour. What is unclear is what type of behaviour they imply for the real wage. One may generally say that these theories involve shifts in the demand side of the labour market, so the real wage rises with employment and output. If so, these theories should give rise to pro-cyclical real wages.

1.2.6 Policy Analysis in the AD-AS Model

Time now to think more systematically about the effects of aggregate demand policy. We shall consider a government spending increase $(dG > 0)$ that has a pure demand-side effect. (We ignore the possible supply-side effects of this policy.) The effects may be logically broken down as follows:

- Textbook multiplier effect at the initial interest rate, $dY^D = \frac{dG}{1-c}$, causing a shift of the IS curve (1.16) right by that amount.
- A rise of the interest rate to clear the money market (thus, the LM 1.17 is involved):

$$dY^D = \frac{dG + I'(.)x(\partial r/\partial Y)dY^D}{1-c} \quad \text{or} \quad dY^D = \frac{dG/(1-c)}{1-I'(.)x(\partial r/\partial Y)dY^D}$$

- As $I'(.) < 0$, $\partial r/\partial Y > 0$, the (negative) second-stage involved here dampens the initial expansion in demand; this is the textbook 'crowding-out' effect; the combined two effects (initial and first crowding-out) are shown by the horizontal segment AB in the AD-AS Figure 1.4.
- The final effect brings together the AS curve, which we re-express as the price level as a function of Y given P^e : $P = (Y^S)^{-1}(Y; P^e)$; this informs how much the price level goes up when output is rising, given a certain level of expectations. Thus:

$$dY = \frac{dG + I'(.)x(\partial r/\partial Y)dY + (\partial r/\partial(M/P))(-M/P^2)x[\partial(Y^S)^{-1}(.)/\partial Y]dY}{1-c}$$

- As $I'(.) < 0$, $\partial r/\partial(M/P) < 0$, this additional effect further reduces the impact of G on output: a second-round crowding out, due to fact that demand raises prices as well as real output (which is less than if prices had not increased); this is BC in Figure 1.4.
- The final effect considers the gradual adjustment of expectations to a point where they are correct: $P/P^e = 1$. Hence, in the limit (long run), $Y^S = Y^S(1) = \bar{Y}$ becomes vertical and $(Y^S)^{-1}$ flat, therefore $\partial(Y^S)^{-1}(.)/\partial Y \to \infty$; rearranging we see that $dY \to 0$. We have now moved to point D: the demand expansion is entirely ineffective in terms of aggregate output, and has only affected the price level. Note however that the fiscal expansion will have altered the composition of output: There will be more government-procured output (G) and less investment. Consumption will have stayed the same. (Why?) Intuitively, this effect arises because prices and wages begin to rise in an overheated economy, setting in motion the 'wage-price spiral' that will be

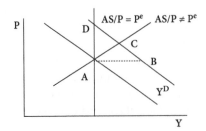

Figure 1.4. Effects of an AD expansion

explained more below. As prices rise, workers realize that their wages decline in real terms and therefore are more reluctant to put in extra hours; as wages and other costs rise, businesses reduce output to some extent and let prices rise. The net effect is that the price level rises and output drops back to normal or 'natural'.

A monetary expansion works in a similar fashion except that it does not involve the first of the above effects. It starts with a fall in the interest rate caused by the rise in M/P. At the end, its effect is more clear-cut in the sense that it involves monetary neutrality: When expectations have caught up, P, P^e, and W will have all risen by the same percentage as M, leaving output and the (real) interest rate unaffected.

Supply-side shocks (resulting from supply-side policies such as tax reductions, as well as productivity changes, institutional change, oil price rises, or simply purely exogenous weather changes) will have permanent effects on real output, no matter what the shape of AS is, as can be seen with reference to Figure 1.5. For simplicity, the effects of only favourable shocks on supply are shown, and only in the case of a vertical AS. All favourable supply shocks result in a higher output and a lower price level (or more realistically, a lower inflation rate), whether one has a vertical or upward-sloping AS in mind.

1.3 From the AS to the Phillips Curve

The Phillips Curve is an inverse relation between inflation and the unemployment rate (better: its deviations from the 'natural' or 'structural' rate). It was the main framework in which the central debates of macroeconomics were cast in the 1960s and 1970s, but a modern form of it continues to inform current debates. This section reviews the basic formulations of Phillips Curve, before reviewing the policy implications arising from its traditional and modern versions.

1.3.1 The Traditional Phillips Curve: A Dynamic Version of the AS

In a landmark paper claimed to be the most widely cited economics article so far, Phillips (1958) uncovered a statistical negative relationship between (nominal) *wage* inflation and unemployment with UK data, 1861–1913. This relationship was remarkably robust, being both structurally stable and showing a good out-of-sample fit (see also Lipsey, 1960). Yet, it was just a statistical relationship without any theoretical foundation. One may think of a reason for this correlation: a lower unemployment puts upward pressure on wage growth as workers become more assertive. Subsequently, Samuelson and Solow (1960) connected

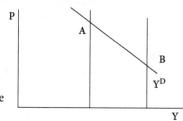

Figure 1.5. Effects of favourable supply-side shocks

unemployment to price (as opposed to wage) inflation and provided a theoretical explanation. Lower unemployment fuels wage growth and therefore price inflation; conversely, higher inflation and prices erode the real wage of workers, therefore firms are willing to hire more and unemployment decreases. Hence, the Phillips Curve now became a theory, suggesting an inverse relationship of unemployment against (price) inflation. In formal terms:

$$\pi = -au + bz \tag{1.20}$$

where π is the inflation rate and u the unemployment rate (per cent); z are all the supply-side factors that shift the AS curve. As written, z shows the *unfavourable* supply-side developments such as: cost surges due to greater firm or worker monopoly power, declines in productivity, higher imported goods prices (including oil, other energy, raw materials, even food prices), higher taxation, non-business-friendly changes in the institutional/regulatory framework, etc. This equation is essentially a dynamic version of the AS curve (1.12), assumed linear for simplicity: Instead of the price level, we have its growth rate (the inflation rate) and instead of output supply, we have the unemployment rate; the two are closely (inversely) related via Okun's law discussed above. Expectations are fixed and for simplicity have been dropped.

The Philips Curve (1.20) is a structural relation that arises from the supply side of the economy (from 'deep' fundamentals such as labour supply-demand, productivity and costs, resource availability and input—energy, raw materials—prices, institutional and market structure, taxation, and so on). In this simple form, it provides a simple but powerful menu of options for government. Generally, governments wish to have as little as possible of both inflation and unemployment, as both of these impose costs on the macroeconomy (for reasons that will be explained in Chapters 3 and 4). Equation (1.20) shows a trade-off between the two 'bads', implying options for the governments but also constraints: Any government can have as little as it desires of the one providing it is prepared to tolerate more of the other. Ultimately, where government positions itself on this trade-off depends on its preferences (or societal preferences). A more (politically) Keynesian or left-wing government will perhaps choose less unemployment and more inflation, a more conservative government the opposite. The policy instrument that allows government to select its chosen point on (1.20) is AD policy (fiscal and/or monetary policy).

1.3.2 Expectations and the Modern Phillips Curve

By the late 1960s, many academic economists were becoming increasingly unhappy with the traditional formulation of the Phillips Curve. The reasons were twofold, both analytical and logical difficulties with it, and also an emerging breakdown in its statistical performance. Under the influence of Friedman (1968), Phelps (1968) and others, two major developments took place. First, instead of simple unemployment, its deviation from the natural rate (u^N) entered (1.20); this was meant to capture all the supply-side factors (z) in a concise way. Secondly, an expectations term was added, as these expectations guide wage inflation which in turn feeds into price inflation (see below). We therefore get:

$$\pi = -a(u - u^N) + c\pi^e + v \tag{1.20'}$$

It is a moot point whether the term v is a pure error term or whether it captures some systematic factors shifting (1.20'), such as the rate of productivity growth. If the latter is the case, then this causes problems in econometric identification because these factors will also influence u^N; see Ball and Mankiw (2002).

Guided by (1.20'), traditional literature made the intuitive (but now old-fashioned) distinction between 'cost-push' and 'demand-pull' surges of inflation. Those that were due to shifts in PC under the influence of z (alternatively: changes in the natural rate, u^N), these were cost factors 'pushing' prices higher from the ground up; and those that were due to moving along the PC, these were due to changes in demand ('pulling' prices from above by policy measures). The possibility of shifts in the PC under the influence of the supply-side factors can cause both inflation and unemployment to change in the same direction, something not possible under (1.20) which just allows for a trade-off. The unhappy coincidence of both inflation and unemployment going up is termed stag(nation-in) flation. The emergence of stagflation in the late 1960s and 1970s, following a near thirty-year happy spell of low inflation and unemployment, was one of the primary motivations of the development of (1.20').

The expectations term $c\pi^e$ is the second, and even more momentous, difference between (1.20) and (1.20'). This term was meant to capture yet another source of inflation, 'built-in' inflation due to the 'wage-price' spiral. Consider an initial exogenous rise in inflation (for whatever reason). Workers will see a fall in the purchasing power of their wages, prompting them to go for higher wage increases next period. These wage increases will however erode profit margins for the firms, which will try to pass them on to higher prices; and so on. A wage-price dynamic then develops which locks in any initial surge in inflation; it works like successive shifts upwards of the AS curve, with the potential however to go on for ever if unchecked. Inflationary expectations enter (1.20') as a good indicator of this process; if inflation is expected to be high next period, there will be higher wage claims to compensate for that; those will feed into higher inflation. Initially, it was assumed that $0 < c < 1$, but the $c < 1$ part was criticized as giving rise to 'money illusion': even if expectations are correct, wage inflation will be (by assumption) lower; the fact that real-wage inflation is $w - w_{-1} - \pi = (c - 1)\pi < 0$ (under correct inflationary expectations) implies that real wages will be declining indefinitely, and workers will not notice. Mistaking nominal values for the corresponding real ones is the essence of 'money illusion' and is present if $c < 1$. To avoid this implausible theoretical premise, we impose $c = 1$, so the Phillips Curve takes its modern form:

$$\pi - \pi^e = -a(u - u^N) + v \tag{1.20''}$$

The *expectations-augmented Phillips Curve* (1.20'') has played an absolutely central role in the development of modern macroeconomics. It is crucial in understanding such key policy debates as the Policy Ineffectiveness Proposition (Chapter 2), the time inconsistency problem related to discretionary policy and the institutional changes that were prompted by this debate (Chapter 7), etc. Because of this importance, its micro-foundations have been further investigated; we shall review the formulation due to Lucas (Chapter 2) and a formulation arising out of staggered wage and/or price setting by the spirit of the New Keynesian school of thought (Chapter 3). The critical feature that is responsible for all the theoretical results just mentioned is the 'linear homogeneity' assumption, $c = 1$.

1.3.3 Policy Implications of the Phillips Curve

Obviously, the exact implications of the Phillips Curve for policy hinge on how expectations evolve and what assumptions we make in this respect. A number of *expectations formation mechanisms* have been explored in the literature. The simplest is to assume that expectations are constant. In this case, the equation gives a nice trade-off between inflation and unemployment, essentially the same as under the simple Phillips Curve (1.20). In Figure 1.6, every line is drawn for a given level of inflation expectations. Though constant expectations are of course unrealistic, they were not a bad approximation of what actually happened in the era of low inflation. Inflation in industrialized economies was not outside the 2–5 per cent range during most of the 1950s and 1960s, the heyday of PC-type of thinking. Many governments used to pursue policies of near-full employment, until the economy overheated and inflation tended to rise (and external constraints were also encountered). Then, governments would pull the brakes and try to move lower down the curve. This was termed a 'go-stop cycle'.

Allowing for changing expectations implies shifts of the curve because of the wage-price spiral; e.g. higher inflationary expectations mean also higher inflation, via higher wages, so the curve shifts up and to the right. Simple 'backward-looking expectations' are a simple hypothesis of how expectations evolve. Let us assume that expectations equal inflation in the last period—in other words, $\pi^e = \pi_{-1}$. Then, suppressing v, we have:

$$\pi - \pi_{-1} = -a(u - u^N)$$

It is the *difference* in inflation rates that is now inversely related to unemployment. To see what this means, consider a policy experiment of reducing unemployment at the cost of some extra inflation (Figure 1.6). Firms see the real wage they pay (W/P) become eroded, marginal costs reduced, and are happy to increase employment and produce more, while that lasts—A to B in the Figure. For a period or so (until expectations are revised), the gains on the unemployment front are sustainable without much trouble; after that, however, expectations are revised, and workers demand higher wages. With such higher wages, firms cut production back to normal, and unemployment returns to normal—this is represented by a parallel shift from PC to PC' and a horizontal move as shown by the arrow (B to B'). To sustain the reduction in unemployment further, the government must engineer a further increase in inflation up along PC' (B' to C), which in due course will come to be expected by wage setters, further shifting PC' to PC", etc. This policy experiment, in other words, moves the economy along the spiral shown by the arrows in Figure 1.6. This is the

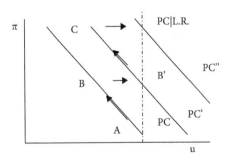

Figure 1.6. The Phillips Curve

wage-price spiral at work; for more details see Blanchard (1986). Furthermore, a spiral of the same kind could be set in motion by an adverse supply shock such as those shifting the AS up and to the left—a productivity slowdown, in particular relative to other economies; an increase in markups by firms or union militancy in claiming higher wages; an oil price rise. Such developments will result in a shift right of the PC (say to PC'), with rising unemployment in the first instance at the same rate of inflation. If subsequently the government attempts—mistakenly—to correct the supply-side developments and support the previous lower unemployment rate with expansionary aggregate demand policies, much the same spiral upwards will result.

Thus, the main message of this analysis is that in the long run we move vertically upwards along the PC|L.R. of Figure 1.6, with only temporary and rather trivial deviations of unemployment from its structural level. Any sustained aggregate demand expansion aiming for an unemployment rate permanently lower than the natural rate will not produce just higher but stable inflation; it will result in inflation spiralling out of control. Thus, the trade-off now disappears: The expectations-augmented (long-run) Phillips Curve is vertical at the structural level of unemployment, which cannot be manipulated by aggregate demand policies.

As the price for low unemployment is sky-rocketing inflation, an outcome that no government is normally prepared to tolerate, the only option for keeping inflation stable is to maintain unemployment at its structural/natural rate. For this reason, this is termed NAIRU (Non-Accelerating Inflation Rate of Unemployment), a name that has caught on in academic as well as policy debates. This argument was the basis for the Monetarists' (and in particular, Friedman's 1968) critique of Keynesian stabilization policies, associated with more traditional versions of the Phillips Curve. The Monetarists used a hypothesis known as Adaptive Expectations, a more sophisticated version of backward-looking expectations, to highlight their argument. But the policy implications were much the same. We shall review Adaptive Expectations in Chapter 2, before reviewing the modern theory of expectations formation, the Rational Expectations Hypothesis in more detail. While the policy implications of both are quite similar (essentially that there is no meaningful Phillips Curve even in the short run), the analytical implications of the latter are much more far-reaching.

A key implication of the foregoing analysis is that unemployment cannot deviate for long (under any plausible expectations hypothesis) from its structural/natural level, which is entirely supply-side determined. This has the powerful consequence that aggregate demand policy can only be useful for (short-run) stabilization purposes, but cannot do anything useful about long-run levels of unemployment, or indeed output or economic welfare. Instead, if you want to deliver sustainable improvements in the latter, you need to employ supply-side policies. As stated, this appears to be the position of the vast majority of the academic economists today; one cannot help pointing out the marked contrast with the position of Keynes who insisted (in the very different circumstances of the 1930s Great Depression) that aggregate demand policies are all-powerful.

We close this sub-section with two policy implications that are broadly in line with this analysis. First, Friedman's 'k-per cent rule' for expansion of the monetary base. Suppose that the monetary base (high-powered money) is expanding at rate x per cent per year, with the growth rate of real GDP in the economy assumed to equal k per cent. The money growth rate of x per cent can be trivially decomposed into two portions, k per cent and

$(x - k)$ per cent. The former will be 'used' to cover any new transactions needs of the economy due to growth, but the latter will be purely inflationary (excess money will be created). Friedman's point is that, in order to achieve zero inflation, the rate of growth of monetary expansion must be $x = k$ per cent, the money growth rate should equal that of real GDP. A second point has to do with the rate of growth of real wages. For reasons that will become clearer in Chapter 4 on unemployment, this can only be equal to the rate of productivity growth in the economy. Any real wage growth higher than that will amount effectively to an adverse shift of the Phillips Curve (in whatever version), and will result sooner or later to a rise in structural unemployment, inflation, and the loss of external competitiveness.

1.3.4 The Phillips Curve and the NAIRU: Discussion

Let us conclude with some empirical observations about the NAIRU. Ball and Mankiw (2002) provide a good review of all theory related to the Phillips Curve, NAIRU, and problems of its econometric estimation. In addition, they provide estimates of the NAIRU for the US, 1960–2000. They argue that 'the estimated NAIRU is 5.4% in 1960, peaks at 6.8% in 1979 and falls to 4.9% in 2000' (Ball and Mankiw, 2002, p. 123). The fall of the NAIRU around 2000 is an issue on which a firm answer does not exist; possible suggestions relate to demographics, the rate of productivity growth, and more intriguingly but also perhaps importantly, rates of imprisonment and the generosity of welfare support for the disabled; on these, see the 'Guidance for Further Study' section. In Chapter 4 on unemployment, we shall consider at length various explanations for high unemployment and the NAIRU, but in a way that is disconnected from inflation and the Phillips Curve.

Other estimates for the US are provided in Gordon (1997), where it is argued that the NAIRU fluctuates considerably, with the late 1970s to mid-1980s seeing a NAIRU of perhaps around 6.5 per cent and the mid-1990s a NAIRU of about one percentage point less. A lively and wide-ranging exchange is the one contained in Solow, Taylor, with Friedman (1998). Among the contributors, John Taylor is perhaps the most forthright proponent of the orthodox view of a (vertical in the long run but not the short run) Phillips Curve and a NAIRU of about 6 per cent in the US (given as a historical average, not based on any underlying model). More recently, Watson (2014) estimates that the NAIRU in the US may have risen since 2007 by as much as 1 per cent; this is because unemployment has risen without any reduction in inflation. The reasons for this increase are not well understood, but may be related to the 'jobless growth' and 'secular stagnation hypotheses' to be discussed in Chapters 4 and 9.

The idea of a vertical PC is vehemently criticized by James Galbraith who points out that there appear so many shifts in the PC in US post-war history as to make the entire concept meaningless. Likewise, Galbraith (1997) presents a wholesale criticism of the (non-existent, in his view) theoretical foundation of the Phillips Curve, short- and long-run, as well as of the NAIRU. More subtly, Robert Solow criticizes the NAIRU on three grounds; first, that the concept is not precisely determined in the data (Staiger et al., 1997, estimate that the US NAIRU in 1990 might be anywhere between 5 per cent to 7 per cent); second, that the NAIRU may itself be endogenous and not a 'structural bedrock' (possibly because of 'hysteresis'—see Chapter 4); and third because there may be asymmetries in this endogenous adjustment of the NAIRU, so that disinflation may raise the NAIRU by more than inflation would lower it (see Ball, 1997). Finally, the verticality of the Phillips Curve even in the long run is also questioned by Eisner (1997), Fair (2000), and more recently Karanassou et al. (2003). However, there was a powerful recent rejoinder that 'the Phillips Curve is Alive and Well' by Gordon (2013); he estimates the NAIRU to have risen since 2007 from 4.8 to 6.5 per cent.

In two thought-provoking papers, Akerlof et al. (1996, 2000) argue that the Phillips Curve may be highly non-linear. At very low inflation rates (< 2 per cent) in particular, there may be a permanent trade-off between inflation and unemployment. Figure 3 of the 1996 paper and figure 7 of the 2000 paper show that, as inflation rises from 0 to 2 per cent, unemployment falls permanently by as much as 4–5 per cent. This is because inflation works to facilitate real wage adjustment (downward in particular), as workers generally have a higher tolerance for real wage cuts than nominal ones. But higher inflation rates may not translate into reduction in unemployment so readily. Relatedly, there is evidence (Akerlof et al., 2000) of some money illusion. Workers may not be sure or notice who is better off: a worker with a 2 per cent rise in nominal wages and 0 per cent inflation, or one with a 5 per cent rise in nominal wages and 3 per cent inflation; and that a worker may be more prepared to accept a wage increase of 1 per cent when inflation is 2 per cent, than a wage cut of 1 per cent when the inflation rate is zero.

So, where does this all leave us? Following Akerlof's (2002) Nobel lecture, a partial summary may emphasize three elements:

- The imprecision of the estimates of the NAIRU;
- Asymmetrically rigid nominal wages (downward-sticky);
- Evidence of money illusion at low inflation.

This perhaps suggests a convex-shaped PC even in the long run, not a vertical one. There may be considerable trade-off to be explored by policy at high unemployment/low inflation but not at a low unemployment rate/high inflation. In any case, the NAIRU should be treated with caution for practical policy-making purposes.

1.4 A Brief Story of Macroeconomics

One good way of appreciating current ideas, theories, and policy dilemmas is by reviewing how we have got here, how previous generations of theorists framed theoretical problems and the solutions they have provided. Symbolically, the beginning of macroeconomics is often considered to be the publication in 1936 of Keynes's *General Theory of Employment, Interest and Money* (Keynes 1973). In reality, however, the story of macroeconomics begins in the early twentieth century.[13] Our aim here is to give the general flavour of the debates, not to provide any complete history of the discipline.

---

[13] The title of this section is inspired by Gombrich's (1989) very enjoyable and readable *The Story of Art* combined with Hawking's (1989) equally enjoyable (and intriguing) *A Brief History of Time.*

1.4.1 The 'Classics'

Before Keynes, there was a reasonable amount of sophisticated macroeconomic thinking in areas such as monetary theory and business cycles (by theorists such as Irving Fisher, Knut Wicksell, Alfred Pigou, and many others); but it is fair to say that an integrated framework was lacking.[14] All in all, macroeconomics proper had not yet come into being. At the danger of over-generalizing (or caricaturing), we may say that the general mindset of pre-Keynesians ('Classics' in Keynes's terminology) was characterized by a few simple tenets:

- A general belief in the ability of the market mechanism to correct its weaknesses—in particular, unemployment, business cycle, or poverty were not deemed problems amenable to public policy. In the same spirit, the appropriate role of the state (or 'government') in economic life was thought to be minimal ('government as night guard', fulfilling only basic defence/security/justice functions).
- Belief in the 'Quantity theory of money': $VM = PQ$. V is the velocity of circulation of money: when it changes hands, each pound coin generates £1 worth of transactions, thus if it changes hands on average ten times a year, the same pound coin generates £10 worth of transactions each year. This velocity is behaviourally and institutionally determined: it depends (inversely) on the fraction of their financial wealth that individuals keep as cash, and on the fraction of their deposits banks keep as reserves in cash form. In other words, the factors that determine velocity are closely related to those that determine the money multiplier through fractional reserve banking (but V is not the money multiplier). Thus, VM on the left-hand side is the total capacity of the available money supply to generate or facilitate transactions. PQ on the right-hand side is nominal transactions, P(rice level) times Q (total transactions). Q will include both new goods and services produced within the year and also transactions in second-hand goods. Since we are more interested in the determination of GDP than total transactions, theorists made the bold assumption that the two are proportional, so that on the right-hand side we have nominal income: PY (times an unimportant constant). A final, quite 'strong', and controversial assumption is that real output Y is exogenously determined by the supply side and is not amenable to monetary policy. Under these assumptions, the 'quantity theory' asserts that the monetary impulses are translated into price changes in equal proportion; in other words, the 'quantity theory' upholds monetary neutrality and is in the spirit of the real-monetary dichotomy. Of course, no one would propose such a crude theory today. But its logic, and the implications spelt out below, would be accepted by some (e.g. Monetarists, New Classicals) even for the short run and by many for the long run.
- Belief in 'Say's Law' (after the French nineteenth-century economist J.B. Say): supply creates its own demand. For output to be generated, both supply and demand must be created (and in equilibrium, they equal each other). But a key question is, which one of the two is the real driver? (It is like saying, it takes two to tango, but who is the

---

[14] For a nicely readable history of macroeconomics, one could consult Backhouse (2002). Backhouse shows how much sophisticated macroeconomic thought there was between the wars.

better dancer?) This doctrine gives a clear answer: supply. This has powerful policy implications as to what kind of policies should be put in place. General opinion in academic macroeconomics is that Say's Law does not necessarily apply in the short run, but does apply in the long run. For improvement of living standards over generations, there ought to be the proper supply conditions in place (broadly interpreted, to include human capital, productivity, technology, entrepreneurship, 'institutions'); demand (decisions to spend, either by government or the private sector) will then follow. In other words, Say's Law coincides with the thinking behind the vertical long-run AS and Phillips Curves.

The policy corollary from all of this is that there is little that government policy can do to stabilize the economy (or to provide public services or alleviate poverty). The best government can do is maintain stable macroeconomic conditions. To do so, it should maintain sound public finances by avoiding deficits and debts; and maintain stable monetary conditions (avoiding inflation) by a tight control on money. Practically, this was achieved by adherence to the 'Gold Standard', an arrangement by which individual currencies were fixed ('pegged') in terms of gold; the monetary authority was deprived of the important tool of devaluations or revaluations, but exchange rate uncertainty was avoided. The Gold Standard was quite widespread in the early twentieth century, but was later (1920s) gradually abandoned as the discipline it required was deemed too challenging when the economic climate worsened.

1.4.2 Keynes

In the wake of the Great Depression of the late 1920s and 1930s, with its serious economic troubles (unemployment upwards of 30 per cent in some key industrial economies like the US and Germany, huge financial upheavals, bankruptcies, and drop in production), Keynes comes to the conclusion that at the root of the problem lies a failure in aggregate demand (AD). What is being produced needs also to be bought by consumers, firms, or government; if that is not the case, then output suffers; that was the root cause of the malaise in Keynes's view. Such ideas flew in the face of then generally accepted doctrines. Keynes dismisses ideas such as an essentially supply-side determined real economy or monetary neutrality; Keynes argues that these may hold in special situations, but not generally. His theory, mainly expounded in his *General Theory of Employment Interest and Money* of 1936 (Keynes, 1973), aims to be just that: more general.

More broadly, the market economy lacks self-correcting mechanisms in some situations, such as for example the 'liquidity trap' (i.e. the horizontal segment of the LM curve). As a result, it is desirable, indeed necessary, to use AD policies for stabilization purposes. For this purpose, government spending is an appropriate policy tool as it is likely to have multiple effects on real output. Expansionary fiscal policies, mainly rises in government spending causing government deficits, could/should be used to get economies moving again. Keynes in fact favoured fiscal over monetary policy as a way of getting out of the Great Depression, because of the then prevailing liquidity trap (very low interest rates that could not be pushed lower by expansionary monetary policy). Finally, and as a corollary, with Keynes, proper macro thought is established, with a coherent analytical framework to back up the main ideas; a framework, furthermore, that lends itself to quantification and empirical measurement. Keynes gives a great impetus to further development of National Income Accounting.

As mentioned, Keynes was hugely important for the critical development, indeed the birth of macroeconomics;[15] there is general talk of a 'Keynesian revolution'. These few lines here cannot even begin to do justice to him, but simply aim to convey the flavour of his ideas. Those ideas were widely seen as challenging prevailing orthodoxy in a huge way, and laid the basis for the proper development of the subject. Subsequent generations of theorists sought to refine these ideas; in the process, these ideas have also altered in subtle but important ways.

1.4.3 The Keynesian-Neoclassical Synthesis

The general thrust in the work of the post-war generation of macroeconomists was to refine and crystallize Keynes's ideas, and to integrate them better with the rest of economics. Early on, Keynes's thinking was formally summarized (or is assumed to be summarized ...) by the 'IS-LM' framework developed by Hicks (1937) and Hansen (1949). One general objective of this research programme was to provide an analysis of the supply side that Keynes seemingly ignored, and to bring the price level into the picture. The AD-AS model integrates all these features. The AD captures the demand side of the economy, with IS-LM at its core; AS captures the supply side. So, a balance between the treatments of demand and supply emerges. A related objective was to synthesize macro analysis (aggregative models) with micro ('sectoral' models). Starting from basic (micro) economic principles, theories of the main behavioural equations underpinning the model were developed. Modigliani (1966) and Friedman (1956) modelled consumption on consumers' lifetime resources (the former) and on 'permanent' (i.e. permanently sustainable) income (the latter). Jorgenson (1963) developed a model of investment starting from a theory of capital that emphasizes the 'rental cost' of owning capital; Tobin (1958) developed the theory of money demand as the riskless part of optimal portfolios. These 'micro-founded' theories were used to provide deeper theoretical foundations for key elements of aggregate demand (the 'sectoral' models) and therefore became integral parts of the overall macroeconomic model.

In parallel with the development of macroeconomic theory, under the lead of Tinbergen and others (see Klein, 2004), econometrics was also being developed. There are close links between macroeconomics and econometric practice. Attempts were made to empirically assess the various aspects of models/theories using large and complex macro-econometric models, estimated in the large 'mainframe' computers of those times; in some of them, hundreds of behavioural equations like consumption functions, money demand, investment, labour demand and supplies, Phillips Curve, etc., all elaborated in great detail, were estimated. Such models were first developed in the 1960s and 1970s in the US, later on in the UK and elsewhere (see Fernández-Villaverde, 2008). These days such models have been

---

[15] The term 'macroeconomics' first appears sometime in the 1940s.

largely replaced by sophisticated medium-sized models focused primarily on the business cycle and estimated on powerful personal computers.

In terms of the effectiveness of AD policy, the 'Keynesian-neoclassical synthesis' is halfway (schematically speaking) between the monetary neutrality of the 'Classics' and Keynes's belief in an entirely AD-determined real output. The 'Keynesian-neoclassical synthesis' is a hybrid position as it argues that output can be influenced by demand, providing the policy-maker can tolerate the resulting rise in the price level. In these models, the AS curve is upward sloping, presumably because of some price and wage rigidity; this gives scope to stabilization policy to deliver output gains alongside higher prices. 'Keynesianism' became synonymous with an activist management of the macroeconomy based on aggregate demand policies, with quite broad goals in mind, including securing a high growth rate and eliminating unemployment. As we shall see, the scope of such AD-based policies drastically diminished over time; but that was later. In wider policy circles, in public discourse, and other social sciences, the term 'Keynesianism' seems to have taken an even wider, political connotation, encompassing a high presence of government in economic life, providing full employment and even affordable housing and other social services via the welfare state (see e.g. the way the term is used in the influential Mann, 2013, Chapter 6).

In general, in the early post-war years, there was optimism that there can be employment for all. This seems to be borne out by the data, as for thirtry years after World War II (1945–75—'les trentes glorieuses', the 'thirty glorious ones' as they came to be known in France), western industrialized economies enjoyed high rates of growth with low unemployment and inflation. However, gradually, this optimism gets watered down to the belief that, by AD policies, unemployment can be stabilized around an exogenous, supply-side 'natural rate'—but it cannot be entirely eliminated. Permanent reductions in unemployment require supply-side policies. This is the belief initially of the Monetarists, later on it wins over the mainstream of the profession. So, the key debate shifts to the question of whether AD policies can help stabilize (as opposed to 'eliminate') unemployment.

Emphasis in analysis shifts gradually to the Phillips Curve. The Phillips Curve framework relates employment to inflation (both variables so far neglected). The consensus of the profession in early years was that it was non-vertical, leaving a well-defined output-inflation trade-off which policy-makers can use: the policy-maker can reduce unemployment by accepting some more (but steady) inflation. Towards the early 1970s, it is recognized that wage pressures may shift the Phillips Curve out, making it less 'pleasant' to society and the policy-maker. To avert this, the fight against unemployment is supplemented by wage/price controls for a while. Furthermore, as unemployment gradually rises to altogether new levels in the 1970s and 1980s, the view is established that most of unemployment is structural or natural, determined only by the supply side of the market and not by aggregate demand; the view espoused first only by the 'Monetarists' as a minority, then winning over the profession. In general, in the 1970s, both unemployment and inflation rise ('stag-flation') as a result of oil price shocks (1973 and 1979), productivity slowdown, and erratic policies. This development goes against the spirit of the simple Phillips Curve (which predicts the two moving in opposite directions). Such real-world developments caused a lot of theoretical soul-searching in the late 1960s and 1970s.

It was realized that the simple Phillips Curve fails to incorporate the 'wage-price' spiral, whereby price increases fuel wage increases as workers try to protect their living standards, and wage increases are passed over to prices, as firms try to maintain their own profit margins. Once developed, therefore, this wage-price spiral is self-perpetuating; its effect is that inflation becomes firmly entrenched. Various theories on the political economy of monetary policy developed in the late 1970s and 1980s and major institutional changes that followed in subsequent years (independence of Central Banks, inflation targeting, etc.) were motivated by the need to break this entrenched inflation. We shall review these theories in Chapter 7.

Due to these shocks (oil, productivity) and policy errors and reversals, the 1970s is characterized by great macroeconomic volatility. In this climate of uncertainty, where previously accepted models seem not to work any longer, Monetarists and later the New Classicals become the dominant schools of thought. This shift is also fuelled by the perception that previously standard theory (IS-LM, AD-AS models, Phillips Curve) are full of internal contradictions. Generally, these models are derived by plausible-looking but arbitrarily postulated ('ad-hoc') assumptions that are not based explicitly on any theory of individual behaviour (utility maximization for individuals, profit maximization for firms). The 'Lucas critique', reviewed in the next chapter, warns us that such relations are likely to break down when policy changes.

Expectations of inflation gradually become important in Phillips Curve analyses. In earlier times (1950s and 1960s) inflation expectations were not important because of the then prevailing low and stable inflation. But this could no longer be true in the increasing inflationary and volatile environment of the late 1960s and 1970s. Additionally, inflation expectations are important as an indicator of the wage-price spiral outlined above. Inflationary expectations guide future wage negotiations, therefore are indicative of future wages. As such expectations rise, the traditional simple PC shifts right. It became gradually accepted that these inflationary rises and right-shifts of the PC eventually gave rise to a long-run, vertical PC, as first pointed out by the Monetarists. A vertical PC is a landmark result in the history of macroeconomics. The ways by which expectations are formed and their implications become an active area of research in the late 1960s and 1970s. The theory of 'Rational Expectations' is proposed by the New Classicals and gradually becomes the benchmark theory. Together with the vertical AS or PC, it has the startling policy implication that AD-based stabilization is totally ineffective, the 'Policy Ineffectiveness Proposition', to be reviewed in Chapter 2.

In conclusion, we may say that the position of the later Keynesian-neoclassical synthesis theorists, before the Monetarists and New Classicals took over from about 1970 onwards, is that it is only in the short run, while prices and wages are fixed, that the AS is upward-sloping. In the long run, when wage/price flexibility is restored, the AS is vertical: Monetary neutrality holds and the output is supply-side determined in that horizon. Likewise, the Phillips Curve may offer some policy options for a little while, but in the long run it is vertical: Unemployment is supply-side determined at its 'natural or structural' rate. It follows that, while there is scope for AD-driven stabilization policy (to stabilize growth and/or unemployment around their supply-side determined averages), any improvements in the macroeconomy in the long run, over decades and generations, would have to engineered via intelligent supply-side policies (education and training to promote human capital, research and training to spur technological innovation, a cleverly designed tax system, a favourable business and institutional environment). These are themes that still run through all the debates in macroeconomics. It is probably fair to say that the average opinion among mainstream academic economists even today about policy is close to that of the late 'Keynesian-neoclassical synthesis' school.

1.4.4 The Monetarists

Monetarists, as they came to be known, with Milton Friedman as figurehead, is a school of thought that achieved a lot of prominence towards the late 1960s and 1970s. Their influence extended well beyond academia and into policy and political circles. Initially, in the 1950s and early 1960s, they work within the dominant IS-LM framework of the day. Analytically, they place a strong emphasis on an empirically stable money demand (which held true till about the mid-1970s, but then broke down because of financial innovation). Shocks to the money supply are the most important shocks in aggregate demand, whereas other AD shocks are next to negligible (hence the name 'Monetarism'). But Monetarists never embraced the spirit of IS-LM, thinking of it as a framework for the short run, which describes developments when the economy is away from the purely supply-side deter- mined 'natural rate of output'. Their reservations against IS-LM are twofold.

First, they develop a line of argument to show that the LM is vertical, hence fiscal policy is totally ineffective, while monetary policy is the only one that can potentially affect economic activity. They begin with a stable money demand function of the form: $M^d = Pf(Y, i)$, $f_Y > 0$, $f_i < 0$, with money market clearing $M^d = M^s \equiv M$; this is then coupled with the Fischer equation that decomposes nominal interest rate as the sum of the real interest rate plus expected inflation, $I = r + \pi^e$. Furthermore, the recognition that the real interest rate is determined by the 'deep' macroeconomic system (productivity, profitability, willingness to invest and save, etc. and not easily amenable to AD policy) and does not change much anyway, leads to an equation of the form: $M = Pf(Y, \pi^e)$, where the real interest rate has been suppressed as roughly constant and not amenable to policy. With the further assumptions that the elasticity with respect to the expected inflation rate is not all that great, and, crucially, that real output (Y) is exogenously, supply-side determined, leads to an equation like: $M = PYf$, where f is just a constant now. This equation is in the form of the 'quantity theory of money' equation discussed above. Hence, there is a direct connection of money supply to the price level, without real output being affected, i.e. monetary neutrality holds. As a result, inflation is 'everywhere and always a monetary phenomenon' (Friedman, 1963). The policy implication of this memorable phrase is that, in order to control inflation, one should keep a tight leash over the rate of growth of money supply; this was put in practice by Mrs Thatcher's Conservative governments (from 1979 on for a few years), with only partial success (Cobham, 2002).

Their second reservation against activist policy concerns the inability of monetary policy to meaningfully affect real output, due to 'long and variable lags' with which policy is formulated and implemented. Recent empirical evidence has vindicated them: it suggests that it may be a year before monetary policy starts having real effects (see Chapter 7). Hence, their assault on AD-based policies is total: fiscal policy is ineffective due to the vertical LM curve, while systematic monetary policy fails to systematically and meaning- fully affect real activity, imparting only 'noise' and uncertainty into the system.

From the 1960s onwards, the debate is increasingly couched in terms of the Phillips Curve. Monetarists argue forcefully that it must be augmented with expected inflation, with a unitary coefficient: $U = F(\pi - \pi^e)$, with $F' < 0$. Expectations are meant to capture the shifts in the Phillips Curve due to the wage-price spiral, as mentioned. The next piece in the jigsaw concerns expectations formation—how agents form their expectations; this is important, as workers try to forecast the future cost of living and react in the labour market, setting in motion the wage-price spiral. Monetarists propose the theory of 'Adaptive Expectations' (to be reviewed in the next chapter)—errors get gradually corrected, but in the end expectations fully converge to actual outcomes. The powerful implication of an expectations-augmented Phillips Curve (which depends, crucially, only on $\pi - \pi^e$, the unforeseen part of inflation) coupled with Adaptive Expectations is that the PC is essentially vertical, at least in the long run—but the short run is very short, to the point of being meaningless. Any activist policy will only result in runaway inflation. Thus, the PC is characterized by the Non-Accelerating Inflation Rate of Unemployment (NAIRU)—essentially a Natural Rate of Unemployment. While monetary expansion may raise real output in the very short run, the cost of (runaway) inflation is overwhelming.

In conclusion, we see that Monetarists begin to work within the accepted framework in the early post-war years, without fully accepting it. Gradually, they move to a yet more radical position which dispenses entirely with any remaining vestiges of the Keynesian-neoclassical synthesis and emphasize concepts such as the 'natural rate' of unemployment, a vertical Phillips Curve, and the ineffectiveness of AD-based stabilization policies. There is more to Monetarism than these propositions (see the papers in the 'Notes on the Literature' section, particularly DeLong, 2000). The role of expectations, 'credibility', and the question of the monetary policy institutional architecture are discussed, ideas and insights that have become standard in monetary theory since, and have profoundly influenced actual policy-making (see Chapter 7). Moreover, Monetarism became influential among practical policy-makers and politicians, notably Mrs Thatcher and her governments in Britain; hence, a political Monetarism strand may be discerned, alongside Monetarism as a purely macroeconomic doctrine, and in parallel with the political Keynesianism discussed above.

1.4.5 The 'New Classicals'

In the confusing 1970s, with disquiet about the deep foundations of the Keynesian-neoclassical synthesis and about the empirical performance of such models, and uncertain macroeconomic environment (oil price shocks, erratic policies, social strife), the mainstream gradually turns towards the New Classicals. (This is a distinct school of thought from both the 'classics' and neoclassical theory in general.) They represent a complete and radical departure from all previous schools in terms both of theory and policy propositions. First, they emphasize that agents optimize along the lines suggested by microeconomics, so any macro theory must be based on such 'deep' reasoning and logic rather than arbitrary assumptions, however plausible. Arbitrary assumptions, such as a constant marginal propensity to consume (of whatever value), may look plausible but are subject to changes when circumstances change; so the validity of such assumptions may depend on specific contexts and situations and may not be general. Behaviour must be explained by appeal to deep fundamentals such as utility or profit maximization. For instance, the modelling of consumption should be based on maximization of intertemporal utility subject to budget and borrowing constraints, uncertainty, etc.

Secondly, they contend that prices and wages are sufficiently flexible, allowing markets to clear. If so, agents (firms—individuals) are always on their demand and supply curves, meaning that they are doing the best for themselves, given the circumstances they face (productivity and wages, competition, price of raw materials, etc.). This has serious implications for the way we view important aspects of the market mechanism like business cycles or unemployment. According to the NCs, such phenomena must be viewed as the best response of the private sector to exogenous developments like productivity shocks (due to technology, training and skills, or organizational changes) and other various real shocks (due to taxation, energy and raw materials prices, or simply climate changes). In particular, unemployment is voluntary and reflects people's choice of work hours based on the market wage, which in turn depends on productivity. Practically speaking, an unemployed person is unemployed not because there was no demand for what they were doing, but because they choose not to take up any employment on offer. If the employment on offer pays little, this is unfortunate but reflects the conditions in the market at the moment (e.g. low productivity). This is a proposition that is of course highly controversial. The bottom line is that both business cycles and unemployment are surely painful, but they do reflect the best agents can do given circumstances beyond their control. This ties with their overall belief that the market mechanism is self-regulated (if the outcomes reflect the individuals' best choices, then there is little that an outside agent like the government can do). It also goes along with their beliefs about the 'efficiency' of financial markets, i.e. the belief that they can quantify and price risk accurately and handle it in mutually beneficial ways (as in insurance markets).

Finally, there is strong emphasis on 'Rational Expectations' as a theory of expectations formation. Agents utilize all available information in predicting the future; they do not predict accurately, but they make expectational errors (mistakes) that are on average zero (you neither systematically under-predict nor systematically over-predict) and show no persistent or otherwise systematic pattern at all—they are completely random and average zero. If they are not, they provide useful information to market agents. Looking at past mistakes you can learn, and by learning you are able to eliminate non-intelligent (non-random) mistakes—and all this happens instantaneously.

An intermediate result, the 'Lucas supply function', suggests that only price surprises (i.e. deviations of prices from expected values) can affect output. This provides theoretical underpinnings for the expectations-augmented Phillips Curve: Unemployment is related to unexpected inflation, not inflation itself. This 'Lucas supply function' (which is in essence an alternative form of the expectations-augmented Phillips Curve) and rational expect-ations jointly imply that the average unemployment rate is supply-side determined—and the deviations from it are random in a way that AD policy cannot fix. This result leads to the conclusion that *only unanticipated* money supply and monetary policy can have real effects; as the *unanticipated* part of monetary policy is completely random (this is a consequence of the fact that expectations are assumed rational in a specific sense), this then leads directly to policy ineffectiveness (see below). As a corollary, this line of reasoning develops an approach to business cycles originating from imperfect information.

Another key result is the 'Lucas critique'—the proposition that the moment the policy-maker attempts to exploit any empirical regularity for delivering output gains, this regularity is likely to break down. This is because, by taking action, the government interferes with the structure of the economic system. Though indirectly, this result advises against government economic action, hence it can be included among the six Policy Ineffectiveness Results reviewed in section 1.5. It also strongly suggests building economic theories on explicit 'micro-foundations' (consumer-firm optimization), as this is a robust, unalterable basis on which to build theories. In sum, the New Classicals have had a profound influence on academic macroeconomics, that is, on the way research (theoretical or empirical) is done in universities. But their influence outside this sphere is limited; they never had the ear of policy-makers in the way Monetarists did. We review their ideas in more detail in Chapter 2.

1.4.6   The New Keynesians

The New Keynesian research programme, active from the late 1970s and lasting into the 1990s, aimed at reviving some of the insights of older Keynesians, particularly on the desirability of AD-based stabilization, taking however on board the methodological innovations of the New Classicals on what constitutes sound economic theorizing. They therefore accept that the private sector is intelligent (i.e. the Rational Expectations Hypothesis) and that it optimizes, therefore the need to build models from 'deep fundamentals' according to microeconomics, rather than simply following naïve, ad-hoc assumptions of behaviour. Their key departure from New Classical premises is their belief that, because of wage/price rigidities, adjustment costs, or lack of information or coordination, markets do not always clear in the way that New Classicals would have us believe. Thus, it does not follow that agents think that their situation is the best that could be under the circumstances; the market economy is generally *not* 'Pareto optimal'. This leaves room for governmental corrective policy.

In particular, they support the scope for Aggregate Demand-based stabilization by emphasizing nominal wage or price rigidities (underpinning an upward-sloping AD). Accepting the New Classicals' logic, though, such rigidities are not merely to be assumed, but must be shown to be the best reaction of agents (firms for price rigidities, workers/firms for wage rigidities) to economic incentives they face, such as costs of revising prices, costs of information acquisition, nature of markets, etc. So, considerable effort goes into the investigation of the nature, causes, and effects of wage and price rigidities. 'Menu costs' is one such type of rigidities called 'nominal' price stickiness: they are the costs of price or wage adjustment that are constant irrespective of the amount of the actual change, such as costs of compiling and printing new price catalogues, etc. A separate category of costs is 'real' price (and wage) rigidities, due to costs of informing customers, negotiating with unions or 'efficiency wages' (for wages), etc; they are proportional to the changes. These 'real' rigidities are not directly the source of why markets do not clear but act in a subsidiary role: They exacerbate the role of 'nominal' rigidities.[16] We review all these issues in detail in Chapter 3; labour market-related real rigidities will be reviewed in Chapter 4.

---

[16] In contrast, the New Classicals emphasize wage/price flexibility and therefore do not accept nominal rigidities. The question of whether their logic is compatible with real rigidities is more moot.

At the same time, there is acceptance of the importance of the supply side, particularly for there ceased to be an active long run. Hence, monetary policy can be used for short-run stabilization, but for longer run gains in living standards, one must employ supply-side policies. Although the New Keynesians have programmes of research since about the mid-1990s, their broad conclusions are reflected in the general outlook of mainstream macro-economists today.

1.4.7 Supply-Side Economics

Over the years, the consensus has emerged that the long-run development of living standards and long-run unemployment are decided by real developments on the supply side of the economy and not by AD policies of any kind. As such, all current schools of thought would ascribe a major role to such analysis. They would emphasize ways of shifting the labour demand and supply schedules right (L^D: by enhancing productivity; reducing taxes, increasing competition in the market place or deregulation; L^S: by again reducing taxation, unemployment benefits, welfare-to-work programmes, or simply curbing union power). These are often controversial propositions; we shall review some of them in Chapter 4 on unemployment. Given the labour supply, they also argue that productivity growth would 'translate' the same labour into more output. This can be done with the adoption of better technology, fostered by research and development by firms (R&D), investment by domestic and foreign firms (FDI), improvement of education and skills of the workforce ('human capital'), other measures of improving labour productivity (better practices, etc.), and better organization. Obviously, given the controversial nature of some of these arguments and propositions, different schools of thought and different policy-makers would pursue them in different degrees and ways. A number of macroeconomists, e.g. Feldstein (2008), have articulated such policy proposals based on sound economic analysis.

The 'supply-side' school are rather extreme proponents of supply-side initiatives. They emphasize the need to reduce taxes in order to provide incentives to workers to supply more work and to firms to demand more labour. They often mention a 'Laffer curve', which suggests that, as the tax rate rises, total tax receipts initially rise but then drop as people/firms are discouraged from work or from hiring more labour. Supply-siders seem to suggest (without much hard evidence) that many economies are located on the declining part of the Laffer curve; the implication is that, if the tax rate *decreases*, *more* tax revenues will in fact be collected. Many of these ideas have a political and ideological background, coming from people who would like to see the state sector's economic role decrease. Often, their analyses are thin, to the point that some of them have been called 'airport economics' (resembling those books with silver letters on the cover). Krugman (1994) provides an amusing as well as informative and critical account of the (mainly American) supply-side school and its ramifications.

Despite these shortcomings, some supply-siders have had a serious influence on governments. One area where some of their ideas are influential is their 'flat-tax' proposals, according to which a country would benefit from a low and fixed income tax rate (which should not increase with income); as such, these proposals should be more properly called 'flat and low-tax' proposals. Some countries, particularly in Eastern Europe, have adopted them; there is as yet no clear-cut assessment of their effects. Apart from the effects on inequality, one reason why one could be sceptical towards them is that, in principle, if a country adopts a low and flat-tax rate, it may see its activity thrive as businesses may flock into it from other countries; but if all countries adopt such low rates, there will not be any influx of capital and businesses, only tax receipts will decline with disastrous effects on the public service provision.

1.5 Six 'Policy Ineffectiveness Results'

Thus, there is an ongoing academic (and public, even political) battle between those who argue that the market mechanism is self-regulated and advise against government intervention; and those who broadly argue in favour of government intervention and stabilization of the macroeconomy. The debate on whether Aggregate Demand policies can be useful for stabilization purposes may be seen as part of this wider debate. It may be fair to say that the bulk of the academic economics profession seems to support the idea that there is a role for AD policy at least for short-run stabilization purposes.

Six 'Policy Ineffectiveness Results'—four theoretical and two empirical ones—summarize the sceptical position against activist government intervention, particularly AD-based:

- The (main) 'Policy Ineffectiveness Proposition'. Articulated by the New Classical School in the early 1970s, it asserts that under some conditions AD-based stabilization is ineffective; New Keynesians and others have criticized it on the grounds that one of its key assumptions, namely wage and price flexibility, is implausible. It will be reviewed in Chapter 2.
- The 'Lucas Critique'. Articulated by Robert Lucas, a leading New Classicist, in 1976, it asserts that, when government intervenes in the economy, it fundamentally changes its structure and therefore the consequences of its actions are not the intended ones. It will also be reviewed in Chapter 2.
- 'Time inconsistency of optimal discretionary policy'. Again the intellectual child of the New Classicals, it suggests that when government uses AD policies freely (with 'discretion'), it has an incentive to settle for short-termist, populist plans and produce chronic inflation. First articulated in the late 1970s, and the subject of much debate and development in the 1980s, it had as a by-product the development of the new field of Political (Macro)Economics. It will be reviewed in Chapter 7 on monetary policy.
- The 'Ricardian Equivalence Proposition'. Originally attributed to the classical Anglo-Portuguese economist David Ricardo, and formally proposed by Robert Barro in 1974, it suggests that tax-induced changes in budget deficits are ineffective in changing real output. Its critics have attacked its many underlying assumptions as unrealistic. It will be reviewed in Chapter 8 on fiscal policy.
- It has been observed empirically, mainly by Christina Romer, that the US economy may not have been more stable in the post-World War II years than in the pre-World War II period despite big advances in economic theory and institutional arrangements. It casts a sceptical eye on the value of modern macroeconomic theory and

policy. While the subject of controversy, this proposition has forced us to re-examine the methods by which the data are constructed, and the role of policies and institutions (like the Central Bank) in stabilizing the economy. See the 'Guidance for Further Study' section in Chapter 6 on business cycle for more information.

- It has been observed by Jones (1995) that the US growth rate has been fairly stable in the last forty years despite many policy changes during that time; hence it may not be responsive to policy after all. See the 'Guidance for Further Study' section in Chapter 9 on growth.

Most academic economists do not believe fully (or often not at all) these propositions. Thus, these results are controversial and by no means conclusive. But anybody who is prepared to defend Aggregate Demand-based macroeconomic stabilization or a wider role for government policy must be able to have a response to them. The value of these propositions is that they prompt us to think harder, examine the underlying assumptions more carefully, and in general sharpen the arguments on both sides of the debate.

1.6 On the Theory of Policy-Making: Targets and Instruments; Rules

While the bulk of macroeconomics has been concerned with substantive issues (What theories and models best explain reality? Does policy work? etc.), a separate strand of literature is concerned with the properties of policy-making in a more abstract sense. It is worth visiting the basics here to gain another perspective about what policy can, or cannot, achieve; this is the subject of this section. It is useful to begin with terminology.

1.6.1 Terminology; Impulse Responses

We postulate that workings of the macroeconomy are summarized by a generic system of equations:

$$
\underset{[nxn]}{B_0}\ \underset{[nx1]}{Y_t} = \underset{[nxk]}{B_1}\ \underset{[nx1]}{Y_{t-1}} + \underset{[nxn]}{B_2}\ \underset{[nx1]}{Y_{t-2}} + \ldots + \underset{[nxn]}{B_m}\ \underset{[nx1]}{Y_{t-m}} +
$$
$$
+ \underset{[nxk]}{C_0}\ \underset{[kx1]}{X_t} + \underset{[nxk]}{C_1}\ \underset{[kx1]}{X_{t-1}} + \ldots + \underset{[nxk]}{C_p}\ \underset{[kx1]}{X_{t-p}} + \underset{[nx1]}{U_t} \tag{1.21}
$$

In a nutshell, an economy's n endogenous variables (the Ys) are determined jointly in an interdependent system of n equations. Among the n equations, structural (or 'behavioural') equations may include consumption and investment functions, money demand, output supply, etc. Some of the n equations may be policy functions like a 'Taylor rule' for monetary policy, a rule by which government sets its budget deficit, etc. Some others may be identities, i.e. they provide definitions of variables, or equilibrium conditions like the National Income Accounting equation $Y = C + I + G$, etc. The Ys are the endogenous variables and include output, unemployment, consumption, investment, interest rates, price level/inflation..., the list goes on. The explanatory variables on the RHS include m lags of the endogenous variables. Such lags capture dynamics and are important in various contexts like growth theory, business cycles, and others. The RHS also includes k exogenous variables, Xs. Such variables may be the purely exogenous policy instruments (those that are not hypothesized to depend on the state of the economy—those that do so are 'endogenized' via the 'Taylor rule' or budget deficit rule) and other exogenous variables like foreign output and oil/raw materials prices. We also have p lags of the Xs on the RHS. Finally, we have n error terms (the Us). (Identities and equilibrium conditions do not include error terms.) Note the obvious, the above equation is a matrix one: the coefficients $B_0, B_1 \ldots, B_m, C_0 \ldots, C_p$ are conformable matrices, in which some of the entries may be 0. The dimensions of the matrices are indicated below them.

A notable omission from (1.21) is the currently expected value of future variables, e.g. $E_t Y_{t+1}, E_t Y_{t+2}, \ldots, E_t X_{t+1}, E_t X_{t+2}, \ldots$ These enter because expectations of the future (incomes, prices, costs, world trade, etc., etc.) profoundly affect current behaviour. For this reason, the models of expectations and their development occupy a prominent place in macroeconomic theory; they will be reviewed in Chapter 2, as will be the solutions of equations like (1.21) when expectations are incorporated. See also Chapter 5 for more on dynamical systems and Chapter 6 on the econometric formulation of systems like (1.22) (the 'Structural Vector AutoRegressions', SVARs).

The equilibrium values of Ys, given current and past Xs and also the history of Y (i.e. past Ys), are given by inverting B_0:

$$
\begin{aligned}
\underset{[n\times1]}{Y_t} = \underset{[n\times n]}{B_0^{-1}} \Big(&\underset{[n\times k]}{B_1} \underset{[n\times1]}{Y_{t-1}} + \underset{[n\times n]}{B_2} \underset{[n\times1]}{Y_{t-2}} + \ldots + \underset{[n\times n]}{B_m} \underset{[n\times1]}{Y_{t-m}} + \underset{[n\times k]}{C_0} \underset{[k\times1]}{X_t} \\
&+ \underset{[n\times k]}{C_1} \underset{[k\times1]}{X_{t-1}} + \ldots + \underset{[n\times k]}{C_p} \underset{[k\times1]}{X_{t-p}} + \underset{[n\times1]}{U_t} \Big)
\end{aligned}
\tag{1.22}
$$

Equation (1.22) is the 'reduced form' of (1.21). To see what this equation implies, let us make some simplifications for argument's sake:

- Assume first that all of Y_t, X_t, and U_t are unidimensional [1x1];
- There are no lags of X involved, all the dynamics is captured by the lags of Y;
- The dynamic structure is given by a simple, first-order Autoregressive structure (AR1).

Thus, (1.22) simplifies to:

$$
Y_t = BY_{t-1} + CX_t + V_t
$$
$$
0 < B < 1
\tag{1.23}
$$

Two questions may be asked of (1.23):

- What are the effects on Y_t now and in the future of a one-off rise in the exogenous variable X_t; because this is one-off, it is often considered as a shock at time t, so it is captured by V_t, which rises. By the 'recursive substitution' method to be considered in Chapter 2, we can calculate the following:

$$
\frac{\partial Y_t}{\partial V_t} = 1, \quad \frac{\partial Y_{t+1}}{\partial V_t} = B, \quad \frac{\partial Y_{t+2}}{\partial V_t} = B^2, \quad \ldots, \quad \frac{\partial Y_{t+p}}{\partial V_t} = B^p
$$

These dynamic multipliers are called 'Impulse Response Functions' (IRF). We observe that they show 'persistence', i.e. the effect of a one-off shock now lasts for some time; it shows gradual decay, starting from 1 (the contemporaneous effect, which is the strongest) and asymptotically $(p \to \infty)$ die away $(B^p \to 0)$.

- We may also consider the effects of a permanent rise in X from t onwards. This can be thought of as a series of equal shocks on $X_t, X_{t+1}, \ldots, X_{t+m}, \ldots$ The difference from the previous IRF is that a Y_{t+1} (for instance) will be affected by both the contemporaneous shock (X_{t+1}) but also from the effect of a changed Y_t:

$$\frac{dY_{t+1}}{dX_t}\bigg|_{permanent} = \frac{\partial Y_{t+1}}{\partial X_{t+1}} + \frac{\partial Y_{t+1}}{\partial Y_t}\frac{\partial Y_t}{\partial X_t} = C + CB$$

Continuing the same logic, we get:

$$\frac{dY_{t+2}}{dX_t}\bigg|_{permanent} = C + CB + CB^2, \quad \frac{dY_{t+p}}{dX_t}\bigg|_{permanent} = C + CB + CB^2 + \ldots + CB^p$$

In the limit, we have:

$$\lim_{p\to\infty}\frac{dY_{t+p}}{dX_t}\bigg|_{permanent} = C + CB + CB^2 + \ldots = C\frac{1}{1-B}$$

In other words, in this case the IRF becomes the familiar steady-state multiplier. To gain intuition, note that it corresponds to the derivate dY/dX of the simple static equation $AY = CX$, where $A = 1 - B$.

The IRFs corresponding to the fuller system (1.22) with its higher dimensions and complex dynamics follow the same logic, but the resulting expressions will be more cumbersome. A good introduction to the relevant methods is found in Hamilton (1994). In practice, the solutions to the IRFs are quite computer-based and routinely given by most econometric software packages.

1.6.2 The Relation between Targets and Instruments; the Tinbergen Theorem

The first result to be obtained here is the 'Tinbergen targets-instruments theorem', after the Dutch economist (and Nobel prize recipient) Jan Tinbergen. Use for simplicity the static version of equation (1.21), $AY = DX$, where $A \equiv [B_0 - B_1 - B_2 - \ldots - B_m]$, $D \equiv [C_0 + C_1 + C_2 + \ldots + C_p]$ and let error terms disappear $(V = 0)$; let there be more than one variable of each type, $n, k > 1$; let also all Xs denote 'independent' policy instruments (variables that the policy-maker can directly and fully control like the money supply or interest rates, government spending, etc.). The endogenous variables take equilibrium values by the 'reduced form equations'; in the simple case considered here:

$$\underset{[nx1]}{Y} = \underset{[nxn]}{A^{-1}} \underset{[nxk]}{D} \underset{[kx1]}{X} \tag{1.24}$$

This is telling us simply how the endogenous variables are determined by the use of policy instruments. Let also the policy-maker care about achieving specific values for the Ys: full employment, specific values for output growth and inflation rates, a balance of payments target, etc. Such values for the endogenous variables are called 'targets'—let them be indicated by Y*. In order for the Ys to attain their target values Y*, the policy instruments need to take appropriate values (X*). Those may be found by effectively standing the equation on its head, and inverting to write:

$$\underset{[kx1]}{X^*} = \underset{[nxk]}{D^{-1}}\ \underset{[nxn]}{A}\ \underset{[nx1]}{Y^*} \tag{1.24'}$$

It is useful to remind ourselves that the matrix D gives the effect of the Xs on the Ys; it is essentially the steady-state version of the C matrix we saw above. Now, the inversion of D causes a problem. We can distinguish between three cases:

- k < n: Fewer policy instruments than targets. In this case D cannot be inverted, and the targets Y* cannot all be attained.
- k = n, equal number of targets and instruments. In this case, the Y*s can all be attained exactly, and the appropriate instrument values X* are uniquely specified.
- Finally, consider the case of more instruments than targets, k > n. Technically, D cannot be inverted, but economically there is no problem: There is more than one combination of Xs that delivers exactly the same combination of targets Y*. In jargon, the policy-maker has some 'degrees of freedom' in setting their instruments.

We may summarize by the following:

> Tinbergen targets-instruments theorem: To attain n targets fully, the policy-maker needs to have at least as many independent instruments as policy targets (see Klein, 2004).

Consider the examples furnished by the closed and open-economy IS-LM and AD-AS models. Imagine that government sets its spending, taxes, and interest rate (i.e. it has three instruments). To start with, if there is only one target, say output, it can be comfortably met (with a spare two degrees of freedom). However, if the government wants to maintain budget balance as well, this eliminates one degree of freedom (because an extra target is added). Furthermore, if the price level/inflation is also targeted, then that eliminates all degrees of freedom. The government can achieve the output, inflation, and budgetary targets exactly; this uniquely determines the appropriate levels for the instruments. Imagine however that the government also wants to maintain a fixed exchange rate—another target. In order not to destabilize foreign exchange markets, the interest rate needs to be set at an appropriate level. This is effectively an extra target, violating the conditions of the Tinbergen theorem: there are now four targets with only three instruments.

1.6.3 Policy Optimization; Feedback Rules; Assignment Rules

The problem just highlighted is not hypothetical, it is in fact a common real-world situation. Typically, governments have too few instruments for their targets; the targets cannot all be attained. In this case, some hard dilemmas emerge. (The world is an interesting place!) Which targets will be sacrificed? Or, will all be partly satisfied and partly sacrificed? It depends on the government's preferences. Formally, government will have a utility function penalizing deviations from targets, which works like the individual's utility function, with the structure of the economy acting given by (1.21) as a constraint, much like the individual's budget constraint. As an example, consider that the system (1.21) is made up of only one relation, the traditional downward-sloping Phillips Curve (1.20). It may be thought of as a constraint on government, a trade-off between the two 'bads' of inflation and unemployment. Government is assumed to aim for targets of inflation, presumably 0, and unemployment, u^*. Both cannot both be fully satisfied because there is only one instrument ('the' AD policy). To determine a preferred combination, government will be guided by its utility function which may take the form:[17]

$$U_G = -\alpha\pi^2 - \beta(u - u^*)^2 \tag{1.25}$$

This weighs by $\alpha > 0$ the aversion to inflation and by $\beta > 0$ the aversion to unemployment. Thus, the preferred and achievable combination will be given by the tangency of the Phillips Curve with its indifference curve between the two 'bads'. Such an optimization by government will be considered in Chapter 7 on monetary policy. Note that for reasons that will be explained there, the target unemployment rate may be lower than the natural rate, $u^* < u_N$.

Such a generic formulation of the government's optimization problem (maximize utility such as 1.26—alternatively, minimize loss—subject to the structure of the economy as encapsulated in generic form in equation 1.22) is called 'optimal control'. It results in optimal policy rules that set the instruments at appropriate levels; they give the optimal value of each instrument given the preferences of the policy-makers and the state and history of the economy. Such rules are called 'feedback rules', because the current state of the economy and its history 'feed back' into the optimal instruments. Such rules are in general quite complex. Hence, some researchers are looking for 'simple (feedback) rules' i.e. a subset of feedback rules which, though not fully optimal, will have the great benefit of being simple, intuitive, and widely understood. It is fair to say, though, that no consensus has emerged yet in this quest. The interested reader may consult Currie and Levine (1985) and the follow-up literature, e.g. Benigno and Woodford (2004), for a more technical treatment. More discussion of these issues with a special focus on monetary policy and the 'Taylor rule' will be presented in Chapter 7.

In real-world situations like the one discussed in the context of the open-economy AD-AS model, government may use 'assignment rules'. Intuitively, but quite arbitrarily from a theory point of view, they may assign a specific instrument to the exclusive task of achieving a specific target. Such an assignment rule of some prominence is the so-called 'Mundell' rule whereby fiscal policy is assigned to domestic targets (output and/or inflation) and monetary policy is assigned the target of maintaining the required exchange rate parity. This was used explicitly some time ago, but it sheds light on modern-world situations, too: monetary policy needs to be devoted to the external target if fixed exchange rates are to be maintained. With increasing international capital mobility resulting from

---

[17] This objective is sometimes stated equivalently as 'minimize the loss function': $L_G = \alpha\pi^2 + \beta(u - u^*)^2$

globalization, the maintenance of a stable exchange rate becomes more pressing; monetary policy is progressively losing any ability to take care of any domestic considerations. In the limit, currency union (i.e. the absolute fixity of the exchange rate) means the complete abandonment of monetary policy by individual countries and its transfer to a Central Bank—e.g. the European Central Bank in the case of European Monetary Union. Thus, the policy architecture in a currency union such as EMU is at heart an extreme application of the Mundell assignment rule. Another real-world assignment rule is effectively implied by inflation targeting, to be considered in Chapter 7: monetary policy is exclusively assigned the task of keeping inflation low. This leaves output/unemployment targets to be cared for by fiscal policy alone.

1.6.4 Intermediate Targets and Indicators

Apart from targets and instruments, we may distinguish a third category of variables, the 'intermediate targets' (or the similar designations of 'indicators', or 'informational variables'). Such variables are not targets themselves, but they are used in an auxiliary way to guide policy (setting of the instruments), if they are thought to be closely connected with the targets and if they are available swiftly, before the targets themselves are revealed. An example here would be the use of money as an indicator for interest rate setting. For example, the European Central Bank has as its main target low inflation and price stability, yet it also pays attention to money supply (a secondary or intermediate 'target') because such data are readily available and closely connected with inflation. The 'leading indicators' of the business cycle, variables that give us advance warning of recessions (see Chapter 6), may also be thought of as a type of informational variable. The 'forward guidance' that Central Banks provide these days (to be discussed in Chapter 7) similarly make use of indicators and other informational variables.

1.7 Looking Ahead: The Structure of the Book

Our discussion of the main building blocks of the AD-AS model gives us a good idea of what lies ahead. Chapters 2 and 3 examine the basic tenets of the two main macroeconomic schools of thought, in modern times, namely the New Classicals and the New Keynesians. We then move on to issues. Inflation and the modern foundations of the Phillips Curve provided by New Keynesians are also in Chapter 3. Unemployment is considered in Chapter 4, with emphasis on its long-term determinants, supply-side considerations, and labour market institutions. In Chapter 5, we introduce the basic models of dynamic macroeconomics: intertemporal optimization, the Ramsey model, the overlapping-generations model, and their policy prescriptions. In Chapter 6, we turn to short-term considerations while discussing business cycles. Debates on monetary policy are reviewed in Chapter 7, while fiscal policy is in Chapter 8. In Chapter 9 on growth, we return once again to long-term considerations and supply-side issues. Chapter 10 introduces a topic that traditionally was not thought to belong to the macro curriculum, but its recent rising tendency makes inequality one of the most pressing public policy issues. Finally,

Chapter 11 sheds more light on (what used to be called) sectoral analyses, considering the modern theory (or -ies) of consumption, saving, and investment; again, policy implications are highlighted.

Notes on the Literature

A number of articles exist that provide partial summaries of the progress of macroeconomics since the times of Keynes and a review of the modern state of play; among them, Mankiw (1990, 2006), Blanchard (2000, the most technical of all), Greenwald and Stiglitz (1988), and Woodford (2000). Blinder (1997) gives a useful summary of the core beliefs of most academic contemporary macro-economists. Snowdon and Vane (2005) presents a panorama of the history of macroeconomics, parallel but more extensive to the one given here. The May 1997 issue of the *American Economic Review* is dedicated to the question 'Is there a core of practical macroeconomics that we should all believe in?', with contributions by Solow, Taylor, Eichenbaum, Blinder, and Blanchard. Romer and Romer (2002) relate the evolution of ideas to developments on the policy front. Blanchard (2009) provides a review of the 'state of macro', which is interesting as it came soon after the 2007–9 financial crisis; he passes a positive verdict overall, saying 'the state of macro is good'. Against that, Stiglitz (2015) comes to the assessment that 'macro needs to be reconstructed' in order for it to be more fruitful for policy. To review the vintage debates on stabilization policy, one can visit Friedman (1968, 1977) and Modigliani (1977). Tobin (1993) is good summary of the 'old' (first post-war generation) Keynesian school. For an overview and assessment of Monetarism, see Johnson (1971), Laidler (1981), and DeLong (2000), the latter emphasizing its lasting legacy on the institutional architecture of monetary policy. Sleeman (2011) is on the history of the Phillips Curve. More references on the New Classicals and New Keynesians will be given in Chapters 2 and 3.

Guidance for Further Study

On the NAIRU

As mentioned in sub-section 1.3.4), Mankiw and Ball (2002) estimate that in the US the NAIRU was 5.4% in 1960, peaking at 6.8% in 1979, falling to 4.9% in 2000. They consider three possibly relevant factors.

(a) Demographics: After World War II, fertility in the US rose briefly, then subsided, producing what is called 'the baby-boom generation' (those born roughly between 1945 and 1955). Can this fact provide an explanation for the NAIRU pattern highlighted?

(b) Rates of imprisonment and welfare support for disability. During the late 1990s, rates of imprisonment increased and support for disability became in general more generous. How can these factors provide an explanation for falling unemployment? Is this effect quantitatively significant?

(c) The (so-called) New Economy (globalization, the internet, flexible work, etc). What is the possible effect of these developments on NAIRU according to the article? What is your own view?

The quest for the Phillips Curve continues

The Economist published an article on 1 November 2017 which showed data on the PC: https://www.economist.com/blogs/graphicdetail/2017/11/daily-chart?fsrc=scn/li/te/bl/ed. What conclusions do you draw from this? How has the PC evolved over the years according to this graph? Has the relationship disappeared recently as the legend in the graph claims?

Determinants of the 'labour wedge'

Equation (1.8') or (1.8") stipulates an equality between the marginal rate of substitution between labour and consumption (MRS) and the real wage (w), $-\frac{U_L}{U_C} = \frac{W}{P}$. In fact, this is a simplification, for two reasons. First, households will equate their MRS with the after-tax real wage, $-\frac{U_L}{U_C} = (1-t)\frac{W}{P}$, where t is the income tax rate (abstracting from other forms of taxation); secondly, firms will equate the marginal product of labour (MPL) with the real wage, MPL = W/P. So, overall, we must have: $-\frac{U_L}{U_C} = (1-t)MPL$. The 'labour wedge' is the discrepancy MPL-MRS in the real data. The (notional) equality $-\frac{U_L}{U_C} = (1-t)\frac{W}{P} = (1-t)MPL$ helps us to pin down the sources of the discrepancy. If the left equality fails, it is because of monopoly power on behalf of households; if the right equality fails, it is monopoly power by firms; and finally, we have the effects of taxes. Review Karabarbounis (2014) and Shimer (2009): what do these studies find to be the main sources of the labour wedge?

A new macroeconomic data architecture

GDP (and similar statistics) provide very useful information on economic activity. Yet, their limitations are also serious: they do not record non-market activity such as home production, or record imperfectly others, such as government and charitable services; they do not record the quality of goods (cars or computers today are not the same as those thirty years ago, yet this is not reflected in the statistics); they do not account for the quality of the environment, or indeed for the general quality of life, social welfare, or a sense of happiness and well-being by individuals. Recently, efforts have been made and proposals put forward to rectify these deficiencies of the data. For example, a 'Commission on the Measurement of Economic Performance and Social Progress' (a Committee headed by Nobel Laureates Amartya Sen and Joseph Stiglitz) was established to address these issues (see Stiglitz, 2009); the Committee reported its findings and made its recommendations in September 2009. Proposals have also been made to incorporate measures of environmental sustainability and social welfare in the UN National Accounts in the volume edited by Jorgenson et al. (2014). Get hold of the Committee report and this volume and discuss more concretely the proposals they make for extending the measures of economic activity to account for (a) economic sustainability, (b) social welfare.

Blogs: DeLong, Krugman, Wren-Lewis

The internet is full of information, a lot of it useful and a lot of it junk. Among the most useful resources may be the blogs of knowledgeable people such as the three top macroeconomists mentioned in the heading (among many others of course). The usefulness of their blogs lies in the fact that they are to the point (often more policy-relevant than elaborate economic analyses), concise, and timely (they do not need to go through the usual journal publications cycle which often takes years). And they are good! As samples, you are invited to read:

- Brad DeLong's 'Lunchtime Must-Read: Roger Farmer: NAIRU Theory—Closer to Religion than Science' (http://equitablegrowth.org/2014/10/06/lunchtime-must-read-roger-farmer-nairu-theory-closer-religion-science/);
- Paul Krugman's 'What I Mean When I Talk About IS-LM (Wonkish)' (http://krugman.blogs.nytimes.com/2014/03/28/what-i-mean-when-i-talk-about-is-lm-wonkish/)
- Simon Wren-Lewis's 'Speaking as an Old New Keynesian . . .' (http://mainlymacro.blogspot.co.uk/2014/02/speaking-as-old-new-keynesian.html);

These posts tackle material that is closely related to what we have been discussing in this chapter. How does this material compare with what you have been learning here? Is there anything that you feel you need to revise after reading these posts?

More blogs: on appropriate models for policy advice

What is the appropriate structure of a policy-relevant macro model—how much detail should it have? Should it be rigorously microfounded, as 'highbrow' theorists would maintain? Should one work within well-defined intellectual paradigms (like 'mainstream' or 'heterodox' macroeconomics) or fish for insights from any source such insights can be obtained ('eclectic')? Read the following three posts and make up your own mind:

- Paul Krugman's 'The Excluded Middlebrow (Wonkish)' (http://krugman.blogs.nytimes.com/2014/02/09/the-excluded-middlebrow-wonkish/?_php=true&_type=blogs&_r=0);
- Simon Wren-Lewis's 'What Place do Applied Middlebrow Models have?' (http://mainlymacro.blogspot.gr/2014/03/what-place-do-applied-middlebrow-models.html?utm_source=feedburner&utm_medium=feed&utm_campaign=Feed:+MainlyMacro+(mainly+macro);
- Dani Rodrik's 'What is Wrong (and Right) in Economics?' (http://rodrik.typepad.com/dani_rodriks_weblog/2013/05/what-is-wrong-and-right-in-economics.html).

Blogs III—on the causes of recent malaise

Is it demand or supply that is lacking for the sluggish growth or stagnation that we have been experiencing in recent years according to Summers? Or is it supply that is the problem, as Blanchard suggests? Or maybe simply the lack of investment, as Sachs argues? Where do you stand on this debate?

- Laurence Summers on why the economy is broken—and how to fix it, interview given in January 2014; http://larrysummers.com/2014/01/14/summers-on-why-the-economy-is-broken-and-how-to-fix-it/
- Olivier Blanchard: 'As Demand Improves, Time to Focus More on Supply', iMFdirect, http://blog-imfdirect.imf.org/2014/04/08/as-demand-improves-time-to-focus-more-on-supply/
- Jeffrey Sachs: 'A New Macroeconomic Strategy, Project Syndicate', http://www.project-syndicate.org/commentary/declining-investment-in-rich-countries-by-jeffrey-d-sachs-2014-10

References

Akerlof, G.A. (2002): Behavioral Macroeconomics and Macroeconomic Behavior, *American Economic Review*, 92(3), 411–33.

Akerlof, G.A., W.T. Dickens, and G.L. Perry (1996): The Macroeconomics of Low Inflation, *Brookings Papers on Economic Activity*, 27(1), 1–76.

Akerlof, G.A., W.T. Dickens, and G.L. Perry (2000): Near-Rational Wage and Price Setting and the Long-Run Phillips Curve, *Brookings Papers on Economic Activity*, 31(1), 1–60.

Antras, P. (2004): Is the U.S. Aggregate Production Function Cobb-Douglas? New Estimates of the Elasticity of Substitution, *B.E. Journal of Macroeconomics*, 4 (1) (April), 1–36.

Arrow, K.J., H.B. Chenery, B.S. Minhas, and R.M. Solow (1961): Capital-Labor Substitution and Economic Efficiency, *Review of Economics and Statistics*, 43(3), 225–50.

Backhouse, R.E. (2002): *The Penguin History of Economics*, London: Penguin.

Ball, L. (1997): Disinflation and the NAIRU, in C.D. Romer and D.H. Romer (eds), *Reducing Inflation: Motivation and Strategy*, Cambridge, MA: NBER Books, 167–94.

Ball, L., and N.G. Mankiw (2002): The NAIRU in Theory and Practice, *Journal of Economic Perspectives*, 16(4) (Fall), 115–36.

Barnes, S., S. Price, and M. Sebastia-Barriel (2006): The Elasticity of Substitution: Evidence from a UK Firm-Level Data Set, Bank of England, mimeo.

Benigno, P., and M. Woodford (2004): Optimal Monetary and Fiscal Policy: A Linear-Quadratic Approach, *NBER Macroeconomics Annual*, 2003(18), 271–364.

Blanchard, O.J. (1986): The Wage Price Spiral, *Quarterly Journal of Economics*, 101(406) (August), 545–65.

Blanchard, O.J. (2000): What do we Know about Macroeconomics that Fisher and Wicksell Did Not?, *Quarterly Journal of Economics*, 115(4) (November), 1375–1409.

Blanchard, O.J. (2009): The State of Macro, *Annual Review of Economics*, 1(1), 209–28.

Blinder, A.S. (1997): Is there a Core of Practical Macroeconomics that we Should All Believe?, *American Economic Review Papers and Proceedings*, 87(2) (May), 240–3.

Blundell, R., A. Bozio, and G. Laroque (2011): Labor Supply and the Extensive Margin, *American Economic Review*, 101(3), 482–6.

Blundell, R., A. Bozio, and G. Laroque (2013): Extensive and Intensive Margins of Labour Supply: Working Hours in the US, UK and France, *Fiscal Studies*, 34(1) (March), 1–29.

Burmeister, E., and A.R. Dobell (1970): *Mathematical Theories of Economic Growth*, London: Collier Macmillan.

Case, K.E., J.M. Quigley, and R.J. Shiller (2005): Comparing Wealth Effects: The Stock Market versus the Housing Market, *B.E. Journal of Macroeconomics*, 5(1), 1–34.

Chetty, R., A. Guren, D. Manoli, and A. Weber (2011): Are Micro and Macro Labor Elasticities Consistent? A Review of Evidence on the Intensive and Extensive Margins, *American Economic Review Papers and Proceedings*, 101(2), 471–5.

Chirinko, R.S. (1993): Business Fixed Investment Spending: Modeling Strategies, Empirical Results, and Policy Implications, *Journal of Economic Literature*, 31(4), 1875–1911.

Chirinko, R.S. (2008). σ: The Long and Short of it, *Journal of Macroeconomics*, 30(2), 671–86.

Chirinko R.S., S.M. Fazzari, and A.P. Meyer (2004): That Elusive Elasticity: A Long-Panel Approach to Estimating the Capital-Labor Substitution Elasticity, CesIfo WP No. 1240, July.

Christiano, L.J., M. Trabandt, and K. Walentin (2010): Involuntary Unemployment and the Business Cycle, NBER Working Papers No. 15801.

Cobham, D. (2002): *The Making of Monetary Policy in the UK, 1975–2000*, Chichester: Wiley.

Cuaresma, J. Crespo (2003): Okun's Law Revisited, Oxford Bulletin of Economics and Statistics, 65(4) (September), 439–51.

Currie, D., and P. Levine (1985): Macroeconomic Policy Design in an Interdependent World, in W.H. Buiter and R.C. Marston (eds), *International Economic Policy Coordination*, Cambridge, MA: Cambridge University Press for NBER, 228–73.

DeLong J.B. (2000): The Triumph of Monetarism? *Journal of Economic Perspectives*, 14(1) (Winter), 83–94.

Duffy, J., and C. Papageorgiou (2000): A Cross-Country Empirical Investigation of the Aggregate Production Function Specification, *Journal of Economic Growth*, 5, 87–120.

Eisner, R. (1997): A New View of the NAIRU, in P. Davidson and J. Kregel (eds), *Improving the Global Economy: Keynesianism and the Growth in Output and Employment*, Brookfield, VT: Edward Elgar Publishers.

Erosa, A., L. Fuster, and G. Kambourov (2016): Towards a Micro-Founded Theory of Aggregate Labor Supply, *Review of Economics and Statistics*, 83(3), 1001–39.

Fair, R.C. (2000): Testing the NAIRU Model for the United States, *Review of Economics and Statistics*, 82(1) (February), 64–71.

Feldstein, M. (2008): Effects of Taxes on Economic Behavior, *The National Tax Journal*, 61(1) (March), 131–9.

Fernández-Villaverde, J. (2008): Horizons of Understanding: A Review of Ray Fair's Estimating How the Macroeconomy Works, *Journal of Economic Literature*, 46(3) (September), 685–703.

Fiorito, R., and G. Zanella (2012): The Anatomy of the Aggregate Labor Supply Elasticity, *Review of Economic Dynamics*, 15(2) (April), 171–87.

Freeman, D. (2001): Panel Tests of Okun's Law for Ten Industrial Countries, *Economic Inquiry*, 39(4) (October), 511–23.

Friedman, M. (1956): *A Theory of the Consumption Function*, Princeton: Princeton University Press.

Friedman, M. (1963): *Inflation Causes and Consequences*, Bombay and New York: Asia Publishing House.

Friedman, M. (1968): On the Role of Monetary Policy, *American Economic Review*, 58(1) (March), 1–17.

Friedman, M. (1977): Inflation and Unemployment: Nobel Lecture, *Journal of Political Economy*, 85, 451–72.

Galbraith, J.K. (1997): Time to Ditch the NAIRU, *Journal of Economic Perspectives*, 11(1) (Winter), 93–108.

Gombrich, E. (1989): *The Story of Art* (15th ed.), London: Phaidon.

Gordon, R.J. (1997): The Time-Varying NAIRU and its Implications for Economic Policy, *Journal of Economic Perspectives*, 11(1) (Winter), 11–32.

Gordon, R.J. (2010): Okun's Law and Productivity Innovations, *American Economic Review Papers and Proceedings*, 100 (May), 11–15.

Gordon, R.J. (2013): The Phillips Curve is Alive and Well: Inflation and the NAIRU During the Slow Recovery, NBER WP No. 19390.

Greenwald, B. and J. Stiglitz (1988): Examining Alternative Macroeconomic Theories, *Brooking Papers on Economic Activity*, 1988(1), 207–70.

Hamilton, J.D. (1994): *Time Series Analysis*, Princeton: Princeton UP.

Hansen, A.H. (1949): Monetary Theory and Fiscal Policy, New York: McGraw-Hill Book.

Hawking, S. (1989): *A Brief History of Time*, London: Bantam Books.

Hicks, J. (1937): Mr Keynes and the Classics: A Suggested Interpretation, *Econometrica*, 5(2), 147–59.

Johnson, H.G. (1971): The Keynesian Revolution and the Monetarist Counter-Revolution, *American Economic Review*, 61(2), 91–106.

Jones, C (1995): Time Series Tests of Endogenous Growth Models, *Quarterly Journal of Economics*, 110 (May), 495–525.

Jorgenson, D. (1963): Capital Theory and Investment Behavior, *American Economic Review*, 53(2), 247–59.

Jorgenson, D.W., J.S. Landefeld, and P. Schreyer (eds) (2014): *Measuring Economic Sustainability and Progress*, Boston: NBER.

Karabarbounis, L. (2014): The Labor Wedge: MRS vs. MPN, *Review of Economic Dynamics*, 17, 206–23.

Karabarbounis, L., and B. Neiman (2014): The Global Decline of the Labor Share, *Quarterly Journal of Economics*, 129(1) (February), 61–103.

Karanassou, M., H. Sala, and D.J. Snower (2003): The European Phillips Curve: Does the NAIRU Exist?, IZA (Institute for the Study of Labor) DP No. 876, Bonn.

Keynes, J.M. (1973): *The General Theory of Employment, Interest and Money* (1st publ. 1936), London: Macmillan.

Kimball, M.S., and M.D. Shapiro (2008): Labor Supply: Are the Income and Substitution Effects Both Large or Both Small?, NBER Working Papers No. 14208.

King, R.G., and S.T. Rebelo (1999): Resuscitating Real Business Cycles, in J. B. Taylor and M. Woodford (eds), *Handbook of Macroeconomics*, i. 927–1007, Amsterdam: Elsevier.

King, R.G., C.I. Plosser, and S.T. Rebelo (1988): Production, Growth, and Business Cycles: I. The Basic Neoclassical Model, *Journal of Monetary Economics*, 21(2–3), 195–232.

Klein, L. (2004): The Contribution of Jan Tinbergen to Economic Science, *De Economist*, 152(2), 155.

Klump, R. and H. Preissler (2000): CES Production Functions and Economic Growth, *Scandinavian Journal of Economics*, 102 (March), 41–56.

Klump, R., P. McAdam, and A. Willman (2012): The Normalized CES Production Function: Theory and Empirics, *Journal of Economic Surveys*, 26(5), 769–99.

Krugman, P. (1994): *Peddling Prosperity*, New Yor: W.W. Norton.

Laidler, D. (1981): Monetarism: An Interpretation and an Assessment, *Economic Journal*, 91 (March), 1–21.

Lee, J. (2000): The Robustness of Okun's Law: Evidence from OECD Countries, *Journal of Macroeconomics*, 22(2), 331–56.

Leon-Ledesma, M., P. McAdam, and A. Willman (2010): Identifying the Elasticity of Substitution with Biased Technical Change, *American Economic Review*, 100(4) (September), 1330–57.

Lipsey, R.G. (1960): The Relation between Unemployment and the Rate of Change in Money Wages in the United Kingdom, 1862–1957: A Further Analysis, *Economica*, 27(105), 1–31.

Mankiw, N. (1990): A Quick Refresher Course in Macroeconomics, *Journal of Economic Literature*, 28(4) (December), 1645–60.

Mankiw, N.G. (2006): The Macroeconomist as Scientist and Engineer, *Journal of Economic Perspectives*, 20(4), 29–46.

Mankiw, N.G., and L. Ball (2002): The NAIRU in Theory and Practice, *Journal of Economic Perspectives*, 16 (Fall), 115–36.

Mann, M. (2013): *The Sources of Social Power*, iv. *Globalizations, 1945–2011*, New York: Cambridge University Press.

Modigliani, F. (1966): The Life-Cycle Hypothesis of Saving, the Demand for Wealth and the Supply of Capital, *Social Research*, 33, 160–217.

Modigliani, F. (1977): The Monetarist Controversy or, Should we Forsake Stabilisation Policies? *American Economic Review*, 67(1) (March), 1–19.

Ohanian, L.E. and A. Raffo (2012): Aggregate Hours Worked in OECD Countries: New Measurement and Implications for Business Cycles, *Journal of Monetary Economics*, 59(1), 40–56.

Okun, A.M. (1965): The Gap between Actual and Potential Output, in E.S. Phelps (ed.), *Problems of the Modern Economy*, , New York: Norton, 287–96.

Phelps, E.S. (1968): Money-Wage Dynamics and Labor Market Equilibrium, *Journal of Political Economy*, 76(S4), 678–711.

Phillips, A. W. (1958): The Relationship between Unemployment and the Rate of Change of Money Wages in the United Kingdom 1861–1957, *Economica*, 25(100), 283–99.

Prachowny, M.F.J. (1993): Okun's Law: Theoretical Foundations and Revised Estimates, *Review of Economics and Statistics*, 75(2) (May), 331–6.

Poterba, J. (2000): Stock Market Wealth and Consumption, *Journal of Economic Perspectives*, 14(2) (Spring), 99–118.

Prescott, E.C. (2004): Why do Americans Work So Much More than Europeans? *Federal Reserve Bank of Minneapolis Quarterly Review*, 28(1), 2–13.

Rogerson, R., and M. Keane (2012): Micro and Macro Labor Supply Elasticities: A Reassessment of Conventional Wisdom, *Journal of Economic Literature*, 50(2) (June), 464–76.

Romer, D. (2000): Keynesian Macroeconomics without the LM Curve, *Journal of Economic Perspectives*, 14(2) (Spring), 149–69.

Romer, C., and D. Romer (2002): The Evolution of Economic Understanding and Postwar Stabilization Policy, *Proceedings*, Kansas City: Federal Reserve Bank of Kansas City, 11–78.

Samuelson, P.A. (1962): Parable and Realism in Capital Theory: The Surrogate Production Function, *Review of Economic Studies*, 29(3) (June), 193–206.

Samuelson, P.A., and R.M. Solow (1960): Analytical Aspects of Anti-Inflation Policy, *American Economic Review Papers and Proceedings*, 50(2), 177–94.

Shimer, R. (2009): Convergence in Macroeconomics: The Labor Wedge, *American Economic Journal: Macroeconomics*, 1(1), 280–97.

Sleeman, G. (2011): The Phillips Curve: A Rushed Job? *Journal of Economic Perspectives*, 25(1) (Winter), 223–38.

Snowdon, B., and H. Vane (2005): *Modern Macroeconomics*, Cheltenham: Edward Elgar.

Solow, R.M., J.B. Taylor, with B.M. Friedman (1998): *Inflation, Unemployment, and Monetary Policy*, Proceedings of the 1995 Alvin Hansen Symposium at Harvard University (Solow and Taylor contributors with Friedman editor), Cambridge, MA: MIT Press.

Staiger, D., J.H. Stock, and M.W. Watson (1997): The NAIRU, Unemployment and Monetary Policy, *Journal of Economic Perspectives*, 11(1) (Winter), 33–49.

Stiglitz, J.E. (2009): GDP Fetishism, *The Economists' Voice*, 6(8), Article 5.

Stiglitz, J. (2015): Reconstructing Macroeconomic Theory to Manage Economic Policy, in E. Laurent, J. Le Cacheux, and D. Jasper (eds), *Fruitful Economics: Papers in Honor of and by Jean-Paul Fitoussi*, London: Palgrave, 20–56.

Tobin, J. (1958): Liquidity Preference as Behavior towards Risk, *Review of Economic Studies*, 25(1), 65–86.

Tobin, J. (1993): Price Flexibility and Output Stability: An Old Keynesian View, *Journal of Economic Perspectives*, 7(1) (Winter), 45–65.

Watson M.W. (2014): Inflation Persistence, the NAIRU, and the Great Recession, *American Economic Review*, 104(5) (May), 31–6.

Woodford, M. (2000): Revolution and Evolution in Twentieth-Century Macroeconomics, in P. Gifford (ed.), *Frontiers of the Mind in the Twenty-First Century*, Cambridge, MA: Harvard University Press—mimeo available on Woodford's website.

Woodford, M. (2010): Financial Intermediation and Macroeconomic Analysis, *Journal of Economic Perspectives*, 24, 4 (Fall), 21–44.

2

The Rational Expectations Hypothesis and the New Classicals

2.1 Introduction

The New Classical (NC) school of thought was a very radical research programme that emerged in the 1970s, and is usually associated with Robert Lucas Jr., Thomas Sargent, Neil Wallace, Edward Prescott, and others. It arose as a reaction to two sets of developments. First, there was discontent with (what was perceived as) naïve and ad hoc theorizing on the part of the mainstream Keynesian-Neoclassical synthesis school of the day. In models in that vein, there were typically Keynesian consumption functions of the type $C = a + bY$, with fixed a and b parameters, or postulated Phillips Curves (without or without expectations). These were all viewed with suspicion as not being derived from any deeper foundations and liable to change if the economic environment changes, hence as inadequate bases for sound policy advice. Second, the empirical performance of such models began breaking down in the 1970s, with erratic and high inflation and unemployment, etc. Similar in policy propositions to the earlier Monetarist School associated with Milton Friedman and others, the NCs (a) pushed the policy propositions to their logical conclusions, (b) had much more far-reaching implications for macroeconomic theory than the Monetarists.

NCs begin with three fundamental tenets:

- First, optimizing agents. Much as microeconomics suggests, all agents maximize (intertemporal) welfare or profits, subject to all the constraints that apply to them, including budget constraints, the market wages/prices, the product/labour/financial market structure, existing technology, raw materials and energy prices, etc. In other words, they determine their behaviour (patterns of consumption, labour supply in the case of individuals, labour demand in the case of firms, investment) so as to maximize their objective function subject to all applicable constraints. Their demand and supply curves in all markets embody this optimization. Thus, they do the best for themselves given elements in their environment beyond their control. This has the strong theoretical implication that any proposed theory of behaviour (e.g. a consumption function) cannot simply be assumed to hold, even if it looks plausible and apparent in the data; it must, instead, be carefully justified given 'first principles' (i.e. optimizing behaviour). Any proposed behavioural model should make sense from the individuals' point of view, otherwise (paraphrasing Lucas) it will be as if we are assuming that people leave 'dollar bills lying on the sidewalk' (i.e. unexploited opportunities). If crude behavioural assumptions are made, the theoretician is in danger of assuming a type of behaviour that depends on policies or institutions and may be liable to change when these change—as 'the Lucas critique', to be reviewed in Section 2.10, warns us.

Theory of Macroeconomic Policy. Christopher Tsoukis, Oxford University Press (2020). © Christopher Tsoukis.
DOI: 10.1093/oso/9780198825371.003.0002

- Secondly, market clearing, associated with price and wage flexibility. The theory here draws on the theory of general equilibrium: agents' optimization leads to well defined (and 'well-behaved') individual supplies and demands for goods and supply of labour; individual demands and supplies are further aggregated giving rise to market demands and supplies. The key assumption here is dual: equilibrium prices/wages exist such that demand and supply are equal in each market (on average, allowing excess demands and supplies that are entirely random). Additionally, wages and prices are flexible and gravitate towards equilibrium, thus facilitating 'market clearing' (equality between supply and demand). Hence, every market participant finds themselves on their demand or supply schedule, i.e. at a point which is consistent with their optimization, at the prices and wages they face.

Thus, there is no persistent excess demand or supply. In other words, barring completely random and unsystematic errors, we do not encounter empty shelves (excess demand), nor do firms keep piling up unwanted stock (excess supply). Surely, firms would have adjusted prices and/or quantities in both cases, given enough time. Equivalently, all market participants will be on their demand and supply curves (i.e. doing the best for themselves given prices and costs they cannot influence). This proposition is considerably stronger than it may at first appear, because it applies to all markets. There is a large number of markets, with complex interdependencies between them (e.g. spending decisions have repercussions on many other spending decisions, the decision how much to work, financial investment, etc.), and 'deep' uncertainty about future developments (on which many of our current decisions depend), yet there exists a vector of prices such that all markets simultaneously clear. This proposition is supported by the general equilibrium branch of microeconomics.

Furthermore, being on their demand and supply curves embodying optimal behaviour, no agent has any incentive to change their behaviour. We are in a Pareto-optimal world. Since agents do the best they can for themselves, given the circumstances, this line of reasoning deprives the government of any scope; we explore the implications of that for stabilization policy in Chapter 6 on business cycles. These ideas have a further very strong implication specifically in regard to the labour market. If all agents are on their supply and demand, as suggested, they all are doing the best for themselves, and hence employment decisions leave both firms and individuals 'happy'. In other words, all unemployment is voluntary! People stay at home (part or all of their time) because the real wage is not high enough to persuade them to trade labour for leisure. Note the inverted commas around 'happy'. The word does not mean that total happiness (whatever that may mean) has been achieved, nor that the individual would not have been happier in another situation which would involve a higher real wage and more hours at work. 'Happy' only means that the person is doing the best for him/herself *under the circumstances*; they may partly prefer leisure (minding the household and children, or pursuing hobbies or whatever else leisure implies) rather than working at a low wage and consuming little. Obviously, this view of unemployment has attracted a lot of criticism. We review issues related to unemployment in Chapter 4, while in Chapter 6 on business cycles, we juxtapose the New Classical and the New Keynesian models of the labour market.

- The third key tenet is the Rational Expectations Hypothesis (REH). This very bold assumption arose as a reaction against the pitfalls of the other expectational hypotheses. It is made not because of its realism, but because of its obvious theoretical appeal. First, a correct answer or guess (even on average) is only one, whereas wrong ones may be millions. So, if we were to assume that people make mistakes, what mistake do they exactly make? In other words, Rational Expectations is the natural theoretical benchmark. Second, one cannot derive theories and policy implications on the basis of systematically wrong expectations and systematic ability of governments to fool them! Surely, if we want to make the theoretical case for meaningful policies, we have to seek more secure theoretical foundations. Hence the need to use REH only as a theoretical benchmark that forces us to think harder. Additionally, the REH is important for the existence of general equilibrium, as it supplies an 'objective anchor' (in the sense that it is consistent with the macroeconomic system) that guides behaviour. The main idea of REH is reviewed in Section 2.2; criticisms of it are in Section 2.11. In Section 2.3, we review some implications (and violations) of REH for financial market 'efficiency'.

Two important policy propositions follow from these premises, namely the Policy Ineffectiveness Proposition (PIP); and the 'Lucas critique'; we review them in Sections 2.5/2.6 and 2.10, respectively. Some intermediate results and models that support the basic ideas such as the 'island' model and the 'surprise' supply function are considered in Section 2.4.

2.2 The Rational Expectations Hypothesis (REH)

2.2.1 Early Expectations-Formation Mechanisms

As mentioned, the REH arose out of the dissatisfaction with the other expectational hypotheses. To appreciate this point, we review briefly the main hypotheses that had been postulated prior to the emergence of REH. For simplicity, we refer to inflationary expectations, but the mechanisms obviously apply to all other variables of interest. Let P_t be the price level at time t and $\pi_t \equiv ((P_t - P_{t-1})/P_{t-1}$ the inflation rate. Let π_t^e be the expectation of π_t made at the end of period $t - 1$, based on any information that was available then (obviously, π_t is not known at that point).

The following simple expectations-formation mechanisms have been proposed:

- Simple backward-looking expectations $\pi_t^e = \pi_{t-1}$: crude, but perhaps plausible under conditions of low and sluggish inflation.
- Regressive expectations, $\pi_t^e = \pi + \lambda(\pi_{t-1} - \pi)$, where $0 < \lambda < 1$ is parameter that controls adjustment: inflation expectations are a weighted average of an inflationary long-run benchmark (π) (with weight $1 - \lambda$) and historical (past) inflation (weighted by λ). Put otherwise, a fraction $(1 - \lambda)$ of the discrepancy between past inflation and the benchmark π is eliminated every period (while a fraction λ of the discrepancy remains). If a shock occurs that causes inflation to deviate from π, expectations will initially be affected but will gradually converge back ('regress') to π (note $\lambda < 1$).

2.2.2 Adaptive Expectations

Adaptive expectations (Cagan, 1956) is a more sophisticated version of the above. It begins with the equation:

$$\pi_t^e = \pi_{t-1}^e + \lambda(\pi_{t-1} - \pi_{t-1}^e) = (1 - \lambda)\pi_{t-1}^e + \lambda\pi_{t-1} \tag{2.1}$$

Inflationary expectations are based on last period's expectations, except that they adapt by a factor proportional to last period's error (actual minus expected); in other words, a fraction $0 < \lambda < 1$ of past errors is corrected every period. An alternative interpretation is that expectations currently are a weighted average of past expectations and past actual inflation. Whichever interpretation one prefers, it is clear that expectations are backward-looking and evolve gradually (adapt) under the influence of actual outcomes.

To see this more clearly, one can use a technique called iterated backward substitution. Shift the above equation one period back (e.g. t becomes $t - 1$, etc.) to get:

$$\pi_{t-1}^e = (1 - \lambda)\pi_{t-2}^e + \lambda\pi_{t-2} \tag{2.1'}$$

Then insert into (2.1), to get:

$$\pi_t^e = (1 - \lambda)\big((1 - \lambda)\pi_{t-2}^e + \lambda\pi_{t-2}\big) + \lambda\pi_{t-1} \tag{2.2}$$

As is easily seen, we have now managed to introduce the inflation dated $t - 2$ in the equation. Then, shift (2.1) two periods back and insert where π^e_{t-2} appears, and so on, to obtain:

$$\pi_t^e = \lambda\sum_{i=0}^{\infty} (1 - \lambda)^i\pi_{t-1-i} \tag{2.3}$$

Expectations are a weighted average of past observations of inflation (note: stretching into the infinite past), where, because $(1 - \lambda) < 1$, the weight declines with time: the observations of the more distant past matter less for forming expectations today. Thus, the Adaptive Expectations Hypothesis postulates that, for expectations today, all past history of the relevant series matter, and in a plausibly declining order. Moreover, the mechanism is consistent with the plausible idea that expectations gradually converge to actual values. Consider a situation where up to time T, say, inflation is a constant $\bar{\pi}$ but from then on it unexpectedly and permanently jumps to a new value $\tilde{\pi} > \bar{\pi}$. Feeding this information into the formula, the pattern of expectations in Figure 2.1 emerges. (The Figure illustrates the

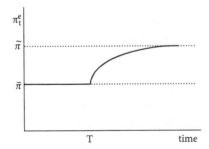

Figure 2.1. Adaptive expectations: an illustration

thought experiment described in the text. The dashed lines are actual values for inflation, whereas the solid line represents expectations.)

The Adaptive Expectations hypothesis has a number of appealing properties. It is an intuitive formula (correction of a fraction of past mistakes, the remote past weighing less on current beliefs); it is optimal under some cases in the process that generates π_t in the sense that it minimizes the mean square of expectational errors. But careful consideration also reveals a number of pitfalls. There is no theory as to what determines λ—it is an arbitrary parameter. Equation (2.1) only looks only at the history of inflation itself; any other relevant information is entirely ignored. Why not look at other series, too, and any other relevant information? For example, when a new government takes office, or whenever unexpected shocks occur, those will likely have a bearing on future inflation; such information is by construction excluded from (2.1). Relatedly and perhaps more seriously, this expectations-formation mechanism allows for systematic mistakes. While adjustment occurs (from time T till expectations catch up with actual inflation), there is in fact a systematic pattern of mistakes: a mistake in a certain direction (above, an under-estimate) implies that there will be more of the same kind. This is a grave flaw in the theory, as agents are surely intelligent enough to learn from such cases of persistent mistakes; and by learning, it is plausible to think that they eliminate such mistakes.[1] Persistent mistakes happen of course because agents look only at the past history of inflation and no other information that might have given, for example, a better idea where the new level of inflation stands. The idea that agents exploit *all available information* in forming expectations, including but not only the history of the relevant series, led to the successor theory, the Rational Expectations Hypothesis, reviewed next.

2.2.3 The Rational Expectations Hypothesis

The Rational Expectations Hypothesis was developed and first explored by Muth (1961). According to this hypothesis, the subjective expectation of the typical agent equals the mathematical mean arising from the model of the economy that agent is using, conditional on the information set they are assumed to possess (I_t). For example, in the case of inflation, $\pi_t^e = E(\pi_t/I_t)$. The content of the information set depends on the context, i.e. on when expectations were taken: if at time t, then we indicate this by I_t (this is all info available at t), if at $t-1$ we indicate by I_{t-1} (all info available at end of $t-1$) etc. A convenient shorthand is to indicate by a subscript to E the time when expectations were taken, i.e. $E_{t-1}\pi_t \equiv E(\pi_t/I_{t-1})$. This is standard practice, and we shall follow it here.

The key properties of REH are as follows. The theory allows expectations errors (of course), but systematic errors of any kind are not allowed. This key property boils down to two requirements. Expectations must be 'on average correct', neither systematically over- nor under-predicting. Furthermore, there must be 'no systematic part' in the errors, as intelligent agents will learn from this systematic part and, in doing so, will eliminate it; in

---

[1] This does not of course mean that persistent mistakes do not happen, but to have a theory that asserts that such mistakes *always* happen during transitions is surely wrong, because transitions are very frequent. On the other hand, Rational Expectations are an equally strong assumption—for the opposite reasons. An acceptable middle way is the theories of bounded rationality and learning—see later in this chapter.

effect, the errors must be entirely random. Formally, if $u_t \equiv \pi_t - E_{t-1}\pi_t$ is the expectations error, the first property requires $E(u_t) = 0$ (mean zero) and the second $E(u_t u_{t+s}) = 0$, for $s \neq 0$ (mistakes are entirely uncorrelated across time).

Moreover, REH addresses the 'look only at the history of one variable' property of Adaptive Expectations by postulating the opposite: 'look-at-everything'. Expectations are formed on the basis of all information available to the agents. (Information can never be harmful, irrelevant information is simply discarded; the implicit assumption here is that the available information is always factually correct, incorrect information—now called 'fake news'—naturally leads to mistakes but should not properly be called information, and is not in I). Thus, agents do not look only at the history of a series or even all the series: all currently available information that may not yet be reflected into historical series is taken into account.

Rational Expectations are 'model-consistent'; expectations are consistent with the model agents are using to understand the macroeconomic system. This property is a logical requirement. (Imagine the opposite assumption that subjective beliefs and estimates of people are different than the predictions made by the model the same people are using!) Apart from being appealing, model-consistency is very convenient analytically. From a modelling point of view, you generate the (subjective) expectations by taking the math-ematical expectations (means) of the variables of the macro system, and you handle them both (subjective and mathematical expectations) pretty much the same. Furthermore, focusing on a unique (the model-consistent or on-average-correct) expectation implies that expectations can be coordinated and beliefs shared; further, that helps the system attain equilibrium through coordination of actions. In other words, RE helps general equilibrium to be attained even in the face of the uncertainty that saddles the economic system (see Kantor, 1979).

At the same time, REH is not devoid of logical difficulties:[2] no algorithm is proposed by which agents actually arrive at specific numbers. Furthermore, do agents know 'the' structure of the system? Even if they do, do they have the cognitive ability to take mathematical means of lots of variables in complex systems? Obviously, REH assumes a huge amount of information (to know the 'true' model) and cognitive ability (to process such a very complex model) on the part of agents. Partially in response to these difficulties, models of learning have developed; some of them ask, does REH arise as a result of learning? The theoretical answers to this question are mixed. Section 2.11 further discusses the properties of RE and highlights further logical difficulties, related to the plausibility of RE under costly information acquisition, plausibility of REH as an approximation to the properties of an economy (as opposed, say to Adaptive Expectations), and the complexity of the tasks involved in forming REH. In response to these, theories of 'bounded ration-ality' have developed (the key idea is that we do our best under our limited cognitive abilities), but without as yet having come to an agreement about the key cognitive limitation or the key mechanisms we use in order to form expectations.

REH remains the benchmark expectational assumption in standard macroeconomic modelling (unless you focus specifically on some other mechanism, e.g. learning). The reason for this appeal is threefold. In any question, there is (normally) one correct answer

---

[2] See Lovell (1986) for empirical tests of the REH.

but millions of wrong ones. If you are to assume that agents make (systematic) mistakes, what are those? So, hypothesizing the 'correct answer' (i.e. non-systematic errors) is the obvious benchmark for theory. Relatedly, the literature on bounded rationality has not, as mentioned, come to much agreement on the best way forward. Finally, if you are to form policy advice, you might as well base it on the assumption that there is an intelligent private sector out there (in the sense described by REH) rather than a daft one that can be fooled and manipulated (even if, on occasion, that may be the case!).

2.3 Implications of REH: Efficient Markets, 'News', and 'Bubbles'

2.3.1 Market Efficiency

Before moving on to the other ideas of the New Classicals, it is worth highlighting some implications of Rational Expectations that are not organically linked to the NCs. Some of these ideas are relevant to financial markets, in particular. One implication of this hypothesis is that no one possesses any formula for making 'smart money' based on the information that is publicly available; i.e. if p^*_t is the general market expectation or estimate of a commodity or a share price before the actual price p_t is revealed, no one can come up with a formula that delivers an estimate p^{**}_t that is systematically closer to the actual price than p^*_t. So, no one possesses any rule for outwitting the others and making extra money as a result or any rule to exploit better the available information than the general market participants are able to. Thus, one further implication of REH is that market prices 'fully reflect all available information' (one cannot make any better use of this information). This is called the 'efficient markets hypothesis', initiated by Fama (1970); see Fama (2014) and Shiller (2014) for recent reviews.[3] If prices fully reflect all available information, the argument can be taken one step further to the broader conclusion that financial assets are appropriately priced. The crises of 2007–8 that started with the 'sub-prime market' mortgage lending and the realization that banks had accumulated loads of 'toxic' assets that no one knew how to appropriately price, brought a rude awakening to that belief. In recent years, the field of behavioural finance (Shleifer, 2000; Shiller, 2003, 2014) challenges many of the key results of the theory of finance based on the rationality postulate.

A related implication of REH worth highlighting concerns the effects of anticipations and 'news'. As expectations are forward looking, agents will try to forecast future developments, policies, state of the economy as best they can. Consider a simple model of the stock market:

$$r = \frac{D_t + E_t \Delta V_{t+1}}{V_t} \tag{2.4}$$

r: The real interest rate (assumed constant for simplicity—but this can be relaxed);

D_t: Dividend obtainable from holding a typical unit of equity during period t;

---

[3] This can be seen more clearly if we interpret p as price of an asset and p* as its expectation based on underlying supply and demand for the asset, profitability and productivity of the firm associated with it, etc., in one word the 'fundamentals' of the asset. Further, if u is 'noise' (completely random movement of the price), then we can write: price of the asset = fundamentals + noise. The efficient market hypothesis asserts that the price fully reflects all knowledge about the fundamentals.

V_t: The value, or price, of such a typical unit of equity (indicative also of the price, or index, of the whole stock market) at the beginning of period t;

Δ: The 'difference operator' is defined as: $\Delta V_{t+1} \equiv V_{t+1} - V_t$;

E_t: Expectations held at the beginning of time t.

The real interest rate on the LHS is the rate of return from holding a riskless asset such as a government bond. The RHS of this equation is the rate of return from holding a unit of stock (equity) during period t: it is made up of the dividend (an explicit return), plus the expected 'capital gain' (the expected rise in price of this unit of equity, an implicit type of return), both as percentages over the current equity price (V). This equation then states that these rates of return should be equalized. This equality is brought about by arbitrage, the riskless buying and selling: if the rate of return obtainable from equity is higher than elsewhere, investors will buy equity, raising its current price. Given the dividend and future expected price (V_{t+1}), this will lower the return from equity. The opposite will happen if the rate of return from equity is less than the real interest rate. In practice, the equality may not hold exactly since 'arbitrage' will be imperfect, as there is risk involved in buying and selling.[4] If so, market participants may wish to hold equity only if the rate of return on the risky asset is on average higher than the riskless rate (r):

$$r + RP = \frac{D_t + E_t \Delta V_{t+1}}{V_t} \qquad (2.4')$$

This 'risk premium' will be positive, $RP > 0$ (and not necessarily constant), because of risk aversion, as those familiar with portfolio theory will know. Such an equation then may characterize not only the returns from equity but also all other financial assets, like bonds of different maturities (the 'term structure of interest rates', to be reviewed in Chapter 8), and even exchange rates of foreign currencies. This is the crucial feature. Equation (2.4') and what follows applies to all prices, notably those of financial assets, that can adjust (or 'jump') instantaneously.

For our purposes here, we assume $RP = 0$ (arbitrage is perfect). This equation is trivially rearranged as:

$$(1 + r)V_t = D_t + E_t V_{t+1} \qquad (2.5)$$

Note an intriguing feature of this equation: the dividend (D) aside, the expected value next period is higher by a factor $1 + r(> 1)$ than the current value (V_t). This will be true of the next period, and the period after, and so on. Continuing with this logic, we find that this process is 'unstable', it implies an equity value that grows geometrically over time. This cannot be right; to disallow that, we 'solve the equation forward' by a method called 'iterated substitution'—we used the same method above in a backward manner, now it is forward. Shift (2.5) above forward and take expectations, to get:

$$(1 + r)E_t V_{t+1} = E_t D_{t+1} + E_t V_{t+2} \qquad (2.5')$$

---

[4] For this reason arbitrage may not be the appropriate term here. A better term for buying and selling when risk is involved is 'speculation'.

Solve for $E_t V_{t+1}$ and substitute into (2.5), to get:

$$V_t = \frac{D_t}{1+r} + \frac{E_t D_{t+1}}{(1+r)^2} + \frac{E_t V_{t+2}}{(1+r)^2}$$

Repeating for t+2, etc. (always taking expectations at the beginning of t, i.e. E_t), we finally get:

$$V_t = \frac{D_t}{1+r} + \frac{E_t D_{t+1}}{(1+r)^2} + \frac{E_t D_{t+2}}{(1+r)^2} + \ldots = \frac{1}{1+r}\left[\sum_{s=t}^{\infty}(1+r)^{-(s-t)}E_t D_s\right] \qquad (2.6)$$

Thus, the bond price is the present value of all expected future dividends. This equation states that the price of a share just reflects the benefits investors get from it in perpetuity (the dividends). This equation is widely taken to be the statement of market efficiency: financial prices fully and justly reflect the underlying 'fundamentals', through arbitrage (buying and selling looking for profitable opportunities). V_t cannot differ from the RHS of (2.6) as this will imply 'smart money' to be made by the correct strategy (buying or selling, depending on the direction of the inequality). These profitable opportunities have already been exploited, and the equality is (assumed to have been) restored.

2.3.2 Anticipations and News

To illustrate (2.6), consider a few examples. First, an asset pays a constant dividend of $D = 5$ for ever (for all t); as the dividend is constant, so will be its price, therefore $V = 5/r$. (Can you explain why?) Assume now that starting at $t = t_0$, it becomes known that the dividend changes to $D = 10$ with immediate effect. This new information is entirely unexpected (note this); let's call it 'news'. What will be the new price? One might be tempted to calculate at what price the equity was bought, and work it from there. But: bygones are bygones! Equation (2.6) tells us that all that we look at is the future (dividends); this formulation and the REH that is associated with it are 'forward looking'.[5] Looking to the future and equating (by arbitrage), we simply get a new price $V_t = 10/r$ for $t \geq t_0$. At time $t = t_0$, those fortunate enough to hold this equity will enjoy an entirely unexpected capital gain of $(10-5)/r$.

Now consider what will happen if this change of dividend is anticipated at t_0 to happen at a future time T, at which D will rise to 10 permanently; until then, $D = 5$. News of this breaks at $t = t_0 < T$. We assume schematically that markets had no idea of that change before t_0; at t_0, anticipation of this becomes wide. Before t_0, $V_t = 5/r$ (for $t < t_0$) by previous reasoning. The question now is what will happen to V from $t = t_0$ onwards. Applying formula (2.6), we have:

$$V_{t_0} = \frac{\displaystyle\sum_{s=t_0}^{T-1}(1+r)^{-(s-t_0)}E_{t_0}D_s + \sum_{s=T}^{\infty}(1+r)^{-(s-t_0)}E_{t_0}D_s}{1+r}$$

$$= \frac{5\displaystyle\sum_{s=t_0}^{T-1}(1+r)^{-(s-t_0)} + 10\sum_{s=T}^{\infty}(1+r)^{-(s-t_0)}}{1+r} \qquad (2.7)$$

---

[5] This is to be contrasted with Adaptive Expectations which is 'backward-looking' as is evident in (2.3).

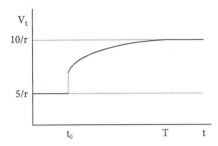

Figure 2.2. Time profile of a 'jump' variable

The plot of this V is given in Figure 2.2.[6]

There are several noteworthy features here: $V = 10/r$ from time T onwards. For time $t_0 < t < T$, we have $5/r < V < 10/r$. Furthermore, as time progresses (as t gets closer to T), the first term on the RHS in (2.7) that 'anchors' V to $5/r$ becomes progressively smaller, and the term that anchors V to $10/r$ progressively larger. Thus, V gradually rises as shown. In other words, V_t for $t_0 < t < T$ can be written as a weighted average $\alpha_t 5/r + (1 - \alpha_t)10/r$, with the weight α_t depending on t. If it is closer to t_0, then α_t is larger (the price has not yet adjusted upwards much and V is tied more to the old price), if t is closer to T then the new price matters more (α_t low).

The main point however is, during the transition, the rate of return from holding the asset (including dividend and capital gains) is r. The only time when the rate of return from holding the asset exceeds r is t_0, showing in the graph by a discrete jump in V at time t_0. (Note that the V is a financial asset price where a discrete jump is possible, as mentioned; it is not any price such as the general price level where such a jump is impossible.) The jump should happen one instant (NOT one period) after the anticipation of a future higher D arises at the beginning of period $t = t_0$; it is essentially the difference between the old value of equity and the new one after the anticipation of a higher future dividend. Denoting by V^+ the value of the stock one instant after the jump and taking account of (2.7), the 'jump' is:

$$V^+_{t_0} - V_{t_0} = \frac{5\sum_{s=t_0}^{T-1}(1+r)^{-(s-t_0)} + 10\sum_{s=T}^{\infty}(1+r)^{-(s-t_0)} - 5\sum_{s=t_0}^{\infty}(1+r)^{-(s-t_0)}}{1+r}$$

$$= (10-5)\frac{\sum_{s=T}^{\infty}(1+r)^{-(s-t_0)}}{1+r} \tag{2.8}$$

This jump will be smaller the further away in the future the anticipated dividend rise takes effect (that is, the higher is $T - t_0$).

A further, subtler, observation is that the jump occurs at $t = t_0$, the time when the news of the higher future dividend first breaks—and only then. In particular, there will not be any jump at T (or any other time except t_0). Why? Well, market participants know that at

---

[6] Note that, as time is discrete $(t = 1, 2, 3, ...)$, the graph should be discrete points. The line shown smoothly connects these points. The same graph can be derived by (continuous-time) differential equations (not used in this book).

time t = T, the equity price will be $V_T = 10/r$. One period earlier, applying formula (2.7) for t = T − 1 (i.e. setting T − 1 where there is t_0 in 2.7), this price should be:

$$V_{T-1} = \frac{\sum_{s=T-1}^{T-1} (1+r)^{-(s-T+1)} E_{T-1}D_s + \sum_{s=T}^{\infty} (1+r)^{-(s-T+1)} E_{T-1}D_s}{1+r}$$

$$= \frac{5 + 10\sum_{s=T}^{\infty} (1+r)^{-(s-T+1)}}{1+r}$$ (2.7')

Since $E_{T-1}V_T = \frac{1}{1+r}10\sum_{s=T}^{\infty}(1+r)^{-(s-T)} = 10\sum_{s=T}^{\infty}(1+r)^{-(s-T+1)}$, (2.7') may be written as:

$$V_{T-1} = \frac{D_{T-1} + E_{T-1}V_T}{1+r}$$ (2.7")

Equations (2.4) and (2.7") are the same (just change T − 1 to t in the latter), thus showing that the rate of return obtainable at time t equals r. The graphical equivalent of this is the absence of any jump between T − 1 and T. If the price V_{T-1} were to be lower than that, so that there would be a discrete jump between T − 1 and T (a rate of return greater than r), market participants would anticipate that (as there is no new information arising at T − 1). Driven by the opportunity of an abnormally high capital gain, they would buy this equity, driving the V_{T-1} price up until it is equal to the above formula (and on the graph), eliminating the discrete jump. Continuing with this logic to all time $t_0 < t < T$, we end up concluding that the jump is only possible at the time when new information, 'news', arises—here, at t_0.

Note that a jump could recur in the future IF new information emerges again. For example, if mid-way between t_0 and T it emerges that D will not rise to 10 but to 12 (again at T), there will be another jump right at that moment, to the new higher trajectory guided by D = 12. Or, if the news breaks that the rise in D will not be to 10 but to 8 after all, the new jump will be downwards, to a lower trajectory, at that very time (a 'correction'). Finally, consider a hypothetical scenario where news breaks at t_0 of a rise in D to10, but the jump at that time is smaller than one would be led to believe on the basis of the above graph and the foregoing analysis. What may have happened? One explanation might be that the theory is wrong! But the above is little more than simple logic, so unlikely to be entirely wrong. Another possibility is that in fact, the 'news' at t_0 may not be entirely new. If, say, the market had already come to anticipate at a time prior to t_0 a rise in D_T to 8, they would have already incorporated that in price (bidding it up), by having possibly caused a jump in the price at an earlier date. At t_0, the true news is a rise in D of 10 − 8, not 10 − 5. Hence, the jump will be smaller than the one shown above. Or imagine, to confuse matters more, that the 'news' at t_0 of a future D = 10 is accompanied by a jump downwards, not upwards. Since this is really intriguing, the (economic) detective Hercule Poirot is called, who soon discovers that, prior to t_0, news had broken that D would rise to 12 at T; this had already been built into the price of V. Then, at t_0, this expectation was revised to D = 10, to take effect again at T. In other words, the true 'news' at t_0 was not 10 − 5 but 10 − 12 < 0, i.e. (downward) news, causing the downward jump. Thus, to determine what is going on in financial markets, one does not need only to keep in touch with current announcements and news (news about future policies, character of policy-makers, business news, even statistics releases and new data from statistical offices which show the state of play of the economy and are eagerly awaited by markets) but also to gauge how much of the (supposed) new information is truly new and how much had already been 'discounted', i.e. was already incorporated into the price at the time that the new(-ish) information arose.

2.3.3 Bubbles

'Bubbles' are the decoupling of asset prices from fundamentals. The idea applies to all types of asset price, from stock prices to house prices to exchange rates. Schematically, it is the failure of (2.4) or (2.6) to hold. If you thought that risk premia are also relevant, you could add PR > 0 as in (2.4') and take it from there. Here, the dividend D is the fundamental, but in wider contexts one may think of firms' profitability or productivity; the capacity of houses to confer housing services; etc. in other contexts. The reason why a bubble may arise can be seen with reference to (2.4). Imagine for a moment that the equality does not hold, and that investing in shares gives a higher rate of return: $r < \frac{D_t + E_t \Delta V_{t+1}}{V_t}$. The investor is thus not indifferent between the riskless asset and shares; rather, they will have an incentive to buy shares. By doing so, they will cause next period's asset price (V_{t+1}) to rise, generating an even greater rate of return from the share. More buying will ensue, with a greater rise in the share price, etc. In this way, the share price (V) will become disconnected from the fundamentals indicated by the dividend and the real interest rate. The price will be sustained at a high level as long as everyone believes that everyone else is buying. In real-world incidents, usually a climate of frenzy develops, all information is blown out of proportion, rumours circulate often with an intention of influencing the market. Eventually, it will be realized that the price has risen too much; panic-selling will ensue and the price will fall fast: the bubble has 'popped'. Those who bought cheap and sold high, those who managed to sell in time, will have made money; those who bought expensive, in Kindleberger's (1985) memorable phrase, those who 'bought the rumour and sold the fact', will experience an opposite change in their balance sheet. One message of equation (2.6) is this: as long as the share price is as dictated by the RHS of (2.6), the stock market is like the goose that lays the golden eggs. It allows agents with savings to spare to invest in firms, allowing them to produce profits that will be remitted back to investors via dividends; everybody gains. If the price of shares is disconnected from the RHS of (2.6), particularly if (2.6) fails for prolonged periods of time, then the stock market becomes a casino: a zero-sum game, where your losses are my gains (or vice versa!).

There have been various episodes where stock market bubbles have formed and then crashed, perhaps the most (in)famous being that of the 1920s in the US, culminating in the 'great crash' of 1929; we discuss that in Chapter 6 on business cycles. But that does not mean that all the rest of the time equations (2.4) or (2.6) clearly hold. The interested reader is invited to look up figure (1) of Shiller (2014; updating his earlier 1981), showing the actual US stock market price and two theoretical benchmarks constructed using the RHS of equation (2.6) (under two different assumptions about future dividends—econometrics in this area uses a fair amount of assumptions in constructing an empirical analogue of the RHS of 2.6 as that involves the future). Shiller (2014) shows that, whatever the 'true' theoretical benchmark, it is clear that the US stock market price has repeatedly veered off it, and in a protracted and persistent way. Such evidence has given rise to extensive econometric testing of the efficient market hypothesis. This hypothesis surely allows random deviations from equality in (2.6); the real question is which deviations can be thought of as 'random' (hence consistent with the theory) and which 'persistent' (and inconsistent).

One way of testing the market efficiency hypothesis is to test whether share price changes are purely random and unforecastable. This is because, as current prices embody (i.e. fully reflect) all available current information, any changes in those prices will be the result of new information that will emerge beyond t, which is by definition unforecastable; hence, price changes are the same. So, one test is to regress stock market changes on any variable that is publicly available at time t. Market efficiency will be accepted if the coefficients of such regressors are not significantly different from zero. Even if market efficiency is rejected, if the proportion of the stock price movement that is explained is small, one concludes that the model is a good approximation to reality. Further description of the many other tests and their variants that have been used is beyond the scope of this; see Shiller (2014) for a portal into this literature. But it seems that after many years where the null hypothesis in many people's minds was market efficiency, now a switch has taken place; most people would argue that the market is not 'rational' and 'efficient' in the strict sense, unless it is otherwise proved. Now, most people would admit that important psychological and sociological processes guide market participants, such as serious cognitive limitations, rat races (I am more motivated by my desire to be more successful than you than by the need to provide for my family), framing (the way you present an issue matters), 'bandwagon', 'herding', and 'contagion' effects (do as the others do, even if you don't understand why!), among many others. These have given rise to the blossoming area of Behavioural Finance and Behavioural Economics more generally. Some of these issues will be explored further later on in this chapter.

2.4 The Lucas 'Island' Model and the 'Surprise' Supply Function

The Lucas (1972, 1973) model delivers an AS function whereby real output supply depends only on price 'surprises', i.e. only the unexpected portion of price movements. This supply function plays a key role in all modern macroeconomic theory: It underpins the development of the Policy Ineffectiveness Proposition (see Section 2.5), it underlies much monetary policy analysis and the arguments on its (lack of) credibility that are behind major institutional developments in the last 20 years or so (see Chapter 7). Hence, it is worth developing it in some length, in order to gain an understanding of the premises on which it rests. Comments on its significance follow at the end of this section.

The world is assumed to be made of individual consumer-producers (e.g. farmers). Each such individual or household lives on an island (or farm) with limited information as to what happens outside—in particular, the individual price P_i is observable but the economy-wide price level P is unknown and imperfectly estimated. There are two steps to the overall argument. One is to show that the producer adjusts output according to the relative price of his/her goods; changes in the price level that affect all nominal prices equi-proportionately (and thus leave relative prices unaffected) do not induce any change in quantities. Then, we show how the producer makes an inference about the general price level based on his own, fully observed good price P_i.

Let the producer i maximize instantaneous utility depending on consumption and inversely on labour:

$$\text{Max} \quad U_i = C_i - \frac{1}{\gamma}L_i^\gamma, \quad \gamma > 1$$

Subject to:

- The production function: $Y_i = L_i$. For simplicity, this production function suggests that output is directly proportional to labour; parameter $\gamma > 1$ measures the disutility of labour.
- An 'eat as much as you work' constraint: $PC_i = P_iL_i$. Consumption is a bundle made up of all goods, hence its price is the price level P; but the product of labour is valued by the price of the individual good it produces (P_i). C_i is the individual's consumption of a basket of goods, which costs the price level P per unit. On the other hand, the individual producer produces a good that is priced P_i.

Inserting the two constraints in the maximand, the problem becomes:

$$\max{}_{L_i} U_i = \frac{P_iL_i}{P} - \frac{1}{\gamma}L_i^\gamma$$

This is to be maximized by an appropriate labour supply, L_i. The First-Order Condition is:

$$\frac{P_i}{P} = L_i^{\gamma-1}, \quad \gamma > 1. \tag{2.9}$$

The real price of good i is equated to the marginal product of labour of the relevant producer. This can then be solved for the optimal amount of labour, which in logs— denoted by lower-case letters—is:

$$l_i = \frac{1}{\gamma - 1}(p_i - p) \tag{2.10}$$

We have two considerations here. A higher relative price of my good (i) gives me an incentive to work harder; but this is tempered by the disutility of labour, γ. But the problem is that the aggregate price level is unobservable to the individual agent/farmer/islander (i), so the exact relative price $p_i - p$ is not accurately known.

If we let $z_i \equiv p_i - p(= \log(P_i/P))$ be the economically important relative price, we can decompose the observable individual price into the unimportant general price level and the important but unobservable relative price trivially as:

$$p_i = p + z_i \tag{2.11}$$

The price level is unimportant because its change signifies only a rescaling of prices (e.g. if all—ALL—prices and wages double or go up by 30 per cent, my living standards do not change). But if the relative price changes, the individual now has an incentive to change their behaviour, e.g. by working overtime (if the relative price of the good I am selling rises, my corresponding opportunity cost of leisure goes up). But though p_i is observed, its decomposition into p and z_i is not.

The producer faces a 'signal extraction' problem, a problem of decomposing a certain 'sound' into a meaningful 'signal' and an unimportant 'noise'. Suppose that p_i shows some change. To what extent is this attributable to 'noise' p (noise in the sense that it is economically irrelevant, it just confuses things) or the important 'signal' $z_i \equiv p_i - p$. If the individual price (p_i) has changed because the price level (p) has changed, the individual will not change any of their behaviour, if, instead, the important relative price (z_i) has changed, the individual will reconsider their behaviour. It thus becomes critical to try and estimate how much of the change in p_i is to be attributed to changes in p and how much to changes in z_i—this is the nature of the 'signal extraction problem'. In other words, agents try to predict z_i on the basis of their observation of p_i, the information they have.

Motivated by physics, the signal extraction (estimate of z_i) is based on the following relation:

$$E(z_i/p_i) = \theta(p_i - E(p)) \tag{2.12}$$

This is the best estimate of z_i based on available information (p_i). (The mean E here is meant as a best prediction, not as an average over the individuals i.) The (log) ratio $p_i - E(p)$ is what appears to be the relative price (z_i)—in physical terms, this is the 'sound'. But how much faith should we have in this estimate? What is the meaningful 'signal' out of this sound? The answer depends on the parameter θ, which brings historical experience to bear upon this estimate. This parameter turns out to be:

$$0 < \theta \equiv \frac{V_z}{V_z + V_P} < 1.$$

Vz and Vp are the variances of z and p, respectively; they are assumed to be known from experience. If p is very 'noisy' (with a high variance V_p), θ is low. Then, an increase (say) in p_i is more likely to have been generated by an increase in p rather than z_i, as the former varies more than the latter. Then, the best estimate of z_i is not updated greatly even if the relative price ($p_i - E(p)$) appears to have changed. If V_z (variance of z) is high, θ is high, and the change in p_i is attributed more to z_i.

Hence, noting the production function $Y_i = L_i$ and that labour supply depends on relative price in (2.10), individual output supply becomes:

$$y_i = b(p_i - E(p)), \quad b \equiv \frac{\theta}{\gamma - 1} > 0. \tag{2.10'}$$

Aggregating over all i, we get (dropping individual subscripts):

$$y = b(p - E(p)) \tag{2.13}$$

This is the Lucas supply function: Only price *surprises* (deviations from the expected price level) matter for aggregate output. This is because individuals' labour supply is motivated by relative price 'signals' that are in turn proportional to the unexpected portion of prices.

This 'surprise' AS curve parallels, and underpins, the expectations-augmented Phillips Curve. To show this, we need two observations. First, 'structural' or 'normal' output may be thought to be the level that arises when all markets clear—there are no price surprises, $p = E(p)$. Thus, y in (2.13) is best interpreted as the (percentage) deviation of output from that level, i.e. the negative of the output gap. Secondly, by Okun's law (see Chapter 1), y is inversely related to deviations of unemployment from its 'natural' or 'structural' rate, so that $y = \alpha(U - U^N)$, $\alpha < 0$. Then, (2.13) may be re-expressed as:

$$U - U^N = c(p - Ep), \quad c \equiv b/\alpha < 0 \tag{2.13'}$$

This is essentially the expectations-augmented Phillips Curve; noting that the inflation rate is defined as $\pi_t \equiv p_t - p_{t-1}$ and $E(\pi_t) \equiv (E(p_t - p_{t-1})$ and because p_{t-1} is known with certainty $(p_{t-1} = Ep_{t-1})$ therefore $\pi_t - E(\pi_t) = p_t - Ep_t$. (2.13) and (2.13') have the same policy implications (depending in both cases on how expectations are formed) and comparable places in the history of macroeconomic ideas. We return to the issue of empirical support for this model in the last section.

The intuitive appeal of the Lucas 'surprise' supply function arises from the fact that it explains with a rigorous reasoning two, seemingly contradictory, observations (see Goodfriend and King, 1997). Nominal prices tend to rise more rapidly during expansionary phases of the business cycle than they do in the trough, as in the former case, trend inflation (evidenced in Ep) and price surprises work in the same direction, while in a downturn, the negative price surprises mitigate the trend inflation. So, the rate of change (inflation) behaves pro-cyclically. In the short run (which may be very short), there is a Phillips Curve: high inflation coincides with low unemployment. On the other hand, inflation and unemployment are unrelated in the long run, as price expectations catch up with the actual. In other words, there is a Phillips Curve only in the short run and only as far as unexpected inflation is concerned.

The full implications of the Lucas supply function (2.13) emerge when it is combined with the Rational Expectations Hypothesis, which implies that there is really no meaningful short run. This leads to the Policy Ineffectiveness Proposition, reviewed next.

2.5. The Policy Ineffectiveness Proposition (PIP): The Core Idea

The PIP builds on the Lucas supply function and Rational Expectations. The former says that only unanticipated prices matter for output, while the latter affirms that such errors in prediction are of necessity completely random. Hence, aggregate demand policies fail to meaningfully affect a supply-side determined output. Section 2.6 develops PIP in detail; in this section, we give an intuitive, diagrammatic presentation. Recall the familiar AD-AS diagram (Figure 2.3).

The AD and AS curves are standard. The only feature that needs a comment here is that the short-run AS curve is based on a given nominal wage (w); in turn, the nominal wage is affected by the expected price as workers try to maintain a standard of living. In turn, a higher wage incentivizes firms to raise prices as they try to maintain profit margins. When the wage rises, the AS shifts up, implying that a given level of output is now accompanied by a higher price level. Thus, the dependence of the s.r. AS on wage and expected price encapsulates the 'wage-price spiral'—price rises feeding into wages feeding into prices, etc. Initial equilibrium A is made up of AD and AS with an initial wage level $w^0 = p^0$, equal to the initial price level (both are in logs, and the negotiated real wage is assumed to equal 1, so that $w_0 - p_0 = 0$). Equilibrium output is Y^*. Let us assume that the policy-maker

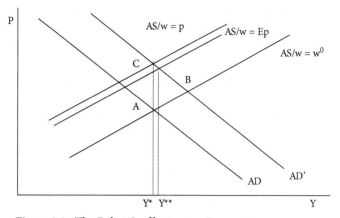

Figure 2.3. The Policy Ineffectiveness Proposition

thinks of Y* as too low, and decides to raise it by expansionary aggregate demand policies (AD to AD').[7]

The critical factor is how the price setters will react to this intention. Two polar cases emerge. If they keep wages fixed (for whatever reason), then point B arises, and the demand-led expansion succeeds (with somewhat higher prices). Note that, at B, the workers will have lost purchasing power as $p_B > p_0 = w_0$. If, on the other hand, the nominal wage is immediately renegotiated to somehow match fully the rise in price, $w = p$, AS shifts by the same distance as the AD, point C emerges, and Y* is restored. In practice, the resulting rise in price is to an extent random, and the rise in wages can only match it in an expected sense. There will be a forecast error, which will be reflected on a final real wage $w - p$ that differs randomly from $w^0 - p^0 = 0$, and consequently a resulting Y** that differs randomly from Y*. But, a key point, under the REH, the deviations $w - p$ and Y** − Y* will be entirely random. So, the expansion will have failed to all intents and purposes, because there is no systematic pattern in its results (Y** − Y* will be purely random, possibly negative). This is in essence the PIP.

We might ask, will things be any different if this AD policy had a more systematic character? So, let us think of a simple stabilization policy rule. Let us assume that monetary policy reacts to past output developments, as in:

$$m_t = -\alpha y_{t-1} + v_t, \quad \alpha > 1, \tag{2.14}$$

where both the money supply (m_t) and output (y_t) are in deviations from their average levels. Accordingly, monetary policy attempts to stabilize output by reacting to past output; there is also a random component of policy, v_t, because policy-makers do not succeed in carrying out exactly their intentions (because of administrative difficulties and imperfections, or because the instrument of policy—here, the money supply—is itself

---

[7] Y* may be a low level of output caused by a recession. Alternatively, Y* may be the 'natural rate of output' but the policy-maker may want to expand from that. The natural rate of output is often considered to be too low because the real world is characterized by monopolistic power. Any movement away from perfect competition lowers economic welfare. Hence, the policy-maker may wish to increase output above Y* by an aggregate demand expansion.

imperfectly controlled).[8] The monetary authority's aim is to stabilize, or 'fine-tune', the economy, i.e. to lift it out of stagnation (overheating) by a monetary expansion (contraction). The monetary authority reacts negatively (note the negative coefficient) to last period's developments in y because, by the autocorrelation typically present in this series, high (low) values of y_{t-1} are likely to be succeeded by high (low) values of y_t, hence y_{t-1} provides a good indicator of what y_t might look like (without intervention). Hence, the monetary authority reacts to y_{t-1}; parameter α indicates the sensitivity of this reaction. Crucially, α is publicly known as it summarizes an important aspect of the monetary authority's behaviour and is institutionally ingrained. The crucial question now is, does this kind of stabilization policy work? Does it deliver effective stabilization, against the predictions of the PIP?

Let us follow the reasoning behind the PIP. Starting from $y_{t-1} = 0$ (output at its baseline Y*) that is deemed too low (say), the policy-maker decides to engineer an expansion during t. The snag, though, is that wage setters who signed their contracts at the end of $t-1$ knew both the general policy thinking (parameter α) and the conditions prevailing then (y_{t-1}). They could in effect gauge the entire policy stance for t except for random errors (policy-related error v_t, or error from whatever other source). This will guide their wage negotiations. In effect, w = Ep, where E here indicates expectations taken at the end of $t-1$. Thus, $y_t = Y^{**} - Y^*$ will emerge, and the policy fails; except random deviations, the same output arises. Things will be no different from above where we considered a simple, one-off AD expansion (instead of a rule as here). Not only that, but the monetary authority will have injected an extra source of uncertainty into the system (the policy error v). The policy corollary of PIP is that demand-led stabilization fails, output is at all times supply-determined and the policy–maker is best advised to follow a rule of steady money growth in line with the economy's transaction needs. In this way, unnecessary uncertainty will be avoided.

Section 2.6 elaborates on this argument; Section 2.7 deals with a powerful criticism of the PIP by the first generation of New Keynesians in the 1970s. They adopted the RE hypothesis, not because of its realism but mainly because it would be erroneous to offer policy advice on the basis of an unintelligent private sector. But they attacked the market clearing assumption: Because of wage contracts that fix the wages for considerable lengths of time, the labour market may not clear (in any case, not continuously). As a result, this generation of theorists focused on the effects of wage contracts on the effectiveness of monetary policy, in particular contracts of duration of more than one period. For concreteness, we could think of 'odd' unions/firms who sign wage contracts at the end of odd periods of time $(t-1, t-3,$ etc.) for the two periods ahead, and 'even' unions/firms that sign at the end of t, $t-2$, etc.

What happens if, in the above example, some of the unions/firms signed their contracts and fixed wages at the end of $t-2$ for t? They would have known the policy thinking and parameter α but not the overall policy stance because they could not have known y_{t-1} at the end of $t-2$. Hence, they fail to sign wages for t to match the rise in p. In fact, there will not only be a random policy error, but there will also be a whole systematic component of policy missed, that part of the expansion formulated on the knowledge of y_{t-1}. The AS will

---

[8] Since v causes money supply to increase relative to the transactions needs of this economy, we could think of 'v' as standing for 'velocity' (of circulation).

not shift back all the way, and policy here will have delivered a real expansion. This type of result, thus, rests on an informational advantage of government over some of the wage setters (the knowledge of y_{t-1}). This, in turn, crucially depends on wage rigidity.

2.6 The PIP in More Detail

The classic paper on this is Sargent and Wallace (1975). The analysis proceeds as follows. Let a simple Aggregate Demand equation be:

$$y = m - p \tag{2.15}$$

This lets output demand be proportional to the real money supply, in obvious notation. This can be interpreted as a reduced-form equation coming out of the IS-LM system; it is also compatible with the 'quantity theory' of money. Unimportant constants are suppressed. Combined with the Lucas supply function (2.13), it gives:

$$m = (1 + b)p - bEp \tag{2.16}$$

Taking expectations (remember that subjective and mathematical expectations coincide under the REH):

$$E(m) = (1 + b)Ep - bEp = E(p) \tag{2.16'}$$

Expected (systematic) money developments feed only into systematic price movements (this is the essence of Em = Ep). Furthermore, from (2.16), we can express prices as a weighted average of actual and expected money with weights $1 - B$ and $0 < B < 1$, respectively, where $B \equiv \frac{b}{1+b} < 1$:

$$p = \frac{1}{1 + b}(m + bEm) \tag{2.17}$$

Hence, from AD (2.15) we have:

$$y = m - p = B(m - Em), \quad B \equiv \frac{b}{1 + b} < 1 \tag{2.18}$$

That is, only a fraction of the monetary policy stance has a bearing on real output, which is that portion that reflects unanticipated monetary policy. (It is worth remembering that lower-cases are logs, so that m-Em is a percentage portion of m.) The rest of the impact is on prices, i.e.:

$$p - Ep = (1 - B)(m - Em) \tag{2.19}$$

What we keep from this is (2.18): only *unanticipated* money (that part of monetary policy about which we are mistaken) matters for output (deviations from normal) and therefore stabilization policy. Coupled with Rational Expectations, we have that this mistake about policy is entirely random and cannot be manipulated in any way by the policy-maker. Hence, neither can systematic policy do anything to prop up or stabilize income, nor can unsystematic policy (i.e. random shocks) be used in any meaningful way: This is the Policy Ineffectiveness Proposition.

Not only that, but by trying to manipulate y by changing m frequently, the monetary authority will increase the variance of the monetary policy shocks, add more uncertainty into the system, and do more harm than good. To see this more formally, and to connect more with the previous section, add a policy rule like (2.14) above ($m_t = -\alpha y_{t-1} + v_t$) and carry out the derivations again: The same result emerges. More policy activism will likely be accompanied by more uncertainty as well (more v), so that the variance of the system as a whole rises but on average output remains the same.

2.7 Staggered Wages and Stabilization Policy: A Baseline Model

It is however a general view that the world is not characterized by such a high degree of wage and price flexibility as is required for markets to clear continually—this is the topic of much of the New Keynesian literature to be reviewed in Chapter 3. In particular, a set of models (the 'first-generation' New Keynesian models of the 1970s) argued that wages are often set for more than one period by multi-period contracts, so that they do not adjust fast enough to monetary policy impulses to render them neutral.[9] This section reviews this argument by adapting Fischer (1977). It is assumed that wage contracts last for two periods: half of them are signed in even and the other half in odd periods. Importantly, the wages that are negotiated are not fixed for the two periods, but are stipulated such that the expected real wage be constant.[10] But the key point is that it takes two periods until a certain contract is renegotiated; during that time, it is unaltered, imparting some wage rigidity into the system. Thus, for example, the contracts signed at the end of period $(t - 1)$ for periods t and $t + 1$ are:

$$w_t^{t-1} = \omega + E_{t-1}p_t \quad \text{and} \quad w_{t+1}^{t-1} = \omega + E_{t-1}p_{t+1} \qquad (2.20)$$

Superscripts indicate the period at the end of which the relevant wage was signed. ω is the targeted real wage and will be set at zero in what follows. At any time, the average wage is the average of wages signed by negotiations one and two periods ago. Hence, the average real wage in period t is:

$$w_t - p_t = 0.5(w_t^{t-1} + w_t^{t-2}) - p_t = 0.5(E_{t-1}p_t + E_{t-2}p_t) - p_t \qquad (2.21)$$

The Lucas supply function in this setup is more akin to a labour demand curve, with employment equalized to output; in turn, employment depends negatively on the real wage. There is also a supply-side error term u_t with an MA structure:[11]

$$y_t = -b(p_t - w_t) + u_t + \rho u_{t-1} = b(p_t - 0.5^*E_{t-1}p_t - 0.5^*E_{t-2}p_t) + u_t + \rho u_{t-1} \quad (2.22)$$

---

[9] The earlier literature on 'implicit contracts' (see Azariadis, 1975, among others) attributed such contractual length to the risk aversion by workers and the willingness by firms to extend insurance to them by stabilizing the wages somewhat and letting the residual variability be taken up by employment.

[10] In jargon, nominal wages are predetermined—their path outlined at the beginning according to expectations held then—but not fixed across the two periods of the contract. Contrast this with the Taylor model later in the chapter.

[11] In fact, it turns out that meaningful stabilization is possible even if the error process in the Lucas supply function has no MA structure at all (i.e. if $\rho = 0$); the only assumption needed is that monetary policy responds to past shocks—see Fischer (1977). But this structure would beg the question, why would monetary policy respond to past shocks in the first place, and why would it end up stabilizing a shock that is not bothering output at t. In other words, the autoregressive structure is there simply to motivate the need for output stabilization.

u_t now is an exogenous supply shock to output. Note that the Moving Average structure of this error term makes output autocorrelated; this has implications for stabilization policy that will be commented below. Output demand (2.15), repeated below, is:

$$y_t = m_t - p_t \tag{2.15}$$

Finally, the stabilization rule (2.14) is simplified to:

$$m_t = -\alpha u_{t-1} + v_t \tag{2.14'}$$

$\alpha > 0$ is the crucial parameter in the monetary policy 'reaction function',[12] while v_t is the monetary policy error. This is a simplified version of (2.14) in that only the past supply shock is assumed to be stabilized without loss of generality—we could put 'y' instead of 'u' above without the argument losing force, but with more complication. The MA error structure and autocorrelated structure of output y implies that it is meaningful to act 'against' the past shock u_{t-1}, as this affects current output. It is more realistic to assume that the policy-maker acts against the past rather than the current shock as the latter may not be observed immediately.

Combining the Lucas supply equation (2.13), the policy rule (2.14'), and the AD equation (2.15), we get the following equation determining the price level:

$$p_t = -\alpha u_{t-1} + v_t - b(p_t - 0.5{*}E_{t-1}p_t - 0.5{*}E_{t-2}p_t) - u_t - \rho u_{t-1} \tag{2.23}$$

This equation is particularly useful in what follows. Taking expectations at the end of t − 2, we have:

$$\begin{aligned} E_{t-2}p_t = {} & -\alpha E_{t-2}u_{t-1} + E_{t-2}v_t - b(E_{t-2}p_t - 0.5{*}E_{t-2}E_{t-1}p_t - 0.5{*}E_{t-2}p_t) \\ & - E_{t-2}(u_t + \rho u_{t-1}) \end{aligned} \tag{2.23'}$$

Now, the 'law of iterated expectations' states that

$$E_{t-2}E_{t-1}p_t = E_{t-2}p_t. \tag{2.24}$$

My expectation at (t − 2) of what I will expect at (t − 1) about p_t is simply my expectation at (t − 2) of p_t. If that were not the case, I would be expecting at (t − 2) to revise my view of p_t next period (t − 1) in a certain direction—but that revision, though expected, is not incorporated into my views at (t − 2). In that case, it would surely be rational to incorporate that into my belief about p_t straight from the beginning (t − 2)! Plugging this 'law of iterated expectations' (2.24) into (2.23'), and since neither u_t nor u_{t-1} were known at t − 1 ($E_{t-2}u_t = E_{t-2}u_{t-1} = 0$; similarly with the v_t shock), we have:

$$E_{t-2}p_t = 0 \tag{2.25a}$$

Price expectations for t two periods in advance were nil. The reason is simple: no relevant shocks were known at that period. Since everything is expressed as deviations from trend, this means at t − 2, P_t was expected to be on the trend.

---

[12] Notice that, as is customary, various constants have been dropped for ease—they do not add much to the analysis. This amounts to saying that both output and money must be construed as deviations from some 'normal' or structural (entirely supply-side determined) benchmark level.

This is not the case, however, with expectations formed one period in advance, as these would take into account the $(t-1)$ shock and the monetary policy stance in t. Taking again expectations from (2.23)—but this time taking account of everything known at the end of period $t-1$:

$$E_{t-1}p_t = -\alpha u_{t-1} - b(E_{t-1}p_t + E_{t-1}E_{t-2}p_t)/2 - \rho u_{t-1} \tag{2.25b}$$

Note that $E_{t-1}v_t = 0$. Now, another law of expectations states that:

$$E_{t-1}E_{t-2}p_t = E_{t-2}p_t$$

In words, at $(t-1)$ I knew for a fact what my previous year's expectation was (in this case: fixed -0). Hence, (2.25b) becomes:

$$E_{t-1}p_t = -\frac{\alpha + \rho}{1 + b/2}u_{t-1} \tag{2.25b'}$$

Substituting all relevant information—the Lucas-type supply (2.22), demand (2.15), policy (2.14), and expectations (2.25b'), we get:

$$y_t = b(-\alpha u_{t-1} + v_t - y_t + \frac{\alpha + \rho}{2(1 + b/2)}u_{t-1}) + u_t + \rho u_{t-1}$$

Collecting terms, we have:

$$y_t = \frac{u_t + bv_t + \beta(2\rho - \alpha b)u_{t-1}}{1 + b}, \quad \beta \equiv \frac{1 + b}{2(1 + b/2)} > 0 \tag{2.26}$$

Last period's shock now has real effects this period, as the coefficient of u_{t-1} is non-zero. As argued, policy is meaningful in offsetting last period's shock (the coefficient of u_{t-1} decreases with the strength of policy indicated by α). The policy captured by (2.14') is stabilizing in the sense that it reduces the variance of y, as can be easily seen by taking the variance of (2.26).

Moreover, policy should be optimally set to

$$\alpha = 2\rho/b,$$

in which case the past period's shock is completely offset. This is the best policy can do in this setup. The properties of this type of 'monetary policy rule' are that policy should be more 'activist' (i.e. more responsive to past shocks as indicated by α):

- the more the effect of the past shock on output today (ρ);[13]
- and the less sensitive output is to monetary policy shocks (b), because in this case smaller-size monetary impulses are needed to generate an output thrust of a certain size.[14]

---

[13] We can now substantiate the claim made earlier, namely that if a past period's shock does not impinge on current output, then there is no point doing stabilization work against them—just see what happens with $\rho = 0$.

[14] The interested reader can pursue various possibilities as an exercise. The idea is this: a low responsiveness of output to the real wage (low b in 2.22) necessitates larger monetary policy changes. In discussing (2.22), though, we noted that this responsiveness depends adversely on the degree of 'noise' in the price level (i.e. a high V_p implies a low b). Assume, as instructed by the signal extraction problem, that $b = b(V_p)$, with $b'(V_p) < 0$. Take the variances of the price level (2.23) and output (2.26). How are these affected by policy activism (α), taking into

Finally, we have emphasized here stabilization against a supply shock only. Taylor (1979) among others shows that such meaningful stabilization can be undertaken with a demand shock as well—e.g. a shock in the AD equation (2.25).

This argument then suggests that PIP does not hold, not as a result of the breakdown of Rational Expectations (which is upheld) but because of the breakdown of the assumption that markets continually clear. Fischer (1977) carries home this point in an emphatic way: he uses a more general policy reaction function than the one above, by letting the current money supply m_t respond to shocks even further back. Importantly, the parameters showing the sensitivity of policy to any shock beyond the one last period fail to show up in the final output equation (Fischer, 1977, p. 248). In other words, in order to be meaningful, policy needs to react only to shocks as far back as the length of the wage contracts. This is because developments that took place further in the past have been known by all wage setters of the current wages, and policy actions based on such developments have already been embedded in all currently valid wages. Thus, it is not the 'sophisticated' policy that reacts to past shocks that makes the PIP fail but the existence of wage rigidity in the form of multi-period (staggered) wage contracts. The implication is that wage flexibility (single-period contracts) entails the PIP.

2.8 Wage and Price Inertia and Stabilization Policy: Further Issues

Taylor (1979) examines essentially the same structure, except that wages are now not simply predetermined during the contract, but fixed, which is a stronger proposition. The newly set (and lasting two periods) contract wage has been determined with reference both to what earlier contracts set and to what future conditions (future contracts as well as future excess demand) are expected to be. In other words, there is a balance between 'backward-looking' and 'forward-looking' dynamics in the newly set wage.[15] The economy-wide wage is the average of the wages set this and last periods. In this setup, money (that is, money market-related as well as policy-related shocks) now has long-lasting effects on output (see also Blanchard and Fischer, 1989)—in contrast to the Fischer (1977) model reviewed above, in which current money supply only affects current output. The important message here is, the greater the degree of wage inertia, the greater the scope for monetary policy to affect output.

Let us take a moment to think through this. The main reason is that in the Taylor (1979) structure, there is a greater degree of wage inertia, so that labour market clearing occurs only sluggishly after new shocks. The degree of wage inertia depends mainly on two factors: the balance between backward and forward-looking elements in new wage setting (obviously, more of the former enhances inertia, while the latter helps determine a wage that responds quickly to expected developments); and the degree of 'monetary policy accommodation'. (The latter is the degree to which the monetary authority is prepared to increase money supply so as to accommodate—and not restrain—the rise in wages and

account the dependence of b on V_p? What is the optimal policy rule now? Is it qualitatively different than the rule above ($a = 2\rho/b$)? See also Section 2.9.

[15] The analysis of Taylor (1979) anticipates the Calvo (1983) model of inflation, reviewed in Chapter 3.

prices; from the simple AD equation $y = m - p$, if p rises, full accommodation implies m rising to the same extent, whereas restrain t means m not rising, in which case y falls.) Such accommodation obviously helps make the real wage more persistent and respond less quickly to labour market discrepancies. In this model, wage inertia delivers a degree of wage stability, with the residual variability being taken up by employment and output stability. Hence, there is a trade-off between the two types of stability—wage and output stability. Taylor (1979) argues that short contract lengths (of about a year, much as observed in reality) deliver empirically plausible output persistence. In parallel to wage inertia, Blanchard (1983) considers delays and staggering in price setting; he shows that empirically plausible lags of a month or so can generate considerable price level inertia and long-lasting real effects of a monetary expansion.

As is clear from the above analyses, monetary policy can have stabilizing (potentially long-lasting) effects not because anybody is fooled, but because not enough information about future policy actions is available when some of the contracts are signed. In other words, single-period contracts take us back to the PIP. In fact, as Fischer (1977) argues, there are mechanisms of wage determination that can replicate the effects of single-period contracts, though the length of the actual contract is longer. Consider an 'indexing' mechanism of the type:

$$w_t^{t-2} = E_{t-1}p_t$$

Under this scheme, the wage for t stipulated at the end of $(t - 2)$—when the contract is signed—envisages adjusting (indexing) the nominal wage for t at the end of $(t - 1)$—i.e. mid-contract—to reflect the then expected price level.[16] In other words, mid-contract, the wage is to be adjusted but only as far as accommodating any expected rises in the prices level at that point; no real gains are to be made. Note that the simpler contract seen above (2.20) would have stipulated $w_t^{t-2} = E_{t-2}p_t$. From an analytical point of view, this is exactly like signing single-period contracts (at the end of each period sign for the period ahead), and PIP is restored. But this mechanism is hard to carry out and has not generally been used in practice. Instead, a type of contract that has often been used specifies that the wage for the second year of the contract be adjusted by the inflation of the first period:

$$w_t^{t-2} = w_{t-1}^{t-2} + p_{t-1} - p_{t-2} \tag{2.27}$$

This 'indexing' mechanism has had some practical application mainly in the 1980s in Europe. While the first-period wage is indexed on the expected price level for $(t - 1)$, the second period adjusts the first wage (of $t - 1$) upwards by the inflation rate of the last year. To see this more clearly, write the above in levels (dropping the superscripts):

$$W_t = W_{t-1}(1 + \pi_{t-1})$$

π here is the inflation rate. The nominal wage is adjusted proportionately upwards to cover any losses due to inflation. Such contracts have been in widespread use in many countries during times of high inflation, but have subsided with the taming of inflation since the

---

[16] Hence, the nominal wage for t is also predetermined, but in a weaker sense than the earlier predetermination which envisaged putting a number on paper for w_t at the beginning of the contract.

mid-1990s. They obviously generate wage inertia that allows the monetary policy to have real effects (see Gray, 1976); but they also have in-built an inflation inertia, so dismantling them was widely seen as necessary in the battle against inflation. We return to price inertia in Chapter 3.

2.9 Other Criticisms of the PIP

A criticism that has been levelled against the Lucas supply function is that it does not admit any serial correlation, or persistence, of output. The expectational errors involved in it are purely random (no systematic pattern or persistence can be detected in them since Rational Expectations is assumed), and therefore do not lend output any such pattern.[17] But this is at odds with empirical evidence which strongly shows such a pattern to exist in the data (see Chapter 6 on Business Cycles), and therefore the Lucas supply function cannot be a meaningful basis for business cycles research. This deficiency can be amended by augmenting the Lucas function (2.13) as follows:

$$y_t = b(p_t - E_{t-1}(p_t)) + \rho_1 y_{t-1} + u_t, \quad \text{with } u_t = \rho_2 u_{t-1} + v_t, \text{and } 0 \leq \rho_1, \rho_2 < 1$$

The u_t is now an error term which has an autoregressive structure—it is made up of past primary shocks v_{t-i} which are more heavily discounted the further away in the past they took place (larger i). Non-zero autoregressive parameters guarantee that output y shows a degree of persistence as the data show. However, any of these autoregressive structures is assumed and not derived from well-understood mechanisms and processes. One can still investigate the capability of monetary policy with these additional mechanisms. It is easy to show that with $\rho_1 > 0$ (which is in fact a more general statement than $\rho_2 > 0$), the PIP is upheld with one-period contracts.[18] The output autoregressive pattern matters, however, when it interacts with multi-period contracts, and might exacerbate the effects of wage inertia because wage setters have more information about what future monetary policy will look like due to output persistence; but this issue appears not to have been researched very thoroughly.

An empirically testable implication of the Lucas supply function is that, in economies characterized by erratic monetary conditions, output responses to specific unexpected aggregate demand developments (m − Em) are more muted; this is because b and θ depend inversely on the variance of nominal aggregate demand V_p. An interesting implication is that real output would respond less to a monetary development (e.g. a given percentage monetary expansion), the more inflationary the overall environment. Lucas (1973) provides cross-country evidence that this is indeed the case. However, Ball et al. (1988) showed that this implication can be obtained from a model with price stickiness, which is in many ways different than the Lucas model and which does not have firms respond to unexpected price shocks only. Barro (1977, 1978) has tested the proposition that $y = B(m - Em)$, which is a fundamental building block of the argument,

---

[17] As we saw, in (2.22) we added arbitrarily an MA structure that induces a weak form of autocorrelation for y_t, in order to motivate the use of stabilization policy.
[18] Sargent and Wallace (1975) derive this result.

with favourable results. However, the response of output did not appear to go via $p - Ep$, as theory predicts. Additionally, even if $p - Ep$ changes, we need a highly elastic labour supply for those changes to be translated into the sizeable labour/output fluctuations that we observe, something that is not verified by the evidence (see Chapter 6 on business cycles and Chapter 1 for more on the labour supply elasticity).

Continuing on empirical evidence and econometric methodology, there are two broader points. Since neither Em nor Ep are observable, any test of the Lucas supply function will be a joint test of two hypotheses: first, that only unanticipated money influences real output and, second, an auxiliary expectational hypothesis. It is very difficult, if not impossible, for these tests to distinguish between the two hypotheses and reject one while accepting the other. Thus, any failure of $y = b(p - Ep)$ or $y = B(m - Em)$ cannot safely be attributed to the failure of theory or the REH. From an even broader perspective, Sargent (1976) has pointed out the 'observational equivalence' of broad classes of theoretical models, including (New) Classical and (New) Keynesian models. His analysis shows how very different models eventually boil down to (qualitatively) identical reduced-form, estimable equations; thus, it is impossible to interpret whether the estimated equation is consistent with one or the other model. An example is given in the next section.

Naturally, the implication of individual optimization and market clearing that agents are doing the best for themselves and therefore any employed resources are voluntarily unemployed (given the environment) has been criticized by theorists of more Keynesian persuasions. Old Keynesians like Tobin (1993) would argue that, if the unemployment of people may possibly be characterized as stemming from their own decisions, the unemployment of machines that accompanies human unemployment (idle capacity during recessions) surely cannot be! Furthermore, research on business cycles shows that most of the variation in total hours of employment comes from people moving in and out of work rather than workers marginally adjusting their hours (see Chapters 1 and 6). This makes it somewhat harder to argue that all employment fluctuations happen along (individual) labour supply curves; there is considerable movement in and out of employment altogether. We shall see in Chapter 6 how this lineage of theories has adapted to account for this possibility.

Finally, and not least, two more substantive points. In his critical review, Buiter (1980) notes that PIP depends on an aggregate demand equation like (2.15) which relates AD to the real money supply directly—and nothing else. In a more realistic model, however, AD affects consumption/saving and investment behaviour and portfolio decisions; fiscal and monetary policy will affect these even without price and wage rigidities. It is unclear whether the PIP will hold under such more complex structures. In defence of the theory, the above model aims to capture the essence of the macroeconomy while maintaining tractability. Secondly, we should mention a weakness of the theory from a wider perspective, made by Iversen and Soskice (2006): the PIP serves as a warning that systematic stabilization policy does not work, that it should not be carried out. But stabilization policies are used, and to varying degrees by different governments. This theory then does not explain what determines whether governments actually carry out stabilization policy, and to what extent. Whether one agrees with it or not, it is a normative theory but not a positive one; so argue Iversen and Soskice (2006). Again, a response would be that the theory does make testable predictions (i.e. it is not only a normative proposition), i.e. that stabilization policy does not work. It is up to empirical work to verify or reject these predictions.

2.10 The Lucas Critique

We now review the celebrated Lucas (1976) critique of interventionist government policy, which is an indispensable part of the set of ideas associated with the New Classicals. Lucas criticized the standard practice of the day which postulated plausible, but theoretically shaky, econometric models, estimated them, and on that basis offered policy advice on the output effects of government instruments like government spending or taxes. Lucas's main point was that if government tried to act on this advice, the macroeconomic system (on which this advice was based) would profoundly change, making this advice invalid. The reason is that the behavioural equations that make up the macroeconomic system (consumption, investment, money demand, labour demand, and so on) depend on the perception that agents have about the government's behaviour. Thus, any change in government policy would be perceived by agents (firms, households) who would in general adjust their behaviour. They would respond to the new government spending, or taxes, or money supply, in a different way than they had done hitherto. In doing so, they will alter the very structure of the system on the basis of which policy advice is offered, and make the policy change ineffective (or even detrimental).

More formally, following Ljungqvist (2008), let the macroeconomic system be described by a system of n equations (assumed linear) of the form:

$$y_{t+1} = f(y_t, x_t, e_t; \theta) \tag{2.28}$$

Where y_t is an nx1 vector of variables that describe the state of the system (output, consumption, capital stock, labour supply, investment dynamics, and so forth), x_t are the policy variables (money supply, government spending, etc.), e_t are exogenous variables (such as world trade, oil prices) and shocks (weather, technology shocks, etc.). These equations and the f(.) functions will include all the behavioural equations characterizing the economy and identities; e.g. the dynamics of consumption, capital accumulation, labour supply, national income accounting, are all included.[19] The behavioural equations among these will essentially derive from the agents' optimization problems, i.e. they will be the first-order conditions. The key point here is that the agents' first-order conditions, and therefore the f(.) functions, depend on the processes that drive the policy (x) and exogenous variables (e). For example, the exogenous variables may be assumed to be characterized by autoregressive patterns, and policy variables are governed by policy rules like the stabilization rule (2.14) above. All the relevant structural parameters of these processes (such as autocorrelation coefficients, and policy parameters like α in equation 2.14) are collected in the set θ. Any change in the form or the properties of the policy rules (and the processes that drive the exogenous variables) will alter the form of the f(.) functions. Why? Because any such change will force agents to recalculate their optimal strategies, i.e. to recalculate their first-order conditions that underpin the system of equations (2.28). An example may be a change in the degree of stabilization α in (2.14). If the government were to become more interventionist, i.e. α were to increase, the money supply would become more volatile. (Note that even if a more activist stabilization policy 2.14' manages to reduce the variance of output in 2.26, the variance of money supply in 2.14' would likely

---

[19] The accounting identities include no error terms.

increase; – why?) So, agents would realize that the volatility of the monetary system has increased. This may induce agents to recalculate the amount of cash reserves they hold in the bank, the frequency of wage or price increases (thus changing the extent of wage-price rigidity), the rules for calculating optimal portfolios as risk premia will have changed, etc. These changes would be reflected in a change in θ; so a change in government behaviour will have changed the structure of the system.

Econometric estimation of (2.28) will of necessity be based on a finite sample in which the policy stance was of a certain type. Let us assume that the estimated (2.28) is

$$\hat{y}_{t+1} = F(y_t, x_t, e_t; \theta_0); \tag{2.28'}$$

the estimated F(.) function reflects the specific form that the f(.) functions had when $\theta = \theta_0$, reflecting the policy stance in place during the time of the sample. It is erroneous, Lucas (1976) argues, to treat the estimated (2.28') as a 'deep' structural equation and offer policy advice. If this advice is to follow a different policy stance than the one underpins the estimated θ_0 parameters, the form of the f(.) functions will change, rendering the policy advice useless.[20]

Let us see the point through a more concrete example. Let the monetary authority follow a countercyclical policy rule similar in spirit to rule (2.14),

$$m_t = \mu_0 + \mu_1 m_{t-1} - \mu_2 y_{t-1} + e_t, \tag{2.29}$$

where the key parameter is $\mu_2 > 0$ (akin to α in equation 2.14); e_t is the error in policy formulation (the money supply was, and is, an imperfectly controlled instrument). Furthermore, output is entirely demand-determined, but importantly, by unexpected monetary developments only, as the New Classicals have emphasized, as in (2.18):

$$y_t = B(m_t - E_{t-1}m_t) = Be_t \tag{2.30}$$

(as $E_{t-1}m_t = \mu_0 + \mu_1 m_{t-1} - \mu_2 y_{t-1}$). Now, (2.29) does show a certain correlation between money and output, but it is the latter that drives the former (because of the policy rule) and not the other way around (by the reasoning of the New Classicals). Unaware of that, the econometrician may attempt to estimate the distributed-lag observable equation:

$$y_t = B\left[m_t - \mu_0 - \mu_1 m_{t-1} + \mu_2 y_{t-1}\right] + u_t \tag{2.31}$$

Note that (2.30) is an estimable reduced-form equation consistent with both (2.30) and with an IS-LM type of model where money influences real output: This is an instance of Sargent's (1976) observational equivalence of different models, mentioned above. The unsuspecting econometrician then may interpret (2.31) as deriving from an IS-LM-type model.

They take this to the data and estimate the parameters; s/he interprets it to show a long-run relationship between money and output, with causality from money to output. On the basis of (2.31), s/he furthermore advises the government on the long-run Keynesian 'multiplier' $dy/dm = (B(1 - \mu_1)/(1 - B\mu_2))$. (A New Classical would have known that this is not true all along, but this is a criticism of naïve econometric practice and policy

---

[20] More generally, x also includes non-policy exogenous variables (e.g. international trade). Any change in the processes that drive these variables will also prompt agents' re-optimization and change of behaviour.

advice.) If on this basis the government decides that monetary policy works (it delivers the real output changes that it intends to), it might embark on a new policy regime of more activist stabilization (a higher μ_2). The government implements the new policy, but finds that the policy does not work as intended, the expansion of money during the recession does not have the predicted effects. The supposed effect of the activist monetary policy does not materialize. Agents have realized that a new policy regime is in place, and have adjusted their behaviour. In particular, the greater variability of m_t (because of more activist stabilization) adds more noise into the system, and dampens the individual output responses: B has fallen. (Remember that $\partial B/\partial \mathrm{Var}(m - Em) < 0$.) Thus, the earlier econometric advice was erroneous because the estimated model did not take into account that the parameters themselves depended on the policy regime in place.

The most often quoted example is the breakdown of the naïve Phillips Curve. We know that the true Phillips Curve (2.13') involves expected prices or inflation. Now, imagine an econometrician who estimates (2.13') with a sample during which monetary policy produced a constant average inflation rate of, say, 5 per cent. Thus, expectations of inflation were constant (5 per cent) and might have been incorporated as a constant in the estimated (2.13'). If the policy advice was to expand money (say), this would reduce unemployment temporarily, but it would also increase expected prices, which had been treated as constant—the naïve Phillips Curve would shift upwards. Thus, the equation will break down (will no longer be empirically successful), rendering the policy advice useless. The shifts in the Phillips Curve in the 1960s and 1970s and the emergence finally of no relationship between inflation and unemployment may be a real-world application of the Lucas critique.

A third example is provided by the possible breakdown of the Keynesian multiplier in the case of tax cuts. Such cuts stimulate output in an IS-LM world, with a naïve Keynesian consumption function; when intertemporal choice is taken into account, however, these tax cuts may instead be saved rather than consumed. Thinking that tax cuts are expansionary, a naïve policy-maker may embark on higher deficits which will however fail to stimulate the economy (as agents save the tax rebates). This is the essence of the 'Ricardian Equivalence Proposition', included among the six 'policy ineffectiveness results' in Chapter 1 and reviewed in more detail in Chapter 8 on fiscal policy. In other words, this proposition may be seen as an application of the Lucas critique. In addition, in some ways the 'Time Inconsistency Proposition', another one of the ineffectiveness results to be further analysed in Chapter 7 on monetary policy, may also be considered an application of the Lucas critique.

In conclusion, the Lucas critique is a powerful indictment of dubious econometric practice. It warns us against estimation across time periods where different policy regimes were in place, cautions us against out-of-sample predictions, and directs us to do structural stability tests in our estimated relations. It is also a warning against activist stabilization policy. The critique calls for theory built explicitly on optimization principles by the private sector, rather than spurious empirical behavioural relations, and econometric estimation of the optimality conditions themselves. Thus, the Lucas critique has acted not only as a criticism of policy but has also profoundly affected the direction of subsequent research.

It is questionable, however, how relevant it is from a practical point of view. Its validity is arguably more long-term, but quite possibly less relevant for short-term predictions. Furthermore, it may be argued that pursuing logical rigour ('internal consistency') in building theories may not be the only, or even sometimes the most important, criterion in judging the success of them. What is termed 'external relevance' is also called for, i.e. the ability of theories to give useful, clear-cut, but also reasonably simple empirically testable predictions (and policy prescriptions). What may be called for is a variety of approaches and a certain degree of eclecticism, where the quest for 'deep structural foundations' in theoretical work may depend on the problem at hand (see Buiter, 1980).

2.11 Criticisms of Rational Expectations and Bounded Rationality

2.11.1 How Much Information?

We saw that the Rational Expectations Hypothesis (REH) implies (by definition) that expectations equal actual plus a zero-mean error term (a 'noise'). Thus, for instance for prices:

$$p_t^* = E(p_t/I_t), \quad \text{so} \quad p_t = p_t^* + u_t$$

where the star indicates the subjective expectation, $E(./I)$ is the mathematical expectation subject to the available information I_t, and u_t is the zero-mean error term. The REH requires minimally that agents know the true structure of the model that characterizes the economy including its parameters, and use that structure on which to base their expectations. These are very strong requirements, and are a basis of forceful criticism of REH (see Buiter, 1980).

Market outcomes (are assumed to) reflect all available information, but what determines how much information becomes available? This is usually taken as a given; but the information is the product of costly search and investigation. How much information will there be? This question has been tackled by Grossman and Stiglitz (1980) who start from the observation that information acquisition is in general costly, therefore agents who possess information have paid a cost, and expect to be rewarded for that. This implies that, in equilibrium, informed agents must be able to better anticipate the market outcome. If p_t^* is the expectation of the uninformed traders and p_t^{**} that of the informed, the latter must be sufficiently closer to the market outcome p_t systematically for the informed to recoup the cost of acquiring information (c—fixed by assumption). This implies that the market price can never fully reflect all available information, if information is costly. More broadly, Grossman and Stiglitz (1980) highlight a fundamental trade-off between the cost of information acquisition and processing, and the benefit of being better informed.

It is worth seeing these issues a little more closely and formally. Let there be two kinds of agents, the informed (**) and the uninformed (*). Let the former know the fundamentals with accuracy (call their expected price p**), whereas the latter have a fuzzier idea and expect p*, where (suppressing time-subscripts from now on):

$$p^* = p^{**} + e, \tag{2.32}$$

where e is error by which understanding of the fundamentals by the uninformed and the informed differs. This error has a mean of zero ($Ee = 0$) but its variance, $Var(e) > 0$, is a reflection of the fuzziness in the expectations of the uninformed. Now, the supply of an asset is,

$$S = \alpha p + u \qquad (2.33)$$

where u is a random shock (the source of all uncertainty); this is equated with demand:

$$D = \lambda(\beta - \gamma p^{**}) + (1 - \lambda)(\beta - \gamma p^*) \qquad (2.34)$$

Demand comes from two market segments (informed-uninformed), in both of which demand is inversely related to the expectations of the price (before it is realized). λ is the proportion of the informed and $(1 - \lambda)$ of the uninformed agents. In this model, α, β, and γ are the known fundamentals and u is an exogenous supply shock.[21] Since e reflects the lack of information of the uninformed, using (2.32), we get:

$$D = \lambda(\beta - \gamma p^{**}) + (1 - \lambda)(\beta - \gamma p^{**} - \gamma e) \qquad (2.34')$$

Equating supply (2.33) and demand (2.34') and taking expectations establishes that:

$$p^{**} = \beta/(\alpha + \gamma) \qquad (2.35)$$

This would have been the price if there was perfect knowledge ('perfect foresight'). The expectation of the informed accurately reflects the fundamentals of supply and demand. On the other hand, the actual price follows from (2.33) and (2.34') with the use of (2.35):

$$p = \beta/(\alpha + \gamma) - u/\alpha - (1 - \lambda)\gamma e/\alpha \qquad (2.35')$$

Now, here is an important point. As in standard Rational Expectations models, the price reflects the fundamentals and the shock u, but on top of that it is also affected by the 'fuzziness' term e. Thus, it cannot fully reflect the fundamentals in the sense asserted by the REH and the Efficient Markets Hypothesis. In turn, this term must have the following property: the margin by which the informed beat the market may be thought to depend on the variance of $e = p^{**} - p^*$ (as the mean of e is zero), divided by the amount of agents sharing the spoils (the informed, λ). If this then is to be equalized to the cost of acquiring information (c), we have that:

$$Var(e) = \lambda c$$

Hence, the understanding of the informed must be sufficiently better (that of the uninformed sufficiently fuzzier—higher Var(e)) the higher is the proportion of the informed— because then the price deviates less from fundamental; and the greater the cost of information—in which case they need to beat the rest of the market by a bigger margin.

The only case by which REH and efficient markets are recovered is when there are only informed agents ($\lambda = 1$); in other words, when information is costless, an implicit assumption of the efficient market hypothesis. But then, disconcerting possibilities may arise. If all prices are informationally efficient, no one has any incentive to acquire information, so what information does the market reflect? Another intriguing outcome is that there will be no trade![22] For more on such logical loopholes see Grossman (1976).

---

[21] It is a moot point whether u should be considered part of the 'fundamentals'. More accurately, its variance is part of the fundamentals.

[22] Trade may arise because of the difference in tastes—I like more an asset e.g. a house than you do, hence we trade—or difference in endowments—I have more of an asset than I want to keep, and the opposite occurs to

We conclude that there *must* be some uninformed traders, $\lambda < 1$. If so, competitive markets can never be 'informationally efficient'.

Haltiwanger and Waldman (1985) investigate further the effects of agent heterogeneity (informed-uninformed). In their model, there are the sophisticated agents who make predictions along the lines of REH and the simpler ones that use adaptive expectations and rules of thumb; for example, in forecasting inflation. The question is, will the overall market behaviour be shaped by the first or second group? The answer is that the second group dominates. The forecast of inflation will have a persistence that is generated from the adaptive mechanism. Hence, the existence of some rational agents is not enough to 'push' the entire market outcome to a type of those envisaged by REH. Persistence of errors remains.

2.11.2 Learning and the REH

One might therefore be inclined to conclude that agent heterogeneity (informed-uninformed) must be allowed, and this is something that makes common sense. But this is not an entirely satisfactory state of affairs either, as DeCanio (1979) shows. As before, let p^{**} be the rationally expected price level, and p^* any other expectation, such as based on adaptive, rule-of-thumb reasoning (e.g., an increase of 5 per cent expected every period), or any other. Now, if some people hold p^{**} and some p^*, the eventual market price will be somewhere between the two (neither of the two exactly). But in this case, p^{**} will not be realized as a price and therefore it will not be RE (remember, RE requires that expectations be model-consistent and therefore self-fulfilling). Thus, the REH seems to require that everybody must know not only the structure of the system but also what everybody else is thinking. If not, RE will not arise.

These analyses lead then naturally to how information is gradually acquired; this process is called 'learning' (in technical jargon as well as in everyday parlance!). The literature has analysed a variety of approaches; one of the main questions is, does learning give rise gradually to rational expectations? If yes, that would be a validation of the REH and would imply that the REH is a useful approximation of what happens in the long run, when sufficient learning has taken place. Whereas if not, that would be another nail in the coffin of REH. However, the literature does not speak with one voice. For example, Cyert and DeGroot (1974) investigate learning in the context of a dynamic demand-and-supply ('cobweb') model and generally find that, with learning, expectations converge to rational; while DeCanio (1979) gives a rather ambiguous answer. As Simon (1978) warns, there may be rationality in terms of how we acquire and use information (rationality as a process), but that does not necessarily coincide with rationality as an end result, a specific 'rational' outcome (which is what the REH assumes). Incidentally, Simon (1978) argues that rationality is a postulate largely shared by other social disciplines.

---

you—or difference in beliefs; the analysis centres entirely on the third possibility. Barring the first two possibilities, if all agents are fully informed, they will all supply or demand the assets in an identical way, hence there will be no trade. No trade also arises when the cost of acquiring information is so great that no one can recoup this cost—resulting again in identical behaviour.

Further analyses of 'adaptive learning' relax the very strong assumption of REH that agents know the true structure of the economic system. This literature assumes that there are aspects of the model known to agents (e.g. that it is linear), and others that are not, e.g. the exact value of linear coefficients or the properties of the exogenous error terms (e.g. serial correlation). Agents gradually learn about these aspects of the economic model. They are assumed to have a 'prior' view (however given) and then update it (using perhaps least squares) as new data come in.[23] The forecasts they build conditional on their knowledge at any point are not in a formal sense 'rational' because agents do not know the system exactly; they keep updating their guesses as new information comes in (adaptive learning). Forecasts built in such a way may or may not converge to the (formal) Rational Expectations. Good introductions to this literature with some basic results and further references are Honkapohja (1993) and Evans and Honkapohja (2009). Apart from its appeal, adaptive learning can provide a criterion of selection in the cases when Rational Expectations yields multiple equilibria.[24] Those equilibria that are 'expectationally stable' (i.e. can be approached by adaptive learning) may be kept while the others discarded.

2.11.3 'Bounded Rationality' and Behavioural Macroeconomics

Learning naturally leads to the broader idea of Bounded Rationality, the idea that agents do not possess the immense calculation powers that the REH assumes; but they are still assumed to use the capabilities they have (see Conlisk, 1996, and Simon, 1987, for good introductions). This is a major direction toward which Economics and Financial Economics has turned in recent years. To organize our thinking, it is useful to define 'rationality', beyond the narrow(er) concept of 'rational expectations'. In fact, a clear definition is not easy to find. In the mind of this author, in economics, 'full' rationality implies:

(a) clear preferences or objectives;
(b) a cognitive ability to determine the best strategy to achieve the objectives as best as possible;
(c) discipline to self-enforce this strategy;
(d) and finally, as a minimum requirement, there must not be systematic errors and mistakes.

It is easy to think of instances and reasons why each of these fails. Part (a) suggests that, e.g. when I am given a menu in a restaurant, I know what I want (given my preferences, the prices, etc.). There is no ambivalence (ehhm, hmm . . . , which one, . . .) or prevarication (can you please give me five minutes more to decide); i.e. all these every-day situations are strictly speaking violations of rationality. And if we do not know clearly our mind in front

---

[23] Thus, this approach has affinities with the notion of Bayesian statistics; see Cyert and DeGroot (1974).
[24] Multiplicity of solutions (i.e. that any model may admit more than one solutions) may in some cases be a strength of a theory, but may also be thought of as a problem: the said model does not yield concrete predictions. REH generates such instances of multiple solutions. This 'non-uniqueness' or 'indeterminacy' problem of REH has attracted considerable attention—see e.g. McCallum (1983). 'Bubbles' in assets markets may be thought of as an instance of multiple solutions.

of a restaurant menu, one can imagine the degree of clarity when more complex dilemmas are involved. There are even more important reasons to think why part (b) may fail, such as the sheer complexity of the tasks involved, our inherently limited cognitive abilities, and the costs associated with structured reasoning. Part (c) fails e.g. when we decide that we will go to the gym (or start a diet, or start saving, etc.) on Monday, but when Monday comes, we change our mind (without circumstances having changed). This is the problem of 'time inconsistency of optimal decisions'; we shall encounter it in Chapter 7 in relation to monetary policy and in Chapter 11 in relation to the form of discounting associated with intertemporal decision-making. In relation to part (d), there is substantial evidence from experimental economics and psychology that people make systematic and substantial reasoning errors and are thus subject to 'biases' (Conlisk, 1996; Ariely, 2008; Kahneman, 2012), while of course being 'rational' in some dimensions. The errors and biases depend on experience, the extent of deliberation costs, the complexity of tasks, incentives, etc., but they do seem a permanent feature of life. Additionally, there are some instances which may or may not be compatible with rationality, e.g. prevarication and procrastination. We might take some time to consider our best choices and strategies; further, we may wait for more information to emerge; but beyond these reasons, rationality suggests that there should not be any further delay in decision-making. What about regret? Does it reflect genuine new information that has arisen from following a certain strategy? Or does it reflect simply inconsistent preferences? The former is compatible with rationality, the latter not. Finally, what about fashion? Or status-seeking from impressing others (e.g., showing my gold watch)? Traditionally, it was thought that the 'neoclassical' utility function only had individual consumption as an argument (thus was incompatible with fashion or status, which take into account what others do); but recently, 'other-regarding' preferences have become commonplace. We dwell on those below and in Chapter 11.[25]

In all, 'full' rationality seems impossible to attain. Our rationality is bounded in various ways. We often use 'rules of thumb' like the Keynesian consumption function: I consume a constant fraction of my income, no matter what the interest rate or what my predictions about the future are, etc., if I have found from experience that such rules are 'good enough'. Or we may reason about a problem 'heuristically', by analogy to simple and more manageable problems. This may sometimes lead to fallacies when the analogies and metaphors are fundamentally erroneous. For example, we often think of the aggregate economy as a big business; this may sometimes lead to useful reasoning and sometimes to misleading conclusions (the 'fallacy of composition'). Experience and judgement should guide us in using appropriate analogies, metaphors, and heuristics. In a more intelligent manner, we may follow Akerlof and Yellen (1985) in assuming 'near-rationality', i.e. that we get it 'about right', but perhaps not *exactly* right. We eliminate the mistakes of 'first order' but choose to live with those of 'second order', particularly when the costs of eliminating them are large.[26] Akerlof and Yellen (1985) show that the aggregate effects of even 'small' such errors can be substantial because of the externalities involved; this is

---

[25] What about boredom? Is that compatible with rationality? To frame the question, consider that time is limited (16 or so hours per day after sleep) but uses of it multiple and competing—work, looking after the family, study, catching up with friends, sports, other hobbies, etc, etc. There is no time to get bored—says the theory! So, what do you think?

[26] This idea is close to the idea of 'satisficing' (Simon, 1987) that postulates that we try to achieve a level of utility that is 'good enough', rather than maximizing utility.

one of the major themes of New Keynesian macroeconomics, to be reviewed in Chapter 3. Yet another practice may be that we break complex tasks (arbitrarily) into more manageable components. For example, at the beginning of his/her adult life, a young person may face the dual problem of what profession to choose (assume that the only criterion is to maximize their living standards—there are no likes and dislikes) and where to settle. Imagine that there are 1, 2, . . . , N professions to choose from, and 1, 2, . . . , M countries. The fully rational procedure is to estimate the living standards of all N professions in all of the M countries—thus, to make NM calculations. Well, I don't think that any of us has done that. Instead, many of us have first chosen a profession (say k), and then asked, what country is best for profession k? Or, we may have started from a country, and again, subject to that choice, we select a profession. Similarly for firms: firms typically have to decide on optimal capacity (from investment and labour hire) and a price to sell their product (and many other things besides). But the simultaneous calculation of optimal capital, labour, and prices is extremely hard even for the most technically sophisticated economists, let alone for lesser mortals. So, firms may at a first stage decide on their capacity, and subject to the given capacity, to decide on the product price and output that maximizes their revenue. This breaking down of complex calculations into simpler, intuitive but arbitrarily staged tasks is called 'hierarchical decomposition' in reasoning (Ermini, 1991). Thus, all these instances of bounded rationality (rules of thumb, heuristics, near-rationality, hierarchical decomposition) have potentially important macroeconomic implications.

Bounded rationality borders the field of behavioural economics. There has long been an unease among some economic theorists about anomalies induced by the rational theory of choice of standard (micro)economics, e.g. the 'Elsberg' and 'Allais paradoxes' (see e.g. Biswas, 1997, for a succinct introduction). Likewise, the field of experimental economics, very active in the last 30 years or so, has pointed out numerous divergences between actual behaviour (as exhibited in experimental setups) and theory. These paradoxes, anomalies, and contradictions have led to the introduction of psychological elements into neoclassical economic theory, and have resulted into such theories and ideas as prospect theory, loss and inequity aversion, herding behaviour, the 'framing' hypothesis, non-exponential discounting in intertemporal choice, etc., all deviating in one way or other from standard economic theory. These models of behavioural economics (which we will not review in detail) assume that our finite cognitive abilities and psychological processes induce systematic patterns of deviation from the behaviour based on the rationality postulate; in so doing, they border the theories of bounded rationality but also psychology and sociology (see Simon, 1978, 1987; Rabin, 1998; Cohen and Dickens, 2002; Ariely, 2008; Etzioni, 2010).

Macroeconomics has started taking into account such developments. Work has proceeded along two broad dimensions. A first strand analyses the effects on the macroeconomy of boundedly rational expectations; while a second strand takes into account social influences and interactions among individuals. Other analyses simply assume that expectations (and the decisions based on them) are guided by 'animal spirits' (the term coined by Keynes) as well as the other factors that theory emphasizes—see Akerlof and Shiller (2009).[27] But just assuming that expectations (and decisions) are dictated by a whim or

---

[27] Cohen and Dickens (2002) argue that behavioural economics may be founded on the arguments of evolutionary psychology: The key aspects of (bounded) rationality may be those that have given the human race the best chances of survival; the others may be discarded.

even by informal intuition or other intricate psychological processes ('animal spirits') does not amount to a theory of expectations: one should specify the thought processes that lead to them. Some progress in this respect is done by DeGrauwe (2011) who shows how simple (not fully 'rational') forecasting rules can generate waves of optimism and pessimism that are characterized by autocorrelation of forecasting errors (in contradiction to REH). The implications of bounded rationality for macroeconomics are further explored in Akerlof and Shiller (2009), Ng (2005), Fehr and Tyran (2005), and De Grauwe (2012).

A second line of developments in macroeconomics is to incorporate other-regarding preferences and social interactions, as mentioned. These were excluded from traditional ('neoclassical') economics.[28] Akerlof (2007) argues that the introduction of 'norms' of expected behaviour (something not allowed by REH) suffices to bring down many of the major results of standard macroeconomics, including the PIP and Ricardian Equivalence. Furthermore, there is a blossoming literature that argues that individuals are motivated not only by their own individual welfare (the basic postulates of the rational and selfish 'homo economicus') but also by what happens around them: These 'other-regarding' preferences are introduced into their individual utility functions by generally allowing utility to depend not only on the own consumption but also on the consumption of society at large. Feelings of altruism and fairness imply that societal consumption exerts a positive influence on my utility; feelings of envy and status-seeking, on the other hand, imply that societal consumption exerts a negative influence on the individual's utility (via e.g. a relative position argument in the utility): given my individual utility, a rise in societal consumption affects me negatively as it worsens my relative position. E.g., the status motive makes me work hard so as to gain utility from both my consumption in absolute terms and by a rise in my relative position. As a result, the labour effort and growth rise. But others do the same (work hard), so the relative position effect ultimately disappears. What remains from such 'rat races' is perhaps a suboptimal level of labour supply and a rise in inequality, as the extra work may have variable productivity. It is a moot point whether such motives constitute a violation of rationality. Rationality is fully consistent with anything in the utility function, only the sovereign individual can decide that; at the same time, there is a violation of rationality if the deeper motive for status-seeking is because the individual is not really sure whether s/he has truly optimized. (Do I know whether I have made the best of my life's circumstances? Perhaps a rough and ready way for checking is by looking at my neighbour.)

All such 'other-regarding' preferences have important implications for macro outcomes, as they introduce social interactions that would not be present otherwise; in turn, those result in 'social multipliers' effects amplified by the presence of interactions. From the many references, one may select Bowles (1998, 2004), Manski (2000), Clark et al. (2008),

---

[28] Following Manski (2000), we may define 'neoclassical' as the economics that is based on four fundamental concepts: Optimization (maximization of an objective subject to all the relevant constraints) leading to optimal behaviour including demand and supply schedules, budget constraints (a subset of the constraints), equilibrium, and expectations. Additionally, there is 'methodological individualism', reliance on the individual as the decision-making unit (i.e. not class or 'society'). Also, the 'homo economicus' was assumed to be selfishly interested in their own individual consumption and welfare. Other-regarding preferences and social interactions, such as altruism and status, are one of the important directions of the 'post-neoclassical' (macro)economics; see Colander (2000).

and Scheinkman (2008) as portals into this literature. Schelling (1978) is an important early exponent of effects of social interactions, such as the (unwanted) segregation of communities. On status and 'keeping up with the Joneses', see the partial survey in Tsoukis and Tournemaine (2013). The basic idea has also been extended to the importance of status in jobs (see Tournemaine and Tsoukis, 2009) and the choice of education (as this also affects relative position and confers status—Tournemaine and Tsoukis, 2015). Even broader (and fascinating!) themes along the lines of social interactions with macroeconomic implications include the economics of fairness and preference for redistribution (Benabou and Tirole, 2006), identity (Akerlof and Kranton, 2005, 2010), social structure (Granovetter, 2005), social capital (Sobel, 2002), culture (Guiso et al., 2006), and even religion (McCleary and Barro, 2006). We return to some of these themes in Chapter 10.

In conclusion, the criticisms of the rationality postulate and REH have led to quite powerful theories of bounded rationality and behavioural economics. But these new developments are disparate as much as exciting: There seems to be as yet no clear-cut alternative. Thus, while individual aspects of bounded rationality and behavioural patterns continue to be investigated actively in the research literature, both rationality and REH continue to be used as benchmarks in macroeconomics. In relation to REH in particular, its enduring popularity is due to its conceptual clarity, the lack of any clear alternative, and the need to formulate theory and policy advice on the presumption that the private sector is intelligent rather than prone to systematic errors and manipulation. At the same time, exciting new developments occur in various branches of economics (macro, micro, experiments) that incorporate psychology, politics, sociology into basic theory.

Notes on the Literature

The REH and New Classicals have generated an enormous amount of literature. Accessible overall reviews are the thematic textbooks of Begg (1982), Attfield et al. (1991), Holden et al. (1985), and Pesaran (1987) focusing on REH; while the critical reviews of Hoover (1990) and Buiter (1980) focus on New Classical thinking more broadly. The REH was first proposed and explored by Muth (1961); Kantor (1979) critically reviews the REH, placing it in context within the history of macroeconomic thought. The PIP was first developed by Lucas (1972) and Sargent and Wallace (1975); see Maddock and Carter (1982) for a review. Lucas (1973) is the source for the 'island model' and the 'surprise supply function', while Lucas (1976) is the classic source for the eponymous critique. On bounded rationality and learning, see Conlisk (1996) in the first instance, and (the much more technical) Honkapohja (1993) and Evans and Honkapohja (2009). Further technical issues on REH, including bubbles and non-uniqueness are reviewed in the advanced textbooks by Blanchard and Fischer (1989, chapter 5), Turnovsky (1995, chapters 3–6), and Minford and Peel (2002, part IV). Finally, a number of resources were given above on bounded rationality, behavioural economics with applications to macroeconomics, and extensions in other exciting dimensions. The succinct introduction by Baddeley (2017) and the popularized accounts of Ariely (2008), Kahneman (2012), among others, are recommended as portals. Quoting the great Paul Samuelson, we wish the interested reader, *bon appetit!*

Guidance for Further Study

Two recent volumes

De Grauwe (2012) and Frydman and Phelps (2013)—the latter may be more indicative of average opinion as the proceedings of a conference—are bold attempts to delineate what might need changing in various areas of macroeconomics, such as the Phillips Curve and the economics of the 'natural rate' of unemployment, wage and price setting, policy-making, or macro-finance. What do you make of all this? What areas of macroeconomics are most in need of revision?

On neuroeconomics

Modern economic theory has on the whole been built on premises of logic as opposed to evidence (seeking more pure logic and internal consistency than external relevance—at least this is my own opinion). In particular, microeconomics assumes that the individual is rational, maximizing a (logical) construct called utility (of which we have no direct evidence), subject to constraints. It has not yet been possible, however, to link that with any more concrete understanding of the physiology of the brain or of decision and thought processes. Starting from the findings of neuroscience, neuroeconomics is a new field that attempts to do just that: tell us how the individual actually thinks and decides. If the conclusions become accepted, the neuroscientist economist will displace the logician and mathematician economist, with potentially far-reaching implications for the entire body of (macro)economic theory. A recent book of neuroeconomics, Glimcher (2010), has created a bit of a stir, offering a lot of promise. Read the reviews of the book by Shiller (2011) and Camerer (2013); would you think that a revolution in (macro)economic theorizing is in the offing?

On the missing motivation in macroeconomics

In his critical review of the literature on socially influenced preferences, Manski (2000) argues that neoclassical economics has been built around four central concepts: preferences (embodied in 'utility' to be maximized), budget constraints, equilibrium, and expectations; see also Colander (2000). He argues that one can go a long way with just these very flexible concepts, and nothing else (such as 'other-regarding' preferences) needs to be introduced. Against that, Akerlof (2007) forcefully argues that 'norms' of behaviour, that may partly be socially influenced and partly individual, are central to resolving a number of macroeconomic results which no one believes in. What are in your view such 'norms' of behaviour and how are they formed? What are their macroeconomic effects?

On economics and psychology

Do you value more a (potential) loss than a gain in a bet? How confident are you of your answers to a quiz? Do you think fast or slow? Is there a merit in either? A recent book by Daniel Kahneman (2012) summarizes the path-breaking research he and his late colleague Amos Tversky have done in analysing the above questions. After reading the book, answer the above questions and explain why you are giving these answers.

On the nature of rationality

We keep talking about 'rationality', rational decision-making, as if it is an activity based entirely on cold calculation and devoid of any emotional content. But things may not be so clear-cut. First, it may not be entirely possible to isolate emotion from decision-making: e.g., when I am told that 'this item is of good quality but expensive' but 'the other is of lower quality but less expensive', theory says that I make a calculation based on marginal utilities and prices to decide which one to buy. But in practice, I may need will-power and power of decision to go for one of the two; after my 'rational' self weighs the option, the 'emotional' self is also needed in order to proceed to the decision. Furthermore, it has been argued by the German economist and sociologist Max Weber that there is a distinction between 'instrumental' and 'expressive' rationality; the former concerns the cold calculations, the latter the consideration of the deepest values that motivate us; both are distinct aspects of the same rational human being. Witztum (2012) in fact has argued that this Weberian distinction helps reconcile the inconsistency between 'selfish' utility and utility that incorporates social and other-regarding preferences. What does 'rationality' mean for you? Is it close to any of the above notions? What is in your own utility function? (OK, you don't need to tell anyone . . .)

References

Akerlof, G.A. (2007): The Missing Motivation in Macroeconomics, *American Economic Review*, 97(1) (March), 5–36.

Akerlof, G.A., and R.E. Kranton (2005): Identity and the Economics of Organizations, *Journal of Economic Perspectives*, 19(1), 9–32.

Akerlof, G.A., and R.E. Kranton (2010): *Identity Economics: How our Identities Shape our Work, Wages, and Well-Being*, Princeton: Princeton University Press.

Akerlof, G.A., and R.J. Shiller (2009): *Animal Spirits: How Human Psychology Drives the Economy, and Why it Matters for Global Capitalism*, Princeton: Princeton University Press.

Akerlof, G.A., and J. Yellen (1985): A Near-Rational Model of the Business Cycle, with Wage and Price Inertia, *Quarterly Journal of Economics*, 100 (supplement), 823–38.

Ariely, D. (2008): *Predictably Irrational: The Hidden Forces that Shape our Decisions*, New York: HarperCollins.

Attfield, C., D. Demery and N. Duck (1991): *Rational Expectations in Macroeconomics: An Introduction to Theory and Evidence*, 2nd ed., Oxford: Wiley-Blackwell.

Azariadis, C. (1975): Implicit Contracts and Underemployment Equilibria, *Journal of Political Economy*, 83, 1183–1202.

Baddeley, M. (2017): *Behavioural Economics: A Very Short Introduction*, Oxford: Oxford University Press.

Ball L., N.G. Mankiw, and D. Romer (1988): The New Keynesian Economics and the Output-Inflation Tradeoff, *Brookings Papers on Economic Activity*, 1, 1–65.

Barro, R. (1977): Unanticipated Monetary Growth and Unemployment in the United States, *American Economic Review*, 67, 101–15.

Barro, R. (1978): Unanticipated Money, Output and the Price Level in the United States, *Journal of Political Economy*, 86, 549–80.

Begg, D. (1982): *The Rational Expectations Revolution in Macroeconomics: Theories and Evidence*, Baltimore: Johns Hopkins University Press.

Bénabou, R., and J. Tirole (2006): Belief in a Just World and Redistributive Politics, *Quarterly Journal of Economics*, 121(2), 699–746.

Biswas, T. (1997): *Decision-Making under Uncertainty*, New York: Macmillan.

Blanchard, O.J. (1983): Price Asynchronization and Price-Level Inertia, in R. Dornbusch and M.H. Simonsen (eds), *Inflation, Debt and Indexation*, Cambridge, MA: MIT Press; reprinted in Mankiw and Romer (1991, vol. 1).

Blanchard, O.J., and S. Fischer (1989): *Lectures on Macroeconomics*, Cambridge, MA: MIT Press.

Bowles, S. (1998): Endogenous Preferences: The Cultural Consequences of Markets and Other Economic Institutions, *Journal of Economic Literature*, 36(1), 75–111.

Bowles, S. (2004): *Microeconomics: Behavior, Institutions and Evolutions*, Princeton: Princeton University Press

Buiter, W.H. (1980): The Macroeconomics of Dr. Pangloss: A Critical Survey of the New Classical Macroeconomics, *Economic Journal*, 90(357) (March), 34–50.

Cagan, P. (1956): The Monetary Dynamics of Hyperinflation, in M. Friedman (ed.), *Studies in the Quantity Theory of Money*, Chicago: University of Chicago Press, 25–117.

Calvo, G. (1983): Staggered Prices in a Utility-Maximizing Framework, *Journal of Monetary Economics*, 12 (November), 383–98.

Camerer, C.F. (2013): A Review Essay about Foundations of Neuroeconomic Analysis by Paul Glimcher, *Journal of Economic Literature*, 51(4) (December), 1155–82.

Clark, A.E., P. Frijters, and M.A. Shields (2008): Relative Income, Happiness, and Utility: An Explanation for the Easterlin Paradox and Other Puzzles, *Journal of Economic Literature*, 46(1) (March), 95–144.

Cohen, J.L., and W.T. Dickens (2002): A Foundation for Behavioral Economics, *American Economic Review*, 92(2) (May, Papers and Proceedings), 335–8.

Colander, D. (2000): The Death of Neoclassical Economics, *Journal of the History of Economic Thought*, 22(2), 127–43.

Conlisk, J. (1996): Why Bounded Rationality? *Journal of Economic Literature*, 34(2) (June), 669–700.

Cyert, R.M., and M.H. DeGroot (1974): Rational Expectations and Bayesian Analysis, *Journal of Political Economy*, 82(3) (May), 521–36.

De Grauwe, P. (2011): Animal Spirits and Monetary Policy, *Economic Theory*, 47(2–3), 423–57.

De Grauwe, P. (2012): *Lectures on Behavioral Macroeconomics*, Princeton: Princeton University Press.

DeCanio, S.J. (1979): Rational Expectations and Learning from Experience, *Quarterly Journal of Economics*, 93(1) (February), 47–57.

Ermini, L. (1991): Hierarchical Decomposition in Economic Analysis, in R. Frantz, H. Singh and J. Gerber (eds), *Behavioral Decision Making: Handbook of Behavioral Economics*, Greenwich, CT: JAI Press, iiB. 547–62.

Etzioni, A. (2010): Behavioral Economics: A Methodological Note, *Journal of Economic Psychology*, 31, 51–4.

Evans, G.W., and S. Honkapohja (2009): Learning and Macroeconomics, *Annual Review of Economics*, 1(1), 421–51, 05.

Fama, E. (1970): Efficient Capital Markets: A Review of Theory and Empirical Work, *Journal of Finance*, 25(2) (May), 383–417.

Fama, E.F. (2014): Two Pillars of Asset Pricing, *American Economic Review*, 104(6) (June), 1467–85.

Fehr, E. and J.-R. Tyran (2005): Individual Irrationality and Aggregate Outcomes, *Journal of Economic Perspectives*, 19(4), 43–66.

Fischer, S. (1977): Long-Term Contracts, Rational Expectations, and the Optimal Money Supply Rule, *Journal of Political Economy*, 85(1), 191–205.

Frydman, R., and E.S. Phelps (eds) (2013): *Rethinking Expectations: The Way Forward for Macroeconomics*, Princeton: Princeton University Press.

Glimcher, P.W. (2010): *Foundations of Neuroeconomic Analysis*, Oxford: Oxford University Press.

Goodfriend, M., and R. King (1997): The New Neoclassical Synthesis and the Role of Monetary Policy, in B.S. Bernanke and J. Rotemberg (eds), *NBER Macroeconomics Annual 1997* (vol. 12), Cambridge, MA: MIT Press, 231–96.

Granovetter, M. (2005): The Impact of Social Structure on Economic Outcomes, *Journal of Economic Perspectives*, 19(1), 33–50.

Gray, J.A. (1976): Wage Indexation: A Macroeconomic Approach, *Journal of Monetary Economics*, 3 (April), 221–35.

Grossman, S.J. (1976): On the Efficiency of Competitive Stock Markets Where Traders have Diverse Information, *Journal of Finance*, 31: 573–85.

Grossman, S.J., and J.E. Stiglitz (1980): On the Impossibility of Informationally Efficient Markets, *American Economic Review*, 70(3) (June), 393–408.

Guiso, L., P. Sapienza, and L. Zingales (2006): Does Culture Affect Economic Outcomes? *Journal of Economic Perspectives*, 20(2), 23–48.

Haltiwanger, J., and M. Waldman (1985): Rational Expectations and the Limits of Rationality: An Analysis of Heterogeneity, *American Economic Review*, 75(3), 326–40.

Holden, K., D. Peel, and J. Thompson (1985): *Expectations: Theory and Evidence*, Houndmills: Macmillan.

Honkapohja, S. (1993): Adaptive Learning and Bounded Rationality: An Introduction to Basic Concepts, *European Economic Review*, 37, 587–94.

Hoover, K.D. (1990): *The New Classical Macroeconomics*, Oxford: Wiley-Blackwell.

Iversen, T., and D. Soskice (2006): New Macroeconomics and Political Science, *Annual Review of Political Science*, 9, 425–53.

Kahneman, D. (2012): *Thinking, Fast and Slow*, London: Penguin books.

Kantor, B. (1979): Rational Expectations and Economic Thought, *Journal of Economic Literature*, 17(4) (December), 1422–41.

Kindleberger, C.P. (1996): *Manias, Panics, and Crashes: A History of Financial Crises*, 3rd ed., New York: Wiley.

Ljungqvist, L. (2008): Lucas Critique, in S.N. Durlauf and L.E. Blume (eds), *The New Palgrave Dictionary of Economics*, 2nd ed., Basingstoke: Palgrave Macmillan.

Lovell, M.C. (1986): Tests of the Rational Expectations Hypothesis, *American Economic Review*, 76(1) (March), 110–24.

Lucas, R.E., Jnr. (1972): Expectations and the Neutrality of Money, *Journal of Economic Theory*, 4, 103–24.

Lucas, R.E., Jnr. (1973): Some International Evidence on Output-Inflation Trade-Offs, *American Economic Review*, 63, 326–34.

Lucas, R.E., Jnr. (1976): Econometric Policy Evaluation: A Critique, in K. Brunner and A.H. Meltzer (eds), *The Phillips Curve and Labor Markets*, Carnegie-Rochester Series on Public Policy, 1, Rochester, NY: Journal of Monetary Economics, 9–46.

McCallum, R.T. (1983): On Non-Uniqueness in Rational Expectations Models: An Attempt at Perspective, *Journal of Monetary Economics*, 11, 139–68.

Maddock, R., and M. Carter (1982): A Child's Guide to Rational Expectations, *Journal of Economic Literature*, 20 (March), 39–51.

Mankiw, N.G., and D. Romer (1991): *New Keynesian Economics: Imperfect Competition and Sticky Prices*, Cambridge, MA: MIT Press.

Manski, C.F. (2000): Economic Analysis of Social Interactions, *Journal of Economic Perspectives*, 14(3) (Summer), 115–36.

McCleary, R.M., and R.J. Barro (2006): Religion and Economy, *Journal of Economic Perspectives*, 20(2), 49–72.

Minford, P., and D. Peel (2002): *Advanced Macroeconomics: A Primer*, London: E. Elgar.

Muth, J.F. (1961): Rational Expectations and tide Theory of Price Movements, *Econometrica*, 29 (July), 315–35.

Ng, Y.-K. (2005): Policy Implications of Behavioural Economics: With Special Reference to the Optimal Level of Public Spending, *Australian Economic Review*, 38(3), 298–306.

Pesaran, M.H. (1987): *The Limits to Rational Expectations*, Oxford: Blackwell.

Rabin, M. (1998): Psychology and Economics, *Journal of Economic Literature*, 36(1), 11–46.

Sargent, T.J. (1976): The Observational Equivalence of Natural and Unnatural Rate Theories of Macroeconomics, *Journal of Political Economy*, 84(3) (June), 631–40.

Sargent T.J., and N. Wallace (1975): Rational Expectations, the Optimal Monetary Instrument and the Optimal Money Supply Rule, *Journal of Political Economy*, 83, 241–57.

Scheinkman, J.A. (2008): Social interactions (theory), in S.N. Durlauf and L.E. Blume (eds), *The New Palgrave Dictionary of Economics*, 2nd ed., London: Macmillan.

Schelling, T.C. (1978): *Micromotives and Macrobehavior*, New York: W.W. Norton.

Shiller (2003): From Efficient Markets Theory to Behavioral Finance, *Journal of Economic Perspectives*, 17(1) (Winter), 83–104.

Shiller, R.J. (2011): The Neuroeconomics Revolution, Project syndicate, 21 November; https://www.project-syndicate.org/commentary/the-neuroeconomics-revolution

Shiller, R.J. (2014): Speculative Asset Prices, *American Economic Review*, 104(6) (June), 1486–1517.

Shleifer, A. (2000): *Inefficient Markets: An Introduction to Behavioral Finance*, New York: Oxford University Press.

Simon, H. (1978): Rationality as Process and as Product of Thought, *American Economic Review*, 68 (May), 1–16.

Simon, H. (1987): Behavioral Economics, in J. Eatwell, M. Milgate, and P. Newman (eds), *The New Palgrave: A Dictionary of Economics*, 1st ed., London: Macmillan 221–4.

Sobel, J. (2002): Can we Trust Social Capital? *Journal of Economic Literature*, 40(1), 139–54.

Taylor, J.B. (1979): Staggered Wage Setting in a Macro Model, *American Economic Review*, 69 (May), 108–13.

Tobin, J. (1993): An Old Keynesian Counterattacks, *Eastern Economic Journal*, 18(4) (Fall), 387–400; reprinted as chapter 2 in his *Full Employment and Growth*, London: E. Elgar, 1996.

Tournemaine, F., and C. Tsoukis (2009): Status Jobs, Human Capital, and Growth, *Oxford Economic Papers*, 61(3) (July), 467–93.

Tournemaine, F., and C. Tsoukis (2015): Public Expenditures, Growth and Distribution in a Mixed Regime of Education with a Status Motive, *Journal of Public Economic Theory*, 17(5) (October), 673–701.

Tsoukis, C., and F. Tournemaine (2013): Status in a Canonical Macro Model: Status, Growth, and Inequality, *The Manchester School*, 81(S2), 65–92.

Turnovsky, S.J. (1995): *Methods of Macroeconomic Dynamics*, Cambridge, MA: MIT Press.

Witztum, A. (2012): Social Dimensions of Individualistic Rationality, *American Journal of Economics and Sociology*, 71(2) (April), 377–406.

3

New Keynesians and Inflation

3.1 Introduction

The New Keynesian school of thought attempts to revitalize many of the insights usually associated with Keynes and his followers, without succumbing to the capital sins (according to the New Classicals) of ad hoc theorizing, arbitrary behavioural assumptions, and policy conclusions founded on the ability by government to systematically fool the private sector. So, New Keynesians share the belief that sound theories should be constructed starting from agent optimization and micro-foundations. They also, except in special circumstances, work with Rational Expectations. But they take issue with two of the fundamental traits of NCs: namely the belief that markets clear and therefore all unemployment must be seen as essentially voluntary; and secondly, the inability of AD policy to meaningfully affect output. Instead, New Keynesians start from the observation that involuntary unemployment is prevalent and often widespread, with people willing to work at the going wage but unable to find a job; and from the widely held observation and belief that governments can affect the working of the macroeconomy via the systematic use of monetary and fiscal policies. As in many other areas of analysis, what appears at first sight to be a well-defined school is in fact lots of like-minded, but individual voices, so total uniformity should not be expected. Various theorists attribute different degrees of importance to the various elements that 'the' New Keynesian school emphasizes. Many of the New Keynesians' analyses (as is also true of the New Classicals) have been assimilated into other areas, e.g. in the analyses of labour or credit markets, fiscal policy, monetary policy, and growth; therefore we shall be touching upon such themes at various places in this book, without necessarily labelling such themes as 'Keynesian'.

Keynesian models take issue with various aspects of the 'Walrasian' macroeconomic model that underpins New Classical economics (see Romer, 1993). Walrasian is a model characterized by perfect competition, instantaneous and costless price and wage adjustment so that all markets clear, no externalities, and perfect information. New Keynesian analyses introduce 'frictions', i.e. deviations from these benchmark assumptions. A large part of New Keynesian analyses is concerned with imperfect competition in goods and/or labour markets. Firms often enjoy some degree of monopoly power in their markets, depending on the degree of specialization of the product and degree of differentiation from similar goods, and more practically on market share. Monopoly power exists also in the labour market, by either firms (in which case it should be more strictly called 'monopsony'), or associations of workers (trade unions), or for other reasons called 'efficiency wages'. Many of these analyses will be considered in Chapter 4 on unemployment, but a generic analysis of imperfect competition and its effects will be given in Section 3.2.

Another objective of the New Keynesians is to analyse why monetary policy has real effects, as the evidence shows. To put things into perspective, recall that the 'Classics' and Monetarists (in a more nuanced way) believe in monetary neutrality: money has no effect

Theory of Macroeconomic Policy. Christopher Tsoukis, Oxford University Press (2020). © Christopher Tsoukis.
DOI: 10.1093/oso/9780198825371.003.0003

on relative prices and real quantities. The New Classicals also argue that monetary policy does not have real effects except to the extent that it is unanticipated (which is unsystematic, under Rational Expectations). So, both Monetarists and New Classicals believe in more sophisticated versions of monetary neutrality. As will become clearer in this chapter, imperfect competition does not help to break down monetary neutrality. The main effect of imperfect competition is to alter the demand and supply curves, particularly the long-run, 'natural', or 'structural' rate of unemployment and the associated level of output. In other words it has 'real' effects; but it does not in general imply that the amount of nominal money in circulation affects real output. To arrive at this result, the New Keynesians refute another key assumption of the Walrasian model, that of costless and instantaneous price and wage adjustment and market clearing. We saw in Chapter 2 how the first generation of New Keynesians refuted the Policy Ineffectiveness Proposition by introducing staggered wage contracts. Section 3.6 of this chapter elaborates on some of these themes, analysing the structure and effects of wage contracts. A second wave of New Keynesian models, developed in the 1980s and 1990s, attack the PIP directly by assuming that there are 'nominal frictions', costs associated with price adjustment. In Section 3.3, we shall see how such 'menu costs' (as they are called in jargon) generate enough price stickiness to break the monetary neutrality. Menu costs generate price rigidity at an individual level, but does this carry over to the aggregate price level, or does it get 'washed out' by some logic of large numbers? Section 3.4 deals with that question, while Section 3.5 discusses the empirical evidence on the costs of price adjustment and price stickiness. Section 3.6 analyses wage contracts, as mentioned. Section 3.7 gives an overview of new directions in research focusing on strategic complementarities, coordination failures, and multiple equilibria. Section 3.8 introduces inflation, its costs, and early theories. As inflation is an issue more closely associated with the New Keynesians than with any other school of thought, the New Keynesians have developed a model of inflation reviewed in Section 3.9. Finally, Section 3.10 places this model of inflation in the context of a 'bare-bones', three-equation macro model and discusses its implications.

3.2 Wage and Price Setting under Monopolistic Competition

The purpose of this section is to review the theory of price and wage setting that is a background to the analysis of wage and price rigidities. It is also indispensable for understanding unemployment and will therefore be used in Chapter 4. The wage-price is essentially a reinterpretation of the labour demand-and-supply framework reviewed in Chapter 1. In recent years, the wage-price setting framework has replaced the labour demand-supply framework as a workhorse model, as it is more intuitive than labour demand-supply; labour supply in particular relies heavily on the notion of supply elasticity, while in practice many workers just want to work 'normal hours'. The theory-derived labour supply is based on individual optimization based on the presumption that the worker is in employment, while as we have seen most of the variation in hours comes from the 'external margin' (movement in and out of employment) as opposed to the 'internal margin' (adjustment of individual hours). Workers often bargain about wages by forming associations ('trade unions'), something not allowed in the labour supply; and the labour supply-demand framework has difficulty accommodating involuntary unemployment unless it is assumed that a rigidly high wage prevents market clearing (indefinitely). The wage-price setting framework cuts through all these difficulties. It is agnostic on whether the adjustment is along the 'internal' or 'external' margin, on what the supply elasticities are, on whether there are trade unions or not, and on whether unemployment is voluntary or involuntary. It is compatible with any of these possibilities, and it does not take any stand on any of these questions. It can more easily accommodate features and 'institutions' of the labour market, such as the welfare state and trade unions, that will be the subject of analysis in Chapter 4.

In the wage-price setting framework, firms are assumed to maximize profits and workers to maximize utility. But instead of having labour (demand or supply) as their decision variable, the two parties now decide on different variables: Firms set their individual prices, while workers set (unilaterally, for a start) their individual wages. In the process, firms form a real wage they are prepared to offer to workers, whereas workers form a real wage that they wish to claim for their labour effort. In the labour market, however, there is only one real wage, so the real wage that comes from either side of the market must be consistent with each other; (un)employment is the variable that facilitates the adjustment that brings about this equality.

In what follows, we give first a review of monopolistic competition and its importance in various contexts, and then proceed to derive the wage-price setting framework from the labour demand-supply model.

3.2.1 Monopolistic Competition, the Dixit-Stiglitz (1977) Framework, and Product Demand

Models of imperfect competition involve the idea that real-world markets may be different from the perfectly competitive paradigm. Traditionally, imperfectly competitive product markets have been categorized as *monopolistic* (here, the size of firms and product differentiation are rather small and the number of firms large, as in e.g. the restaurant sector), *oligopolistic* (with bigger size, smaller numbers of firms and greater product differentiation, as in e.g. the car market), and finally *monopolies* (whereby only one firm exists in the sector, e.g. the formerly public owned utilities). As mentioned briefly in Chapter 1, we may think of perfect competition and pure monopoly as the limits either end of monopolistic competition, so these polar extremes can be seen as special cases of the monopolistic framework. Models of oligopoly, however, are hard to tackle analytically, as they explicitly deal with the strategic interactions between oligopolists (each one's reactions depend explicitly on the others', a feature absent in monopolistically competitive analysis) and are therefore carried out with the aid of game theory.

Therefore, macroeconomics relies on monopolistic competition as a generic model of imperfect competition. Monopolistic competition is harder to treat analytically than either perfect competition or monopoly, hence its belated entry into macroeconomic theory. One approach, pioneered by Dixit and Stiglitz (1977), assumes that there are n firms in the economy, each producing a differentiated good. All of the n goods have constant pair-wise elasticities of substitution in utility; in other words, symmetry is assumed between the monopolistic firms. For example, goods may all be rather like different types of soap (with a high degree of substitutability), or newspapers (where substitutability is presumably less). We can therefore refer to each individual good as an individual variety.

The Dixit-Stiglitz (1977) approach is to aggregate all individual goods $j = 1, 2, ..., n$ into a bundle using a Constant Elasticity of Substitution-type function (where i is the typical consumer and the quantities are their consumption of each variety):

$$C_i = \left[\frac{\sum_{j=1}^{n} C_{ij}^{(\theta-1)/\theta}}{n^{1/\theta}} \right]^{\theta/(\theta-1)}, \quad \theta \geq 1 \tag{3.1}$$

Intuitively, each individual variety (j) is subject to a diminishing return in its contribution to the bundle (increasing a variety on its own increases the bundle but less than one-to-one), but the overall bundle maintains constant returns (if you double all varieties, the bundle will double). The averaging over n (note the exponent) is such as to maintain consistency.[1] It implies that the number of varieties (n) does not matter; it is only the quantities that matter.[2] θ is the elasticity of substitution.

If the price of the individual varieties is P_j, $j = 1, 2, ..., n$, then the price level of the bundle is:

$$P = \left[\frac{\sum_{j=1}^{n} P_j^{1-\theta}}{n} \right]^{1/(1-\theta)} \tag{3.2}$$

Note that there are no individual-specific subscripts (i) as these prices apply to all consumers. In terms of economic interpretation, the price level is the minimum expenditure required to purchase one unit of the bundle C_i. The CES function (3.1) boils down to Cobb-Douglas and the price level becomes a geometric average (log-average) in the special case of a unitary elasticity of substitution ($\theta = 1$). In this setup, the demand for the individual variety (j) by any consumer i is given by:

$$C_{ij} = \left(\frac{P_j}{P} \right)^{-\theta} \frac{C_i}{n} \tag{3.3}$$

---

[1] Imagine that each variety is simply 'one-nth' of the bundle, $C_{ij} = C_i/n$ for all j. Can you check that the formula holds?

[2] We could envisage a 'taste for variety', whereby the number of varieties enriches the bundle. (Crudely speaking, £10 would make a richer bundle if it were spent on 10 different varieties of £1 each than on 5 varieties of £2 each, and that would be better still than spending all £10 on a single variety). Taste for variety can be captured by a parameter $0 \leq \varepsilon < 1$ in the following generalization of (3.1):

$$C_i = n^{\varepsilon} \left[\frac{\sum_{j=1}^{n} C_{ij}^{(\theta-1)/\theta}}{n^{1/\theta}} \right]^{\theta/(\theta-1)}.$$

(You can confirm this by maximizing C_i in 3.1 using C_{ij} as the choice variable, subject to the price level 3.2.) The interpretation of (3.3) is that individual demand starts from an average amount $(= C_i/n)$ over all varieties as a basis, and then adjusts this depending on the relative price and θ. With (3.3), the nominal value of the bundle equals:

$$\sum_{j=1}^{n} C_{ij}P_j = C_iP \tag{3.4}$$

The sum of optimal (i.e. according to 3.3) expenditures on individual varieties equals the bundle times its price (price level).

The great analytical convenience of the Dixit-Stiglitz framework is that it greatly simplifies the optimization by the individual consumer. Imagine that the latter has a separable utility function of the form:

$$U_i = U_i\left(U_i^C(C_{i1}, C_{i2}, ..., C_{ij}, ..., C_{in}); L_i\right) \tag{3.5a}$$

Where utility depends on the separable consumption-related sub-utility $(U^C_i(.))$ and other elements such as labour (L_i), etc. If there is constant elasticity of substitution between the varieties, then the utility can be equivalently written as:

$$U_i = U_i\left(U_i^C(C_i); L_i\right) \tag{3.5b}$$

where C_i is the bundle defined in (3.1). Then, instead of maximizing utility (3.5a) with all the varieties and leisure as choice variables subject to a budget constraint of the form:

$$\text{Income} = \Sigma C_{ij}P_i,$$

the individual maximizes utility (3.5b) with only two choice variables, the bundle and leisure, subject to a constraint of the form:

$$\text{Income} = C_iP.$$

By assumption, the two utilities are the same; and by (3.4), the two budget constraints are also the same. Hence, the two approaches are equivalent, but there is a considerable gain in terms of simplification from using the latter. Once the bundle C_i has been determined, we can then determine the quantities of the individual varieties via (3.3). In other words, a form of 'two-stage budgeting' applies, where bundles are determined first, then subject to those, individual varieties are obtained; rather than everything being determined at once. The downside to this big gain in tractability is the restrictions the framework imposes: Equation (3.3) in particular suggests that everyone, rich or poor, consumes individual varieties in the same proportions. So, this framework should not be used to model individual consumption, but it can be useful in macroeconomics as it enables us to keep track of aggregates while maintaining a consistent framework of individual choice.

Turning to individual varieties (3.3), aggregating over I consumers ($i = 1, 2, ..., I$), we obtain market demand for those varieties:

$$C_j^D \equiv \sum_{i=1}^{I} C_{ij} = \left(\frac{P_j}{P}\right)^{-\theta} \frac{C}{n} \qquad (3.6)$$

where aggregate consumption is defined as the sum of all individual-consumer bundles:

$$C \equiv \sum_{i=1}^{I} C_i$$

Finally, in analogy to (3.6),[3] we can then postulate the market demand for those varieties as:

$$Y_j^D = \left(\frac{P_j}{P}\right)^{-\theta} \frac{Y}{n} \qquad (3.6')$$

where Y is real aggregate output. (3.6') is a parametric version of the setup of Chapter 1 (see Section 1.4, equation 1.4 and below). Each firm's demand inversely depends on its relative price; if all firms had equal prices (i.e. unitary relative prices), they would all share the market equally (by Y/n). The elasticity of demand equals θ (= e in the notation of Chapter 1); furthermore, the monopoly markup (μ) that the firm that produces any individual variety is able to command (see again Chapter 1) also depends on this parameter: We have that

$$1 + \mu \equiv \frac{\theta}{\theta - 1} \geq 1 \qquad (3.7)$$

under perfect competition ($\theta \to \infty$), $\mu \to 0$ and the demand curve is horizontal. (The graph is left as an exercise.) Because any individual variety has perfect substitutes, no producer has any incentive to deviate from the market price ('price taker'). Under monopolistic competition, the product is somewhat differentiated, so the producer maintains some customer loyalty: the demand curve is downward sloping and the producer is able to set their own price (providing they will be happy to serve the associated quantity demanded)—'price setters'.

The final preliminary building block concerns the marginal revenue product (MRP) of the individual firm. In order to be able to sell one more unit, the producer needs to lower the price not only of the extra unit but all the units they are selling. Hence, they get some extra revenue by selling one more unit, but this is less than the price. Formally, the change in revenue when a unit of output of firm j changes is:

$$d(P_j Y_j)/dY_j = P_j \left[1 + \frac{\partial P_j}{\partial Y_j} \frac{Y_j}{P_j}\right] = P_j \frac{\theta - 1}{\theta} = \frac{P_j}{1 + \mu} \qquad (3.8)$$

---

[3] To go from (3.6) to (3.6'), one must assume that all other components of demand, such as investment, government spending and net exports are made up by the same varieties structured in the same way as consumption.

In a conventional (P_j, Y_j) graph, the MRP is steeper than and below the product demand curve (except in the special case of perfect competition).

There are at least three main reasons why imperfect competition matters. First, as we saw in the first chapter (see e.g. equations 1.6 and 1.6'), all else equal, a firm operating in an environment characterized by greater monopoly power would be tempted to exploit its position by raising prices above marginal costs by a higher markup. If so, with a given quantity of nominal money or *nominal* aggregate demand, this economy will have a lower level of real money (M/P), *real* aggregate demand and output. Thus, and again all else equal, this economy will experience a greater degree of unemployment. Likewise, in the labour market, existence of monopolistic sellers of labour, like unions, and other deviations from the perfectly competitive framework such as efficiency wages, unemployment benefits, etc., mean that we are in general away from the point where the competitive demand and supply curves meet. Thus, although the individuals do their best under the circumstances (that is, the individual optimality conditions hold), the resulting aggregate equilibrium involves involuntary unemployment and a level of output that is lower than socially optimal.

Secondly, but equally importantly, imperfect competition matters because of the real effects of nominal aggregate demand changes in such environments. Practically speaking, this makes monetary policy effective. However, the assumption of imperfect competition alone is not capable of delivering the result of monetary non-neutrality. In this respect, imperfect competition does not differ from perfect competition. An additional assumption is required; namely, that price adjustment is costly, as firms have to reprint catalogues ('menus') and labels, and risk upsetting customers. But such costs are usually small, and would normally not be enough to impede price adjustments if the benefits to firms from such adjustments were considerable. The importance of the monopolistic competition assumption is that the benefits from adjustment to individual firms may be much smaller, so that the price adjustment costs may exceed the benefits from adjustment. Hence, with the dual assumption of imperfect competition and 'menu costs', monetary neutrality breaks down, nominal aggregate demand changes have real effects, and monetary policy can be used for stabilization purposes.

A last reason has to do with fiscal policy and a version of the Keynesian multiplier developed by the New Keynesians, reviewed in Chapter 8. Under imperfect competition, the higher the monopoly power, the higher firms' profits. When ultimately remitted to the personal sector, such profits naturally influence consumption, causing a rise in output and further rises in profits. This gives rise to a (modified) Keynesian multiplier, whereby public expenditures generate higher output, profits, greater consumption, further demand and output, profits, and so on. It will be shown that under perfect competition profits are zero, and as a consequence this kind of multiplier process does not exist.

3.2.2 Price Setting

We assume that the firm is monopolistic in the goods market, but competitive in the labour market. This practically means that the firm has some price-setting power regarding its own price P_j, but it only takes the market wage W as given without influencing it. The typical firm (j) selects its labour so as to maximize revenue $P_j Y_j - W L_j$ subject to its simplified production function $Y_j = Y(L_j)$. Due to diminishing marginal product, the marginal product of labour, $MPL_j \equiv \partial Y_j / \partial L_j$, depends negatively on L_j. There is no capital here. Formally:

$$\text{Max}_{Lj} \; P_j Y_j - W L_j \quad \text{s.t.} \quad Y_j = Y(L_j)$$

This optimization is nothing but (3.8) taken one step further. It results in:

$$P_j \left[1 + \frac{\partial P_j}{\partial Y_j} \frac{Y_j}{P_j} \right] \frac{\partial Y_j}{\partial L_j} - W = 0$$

Therefore, we have the following pricing rule:

$$\frac{P_j}{P} = \frac{W}{P} \frac{1 + \mu}{MPL_j} \tag{3.9}$$

Hence, the individual relative price must be set at such a level as to cover the real wage (W/P) adjusted by the marginal product of labour. Alternatively, we may think of (W/P)/MPL_j as the marginal cost, the cost of an hour of labour divided by how many units this labour produces, therefore the marginal cost of an additional unit of product.[4] The importance of monopolistic competition is manifested in the monopoly power markup (μ), which increases the individual price above its marginal cost. The other side of the same coin is that it decreases equilibrium employment and output, as will be shown below.

In order to proceed, we employ a simple parametric production function:

$$Y_j = A L_j^\alpha, \quad 0 < \alpha < 1 \tag{3.10}$$

This gives individual product supply of firm j as a function of the labour that it employs and also of technology (A). Parameter $0 < \alpha < 1$ is a measure of how fast the diminishing product 'kicks in'. The marginal product of labour (MPL) equals $MPL(L_j) = \alpha A L_j^{\alpha-1}$ and is falling in total labour hours.[5] If we think of the marginal cost of producing an additional unit of output as (W/P)/MPL, α indicates how fast such a cost rises with output. Introducing this information into (3.9), we get:

$$P_j/P = (1 + \mu) \frac{W/P}{\alpha A L_j^{\alpha-1}} = (1 + \mu) \frac{W/P}{\alpha A^{1/\alpha} Y_j^{(\alpha-1)/\alpha}} \tag{3.11}$$

The second equality follows by replacing L_j by Y_j. Using (3.6') and sorting out, we get:

$$P_j/P = \left[\frac{1 + \mu}{\alpha^\alpha A} (W/P)^\alpha (Y/n)^{(1-\alpha)} \right]^b, \quad 0 < b \equiv \frac{1}{(1 - \theta)\alpha + \theta} \leq 1 \tag{3.11'}$$

---

[4] This is commonly referred to as 'unit labour cost'.
[5] Note that although the labour supplied by any individual household i is a fraction of their time ($L_i < 1$), the hours required by any firm j is assumed to be drawn from several workers, so that $L_j > 1$ and diminishing returns apply.

With $\theta \geq 1$, we also have $0 < b \leq 1$. Blanchard and Kiyotaki (1987) derive a slightly different version of (3.11'). Accordingly, the optimal relative price for firm i is essentially a (geometric) average of the real wage the firm faces (i.e. its variable cost) and the average real output demand per firm (Y/n). Under non-diminishing MPL ($\alpha = 1$), aggregate demand does not matter because the marginal product of labour does not fall with it; in terms of the individual-firm supply function, as the diminishing returns to labour kick in (α falls), the supply curve becomes steeper. As a result, two parameter changes occur: the relative role of demand in determining the real price is strengthened; and the relative price is more sensitive to both wage costs and product demand—$b > 0$ increases. Finally, a note on the role of the elasticity of demand with respect to its relative price (θ); this is twofold. First, it determines the monopoly markup (μ). Second, b on the RHS of (3.11') and the optimal relative price fall with θ. (Intuitively, as demand for good j becomes flatter, variations in production or in costs are accompanied by smaller variations in the real price.)

3.2.3 Wage Setting

We now turn to wage setting. This is essentially a recasting of the labour supply equation in Chapter 1 with a slight twist. Here, we abandon the assumption of a single-type, homogeneous work. We assume instead that there is a large amount of different skills or types of labour, with a degree of substitutability among them of $\sigma \geq 1$. Each individual i (possessing uniquely the skill i) faces a labour demand curve by firms as follows:

$$L_i = (Y/n)^\alpha (W_i/W)^{-\sigma} \qquad (3.12)$$

Accordingly, the demand for labour of type i depends, first, on aggregate demand and production; with greater diminishing returns to labour (higher α), any given level of output requires more labour. Second, individual-type labour demand also depends on the relative wage of skill j with elasticity σ.

In this economy, the individual i will find it optimal to require the following relative wage in the market (as with firms, monopolistic competition in the labour market among workers with imperfectly substitutable attributes enables them to set individual prices that could differ from the average)—see Blanchard (1986) and Blanchard and Kiyotaki (1987) for details:

$$W_i/W = B\left[(1+v)(W/P)^{-1}(Y/n)^{\alpha\beta}\right]^{\frac{1}{1+\sigma/\beta}} \qquad (3.13)$$

$B > 0$ is an unimportant constant. In analogy with the optimal price equation (3.9), the optimal relative wage is influenced by two factors, the real wage (inversely, because it is a higher price level relative to wage that persuades workers to go for higher wages); and the average output Y/n (because that influences positively labour demand). Again, there are two parameters of interest. First, the elasticity of labour demand is given by the substitutability between the various types of labour (σ); $v \equiv \sigma/(\sigma - 1) - 1$ is the markup that individual wage setters require over the general wage rate W because of their monopoly power on skills. As labour tends to become more homogenized (σ increases), individual workers have less and less bargaining power, and their markup over the average wage rate falls. As well as decreasing the markup, a rise in σ flattens the labour demand curve, so that the real wage variation due to any changes is dampened. Second, β indicates the elasticity of marginal disutility of work with respect to work (employment) itself. In plain English, the higher β is, the higher is the extra disutility from the loss of a certain amount of leisure, and therefore the higher is the relative wage individual i requires as compensation, and the greater its variation when aggregate demand for labour (given by Y/n) changes. As an exercise, the reader is invited to clarify the relationship of β with the Frisch elasticity of labour supply (η) introduced in Chapter 1.

3.2.4 Symmetric Equilibrium

In the real world, there will be lots of firm- or person-specific characteristics that might allow a variation in individual prices/wages around their means, but in our simplified macro framework, we are not interested in such heterogeneity. So, we resort to the analytical simplification of 'symmetric equilibrium', whereby all individual prices/wages are assumed to be equal among themselves and to their respective means; individual outputs are equal to average output Y/n. In plain English again, this allows us to think of all firms/workers as identical. (Alternatively stated, we concentrate only on the typical firm/worker.) But we do keep the results of their monopolistic behaviour, namely the markup of prices over wages and of wages over prices. As this cannot be true of all firms and workers (not all prices/wages can be above their means), we shall see that this feature simply raises the average price and wage and reduces output.

In this symmetric situation (alternatively: for the average firm), the relative price is one; imposing that on (3.9) and rearranging, we get:

$$W/P = \alpha \left(\frac{A}{1+\mu} \right)^{1/\alpha} (Y/n)^{-(1-\alpha)/\alpha} \tag{3.14}$$

This is the (aggregate) price setting equation; in fact, it gives the real wage that emerges out of the price setting of individual firms (hence the name). It is the real wage with which firms are 'happy' in the sense that it is consistent with their optimization. Likewise, imposing unity on relative wages in (3.13), we get:

$$W/P = (1+v)(Y/n)^{\alpha\beta} \tag{3.15}$$

This is the (aggregate) wage setting rule; it is the average real wage consistent with workers' behaviour, hence the wage they would like to claim for the work they provide.[6]

We show the workings of the system in a graph of the real wage against output (which is also a proxy for labour), Figure 3.1. The price-setting equation (3.14), PS for short, is downward-sloping, as more output raises the price level and, given the nominal wage,

---

[6] Dixon (1987) emphasizes the fact that the wage equation may depend on wealth, as higher wealth increases consumption and leisure in proportion to it, and thereby reduces the work effort. But this effect is likely to be small numerically, hence omitted here.

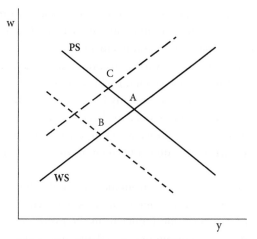

Figure 3.1. Price and wage setting

reduces the real wage that is consistent with firms' behaviour; while the wage-setting one (3.15), WS, is upward-sloping as a more buoyant market encourages workers to go for higher wages. Logs of the real wage ($w \equiv \log(W/P)$) and output ($y \equiv \log(Y/n)$) appear on the axes—as a result, the schedules are represented as straight lines.[7] Aggregate output (equivalently: labour) is the variable that moves us to equilibrium, where the real wages consistent with firms' and workers' behaviour are identical.

The first observation is that, *ceteris paribus*, more monopoly power in the product market (μ) raises the required nominal prices over nominal wages, so that the real wage falls; the PS schedule shifts down/left (broken line). The equilibrium real wage falls together with output; from the production function, the falling output requires less labour, so employment also falls. The same effect arises with another two factors we have not explicitly introduced but work exactly in the same way as the monopoly markup: commodity taxes (such as VAT) and energy price (including oil prices) and raw materials prices all increase prices above marginal labour costs, therefore push up the price level and reduce the real wage. The effects, as with μ, are to shift PS down/left and reduce equilibrium w and y. More pronounced diminishing returns (lower α: a faster falling MPL) make the relative price more responsive to output changes; this results in a steeper PS curve, higher equilibrium P/W ratio (or else, lower real wage), and lower output.

Productivity and technology (A) shift the price schedule <u>right</u>, resulting in a higher real wage and increased output. A question is whether employment rises as well; though there is more output, it is also more productively produced, so does it require more employment? In Chapter 1, while talking about labour demand and supply, we derived an unambiguously positive effect; here, the sign of the effect is ambiguous, depending on parameter values. Under plausible parameter values ($\alpha\beta < 1$), the effect is positive, too. Some people may not be comfortable with the notion of a rise in technology resulting in higher employment; an advantage of the price-wage setting framework is that it allows a more nuanced answer (either effect is in principle possible). The issue is a vexed one and

---

[7] Once again, the wage and price schedules parallel the labour supply and demand curves, respectively. Note that average output can be translated into labour via the production function.

the evidence quite mixed. We discuss the effects of technology further in two places: in Chapter 4 while discussing the determinants of structural unemployment, and in Chapter 5 while talking business cycles and fluctuations.

Finally, more monopoly power by workers (captured by v—due to more differentiated skills) shifts the wage-setting left (broken line). This results in a higher real wage but a fall in output and employment. Again not explicitly introduced, income taxes work exactly as the wage monopoly premium as they reduce the 'take-home pay' out of a given wage, and therefore induce workers to try to increase wages in order to compensate for that loss. We discuss these effects further in the context of unemployment and labour market 'institutions' in Chapter 4.

One important conclusion established from the above is that there is no role for nominal factors (mainly, the money supply). Output may be reduced by the monopoly power inherent in monopolistic competition (either from the firms' or workers' side, or both), and other determinants of equilibrium output, relative prices and the real wage are 'real' factors that have to do with productivity and other aspects of production (e.g. diminishing marginal product), the structure of markets, taxes, and energy prices. As easily seen, the money supply does not feature in either (3.14) or (3.15).

3.3 Menu Costs, Price Stickiness, and Monetary Non-Neutrality

3.3.1 Introduction: 'Nominal' vs. 'Real' Costs of Price Adjustment

The previous section argued that, under monopoly power in either the goods or labour market, equilibrium output is lower than in the perfectly competitive case. But the discussion so far has not dealt with the question of whether, or how, changes in the nominal quantity of money affect real output. In fact, it was established that monopoly power by itself does not break monetary neutrality; equilibrium output may be lower, but it is determined entirely by real factors. The literature on costs of nominal price adjustment (or 'menu costs') investigates the reasons for a central Keynesian tenet: the belief that the quantity of nominal money affects real output. Because of price stickiness, the aggregate price level may not respond one-for-one with movements in nominal money, so that the M/P ratio, and therefore real output, changes for a while, and in particular over the business cycle horizon. Thus, price rigidity (or inertia, or stickiness—the terms will be used interchangeably) emerges as a crucial factor in understanding the real effects of nominal aggregate demand changes (due to various reasons, among them monetary policy). This is a major theme of New Keynesian economics and will be reviewed in this section. The thrust of this literature is to base these arguments on solid micro-foundations, i.e. on optimizing and other attributes of firms, rather than assuming pure ignorance, incompetence, or arbitrary rules of thumb. In other words, the thrust is to avoid the criticism levelled against Keynesian economics by the New Classical economics school, that Keynesian results are based on presumed behaviour by firms and consumers that is incompatible with optimization.

When firms change their individual nominal prices they face two types of cost. One type of cost is a fixed one, irrespective of the magnitude of the change. Firms need first to spend some time thinking through the new optimal price, do their calculations and sums, convene meetings of executives. Then, once they decide, they must print new catalogues and menus (hence 'menu costs'), put new price stickers on individual items, assign new prices to barcodes that are scanned electronically at tills, and so on. Because of a fixed nominal cost involved in this case (fixed in the sense that it does not vary whether you change the price by 1, 5, or 10 per cent, not in the sense that the cost is the same across goods), this type of cost is commonly referred to as 'nominal costs of price adjustment' or 'menu costs'. The main thing is, this cost is incurred once per price change; in order to avoid those, a firm tries to avoid frequent price changes, and price stickiness emerges. The subtle but crucial question that this literature analyses is, are such costs sizeable enough to seriously inhibit price flexibility? There is obviously cost-benefit analysis to be done, on the one side we have 'menu' and similar costs, while on the benefit side, a price change moves a price that is out of step with costs and demand to its optimal level.

Second, firms need to consider the real costs of price adjustment, a subtler concept. They must try not to alienate customers who see the change in the individual price but do not realize (for instance) that the price level and/or competitors' prices have risen in the same proportion. Imagine that a firm anticipates that the price level and its nominal wage costs are going to rise by 10 per cent over a year. At the beginning of the year (1 January), they announce their own price increases of 10 per cent. The firm's real price immediately after the increase will be about 10 per cent higher, even though it is calculated to match the price level increase by the end of the year, because the latter evolves only sluggishly. If by 31 December of last year the firm had a real price that was optimal (profit-maximizing), then its real price over much of the new year will be above its optimal value. Customers again will react along their demand curves, with the inevitable loss of sales and profits. To alleviate these, salesmen and clients must be informed that it is not corporate greed that necessitates these price changes, but reaction to rising costs; this type of information and publicity campaign is a further cost. This type of cost obviously depends on the magnitude of the price increase, as you will only spend some effort informing customers about a sizeable price increase; for this reason, this is referred to as *real* cost of price rigidity. This is a cost of quite a different nature to the 'menu cost'. It increases fast with the magnitude of price change (a greater change alienates more customers, hence it is modelled as quadratic on the magnitude of price change); therefore, if you wish to keep up with, say, inflation or rising wages, you would rather make frequent small changes in your price, as opposed to infrequent large ones induced by menu costs. Hence, this type of cost is generally thought not to be the basis of price inertia.

While the distinction between nominal and real costs of price adjustment may be somewhat blurred in practice (e.g. informing salesmen may be classified as either), it is sufficiently clear conceptually that the two play different roles in the analysis of monetary non-neutrality. To preamble, nominal (or 'menu') costs play the crucial role, but real costs reinforce the effects menu costs have. Costs of price changes, of either type, may plausibly be thought to be rather small; after all, what is the cost of printing new catalogues as a percentage of profits? However, this literature establishes that the gains from changing prices, *from the point of view of individual firms*, may be even smaller, so that it may not be worth changing prices, at least for some time, even in the case of fully rational, optimizing firms. While it may then be individually optimal *not* to change price, the *social costs* from foregone price changes are however non-trivial.

3.3.2 Menu Costs and Price Inertia

Following Mankiw (1985), the menu cost argument proceeds as follows. Let y and p represent the individual firm i's real output and relative price; lower-case letters will denote individual variables (y, p), and upper cases the corresponding aggregate variables (Y, P). Then, let $y = D(p; M/P)$ be a generic expression of equation (3.6'), the demand function facing this firm—see Figure 3.2. M/P is the real money supply, which is a proxy for aggregate demand and output (aggregate output and demand are the same and they both depend on the position of the LM curve, i.e. the real money supply). Monopolistic competition implies that individual demand is downward-sloping and the marginal revenue product (MRP) curve is below it. MC is the marginal cost, rising in the firm's output because (implicitly) working the people and machines more intensively is progressively more costly (because of overtime, increased maintenance, etc.). Initial equilibrium is given by MRP = MC (point A) with output y*; the optimal price p* follows from the demand curve. For ease of comparison, MRP and MC are denoted by thick lines, and D by a thin one.

Now, let an adverse monetary shock happen, decreasing M to M' < M, and shifting D to D' and MRP to MRP'. The new optimal position involves MRP' = MC (point B), with output y**, and new (lower) optimal price p** (projecting B onto D'). The firm now faces the choice of whether to adjust its existing but no longer optimal price p* or not. If it does, it will move to p** and y**. If it does not, the firm will be off the optimal situation, given by B: price will remain at p* and output will be $y' = D'(p^*; M'/P)$, given by the old price at the new demand curve. The million-euro question now is, should the firm bother changing its price to p**, or leave it at p*? Since the money supply or aggregate demand fluctuates every day a little bit, the firm surely has other more important things to do than tinker with its price daily?

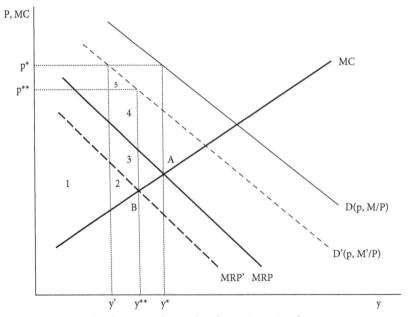

Figure 3.2. Producer surplus under alternative price decisions

Let us consider the benefits of changing or not changing; these can be measured by the producer's surplus. Readers should be reminded that the producer's surplus is the area (triangle) left of the MRP and MC lines. What we need to compare is the surplus attained in the two options that the firm has—inaction: leaving price at p*, to have output y'; price change: moving to the new full optimal situation with price p** and output y**. In both cases, the relevant marginal revenue curve is MRP'. (The old situation arising from point A is obviously no longer relevant.) If we indicate by S(p, y) the surplus arising from a combination of price p and output y, then with reference to Figure 3.2, we have:

$$S(p^{**}, y^{**}) = \text{areas } 1 + 2; \quad S(p^*, y') = \text{area } 1$$

The latter is the area between MRP' and MC, just stopping at y = y'. Therefore, the net gain from changing the price to its new optimal level, i.e. $S(p^{**}, y^{**}) - S(p^*, y')$, is equal to area 2 of producer surplus. This is a triangle, an area made up of two small distances multiplied together, therefore it is of 'second order'. Hence the major result of this literature immediately emerges:

The private (opportunity) cost for a firm from keeping the price unchanged in the face of a reasonably small change in nominal demand is of second-order.

What does this imply about monetary (non-)neutrality? We can answer this after having done the full cost-benefit calculus of inaction or price change. The cost of price change is assumed to be a fixed 'menu cost' m that the firm must pay in order to change its price (irrespective of the magnitude of the change). If, and only if, the surplus derived from the (p**, y**) combination outweighs the surplus derived from (p*, y') by more than m, will the firm abandon its old price p*. We have:

$$\begin{aligned} \textit{Price inaction if} \quad & S(p^{**}, y^{**}) - S(p^*, y') < m \\ \textit{Price change if} \quad & S(p^{**}, y^{**}) - S(p^*, y') > m \end{aligned}$$

(The special case of equality is ignored.) The result that the gain from change is second-order implies then that even near-trivial menu costs will prevent the firm from changing its price. The available evidence on costs of price adjustment is reviewed in the next section; here, suffice it to say that the numerical calculations reported by Blanchard and Kiyotaki (1987) suggest that, for plausible values for parameters like elasticity of demand and marginal cost, a menu cost of the order of a small fraction of 1 per cent of profits would be prohibitive for price adjustment; these are small enough numbers to make the menu cost story plausible.

The importance for the aggregate economy of such individual price stickiness is that prices will fail to adjust by much. As a result, changes in the nominal money supply M, by altering real aggregate demand, will induce real output changes. In other words, output will fall. If, instead, there had not been price stickiness, prices would have fallen (note that p** < p*). As a result, the price level P would have fallen and M/P would not have fallen by as much (or perhaps not at all).

The cost to society from inaction is measured by the sum of producer and consumer surplus. The latter is the triangle left of the (new) D' and MC curves. It can then be established, with reasoning exactly as above, that price inaction (outcome (p*, y')) involves the loss of areas $3 + 4 + 5$ of consumer surplus, compared to the fully optimum (p**, y**). This is to be added to the foregone producer surplus given by area 2 as before, to give the total societal surplus foregone from inaction. This is now a first-order sum (one of the dimensions is not small any longer). Intuitively, this is because output has fallen by more at y' than at y**; price decreases would have cushioned the fall in real demand. Hence, we derive the second important result of this analysis:

Though it may be privately optimal for a firm not to change its price following a change in nominal demand, the social costs of such price inertia are non-negligible.

We return to the issue of the magnitude of menu costs below.

3.3.3 General Equilibrium and Aggregate Demand Externalities

So far, the analysis is only of partial equilibrium; in other words, it centres on a single firm as if it were the only one and ignores the repercussions to, and from, other markets and the wider economy. Taking on board such interactions complicates slightly the analysis, because the pricing decisions of firms affect the real money supply M/P (via the denominator, given the numerator). The behaviour of M/P in turn affects the real price that the individual firm sets (via e.g. the pricing rule 3.11'). Hence, there is a two-way interaction between individual and aggregate price adjustment. To be sure, the individual firm is small enough (remember, it has monopolistic but not oligopolistic power) to legitimately ignore the effects of its own decisions on the general price level. Yet, the behaviour of the unit should be compatible with that of the whole. Incorporating this requirement is what distinguishes general from partial equilibrium analysis.

As before, we focus on symmetric equilibrium: for the typical or average firm, its equilibrium real price will be one—we are not interested much in firm heterogeneity or specific characteristics, and we shall pretend that all firms are identical, and therefore all individual relative prices are unity for all firms (so $p = 1$). Let the initial equilibrium in Figure 3.2 be such a symmetric equilibrium, so that $p^* = 1$. Now, as analysed, a monetary contraction may generate two possibilities, regarding prices: *either* menu costs are strong enough, so that real prices remain at $p^* = 1$ and output falls to y'; firms' profits will fall accordingly. *Or*, menu costs will not be high enough, and firms may wish to set the new optimal real individual prices to $p^{**} < 1$; but this can no longer be an equilibrium—not all firms can have prices below the price level! As gradually firms try to outdo the others and reduce their own prices by more, the price level P will drop. M/P and real demand will rise, and demand will begin shifting back to its old position D. When all the dust clears, demand will be back at D, optimal prices will again be p*, and output—this is crucial—back at y*. In this case, firms' profits will not be affected from the monetary shock, as the pre-shock situation has been restored.

In other words, individual price decisions generate an *aggregate demand externality* emphasized by Blanchard and Kiyotaki (1987). Every drop in any individual price causes an (imperceptible) drop in the price level P; while each firm has every reason to ignore this effect, it is substantial when all firms act in the same way. The effect is external to the firm (not considered in its own calculations) and affects aggregate demand via the P of M/P—hence the name. This aggregate demand externality may be argued to be the wedge between private and social costs of price inertia.

The social costs of price inertia may be explained with reference to the aggregate demand externality of price changes. Following the monetary contraction, the firms may find it optimal to maintain the old prices; if however they were to adjust their prices, this would have the inadvertent effect of reversing the monetary shock.

Privately optimal but socially (or collectively) inferior decisions: this is a running theme of New Keynesian economics that has far greater applicability than just pricing decisions.

3.3.4 'Near Rationality' and Price Stickiness

This argument that the benefit from price adjustment is small (formally: second-order) can be seen from a different perspective with the aid of Figure 3.3. This shows the profit that a firm derives as a function of its individual price. It is assumed that the new demand, D', is in force. Obviously, maximum profits are derived by the optimal price p**. Now, keeping the old price p* is suboptimal for the firm, but, from the graph, it is clear that the foregone profits by keeping p* instead of p** are not so big. Because p** is the optimum, profits in the area around p** do not fall fast as we move away from it. If profits are indicated by Π, then the foregone profits (ΔΠ) are given (by a second-order Taylor approximation) by,

$$\Delta\Pi = (d\Pi/dp) \times \Delta p + d^2\Pi/(dp)^2 \times (\Delta p)^2,$$

where Δ is the symbol of change and the derivatives are evaluated at $p = p^{**}$. But, $d\Pi/dp = 0$ since we have a maximum at $p = p^{**}$, leaving foregone profits as proportional only to the small, second-order term $(dp)^2$.

Akerlof and Yellen (1985), from which this exposition is derived, argue that this argument embodies 'near-rationality' on behalf of firms. When they find themselves in the vicinity, but not exactly on, the optimal point p** (as is the case at p*), the benefits from

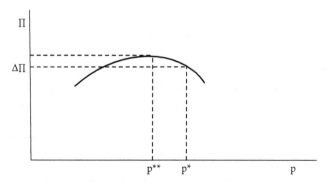

Figure 3.3. Profits under alternative price decisions

further fine-tuning the price (moving to p**) are so small that they are not worth the trouble. In other words, firms optimize but only roughly: they are 'near' rational. On the basis of simple numerical calculations, Akerlof and Yellen (1985) argue that there may be an area of deviation of as much as a few percentage points (up to 5 per cent) away from optimal profits in which a firm will not try to further fine-tune its price. Viewed upside down, this argument suggests that an equal percentage of firms find themselves in this situation. Hence, at any given time, an equal percentage of firms, it is argued, may plausibly fail to adapt optimally to the business cycle.

The argument on near-rationality has a much wider relevance than simply explaining price stickiness. The argument suggests that it does not really pay to aim for the exact optimum, as long as one gets the decision 'basically right'. In the menu cost literature, it is menu costs that deter us from moving to the exact optimum. More broadly, due to cognitive limitations, uncertainty, the complexity of the problem, etc., we may not be looking for the optimum but about an outcome that is 'good enough', as emphasized by the 'satisficing' approach. Thus, the Akerlof-Yellen argument becomes an instance of, indeed the definition of, bounded rationality that we discussed in Chapter 2. In Lucas's (1976) terms, one is rational if one 'does not leave $500 bills on the sidewalk' (i.e. if no opportunities are left unexploited). Instead, one is nearly rational (or boundedly rational) if one exploits the biggest opportunities, leaving small change lying around that is not really worth the trouble picking up.

3.3.5 The Role of Real Rigidities

So far, nothing has been said about real price rigidities, that portion of price stickiness that is due to costs that are proportional to the magnitude of the price change. Though not the critical factor in generating monetary non-neutrality, real rigidities play however an important role in that they reduce the gain from abandoning the old price and moving to the new one. Real rigidities are essentially the losses of profit incurred from moving away from the optimal price; they may be visualized by the aid of Figure 3.3. Let again p* be the initial optimal and equilibrium price, and p** be the new optimal price after M falls. As mentioned, the foregone profits from price inertia will be:

$$\Delta\Pi = d^2\Pi/(dp)^2 \times (p^* - p^{**})^2$$

This is the product of two terms (on the RHS): $d^2\Pi/(dp)^2$ is the loss of profit per 1 per cent (say) of price movement away from optimum; $p^* - p^{**}$ is the optimal response of the relative price to a 1 per cent (say) change in real money supply. Following Ball and Romer (1990), we define the *reciprocal* of the latter term as real rigidity; accordingly, we have a high real rigidity when the optimal price does not respond much to movement in aggregate demand.[8]

How is this related to our discussion? Consider Figure 3.3 again. The discussion above suggested that we have inaction if the foregone profits are outweighed by the menu cost,

---

[8] In fact, Ball and Romer argue that real rigidity rises as $(p^* - p^{**})^2$ falls *and* $|d^2\Pi/(dp)^2|$ rises, but we ignore that here.

$\Delta\Pi < m$, or $d^2\Pi/(dp)^2 \times (p^* - p^{**})^2 < m$. The flip side of the argument is that, for a given menu cost m, and properties of the profit function $d^2\Pi/(dp)^2$ (which may reflect structures of markets, technology, etc), a higher price rigidity makes the range of monetary shocks that fail to induce a price response by firms larger; this is because the required $(p^* - p^{**})^2$ will be smaller for every 1 per cent of change in M. The other side of the same coin is that, for a given monetary shock, the necessary size of menu cost that is prohibitive for price change becomes less. The former argument has implications for the real world, as monetary non-neutrality will be more prevalent with higher real rigidities. The other argument has implications for the theory, as a smaller size of the sufficient menu cost makes this a more plausible theory of price rigidity. We may summarize as follows:

Though real price rigidities do not generate monetary non-neutrality on their own, they can be said to enhance the effects of nominal price rigidities (menu costs). In particular, they increase the range of non-neutral monetary shocks, which will not be followed by price adjustments. They also make the size of menu cost that is sufficient to deliver monetary non-neutrality more plausible.

An obvious factor behind real rigidity is the elasticity of labour supply with respect to the real wage. Following, say, a rise in M by 1 per cent, workers will be happy to supply more labour providing the real wage goes up; this is the reason why MC slopes up in terms of Figure 3.2. The higher the labour supply elasticity, the lower will be the required real wage increase and the flatter the slope of MC. Hence, the slope of MC is an inverse index of real wage rigidity: a flatter MC implies more real rigidity. It can be checked that, with everything else equal, a flatter slope of MC reduces the size of area 2, and therefore makes price inaction more likely. Hence, a higher elasticity of labour supply/higher real rigidity increases the instances of monetary non-neutrality; which is another way of saying that greater price rigidity enhances the effects of nominal rigidities. The numerical simulations that Ball and Romer (1990) confirm that. They also show that a higher degree of real rigidity increases the social costs of price inertia, because the price level is more rigid, which makes M/P and real demand more variable (with a given variability of M).

3.4 Price Rigidity and Price Level Dynamics

We now briefly review a number of issues related to *aggregate* price rigidity, as opposed to individual price stickiness; and asymmetric price adjustment.

3.4.1 Infrequent Price Adjustment and Monetary (Non-)Neutrality

One question following from the above analysis is whether the infrequent individual price changes generate aggregate price level stickiness; and if monetary non-neutrality follows. The key papers here are Caplin and Spulber (1987) and Caplin and Leahy (1991), and the main argument is also summarized in Blanchard (1990). The idea is simple enough: even though individual prices change infrequently, at every time there will be some prices that are changing; so that the aggregate price level evolves gradually over time as if there was no

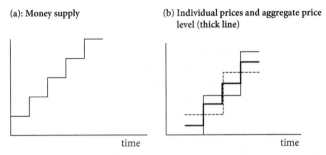

Figure 3.4. Individual price stickiness and aggregate price flexibility

individual price stickiness. For the sake of exposition, we shall make some rather strong assumptions here. Consider Figure 3.4 (a, b):

Panel (a) depicts the money supply, which rises by a fixed amount every period, hence the ladder-type shape. Note the orderly (in jargon: deterministic) pattern of the money changes: there are no shocks, uncertainty, etc. The economy consists of two firms, each adjusting their individual prices every two periods because of the menu cost—the argument is easily generalized to more than two firms. In the second panel, we have the individual prices of the two firms (thin and broken lines): The firms are assumed to want to catch up with inflation only, as real wage costs and demand are assumed constant. Because of infrequent price adjustment, their prices exhibit ladder-type shapes as the money supply does, except that the steps are now bigger and fewer. The two prices average out to the price level, which is the thick line. You have already noticed what happens: the aggregate price level exhibits exactly the same pattern as the money supply. Hence, there is no aggregate price inertia. M/P and real aggregate demand remain constant, and the particular pattern of money supply growth fails to have any real effects.

Caplin and Spulber (1987) conduct their analysis with endogenous timing of price changes, monetary uncertainty (but with monetary shocks that exhibit some regularity), and they let demand be endogenous (dependent on M/P). Firms are also identical. Their results are as above, and are due essentially to the regularity of monetary shocks: Though such shocks may change the picture momentarily, because of their regularity, money in general behaves as in panel (a). Once the regularity assumption is broken, by e.g. admitting a big, unexpected, step-wise increase in money, then monetary non-neutrality is restored (Caplin and Leahy, 1991); this is because the aggregate price level fails to match exactly the movement in M. So, the conclusion of this literature seems to be that, except under special conditions, individual price stickiness does translate into aggregate price level inertia. As aggregate price level adjustment is not as fast or as flexible as the money supply change, real money (M/P) does change and has real output implications.

3.4.2 Asymmetric Price Adjustment

Infrequent individual price adjustment and stickiness have important implications not only about the behaviour of the price level but also about the dispersion of individual prices around the mean. The argument has two parts. The first part is presented in Ball and Mankiw (1995). Assume that the environment is one of a trend inflation (i.e. in general the money supply and the aggregate price level look like in Figure 3.4a, b). At some point, however, there is an unexpected step-wise *change* in money and the price level; after this shock, the ladder-type pattern continues. How should firms react? Well, the answer depends on whether the change is an increase or decrease. In general, as the price level is going up, so is the optimal price of the firm. If a step increase in money and the aggregate price level occurs, so does the optimal price; with the actual price given at the moment the firm suddenly finds itself further away from its optimal. It may therefore decide to precipitate its (upward) price adjustment. Now consider a money and price level decrease. This is working against the trend inflation, which is continuously raising the optimal price and increasing the discrepancy between actual and optimal; the step decrease of money brings the optimal price down and reduces the discrepancy with the actual price. Hence, the firm may actually postpone the price change for longer. In other words, the individual prices respond asymmetrically to money changes under trend inflation, rising faster if there is an increase, whilst staying put if there is a decrease. Hence, a monetary expansion may not have much of an effect on real money balances and output, whereas a monetary contraction will (downwards). Furthermore, a given monetary expansion will have a smaller effect when trend inflation is higher (see Section 2.9 for discussion).

A sequel to this argument is provided by Ball and Mankiw (1994). To understand their argument, observe panel (b) of Figure 3.4. Assume that a firm's optimal price mirrors exactly the money supply; as demand rises, so does the optimal price. Because of infrequent but large individual price adjustment, at any time, there will be firms which are below their optimal prices and others that are above them. Ball and Mankiw (1994) show that, under trend inflation and following a step-wise monetary expansion, those firms that are furthest below their optimal prices will precipitate their price changes, whereas those that are close to them and above them will wait. Hence, the monetary shock alters the distribution of prices asymmetrically; *ceteris paribus*, the firms with the lower prices will have a higher probability of upward adjustment. These are testable implications of the menu cost argument, but unfortunately there has not been much empirical work along these lines.

3.5 Empirical Evidence on the Cost of Price Adjustment and Price Stickiness

3.5.1 Costs of Price Adjustment

Given the importance that theory attributes to costs of price adjustment, it is crucial that we should have an idea about the magnitude and nature of such costs in practice. In a series of papers, a group of researchers investigate the costs of price adjustment for a variety of US firms. In a typical estimate, they find that 'menu costs for the chain drugstore average $0.33 per price change which constitutes about 0.59 per cent of revenues' (Dutta et al., 1999). These costs are comparable to findings from supermarkets (Levy et al., 1997). These costs are not trivial, considering the very tight profit margins under which such retailers operate. In an interesting twist, investigating a large US manufacturing firm with a large network of salesmen, Zbaracki et al. (2004) find that the managerial costs (gathering information, meetings to finalize prices, informing the rest of the firm) are more than six times the physical (menu) costs of price changes, and that the customer costs (informing and convincing customers) are more than 20 times the physical costs. These numbers are substantially (and surprisingly) high, but they also suggest that quadratic (rising with the magnitude of price change) real costs (particularly the customer costs) may be more important than lumpy (i.e. fixed) menu costs. If so, frequent but small changes ought to be the norm, hardly a basis for aggregate price level inertia. So, the evidence from this literature seems rather mixed on the relevance of menu costs in the strict sense.

Using data from a large US supermarket chain, Chen et al. (2008) find evidence of asymmetric price adjustment—more upwards than downwards—in 'small' price increases. The asymmetry lasts for price changes of up to about 10–15 cents, which is about 5 per cent of the average retail supermarket price of about $2.50. This asymmetry seems to be only partially explained by inflation (which induces upward price changes), so it appears to be not well understood. In contrast, Levy et al. (2020) document an asymmetry in the rigidity of nine-ending prices (e.g. $8.99): these prices are upwardly, but not downwardly, rigid. This pattern is not obvious in the non-nine-ending prices and it is counter-intuitive in that inflation, if anything, should push prices upwards. The explanation here appears to be the perception (due to bounded rationality) that nine-ending prices are low (e.g. consumers tend to think that £9.99 is a low price, while £10 is a double-digit, higher, price). Thus, firms are unwilling to break this barrier, in order for price increases not to be noticed, so they tend to keep nine-ending prices longer at that level; whereas they have less difficulty pushing non-nine-ending prices to the immediately higher nine digit (e.g. £9.50 to £9.99).

3.5.2 Evidence on Price Stickiness

Regarding price stickiness, in an early contribution, Cecchetti (1986) estimated that the prices of American magazines change only once a year, showing evidence of stickiness. In the same spirit, Kashyap (1995) found the prices of a dozen goods to last on average more than a year; prices change faster in periods of high inflation. More recently, there has been a debate between Bils and Klenow (2004) and Nakamura and Steinsson (2008) on the extent of individual and aggregate price stickiness. Bils and Klenow (2004) find that individual prices change often—once every 4.3 months—and argue on this basis that the aggregate price level is fairly flexible. Nakamura and Steinsson (2008) show that, once they exclude temporary price cuts, individual prices change infrequently—about every 7–11 months—and therefore argue that the price level is fairly sticky. Obviously, this has direct implications on the ability of monetary policy to deliver real effects.

Kehoe and Midrigan (2015) revisit the issue and aim to find the root of the disagreement. Using US prices, they show that, on the average, prices change indeed change every about four to five months. But about 70 per cent of prices changes are temporary and short-lived, driven by idiocyncratic shocks; these prices return soon to a much stickier 'regular' price (i.e. a benchmark), which is not very responsive to monetary and other aggregate shocks. These underlying 'regular price' benchmarks only change on average about once a year. For this reason, even though micro-prices change frequently, the aggregate price level is sticky. Kehoe and Madrigan (2015) suggest an estimate of the cost of the adjustment of these 'regular' prices as 0.38 per cent of profits. Eichenbaum et al.

(2011) also find evidence of quite inertial reference prices (that reflect main costs and change on average once a year) while actual prices change on average every two weeks (but hover on average around the reference prices). This line of research would suggest, then, that it is not menu-type costs that are responsible for price stickiness; rather, it is the underlying calculations ('reference prices') that are revised infrequently.

The balance of the evidence seems to suggest that there exists price stickiness at both the individual and the aggregate level, even though we (again) do not understand its nature as fully as desirable. All this gives scope for aggregate nominal disturbances, including monetary policy, to affect real output. An interesting by-product of this line of research is the estimated small magnitude of the costs of price adjustment. Whether they be of the order of 0.6 per cent of revenues (Dutta et al., 1999) or 0.4 per cent of profits (Kehoe and Madrigan, 2015), these are small percentages. Of course, they still prevent prices from moving flexibly, as theory informs us that the benefits from getting prices 'exactly right' are also quite small. But there is also an implication here for the costs of inflation. Inflation in general will induce a faster price change, as costs will rise faster. But if the costs of price adjustment are small anyway, this points towards inflation not having great costs in terms of the faster price adjustment it induces. We revisit the costs of inflation below.

3.5.3 New Directions: 'Sticky Information' and 'Rational Inattention'

Another conclusion from the literature is that the nature of the costs of price adjustment and stickiness seems to be multi-faceted and rather complex. There is a variety of reasons why firms are reluctant to change their prices continuously. The costs may vary according to sector, with difference costs in e.g. supermarkets with the myriad of not very expensive products they sell, and different in manufacturing firms which produce fewer, more valuable goods. In the former case, it is literally the costs of changing catalogues and online lists whereas in the latter case, prices need to be calculated carefully and customers to be informed. In any case, because these costs have proved rather elusive, some literature is now suggesting that it is futile to try to pinpoint them exactly. Perhaps it is not literal costs that prevent firms from adjusting frequently, but the boundedly rational strategy of getting it 'about right'. Once this is done, we can leave our prices alone for a little while. This is the argument of 'rational inattention' (Sims, 2003). By a similar argument, prices are sticky simply because management may not have all the required information in 'real time'; it takes considerable time to get the required information to make the recalculation of optimal price. Thus, it may be the 'sticky information' that is the root cause of the sticky prices (Mankiw and Reis, 2002).

3.6 Wage Contracts and Wage Rigidity

3.6.1 Wage Contracts; State- vs. Time-Contingent Adjustment Rules

We now turn to another aspect of rigidity, namely wage rigidity. We saw in Chapter 2 that wage stickiness is due to the existence of wage contracts that are infrequently renegotiated. Wage contracts are a feature of much salaried employment, whether in the public or private sectors.[9] Typically, wage contracts are negotiated between (unions of) employers and unions of employees and last for some time, often a year. As we discussed, wage contracts are a key reason for the breakdown of the Policy Ineffectiveness Proposition; and, on the whole, longer-lasting contracts generate and prolong real effects of nominal shocks (including monetary policy ones). From the perspective of this chapter, such wage rigidity implies a real rigidity (a flatter MC curve) that exacerbates the effects of nominal rigidity (menu costs). Another reason why such rigidity matters is that it affects the inflation dynamics that will be reviewed later on. Blinder and Mankiw (1984) warn against highly aggregative models that mask the underlying multiplicity of sectors and heterogeneity of their wage negotiation practices. In this section, we analyse further issues around these basic themes.

Before proceeding, we digress to explain a key difference between price and wage adjustment. This has to do with the state- and time-contingent adjustment rules. The former are adjustment rules that depend on the state of the variable in question; while the latter depend on time and have a fixed time frequency. Price adjustment seems to be more in the nature of state-contingent adjustment; the firm allows deviations of its price from optimal (due e.g. to a change in costs, demand, etc) up to a point (a 'state'); when the deviation of actual from optimal price reaches a threshold (say 10 per cent) then the firm takes action to adjust the price. This seems to be the typical strategy of price adjustment (though the threshold surely varies and is not easy to ascertain), and so the frequency of price adjustment appears in general variable. On the other hand, wage adjustment takes place at regular intervals (for example, once a year), so it is more in the nature of time-contingent adjustment.[10]

3.6.2 Staggering or Synchronization of Wage Contracts?

Wage inertia is due to mainly to wage contracts; it follows that the length and form of wage contracts is very important both for the effects of aggregate demand policy and for inflationary dynamics. An important issue concerns the form of staggering of wage contracts. Let us assume that all contracts last for two years. Will wage setters all choose to set wages at the same date—e.g. on 1 January of even years (synchronization or 'bunching' of contracts); or will staggering persist, with some signing on the 1 January of even and others of odd years (staggering)? The two different structures will have different effects; e.g. De Fraja (1993) shows that, all else equal, staggering gives rise to higher wages and unemployment than synchronization. Why does staggering exist, as we observe in practice? In what follows, we attempt to shed some light on the logic of staggering.

It may be informative to think about staggering with an analogy drawn from a different context, namely in terms of the holiday structures around various countries in Europe. There are countries like the UK or Germany in which holidays are staggered, and for most people daily routine goes on even during the peak season. There are others (like France or

---

[9] There is of course employment, particularly in the private sector, where there are no contracts and wages vary from one day to the next.

[10] A simple analogy may clarify: If I fill up my petrol tank when the level falls below a certain threshold, I follow a state-contingent adjustment rule. If, on the other hand, I fill up once a week (say), then my rule is time-contingent.

Italy) in which the bulk of holiday-makers go away all together (i.e. in a synchronized way) and which almost literally shut down during August (except in the coastal areas). Naturally, climate plays a role but this observation may suggest that both staggering and synchronization may be Nash equilibria. If everybody goes away in August, there is not much point in staying behind and all businesses shut down. If, on the other hand, the daily routine is normal all year long, everybody has an option on when to go away, and individuals will choose randomly. Thus, both structures (staggering-synchronization) make sense. Because individuals have no private incentive to deviate from the existing norm, either situation can replicate itself. Thus, the answer to why staggering exists may be a hybrid of reasoning at the empirical and the logical levels.[11] Concluding this analogy, as staggering or synchronization of holidays may have important implications in terms of seasonality of (un)employment, frictional unemployment (workers between jobs, etc.) and regional variations in income and wealth, so staggering or synchronization of wages and prices may affect the dynamics of inflation and the real effects of monetary policy.

Fethke and Policano (1986) analyse the conditions under which wage contracts are staggered or synchronized, and parallel analyses are carried out by Ball and Cecchetti (1988) and Ball and Romer (1989) for prices. The former paper centres on the externality that a firm/sector that adjusts wage exerts on the others: by raising their wage, this firm contributes to a rise in the overall wage and price level and a lowering of the real wage in the other sector—see also Ball (1987); this provides an incentive for the other wage setters to move simultaneously, therefore in sync. On the other hand, Ball and Cecchetti's (1988) analysis emphasizes the informational gains from 'waiting to see', so that staggering may be both privately optimal (therefore, a stable Nash equilibrium) and socially optimal. Both analyses seem to converge on the importance of relative vs. aggregate disturbances (recall the Lucas 'island model' of Chapter 2) and the number of firms. Aggregate disturbances favour synchronization as they are common. On the other hand, relative disturbances are by nature asymmetric, so they are more effectively countered by staggering because those firms adjusting their wage will partly cancel out the relative disturbance to the other sector. A large number of firms, moreover, implies that individual firms are small, so there are small gains for observing other individual firms and the externality of individual firms on the aggregate price level is small. So, a large number of firms favours synchronization.

3.6.3 Length of Wage Contracts, Wage Indexing, and Asymmetric Wage Rigidity

A further issue is the length of wage contracts: are they going to be signed for a year, or two years, or what? Gray (1978) emphasizes two costs of signing contracts, one is the transactions costs of contracting (negotiations and effort required to reach and draft the

---

[11] This is to say that the contract structure is a Nash equilibrium. If everybody signs their contracts on a certain date, I should do the same; but by the same reasoning, everybody does the same, and synchronisation emerges as a Nash equilibrium. Likewise, if the signing of contracts occurs at random dates, I may as well choose a random date, and staggering emerges. But then, more than one alternative outcomes may be in principle possible ('multiple equilibria').

agreement), and the other is the deviation from the optimal wage while the contract lasts (the optimal will change as shocks become known). Obviously, the former argues for longer duration of contracts, whereas the latter for shorter contracts; optimal contract length balances the two considerations. So, a greater variability of shocks will be a factor pushing for shorter contracts.

A related issue is the degree of 'indexation' of wage contracts, namely a formula according to which nominal wages adjust in line with the rate of inflation. While in most types of contract the nominal wage is fixed for the duration of the contract (e.g. for a year), it is standard practice for wages to be adjusted for inflation from one contract (or year) to the next—completely or partially. The effects of this mechanism were in a contribution by Gray (1976) of the early generation of New Keynesians. Essentially, indexing fixes the real wage and turns the AS curve vertical. In terms of the MC curve of Figure 3.2, it makes the MC flatter, increasing the degree of real rigidity. Therefore, indexing insulates against the effects of monetary shocks (shifts in AD—from monetary policy, developments in the monetary sector like financial innovation, money demand, etc.), while at the same time it exacerbates the effects of supply-side, real shocks. Hence, the optimal degree of indexation depends on the mix of these two shocks in the real economy, and is in general imperfect (neither zero nor full). We shall discuss the effects of indexing further in relation to inflation dynamics later on.

Finally, it is often thought that nominal wage rigidity may be asymmetric, more downwards than upwards. This insight, originally made by Keynes, may be due to 'money illusion', the (boundedly rational, again!) inability of workers to distinguish between their nominal wages and the purchasing power of those. This downward wage stickiness is at the root of some basic macroeconomic theory; e.g. it is the key idea behind the (simple) Phillips Curve: a higher rate of inflation erodes the real wage and increases employment, something which could not happen with nominal wages getting reduced in the first place. But the supposed nominal wage rigidity at the basis of this argument may not have much empirical foundation after all: Smith (2000) finds that there was not a lot of nominal wage rigidity in the UK in the 1990s *even downward*; if one includes wage rigidity due to contracts and menu costs, only about 9 per cent of employees who stay in the same job had zero pay growth. Smith concludes that 'the UK labour market exhibits surprisingly high nominal flexibility'; and that 'downward rigidity is not large enough to have serious macroeconomic consequences'.

3.7 New Directions: Strategic Complementarities, Coordination Failures, and Multiple Equilibria

In this section, we review some other New Keynesian themes and directions that are somewhat different from the themes we have highlighted so far, namely imperfect competition, price and wage stickiness, and monetary non-neutrality. Specifically, we shall be introducing themes like 'coordination failures', multiple equilibria and the possibilities they open, and 'animal spirits'. It is not that these themes are entirely incompatible with the themes discussed above; it is that they do not presuppose nominal rigidity and do not involve monetary non-neutrality. Their relevance is that (if true) they move the economy away from the situation of 'first-best' Pareto optimality. In that way, they are related to the research programme of the New Keynesians.[12]

3.7.1 Strategic Complementarities and Coordination Failures

To illustrate the concept of strategic complementarity (Cooper and John, 1988) we can work with the pricing framework of sub-section (3.2.2). Consider again equation (3.11'):

$$P_j/P = \left[\frac{1+\mu}{\alpha^\alpha A}(W/P)^\alpha (Y/n)^{(1-\alpha)} \right]^b, \quad 0 < b \equiv \frac{1}{(1-\theta)\alpha + \theta} \leq 1 \qquad (3.11')$$

Let aggregate demand (Y) be proportional to real money balances M/P; let also everything else be constant (markup, μ, real wage, W/P, and the number of firms, n) and be subsumed by a constant k. Then, (3.11') can be rewritten as,

$$P_j/P = k(M/P)^d,$$

where

$$0 < d \equiv (1-\alpha)b = \frac{1-\alpha}{\alpha + \theta(1-\alpha)} < 1 \text{ and } \kappa \equiv \left[\frac{1+\mu}{\alpha^\alpha An^{(1-\alpha)}}(W/P)^\alpha \right]^b;$$

or, by trivially rewriting:

$$P_j/M = k(P/M)^{1-d}. \qquad (3.16)$$

By the fact of d < 1 (justified by the underlying parameters of the pricing rule), the pricing decisions exhibit 'strategic complementarity': a rise of prices by others (exemplified in the aggregate price level, P) prompts the individual firm to also raise its price. If we had d > 1, we would have instead 'strategic substitutability'. Price increases by others induce a price *decrease* by the individual firm (this is less plausible as far as pricing decisions go, but the idea is more widely applicable). One last thing to be remembered is that, in symmetric equilibrium, $P_i = P$.

The situation is depicted in Figure 3.5, following Blanchard and Kiyotaki (1987). The horizontal axis shows log(P/M) and the vertical log(P_i/M). Strategic complementarity implies that the pricing locus (3.16) is upward-sloping, with slope 1 − d < 1. The requirement of symmetric equilibrium ($P_i/M = P/M$ in this context) is depicted by the 45° line. Equilibrium N incorporates three ideas: strategic complementarity in individual price setting, symmetric equilibrium, and as a summary of these two, Nash equilibrium. Nash equilibrium implies that every 'player' (here, firm) does their private optimal or 'best response' to what everybody else is doing (here, they are on the pricing locus, responding

---

[12] Sometimes, this broad agenda of research is called 'Post-Walrasian Macroeconomics' (Colander, 2006).

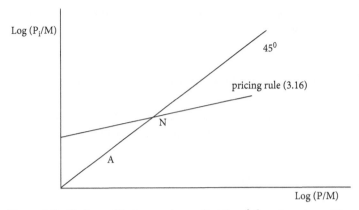

Figure 3.5. Nash equilibrium and coordination failure in price setting

best to price increases); and that the individual actions replicate the existing situation (here, the individual P_i replicates the P to which it responds).

You may ask, so what? Well, N is worse than any other point below it on the 45° line like A, because higher profits are generated by higher demand and output (remember, it is P/M on the axis, so output increases leftwards). But does the individual firm have a private gain in moving to A? Obviously not, since it is not on its best-response price decision line (3.16). Yet, A is socially superior to N. Due to the aggregate demand externality (see sub-section 3.3.3 above) of the price decision, the firm fails to pursue the collective optimal. If, somehow, their actions could be coordinated, they could all decrease their prices equipro-portionately, relative prices would not change, but P would fall, M/P would rise, and a point like A could be attained. So, the prevailing situation is not socially optimal; the loss of a superior outcome (such as A) is due to a failure to coordinate privately optimal actions (Cooper and John, 1988). This is often the case in decentralized economies where every agent pursues their private optimal.

These ideas may be generalized in many contexts. Let us take three examples from real life: queues, driving behaviour, and corruption. Imagine your individual behaviour depending on others' queuing behaviour (at bus stops, etc.). In all probability, it exhibits strategic comple-mentarity: if you observe orderly queues around you, you will also behave in an orderly manner; if everybody jumps the queue, then you will also be inclined to do the same, otherwise you will be left at the end. Likewise with driving behaviour: if everyone drives in an orderly and courteous way, so will you; if others' behaviour is aggressive, you may develop the same strategy in order to (so to speak) survive. Referring to corruption: if you live in an orderly society, where everyone is behaves in a civil manner, so will you; if however, everybody wants 'a little private extra' (i.e. a bribe) to work, you may be inclined (sooner or later) to do the same. You may now be convinced that behaviour in many walks of life (and economy) exhibits strategic complementarity: If P/M in Figure 3.5 is aggression on the roads, or amount of corruption, our private reaction function is upward-sloping: We respond to more corrup-tion, aggression, etc. with increasing our individual degree of corruption, aggression, etc. (The exact slope of the reaction function could be debated and it would certainly differ between individuals, but these are inconsequential details.) If so, and since eventually the aggregate behaviour is made up of individual behaviours, the setup of Figure 3.5 applies fully.

In particular, the Nash equilibrium will not generally be the best possible one from a social point of view. That is most clearly seen with respect to queues. From a social point of view, the rate at which the queue is depleted depends on (say) the capacity of the bus and is given. My gain from jumping the queue entails an equal loss to my fellow passengers (technically, this is a *zero-sum game*). So, more or less, (dis)order at the queue will not make the bus go faster. But, less order may also generate friction, confusion, and anger, and these may be negative externalities from my behaviour that make the Nash equilibrium with imperfect order socially inferior to that of an orderly queue. Similar reasoning applies to all the other examples. A summary may be the following:

Strategic complementarity often implies that socially inferior Nash equilibria may prevail. If somehow private actions could be coordinated, socially better outcomes could be supported.

We shall encounter strategic complementarities again in Chapter 11 when we discuss consumer behaviour; we shall see there that various types of social interaction give rise to such a behaviour. The analysis here serves as a warning that such behaviour leads to socially inferior outcomes. These ideas are also relevant in the quest for appropriate social institutions (norms and culture, as well as formal institutions such as laws) that promote productivity, growth, and overall economic welfare. We return to them in Chapter 9 on growth.

3.7.2 Other Directions: Multiple Equilibria, 'Animal Spirits', and 'Agent-Based' Models

New directions associated with the New Keynesian programme of research centre around the possibility of there being more than one Nash equilibria that are due to 'animal spirits'. The term 'animal spirits' is used in many contexts (e.g. Akerlof and Shiller, 2009), without complete agreement on its meaning. The most common understanding of the term seems to be endogenous waves of optimism and pessimism that induce a two-way causality between the economy and psychology: optimism (pessimism) leads to an increase (decline) in output, and the increase (decline) in output in term intensifies optimism (pessimism) (De Grauwe 2012; De Grauwe and Ji, 2017; Farmer, 2008). These mood-swings are due to the boundedly rational, imperfect cognition by agents of the complex economic system; when things are going well (badly), we tend to project that into the future in a more arbitrary way than the sophisticated calculations hypothesized by rational expectations allow. These psychological mood swings are self-fulfilling as they are validated by the turn of events. Consider the following example.

Consider the representative consumer (denoted i) who follows a simple consumption rule:

$$C_i = c(Y_i + zY_i^e)/2 \qquad (3.17a)$$

whereby consumption is a fraction c of the average of current and expected future income (Y_i and Y_i^e, respectively), the latter weighted by $0 < z < 1$. Future income is assumed to be

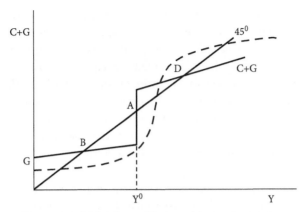

Figure 3.6. Multiple equilibria and 'animal spirits'

forecast accurately but imperfect cognition and psychology imply that the weight on future income depends on the state of the economy:

$$z = \begin{cases} h > 1, & Y_i^e > Y_i^0 \\ 1, & Y_i^e \le Y_i^0 \end{cases} \tag{3.17b}$$

Accordingly, when the future state of the economy is expected to be good, income is weighted by h(igh), while a bad state receives a l(ow) weight. Rational expectations would assume that once we make our best forecast of future income, that would enter with a constant coefficient (which perhaps incorporates a risk premium). Bounded rationality and psychology suggest that we are naturally more cautious (extravagant) when things are going badly (well).

To this simple structure, we now add the standard symmetry assumption ($C_i = C$, $Y_i = Y$, and $Y_i^e = Y^e$ for all i, where the variables without subscripts are aggregate) and the national income accounting: $Y = C + G$, as we have no investment or external sector. We also consider only the 'steady state' where all adjustment has taken place and the dust has settled. This implies that output (etc.) is the same at all times, so that $Y = Y^e$. The situation is depicted in Figure 3.6.

The 45° locus depicts graphically the equality $Y = C + G$. The $C + G$ locus draws equation (consumption 3.17a with b) plus $G > 0$. It exhibits a step and an increase in slope at $Y = Y^0$. With more realistic (and more complicated) assumptions, one could get the smooth 'sigmoid' broken curve, which exhibits much the same basic properties; but to keep the discussion simple, we focus on the simple structure we have described. We get three equilibria, A, B, and D, two of which (B and D) are stable. If they are perturbed, they tend to be re-established, while equilibrium A is unstable: if it is perturbed, we veer off it, towards either B or D.

What insights do we get out of this structure? First, we tend to spend more time at extremes (B or D) rather than in the middle (A). There is indeed evidence that growth rates or the output gap are not normally distributed but exhibit 'fat tails', more occurrences at the extremes than the normal allows (Fagiolo et al., 2008). Secondly, a shock (government spending? the world economy? energy prices? natural event?) that is strong enough to move us away from the region around one of the equilibria towards the other one will have a stronger effect than traditional theory allows for. To the 'fundamental' determinants of outcomes that are traditionally accounted for (technologies, preferences, factor endowments—TPFE for short) we may now add psychology and human behaviour, which exacerbate and distort the outcomes that would be delivered by those fundamentals. Various 'agent-based' models (see Page, 2008) incorporate heterogeneous individuals and firms that exhibit 'agency', i.e. boundedly rational behaviour that practically defies straight-forward description; see the Guidance for Further Study. We return to similar themes in Chapter 6 on business cycles.

All these considerations matter because they undermine the belief in the 'self-regulating' ability of the market economy, a theme emphasized by a whole lineage of schools of thought, reviewed in Chapter 1 and culminating with the New Classical and the 'Real Business Cycles' theorists that will be discussed in Chapter 6 on business cycles. For them, a 'shock' would rock the system temporarily but that will return to the same predetermined trend path over time (see Chapter 6). Instead, a (New) Keynesian would argue that a shock, if sufficiently strong, may rock the system to a new long-run equilibrium. Thus, the economy does not return to its prior condition over time. For example, the financial crisis 2007–9 may have rocked us into a new equilibrium of lower long-run growth rates (i.e. stagnation). All this calls for more policy activism to return the economy to the prior equilibrium.

Other insights that can be gleaned out of multiple equilibria concern the role of history and institutional structure. For instance, the two different equilibria may reflect different stages of development. In the low one, production is low because the market is small because incomes are small because production is low—a circle. In the high one, we have the opposite. Public policy may provide the 'big push' for simultaneous industrialization and development across the entire economy (Murphy et al., 1989). Something like that may have been witnessed in China and other Eastern Asian economies in the 1970s and 1980s. We revisit this theme in Chapter 9 on growth. More broadly: according to traditional theory, the economic outcome is singly determined by the 'fundamentals' (TPFE). Note, singly: all economies with the same TPFE will have the same outcome. There is no differentiation here by, say, history or historically determined institutions, culture, norms. For this reason, traditional neoclassical theory has been criticized as ahistorical. Multiple equilibria allow for history (precise historical path) and institutions (including culture, etc.) to matter by determining which of the equilibria is selected. Thus, history, institutions, and fundamentals all matter (see Krugman, 1991a; and the Guidance for Further Study).[13] These are fascinating themes related to New Keynesian analyses, and dovetailing with analyses of social and behavioural economics (Schelling, 1978; Bowles, 2004) and analyses of 'institutions' in Political Economy (Acemoglu and Robinson, 2013).

---

[13] The idea that the actual course of history shapes current outcomes is called 'path dependence'. This idea has parallels in many other disciplines, including evolutionary biology, physics and mathematics. A similar idea is 'hysteresis' (on which more in Chapter 4 on unemployment) which suggests that the actual historical path shapes the end result (equilibrium). The polar opposite is the standard view in economics that only the fundamentals determine the nature of the equilibrium. A hybrid position might be that both history and fundamentals matter; the exact mix varies and depends on the context.

3.7.3 New Keynesians: Concluding Comments

The whole agenda of New Keynesian economics started from the New Classicals' claim that older Keynesian arguments and policy prescriptions were based on ad hoc assumptions about agents' behaviour and beliefs. New Keynesians strove to put their ideas on a more secure footing, by accepting Rational Expectations and providing more secure micro-foundations of their models. The former should not perhaps be taken as a literal belief in the Rational Expectations doctrine, but as a way of avoiding expectational mistakes as a foundation of Keynesian prescriptions. Micro-foundations also mean behaviour that is firmly based on optimization by households/consumers/workers, and firms.

New Keynesians generate their policy prescriptions by considering a richer set of fundamentals (in addition to TPFE) like market structure (monopolistic competition), costs of price adjustment and price stickiness, and the nature of wage contracts. They are thus able to reaffirm core Keynesian ideas such as the effects of government spending on aggregate demand, and on real output of nominal aggregate demand (monetary non-neutrality). They are also able to provide a whole range of new insights on the pricing decisions by firms, with concomitant implications on inflation and the Phillips Curve (which we review in Section 3.8). Later generations of New Keynesians have also started to develop themes such as bounded or near-rationality, strategic complementarity (or sub-stitutability) of private decisions, and coordination failures, the possibility of multiple equilibria and all their implications (history, path dependence, and hysteresis), animal spirits, the relevance of social interactions, and so on. These are wide-ranging themes with important implications for public policy, institutions, and welfare. There is not as yet any emerging consensus on common approaches and frameworks. But there is no doubt that, in the quest for understanding the complex fabric of economies and societies around us, these insights will prove long-lasting.

Regarding the core ideas of the New Keynesians, an older Keynesian such as Tobin (1993) has reason to remain sceptical. 'Old' Keynesians would not invoke price and wage rigidity as the causes of excess supplies (or occasionally demands) in markets; those may be the results of complex interactions and uncertainty, themes closer to some of the extensions rather than the main themes of New Keynesians, and may be there even with fully flexible prices and wages. According to this view, the New Keynesian framework misses the key interaction and vicious circle between excess supply in the product market, consequent unemployment in the labour market, and reduced purchasing power by workers, inefficient demand, and so on. This is the approach that the so-called 'Disequilibrium school' (Barro and Grossman, 1971; Malinvaud, 1977) pursued. While this approach held some promise among earlier generations of New Keynesians, their failure to explain why prices and wages get stuck at non-market-clearing levels made them lose appeal and such models were thus abandoned.

Another criticism that may be directed towards the New Keynesians is that their emphasis on price stickiness is yesterday's question. Their central argument is that real aggregate demand depends on the quantity of real money balances, M/P. When M changes, with a sticky P, M/P changes, and this moves the equilibria in the standard IS-LM/AD-AS framework. This is now obsolete as the quantity of money (M) is no longer the exogenous policy instrument. First, in the last few years central banks have widely adopted the practice of setting interest rates and letting the money supply be determined endogenously, i.e. they are happy to supply the market with whatever liquidity it needs. M is thus endogenous. Secondly, the 'credit channel' literature (see Chapter 7) has shown that it is the availability of credit as well as money balances that affect demand. Likewise, if aggregate demand shocks are thought to originate more with the real exchange rate EP*/P (E: nominal exchange rate, P*: foreign price level, P: domestic price level) or stock markets or other wealth such as housing (We/P, where We is nominal wealth), both the nominal exchange rate E and nominal wealth W are far more volatile than the price levels, so that it cannot be said that the rigidity of P inhibits the movements of EP*/P or We/P. All these arguments point to the fact that price stickiness loses some of its importance: pricing decisions do determine the aggregate price level P, but aggregate demand is no longer affected by M/P. But price stickiness continues to be important in the New Keynesian analyses of inflation; inflation is important in the 'Taylor rule' (see Chapter 7); thus, as we discuss in the 'three-equation New Keynesian system' in Section 3.9, price rigidity and 'menu costs' remain relevant for macroeconomic outcomes.

3.8 Inflation

We now turn to a somewhat different topic, that of inflation. There are good reasons why the study of inflation is grouped together with New Keynesian macroeconomics: a key point of disagreement between New Keynesians and New Classicals concerns wage and price stickiness and rigidities; the scope for aggregate demand policies is then a corollary of the absence of market clearing induced by wage/price stickiness. But prices and wages are not immutably sticky: they move slowly, but they do move. Any plausible position on the possibility of markets not clearing because of price stickiness, therefore, goes hand-in-hand with a realistic description of the dynamics of price adjustment and inflation.

The New Keynesians have gone down the path of analysing inflation dynamics exactly for this reason. The work, over two decades and more, has been so extensive that the modern approaches to inflation are in the main New Keynesian contributions. In turn, these analyses of inflation have been taken on board and used extensively by modern policy analyses (e.g. Clarida et al., 1999). For all these reasons, if the modern theories of inflation are to be placed next to a school of thought, this ought to be the New Keynesian one.

3.8.1 Post-War Inflation and the 'Great Moderation'

As may be seen from Figure 3.7, inflation was low in the 1950s and 1960s, in the single digits and possibly less than 5 per cent, rising considerably in the 1970s up to the mid-1980s to double digits. From the mid-1980s, a sustained process of reduction took place, initially to single digits, then to inflation almost everywhere in western Europe and the US of around 3 per cent; this process of dis-inflation has been termd 'the great moderation'. This has been mirrored across the world, including developing and high-inflation countries, noting of course that the scale has always been different: many of these countries had very high inflation (see below on 'hyperinflation') which they managed to reduce considerably but not to single digits.

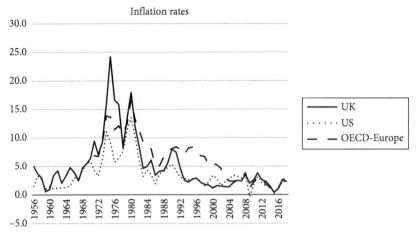

Figure 3.7. Annual inflation rate among selected industrialized economies

3.8.2 Costs of Inflation

Inflation is a variable of acute policy concern, evident in the fact that the monetary policy framework is overall titled 'inflation targeting' (see Chapter 6 on monetary policy); Central Banks in countries such as the UK are mandated to maintain inflation rates around 2 per cent. But why care about inflation in the first place? At a general level, the answer is rather easy: inflation disrupts the workings of the market mechanism, creating uncertainty about future market conditions, costs, etc. But, when trying to specify and concretely estimate these costs, researchers have not been so successful: the costs do not appear to be that high, at least for moderate (single-digit) rates of inflation. Below, we review these costs; their magnitude depends on whether the inflation rate is entirely predictable or not, and so we organize the discussion accordingly.

'Shoe-leather' costs of predictable inflation

Traditionally, the costs of predictable inflation were thought to arise in relation to money holdings: a higher inflation rate increases the nominal interest rate (recall the 'Fisher equation'), so the demand for money decreases. Agents try to economize on money holdings, and they do so by more frequent visits to the bank or cashpoint. (If you spend £10 per day uniformly within the day, you could withdraw £10 from the cashpoint every morning, in which case your average money holdings is £5—initially £10, gradually falling to £0; or you could visit the cashpoint twice a day, withdrawing £5 each time, in which case your average money holdings is £2.50.) Such more frequent visits to the bank may wear out the heels of your shoes, imposing 'shoe-leather' costs. More generally, these are the costs of more frequent transactions necessitated by the higher rate of inflation. Viewed alternatively, if agents try to economize on shoe-leather costs by keeping the same nominal balances, inflation erodes their real value, which is the opportunity cost of holding money.

Furthermore, the analyses of Ball and Mankiw (1994, 1995) reviewed above suggest that the inflation rate affects the dispersion of relative prices. Additional effects of inflation include its effects on a higher frequency of price adjustment implying more menu costs and costs of recalculating new optimal prices and informing customers. But, as the early survey by Driffill et al. (1990) shows, there is reason to believe that the welfare losses due to perfectly anticipated inflation may not be of great empirical importance. More recent studies confirm this: for instance, Burstein and Hellwig (2008) estimate the costs of inflation in terms of the opportunity costs of real balances to be of the order of 1–2 per cent of consumption when inflation rises by 10 per cent. The welfare costs induced by a greater price dispersion are negligible relative to the opportunity cost effect. Lucas's (2000) findings are of the same order of magnitude. We also saw above that the costs of price adjustment seem not to be very sizeable.

Costs of imperfectly predictable inflation and inflation uncertainty

It is an age-old ('folk') piece of knowledge, and verifiable from Figure 3.7, that a higher average rate of inflation implies greater inflation variability.[14] Such inflation variability implies that inflation is unpredictable. In this case, the welfare costs are likely to be considerably higher. How much will the cost of living change within the year? What will be the wages and other costs that my business faces, the real price of my goods (I can determine my own nominal prices, but not the average price level and therefore the real prices—think of the Lucas 'island model' of Chapter 2)? Furthermore, if quantities are affected by this uncertainty over wages and prices, this will compound the overall uncertainty: e.g. how will market demand fluctuate over the year? For this reason, the costs of higher inflation are thought to be much more sizeable (Driffill et al., 1990).

The real question is how these costs compare with the costs in terms of lost output incurred by the tight monetary and fiscal policies, pursued in order to bring inflation under control. Recent literature has looked at the correlation between inflation and growth across time and countries. The (short-run) Phillips Curve implies a positive correlation (higher inflation coincides with lower unemployment therefore less output gap and more output growth, with the causal direction from growth to inflation). But the above arguments imply that inflation hurts output growth, hence a negative correlation, with causality going the opposite way. An influential study by Bruno and Easterly (1998) found no correlation overall between the rates of inflation and real output growth. What they did find is that inflation crises, defined as periods when inflation is above 40 per cent annually, induce sharp growth falls; growth then recovers surprisingly strongly after inflation falls. There are two messages from this: first, the costs of moderate inflation in terms of growth seem to be negligible except in countries or episodes with quite high inflation. Secondly, inflation crises do have serious growth costs but only temporarily; this can be read in an opposite way to suggest that reducing extreme inflation rates does not incur great costs for long.

After controlling for other possible determinants of growth, Barro (1997, chapter 3) presents negative growth-inflation correlations, driven most probably by the experience of countries and times with middle (15–40 per cent) or higher (> 40 per cent) rates of inflation, rather than the low (< 15 per cent) ones. Interestingly, in the same growth regressions with other determinants and the level of inflation, adding the standard deviation of inflation renders them insignificant; casting a question mark over the arguments that it is inflation uncertainty that imposes the highest inflation costs. But Fischer

[14] See e.g. Barro (1997, Chapter 3), which shows a positive correlation between the level and standard deviation of inflation across a wide range of countries and times; and Ascari and Sbordone (2014).

(1993) does find a significantly negative relation between the growth rate and both the inflation rate and the standard deviation of inflation; interestingly, he finds similar results among low- and high-inflation countries. Fischer (1993) also finds that inflation adversely affects productivity growth (the 'Solow residual', see Chapter 9 on growth) and capital accumulation.

On the basis of his numerical estimates, Barro (1997) concludes that increasing the inflation rate by 10 per cent would produce a reduction in the growth rate by 0.3–0.4 per cent per year; over 30 years, this would translate to a level of real GDP lower by 6–9 per cent. Translated into absolute magnitudes (in $bn), Barro rightly argues that these are large sums. The inflation-growth correlations that Fischer (1993, table 10) shows are often less (in absolute value) than −0.1, reaching a maximum of -0.2 in only one of the regressions. If we take the median of his estimates of about -0.03, this means a reduction of inflation by 10 per cent would add about 0.3 per cent of growth; of the same order as in Barro (1997). Similar results are presented in the careful study by Andres and Hernando (1999); their estimates of table 6 imply that a permanent reduction of inflation by 1 per cent increases the present value of income (i.e. the sum of all future income increases appropriately discounted) by about 0.2–0.3 per cent; a little less than in the other studies (which do not discount).

But one has to put these things into perspective. Lowering inflation by 10 per cent would add 6–9 per cent to GDP after 30 years, Barro (1997) argues; this is the equivalent of around three years of medium-to-robust growth (i.e. of the order of 2–3 per cent); but how much austerity would it take, and unemployment and years of low if not negative growth, for that reduction of inflation to be produced among the now mostly developing countries that still feature double-digit inflation rates? In other words, do the gains from low(er) inflation justify the costs imposed by anti-inflationary policies? In the memorable phrase of the older-generation Keynesian James Tobin, how many 'Harberger (welfare) triangles' does it take to fill up an 'Okun (output) gap'? Perhaps the real question is, where is the balance? A sound macroeconomy surely does not need inflation (on the contrary...), but what are we prepared to sacrifice in order to get rid of it, and up to what point? Guided by theory, evidence, sound reasoning, and by their own priors (a little bit), the readers are invited to make up their own mind.

3.8.3 An Optimal Rate of Inflation?

While the details may be a matter of interpretation, the above discussion suggests that inflation may induce costs by disrupting the market mechanism and harming material welfare; we certainly do not want high inflation, whatever 'high' means. On the other hand, there are good grounds to think that we do not want too low inflation, either. Not only because there are (perhaps temporary) costs in terms of the austerity policies required to bring inflation down; but also too low an inflation rate is bad in its own right. First, the officially calculated rate of inflation probably overestimates the true rate of inflation. The Consumer Price Index (or similar price indices), out of which the inflation rate is calculated, does not take into account the improvement in quality of goods. For example, a computer or a car today bears little resemblance to the computer or car of 20 years ago. A middle-range (say) PC of today costs probably the same as the equivalent PC 20 years ago, yet its capabilities are a multiple of those of the earlier-generation product. Failure to account for that imparts an upward bias on the calculated CPI index. If we value now *that* 20 year-old PC (not its modern equivalent), its price would be much lower, perhaps close to zero.[15] If such quality adjustments were taken into account, the true price level (therefore the inflation rate, too) would have been lower than published.[16]

A second reason why we do not want a too low rate of inflation is that that rate affects the average nominal interest rate. The Fisher equation that links the two is:

$$i_t = r_t + E_t \pi_{t+1}, \tag{3.18}$$

whereby the nominal interest rate (i_t) is decomposed into the real interest rate (r_t) and the expected loss of purchasing power due to inflation (π). Now, the real interest rate, the reward to saving and price of borrowing funds, is thought to reflect 'deep' fundamentals in the economy such as productivity and thrift, and does not change much. Hence, a rise in inflation (and its expected rate) will be reflected one-to-one on the nominal rate, at least in the long run. If the inflation rate is low, so will be the nominal rate. This means that the monetary authority will not have much room for manoeuvre should it need to reduce interest rates in order to get an economy out of stagnation. (This has been obvious in recent years, when various monetary authorities might have wished to reduce nominal interest rates but those are stuck at the 'zero lower bound'—ZLB.) The bottomline of the argument is that a higher rate of inflation would have meant higher nominal rates and less danger of them being stuck at the ZLB.

Finally, a lower rate of inflation moves us closer to the possibility of *deflation*, i.e. a negative rate of inflation. Deflation is dangerous because it pushes an economy further and further into stagnation: as prices are expected to become lower, the smart strategy is to postpone consumption till later, reducing demand ever more. Moreover, with a given nominal interest rate, at least for a while, the real interest rate rises, which is bad news for borrowers, mortgage holders, and businesses thinking whether to invest. Finally, the real value of both assets (wealth) and liabilities (debts) rises; the latter however is more dangerous as it brings more agents (households or firms) closer to default.

Thus, there are costs from both high and too low a rate of inflation. On these grounds, one might ask, is there an optimal rate of inflation, one that balances the two types of cost in the best possible way? Unfortunately, theory and evidence provide little guidance as to what that might be. Currently, major Central Banks target an inflation rate of about 2 per cent (most typically and clearly the Bank of England); there are some voices that this is too low, and that it should rise *once only*. Because this would happen with an AD expansion, it is considered a 'Keynesian' measure. The problem would be that, if you change the targeted inflation, what guarantees are there that you will not do it again, even if you promised it this to happen once only? In other words, such a move by monetary authorities would be fraught with problems of credibility (see Chapter 7 on monetary policy), those very problems that took a generation and careful design of monetary policy institutions to rout. For this reason, the targeted 2 per cent rate of inflation is likely to remain for the foreseeable future.

---

[15] Gordon (1990a) estimates that the price of a modern technologically-intensive durable good may be a multiple of the price *now* of its equivalent made a generation ago.

[16] See Reed and Rippy (2012) for an up-to-date account of measurement issues around the cost of living.

3.8.4 Early Theories of Inflation

There has been no shortage of theories on inflation. We can distinguish two phases of the literature: the first, around the period when inflation was high, explored a variety of perspectives on inflation; the second, in the 1980s and 1990s, under the influence of the work of New Keynesians on price and wage stickiness, focused on modelling inflation in a stylized way. In this sub-section and the next, we explore briefly some of the earlier ideas and perspectives; in Section 3.9, we analyse the modern, New Keynesian model of inflation.

Early work (see the survey by Laidler and Parkin, 1975) started from the basic premise that inflation reflects a disequilibrium between aggregate demand and supply. It then explored the reasons why this might be so, relating it to aggregate demand policies, the output gap, productivity, conditions in the labour market, the exchange rate and 'imported' inflation via the price of imported goods, etc. Adopting the consensus position that aggregate demand gravitates in the long run towards the natural rate of output, which is supply-side determined, this analysis leads to the conclusion that inflation <u>in the long run</u> (i.e. that component of inflation which is permanent) ultimately reflects the expansion of money; in popular parlance, too much money chasing too few goods. But that is only in the long run; in the short run, all types of disequilibria and discrepancies between supply and demand matter. Contrast that with Friedman's (1970, p. 24) position that 'inflation is always and everywhere a monetary phenomenon'; this denies any role to any structural (demand-supply) factors and attributes all inflationary developments to variations in the supply of money, even in the short run. Many people would agree that this is a rather extreme position; it may capture only the experiences of 'hyperinflationary' economies—see the models of hyperinflation below.

More structuralist in nature was also the so-called 'Scandinavian' model of inflation, associated with Aukrust (1977) and others (see the survey by Frisch, 1984). The emphasis there was on the open economy (to a large extent, inflation is imported in small, open, and oil-importing, economies), productivity, and the wage-price spiral. The wage-price spiral features also in sociological accounts of inflation (Goldthorpe, 1978; Hirsch and Goldthorpe, 1978), also active during the era of high inflation. The wage-price spiral however takes a social and class-conflict dimension in those theories: employers/capital owners and workers aim to increase their share in national output, and they try to do so by increasing respectively prices and wages; eventually the result is a zero-sum game whose only effect is inflation.

The wage-price spiral takes yet another dimension in the work of Kydland and Prescott (1977) on the pitfalls of discretionary monetary policy-making. Here, there are three parties to the vicious circle of inflation: Wage-setters raise wages as they expect the cost of living to rise, price-setters raise prices as they expect wage costs to rise (so far the story is the standard wage-price spiral), but now there is an account of government policy, too. If the monetary authority were to try to check this inflationary process, they would have to apply contractionary measures, causing a painful recession; if they were to 'accommodate' the inflation by raising the money supply accordingly, the inflation becomes permanent. So, the policy-maker raises money as they expect the private sector to generate inflation, and the latter does so because they expect the policy-maker to accommodate the inflationary tendencies. There is an 'inflation bias' that will not go away as no party has any incentive to unilaterally move away from it. Furthermore, there is always the temptation by the policy-maker to engineer an increase in output (perhaps temporarily); this generates credibility problems for monetary policy, resulting again in inflation. These arguments, reviewed in detail in Chapter 7 on monetary policy, have sparked an intense debate in the literature on the appropriate monetary policy 'architecture' that can alleviate such dis-functionalities, and have profoundly influenced practical policy developments.

Other modern theories centre on the need by government to maintain sound public finances. As we discuss in detail in Chapter 8 on fiscal policy, inflation is a way of alleviating the burden of government debt by reducing its real value (Calvo, 1978); eventually, it acts as a tax whereby government gets hold of a bigger share of national output (and offers it as public services). This situation again generates an inflationary bias, like that due to monetary policy-making, and for similar reasons. A continuation of this argument is the 'unpleasant arithmetic' of Sargent and Wallace (1981) in which persistent government deficits will eventually be monetized (see again Chapter 8), leading to inflation.

3.8.5 Hyperinflation: The Cagan Model

An earlier approach to inflation centred on 'hyperinflation' (see Cagan, 1956). This is a situation of extremely high inflation, from (say) 100 per cent (prices double within a year) to perhaps several hundred per cent: prices multiply within a year. This is an unstable, therefore dangerous situation. As you expect prices to be appreciably higher in a little while, the rational thing is to bring forward consumption, therefore raising demand and pushing inflation still higher. In the era of high inflation, various developing countries had inflation rates which could be classed as hyperinflation; today, few exceptions remain, and those are countries with deep structural problems (acute supply deficiencies, so demand >> supply) and broken public finances (so rampant monetization of government budget deficits). Several European countries experienced hyperinflation in the difficult times of the inter-war years and during World War II.

Hyperinflation is almost always accompanied by rapid money creation; this is because to try and slow down the rate of money creation would cause a deeper recession than the structural problems are already causing. As both money and prices are rising fast, inflation becomes a monetary phenomenon. It is not a monetary phenomenon in Friedman's (1970) sense that causality goes from money to prices and nothing else matters; rather, only in the sense that money and prices are highly correlated, perhaps both caused by the deep structural problems of the economy, so there is no clear causality.

A model that builds on the high money-price correlation is the Cagan (1956) model of hyperinflation. This model proceeds as follows. Demand for real money balances is an inverse function of the nominal interest rate, which is the opportunity cost of holding money:

$$m_t - p_t = \alpha - \beta(r + E_t p_{t+1} - p_t) - v_t \tag{3.19}$$

The logs of money supply and price level are denoted m_t and p_t, respectively; therefore $p_{t+1} - p_t$ is inflation in the year ahead. Furthermore, invoking the Fisher equation (3.18), the nominal interest rate is decomposed into a constant real interest rate (r), assumed constant, and expected inflation. A real higher interest reduces the demand for money as it is its opportunity cost. The term v_t captures 'velocity shocks' of demand (variations in the willingness to hold money due to such factors as changes in transactions technology); e.g. an increase in v_t is defined as any innovation that reduces the need for cash balances, such as increased use of credits cards or the spread of cash dispensers. Finally, imposing instantaneous market clearing, money demand equals money supply at all times (both denoted by m_t). The intuition is that if money supply were to rise above demand for a moment, then the LHS would be greater than the RHS momentarily; immediately, the price level (p_t) rises as agents try to get rid of excess money holdings by spending them; given the long-term expected price level ($E_t p_{t+1}$), this reduces the LHS and increases the RHS, thus restoring equilibrium.

To see the empirical implications of this model, we may use the transformed error term:

$$u_t \equiv -v_t + \beta(p_{t+1} - E_t p_{t+1})$$

which adds the white-noise (under rational expectations) expectations error to the structural shock v_t, to transform (3.19) to:

$$m_t - p_t = \alpha - \beta r - \beta(p_{t+1} - p_t) + u_t \tag{3.19'}$$

In times of hyperinflation, both the (log) nominal money and price level are both integrated of order two (I(2); intuitively: they both rise too fast). In this case, they should co-integrate with a $[1, -1]$ co-integrating vector, so that real money balances ($m_t - p_t$) become an I(1) variable (see Engsted, 1993). With a stationary error term, real money balances ($m_t - p_t$) and inflation ($p_{t+1} - p_t$), which are both I(1), are co-integrated.

Next, we return to (3.19) to see another important implication of this model. Solving (3.19) forward iteratively in the same manner as we did in Chapter 2, we get:

$$p_t = (1 - b) \sum_{i=0}^{\infty} b^i (E_t m_{t+i} + E_t v_{t+i}) - \alpha + \beta r, \quad b \equiv \beta/(1 + \beta) \tag{3.20}$$

This shows the fundamental determinants of the price level in monetary models: that the money supply feeds into the price level is straightforward; a change in transactions technology that reduces the need for cash also raises the price level as it implies an excess of money balances above need; the surplus is spent, raising the demand for goods and the price level (under a given exogenous supply, as is the underlying assumption in this model). A rise in the interest rate that makes us economize on cash balances, as it makes them more costly, will for the same reason raise the price level.

The current price level is a weighted average of all current and future anticipated levels of the money supply and the velocity shock (v_t), with the weights declining for quantities further away in the future.[17] This is because any rise in the money supply (say, at time T) leads to a contemporaneous increase in the price level (p_T); to the extent that this is

---

[17] We should clarify that the velocity shock (v_t) is stationary but it may be forecastable, hence the expectation of its future values is not generally zero. It will be zero in the special white-noise case.

anticipated, this will have led to a rise in inflation one period earlier, $p_T - p_{T-1}$. This will have led to a decline in the demand for real balances at time $T - 1$, which is equivalent to excess money supply; as agents try to get rid of excess balances at $T - 1$, the price level rises then (p_{T-1}). In turn, this causes the same effect at $T - 2$, and so on all the way down to the present (t). So, the price level now and all future price levels between time t and T increase.

To reduce the price level, or inflation, therefore, the policy-maker needs to reduce the present value of all future money supplies (not only the current one), and to be seen to do so. Sargent (1993, chapter 3) argues that some of the inter-war hyperinflations ended rather abruptly when a new monetary regime was instituted that convinced markets that money printing in the future would be lower. Note: in the future. But this rather powerful implication (which, according to Sargent is borne out by the inter-war data) rests on a number of strong assumptions. First perhaps is the assumption of an exogenously (supply-side) determined level of real output; this is the hallmark of all monetarist models. If real output were even partly responsive to demand, then a rise in the money supply would raise real output, not only the price level. Furthermore, the price level is free to react freely to developments in the money supply; yet, the literature on price stickiness makes a powerful case that the price level moves only gradually. Second, the resulting specification for the price level is entirely forward-looking (it depends only on future and not on past money supplies); this raises some empirical and conceptual issues that are discussed in Section 3.9 and in the Chapter 7 on monetary policy, when we evaluate the credibility theories of inflation. And to finish, this formulation bypasses all the issues related to the strategic use of monetary policy; e.g. what happens if the monetary authority intends now to reduce the future money supply but changes its mind later? Again, these issues are discussed in Chapter 7. For all these reasons, one might choose not to believe literally in this monetarist model; rather, to use it only as a rough guide of the relation between the money supply and prices as we approach conditions of (a) full capacity in the economy and (b) very high inflation (and money growth) rates.

3.9 The New Keynesian Model of Inflation

In this section, we develop and discuss the New Keynesian model of inflation; in this, we draw on the survey by Kapetanios et al. (2011). The model is based on price stickiness. It is assumed that there is a large number n of monopolistically competitive firms which revise infrequently their prices because of menu costs. The first to model these infrequent price adjustments was Calvo (1983) and a voluminous subsequent literature with many extensions and variations builds on this. McCallum (1997) calls it 'the closest thing there is to a standard specification'. Clarida et al. (1999) place it at the centre of their influential review of monetary policy. In their recent review of empirical findings on inflation and their implications for macro-modelling, Angeloni et al. (2006) conclude that the Calvo equation is at least as consistent with empirical findings as its alternatives, and continues to play a fruitful role in the theoretical analysis of inflation. Its properties are mirrored in many of the more extended models.

Time is discrete and all price adjustments occur at the beginning of each period. For tractability, the time between consecutive price adjustments is assumed random but exogenous.[18] In each period, a proportion of firms $(1 - \lambda)$, $0 < (1 - \lambda) < 1$, adjust their price; therefore λ is an index of price stickiness. The probability of adjusting after s periods since the last adjustment will be given by the geometric distribution: $f(s) = (1-\lambda)\lambda^s$, i.e. a fraction $(1 - \lambda)\lambda$ of firms will on average adjust one period after the last adjustment, a fraction $(1 - \lambda)\lambda^2$ will adjust two periods after, and so on. Therefore, the mean 'waiting time' between subsequent price adjustments is $\lambda/(1 - \lambda)$.[19]

Because of the large number of firms, this distribution determines the percentage of prices as of time t that were set at time $t - s$ in the past; i.e. a fraction $(1 - \lambda)$ of the current (t) prices have been set this period, a fraction $(1 - \lambda)\lambda$ of prices were set in $t - 1$, a fraction $(1 - \lambda)\lambda^2$ were set in $t - 2$, etc. The price level at t will be approximated in a log-linear way as the sum of all individual prices holding at t:

$$p_t = \frac{1}{n}\sum_i p_t^i, \tag{3.21}$$

where p_t is the price level and p_t^i is the nominal price of firm i, all in logs[20]. As a fraction $(1 - \lambda)\lambda^s$ of current prices was set s times ago, the price level will be:

$$p_t = \frac{1}{n}(1 - \lambda)\sum_{s=0}^{\infty}\lambda^s \bar{p}_{t-s}^i \tag{3.21'}$$

where $\bar{p}_{t-s}^i$ denotes a newly set price. In other words, the price is a backward-looking sum of past newly set prices. Because of price stickiness, only a fraction of prices will change at any time, so that the price level adjusts sluggishly (in the terminology of Chapter 5, it is a 'predetermined' variable).

In setting its new nominal price $\bar{p}_t^i$ at any time—t for concreteness—firm i maximizes expected log profit (Π_t^i). Profit depends on price, $\Pi_t^i = \Pi(p_t^i)$, and is maximized at an optimal price $(\tilde{p}_t^i)$ that takes into account demand, costs, etc. A second-order Taylor expansion of maximal profit around the optimal price is (see Rotemberg, 1982; Ball and Romer, 1990):

$$\Pi(p_t^i) \approx \Pi(\tilde{p}_t^i) + \frac{1}{2}\Pi''(\tilde{p}_t^i)(p_t^i - \tilde{p}_t^i)^2$$

where the double prime indicates the second derivative and the first derivative is zero as the optimal price maximizes profits (by definition; recall also the analysis of sub-section 3.3.4). By profit maximization (as opposed to minimization), we also have $\Pi'' < 0$.

---

[18] This is a time-contingent price adjustment rule (rather than a state-contingent one).

[19] Implicitly, it is menu-type costs (independent of the magnitude of the price change) that are responsible for price stickiness in this model. Nevertheless, Rotemberg (1982, 1996) showed that quadratic costs of price changes (that depend on the magnitude of the change) have similar implications for the aggregate price level to the Calvo (1983) model.

[20] Recalling the proper specification of the price level in (3.2), the price level (3.21) corresponds to the special case of a unitary elasticity of substitution between varieties of goods ($\theta = 1$). If $\theta \neq 1$, (3.21) may be thought of as an approximation of the correct price level.

The forward-looking firm will select its new price that maximizes expected log profits over time:

$$max_{\bar{p}_t^i} \; E_t \sum_{k=0}^{\infty} R^k \left[\Pi(\tilde{p}_{t+k}^i) + \frac{1}{2}\Pi''(\tilde{p}_{t+k}^i)(\bar{p}_t^i - \tilde{p}_{t+k}^i)^2 \right]$$

where $R \equiv 1/(1+r)$ is the discount factor (r being the real interest rate—note $0 < R < 1$) and expectations are taken on the basis of information available at the beginning of period t.[21] Taking the first-order condition with respect to $\bar{p}_t^i$ and combining that with the probability of a newly set price to last k periods until a new revision, assuming $\Pi'' < 0$ to be a constant, we get:

$$\sum_{k=0}^{\infty} (1 - \lambda)(\lambda R)^k (\bar{p}_t^i - E_t\tilde{p}_{t+k}^i) = 0$$

This implies:

$$\bar{p}_t^i = \frac{\displaystyle\sum_{k=0}^{\infty} (\lambda R)^k E_t\tilde{p}_{t+k}^i}{1 - \lambda R}, \tag{3.22}$$

or, shifting back to $t - s$:

$$\bar{p}_{t-s}^i = \frac{\displaystyle\sum_{k=0}^{\infty} (\lambda R)^k E_{t-s}\tilde{p}_{t-s+k}^i}{1 - \lambda R} \tag{3.22'}$$

This is a forward-looking formulation of the new price; it depends on the future optimal prices weighted by the probability that the new price will last that long and by the discount factor. The new price can adjust instantaneously if current and future optimal prices change; it is a 'jump' variable.

We now need to specify expected optimal prices. In the spirit of the imperfect competition literature (see for instance Ball et al., 1988; Blanchard and Kiyotaki, 1987; Dixon and Rankin, 1994), we specify optimal prices as:

$$\tilde{p}_t^i = p_t + \psi y_t, \quad 0 < \psi < 1 \tag{3.23}$$

y_t is percentage excess real demand relative to the normal (or 'trend') output (see Chapter 6). In other words, the optimal price relative to the price level ($\tilde{p}_t^i - p_t$) is higher in conditions of excess demand. ψ is an inverse indicator of real price rigidity: The lower ψ is, the more invariant the relative price is to excess demand—hence there is more rigidity of the real price. It is related to the degree of monopoly power: ψ close to 0 is associated with near-perfect competition, whereas the greater ψ, the greater the degree of monopolistic

---

[21] Note that this discounted sum records profits during the 'life' of new price $\bar{p}_t^i$, so the latter is constant.

power of firms in the Dixit-Stiglitz framework of Section 3.1 (see e.g. Blanchard and Kiyotaki, 1987; Dixon and Rankin, 1994).

Combining the price level (3.21'), the new price (3.22') and the optimal price (3.23), after some tedious factorization, we get:[22]

$$\pi_t \equiv p_t - p_{t-1} = R(1 - \lambda)(1 - \lambda R)\psi \sum_{k=0}^{\infty} R^k E_t y_{t+k} \tag{3.24}$$

Eventually, the forward- and backward-looking dynamics combine into a simple, intuitive, purely forward-looking formulation of inflation (π_t; note that it is entirely different from profit Π). Inflation, a variable that can adjust instantaneously (in contrast to the price level), is fuelled by all the future excess demands, weighted by the discount factor (R). Inflation is also affected by the degree of price stickiness (λ) and the sensitivity of optimal prices to excess demand (ψ); the higher λ and ψ, the more sensitive is current inflation to future excess demand.

One notable feature is the entirely forward-looking nature of the inflation equation (3.24). To see that, we can rewrite it as:

$$\pi_t = R E_t \pi_{t+1} + R(1 - \lambda)(1 - \lambda R)\psi y_t$$

Or, slightly more generally as:

$$\pi_t = \varphi E_t \pi_{t+1} + \Psi y_t, \quad \Psi \equiv R(1 - \lambda)(1 - \lambda R)\psi \tag{3.24'}$$

Inflation depends on the future expected inflation and the current excess demand. Intuitive and simple though it is, this model of inflation has been roundly criticized for its various strong assumptions and drawbacks. We provide here a brief summary of the discussion in Kapetanios et al. (2011) to which the reader may turn for details and the voluminous literature that has built on Calvo (1983). Chadha and Nolan (2004) provide a slightly more advanced, integrative treatment. For the empirical performance of the various models, the reader can consult Mavroeidis et al. (2014) as well as Kapetanios et al. (2011).

- The probability of price adjustment $(1 - \lambda)$ is independent of aggregate demand or idiosyncratic shocks and firms are randomly selected to adjust irrespective of how far away their actual price is relative to the desired one (as argued, pricing in this model is time-contingent). Eichenbaum et al. (2011), criticize the consistency of the Calvo model with key features of the micro-data. They also argue that price adjustment is state-contingent: Prices are much more likely to change the further away the actual price is from the desired price. More recent strands of the follow-up literature extend to state-contingent pricing (e.g. Dotsey and King, 2006; Gertler and Leahy, 2008) but the resulting model is not as tractable. In an early contribution, Romer (1990) endogenized the probability of price adjustment in a Calvo-type setup.

---

[22] To see how this factorization works, it is best to use the 'lag operator' (L). See the Guidance for Further Study.

- The inconsistency of (3.24') with the NAIRU property must be counted as another weakness of the basic model (Gali and Gertler, 1999; Mankiw and Reis, 2002). Recall from Chapter 1 that the NAIRU property implies constant inflation when unemployment equals structural (or 'natural') unemployment. Here, instead of unemployment, we have excess demand for output, defined as: $y_t \equiv (Y_t - Y^*_t)/Y^*_t$, where Y^*_t is a supply-side determined level of capacity output (or 'normal' output).[23] We face a number of possibilities here, none of which is satisfactory:

  o The first possibility is that in the long-run equilibrium, when all the dust has settled, inflation and excess demand are constants (without subscripts), i.e. $\pi_t = E_t\pi_{t+1} = \pi$ and $y_t = y$. Then, (3.24') implies in the long run:

  $$\pi = \frac{\Psi y}{1 - \varphi} \tag{3.25}$$

  In this case, $\pi > 0$ if $y > 0$. If $y = 0$, then inflation goes to zero. There is no inflation in the long run unless there is permanent excess demand. But that would imply that output is permanently above its supply-determined capacity!

  o Assume instead that it is the change in inflation that is constant in the long run and that is zero only at the special case of cyclical unemployment or excess demand being zero—the 'NAIRU property'. Assuming that $\varphi \approx 1$, factorization and rearrangement of (3.24') implies:

  $$E_t\pi_{t+1} - \pi_t = -\Psi y_t$$

  Or, in the long run ($\pi_t - \pi_{t-1} = E_t\pi_{t+1} - \pi_t \equiv \Delta\pi$), we get:

  $$\Delta\pi = -\Psi y$$

  Then inflation increase $\Delta\pi$ increases with $-y$, i.e. excess supply! So, if the equation is brought to a form that (in principle) delivers the NAIRU property, it then has the wrong sign in front of excess demand.

- The empirical performance of the basic model (3.24') is weak. The purely forward-looking nature of this inflation equation implies that inflation shows little persistence, or else it adjusts readily to changes in excess demand. In contrast, in empirical estimation, the lead inflation ($E_t\pi_{t+1}$) is often insignificant, while a lag (π_{t-1}) is invariably strongly significant (Fuhrer and Moore, 1995; Roberts, 1997; Rudd and Whelan, 2006)—something that equations (3.24) or (3.24') do not have. In other words, the data show inflation to have persistence (this is the economic significance of the lag term) which the model does not predict.

- As a result of the lack of persistence in inflation, the inflation equation (3.24') fails to adequately capture important aspects of inflation dynamics. In particular, it fails to give rise to a hump-shaped effects of monetary expansions (see Mankiw and Reis, 2002). For instance, Christiano et al. (2005) find that:

---

[23] We cannot have real output (Y_t) in (3.24') or (3.25) as output trends upwards over time, implying that the inflation rate would increase out of bounds. It should also be clear that excess demand is closely (negatively) correlated with cyclical unemployment ($u_t - u^N_t$). Refer again to Chapter 1 if unclear.

'after an expansionary monetary policy shock,

1. output, consumption, and investment respond in a hump-shaped fashion, peaking after about one and a half years and returning to preshock levels after about three years;

2. inflation responds in a hump-shaped fashion, peaking after about two years;'

(Christiano et al., 2005, pp. 5, 8)

Any purely forward-looking inflation equation such as (3.24') fails to capture that.

To correct these weaknesses, the following generalization of (3.24') is often used:

$$\pi_t = \phi_1 \pi_{t-1} + \phi_2 E_t \pi_{t+1} + \Psi y_t, \quad \Psi \equiv R(1-\lambda)(1-\lambda R)\psi \tag{3.26}$$

An equation like (3.26) is often called the 'New Keynesian Phillips Curve'.

In empirical work, the result that often emerges is $\phi_1 > \phi_2 \geq 0$, where the latter may be insignificant. Note that the presence of the lag is arbitrary from the point of view of the basic model. Kapetanios et al. (2011) survey a number of other strands of the literature aimed at developing an inflation equation like (3.25) that includes a lag. Arguably, the variants that are most promising are: (a) models that include wage stickiness, in the spirit of the wage contracts discussed in Section 3.6, as well as price stickiness; and (b) models of price indexation, where recalculation of optimal prices takes place infrequently, but in the period in-between successive optimal price recalculation, actual prices adjust by the rate of inflation.

Additionally, (3.26) can be consistent with the NAIRU property, under the homogeneity restriction of $\phi_1 + \phi_2 = 1$ and the additional restriction of $0.5 < \phi_1 \equiv 1 - \varphi < 1$ (therefore $0 < \phi_2 = \varphi < 0.5$), so that the lag-lead coefficients sum to one but the lag is the more significant one. Factorization and rearrangement implies:

$$\pi_t - \pi_{t-1} = \frac{\varphi(E_t \pi_{t+1} - \pi_t) + \Psi y_t}{1 - \varphi}$$

In the long run ($\pi_t - \pi_{t-1} = E_t \pi_{t+1} - \pi_t \equiv \Delta\pi$), we get:

$$\Delta\pi = \frac{\Psi y}{1 - 2\varphi} \tag{3.26'}$$

Note that our assumptions imply that $1 - 2\varphi > 0$. So, we have the correct properties: inflation change is fuelled by excess demand; and it is zero when actual output and demand is at capacity or 'normal' level—the NAIRU property.

Finally, it is worth mentioning another generalization of the Calvo setup derived from a combination of micro-foundations and time-contingent price adjustment (e.g. Erceg et al., 2000). There is again a probability λ of a current price staying the same next period; the departure is that the new price set when time for adjustment comes (e.g. t) is:

$$P_t^i = (1+\mu)\frac{\sum_{s=0}^{\infty} E_t\left(\Lambda_{t+s}P_{t+s}mc_{t+s}^i\right)}{\sum_{s=0}^{\infty} E_t\Lambda_{t+s}} \tag{3.23'}$$

This replaces the simpler optimal pricing rule (3.22') with (3.23). This is a forward-looking, weighted sum of future real marginal costs (mc^i) times the price level (P), adjusted by the monopolistic markup (μ). The weights are $\Lambda_{t+s} \equiv R^s \lambda^s MRSU_{t,t+s} P_t^{\theta-1} Y_t$, which are a product of the discount factor (R) and probability of the same price lasting longer (λ), as in the basic model. Then, there is a new element: the marginal rate of substitution in utility (MRSU$_{t,t+s}$), which is the ratio of marginal utilities (MRSU$_{t,t+s} \equiv MU_t/MU_{t+s}$); the effect of this is to turn the objective discounting (R^s) to subjective discounting (R$^s MU_{t+s}/MU_t$); this gives the number of extra 'utils' (rather than pounds) now that are equivalent to one extra 'util' at time t + s. We do this type of adjustment as eventually the extra profits generated from optimal pricing are remitted to individuals for utility-enhancing consumption; and the future utils need to be converted to current utils. The final item in the weight is essentially market demand (P$^{\theta-1}_{t+s}$Y$_{t+s}$). So, the weights give the discounted future market demand in a certain period as a share of the discounted future total. Intuitive and important though it is, this formulation however does not lead to an analytically tractable inflation equation.

The bottomline is that the Calvo (1983) model and its variants are very intuitive but face rather serious empirical difficulties, prominent among which perhaps is the significance of lagged inflation, against the theoretical predictions. Various extensions and generalizations have been pursued in the literature, and the reader is invited to make up their own mind about the relative merits of each. For our purposes, providing we keep these considerations in mind, we may use an inflation equation like (3.24') as reminder of the importance of price stickiness for inflation dynamics. The main message is that, with more stickiness, average inflation is lower (given y, π is lower). In addition, (3.23') suggests that, given the average level of inflation, current price setting is done with an eye more to future demand conditions, therefore current inflation is relatively more responsive to them (as opposed to current demand). We may also keep (3.25) as a workhorse inflation equation; this is what we do in the final Section 3.10, when we analyse the 'three-equation New Keynesian model' of which it forms a part.

3.10 The 'Three-Equation' New Keynesian Model

The New Keynesian system is relevant for short- and medium-run analysis. It parallels the familiar IS-LM and AD-AS models but introduces two modifications. First, the traditional LM curve is replaced by the 'Taylor-rule' briefly introduced in Chapter 1 (see equation 1.17') and further analysed in Chapter 7 on monetary policy. The main reason is that monetary policy these days is done with the interest rate as the policy instrument and not with the money supply (as presumed in LM). Secondly, the static AS curve is replaced by a more dynamic version, which is the New Keynesian Phillips Curve. Thus, the system involves three equations:

- a generalization of IS, equation (1.16) of Chapter 1;
- the Taylor rule, (1.17') of Chapter 1;
- and an inflation equation like (3.26 or 3.26').

An auxiliary, fourth equation (the 'Fisher equation') links the nominal and real interest rates and the inflation rate.

The endogenous variables are real output, the nominal interest rate, and the inflation rate. The model allows enough time for output to change (the 'short-run' horizon), for prices to adjust and inflation dynamics to play out fully (the 'medium run') but takes as given both the institutional structure of labour markets, therefore structural unemployment to be analysed in Chapter 4, and capital, to be analysed in Chapter 9 on growth. Allowing such factors to change would get us into the long run, discussed in Chapter 4 (in relation to unemployment) and Chapter 9 (in relation to output growth). The system is best expounded by simple algebra, rather than diagrams. Dynamics is suppressed and variables are given at their steady-state values (so time subscripts and expectations are suppressed).

The first component is an equation generalizing the IS curve (1.16) in log-linear form:

$$\log Y = \alpha_1 \log(C_0 + G + NX) - \alpha_2 \log(T) - \alpha_3 r, \quad \alpha_1, \alpha_2, \alpha_1 > 0: \qquad (3.27)$$

Current output (in logs, y) is affected by the following:[24]

- Positively by exogenous spending (government spending G, autonomous consumption C_0 capturing wealth effects due to housing or stock markets and consumer psychology or 'confidence', or net exports NX);
- Negatively by taxes T, assumed lump-sum.
- Negatively by the real interest rate r, as this hurts investment.

Next, a simple Taylor rule gives the interest rate that the monetary authority sets:

$$i = i^* + \beta_1 y + \beta_2 (\pi - \bar{\pi}), \quad \beta_1 > 0, \beta_2 > 1 \qquad (3.28)$$

The interest rate set by policy (assumed to be identical to that which applies in markets) evolves around the long-run interest rate (i*—on which more below). Additionally, it is affected positively by:

- 'Cyclical output' or excess demand for output, defined (recall) as $y = (Y - Y^*)/Y^* \approx \log Y - \log Y^*$. The idea is that cyclical output, or output above normal, fuels inflation, so again the interest rate must rise to quell it. Conversely, a negative cyclical output ($y < 0$) signifies a recession (informally speaking here), so that policy must relax (interest rate to fall) in order to help the economy out of it.
- The inflation rate over and above the target inflation rate ($\bar{\pi} > 0$), as the policy-maker results in more stringent monetary policy when inflation is high in order to quell it. The restriction on the coefficient ensures that policy affects the real interest rate in the required direction; see below.

---

[24] From basics, real output (Y) equals real aggregate demand, so we may use the terms interchangeably. The point is that Y differs from the supply side-determined, long-run level Y*. As output can be temporarily different from Y*, the labour supply and work that supports it also differs from its long-run level. Thus, unemployment can temporarily differ from its structural or 'natural' rate; the difference, as we saw in Chapter 1, is 'cyclical unemployment'.

Furthermore, the 'Fischer equation' decomposes the nominal interest rate into the real interest rate (r) and the expected inflation rate:

$$i_t = r_t + E_t \pi_{t+1} \tag{3.29}$$

The nominal interest rate first compensates for the expected loss of purchasing power (the expected inflation rate) and then gives the real return to saving or real payment for borrowing (the real interest rate). In our static framework, this simply boils down to:[25]

$$i = r + \pi \tag{3.29'}$$

The long-run nominal interest rate equals the long run real rate (r*) plus the inflation target:

$$i^* \equiv r^* + \bar{\pi} \tag{3.29''}$$

With (3.29"), the Taylor rule (3.28) becomes:

$$r = r^* + \beta_1 y + (\beta_2 - 1)(\pi - \bar{\pi}) \tag{3.28'}$$

We now see that the assumption $\beta_2 > 1$ ensures that when inflation rises, the real interest rate falls, as is required in order to reduce output demand (3.27) and excess demand (y) and thereby stabilize inflation.

Finally, there is an inflation equation like (3.26'), repeated below. This is the steady-state version of the 'New-Keynesian Phillips Curve':

$$\pi - \pi_{-1} \equiv \Delta\pi = \frac{\Psi y}{1 - 2\varphi}, \quad 0 < \varphi < 0.5 \tag{3.26'}$$

As we have discussed, this equation is consistent with the 'NAIRU property' whereby an excess demand (or positive cyclical output) fuels not the level but the acceleration in inflation. Thus, in the medium run when all inflation dynamics have had time to adjust, the output level settles at 'steady-state' level that is exogenously given by supply-side considerations—denoted y*; otherwise there is runaway inflation. In the steady state, the non-accelerating inflation cyclical unemployment rate and cyclical output will both be zero. In the short run however, we may think that, due to price stickiness, past inflation (π_{-1}) is given for a while. Then, we have a 'Keynesian' Phillips Curve where inflation and output can both temporarily rise:

$$\pi = \pi_{-1} + \frac{\Psi y}{1 - 2\varphi}$$

---

[25] In a closed economy, the real interest rate equalizes output with planned aggregate demand; or, equivalently, it ensures that the equality $I = S + (T - G)$ (expressed in obvious elementary notation) holds.

In the short run (given π_{-1}), output is solved out as (can you verify?):

$$\log Y = \frac{\alpha_1\log(C_0+G+NX) - \alpha_2\log(T) - \alpha_3\left[r^* - \beta_1\log Y^* + (\beta_2-1)(\pi_{-1} - \frac{\Psi\log Y^*}{1-2\varphi} - \bar{\pi})\right]}{1 + \alpha_3\beta_1 + \frac{\alpha_3(\beta_2-1)\Psi}{1-2\varphi}}$$

(3.30)

With excess demand $y \equiv \log Y - \log Y^*$, we can readily solve for inflation and the real interest rate.

We then have the following effects:

- A rise in exogenous spending (G, C_0 or NX) or fall in lump-sum taxation (T) raise output, inflation, and the real and nominal interest rates.
- A rise in exogenous output (Y*) reduces excess demand, inflation, and the real interest rate and thereby raises output.
- A rise in the economy's supply-side-driven long-run interest rate (r*) raises the real interest rate and thereby harms investment and output.

What about labour supply and hours of work? They follow output, so they rise when y is higher; correspondingly, cyclical unemployment is lower.

A key result concerns the effect that price rigidities, nominal and real, have on the impact of exogenous spending on output. Taking the government expenditure multiplier on output, we get:

$$\frac{\partial\log Y}{\partial\log G} = \frac{\alpha_1}{1 + \alpha_3\beta_1 + \frac{\alpha_3(\beta_2-1)\Psi}{1-2\varphi}}$$

(3.31)

Both nominal rigidity (price stickiness, λ) and real rigidity (low ψ) decrease Ψ and thereby increase the effect of demand on output. These are key themes of New Keynesian economics: More price rigidities and stickiness imply that fluctuations in demand have a higher effect on output. In other words, economies with high price rigidities will experience more output volatility as a result of a given variability of exogenous demand; this is because prices and inflation fluctuate less and are therefore less able to neutralize the variability in excess demand. There is a corollary here: price stickiness remains relevant and important even though the real money supply (M/P) is now endogenous. But its importance now manifests itself through the more intricate inflation dynamics. Finally, we also have that the policy willingness to combat inflation (β_1) decreases the effect of demand on output. These are important insights offered by New Keynesian economics. They become visible only after we have replaced the IS-LM-AD-AS traditional framework with the 'three equation framework' of IS-Taylor rule-inflation equation/ Phillips Curve.

In the medium run, where Y settles to its 'steady state' of Y*, things change. Output is obviously entirely supply-determined; from (3.26'), inflation is constant (zero acceleration). From (3.27), since $r = r^*$, inflation must settle to its target ($\bar{\pi}$). The real interest rate is such that it equalizes real output with its supply-side-determined normal, therefore it is solved as:[26]

$$r^* = \frac{\alpha_1 \log(C_0 + G + NX) - \alpha_2 \log(T) - \log Y^*}{\alpha_3} \tag{3.32}$$

We conclude with a weakness of this 'three-equation framework' in comparison to the standard IS-LM-AD-AS one. This weakness is that the dynamics by which we converge to the medium run (Y^*, r^*, $\bar{\pi}$) are not apparent.[27] In Chapter 6, we discuss an extension of this model which derives the IS equation (3.27) from the 'Euler equation' of intertemporal optimization (see Chapter 5) and discuss the resulting dynamics.

Notes on the Literature

The Winter 1993 issue of the *Journal of Economic Perspectives* has a number of reviews on New Keynesian Economics, with contributions by Romer (1993), a comparison of old and new Keynesians by Greenwald and Stiglitz (1993), and a riposte by the old-school Keynesian Tobin (1993), among others. Mankiw (1990), Dixon and Rankin (1994), Dixon (2008), and the sceptical review by Gordon (1990b) could be read beneficially by many, while the books of readings by Mankiw and Romer (1991a, 1991b) and Dixon and Rankin (1995) will be of use to more advanced readers. Early theories of inflation are reviewed by Laidler and Parkin (1975), Aukrust (1977), and the volume of readings collected by Hirsch and Goldthorpe (1978); the perspectives vary considerably. The state of the art on New Keynesian economics is best reviewed in Gali (2015, 2018). The work on the New Keynesian Phillips Curve, building from price rigidities up, is critically reviewed in Kapetanios et al. (2011), while more empirical aspects of it are to be found in Mavroeidis et al. (2014). On costs of inflation, you can get started with the nice early review by Driffill et al. (1990).

Guidance for Further Study

On the optimal degree of price inertia

We mentioned in relation to (3.31) that price inertia increases the fiscal multiplier. This is in line with the traditional Keynesian thinking which emphasizes price rigidity while output varies, in contrast to the neoclassical model that emphasizes fully flexible prices and a constant output (at the supply-side level which we have called Y^* here). However, some Keynesians have challenged the neoclassical

---

[26] We shall see in Chapter 9 that the long-run real interest rate (r^*) equals the marginal product of capital. Obviously, this is inconsistent with (3.31); the inconsistency is resolved by considering that there are more than one interest rates (and corresponding real rates). (3.31) solves for the policy interest rate, while the marginal product of capital determines another (e.g. that on borrowing by firms for investment). But these two interest rates are not independent of each other: As they are likely to have different maturities (typically, the policy rate is for overnight lending by banks, while borrowing by firms is done through financial instruments of longer maturity), a 'term-structure' theory such as the one expounded in Chapter 2, is needed provide the link between the two.

[27] In contrast, in the standard model, given an exogenous money supply, the rise in inflation modifies the real money supply, until medium-run equilibrium is reached. See Chapter 6 for more detail.

position by doubting whether price flexibility in fact brings output stability (DeLong and Summers, 1986). A middle-of-the-road position is that of Chadha (1989) which finds that there is an optimal degree of price flexibility (neither too much nor too little) from the point of view of stabilizing output. Chadha's (1989) arguments balance the effects of changes in the inflation rate and in the price level; we have seen that, in the modern macroeconomic system, there is reason to believe that the price *level* is not that important. Yet, even in the case when only the inflation rate matters, the optimal degree of price inertia may be an intermediate one. We next show why.

Let us have a simplified version of the demand equation (3.27), modified as:

$$\log Y = \log D - \alpha r = \log D - \alpha\beta\pi, \quad \alpha, \beta > 0$$

Lots of unimportant details have been suppressed. As in the model above, particularly (3.28'), inflation raises the real interest rate because of a simple Taylor rule. The inflation equation (3.26') is amended to:

$$\pi = \Psi y + \varepsilon \equiv \Psi(\log Y - \log Y^*) + \varepsilon$$

In this, we have simplified the dynamics (there aren't any) and have added an adverse supply shock ε (e.g. a rise in the oil price or a slowdown in productivity). Combining, the output equation becomes:

$$\log Y = \frac{\log D - \alpha\beta(-\Psi\log Y^* + \varepsilon)}{1 + \alpha\beta\Psi}$$

We are now in a position to see why neither extreme price stickiness nor extreme flexibility are beneficial. The supply-side shocks will move $\log Y^*$ and ε in opposite directions. This is captured schematically by $\log Y^* = -\omega\varepsilon$, where $0 < \omega < 1$ (obeying also $0 < \omega\Psi < 1$) shows the effect of the supply shock (ε) on output in the medium run. Substitute this above and answer the following:

- What is the degree of price flexibility Ψ (or inverse rigidity) that completely neutralizes the shock on output from the supply side? How is it related to ω? Explain.
- Now, consider that demand also varies, entirely independently of supply (the covariance between the two is 0), but that $Var(\log D) = \theta Var(\varepsilon)$, where $\theta > 0$ measures the importance of demand-side shocks relative to supply. Take the variance of $\log Y$ and find the optimal degree of price flexibility (Ψ) from the point of view of minimizing $Var(\log Y)$. How does this optimal Ψ depend on the parameters of the model? In particular, how does the relative importance of the demand shock (θ) affect the optimal price flexibility? Explain.

Output, inflation, and monetary policy

Let us now turn the tables and investigate the role of monetary policy in this very simple model. Solve again for output and inflation, and if you've got it right (and if I've got it right, too!), then you will obtain:

$$\log Y = \frac{\log D - \alpha\beta(1 - \omega\Psi)\varepsilon}{1 + \alpha\beta\Psi}$$

$$\pi = \frac{\Psi\log D + (1 - \omega\Psi)\varepsilon}{1 + \alpha\beta\Psi}$$

- One could begin here by calculating optimal monetary policy (the responsiveness of the policy interest rate to the inflation rate, β), from the point of view of minimizing the variance of output and the variance of inflation (separately). Is the optimal monetary policy the same in both cases? How does it depend on parameters? Explain.
- Now, observe the following: A rise in price flexibility (Ψ) increases the relative importance of the demand shock for inflation but decreases it for output. More importantly, the same happens with monetary policy. A higher β stabilizes output if demand shocks are more predominant but destabilizes it if shocks are more supply-side. It always stabilizes inflation, of course. So, one theme that emerges is that supply shocks are more difficult to deal with, as in that case the same policy stabilizes one variable but destabilizes the other; we shall show that more informally in Chapter 6. Another theme is that price flexibility and monetary policy under predominance of supply shocks generates a kind of Phillips Curve in output and inflation—not levels, but variances! Can you show that formally? This theme of Phillips Curve in variances will be revisited in Chapter 7 on monetary policy. It has powerful implications (focusing monetary policy solely on inflation destabilizes output) that deserve more attention in the literature than they seem to be getting.

Apparent contradiction of forward-looking equations

Ball (1994) has highlighted a puzzling implication of the forward-looking nature of inflation equations like (3.24'). As current inflation depends on future demand, a contractionary monetary policy ('disinflation') announced for the future (assumed fully credible and believed now) will reduce current inflation and therefore, given the rate of monetary expansion (or the Taylor rule described in Section 3.10), it will engineer an expansion now! What do you make of this? One resolution of this apparent contradiction is of course to argue that future disinflations can never be fully credible; so they will not affect current inflation so strongly. Another resolution is offered by Ascari and Rankin (2002) who consider an inflation equation that arises from staggered wage, rather than price, setting. In this case, a future disinflation is unambiguously contractionary now. Why is this so? What is the role of the length of the wage contract, which is optimally chosen, in this result?

History versus expectations

Krugman (1991a) has highlighted an important question: in dynamic models, where typically both lagged and leads of variables appear, is it the lags (the past, 'history') or the leads (the expected future, 'expectations') that are more important in guiding behaviour? More concretely, taking the inflation equation (3.26), let us assume that inflation in the long run is determined by 'fundamentals' such as mainly the supply side (productivity, technology, raw materials, and energy prices, etc). But what guides short-run behaviour? The lags anchor behaviour in the past, which is observable. But the leads introduce different considerations: The future is unknown, so we take expectations. These expectations may have all the nice properties of the Rational Expectations Hypothesis; alternatively, they may suffer from all the biases that Behavioural Economics and Bounded Rationality have highlighted: systematic misperceptions, herding behaviour (I believe what others believe), panic (abrupt changes of 'sentiment' arising out of small observed developments), and various others. In the extreme, behaviour may be affected by entirely irrelevant developments ('sunspots'). Obviously, when behaviour is guided more by the expected future, there is the potential for more volatility. You are invited to read Krugman (1991a). Taking the messages of that paper to our context, particularly the inflation equation (3.26), when is behaviour anchored by the past and when is it dependent on expectations? How does the answer depend on parameter values?

Increasing returns

Increasing returns is a theme emphasized in other contexts such as international trade and geography (Krugman, 1991b); some New Keynesian work is related to it. Increasing returns (to scale) is the idea that a larger scale of production of the economy makes production more efficient, hence lowers the unit costs. We alluded to increasing returns in sub-section 3.7.2. Generally, increasing returns may generate multiple equilibria, such as the ones depicted in Figure 3.6. A greater (lower) scale of the economy reduces (increases) costs, therefore encourages (discourages) more investment and more (less) production. A virtuous (vicious) circle arises. The high equilibrium may mean growth and industrialization, the low one stagnation. Read Krugman (1991b) and Murphy et al. (1989). If you are convinced of the importance of increasing returns, how would you incorporate them into your favourite macro model?

On 'complexity'

'Complexity' may be one of the new directions broadly associated with the work of (some!) New Keynesians. It is a term used to described systems, simulated by computers, that are characterized by the following main features:

- Complex systems are decentralized collections of simple agents, a multitude of independent agents interacting without central control.
- There are interactions at many levels or scales; e.g. the human body is characterized by interactions within each scale at the level of molecules, cells, organs, and interactions between these scales; similarly, there are interactions between the cells of a tree and between trees within a forest; in the economy, we have interactions (e.g.) between employees in a firm, between firms, between sectors, etc;
- The outcome of such interactions is unpredictable a priori; one needs to run the simulations to see what happens.

All natural systems are complex and the same applies in the economy. It is sometimes said that complexity involves a system of systems. 'Complex' is not the same as 'complicated'. The mechanism of a clock is complicated but not complex, as it does not have any of the above characteristics: The components are part of one single mechanism that operates at one scale (the clock, there are no other interactions) and is predictable, it does every time what it is designed to do (except when failing).

One way of summarizing 'complexity' may be to say that it is not unlike 'chaos' (on which see the fascinating introduction by Gleick, 1997), except that it builds it from the 'bottom up' rather than just assuming or describing some aggregate behaviour. In economics, the approaches closest to these ideas are the 'Agent-Based Modelling' and 'Agent-Based Computational Economics', see Page (2008) and Leigh Tesfatsion's webpage: http://www2.econ.iastate.edu/tesfatsi/abmread.htm. If these ideas appeal to you (as they do to me), you are invited to take a look. What do you make of this approach? Is this approach useful in injecting more realism and detail into standard models while retaining a degree of parsimony and tractability?

References

Acemoglu, D., and J.A. Robinson (2013): *Why Nations Fail: The Origins of Power, Prosperity and Poverty*, London: Profile Books.

Akerlof, G.A., and R.J. Shiller (2009): *Animal Spirits: How Human Psychology Drives the Economy and Why it Matters for Global Capitalism*, Princeton: Princeton University Press.

Akerlof, G.A., and J. Yellen (1985): A Near-Rational Model of the Business Cycle, with Wage and Price Inertia, *Quarterly Journal of Economics*, 100 (Suppl.), 823–38; reprinted as chapter 2, in Mankiw and Romer (1991a).

Andres, J., and I. Hernando (1999): Does Inflation Harm Economic Growth? Evidence from the OECD, in M. Feldstein (ed.), *The Costs and Benefits of Price Stability*, Chicago: Chicago University Press for the NBER, 315–48.

Angeloni, I., L. Aucremanne, M. Ehrmann, J. Gali, A. Levin, and F. Smets (2006): New Evidence on Inflation Persistence and Price Stickiness in the Euro Area: Implications for Macro Modeling, *Journal of the European Economic Association*, 4(2–3), 562–74.

Ascari, G., and N. Rankin (2002): Staggered Wages and Output Dynamics under Disinflation, *Journal of Economic Dynamics and Control*, 26(4) (April), 653–80.

Ascari, G., and A.M. Sbordone (2014): The Macroeconomics of Trend Inflation, *Journal of Economic Literature*, 52(3) (September), 679–739.

Aukrust, O. (1977): Inflation in the Open Economy: A Norwegian Model, in L.B. Krause and W. S. Salant (eds), *Worldwide Inflation: Theory and Recent Experience*, Washington, DC: Brookings Institute.

Ball, L. (1987): Externalities from Contract Length, *American Economic Review*, 77(4) (September), 615–29.

Ball, L. (1994): Credible Disinflation with Staggered Price-Setting, *American Economic Review*, 84(1) (March), 282–9.

Ball, L., and S.G. Cecchetti (1988): Imperfect Information and Staggered Price Setting, *American Economic Review*, 78 (December), 999–1018.

Ball, L., and N.G. Mankiw (1994): A Sticky-Price Manifesto, *Carnegie-Rochester Conference Series on Public Policy*, 41 (December), 127–51.

Ball, L., and N.G. Mankiw (1995): Relative-Price Changes as Aggregate Supply Shocks, *Quarterly Journal of Economics*, 110 (February), 161–93.

Ball, L., N.G. Mankiw, and D. Romer (1988): The New Keynesian Economics and the Output-Inflation Tradeoff, *Brookings Papers on Economic Activity*, 1, 1–65; reprinted in Mankiw and Romer, (1991b).

Ball, L., and D. Romer (1989): The Equilibrium and Optimal Timing of Price Changes, *Review of Economic Studies*, 56, 179–98.

Ball, L., and D. Romer (1990): Real Rigidities and the Nonneutrality of Money, *Review of Economic Studies*, 57 (April), 183–203; reprinted as chapter 3, in Mankiw and Romer (1991a).

Barro, R.J. (1997): *Determinants of Economic Growth: A Cross-Country Empirical Study*, Boston: MIT Press.

Barro, R.J., and H. Grossman (1971): A General Disequilibrium Model of Income and Employment, *American Economic Review*, 61(1), 82–93.

Bils, M., and P.J. Klenow (2004): Some Evidence on the Importance of Sticky Prices, *Journal of Political Economy*, 112(5), 947–85.

Blanchard, O.J. (1986): The Wage Price Spiral, *Quarterly Journal of Economics*, 101 (August), 543–65.

Blanchard, O.J. (1990): Why does Money Affect Output? A Survey, in B. M. Friedman and F.H. Hahn (eds), *Handbook of Monetary Economics*, 1st ed., Amsterdam: Elsevier, vol. 2, 779–835.

Blanchard, O.J., and N. Kiyotaki (1987): Monopolistic Competition and the Effects of Aggregate Demand, *American Economic Review*, 77 (September), 647–66; reprinted as chapter 13, in Mankiw and Romer (1991a).

Blinder, A., and N.G. Mankiw (1984): Aggregation and Stabilisation in a Multi-Contract Economy, *Journal of Monetary Economics*, 13, 67–86.

Bowles, S. (2004): *Microeconomics: Behavior, Institutions and Evolutions*, Princeton: Princeton University Press.

Bruno, M., and W. Easterly (1998): Inflation Crises and Long-Run Growth, *Journal of Monetary Economics*, 41(1) (February), 3–26.

Burstein, A., and C. Hellwig (2008): Welfare Costs of Inflation in a Menu Cost Model, *American Economic Review*, 98(2), 438–43.

Cagan, P. (1956): The Monetary Dynamics of Hyperinflation, in M. Friedman (ed.), *Studies in the Quantity Theory of Money*, Chicago: University of Chicago Press, 25–177.

Calvo, G. (1983): Staggered Prices in a Utility-Maximizing Framework, *Journal of Monetary Economics*, 12 (November), 383–98.

Caplin, A.S., and J. Leahy (1991): State-Dependent Pricing and the Dynamics of Money and Output, *Quarterly Journal of Economics*, 106(3) (August), 683–708.

Caplin, A.S. and D.F. Spulber (1987): Menu Costs and the Neutrality of Money, *Quarterly Journal of Economics*, 102(4) (November), 703–26.

Cecchetti, S.G. (1986): The Frequency of Price Adjustment: A Study of Newsstand Prices of Magazines, *Journal of Econometrics*, 31, 255–74.

Chadha, B. (1989): Is Price Flexibility Destabilising? *Journal of Money, Credit and Banking*, 21, 481–97.

Chadha, J.S., and C. Nolan, (2004): Output, Inflation and the New Keynesian Phillips Curve, *International Review of Applied Economics*, 18(3) (July), 271–87.

Chen, H., D. Levy, S. Ray, and M. Bergen (2008): Asymmetric Price Adjustment in the Small, *Journal of Monetary Economics*, 55, 728–37.

Christiano, L.J., M. Eichenbaum, and C.L. Evans (2005): Nominal Rigidities and the Dynamic Effects of a Shock to Monetary Policy, *Journal of Political Economy*, 113(1), 1–45.

Clarida, R., J. Gali, and M. Gertler (1999): The Science of Monetary Policy: A New Keynesian Perspective, *Journal of Economic Literature*, 37 (December), 1661–1707.

Colander, D. (ed.) (2006): *Post Walrasian Macroeconomics: Beyond the Dynamic Stochastic General Equilibrium Model*, Cambridge: Cambridge University Press.

Cooper, R., and A. John (1988): Coordinating Coordination Failures in Keynesian Models, *Quarterly Journal of Economics*, 103(3) (August), 441–63.

DeFraja, J. (1993): Staggered vs. Synchonised Wage Setting in Oligopoly, *European Economic Review*, 37, 1507–22.

De Grauwe, P. (2012): *Lectures on Behavioural Macroeconomics*, Princeton: Princeton University Press.

De Grauwe, P., and Y. Ji (2017): Behavioural Economics is Also Useful in Macroeconomics, Vox: CEPR Policy Portal, 1 November.

DeLong, J.B., and L. Summers, (1986): Is Increased Price Flexibility Stabilizing? *American Economic Review*, 76(5) (December), 1031–44.

Dixit, A., and J. Stiglitz (1977): Monopolistic Competition and Optimum Product Diversity, *American Economic Review*, 67 (June), 297–308.

Dixon, H.D. (1987): A Simple Model of Imperfect Competition with Walrasian Features, *Oxford Economic Papers*, 39, 134–60.

Dixon, H.D. (2008): New Keynesian Macroeconomics, in S.N. Durlauf and L.E. Blume (eds), *The New Palgrave Dictionary of Economics*, London: Palgrave Macmillan, 4552–56.

Dixon, H.D., and N. Rankin (1994): Imperfect Competition and Macroeconomics: A Survey, *Oxford Economic Papers*, 46(2) (April), 171–95; reprinted in Dixon and Rankin (1995).

Dixon, H.D., and N. Rankin (eds) (1995): *The New Macroeconomics: Imperfect Markets and Policy Effectiveness*, Cambridge: Cambridge University Press.

Dotsey, M., and R.G. King (2006): Pricing, Production, and Persistence, *Journal of the European Economic Association*, 4(5) (September), 893–928.

Driffill, J., G.E. Mizon, and A. Ulph (1990): Costs of Iinflation, in: B.M. Friedman and F. H. Hahn (ed.), *Handbook of Monetary Economics*, 1st ed., , Amsterdam: Elsevier, ii. 1013–66.

Dutta, S., M. Bergen, D. Levy, and R. Venable, (1999): Menu Costs, Posted Prices and Multi-Product Retailers, *Journal of Money, Credit and Banking*, 31(4) (November), 683–703.

Eichenbaum, M.S., N. Jaimovich, and S. Rebelo (2011): Reference Prices, Costs, and Nominal Rigidities, *American Economic Review*, 101(1), 234–62.

Engsted, T. (1993): Cointegration and Cagan's Model of Hyperinflation under Rational Expectations, *Journal of Money, Credit and Banking*, 25(3), 350–60.

Ergec, C.J., D.W. Henderson, and A.T. Levin (2000): Optimal Monetary Policy with Staggered Wage and Price Contracts, *Journal of Monetary Economics*, 46(2) (October), 281–313.

Fagiolo, G., M. Napoletano, and A. Roventini (2008): Are Output Growth-Rate Distributions Fat-Tailed? Some Evidence from OECD Countries, *Journal of Applied Econometrics*, 23(5) (August), 639–69.

Farmer, R.E.A. (2008): Animal Spirits, in S.N. Durlauf and L.E. Blume (eds), *The New Palgrave Dictionary of Economics*, London: Palgrave Macmillan, 157–63.

Fethke, G., and A. Policano (1986): Will Wage Setters Ever Stagger Decisions? *Quarterly Journal of Economics*, 101 (November), 867–77.

Fischer, S. (1993): The Role of Macroeconomic Factors in Growth, *Journal of Monetary Economics*, 32(3), 485–512.

Friedman, M. (1970): *The Counter-Revolution in Monetary Theory*, London: Institute of Economic Affairs.

Frisch, H. (1984): *Theories of Inflation*, Cambridge: Cambridge University Press.

Fuhrer, J., and G. Moore (1995): Inflation Persistence, *Quarterly Journal of Economics*, 110(1) (February), 127–59.

Gali, J. (2015): *Monetary Policy, Inflation, and the Business Cycle: An Introduction to the New Keynesian Framework and its Applications*, 2nd ed., Princeton: Princeton University Press.

Gali, J. (2018): The State of New Keynesian Economics: A Partial Assessment, *Journal of Economic Perspectives*, 32(3), 87–112.

Gali, J., and M. Gertler, (1999): Inflation Dynamics: A Structural Econometric Analysis, *Journal of Monetary Economics*, 44(2), 195–222.

Gertler, M., and J. Leahy (2008): A Phillips Curve with an S-s Foundation, *Journal of Political Economy*, 116(3), 533–72.

Gleick, J. (1997): *Chaos: Making a New Science*, new ed., London: Vintage.

Goldthorpe, J.H. (1978): The Current Inflation: Towards a Sociological Account, in Hirsch and Goldthorpe (1978).

Gordon, R.J. (1990a): *The Measurement of Durable Goods Prices*, Chicago: University of Chicago Press.

Gordon, R.J. (1990b): What is New-Keynesian Economics?, *Journal of Economic Literature*, 28(3) (September), 1115–71.

Gray, J.A. (1976): Wage Indexation: A Macroeconomic Approach, *Journal of Monetary Economics*, 2(2), 221–35.

Gray, J.A. (1978): On Indexation and Contract Length, *Journal of Political Economy*, 86(1) (February), 1–18.

Greenwald, B., and J.E. Stiglitz (1993): New and Old Keynesians, *Journal of Economic Perspectives*, 7(1) (Winter), 23–44.

Hirsch, F., and J.H. Goldthorpe (1978): *The Political Economy of Inflation*, London: Martin Robertson.

Kapetanios, G., J. Pearlman, and C. Tsoukis (2011): Elusive Persistence: Wage and Price Rigidities, the New Keynesian Phillips Curve, and Inflation Dynamics, *Journal of Economic Surveys*, 25(4) (September), 737–68.

Kashyap, A.K. (1995): Sticky Prices: New Evidence from Retail Catalogs, *Quarterly Journal of Economics*, 110(1), 245–74.

Kehoe, P., and V. Midrigan (2015): Prices are Sticky After All, *Journal of Monetary Economics*, 75, 35–53.

Krugman, P. (1991a): History versus Expectations, *Quarterly Journal of Economics*, 106(2) (May), 651–67.

Krugman, P. (1991b): Increasing Returns and Economic Geography, *Journal of Political Economy*, 99(3) (June), 483–99.

Kydland, F.E., and E.C. Prescott (1977): Rules Rather than Discretion: The Inconsistency of Optimal Plans, *Journal of Political Economy*, 85(3), 473–91.

Laidler, D., and M. Parkin (1975): Inflation: A Survey, *Economic Journal*, 85(340) (December), 741–809.

Levy, D., S. Dutta, M. Bergen, and R. Venable (1997): The Magnitude of Menu Costs: Direct Evidence from Large U.S. Supermarket Chains, *Quarterly Journal of Economics*, 112 (August), 791–825.

Levy, D., A. Snir, A. Gotler, and H. Chen (2020): Not All Price Endings are Created Equal: Price Points and Asymmetric Price Rigidity, *Journal of Monetary Economics*, forthcoming.

Lucas, R.E. (1976): Econometric Policy Evaluation: A Critique, in K. Brunner and A.H. Meltzer (eds), *The Phillips Curve and Labor Markets*, Chicago: Chicago University Press, 9–46.

Lucas, R.E. (2000): Inflation and Welfare, *Econometrica*, 68(2), 247–74.

McCallum, B.T. (1997): Comment on Rotemberg and Woodford, in B.S. Bernanke and J. Rotemberg (eds), *NBER Macroeconomics Annual 1997*, Cambridge, MA: MIT Press, vol. 12, 355–61.

Malinvaud, E. (1977): *The Theory of Unemployment Reconsidered*, Yrjö Jahnsson lectures, Oxford: Blackwell.

Mankiw, N.G. (1985): Small Menu Costs and Large Business Cycles: A Macroeconomic Model of Monopoly, *Quarterly Journal of Economics*, 100 (May), 529–39; reprinted in Mankiw and Romer (1991a).

Mankiw, N.G. (1990): A Quick Refresher Course in Macroeconomics, *Journal of Economic Literature*, 28(4) (December), 1645–60.

Mankiw, N.G. and R. Reis (2002): Sticky Information versus Sticky Prices: A Proposal to Replace the New Keynesian Phillips Curve, *Quarterly Journal of Economics*, 117(4) (November), 1295–1328.

Mankiw, N.G., and D. Romer (eds) (1991a): *New Keynesian Economics*, i. *Imperfect Competition and Sticky Prices*, Cambridge, MA: MIT Press.

Mankiw, N.G., and D. Romer (eds) (1991b): *New Keynesian Economics*, ii. *Coordination Failures and Real Rigidities*, Cambridge, MA: MIT Press.

Mavroeidis, S., M. Plagborg-Møller, and J.H. Stock (2014): Empirical Evidence on Inflation Expectations in the New Keynesian Phillips Curve, *Journal of Economic Literature*, 52(1), 124–88.

Murphy, K.M., A. Shleifer, and R.W. Vishny (1989): Industrialization and the Big Push, *Journal of Political Economy*, 97(5) (October), 1003–26.

Nakamura, E., and J. Steinsson (2008): Five Facts about Prices: A Reevaluation of Menu Cost Models, *Quarterly Journal of Economics*, 123, 1415–64.

Page, S.E. (2008): Agent-Based Models, in S.N Durlauf and L.E. Blume (eds), *The New Palgrave Dictionary of Economics*, London: Palgrave Macmillan, 47–52.

Reed, S.B., and D.A. Rippy (2012): Consumer Price Index Data Quality: How Accurate is the U.S. CPI? *Beyond the Numbers: Prices and Spending* (online journal published by the US Bureau of Labor Statistics), 1(12) (August).

Roberts, J.M. (1997): Is Inflation Sticky? *Journal of Monetary Economics*, 39 (July), 173–96.

Romer, D. (1990): Staggered Price Setting with Endogenous Frequency of Adjustment, *Economics Letters*, 32(3), 205–10.

Romer, D. (1993): The New Keynesian Synthesis, *Journal of Economic Perspectives*, 7(1) (Winter), 5–23.

Rotemberg, J. (1982): Sticky Prices in the United States, *Journal of Political Economy*, 90 (December), 1187–1211.

Rudd, J., and K. Whelan (2006): Can Rational Expectations Sticky-Price Models Explain Inflation Dynamics? *American Economic Review*, 96(1) (March), 303–20.

Sargent, T.J. (1993): *Rational Expectations and Inflation*, 2nd ed., New York: Harper Collins.

Sargent, T.J., and N. Wallace (1981): Some Unpleasant Monetarist Arithmetic, *Federal Reserve Bank of Minneapolis Quarterly Review*, Fall.

Schelling, T.C. (1978): *Micromotives and Macrobehavior*, New York: Norton.

Sims, C.A. (2003): Implications of Rational Inattention, *Journal of Monetary Economics*, 50(3) (April), 665–90.

Smith, J.C. (2000): Nominal Wage Rigidity in the United Kingdom, *Economic Journal*, 110 (March), C176–95.

Tobin J. (1993): Price Flexibility and Output Stability: An Old Keynesian View, *Journal of Economic Perspectives*, 7(1) (Winter), 45–65.

Zbaracki, M., M. Ritson, D. Levy, S. Dutta, and M. Bergen (2004): Managerial and Customer Costs of Price Adjustment: Direct Evidence from Industrial Markets, *Review of Economics and Statistics*, 86(2) (May), 514–33.

4

Unemployment

4.1 Introduction and Definitions

Unemployment is a vast and hugely important area, at the crossroads between macroeconomics and labour economics. There is no need to elaborate much on the costs of unemployment: psychological, as well as material. Individuals find themselves rejected, poor, and with depreciating skills, while economies waste valuable resources (labour power) and societies become polarized. We need not be concerned with the distinction between voluntary and involuntary unemployment (of which more later). While the costs of the former may safely be presumed to be less than the costs of the latter, it is a common perception that unemployment is at least partly involuntary from the point of view of the individual (i.e. it is not generated by individual decisions or actions), particularly in the long run with which this chapter is mainly concerned. The bottomline is, there are very real and important costs of unemployment. This makes it one of the most talked-about economic variables.

The aim of this chapter is to present various theories and models that help us to understand the emergence and persistence of unemployment. The focus here is on the 'natural' (or 'structural' or 'equilibrium' or whatever else you choose to call it) unemployment rate; i.e. the rate that persists on average for considerable periods of time. We shall not be concerned much about the cyclical ups and downs of unemployment, which will be the focus of Chapter 6, on business cycles. The emphasis here is on the long run. Also, we view things from a macroeconomic perspective, so we are interested to see how headline unemployment is affected by the state of the economy. We shall not take a detailed look into labour markets.

The unemployed are all those outside employment <u>and</u> seeking work. The per cent rate of unemployment is the ratio:

$$u(\%) = \frac{U}{N} \tag{4.1}$$

where U is the number of unemployed and N the number of people that are 'in the labour market'. This leads us to consider who participates in the labour market. The idea is this. The total population (Pop) is made up of:

- the participants in the labour market (N); these are either employed or unemployed;
- plus the 'economically inactive' or 'out of the labour market'.

Theory of Macroeconomic Policy. Christopher Tsoukis, Oxford University Press (2020). © Christopher Tsoukis.
DOI: 10.1093/oso/9780198825371.003.0004

This category includes children (up to 16), retirees and/or elderly (above 64), students, househusbands/wives, and special cases like those in prison. A useful ratio that captures this division is the 'labour market participation rate':

$$n(\%) = \frac{N}{Pop} \tag{4.2}$$

The participation rate increased around the 1970s and 1980s mainly due to the big increase in female participation in the labour market (from housework to employment). More recently, we have been seeing a gradual, small but steady, decline in n, due to more people taking early retirement. This may have been due to increasing unemployment or the increase in the proportion of low-paid jobs. Thus, the unemployment and labour force participation rates may be related. However, we will not have much to say about the latter.[1]

   One note about data: the current, commonly used standardized definition comes from the International Labor Organization (ILO) and data are compiled by all national statistical offices such as the Office for National Statistics (ONS) in the UK and assembled by the European Statistical Authority (Eurostat) and the Organization for Economic Cooperation and Development (OECD) for international comparisons. This common definition and datasets are based on sampling (a sample of people is sent a questionnaire and they classify themselves as unemployed or not) and not by any actual survey of the population.[2] The problems with this methodology include the errors associated with sampling (which however are small as the samples are large) and the fact that individuals in those samples self-classify themselves as unemployed or not (based on guidance), therefore there may be errors or biases in the answers (despite the guidance). In the UK, another methodology exists based on counting those claiming unemployment benefit (or 'Job Seeker's Allowance'); but the problem with this is the individuals eligible for unemployment benefit and those unemployed are not identical. Before we get on with any theory, let us set the scene with a quick survey of facts.

4.2 Aggregate Unemployment over Time: Facts

We present here a brief review of what appear to be some 'stylized facts' about unemployment in the UK and similar advanced economies (members of the OECD) over the last 40 years or so. These developments have inspired a lot of interest and research in both policy and academic circles. The aggregate picture first: Figure 4.1 gives the economy-wide unemployment rates for the US, UK, the average of the OECD economies, and the average for older members of the EU (EU16), 1960–2017. The first striking fact is the evolution over the decades across the entire group. In the early days, up to about the mid-1970s, the unemployment rate was generally stable and fairly low (2–6 per cent); unemployment increased sharply after the mid-1970s, reaching often double digits around the mid-1980s

---

[1] To give some headline figures for the UK, in the summer of 2018, there were about 33.8 million people in the labour force including 1.4 million unemployed, giving an unemployment rate of just above 4 per cent. The inactivity rate, (Pop-N)/Pop or $1 - n$, was about 21 per cent.

[2] In the UK, sampling is done through the 'Labour Force Survey', which asks a sample of 53,000 households and is conducted every three months.

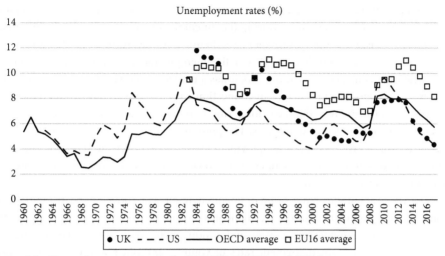

Unemployment rates (%)

Figure 4.1. Unemployment rates in the UK, US, OECD, and EU16

and 1990s—including the UK in the 1980s. There was also some volatility in those rates. Secondly, though the US had generally higher unemployment than most of Europe in the 1960s, its rate subsequently did not increase so sharply and never went above 10 per cent; whereas the European average was well above the US rate for most of the 1980s, 1990s, and 2010s, occasionally going to double digits. This comparison gave rise to much talk of 'Eurosclerosis' (rigidity in European labour markets) particularly in the mid-1990s and has spawned a big debate as to whether any European 'labour market institutions' (laws but also modes of organization in the labour market) are responsible for this; this debate will be reviewed later on. More recently, unemployment increased after the financial crisis of 2007–9, particularly in the UK and US, and in Europe following the sovereign debt crisis in Greece and elsewhere. Finally, unemployment rates have shown a tendency to come down in recent years, with the UK and US for instance currently (Spring 2019) being at around 4 per cent. The European average (EU16) is somewhat higher at about 8 per cent.

Thirdly, the European experience of the last 20 or so years has not been uniform; in fact, each country tells a separate story! Spanish unemployment has been persistently high—in double digits for most of the period, and higher than 20 per cent for a while in the early 1990s and in 2011.[3] More recently (post-2010), Greek unemployment rates of > 25 per cent (> 50 per cent youth unemployment) is an extreme, well-documented case. With a rate less than 5 per cent almost all the time, Japan has the least unemployment among OECD economies; but even there, the unemployment rate was slightly lower in the 1960s than at any time since. So, understanding European unemployment involves understanding the heterogeneity between national unemployment experiences, as well as the overall evolution of (aggregate) European unemployment—a point emphatically made by Blanchard and Wolfers (2000). Relatedly, individual European country labour markets have historically been largely separate, with little mobility across them (Nickell, 1997); although this has changed in recent years in the context of the European Union.

---

[3] Particularly intriguing is the comparison between the Iberian neighbours, Spain, which registered a rate of more than 20 per cent for much of 1985–95, and Portugal, which registered almost one-third of that.

Looking at the larger picture, a further 'stylized fact' becomes evident. Over the very long run (say, over the twentieth century), the unemployment rate does not vary much (technically, it is a stationary variable)—see figure 2 in Layard et al. (1991). Except for historically very brief spells (e.g. the 1930s), the unemployment rate rarely ventures outside the single-digit zone and, after it does so, it has a tendency to revert back to average rates. This is very important in particular in connection with productivity growth and technical progress, as growth over the very long run is driven by productivity improvements generated mainly by technical progress. The point made here is that the levels of productivity or technical progress and unemployment are unrelated over the very long run. Over shorter horizons, things are more unclear. We review the relationship between unemployment and productivity below.

Next, a note about the composition of unemployment. The above aggregate figures quite clearly mask big differences in unemployment within countries across those in short- and long-term unemployment (respectively, of duration < and > than 12 months), male/female unemployment rates, unemployment rates of younger and older workers, regional variations, etc. Moreover, the composition across these divides also varies across countries. Vintage information from Layard et al. (1991), tables 1 and 2, highlights the point.

According to this data, women's unemployment tends to be higher than men's. Also, youth unemployment (below 25 years) tends to be higher than in the total labour market, a point that has reappeared in the last ten years in Europe. Unemployment also varies by duration. In this respect, we can distinguish short-term unemployment (the percentage of those who have been unemployed less than a year) and long-term unemployment (those who have been unemployed more than a year).[4] Additionally, there is generally a lot of diversity in unemployment among ethnic groups in multi-cultural countries. Note that some of these observations may change over time, so they are mentioned here just to make the point that the headline, aggregate unemployment rates we read about (and with which we shall be concerned) mask a lot of heterogeneity along many dimensions. We will not be concerned with the composition of unemployment, which is more in the domain of labour economics—for a panorama of such work see Ashenfelter and Card (1999).

Some of the key issues that the existence of unemployment raises, particularly from a macroeconomic point of view, include the following. What are the determinants of unemployment in the long run, the unemployment rate that exists on average, and has been termed 'natural' or 'structural'? Most of this chapter is about this question. Following Section 3.2 of the last chapter, in Section 4.3 we develop a wage-price setting model, which serves as an organizing framework. This basic framework has been termed 'Walrasian' as it assumes agents that freely interact in the marketplace, without transactions costs, informational asymmetries, or other such 'frictions' disturbing trade. It allows us a first approach to the determination of the real wage and the unemployment rate. A criticism that can be made against this framework, however, is that it only allows unemployment that is 'voluntary'.[5]

---

[4] There is a potential source of confusion here, so we should clarify: The term 'long run' (or long term) applies in two different ways to unemployment. One, elaborated here, refers to the duration of the unemployment spell; the other is the standard distinction between short and long runs (so, the unemployment rate that the system settles to in the long run is the 'natural rate'); which usage applies should be clear from the explanation and the context.

[5] In former times, much used to be made of the distinction between 'voluntary' and 'involuntary' (or 'Keynesian') unemployment; the former being more the result of supply-side factors, while the latter was definitely thought to be the result of demand deficiency. More recently, this distinction is considered not so fruitful, as it

As both firms and workers (in particular) are on their optimal decision schedules, they cannot do any better for themselves given the situation they face (e.g. the real wage). They would like perhaps to enjoy a higher wage, and work more, but given the real wage the market gives them, they are quite happy to work the hours they do, and think that working further is not worth the point. If so, unemployment would be a matter of personal choice. But that cannot be right, though! To put it otherwise, why do the unemployed not offer to do the same jobs as the employed, but at lower wages? There must be other reasons then that move us away from the simple framework of Section 4.3 and make unemployment not a matter of individual choice, and prohibit the unemployed from undercutting the employed. Possible answers include the existence of trade unions and wage bargaining (Section 4.4), and the willingness of firms to offer higher-than-average wages to attract higher-than-average workers (the notion of 'efficiency wages'—Section 4.5). A variation on the theme of 'efficiency wages' is the analysis of 'dual labour markets' of a premium market with good prospects and a market-clearing secondary market; we argue that this approach is useful for the analysis of unemployment but perhaps even more so for the analysis of wage inequality (Section 4.6).

Further deviations from the Walrasian framework are explored in Section 4.8, which approaches the determination of unemployment from the perspective of flows into and out of it, 'job separations' and hiring. The question of relation between productivity and unemployment, in all its twists and turns, occupies us in Section 4.9. Section 4.10 brings all these debates to bear upon the 'European unemployment puzzle'—the question why, following the turbulent 1970s, European unemployment shot up above the US one (while it was lower up to the early 1970s) and why it persisted longer. The question assumes even more relevance if one remembers that the US and Europe have different degrees of liberalization of labour markets (with the UK somewhere in between), so the answer to this question becomes important for the optimal degree of labour market liberalization, too. Finally, Section 4.7 deals with another type of issue, namely the short-run adjustment of unemployment. Here, we shall be concerned with the persistence, or in sharper jargon 'hysteresis', of unemployment. There is also of course the distinction between 'natural' (or 'structural') unemployment and cyclical unemployment, and the relation between the latter and business cycle. With the exception of Section 4.7, which touches on issues of dynamic adjustment, this chapter is almost exclusively concerned with structural unemployment, and we leave cyclical unemployment to the discussion of business cycles in Chapter 6.

4.3 Wage and Price Setting and Implications for Unemployment

4.3.1 The Basic Framework

We begin by presenting a framework that builds on the wage and price setting of Chapter 3; it gives key insights and serves as basis for the development of further themes in subsequent sections. The model we present here is standard; see Blanchard (1986),

characterizes unemployment without telling us much about its causes. The current mainstream thinking is that all structural (or 'natural') unemployment is the result of factors that must be classified as 'supply side', with demand fluctuations being potentially (note: potentially) relevant only for cyclical unemployment.

Blanchard and Katz (1997), Blanchard and Kiyotaki (1987), Nickell and Layard (1999), among others. This framework can also be derived from the labour demand and supply model that we developed in Chapter 1 (see the references there and Manning, 1995). But the wage-price framework has a number of advantages over the L^D-L^S framework:

- It is more intuitive;
- It dispenses with the internal-external margin distinction (see Chapter 1). Labour supply is mostly based on individual optimization, hence it considers mostly the 'internal margin' of the individual adjusting their hours of work; it ignores the 'external margin' of individuals moving in and out of employment altogether. Yet, Kydland and Prescott (1990) King and Rebelo (1999) document the fact that the external margin comprises perhaps two-thirds of the total adjustment of labour hours over the cycle; see Chapter 6 for further discussion. The employment in the wage/price-setting framework below can be interpreted as determined by both the external and internal margins.
- The added advantage of that is that this framework is agnostic about individual labour supply elasticities and bypasses this vexed issue.
- And as a corollary of all that, it is more readily compatible with involuntary unemployment. In the labour demand-supply framework, there are two possibilities: either we are at the intersection of the curves, in which case unemployment is implicitly voluntary, as individuals are on the supply curve therefore their behaviour is optimal given the environment they face (see also Chapter 2); or, the wage is stuck above the equilibrium level, in which case there is involuntary unemployment (labour demand is less than supply); but in this case, one needs to carefully explain why the wage persists at a high level for a long time. The wage-price setting framework bypasses the need for any such explanation.

The price- and wage-setting equations are the following:

$$P_j/P = (1 + \mu) \left(\frac{w(1 + \tau_P)}{MPL} \right)^b y^{1-b} \tag{4.3}$$

This is the relative price of producer j; it follows closely (3.11') of Chapter 3 (note that the coefficient $0 < b < 1$ here is not exactly the same as in 3.11'); w is the real wage, MPL the Marginal Product of Labour, therefore w/MPL is marginal cost. Y is real output as a percentage deviation from normal or 'natural' level; $\mu \geq 0$ is the (possible) monopoly markup that is derived from the degree of specialization; a highly specialized firm may feel that they can raise their prices as there are no close substitutes. More broadly, this markup can also capture other inflationary pressures that do not appear elsewhere such as greater import prices, higher energy/raw materials/food prices, etc.; a rise in any of this would be analytically shown as a rise in μ. τ_P is the indirect (or commodity) tax rate (such as VAT), which raises the final price as the producer tries to shift the cost to the consumer. Note the structure of (4.3): the relative price is a geometric average (with weights b and $1-b$) of cost and demand considerations.

From (3.13), we also get the relative wage quotation of worker i:

$$W_i/W = (1 + v) \frac{R}{w} (1 + \tau_I) y^d \tag{4.4}$$

The relative wage will depend on the markup ($v \geq 0$) that reflects the individual worker's degree of specialization; a highly specialized individual will likely raise their wage. More broadly, the existence of trade unions with their bargaining power may be interpreted as raising the workers' markup. An addition to what we had in Chapter 3 is the 'reservation wage' (R) in relation to the actual real wage (w). The reservation wage is the (hypothetical) wage that would make us indifferent between accepting and rejecting a job; it reflects workers' disutility of work, but also aspirations, ideas of fairness, etc. R is also affected by the institutional setup of the labour market: A more generous employment insurance system (higher and longer-lasting unemployment benefits) may raise the real wage that the individual worker may think of as fair or normal; this is shown as a rise in R. The same goes for employment protection and the minimum wage. The income tax rate (τ_I) reduces the 'take-home pay' out of any nominal wage, and the individual may try to recoup that by raising the nominal wage they demand; hence, this also raises the wage quotation. Finally, a greater output also encourages the workers to claim higher wages (with exponent $d \geq 0$). Naturally, labour markets are not as simple as this description suggests, and not all workers work freelance. In Section 4.4, we shall consider labour markets in which workers bargain with firms through their trade unions; in Section 4.5, we shall consider additional complicating structures originating from the firms' side ('efficiency wages').

As in Chapter 3, we are only interested in what happens to the aggregate economy, or the 'typical firm', and we ignore the variations across firms. Analytically, we consider the 'symmetric equilibrium' in which $P_j = P$ and $W_i = W$; but the gain is that we have already built into the model the monopolistic power that the typical individual or firm has. Introducing these assumptions into (4.3) and (4.4) and rearranging, we get:

$$w = \frac{MPL}{1 + \tau_P} \left((1 + \mu) y^{1-b} \right)^{-1/b} \tag{4.5}$$

$$w = R(1 + v)(1 + \tau_I) y^d \tag{4.6}$$

The interpretation of these two equations is as follows. The first (4.5) gives the real wage consistent with price setting: by raising individual prices, firms also raise the price level and indirectly reduce the real wage; so, (4.5) gives the real wage that results after firms set their prices, given their monopoly power, taxes, and market activity (or demand). The second (4.6) gives the real wage consistent with wage setting. This is the real wage that workers are inclined to claim given such factors as skills, specialization, and markups, aspirations of all kinds (R), taxes, and activity in the market. But obviously, there is only one market real wage; equilibrium requires that these two wages be equalized. This happens by (un)employment that is set at such a level as to achieve consistency between the two equation, i.e. equilibrium.

Blanchflower and Oswald (1994, 1995) have offered empirical support for the wage curve (4.6). Using data from 12 countries, they estimate the following equation:

$$\log w = -0.1 \log(\text{u-rate}) + \text{other terms}$$

where log(u-rate) is the logarithm of the unemployment rate in the worker's area, and the 'other terms' are further characteristics of the worker and his or her sector such as gender, race, age, schooling, and industry or region. The equation, which seems to hold in each country, implies that the unemployment elasticity of pay is -0.1, other things (factors) equal. A hypothetical doubling of the local unemployment rate is associated with a drop in the real wage of 10 per cent.

What about output demand (y), will be asked by the perceptive reader. Demand and the size of the market are exogenous in the short run but endogenous in the long run. Consider a typical business, e.g. a restaurant. When it first makes its business plan for the long term, it decides optimally its capacity and the prices of its products, based on marginal cost considerations, cost of capital (including rent), etc. This means that output and employment in the long run are endogenous; they depend on the businesses' own decisions. If the business faces a more buoyant market, in the long run it may expand, or it may raise its prices, or a combination of the two. Once the restaurant has opened, though, the logic changes. Providing it works below capacity, the restaurant is happy to serve any customer that arrives at their door. If the size of the market falls (or rises while still below capacity), the slack is going to be taken by quantity (turnover) and employment; prices are likely to remain constant or at least slow to respond.

This implies that output demand (y) will be exogenous and shifts the wage and price-setting curves in the short run; but in the medium/long run, about which we are concerned in this chapter, output is endogenously determined. Thus, output is a function of employment; analytically: $y = f(L)$, where $f(.)$ is the production function, with $f'(.) > 0$. While MPL is also a function of labour, it is instructive not to replace it, so that it traces the effects of an exogenous rise in productivity. So, to repeat the main point, in the long run, on which we focus here, output does not appear as a separate argument in the wage and price schedules; rather, it has been substituted out via $y = f(L)$. (To return to our example: all the restaurants in the area make their business plans, they consider how many employees they want depending on the going wage. Potential employees, on the other side of the market, decide whether/how many hours they want to work, again depending on the wage. The two sides meet in the marketplace, and the equilibrium wage and employment are determined. The equilibrium employment then gives the size of the market and demand, which are endogenously determined.)

The situation is depicted in Figure 4.2 which plots the log-real wage (logw) against log-employment (logL). The price schedule is downward-sloping as higher employment and/or output induces firms to raise their prices and thereby erode the real wage. The wage schedule is upward-sloping as a more buoyant market, in terms either of employment or output, encourages workers to go for higher wages. Baseline equilibrium is at A. If we happen not to be at A, say we have a higher real wage than w_E, this would mean that workers claim a wage higher than the one consistent with price setting; i.e. the one that firms are prepared to grant indirectly by setting their prices. Some workers will not find employment at these wages, thus employment and output declines; we therefore 'slide down' the wage schedule until we reach point A.

How do various exogenous factors such as taxes, productivity, etc., affect these schedules? First, consider all factors that raise prices given the wage level; such changes shift the pricing locus *left* (to the broken line), as they reduce the real wage compatible with firms' behaviour. They include:

- Indirect taxes (e.g. VAT) shift the pricing locus left (due to higher prices-lower real wage at every level of income), as shown (from A to B). As a result, both the real wage and employment unambiguously fall;

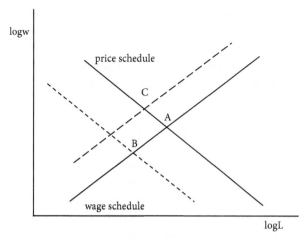

Figure 4.2. Wage and price setting

- Higher import/energy prices shift the price schedule left (A to C);
- The same shift (leftwards by the price schedule) is obtained by a *fall* (or, more realistically, a slowdown in the growth rate) of productivity (MPL); note that a productivity increase shifts the price locus right and *in*creases employment;

Turning to the wage schedule, anything that increases the wage claimed by workers shifts the wage schedule up/left as the real wage compatible with workers' behaviour rises. (This is more intuitive.) Such changes include:

- Any rise in the workers' markups (v) shifts the wage schedule up/left. This includes any rise in the negotiating power of trade unions.
- Any rise in income taxes will have the same effect, as workers try to make up for the loss in earnings power by pushing for a higher wage if they can. A common theme that emerges with respect to all types of tax is that they shift the curves in such a way that employment unambiguously falls (in principle). The effects on the wage are variable. The relevance of taxes for unemployment will be discussed in connection to European unemployment below. We shall see that the evidence shows that the various types of tax all affect unemployment in a similar manner; statistically significantly, but quantitatively rather modestly.
- Any rise in the reservation wage R also shifts the wage schedule up as it induces workers to claim a higher wage. The significance of this for the institutional determinants of unemployment is that various labour market policies and legal/institutional arrangements such as the minimum wage, unemployment insurance, and employment protection may be seen as raising the reservation wage. While the theoretical relevance of these factors is clearcut, and somewhat controversial, their empirical relevance will be evaluated in the discussion below.

4.3.2 Natural or Structural vs. Cyclical Unemployment
and the Role of AD

Figure 4.2 tells us about the overall determinants of unemployment. To relate this information to the unemployment rate, rewrite equation (4.1) as:

$$u\% = \frac{N - L}{N} \approx \log N - \log L. \tag{4.1'}$$

For the purposes of this chapter, the labour force (N) is taken as exogenous. So, the unemployment rate and log(employment) are directly opposite. Equilibrium unemployment increases (in principle) with the monopoly power of firms and workers, taxes of all kinds, and the reservation wage, while it falls with rising productivity. These are obviously the long-run determinants of unemployment, hence the implied rate of unemployment is called (interchangeably) the structural or natural rate of unemployment, or the NAIRU. Whatever we call it, it is clear that this analysis has little to say about the cyclical variations in employment, which will be examined in Chapter 6 on Business Cycles.

Traditionally, there has been a long debate about the relevance of aggregate demand for unemployment—whether unemployment is in essence 'Keynesian', i.e. due to inefficient demand; or whether it is due to characteristics in the labour market only, particularly its supply side ('classical'). Figure 4.2 and the theory behind it make it clear that there is no role for aggregate demand here; equilibrium (natural or structural) unemployment is entirely supply-side determined. This seems to be the mainstream consensus (with important exceptions which we discuss below). And it is difficult to see how it could be otherwise; aggregate demand is a variable that secularly trends upwards, as it is the mirror image of GDP; on the other hand, unemployment does not, as we shall see. Hence, the unemployment rate (an I(0) variable in the language to time-series analysis) cannot be affected by demand (an I(1) variable). Hence, the correlation that would make sense is between the cyclical component of demand and the cyclical component of employment or unemployment (which is not present above). This is examined in Chapter 6, as mentioned.

4.4 Trade Unions and Wage Bargaining

4.4.1 Wage Bargaining: Essentials

The picture of all workers as freelance offering quotes for various job offers is simplistic. Large sections of workers work in firms, organizations, or the public sector in salaried employment. They often organize themselves in trade unions whose mission is to safeguard work conditions and advance pay demands. Their wages are negotiated between the employers and the trade unions. They surely are not determined by workers as individuals, as assumed above. This section presents the theoretical models that describe trade union behaviour and the resulting outcomes. But some of these outcomes are debatable and, in any case, they do need empirical evaluation; this will be presented in a later section.

Trade unions differ across and even within countries along various dimensions. Two important features are union 'density' (the extent of unionization among employees) and 'collective bargaining coverage' (the percentage of firms in which the wages are negotiated

Table 4.1. Trade union profile

	Union density(%)			Collective bargaining coverage(%)		
	60–64	80–87	96–98	60	80	94
Australia	48	49	35	85	85	80
Canada	27	37	36	35	40	36
Finland	35	69	80	95	95	95
Finance	20	16	10	–	85	95
W Germany	34	34	27	90	91	92
Italy	25	45	37	91	85	82
Japan	33	27	22	–	28	21
Netherlands	41	30	24	100	76	85
Portugal	61	57	25	–	70	71
Spain	9	11	18	–	68	78
Sweden	64	83	87	–	–	89
UK	44	53	35	67	70	40
US	27	20	14	29	21	17

Source: Nickell *et al.* (2005), Table 3.

with trade unions (collective bargaining)—the rest are firms which offer wages guided by the market or other considerations). Nickell et al. (2005), table 3, offer information on these features for the 1960s, 1980s, and 1990s. The picture is varied, with unions and unionization being very prominent in Scandinavian countries and much of continental Europe (but with many differences).[6] Unionization (density) is smaller in the so-called Anglo-Saxon world (US, UK, Canada) and Japan. The coverage of negotiated wages confirms the continental European/Anglo-Saxon contrast, of which more later. One important development is that there has been a general tendency for union strength to weaken over the decades in many countries and for the extent of wages that are negotiated with unions to fall. This overall tendency is important when we consider the rise of European unemployment in the 1980s and 1990s.

Unions set the real wage by bargaining with firms, and this implies that, in the context of Figure 4.2, the wage curve is discarded; this is because the wage curve reflects the behaviour of individualized workers. Rather, the real wage is determined by bargaining, and this picks up a point on the price schedule, which remains valid as it is based on firm behaviour. The situation is depicted in Figure 4.3.

There is a variety of bargaining models—see Oswald (1985) for a survey and Manning (1987) for a synthesis. The simplest is the 'monopoly union' model, whereby the union sets the real wage unilaterally to maximize their individual objective function, subject to the firm's behaviour (price schedule or demand for labour). The union's objective function is given by,

$$U = L^{\phi}w, \tag{4.7}$$

i.e. as the product of employment (L) times the real wage for those employed (w). The parameter $\phi > 0$ shows whether the union is concerned more about the real wage than employment (in which case $\phi < 1$) or whether its main aim is to safeguard employment

---

[6] Observe the contrast between the little unionized but highly unemployed Spain of the late 1980s and 1990s, and Portugal, which was fairly highly unionized but had a very different unemployment experience. In this comparison, it is worth bearing in mind the troubled political past in both countries.

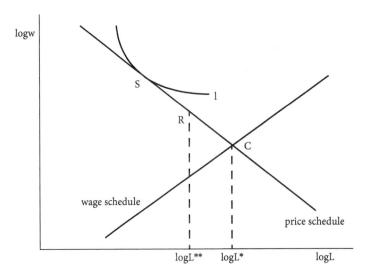

Figure 4.3. Firm-union bargaining

($\phi > 1$).[7] The union's indifference curves are hyperbolas; we depict here the one that is tangent to the pricing locus. This outcome is denoted by S—from Stackelberg equilibrium. This is the equilibrium in a game where one party makes the leading move (the leader—in this case the union) but taking into account the other party's reaction—here, the price schedule, signifying the firm behaviour.[8] This outcome seems not to have any empirical relevance (Nickell, 1990), as it is implausible to assume that the union sets the wage unilaterally. But its appeal is that it coincides with a well-known theoretical concept and that it provides a reference point, the relevance of which will be seen shortly.

Another type of bargain is the 'right-to-manage' model. In this, the firm and union bargain over the real wage, subject to the price curve and then the firm chooses employment. This more realistic model's outcome is depicted as R (from 'right'). Finally, we also depict the competitive outcome (C), which is given by the intersection of the wage and price curves of Figure 4.2.[9] Using the synthetic framework of Manning (1987), it is easy to see that the 'monopoly union' and competitive outcomes are polar extremes, and the 'right-to-manage' model represents a linear combination of them on the price curve. The exact position of R depends on the relative bargaining power of the union, which is pushing it closer to S, and the firm, which is pushing it closer to C.

---

[7] In the special case of $\phi = 1$, the union is assumed to have a 'utilitarian' objective function, whereby individual members' utilities (assumed w) are simply added up (times L). This objective function gives an equal weight to employment and remuneration.

[8] This equilibrium parallels the Nash equilibrium in that each party does their individual best given the behaviour of the other: the union maximizes utility and firm maximizes profit by pricing optimally, with the important difference that the union is the leader here.

[9] The C outcome is not strictly speaking a competitive one, since it embeds some monopoly power by workers and/or firms. But it is atomistic in that each agent acts on their own without any one-to-one strategic interaction in the form of bargaining, or game, with the workers. C corresponds to Friedman's (1968) definition of a 'Walrasian' outcome that underpins the 'natural rate' of unemployment.

4.4.2 A More Formal Model

As the 'right-to-manage' (point R) seems to be the most relevant model, we elaborate more here—in this, we follow Nickell (1990) and Manning (1995). Bargaining is often modelled by letting the two parties follow the 'Nash bargaining solution', which involves the joint maximization of the product,[10]

$$\text{Max}_w \left(L^\phi (w - R) \right)^\delta \Pi^{1-\delta}, \tag{4.8a}$$

s.t. the price curve

$$w = MPL((1 + \mu)L^{\alpha(1-b)})^{(-1/b)} \tag{4.8b}$$

The Nash product in (4.8a) gives the joint gain of the two parties from the successful completion of negotiation, compared to the reference point of the 'outside option' which is the case when negotiations fail. $0 < \delta < 1$ is the bargaining power of the union, so that $1 - \delta$ is the bargaining power of the firm. The maximand that refers to the union, $L(w - R)$, takes into account the 'outside option' of employment elsewhere; we assume for simplicity that the average wage available elsewhere equals the reservation wage R. Π are profits (for the firm the outside option is no activity, so zero profit). (4.8b) differs from the price curve above in that we have omitted taxes ($\tau_p = 0$) and we have substituted y out by a simple production function $y = L^\alpha$.

Taking the derivative of the above with respect to w, and with a little rearrangement, we have:

$$\delta\phi \frac{dL}{dw} L^{-1} + \frac{\delta}{w - R} + (1 - \delta)\frac{d\Pi}{dw}\Pi^{-1} = 0 \tag{4.9}$$

Multiplying through by w, we convert this to,

$$-(\delta\phi\varepsilon_{Lw} + (1 - \delta)\varepsilon_{\Pi w})(w - R) + \delta w = 0. \tag{4.9'}$$

The elasticities shown, both absolute, are the elasticity of employment with respect to the real wage alongside the price curve (what may also be termed the elasticity of labour demand with respect to w), and the elasticity of profits with respect to the real wage, when the price setting rule above is followed. Importantly, both these elasticities are negative, hence the negative sign. From here, with a simple rearrangement, we get an expression for the real wage:

$$w = \bar{\delta}R, \quad \bar{\delta} \equiv \frac{\delta\phi\varepsilon_{Lw} + (1 - \delta)\varepsilon_{\Pi w}}{\delta\phi\varepsilon_{Lw} + (1 - \delta)\varepsilon_{\Pi w} - \delta} > 1 \tag{4.10}$$

---

[10] We must take care not to confuse the Nash <u>equilibrium</u> (the simplest form of strategic <u>non-cooperative</u> interaction) with the Nash <u>bargaining solution</u> (where one-to-one bargaining is involved)—both named after John Nash, but quite different.

So, the real wage is a multiple of the reservation wage R, the multiple determined by absolute elasticities and the bargaining powers of the two parties. This multiple is greater than one under the assumption that the elasticities are high enough and/or that the union cares enough about employment so that the denominator is positive. Importantly, it falls with the absolute value of the elasticity of employment with respect to wage (ε_{Lw})—unions will be cautious if a rise in the wage is to knock off a greater amount of employment. Whether it rises or falls with the union's bargaining power (δ) is a subtler point: It can be seen that the multiple rises with union power if ϕ is low enough (specifically, $\phi < \alpha$), so that the union cares more about the real wage. If ϕ is higher than that, then the union is concerned with the employment implications of its actions and uses its higher influence towards wage moderation.

In this respect, it is worth mentioning the *insider-outsider* model of Gottfries (1992) and Lindbeck and Snower (1986, 2001), which assumes that the union is run by long-serving members who are well established as firm employees. The insiders, or established workers, have a greater value for the firm, because expenditure has been spent to recruit them and they are trained (formally and practically). Insiders cannot undercut them by offering to work for less, because of this differential in value. For this reason, the argument goes, any new unemployment will be felt among the newer employees, or outsiders, the last to have been hired and the first to be laid off. Thus, the older and more established workers who run the union (the insiders) aim for higher wages, safe in the knowledge that it will be the outsiders that suffer the unemployment consequences. If this is the case, ϕ is low so that the union power is geared towards raising wages rather than protecting employment. Such ideas have of course a certain degree of plausibility, and can potentially answer the question, if involuntary unemployment is painful (which it surely is), why does the wage not fall enough to secure employment for all. According to the insiders-outsiders theory, this is because the groups who run the union and who suffer unemployment have (supposedly) divergent interests. But it is rather hard to see these ideas as the fundamental cause of unemployment. There is no compelling evidence that a principle of 'last in, first out' applies in firms (see Nickell, 1990, for a discussion); that is, there is no distinct class of outside workers who suffer the consequences while being divorced from the decisions.

Returning to (4.10), as an illustration, we can derive the elasticities involved from first principles, i.e. using the aggregate price setting curve (4.8b). With the production function $y_i = L_i^\alpha$ and $MPL = \alpha L_i^{\alpha-1}$, we have,

$$\varepsilon_{Lw} = 1/(1 - \alpha).$$

It is also easy to see that, from the price curve above, for firm i, the wage bill is $wL_i = \frac{\alpha}{1+\mu} \frac{P_i}{P} Y_i$, so that aggregate profits under symmetric equilibrium ($P_i = P$) are

$$\Pi = \left(1 - \frac{\alpha}{1+\mu}\right) Y = \frac{1+\mu-\alpha}{\alpha} L^\alpha;$$

thus, the (total) elasticity of profits with respect to w is $\varepsilon_{\Pi w} = \alpha \varepsilon_{Lw}$. In this case, then, the denominator above is

$$\delta \varepsilon_{Lw} + (1 - \delta)\varepsilon_{\Pi w} - 1 = [\delta(1 - \alpha) + 2\alpha - 1]/(1 - \alpha)$$

We assume that this quantity is positive, which essentially means that the production function is elastic enough ($\alpha < 1$ high enough). Combining these pieces of information, the multiple of w over R can be written as:

$$\bar{\delta} = \frac{\delta(1 - \alpha) + \alpha}{(\delta - 1)(1 - \alpha) + \alpha} > 1 \qquad (4.10')$$

But so far, we have considered the alternative wage opportunities (which we have equalized to the reservation wage R) exogenous; yet, in the aggregate economy, this is surely endogenous. As mentioned, R is the average wage available elsewhere. Alternative possibilities are of course employment elsewhere, with probability $(1-u)$ where u is the unemployment rate (per cent), in which case the assumption is that the same real wage w is available; and being unemployed with probability u, when one earns the unemployment benefit. Let us assume that the benefit is B, and that the 'benefit replacement ratio' is $\beta \equiv B/w < 1$. So, R equals a weighted average of these extraneous possibilities,

$$R = (1-u)w + u\beta w. \qquad (4.11)$$

Inserting into (4.10) and solving for u, we have:

$$u = \frac{\bar{\delta} - 1}{\bar{\delta}(1 - \beta)} \qquad (4.12)$$

Accordingly, the equilibrium unemployment rate increases with the w − R multiple (4.10') and the benefit replacement ratio (β). These results are intuitive: The equilibrium wage will rise with union power (δ), if the union cares enough about the wage as opposed to employment, hence this will place us higher up the price setting curve—higher w, lower L. The benefit ratio will have a similar effect as this gives more security in terms of outside options and hence makes unions more inclined for wage increases. In terms of Figure 4.3, then, clearly union activity (if the union cares mostly about wages) and negotiating power shifts the R outcome up and to the left along the price schedule, delivering a higher real wage and lower employment.

Before discussing these models further, we should mention one aspect of wage negotiation ignored so far, which is the level at which negotiations take place: Unions as well as employers' organizations (and therefore negotiations) can be firm-specific, sectoral, or nation-wide, and the bargaining can be more or less centralized. This is obviously important because union strength and the outcomes vary accordingly. A centralized union is more likely to consider the aggregate implications of its decisions and may be more restrained in its wage claims. A small (firm-specific) union, on the other hand, may not consider the employment effects of its decisions, but because of its limited power, those may not be very high anyway. In contrast, fairly but not too centralized unions (like the sectoral ones of the UK) may have both considerable power *and* may be inclined to ignore the wider implications of their actions. Calmfors and Driffill (1988) present cross-country evidence showing that unemployment is lower with very centralized or very decentralized unions, but higher in the countries with a medium degree of centralization (such as the UK with its sectoral unions).[11]

4.4.3 Efficient Firm-Union Bargaining

Starting with MacDonald and Solow (1981), the point has been made that the union-firm negotiations described above are not Pareto efficient: one party could be made better off without the other being harmed. The simplest way to describe the idea is as follows. The structure of the bargaining above is that firms and union jointly maximize the objective

$$\left(L^{\phi}(w-R)\right)^{\delta}\Pi^{1-\delta},$$

subject to the constraint imposed by the price curve. In other words, the union and firm have one free variable to choose (w), and the other (L) follows from the price curve. The price curve is a unilateral optimality condition for the firm, and there is no reason in principle why that could not be negotiated, too. In other words, the union and the firm could, instead, jointly maximize the objective function, by selecting both w and L, without being constrained by the price curve. The former problem imposes one constraint, the latter none, therefore it is the case that the maximized joint utility

$$\left(L^{\phi}(w-R)\right)^{\delta}\Pi^{1-\delta}$$

will be higher in the latter case. It is then possible to distribute the gains between firm and union such that both are better off in comparison to the case of the pre-imposed price curve. Thus, a Pareto improvement can result; this type of bargaining is Pareto optimal (or 'efficient'—no party can be made better off without harming the other).[12]

Thus, this type of bargaining (bargaining over employment as well as the real wage) must be a good thing. It was in fact a widespread belief for some time that such an efficient bargaining would lead to higher employment at any level of the real wage, and even a higher level of employment in comparison to the competitive case. Nickell and Layard (1999) showed this, however, to be a fallacy. Employment will be the same or lower—not higher than under wage bargaining only; only the wage will be higher. The difference with the earlier analyses, such as in MacDonald and Solow (1981) is due to whether one conducts a partial or general equilibrium analysis. In the former, the outside opportunities (and the reservation wage here) are assumed exogenous; in the latter, the outside opportunities are endogenous, given by employment in unions that are symmetric (hence, they pay the same wage and leave the same rate of unemployment in their respective sectors).

---

[11] Of course, equally important is the degree of coordination of actions across unions. Data from Nickell et al. (2005, table 3) show the total degree of coordination (encompassing the full amalgamation into a single union as well as coordination of action across separate unions). This varies across countries, with union action in many European and Japanese being very coordinated and very little so in the 'Anglo-Saxon' countries (US, UK, Canada).

[12] Graphically, the price curve is completely dispensed with; instead, the equilibrium (w, L) outcome will be located on the 'contract curve', the locus of all points of tangency between union indifference curves and firm 'iso-profit' curves. In the partial equilibrium version of the model—see the next paragraph—the contract curve begins from the competitive equilibrium point C and veers off to the northeast (higher both wage and employment). But this changes in a general equilibrium setting.

That there must be unemployment is fairly easy to see: if the reservation wage is $R = (1 - u)w + u\beta w$, as above, then $w - R = u(1 - \beta)w$. We must have $u > 0$, otherwise the union would not be able to improve upon the reservation wage. But the most striking part is that the same or lower level of employment results compared to the 'right-to-manage' model. This is because unions in this case will be more powerful.[13]

There is rather little evidence that firm-union bargaining includes explicit reference to employment (over and above, that is, of conditions) (Nickell, 1990). However, we may not preclude the case that that may happen on occasion, and that firms consult unions particularly at times of great adjustment (layoffs during recessions like the one experienced during late 2008 and 2009). The above analysis warns us that this may be a mixed blessing. The efficient wage bargain model adds interesting twists to our understanding of the behaviour and macroeconomic effects of trade union activity. But ultimately, as an explanation of real-world unemployment developments, it faces the same challenges as the 'right-to-manage' model.

Trade union models offer a line of explanation for unemployment: broadly speaking, unemployment will be higher when/where unionization is stronger and covers a wider segment of the economy. Ultimately, such predictions need to be tested against data and their quantitative significance be evaluated. Work along these lines will be reported below. As we shall see, the main problem such work encounters in explaining the high European unemployment of the 1980s and 1990s is that unionization at that time was declining in relation to earlier decades, when unemployment was lower.

4.5 Efficiency Wages

We now review a class of models called 'efficiency wage models' which argue that firms' pursuit of motivated workers leads them to maintain wages above the competitive level. Famously put to (good) effect by the car manufacturer Henry Ford in the early 1900s, such (unilateral) firm activity possibly decreases employment below the competitive level and contributes to (involuntary) unemployment.[14]

There are a number of reasons why a firm may wish to keep the wage at a level above the competitive level; see Malcomson (1981), Yellen (1984), Krueger and Summers (1988). A firm keeps a wage about the competitive level for a variety of reasons:

- In order to attract high-quality workers when quality is not directly observable;
- To motivate workers to provide more effort;
- Relatedly, such wages persuade workers not to shirk (Shapiro and Stiglitz, 1984), since by shirking they risk getting caught, in which case firing and the lower wage available elsewhere are a painful prospect;

---

[13] Espinosa and Rhee (1989) consider a setup where the firm and union bargain repeatedly (say, every year). This is an interesting extension for two reasons. First, it is a dynamical model of firm-union bargaining. Secondly, it shows that the 'monopoly union' and the 'efficient bargaining' models are special cases of their wider setup: if both parties are sufficiently long-sighted, they can maintain the efficient arrangement; if their horizon is just one period, the monopoly union model prevails. In general, a combination of the outcomes of the two types of bargain will emerge.

[14] Another possible source of terminological confusion should be cleared: The 'efficiency wage' models reviewed in this section have no connection with the 'efficient bargaining' models.

- Higher wages induce workers to stay longer with a company and so turnover decreases; this has the beneficial effect of reducing the hiring (recruitment, training, etc) costs of the firm;
- Another factor is social conventions and fairness norms, not easily explained by the conventional models of rational individualistic behaviour by either firms or workers.

The basic model of Solow (1979) formalizes these insights. Let the production function of firm i be:

$$Y_i = F(E_i L_i) \tag{4.13}$$

The production of firm i depends on its employment (L_i) times the effort (E_i) that its employees put in; so, we have labour in 'quality units', which is the novelty here. This must be distinguished from skill; it is extent to which we 'try hard'. In turn, this determined by a motivation function,

$$E_i = E(w_i - R), \tag{4.14}$$

whereby effort is motivated by a function E(.) of the real wage paid by this firm over and above that available elsewhere (which we here equate to the reservation wage R). We postulate a simple functional form for the effort function,

$$E_i = (w_i - R)^\varepsilon, \quad 0 \le \varepsilon < 1. \tag{4.15}$$

Parameter ε tells us how important effort considerations are in production and helps us keep track of its effects; the polar case of $\varepsilon = 0$ reverts us back to the competitive model (where effort—as distinct from skill—is not a consideration).

The firm aims to maximize profits. (Everything is expressed in real terms and symmetric equilibrium is imposed across firms regarding prices—but not wages.)

$$\text{Max} \quad Y_i - w_i L_i \tag{4.16}$$

The firm chooses the real wage w_i and employment L_i in order to maximize profits, recognizing that output depends on effort, which in turn depends on the wage. At the moment, the reservation wage R is taken as given. The first-order conditions are (where primes (') indicate the first derivatives):

$$\text{w.r.t.} L_i : \quad E_i F'(.) = w_i \tag{4.17a}$$

This is essentially the labour demand of the firm (or the real wage arising from price-setting if we dealt explicitly with pricing by firms), augmented by the new consideration of effort E.

$$\text{w.r.t.} w_i : \quad L_i E_i'(.) F'(.) = L_i \tag{4.17b}$$

This is a new condition, informing us of the level of effort that the firm wants to induce. Straightforward combination of these two conditions (4.17a, b) yields:

$$\frac{E_i' w_i}{E_i} = 1 \qquad (4.18)$$

The firm will offer a real wage such that the elasticity of the effort function with respect to it is unity—a standard result in this literature. To see a specific example, take the specific effort function postulated in (4.15), from which $E_i' = \varepsilon E_i/(w_i - R)$. Combining into the above, the unit-elasticity condition (4.18) becomes:

$$\frac{\varepsilon w_i}{w_i - R} = 1, \quad \text{or} \quad w_i = \frac{R}{1 - \varepsilon} \qquad (4.18')$$

Note that $0 < 1 - \varepsilon \leq 1$. The real wage is a multiple (greater than one) over the reservation wage, rising with the importance of relative wage considerations in inducing effort.

While the reservation wage (R) is exogenous to any specific firm, it is endogenous to the economy as a whole. To incorporate this, we move to a general equilibrium setup, following Summers (1988). As in (4.11), the reservation wage is endogenous and equal to:

$$R = (1 - u)w + u\beta w \qquad (4.11)$$

Furthermore, and assuming symmetry across firms, all firms have the same wage, so that $w_i = w$ for all i. Introducing this information and (4.11) into (4.18'), we finally get:

$$u = \frac{\varepsilon}{1 - \beta} \qquad (4.19)$$

The unemployment rate increases with the importance of effort and the benefit replacement ratio $\beta(< 1)$. The unemployment rate is set at such a level that it creates an effective motivation to those in employment to provide enough effort. This is done by creating a gap between the wage available in employment and the outside option, which is the unemployment benefit. By creating such a gap, unemployment then becomes an effective threat. In the polar case where effort is irrelevant ($\varepsilon = 0$), there is no (involuntary) unemployment.

What about the real wage? This is determined from the labour demand condition (4.17a). For illustration, let the production function (4.13) have the simple form:

$$Y_i = F(E_i L_i) = (E_i L_i)^\alpha \qquad (4.20)$$

In this case, (4.17a) becomes $\alpha Y_i/L_i = w$. Rearranging, recalling that the wage is common across firms, we can aggregate this to:

$$\alpha Y/w = L = 1 - u \qquad (4.21)$$

(The labour force is assumed to have a unit size, so $L = 1 - u$.) Hence, the real wage and unemployment move in the same direction, essentially along a price schedule (or labour demand curve). (Recall that along the price schedule, employment and the real wage are negatively related.) Accordingly, the wage depends positively on unemployment and product demand (Y). As unemployment is higher than in the market-clearing models, the wage is also higher. Thus, efficiency wage considerations deliver both wage rigidity at a higher level than the competitive outcome and higher unemployment. Interestingly, these effects are not easily reconcilable with the wage-price setting Figure 4.2: a shift in the price schedule will produce either higher wages and *employment* or the opposite, but not the mix that efficiency wage theories predict (higher *unemployment* and real wage). In this sense, these models provide genuinely new insights. These models are also consistent with the fact reviewed in the section on technical progress, that structural unemployment is constant while output growth is reflected on the real wage (w and Y are proportional above).

There is a variety of such 'efficiency wage' models, with individual characteristics and more specific implications. On the whole, this class of models can help explain a number of phenomena not explicable by competitive models. Those include the emergence of involuntary unemployment and wage differentials across industries which cannot otherwise be explained by competitive models and their emphasis on skills and productivity alone (Krueger and Summers, 1988).[15] Such models in principle can also explain the phenomenon of 'dual labour markets', analysed in the next section, whereby there is a well-paid sector but with limited employment, and a second one which clears the labour market but with competitive wages. It is less clear, however, whether they can contribute to the understanding of European unemployment. It is also unclear whether these models can connect with cyclical unemployment. Observe that equilibrium unemployment (4.19) is independent of anything that might be thought of as moving the cycle, like aggregate demand or productivity. The extension to 'dual labour markets' presented in Section 4.6 may rectify this weakness.

A variety and extension of this basic setup is provided by the Shapiro and Stiglitz (1984) 'shirking' model which has achieved a certain prominence. The model is rather complicated but a variant of it can be fairly easily incorporated in our context. The main idea is that the firm may be inclined to pay a wage that is higher than the market in order to induce workers not to shirk, or cheat in the marketplace.[16] A worker may be inclined to shirk, or skip work, if they can go undetected, as this involves less work effort. Monitoring is imperfect, so the device that the firm employs to discipline its workers is the sack: if you shirk and get caught, you lose the job and the attractive wage it offers. In order for that method to work, the wage must be attractive enough.

In this case, the production function of firm i (4.13) be modified to:

$$Y_i = F(E_i L_i(1 - s_i)), \quad 0 < s_i < 1 \tag{4.13'}$$

---

[15] In fact, in the Krueger-Summers study, industry dummies (dummy variables aiming to capture specific industry characteristics) are more important than worker age, occupational (proxies for skills), demographic, or geographic characteristics in explaining the inter-industry wage structure (how wages vary across industries) in the US. The fact that such industry dummies alone are very significant is thought to be an indication of industry differentials explicable only by efficiency wages.

[16] This is not too different from the idea that firm wants to induce workers to provide effort—shirking may be thought as no effort (though the worker gets paid), hence no production by that worker.

s_i is the probability of shirking and the fraction of workers of firm i that shirk (i.e. who do not work at all, and do not produce, while still on the payroll of the firm). In the Shapiro-Stiglitz model the worker needs to decide whether they work properly or shirk (an either-or decision), but here we can assume that there is implicitly a probability of shirking, and workers switch randomly from one state to the other. Furthermore, let this probability depend negatively on the wage premium in that firm, $w_i - R$, and positively on the cost of monitoring, c (more difficult monitoring implying more frequent lapses):

$$s_i = s(w_i - R, c), \quad s_i^1(w_i - R, .) < 0, \quad s_i^2(., c) > 0 \tag{4.21}$$

If so, the firm's FOC with respect to employment L_i and the wage, w_i need to change to:

$$(1 - s_i)E_i F'(.) = w_i \tag{4.17a'}$$

$$(1 - s_i)L_i E_i'(.)F'(.) - s_i^1 L_i E_i F'(.) = L_i \tag{4.17b'}$$

where the superscript 1 indicates the derivative of s(.,.) with respect to the wage premium. Combining as before, we get:

$$\frac{[\varepsilon - s_i^1/(1 - s_i)]w_i}{w_i - R} = 1, \quad \text{or} \quad w_i = \frac{R}{1 - [\varepsilon - s_i^1/(1 - s_i)]} \tag{4.22}$$

This is to be compared to (4.18'). Since $s_i^1 < 0$ and $(1 - s_i) > 0$, the wage rate is higher than before (compared to the outside wage R). Following on in the same manner as before, unemployment now becomes,

$$u = \frac{[\varepsilon - s_i^1/(1 - s_i)]}{1 - \beta}. \tag{4.23}$$

Note that the unemployment rate in (4.23) is, by the signs stated in (4.21), higher than in the simpler efficiency wage model (4.19). The new element that this story adds is the higher wage and unemployment due to the need of the firm to maintain the effective threat of the sack as a discipline device. Additionally, the monitoring cost (c) plays a role here. As both s^1 and s increase in absolute value with c, more difficult monitoring implies the need for the firm to maintain a higher differential between the wage and the reservation wage R, and for the market to incur a higher unemployment rate as a result.

4.6 Dual Labour Markets

With the headline unemployment rate in the UK currently (Spring 2019) at about 4 per cent, it may be argued that the main problem in the UK labour markets is not so much unemployment itself; rather, it is the incidence of low-quality jobs in a certain segment of the labour market. 'Zero-hours contracts', low-quality jobs without security, low pay without social provisions such as paid holidays or social insurance may be the everyday reality for some workers.[17] This is not to say that unemployment is no longer a problem; it is, both in the UK and everywhere. But alongside the study of unemployment, one should also make a point of studying the marked differences in pay and job quality between various segments of the labour market. Models of the 'dual labour markets' (e.g. Saint-Paul, 1991, 1992) do that; such models are not new but are currently getting less attention than they deserve. This section is devoted to this type of model and is a little more exploratory than the rest of the chapter.

Not all jobs are the same. In particular, an important difference may be noted between two sectors, or separate labour markets, between which there appears to be little communication. In other words, there appears to be a duality, or market segmentation, in the labour market, between sectors that may be termed (for no reason other than labelling) primary and secondary. A primary sector is made up of 'career jobs', with job security, promotion possibilities, high wages, welfare entitlements like pension rights and holiday allowances, and a relatively high degree of unionization. A secondary market, in contrast, is made up of low-paid, often menial jobs, with casual attachments between firm and worker and job insecurity. Though in reality there may be some differences between the two sectors in terms of required qualifications, with the primary one requiring tertiary education (what Tournemaine and Tsoukis (2009) call 'status jobs'), productivity differences are not necessary to generate such a labour market segmentation. Indeed, a vintage analysis of this situation, due to Bulow and Summers (1986), assumes that the workers in the two sectors are equally productive. The question then that arises is why the secondary workers do not bid down the wages of the primary sector by offering to work at lower wages. The answer is in the spirit of the efficiency wage model: firms in the primary sector want to maintain above-market wages so as to motivate these workers and monitor their performance. It is shown that this results in unemployment as the demand for primary workers is restricted.

Below, we present a simple model in the spirit of Bulow and Summers (1986) to highlight such a situation. Let there be two sectors, 1 and 2, offering wages w_1 and w_2, respectively. Sector 1 is the 'primary' sector that offers a higher wage: $w_1 > w_2$. The reason, as mentioned, is that efficiency wage considerations apply in the first sector, but not the second. Employment in the two sectors is denoted as L_1 and L_2, and with an assumed unit mass of labour force, the unemployment rate is given by $u = 1 - L_1 - L_2$. The only other amendment is to assume an aggregate production function similar in spirit to (4.13):

$$F = A(EL_1)^{\alpha}(L_2)^{1-\alpha} \tag{4.24}$$

Employment in both sectors matters for aggregate output, but in sector 1, effort E also matters, which depends on the wage premium as before. A is a productivity term that can also serve as a proxy for output. Any rise in A signifies an expansion, from whatever source (demand or supply). Each firm receives as remuneration its contribution to aggregate production, so that each firm's first-order conditions (in the primary or secondary markets) coincide with the first-order conditions of the aggregate production function (4.24). Accordingly, following the same steps as those that yielded (4.17a, b), the firm's first order conditions for employment and effort yield a wage premium:

---

[17] Commentators talk of a 'precariat', the workforce in precarious employment. This is the modern-day replacement of the proletariat, the industrial workforce in low-paid but fairly secure employment, emphasized mainly by Marxist analyses.

$$w_1 = \frac{R}{1 - \varepsilon} \tag{4.25}$$

This is very similar to (4.18') which it replaces. The wage now is the typical one in sector 1; the reservation wage, R, however, should take account of employment opportunities in both sectors, if a dismissal from a firm in sector 1 occurs:

$$R = L_1 w_1 + L_2 w_2 + \beta w_1 u \tag{4.26}$$

Since any firm (in either sector) is assumed to be of mass 0, the employment probability in sector 1 remains L_1 (its employment share), while employment probability in sector 2 is L_2. If the individual goes into unemployment (with probability u), then they receive the unemployment benefit, assumed to be a fraction $\beta < 1$ of the sector 1 wage. Combining these two equations, and dividing through by w_2, we get:

$$\omega \equiv w_1/w_2 = \frac{L_1 + L_2/\omega + \beta u}{1 - \varepsilon} \tag{4.27}$$

We call the ratio of the two wages the 'wage premium' and denote it by $\omega(>1)$. The above needs now to be transformed in a straightforward manner as follows.

$$\omega = \frac{L_1 + L_2 + L_2(1/\omega - 1) + \beta u}{1 - \varepsilon} = \frac{1 - u + (1 - u)(L_2/(L_1 + L_2))(1/\omega - 1) + \beta u}{1 - \varepsilon} =$$

$$= \frac{1 - u + (1 - u)(1 + L_1/L_2)^{-1}(1/\omega - 1) + \beta u}{1 - \varepsilon}$$

Furthermore, the firms in the two sectors set employment by equating their marginal product of labour to the respective wages:

$$\alpha F/L_1 = w_1, \quad \text{and} \quad (1 - \alpha)F/L_2 = w_2 \tag{4.28}$$

(The first of these is the same as 4.21 above.) These allow us to write the ratio of labour demands (and levels of employment) in the two sectors as:

$$L_1/L_2 = \alpha(1 - \alpha)^{-1}\omega^{-1} \tag{4.29}$$

Introducing above, we have:

$$\omega = \frac{1 - u + (1 - u)(\omega + \alpha/(1 - \alpha))^{-1}(1 - \omega) + \beta u}{1 - \varepsilon} =$$
$$= \frac{(1 - u)(1 + \alpha/(1 - \alpha))(\omega + \alpha/(1 - \alpha))^{-1} + \beta u}{1 - \varepsilon} \tag{4.30}$$

(4.20) is the first of two key equations in the model. It is expressed in terms of unemployment u and the wage premium ω, which are negatively related. We may call it the 'wage premium' equation, as what underlies it is the need by firms of sector 1 to maintain a wage difference from sector 2 (and from the unemployment benefit), in order to motivate effort. The wage premium is negatively related to unemployment as a higher unemployment rate reduces the reservation wage and requires a smaller wage differential from sector 2—the higher probability of unemployment is by itself enough motivation (or threat) for workers to provide effort. To connect with the analysis of efficiency wages without market segmentation (the analysis of the previous section), there we had a unitary wage premium ($\omega = 1$). The unemployment level of $u = \varepsilon/(1 - \beta)$ in (4.19) immediately results. Here, as $\omega > 1$ rises, the LHS increases while the RHS decreases, therefore the unemployment rate u decreases, too.

To proceed, we need to derive the second key equation. The unemployment rate can be derived from the first order conditions for employment in the production function (4.24) and using (4.28), as follows:

$$1 - u = L_1 + L_2 = \alpha AE^\alpha(L_1/L_2)^\alpha L_2/w_1 + (1 - \alpha)AE^\alpha(L_1/L_2)^\alpha L_2/w_2 =$$
$$= AE^\alpha(L_1/L_2)^\alpha(L_2/w_2)(\alpha/\omega + 1 - \alpha)$$

Furthermore, we need to postulate a wage or labour supply equation:

$$1 - u = L_1 + L_2 = \gamma w_2, \quad \gamma > 0 \tag{4.31}$$

The higher the unemployment rate, the lower will be the wage claimed by workers, with the wage in sector 2 as an indicator. Alternatively, the higher the basic wage (that of sector 2), the greater (is assumed to be) the overall labour supply. Such an equation has not been employed above, because the efficiency wage model, due to its special structure, determines the unemployment rate regardless of what labour supply is. But it is necessary here for the model to close. Introducing (4.31) and the effort function (4.15) for sector 1, $E = (w_1 - R)^\varepsilon$, into (4.30), we get:

$$1 - u = AE^\alpha(\omega)^{-\alpha}(\gamma L_2/(L_1 + L_2))(\alpha/\omega + 1 - \alpha) =$$
$$= A(w_1 - R)^{\varepsilon\alpha}(\omega)^{-\alpha}\gamma(1 + \alpha)^{-1}\omega^{-1})^{-1}(\alpha/\omega + 1 - \alpha)$$

Since, from (4.25), $w_1 - R = \varepsilon w_1$ and we also have $w_1 - R = \varepsilon w_1 = \varepsilon\omega w_2 = \varepsilon\omega(1 - u)/\gamma$ (from 4.31), introducing above, we get the second key equation (after simplifications):

$$(1 - u)^{1-\varepsilon\alpha} = \varepsilon A(1 - \alpha)(\omega)^{\alpha(\varepsilon-1)}\gamma^{1-\varepsilon} \tag{4.32}$$

We may call this the 'labour demand' equation, as labour supply only plays a subsidiary role. The wage premium and the unemployment rate are positively related here (with $\varepsilon < 1$), so the wage premium is negatively related to employment, as in a labour demand or price equation. Intuitively, as a higher premium changes the employment ratio in favour of sector-2 employment, it reduces labour demand and increases the unemployment rate. To facilitate intuition, we may depict the two equations in (ω, u) space in Figure 4.4 below:

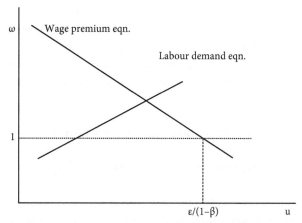

Figure 4.4. The workings of dual labour markets

The equilibrium wage premium and unemployment rate are given by the intersection of the two curves. Some comparative statics results may be that as the importance of the effort function increases (higher ε), both lines shift up; as a result, the wage premium unambiguously rises, but it is unclear what happens to the unemployment rate. (It is useful to contrast this with the earlier model where this effect produced a higher unemployment rate, only and unambiguously.) Furthermore, as labour supply increases (or, more precisely, it becomes more responsive to the wage), γ rises, the labour demand shifts up. The result is less unemployment but a higher wage premium, as firms in sector 1 now try harder to motivate workers.

These results may be combined with the observation that the unemployment rate is less here than in the basic model of efficiency wages of Section 4.5 without duality in the labour market. Note that, in that case, the equilibrium is where the wage premium equation meets the $\omega = 1$ line. So, the dual labour market model suggests that unemployment is cushioned by the existence of the 'secondary' market, but at the cost of more inequality. This accords with intuition: economies, like those of the UK and US, which feature rather deregulated labour markets, with prominent 'secondary' sectors, can also boast lower unemployment but also feature greater wage inequality. But unemployment does exist in this model, too, and it is involuntary in nature. Firms will not hire workers at the lower wage because they want to maintain worker effort and discipline. Thus, the workers of sector 2 (and the unemployed) will not be hired by firms of sector 1, even if they offer to work at lower wages. Another point where this model has an advantage over the basic efficiency wage model of Section 4.5 is its cyclical properties. Any expansion (due to either demand or supply sides) manifested in a rise in A will shift the labour demand schedule upwards, resulting in a higher primary sector wage premium and less unemployment. Thus, unemployment here is counter-cyclical, which is in line with the real world, in contrast to Section 4.5 in which unemployment is constant.

Thus, this model offers a rich framework for the analysis of both unemployment and wage inequality. While segmented or dual labour markets may be part of the overall picture of unemployment, they are perhaps even more interesting as a way of understanding the rising generational gaps in terms of economic prospects (the fate of 'generation X',

Friedman, 2008, or else the 'generation of the 700 Euros' as they are known in Europe). The implications of the model, as Bulow and Summers (1986) emphasize are fairly drastic. There is scope for industrial policy to support the primary sector (aside from the administrative and political difficulties of implementing such a policy) as a source of good wages, and there is also scope for subsidizing good jobs to be offered to disadvantaged workers.

4.7 Dynamic Adjustment Issues

4.7.1 Unemployment Persistence and 'Hysteresis'

The above theories may help explain the incidence of structural unemployment, based on such 'fundamentals' as union power, productivity, taxes, or efficiency wages, but not its evolution. This has become an important issue in the last 30 years, as European unemployment shot up in the late 1970s and early 1980s, grew again in the 1990s, but then dramatically de-escalated later. Did the fundamentals that gave rise to it in the first instance produce such dramatic reversals later on? Or, instead, did the process of unemployment produce complex dynamics out of essentially transitory shocks like the oil price shocks of the 1970s? Such questions put the issue of the dynamic adjustment of unemployment in sharp relief. Two notions are particularly relevant here, persistence and 'hysteresis'. Loosely speaking, persistence of a variable is the sluggish adjustment following some extraneous developments. The other side of the coin of sluggish adjustment is the fact that past shocks continue to have some bearing on this variable, long after the shocks themselves have died out; in other words, their effect persists, hence the name. The 'hysteresis' models of Blanchard and Summers (1986, 1987) take this argument one step further, arguing that the entire past history of unemployment matters—the effect of past shocks never fades away. If so, there are drastic implications for the evolution of unemployment. We now turn to reviewing these concepts and issues briefly. We begin with a digression on persistence.

Structural (or natural or equilibrium) unemployment is determined by the (entirely supply-side) factors underlying wage and price setting. These factors are structural and long-run in nature. The notion of hysteresis began with the recognition that while unemployment had changed by the mid-1980s in a way that looked permanent, none of the possible underlying factors had changed permanently (more on that in Section 4.10). Is it possible that temporary shocks could give rise to a *permanent* rise in equilibrium unemployment? The 'hysteresis' models answer yes; they argue that the protracted adjustment influences equilibrium unemployment permanently. In this section, we review such issues, starting from a more formal explanation of persistence and hysteresis themselves.

4.7.2 A Digression on Persistence and Hysteresis

Persistence of a variable rests on the fact that its current state depends on one or more of its past states. Schematically, let the evolution of variable y_t be described by:

$$y_t = \alpha y_{t-1} + x_t, \quad 0 \leq \alpha \leq 1, \tag{4.33}$$

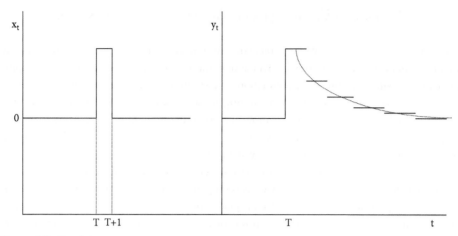

Figure 4.5. Persistence

This is the is the simplest case of persistence, whereby y_t depends only on its immediate past state (y_{t-1}), alongside an exogenous variable x_t; the strength of persistence is given by parameter α.[18] What does this scheme tell us about the evolution of y_t?

To see this, use repeated backward substitution (along the lines described in Chapter 2), to get:

$$y_t = \sum_{i=0}^{\infty} \alpha^i x_{t-i} \qquad (4.34)$$

Let also $x_t = 0$ for all t except T, when it registers a shock for one period, after which it goes back to 0. The graphic evolution of x_t and y_t is given in Figure 4.5.

In Figure 4.5, following the one-period shock in x_t at $t = T$, y_t jumps upwards but its return to base is gradual, showing persistence, because each state depends on the previous one which was above base. (The movements occur along the 'steps' depicted above, which may be thought of as being joined by the smooth curve shown.) If so, the entirely transitory shock that occurred at T continues to have effects even after it has disappeared; the effects themselves die away over time. The speed of adjustment is shown by the steepness of the curve and is regulated by the parameter α: the *greater* α, the *flatter* will be the curve and the slower the adjustment to base; the smaller α, the steeper the curve. Conversely, the higher the persistence, the higher will be the effect of any shock that occurred at T a given number of periods later. There are two extreme cases: $\alpha = 0$ is the case of no persistence at all, when y_t emulates the pattern of x_t exactly; on the other hand, $\alpha = 1$ would deliver a completely horizontal curve for y_t from T onwards (dashed line). This is the case of hysteresis and is of interest because even the transitory shock has a permanent effect on y_t. In other words, hysteresis is an extreme form of persistence. In this case even long-run (or 'steady-state') values are affected by any shock in the past and by all the history of y_t.[19]

---

[18] Econometrically minded people will recognize this scheme as an Autoregression of order 1 (AR(1)).

[19] Hysteresis (= lag in plain English), a term borrowed from physics, is used to describe a system when its equilibrium state depends not only on current exogenous conditions but also on the path that it has followed so far. In the unemployment context, the term is used in the sense of actual unemployment influencing structural

4.7.3 Back to Unemployment: Three Channels of Persistence

There are three channels whereby persistence, and in the extreme case hysteresis, arises in unemployment. First, a temporary adverse demand or supply shock that destroys capital and capacity will mean the associated labour is also out of job; moreover, once capacity is destroyed, there is no easy way of rebuilding it (see Bean, 1989). But this idea has not attracted much attention. Second, a temporary rise in unemployment will imply that more people are now in long-run unemployment (lasting more than a year). This type of unemployment arguably puts less downward pressure on wages; this is because the skills of the long-run unemployed may depreciate faster, or more plausibly, they may become disaffected and less motivated, hence searching less intensively. This means that the necessary wage adjustments will not take place and some of the rise in unemployment will become permanent. Yet another strand of argument builds on the insider-outsider worker distinction mentioned above. Imagine that the insider union membership is all those employed last period. Past unemployment reduces current union membership, and the insiders' union protects only the currently employed. Hence, such a structure helps make any even seemingly temporary increase in unemployment permanent (the last mechanism is central in Blanchard and Summers, 1986).

We can illustrate this model slightly more formally as follows. Let a simple, NAIRU-type Phillips Curve equation be described as follows:

$$\pi_t - \pi_{t-1} = u_t^N - u_t \tag{4.35}$$

and

$$u_t^N = \rho \bar{u}_t^N + (1 - \rho)u_{t-1}, \quad 0 \le \rho \le 1 \tag{4.36}$$

Notation is standard: u and π are the actual unemployment and inflation rates, and u^N is the equilibrium, or 'natural' or 'structural' unemployment rate. The NAIRU-type Phillips Curve (4.354) says that the change in inflation is positively related to cyclical unemployment (equilibrium minus actual). The change in inflation represents all the (temporary) demand impulses on unemployment. Furthermore, (4.36) argues that the natural rate itself (u_t^N) is not invariant but develops over time. It is the linear combination (with weights ρ and $1 - \rho$) of two components: its permanent supply-side determinants $\bar{u}_t^N$, i.e. the underlying unemployment fundamentals that we have been discussing in this chapter, and past actual unemployment weighted by a factor $1 - \rho$. The justification is the one given above: a higher than normal actual unemployment rate may influence the natural rate upwards because capacity is destroyed after a recession, or workers become demotivated, or the group of insiders diminishes and this affects wage negotiations. The value of

---

unemployment and giving rise to its very sluggish dynamical adjustment. Hysteresis is parallel to the notion of 'path dependence', used in engineering, biology, etc. The appeal of these notions is that history matters—that is, the precise path you follow is an important determinant of the long-run equilibrium, over and above such exogenous 'fundamentals' as factor endowments, tastes, geography, or labour market 'institutions' in our context. (But note that hysteresis and history are different words.) Common sense, really, but rather difficult to model formally in economics. In this case, we can write $y_t - y_{t-1} = x_t$: any shock affects the change in y. This is the case of 'random walk' in econometrics, when the current y_t fully 'remembers' all past shocks.

$(1 - \rho)$ depends on the strength of these three effects. Combining (4.35) and (4.36) and rearranging, we have:

$$u_t = \rho \bar{u}_t^N + (1 - \rho)u_{t-1} + \pi_t - \pi_{t-1} \tag{4.37}$$

The current unemployment rate depends on its own lag, the long-run supply-side fundamentals, and demand and supply shocks (evidenced in the evolution of inflation). $1 - \rho$ reveals the extent of persistence. Blanchard and Summers (1986) estimate such an equation for West Germany, France, the UK, and the US for 1953–84; they find a coefficient $1 - \rho$ that for European countries is statistically indistinguishable from unity; it is less than unity for the US. This implies extreme persistence (i.e. hysteresis) in Europe. See Alogoskoufis and Manning (1988) for further evidence and Nickell (1990) for a discussion.

Ball (1999, 2009) provides evidence of hysteresis in unemployment. The key point is that the natural rate in a Phillips equation, of whatever form, is not constant over time, but is affected by past unemployment itself. Furthermore, he argues extensively and rather persuasively, that the changes in the NAIRU were associated with changes in aggregate demand as evidenced in aggregate demand contraction and (dis)inflation. Note that (dis) inflation implies an actual unemployment that deviates from NAIRU; hysteresis implies that this level of employment will influence future levels of the NAIRU. In this way, demand shocks can have a long-lasting effect on unemployment. This is a considerable break with much mainstream theory that views demand shocks as having only a temporary effect on unemployment, and where supply-side stories hold the most promise as explanations of the longer term evolution of unemployment.

Ball (2009) updates the evidence on hysteresis. Using an expectations-augmented Phillips Curve, he shows that disinflation is associated with an unemployment rate higher than the NAIRU. In fact, the estimated Phillips Curve allows him to estimate the NAIRU (actual unemployment is of course observed). By regressing NAIRU on past unemployment, he offers quantitative evidence of hysteresis; although as he stresses, the precise mechanism by which hysteresis operates—whether demoralization or de-skilling of workers, or something else—is not precisely understood. We return to demand versus supply-side explanations of unemployment in Section 4.10.

4.7.4 Wage Adjustment and Unemployment—the Wage Curve vs. the Phillips Curve

We now turn attention to a different set of issues, associated with the persistence of unemployment through the dynamical adjustment of wages. Recall the wage equation (4.6) of Section 4.3.

$$w = R(1 + v)(1 + \tau_1)y^d \tag{4.6}$$

This suggests a relationship between the level of the real wage (w) and real output (y), conditional on the reservation wage (R)—ignoring taxes. The reservation wage, however, is unobservable and is endogenous in general equilibrium, as argued above. So, the empirical specifications vary, depending on how they control for the reservation wage. If one assumes that the reservation wage reflects workers' aspirations among other considerations, and aspirations adapt to the environment with a lag, then we may write in a simple manner $R_t = \lambda w_{t-1}$. According to this, the reservation wage, interpreted as the wage currently assumed normal, follows last period's wage with a factor of proportionality λ. This parameter may reflect such factors as the strength of aspirations, perceptions about productivity growth, and unemployment. Aspirations raise λ; if productivity growth is expected, workers will aim for their wages to increase in line, so λ will rise; a higher unemployment rate will discourage high wage claims, so λ falls. The idea is that workers will aim for an adaptation in their wages in their negotiations, depending on such considerations as the state of output and labour markets. In this case, considering that output and labour market activity is inversely related to unemployment, (4.6) may be approximated by the following linear-dynamic empirical wage equation:

$$w_t = \lambda w_{t-1} - \beta u_t \tag{4.6'}$$

The value of the adjustment parameter λ has been the subject of some controversy (Blanchard and Katz, 1997). Most theories would imply a relationship between the *level* of (log) real wage and u (possibly augmented by dynamics, but such that $\lambda < 1$), and this is the evidence presented by Blanchflower and Oswald (1994, 1995) from regional studies of US and UK states/regions. On the other hand, many macroeconometric studies of the aggregate US and other OECD labour markets suggest that $\lambda = 1$, implying a relationship between the *rate of change* of the real wage (possibly augmented by dynamics, but of the rate of change). The former view is closer to the wage curve, the latter to an expectations-augmented Phillips curve.

Again, the issue is relevant in understanding the great persistence of European labour markets in the face of shocks that occurred in the late 1970s/early 1980s. The difference with the US is marked, as unemployment in the US rose only temporarily. To see what the estimate of λ implies, let the price equation (4.5) of Section 4.3 be approximated in a similar manner as:

$$w_t = \alpha u_t - x_t \tag{4.5'}$$

This is because the real wage consistent with price setting is negatively related to employment, therefore positively to unemployment; x are factors that may decrease the profitability of firms and hence the real wage they are prepared to pay, like higher energy prices, taxes, or interest rates.[20] Introducing price setting (4.5') into the wage equation (4.6'), we get:

$$(\alpha + \beta)u_t = \lambda w_{t-1} + x_t = \lambda \alpha u_{t-1} + x_t - \lambda x_{t-1} \tag{4.38}$$

The second equality results by applying (4.5') once again to the middle part. In the long run, all change will have ceased (a stationary state will have been achieved), so that $u_t = u_{t-1} = u$, and $x_t = x_{t-1} = x$, and:

---

[20] They reduce, that is, the real wage in relation to its very long-run trend, which is determined by productivity, as seen in Section 4.3.

$$(\alpha(1 - \lambda) + \beta)u = (1 - \lambda)x \qquad (4.39)$$

If $\lambda = 1$, the adverse effects manifested in x (e.g. oil prices, taxes) noted above will have no effect on the structural rate of unemployment—no persistence. However, if $\lambda < 1$, a rise in x will increase unemployment permanently—giving rise to hysteresis in unemployment. For the US, Blanchard and Katz (1997) estimate λ to be statistically indistinguishable from unity, so that the US seems to have little persistence. For Europe, they argue that the bulk of the evidence is for $\lambda < 1$, yielding unemployment persistence.

4.8 Stocks, Flows, and Unemployment Duration

4.8.1 Introduction

We now turn attention to a somewhat different approach to (un)employment that has recently gained a lot of attention. The approach focuses on the key distinction between stocks and flows in the labour market, and the duration of unemployment. To motivate this approach, let us point out some limitations of the more standard approach based on wage and price setting. At the core of the more standard approach are the price and wage setting curves, or, in more neoclassical terms, labour demand and supply. When we are at equilibrium in this framework, there is typically some unemployment. Various comments can be made about this unemployment. First, it is not a homogeneous pool of people. Workers differ in skills, abilities, and locations. The unemployed workers will have different histories: some will be longer in unemployment than others; some will be unemployed because their old jobs were permanently destroyed, some others because of only temporary job destruction, others because they are in the process of searching for better opportunities. All this information is lost from the standard 'price-wage setting—homogeneous unemployment' framework. Furthermore, jobs themselves are not homogeneous, they often require specialized skills and are based in different locations, so the matching between workers and jobs is not a frictionless process: Employers do not put a hand in the hat and pull out any worker, so to speak. The process takes time and is costly (because of advertising, interviews, required training for the job, etc.). There is also imperfect information about the pool of workers and jobs 'out there'. When you come up with an offer, you need to decide whether it is good enough, or whether it is worth carrying on the search for a better alternative. Similarly, firms need to select among available workers. For these reasons, a firm needs to calculate carefully whether it wants to create a job; there are subtler considerations to make than the marginal product-wage calculus that we have seen so far (but including it). In other words, there are various departures from the Walrasian framework. Part and parcel with this idea is the existence of vacancies which are incompatible with unemployment in a Walrasian world: if there are unemployed people, why are the vacancies not filled instantaneously?

A final argument concerns the reason why there remain some unemployed workers at the equilibrium (real) wage. Why do these people not offer to work at lower wages—surely that would be better than nothing? The standard model relies on the notion of 'reservation wage', or the wage level that would be barely adequate in getting us out of bed; some people are unemployed because any available jobs offer a wage below the reservation wage. This depends on the value of leisure, welfare provisions, taxes, etc.—all those considerations we saw. But it is a theoretical notion. Instead, the theory sketched here would rely on such concepts as time-consuming and costly job search, imperfect matching, etc. In other words, with its emphasis on flows, unemployment duration, and costly search and matching, the theory sketched here is closer to the ideas about 'natural rate' or 'equilibrium' unemployment outlined by Friedman (1968).

This section will present briefly a model along these lines. We begin with a model of stock and flows, assuming many of these considerations away, or as exogenous and fixed. We then move on to introduce time-consuming matching between workers and firms, and costly job creation.

4.8.2 Stocks and Flows

This sub-section draws on Hall (1979) and Blanchard and Diamond (1992) to present a model of flows in the labour market. The model is arguably very schematic but serves to introduce the framework. Let there be an amount U of unemployed and E of employed workers in the economy, where the total labour force $L = E + U$ is a fixed number. Employed workers flow into unemployment because a fraction $0 < \lambda < 1$ of current jobs are destroyed every period. (The reasons are not explicitly specified at the moment—it is just assumed that they are no longer viable.) At the same time, a number of new jobs are created, so that a fraction $0 < \Theta < 1$ of the unemployed get into employment; thus, a fraction $1 - \Theta$ stay unemployed.[21] There are no inflows into the labour market from new workers, as the size of the labour force L is fixed.

Thus, unemployment next period (subscripted +1) is made up of the new unemployed plus those who do not manage to escape unemployment in the current period (no time subscript):

$$U_{+1} = \lambda E + (1 - \Theta)U = \lambda(L - U) + (1 - \Theta)U \qquad (4.40)$$

Dividing through by L, we can express everything as percentages in the labour force. In the steady state, the unemployment rate is constant ($u_{+1} = u$). We thus have:

$$u(= U/L) = \lambda(1 - u) + (1 - \Theta)u \qquad (4.40')$$

Rearranging, the unemployment rate is:

$$u = \frac{\lambda}{\lambda + \Theta} \qquad (4.41)$$

Accordingly, the unemployment rate increases with the rate of job destruction/separation (λ) and decreases with the rate of job creation/hiring (Θ). This is intuitive: more inflows into employment (Θ) result in less unemployment, and more outflows (λ) in more unemployment. Hall (2005, table 2.2) gives historical averages of $\lambda \approx 1.5$ per cent and $\Theta \approx$

---

[21] In the context of this sub-section, we should more properly be talking about a *job separation* rate (λ) and a *job finding* rate (Θ). But we use the terminology that will be more appropriate in the subsequent sub-sections.

27.5 per cent for the US, 1967–2004. This would imply a 'natural rate' (or equilibrium) unemployment of the order of 5 per cent; but one would need to consider the movements in and out of the labour force in any numerical implementation of the formula.

Both these rates are assumed exogenous and constant here; the next sub-section will aim to endogenize them and relate them to the economic cycle. But we can use this formula for shedding some light in the dynamics of the labour market over the business cycle. The equilibrium unemployment formula (4.41) suggests that during a recession unemployment is high because the job destruction/employment separation (λ) is high and/or because the job creation/employment finding rate (Θ) is low. Hall (2005) revisits the empirical relevance of the two factors and argues that higher unemployment during the downturns is due to lower job creation and hiring by firms, not because of higher job destruction/firing. This is because the empirical performance of hiring/job creation seems to contain more information and potential to explain unemployment. Among the key underlying reasons may be lower productivity, higher hiring costs, or higher real interest rates, but Hall (2005) argues that the same factors do not apply in every recession; see also Shimer (2005).

But proceeding, let us mention one straightforward extension. Assume that there is population growth rate $p > 0$, so that pL new people come into the workforce every period. Assume further that these new workers need to go into unemployment first before getting a job; then, (4.40) changes to:

$$U_{+1} = \lambda(L - U) + (1 - \Theta)U + pL$$

Then, following the same steps as above, noting that $L_{+1} = (1 + p)L$, it can be seen that the unemployment rate changes to:

$$u = \frac{\lambda + p}{\lambda + \Theta + p} \tag{4.41'}$$

Accordingly, all else equal, the population growth rate increases the unemployment rate because there are not enough new jobs created to absorb all the new entrants into the labour market. But of course, the population growth rate may affect the rates of job creation and destruction when those are endogenized, so that, in general equilibrium, p may have secondary effects on the unemployment rate going via λ and Θ.

4.8.3 Job-Worker Matching and the 'Beveridge Curve'

As mentioned, the flows approach aims to shed more light on unemployment by endogenizing the job creation/hiring rate and the duration of unemployment. The basic tool in this effort is the 'matching function'. The idea is that the particular requirements of jobs and workers' skills do not always match. It is assumed that, within every period, there will be m matches between job openings and workers, where m is given by:

$$m = m(uL, vL) \tag{4.42}$$

Accordingly, matches per period increase in both the number of unemployed workers (uL) and vacancies (vL), where v is the 'vacancy ratio' (number of vacant jobs as a percentage of the workforce). The more the unemployed the more intensive the search, hence more matches; and the more openings, the more likely the search is to be successful.[22] For simplicity, this function is assumed to be characterized by constant returns to scale.

Now, the likelihood of a vacant job being filled up is given by:[23]

$$m(uL, vL)/vL = m(u/v, 1) \equiv m(1/\theta), \quad m'(1/\theta) > 0, \quad (4.43a)$$

where $\theta \equiv v/u$ is the vacancy/unemployment ratio. This ratio may also be thought as an index of tightness in the labour market (intuitively speaking: the demand for labour as a ratio over the total labour force). The *higher* is θ, the better the chances for the unemployed and the lower the likelihood of a firm filling a vacancy; put otherwise, the more vacancies per unemployed worker, the less chance that each vacancy will be filled within a week (say). The elasticity of this function with respect to θ itself is negative: $-1 < \mu(\theta) < 0$.

On the other hand, the probability of the unemployed getting into employment—that is job creation, Θ—is:

$$\Theta \equiv m(uL, vL)/uL = m(1/\theta)(v/u) = m(1/\theta)\theta \quad (4.43b)$$

The elasticity of this is $1 + \mu(\theta) > 0$. Under these assumptions, the equilibrium unemployment equation (4.41) above (or its variant 4.41') gives an inverse relation between the unemployment rate and the 'tightness' rate θ, or alternatively, between the unemployment rate and the vacancy ratio, v. This relation is known the 'Beveridge curve' (see Blanchard and Diamond, 1989).

4.8.4 Endogenizing the Real Wage and the Job Creation/Hiring Rate: Intuition

Because of some frictions, primarily hiring and firing costs, that make a firm's decision to fire a worker not a trivial one, existing jobs attract what we call 'rents'. Holding a job has a value above the value of the best alternative activity; this is true of both firms and workers. For firms, because of the whole process associated with hiring (involving advertising, selecting, and training), there is a surplus between the value of a filled existing position (or job) over and above the marginal revenue product of that same position, even adjusted for the monopoly power of firm. Likewise, for workers, there is a surplus between the wage and the reservation wage or value of leisure. Therefore, those seeking jobs are prepared to spend some time looking for jobs, even if that involves being unemployed for a while. The prospect of a job paying above the reservation wage (as all do because of rents) makes this worthwhile. Since there is a surplus for both worker and firm, there is a question of how to split it, or in other words, what value the wage should have. Here, it is assumed that the firm and the worker engage in bilateral bargaining, and obtain the Nash solution (not the

---

[22] It is worth pointing out the formal similarity between the matching function and the aggregate production function: the unemployed and the vacant jobs combine (somehow) to 'produce' successful matches.
[23] In this formula, we shall make use of the constant returns-to-scale property.

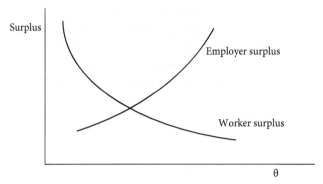

Figure 4.6. Employer and worker surpluses from a given job

Nash equilibrium, which is a non-cooperative game concept): They agree on a wage such as to (jointly) maximize the product of surpluses of each party.

From this process, apart from the determination of the real wage, an endogenous hiring rate also results. To see this, consider the Figure 4.6, due to Hall (2005). The firm's surplus from a job opening (generally, disregarding the fact that this may be different to employer and employee) is plotted against the job finding (or hiring) rate (which we approximate by the job creation rate Θ above—but we can use θ and Θ interchangeably as they are positively related by 4.43b). As the surplus rises, the employer is prepared to make more recruitment effort. Hence the locus showing relation between the employer's surplus and the hiring rate is upward-sloping.

For the worker, the surplus can be thought of as the gap between wage and the Reservation wage (R). As before, R equals the expected wage available elsewhere; this is: probability of unemployment × unemployment benefit + wage elsewhere × probability of employment elsewhere. For the worker, the opposite reasoning to that of the firm applies. As the job finding rate increases, the value of a given job offer declines: if it is easier to get jobs, I don't think so highly of any particular offer. Therefore, the surplus from a specific wage offer also declines: the employee surplus-hiring rate line is downward-sloping. By determining an appropriate wage, the Nash solution ensures that in equilibrium we are at the intersection of the two curves. This endogenizes the job finding rate, alongside the wage rate. A formal analysis follows in the next sub-section.

4.8.5 Endogenous Wage and Job Creation: A Formal Analysis

This sub-section formalizes the ideas just presented, drawing mainly on Pissarides (2000, chapter 1). First, let us present some notation. Let V_J, V_V, V_E, and V_U represent the value to the firm of an occupied and a vacant job (the first two) and the value to the worker of being employed and unemployed (the last two). These values represent 'asset values' of each respective state; as if, in other words, the firm or workers 'packaged' all the claims on the earnings on the job or state in question into a bond or other asset and traded this bond or asset in financial markets. Each value V would be the price that the respective asset commanded in the market.

Since these are asset prices, they are then linked to other asset prices by arbitrage (riskless buying and selling to get the highest return). In particular, let there be a constant, riskless real rate of interest (available on savings accounts); this will be the opportunity cost of the capital that any investor would commit in buying the various assets mentioned above. The value of any financial asset would be linked to this real rate by the following generic formula:

$$r = \frac{D + \dot{V}}{V} \tag{4.44}$$

The riskless rate of interest (the opportunity cost of the asset) is equal to the dividend the asset pays (D) plus its change of value in the market (or else, capital gain—dotted V), all expressed as a percentage over the value of the asset itself. In the analysis we are pursuing, there will be no capital gain ($\dot{V} = 0$) as we are considering the steady state where all change stops. The 'dividend' though will be made of two parts, the current earnings of the job or state, plus a part that arises from a change in state. As the states come in two mutually exclusive pairs (occupied vs. vacant jobs, and employed vs. unemployed), if a state were to change, the (notional) asset associated with that state would cease to be traded and the owner of the asset would be automatically issued the asset associated with the other state. Thus, if say the unemployed became employed, the owner of the asset associated with the state 'unemployed' would automatically lose that and acquire the asset associated with 'employed'. So, this part of the dividend would be the probability that that state may change times the change in value that would result if that were the case.

Let us begin with the value of a vacancy, V_V. This is given by:

$$rV_V = -c + m(1/\theta)(V_J - V_V) \tag{4.45}$$

The 'dividend' here is made up of a cost (with a negative sign) of search, c, plus the probability of a filling of the vacancy ($m(1/\theta)$) times the change in the asset value from the transition between states (vacancy to occupied job). In equilibrium, moreover, the value of a vacancy is driven down to zero because it is always possible (costlessly) for a firm to create more vacant jobs. So, with $V_V = 0$, the value of an occupied job must satisfy:

$$V_J = c/m(1/\theta) \tag{4.45'}$$

The value of a filled job essentially derives from the fact that there is a cost associated with search (c) divided by the ease by which the vacancy can be filled ($m(1/\theta)$). Thus, a greater firm-search cost raises the value of job (as essentially this cost has been paid by the firm), while easier matching implies that the vacancy state can be changed more easily, hence the investment required (so to speak) for creating a filled job falls together with its value. In other words, the expected value of the job for the firm equals the expected value of searching for it to be filled.

In turn, the asset value of a job satisfies:

$$rV_J = p - w + \lambda(V_V - V_J) \tag{4.46}$$

In analogous fashion as before, the value of a job is such that the opportunity cost of the asset (real interest on the required capital) is equalized to the 'dividend' made up of the price of the good produced from one unit of work (p—not the population growth rate as above) minus the real wage (w) plus the (exogenous and constant) probability of job destruction (λ) times the associated change in value. (Implicitly, it is assumed that each worker produces one unit of good worth a constant relative price p; but analytically, p has the same place as the marginal product of labour; p is exogenous, but w will be determined endogenously later.) Rearranging:

$$V_J = \frac{p - w}{r + \lambda} \qquad (4.46')$$

Essentially we have integrated forward into time; therefore, the value of the job equals the firm profit (p − w) divided by the discount rate r, augmented by the probability that the state may cease to apply (job destruction and separation probability, λ).[24]

Combining (4.45') and (4.46'), we have:

$$p - w = \frac{(r + \lambda)c}{m(1/\theta)} \qquad (4.47)$$

This equation is called the job creation condition. It gives an expression for the surplus the firm derives from the job. Analytically, it replaces the traditional price-setting curve of the Walrasian model of Section 4.3. In competitive equilibrium, p would be equalized to w plus any exogenous monopoly markup. Here, the markup is endogenized with reference to costly job search and matching. Because of costly search, once created, the job is worth more to the firm than the flow of profit (p − w). The cost of search divided by the rate by which jobs are filled and the cost ceases to apply (m) essentially determine the wedge between p and w and the surplus, or rent, that this filled job confers to the firm. Perhaps the most intuitive way of seeing this is by rewriting it as the following, which we may call the 'job creation condition':

$$\frac{p - w}{r + \lambda} = \frac{c}{m(1/\theta)} \qquad (4.47')$$

On the left-hand side, we have the present value of all the surpluses to the firm derived while the job exists. On the right-hand side, we have the present value of the cost of search, as m is the rate at which this cost is expected to disappear. Going back to (4.47), the ease by which a vacancy is filled (m) decreases this surplus because it means that the cost of search (c) will be applied for a smaller period of time. The search cost increases the surplus, while the augmented discount rate increases it. But there are two unknowns to be determined here, the wage rate and the 'tightness' ratio θ. The rest of the analysis aims to determine them.

Turning attention to the worker, we have the following value for the state of unemployment:

---

[24] Such 'death rates' (here, it is the death of a job) generally augment the discount rate as they effectively mean that we discount the future more heavily.

$$rV_U = z + \Theta(V_E - V_U) \tag{4.48}$$

z is the net return that the worker enjoys during search—the value of leisure plus unemployment benefit plus the wage from any odd jobs minus any search costs. This is augmented by the gains from any transition between states. In other words, this formula follows exactly the pattern set out above.[25] The value of employment is:

$$rV_E = w + \lambda(V_U - V_E) \tag{4.49}$$

The return to employment is equalized to the wage rate plus the probability of job destruction/separation, times the associated change in asset value. The rent that the job confers to the worker is the difference between the value of employed and the value of unemployed. From (4.48) and (4.49), this is:

$$r(V_E - V_U) = w - z - (\lambda + \Theta)(V_E - V_U) \tag{4.50}$$

or

$$V_E - V_U = \frac{w - z}{r + \lambda + \Theta} \tag{4.50'}$$

In a similar manner as above, the value of employment over unemployment equals the wage minus the value of leisure discounted by the interest rate and the rate of job destruction (λ) and the rate of the unemployed finding a job (Θ).

The wage rate, as mentioned, is determined by the Nash solution, i.e. joint maximization of the respective rents through bargaining. In other words, the firm and the worker engage in bilateral negotiations so as to maximize the worker's rent (value of work minus value of unemployment, which is the worker's fall-back position—$V_E - V_U$) times the value of the job for the firm minus the value of the vacancy ($V_J - V_V$, but note that $V_V = 0$). Hence, the firm and worker jointly negotiate a wage such as to maximize:

$$\text{Max}_w \quad (V_J)^{1-\beta}(V_E - V_U)^\beta$$

In this, $0 < \beta < 1$ is the bargaining power of the worker and $(1 - \beta)$ of the firm. The first-order condition yields:

$$V_E - V_U = \beta(V_J + V_E - V_U) \tag{4.51}$$

The negotiated wage is such that the rent enjoyed by the worker turns out to be a fraction β (the worker's negotiating power) of the total rents enjoyed by both firm and worker. Substituting out from (4.46'), (4.47), and (4.50), we have:

---

[25] Since unemployment always confers this value, the worker will not take up a job unless the wage is higher than this. That is, z now becomes the worker's reservation wage.

$$(1 - \beta)\frac{w - z}{r + \lambda + \Theta} = \beta\frac{p - w}{r + \lambda} \tag{4.52}$$

or

$$w = \frac{(1 - \beta)(r + \lambda)z + \beta p(r + \lambda + \Theta)}{r + \lambda + \beta\Theta} \tag{4.52'}$$

Accordingly, the real wage is a quasi-average of the return enjoyed by leisure, z, and the value of the product (or marginal product of labour), p. It is instructive to rewrite this as:

$$w = p + \frac{(1 - \beta)(r + \lambda)(z - p)}{r + \lambda + \beta\Theta} \tag{4.52''}$$

This equation replaces the wage-setting curve of the Walrasian model of Section 4.3—but we may still call it the wage curve. Since $z - p < 0$ (by a plausible assumption), the wage is dragged down from the value of product (or marginal product of labour) because the worker's fall-back position is less attractive, so they are prepared to give way. As we have seen, the fact that $p > w$ is necessary for the firm to cover its search costs and engage in the search/hiring process in the first place.

We are now ready to put the model together. There are three key equations, repeated below: the Beveridge curve,

$$u = \frac{\lambda}{\lambda + \Theta}, \tag{4.41}$$

the job creation condition,

$$p - w = \frac{(r + \lambda)c}{m(1/\theta)}, \tag{4.47'}$$

and the wage curve,

$$w = p + \frac{(1 - \beta)(r + \lambda)(z - p)}{r + \lambda + \beta\Theta}. \tag{4.52''}$$

The unknowns are u, w, and θ, with $\Theta = m(1/\theta)\theta$ from (4.43b). Under an exogenous product price (and marginal product of labour, p), we may use the job creation and wage equations (in lieu of the price and wage equations of the traditional model) to determine the real wage $w - p$ and the tightness (θ), and then use the Beveridge curve to determine the unemployment rate, u. Having done that, we recover the vacancy ratio from the definition $v = u\theta$. The workings of the system are depicted in Figure 4.7 in $(w - p, \theta)$ space.

The job creation condition is downward-sloping essentially because a higher tightness makes it more difficult for a vacancy to be filled and decreases the rate (m) at which that happens; hence the $p - w$ wedge and surplus need to rise—given a p, the real wage needs to fall. The curve shifts *down* (to the broken line) with a rise in the discount rate (r) and the separation/job destruction rate (λ) because those augment the $p - w$ wedge (and decrease

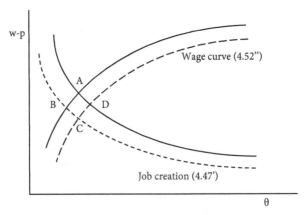

Figure 4.7. Flow labour market equilibrium

$w - p$). For the same reason, so does the search cost by the firm (c). The wage curve is upward-sloping because, with a higher rate of job finding Θ, the weight put on the return to leisure z in the wage negotiation is smaller. Put otherwise, the worker is in a better bargaining position and demands a higher wage. A *reduction* in outside returns z obviously shifts this line *down* (to the broken line), as does a rise in the effective discount rate $(r + \lambda)$, and more bargaining power for the firm $(1 - \beta)$ —recall that $z - p < 0$ by assumption. Thus, a rise in search costs by the firm (A to B) brings about a lower real wage $(w - p)$ and a less tight labour market (less demand for labour and less vacancies). A rise in the effective discount rate (A to C) brings about a lower $w - p$, with ambiguous effects on tightness. More bargaining power for the firm $(1 - \beta$ —A to D) brings about a lower $w - p$ and a tighter labour market. Finally, a rise in productivity, manifested in a rise in the (marginal) product of labour (p) shifts down the wage curve (A to D), with similar effects as the firm's bargaining power. But while $w - p$ falls, it should be clear from (4.52") that the wage proper (w) rises.[26]

The effects on the unemployment rate become obvious if we think that u and the rate of job finding Θ (therefore tightness and θ) are inversely related by the Beveridge curve (4.41): more inflows into employment result in less unemployment. Hence, more search costs by the firm, for instance, result in more unemployment. More bargaining power for the firm, by bringing down the real wage, increases the demand for labour and reduces unemployment.

Things would be slightly more involved if, in line with more standard formulations, we assumed diminishing marginal returns—a marginal product of labour that declines with labour, i.e. $p = p((1 - u)L)$, with $p' < 0$ hence $dp/du > 0$. In this case, any effect that would raise, say, the unemployment rate, would also raise the marginal product of labour p, triggering secondary effects. In particular, the real wage would rise, shifting the job creation and wage curves upwards.

How do these results compare with those of the more standard models, like the wage-price setting? This is richer in terms of considerations paid to flows and the job destruction/separation and the job creation rates. Search costs and vacancies are also something

---

[26] We have been calling $w - p$ the 'real wage'; this is a convenient but imprecise shortcut. The precise statement would be that w, like everything in this section, is real; $w - p$ is the wedge between the real wage and the real marginal product of labour; so, a rise in productivity unambiguously raises the real wage w.

not considered by the standard model, so this model enhances our understanding on these fronts. At the same time, other considerations are lost, like institutional factors such as the welfare state, unions, and taxes (except in the inclusion of some of them in z in a rudimentary form). Also, product market conditions, elasticity, and monopoly power, and the production technology of the firm are absent, except what can be salvaged via the exogenous marginal product of labour p. Of the results obtained, most are intuitive; of those that can be directly compared with the standard model, some are in line with it and some are not. For instance, the bargaining power of the firm lowers the real wage and increases tightness (θ) and decreases unemployment. This is the same as that obtained in the trade union model (Section 4.4) where more bargaining power of the firm pushes us towards the competitive outcome C in Figure 4.3. But the negotiations and bargaining power of this section are not really related to the negotiations between a firm and the union; rather, they are the bilateral negotiations between a firm and an individual potential employee. In this respect, the bargaining power is more akin to the monopolistic power of the individual worker (v) in the basic wage-price setting framework of Section 4.3. But in that framework, let us recall, a rise in the monopoly power of the firm in product markets unambiguously reduces the real wage and increases unemployment. While the effect on the real wage is the same as here, the effect on unemployment is the opposite.

As mentioned, this model has now become the dominant, 'canonical' framework for macro-labour market analysis. The instigators of the approach, Peter Diamond, Dale Mortensen, and Christopher Pissarides have shared a Nobel Prize in Economics. Indeed, the model advances our understanding of labour market flows and brings in a variety of considerations that are not present in other models. There are numerous applications in a busy literature that cannot be surveyed in any detail here; e.g. Pissarides (2013) studies the unemployment during the 'Great Recession' (2007–9) by applying the analysis related to the Beveridge Curve. Nevertheless, one may wonder whether, at a time of online searches and abundant information, an approach built exactly on costly and time-consuming search can be really fruitful. Is the incidence of high unemployment really the result of lack of information on either side of the market and the mismatch between available jobs and the characteristics of candidates? This scepticism is mirrored in some prominent studies. Shimer (2005) finds that the model performs poorly in predicting the behaviour of vacancies, unemployment, and the real wage over the business cycle; which is precisely the focus and supposed strength of the model, one might add. Shimer (2005) argues that the main weakness of the model is the assumption of a flexible real wage and the absence of any wage rigidity. Using US data, Sahin et al. (2014) find that job-candidate mismatch can only explain at most one-third of the variation in the unemployment rate. This is not negligible and suggests a useful role for this model in the analysis of unemployment; at the same time, it suggests that there is a role, perhaps substantial, for other models, too.

4.9 Technical Progress and Unemployment

We now turn to the vexed issue of technological progress and unemployment. The issue is quite topical, as we hear reports that the internet- and artificial intelligence-based progress is about to generate automation, robotization, etc, with the large-scale loss of jobs in a wide range of industries. The state of the art of theory on this front may not be as developed as we would like it to be. In this section, we review what theory there is on the topic; we arrange discussion according to horizons, from the (very) long, to the medium, and to the short run.

4.9.1 Technology and Unemployment in the Long Run

The starting point is again the standard price and wage setting schedules of Section 4.3, repeated below (without taxes):

$$w = MPL[(1 + \mu)y^{1-b}]^{-1/b} \qquad (4.5)$$

$$w = R(1 + v)(y)^d \qquad (4.6)$$

Changes in technology (and productivity more generally) manifest themselves in rises in the marginal product of labour (MPL). In terms of Figure 4.2, this implies that the price schedule (4.5) shifts right. The result is that both the real wage and employment increase. In other words, rises in productivity including technology benefit employment (and reduce unemployment) and also the real wage (increase it) because essentially firms can afford to offer greater real wages and/or hire more people without reducing profit margins. So, technical progress, and a rise in productivity more generally, are good developments. On the other hand, this result conflicts with casual observation, which suggests that every time a firm improves its technology, it most likely sheds some of its workforce.[27] Another problem with the above result is that productivity and technology have improved quite dramatically over the last two centuries in industrial countries (more precisely, since the Industrial Revolution in the last quarter of the eighteenth century); however, increases in employment surely cannot have been so dramatic, as the population of industrialized countries has been rather stationary in the last few decades of the twentieth century. Is there a way of reconciling the theoretical result with the casual observation mentioned above and the intriguing realization that employment, unlike productivity, cannot keep growing forever?

Let us go back to basics. Let us start from the observation that a rise in technology or productivity may be 'used' in different ways.[28] If we schematically write:

$$Y = T \times L,$$

i.e. output = technology × employment (given a constant capital stock), then a rise in technology T could produce the following two polar results:

---

[27] This observation has prompted many movements of workers to oppose, sometimes by violent action, the implementation of new technology by their firms—see Saint-Paul (1998).

[28] Productivity is a more general term than technology, which it encompasses. Besides technology, productivity is affected by such factors as quality of human capital, education, and skills; structure and organization in the private sector; quality of public services. Of these, technology is the factor most likely to deliver sustainable increases in productivity over long periods of time. For this reason, we shall focus on technology in the rest of this section; but many of the considerations here could be made with reference to productivity more generally.

(a) A fall in employment by an equal percentage as the technical progress, while keeping output constant (formally: $dL/L = -dT/T$, while $dY = 0$);

(b) A rise in output by an equal percentage as the technical progress, while keeping employment constant (formally: $dY/Y = dT/T$, while $dL = 0$).

There may of course be any number of intermediate cases which would combine a partial rise in output (less than equiproportional to technical progress) with a fall in employment (again, less than equiproportional to the rise in T).

Which view may be closer to reality? Here, it may be useful to distinguish between two perspectives:

- That of a firm which has given more or less output targets (at least in the short run), determined by its perception of market share, etc. If so, technological growth will lead to economizing on labour. If one then adopts the firm manager's viewpoint, one might be more inclined towards view (a)—employment is hurt;
- The aggregate economy's perspective, which may hold that output is flexible as the economy grows over time. (Hence, this is a longer run perspective.) As will be seen in Chapter 9 on growth, technical progress causes many firms and industrial processes to become obsolete and close over time. At the same time, lots of innovations occur (this is the way by which technological advances manifest themselves), and new firms spring up to put them in practice.[29] The net effect is that the number of firms and aggregate output do expand over time, although with humps and bumps, not smoothly. Thus, from an aggregate point of view, there are no fixed output targets over the long run; if so, one would be more inclined towards view (b)—the gains in technology are used to augment output with minimal effects on employment.

Empirically, one can consider the level of technology (the cutting edge, state-of-the-art technology), the unemployment rate, and the real wage over time for the twentieth century. Technology can be proxied by the output per person. Output per person shows a very distinct and clear trend over time. For example, over the last 100 years, output-per-person has increased by an order of 10. This of course reflects the accumulation of capital as well, but part of the growth is due to technical progress as well. If one looks at the unemployment rate, though, there is clearly no trend over the very long run—unemployment fluctuates around the 5–10 per cent levels most of the time (with well-known exceptions like in the Great Depression in the 1930s and other more limited incidents). Of course, a 5 per cent unemployment rate is very different from a 10 per cent one, the human suffering involved much greater in the latter case, but for the purposes of our discussion, one fact is clear: the unemployment rate shows no trend over time, so it cannot basically be associated with the level of technology. Given enough time, the unemployed will find their ways towards new opportunities for employment (the economy grows most of the time), so employment does not suffer. The clear trend in technology, the manifold improvement in it over the decades, is mirrored in other variables, notably real output, the real wage, and (to a much lesser extent) a decline in hours worked. In other words, the technical

---

[29] There is thus a process of 'creative destruction' according to the prominent twentieth-century Austrian economist Joseph Schumpeter—creation through destruction of the old. More in Chapter 9 on growth.

sophistication of industrial societies has been mirrored in rises in living standards, the average real wage, and a decline in hours (a 40-hour week, holidays, etc, in the place of the 70-hour week common at the early twentieth century).

This suggests a picture whereby the unemployment rate u remains roughly constant over time, and where the real wage w grows perpetually. In terms of the price-wage setting (4.5–6), let MPL grow at the exogenous rate of technical progress g over time, so that $MPL_t = (1 + g)^t MPL_0$, and the real wage grow at rate g^w, i.e. $w_t = (1 + g^w)^t w_0$, and $w_t = (1 + g^w)w_{t-1}$. If we further assume that the reservation wage is simply the wage last period $(R_t = w_{t-1})$ as in Section 4.7 above, and if we replace y_t by $1 - u_t$,[30] the system is rewritten as:

$$w_t = MPL_t \left[(1 + \mu)(1 - u_t)^{1-b}\right]^{-1/b} \tag{4.53}$$

$$w_t = w_{t-1}(1 + v)(1 - u_t)^d = \frac{w_t}{1 + g^w}(1 + v)(1 - u_t)^d \tag{4.54}$$

We can solve the system by starting from the wage equation (4.54), in which the real wage cancels out across the two sides, essentially because the wage on the left-hand side also affects the reservation wage on the right-hand side. As the rate of growth of the wage g^w is constant across time (in the steady state), so is the unemployment rate u. Furthermore, from the price-setting equation (4.53), we get that the real wage is proportional to MPL, with unemployment and firms' markup providing a constant factor of proportionality. Now, if w and MPL are proportional at all times, they must grow at a common rate, i.e. $g = g^w$. In other words, the real wage absorbs all the technological gains, without employment being affected. It grows at the same rate g as real output, and the 'wage bill' wL remains a constant fraction over real output; therefore, the profit rate also remains constant.

In terms of Figure 4.2, the technical progress shifts the price curve up (and right), moving us up the wage curve. But workers are aware of this technical progress and incorporate it into their reservation wage. As that is updated, the wage curve also shifts up (and left), so that eventually we are moving vertically up from point A—to point LR (= long run) in Figure 4.8: The real wage increases, but there is no effect on employment or unemployment. From the wage equation (4.54), we can solve in a straightforward manner for the unemployment rate, which is seen to be affected negatively by the exogenous rate of technical progress g and positively by the workers' monopoly power and markup in their services v. So, the level of technological sophistication is not related to unemployment, but its rate of growth reduces unemployment—as it effectively reduces the reservation wage. In turn, from the price equation (4.53), the unemployment rate and firms' monopoly power and markup determine the ratio of real wage to productivity— the higher the markup, the lower this ratio, and the higher the unemployment, the higher the ratio.

---

[30] Strictly speaking, it should not be the real output itself that should enter the price- and wage-setting equations, but the output gap, the difference between actual minus natural output.

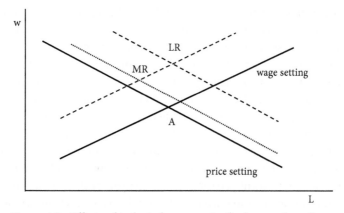

Figure 4.8. Effects of technical progress in the long and medium runs

So, where does this introductory discussion leave us? The aggregate, economy-wide perspective seems to make sense on theoretical grounds (after considering 'creative destruction' and the price-setting framework) and is more in line with facts.[31] So, an initial conclusion must be that from an aggregate point of view, technology is used in expanding output, at least over the long run, while not affecting unemployment much. Does this mean that technical progress does not impinge on unemployment *at all*? No, before one forms a reasonably full picture, one needs to consider at least three other perspectives: different horizons like the medium and short runs; the effects of the rate of growth of technology; and the effects of 'skills biased' technical progress.

4.9.2 The 'Medium' Run

In the medium run, there may develop some problems that have been similar to the persistence of unemployment in Europe, see Blanchard (1997). We saw above that the exogenous growth rate of technology is incorporated into workers' aspirations and wage claims via the continual updating of the reservation wage. But what happens if workers get it wrong—if they misperceive for a while this rate of growth of technology and of the economy as a whole? The question is relevant to the European experience. After about a generation of glorious growth in the aftermath of World War II (*les trentes années glorieuses*, 1945–75), growth in Europe markedly slowed down from the mid-1970s. But that may not have been apparent to workers who may have continued for some time to conduct wage negotiations on the erroneous belief that growth continued at its high pace. What happens then? Figure 4.8 has the answer. From the initial point A, let the wage curve shift upwards by the same amount as before, reflecting workers' belief that growth continues as before. But the growth rate of technology is now less, and thus the price-setting curve has shifted upwards by less than before. Point MR (= medium run) results: the wage has increased by less than if the growth had not slowed down (i.e. if we were at

---

[31] As an aside to that, we could mention that, to think of the economy like a giant big firm (leading us to reason that technical progress hurts unemployment) would be a rather misleading argument. This would be a *fallacy of composition*. Sometimes (but not always) it is wrong to perceive of the economy as a giant firm or giant consumer—this would cause us to be misled in our conclusions. The above arguments are an example of this.

LR), but employment has fallen from its level at A and LR. Simple geometry also establishes that if the wage claims had been in line with actual, not perceived, growth, the wage curve would have shifted by less, the wage would have increased by even less but unemployment would have stayed constant, and this will surely be how things will develop given enough time. And there is a further twist, namely that the wage at MR is less than at LR; if workers tried to compensate for that by pushing for further wage claims (shifting the wage curve further upwards), employment would have fallen even further. The upshot is: the unsustainable wage claims by workers mean that employment has fallen. This may explain some of the European experience of high unemployment in the 1980s, as workers were possibly making unsustainable wage claims. The problem with this line of reasoning is of course why high unemployment persisted for the best part of 20 years, a period which was surely enough time for workers to learn to make sustainable wage claims. Hoon and Phelps (1997) gives support to this line of argument: With data from the G7 countries, they report a strong positive association between the change in unemployment and the slow-down in productivity growth. But on the whole, the evidence seems mixed: Muscatelli and Tirelli (2001) find a negative correlation between growth and unemployment for five developed economies while Mortensen (2005) finds no relation; see the last paper for further discussion.

4.9.3 The Short Run and Other Issues

In the short run, things are very unclear. To reflect on this, the empirical literature is very mixed, see for instance the partial reviews of Saint-Paul (1998) and Trehan (2003). The problem here is that the two perspectives we distinguished above both are relevant in the short run. In a nutshell, technical progress enables some firms to economize on labour, while others close because they have been made obsolete by the new technology. So employment suffers. At the same time, some jobs emerge, but this process takes time, so the balance on employment is unclear. In general, the new jobs that emerge will not be in the same sectors or even regions as the old jobs. Thus, costly retraining and relocation is required for the redundant workers to be absorbed in the new jobs, and that is not always easy. For instance, in the late 1970s and 1980s, much of heavy industry in Britain (coal, iron, shipbuilding, etc.) closed down. These industries were heavily concentrated in the north of the country. Starting from the 1980s, however, new jobs were created in the emerging sectors of services, catering, IT, also in established ones like finance, etc. These jobs were however mostly in the south of the country. Due to the high retraining and relocation costs, the North of England lost an entire generation in unemployment. Such reallocations are more turbulent the faster the *rate of growth* of technical progress (as opposed to its level). The 'sectoral shifts hypothesis' (Lilien, 1982) suggests that sectoral reallocations are responsible for unemployment because of the above reasoning. This line of explanation for unemployment has now fallen out of fashion but deserves more attention. These ideas are not far away from the effects suggested by 'Schumpeterian growth' and 'creative destruction'. The policy implication is that retraining and mobility of workers is important in order to minimize the inevitable sectoral reallocation that occurs in market economies. In relation to Europe, such mobility between jobs has been argued to be inhibited by social security provisions (Lazear, 1990; Addison and Grosso, 1996), hiring and firing costs (Bentolila and Bertola, 1990), and other arrangements in the labour markets; we review those in more detail in the next section.

Finally, one needs to consider the fact that technical progress does not affect all jobs and firms equally. Above, we assumed that technology determines 'the' marginal product of labour. What if there are, though, various types of jobs whose marginal products are not equally affected by technology? The 'skills-biased technical progress hypothesis' (e.g. Blanchard and Katz, 1997; Autor et al., 2006; Violante, 2008) starts from the premises that technology affects in a favourable way the productivity and the demand for the skilled workers, those that possess the skills, education, and human capital required to fully utilize the new technologies, while it leaves the unskilled largely unaffected. If this is the case, then the labour demand for the skilled should rise over time, whereas the demand for the unskilled is not affected by the technologies and remains stagnant. This may be a cause for two effects: the rising wage inequality observed in recent decades (which will be discussed in Chapter 10),[32] and the emergence or deepening of the dual labour markets discussed in Section 4.6. In this case, unemployment may rise first among the unskilled sector, and then in the entire economy. But the empirical relevance of this is not clear: For instance, Nickell and Layard (1999, section 9) review the evidence and conclude that such biased technical progress can explain the big wage differentials in the UK and US but not unemployment in the OECD economies in general. See Autor (2010) and Goos et al. (2014) for more recent thinking and evidence on this topic, which emphasizes the polarization in the labour markets.

4.10 The European Unemployment Puzzle: 'Shocks' vs. 'Institutions'

We now turn to reviewing the debates and associated empirical issues surrounding the rise in the European unemployment rate in the last 40 years. As mentioned in Section 4.2, European unemployment tended to be higher than the US level post-1975, whereas earlier the opposite was the case. This has raised questions and criticisms on whether the European labour markets were too rigid; rigidity and 'Eurosclerosis' were very much the buzzwords in the 1980s and 1990s.

Did Europe have too generous unemployment insurance (unemployment benefits), or employment protection and similar legal and institutional frameworks? Did such provisions discourage labour supply and impede the smooth functioning of labour markets? Did employment protection protect workers in times of recession (as was intended) but discourage businesses from hiring workers in good times (as they would not be able then to lay them off when times turned more difficult)? Did European trade unions, in their efforts to protect worker interests, push wages too high? Did European countries have too high taxation?

These are the questions that will occupy us in this section. Obviously, the answers can be controversial. On the one side of the argument, labour market rigidity can stifle market potential; on the other, too much liberalization (often called 'neoliberalism') can harm workers' interests. But it is also important to 'get things right' and put in place sound

---

[32] Such skills-biased technical progress is said to raise the 'college premium', the difference in the wages of those with university education and those without.

institutional frameworks and labour market structures that foster employment. If such 'institutions' matter and you ignore that, you end up with high unemployment; if they do not but policy-makers pursue market liberalization programmes in vain, they will just end up with inequality and poverty.

4.10.1 Taxation

One argument that has been advanced is that Europe has too much taxation. A good review of the state-of-the art knowledge on the effects of taxes in the labour market is Nickell et al. (2005). As mentioned, there are two types of taxes, income and consumption taxes, while a third (payroll taxes) includes taxes such as national insurance contributions by both employee and employer. In his review, Nickell (1997) concludes that there is very little evidence that individual types of tax have any differential effects, hence they are lumped as follows:

$$\frac{W(1 - t_1)(1 - t_2)}{P(1 + t_3)} \approx w(1 - T), \quad T \equiv t_1 + t_2 + t_3$$

Income (t_1) and payroll (t_2) taxes reduce the net take-home pay, while consumption taxes (t_3) raise the price level. The total effect of these taxes, when lumped, is to reduce the net take-home pay by their sum T (approximately). The sum of the rates of tax T is often called the 'tax wedge'.

All types of tax may be thought of as shifting the wage curve up and to the left, as workers try to shoulder some of the tax burden off to firms, tending to produce a higher real before-tax wage and lower employment. The empirical task is to determine the empirical magnitude of the rise in w and fall in L. Nickell et al. (2005) reviews existing empirical studies of the effects of the tax wedge T. There seems to be a reasonable consensus that a rise, say, of T by 10 per cent increases unemployment by about 2 per cent and a rise in T by 1 per cent increases total labour costs for firms by probably about 0.5 per cent. As Nickell et al. (2005) argues, these numbers are considerable but not dramatic.

The effects of taxation on the labour market is a rather complicated issue, reflecting in part the complicated nature of most tax systems themselves. Just as a reminder of these complexities, consider two additional issues. First, these taxes have been assumed above to be flat-rate, but in practice they are progressive (the higher the income, the higher is the tax rate that applies); progressivity may also play a role. Second, the tax rate, alongside other social security provisions, affects not only the flows from employment to unemployment, but also from employment to outside the labour market altogether, which may happen e.g. when a higher tax (allowance) persuades someone to take early retirement.

How do tax considerations fare in explaining the rise of post-1980 unemployment, particularly European? Nickell et al. (2005, table 2) gives an idea of the tax wedge in industrialized economies. Two contrasts seem to stand out. Across countries, continental Europe tends to have higher tax rates than the 'Anglo-Saxon' ones. Over time, T rose from typical values of 40–50 per cent and 30 per cent for the two groups in the 1960s, to higher by at least 10 per cent in all cases in the late 1980s; they have fallen a little since then. If a rise in

T by 10 per cent produces a rise in the unemployment rate by 2 per cent, this is not an adequate explanation for either the general rise in unemployment in the 1980s or the difference between European and US unemployment rates, as both the overall rise and the difference have been greater than 2–3 per cent. Hence, we now turn to reviewing other possible explanations.[33]

4.10.2 The Rise in European Unemployment: Demand- vs. Supply-Side Explanations

There has been no shortage of possible explanations for European unemployment—good overviews of the debate are given in Blanchard and Summers (1986), Alogoskoufis et al. (1995), and Nickell and Layard (1999). The culprits may broadly be categorized as demand- and supply-side exogenous developments. On the demand side, after the pretty chaotic 1970s, there came restrictive demand policies in many countries in order to combat inflation. In the US, there was the monetary-policy-led so-called Volcker disinflation 1979–81 (from the then Fed chairman Paul Volcker); in the UK, there was the new conservative government of Margaret Thatcher, 1979 onwards, ushering in a completely new philosophy and methodology on how to conduct monetary policy; in continental Europe, various member-countries of the European Monetary System (including France and Belgium) embarked in restrictive fiscal and monetary policies in order to meet the requirement of the system (basically, to shore up the exchange rates). Often, but not exclusively, the restrictive policy stance manifested itself in high real interest rates. So, the 1980s were a period of fiscal and monetary retrenchment—see Ball (1999) for a discussion of policy developments in the 1980s.[34]

The problem with such demand-side explanations, in the eyes of many, is that they were essentially one-off developments (the shift to the new policy regime was only once), whereas unemployment rose permanently; and, as Blanchard and Summers (1986) note, they were not accompanied by any great disinflation (inflation did not come down until the 1990s), so there must have been something structural and supply-side in the rise of unemployment. Ball (1999) is a notable exception which challenges the conventional wisdom that the structural unemployment rate is entirely supply-side. It argues that unemployment rose permanently in those countries (mainly in Europe) which continued to pursue contractionary policies in the face of the recession in the early 1980s; in contrast, those countries that reverted to expansion after the initial disinflationary policy shock managed to have only short-run increases in unemployment. The Ball (1999) argument of the longer term relevance of demand shocks on unemployment is in rather sharp contrast to much current mainstream theory that emphasizes only supply-side factors. This story is underpinned on more recent evidence by the same author (Ball, 2009) on hysteresis.

---

[33] It is interesting to observe that there was a spate of OECD-sponsored papers in the 1990s arguing forcefully the case of taxes harming employment and (implicitly) for reducing them—see Nickell (2005) for references.

[34] With the notable exception of expansionary fiscal policy in the US under President Ronald Reagan (1980–8). The peculiar combination of restrictive monetary policy and expansionary fiscal policy has been termed Reaganomics—and may have been responsible for high interest rates, overvalued dollar, and ballooning US budget and current account deficits. Most of this policy mix was contractionary for the US; for Europe, the overvalued dollar was good news but the capital flows towards the US due to high interest rates were not good for firm profitability and employment.

The current mainstream position on the relevance of supply-side factors for structural unemployment goes as far back as Bruno and Sachs (1985). One supply-side development was the dual oil price increases, which occurred in 1973 and 1979 but were rather short-lived ('shocks'). So, to argue that this explains unemployment in the 1980s and 1990s, one has to explain carefully such a long persistence of unemployment; how such a shock had effects almost 20 years later. Another shock that occurred was the slowdown in product-ivity growth that occurred at around 1975; this line of explanation meets similar difficulties as the oil price shock explanation. For this reason, yet another line of explanation emphasizes the relevance of 'labour market institutions'; by being permanent, such insti-tutions perhaps hold the promise of offering a convincing explanation. Or do they? Below, we take up each in turn.

4.10.3 'Eurosclerosis' and the Shocks vs. Institutions Debate

The important labour market 'institutions', or institutional arrangements, include trade union power, social security provisions like unemployment benefits, employment protec-tion, and minimum wages. An additional feature is taxes, which we have commented upon above. We have also commented on unions and unemployment benefits. Employment protection are various restrictions on the amount of layoffs as a percentage of its labour force each firm can do within a certain period of time. These restrictions aim to protect workers but can potentially harm employment as the firms may be reluctant to hire in good times in the knowledge that they will not be able to lay workers off in a downturn. Equally, minimum wages aim to give workers a decent wage but may harm unemployment by pushing up the wage level. Yet another feature is 'active labour market policies' like the welfare-to-work programmes in the UK which assist retraining and re-entry into employ-ment. Such 'institutions' are long-standing features so hold the potential to explain unemployment over a couple decades. But there are also criticisms, starting from the need to empirically quantify these supposed effects of institutions. Thorough investigations have been carried out by numerous studies including Nickell (1997), Nickell and Layard (1999), Nickell et al. (2005), and Blanchard and Wolfers (2000), which the interested reader should consult in the first place.

There appears indeed some evidence that these arrangements harm employment (and total labour force participation). Nickell (1997), in line with Nickell and Layard (1999), concludes that the factors that affect unemployment are the degree of unionization and the absence of effective central coordination in wage bargaining; generous and long-lasting unemployment benefits, whereas active labour market policies reduce unemployment; and taxes as mentioned in the previous sub-section. Factors that do *not affect* unemployment are employment protection and upholding labour standards; shifts in labour demand in favour of skilled workers; and minimum wages.

In general, most labour market institutions are thought to discourage labour market adjustment to competitive outcomes and thereby promote wage rigidity. So, their discus-sion borders the discussion of the related (and politically more charged) issue of rigid European labour markets and 'Eurosclerosis'. Among the prominent supporters of the thesis that 'rigid' (mainly continental) European markets are largely responsible for European unemployment are Siebert (1997), Ljungqvist and Sargent (1998), Addison and Siebert (1999). In addition, Addison and Siebert (1999) praise the UK's 'flexible wage' economy. As mentioned, Nickell (1997) and Nickel and Layard (1999) seem to be more cautious, though not denying an important role for these institutions. For example, noting that the evidence is mixed both among countries and among the individual institutions listed above, Nickell (1997, p. 73) concludes: 'It is clear that the broad-brush analysis that says that European unemployment is high because European labor markets are "rigid" is too vague and probably misleading.' Mortensen (2005) also finds a weak positive correlation between unemployment and employment protection policies among 28 European countries (1992–2003).

Aside from empirical significance, there are several criticisms against the relevance of 'institutions'. First, the skeptical review by Howell et al. (2007) points out a number of difficulties in all this line of literature:

- Reverse causality—if unemployment benefits and unemployment rates are positively correlated, might it be the case that this is because the generosity of the system rises in the times of hardship?
- Fragility of reported estimates—with the significance of coefficients changing drastically when a specification changes even slightly, and different versions of the same paper contain a number of radically different conclusions;
- Endogeneity of the institutional indices that capture the strength of these institutions and are therefore absolutely central to empirical work—but their construction inevitably is as much a matter of judgement as fact.

These difficulties are present in all empirical work but perhaps here more than elsewhere. In the mind of this author, it would be wrong to argue that they invalidate completely the empirical findings reported above; but the contribution of Howell et al. (2007) is to remind us that no empirical conclusions are 'watertight' and that, as a result, such explanations of unemployment are not free of built-in assumptions and judgement.

Secondly, these institutional arrangements have been present for a long time, from the low-unemployment 1960s through the 1980s and 1990s till now—yet the unemployment experience has varied markedly (Blanchard and Wolfers, 2000). Moreover, institutions such as trade unions and employment protection were generally stronger in the 1960s when unemployment was lower, and weaker in the 1980s or 1990s, when unemployment was high. Yet a third difficulty, noted both by Nickell (1997) and Blanchard and Wolfers (2000) is that there is not enough heterogeneity of such arrangements across European countries to explain the heterogeneous unemployment experiences of these countries.

If the explanation of European unemployment based on 'institutions' fails, an alternative line of reasoning would centre on 'shocks'. The 1970s were a decade of shocks and overall macroeconomic turbulence. Among others, there were two oil price shocks (1973 and 1979), a widely suspected productivity slowdown around 1975, and contractionary macroeconomic policy shocks, that were motivated by the need to reduce inflation and were evident in a rise in real interest rates. As we have seen, the first two of these shift the schedules of Figure 4.4 in such a way that employment falls and unemployment rises. A contractionary policy/demand shock causes unemployment to rise in the short run, but most analysts (with the exception of Ball, 1999) would argue that its effect disappears in the medium to long run.

Could such shocks have caused unemployment therefore, instead of the 'institutions' that much of the literature has considered? The difficulty with pursuing this line of reasoning is that these shocks were essentially one-off, temporary occurrences in the 1970s, yet unemployment was high 10 and 20 years later. How could unemployment be so persistent? How is it possible that labour markets did not adjust to such shocks? These observations and difficulties have led Blanchard and Wolfers (2000) to suggest that it is not the labour market 'institutions' per se that are responsible, but the conjunction of shocks with the shocks of the late 1970s and early 1980s. In other words, the labour market arrangements were sustainable and appropriate until the need for adjustment arose because of those shocks; at which point, labour market adjustment was inhibited by the inflexibility built into the labour market by these institutions. Blanchard and Wolfers (2000) present fairly convincing evidence along these lines. See also Fitoussi et al. (2000) and Howell et al. (2007).

In an important rejoinder, Nickell et al. (2005) re-evaluate the evidence. Their results are worth quoting at some length as they are informative about institutions, but also because they do not find the interaction that Blanchard and Wolfers (2000) found:

'So given the dramatic rise in European unemployment from the 1960s to the 1980s and early 1990s, how much of an overall explanation do our institutional variables provide? Consider the period from the 1960s to 1990–95. Over this period, the unemployment rate in Europe, as captured by the European OECD countries considered here, rose by around 6.8 percentage points. How much of this increase do our institutional variables explain? [. . . T]he answer is around 55 per cent.

. . .

So what proportions of this latter figure are contributed by the different types of institution? Changes in the benefit system are the most important, contributing 39 per cent. Increases in labour taxes generate 26 per cent, shifts in the union variables are responsible for 19 per cent and movements in employment protection law contribute 16 per cent. So the combination of benefits and taxes are responsible for two-thirds of that part of the long-term rise in European unemployment that our institutions explain.

[. . . I]interactions between . . . these institutions and shocks . . . makes no significant additional contribution to our understanding of OECD unemployment changes.'

Nickell et al. (2005, Conclusions)

As always, the reader is invited to make up their own mind!

Notes on the Literature

The macroeconomics of unemployment and labour markets in general is a vast subject. We may distinguish two phases of the literature: the earlier one, with a lot of emphasis on formal modelling (unions, wage equations, etc.); and a later one, dominated by the experience of European unemployment, institutions, and the possible effects of market liberalization. Good places to start, regarding the former, are Nickell (1990), Layard et al. (1991), and Manning (1995), all of which place the debates on unemployment in the wider context of macroeconomic debates (Nickell is by far the most detailed). About the shocks vs. institutions debate on European unemployment, good reviews are by Saint-Paul (2004) and Blanchard (2006). The current debates on the polarization of labour markets are introduced by Autor (2010). A description of institutions with good background discussions are provided in Bean (1994), Nickell and Layard (1999) and Calmfors and Holmlund (2000). For the flows approach, Hall (1979) is a key paper; Mortensen and Pissarides (1994) and Pissarides (2000) are good introductions.

Guidance for Further Study

Minimum wages

Minimum wages are thought to be another of the institutions that aim to protect workers yet raise wages and unemployment. However, the evidence is not overwhelming. If anything, they raise the wages at the bottom end of the distribution, leaving the others unaffected and having limited effects on employment. See the early study by Dolado et al. (1996), Draca et al. (2008) for the UK experience, and IZA (2014) for the German experience.

Implications of all these analyses

How can unemployment be practically reduced? The interested reader is invited to see the analyses by Van Reenen (2008) on the 'welfare-to-work' programmes and Saint-Paul (2008) on the trade-off between measures that promote the (European) 'social model' and those that promote efficiency. Blanchard and Giavazzi (2003) consider the effects of liberalization or deregulation in goods and labour markets.

Labour market segments

We have mentioned above the fact that the headline unemployment rate masks differences between different segments of the labour market. The male-female unemployment rate differential has attracted some analysis; see Blau and Khan (1996) and Azmat, Guell and Manning (2006) for portals into this literature.

Technical progress, structural change, and unemployment

There is talk that the fast progress of internet- and artificial intelligence-based automation is now threatening jobs big time. Of course, predictions here are not safe. But our best forecasts about what is in store are described in a report by the *Guardian* (2019). Of course, as with all structural change, Information Technology (IT) will not only destroy jobs but will also create jobs, particularly in those countries that are 'IT-literate'; see OECD (2019) on the state of IT literacy in various countries. But the net effect of IT on jobs is very likely to be negative; this is because the jobs that will be destroyed will be labour-intensive (manual workers, professional drivers, bank clerks) and therefore many; while the jobs that will be created (analysts, programmers) will be based on economies of scale and network externalities (a small number of programmers for the entire network) and therefore few. If so, we are likely to see a great polarization of the labour market (Autor, 2010), with some well-paid jobs among a sea of low-paid or unemployed. The ethical and moral implications of such predictions are highlighted in Skidelsky (2019). Summers (2014) considers where major new sources of employment can be found for the jobs that are threatened by automation (in the care for ageing populations?). Finally, Rogerson (2008) considers another dimension in the differences between the US and European unemployment, namely structural change and in particular the differences in the wage sector.

References

Addison, J.T. and J.-L. Grosso (1996): Job Security Provisions and Employment: Revised Estimates, *Industrial Relations: A Journal of Economy and Society*, 35 (October), 585–603.

Addison, J., and S. Siebert (1999): Regulating European Labour Markets: More costs than benefits? Institute of International Economics Hobart Paper No. 183.

Alogoskoufis, G., and A. Manning (1988): Wage Setting and Unemployment Persistence in Europe, Japan, and the USA, *European Economic Review*, 32, 698–706.

Alogoskoufis, G., C. Bean, G. Bertola, D. Cohen, and G. Saint-Paul, Gilles (1995): *Unemployment: Choices for Europe*, Monitoring European Integration 5, London: Centre for Economic Policy Research.

Ashenfelter, O., and D. Card (eds) (1999): *Handbook of Labor Economics*, Amsterdam: North-Holland.

Autor, D. (2010): *The Polarization of Job Opportunities in the U.S. Labor Market: Implications for Employment and Earnings*, The Hamilton Project, Washington, DC: Center for American Progress, April; https://economics.mit.edu/files/5554

Autor, D.H., L.F. Katz, and M.S. Kearney (2006): The Polarization of the US Labor Market, *American Economic Review*, 96(2), 189–94.

Azmat, G., M. Guell, and A. Manning (2006): Gender Gaps in Unemployment Rates in OECD Countries, *Journal of Labor Economics*, 24(1), 1–37.

Ball, L. (1999): Aggregate Demand and Long-Run Unemployment, *Brookings Papers on Economic Activity*, 2, 189–251.

Ball, L.M. (2009): Hysteresis in Unemployment: Old and New Evidence, NBER Working Paper No. 14818, March.

Bean, C. (1989): Capital Shortages and Persistent Unemployment, *Economic Policy*, 8 (April), 12–53.

Bean, C. (1994): European Unemployment: A Survey, *Journal of Economic Literature*, 32, 573–619.

Bentolila, S., and G. Bertola (1990): Firing Costs and Labor Demand in Europe: How Bad is Eurosclerosis? *Review of Economic Studies*, 57(3), 381–402.

Blanchard, O.J. (1986): The Wage Price Spiral, *Quarterly Journal of Economics*, 101 (August), 543–65.

Blanchard, O.J. (1997): The Medium Run, *Brookings Papers on Economic Activity*, 2, 89–158.

Blanchard, O.J. (2006): European Unemployment: The Evolution of Facts and Ideas, *Economic Policy*, 21(45) (January), 5–59.

Blanchard, O.J., and P.A. Diamond (1989): The Beveridge Curve, *Brookings Papers on Economic Activity*, 20 (1), 1–76.

Blanchard, O.J., and P. Diamond (1992): The Flow Approach to Labor Markets, *American Economic Review*, 82(2) (May), 354–9.

Blanchard, O., and F. Giavazzi (2003): Macroeconomic Effects of Regulation and Deregulation in Goods and Labor Markets, *Quarterly Journal of Economics*, 118(3) (August), 879–907.

Blanchard, O.J., and L.F. Katz (1997): What we Know and Do Not Know about the Natural Rate of Unemployment, *Journal of Economic Perspectives*, 11(3) (Summer), 51–72.

Blanchard, O.J., and N. Kiyotaki (1987): Monopolistic Competition and the Effects of Aggregate Demand, *American Economic Review*, 77 (September), 647–66.

Blanchard, O.J., and L. Summers (1986): Hysteresis and the European Unemployment Problem, in S. Fischer (ed.), *NBER Macroeconomics Annual*, Boston: National Bureau of Economic Research, 19–50.

Blanchard, O.J., and L. Summers (1987): Hysteresis in Unemployment, *European Economic Review*, 31(1–2), 288–95.

Blanchard, O.J., and J. Wolfers (2000): The Role of Shocks and Institutions in the Rise of European Unemployment: The Aggregate Evidence, *Economic Journal*, 110 (March), C1–33.

Blanchflower, D.G., and A.J. Oswald (1994): Estimating a Wage Curve for Britain: 1973–90, *Economic Journal*, 104(426), 1025–43.

Blanchflower, D.G., and A.J. Oswald (1995): The Wage Curve, *Journal of Economic Perspectives*, 9(3) (Summer), 153–67.

Blau, F.D., and L.M. Kahn (1996): International Differences in Male Wage Inequality: Institutions versus Market Forces, *Journal of Political Economy*, 104(4), 791–837.

Bruno, M., and J. Sachs (1985): *The Economics of Worldwide Stagflation*, Oxford: Basil Blackwell.

Bulow, J., and L. Summers (1986): A Theory of Dual Labor Markets with Application to Industrial Policy, Discrimination and Keynesian Unemployment, *Journal of Labor Economics*, 4(3), 376–414.

Calmfors, L., and B. Holmlund (2000): Unemployment and Economic Growth: A Partial Survey, *Swedish Economic Policy Review*, 7(1), 107–53.

Calmfors, L., and J. Driffill (1988): Centralisation of Wage Bargaining and Macroeconomic Performance, *Economic Policy*, 6, 13–61.

Dolado, J., F. Kramarz, S. Machin, A. Manning, D. Margolis, and C. Teulings (1996): The Economic Impact of Minimum Wages in Europe, *Economic Policy*, 11(23) (October), 317–72.

Draca, M., R. Dickens, and R. Vaitilingam (2008): The National Minimum Wage: The Evidence of its Impact on Jobs and Inequality, September, LSE CEP Policy Analysis No. 006, http://cep.lse.ac.uk/pubs/download/pa006.pdf

Espinosa, M.P., and C.-Y. Rhee (1989): Efficient Wage Bargaining as a Repeated Game, *Quarterly Journal of Economics*, 104, 565–88.

Fitoussi, J-P., Jestaz, D., Phelps, E.S., and Zoega, G. (2000): Roots of the Recent Recoveries: Labor Reforms or Private Sector Forces? *Brookings Papers on Economic Activity*, 1, 237–91.

Friedman, M. (1968): On the Role of Monetary Policy, *American Economic Review*, 58(1) (March), 1–17.

Friedman, T.L. (2008): The Real Generation X, *New York Times*, 7 December.

Goos, M., A. Manning, and A. Salomons (2014): Explaining Job Polarization: Routine-Biased Technological Change and Offshoring, *American Economic Review*, 104(8), 2509–26.

Gottfries, N. (1992): Insiders, Outsiders, and Nominal Wage Contracts, *Journal of Political Economy*, 100(2) (February), 252–70.

Guardian (2019): Automation Threatens 1.5 Million Workers in Britain, Says ONS, 25 March; https://www.theguardian.com/money/2019/mar/25/automation-threatens-15-million-workers-britain-says-ons?CMP=Share_AndroidApp_Gmail

Hall, R.E. (1979): A Theory of the Natural Unemployment Rate and the Duration of Unemployment, *Journal of Monetary Economics*, 5, 153–69.

Hall, R.E. (2005): Job Loss, Job Finding, and Unemployment in the U.S. Economy over the Past Fifty Years, in M. Gertler and K. Rogoff (eds), *NBER Macroeconomics Annual 2005*, (Boston: NBER, 101–37.

Hoon, H.T., and E.S. Phelps (1997): Growth, Wealth, and the Natural Rate: Is Europe's Job Crisis a Growth Crisis? *European Economic Review*, 41, 549–57.

Howell, D.R., D. Baker, A. Glyn, and J. Schmitt (2007): Are Protective Labor Market Institutions at the Root of Unemployment? A Critical Review of the Evidence, *Capitalism and Society*, 2(1), Article 1.

IZA—Institute for the Study of Labor (2014): Germany's Minimum Wage Experiment: Independent Scientific Evaluation Needed, IZA Compact, March, http://ftp.iza.org/com pacts/iza_compact_en_46.pdf

King, R.G., and S.T. Rebelo (1999): Resuscitating Real Business Cycles, in M. Woodford and J. Taylor (eds), *Handbook of Macroeconomics*, Amsterdam: Elsevier, 927–1007.

Krueger, A., and L. Summers (1988): Efficiency Wages and the Inter-Industry Wage Structure, *Econometrica*, 56 (March), 259–93.

Kydland, F., and E. Prescott (1990): Business Cycles: Real Facts and a Monetary Myth, *Quarterly Review, Federal Reserve Bank of Minneapolis*, 14(2) (Spring), 3–18.

Layard, R., S. Nickell, and R. Jackman (1991): *Unemployment: Macroeconomic Performance and the Labour Market*, Oxford: Oxford University Press.

Lazear, E.P. (1990): Job Security Provisions and Employment, *Quarterly Journal of Economics*, 105(3) (August), 699–726.

Lilien, D.M. (1982): Sectoral Shifts and Cyclical Unemployment, *Journal of Political Economy*, 90(4) (August), 777–93.

Lindbeck, A., and D. Snower (1986): Wage Setting, Employment, and Insider-Outsider Relations, *American Economic Review*, 76, 235–9.

Lindbeck, A., and D.J. Snower (2001): Insiders versus Outsiders, *Journal of Economic Perspectives*, 15(1) (Winter), 165–88.

Ljungqvist, L., and T.J. Sargent (1998): The European Unemployment Dilemma, *Journal of Political Economy*, 106(3), 514–50.

MacDonald, I., and R. Solow (1981): Wage Bargaining and Employment, *American Economic Review*, 71 (December), 896–908.

Malcomson, J.M. (1981): Unemployment and the Efficiency Wage Hypothesis, *Economic Journal*, 91, 848–66.

Manning, A. (1987): An Integration of Trade Union Models in a Sequential Bargaining Framework, *Economic Journal*, 97, 121–39.

Manning, A. (1995): Developments in Labour Market Theory and their Implications for Macroeconomic Policy, *Scottish Journal of Political Economy*, 42(3) (August), 250–66.

Mortensen, D.T. (2005): Alfred Marshall Lecture: Growth, Unemployment, and Labor Market Policy, *Journal of the European Economic Association*, 3(2–3) (April–May), 236–58.

Mortensen, D.T., and C.A. Pissarides (1994): Job Creation and Job Destruction in the Theory of Unemployment, *Review of Economic Studies*, 61(3), 397–415.

Muscatelli, V.A., and P. Tirelli (2001): Unemployment and Growth: Some Empirical Evidence from Structural Time Series Models, *Applied Economics*, 33(8), 1083–8.

Nickell, S. (1990): Unemployment: A Survey, *Economic Journal*, 100 (June), 391–439.

Nickell, S. (1997): Unemployment and Labor Market Rigidities: Europe versus North America, *Journal of Economic Perspectives*, 11(3) (Summer), 55–74.

Nickell, S., and R. Layard (1999): Labour Market Institutions and Economic Performance, in O. Ashenfelter and D. Card (eds), *Handbook of Labor Economics*, Amsterdam: North-Holland, vol. 3C, 3028–84.

Nickell, S., L. Nunziata, and W. Ochel (2005): Unemployment in the OECD since the 1960s. What do we Know?, Economic Journal, 115(500) (January), 1–27.

OECD (2019): *Skills Outlook 2019, Thriving in a Digital World*; http://www.oecd.org/education/oecd-skills-outlook-2019-df80bc12-en.htm

Oswald, A. (1985): The Economic Theory of Trade Unions: An Introductory Survey, *Scandinavian Journal of Economics*, 87, 160–93.

Pissarides, C.A. (2000): *Equilibrium Unemployment Theory*, 2nd ed., Boston: MIT Press.

Pissarides, C.A. (2013): Unemployment in the Great Recession, *Economica*, 80, 385–403.

Rogerson, R. (2008): Structural Transformation and the Deterioration of European Labor Market Outcomes, *Journal of Political Economy*, 116(2) (April), 235–59.

Şahin, A, J. Song, G. Topa, and G.L. Violante (2014): Mismatch Unemployment, *American Economic Review*, 104(11), 3529–64.

Saint-Paul, G. (1991): Dynamic Labor Demand with Dual Labor Markets, *Economics Letters*, 36(2) (June), 219–22.

Saint-Paul, G. (1992): Explaining the Cyclical Behavior of Labor Market Flows: A Dual Perspective, *Economics Letters*, 39(3) (July), 339–43.

Saint-Paul, G. (1998): Does Technical Progress Create Unemployment?, *European Investment Bank Papers*, 3(1), 55–64.

Saint-Paul, G. (2008): Alternative Strategies for Fighting Unemployment: Lessons from the European Experience, *World Economics*, 9(1) (January), 35–55.

Saint-Paul, G. (2004): Why are European Countries Diverging in their Unemployment Experience? *Journal of Economic Perspectives*, 18(4) (Fall), 49–68.

Shapiro, C., and J. Stiglitz (1984): Equilibrium Unemployment as a Worker-Discipline Device, *American Economic Review*, 74 (June), 433–44.

Shimer, Robert (2005): The Cyclical Behavior of Equilibrium Unemployment and Vacancies, *American Economic Review*, 95(1), 24–49.

Siebert, H. (1997): Labor Market Rigidities: At the Root of Unemployment in Europe, *Journal of Economic Perspectives*, 11(3) (Summer), 37–54.

Skidelsky, R. (2019): The AI Road to Serfdom?, Project Syndicate, 21 February; https://www.project-syndicate.org/commentary/automation-may-not-boost-worker-income-by-robert-skidelsky-2019-02

Solow, R. (1979): Another Possible Source of Wage Stickiness, *Journal of Macroeconomics*, 1 (Winter), 79–82.

Summers, L (1988): Relative Wages, Efficiency Wages, and Keynesian Unemployment, *American Economic Review*, 78(2) (May), 383–8.

Summers, L.H. (2014): The Economic Challenge of the Future: Jobs, http://larrysummers.com/2014/07/07/the-economic-challenge-of-the-future-jobs/

Tournemaine, F., and C. Tsoukis (2009): Status Jobs, Human Capital, and Growth, *Oxford Economic Papers*, 61(3) (July), 467–93.

Trehan, B (2003): Productivity Shocks and the Unemployment Rate, *Federal Reserve Bank of San Fransisco Review*, 13–27.

Van Reenen, J. (2008): Big Ideas: Unemployment and Welfare to Work, *CentrePiece—LSE CEP*, 248 (Spring 2008), 2–3.

Violante, G.L. (2008): Skill-Biased Technical Change, in S. Durlauf and L. Blume (eds), *The New Palgrave Dictionary of Economics*, 2nd ed., London: Macmillan, 5938–41.

Yellen, J. (1984): Efficiency-Wages Models of Unemployment, *American Economic Review*, 74 (May), 200–5.

5

Introduction to Dynamic Macroeconomics

This chapter introduces the main concepts and models of macroeconomic dynamics. Having absorbed the lessons of the New Classicals, modern macroeconomic theory is based on the principles of consumer rationality (clear objectives), optimizing behaviour derived from micro-foundations (utility/profit maximization subject to well-specified constraints that describe fully the environment in which the agent operates), and forward-looking behaviour (the utility/profits over the entire life matters). In terms of dynamic macroeconomics, these principles make intertemporal optimization central. Prices/wages are flexible and markets clear: The models of this chapter abstract entirely from New-Keynesian themes (which are reintroduced in some models of business cycles).

In Section 5.1, we introduce some background concepts required in the study of dynamics. Building on this, in Section 5.2, we review a workhorse model of modern dynamic macroeconomics. It is the 'Ramsey model' (or 'Ramsey-Cass-Koopmans' model) and assumes an infinitely lived, intertemporally optimizing, representative agent. As we shall see, the model gives useful results related to the deep structure of the economy; it is also used in policy design and evaluation. In Section 5.3, we extend this model to introduce a more realistic picture of investment based on adjustment costs. Then, in Section 5.4, we analyse money and monetary policy. Finally, in Section 5.5, we change tack and consider a model of 'overlapping generations' who live finite lives; apart from realism, this model is indispensable in studying issues where age structure and demographics are critical, such as government debt and pensions.

5.1 Introduction to Dynamic Optimization

In this section, we introduce some background concepts required in the study of dynamics. The setup is based on a single representative household who lives forever and is the decision-making unit. Its problem is to select its consumption path across its lifetime so as to maximize lifetime utility, subject to the constraints it faces; in other words, the representative agent (household) 'optimizes intertemporally'. Physical capital is the only asset in this model. We abstract from financial assets and the financial structure of the economy; in this way, we focus on production with the minimum analytical apparatus. Aspects of the financial structure will be considered in Chapter 6 in relation to the stock market and Chapter 8 in relation to monetary policy. All capital, as well as labour, belongs to households that rent it to firms to produce. Due to the large number of both firms and households, the rental markets of both capital and labour are perfectly competitive.[1] Until

---

[1] The assumption of a firm that is distinct from the household or individual is in line with the distinction between the firm and its ownership. The assumption that the household, and not the firm, owns the capital and rents it to the firm may appear less realistic; alternatively, we could assume that the firm owns capital and remits

Theory of Macroeconomic Policy. Christopher Tsoukis, Oxford University Press (2020). © Christopher Tsoukis.
DOI: 10.1093/oso/9780198825371.003.0005

we note otherwise, everything is real in this model, including the interest rate; the price level or inflation do not appear.[2]

5.1.1 Methodological Considerations

Dynamic models can be based on either discrete or continuous time. In the former, time takes an integer value $(t = 0, 1, 2, ...)$ while in the latter, time is the real line. Different optimization methods lend themselves to discrete or continuous time: models of continuous time can be solved using the Optimal Control methods, whereas models in discrete time are often solved using a method called Dynamic Programming. The latter is more involved but also more flexible as it can handle stochastic setups. We shall use discrete time here (as we do throughout the book) but we forgo the use of Dynamic Programming; instead, we use an optimization method that resembles as closely as possible static optimization which is slightly more intuitive and does not make taxing technical demands on the reader (the cost will be that it is slightly cumbersome).

Within discrete time, a choice needs to be made concerning the timing of the variables. While flow variables like output, consumption, incomes, investment, and many others, occur and are measured during a specified period (so e.g. C_t is consumption during period t), stock variables like assets and capital are gradually accumulated but measured at a specific point in time. So, the stock of capital active within 2017 can be measured either on 1 January or 31 December 2017, using 'beginning' or 'end-of-period' notation. We shall adopt the 'beginning-of-period' convention: Stocks are measured on 1 January of year t and that is the stock relevant to production during year t. There are subtle differences that result from the convention that has been adopted, but once the basic setup is sound and consistent, one should not get too distracted by details.

5.1.2 Lifetime Utility Maximization

We now describe the behaviour of the representative household, which is the decision-making unit. This household has an exogenous endowment of resources: some initial physical capital obtained from mother earth at the beginning of time and time itself. They also have clear-cut preferences (as a rational agent), formalized in a utility function.

---

profits to households. As long as factor markets (capital and labour) are competitive, the two setups yield equivalent results: see Barro and Sala-i-Martin (1995, chapter 2). The setup here is simpler.

[2] It will of course be objected that both the single, representative-agent and the infinite-life assumptions are absurd. The first is more easily justified: the representative agent is 'society' itself, or a society in which all agents are identical. In other words, this model by construction aims to analyse the behaviour of the average, while completely ignoring distributional issues. There are two justifications for the second assumption: first, analytical convenience: one can have instead a model of 'overlapping generations' which live finite lifetimes as in Section 5.5, which will be more complex. The other reason is that, due to discounting, the practical horizon of the model is not infinite; e.g. after 30 periods, which is not too far off a realistic working life, discounting is quite heavy, even with a small discount rate, so that discounted values become rather small; e.g. with a $\rho = 0.02$ $(= 2\%)$, $(1 + \rho)^{-30} \approx 0.55$ and with $\rho = 0.04$, $(1 + \rho)^{-30} \approx 0.31$.

A useful analytical device is to postulate a 'unit mass' of both households and firms.[3] We shall make a notational distinction between:

- Aggregate variables indicated by capital letters; e.g. C_t is aggregate consumption in period t; due to the unit mass of households, this also equals consumption per household;
- And the corresponding per capita quantities, e.g. c_t; this differs from C_t as household size changes.

The household size is denoted n_t; due again to the unit mass of households, this also equals the total population in the economy. It is assumed to grow at rate $\eta \geq 0$, i.e. $\eta = (n_{t-1} - n_t)/n_{t-1}$ for all t, with $n_0 = 1$. So, per capita and aggregate consumption are linked by $c_t = C_t/n_t$. It is important to note that unemployment is assumed away; also, there is no childhood or retirement. Therefore, available total labour supply equals population times the amount of work that the representative individual chooses to offer.

Formally, the household maximizes lifetime utility U_0:

$$U_0 \equiv \sum_{t=0}^{\infty} (1+\rho)^{-t} u(c_t, l_t, n_t), \quad 0 < l_t < 1 \tag{5.1}$$

This is made up of the sum of period utilities (denoted by u(.)) from the beginning of history (t = 0) till the end of time (t → ∞). The sum is discounted: $\rho > 0$ is the rate of time preference: it subjectively discounts sums of future utility in much the same way as the real interest rate discounts future monetary sums. It is a measure of impatience: a higher ρ implies that future utility sums are discounted more heavily and the individual derives more utility in the near future. Utility in each period, $u(c_t, l_t, n_t)$, involves private per capita consumption c_t and leisure (per person) $1 - l_t$, as work is l_t. The units of time have been chosen such that the individual's total labour endowment is one (one period), and this is allocated between labour and leisure. We also let the size of the household size, n_t, affect utility as discussed in the next sub-section.[4]

The literature has used different specifications of period utility. The additive specification below is quite common as well as simple and informative:

$$U_0 = \sum_{t=0}^{\infty} (1+\rho)^{-t} \left(\frac{c_t^{1-1/\sigma}}{1 - 1/\sigma} - l_t^{\theta} \right) n_t^{\varphi}, \quad \sigma > 0, \sigma \neq 1 \tag{5.1'}$$

A number of parameters are involved here:

- $\sigma > 0$ is the intertemporal elasticity of substitution; it tells us how much the household alters its intertemporal profile of consumption when the incentives (interest rate and rate of time preference) change; more on this later. Empirically, it has been found that

---

[3] This implies that their number is not one, but equal to the number of points that a unit segment contains, i.e. infinite. This device implies that the aggregate and per-firm or per-household variables are the same, since (e.g.) aggregate capital = capital per firm × no. of firms = capital per firm × 1.

[4] It may be asked whether the optimization calculation should be performed only once and when (at t = 0?) or every period. The answer turns out to be that, due to the geometric nature of the discounting scheme, the resulting intertemporal consumption plan will be 'time-consistent': the same plan will result every time the optimization is carried out, so this only needs to take place once, at the beginning of time. The same time-consistency result is obtained if, in continuous time, the discounting scheme is the continuous-time analogue, i.e. the (negative) exponential. See the Guidance for Further Study for information on non-geometric discounting.

this is below unity (Hall, 1988; Havranek et al., 2013) although estimates differ.[5] Attanasio and Weber (2010, section 3) consider 0.6–0.8 as a plausible range. Therefore, we shall assume that $0 < \sigma < 1$.[6] Note that, though not empirically supported, the benchmark case of $\sigma = 1$ is often used in the literature, as then utility simplifies to:

$$U_0 = \sum_{t=0}^{\infty} (1+\rho)^{-t} (\log c_t - \theta l_t + \varphi \log n_t), \quad \sigma = 1 \tag{5.1''}$$

- $\theta > 0$ is the elasticity of leisure, capturing the disutility of work; see the discussion about the Frisch elasticity of labour supply in Chapter 1 for more information.
- $0 \le \varphi \le 1$ parameterizes the extent to which family size matters for the total utility of the entire family. There are arguments that $\varphi = 0$ (family size does not matter) and that $\varphi = 1$ (a family with three children is three times happier than a family of one child). Perhaps both extremes are off the mark, so we allow them both as well as all intermediate values. Another way to view this is to suggest that a proportion $1 - \varphi$ is children (i.e. new entrants) who do not increase any existing family's welfare (such as immigrants). Therefore, one use of φ is to track the effects of immigration, which will be $(1 - \varphi)$ per cent of population growth.

5.1.3 The Household Budget Constraint and the Aggregate Resource Constraint (National Income Accounting)

Aggregate output is divided between consumption and investment (think of a farmer who divides their crop between consumption and seeds for future planting). In a more realistic setup, there would be a government/public sector which would collect taxes and use them for spending; both are suppressed for now. Also, the economy is closed, so there is no foreign trade. This results in the simplified National Income Accounting equation:

$$Y_t = C_t + I_t \tag{5.2}$$

This applies, let us remember, at the household level as well.

Physical capital is built according to the capital accumulation equation:

$$K_{t+1} = I_t + (1 - \delta)K_t \tag{5.3}$$

Where I is gross investment and $0 < \delta < 1$ is the depreciation rate of physical capital.[7] This applies to both the aggregate and the household level and says that net capital accumulation during period t $(K_{t+1} - K_t)$ equals gross investment minus depreciation occurring

---

[5] The 'meta-study' by Havranek et al. (2013) finds a mean elasticity of intertemporal substitution of 0.5; but there is heterogeneity across households: poor households substitute consumption across time periods less easily because their consumption is in greater proportion made up of necessities, which are difficult to substitute intertemporally. A higher participation in the stock market also enables greater substitution; and micro-studies show greater elasticities than macro-studies.

[6] $1/\sigma$ equals the coefficient of 'relative risk aversion', hence this specification is called the Constant Relative Risk Aversion (CRRA) utility. We do not emphasize this interpretation in this book.

[7] This is the expenditure required to fix the wear and tear of physical capital. We review depreciation more thoroughly in Chapter 11 (Section 11.3). As a ball-park figure, that may be of the order of 2.5 per cent per year for office buildings, while it will likely be 5–10 per cent for plant (factory buildings), machinery, and vehicles.

during the period. (5.2) and (5.3) can be combined into the following period-by-period resource constraint of this economy:

$$C_t + K_{t+1} - (1 - \delta)K_t = Y_t = r_t K_t + w_t L_t \tag{5.4}$$

On the right-hand side, we have income earned by each factor of production—capital (rK) and labour (wK); more on these later. On the left-hand side, we have the uses of these resources: consumption plus gross investment (= net increase in physical capital + replacement of depreciating capital, δK_t). Note the implicit assumption that both physical capital and consumption are made up of essentially the same material (a crop; or maybe just 'material'), so one can be changed immediately and costlessly into the other (while obeying the resource constraint) if that is dictated by optimal planning.

5.1.4 The Intertemporal Budget Constraint

(5.4) applies every period t and constrains the amount available for private consumption (C). But using borrowing or lending (on which more below), a household may be able to shift resources between periods, e.g. they may consume more than earning by borrowing against future resources or earn more than consuming and save the difference for the future. In other words, if borrowers and lenders are available contemporaneously, a resource constraint need not apply in each and every period; rather, the household is constrained to match resources and uses of them only intertemporally, across the entire (infinite) life or history. The real constraint is only a lifetime one, which may be derived by consolidating the period-by-period budget constraint (5.4); first rewrite it as:

$$K_{t+1} = (1 + r_t - \delta)K_t + w_t L_t - C_t \tag{5.4'}$$

We see that the interest rate and the depreciation rate are consolidated into a composite discount factor that discounts future sums. This holds for any time t; for instance, for the initial period 0 as:

$$\frac{K_1 - w_0 L_0 + C_0}{(1 + r_0 - \delta)} = K_0$$

For period 1, it will be:

$$\frac{K_2 - w_1 L_1 + C_1}{(1 + r_1 - \delta)} = K_1$$

Inserting this into the period 0 constraint to replace K_1, we get:

$$\frac{\frac{K_2 - w_1 L_1 + C_1}{(1 + r_1 - \delta)} - w_0 L_0 + C_0}{(1 + r_0 - \delta)} = K_0$$

Continuing this 'forward iteration' in the same way (i.e. shifting the time-subscript one period ahead at a time and substituting into the existing constraint—much as we did in Chapter 2, but now we allow for a variable real interest rate), we finally obtain:

$$K_\infty R_\infty^{-1} + \sum_{t=0}^{\infty} R_t^{-1} C_t = (1 + r_0 - \delta)K_0 + \sum_{t=0}^{\infty} R_t^{-1} w_t L_t \tag{5.5}$$

Where $K_\infty \equiv lim_{t\to\infty}K_t$, $R_\infty \equiv lim_{t\to\infty}R_t$ and $R_{t+1} \equiv (1+r_{t+1} - \delta)R_t$, $t = 0, 1, 2, .., \infty$, $R_0 \equiv 1$, is the product of all the depreciation-adjusted interest rates $(1+r - \delta)$; the reciprocal of that is the effective discount factor (it generates the present value at period 0 of sums at t). The depreciation rate works as a reduction on the gross interest rate as the owner of capital needs to repair the wear-and tear out of the return (r) they receive. The intertemporal resources of this economy are given on the right-hand side: endowed capital (K_0) augmented by the interest net of depreciation obtainable in the first period plus the present value of all future labour income. The uses are on the left-hand side: consumption, plus any capital left at the end of history.

Before we dwell on (5.5), a comment is in order on $K_\infty R_\infty^{-1} \equiv lim_{t\to\infty}K_t R_t^{-1}$, which is capital (discounted) at the very end of history (when, say, the sun will be extinguished). This is to say that, at that point, capital will be completely useless; what use will it have when all life on earth ceases to exist? Hence, optimal planning dictates that, at that point, no physical capital should be left, as that will be wasted; all physical capital will need to have been converted to consumption that confers utility at earlier dates. (Remember the assumption that capital and consumption are physically interchangeable.) Equally, capital cannot be negative. Thus, optimal planning will require that:

$$K_\infty R_\infty^{-1} \equiv lim_{t\to\infty}K_t R_t^{-1} = 0 \tag{5.6}$$

This equation is called a 'transversality condition'. We discuss it more in sub-section 5.1.9. With this, (5.5) finally becomes:

$$\sum_{t=0}^{\infty}R_t^{-1}C_t = (1+r_0 - \delta)K_0 + \sum_{t=0}^{\infty}R_t^{-1}w_tL_t \tag{5.7}$$

Apart from cumulating over the lifetime, the difference between (5.4') and (5.7) is that the latter emphasizes the *ultimate* sources and uses of funds: on the right-hand side, endowed capital plus accumulated labour earnings over history; on the left-hand side, consumption. Capital and interest incomes have been dropped out of (5.7), though they are present in (5.4'), as they are merely the vehicles for shifting resources between periods (if you reduce consumption now, you can accumulate more capital and therefore have more consumption later).

Turning this to per capita quantities, we have an analogous situation. Recall that population and labour at time 0 is $n_0 = 1$, thereafter it increases at rate $\eta \geq 0$ and $L_t = l_t \times n_t$ and $C_t = c_t \times n_t$; while the real wage, w_t, is the same for every individual:

$$\sum_{t=0}^{\infty}R_t^{-1}(1+\eta)^t c_t = (1+r_0 - \delta)k_0 + \sum_{t=0}^{\infty}R_t^{-1}(1+\eta)^t w_t l_t \tag{5.8}$$

We are now able to revisit the representative household's problem: it is to maximize intertemporal utility (5.1) subject to the intertemporal budget constraint (5.8), by selecting the appropriate per capita labour supply and consumption in all periods; formally:

$$\text{Max}_{c(t), l(t)} \quad U_0 = \sum_{t=0}^{\infty}(1+\rho)^{-t}u(c_t, l_t, n_t),$$
$$\text{Subject to}: \quad \sum_{t=0}^{\infty}R_t^{-1}(1+\eta)^t c_t = (1+r_0 - \delta)k_0 + \sum_{t=0}^{\infty}R_t^{-1}(1+\eta)^t w_t l_t$$

Thinking more intuitively, the individual needs to solve a problem akin to that of a person cast out on a remote island on their own (Robinson Crusoe?). This person has a limited time resource in which there is a lot of pressing stuff to do—Robinson is never bored! First choice: labour supply. He needs to work enough in order to survive, on the other hand he needs to have some rest in order not to drive himself to exhaustion. Second choice: consumption versus capital accumulation. In his chosen labour time, Robinson needs to catch enough fish to survive; in order for him to escape hunger for good, he can devote some of his time to making a net by which he can catch more fish; this involves foregoing some consumption now in order to have more of it later— investment. Third choice: fish versus meat (e.g. hunting); this obviously depends on his preferences and the relative availability of each type of food; but this option is not present here as we have only one consumption good. Optimization means that Robinson must have it 'just right', given the specifics of his environment (how easy it is to catch fish, how much sleep he needs, etc.). Aside from the conventions of this imaginary story (e.g., instead of sleep, read: individual or family time, hobbies, enter- tainment), are these not some of the key dilemmas that any society faces in its quest for prosperity?

5.1.5 First-Order Conditions and the 'Euler Equation'

Optimization can be carried out by forming and maximizing the dynamic Lagrangean, Λ_0:

$$\text{Max}_{c(t),\,l(t)} \quad \Lambda_0 \equiv \sum_{t=0}^{\infty} (1+\rho)^{-t} u(c_t, l_t, n_t) +$$
$$+ \lambda \left[-\sum_{t=0}^{\infty} R_t^{-1} (1+\eta)^t c_t + (1+r_0-\delta)k_0 + \sum_{t=0}^{\infty} R_t^{-1}(1+\eta)^t w_t\, l_t \right], \qquad (5.9)$$

where λ is the dynamic Lagrange multiplier. Maximization of (5.9) is to take place by choice of the sequence of c_t and l_t, for all $t = 0, 1, 2, ..., \infty$.[8] We therefore obtain $2t$ first- order conditions (FOCs); to economize on space, we can derive the condition for a *typical* c_t and a typical l_t:

$$\frac{\partial \Lambda_0}{\partial c_t} = (1+\rho)^{-t} \frac{\partial u(c_t, l_t, n_t)}{\partial c_t} - \lambda R_t^{-1}(1+\eta)^t = 0 \qquad (5.10)$$

This equates the marginal utility of an extra unit of c_t with its opportunity cost in terms of lifetime resources valued at the marginal utility of those resources (λ). Using the specific functional form (5.1'):

$$(1+\rho)^{-t} c_t^{-\frac{1}{\sigma}} (1+\eta)^{\varphi t} = \lambda R_t^{-1}(1+\eta)^t \qquad (5.10')$$

Note the way population growth works: to the extent that the newborn are loved (φ), η effectively decreases the rate of time preference (the aversion to the future is mitigated by the offspring we care about); and because all the new generation (including immi- grants) are productive, η also effectively decreases the objective discount rate (the interest rate).

---

[8] An implicit restriction is that neither consumption nor capital can be negative.

The way to get rid of the Lagrange multiplier λ in (5.10) is by writing it for both t and $t+1$ and dividing the two by parts to get:

$$(1+\rho)^{-1}\frac{\frac{\partial u(c_{t+1},l_{t+1},n_{t+1})}{\partial c_{t+1}}}{\frac{\partial u(c_t,l_t,n_t)}{\partial c_t}} = \frac{\lambda R_{t+1}^{-1}(1+\eta)^{t+1}}{\lambda R_t^{-1}(1+\eta)^t} = \frac{1+\eta}{1+r_{t+1}-\delta} \tag{5.11}$$

This is the celebrated 'Euler equation' of consumption; it is a cornerstone of dynamic macroeconomics. There are three different ways of shedding light on this formula:

- The first is called a 'perturbation argument', similar to that in static optimization (if you are at the top of the hill, moving one step left or right does not change your altitude to a first-order approximation). Similarly, if you have devised a lifetime profile of consumption such as to maximize lifetime utility U_0, a small perturbation to it should leave U_0 approximately unaffected; for instance, if you cut down consumption at t, saving-investing (the same in this model) the proceeds and consuming the resulting extra resources at $t+1$, U_0 should be unaltered. If you cut down c_t by £1, you lose $(1+\rho)^{-t}\frac{\partial u(c_t,l_t,n_t)}{\partial c_t}$, while you gain $\frac{1+\eta}{1+r_{t+1}-\delta}$ extra resources next period (as a household), each £1 of which yields a marginal utility of $(1+\rho)^{-t-1}\frac{\partial u(c_{t+1},l_{t+1},n_{t+1})}{\partial c_{t+1}}$. Equating the two (loss and gain), yields (5.11).
- Considering c_t and c_{t+1} as distinct goods, the optimal lifetime plan equalizes their marginal rate of substitution (the left-hand side of 5.11) with the marginal rate of transformation (the relative cost in terms of lifetime resources—the right-hand side).
- Finally, the optimal lifetime plan equates the marginal return to current consumption with that of saving; the former is again the left-hand side of (5.11) as by foregoing a unit of consumption next period $(t+1)$ and somehow moving it now (t), utility will rise at a rate of $\dfrac{\frac{\partial u(c_t,l_t,n_t)}{\partial c_t}}{(1+\rho)^{-1}\frac{\partial u(c_{t+1},l_{t+1},n_{t+1})}{\partial c_{t+1}}}$, while the return to saving-investment (allowing for depreciation and population growth) is $\frac{1+r_{t+1}-\delta}{1+\eta}$.

The key point is that optimality, 'getting it right', requires (5.11) to be satisfied. If it is not, the rational agent will revise the plan and transfer resources across time in obvious ways until the equation is restored.[9]

With the specific functional form (5.1'), after rearranging, we get:

$$\left(\frac{c_{t+1}}{c_t}\right)^{-1/\sigma} = \frac{(1+\rho)(1+\eta)^{1-\varphi}}{(1+r_{t+1}-\delta)} \tag{5.11'}$$

Note that the population growth rate enters here if $\varphi < 1$, i.e. if the utility of the family is less than proportional to its size. We next take logs, noting $log(1+\rho) \approx \rho$, $log(1+\eta) \approx \eta$, $log(1+r_{t+1}-\delta) \approx r_{t+1}-\delta$, as ρ, η, r_{t+1}, $\delta > 0$ are all small. So:

---

[9] Exercise for the reader: can you think how the plan should be revised if, say, the left-hand side of (5.11) is greater than the right-hand side?

$$g_t^{pc} \equiv \frac{c_{t+1} - c_t}{c_t} \approx log\left(\frac{c_{t+1}}{c_t}\right) = \sigma[r_{t+1} - \delta - \rho - (1 - \varphi)\eta] \qquad (5.12)$$

This equation is sometimes known as the 'Keynes-Ramsey rule' of (per capita) consumption growth (g^{pc}). It suggests that consumption growth rate responds to a balance of two motives:

- the incentive to save and invest, i.e. the interest rate;
- then the various disincentives:
  - The rate of depreciation (δ) that reduces the net proceeds from investment;
  - The rate of time preference (ρ), which is a measure of impatience and argues for consumption now rather than later;

Finally, the adjusted population growth, $(1 - \varphi)\eta$, appears. To understand this, note from the consumption side (left-hand side of 5.10') that the loved offspring require forward planning and therefore more patience; while the entire new generation growth rate effectively reduces the interest rate, as discussed in relation to (5.10'). Population size becomes irrelevant if the welfare of the family is exactly proportional to its size ($\varphi = 1$).

The elasticity of substitution (σ) tells us how responsive the agent (household) is to these considerations.

Under the assumption that the real interest rate is constant, the consumption growth rate will also be constant (without time-subscripts), so in this case we get:

$$g^{pc} = log\left(\frac{c_{t+1}}{c_t}\right) = \sigma[r - \delta - \rho - (1 - \varphi)\eta] \qquad (5.12')$$

Let us now see how the 'Keynes-Ramsey rule' (5.12) works; consider Figure 5.1. The graph depicts two hypothetical time profiles (linearized) of consumption (thin lines) of two agents (1,2) who share the same income profile over the lifetime (y_t—the thick line); c^1 may result from a higher $r - \delta - \rho - (1 - \varphi)\eta$ than the one that has generated c^2 (i.e. the balance of incentives to save-invest versus those to consume is higher for c^1 than for c^2) or

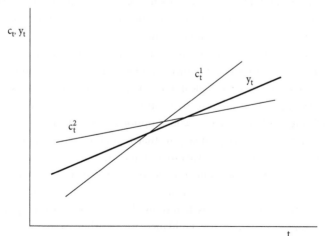

Figure 5.1. Consumption and income profiles

the balance of incentives $(r - \delta - \rho - (1 - \varphi)\eta)$ is the same but the agent behind c^1 responds more to them than the c^2 one (i.e. the rate of intertemporal substitution in consumption, σ, is higher). In either case, c^1 starts with a lower early consumption and later grows more than c^2; such that the consumption in both cases just exhausts the same lifetime resources in a present-value sense.

For both agents, saving equals $y_t - c_t$. We observe that the patient agent 1 saves early on $(y_t - c^1_t > 0)$, accumulates wealth (K) and gradually generates a higher disposable income because of a higher capital income (rK) that allows them to finance a consumption that is higher than disposable income in later life. In contrast, the agent who for whatever reason is inclined to spend more early on, dis-saves or borrows $(y_t - c^2_t < 0)$ against future resources; later, their consumption is less than income so that they are able to repay their debts (accumulated loans). In real life, of course, income and consumption profiles are both likely to be richer; we start with low incomes, then earn during the working life, then income drops in retirement; the lifetime consumption profile is also likely to mirror this 'hump-shaped' profile of income. Such profiles of income and consumption are allowed in the 'life-cycle' model of consumption reviewed in Chapter 11.

The 'Euler-Keynes-Ramsey' consumption equation (5.12) and its variants have been soundly rejected empirically—see Caroll (2001) and Ascari et al. (2016) for information and suggestions as to what may be missing. Despite its limited degree of realism, however, the model has enough intuitive appeal to make it a centrepiece of macroeconomic dynamics. Business cycles and short-run policy analysis use it to motivate general output dynamics by substituting consumption out using the NIA equation (5.4). Out of this has sprung a 'micro-founded IS' model. But again, this 'output-Euler' equation has run into empirical problems (Fuhrer and Rudebusch, 2004; Ascari et al., 2016). The theory of growth to be reviewed in Chapter 9 uses (5.12) to motivate long-term output growth. Typically, it assumes a representative agent, as here; it also often focuses on a closed economy. Therefore, lending and borrowing is not possible (as there is no one else to borrow from or lend to, either inside the country or from any other country) and as a result the consumption and income profiles cannot deviate from each other. In that case, the consumption dynamics in fact drive the income dynamics, and the factors behind $r - \delta - \rho - (1 - \varphi)\eta$ (as well as others) become the key determinants of growth.

In an open economy, there can be borrowing or lending from abroad, so even with a representative agent the consumption and income profiles can deviate from one another. In fact, the difference $Y_t - C_t - I_t$ reflects the trade balance, and a theory of external balances builds on this. Finally, dispensing with the representative agent and allowing for agent heterogeneity can introduce borrowing and lending even in a closed economy. But this setup needs to overcome some logical difficulties. Consider the simplest setup of agents 1 and 2 with consumption profiles exactly as above, where one borrows and the other one lends early on. Time is infinite; after the consumption crosses income at whatever direction and at whatever point, it is going to stay in that regime for an infinite amount of time. Thus, if one agent is accumulating wealth in later life (agent 1 above), s/he will grow infinitely wealthy; if s/he is accumulating loans (the case of 2), their net worth will eventually drop to zero. Thus, agent 1 will eventually own the entire economy. The model of agent heterogeneity of Krusell and Smith (1998) avoids such pitfalls but things become quite complicated. See the Guidance for Further Study for more on agent heterogeneity.

5.1.6 The Labour-Leisure Choice

We now turn attention to the second first-order condition on the optimal labour choice:

$$\frac{\partial \Lambda_0}{\partial l_t} = (1+\rho)^{-t} \frac{\partial u(c_t, l_t, n_t)}{\partial l_t} + \lambda R_t^{-1} w_t (1+\eta)^t = 0 \tag{5.13}$$

This equates the marginal disutility of an extra unit of labour at t with its marginal contribution to lifetime resources times λ. Division of (5.13') by (5.10) and a slight rearrangement yields:

$$\frac{\partial u(c_t, l_t, n_t)}{\partial l_t} = w_t \frac{\partial u(c_t, l_t, n_t)}{\partial c_t} \tag{5.14}$$

In contrast to (5.11), (5.14) is an intra-temporal optimality condition (i.e. not a dynamic one). It equates the marginal cost of labour (or marginal utility of leisure) on the left-hand side with the marginal contribution of labour on the right-hand side: the real wage (hourly pay) times the marginal utility of that pay so as to turn everything into (marginal) utility. It is also easy to see this slightly differently. Recall that the real wage is the relative price (opportunity cost) of leisure. Therefore, (5.14) equates the marginal rate of substitution between the two goods (leisure—the negative of work—and consumption) and the marginal rate of transformation between them (the real wage). Using the specific functional form:

$$\theta l_t^{\theta-1} = w_t c_t^{-\frac{1}{\sigma}} \tag{5.14'}$$

This ties labour with the concurrent real wage and consumption. To see what this implies, imagine that there is an increase in the real wage fuelled by a productivity rise. Labour (or leisure) will respond but without a fuller model that tells us how consumption responds to this change and without further assumptions on θ, it remains an open question whether labour increases (a switch away from leisure—i.e. the substitution effect predominates) or whether the greater income translates into more leisure (as well as consumption—i.e. the income effect predominates). We consider the empirical evidence on this question in Chapter 6 on business cycles.[10]

5.1.7 Consumption and Saving: A First Pass

We are now in a position to gain some intuition about this model and some first predictions regarding consumption and saving. Consider the implications of the intertemporal budget constraint (5.7) for the level of consumption. Imagine that aggregate/household consumption (C) grows at a constant rate $g \geq 0$ per period. Assume also that the interest rate is constant, $r_t = r$ for all t. If so, we have:

---

[10] An uncomfortable implication of (5.14) may be noticed in relation to growth. If the real wage and/or consumption grow perpetually, except in a special case (where the two growth rates cancel out), labour will be growing, too. But this cannot happen as labour is bounded by $l_t < 1$. For this reason, the additively separable utility (5.1) in c_t and l_t is not admissible in a growth context (see Chapter 1); but it is simpler, hence chosen here.

$$C_0 \sum_{t=0}^{\infty} (1+r-\delta)^{-t}(1+g)^t = (1+r-\delta)K_0 + \sum_{t=0}^{\infty} (1+r-\delta)^{-t}w_t L_t$$

Or:

$$C_0 = \Psi[K_0 + H_0] \tag{5.7'}$$

Where H_0 is 'human wealth'—the present value of intertemporal labour income:

$$H_0 \equiv \frac{1}{(1+r-\delta)} \sum_{t=0}^{\infty} (1+r-\delta)^{-t}w_t L_t \tag{5.15}$$

and Ψ is the marginal propensity to consume out of lifetime resources:

$$0 < \Psi = r - \delta - g < 1 \tag{5.16}$$

The level of consumption in each period is a fraction Ψ of lifetime resources: the capital endowment K_0 and human wealth H_0.[11] The intuition here is that, if the household were able to put all their resources, human and non-human, in a bank, they would get interest at rate r; this would finance their consumption, after taking out enough to fix depreciation and provide for capital accumulation. We make the standard assumption $r - \delta - g > 0$. The interest rate and discount rate exert multiple effects on this propensity to consume; all these points will be further analysed below.

Now consider the 'Keynes-Ramsey' rule of consumption growth (5.12'); it gives per-capita consumption growth, $g^{pc} = g - \eta$. Thus, the marginal propensity to consume becomes:

$$\Psi = r - \delta - g = (1-\sigma)(r-\delta) + \sigma\rho - \eta[1 - \sigma(1-\varphi)] \tag{5.16'}$$

We have the following effects:

- The rate of time preference increases the propensity to spend now as it indicates impatience;
- The rate of population growth decreases spending out of a given amount of lifetime resources as there are more mouths to feed out of those given resources. $\eta[1 - \sigma(1-\varphi)]$ is the wedge that population growth drives between aggregate and per capita consumption growth as planned by Keynes-Ramsey (5.12').
- The depreciation-adjusted real interest rate elicits two effects. As the relative price (opportunity cost) of consumption at t versus that at t + 1, the interest rate exerts both a substitution and an income effect, in line with standard theory. A rise in r (consumption at t + 1 becoming relatively cheaper), switches consumption away from early consumption (that is the effect introduced by $-\sigma(r-\delta)$) but also generates more overall resources (the income effect), thus permitting more current consumption (the positive $r - \delta$ part).

---

[11] More accurately, (5.7") asserts that all human wealth is consumed by the infinite future whereas the capital that we get from mother-nature is not consumed but returned intact at the end; only the flow services of it are consumed. (But in discounted terms it gets to zero, so that the transversality condition is respected.) Of course, whether nature remains intact at the end of human history or not is another matter.

- The depreciation-adjusted real interest rate also generates a third effect that is not included in Ψ but only in the intertemporal labour income, H_0. As this affects the discount rate, a rise in r discounts future labour income more heavily (all else equal), and therefore reduces H_0—a wealth effect.

Consider now human capital (5.15); assume that the real wage follows a constant rate of growth equal to the per capita consumption growth rate, as is standard.[12] We thus have $H_0 \approx \frac{w_0 L_0}{r-\delta-g}$. Thus, consumption (5.7') becomes:

$$C_0 = (r - \delta - g)K_0 + w_0 L_0 \tag{5.7''}$$

This is a general result: consumption equals the net capital income, $(r - \delta)K$, minus the funds required for investment (gK) plus the labour income. Finally, a note on saving: Since aggregate disposable income is $(r - \delta)K + wL$, this is:

$$S_0 = (r - \delta)K_0 + w_0 L_0 - C_0 = gK_0 \tag{5.17}$$

In this closed economy model, saving equals investment. The formula brings out the close relation between saving and growth.

5.1.8 Production

Firms rent capital and labour from households in order to produce. All markets are fully competitive. The representative firm produces output by the following production function:

$$Y_t = F(K_t, L_t, A_t) \tag{5.18}$$

with all the usual properties (the 'Inada conditions' discussed in Chapter 1), namely constant returns to scale across both factors (physical capital, K_t, and labour, L_t) and a diminishing marginal product of each factor taken separately. Productivity, A_t, has also been discussed in Chapter 1 and will be discussed further below.

Households, the owners of both capital and labour, supply both to the firm in perfectly competitive markets. In order to maximize profit, the firm should demand both factors of production up to the point where their marginal products are equalized with factor prices (see Chapter 1):

$$r_t = F_K(K_t, L_t, A_t) \equiv \partial F(K_t, L_t, A_t)/\partial K_t \tag{5.19a}$$

and

$$w_t = F_L(K_t, L_t, A_t) \equiv \partial F(K_t, L_t, A_t)/\partial L_t \tag{5.19b}$$

where r_t and w_t are the real interest rate and the real wage, respectively. From now on, the shorthand notation F_K and F_L will be used but do let us keep in mind that both these

---

[12] This is a standard assumption, see later in this chapter and Chapters 4 and 9.

quantities depend on all K_t, L_t, and A_t. Because of the properties of the production function (constant returns and the resulting Euler theorem), we have:

$$Y_t = F(K_t, L_t, A_t) = F_K K_t + F_L L_t = r_t K_t + w_t L_t \qquad (5.20)$$

Due to constant returns, the output of the economy, from the incomes side, is equal to payments to capital and to labour. As firms are assumed perfectly competitive, the payment to capital does not involve any payment beyond the competitive interest rate (i.e. there are no 'supernormal profits'); likewise, the wage is the perfectly competitive one (equal to the marginal product of capital).

5.1.9 The Transversality Condition and the 'No Ponzi-Game' Condition

Before proceeding, we shed a little more light on the transversality condition (5.6). The logic of intertemporal planning requires that, at the end of the horizon, there should be no capital left if capital is valued at that point:

$$lim_{t \to \infty} (1 + \rho)^{-t} \frac{\partial u(.)}{\partial c_t} k_t = 0$$

As capital can in principle be turned to consumption, it is valued by the marginal utility of consumption appropriately discounted to establish a present value. Accordingly, capital should asymptotically go to zero if it is valuable, but it can be accumulated for ever if it is not valuable (note than only one of $(1 + \rho)^{-t} \frac{\partial u(.)}{\partial c_t}$ or k_t should tend to zero, not both). Using (5.10), we then get $lim_{t \to \infty} \lambda R_t^{-1} K_t = 0$ and since λ is constant, we have (5.6). Moreover, as R_t grows (declines) at rate $-(r - \delta)$, while K_t in the long run grows at rate $g + \eta$ (see sub-section 5.2.2 below), the above implies:

$$r - \delta - g - \eta > 0 \qquad (5.21)$$

This justifies the assumptions made above.

The transversality condition is closely linked to the 'no Ponzi-game' condition which takes the form:

$$lim_{t \to \infty} R_t^{-1} \Omega_t = 0$$

where Ω_t are the assets of the household. So far these have been assumed to consist only of physical capital which is non-negative; but when financial assets are distinct from physical assets (through the financial system), then assets can be negative (debt). So, both inequalities associated with the above become meaningful: The inequality $lim_{t \to \infty} R_t^{-1} \Omega_t < 0$ continues to imply that the household will not leave positive assets that could have been used to augment consumption; but $lim_{t \to \infty} R_t^{-1} \Omega_t > 0$ is now not trivial but implies that other parties will not allow the household debts at the end of history that could have been used by other parties to finance their consumption. As we discuss in Chapter 8 on fiscal policy and government debt (where this is used to restrain the government's excessive borrowing), this implies that debts (or assets) should grow at a rate less than the adjusted interest rate $(r - \delta)$. This further implies that debts in particular should not be rolled over indefinitely (by raising new borrowing to finance interest payments); rather, at least some of the interest on outstanding debt should be payed from own means. Various schemes exist whereby interest is paid by entirely new debt (raised by conning the naïve), such as the 'pyramids' or the scheme once devised by the eponymous (or notorious) Ponzi guy; all such schemes are illegal. The 'no Ponzi-game' condition rules them out. The issue is linked to the question of dynamic efficiency discussed in the next section.

5.2 The Ramsey Model

5.2.1 The Setup

Based on the preliminary analysis of Section 5.1, this section reviews a workhorse model based on an infinitely lived, intertemporally optimizing, representative agent. Often called the 'Ramsey model' (from its first development in Ramsey, 1928), it was further refined by Cass (1965) and Koopmans (1965). The standard version of the model adopts the setup of Section 5.1 with three modifications. First, there is no disutility of labour: $\theta = 1$. If so, it is obvious that the second FOC (5.13 or 5.14) is redundant; and since work involves no psychic costs, we work the entire available time, so $l_{it} = 1$ for all i and t; and the labour supply equals the (working) population, $L_t = n_t(\times 1)$. Furthermore, it is assumed that in the background there is a process of exogenous productivity growth. It is useful to think of this as technology (indicated here by A_t) that grows at the constant rate g_A. The reason for introducing this element is partly realism, partly the need to ensure that there is ongoing growth and improvement of living standards even in the long run (a realistic feature).[13]

Lastly, productivity is assumed to be 'labour-augmenting' (see Chapter 1), so that the aggregate production function (5.18) takes the slightly more restrictive form:

$$Y_t = F(K_t, A_t L_t) \tag{5.18'}$$

This production function involves constant returns across its two arguments, capital and 'efficiency-adjusted labour units' ($A_t L_t$); this represents quality-adjusted labour and has a key place in what follows. Diminishing marginal products apply to both K_t and $A_t L_t$ individually. All markets (and firms in them) are assumed to be perfectly competitive, as before, so the interest rate and wage equal their marginal products, see (5.12a, b).

Therefore, the setup is as follows:

$$\text{Max}_{c(t)} \quad U_0 = \sum_{t=1}^{\infty}(1+\rho)^{-t}\frac{c_t^{1-1/\sigma}}{1-1/\sigma}n_t^{\varphi},$$

$$\text{Subject to :} \quad \sum_{t=1}^{\infty}R_t^{-1}(1+\eta)^t c_t = k_0 + \sum_{t=1}^{\infty}R_t^{-1}(1+\eta)^t w_t$$

The wage is given to the household. The only FOC now is Euler-Keynes-Ramsey rule (5.12). The aggregate resource constraint is (5.4). Finally, the production-related FOCs (5.19a, b) also remain valid but need to be applied to the production function (5.18').

---

[13] This model will also be briefly reviewed in Chapter 9 in the context of growth. The assumption of an exogenous technical progress, about which the model has nothing to say, is an analytical device that allowed early models to focus on more tractable issues. Later theoretical developments endogenize the rate of technical progress.

The model is then transformed into variables couched in 'efficiency labour units', indicated by hats, as follows:

$$\hat{k}_t \equiv \frac{K_t}{A_t L_t} = \frac{k_t}{A_t}, \tag{5.22a}$$

$$\hat{c}_t \equiv \frac{C_t}{A_t L_t} = \frac{c_t}{A_t} \tag{5.22b}$$

(Where it should be remembered that lower-cases are the per capita variables, e.g. $k_t = \frac{K_t}{L_t}$.) The idea is to anchor everything onto the fundamental driver of living standards, the quality-adjusted labour.

Recalling that $L_t = n_t$ (as individual work is one unit) and that $\log(\frac{\hat{c}_{t+1}}{\hat{c}_t}) = \log(\frac{c_{t+1}}{c_t}) - \log(\frac{A_{t+1}}{A_t})$, the FOC (5.12) is rewritten in terms of the transformed variables (5.22a, b):

$$\log\left(\frac{\hat{c}_{t+1}}{\hat{c}_t}\right) = \log\left(\frac{c_{t+1}}{c_t}\right) - \log\left(\frac{A_{t+1}}{A_t}\right) = \sigma[r_{t+1} - \delta - \rho - (1-\varphi)\eta] - g_A \tag{5.23}$$

Additionally, by division by $A_t L_t$, the resource constraint (5.4) is transformed to:

$$\hat{y}_t = \hat{c}_t + \hat{k}_{t+1} - (1 - \delta - \eta - g_A)\hat{k}_t \tag{5.24}$$

(5.24) retains the same form as (5.4) except that now the population and productivity growth rates effectively augment the depreciation rate. The best way to make sense of this is to think of g_A as 'economic depreciation', the rate at which equipment becomes obsolete as it ceases to be 'cutting edge' (not because of physical depreciation, the rate of which is captured by δ). Let us use an analogy. Think of $\hat{k}_t$ as the ratio of cutting-edge computers per student that a university maintains. The investment expenditure by the university then aims to fulfil four objectives. First, the replacement of machines that break down; this is an expenditure at rate δ of existing computers. Secondly, the maintenance of the same standard of computing across all students; this requires endowing all new students with the same amount of computers as everyone else, involving an expenditure at rate η of existing computers. Thirdly, the replacement of all machines that may still be functioning but are no longer cutting-edge; an expenditure at rate g_A. Fourthly, any remaining resources go towards improving the standard of computing, $\hat{k}_{t+1} - \hat{k}_t$.

Moreover, exploiting the constant-returns assumption of the production function (5.18'), that can be rewritten as:

$$\hat{y}_t \equiv Y_t / A_t L_t = F(\frac{K_t}{A_t n_t}, 1) \equiv f(\hat{k}_t) \tag{5.25}$$

Two final pieces of necessary information flow from the above: Since (with $L_t = n_t$),

$$F(K_t, A_t L_t) = A_t n_t F(\frac{K_t}{A_t n_t}, 1) \equiv A_t n_t f(\hat{k}_t),$$

the derivatives are:

$$F_K(K_t, A_t L_t) = A_t n_t F_K\left(\hat{k}_t\right) = A_t n_t f_{\hat{k}}\left(\hat{k}_t\right) \frac{1}{A_t n_t} = f'(\hat{k}_t)$$

And similarly (with $L_t = n_t$)

$$F_L(K_t, A_t n_t) = A_t F\left(\hat{k}_t\right) + A_t n_t F_L\left(\hat{k}_t\right) = A_t f\left(\hat{k}_t\right) - A_t n_t f_{\hat{k}}\left(\hat{k}_t\right) \frac{A_t K_t}{(A_t n_t)^2} =$$

$$= A_t \left[f\left(\hat{k}_t\right) - f_{\hat{k}}\left(\hat{k}_t\right)\hat{k}_t\right]$$

With these results, the FOC (5.19a, b) now take the form:

$$r_t = f'(\hat{k}_t) \tag{5.26a}$$

and

$$w_t/A_t = f\left(\hat{k}_t\right) - f'\left(\hat{k}_t\right)\hat{k}_t \tag{5.26b}$$

The latter is best couched in terms of wage in efficiency units (w_t/A_t). Roughly speaking, $f\left(\hat{k}_t\right)$ is output while $f_{\hat{k}}\left(\hat{k}_t\right)\hat{k}_t$ is capital times its return; the difference is the wage. As we shall see later, in the long-run stationary state, $\hat{k}_t$ will be constant, therefore so will be the wage in terms of productivity, w_t/A_t; the (unadjusted) wage will trend upwards in line with productivity at rate g_A. We have the following important intermediate result:

Result 1: If productivity is labour-augmenting, in the long run, the real wage will be growing at the rate of productivity growth.

This result has important implications for the relation between productivity and unemployment/living standards (as has already been mentioned in Chapter 4); and for growth in general (Chapter 9). At the heart of this result lies the intuitive observation that, with F(.) a constant returns function (homogeneous of degree 1), both $f\left(\hat{k}_t\right)$ and $f_{\hat{k}}\left(\hat{k}_t\right)$ will be homogeneous of degree 0. To proceed, we shall assume the quasi-Cobb-Douglas form for the production function, which replaces (5.18'):

$$f\left(\hat{k}_t\right) = \hat{k}_t^\alpha, \quad 0 < \alpha < 1 \tag{5.27a}$$

The marginal product is:

$$f'\left(\hat{k}_t\right) = \alpha \hat{k}_t \,\alpha^{-1} \tag{5.27b}$$

As with all marginal products, this is positive and monotonically declining with $\hat{k}_t$.
    Time to put everything together. With (5.26a, 5.27a, b), (5.23) and (5.24) become:

$$\log\left(\frac{\hat{c}_{t+1}}{\hat{c}_t}\right) = \sigma\left[\alpha \hat{k}_{t+1}^{\alpha-1} - \delta - \rho - (1 - \varphi)\eta\right] - g_A, \tag{5.23'}$$

and

$$\hat{c}_t + \hat{k}_{t+1} - (1 - \delta - \eta - g_A)\hat{k}_t = \hat{k}_t^\alpha \tag{5.24'}$$

Equations (5.23')—consumption growth—and (5.24')—the aggregate resource constraint—form the backbone of the Ramsey model. They are a non-linear 2 × 2 difference equation system in two variables, $\hat{c}_t$ and $\hat{k}_t$. As is standard, the model is solved in two stages. First, we consider the long-run 'steady state'; then, we consider 'dynamics', i.e. how the system approaches the said steady state from any initial arbitrary position. Our discussion will be partitioned accordingly.

5.2.2 The Steady State and the 'Balanced-Growth Path'

The steady state is the state approached by the system in the long run, when all adjustment has taken place and all the dust has settled, so to speak; there will be no more movement until/unless some exogenous change takes place. Formally, it is the state that emerges when the two variables in (5.23', 5.24') remain constant:

$$\hat{c}_{t-1} = \hat{c}_t = \hat{c}_{t+1} = \hat{c} \quad \text{and} \quad \hat{k}_{t-1} = \hat{k}_t = \hat{k}_{t+1} = \hat{k} \quad \text{for all t}$$

Other variables that depend on these will also be constant; yet others will be growing at a constant rate. From (5.26a) and (5.27b), output in efficiency units $(\hat{y}_t)$ and the real interest rate will be constant, too. From (5.27a, b) and (5.26b), the productivity-adjusted real wage, w_t/A_t will also be constant, as implied by Result 1. Therefore, per capita variables $(y_{it}, c_{it}, k_{it}$ and the real wage (w_t) all grow at the same constant rate (which turns out to be g_A),[14] while their aggregate counterparts (C_t, K_t) grow at rate $g_A + \eta$. (Ensure you understand why.) This state, at which growth rates are common across variables so that ratios are kept constant, is called the 'Balanced-Growth Path'. Thus:

Result 2: In the Ramsey model, in the steady state (long run):

All efficiency-adjusted variables like (5.22a, b), the real interest rate and the productivity-adjusted real wage (w/A) are constant;

All per-capita variables and the real wage trend upwards at rate g_A;

All aggregate variables trend upwards at rate $g_A + \eta$.

In other words, as mentioned, g_A is crucial in shaping living standards in the long run. With $\hat{c}_t = \hat{c}$ and $\hat{k}_t = \hat{k}$ for all t (dropping time-subscripts), the above system reads:

$$0 = \sigma[\alpha \hat{k}^{\alpha-1} - \delta - \rho - (1 - \varphi)\eta] - g_A \tag{5.28}$$

and

$$\hat{k}^\alpha = \hat{c} + (\delta + \eta + g_A)\hat{k} \tag{5.29}$$

The system is depicted graphically in Figure 5.2. (5.28) is vertical as it does not depend on the level of consumption; while the shape of (5.29) will become clearer below. Point A, $(\hat{c}^*, \hat{k}^*)$, signifies long-run equilibrium (starred variables).

These two equations can be explicitly solved sequentially; first (5.28) for $\hat{k}^*$, then conditional on that, (5.29) can be solved for $\hat{c}^*$. It is also informative to recall that the real interest rate is $r = \alpha \hat{k}^{\alpha-1}$ and solve for r:

$$r^* = \delta + \rho + (1 - \varphi)\eta + g_A/\sigma \tag{5.30}$$

---

[14] In other words, this equals the rate that we called g in Section 5.1.

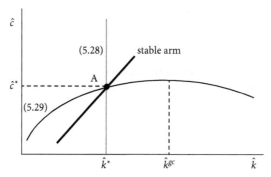

Figure 5.2. The steady state of the Ramsey model

Result 3: In the long run, the real interest rate in the Ramsey model is determined by:
The subjective discount rate and impatience (ρ), as the saver needs to be rewarded for postponing consumption;

The depreciation rate (δ), as the capital holder replaces wear and tear of their capital out of the return to it;

Population growth (η) as there is demand for borrowing against future labour income;

Productivity growth (g_A) as again there is future growth in labour incomes.

Next, we solve for the steady-state level of capita in efficiency units, $\hat{k}^*$:

$$\hat{k}^* = \left(\frac{\alpha}{\delta + \rho + (1 - \varphi)\eta + g_A/\sigma} \right)^{1/(1-\alpha)} \tag{5.31}$$

As the adjusted level of capital depends inversely on the real interest rate and adjusted output depends directly on it, the same factors that increase the interest rate now decrease long-run capital and output (in efficiency units) and living standards:

Result 4: In the long run, efficiency-adjusted capital and living standards will be *lower* the higher are:
The subjective discount rate as a measure of impatience in consumption (ρ);
The depreciation rate (δ);
The population growth rate (η);
The exogenous productivity growth rate (g_A).

These results are of interest lately in relation to the population growth rate. In all industrialized economies, the population growth rate is invariably at historically low levels. At the same time, the (real) interest rate is also very low and there is normally an abundance of capital. Perhaps as a result of the low interest rate (and marginal product of capital), there is currently rather little growth (what some have begun to call 'secular stagnation'). Equations (5.30) and (5.31) tell us that all these phenomena are linked, without however telling us what explains what (the question of 'causality'). We return to these issues in Chapter 9 when we discuss the 'secular stagnation hypothesis'.

Furthermore, from (5.29), consumption is given by:

$$\hat{c}^* = \hat{k}^{*\alpha} - (\delta + \eta + g_A)\hat{k}^* \tag{5.32}$$

Steady-state consumption is what is left from production after the investment expenditure required by depreciation (both physical and 'economic') and population growth. From (5.28'), the common growth rate is:

$$g = g_A = \sigma\left[\alpha\hat{k}^{\alpha-1} - \delta - \rho - (1-\varphi)\eta\right] \tag{5.33}$$

5.2.3 The 'Golden Rule' Level of Capital

It may be asked whether steady-state consumption could be increased or decreased by some kind of policy; how does it compare with the maximum potential level of consumption? That is given by maximising (5.32):

$$\text{Max}_{\hat{k}} \quad \hat{c} = \hat{k}^{\alpha} - (\delta + \eta + g_A)\hat{k}$$

The level of capital that maximizes consumption is called the 'golden-rule' capital level, denoted by superscript 'gr':

$$\hat{k}^{gr} = \left(\frac{\alpha}{\delta + \eta + g_A}\right)^{1/(1-\alpha)} \tag{5.34}$$

Comparing the steady-state and golden-rule levels of capital, $\hat{k}^*$ in (5.31) with $\hat{k}^{gr}$ in (5.34), we find that:

$$\hat{k}^* \underset{<}{\overset{>}{\gtrless}} \hat{k}^{gr} \tag{5.35}$$

if

$$\left(\frac{\alpha}{\delta + \rho + (1-\varphi)\eta + g_A/\sigma}\right)^{1/(1-\alpha)} \underset{<}{\overset{>}{\gtrless}} \left(\frac{\alpha}{\delta + \eta + g_A}\right)^{1/(1-\alpha)}$$

Note that the implication of the transversality condition (5.21) with the growth rate (5.33) and $r = \alpha\hat{k}^{\alpha-1}$ imply that $\delta + \rho + (1-\varphi)\eta + \frac{g_A}{\sigma} - (\delta + \eta + g_A) > 0$, therefore we get:

Result 5: The equilibrium capital stock is lower than the 'golden-rule' level: $\hat{k}^* < \hat{k}^{gr}$ [15]

Result 5 is standard and is reflected in Figure 5.2. The main driver of it is the transversality condition and its implication (5.21). The steady-state level of capital should be sufficiently low as to induce a high enough interest rate for the transversality condition to hold via sufficient discounting of the future capital stock.

---

[15] In parallel to the 'golden rule' $\hat{k}^{gr}$, the equilibrium $\hat{k}^*$ is called the 'modified golden rule' capital.

5.2.4 Dynamic Efficiency

As mentioned, the inequality $\hat{k}* < \hat{k}^{gr}$ implies that we cannot increase consumption simply by switching existing capital into consumption; there is no way existing resources can be reallocated so as to increase consumption and welfare. This property is called 'dynamic efficiency' and is a precondition (necessary but not sufficient) for overall Pareto optimality (which we discuss later).[16] It is a property of the steady state of the Ramsey model, so we can restate Result 5 as:

Result 5': In the Ramsey model, dynamic efficiency holds in the steady state.

Dynamic efficiency is a desirable property because its absence implies that welfare is unnecessarily low and because its presence rules out asset bubbles (see Chapter 2). As we mentioned above, the transversality condition $r - \delta - \eta - g > 0$ eliminates Ponzi schemes, worthless assets that rely on new buyers (who arrive at rate η and are g per cent richer than previous buyers) in order to provide a return to previous buyers. The inequality implies that Ponzi-type of finance cannot generate a normal rate of return $(r - \delta)$, guaranteeing dynamic efficiency. The same condition also eliminates bubbles in some productive assets such as housing; inefficiency leaves the door open to bubbles. See the Guidance for Further Study for more implications. Though present in the Ramsey model, dynamic efficiency is by no means general: as we shall see later, it may break down in the 'overlapping-generations' model. Thus, it is an open question that must be examined empirically.

In a seminal paper, Abel et al. (1989) have examined dynamic efficiency empirically. To derive a testable implication, they start from (5.35) with (5.34). For any level of the capital stock, not necessarily long-run equilibrium, the dynamic efficiency condition can be re-expressed as:

$$\hat{k}^{1-\alpha} < \left(\hat{k}^{gr}\right)^{1-\alpha} = \frac{\alpha}{\delta + \eta + g_A}$$

or

$$\alpha\hat{k}^{\alpha-1} > \alpha\left(\hat{k}^{gr}\right)^{\alpha-1} = \delta + \eta + g_A$$

Noting that $\alpha\hat{k}^{\alpha-1} = f'\left(\hat{k}\right) = r$, this translates to:

$$r - \delta > \eta + g_A = \eta + g \tag{5.21'}$$

Thus, we get precisely (5.21), the condition that underpins the transversality condition: The depreciation-adjusted real interest should be greater than the growth rate of the economy which is made up of productivity-driven per capita growth and population growth. However, a difficulty with direct application of (5.21) is that there are many interest rates in the economy and in conditions of uncertainty it is unclear which one to use.

---

[16] Once upon a time, a lay person in a developing economy told me something that helps put this idea in plain English: dynamic INefficiency occurs when 'you have a fridge but nothing to put in it'; i.e. too much capital and too little consumption. It would be beneficial to reduce one and increase the other. In the real world, this is not immediately possible; but in the long run, it is possible to switch resources between sectors, as the model allows.

Abel et al. (1989) show that (5.21) is equivalent to the condition that the capital income be greater than investment inclusive of depreciation; intuitively, the condition is $rK > (\eta + g + \delta)K$, with $\eta + g_A$ being the overall growth rate of the economy and therefore net investment (= capital accumulation). On the basis of this modified condition, Abel et al. (1989) find that dynamic efficiency holds for the US in 1926–85 and for the UK, France, Germany, Italy, Canada, and Japan between 1960 and 1984.

5.2.5 Dynamics

The dynamics of the model involve the explicit solution of equations (5.23') and (5.24') in consumption and capital. First, we log-linearize the variables around their steady-state solutions, $\hat{k}^*$ and $\hat{c}^*$, also trivially adding and subtracting as required, as follows:

$$
\begin{aligned}
&log\hat{c}_{t+1} - log\hat{c}^* - (log\hat{c}_t - log\hat{c}^*) = \\
&\sigma\left[\alpha\hat{k}^{*(\alpha-1)} + (\alpha - 1)\hat{k}^{*(\alpha-1)}(\hat{k}_{t+1} - \hat{k}^*)/\hat{k}^* - \delta - \rho - (1 - \varphi)\eta\right] - g_A
\end{aligned}
\tag{5.36}
$$

and

$$
\begin{aligned}
&\hat{k}^{*\alpha} + \alpha\hat{k}^{*\alpha}\left(\hat{k}_t - \hat{k}^*\right)/\hat{k}^* = \\
&\hat{c}^*[1 + \frac{\hat{c}_t - \hat{c}^*}{\hat{c}^*}] + \hat{k}^*[1 + \frac{\hat{k}_{t+1} - \hat{k}^*}{\hat{k}^*}] - (1 - \delta - \eta - g_A)\hat{k}^*[1 + \frac{\hat{k}_t - \hat{k}^*}{\hat{k}^*}]
\end{aligned}
\tag{5.37}
$$

Then, notice that a number of terms cancel out via the steady-state version of the equations, (5.28) and (5.29). Also note that $\frac{\hat{c}_t - \hat{c}^*}{\hat{c}} \approx log\hat{c}_t - log\hat{c}^*$. Incorporating this information, we are able to express the system in two linear equations in log-deviations of the variables from their steady-state values. In matrix form, the system is:

$$
\begin{aligned}
&\begin{bmatrix} 1 & -\sigma(\alpha - 1)\hat{k}^{*(\alpha-1)} \\ 0 & \hat{k}^* \end{bmatrix} \begin{bmatrix} log\hat{c}_{t+1} - log\hat{c}^* \\ log\hat{k}_{t+1} - log\hat{k}^* \end{bmatrix} = \\
&= \begin{bmatrix} 1 & 0 \\ -\hat{c}^* & (1 + \alpha - \delta - \eta - g_A)\hat{k}^{*\alpha} \end{bmatrix} \begin{bmatrix} log\hat{c}_t - log\hat{c}^* \\ log\hat{k}_t - log\hat{k}^* \end{bmatrix}
\end{aligned}
\tag{5.38}
$$

The dynamic properties of the system depend on its eigenvalues. In order not to disrupt the flow, some details are relegated to Appendix 5A. The gist of the argument is that the equilibrium is a 'saddle point', the hallmark of which is two positive eigenvalues either side of unity. From any arbitrary starting point, there is a single path, the 'stable arm' (SA—the thicker line in Figure 5.2) that converges to equilibrium; any other path either implodes to zero capital or involves a capital stock that increases unsustainably and violates the transversality condition. In order to jump on to SA from any arbitrary initial point, it is required that one variable should be 'pre-determined' and unable to make instantaneous changes; here this is the capital stock, as it is a stock variable evolving only sluggishly. The other variable should be a 'jump' variable, freely able to change instantaneously, such as consumption here.[17]

---

[17] In fact, this rule generalizes to more than two equations and variables (see Blanchard and Khan, 1980). In a system of n equation with m unstable (> 1) eigenvalues, where n > m, there is a unique solution iff (necessary and sufficient condition) the system has exactly n − m 'predetermined' and m 'jump' variables. Intuitively, the 'predetermined' variables are assigned to the stable eigenvalues and dynamics that are solved backwards, giving

Any changes induced by the parameters of the model (the exogenous 'drivers), such as those that determine the steady state capital in (5.32), will generally involve a discrete jump only at the time they occur (or at the time they become public knowledge); thereafter, the new steady state will be approached gradually and smoothly without any further discrete jumps. Similarly, as explained in Chapter 2, this is a standard property of Rational Expectations models and is very relevant when one deals with asset prices such as the stock market, exchange rates, or interest rates (which reflect inversely bond prices). If you see a discrete jump at any point, it must have been driven by some new piece of information revealed at that point in time.

5.2.6 Welfare and the 'Command Optimum'

Let us take stock of what we have accomplished so far. We have assumed a market economy under the assumption that households own capital and labour that they rent to firms. Alternatively, we could analyse a market economy in which households own the firm and labour; in turn, firms own the capital and remit profits to households. Under the assumptions utilized so far, namely that consumption and capital are interchangeable and that there is perfect competition, that environment is 'observationally equivalent' (it produces the same outcomes) with the case analysed here; we shall see later an instance where the first assumption fails. But both cases are versions of the market economy, where firms are independent entities motivated by profit maximization.

It may be asked whether this type of economy achieves the highest possible welfare for individuals (or families or households). To answer, we compare the welfare achieved in this setup with that under a different setup in which all resources are mobilized directly by a planning agency solely for the purpose of welfare maximization, without firms interfering as independent entities. Directed by a 'central planner' or 'benevolent dictator' (various names have been given to this planning agency), this is then a 'command optimum' and is to be contrasted with the (market) 'equilibrium' analysed in the earlier sections. It must be emphasized that the command optimum is a completely hypothetical scenario and in no way a realistic prospect. Its use is that the outcomes achieved under it are, by construction, Pareto optimal; hence, it is a benchmark against which the outcomes of the market equilibrium are to be measured.[18]

---

us the history of the system (e.g. past accumulation of capital). The 'jump' variables are assigned to the unstable eigenvalues and dynamics that need to be 'solved forward', thus being dependent on future expectations of exogenous drivers (e.g. productivity, future policies). The dynamics of the predetermined variables (here capital) evolve according to history and what the current jump variable (here consumption) is doing; the dynamics of the jump variables depend on the current state of the system (predetermined variables) and future expectations. Of course, all dynamics are determined jointly. The keen reader may have noticed the interesting parallels with the idea of cointegration in econometrics. Finally, in two-variable continuous-time models, saddle-point stability arises when the two eigenvalues are either side of zero.

[18] The countries of the Soviet-led Communist bloc of the Cold-War era had structured their economies in a command type of way, with a central planning agency dictating the essentials of all economic activity. Analysis of those economies is beyond the scope of this book; a consensus view is that, despite an early rapid industrialization, these experiments progressively led to stagnation. One possibility is dynamic inefficiency; there was too much capital accumulation at the expense of consumption and living standards, which progressively led to demotivation and demoralization.

By mobilizing resources directly, particularly the resource constraint in per capita period-by-period form, the central planner faces the following problem:

$$\text{Max}_{k(t)} \quad U_0 = \sum_{t=1}^{\infty} (1+\rho)^{-t} \frac{\left(k_t^{\alpha} - k_{t+1}(1+\eta) + (1-\delta)k_t\right)^{1-1/\sigma}}{1 - 1/\sigma} n_t^{\varphi},$$

The first-order condition is:

$$(1+\rho)^{-(t+1)} c_{t+1}^{-\frac{1}{\sigma}} (1+\eta)^{\varphi(t+1)} \left(\alpha k_{t+1}^{\alpha-1} + (1-\delta)\right) = (1+\rho)^{-t} c_t^{-\frac{1}{\sigma}} (1+\eta)(1+\eta)^{\varphi t}$$

Rearranging, we get:

$$\left(\frac{c_{t+1}}{c_t}\right)^{-1/\sigma} = \frac{(1+\rho)(1+\eta)^{1-\varphi}}{(1+\alpha k_{t+1}^{\alpha-1} - \delta)}$$

Noting that under the decentralized equilibrium we have $r_{t+1} = \alpha k_{t+1}^{\alpha-1}$, the above is exactly the same as the FOC (5.11'), and the resource constraint is the same; hence, the rest of the analysis (equilibrium capital, output, and consumption) goes through as before. The result also generalizes to the case of flexible labour supply:

Result 6: Relation between the command optimum and decentralized equilibrium: under the standard assumptions of the 'First Theorem of Welfare Economics' and when consumption and capital are the same good, the two setups produce exactly the same outcomes.

The major implication is that under the said assumptions, the decentralized equilibrium is Pareto optimal. But we must not lose sight, as is often done, of how strong the assumptions of the 'First Welfare Theorem' are: perfect competition, no externalities or public goods, no missing markets, and full information. Additionally, we have a production function with constant returns to scale and diminishing marginal products. These assumptions are so strong that they are likely to be violated in the real world. If so, the decentralized equilibrium may well be Pareto-suboptimal.

5.3 Investment and the Equity Price of the Firm

5.3.1 Capital Adjustment Costs, Profit Maximization, and the User Cost of Capital

So far, we have assumed a capital stock that adjusts passively to the demand for goods dictated by consumption. We now want to discuss investment not as passive but as a co-driver of the capital accumulation process. In order to do so, we change the setup slightly: Firms own the capital (rather than renting it from households as before); in turn, households as shareholders own the firms. This setup allows a richer development of the cost of capital. In the previous section, this simply equals the (real) interest rate minus the depreciation rate, but it disregards elements such as capital gains; incorporation of these elements leads to the important concept of the 'user cost of capital'. This setup also incorporates adjustment costs in investment. In this section, we present the basic model; we defer a fuller discussion of the theory and the empirical evidence related to both investment and housing until Chapter 11.

The cost of investment is an important part of the analytics: It is made up of two components: the first is the amount of capital to be installed; the second is installation or adjustment costs that depend on the level of investment relative to already installed capital. For simplicity, adjustment costs take the quadratic form: $i_t\varphi(i_t/k_t)$, where $\varphi > 0$ measures the significance of such costs; these costs rise with investment itself but also as the investment increases in relation to existing capital. The idea is that a very small amount of investment requires next to no labour costs for installation, whereas more substantial investment costs more to install per unit of investment or causes more disruption. Hence, total investment costs $i_t(1 + \varphi i_t/k_t)$: the investment itself plus the adjustment costs. As is standard, investment is related to capital accumulation via the identity:

$$i_t = k_{t+1} - (1 - \delta)k_t \tag{5.39}$$

Investment is made up of net addition to capital plus the depreciation expenditure. To simplify, we disregard technical progress and population growth and assume a constant real interest rate, r.

The firm maximizes its intertemporal real profitability net of investment costs, by choosing optimally its capital accumulation and time profile of capital. It is assumed to finance its investment from retained profits (so, finance, bank loans, etc., are irrelevant here). Profits are distributed to shareholders (households) as dividend payments, but this is not important here; what is important is that the firm, as an independent entity, aims to maximize profits. Lower-case letters here represent the typical firm's quantities (we avoid subscripts to avoid further clatter). Thus, the problem is to maximize the present value of profits—output net of the wage bill $(w_t l_t)$ and total investment costs:

$$\text{Max}_{i(t),\,l(t)} \sum_{t=1}^{\infty} R_t^{-1} \left[F(k_t, l_t) - w_t l_t - i_t \left(1 + \varphi \frac{i_t}{k_t} \right) \right],$$

$$\text{Subject to}: \quad i_t = k_{t+1} - (1 - \delta)k_t$$

A standard production function without technical progress, $y_t = F(k_t, l_t)$, has already been used to replace output. The relative price of the firm's good is unity, reflecting its typical nature. So, the firm selects the sequence of investment and labour over time in order to maximize its intertemporal profits.

We form the dynamic Lagrangean by incorporating the period capital accumulation into the maximand:[19]

$\text{Max}_{i(t),\,l(t),\,k(t)}$

$$V \equiv \sum_{t=1}^{\infty} R_t^{-1} \left[F(k_t, l_t) - w_t l_t - i_t \left(1 + \varphi \frac{i_t}{k_t} \right) + q_t(i_t - k_{t+1} + (1 - \delta)k_t) \right]$$

---

[19] In continuous time, this dynamic Langrangean is known as the 'current-value Hamiltonian'.

The Langrange multiplier q_t is the 'shadow price' (value) of installed capital—the marginal intertemporal profit net of the adjustment/installation costs arising from installing an extra unit of capital. The appropriate transversality condition is:

$$lim_{t \to \infty} R_t^{-1} q_t k_t = 0$$

This states that asymptotically capital should be accumulated to the point that its present-value shadow price should tend to zero; unless capital itself is driven to zero asymptotically ($k_\infty = 0$).

There are two intra-temporal first-order conditions (that do not involve dynamics). First, setting $\partial V / \partial l_t = 0$, we get the standard equation of the wage with the marginal product of labour:

$$w_t = F_l(k_t, l_t) \tag{5.40a}$$

Second, from $\partial V / \partial i_t = 0$, we get the optimal investment policy as follows:

$$1 + 2\varphi \frac{i_t}{k_t} = q_t \tag{5.40b}$$

This equates the marginal cost of an additional unit of capital inclusive of adjustment costs (on the left-hand side) with the marginal additional profits derived from this unit (the shadow price on the right-hand side). The equality determines optimal investment (proportional to installed capital) as a function of the shadow price of capital only: $\frac{i_t}{k_t} = \frac{q_t - 1}{2\varphi}$. The shadow price (q) is of course unobservable, so in Chapter 11 we shall review the available approaches that proxy it in empirical work.

In addition, from $\partial V / \partial k_t = 0$, there is a third, dynamic equation:

$$(1 + r)^{-1} \left[F_k(k_t, l_t) + \varphi \left(\frac{i_t}{k_t} \right)^2 + q_t(1 - \delta) \right] = q_{t-1} \tag{5.41}$$

This uses $R_t^{-1} = R_{t-1}^{-1}(1 + r)^{-1}$ with a constant interest rate. We can rewrite (5.41) in two or three different ways, starting from this:

$$\Pi_k(k_t, l_t) = q_{t-1}(1 + r) - q_t(1 - \delta) \approx q_{t-1}[r + \delta - (q_t - q_{t-1})/q_{t-1}]$$

where we define $\Pi_k(k_t, l_t) \equiv F_k(k_t, l_t) + \varphi \left(\frac{i_t}{k_t} \right)^2$ to be the marginal profit inclusive of the (beneficial) effect of an extra unit of installed capital in decreasing adjustment costs (but because this effect is small, it can be ignored) but exclusive of capital adjustment costs. Also, we could allow for a non-unitary relative price of the firms' product, so it should be the marginal revenue product (which may include a markup if the product market is monopolistic) instead of simply the marginal product (F_k). Finally, the tax rate on firm revenues could also be included (see the Guidance for Further Study). With these reminders, we can call $\Pi_k(k_t, l_t)$ the marginal profit from an extra unit of capital.

The term $q_{t-1}[r + \delta - (q_t - q_{t-1})/q_{t-1}]$ on the right is the 'user cost of capital' (UCK). As mentioned, this is cost of capital that incorporates depreciation and capital gains. If we think of q_{t-1} as the price of a unit of capital, the per-period cost of capital is interest on this plus depreciation costs that need to be fixed minus the capital gains, the percentage increase in the price of this capital. This user cost represents the flow cost of capital, the effective cost of buying one unit and selling it the next period; namely, interest on the loan (alternatively, the interest foregone on the financial capital that is tied there) plus the depreciation bill minus the gain in price. So, owning a unit of capital effectively costs the firm the UCK per period. The optimality condition dictates that the UCK should equal the marginal (revenue) product of capital or marginal profit.

A second way to interpret (5.41) is by rewriting it as:

$$r = \frac{\Pi_k(k_t, l_t)}{q_{t-1}} - \delta + \frac{q_t - q_{t-1}}{q_{t-1}}$$

This condition equalizes two rates of return: On the left-hand side is the market interest rate (r) available in the financial market; on the right-hand side is the rate obtainable from owning a unit of capital: the marginal profit as a percentage of the price of capital minus the depreciation rate plus proportional capital gains; this is the net effective rate of return to capital. Equilibrium in the financial markets occurs when no asset yields any predictable excess return; if it were so, financial investments should flow between assets, adjusting prices and rates of return, until, in equilibrium, the rates of return are equalized.[20]

5.3.2 Digression on Asset Prices

There is a third way of expressing (5.41) which is informative from the point of view of understanding asset prices. To see that, rewrite (5.41) as:

$$q_{t-1} \approx \frac{\Pi_k(k_t, l_t) + q_t}{(1 + r + \delta)} \tag{5.41'}$$

Consider now the interpretation of q_{t-1} as the stock market price of a unit of capital k_t.[21] This equals the marginal profit within a period (discounted) plus the discounted value of the same price at the end of the next period. This is in fact a general condition underlying asset pricing. Consider, e.g., q being a bond price: then this price in a certain period (e.g. $t - 1$) is the dividend (flow profit) that this bond entitles the owner to for one period plus the discounted price next period (obtainable for instance when this asset might be sold).

But the asset may be kept for more than one period. To see then what this implies intertemporally, we 'solve (5.41') forward' by repeated substitution as before, to obtain:[22]

$$q_t = \sum_{s=1}^{\infty} \frac{\Pi_k(k_{t+s}, l_{t+s})}{(1 + r + \delta)^s} \tag{5.42}$$

We now see more concretely that q is the present value of the marginal profits generated by a unit of new capital (investment) installed at the beginning of the planning period. The

---

[20] We have taken q to be the stock market price of a unit of capital; we are being rather informal here—see Chapter 11 for more rigorous detail.

[21] Under our timing conventions, this will be the stock market price on 31 December of the capital measured on 1 January of the next year (i.e. next day)—as mentioned, timing conventions can be slightly confusing but need not distract us.

[22] We also use the transversality condition which, given that asymptotically capital will be non-zero, implies: $\lim_{t \to \infty} R_t^{-1} q_t = 0$.

appropriate discount factor takes into account both the interest rate (cost of shifting funds across time) but also the depreciation rate (as this erodes capital).[23]

5.3.3 Summary

Analytically, the model is summarized by the user cost equation (5.40b) with the investment accounting equation (5.39) and the dynamic optimality condition (5.41). Let us see some implications of the model. Consider first a specification where (unlike here) investment in levels (not proportional) is related to q, $I_t = I(q_{t-1})$.[24] If so, the firm keeps accumulating capital until, in the steady state, q is equal to unity; then all investment ceases and the steady-state level of capital is implicitly given from the requirement that $\Pi_k(k_t, l_t) = r + \delta$. So, the steady state is the same as in the simple model of investment of the earlier section. But in the model here where adjustment costs depend on proportional investment, a more interesting scenario emerges. In the steady state, i/k is constant, so the representative firm (and the economy and all its variables) grows at a constant rate (g). From (5.39) and (5.40b), we have:

$$g \equiv \frac{k_{t+1} - k_t}{k_t} = \frac{i_t}{k_t} - \delta = \frac{q-1}{2\varphi} - \delta \tag{5.43a}$$

Additionally, with both q and Π_k constant (it is a zero-returns-to-scale function, as $\Pi(.)$ is assumed constant returns in k, therefore Π_k does not grow in the long run), (5.41) gives:

$$q = \frac{\Pi_k}{r + \delta} \tag{5.43b}$$

This is essentially the steady-state version of (5.42). The stock market value of the firm (average per unit of capital) is the present value of marginal profit. The steady-state equations (5.43a, b) are depicted in Figure 5.3 in (q, g) space.

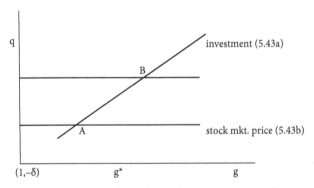

Figure 5.3. Stock market value and investment/growth

---

[23] The reader may be confused why $r + \delta$ appears in the user cost, but in the Ramsey model we had $r - \delta$. This is due to the difference in perspective. In the Ramsey model, $r - \delta$ is the rate of return (net of depreciation) available to the owner of capital/saver. Here, $r + \delta$ are both costs to the firm from owning capital; in addition to depreciation, there is the cost of borrowing or opportunity cost of tied resources.
[24] As we shall see in Chapter 11, such a theory is 'Tobin's (average) q'.

It is straightforward to see that:

Result 7: In the long run, the stock market of the firm and the growth rate:

Increase with the marginal profit of capital (indicated by a shift up of the 5.43b line in Figure 5.3, so that equilibrium moves from A to B);

Decrease with taxation (that implicitly decreases the marginal revenue product of capital);
Decrease with the real interest rate;

Decrease with the depreciation rate—this exerts a dual effect on the growth rate, so think carefully how each line shifts.

The dynamics of the system are simple, essentially governed by the one-variable difference equation (5.42); investment depends on but does not affect q. Imagine now that profitability rises permanently, e.g. in an industry (IT?) that experiences a sudden technical innovation in year t. The model has no transitional dynamics: q jumps up, immediately at the time that the improvement in profits becomes public news, and permanently. If the increase is a fixed amount $\Delta\Pi_k$, we may use (5.43b) to get at time t:

$$\Delta q_t = \frac{\Delta\Pi_k}{r+\delta}$$

In this way, the rise in marginal profit will be matched immediately by a rise in the user cost via the rise in q; but there will not be any (expected) capital gains as the jump in the stock price will be instantaneous and complete; there will be no further movement.

But the absence of any dynamics of transition is rather simplistic. Though this is not in the model, one may realistically hypothesize that investment responds partly to this year's stock market and partly to last year's investment (with $0 < \gamma < 1$). This is the 'time to build' specification of Kydland and Prescott (1982) and Altug (1989) which suggests that investment projects take time, so what was going on last year will partly continue this year; this obviously builds an element of inertia in the investment process and thereby the whole system:

$$1 + 2\varphi\frac{i_t}{k_t} = \gamma q_t + (1 - \gamma)\frac{i_{t-1}}{k_{t-1}} \tag{5.44}$$

(5.44) is an expanded version of (5.40b) in which a fraction γ of investment is based on profitability considerations embodied in q and a fraction $1 - \gamma$ is simply the left-over work from past investment. Thus, in (5.41') and (5.44), we now have a truly dynamic 2×2 system in q_t and $g_t (= i_t/k_t)$. Appendix 5B more formally illustrates the dynamics in this case. Under some range of the parameters, we shall have both an initial, instantaneous jump in q_t and some subsequent upward adjustment. So, the higher marginal profit will be matched by a higher user cost due to a higher price of capital q, alongside the anticipated capital gains after the innovation becomes public news and till the adjustment to the new long-run equilibrium is complete. Same (observationally equivalent) effects will be obtained if we have a new tax rate on the firm turnover that decreases its marginal profit. The reader is invited to consider the effect of a rise in the interest rate brought about by monetary policy.

5.3.4 Consumption and Investment Combined

We end this section by briefly bringing this analysis together with the analysis of consumption obtained in the Ramsey model; we follow Barro and Sala-i-Martin (1992) here. The household side of the economy is given in the same way as before; the profits are remitted to households but households treat them as residual as they do not control the firms; hence, the household optimization remains unchanged. The end result is that the Keynes-Ramsey rule (5.12') holds unaltered; it effectively gives the saving (S) that underpins growth. Consider it in the steady state without productivity or population growth:

$$g = \sigma[r - \delta - \rho] \tag{5.45a}$$

While the investment-production side is summarized by (5.43a, b):

$$g = \frac{\frac{\Pi_k}{r+\delta} - 1}{2\varphi} - \delta \tag{5.45b}$$

We plot (5.45a,b—labelled S(aving) and I(nvestment)) in Figure 5.4 in (r, g) space.

The S locus is upward-sloping as it depicts saving-financed growth, which depends positively on the return to it—the interest rate; the I locus is negatively sloped as the interest rate reduces the present value of profits, the stock market value of the firm, and hence investment and growth. Viewed in this way, the framework gives equilibrium growth and interest rate (g*, r*) in a closed economy, or (analytically the same thing) an integrated global economy. Since these loci essentially give saving and investment (which underpin growth from the two sides), Figure 5.4 gives us an analysis of the alternative goods market equilibrium condition (S = I).

Finally, we can use this framework to gain insights about the open economy, although a thorough treatment of this vast topic would require another book. Assume now that the economy in question is an open one, with fully integrated capital markets with the rest of the world; the implication is that it adheres to the world interest rate, r^w, otherwise unsustainable capital flows will ensue.[25] Assume also that the world interest rate is lower

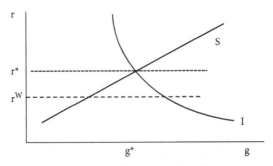

Figure 5.4. The saving-investment relationship in closed and open economies

---

[25] We ignore here the exchange rate movements and the wedge those may provide between the domestic and world interest rates.

than the one at which a closed economy would clear its goods market, $r^w < r^*$. It can be seen that at r^w, $I > S$, so the economy in question experiences a current account deficit (as can be verified from goods market equilibrium, $CA = S - I < 0$). The reader is invited to analyse the effects on the external deficit of the various changes considered in Result 7.

5.4 Money and Intertemporal Optimization: The Sidrauski Model

5.4.1 The Setup

We now introduce money into the Ramsey model of Section 5.2 based on Sidrauski (1967). The model integrates money into the real side of the economy and is designed to answer questions related to monetary policy and to the determination of the price level and inflation. Underlying all this are of course more fundamental questions such as why money exists and why we hold it; all these and many others are analysed in depth in Monetary Economics to which the interested reader is directed. In macroeconomic models of money such as the one here, the starting question is how to introduce money. Two avenues have been followed, a 'cash-in-advance' whereby cash is required ahead of any transaction, which is beyond our scope; and the 'money in the utility function' approach of the Sidrauski model, which we follow and which is the main innovation in what follows compared to the Ramsey model. Otherwise, the model here is based on an infinitely lived, intertemporally optimising, representative agent, i.e. the same setup as underlying the Ramsey model. So, we adopt here all the notation and assumptions of Section 5.2. To simplify further, we also assume that there is neither population nor productivity growth (population is normalized to 1), nor depreciation ($\delta = 0$). Prices (and implicitly, wages) are fully flexible.

The representative agent/family maximizes intertemporal utility:

$$\text{Max}_{c(t),\, m(t)} \qquad U_0 = \sum_{t=1}^{\infty} (1+\rho)^{-t} u(c_t, m_t)$$

Period utility u(.) depends in a general form on real consumption (c_t) and the real quantity of money (m_t), with the usual assumptions of positive but diminishing utility in each argument and complementarity between the two:

$$u_c > 0, \quad u_{cc} < 0, \quad u_m > 0, \quad u_{mm} < 0, \quad u_{cm} > 0$$

The justification for money to enter utility is that the individual values the 'liquidity services' of money, i.e. the fact that it facilitates transactions. The maximization is subject to the following period-by-period budget constraint:

$$w_t + rk_t = c_t + k_{t+1} - k_t + (M_{t+1} - M_t)/P_t \tag{5.46}$$

The sources of income, labour (with labour supply fixed at 1) and capital, are shown on the left-hand side; while the uses are shown on the right-hand side. Income is allocated between consumption, capital accumulation plus accumulation of nominal money, M_t, divided by the price level, P_t, so as to find the real value of money accumulation.[26] Noting

---

[26] Why do we write $(M_{t+1} - M_t)/P_t$ and not $m_{t+1} - m_t$ as the real cost of money accumulation? This is so as to highlight the opportunity cost of money—inflation. For other assets like capital, the inflation rate implicitly

the relation between real and nominal money, $m_t \equiv M_t/P_t$, the definition of inflation, $\pi_t \equiv \frac{(P_{t+1}-P_t)}{P_t}$, and the trivial development:

$$\frac{M_{t+1}}{P_t} = \frac{M_{t+1}}{P_{t+1}}\frac{P_{t+1}}{P_t} = m_{t+1}(1+\pi_t),$$

the constraint (5.46) can be re-expressed as:

$$w_t + rk_t = c_t + k_{t+1} - k_t + m_{t+1}(1+\pi_t) - m_t \tag{5.46'}$$

In this formulation, we have two additional uses of resources, which is to accumulate real money, plus to pay the cost of holding money incurred by inflation in the form of $m\pi$; this is because nominal money holdings lose purchasing power every year at the rate of inflation. Next, we introduce nominal interest rate (i_t) via the 'Fisher equation' with a constant real interest rate (r):

$$i_t = r + \pi_t \tag{5.47}$$

The Fisher equation states that the nominal interest rate should first compensate the owner of any asset for the loss of purchasing power due to inflation while they are holding the asset; the remainder is the real rate of return available to the saver and incurred by the borrower. In line with the conclusions of the Ramsey and the investment models, the real rate of return embodies deep fundamentals like productivity, the rate of time preference, the depreciation rate, the cost of investment, etc.

We use the approximation $m_{t+1}\pi_t \approx m_t\pi_t = m_t(i_t - r)$ and define total real assets as: $a_t \equiv k_t + m_t$. With all this information, we obtain the modified constraint:

$$w_t + ra_t = c_t + a_{t+1} - a_t + m_t i_t \tag{5.46''}$$

In this formulation, income from labour and total assets (ra_t) is spent on consumption, asset accumulation, and interest on money holdings. Money holdings do not incur any nominal cost or reward but are subject to the opportunity cost of foregoing the return available on other assets (the real interest rate, r) and they lose purchasing power at rate π_t, as mentioned. Put together, these make up the nominal interest rate which becomes a user cost of holding money, so $m_t i_t$ is effectively the rental cost of these money holdings.

Summing this period constraint forward as we did above with capital but now with real assets, we obtain the following intertemporal constraint:

$$\sum_{t=1}^{\infty} R_t^{-1}(c_t + m_t i_t) = a_0 + \sum_{t=1}^{\infty} R_t^{-1} w_t \tag{5.47}$$

As before, the lifetime income (made up of assets at the beginning of history, a_0, plus lifetime labour income) is allocated between consumption (price: 1) and money holdings (rental price: i_t). The household maximizes intertemporal utility subject to (5.47) with respect to the sequence of c_t and m_t. Note that we have brought the intertemporal constraint (5.47) in exactly the same form as (5.5). Therefore, the first-order conditions can be obtained in the same spirit as in Section 5.2.

---

drives a wedge between the nominal and real returns. An additional reason is that the nominal money supply (M) and its growth rate are determined by the policy-making authorities and exogenous to the model.

In analogy to (5.9), the dynamic Lagrangean is formed as:

$$\text{Max}_{c(t),\, m(t)} \quad \sum_{t=1}^{\infty}(1+\rho)^{-t}u(c_t, m_t) + \lambda\left[-\sum_{t=1}^{\infty}R_t^{-1}(c_t + m_t i_t) + a_0 + \sum_{t=1}^{\infty}R_t^{-1}w_t\right]$$

The first (intertemporal) FOC is essentially the same as (5.10):

$$(1+\rho)^{-t}\frac{\partial u(c_t, m_t)}{\partial c_t} = \lambda R_t^{-1} \tag{5.48}$$

This leads to something similar to (5.21):

$$\frac{\frac{\partial u(c_{t+1}, m_{t+1})}{\partial c_{t+1}}}{\frac{\partial u(c_t, m_t)}{\partial c_t}} = \frac{1+\rho}{1+r} \tag{5.48'}$$

If a parametric specification were used to substitute the marginal utility of consumption out, one would obtain a version of the Euler of consumption growth (5.11).

But the main focus of this model is on the second, intra-temporal FOC with respect to m_t, which determines the optimal money holdings in relation to consumption:

$$(1+\rho)^{-t}\frac{\partial u(c_t, m_t)}{\partial m_t} = \lambda R_t^{-1} i_t \tag{5.49}$$

The subjectively discounted marginal utility of money equals its discounted opportunity/ user cost times the Lagrange multiplier (λ). Using (5.48), we can rewrite:

$$\frac{\partial u(c_t, m_t)}{\partial m_t} = \frac{\partial u(c_t, m_t)}{\partial c_t} i_t \tag{5.49'}$$

The marginal utility of money equals the opportunity cost of money, evaluated in terms of welfare by the marginal utility of consumption. Under standard assumptions on utility, implicitly this yields a money demand of the form:

$$m_t = m(c_t, i_t), \quad m_c(.) > 0, \quad m_i(.) < 0$$

The main implications of the model arise from considering the steady state. The increase in nominal money can be written as:

$$\frac{M_{t+1} - M_t}{P_t} = \frac{M_{t+1} - M_t}{M_t}\frac{M_t}{P_t} \equiv \mu m_t$$

where μ is the rate of nominal money growth, assumed here to be constant and entirely determined by the monetary authority.[27] We also know that:

$$\frac{M_{t+1} - M_t}{P_t} = m_{t+1}(1+\pi_t) - m_t$$

---

[27] As we know from elementary Macro and we shall see in Chapter 7, the workings of the banking and financial sector partly determine the rate of monetary expansion, particularly of the broad money; also, modern Central Banks fix interest rates rather than the nominal money supply. But these objections are ignored here.

In the steady state, all real variables are assumed constant: $k_t = k$, $c_t = c$, $m_t = m$, $\pi_t = \pi$, for all t. Combining the two equations above using this information, we get that:

$$\pi = \mu$$

In the steady state, inflation is an entirely monetary phenomenon, in the sense that the inflation rate equals the (exogenous: policy determined) rate of nominal money expansion. Furthermore, since

$$\frac{\partial u(c_{t+1}, m_{t+1})}{\partial c_{t+1}} = \frac{\partial u(c_t, m_t)}{\partial c_t} = \frac{\partial u(c, m)}{\partial c},$$

from the Euler equation (5.48') and the profit-maximization condition (5.19a), we get:

$$f'(k) = r = \rho$$

The marginal product of capital ($f'(k)$) is equal to the real interest rate and that in turn to the rate of time preference, as before; if we had allowed for population growth and exogenous productivity growth, the equation would be exactly as in (5.22). But the key point is that the real interest rate and capital are not affected by monetary policy at all in the steady state. Moreover, neither does the level of nominal money in circulation nor its rate of growth affect the real side of the economy: level of capital, real interest rate, output, or consumption. The fact that the level of money does not affect the real side of the economy is called 'neutrality of money'; the fact that the growth rate of money is equally neutral is called 'superneutrality':[28]

Result 8: In the standard Sidrauski model, in the steady state:
(a) Money is superneutral (as well as neutral);
(b) The rate of money growth determines the inflation rate one-for-one.

A second implication is the celebrated 'Friedman (1969) rule': the departure point is that, for society as a whole, the marginal cost of creating additional money is (very close to) zero; you can produce banknotes at a very low marginal cost compared to their value. Therefore, in their quest to maximize welfare, the authorities should produce so much money such that:

Marginal social benefit = marginal social cost = 0

where the marginal social benefit equals the marginal utility of money (assuming away externalities).[29] It follows that the monetary policy-maker should create money to the point where marginal utility is zero, and this implies from (5.49'):

$$\frac{\partial u(c, m)}{\partial m} = \frac{\partial u(c, m)}{\partial c} i = 0 \qquad (5.50)$$

---

[28] Reis (2007) investigates the conditions underlying neutrality and superneutrality more thoroughly. Neutrality is always upheld while superneutrality holds as long as the money supply expands at a constant rate (μ); which is an assumption underpinning Result 8a (the Sidrauski superneutrality result). Note that, in both cases, price and wage flexibility is presumed.

[29] Note that the individual sets $u_c = i.u_m$, as the interest rate is given to them; but this interest rate is endogenous socially, so it cannot be the guide to policy. Instead, the policy-maker is guided by the more fundamental equality MSB = MSC(= 0).

Since $u_c > 0$ due to the usual assumption of non-satiation in consumption, the nominal interest rate (i) should be set to zero and this further implies from the Fisher equation (5.47):

$$i = r + \pi = r + \mu = 0$$

or

$$\mu = \pi = -r < 0$$

The monetary growth rate should be negative: there should be deflation equal to minus the real interest rate. This is the 'Friedman rule' of monetary policy (Friedman, 1969).[30] It is motivated by the need to provide a useful but costless good (money) to the point of satiation. See Schmitt-Grohe and Uribe (2010) for further analysis.

Result 9: The 'Friedman rule': the rates of nominal money growth and inflation should be negative and equal to minus the real interest rate.

Under this rule, there will be disinflation over time and the price level will be approaching zero; commensurately, the quantity of nominal money will be declining, thus reducing the costs of producing this intrinsically useless good (piece of metal or paper that has no other use). So, the more general rationale for the Friedman rule is that it leads us towards a cashless economy such as in the Ramsey world, where there is no money; the economy will then be approaching Pareto optimality (if the assumptions underpinning optimality in Ramsey hold).

5.4.2 The 'Friedman Rule' and Monetary Policy

The Friedman rule suggests that the instrument of monetary policy should be the nominal interest rate (set to zero, $i = r + \pi = r + \mu = 0$). However, for a long while monetary policy used to rely on money supply as its instrument, i.e. it determined a path of a monetary aggregate. This followed another reasoning made by Friedman (1956) that money supply and output were in a stable proportional relationship that depended on money demand. Evidence in the 1960s and 1970s suggested the existence of a stable money demand function, linking money and other key macroeconomic variables (output, the price level, interest rates, or variants of them). However, by the early 1990s, serious scepticism had arisen about the existence of such a stable money demand function. At the root of this scepticism were the sweeping financial innovations from the 1980s onwards; these have reduced any narrow money-GDP ratio as we need less cash balances for transactions (with credit cards, internet banking, etc.) but increased any broad money-GDP ratio. Furthermore, it has been found that significant effects of monetary policy actions on aggregate activity were manifested through changes in the interest rate(s) rather than the quantity of money; see Ireland (2009). As a result of all this reasoning and evidence,

---

[30] This is not the same as Friedman's 'k-per cent rule' which states that the monetary growth rate should be a constant (k per cent) no matter what the phase of the economy is (recession or expansion); see Chapter 1 and Chapter 6 on business cycles.

monetary policy since the 1990s has abandoned using the quantity of money as the instrument of policy and has adopted (an) interest rate as the policy instrument. It is argued (Woodford, 2000) that such an interest rate-based policy is the appropriate one for the 'cashless economy' arising from the use of the modern transactions technology. As we discuss in Chapter 7, this is how Central Banks target inflation; and this is what the 'Taylor rule' is based on.

In a sense, then, modern monetary policy has come round from a rule based on a stable monetary aggregate à la Friedman (1956) to a Friedman (1969) rule based on (zero) interest rates. Yet, Friedman's reasoning is not followed entirely: while it suggests that nominal interest rates should be zero and inflation rates negative, typically monetary authorities target an inflation rate slightly above zero (about 2 per cent). The background argument is that the Friedman rule relies heavily on the assumptions of the underlying Sidrauski model which are very special indeed (the 'money-in-utility' specification, infinite lives, price flexibility, lack of distortionary taxation); if any of these and other assumptions fail, as they do in real life, then the Friedman rule is an interesting benchmark but not necessarily optimal. As we discussed in Chapter 3, some more specific considerations about the optimal rate of inflation include:

- The true inflation rate is lower than the measured one (so that a measured inflation rate 2 per cent implies a true one close to zero);
- The nominal interest rate should be above zero, so as to have some room for policy expansion (by reducing it);
- A positive (but low) inflation rate is necessary for the adjustment of real wages.

5.5 Overlapping Generations Models

5.5.1 The Setup

Overlapping generations models, originally due to Samuelson (1958) and anticipated by Allais (1947), amend the obvious unrealistic feature of the Ramsey model of infinite lives. As mentioned, there are issues for which this obviously wrong assumption does not matter and the Ramsey model yields valuable conclusions in a tractable way. But there are other issues such as saving, much of which is done for retirement, or debt and social insurance, for which the infinite life assumption is outright misleading. By introducing finite lives and generations that overlap at different stages, the model introduced here is able to offer new insights. The simplest version of the model assumes that each generation lives for two periods, the 'young age' when the typical individual of this generation works and the 'old age' when the individual/generation is retired. Two generations are concurrently alive, the old and the young. One variant of the model assumes lives of three periods, very young, young, and old age; this allows for borrowing during the very young age with low income. But the complexity increases exponentially with every additional element, so treatment of this and other versions are left as an exercise to the interested reader (see Guidance for Further Study).

There are two generations alive, each of which lives for two periods—young and old. All variables will be super-scripted accordingly, e.g. consumption $c_{t-1}{}^y, c_t{}^o, c_t{}^y$ is that of the young at $t-1$ and the old at t (these two are in the same cohort) and the young at t, etc; and similarly with all variables. Aggregate variables will be shown with capital letters. The size of the generation that is born (young) at t (generation-t) is n_t and that of the generation born at $t+1$ is n_{t+1}; as before, the growth rate of n_t is $\eta \geq 0$. Aggregate population is $N_t = n_{t-1} + n_t$ (the young and the 'former young', born in $t-1$) and it is easy to check that it also grows at rate η. Straightforward division suggests that the proportion of the young in the population is $n_t/N_t = (1+\eta)/(2+\eta)$ whereas the old is $n_{t-1}/N_t = 1/(2+\eta)$; the higher the growth rate of the population the more relatively numerous are the young; the structure of the demographic pyramid and the growth rate of the population are closely linked.

All agents provide one unit of labour inelastically at their young age only; in the old age they are retired and consume the saving they have accumulated. As before, we assume that individuals own capital that they rent to firms; but the same results would be derived from a setup in which firms own the capital. The model only allows saving from a young age to old through capital accumulation but does not allow borrowing: Financial markets do not exist. In the absence of financial markets, production is the only channel through which the generations are economically linked.

In analogy to the setup of Sections 5.1 and 5.2, at the beginning of its life, the representative agent of each generation (say, born at t) maximizes their intertemporal utility:

$$U_t \equiv u(c_t^y) + (1+\rho)^{-1}u(c_{t+1}^o) \tag{5.51}$$

The newly born receive no endowment, so the only income of the young is labour (earning the exogenous market wage, w_t); it is allocated between consumption and capital accumulation which is the only form of saving. Thus, the period-t budget constraint of generation-t is:[31]

$$k_{t+1}^o + c_t^y = w_t \tag{5.52a}$$

In the following period, the old dis-save and leave zero assets;[32] they consume the capital they have accumulated plus the capital income they receive from it (before the capital is consumed)—the interest rate being variable here. The period-$t+1$ constraint of generation-t is:

$$k_{t+1}^o(1+r_{t+1}) = c_{t+1}^o \tag{5.52b}$$

Consolidating (5.52a, b), we obtain the lifetime budget constraint for generation-t:

$$\frac{c_{t+1}^o}{1+r_{t+1}} + c_t^y = w_t \tag{5.53}$$

---

[31] A note on timing: the saving accumulated at the end of youth (end of t) buys capital at the next instant, i.e. beginning of $t+1$. Thus, there is no interest in (5.52a). Interest on this saving accrues during period $t+1$, so it appears in (5.52b).

[32] An important assumption is that there are no bequests left from the old to the young. Thus, the old consume all their resources by the end of their lives, the young receive no endowments and there are no intergenerational linkages. The absence of bequests is an unrealistic but convenient assumption with important implications; it is rectified in more elaborate versions of the model; see the Guidance for Further Study.

Present and future discounted consumption equal the labour income of the young. At time t, this generation plan their consumption over their lifetime (c_t^y and c_t^o) in order to maximize lifetime utility (5.51) subject to the lifetime budget constraint (5.53). The resulting Euler equation, derived by substituting c_t^y out in (5.51) via (5.53) and maximizing with respect to c_{t+1}^o, is:

$$u'(c_t^y) = \frac{1+r_{t+1}}{1+\rho} u'(c_{t+1}^o)$$
(5.54)

This is a special version of (5.11), with two-period lives and no depreciation and zero population growth within the generation. As before, utility is $u(c_t) = \frac{c_t^{1-1/\sigma}}{1-1/\sigma}$. With this, we obtain:

$$c_{t+1}^o = \left(\frac{1+r_{t+1}}{1+\rho}\right)^\sigma c_t^y$$
(5.54')

This is the Keynes-Ramsey rule (5.11') adapted to the present context. Next, we introduce this information into the lifetime budget constraint to solve explicitly for consumption in each period:

$$c_t^y = \gamma_t w_t,$$
(5.55a)

$$\frac{c_{t+1}^o}{1+r_{t+1}} = (1-\gamma_t)w_t$$
(5.55b)

The two consumptions (the later one appropriately discounted) are fractions of lifetime labour income which is simply the wage earned in early life. The marginal propensity to consume out of income (γ_t) is:

$$0 < \gamma_t \equiv \frac{(1+r_{t+1})^{1-\sigma}(1+\rho)^\sigma}{1+(1+r_{t+1})^{1-\sigma}(1+\rho)^\sigma} < 1$$
(5.56)

Early consumption increases with impatience (ρ). The rate of return (future interest rate) accruing next period to current saving exerts an ambiguous effect, depending on whether the income or substitution effect dominates ($\sigma < 1$ or $\sigma > 1$, respectively); in the benchmark case of logarithmic utility ($\sigma = 1$) the two cancel out. Thus, the degree of flexibility in adjusting the plans to incentives (σ) is important. Discounted later-life consumption is essentially the mirror image of the early consumption.

Saving, that takes place in the early period, is only done by the acquisition of capital and is:

$$k_{t+1}^o = w_t - c_t^y = s_t w_t$$

where the propensity to save is the mirror image of the propensity to spend:

$$0 < s_t \equiv 1 - \gamma_t < 1$$

Turning now to the aggregate budget constraint, this is the sum of the budget constraints of the two generations, (5.52a) and (5.52b) shifted one period earlier, and both adjusted by cohort size. For period t, the national variables (in capitals) are:

$$Y_t = n_{t-1}k_t^o r_t + n_t w_t = n_{t-1}c_t^o + n_t c_t^y + n_t k_{t+1}^o - n_{t-1}k_t^o = C_t + K_{t+1} - K_t$$
(5.57)

Accordingly, national GDP equals the capital incomes (of the old) and the labour incomes (of the young) and these in turn equal consumption and capital accumulation—made up of the building capital of the young and the de-cumulation of the old (who will have consumed all their assets at the end of their lives). In other words, in this model, all asset accumulation happens within a lifetime and no assets are passed on between generations. But physical capital is not destroyed, merely sold by the old generation which consumes the proceeds, to the young. For example, aggregate capital at the beginning of $t + 1$ equals the capital of the then old, $K_{t+1} = n_t k^o_{t+1}$. Of that, a part $K_t = n_{t-1} k^o_t$ will have been bought from the previous generation in time t and the rest built by investment. We return to this issue shortly.

5.5.2 Implications for Aggregate Saving and the Growth Rate

Aggregate saving is of considerable interest, as will be discussed in Chapter 11. Here, in a closed economy without any government sector, aggregate saving equals investment, $K_{t+1} - K_t$. As mentioned, this also equals the acquisition of assets by the productive generation minus the consumption (liquidation) of the assets of the retired generation:

$$K_{t+1} - K_t = n_t k^o_{t+1} - n_{t-1} k^o_t = n_t (1 - \gamma_t) w_t - n_{t-1} (1 - \gamma_{t-1}) w_{t-1}$$

There is no guarantee as to whether this is positive or negative. But it is easy to see that it is higher the greater the population growth rate, the greater the growth rate of the economy (an effect that goes via the real wage available to the different cohorts—whether the growth rate is due to productivity improvement or due to other reasons), and the rate of time preference as impatience increases the marginal propensity to spend (γ_t). The interest rate exerts an ambiguous effect for reasons discussed earlier. These are useful perspectives to keep in mind when in Chapter 11 we discuss the empirical determinants of saving.

Result 10: Aggregate saving in the basic OLG model: increases with the population growth rate and the growth rate of the economy; decreases with the rate of time preference.

It is also informative to inspect the growth rate of aggregate capital:

$$\frac{K_{t+1} - K_t}{K_t} = \frac{n_t (1 - \gamma_t) w_t - n_{t-1} (1 - \gamma_{t-1}) w_{t-1}}{n_t w_t}$$

In the steady state (when $\gamma_t = \gamma_{t-1} = \gamma$), we get:

$$\frac{K_{t+1} - K_t}{K_t} = (1 - \gamma) \left[1 - \frac{n_{t-1} w_{t-1}}{n_t w_t} \right] \approx (1 - \gamma) \left[\eta + \frac{w_t - w_{t-1}}{w_{t-1}} \right]$$

So, three sets of factors affect the growth rate: the individual propensity to save ($s = 1 - \gamma$), embodying the return to saving, the time preference/impatience rate, and intertemporal substitution; the population growth rate ($\eta \equiv \frac{n_t}{n_{t-1}} - 1$); and the productivity growth rate implicit in the growth rate of the market wage (w).

5.5.3 Production

We next turn to production. Here, things are the same as in the Ramsey model. Households rent their capital and labour to firms and get the market interest and wage rates. Again, we shall transform variables to per capita, efficiency units through division by $A_t N_t$ (reminder: $\hat{k}_t \equiv \frac{K_t}{A_t N_t}$ and similarly for the other variables). The production function is:

$$\hat{y}_t = f\left(\hat{k}_t\right) = \hat{k}_t^\alpha \tag{5.58}$$

with the productivity-adjusted wage:

$$\frac{w_t}{A_t} = f\left(\hat{k}_t\right) - f'\left(\hat{k}_t\right)\hat{k}_t = (1-\alpha)\hat{k}_t^\alpha \tag{5.59a}$$

and interest rate:

$$r_t = f'\left(\hat{k}_t\right) = \alpha\hat{k}_t^{\alpha-1} \tag{5.59b}$$

Equations (5.59a, b) repeat (5.26a, b). Furthermore, the aggregate resource constraint (5.57) is readily turned to efficiency units:

$$\hat{y}_t = \hat{c}_t + \hat{k}_{t+1}(1+g_A)(1+\eta) - \hat{k}_t \tag{5.57'}$$

This is essentially (5.24) with an inconsequential modification.

Using information developed above, capital at $t+1$ is:

$$K_{t+1} = n_t k_{t+1}^o = n_t s_t w_t$$

Division by $N_t A_t$ to turn this into efficiency units, noting $\frac{n_t}{N_t} = \frac{1+\eta}{2+\eta}$, and use of (5.59a) yields:

$$\hat{k}_{t+1}(1+\eta)(1+g_A) = \frac{1+\eta}{2+\eta} s_t (1-\alpha)\hat{k}_t\alpha$$

Using (5.56) and (5.59b), we also have:

$$s_t = \left(1-y_t\right) = \frac{1}{1+\left(1+\alpha\hat{k}_t^{\alpha-1}\right)^{1-\sigma}(1+\rho)^\sigma}$$

The combination of the last two equations gives:

$$\hat{k}_{t+1}(1+\eta)(1+g_A) = \frac{1+\eta}{2+\eta}\frac{1-\alpha}{1+\left(1+\alpha\hat{k}_t^{\alpha-1}\right)^{1-\sigma}(1+\rho)^\sigma}\hat{k}_t\alpha \tag{5.60}$$

This is a non-linear equation in capital (in per capita, efficiency units). The steady state involves a constant $\hat{k}_t = \hat{k}^* > 0$ for all t:[33]

---

[33] In fact, there may be more than one equilibrium, some of which may be stable and others unstable; there is also of course the trivial equilibrium of $\hat{k} = 0$ which we ignore. Note also that the quantity κ depends on the equilibrium capital stock and thus will be different for each solution. Appendix 5.C briefly discusses the stability properties of any solution.

$$\hat{k}^* = \frac{1}{(1+g_A)(2+\eta)} \frac{1-\alpha}{1 + \left(1 + \alpha \hat{k}^{*\alpha} - 1\right)^{1-\sigma}(1+\rho)^\sigma} \hat{k}^{*\alpha} \tag{5.61}$$

Once we determine equilibrium capital $\hat{k}^*$, equilibrium output and all the other variables are immediately read off this, e.g. through $\hat{y}^* = \hat{k}^{*\alpha}$. The problem is that there may be more than one equilibrium, whose properties are not easy to ascertain. To proceed, we can invoke the 'correspondence principle' due to Samuelson (1947); this states that the 'comparative statics' and the dynamics of a model are linked. In our context, this implies that, if a solution is stable, then we can use this property to ascertain its 'comparative statics'—the effect of parameters on equilibrium capital given by that solution.

Stability of an equilibrium $\hat{k}^*$ requires that, around it, we must have:

$$\kappa \equiv \frac{d\hat{k}_{t+1}}{d\hat{k}_t}\Big|_{\hat{k}_t^* = \hat{k}_{t+1}^* = \hat{k}^*} < 1$$

Intuitively, this implies that any movement in $\hat{k}_t$ away from equilibrium elicits a less than one-for-one movement in $\hat{k}_{t+1}$, therefore the whole movement eventually dies down.[34] From (5.60), evaluating the derivative at equilibrium, we see that this requires:

$$\kappa = \alpha \left[1 + \frac{1-\alpha}{\alpha}(1-\sigma) \frac{(1+\alpha \hat{k}^*\alpha - 1)^{1-\sigma}(1+\rho)^\sigma}{1 + (1+\alpha \hat{k}^*\alpha - 1)^{1-\sigma}(1+\rho)^\sigma} \frac{\alpha \hat{k}^*\alpha - 1}{1 + \alpha \hat{k}^*\alpha - 1} \right] < 1 \tag{5.62}$$

Now, assume that a certain equilibrium $\hat{k}^*$ is stable; how is it affected by the parameters of interest such as the population growth rate (η), the productivity/technology growth rate (g_A), or the rate of time preference (ρ)? Totally differentiating (5.62), we obtain:

$$\frac{d\hat{k}^*}{dg_A} = -\frac{\hat{k}^*}{(1-\kappa)(1+g_A)}$$

We see that the condition $\kappa < 1$ that is required for stability is also critical for signing the effect of this parameter; this is an application of the 'correspondence principle'. Similar expressions and the same sign would be obtained with respect to the other parameters of interest—the reader is invited to verify the following results:

Result 11: Capital intensity and output in the overlapping generations model decrease with:
the population growth rate,
the rate of productivity/technological progress, and
the rate of time preference.

The first two reduce the steady-state capitalization (per capita capital stock in efficiency units) as they require a higher maintenance bill before additional accumulation takes place; the rate of time preference implies higher consumption due to greater impatience and leads to the same effect.[35] All these results are the same as in the Ramsey model.

---

[34] See Appendix 5.C for more on the stability properties of any solution.
[35] Note of course that, although a higher g_A leads to a lower $\hat{k}^*$, it still implies a higher growth rate of per capita capital and output (K/N and Y/N; i.e. not in efficiency units) as noted in the Ramsey model.

5.5.4 Overlapping Generations and Dynamic (In)Efficiency

One important difference between the Ramsey and OLG models concerns the possibility for dynamic inefficiency. Recall that the 'golden rule' capital stock is the one that maximizes consumption (always in per capita, efficiency units). As in the Ramsey model, this can be obtained from the national income accounting equation (5.57') in the steady state (with $\delta = 0$):

$$\hat{k}^{*\alpha} = \hat{c}^* + \hat{k}^*(\eta + g_A) \tag{5.63}$$

Maximization of $\hat{c}^*$ with respect to $\hat{k}^*$ results in the following levels (superscripted 'gr'):

$$r^{gr} = \alpha\left(\hat{k}^{gr}\right)^{\alpha-1} = \eta + g_A \tag{5.64}$$

To see the possibilities that arise, rewrite the equilibrium capital (5.61) as:

$$r^* = \alpha\hat{k}^{*\alpha-1} = (1+g_A)(2+\eta)\left[1 + \left(1+r^*\right)^{1-\sigma}(1+\rho)^{\sigma}\right]\frac{\alpha}{1-\alpha} \tag{5.61'}$$

Or linearizing the right-hand side and rearranging:

$$r^* \approx \frac{\alpha[4 + g_A + \eta + \sigma\rho]}{1 - \alpha - \alpha(1 - \sigma)} \tag{5.65}$$

Comparing (5.64) with (5.65), with a small enough α, we have $r^* < r^{gr}$, therefore $\hat{k}^* > \hat{k}^{gr}$, so dynamic efficiency potentially arises. It is rather unlikely, though. Even with $\sigma = 1$, the limit of what can be considered realistic, we would need to have an α much less than 0.33, which is the ball-park value typically assumed as the contribution of capital in a Cobb-Douglas production function; this is because η and g_A, being small fractions, are whole orders of magnitude lower than 4. Hence, in our context, dynamic inefficiency is possible but unlikely; in other OLG setups however, inefficiency arises more naturally. As dynamic efficiency is a prerequisite for Pareto efficiency, and this possibly fails here, it follows that the OLG setup may be Pareto inefficient, too.

Result 12: In the OLG model, dynamic inefficiency potentially arises, leading to overall Pareto inefficiency.

The possibility of dynamic inefficiency predicted by OLG makes the empirical testing of the question even more pressing; see the Guidance for Further Study.

5.5.5 Overlapping Generations and Social Insurance

OLG models are well suited to study of social insurance and pension systems. Such models share with the Ramsey model the idea that individuals plan for the future in a rational way according to their utility function and the relevant constraints, taking into account impatience (rate of time preference). But OLG models add some basic realism about lifetimes (a retirement stage), which the Ramsey model with the infinite lives lacks. In this concluding sub-section, we examine social insurance in an OLG framework.

Though adequate pensions and a decent standard of living in later life are important, in practice individuals may not be trusted to save 'enough' for old age; as anyone in their middle or later age remembers, saving for retirement was not the top priority when one started a career! Aside from myopia, saving for retirement requires commitment, sophistication, and resources that many people do not have. Myopia, lack of self-discipline and commitment, or lack of financial awareness, all imply that the optimality conditions of the OLG or Ramsey models will be violated. The result may be poverty during retirement and old age.

For these reasons, there is potentially a role for the state in organizing and operating social insurance. Individuals pay contributions to the state (or a state-run system or, increasingly often, private providers) when young and receive a pension in old age. Pension systems are classified as 'Fully funded' (FF) systems where the pensions that are paid come from the contributions made in the young age of the same generation after investment (by the social insurance provider, state or private); individuals pay contributions into a personal 'pot' which is liquidated during retirement and the amount of the pension depends on the value of this personally accumulated pot. The alternative is 'Pay as you go' (PAYG) systems, whereby the contributions of the young pay for the pensions of the old generation concurrently; the value of the pensions received by the old depends on the number and contributions of the current younger generation. In other words, FF systems involve transfers across time but not across generations whereas PAYG systems are the opposite. Next, we examine analytically the two systems.

'Fully funded' social insurance (FF)

We use the OLG model with a slight modification: individuals do not own all the capital of firms; part of the capital is owned by pension funds. The part that individuals own in $t + 1$ (acquired in the productive young age) continues to be denoted k_{t+1}^o; additionally, individuals pay a contribution d_t to a pension fund in their youth. So, the budget constraint of the young (5.52a) is modified to:

$$k_{t+1}^o + d_t + c_t^y = w_t \tag{5.66a}$$

The key feature of the system is that the transfer of funds happens across time within each generation; there are no financial linkages between generations. The insurance provider (pension fund) invests the contributions d_t; the easiest is to assume that they also buy firm capital, denoted k_{t+1}^s, so the individual 'pot' that is formed is $d_t = k_{t+1}^s$. In $t + 1$, the insurance provider receives interest on its investment which it pays out together with the liquidation of the 'pot', so the pension paid out equals $k_{t+1}^s(1 + r_{t+1})$. In other words, the system does extra saving on behalf of the individuals. Hence, the budget constraint of the old (5.52b) is modified to:

$$(k_{t+1}^o + k_{t+1}^s)(1 + r_{t+1}) = c_{t+1}^o \tag{5.66b}$$

Now, if we define the total amount of assets owned in period $t + 1$ either directly by individuals or indirectly on their behalf by pension funds (their personal 'pot') as $k_{t+1} \equiv k_{t+1}^o + k_{t+1}^s$, and noting $d_t = k_{t+1}^s$, the period budget constraints (5.66a, b) are rewritten as:

$$k_{t+1} + c_t^y = w_t, \tag{5.66a'}$$

$$k_{t+1}(1+r_{t+1}) = c^o_{t+1} \tag{5.66b'}$$

In other words, except for an inconsequential renaming of capital from to k^o_{t+1} to k_{t+1} (and from k^o_t to k_t, etc.) nothing else changes from (5.52a, b). Utility continues as before, and the budget constraints are the essentially same; therefore, the optimality conditions will be the same and so will be the aggregate resource constraint. The system will behave exactly as before in both dynamics and the steady state, with the same amount of (total) capital and consumption as before in both periods, for all generations; the only change is that part of the capital stock will now be held by the social insurance provider on individuals' behalf. Thus, this system does nothing else except enforce the optimality conditions of the OLG model: It does the forward planning on behalf of the individuals and commits them to it; and all that in a way that does not distort the aggregate outcomes.

'Pay as you go' (PAYG) social insurance

Things are different with PAYG. Here, the pensions of the old, p_t, are paid from the contributions of the young; as mentioned, the transfer is now across generations within each period and there are no investments made by the system. To balance its books, taking into account cohort numbers, the system pays:

$$n_{t-1}p_t = n_t d_t \tag{5.67}$$

Thus, the budget constraints in the two periods of life for generation-t (5.52a, b) are modified to:

$$k^o_{t+1} + d_t + c^y_t = w_t \tag{5.68a}$$

$$c^o_{t+1} = k^o_{t+1}(1+r_{t+1}) + p_{t+1} = k^o_{t+1}(1+r_{t+1}) + n_{t+1}d_{t+1}/n_t \tag{5.68b}$$

For simplicity, let us assume that the per capita contribution is constant, so that $d_t = d$ for all t.[36] So, as before, the individual maximizes:

$$U_t \equiv u(c^y_t) + (1+\rho)^{-1}u(c^o_{t+1})$$

Subject to:

$$k^o_{t+1} + d + c^y_t = w_t \tag{5.68a'}$$

$$c^o_{t+1} = k^o_{t+1}(1+r_{t+1}) + (1+n)d \tag{5.68b'}$$

Intuitively, the individual forgoes an amount d that they would have invested themselves earning the interest rate, and instead the system 'invests' it for them, giving them a rate of return equal to the population growth rate (ratio of aggregate contributions to aggregate pensions). Consolidate (5.68a', b') into an intertemporal constraint to get:

$$\frac{c^o_{t+1}}{1+r_{t+1}} + c^y_t = w_t - \frac{(r_{t+1}-n)d}{1+r_{t+1}} \tag{5.69}$$

[36] In practice, contributions are more likely to be proportional to earnings; but treatment of this (harder) case is left as an exercise to the reader.

This replaces the original intertemporal budget constraint (5.53). So, the individual is better/worse off with PAYG social insurance than if they were left on their own if the population growth rate is higher/lower than the interest rate; in a nutshell, PAYG works if the population growth rate is sufficiently high. The same Euler condition as before

$$\left(u'(c_t^y) = \frac{1+r_{t+1}}{1+\rho} u'(c_{t+1}^o) \right)$$

now leads to:

$$c_t^y = \gamma_t \left[w_t - \frac{(r_{t+1} - \eta)d}{1+r_{t+1}} \right], \tag{5.70a}$$

$$\frac{c_{t+1}^o}{1+r_{t+1}} = (1 - \gamma_t) \left[w_t - \frac{(r_{t+1} - \eta)d}{1+r_{t+1}} \right] \tag{5.70b}$$

(5.70a, b) replace (5.55a, b). Following exactly the steps taken before, we now get:

$$\hat{k}_{t+1} = \frac{1}{(2+\eta)(1+g_A)} \frac{1}{1 + \left(1+\alpha\hat{k}_t^{\alpha-1}\right)^{1-\sigma}(1+\rho)^\sigma} \left[(1-\alpha)\hat{k}_t^\alpha - \frac{\left(\alpha\hat{k}_t^{\alpha-1} - \eta\right)d}{1+\alpha\hat{k}_t^{\alpha-1}} \right]$$

For convenience, let us assume that contributions d are proportional to the steady state capital, $d = \omega\hat{k}^{**}$ (the steady-state values of this model are denoted by **). Substituting into the steady-state version of the above, it is convenient to solve for the interest rate, $r^{**} = \alpha\hat{k}^{**\alpha-1}$:

$$(1+g_A)(2+\eta)\left[1 + (1+r^{**})^{1-\sigma}(1+\rho)^\sigma\right] = \left[\frac{(1-\alpha)r^{**}}{\alpha} - \frac{(r^{**} - \eta)\omega}{1+r^{**}} \right]$$

Ignoring the $1+r^{**}$ denominator on the far right, we get:

$$r^{**} \approx \frac{\alpha[4 + g_A + \eta + \sigma\rho + \eta\omega]}{1 - 2\alpha - \alpha(1 - \sigma)} > r^* \tag{5.71}$$

Comparing r^{**} to r^* in (5.65), we see that, with an α sufficiently low to ensure a positive denominator, the interest rate is higher and capital stock lower under PAYG social insurance than without any insurance. Providing that dynamic efficiency holds, welfare is reduced in relation either to no insurance at all or (the same thing) to an FF system. But if there is INefficiency, then the intriguing possibility arises that PAYG systems might actually improve welfare (as they decrease capital); see the Guidance for Further Study.

In practice, FF systems are called 'defined contributions' as you know what you pay in but do not know what you get out (to put it with a mild dose of cynicism), as the contributions are then invested in the stock market and the pension to be derived depends on how the stock market is doing at the time when the 'pot' is liquidated. The alternative is the 'defined benefits' system, which is a stronger version of PAYG in the sense that the pension is a fixed proportion of the end-career wage; this proportion is called the 'replacement ratio', whose average for the OECD economies is around 50 per cent. So, the insurance system faces a constraint of the type (with a replacement ratio of 0.5) $n_{t-1}p_t = 0.5n_{t-1}w_{t-1} = n_t d_t$. In practice, d_t will be proportional to current wages (w_t), so this budget constraint will be satisfied when there are healthy demographics and a strong per capita growth rate of the economy (implicit in wage growth). Under these conditions, a PAYG system is financially healthy and permits inter-generational solidarity; it is as if the younger generation tells the older 'you brought us up, now it is our turn for us to support you'. So, when the system is healthy, rather little attention is paid to its adverse effects—reduced capital and welfare compared to its absence or with FF.

The problem is that the weak demographics of almost all industrialized economies and slow growth have put the financial viability of social insurance systems into serious question. As a result, a mixture of responses has been adopted: pensions tend to be reduced (e.g. in 'defined benefits' systems the benefit tends to become the career-average wage, rather than the end-career); working lives tend to lengthen (pensionable age for the author's generation in the UK is 67 with the tendency to rise); and there is a tendency for systems to switch away from PAYG to FF; e.g. in the UK, practically all employees outside the state sector are now subject to 'defined contributions'/FF schemes, and there is pressure for state-sponsored schemes to also switch to 'defined contributions'. Finally, immigration, a vexed issue politically, may in fact be a substitute for the weak demographics and shores up the finances of social insurance, as typically immigrants are young and economically active and pay contributions without drawing pensions.

Notes on the Literature

The Ramsey (1928)/Cass (1965)/Koopmans (1965) model is now standard fare and well explained in practically all advanced macro texts. So is the OLG model, launched by the celebrated Samuelson (1958) article, but also anticipated by Allais (1947) and elaborated by Diamond (1965); see Weil (2008) for a useful review. The hybrid Ramsey-OLG model by Yaari (1965), Blanchard (1985), and Weil (1989) is introduced briefly below. On investment, we shall have more to say in Chapter 11, so we mention more sources there; Hayashi (1982) is a good introduction to the modern theory, bringing together the concepts of investment, user cost, marginal and average q. For a peek at state-of-the-art theory, one should become acquainted with the burgeoning and very technical 'heterogeneous agents' literature, nicely surveyed by Heathcote et al. (2009).

On the mathematical background: A rather thorough familiarity with Chiang (1984, 1992) is the minimum required for anyone aiming to get to grips with macro dynamics, indeed all modern macroeconomic theory. For anyone armed with that, most graduate macro texts are within reach. Beyond that, one could consult Sydsaeter et al. (2005) and Sundaram (1996), before being in a position to tackle the most technical advanced macro texts such as Lucas et al. (1989) and Ljungqvist and Sargent (2000). At a more accessible level, Turnovsky (1995) covers much of the material of this Chapter in continuous time. Azariadis (1993) offers a useful advanced treatment of non-linear dynamic models.

Guidance for Further Study

Heterogeneity

The first generation of dynamic micro-founded macro models were based on a representative agent, either an infinite-lived one (Ramsey model) or a representative of each generation (OLG); there was also a representative firm; and these are the models we have reviewed in this chapter. Introducing heterogeneous agents and firms was not thought important and was also technically demanding. Gradually, however, the importance of heterogeneity became obvious: agents differ in initial wealth and/or ability and motivation and/or preferences and/or the shocks they face (e.g. unemployment or illness) against which they may be unable to fully insure. Meanwhile, advances in mathematical and computational methods allowed the complex aggregation involved in going from individual optimality conditions and behaviour to aggregate outcomes. Heterogeneity allows tackling important issues such as inequality, the uncertainty experienced at the individual level (much larger than the aggregate) and hence welfare, and richer public policy conclusions. Models with complete insurance are simpler as somehow the individual risk 'washes out' in the aggregate; the much more realistic models with imperfect insurance are much more complex, however, as aggregate output and its distribution are interdependent and evolve jointly over time. This is already a very rich and fast-expanding literature; the nice survey by Heathcote et al. (2009) is a good portal into it.

OLG models are instrumental for 'generational accounting'

This important concept has been pioneered by the American economist Laurence Kotlikoff (1992) and his co-authors; see e.g. Auerbach et al. (1994). This approach aims to estimate the tax burden (net of taxes) each generation now and in the future will shoulder. It proceeds by estimating the lifetime tax burden, appropriately discounted, of the current adults (call it T) and subtracting this from the 'fiscal gap', an estimate of the intertemporal government expenses minus revenues, again appropriately discounted; the difference: 'fiscal gap' – T represents the tax burden the future adults will be called to shoulder over their lives. As such, generational accounting is closely linked to public finances and their sustainability. Of course, to estimate intertemporal values, one needs to make 'heroic' assumptions about future public expenditure plans, GDP, etc., all of which can change dramatically. Also, one needs to select appropriate discount rates and estimates are very sensitive to them (a problem that also plagues social insurance providers who need to estimate current and future receipts and payments). And of course one would need to know how much each generation benefits from public services, as well, and ideally subtract this from the intertemporal tax burden (T). For these reasons, generational accounting has attracted criticism (e.g. Galbraith et al., 2009). So, while perhaps one may not fully trust the fine details of such exercises, a rough idea of how each generation fares may be informative at a time when (the general suspicion is) that the current young generation cannot hope to be better off than the previous one for the first time in recent history (stagnation, changing national insurance systems, rising cost of housing, and whatnot). See Kotlikoff (1992) for more details from the originator of the idea and Gokhale and Smetters (2006) for an update. What do you make of it?

Hybrid Ramsey-OLG models

A strand of models assume generations that live many periods but have a constant probability of death (due to Yaari, 1965—somewhat more realistic than either the infinite horizon or the lives of fixed length, but not entirely true); new generations arrive at a constant birth rate. These models allow aggregation over cohorts as the fixed birth/death rates work analytically in the same way as discounting. In one version of the model (Blanchard, 1985) the birth and death rates are equal, so that population is constant. In another version (Weil, 1989), generations live forever and new generations arrive at a constant rate; it is argued that the essential properties of OLG models are due to birth and not death. These models derive aggregate consumption dynamics which are similar to the Ramsey-type Euler equation but with a twist and combine this with the aggregate resources constraint of the

Ramsey model. Derive these two equations for either version of the model. How does equilibrium differ from the Ramsey case? What are the effects of important parameters such as the rate of growth of population or the rate of time preference? How do they differ from the Ramsey setup?

Dynamic (in)efficiency

There has not been much work since the seminal paper by Abel et al. (1989) on this important question. Dynamic inefficiency, if true, could have very serious implications: First, on 'secular stagnation' from which Japan has suffered for 20 and more years and western economies may be sliding into (see the discussions in various places of this book)—if an economy has over-accumulated capital, why would it grow further (think of the Euler equation with a low interest rate); there is the potential for asset bubbles (Tirole, 1985)—if the marginal product and dividend on capital are low, you are forced to seek capital gains, driving prices higher, e.g. in housing or land, which would transfer resources from the younger generations to the older who typically own these assets; and firms may be giving investors less for their money than they demand from them for further investment, thus destroying shareholder value. These and other implications are discussed in as yet unpublished research by Geerolf (2017) which provides updated empirical work and finds that inefficiency is more likely than we thought. If so, there are important policy implications, one of which is the desirability of PAYG social insurance, which would reduce equilibrium capital.

Bequests in the OLG model

The basic model presented here assumes that parents (the old generation) do not care at all for their children (the young); however, parents leave bequests at the end of their lives motivated by the fact that they love their offspring. These bequests create linkages between the generations; in the limit, if parents love the children like themselves, it is as if they live forever through their children, so that the OLG model approaches the infinite-horizon model. In reality, we may be somewhere in-between the basic OLG model without bequests and infinite horizons. Bequests and concomitant linkages between generations have implications for a number of issues, e.g. the effects of fiscal policy, discussed in Chapter 8. Another issue that can be meaningfully addressed when bequests exist is the extent to which capital accumulation is due to saving within a lifetime period and to what extent it is due to bequests between the generations. These are important questions for income inequality and social mobility; we return to them in Chapter 10 on Inequality. An early investigation by Kotlikoff and Summers (1981) suggested that the wealth passed on as inter-generational transfers (bequests) made up the vast majority of total accumulated wealth in the US. Of the total of $3.9tr of wealth in 1974, $3.15tr was transfer wealth and only $0.7tr was wealth accumulated within the lifetime. While estimates like these continue to be re-examined, they do suggest that the model without bequests is rather seriously lacking. There are of course important implications for (in)equality and a strong argument arises for inheritance taxes.

OLG-3

Naturally, allowing for only two-period lives is very restrictive. Models do exist that allow for three-period lives: the low-income young, the high-income middle-aged, and the pensioners (children are not economically active in their own right); so three generations are concurrently alive. Such frameworks can deal with a much richer set of issues such as borrowing by the young (who overlap with the immediately older generation for two periods, so they can repay the loan later, something not possible in the basic model), age-related income distribution, the resulting aggregate saving pattern, asset bubbles, and more. The problem is that the complication rises greatly with the additional, third cohort. Consult Raurich and Seegmuller (2017) for an interesting recent paper along these lines and portal into this literature. See also Chapter 11 for further discussion.

Immigration and social insurance

As mentioned, immigrants, who are typically young and economically active, may be useful in supporting the finances of social security in OECD economies that feature 'demographic deficit' (most of them). For recent estimates of the fiscal implications of immigration see Storesletten (2003) and Ben-Gad (2017).

Demographics and social insurance

As mentioned, most developed economies have seen their pension systems come under serious financial strain in recent years, which is a combination of a number of factors: first, a 'demographic deficit', lower population growth rates due to lower fertility rates and especially longer lives (with longer retirement); second, a more transitory but important demographic factor is that the 'baby boom' post-war generation is now retiring; thirdly, the economic stagnation after the 2007–9 'great recession' leading to lower contributions; lastly, also economic, the lower interest rates and returns for the providers' financial investment. The Paris-based Organization for Economic Cooperation and Development (OECD) continually monitors the pensions systems and their viability in member states and the efforts made to address the difficulties. See OECD (2017) for a recent report.

Money demand with changing transactions technology

Even though monetary policy has now switched to the interest rate as the policy instrument, the relation between monetary aggregates and economic fundamentals (the money demand function) continues to be of interest. Some recent work suggests that a stable relationship is to be found if one models not any monetary aggregate on its own but a combination of aggregates (narrow and broad money) called a 'Divisia index' whose opportunity cost is correspondingly an index of interest rates; e.g. Belongia and Ireland (2017) suggest that such a measure exhibits a stable money demand function. However, financial innovation continues in a fast pace, with internet banking (etc.) that further weakens the use of money; so, more time and data are required in order to see whether this approach is indeed stable.

APPENDIX 5A
Saddle-Point Stability of Linear, 2 × 2 Difference Equation Systems

We illustrate saddle-point stability with system (5.38) which is repeated here:

$$\begin{bmatrix} log\hat{c}_{t+1} - log\hat{c}^* \\ log\hat{k}_{t+1} - log\hat{k}^* \end{bmatrix} = D \begin{bmatrix} log\hat{c}_t - log\hat{c}^* \\ log\hat{k}_t - log\hat{k}^* \end{bmatrix}$$

Where

$$D \equiv \begin{bmatrix} 1 & -\sigma(\alpha-1)\hat{k}^{*(\alpha-1)} \\ 0 & \hat{k}^* \end{bmatrix}^{-1} \begin{bmatrix} 1 & 0 \\ -\hat{c}^* & (1+\alpha-\delta-\eta-g_A)\hat{k}^{*\alpha} \end{bmatrix} =$$

$$= \frac{1}{\hat{k}^*} \begin{bmatrix} \hat{k}^* - \hat{c}^*(\alpha-1)\hat{k}^{*(\alpha-1)} & (\alpha-1)\hat{k}^{*(\alpha-1)}(1+\alpha-\delta-\eta-g_A)\hat{k}^{*\alpha} \\ -\hat{c}^* & (1+\alpha-\delta-\eta-g_A)\hat{k}^{*\alpha} \end{bmatrix}$$

as we have:

$$\begin{bmatrix} 1 & -\sigma(\alpha-1)\hat{k}^{*(\alpha-1)} \\ 0 & \hat{k}^* \end{bmatrix}^{-1} = \frac{1}{\hat{k}^*} \begin{bmatrix} \hat{k}^* & \sigma(\alpha-1)\hat{k}^{*(\alpha-1)} \\ 0 & 1 \end{bmatrix}$$

The trace and determinant of D are:

$$trD = \frac{1}{\hat{k}^*}\left[\hat{k}^* - \hat{c}^*\sigma(\alpha-1)\hat{k}^{*(\alpha-1)} + (1+\alpha-\delta-\eta-g_A)\hat{k}^{*\alpha}\right] > 0$$

And

$$detD = (1+\alpha-\delta-\eta-g_A)\hat{k}^{*\alpha} > 0$$

The eigenvalues are given by:

$$\lambda_{1,2} = \frac{trD \pm \sqrt{(trD)^2 - 4detD}}{2}$$

$$\text{As } \sqrt{(trD)^2 - 4detD} > \frac{1}{\hat{k}^*}\left[\hat{k}^* - \hat{c}^*\sigma(\alpha-1)\hat{k}^{*(\alpha-1)} - (1+\alpha-\delta-\eta-g_A)\hat{k}^{*\alpha}\right]$$

As may be checked, we have:

$$\lambda_1 > \frac{1}{\hat{k}^*}\left[\hat{k}^* - \hat{c}^*\sigma(\alpha-1)\hat{k}^{*(\alpha-1)}\right] > 1,$$

$$\text{as } \sqrt{(trD)^2 - 4detD} > \frac{1}{\hat{k}^*}\left[-\hat{c}^*\sigma(\alpha-1)\hat{k}^{*(\alpha-1)} + (1+\alpha-\delta-\eta-g_A)\hat{k}^{*\alpha}\right].$$

It follows that:

$$\lambda_2 < 1/2$$

Hence, the two eigenvalues are either side of unity, as stated. To verify the slope of the stable arm, note that each of the eigenvalues, λ_i, $i = 1, 2$, by definition satisfies:

$$0 = (D - \lambda_i I_2)\begin{bmatrix} q_c^i \\ q_k^i \end{bmatrix}$$

Where I_2 is the 2 × 2 unit matrix, and $[q_c^i, q_k^i]$ is the eigenvector associated with eigenvalue i. Note that the above involves two equations for each i, as the matrices are 2 × 2. The vector of the variables as they evolve along the stable arm is given by the eigenvector associated with λ_2; choosing the upper equation, we have:

$$0 = \left[1 - \hat{c}^*\sigma(\alpha-1)\hat{k}^{*(\alpha-1)}/\hat{k}^* - \lambda_2 \quad \sigma(\alpha-1)\hat{k}^{*(\alpha-1)}(1+\alpha-\delta-\eta-g_A)\hat{k}^{*\alpha}\right]\begin{bmatrix} q_c^i \\ q_k^i \end{bmatrix}$$

Since $1 - \lambda_2 > 0$, and $\alpha - 1 < 0$, we readily see that $q_c^2/q_k^2 > 0$; the variables are positively correlated alongside the stable arm which is upward-sloping in $(\hat{k}_t, \hat{c}_t)$ space, as shown in Figure 5.2. In other words, the variables are positively correlated during transition. When the steady-state equilibrium changes for whatever reason, consumption (only) jumps instantaneously from its initial position onto the stable arm that passes from the new equilibrium. After the initial jump, the variables gradually move along the stable arm towards the new equilibrium.

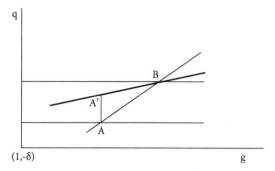

Figure 5B.1. Stock market value and investment/growth under 'time to build'

APPENDIX 5B
Adjustment Costs, 'Time to Build', and the Dynamics of the Stock Market Price and Investment

We now briefly discuss the dynamics of the investment-stock market price model with the richer formulation of investment (5.44), repeated below:

$$1 + 2\varphi \frac{i_t}{k_t} = \gamma q_t + (1 - \gamma) 2\varphi \frac{i_{t-1}}{k_{t-1}} \tag{5.44}$$

For $0 < \gamma < 1$, this introduces some autocorrelation and persistence in investment, intended to capture the 'time-to-build' property of investment; accordingly, current investment depends on a weighted average of the cost of capital (q) and past investment. As before, we also have the stock market equation (5.41') with $\Pi_k(k_t, l_t) \equiv F_k + \varphi \left(\frac{i_t}{k_t}\right)^2$:

$$q_{t-1} = \frac{F_k + \varphi \left(\frac{i_t}{k_t}\right)^2 + q_t}{(1 + r + \delta)} \tag{5.41''}$$

To make it more interesting, we have reintroduced the marginal product of capital (assumed constant) and the effect of capital on adjustment costs instead of the marginal profit.

Next, using $\frac{i_t}{k_t} = g_t + \delta$, where g is the growth rate of capital, we rewrite (5.44) as:

$$1 + 2\varphi(g_t + \delta) = \gamma q_t + (1 - \gamma) 2\varphi(g_{t-1} + \delta) \tag{5.B.1}$$

We can also linearize around the steady state:

$$\left(\frac{i_t}{k_t}\right)^2 \equiv (g_t)^2 \approx (g_t + \delta)^2 \approx (g + \delta)^2 + 2(g + \delta)g_t$$

With this information, (5.41'') becomes:

$$q_{t-1} = \frac{F_k + \varphi(g + \delta)^2 + 2\varphi(g + \delta)g_t + q_t}{(1 + r + \delta)} \tag{5.B.2}$$

Equations (5.B.1, 2) are a linear, 2×2 system of difference equations as that analysed in Appendix 5A. To proceed, we re-write the variables as deviations (tildes) from the steady-state values (without subscripts). In matrix formulation, the system is:

$$\begin{bmatrix} 1 & 2\varphi(g + \delta) \\ -\gamma/2\varphi & 1 \end{bmatrix} \begin{bmatrix} \tilde{q}_t \\ \tilde{g}_t \end{bmatrix} = \begin{bmatrix} (1 + r + \delta) & 0 \\ 0 & (1 - \gamma) \end{bmatrix} \begin{bmatrix} \tilde{q}_{t-1} \\ \tilde{g}_{t-1} \end{bmatrix},$$

where $\tilde{q}_t \equiv q_t - q$, and similarly for g_t. Using the terminology of Appendix 5A, we have:

$$D \equiv \begin{bmatrix} 1 & 2\varphi(g+\delta) \\ -\gamma/2\varphi & 1 \end{bmatrix}^{-1} \begin{bmatrix} (1+r+\delta) & 0 \\ 0 & (1-\gamma) \end{bmatrix} =$$

$$= \frac{1}{1+\gamma(g+\delta)} \begin{bmatrix} 1 & -2\varphi(g+\delta) \\ \frac{\gamma}{2\varphi} & 1 \end{bmatrix} \begin{bmatrix} (1+r+\delta) & 0 \\ 0 & (1-\gamma) \end{bmatrix} =$$

$$= \frac{1}{1+\gamma(g+\delta)} \begin{bmatrix} 1+r+\delta & -2\varphi(g+\delta)(1-\gamma)2\varphi \\ (1+r+\delta)\gamma/2\varphi & (1-\gamma) \end{bmatrix}$$

And

$$detD = (1+r+\delta)2\varphi(1-\gamma) > 0$$

$$trD = \frac{1+r+\delta+(1-\gamma)2\varphi}{1+\gamma(g+\delta)}$$

The eigenvalues are given by:

$$\lambda_{1,2} = \frac{trD \pm \sqrt{(trD)^2 - 4detD}}{2}$$

If there is no 'time to build' specification ($\gamma = 1$), then we only get one eigenvalue that is higher than 1 (if $g < r$) that needs to be solved forward as in the text, giving the q as the forward sum of future marginal profits. With 'time to build' ($\gamma < 1$), we get two eigenvalues. It is easy to think of parameter values that make these eigenvalues either side of 1, yielding a saddle-point equilibrium.

The situation is depicted in Figure 5B.1; initial equilibrium is A. Consider the effects of an one-off technical innovation or productivity improvement. In Figure 5B.1, as in Figure 5.3, the stock market price line shifts up, yielding the new equilibrium B. How do we approach this? It can be easily checked as before that the stable arm is positively sloped (the thick line). For stability, we need one (free to) 'jump' variable, readily given by q which is an asset price. The level of capital is for sure 'predetermined', unable to jump instantaneously; it is a moot point of how to characterize its growth rate (investment). We assume that g is predetermined, evolving sluggishly in view of the adjustment costs associated with it. At the instant ($t = t_0$) when the innovation becomes public news (and only then), we have a discrete jump of the stock price q, from A to A', which is only part of the long-term adjustment. Investment, g, does not respond instantaneously. Thereafter ($t > t_0$), q rises further towards B; investment picks up gradually towards its new steady-state level (recall the inertia due to 'time to build'). Hence, the rise in the marginal profit is matched by a higher user cost which is

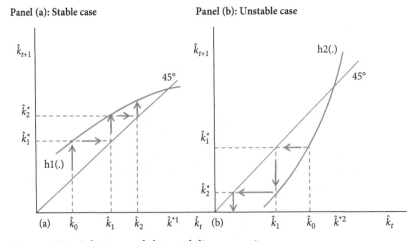

Figure 5C.1. Solutions and their stability properties

made up of a higher stock price, but is mitigated by the anticipated capital gains. The adjustment is faster in the beginning, gradually slowing down towards B; so capital gains are strong early on and milder later on. Profitability inclusive of the effect of capital on adjustment costs, $F_k + \varphi\left(\frac{i_t}{k_t}\right)^2$, rises even beyond the initial rise at $t = t_0$; this generates an upward movement in q and a decline in the capital gains, so there is a two-fold rise in the user cost that matches the rise in the adjustment cost-inclusive marginal profit.

APPENDIX 5C
On the Stability Properties of Non-Linear Difference Equations

In this Appendix, we illustrate the stability properties of single-variable, non-linear difference equations like (5.60). Such an equation takes the general form:

$$\hat{k}_{t+1} = h(\hat{k}_t)$$

As mentioned in the text, there may be more than one solutions, whose stability properties vary; two families of solutions are shown graphically in Figure (5C.1) in $(\hat{k}_t, \hat{k}_{t+1})$ space:

Panels (a) and (b) represent a stable and an unstable case; these may be present in the same function h(.) even multiple times, depending on how many equilibria exist; h1(.) and h2(.) may therefore be interpreted as different functions or different segments of the same function. The 45° is the graphical equivalent of equality, as in (any) equilibrium, $\hat{k}_{t+1} = \hat{k}_t = h(\hat{k}_t)$. Function h1(.) is flatter than 45° (in the vicinity of the equilibrium) as $\kappa_1 < 1$, while the opposite is true for h2(.), where $\kappa_2 > 1$.

In panel (a), stability is illustrated by the arrows which trace the adjustment in capital from a hypothetical starting point $\hat{k}_0 < \hat{k}^{*1}$. Apply h1(.) to see where we are next period, i.e. $\hat{k}_1 = h1(\hat{k}_0)$. Now apply the 45° line to see the starting point for the following iteration. The following period, apply h1(.) again to get $\hat{k}_2 = h1(\hat{k}_1)$; then, $\hat{k}_2$ becomes the starting point; and we continue in the same way. The key point is that, in this case, the iterations become progressively smaller (infinitely so) and we approach equilibrium $\hat{k}^{*1}$. The same happens if we happen to start at a level of capital above $\hat{k}^{*1}$; illustration is left as an exercise to the reader. Thus, $\hat{k}^{*1}$ is stable. Things are quite different with h2(.) which is steeper than 45°. Again, starting from an arbitrary starting point $\hat{k}_0 < \hat{k}^{*2}$, we trace the adjustment to $\hat{k}_1$, $\hat{k}_2$, etc. We see that in fact capital withers away to zero. The same conclusion applies if the starting point were $\hat{k}_0 > \hat{k}^{*2}$, were capital would diverge more and more from equilibrium towards infinity. Thus, $\hat{k}^{*2}$ is unstable.

So, the 'cookbook' procedure is as follows:

- Take the dynamic equation such as $\hat{k}_{t+1} = h(\hat{k}_t)$; plot the $h(\hat{k}_t)$ function and the 45° line in a $(\hat{k}_{t+1}, \hat{k}_t)$ graph; check for equilibrium/a (intersection/s of the two lines);
- For *each* equilibrium $\hat{k}_i^*$, check whether

$$\kappa_i \equiv \frac{dh(\hat{k}_t)}{d\hat{k}_t}\Big|_{\hat{k}_t = \hat{k}_{t+1} = \hat{k}_i^*} = \frac{d\hat{k}_{t+1}}{d\hat{k}_t}\Big|_{\hat{k}_t = \hat{k}_{t+1} = \hat{k}_i^*} < 1 \text{ or } > 1;$$

- The equilibrium/a with $\kappa_i < 1$ is/are stable.

In fact, κ is also informative in other respects. Note, the arguments below apply to any stable equilibrium only ($\kappa < 1$). Start from a first-order linearization of $h(\hat{k}_t)$ around an equilibrium $\hat{k}_i^*$:

$$\hat{k}_{t+1} = \hat{k}_i^* + \kappa_i(\hat{k}_t - \hat{k}_i^*)$$

This can be rewritten as a 'partial adjustment' equation:

$$\hat{k}_{t+1} - \hat{k}_t = (1 - \kappa_i)(\hat{k}_t - \hat{k}_i^*)$$

Each period, the movement in $\hat{k}_t(\hat{k}_{t+1} - \hat{k}_t)$ will be proportional to (i.e. partially adjust to) the discrepancy from equilibrium $(\hat{k}_t - \hat{k}_i^*)$. In other words, each period, the variable will move to eliminate a fraction $1 - \kappa_i$ of this discrepancy. Thus, $1 - \kappa_i$ is also the speed of adjustment of $\hat{k}_t$. Finally, consider a position $\hat{k}_0$ that the variable had at t = 0.[37] Adapting the above, we have:

$$\hat{k}_1 = (1 - \kappa_i)\,\hat{k}_i^* + \kappa_i \hat{k}_0$$
$$\hat{k}_2 = (1 - \kappa_i)\,\hat{k}_i^* + \kappa_i \hat{k}_1 = (1 - \kappa_i)\,\hat{k}_i^* + \kappa_i(1 - \kappa_i)\,\hat{k}_i^* + \kappa_i^2 \hat{k}_0$$
$$....$$
$$\hat{k}_t = (1 - \kappa_i)\left[1 + \kappa_i + \kappa_i^2 + \cdots + \kappa_i^{t-1}\right]\hat{k}_i^* + \kappa_i^t \hat{k}_0$$

From the properties of the geometric series, we have that $(1 - \kappa_i)\left[1 + \kappa_i + \kappa_i^2 + \cdots + \kappa_i^{t-1}\right] = 1 - \kappa_i^t$. So, after t periods, our variable will be a linear combination of the equilibrium (end state) and the initial condition ($\hat{k}_0$), with weights $1 - \kappa_i^t < 1$ and $\kappa_i^t < 1$, respectively. How close will $\hat{k}_t$ be to the equilibrium and how close to its initial position? How far will it have travelled? That depends on two factors: time (t) as κ_i^t declines with t (recall that $\kappa_i < 1$); and the speed of adjustment $1 - \kappa_i$ (so, inversely on κ_i). Recall also that κ_i depends on the parameters of the model, so its structure also determines speed and position at any time t.

References

Abel, A.B., N.G. Mankiw, L.H. Summers, and R. Zeckhauser (1989): Assessing Dynamic Efficiency: Theory and Evidence, *Review of Economic Studies*, 56(1), 1–20.

Allais, M. (1947): *Economie et interet*. Paris: Imprimerie Nationale.

Altug, S. (1989): Time-to-Build and Aggregate Fluctuations: Some New Evidence, *International Economic Review*, 30, 889–920.

Ascari, G., L.M. Magnusson, and S. Mavroeidis (2016): *Empirical Evidence on the Euler Equation for Consumption and Output in the US*, University of Oxford, mimeo, July.

Attanasio O.P., and G. Weber (2010): Consumption and Saving: Models of Intertemporal Allocation and their Implications for Public Policy, *Journal of Economic Literature*, 48(3) (September), 693–751.

Auerbach, A.J., J. Gokhale, and L.J. Kotlikoff (1994): Generational Accounting: A Meaningful Way to Evaluate Fiscal Policy, *Journal of Economic Perspectives*, 8(1) (Winter), 73–94.

Azariadis, C. (1993): *Intertemporal Macroeconomics*, Oxford: Wiley-Blackwell.

Barro, R.J., and J. Sala-i-Martin (1992): Public Finance in Models of Economic Growth, *Review of Economic Studies*, 59(4), 645–61.

Barro, R.J., and J. Sala-i-Martin (1995): *Economic Growth*, New York: McGraw-Hill.

Belongia, M.T., and P.N. Ireland (2017): The Demand for Divisia Money: Theory and Evidence, Boston College Working Papers in Economics 937.

Ben-Gad, M. (2017): On the Political Economy of Deficit Bias and Immigration. *Economic Journal*, 128(614) (September), 2191–2221.

Blanchard, O.J. (1985): Debt, Deficits, and Finite Horizons, *Journal of Political Economy*, 93(2), 223–47.

Blanchard, O.J., and C.M. Kahn (1980): The Solution of Linear Difference Models under Rational Expectations, *Econometrica*, 48(5) (July), 1305–11.

---

[37] This argument is correct under the assumption that $\hat{k}_0$ is not far away from $\hat{k}_i^*$.

Carroll, C.D. (2001): Death to the Log-Linearized Consumption Euler Equation! (And Very Poor Health to the Second-Order Approximation), *Advances in Macroeconomics (B.E. Journal of Macroeconomics)*, 1:(1) (November), Article 6.

Cass, D. (1965): Optimum Growth in an Aggregative Model of Capital Accumulation, *Review of Economic Studies*, 32(3), 233–40.

Chiang, A. (1984): *Fundamental Methods of Mathematical Economics*, 3rd ed., New York: McGraw-Hill.

Chiang, A. (1992): *Elements of Dynamic Optimization*, New York: McGraw-Hill.

Diamond, P. (1965): National Debt in a Neoclassical Growth Model, *American Economic Review*, 55(5), 1126–50.

Friedman, M. (1956): The Quantity Theory of Money: A Restatement, in M. Friedman (ed.), *Studies in the Quantity Theory of Money*, Chicago: University of Chicago Press, 3–21.

Friedman, M. (1969): *The Optimum Quantity of Money*, London: Macmillan.

Fuhrer, J., and G. Rudebusch (2004): Estimating the Euler Equation for Output, *Journal of Monetary Economics*, 51(6), 1133–53.

Galbraith, J.K., L.R. Wray, and W. Mosler (2009): *The Case Against Intergenerational Accounting: The Accounting Campaign Against Social Security and Medicare*, Public Policy Brief, No. 98, Annandale-on-Hudson, NY: The Levy Economics Institute of Bard College.

Geerolf, F. (2017): *Reassessing Dynamic Efficiency*, UCAL mimeo, July.

Gokhale, J., and K.A. Smetters (2006): Fiscal and Generational Imbalances: An Update, in J.M. Poterba (ed.), *Tax Policy and the Economy*, Boston: MIT Press, 193–223.

Hall, R.E. (1988): Intertemporal Substitution in Consumption, *Journal of Political Economy*, 96(2), 339–57.

Havranek, T., R. Horvath, Z. Irsova, and M. Rusnak (2013): Cross-Country Heterogeneity in Intertemporal Substitution, IES Working Paper 11/2013, Charles University.

Hayashi, F. (1982): Tobin's Marginal q and Average q: A Neoclassical Interpretation. *Econometrica*, 50, 213–24.

Heathcote, J., K. Storesletten, and G.L. Violante (2009): Quantitative Macroeconomics with Heterogeneous Households, *Annual Review of Economics*, 1, 319–54.

Ireland, P.N. (2009): On the Welfare Cost of Inflation and the Recent Behavior of Money Demand, *American Economic Review*, 99(3), 1040–52.

Koopmans, T.C. (1965): On the Concept of Optimal Economic Growth, in *The Economic Approach to Development Planning*, Chicago: Rand McNally, 225–87.

Kotlikoff, L.J. (1992): *Generational Accounting: Knowing Who Pays, and When, for What we Spend*, New York: Free Press (Macmillan).

Kotlikoff, L.J., and L.H. Summers (1981): The Role of Intergenerational Transfers in Aggregate Capital Accumulation, *Journal of Political Economy*, 89(4), 706–32.

Krusell, P., and A.A. Smith, Jr. (1998): Income and Wealth Heterogeneity in the Macroeconomy, *Journal of Political Economy*, 106(5) (October), 867–96.

Kydland, F., and E. Prescott (1982): Time to Build and Aggregate Fluctuations, *Econometrica*, 50 (November), 1345–70.

Ljunngqvist, L., and T.J. Sargent (2000): *Recursive Macroeconomic Theory*, Boston: MIT Press.

Lucas, R.E., N.L. Stokey, with E.C. Prescott (1989): *Recursive Methods in Economic Dynamics*, Cambridge, MA: Harvard University Press.

OECD (2017): *Pension Markets in Focus*, Paris: OECD.

Ramsey, F.P. (1928): A Mathematical Theory of Saving, *Economic Journal*, 38(152), 543–59.

Raurich, X., and T. Seegmuller (2017): *Income Distribution by Age Group and Productive Bubbles*, AMSE Working Papers 1740, Marseille, France: Aix-Marseille School of Economics.

Reis, R. (2007): The Analytics of Monetary Non-Neutrality in the Sidrauski Model, *Economics Letters*, 94(1) (January), 129–35.

Samuelson, P.A. (1947): *Foundations of Economic Analysis*, Cambridge, MA: Harvard University Press.

Samuelson, P.A. (1958): An Exact Consumption-Loan Model of Interest with or without the Social Contrivance of Money, *Journal of Political Economy*, 66(6), 467–82.

Schmitt-Grohe, S., and M. Uribe (2010): The Optimal Rate of Inflation, in B.M. Friedman and M. Woodford (eds), *Handbook of Monetary Economics*, Amsterdam: Elsevier, iiiB, 653–722.

Sidrauski, M. (1967): Rational Choice and Patterns of Growth in a Monetary Economy, *American Economic Review*, 57(2), 534–44.

Storesletten, K. (2003): Fiscal Implications of Immigration: A Net Present Value Calculation, *Scandinavian Journal of Economics*, 105, 487–506.

Sundaram, R.K. (1996): *A First Course in Optimization Theory*, Cambridge: Cambridge University Press.

Sydsaeter, K., P. Hammond, A. Seierstad, and A. Strom (2005): *Further Mathematics for Economic Analysis*, Harlow: Prentice Hall.

Tirole, J. (1985): Asset Bubbles and Overlapping Generations, *Econometrica*, 53, 1071–1100.

Turnovsky, S.J. (1995): *Methods of Macroeconomic Dynamics*, Cambridge, MA: MIT Press.

Weil, P. (1989): Overlapping Families of Infinitely-Lived Agents, *Journal of Public Economics*, 38(2), 183–98.

Weil, P. (2008): Overlapping Generations: The First Jubilee, *Journal of Economic Perspectives*, 22(4) (Fal), 115–34.

Woodford, M. (2000): Monetary Policy in a World Without Money, *International Finance*, 3(2), 229–60.

Yaari, M. (1965): Uncertain Lifetime, Life Insurance, and the Theory of the Consumer, *Review of Economic Studies*, 32, 137–50.

6

Business Cycles and Stabilization Policy

6.1 Introduction to Business Cycles

6.1.1 Introduction

Business cycles are recurrent ups and downs in economic activity ('business'); they are equivalently called 'economic fluctuations'. If we look at the time profile of the real GDP (RGDP) of just about any country, two striking observations are immediately made (see Figure 6.1 for a few industrialized economies). First, RGDP tends to grow secularly, allowing for considerable improvements (in many cases) in living standards over generations. Secondly, the time profile of RGDP is not smooth, but is characterized by temporary ups and downs. These show some (imperfect) regularity—e.g. output may be relatively high or low for a few quarters in a row. These movements are the business cycles. Finally, there are also movements that appear to be completely erratic; such movements, are said to be pure 'noise'.[1]

The first question that emerges in business cycle analysis is how to determine and isolate the business cycle component of the RGDP time profile from both the long-term developments and the erratic noise. Here, three approaches have been followed, which we can call the NBER approach (from the US National Bureau of Economic Research), the detrending approach, and the differencing approach. Traditional study of the business cycle at the NBER in the US, going at least as far back as Burns and Mitchell (1946) and still pursued today, proceeds by inspecting the data and judging (by a variety of methods, including visual) when peaks and troughs occur (the terminology will be systematized a little later). These are points at which increases in RGDP give way to slowdowns, or vice versa—much like the (local) maximum and minimum points in maths.

When analysing peaks and troughs, NBER analysts take into account the behaviour of a variety of aggregate and sectoral indices of economic activity (RGDP, employment, real consumption, investment, etc., at both aggregate and sectoral levels).[2] This method of characterizing cycles has produced a full history of US peaks and troughs for the last 150 years. But the NBER uses this type of analysis not only for historical purposes, but also in order to forecast—to the extent possible—future turnarounds. To do this, they use the historical record to identify a list of variables that precede (or 'lead') the cycle. By compiling and inspecting the behaviour of a list of 'leading indicators' (variables such as various components of GDP, housing starts, and new car registrations), they are able to detect advance signs of impending turnarounds. A useful, and succinct, introduction to NBER

---

[1] Like the noise heard on the radio or TV when the reception is not good. The distinction here, as in the discussion of the Lucas 'island' model in Chapter 2, is between 'signals', systematic patterns, and 'noise', completely erratic and uninformative movements.

[2] See <http://www.nber.org/cycles/recessions.html>

Theory of Macroeconomic Policy. Christopher Tsoukis, Oxford University Press (2020). © Christopher Tsoukis.
DOI: 10.1093/oso/9780198825371.003.0006

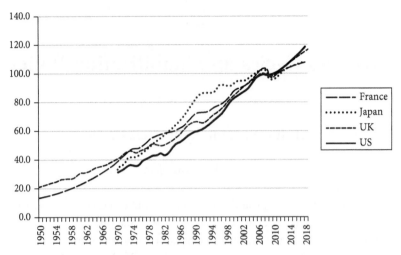

Figure 6.1. Real GDP for selected industrial economies

Notes: Real Gross Domestic Product (index, 2010 = 100).

Source: OECD (expenditure method, volume). Because all the indices equal 100 in 2010, the series do not give information about cross-country comparisons; the graph is only meant to show the evolution of individual series across time.

practices and comparison with other methods of detecting cycles is given by Stock and Watson (1999); see their earlier Stock and Watson (1989) paper for a description of vintage work. Now, the practice has spread: the OECD compiles a 'Composite Leading Indicator' for each country.[3]

The second, de-trending method proceeds by distinguishing and identifying the trend and business cycle components of RGDP. We can imagine the long-term movements of GDP occurring along a smooth line, such as the 'line of best fit' provided by econometrics—this line is said to represent trend RGDP. Figure 6.2 plots the US actual and trend real GDP— both logged; the trend line is the broken line. If Y is actual RGDP, the business cycle component (or 'output gap') is defined as $Ygap \equiv Y^* - Y$ (where $Y^* \equiv$ Trend Y).[4] Ygap is positive when the economy is producing below its long-run sustainable level and negative when, temporarily, the economy is working on, as it were, overdrive (because people and capital are working overtime, in a way that cannot be sustainable in the long run). Actually, it makes more sense to define the output gap in percentage terms, i.e.

$$ygap \equiv (Y^* - Y)/Y^* \approx y^* - y,$$

where $y \equiv \log Y$, and $y^* \equiv \log(\text{Trend}Y)$. Another oft-used concept is the 'de-trended output', output net of the trend, $Y^{dt} \equiv Y - Y^*$; in percentage terms, $y^{dt} \equiv (Y - Y^*)/Y^*$. Clearly, $y^{dt} = -ygap$. This is shown in Figure 6.3 for the US; it clearly shows an (imperfect) periodical pattern.[5]

---

[3] See the St Louis Fed page <http://research.stlouisfed.org/fred2/categories/33077> for more information related to the US.

[4] Relating to the discussion in Section 1.8, trend output is the 'natural rate of output' as it evolves over time; and the output gap in percentage terms (ygap) is exactly as in equation (1.11).

[5] The Figures here are based on annual data. If we had used quarterly or monthly data instead, we would have also observed 'seasonal cycles', variations according to season; typically, business is better around Christmas or summer, and less good during winter; see Cecchetti and Schoenholtz (2014).

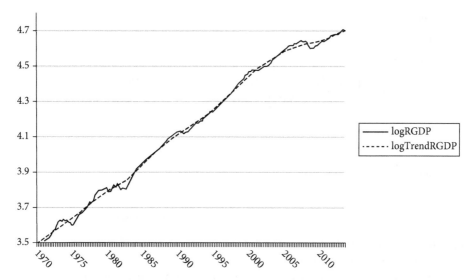

Figure 6.2. Actual and trend US real GDP

Notes: Actual andd trend US Real GDP (both logged).

Source: Bureau of Economic Analysis. Data accessed 16/7/2014. The trend series is constructed in the same way as in Figure 6.3. Note that because of the log scale of the variables, a certain distance on the vertical axis translates into a certain percentage change in the variable (as opposed to a given absolute increase) – e.g. from 3.7 to 3.9 represents the same percentage increase as from 4.3 to 4.5 (can you explain why?).

The third method, called differencing, involves constructing the growth rates of series like the RGDP or any other trending series of interest such as the price level (the RGDP growth rate and the inflation rate, respectively). Most commentators in public discourse look at the growth rate of real GDP rather than the output gap which involves de-trending output by elaborate methods. The industrialized world has experienced an average rate of GDP growth in the post-World War II years of about 3 per cent. Any rate similar to that or higher (such as those experienced during much of the 1990s) is considered to be a healthy, booming rate of growth; anything below that, but positive, is a slowdown. (But note that these designations are not appropriate for emerging economies, several of which have experienced growth rates of 6, 8, or 10 per cent for many years in a row.) Many statistical offices classify a recession as a period of two or more successive quarters (six months or more) of falling output (negative growth); but that is not exactly the NBER approach (see below). A really severe recession is called a depression, such as the one that occurred in the inter-war years (from about 1929 and well into the 1930s—the 'Great Depression'). The last section of this chapter gives an informal account of major episodes such as this.

Figure 6.3 gives a first visual impression of how the three methods work when applied to the US RGDP. Shown are the growth rate of actual output as well as the (per cent) de-trended output; the two are positively correlated but only weakly; their correlation coefficient is r = 0.23. The key point here is that the two series in general have quite different statistical properties. Shown also are the recessions determined by NBER; they capture most of the episodes of strong negative growth and a big output gap as determined by de-trending. So, in practice, there is a considerable degree of (but not full) agreement between the three methods.

These two features neatly define the agenda of much of modern macroeconomics. The growth rate of Y*, trend real output, is studied by Growth Theory reviewed in Chapter 9

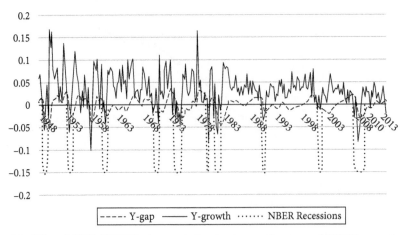

Figure 6.3. US real GDP (RGDP): de-trended output, growth rate, and NBER recessions

Note: US RGDP is a seasonally adjusted index.

Source: US Bureau of Economic Analysis (BEA). De-trended Y is given in percentage terms, i.e. $(Y-Y^*)/Y^*$; the trend is calculated with the Hodrick-Prescott filter, $l=1600$. The (seasonally-adjusted) growth rate is given by the BEA (not calculated). 'NBER Recessions' is the dates of the recessions as given by NBER (see their website - accessed July 2014).

and is widely thought to be determined by supply-side factors only. The output gap is studied by (various) models of business cycles—the subject of this chapter as well as of much of intermediate macroeconomics. Stabilization policy is the set of policies that aims to smooth the cycle as much as possible. Business cycles are potentially caused by the interaction of both demand and supply factors, with the exact mix a matter of debate. The key point here is that, whereas long-run growth theory and policy is only about supply, the study of business cycles and stabilization policy potentially gives a prominent role to Aggregate Demand (as well as Supply).

6.1.2 Terminology

Time now to introduce some more precise terminology. Consider Figure 6.4 which shows an imaginary de-trended output line (in per cent, i.e. $(Y-Y^*)/Y^*$):

The local maxima A and C are called peaks, and the minima B and D are troughs; the distance between any of these pairs (peak to peak or trough to trough) is the time length (or 'period') of a typical cycle. The inverse of length is called frequency; obviously, the shorter the cycles, the greater their frequency. The cycle can be divided into two phases. The areas of accelerating output are called booms; they are followed by slowdowns (during which output may not necessarily be falling, it may only be rising at a slower rate than the trend, so that de-trended output is falling). After a trough, output will be getting into an accelerating phase again. King and Rebelo (1999) define the cycle as any stochastic movement with periodicity less than 32 quarters (eight years); any developments of longer duration are characterized as trends and should be filtered out with de-trending. The study of such developments belongs to the domain of Growth Theory (as opposed to business cycles). Others however define the business cycle periodicity slightly differently; in most people's minds, a typical cycle is two to five years long. We may take the King-Rebelo eight-year cycle duration as the upper limit of the length of the cycle.

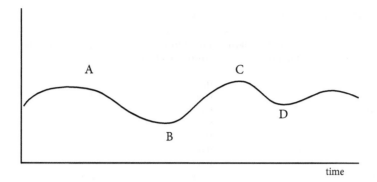

Figure 6.4. Per cent de-trended real output and the phases of the cycle

The cycle is not of course manifested only in GDP or its growth rate. All major macroeconomic variables, such as employment, consumption, investment, interest rates, inflation, sales, house prices, asset prices like stock market prices, and more, are affected by it. Many series boom at about the same time as does output; positive correlation of a certain series with output, or its growth rate, indicates that the series in question is 'procyclical'. Most series are pro-cyclical: typical examples include consumption, inflation, sales, and employment. 'Counter-cyclical' are those series that are negatively correlated with output; examples being unemployment and (perhaps) interest rates. Sometimes, statistical analysis shows some variables to be largely a-cyclical, i.e. not much affected; an example is often shown to be the (real) wage.

The exact timing of boom and slowdown is another dimension of classification of variables. Those variables whose cycle precedes that of output (whether pro- or counter-cyclical) are called 'leading'. Famously, money and employment are among those; the NBER's list of 'leading indicators' includes many more. As mentioned, the importance of timing (and the leading variables, in particular) is that such variables can help us forecast output cycles. 'Lagging' is an even more obvious name for those that peak after output, like often consumption, wages, and inflation. A word of caution: because of the cycle's lack of exact regularity, the statistical analyses that aim to classify variables as pro- or counter-cyclical and leading or lagging often provide conflicting or debatable results, based as they are on different time periods and different countries. With this in mind, the next sub-section proceeds to show some, more or less widely, accepted 'stylized facts' about the properties of the business cycle.

6.1.3 'Stylized Facts' of Business Cycles: Old and New

Following King and Rebelo (1999), we now summarize what are thought to be the (reasonably) well established empirical regularities and 'stylized facts' of business cycles—see Table 6.1. Most macroeconomic time series are pro-cyclical (move together with output, Y) and highly persistent (note the auto-correlation coefficients of the order of 0.7–0.8, sometimes more). Series that are quite weakly (pro-)cyclical or mostly a-cyclical are the real wage (w) and government spending (not shown). The capital stock is also mostly a-cyclical but it is more intensively utilized in booms (the 'capital utilization rate' is pro-cyclical and more volatile than other series). The real interest rate (r) is counter-cyclical, probably because of the subtracted inflation expectations which is pro-cyclical (note the Fisher relation $r_t = i_i - E_t\pi_{t+1}$, where i is the nominal interest rate, π inflation and

Table 6.1. Key properties of US business cycles

	Standard Deviation	Relative Standard Deviation	First Order Auto-correlation	Contemporaneous Correlation with Output
Y	1.81	1.00	0.84	1.00
C	1.35	0.74	0.80	0.88
I	5.30	2.93	0.87	0.80
N	1.79	0.99	0.88	0.88
Y/N	1.02	0.56	0.74	0.55
w	0.68	0.38	0.66	0.12
r	0.30	0.16	0.60	−0.35
A	0.98	0.54	0.74	0.78

Notes: This is Table 1 of King and Rebelo (1999). The notation will be explained in the discussion below.

E_t takes expectations of next-period variables based on time-t information—the expectations operator).

The volatility of individual series, measured by the standard deviation, varies. Non-durable consumption (not shown) and total consumption (C) are less volatile than output; durable consumption however is considerably more volatile (not shown). So is investment (I, about three times the output volatility). Total employment (hours worked, N) is as volatile as output itself; average productivity (output per hour worked, Y/N) less so. A notable fact, mentioned in Chapter 1, is that most of the volatility in total hours of employment comes from changes in employed people moving in and out of unemployment (the 'extensive margin') and not in the hours offered by individual workers (the 'intensive margin') as the basic models assume. Finally, total factor productivity (the 'Solow residual', A) is pro-cyclical and as volatile as output, lending at least first-sight support to theories that emphasize productivity shocks as the primary drivers of the cycle; this point will be extensively discussed below.

As Backus et al. (1995) show, these properties are generally shared across the industrialized economies; and the series of each country is generally positively correlated with the counterpart series of the US, so there is positive co-movement of the key series across countries and the cycles are internationally aligned. However, note the qualification 'generally' (as in all discussions of stylized facts and empirical regularities). The details differ across countries, so the more closely one looks, the more confusing the picture gets; yet, these country variations do not alter the basic messages. The international alignment of cycles may be expected to rise with globalization and regional integration processes (such as European integration).

Since the financial crisis of 2008–9, new observations have been made that have traditionally been less emphasized (or not at all). One such finding is that post-World War II there has been an increasing tendency for sharp downturns and slow recoveries. See the Guidance for Further Study (e.g. C. Romer, 1999; Comin and Gertler, 2006) for varied thinking on this. In a seminal recent piece, Jorda et al. (2016) offer another line of explanation that emphasizes the role of credit in the structure of business cycles. They begin (section 1) with this observation:

> [T]he 'financial hockey stick': the ratio of aggregate private credit, as shown by bank lending, to income in advanced economies has surged to unprecedented levels over the second half of the 20th century. [...With] this 'great leveraging', key business cycle moments have become increasingly correlated with financial variables.

There is greater synchronization (correlation of growth rates) between output and credit post-World War II than pre-World War II. Jorda et al. continue on the implications:

> Higher debt goes hand in hand with worse tail events.... [L]everaged economies are more at risk of steeper downturns and slower recoveries, often these taking the form of financial crisis recessions.

This work presents novel and important evidence on the effect that the increased 'leveraging' (credit-GDP ratio) of modern economies has on their business cycles. It also provides a clear hypothesis (to be tested) as to why we are seeing sharper downturns and slower recoveries. These findings are bound to generate lots of follow-up research.

6.1.4 Further Discussion: De-Trending, Filtering, ... Are All Cycles Alike?

Further observations can be made, regarding both the trend and the cycle. Since the (typical) economy is thought to be growing at largely constant percentage rates in the long run (of the order of 2–3 per cent in the western world during the most part of the post-war period), the trend line is an exponential rather than a straight line. Second, and somewhat less obviously, as Y^* grows over time, so does the magnitude of the cycles; this is reflected in the magnitude of the average output gap or de-trended output, which generally increases as the scale of the economy increases. For this reason, GDP and related series are usually converted to logs, typically denoted by lower-case letters. This turns exponential lines like that of Y^* into straight lines; and turns the output gap or de-trended output into percentage terms (i.e. de-trended $y \equiv y - y^* \approx (Y^* - Y)/Y^*$), which is usually independent of the scale of the economy, so it does not secularly grow over time.

In business cycle-related research, the trend line is commonly obtained by a technique known as the Hodrick-Prescott filter (1997). Alternatives are proposed by Baxter and King (1999): the 'band-pass filter', see also Stock and Watson (1999); and Mise et al. (2005) who examine the properties of the HP in finite samples and consider appropriate adjustments. These filters are applied to the (log) levels data, gaps (actual-trend) are calculated and statistical analysis proceeds from there (see the next section). It is worth keeping in mind three points: that with notable exceptions such as Stock and Watson (1999) and Harvey and Trimbur (2008), there do not appear to be many studies that undertake a thorough comparison of the results of applying the three methods of characterizing cycles (NBER, de-trending, differencing); that in most cases, the exact method does not matter much for the results but there may be exceptions to this (analysis of the price level series may be a case in point—see below); finally, that de-trending is the favourite of business cycles analysts but many econometricians and others remain deeply sceptical about de-trending (see e.g. DeLong, 2012).

The decomposition of output into a trend and a cyclical component is not as clear-cut as might be thought; the two may in fact be inter-related. In other words, trend and cycle may interact (see Nelson and Plosser, 1982; Comin and Gertler, 2006; and other suggestions in the Guidance for Further Study), which is an intuitive conclusion to arrive at since it is the same economy producing both, anyway. Thus, fitting a trend, with whatever method, involves judgement and it is an art as well as science. Furthermore, the distinction made above between Growth and Business Cycle Theory rests conceptually on the distinction and *lack of interaction* between trend and cycle. If the cycle possibly interferes with growth, and vice versa, should we not study them together? Perhaps we should, but this would make progress extremely difficult; for us, the distinction between trend and cycle provides a neat and tractable methodological principle which we shall follow even if it is not literally true.

A final remark. Business cycles are recurrent phenomena but not with a perfect periodicity (as mentioned twice already). Casual visual inspection of the time profile of GDP for any time period of any country convinces us that no cycle is exactly the same as another, at least in terms of timing. Indeed, there are arguments that no two cycles are alike (see Gordon, 1986). Against that, one can counter that, for any given economy, the underlying economic system, despite its fluidity, is largely the same (at least for neighbouring time periods), only developments on the surface or shocks vary; 'business cycles are all alike', in the words of Lucas (1977). For this reason, a good approach to studying cycles may be dual. A variety of formal models aim to build a unified theory of cycles (despite their many differences); they are based on the principle that there is a common underlying economic structure that produces cycles (much like a common DNA structure that produces humans with all their differences in appearance). At the same time, a more historical approach would approach each cycle as a case study in order to identify similarities or differences with other episodes. The two approaches are complementary, something reflected in this chapter. We begin by reviewing some early formal models.

6.2 Early Approaches: Multiplier-Accelerator Interactions, Goodwin Cycles, Kuznets Cycles, and Kondratieff Waves

We first review some early approaches. The first two, the 'multiplier-accelerator' and Goodwin models, are almost entirely demand-led, giving little or no role to supply-side factors. A third approach, named after the Russian economist Kondratieff, is less remembered today by mainstream economists but worth keeping in mind.

6.2.1 The Multiplier-Accelerator Model

First developed by Samuelson (1939), the 'multiplier-accelerator' hypothesis is based on the old Keynesian idea that business cycles may be due to the interactions between the dynamics of investment and consumption. It is nicely reviewed in Allen (1956, chapter 7) and Blanchard (1981), which we follow here.

Let consumption be of the naïve Keynesian form,

$$C_t = c_1 Y_t + c_2 Y_{t-1}, \tag{6.1}$$

whereby consumption at t is a fraction of current and past output (with different marginal propensities c_1 and c_2, with $0 < c_1, c_2, c_1 + c_2 < 1$). This is very similar to the textbook

Keynesian consumption function, with the addition of past output, which plays a significant role as we shall see. This part of the model is the 'multiplier' part, based as it is on the
Keynesian consumption function (see Chapter 8 on fiscal policy).

Investment depends simply on the increase in output; the implicit assumption is that
output is proportional to physical capital, $Y = AK$ (see Chapter 9 on Growth), so that the
increase in output necessitates an increase in investment, which is only completed with a
lag due to delays in construction. We have in general:

$$I_t = v(Y_{t-1} - Y_{t-2}), \quad v > 0 \tag{6.2}$$

This is the 'accelerator' part, whereby an increase in output accelerates investment after
one period.

Finally, the model is completed with the National Income Accounting equation (for a
closed economy):

$$Y_t = C_t + I_t + G_t \tag{6.3}$$

Combining (6.1), (6.2), and (6.3), we get:

$$Y_t = \frac{(v + c_2)Y_{t-1} - vY_{t-2} + G_t}{1 - c_1} \tag{6.4}$$

Note the coefficient on government spending, which is greater than one, in line with the
textbook Keynesian multiplier. This is a 'difference equation' (whereby output depends on
its lags as well as exogenous processes, like government spending here) of second order. It
may imply oscillations of various kinds in output depending on the values of the parameters; description of these oscillations are found in Samuelson's original article, Allen
(1956); see also Sargent (1987, chapter 2) for a general analysis of second-order difference
equations. The main policy implication of this model is clear: government should engage in
aggregate demand-based stabilization policy; government spending, G_t, should be counter-
cyclical (be low when Y is high, and vice versa) in such a way as to dampen these
oscillations as much as possible. Alternatively, one could devise subsidies to investment
to support it counter-cyclically (i.e. encourage it to be more than implied by equation (6.2)
in bad years and be less than (6.2) in the good ones) in such a way as to make $v = 0$ in (6.2)
after considering both the market and policy effects.

An important feature of the above is that the coefficient of Y_{t-1} is higher and of opposite
sign to that of Y_{t-2}; there is some evidence that a process of this kind is in line with
empirical evidence on the behaviour of (de-trended) US output; see Blanchard (1981) and
McCallum (1989). But of course the model can be roundly criticized from the point of view
of someone who believes that agents do not follow arbitrary rules of thumb-type of
behaviour but optimize, particularly in a forward-looking manner (the above are entirely
backward-looking). Blanchard (1981) has examined whether the above deviate fundamentally from the modern theories of consumption and investment. Consumption as given
above implies that the change in consumption is forecastable (if output is, too), whereas the
modern theory of consumption (or, at least, some version of it) implies that, because of
intertemporal optimization and consumption smoothing over time, changes in

consumption should occur only because of *unanticipated* shocks; see Chapter 11. To the extent that this is true, then, 'the multiplier is dead', in Blanchard's words. The accelerator part fares better, because the modern theory of investment allows for forecastable movements in investment, as is the case here. A generalization of the investment model along the 'accelerator' lines has found strong empirical support, particularly in studies related to the developing world (see Chapter 11).

Another distinguishing feature of the above approach is its complete emphasis on demand shocks (at least in its simplest form). There is a grave omission of productivity and supply-side shocks in general which have been emphasized by the 'Real Business Cycles' approach, to which we shall shortly turn.

6.2.2 Goodwin Cycles

Goodwin cycles are another strand of early models that are Keynesian in spirit. In fact, Richard Goodwin, a mathematician and economist, is the author of a range of models of cycles, some with a Marxist flavour to them. The first model, due to Goodwin (1951), is essentially another model of the multiplier-acceleration interaction, with a couple of additions: a concept of a desired, or target, capital stock, K^*, and a non-linearity in investment. It may be summarized by the following variant of the above system, with slight modifications:

$$C_t = C_0 + c_1 Y_t, \qquad (6.1')$$

$$K_t^* = \psi Y_t + \alpha t, \quad \psi > 0, \qquad (6.5)$$

(6.1') is the textbook consumption function while (6.5) introduces the desired capital stock, K^*; this increases at the exogenous rate α. We may think of α as the exogenous rate of technical progress that requires a certain rate of capital increase (technical progress may be 'embodied', as will be discussed in Chapter 9). Furthermore, the more output rises, the greater will be the desired capital stock so as to take advantage of the expanding market; this is captured by ψ.

Actual capital stock evolves by investment (there is no depreciation),

$$K_t - K_{t-1} = I_t. \qquad (6.6)$$

Investment may take one of three values, H(igh) or L(ow) or α, so $I_t = H, L, \alpha$. Let these values be on either side of α:

$$0 < L < \alpha < H < 1.$$

The key assumption is that when $K_t > K_t^*$, investment will take the H value (it will be high so as for the capital stock to catch up with the desired); when the inequality goes the other way, investment will be L (capital will grow slowly to gradually adjust downwards to the desired level); when actual and desired capital coincide, investment will be α. Finally, the National Income Accounting equation (6.3) completes the model.

Thus, in a good (H) and bad (L) year, output will be as follows, respectively (where the intermediate value with $I_t = \alpha$ is omitted)—to see this, combine (6.1'), (6.3), and the information about investment:

$$Y_t^H = \frac{C_0 + H}{1 - c_1} > Y_t^L = \frac{C_0 + L}{1 - c_1} \tag{6.7}$$

Note that these values are constant. Note also that they do not depend on the capital stock, actual or desired. This is a weakness of this model, which, in the spirit of early Keynesian models, let all output be demand-determined and neglected supply. Accordingly, at any t, the desired capital stock will take either of the two values:

$$K_t^* = \psi \frac{C_0 + H}{1 - c_1} + \alpha t \tag{6.8a}$$

or

$$K_t^* = \psi \frac{C_0 + L}{1 - c_1} + \alpha t \tag{6.8b}$$

On average it will increase at rate α.[6] On the other hand, the actual capital stock will increase at rate H in a good year, and L in a bad year.

Here is the logic of the model. Let us start from a situation of a shortfall of actual capital (in the sense that it is less than desired, $K_t < K_t^*$). Then investment will be H and actual capital (K) will be growing at rate $H > \alpha =$ the growth rate of desired, K^*. At some point, K will catch up with K^*. Then investment falls first to α, then to L (as it is easy to check). The level of K^* will show a one-off fall from

$$K_t^* = \psi \frac{C_0 + H}{1 - c_1} + \alpha t$$

to

$$K_t^* = \psi \frac{C_0 + L}{1 - c_1} + \alpha t;$$

the situation then develops into $K^* < K$ (note that the actual capital stock is never destroyed even partially—zero depreciation is assumed). From this point on, investment will be L, K will grow at a low rate until K^* catches up with it, at which point investment will switch to α, then to H, there will be again a shortfall of actual capital, and we start all over again.

Thus, we get perpetual cycles or oscillations that do not fizzle out; the cycles are said to be endogenous or perpetual. There is also a 'happy' equilibrium in which $K = K^*$ and both grow at rate α all the time without fluctuations; but it is unstable, and any little shock will rock the system into perpetual motion. This model of endogenous fluctuations is in sharp

---

[6] Note that to say that it grows at rate α is loose terminology, as α is not strictly speaking a growth rate.

contrast to the standard multiplier-accelerator model, in which oscillations eventually die out, so every so often there must be a new shock that puts the system into motion; and it is in even greater contrast with the modern theories of the cycles which assume that shocks occur all the time. The policy implication is that AD-based stabilization is desirable. But note a subtle difference with the multiplier-accelerator model. Here, the slowing investment after the peak of the cycle performs a necessary function, as firms correct their earlier investment over-drive (this is captured by the $K^* < K$ that now develops). Stabilization may well be desirable but investment should not be prevented from performing this correcting function; thus, the counter-cyclical investment subsidies that are implied by the multiplier-accelerator model are quite inappropriate here. This theme, of whether investment should be supported counter-cyclically or be allowed to engage in necessary rebalancing is explored in a recent paper by Beaudry et al. (2014).[7]

One possible extension to the Goodwin (1951) model is to introduce inventories in this model. A rather neglected aspect of business cycles, inventories (or stocks) may be important in their propagation, judging by the fact that inventories are pro-cyclical and very volatile. There are various reasons why firms accumulate inventories, some planned and some not: among the former is the motive to smooth production over the seasonal or even the business cycle; on the other hand, unwanted accumulation (or decumulation) occurs when demand falls short (or above) actual production. If we introduce output supply in the above model which would be linked to actual capital, we can argue that, as capital falls short of its desired level, actual production falls below demand, the stock of inventories declines as the firm tries to meet some of the expenditure with previously made stock; when output turns high, stocks are already low and the firm spends extra in order to replenish them. But when there is a downturn, businesses will stop accumulating inventories; the fact that this item of expenditure is cut down may increase the depth and duration of the downturn. Galbraith (1975, chapter 10) attributes to change in inventories a vital role in the transmission from the stock market crash of 1929 in the US to the Great Depression from 1930 onwards. See Blinder and Maccini (1991) and Cesaroni et al. (2011) for introductions into this important but rather neglected corner of business cycles research. We return to inventories in Chapter 11.

In later work, Goodwin introduced refinements to his model, one of which is to allow investment to respond to both current and past changes in output. The former are in line with the accelerator model; the latter are rationalized by the fact that there may be some time lag between an initial decision to invest and the actual building of investment, due to implementation lags. This is idea that investment 'takes time to build' discussed in Chapter 5. It has found an echo in more modern literature, including the paper credited by many to have kick-started the modern 'Real Business Cycles' literature (Kydland and Prescott, 1982; and also Altug, 1989).[8]

A weakness of Goodwin (1951) and its variants is that they completely neglect supply; all the focus is on demand. In particular, there is no connection between actual capital and output, while both are variables in the model. Some resolution of this difficulty is done by a

---

[7] A distant echo of the Goodwin (1951) model may be found in Evans et al. (1998) in which the cycle is caused by alternating phases of high and low investment.

[8] Shleifer (1986) analyses the interaction between aggregate demand and innovation by firms that produces 'implementation cycles'.

later Goodwin (1967) model, which also results in endogenous fluctuations but of a different nature. There is a Leontieff production function (capital and labour are in strict proportions between themselves and with output). There is also an equation akin to a Phillips Curve, or a wage equation: when employment (L) is high, real wages (w) rise, when it is low they fall. Let us begin with a high employment rate; wages are rising. The labour share, wL/Y is also rising. Workers are assumed to consume all their income, while all the saving comes from the capitalists' share in output (a standard assumption in many Heterodox or Marxist macroeconomic models; something in line with empirical evidence, see Chapter 11). As the labour share increases, saving and investment declines; output also declines, and with it employment, wages, and the labour share. When the labour share has fallen and the capital share rises, saving and investment begin again, putting in motion the reverse process of rising output, employment, and labour share; and so on, into a perpetual motion.

The logic of various of these models is best described by the 'Lotka-Volterra' dynamic equations that have been used in evolutionary biology to describe predator-prey dynamics. (Have you seen the screen saver in which sharks chase and eat small fish?—It is the visual analogue of this! If there are too many sharks, the fish get eaten; sharks starve and begin to decline in number. As that happens, the stock of fish gets replenished, so the shark population begins to grow; and so on.) The wider point is that these models introduce endogenous fluctuations and do not rely on a continual battering of the economy by shocks whose nature remains fuzzy. These and other similar models (see Allen, 1956, chapter 7; and Krugman, 1996, chapter 7) are dealt with by some macroeconomic models that rely on non-linear and 'chaos' mathematical methods; we describe these briefly below.

6.2.3 Kuznets Cycles and Kondratieff Waves

In the 1920s, the Russian economist Nikolai Kondratieff observed that the world economy is characterized by a mixture of long cycles ('waves') of length of about 30–40 years, and shorter cycles; the longer cycles now bear his name. Independently, the American economist, statistician, and historian of growth (for which he was awarded the Nobel Prize in Economics) Simon Kuznets has talked about intermediate cycles of 15–20 years. Such ideas are in line with mathematical theory which analyses any arbitrary periodic process into constituent cycles of different frequencies ('Fourier analysis'). The problem is that the existence of such long cycles (or 'long swings') cannot be conclusively established, one reason being that we do not have as yet the span of data that would allow us to do so; to detect such cycles with confidence, we would need hundreds of years of data, while historical GDP series only go as far back as the nineteenth century. Economic historians and historical sociologists (Wallerstein, 2004) may argue that such cycles are generated by big technological revolutions and other such momentous events (e.g., the industrial revolution of the late eighteenth century, the 'second' industrial revolution around the beginning of the twentieth century based on the introduction of the internal combustion engine and electrification, World War II, etc.). Mainly because of such difficulties Kuznets and Kondratieff cycles are not much used in economics. Yet, such ideas are not without appeal: e.g. as mentioned in Chapter 1, the years 1945–75 were 'glorious' years of high growth, little unemployment or inflation; the next 30, roughly up to the crisis of 2007–9, were so-so; from then on, the talk in town is of sluggish growth or even perpetual stagnation. So, we begin to see long (30-year) cycles. Thinking broadly, one could ask: does globalization, the onset of the internet, or climate change herald a new such cycle? These remain open questions.

6.2.4 Non-Linear and Chaotic Models

A distinct class of models of cycles relies on non-linear and 'chaos' mathematics. 'Chaos' is a branch of mathematics with wide applications in physics, biology, meteorology, and other natural sciences (see e.g. Gleick, 1998, for a very readable introduction). Among the hallmarks of chaotic systems are two features: (a) patterns of endogenous cycles of the variables of the system that are so complex as to appear stochastic (driven by random shocks, see the next sub-section); (b) non-linear reliance on the parameters of the system. The latter feature often implies that if you vary a parameter within some range, only marginal changes in the cyclical patterns of the series emerge; but if you reach a critical value, any further change of the parameter may result in a drastic alteration of the behaviour of the series. Such a change is called a 'bifurcation'.

Beyond these broad features, however, the models are very wide-ranging, and that is reflected in the economic applications of the theory. Applications include the 'animal spirits' driving investment in Farmer and Guo (1994); the investment-driven cycles of Evans et al. (1998); the change of regimes between Solovian (capital accumulation-driven) and 'endogenous' (innovation-driven) growth in Matsuyama (2001); and many more that draw inspiration from all corners of the literature, from Goodwin to neoclassical to 'Schumpeterian' models (see Chapter 9). The interested reader may consult the readable surveys of methods and models in Baumol and Benhabib (1989), Boldrin and Woodford (1990), Benhabib and Rustichini (1994), and Barnett and He (2002). For the more determined, the heavier tomes of Brock et al. (1991), Azariadis (1993), and Gandolfo (1996) will provide plenty of food for thought.

Themes that keep reappearing in this strand of theory are (a) increasing returns to scale in production, (b) self-fulfilling expectations, and (c) externalities and/or monopolistic competition. Many of these are themes that we have seen in Chapter 3 on New Keynesians. Upon reflection, none of them is surprising: We shall see in the theory of growth (Chapter 9), that the returns to scale represent a 'knife-edge' condition; any deviation from constant returns can alters drastically the nature of the models. Patterns of cyclical fluctuations may likewise be very different when constant or increasing returns apply. The importance of self-fulfilling expectations (or 'prophecies') is not surprising, either. We know expectations are important, and they can drive the model in any direction if the expectations are not anchored on fundamentals. For example, if an investor thinks (for whatever unfounded reason) that the market is good, they will invest and hire; and if there are enough such investors, the market will turn out to be good. (Note that even in self-fulfilling expectations, the expectations themselves are model-consistent, as they turn out to be true. But it is the expectations that drive outcomes, and not the other way around.) Because such expectations are formed on a whim, sometimes they are called 'animal spirits' (as in Farmer and Guo, 1994); alternatively, they are said to be driven by 'sunspots' (physical phenomena that are completely exogenous and unrelated to human affairs).

Finally, externalities and monopolistic competition generate conditions under which the actions of one agent have effects on others (unplanned because of externalities, planned because of the multiplier effects associated with monopolistic competition, as will be discussed in Chapter 8). With these effects, the ensuing coordination of agents may result into endogenous cyclical patterns.

Exciting as they are, such models, and the models of endogenous fluctuations more generally, remain at the fringes of mainstream macroeconomics. Reasons why this is so (aside from the technical complexities that are involved) are their very disparate nature, the difficulty in empirically verifying them (or even distinguishing the implications of one from another), and their unclear policy implications. Yet, at the time when there is some theoretical soul-searching following the 'Great Recession' of 2007–9 (see below), it seems that macroeconomics would benefit from a greater fusion between some of these models and more mainstream business cycles research.

6.2.5 Shocks and Propagation

The models we have seen on the whole produce endogenous fluctuation in the sense that, once they are set in motion, such fluctuations do not stop (much like the movement of the planets and the moon). In contrast, most modern work on cycles relies on the existence of (hypothesized and unobservable) shocks that move the economic system; without any such shocks, there would be no fluctuations (much like a boat that tilts sideways only because waves hit it). The modern approach makes an important distinction between shocks and propagating mechanisms. Shocks are exogenous and unforeseen developments that affect agents' behaviour; propagating mechanisms are essentially the mechanisms of the economic system that magnify or alter the effects of shocks. Examples of shocks are natural shocks such as good/bad weather or natural disasters; exogenous new developments in demand-related policies such as monetary, government spending, or tax policies; the state of the world economy is also a shock for any individual country; supply shocks include (again) tax policies or subsidies, changes in the price of oil/energy/raw materials; developments on labour market legislation, regulatory regimes, trade, or competition policy; broader institutional changes in business or government; productivity shocks, such as those arising out of new technological breakthroughs but also from better organization, skills, or human capital. Such changes constitute shocks only once (when they first occur), but they may influence behaviour long after that.

As shocks are completely unpredictable, they are completely random and without any pattern (this is almost the definition of shocks); e.g. the shock called 'abnormal weather' (the deviation of weather from the seasonal average, a kind of 'weather gap') shows no pattern—it is perhaps determined by the throw of the dice by some Higher Power. Yet, cycles do seem to have a pattern: Table 6.1 shows that most macroeconomic series are positively auto-correlated: The typical e.g. GDP cycle implies that it takes a few periods before the boom is succeeded by a slowdown, and vice versa. So, there is a pattern: if output is high (low) now, it is likely that it is going to be high (low) next period, too. Yet, shocks are by definition without any pattern (no auto-correlation). The propagation mechanisms are those economic structures that convert the completely random (and unobservable) shocks to more predictable (and observed) patterns in the macroeconomic variables.

As there is potentially a multitude of shocks, it is useful to think of them in big broad categories. One distinction is between nominal and real shocks; the former include money supply policy and/or changes in nominal wages and prices separately, while the latter are all the others, prominently featuring productivity shocks among them. The significance of this distinction lies partly in its policy implications: if shocks are predominantly real they must be countered by supply-side policies, while nominal shocks leave room for employing aggregate demand policies for stabilization. A further sub-categorization would distinguish between demand-led real shocks (government spending, taxes, the world demand for our exports) and supply-side shocks (productivity, input prices, structural changes). The identification of propagation mechanisms also has important policy implications. The next section will introduce two (families of) theories that deal with the kinds of shocks hitting the economy and the propagation mechanisms.

6.3 Two Views of the Cycle

This section gives an overview of the modern approaches to business cycles. The main schools of thought are: first, the Real Business Cycle (RBC) theorists, who are an offshoot of the New Classicals (NC) discussed in Chapter 2; secondly, the New Keynesians, who are the modern advocates (though in modified and nuanced ways) of the ideas of John Maynard Keynes—discussed in Chapter 3; and the 'DSGE approach' which is a fusion of the two. For ease of exposition, there is a (very) limited review of some ideas already discussed in Chapters 1–3.

The primary questions in modern business cycle research are, what are the most important shocks hitting an economy; and what are the most important propagating mechanisms—the most salient characteristics of a typical modern industrialized economy that convert random shocks into a patterned evolution of the key macroeconomic series? We broadly organize our discussions along these lines. The exposition in this section is more informal, relying on diagrammatic exposition based on traditional models (labour demand-supply, IS-LM, and AD-AS); the interested reader can easily recast the analysis into the wage-price setting and the 'three-equation New Keynesian' model of Chapter 3.

6.3.1 Real Business Cycles, New Keynesians, and the DSGE Approach

Let us begin with the NC/RBC theorists, whose doctrines are in some ways theoretically (but not necessarily intuitively) more straightforward. As explained in Chapter 2, this school believes that economic systems are characterized by rational and optimizing agents (individuals or firms), who behave according to the optimization principles of standard economic theory. In doing so, they utilize all the information that is available to them. For example, when individuals decide on the demand for a certain good, they aim to maximize their utility subject to the budget constraints based on their incomes and the relative prices of various goods. When firms decide how many workers to hire, they solve their maximization problem, subject to a well-defined production function, the market real wage, and the demand (schedule) for their good (among other things). Similar calculations (based on our preferences for leisure and consumption, and the real wage) underlie our decisions to provide work. Because of explicit reliance on individual optimization, the NC/RBC models are based on Microeconomics. Apart from the logical and coherent sense that such micro-foundations make, the NC/RBCs claim that they also constitute a sounder basis for model building. To summarize the NCM/RBC position somewhat schematically, following Mankiw (1989), this school envisages an economy that consists of markets that work (and clear) like those in the microeconomics textbook. From the First Theorem of Welfare Economics, such a world is Pareto optimal.[9]

NC/RBC theorists also assert that individuals and firms interact in markets which clear, i.e. which work sufficiently well that equilibrium prices and quantities are arrived at. This further means that supply eventually equals demand in any market, and that no side is frustrated, i.e. unable to buy or sell at the going price even if it wanted to. Of course, we all have encountered a case when our local bakery has run out of bread, so one party (customer) is willing to transact more at the going price but is simply unable to. Equally surely, every shop is at times left with unsold merchandise. But this must happen occasionally and by mistake, otherwise the bakery would not be maximizing its profit; it is not rational either to be left with unsold output or to turn customers away systematically. On average, it is setting a price at which both the bakery and the customer are willing to transact the same quantities. The assumption of market clearing rests squarely on price and wage flexibility that delivers equilibrium in any market.

This school also emphasizes traditionally that, whenever expectations of the future are involved, agents form them rationally, i.e. they do not make any systematic mistakes. They may occasionally over- or under-predict but on average they 'get it right'; furthermore, their mistakes are completely random, so that no pattern in them is discernible, and that no improvement on their forecasts can be made without any new information. Such forecasts are called model-consistent, as they are assumed to be (on average) equal to the outcomes of the model's own endogenous variables. Again, the obvious criticism is that such forecasts may be quite impossible to develop. But this assumption is adopted because of the lack of any well-defined alternative. An answer (or forecast) that is correct is unique, but there exist an infinite number of erroneous ones; which one do we choose as the basis on which to build our models? Moreover, building theories on the assumption that agents make systematic mistakes is not only unacceptable but also an unfruitful basis on which to develop policy suggestions. As we saw in Chapter 2, modern research attempts to relax the assumption of Rational Expectations by introducing gradual learning on the part of agents (as opposed to making unbiased forecasts from the beginning) and elements of Bounded Rationality (whereby agents' reasoning is limited in some well-specified ways).

As the name suggests (Real BCs), this school emphasizes the predominance of real shocks for business cycles, particularly productivity shocks. McCallum (1989) has distinguished between a weak-version and a strong-version of RBC models. The former accept that other shocks exist that have only minor influences on the evolution of real variables, while the stronger version would deny any such influences at all. In general, and in line with NC thinking, RBCs advocate that money is neutral, in the sense that an increase in it

---

[9] Named after the nineteenth-century Swiss economist Wilfredo Pareto, Pareto optimality is the idea that an economic outcome cannot improve from the point of view of one, or some, agents without some other(s) becoming worse off. Loosely speaking, a situation or outcome is Pareto-optimal if it involves no wastage. It is a condition of economic efficiency; it is also the formal analogue of Adam Smith's 'invisible hand' idea.

will just raise all nominal prices and wages at the same proportion, and leave real quantities unaltered. Money may not be neutral only to the extent that it is unanticipated, i.e. incorrectly anticipated, but this cannot be the case on average (otherwise we would be systematically mistaken). The result of these two beliefs is that Aggregate Demand policies cannot have any effect on output or any meaningful role to play in stabilization; the only polices that can work are supply-side ones. The predominance of productivity shocks is challenged by the NKs, who would argue that monetary influences are the important in the economy, but would leave the door open for other developments, particularly real shocks.

The New Keynesians are not a homogeneous group (even less homogeneous than NC/RBCs); their basic aim is to refute the most extreme NC doctrines and restore some of Keynes's (1936) insights, particularly in relation to the desirability of AD-based stabilization. They believe that the real world does not quite work in the way the RBCs' elegant theoretical formulations suggest. However, in their quest to provide rigorous foundations that can withstand the Lucas (1976) critique, they accept micro-foundations and Rational Expectations as the only logical basis for model-building and sound policy advice. Their main deviation from NCs and RBCs is their assumption that markets fail to clear in some cases, in a way that is consistent with underlying optimization by agents. They show how (nominal) price rigidities and (real) wage rigidities, which prevent goods and labour markets from clearing, can result from the actions of both rational firms (which cannot change prices continuously because of the costs involved in doing so) and rational trade unions (which fix wages in bargaining with firms by contracts which stipulate a fixed wage for some time). NKs point out the significance of these real-world features for the (non)-neutrality of money, for the emergence of structural unemployment, and for the relevance of monetary stabilization policy. Although many of these rigidities disappear in the long run, some of their effects may be long-lasting (though not money non-neutrality).

NKs attribute a lot of importance to monetary shocks (those arising from policy, but also from institutional changes like the financial liberalization of the 1980s and behavioural changes like changes in money demand). Coupled with non-neutrality, this thinking then leads to the relevance of monetary, and more generally Aggregate Demand, policies: There is scope for such stabilization policies that can alleviate the cycles in output and unemployment. It should be noted, however, that in contrast to earlier Keynesian thinking (that of Keynes himself but also of the 1950s and 1960s generations of Keynesians), they do not advocate such polices in order to wipe unemployment out completely, as much of it is structural and due to institutional and systemic factors which are then amenable only to supply-side policies and reforms (as discussed in Chapter 4); rather, the aim of policy should be more modest but still important: to stabilize unemployment around its structural rate and output around its trend.

In recent years, the RBC and New Keynesian schools have fused into a single approach, called the 'DSGE' (Dynamic Stochastic General Equilibrium) models. From the RBC tradition they borrow the methodology (equilibrium approach with detailed modelling of micro-foundations, matching empirical statistics with theoretical predictions, reliance on advanced mathematical/analytical methods and computing) and the prominence of supply-side shocks; from the NK tradition they keep the non-market clearing feature via wage/price rigidity while they also incorporate some demand-side shocks. Importantly, because of the lack of market clearing, the world they describe is not Pareto optimal, thus scope exists for government stabilization policy (which is in general 'welfare improving').

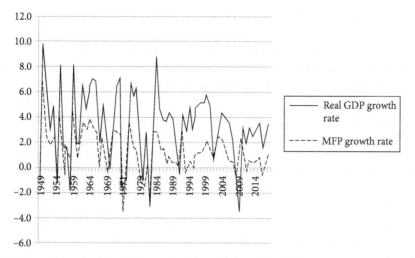

Figure 6.5. Multifactor productivity and Real GDP growth in the US
Source: US Bureau of Labor Statistics, MFP page (data accessed 11/5/2019). Data is annual.

6.3.2 Productivity Shocks as Drivers of Cycles

As mentioned, the origin of shocks is an important point of contention between the RBCs and the New Keynesians. RBCs emphasize the prevalence of real shocks, particularly productivity shocks, which include: changes in skills, education, and human capital; technology; the institutional and legal framework, organization; product and labour market regulation; the international trade regime, etc.[10] Using US data, Prescott (1986) uncovered some important evidence that underpins the RBC position: real GDP growth is closely correlated with the growth rate of 'Total Factor Productivity (TFP)', otherwise also known as the 'Solow residual' (Solow, 1957). The 'Solow residual' is a measure of real output growth that occurs over and above the accumulation of tangible factors of production (capital and labour). It therefore (supposedly) captures all the contributions to output growth from non-tangible factors, i.e. (exogenous) productivity. The main point of the RBC theory is that the close correlation between the Solow residual and real output growth is strong evidence pointing to shocks in productivity growth as the main driver of fluctuations in output growth; see Mankiw (1989). To present the point, Figure 6.5 plots 'multifactor productivity (MFP)' and output in the US (both in annual growth rates), 1949–2018.[11] The correlation is striking: It is 0.79 for the entire sample, dropping somewhat in the latter part (1985–2018) but still a strong 0.53. The RBCs' point seems unassailable.

But there are conceptual difficulties both with the notion of 'productivity shocks' as such and with the Solow residual as an indicator of it. First, all shocks have a mean of zero, thus there are by definition both positive and negative shocks; but what do 'negative productivity shocks' mean? Can productivity be reversed? One answer here is that negative values

[10] By 'productivity' we mean here 'exogenous productivity', the 'A' in the production function ($Y = AK^{\alpha}L^{1-\alpha}$)—not the marginal product of labour or capital. The main argument of the RBC school is that A is time-varying and in particular, pro-cyclical.

[11] The terms MFP growth, TFP growth, and Solow residual can be used interchangeably; MFP seems to be the term now used by statistical offices (e.g. BLS in the US or the OECD).

of the Solow residual do not indicate technological or productivity regress, but a slowdown in its rate of growth.[12] Secondly, what are these shocks? How often do we observe a development that we can confidently call a productivity shock? The answer here is that there are myriad such shocks; each of these changes may be of negligible size, but together they amount to a sizeable component of real GDP growth.[13] All these points have attracted attention and debate in the literature, see Mankiw (1989). Furthermore, such a multiplicity of tiny shocks will of necessity be of all different kinds; since our models allow for only very few categories of shocks (two or three, typically), we often have to put shocks such as technological breakthroughs, trade liberalization developments, or organizational changes together under the category 'productivity shocks'. Yet, these shocks may work in very different ways; something that will be missed in any model that lumps them all under two or three broad categories.

New Keynesians have also criticized the argument that the correlation evident in Figure 6.5 implies that productivity shocks are the main drivers of the cycles: they argue that the true contribution of both labour and capital vary (pro-cyclically) and cannot easily be measured. Businesses may not reduce labour during downturns as much as is optimal, either because of labour market regulations, or because of solidarity with the workforce, or labour adjustment costs; instead they 'hoard labour' even though it may not be utilized fully, in anticipation of better times in the future (see Biddle, 2014). Similarly, firms do not scrap capital in a downturn but utilize it less intensively, so the 'capital utilization rate' falls (Basu, 1996). As a result of both labour hoarding and a variable capital utilization rate, the true (fully utilized) 'K' and 'L' of the production function will be more pro-cyclical than the statistically measured capital and labour. Thus, the Solow residual, calculated as $\log Y_t - \alpha \log K_t - (1-\alpha)L_t$ (with the K and L as measured in statistics), is very pro-cyclical but is not a true reflection of $\log A_t$; the true $\log A_t$ should be calculated with the true 'K' and 'L' and will be a lot less pro-cyclical than the residual shown in Figure 6.5.[14] King and Rebelo (1999) shows how the RBC programme of research survives this criticism: various studies have constructed proper Solow residuals, which are less cyclical, but the associated models feature stronger propagation mechanisms.[15] Thus, the models are able to match the business cycles stylized facts.

6.3.3 A Digression: Why is it Important to Know the Origin of the Shocks?

From a policy perspective, the ultimate goal is to design appropriate stabilization policy such that the cycle is 'ironed out' and output follows the smooth trend line. In order to fulfil this goal, business cycles analysis must ascertain the origins of shocks, the fundamental causes of the cycles. RBCs argue strongly in favour of productivity shocks, while NKs assert

---

[12] Even RBC theorists themselves (see e.g. Rebelo, 2005) acknowledge the difficulty of envisaging negative productivity shocks. The adjustments done to refine the 'Solow residual' as an indication of productivity (see below) also result in a diminished probability of negative productivity shocks.

[13] The analogy here is that cars moving in the same direction produce traffic.

[14] To avoid confusion, note that Figure 6.5 gives both output and the residual in growth terms, as is standard practice.

[15] Labour and capital are not able to be adjusted marginally; rather, individual workers or units of capital move in and out of employment. So, the implied residual is smaller but its implications are larger.

the predominance of Aggregate Demand shocks. But why is it important to know the origin of the shocks? Because, in principle, any shocks that originate in the demand side of the economy (say, changes in consumer spending, investment, credit conditions, foreign demand for exports, etc.) can in principle be countered by appropriate AD policies. But any shocks that originate in supply (changes in labour market conditions, organization, technology, other productivity, regulations) may be more difficult to counter by AD policies. This point is made in Figure 6.6 using the standard AD-AS model:

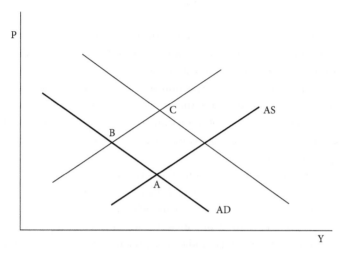

Figure 6.6. Different shocks in the AD-AS diagram

Consider an aggregate demand shock that moves the AD curve (not shown). This is in principle reversible by a policy that moves the AD curve back to its original position. Things are conceptually clear here: the policy must be the reverse, i.e. an aggregate demand policy in the opposite direction from that of the shock. If, say, a stagnating world income decreases exports, this calls for an AD expansion to counter the original shock. But the situation is more intriguing with supply shocks. Let there be an adverse supply shock (e.g. an oil price increase) that shifts the AS curve up (to the thin line), and moves us from the original position A to B. There is now a policy dilemma: if you do not engage in any AD policy, the economy stays in recession and with higher prices (point B); if you do respond by expanding AD, moving the economy to C, you could in principle reverse the recession but you raise prices further. This dilemma was said to exist in the UK around 2011 when inflation was high and the economy in a low-output situation. There were calls for monetary policy to 'ease' (expand) to help the economy out of the recession; something that happened but only with some delay (critics argue). One of the reasons cited then by the Bank of England for its reluctance to engage in (more) expansionary monetary policy in the middle of a recession was that inflation was imported (high oil and food prices) and would have been made worse by the monetary expansion. In other words, the argument was that the economy, having suffered an adverse supply shock, was at a point like B, and an AD expansion would worsen things on the inflation front.

The degree to which the Central Bank reacts to an adverse shock is called the 'degree of monetary accommodation'—thus, at B this degree is zero, whereas if we arrive at C, the shock has been fully accommodated.

6.3.4 Model Calibration and Other Methodological Innovations of RBCs

A distinctive feature of RBC theories is their methodological innovations. When it comes to testing against data and providing quantitative information on aspects of theories (e.g. on multipliers or elasticities), most economic theories resort to (classical) econometrics. Going back to basics, suppose that we want to test the Keynesian consumption function:

$$C_t = C_0 + c_1 Y_t + u_t, \tag{6.1''}$$

where the notation is as before and u_t is an error term (with the usual properties). Using actual data on C_t and Y_t, econometrics allows us to directly estimate C_0 and c_1 and to perform an overall test of the empirical fit of this theory. This is based on specific diagnostic checks as well as on an inspection of the estimated values of C_0 and c_1 and conformity with basic postulates of the theory. For example, we must find the estimated values to be $C_0 > 0$ and $0 > c > 1$; if not, something is wrong with the theory. The important point about econometric methodology is that it gives us tools and tests by which we can formally accept or reject a theory.

The RBC theorists proceed in a very different way, based on simulations. They construct model economies that work according to their theories, based on micro-foundations. From previous empirical studies, they supply their models with estimates of crucial parameters, like the rate of time preference (how impatient we are when choosing between current and future consumption), the parameters indicating preferences on consumption versus leisure, the shares of labour and capital in firms' production function, the rate of capital depreciation, etc. For argument's sake, suppose that their model consists of two equations, the Keynesian consumption (1'') (though they would readily discard it in favour of the micro-based theory of intertemporal choice of consumption and leisure), and the National Income Accounting identity (6.3):

$$Y_t = C_t + I_t + G_t \tag{6.3}$$

There is no error term here as this is an identity holding precisely. For simplicity, let us assume that government spending is a constant fraction g of GDP, $G_t = \gamma Y_t$, and that there is no investment, $I_t = 0$. Inserting (6.1'') and this information into (6.3) and solving, we have:

$$Y_t = \frac{C_0 + u_t}{1 - c_1 - \gamma}, \qquad C_t = \frac{1 - \gamma}{1 - c_1 - \gamma}(C_0 + u_t) \tag{6.9}$$

We can easily calculate that,

$$E(Y_t) = \frac{C_0}{1 - c_1 - \gamma}, \qquad Var(Y_t) = \frac{Var(u_t)}{(1 - c_1 - \gamma)^2}, \tag{6.10a}$$

$$E(C_t) = \frac{1 - \gamma}{1 - c_1 - \gamma} C_0, \qquad Var(C_t) = \left(\frac{1 - \gamma}{1 - c_1 - \gamma}\right)^2 Var(u_t), \tag{6.10b}$$

$$Corr(Y_t, C_t) = 1 - \gamma \tag{6.10c}$$

Naturally, analytical solutions are available in this simple example because it is linear; in the complex RBC models, the calculations are numerical, but the logic is the same.

RBCs would take estimates of C_0, c, and γ from previous studies. They would then supply random data on the error term u_t from a computer-based 'random number generator' (an electronic form of throwing dice) which would have mean zero and a certain variance, $Var(u_t)$, that can be controlled. In fact, they set $Var(u_t)$ such that the calculated $Var(Y_t)$ matches exactly the variance of real-data Y (usually de-trended)—this is called calibration. RBC theorists then proceed to ask whether the properties of the constructed and actual C are similar. In particular, this line of research examines whether the moments such as $Var(C)$ and $Corr(Y, C)$ implied by the models on the basis of the selected $Var(u_t)$ are similar with those in the actual data (usually de-trended) as given in Table 6.1.[16]

Such methodology is novel, and a whole lot more demanding and thorough than that of econometrics, based as it is not on an estimate of a single coefficient, but on a more thorough examination of the properties of the constructed series (which may be numerous). In other words, for a theory to pass the test, more stringent requirements must be met than in the classical methodology. This methodology, however, also suffers from serious drawbacks (in many people's eyes); for a thoroughly sceptical review, the reader could consult Hoover (1988). The main problem is that a theory never passes any test rigorously. Unlike econometrics, no critical values (of variances, correlation coefficients, etc.) are given so as to say whether those found are close enough to the actual ones and whether the underlying theory is 'good' (enough) or not.

Furthermore, it is not clear how to deal with theoretical trade-offs; any aspect of the model that improves some features of the calculated series may worsen some other features; in this case, it is very hard to tell whether the new aspect has improved things overall or not. Furthermore, the artificially constructed variables from widely different model economies are often hardly distinguishable. This problem is called 'observational equivalence' of models, which is the property that very different models and theories boil down to similar quantitative predictions. Any RBC theorist would be quick to point out here that the same problem plagues classical econometrics and Keynesian models (Sargent and Wallace, 1976). Even so, it is hard to escape the conclusion that, valid though the simulation approach is as a complementary approach for quantifying and testing economic theories, it can only work in parallel with econometrics and not on its own. The fact that it cannot provide estimates of parameters but that it must rely on previous econometric studies can only strengthen this conclusion.

6.3.5 The Real Business Cycles Model: Diagrammatic Analysis

Let us first illustrate the logic of a basic Real Business Cycles (RBC) model. We start from the labour market, as this is fundamental for supply, which is fundamental for the entire model. Consider the model of the labour market reviewed in Chapter 1—repeated as Figure 6.7 here. The real wage W/P is plotted against employment (hours worked)

---

[16] With $\gamma, c_1 < 1$, equations (6.9) predict that consumption is less volatile than GDP, $Var(C_t)/Var(Y_t) = (1-\gamma)^2 < 1$; this corresponds to the information given in Table 6.1 (ratio of standard deviations = 0.74). So, the toy economy we have constructed here passes a (very) first test!

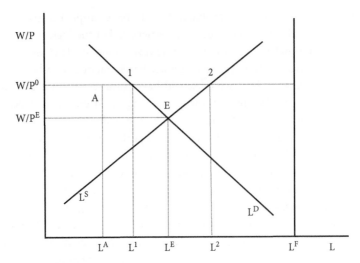

Figure 6.7. The labour market

L. The total possible employment is denoted L^F. Labour demand L^D gives the labour required by firms at each real wage such that profits be maximized (at this given wage). Likewise, labour supply L^S gives individuals' total offer for work at each wage, given all the underlying calculus based on preferences over leisure and consumption, the remuneration to work, etc. If the market's functioning is uninhibited, then equilibrium E will be established; employment L^E and unemployment $L^F - L^E$ will result. According to New Classicals, all of this unemployment must be considered voluntary: as employment is given by the intersection of L^D and L^S, both firms and, importantly, individuals are happy to employ/offer L^E hours of labour at wage $(W/P)^E$. The resulting unemployment $L^F - L^E$ is in the nature of voluntary unemployment: they choose to take that as leisure in a broad sense. At this wage, it is worth devoting more time to family, study, or hobby, as well as strict leisure. To some extent also, $L^F - L^E$ may represent hours of work foregone because the precise skills required by firms, or the location of jobs, do not match those offered by workers; at this wage, it might not be worth the workers' effort for retraining or relocating. This does not mean that equilibrium E is the best of all possible worlds, but it does mean that this is the best available to the economy given its resource endowments, exogenous productivity, preferences, etc. Individuals would be better off being at any point on their L^S schedule higher than that given by $(W/P)^E$, but the combination of $(W/P)^E$, L^E is the best *possible*. The main point is, any hours to the right of the labour supply curve represent hours that workers have chosen not to offer; L^E may be considered as full employment and $L^F - L^E$ represents 'natural unemployment'.

Having determined the hours that are worked, we then translate this into output produced using the production function $F(K,L)$ discussed in Chapter 1—note that K is taken as fixed,[17] so F(L) becomes only a function of L. At $L = L^E$, in particular, we have:

$$Y^E = F(L^E) \tag{6.11}$$

---

[17] Much of business cycles research de-emphasizes capital as a driver of cycles (though capital exists in the models as a variable). The rationale for this is that K (but not its rate of utilization) shows little variation over the cycle.

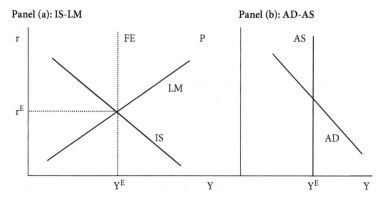

Figure 6.8. Equilibrium output and real interest rate in the RBC model

This output level (Y^E) corresponds to 'full employment' (FE) output. It may be thought of as the output level on the trend line. It is shown in the IS-LM and the AD-AS graphs, in Figure 6.8a, b.

The logic of RBC models is this: starting from the labour market, firms decide labour demand, individuals decide labour supply, and an equilibrium is reached. Knowing L^E, Y^E is determined. One then goes to IS-LM. Demand passively responds to the supply-side determined level of real output (Y^E): The position of IS effectively determines the equilibrium real interest rate (r^E). The price level is determined residually: from the money market equilibrium, we know that $M/P = M^D(Y, r)$, where $M^D(.)$ is real money demand. Knowing output and the interest rate (Y^E, r^E), and with the money supply exogenously set by the monetary authority, the price level follows. It is such that solves the equation:

$$P = M/M^D(Y^E, r^E) \qquad (6.12)$$

At the heart of this system is money neutrality. All the real variables have been determined either by the supply side alone (Y^E) or a combination of AD and AS (r^E). We can also recast much of this analysis in terms of the AD-AS graph, with AS inelastically fixed at $Y = Y^E$. (The AD-AS analysis is simply an alternative in this model.) The IS and LM will combine into the AD schedule. The price level and real interest rate are such that demand equals supply at the Y^E level of output.

RBC models have analysed the effects of various exogenous changes, as follows. The changes are not shown but the reader is invited to verify diagrammatically:

- A rise in productivity will shift L^D out and raise both L^E and $(W/P)^E$ in the labour market. Y^E, will rise, too, for a double reason: both of the rise in L^E and an (implicit) change in $Y = F(L)$—an increase in Y for every level of L. In the IS-LM model, neither IS nor LM will change. The intersection of FE (which has increased) and IS will produce a lower r^E. Thus, the real interest rate has fallen as productivity has risen. The intuition is obtained from considering the alternative output market equilibrium condition, injections = leakages, or $I(r) + G + X = S(Y, r) + T(Y) + Im(Y)$— augmented by the government and external sectors and in obvious notation. Since Y and all leakages rise, the interest rate must fall to encourage an increase in investment. In the AD-AS diagram, AD has not changed but AS has shifted right; the equilibrium price level falls. Given M, this will reduce real balances (M/P) and shift the LM right, so that the intersection of IS and LM again occurs at the new, higher, Y^E and lower r^E.

- A rise in government spending does not alter any of L^D or L^S, hence neither L^E nor Y^E nor AS change. The IS and AD shift right. The price level rises, so that M/P falls and the LM shift left, such that the new intersection of IS and LM occurs at the same Y^E as before. The interest rate r^E has risen, and this is the only real change in the model. The reader is invited to explain why, again with reference to the output equilibrium condition $I + G + X = S + T + Im$.

- A rise in lump-sum taxation will have qualitatively the opposite effects of a rise in G— but the quantitative details will change. Other, proportional, forms of taxation will also affect behaviour (labour supply or demand, etc.); more formally, they will 'distort' the decisions taken by the private sector. We defer discussion of fiscal policy to Chapter 8.

- A rise in money supply will shift the LM right (will raise M/P). But the price level must obey (6.12). Given Y^E and r^E that are determined prior to the price level and are unchanged, P will simply rise in an equal proportion to M; this is because AD has the tendency to rise but supply is fixed.[18] We can also show the same point diagrammatically: The unchanged FE and IS lines will mean that their intersection does not change. With the rise in M (and M/P), the LM temporarily shifts right and out of intersection; the equiproportionate rise in P, however, restores M/P to its initial level and LM to its initial position. Nothing real changes in this model, including the real interest rate and the real money supply. Only (all) prices and wage change equiproportionately; monetary neutrality holds.

6.3.6 The New Keynesian Model: Diagrammatic Analysis

New Keynesians (NK) would agree that the RBC model describes the world in the long run. However, the short-run behaviour of the economy is quite different and is described by the NK model. This model has exactly the same diagrams as the RBC one, with a couple of key differences. Both differences arise from the NKs' rebuttal of the market-clearing assumption that underlies the RBC reasoning. Lack of market clearing implies that the real wage fails to move to its equilibrium level. This changes the way one views the labour market. Referring again to Figure 6.7, let us say that for whatever reason the real wage is stuck at $(W/P)^0$. In this case, $L^D \neq L^S$ and employment is given by the short side of the market $(L^1 = L^D(W/P^0))$; employment is determined by labour demand regardless of supply. At that point, the total unemployment $L^F - L^1$ may be decomposed as $L^F - L^2$ (voluntary), where $L^2 = L^S(W/P^0)$, and $L^2 - L^1$ (involuntary) unemployment. In fact, as we shall see later, actual labour demand (L^A) may be even less than L^1. Therefore, NKs argue that there

---

[18] That output and the real interest rate are determined 'prior' to the price level means that they are more fundamental. They are due to the deeper structure of the system and therefore they affect, but are unaffected by (i.e. 'exogenous to') the price level.

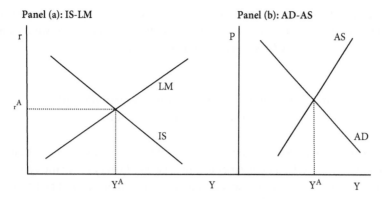

Figure 6.9. Equilibrium output and real interest rate in the NK model

is involuntary unemployment.[19] The implied market failure (obstacle to market clearing) necessitates government intervention with Aggregate Demand policies to correct it.

The other difference brought about by wage-price rigidity is an upward-sloping AS curve. As demand increases, some firms may increase prices while others may fix prices for a while and let output absorb the variation in demand.[20] Thus, the price level and output will be positively correlated, giving an upward-sloping AS curve. This is depicted in Figure 6.9a, b.

Other than the two exceptions mentioned (lack of equilibrium in the labour market and an upward-sloping AS), the economic system envisaged by the New Keynesians consists of exactly the same equations as the RBC model. But now, wage and price rigidity reverses the logic. The world begins with demand—the IS-LM and the AD-AS diagrams with an upward-sloping AS curve. As is standard, these two diagrams determine a level of output (Y^A). This will then be translated into required labour via the inverse production function:

$$L^A = F^{-1}(Y^A)$$

This gives the labour required to produce the output determined in the demand side of the economy. Labour demand then is a 'derived demand for labour', depending on the sales the firm is able to have and entirely unrelated to issues like marginal productivity and cost. In terms of Figure 6.7, we shall have $L^F - L^2$ voluntary unemployment (due to individual choice) and $L^2 - L^A$ involuntary unemployment.

As mentioned, $L^A \leq L^1 = L^D(W/P^0)$, i.e. the required labour may be less than the labour demand schedule at the prevailing real wage. This is because, if the real wage is given by $(W/P)^0$, the firm is happy to meet all the demand up to the point where the marginal product of labour just about equals the given real wage (i.e. L^1); the firm will not employ more people than that as it will be making losses. The labour demand schedule, therefore, becomes a boundary, the firm will be to the left of it at a point determined by demand. Thus, demand is a determining factor for (un)employment. In the long run of course, the firm will be choosing its production and labour demand based on marginal cost

---

[19] As discussed in Chapter 4, the voluntary-involuntary unemployment distinction is not emphasized any longer; this is partly because the boundary between the two is not as clear-cut as the distinction implies.
[20] Compare this key point with the RBCs' reasoning: firms flexibly adjust prices so as to fix output at the profit-maximization level (Y^E in Figure 6.8b); thus, the AS curve is vertical at Y^E.

considerations, thus will choose to be on L^D; and prices and wages will adjust until full employment (L^E) is arrived at. In the long run, even the New Keynesians would admit that the world works as the New Classicals/RBS theorists describe.[21]

6.3.7 Debates I: Labour Supply Elasticity and the Variability of Employment

One major issue with the RBC reasoning is the extent of the adjustment of labour over the cycle. We saw in Table 6.1 that the variability of total employment over the cycle is roughly equal to that of output. Are RBC models consistent with that 'stylized fact'? The starting point is that labour demand (L^D) is a positive function of productivity; in a nutshell, with higher productivity, the firm can offer higher wages without endangering profit margins, therefore L^D shifts up and right (see Chapters 1 and 3 for the parallel analysis of wage-price setting). RBCs attribute a key role to fluctuations in productivity (growth) in generating the cycle. Referring to Figure 6.7, fluctuations in productivity move the L^D curve about, therefore the equilibrium point moves up and down the labour supply function (L^S). Thus, for the equilibrium labour hours (L^E) to be variable enough, L^S must be sufficiently responsive (flat) to changes in the real wage. The New Keynesians' criticism is that labour supply is not so responsive to the real wage; see Manning (1995). One response is that there is an important difference between permanent and temporary changes in the real wage. As we saw in Chapter 1, while permanent increases in the real wage are thought to leave employment basically unaltered, temporary increases in the real wage may be numerically stronger. This is because of the 'intertemporal substitutability of leisure/labour', the elasticity by which one can substitute future leisure for current (i.e. work temporarily more now) in response to a temporary rise in the real wage. The problem is that, for RBC models to generate sufficient variability of hours worked, a highly implausible such elasticity must be assumed (way above unity), whereas available estimates suggest unity or below; see King and Rebelo (1999) and Nickell (1990). With the empirically estimated elasticity, the variance of employment predicted by the RBC model is much lower than what is observed.

RBC theorists have responded in a number of ways: One strand of models postulates 'indivisible labour' (Hansen, 1985). This model assumes that many workers move in and out of employment over the cycle, rather than simply adjusting their labour supply fractionally; in this way, the predicted variability of labour over the cycle is larger. These assumptions are in line with the observation made in Chapter 1 that about two-thirds of the total variation in hours worked between cycles is due to workers moving in and out of employment altogether (the 'extensive margin' of adjustment for firms), and about one-third due to existing employees adjusting their hours (via overtime or part-time work, the 'intensive margin'). This insight has also helped refine the Solow residual against the 'labour hoarding' criticism. But the Hansen (1985) model is rather less plausible in the other assumptions it makes: that the workers enjoy full insurance by firms and the

---

[21] To give a concrete example, imagine a restaurant. In day-to-day business, it meets any demand to the left of L^D which is a capacity constraint. In the long run, things will be as in the 'business plan' which stipulates employment based on prices, costs, etc.—this is L^D. And if prices and wages are too high, they will gradually adjust to the level given by $(W/P)^E$.

selection of who is unemployed during a recession is made randomly. To rectify these unrealistic assumptions would involve admitting that some unemployment is involuntary, and this would go against the spirit of the RBC approach.

Another extension of the basic model is to introduce home production (cooking, cleaning, child-minding, growing own vegetables) alongside more standard economic activity (see Benhabib et al., 1991; and Greenwood and Hercowitz, 1991). Their motivation was that home-work (non-market activity) is large both in terms of time worked and output and that it is substitutable with ordinary market activity (a higher wage provides an incentive to work longer hours and buy food/cleaning/child-minding services from the market). This extension is shown to improve the quantitative performance of the model.

6.3.8 Debates II: The Cyclicality of the Real Wage and Inflation and the Role of Money

Now, let us explore the cyclicality of key variables according to different views; consider again the labour market depicted in Figure 6.10, with initial point A. A favourable productivity shock shifts L^D out, resulting in both higher employment and real wage (point B). So, both these variables are predicted by the RBC model to be pro-cyclical. In contrast, the NK model assumes some wage or price rigidity. If, say, an AD shock has occurred which raises the price level, and workers are prevented from raising their nominal wages by fixed contracts, they will be offering the same amount of labour even at a lower real wage, indicating an effective shift right of labour supply. If so, point C results: while employment is still pro-cyclical, the real wage is now counter-cyclical.

So, the cyclical behaviour of W/P emerges as a test between the two theories. Which theory do the data support? Empirical studies do not always give a clear picture, but according to Table 6.1 and similar findings, the real wage is pro-cyclical (but very mildly so), thus appearing to validate the RBC view. Partly in response to this, the NKs over the years have turned away from theories that emphasize wage stickiness to those emphasizing price stickiness more, which could result in a pro-cyclical real wage. Consequently, the cyclicality of the real wage ceases to be such a decisive test.

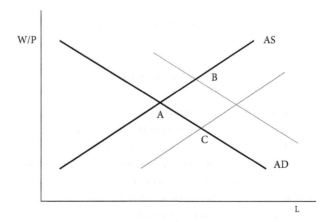

Figure 6.10. Productivity shocks, price stickiness and the real wage

Another way of ascertaining whether the shocks are primarily demand or supply would be by looking at the cyclical behaviour of prices and inflation. The standard AD-AS model (Figure 6.9b) suggests that the price level will be counter-cyclical if the primary shocks are the productivity ones, while with AD shocks, prices will be pro-cyclical. What do the data support? Here, ambiguities emerge when we talk about the rate of change of the price level (inflation) as opposed to the price level. Indeed, Cooley and Ohanian (1991) find that prices are counter-cyclical, lending support to productivity shocks as a driver of cycles; but Chadha and Prasad (1994) find that de-trended prices are counter-cyclical but inflation is pro-cyclical. Thus, no agreement (and rather little research) exists on this important aspect of the theory.

One among the most important points of debate is the role of money. If monetary shocks have real effects, then monetary policy can also have real effects and thus a useful role in stabilization. An RBC theorist would observe that nothing in Figures 6.7 or 6.8a depends on P: The wage W/P is in real terms, which is very different from P itself. The production function also involves only real variables (L and Y). The supply side of the economy is cast entirely in real terms, and the AS curve is vertical—at all times. Hence, money is neutral, it only affects prices (equiproportionately) and not real variables. The NK position is of course that neutrality breaks down (only in the short run) because of the positive slope of the short-run AS curve, which is due in turn to price and wage stickiness. This view refutes the neutrality of money and cites the evidence: money is found in the data to be pro-cyclical and leading. If money is neutral, how can it be systematically correlated with output in that way? RBC theorists respond by considering money as being endogenously generated by the banking sector (King and Plosser, 1984; Kydland and Prescott, 1990). Because of an endogenous 'money multiplier', (broad) money supply responds endogenously to output because of adjustment in both the personal and banking sectors, without however implying any monetary non-neutrality that could be exploited for stabilization purposes. Thus, the RBC theorists have in mind a concept of 'reverse causation'. Much as Christmas gifts are correlated and precede Christmas without of course causing it, so does money correlate and precede, but without causing, output.

6.4 A Basic Real Business Cycles Model

In this section, we turn to a simple, formal RBC model of cycles.

6.4.1 Introduction

Initiated by Kydland and Prescott (1982) and Long and Plosser (1983), the 'Real Business Cycles' approach (RBC) is the offshoot mainly of the New Classicals' to modelling business cycles. As such, it is predicated on the assumptions of individual rationality and optimization, market clearing (though more recent approaches have begun to introduce price/wage rigidities and lack of market clearing). RBC theorists argue that the business cycles are the best response (though not a painless response) of the private sector to exogenous shocks hitting the economy. As such, the RBC approach shares the predisposition of the New Classicals against government intervention and systematic aggregate demand-based stabilization of the cycle. In fact, much of the thrust of the RBC theories is to show the predominance of productivity shocks (a supply-side shock), against which demand stabilization policies are rather powerless. RBCs attribute no or very little importance to monetary shocks of any kind as drivers to the cycle.

Methodologically, the RBC approach has relied on explicit micro-foundations incorporating intertemporal optimization and dynamics, allowing for shocks, uncertainty, and general equilibrium effects. Micro-foundations and dynamic optimization require quite advanced mathematical methods, but the models cannot be solved analytically, so numerical and computational methods are heavily relied upon to deliver concrete results. Despite the many potential criticisms, the approach has offered considerable substantive and methodological advances in our understanding of the business cycles and macroeconomic modelling in general. We now turn to building a very sketchy model to illustrate how business cycles can emerge out of simple productivity shocks. Our interest is only to give a flavour of this approach and not present any complete account of these models; for such surveys, the reader may consult (in the first instance) King and Rebelo (1999—perhaps the best all-round introduction), King et al. (1988a, b), the papers in Cooley (1995), and McCallum (1989). Though RBC models have faded as an active research programme (supplanted now by the DSGE programme), a reassessment is offered by Rebelo (2005) and McGrattan and Prescott (2014).

6.4.2 A Prototype RBC Model

As mentioned, RBC models start from individuals' and firms' optimization problems, therefore they take on board all the analysis of Chapter 5. To make progress, some more specific structure needs to be assumed, as follows. Production takes the Cobb-Douglas form:

$$Y_t = A_t K_{t-1}^\alpha L_t^{1-\alpha} \tag{6.13}$$

This is a parametric example of the production function (5.18) or (5.18'), with end-of-period specification for capital (so K_{t-1} is the level of capital available to the economy at time t).[22] The only addition is the time-varying productivity, A_t. Furthermore, utility is a logarithmic version of (5.1), without population growth:

$$U = \sum_{t=1}^{\infty} (1+\rho)^{-t} u(C_t, 1-L_t) \equiv \sum_{t=1}^{\infty} (1+\rho)^{-t} [\log C_t + \theta \log(1-L_t)] \tag{6.14}$$

$0 < L_t < 1$ is labour, therefore $1 - L_t$ is leisure; $0 < \rho < 1$ is the rate of time preference (subjective rate of discount). Since we are not interested in replicating long-run growth

---

[22] One generally neglected issue is capacity utilization. The quantity of output generated by (6.11') reflects the maximum, but not all of that may be used; for whatever reason, there generally exists spare capacity. The (rate of) capacity utilization is the ratio of actual to capacity (maximum) output. As Corrado and Mattey (1997) explain, the rate of capacity utilization in the manufacturing sector is highly correlated with real output growth in the US (with a coefficient of 0.9!). Why and how much spare capacity do businesses choose to have? And how do they vary that over the cycle? It is probably fair to say that business cycles research should generally investigate these questions more.

(the data consist of filtered series that extract the business cycle component and disregard the long-run growth component), we assume that there is 100 per cent depreciation of physical capital within the period ($\delta = 1$, instead of the more empirically plausible rough figure of 10 per cent per year), so that the capital accumulation equation (5.3) reduces to:

$$K_t = I_t \tag{6.15}$$

In other words, no capital survives beyond one period, so all the capital we have is the current investment. An important strand of RBC research has investigated the effects of government spending, so we include it here as a constant fraction ($0 < \gamma < 1$) of output. To keep the analysis simple, the public services that this expenditure buys are not included in utility (counterfactually). Including public spending but excluding net exports, the National Income Accounting equation is:

$$Y_t = C_t + K_t + \gamma Y_t \tag{6.16}$$

These assumptions permit one to obtain simple analytical solutions to the model (see McCallum, 1989, which is mostly followed here).[23] So, the agent's problem is to maximize intertemporal utility (6.14), subject to an appropriate intertemporal budget constraint and equations (6.13) and (6.14–15) as descriptors of the economic environment.

As we saw in Chapter 5, the solution to this problem is characterized by two equations. First, the Euler equation (5.11') which gives consumption dynamics; with zero population growth ($\eta = 0$) and logarithmic growth ($\sigma = 1$), this becomes:

$$\frac{\partial U/\partial C_t}{\partial U/\partial C_{t+1}} = \frac{1 + r_{t+1} - \delta}{1 + \rho} \tag{6.17}$$

And the labour-leisure optimal choice condition (5.14), which in this context is:

$$-\frac{\partial U/\partial L_t}{\partial U/\partial C_t} = W_t \tag{6.18}$$

In our context, because of logarithmic utility, the consumption and substitution effects of any rise in the productivity on labour supply cancel out and labour turns out to be constant; we indicate it by L (which is endogenous). Furthermore, from the NIA equation (6.16), we may write,

$$K_t = \phi Y_t/(1-\gamma), \tag{6.19a}$$

$$C_t = (1-\phi) Y_t/(1-\gamma), \tag{6.19b}$$

---

[23] Without these restrictive assumptions, RBC models tend to become very complicated and analytical solutions are not available. In that case, one may proceed in two alternative ways: either to log-linearize the model around the steady states using basically Taylor approximations (see King et al., 1988a, b; and Campbell, 1994); or to use computer-heavy numerical methods.

where ϕ is investment's share in output, which turns out to be:

$$\phi \equiv \frac{\alpha}{1+\rho}$$

This share depends positively on capital's contribution to production (α): the higher this is, the more it is worth to forego current consumption in favour of future one; and inversely on the rate of time preference ρ: the higher this is, the less will future consumption be valued, therefore the less valuable will be investment for the future.

Substituting the production function for Y_t in the solution to capital in (6.19a) and taking logs (which are indicated by lower cases), we have (note the difference between parameter α and technology a_t):

$$k_t = \log(\phi/(1-\gamma)) + \alpha k_{t-1} + (1-\alpha)\log L + a_t \tag{6.20}$$

With the lag coefficient of $0 < \alpha < 1$, we have arrived at a dynamic equation of capital which shows endogenous persistence, i.e. even if the productivity level is a purely random shock, capital does show some pattern. In addition, productivity may be plausibly thought to show some exogenous persistence of its own, i.e. it may be hypothesized to be:

$$a_t = \beta a_{t-1} + \varepsilon_t, \tag{6.21}$$

where $0 < \beta < 1$ and ε_t is the statistical innovation in technology, over and above last period's influence. Introducing into (6.20), the solution of capital may be rewritten as:[24]

$$k_t = (1-\beta)\{\log(\phi L/(1-\gamma))\} + (\alpha+\beta)k_{t-1} - \alpha\beta k_{t-2} + \varepsilon_t \tag{6.22}$$

Log-capital then becomes an AR(2) process; so does output from the production function (6.13) and consumption (from 6.19b). There is evidence (Blanchard, 1981; Christiano et al., 2005) that such processes seem to characterize adequately the behaviour of de-trended US output and consumption.

6.4.3 Productivity and Labour Supply

Equation (6.22) embodies a key prediction of RBC models, namely that labour supply and output respond in the same direction to a productivity or technology shock (ε_t). The underlying intuition comes from the labour-leisure choice, equation (6.18): when the productivity of labour rises (and therefore the real wage), the opportunity cost of leisure rises. The optimal response is to raise labour and reduce leisure; as output rises with a positive productivity shock, the RBC model predicts a pro-cyclical labour supply. Most researchers would accept that; but Gali (1999) finds that labour supply falls in the short run in response to a positive technological shock (a form of positive productivity shock). Note

---

[24] This involves substituting the production function (6.13) into the solution for capital (6.20 with 6.21), shifting back once by multiplying through by β (i.e., obtaining an equation of the form $\beta k_t = ...$) and subtracting the latter from the former (obtaining $k_t - \beta k_{t-1} = ...$).

that this effect is entirely labour supply and it is not due to the fact that the firm now requires a small labour input: it is generated because the wealth effect of the shock (a higher wage, therefore more resources, pushing for more leisure) may be greater than the substitution effect (a high opportunity cost of leisure, pushing for more labour). Gali's finding has sparked a lively debate in the literature, which cannot be reviewed here.[25] See Christiano et al. (2004) for the opposite view (that positive productivity shocks increase employment) and Rebelo (2005) for a review. Kimball et al. (2006) make a careful estimate of aggregate technological shocks; they argue that both employment and output may fall slightly in the short run, following a positive technology shock. They conclude by showing the relevance of sticky prices for this result.

6.4.4 Open Questions and Issues

The RBC strand of models has been a very successful programme of research. It began as a peculiar and marginal type of models, rose to become 'orthodoxy', and then later got supplanted by the newer generation of 'DSGE' models, as we explain below. During this trajectory, it has paved the way for important methodological innovations in macroeconomic modelling and has highlighted numerous issues, some of which are still being debated. Among those that remain open, we can list the following:

- The nature and effects of productivity shocks. We have discussed at length at various places the controversy over the nature of such shocks, their connection to the Solow residual, and their effect on employment; it continues to be an area of active research.
- The persistence of endogenous variables. The persistence that the system endogenously generates (as opposed to assuming it from the exogenous productivity process) is rather limited: If one sets $\beta = 0$ above, all the persistence comes from capital's share in production (α), which, on the basis of capital's share in output may be argued to be of the order of 0.3. Hence, the endogenously generated persistence is limited (Cogley and Nason, 1995). This endogenous persistence may increase in models that take into account labour hoarding and a variable capital utilization rate, as discussed above (King and Rebelo, 1999).
- Other open questions include the behaviour of asset prices over the cycle (the 'equity premium puzzle', see Chapter 11); questions of whether the model can explain the emergence and the propagation of the Great Depression (1929–1930s) and the recent 'Great Recession' (2007–9)—see Christiano et al. (2015); and the relevance of other shocks such as fiscal or oil price shocks.[26]
- Further open questions and issues have been discussed in the context of the newer generation 'DSGE' models, to which we now turn.

---

[25] I remember examining a Ph.D. thesis some time ago which quoted upwards of 100 empirical studies on the issue. They were roughly equally divided in their findings on whether labour supply increases or decreases after positive productivity shocks.

[26] Benassy (1995) introduces money and wage contracts in a tractable fashion in an otherwise archetypal RBC model, thus forming a bridge between models based on optimizing agents and models with 'frictions' and more Keynesian features.

6.5 The RBC/New Keynesian Synthesis and the DSGE Model

As mentioned, the RBC programme of research has now given way to the newer generation of models that synthesize much of the methodology of those models with some insights of New Keynesians, predominantly (nominal) price and wage stickiness. These models are called 'Dynamic Stochastic General Equilibrium' models (DSGE). Though they also rely on calibration, one major difference from RBC models is they are able to evaluate the empirical performance of alternative models using advanced econometrics (Maximum Likelihood estimation) and do not rely simply on judgement as the RBC models do; see Fernandez-Villaverde (2010) for a review of DSGE econometrics. Other extensions concern the existence of heterogeneous agents, as opposed to a single representative agent hypothesized in much RBC work, and an in-depth treatment of the financial sector along the lines explored in Chapter 7 on monetary policy.

Begun with Rotemberg and Woodford (1997) and Clarida et al. (1999), DSGE models have now become a kind of common language with which many macroeconomists communicate. Research departments in Central Banks are busy producing such models (but it is unclear how much they trust them). Other prominent exponents of this strand are Christiano et al. (2005), and Smets and Wouters (2007). Though details differ, these models share a common core, reviewed next.

6.5.1 A Basic DSGE Model

In its essentials, the core of the DSGE model follows the 'three-equation New Keynesian model' of Chapter 3 with the addition that the IS equation (3.27) is 'micro-founded'. It is based on the Euler equation (5.11') or (6.17) with the addition of 'habits' in consumption, so as for it to have a richer lag structure. This IS equation is simply stated here; it is fully derived in Appendix 6A at the end of this chapter:

$$y_t = (1-\Phi)E_t y_{t+1} + \Phi y_{t-1} - \sigma(1-\phi)(E_t r_{t+1} r_{t+1} + \phi - \rho) + \Gamma_t \qquad (6.23)$$

Γ_t is a government spending shock, whose exact composition is given in Appendix 6A. $E_t(.)$ is the 'expectations operator'. Current output is negatively related to the real interest rate. It also depends on its own lag and its expected lead $(E_t(y_{t+1}))$ which provides a kind of anchor: it may be thought of as showing the level at which output is normally expected to be. The existence of habits (captured by ϕ) results in a wish for growth, therefore saving rises and current consumption and output falls.

Next is the New Keynesian Phillips Curve (or simply inflation equation) (3.26) with the 'homogeneity restriction' $\phi_1 + \phi_2 = 1$:

$$\pi_t = (1-\Theta)E_t \pi_{t+1} + \Theta \pi_{t-1} + \Psi(y_t - \bar{y}_t) + v_t \qquad (6.24)$$

To relate to (3.26), note that $\Theta \equiv \phi_1$; output enters in a de-trended form (deviation from log-trend output, $\bar{y}_t$) and there is an added price shock (arising e.g. from higher oil or raw materials prices or a stronger monopoly power), v_t. Furthermore, we have:

$$i_t = (1-\omega)\bar{i} + \omega i_{t-1} + (1-\omega)\eta_y(y_{t-1} - \bar{y}_{t-1}) + \eta_\pi(\pi_t - \pi^*) + \zeta_t \qquad (6.25)$$

Equation (6.25) is the 'Taylor rule' of monetary policy (3.28), to be further discussed in Chapter 7, with some additions. It shows how the nominal interest rate i_t, which is the exogenous policy instrument, is set by Central Banks; i.e., anchored around its long-run level $(\bar{i})$, it varies with reference to de-trended output and the inflation deviation from its target (π^*). For tractability, it is past output that is the indicator for the state of the economy; it may be rationalized by the fact that output data only come out with a lag (of about three months or so). There is also a monetary policy shock, ζ_t. Such an equation describes quite well actual policy-making, although no monetary policy-maker admits to following it. We must impose $\eta_\pi > 1$ for consistency. The parameter $0 < \omega < 1$ represents the degree of interest rate smoothing—the degree to which any changes in the base interest rate desired by the Central Bank are phased in gradually so as not to unsettle markets. To show things in a tractable way, though, we assume in what follows that $\omega = 0$ (no interest rate smoothing).

6.5.2 Solution

The real interest rate (given by the 'Fisher equation') may be approximated as:

$$r_t \equiv i_t - E_t\pi_{t+1} \approx i_t - \pi_t \tag{6.26}$$

With (6.26), the Taylor rule (6.25) with $\omega = 0$ can be re-expressed as:

$$r_t = \bar{i} + (\eta_\pi - 1)\pi_t + \eta_y(y_{t-1} - \bar{y}_{t-1}) - \eta_\pi\pi^* + \zeta_t \tag{6.26'}$$

First, we explore the long-run properties of the model. De-trended output is zero; the lead-lag structure of output in equation (6.23) and inflation in equation (6.24) can be factorized into differences which are eliminated in the long run; government spending g_t is assumed entirely transitory (therefore also eliminated in the long run); and inflation returns to its target (π^*). It is also instructive to inspect the long-run nominal interest. Using the above information, we get:

$$\bar{i} = \rho - \phi + \pi^* \tag{6.27}$$

From the Fisher equation (6.26), the long-run nominal interest rate is the sum of the long-run real interest rate and inflation. The former (the first two items) is obtained from (6.23) and follows essentially the logic of the Euler equation. The first item is the discount rate, which reflects impatience and must be therefore be rewarded for saving to take place. As seen from equation (6.23), the desire to improve on past consumption via 'habits', captured by ϕ, works in the opposite way to ρ as it increases saving therefore necessitates less reward. Finally, the long-run inflation is simply the inflation target.

In the short run, though, the interest rate can deviate from (6.27). Inserting (6.27) into (6.26'), the system (6.23-24, 6.26') becomes:

$$y_t = (1-\Phi)E_ty_{t+1} + \Phi y_{t-1} - \sigma(1-\phi)(E_tr_{t+1} + \phi - \rho) + \Gamma_t \tag{6.23}$$

$$\pi_t = (1-\Theta)E_t\pi_{t+1} + \Theta\pi_{t-1} + \psi(y_t - \bar{y}_t) + v_t \tag{6.24}$$

$$r_t = \rho - \phi + (\eta_\pi - 1)(\pi_t - \pi^*) + \eta_y(y_{t-1} - \bar{y}_{t-1})r_t + \zeta_t \tag{6.28}$$

This is a 3×3 dynamic system with y_t, π_t, and r_t as the endogenous variables, and γ_t, v_t, ζ_t, and $\bar{y}_t$ as the exogenous shocks (two of them policy-related). The inflation target π^* and various parameters also play important roles. In principle, the system can be analysed along the lines described in Appendix 5A but applied to a 3×3 system; the general treatment is found in Blanchard and Khan (1980). As an explicit analytical solution is very hard to obtain, in practice, the solutions are computer-based and the most common econometric software packages and routines can solve these out. The logic follows the treatment of equation (1.21) of Chapter 1: first, the reduced-form of the system is found, then Impulse Responses (IRs) are obtained.

As an application, let us think of a one-off monetary shock at a particular time t (a rise in the nominal rate above the value that would prevail normally, ζ_t) and consider how this affects output from t onwards—schematically, at time $t + s$, with s = 0, 1, 2, 3, ... Typically, the effect is long-lasting: The output response is 'persistent' (even though the monetary shock is one-off) in the sense that the effect dies away only gradually (see the discussion in Appendix 5C). As a result, the output series will be serially correlated. In empirical work, IRs of monetary shocks often appear to be hump-shaped, i.e. the strongest effect of the shocks takes place not contemporaneously but a few periods after the shock; see e.g. Christiano et al. (2005).

6.5.3 Other Directions and Open Questions

- More sophisticated models of price frictions: The 'canonical' three-equation DSGE model (Euler-IS equation, NK Phillips Curve, Taylor rule) is effectively a real model augmented with an inflation equation. The derivation of the latter is based on infrequent, and uncertain, price setting. But the riskiness involved here sits uneasily with the uncertainty elsewhere in the model: the Euler equation does not take into account uncertainty on the pricing front. (In other words, it assumes that a firm takes decisions on capital accumulation or employment assuming away the uncertainty involved in prices; that may be so to a first approximation—perhaps—but it is surely not accurate.) Danziger (1999) considers a unified, but complex, model of uncertainty. Other models make more tractable steps in integrating the real aspects of the model with sophisticated inflation equations. See for instance Christiano et al. (2005); Ercec et al. (2000).
- The 'credit channel' and financial frictions: The Great Recession of 2007–9 has put in sharp relief the role of the financial system in the emergence and propagation of cycles. Thus, a lot of business cycles research is taking on board the insights of the literature on the 'credit channel', to be reviewed in Chapter 7. For surveys of DSGE models with 'financial frictions' see Christiano et al. (2015) and Gertler and Kiyotaki (2010); for a more recent contribution, Brunnermeier and Sannikov (2014). Gertler and Karadi (2011) consider a DSGE model with financial frictions and unconventional monetary policy in particular (lending from the Central Bank which holds riskless government debt and is therefore not balance-sheet constrained, unlike private banks).

- Unemployment: The Great Recession has also caused a rise in unemployment. In response to this, some DSGE models have incorporated (involuntary) unemployment, which is generated by search frictions in the labour market; see Gali et al. (2012) and Christiano et al. (2010).
- 'News': Following the lead of Beaudry and Portier (2006), an expanding literature analyses the role of 'news' as drivers of business cycles. In much of this literature, 'news' refers to advance signals that convey (imperfect) information about future shocks before these actually take effect (Jaimovich and Rebelo, 2009; Schmitt-Grohe and Uribe, 2012; Karnizova, 2010; Khan and Tsoukalas, 2012; Milani and Treadwell, 2012). These signals are modelled via additional shocks; however, their relation to the fundamental shocks (demand, productivity, etc.) is rather unclear. The conceptual issues related to such additional shocks ('noise' in agents' expectations vs. correct fundamentals-driven changes in expectations) and issues of identification are discussed in Blanchard et al. (2013).
- The fiscal multiplier: Investigation of fiscal policy, with a focus on ascertaining the magnitude of the fiscal multiplier is also an active area of research in the context of DSGE models (Cogan et al., 2010; Mountfort and Uhlig, 2009; Zubairy, 2013). Fiscal policy will be discussed in Chapter 8.
- Fine-tuning or thinking big? It is fair to say that, on the whole, the 'Great Recession' (2007–9, on which more in the next section) has caught researchers and analysts unaware. As a result, it has provoked some deep soul-searching in some quarters and criticism of both research and policy-making. Even prior to the Great Recession, there had been talk of a 'jobless recovery' after the slowdown of around 2000. More broadly, the possibility that the recovery may not place us onto the same trend as before is a possibility that most modern business cycles research cannot account for. Caballero (2010) criticizes the currently prevailing (i.e. DSGE) models as preoccupied with 'second-order' refinements and extensions on an essentially standard structure; but the crisis revealed our 'first-order' ignorance about the world, therefore we ought to be more experimental with models and formulate and test a wider range of ideas; see also Kocherlakota (2010) who gives a critical overview of the current state of macroeconomics. Likewise, Summers (2014) argues that policy should not confine itself with fine-tuning output around a 'given trend' (recall the ambiguities in estimating it); rather, it should attempt to solve the emerging pressing issues: supporting employment, avoiding 'secular stagnation' (Summers, 2014) and a repeat of the crisis. Such criticisms are potentially game-changing; time will tell how much water they will carry, but they do reflect some uneasiness about the currently prevailing mindset.

6.6 Structural Vector Autoregressions (SVARs)

Vector AutoRegressions (VARs) are small, formal systems that purport to capture the inter-related dynamics of a set of variables. VARs have proved quite useful in business cycles-related research as they are able to give precise answers about the relative importance of the exogenous drivers of the cycles (via 'Forecast Error Variance Decomposition'); and because they allow estimation of the 'Impulse Responses' (the effects of shocks on the endogenous variables over time). Here, we give an introduction to SVARs and their identification; Section 1.6 of Chapter 1 serves as a useful background.

For concreteness, consider the VAR—the econometric analogue of equation (1.22):

$$Y_t = A_1 Y_{t-1} + A_2 Y_{t-2} + \ldots + A_k Y_{t-k} + u_t \qquad (6.29)$$

where Y is a $(n \times 1)$ vector of endogenous variables, each of $A_1, A_2, \ldots, A_k$ is an $(n \times n)$ matrix of coefficients, and u is a commensurate $(n \times 1)$ vector of residuals. More often than not, the dimension (n) of the system is not great—three to five variables—and k is estimated by an information criterion (e.g. Akaike)—typically $k = 1$ or 2 with annual data.[27] The usefulness of (6.29) is that it allows estimation of the dynamics of these n variables without reference to any other variable—it is a closed system. But extensions of (6.28) to exogenous regressors (not included in Y) are considered in 'open VARs'.

The residuals from the VAR (u_t) are the statistical innovations in the variables Y_t. But these cannot be given a straightforward economic interpretation. The reason is that (6.29) assumes in effect that each of the Y_t is affected by past values of itself and the other Ys, and contemporaneous exogenous shocks; no contemporaneous interaction between the Ys is allowed.[28] That cannot be true in economic systems, though. Hence, economic systems must be represented by a system like this:

$$BY_t = D_1 Y_{t-1} + D_2 Y_{t-2} + \ldots + D_k Y_{t-k} + e_t \qquad (6.30)$$

The matrices here are also of the same dimension $(n \times n)$ as the As. But (6.30) crucially differs from (6.29) because the B matrix allows contemporaneous interaction of the Ys. The $(n \times 1)$ vector of error terms here, e_t, are the mutually uncorrelated ('orthogonal') economic shocks: productivity, demand, pricing, etc. that theory emphasizes. Exactly n of them (equal to the number of equations) can be identified. Which ones are allowed to enter is a matter of judgement: the modeller first chooses the dimensions of the system (n) and the variables, then needs to decide what shocks are most likely to affect these variables on the basis of theory. For example, if the VAR is made up of output (gap), inflation, and unemployment, the obvious shocks are demand, productivity, and a pricing shock (think of the shocks that would appear in an AD, an NK inflation, and a labour demand equation). If the VAR involves output, interest rates, and inflation, then the shocks should be interpreted as related to monetary policy, other AD, and pricing shock.

The question is how to derive (identify) the economic shocks e_t from the estimated u_t. (Note that it is 6.29 that is estimated, not 6.30.) 'Structural VARs' (SVARs) allow us to do that; in fact, there are several methods by which this can be accomplished. To see how they work, let us introduce the inverse of B, $\beta \equiv B^{-1}$, and pre-multiply (6.30) by that, to get:

$$\beta B Y_t = \beta D_1 Y_{t-1} + \beta D_2 Y_{t-2} + \ldots + \beta D_k Y_{t-k} + \beta e_t \qquad (6.30')$$

---

[27] k is small in order to avoid over-parameterization of the system: note that each matrix A contains $n \times n$ coefficients, and there are k of them, so one needs very long series in order to preserve degrees of freedom.

[28] Formally, (6.29) is the 'reduced-form' version of (6.30). As a result, each of the estimated residuals $u^i_t, i = 1, 2, \ldots, n$, is a combination of economic shocks e^i_t.

If we call $A_m = \beta D_m$, $m = 1, 2, ..., k$ and if $u_t = \beta e_t$, then (6.29) and (6.30') are identical. This allows us to estimate matrix B. The variance-covariance matrix of u_t and e_t are linked by:

$$V \equiv E(u_t u_t') = \beta E(e_t e_t')\beta' = \beta I \beta' = \beta \beta' \tag{6.31}$$

The variance of the residuals, $V \equiv E(u_t u_t')$, is estimated; as it is symmetric, it involves $n \times (n+1)/2$ free coefficients to be estimated—n on the diagonal $+ n \times (n-1)/2$ off the diagonal. On the other hand, the economic shocks e_t (by assumption) have a unit variance each and are mutually orthogonal; their variance-covariance matrix is the identity matrix of size $(n \times n)$.

Having estimated $V \equiv E(u_t u_t')$, (6.31) allows us to work out the elements of the β matrix if we postulate a number of restrictions on them ('identifying restrictions'). The various methods of estimating β differ by the identifying restrictions they place. One method involves considering the pattern by which shocks affect variables contemporaneously. For a concrete example, consider a 5×5 VAR in money supply, employment, output, wages, and prices (the order is important). The shocks e_t will then be a monetary shock, other AD shock, wage, price, and productivity shocks. The β matrix with identifying restrictions takes the form:

$$\beta = \begin{bmatrix} 1 & 0 & 0 & 0 & 0 \\ 0 & 1 & * & * & 0 \\ * & 0 & 1 & 0 & * \\ 0 & 0 & * & 1 & * \\ * & 0 & 0 & 0 & 1 \end{bmatrix}$$

The 1s on the diagonal simply say that the shocks affect the own variable one-for-one contemporaneously. The 0s are effects that theory suggests are very weak so as to be assumed away; these are the identifying restrictions. The '*' are the entries that can be calculated from the estimates of $V \equiv E(u_t u_t')$; their number must be $n \times (n+1)/2$ for the method to work.

For instance, the first row effectively gives us the equation:

$$u_t^1 = \sum_i \beta_{1i} e_t^i$$

i.e. how the statistical innovation (residual) to the money variable (u^1) is affected by all five economic shocks (the e^is). The off-diagonal 0s in the first row (the β_{1i}, $i = 2, ..., 5$) suggest that monetary policy (exogenously set by the Central Bank) does not respond to the other economic shocks (this is for argument's sake). The '*' are the entries of the matrix that can be freely estimated from (6.31) once these identifying restrictions have been incorporated. Typically, econometric packages allow us to place those restrictions.

Other identification methods rely on other restrictions. The method of 'Choleski decomposition' assumes that there is an ordering of exogeneity among the shocks; e.g. u^1 is only affected by e^1, u^2 is only affected by e^1 and e^2, u^3 by e^1, e^2, and e^3, and all the way to u^k which is the least exogenous (most endogenous) that is affected by all shocks. In effect, the β matrix is lower-triangular—has zeros everywhere above the diagonal. The task of the modeller is to think carefully which economic shocks can be placed in that order. Yet another method places only long-run identifying restrictions, in line with the view that theory can inform us only about long-run relations, whereas the data should be allowed to pick up freely any short-run dynamics.

Once matrix β has been definitized (partly by identifying restrictions/assumptions and partly estimation), we have in effect got (6.30'). By the $D_m = BA_m$ and $B = \beta^{-1}$ transformations, we recover (6.30). From there, we can trace the effects of e^i_t's on all the Y_t's over time (the 'Impulse Response Functions'), and we can also decompose the variances of Ys into the constituent shocks, to ascertain how important each shock is as a driver of a particular variable ('Forecast Error Variance Decomposition').

As mentioned, VARs and SVARs continue to be quite useful in business cycle research; the interested reader should consult Stock and Watson (2001) and Christiano et al. (2007) for introductions to VARs, SVARs, and long-run identifying restrictions, respectively. Against that, there has been criticism that they cannot uniquely identify economic shocks, therefore their true value in identifying the drivers of cycles is questionable (Chari et al., 2008). We have seen that this is a pressing issue in some areas, e.g. when identifying the productivity shocks and their effects. Partly in response to that, Fernández-Villaverde et al. (2007) have carefully considered the conditions under which the residuals of (6.29) uniquely identify the economic shocks of (6.30). A necessary condition, of course, is that the number of u's and e's must be the same, but there is a lot more to say than that!

6.7 Episodes

In this final section, we change course and review briefly the major macroeconomic business-cycle type of episodes that the industrialized world has faced in the last 100 years or so. The aim is to supplement the formal analyses given above with some historical context, without aiming to be anywhere near exhaustive; the interested reader should refer to more specialist literature.

6.7.1 The Great Depression

The Great Depression refers to the major recession that ensued in most industrialized economies (US, Germany, UK, France) from about 1929 into the 1930s, lasting often right up to the onset of World War II. Talking about the US experience, Galbraith (1975, chapter 10) sums up its severity quite powerfully:

> After the Great Crash came the Great Depression which lasted, with varying severity, for ten years. In 1933, Gross National Product (total production of the economy) was nearly a third less than in 1929. Not until 1937 did the physical volume of production recover to the levels of 1929, and then it promptly slipped back again. Until 1941 the dollar value of production remained below 1929. Between 1930 and 1940 only once, in 1937, did the average number of unemployed during the year drop below eight million. In 1933 nearly thirteen million were out of work, or about one in every four in the labour force. In 1938 one person in five was still out of work.   (Galbraith, 1975, p. 186)

So, a lost decade and more in terms of industrial production, with unemployment rates of upwards of 20 per cent for much of the time (Temin, 1991). This experience was mirrored by the other economies mentioned above, if in a slightly milder form. But why remember this episode more than 80 years later? For at least three serious reasons: first, it is part of a very turbulent period of European, indeed world, history—some analysts would even claim that it forms a continuum with the two world wars that frame it at either end, and that it really was instrumental in causing World War II. Second, it offers valuable lessons for economic policy, on what to do and what to avoid—though there is no agreement on what exactly these lessons are! And third, this episode is a litmus test for economic theories—because if our theories are unable to explain this episode, they fail a crucial practical test.

Our purpose is to give a flavour of the theories that have been proposed to explain the Great Depression as a way of connecting historical experience with the theories examined here. A good gateway into the relevant debates and literatures is the lectures by Temin (1991), while the volume by Feinstein et al. (1997) focuses on the European experience and Kindleberger (1973) provides an in-depth historical treatment.

One clear line of explanation is provided by Temin (1991), who argues that the Great Depression is the result of a 'deflationary' (= contractionary) bias in fiscal and monetary policy during the 1930s among the countries in question. In fact, this contractionary bias is more than the sum of its parts, as the international exchange system (the inter-war 'Gold Standard') imparted an inflationary bias itself, over and above what individual policy-makers were aiming to do. The key idea was that currencies were fixed in value against gold, and that implied parities between currencies themselves. This system existed before World War I. The problem was that World War I disrupted the advanced industrialized economies, and rendered the old gold parities obsolete; yet policy-makers decided to return to the Gold Standard after the war and, worse, at wrong parities. In theory, if your parity was too low (meaning an undervalued currency), you would run a trade balance surplus, earning gold and other foreign currency payments. This would (or should) increase your money supply, causing inflation and the deterioration of the trade balance. Conversely, if your currency was overvalued, at a parity above its real value, you would run a trade deficit, which would deplete your gold reserves. This w/should induce you to decrease your money supply (a contractionary policy), but you should also reduce domestic 'absorption' (= demand) in order to reduce the deficit and the drainage of gold reserves. The problem is the asymmetry in the workings of the system. For the surplus countries, the 'should' (cause an increase in money supply and inflation) does not materialize, whereas for the deficit countries, the 'should' is more readily translated into a deflationary/contractionary stance. Thus, on balance, there is contractionary aggregate demand policy across countries. Beyond that, individual countries had their own reasons for pursuing contractionary policies: the US in order to combat the speculative frenzy of the 1920s, and Germany in order to combat its own structural problems, including worries about World War I reparation payments. And behind all this was the 'Classical' mindset that we described in Chapter 1: the paramount goal was sound money, the market economy had self-equilibrating mechanisms, etc. Based more on ideology and dogma than cool-headed analysis and hard evidence, these beliefs were however pervasive, as is agreed by Galbraith (1975, chapter 10) and Temin (1991, chapter 1). Thus, one influential line of argument is that the Depression was due to a sustained deflationary stance, with a misconceived system of international exchanges providing the overarching impetus for it.

The contractionary stance is blamed by other analysts as well, who however disagree on other aspects of the analysis. The influential volume by Friedman and Swartz (1963) puts the blame on bank crises and crashes that occurred in various waves from 1930 onwards. This induced both the public and banks themselves (the surviving ones, that is!) to hold more cash in proportion to deposits, and therefore reduced the 'money multiplier' (see Chapter 7). This implied an effectively contractionary monetary stance, even if not one induced by policy as such. This idea is criticized by Temin (1991, chapter 2) which argues that such bank crashes are on the whole endogenous (why would banks fail if not because the macroeconomy worsens?—except for the odd fluke) and should be more symptoms rather than causes of the malaise.

Bernanke (1983) has argued that the banking crises caused 'credit rationing', i.e. a drying up of credit by banks as the economic climate became more uncertain and banks became less willing to take risks. In this, he reflected a busy literature of the 1980s, and anticipated the literature on the 'credit channel' of monetary policy transmission, that will also be reviewed in Chapter 7. According to this line of reasoning, it was the retail banks of mass everyday banking that were mainly affected and reduced credit, and the small business, self-employed, and agricultural sector that was most severely hit as a result (the agricultural sector's plight having been immortalized in Steinbeck's *The Grapes of Wrath*). Temin (1991, chapter 2), though, contests this line of reasoning on statistical grounds. The debates continue (see Kehoe and McGrattan, 2002; and Romer and Romer, 2013, for recent contributions).

The Depression also afflicted much of Europe outside the countries mentioned above, though there is the customary country heterogeneity and diversity of experience; see Feinstein et al. (1997) for a comprehensive description. Between 1929 and 1932, industrial production fell by almost 40 per cent in Poland, Austria, and Germany, the countries worst afflicted in the continent (by about 10 per cent in the UK and almost 50 per cent in the US). Bank failures were widespread in Austria and Germany, less so elsewhere. A casualty of the turbulent times was the Gold Standard: The first country to abandon it was the UK (1931); by 1932, the system had practically ceased to exist.

Two other features are worth mentioning. The latter part of the 1920s saw an unprecedented speculative frenzy develop in the US. It is clear that the stock market prices went into a bubble, with all the malpractices that this entails or encourages (see Galbraith, 1975). Eventually, the stock market crashed in October 1929 (the 'Great Crash'). What is not clear is whether and how the Crash was connected to the Great Depression. One argument (Temin, 1991) is that that there is no connection, supported by the fact that in October 1987 there was a stock market crash of an equal magnitude, yet the real economy did not suffer on that occasion. Galbraith (1975) argues that the crash generated cash flow problems (again emphasized by the 'credit channel') that eventually snowballed into cuts in inventory accumulation, investment, and luxury goods as the financial sector's difficulties gradually were transmitted into the 'real' economy. In this, we find a number of the mechanisms or model of cycles at work: cash flow and financial difficulties—the credit channel; inventory accumulation slowing down—Goodwin cycles; investment cuts and production slow-down—multiplier-accelerator. In addition, Galbraith offers ideas that sound surprisingly modern and relevant. In the inter-war years, the income distribution in the US became more unequal; as mass incomes fell behind, aggregate demand was disproportionately sustained by investment and by luxury consumption by the well-off.

In times of crisis, these are the items of spending that are more hit as they as the more income-elastic, so to speak. With the rise in income inequality witnessed in our times, these suggestions sound rather prescient (see the discussion on 'secular stagnation' in Chapter 9 on growth and Chapter 10 on inequality).

One last feature of the Great Depression merits a mention. During much of the 1930s, the price level in the US and elsewhere was falling—a *de*flation (negative rate of inflation). This aggravated the contractionary policy stance. There are at least three serious reasons why a deflation is bad. First, as prices fall, it is worth waiting till later to make purchases, so aggregate spending falls. Second, and relatedly, what matters to businesses, borrower,s and mortgage holders alike is the real interest rate ($i - \pi$ —ignoring expectations of inflation). If the inflation rate $\pi < 0$, the real interest rate and the real cost of borrowing rise; the consequences on borrowing and therefore spending are adverse. Finally, as prices fall, the real value of all wealth and liabilities (loans, mortgages, etc.) rises. Because of an asymmetry similar to the one discussed above in relation to the Gold Exchange, a rising real value of wealth may not greatly induce a rise in consumption; however, those with rising liabilities will definitely cut down on spending as they try to shore up their finances. As a result of all these, a *de*flation (negative inflation) can have a drastic adverse effect on spending. All these themes and aspects of the Great Depression are not only relevant for evaluating (macro)economic theories but also offer lessons for understanding the world around us in the aftermath of the Great Recession (2007–9).

6.7.2 Post-World War II

The first 30-odd year after World War II were years of relative (macroeconomic) plain sailing. Europe in particular kept very busy reconstructing itself; as a result, there were high rates of growth and per capita income rose fast, at least in Western Europe. (A description of what happened in the communist Eastern Europe and the Soviet Union is outside the scope of this narrative.) The growth experience of west Europe during 1945–75, rising from a low base following the war and towards prosperity at the end may be well described by the Solow Growth Model and the catch-up or convergence that it implies, all reviewed in Chapter 9. Other factors that underpinned the 30-year boom apart from post-war reconstruction were the resurgence of trade after the protectionist 1930s, more educated workforces, and the generalized use of technologies such as electricity and the internal combustion engine. Meanwhile, despite (or because of?) the high growth rates, inflation and unemployment were low and income inequality was steadily declining. To be sure, there were serious obstacles to be overcome before reconstruction got seriously under way; and there were the occasional balance of payments or exchange rates crises throughout this period; but the macroeconomic climate remained quite benign, at least in comparison to what the next 30 years would bring. For this, the 30 years 1945–75 have been termed by the French 'Les trentes années glorieuses' (the thirty glorious years).

In sharp contrast, the 1970s was a particularly turbulent period. The inflation rate rose to double digits in countries like the US and UK (peaking at 26 per cent in 1975 in the UK) that never knew more than 3-4 per cent inflation in the generation before. A variety of reasons may be responsible for this, and this author remains rather agnostic (and not quite knowledgeable enough!) about the exact mechanisms at work. Some would argue that the

Vietnam War, with the huge budget deficits in the US required to finance it, generated pressures for the deficits to be monetized and therefore inflation. As the US was a pivotal country in the dollar–gold exchange rate system (the 'Bretton Woods arrangement'), this may not be unrelated to the eventual demise of Bretton Woods and the onset of flexible exchange rates in 1973. Further, there were two oil price shocks in 1973 and 1979, largely exogenous to the macroeconomic system as they were caused by the politics of the Middle East. In addition, there was a lot of policy uncertainty and social strife, particularly in the UK, which culminated in the 'winter of discontent' (1978–9). We return to the oil shocks below.

There is evidence that around the mid-1970s, the rate of productivity growth slowed down; following Greenwood and Yorukoglu (1997), we can term this 'the 1974 effect'. We saw in Chapter 4 some possible effects: the productivity slowdown is one of the shocks considered in the shocks vs. institutions debate; if wage growth failed to adjust, the result may have been a rise in unemployment in the medium term. Greenwood and Yorukoglu (1997) argue that 1974 represents an even more important watershed, the dawn of a new industrial revolution based on information technology. They show evidence that technological innovation accelerated around that time; this takes the form of declining prices of goods that embody these technologies; the prices of these goods decline rapidly in periods of high innovation (e.g. consider the price of a car of a given class: if it is the same today as it was ten years ago, the real price—i.e. quality-adjusted—will be lower now as simply the car today is better than the car of ten years ago). There are two implications of this accelerated technical progress: the demand for skilled jobs rises and so does inequality (which indeed began to increase about the same time—see Chapter 10). Furthermore, adopting new technologies requires investment in human capital that is costly in terms of time; the long-run advance in labour productivity temporarily pauses as economic agents undertake the necessary (unmeasured) investment in human capital and information required to make the most of the new technologies. Greenwood and Yorukoglu (1997) present a simple argument that unifies various pieces of evidence (falling prices of technologically based goods, increasing inequality, productivity slowdown) but we need to wait and see whether their bold thesis that a new wave of industrial revolution began in the 1970s stands the test of time. On many of these themes, see Chapter 9 on growth.

As a result of high (and erratic) inflation in the 1970s, monetary policy-makers in the US and UK gradually determined to adopt a more contractionary stance in order to bring it under control; this coincided with the change in the political climate in the two countries, with the ascent to power of Mrs Thatcher in the UK (1979) and President Reagan in the US (1980). Broadly speaking, they were both avowedly pro-market and were elected with a platform of liberalizing markets, controlling inflation, and reducing the size of the state. Technically, monetary policy shifted only in operating procedures, a shift from interest rate to money stock targeting. This masked, however, a turn towards a more contractionary stance. In the US, the new Fed Chairman Paul Volcker initiated this stance in 1979, slowed down in 1980, and proceeded in a second wave of contraction in 1981–2. By 1982, this had reduced inflation from 10 per cent in 1979 to under 5 per cent in 1982, most of the gains being achieved in 1982. At the same time, unemployment rose from 5.8 per cent in 1979 to just under 10 per cent in 1982. As we discussed in Chapter 4, the gradual tightening has been credited by Ball (1999) for the lower and less persistent increase in unemployment than in Europe. In the UK, these developments were mirrored by a policy stance that has

become known as (political) monetarism. The key point is that the 1980s were characterized by high unemployment; that led to a decline in inflation to levels of 2–3 per cent in
leading industrialized economies by the mid-1990s (the 'great moderation' of inflation).

As the 1980s wore on, in the UK there developed a housing market-led boom around
1988. In order to correct the possible bubble, and in order to sustain an agreed exchange
rate when the UK pound entered in 1990 the European Monetary System (a precursor to
European Monetary Union), monetary policy progressively tightened. From the autumn of
1990 till 1992, this induced a recession in the UK. To some extent, this recession mirrored
the recession of 1990–1 in the US. This was led by a slowdown in consumer spending
(a shift left of AD); this is a key item in national spending, so it has important effects on
aggregate demand both contemporaneously and over time (recovery is slow) (see
Blanchard, 1993). What is not so clear is why consumption slowed down. Two leading
hypotheses are, first, that the slowdown reflected reduced expectations of lifetime incomes
(i.e. the slowdown was ultimately endogenous but reflecting expectations of future
incomes, not current incomes). The second hypothesis is that the consumption slowdown
reflected a change in the mood of consumers, either because of political turmoil (Iraqi
invasion of Kuwait in 1990 leading to the first Gulf War of 1991), or a sudden realization by
the personal sector that it is excessively indebted, or some kind of credit crunch. To the
extent that the change of mood was unrelated to other developments and was mostly
psychological, it can be called (changes in) 'animal spirits'—see Chapter 3 and the
Guidance below.

The 1990s and early 2000s were on the whole good economic times for the advanced
industrialized economies. There was much talk of the emerging 'new' economy, which was
heavily internet-based. There occurred a flurry of activity by internet-based companies (the
'dot.coms'), which however were not always successful. A dotcom stock market bubble
developed in the late 1990s, followed by a crash: NASDAQ, the technology-heavy US stock
market index, doubled between 1999 and April 2000, then lost 25 per cent of its value in a
month. The majority of the dotcoms ceased trading, many having never made a profit and
in the process devouring the venture capital available to them ('dot.bombs'). The nature of
the 'new(?) economy' will be discussed in Chapter 9 in the context of technical progress. To
the extent that the IT-related technological growth is real (this author believes that it is real
and far-reaching), then it represents a shift right of the AS curve; it is unclear, though, how
it affects the labour market. In any case, the euphoric mood continued for much of the
2000s but was shattered by the 'Great Recession' of 2007–9, to which we turn after
digressions on Japan and oil.

6.7.3 Japan's 'Lost Decade'

An interesting ongoing episode from a macro policy point of view is the Japanese
experience since 1990. Following a period of hectic post-war expansion starting from a
pretty low base, during which Japan became one of the richest economies in the world,
Japan's economy came to a sudden halt in the 1990s. In 1991, an asset price bubble burst,
leaving behind deep scars: excessive leverage by banks and the private sector and many
'zombie' private enterprises unable to overcome the vicious circle of debt–losses–yet more
debt. Positive nominal GDP growth continued for a while, but it was sluggish and

unemployment was rising. (Note that in Japan unemployment rates of the order of 4 per cent are considered high.) Analysts point to an output gap (potential-actual GDP) from the early 1990s on. The sense of stagnation prompted a variety of responses, all without great results. Monetary policy eased until the low interest rates hit the floor of zero; there has been talk of (the re-emergence of) a 'liquidity trap' whereby extra money is just hoarded by the private sector (as deposits offer next to no interest) and has no real effect (see Krugman, 1998; Kuttner and Posen, 2001; and McCallum, 2003). This experience anticipates the situation various western Central Banks find themselves 20 years later, as we discuss in Chapter 7 on monetary policy. Fiscal policy has been expansionary, giving rise to deficits that over the years have produced one of the highest debt-GDP ratios in the world; in 2013, it stood at more than 200 per cent. Despite its size, this public debt seems quite benign so far, held domestically by a saving-prone, ageing population. To shore up public finances, the Japanese government raised consumption tax rates in 1997, which worsened the recession and in fact decreased government revenues. The government raised the sales tax in 1997 for the purpose of balancing its budget. After this, the economy sank into outright recession; the nominal GDP growth rate was negative for most of the five years after the tax hike. Further damage was done with the onset of the 'Great Recession' (see below): by 2013, nominal GDP was at the same level as 1991 while the Nikkei 225 stock market index was at a third of its peak. There has been much talk of Japan's 'lost decade', but it begins to feel a lot longer than that. The perception that individual policies do not work has led Prime Minister Abe to a concerted policy ('Abenomics') of fiscal stimulus, monetary easing, and structural reforms; time will tell how successful this package is.

6.7.4 Oil and the Macroeconomy

There is broad agreement that the oil price shocks of 1973 and 1979 have caused 'stagflation'—the combination of stagnation and inflation. This merits a digression on the effects of oil prices on economic activity. Oil and gas are among the main sources of energy in modern economies, and as such their availability and price should be important for economic activity (environmental concerns aside). There are two very big questions to be asked. What are the effects of limits in the supply of a non-renewable, finite resource in the very long-run growth prospects of any economy? This is fuelled by a discussion, in some circles, about 'peak oil', the idea that oil production has peaked or will peak soon (in the next 10–20 years), after which supply will decline, with all the pressures that will put on an energy-hungry planet. These arguments become important as there is as yet no renewable, clean form of energy available in sizeable quantities. Even more broadly, it is argued, the finite size of the planet and its resources will put a ceiling to the material prosperity of its inhabitants (the 'limits to growth'). We shall not dwell on these arguments here; we shall review some of them briefly in Chapter 9 in the context of the discussion on 'secular stagnation' and very-long run growth prospects.

The second big question concerns the relation of oil prices with the business cycles. To this end, we show growth rates of the US real GDP and of the oil price (US$ per barrel), 1988–2018 in Figure 6.11. A couple of observations are noteworthy. The nominal oil price is much more volatile but has also recorded a much higher average annual growth

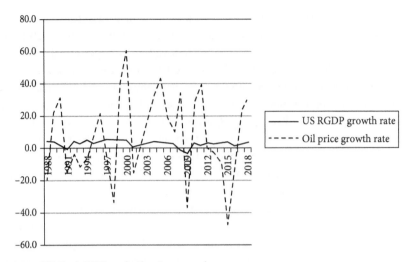

Figure 6.11. US Real GDP and oil price growth rates

Source: St Louis Fed: (https://fred.stlouisfed.org/series/ACOILBRENTEU), annual data. The oil price is of the 'Crude Brent' variety - Europe, dollars per barrel. Data accessed 11/5/2019

rate (7.7 per cent) than the US real GDP (2.9 per cent) over this period.[29] The correlation with the US real GDP growth rate is 0.24. Recall that a rise in the oil price represents an adverse supply shock, so if it is driver of the cycle, the correlation should be negative. The positive correlation is an indication of a demand-side effect (causality running from the world economy as a demand shifter to the oil price) rather than a supply-side effect (with the reverse causality of a supply-shifting oil price).

Blanchard and Gali (2007) have identified four major oil price shocks in the last 50 years or so, namely in 1973, 1979, 2000, and 2003. As mentioned, the consensus view (see e.g. Hamilton, 1983, 1996) is that the oil hikes of the 1970s caused inflation and a slowdown of economic activity (in real terms). Though these effects vary between countries, 'stagflation' seems to have been the overall effect. If so, and if as commonly argued they were entirely exogenous (to the economy: i.e. political), the oil price shocks of the 1970s represent the archetypal 'leftwards AS curve shifts'.

A major revision in the 'oil price shocks cause stagflation' thesis is represented by Blanchard and Gali (2010) who compare the effects of more recent with earlier oil price shocks. They show that the effects of oil price rises since 2000 have been much less severe than the effects of the price rises in the 1970s. The effects have also varied between countries. They provide evidence that the plausible reasons that account for this much diminished effect of more recent oil hikes are:

- Smaller shares of oil in production as economies have learnt to become more fuel-efficient following the earlier price shocks;
- More flexible labour markets, able to adjust in the face of these shocks;
- Better monetary policy;
- They also argue that the effects of oil price shocks in the 1970s must have coincided in time with large shocks of a different nature, an argument in line with those presented in the 'shocks vs. institutions' debate on European unemployment reviewed in Chapter 4.

[29] It should be borne in mind that, as the general price index has been rising, the real oil price has risen less than shown here; but it is likely that even in real terms, oil prices have been rising faster than real GDP.

A rejoinder to this debate is Hamilton (2009). It compares the oil prices rises in 2007–8 and earlier oil price shocks and their effects. Whereas previous oil price shocks were primarily caused by physical disruptions of supply, it is argued that the price rise of 2007–8 was caused by strong demand combined with a stagnating world production. Although the causes were different, the consequences for the economy appear to have been similar to those observed in earlier episodes, with significant effects on consumption spending. Hamilton (2009) concludes that the period 2007Q4–2008Q3 should be added to the list of US recessions to which oil prices appear to have substantially contributed.

The effects of oil prices increases on economic activity remain an important topic, more so in policy circles, whereas academic circles (it may be argued) do not pay the topic its due attention. One major difficulty is that the proper assessment of both causes (as they may be affected by the state of the economy as well as politics, therefore they are in general endogenous) and effects of oil prices requires a proper construction of a demand and supply system of oil—a tall order; see Dees et al. (2007) and Kilian (2014) for such structural empirical models of the oil market. The possible two-way causality between the macroeconomy and oil prices is explored in Barsky and Kilian (2004). Furthermore, oil price rises may have asymmetric effects: For instance, Andreopoulos (2009) shows that oil price increases lead to falls in employment, whilst, whenever there is growth of employment during expansions, this is more likely to have had other causes than (real) oil price declines. The wider macroeconomic climate plays a role: Van Robays (2012) shows that higher macroeconomic uncertainty tends to increase the impact on oil price of shocks in oil production. This may be due to lower price elasticity of both oil demand and supply during uncertain times. Accordingly, heightened uncertainty about the macroeconomic outlook can lead to oil price volatility. It is additionally shown that the impact of oil shocks on economic activity appears to be significantly reinforced by uncertainty. One concluding thought: because of its policy relevance and because of the currently rather high degree of uncertainty surrounding the macroeconomics of oil, we should be seeing an increase in related research in the future.

6.7.5 The 'Great Recession' (2007–9) and After

There is a widespread perception that the Great Recession was a watershed; nothing is the same after it. The 'Great Recession' refers to the crisis that erupted in about 2008, with 2007 as a 'preparatory' year during which the storm was brewing. Much of the world was technically in recession in 2008–9, with a relapse in several countries (including the UK) during 2011–12 (a 'douple dip'). The crisis seems to have hit the western world disproportionately, as the global economy only briefly went into recession in 2009. But countries like the UK have suffered; there is a perception of a lost decade, it has taken the best part of a decade for living standards to go back to the heights of 2007. Rising unemployment, high indebtedness of the banking and private sectors, rising inequality, and sluggish stock markets are parts of the immediate legacy of the crisis. Public debt rose in the UK and elsewhere due to public interventions in the financial system; the need to put public finances in order has led to 'austerity policies' that have persisted since.

The initial trigger (though not the deeper cause) of the recession came from the 'subprime' mortgage market in the US: a highly unregulated, risky market with $1.3tr of outstanding loans in Spring 2007 (>10 per cent of US GDP). Lots of borrowers of low credit-worthiness got loans that would not have been available in a more tightly regulated mortgage market. The availability of loans led to a house price bubble in many areas of the US. But bubbles eventually burst and so did the housing bubble of the mid-2000s. As house prices began to decline, many home-owners found themselves with negative equity (the value of the house was less than the mortgage on it) and in financial distress, unable to meet the interest payments. 'Foreclosures' (requisitions by banks and sales in auctions) of these properties resulted, leading to further downward pressures on house prices. Apart from the social distress this process causes, it also started creating losses for lending institutions as a rising share of their assets (loans) began to be 'non-performing'.

In parallel with the unsafe practices regarding loan provision, various financial institutions engaged in unsound financial management; much of this was made possible by the new instruments made available through financial innovation and was driven by the desire to get big fast. Such processes and financial instruments were 'securitization' and 'collaterilized debt obligations' (CDOs): For instance, some mortgage lenders would sell on their assets (loans) to other lenders. This was done with the use of CDOs and rather intricate and hard-to-regulate practices. In the words of one commentator, Peston (2008), mortgages were 'sliced, diced, repackaged, sold and resold'. Such practices seem to have been motivated by the need of mortgage lenders to reduce their individual risk by spreading it around; and by the desire for fast growth. Instead of obtaining funds from retail deposits as was the traditional practice, they would acquire cash to be used as fresh loan advances by selling the mortgages they held. But such practices look like being on a bicycle: stable as long as you keep going, otherwise you fall. With hindsight, there is a wide consensus that such financial practices and instruments were toxic, but they were not confined to the sub-prime mortgage or indeed the US; before they unravelled, they fuelled easy credit and economic growth in many developed economies. The UK personal sector amassed a record £1.4tr of debts as banks loosened their lending criteria. With the unsafe practices related to the 'sub-prime' market, we now have two dimensions of risky behaviour.

One serious problem with instruments such as CDOs is that their pricing is extremely complex; the prices of individual instruments depends on many contingencies, and there are intricate linkages between the prices of individual instruments. Serious doubts have been expressed as to whether anyone (*anyone*) really understood them; what seems to have kept them going was a belief in the self-equilibrating powers of the market and of the ability of the 'invisible hand' to deliver fair outcomes. But when difficulties arose, no one knew how to price these new and complex instruments, giving rise to yet another dimension of uncertainty.

Gradually, it dawned on market participants that the process was flawed and that some of the key financial products could not be priced with any confidence; meaning that financial institutions worldwide had huge 'black holes' in their balance sheets. Key date here: 9 August 2007, when BNP Paribas makes such an announcement. Financial markets freeze, spooked also by the sub-prime crisis in America; policy-makers such as the US Federal Reserve and the European Central Bank begin emergency procedures—inadequate, as was to be shown by later developments. The US Dow Jones Industrial Average slumps. As a result, financial institutions begin to stop lending to one another because they need all the cash they can get to plug holes in their own balance sheets, and because they do not know whether the other party is in good financial health, so they do not want to risk losses. 'Liquidity' is drying up; a 'credit crunch' emerges (themes to be taken up in Chapter 7).

Northern Rock, a leading UK Building Society, did not have exposure to sub-prime market related products, but is a main example of the high-risk strategy of drawing funds for the mortgages it advances not only via retail deposits (about 15 per cent of its assets), but mainly via money markets. As mentioned, the process works when financial markets are awash with liquidity, but not now that money markets are drying up. In early September 2007, Northern Rock finds itself in great difficulty, and requests emergency liquidity from the Bank of England (in its capacity as the commercial banking system's 'lender of last resort'). This is not effective, so word spreads that NR is 'insolvent', i.e. it is unable to meet its obligations and return all their money back to its depositors. Depositors queue to withdraw their deposits, but this is impossible, as only a fraction of deposits is kept in liquid (cash reserves) form, even in the healthiest of banks (cf. the 'money multiplier'). A 'bank run' develops as depositors realize that the first few will get their money back, the rest nothing. The bank fails (13 September 2007). Bank runs would bring down any financial institution (even the healthiest one), but they do not happen in normal times (the last one before NR happened in 1861—this is *eighteen* 61!). The bank run ends four days later, when the Treasury, fearing damage to the reputation of the whole UK financial system, guarantees the majority of deposits in UK banks. Bank of England lends £30bn to NR, with guarantees from the Treasury: Effectively, it is the taxpayer that injects new capital into it ('bails it out'). NR is fully nationalized six months later.

September 2007–August 2008 is a period of great unease, as major banks (Merrill Lynch, Citigroup, Bear Stearns in the US) report heavy losses, are rescued at the last minute, and lose their chiefs. Financial markets increasingly dry up; stock markets remain uneasy. The credit crunch now begins to have an effect on the real economy: housing markets slow down, housebuilding suffers, and consumers become more cautious. The US economy is officially (i.e. according to NBER dating) in recession from March 2008. Monetary authorities begin, rather cautiously, a 'monetary expansion' to help the economy. In the UK, the Bank of England has been criticized as slow to respond by reducing interest rates; its answer has been that it feared inflation from rising food prices (an adverse supply shock, which poses policy dilemmas as we have seen). However, there is a concerted action by major Central Banks (US Fed, BoE, ECB, Bank of Canada, Swiss National Bank) to inject liquidity into international markets; the numbers are mind-boggling: $50bn on 12 December 2007 and further sums on 11 March 2008, $400bn by the Fed alone. The US government is forced to bail out major mortgage lending institutions (Fannie May and Freddie Mac). The crisis takes an even more dramatic turn in March 2008 when Wall Street bank Bear Stearns was saved from bankruptcy by its bigger rival JP Morgan in a rescue orchestrated by the Federal Reserve.

Stock markets become increasingly nervous in the summer of 2008 ('bear-ish markets'). The London stock market moves into bear territory in July. The plunge in the FTSE 100 to 5,261 on 11 July means the index of Britain's top-100 companies had fallen more than 20 per cent since its peak—the definition of a bear market. The losses are mainly driven by housebuilding companies, banks, and retailers. But despite problems in the US and Europe, the world economy (mainly: China and the other 'Next 11', N11) are still going strong. Perhaps as a result of this, oil prices hit new records (about $135 a barrel in August 2008); adding to the above fear of inflation noted by the Bank of England.

The whole process came to the crunch in Autumn 2008, when US and European (hence: global) financial markets very nearly went into meltdown. The US government under President G.W. Bush decides that it cannot forever bail out financial institutions and that none of them is 'too big to fail': US investment bank Lehman Brothers fails (goes bankrupt) on 14 September 2008. Panic ensues; a full financial crisis develops, engulfing also the City of London with the loss of thousands of jobs. The weekend around 12 October 2008 is widely acknowledged as the critical point, when financial markets stared into the abyss. This galvanizes policy-makers into action; the government of Gordon Brown with Chancellor Alistair Darling in the UK is credited with providing leadership: £37bn is injected by the government into major UK banks ('recapitalization' of the Royal Bank of Scotland, Halifax Bank of Scotland, and Lloyds TSB) in order for them to avoid bankruptcy; a second, much bolder, package is unveiled in mid-January 2009. The pound takes a bad hit (late 2008). In the US, a 'bail out' package of around $700bn to recapitalize banks was approved by both Houses of Congress at the end of November 2008.

The crisis now engulfs fully both the financial and real spheres of the economy. Unemployment rises. In April 2009, it stood at 2.25m unemployed in the UK (on the most acceptable definition), around 7.5 per cent of the labour force. The housing sector continues to be affected, the retail sector remains sluggish for quite a while. (This sector is thought to be a 'bellweather', giving reliable signs of where the economy is heading.) In the US, the crisis also spreads to the car (automobiles) industry, which faces long-standing issues of over-supply worldwide anyway. Large-scale restructuring takes place (GM and Chrysler fail in the US despite government support); similar problems appear in the UK.

To revive the struggling economies, successive US governments assemble two fiscal 'stimulus' packages (expansionary fiscal policy), first a package of $168bn of tax cuts under President G.W. Bush, and then a package of $789bn finally agreed by Congress in February 2009 under the stewardship of the newly elected President Obama. The latter package, two-thirds spending and one-third tax cuts, includes extra spending on unemployment benefits, education, health, infrastructure building, high technology adoption, and the environment. Such initiatives represent 'expansionary fiscal policy' measures and aim to revive the economy via the Keynesian multiplier. Major initiatives like that are always subject to controversy; the effectiveness of the 'Obama stimulus plan' and associated criticisms will be discussed in Chapter 8 on fiscal policy.

In the UK, monetary policy begins to ease: interest rates begin to substantially fall by early October 2008 (from 5 per cent), falling gradually to 0.5 per cent in early March 2009. A similar pattern is followed by the US Fed. Yet economies are slow to pick up. The problem that such monetary authorities face in their effort to boost the macroeconomy, once nominal interest rates go close to zero (the 'zero lower bound), is that they cannot be reduced any further, so monetary policy cannot ease any more with conventional methods. So, the US and UK Central Banks expand the money supply by creating electronic money ('Quantitative Easing'). They buy assets (government and good quality private bonds—the latter in the US only) from banks and pay for those by crediting the commercial banks' accounts in the Central Banks; thus, the money created is only in book entries (electronic, without any physical money printing). With their finances so shored up, (the hope is that) the commercial banks would begin to lend to the private sector, boosting the economy. See Chapter 7.

In terms of fiscal policy, a fiscal 'stimulus package' was unveiled in the UK budget in early April 2009. With the bailout plans, government budget deficit (government outlays-revenues) rose to 15 per cent of UK GDP—from around 5 per cent in 2008. Public sector debt (accumulated deficits with interest) rose to about 80 per cent in 2012/13, from 37 per cent in 2008. As a response, the Conservative-Liberal Democrat coalition government embarked on a programme of cutting the budget deficit ('austerity'), which has generated major controversy. The government maintains that the deficit should be cut and there is no other way, while critics (Krugman, 2013, being among the most vocal) argue that austerity is self-defeating, as the recession or slowdown hits public finances. We shall be discussing such fiscal policies and associated dilemmas further in Chapter 8.

One ramification of the recession is the European sovereign debt crisis that started in Greece in 2010 and spread to much of the southern periphery of the EU.[30] The connection may have been more direct (failed banks that needed bailing out brought down the government finances with them—the case of Ireland) or more indirect (the recession and its effect on public finances exposed chronic deficits and other pathologies—the case of Greece). Being members of the Eurozone, all these countries found themselves having to follow austerity paths, as the exchange rate instrument is not available to them. In general, there has been no fiscal stimulus in continental Europe (there has been some monetary policy easing by the ECB and generous loans—'bailout packages'—to the ailing econ-omies); is it so perhaps because the extra spending would find its way towards imports (the Keynesian multiplier is less in open economies)? If so, there is scope for a coordinated fiscal expansion at a central level, as well as a further relaxation of the monetary stance of the ECB. In general, the situation where some Eurozone countries find themselves, following deficit-reduction policies in the face of recession and high unemployment and without being able to change their exchange rates, brings uncanny echoes of the Great Depression when some countries doggedly defended the defunct Gold Standard.

Turning now to the effects of the Great Recession, the first theme is its very substantial, and very persistent costs. In countries like the UK, nominal incomes stagnated for nearly ten years; with inflation at about 2–3 per cent (in the UK), the result was that real incomes went back to the level of the early 2000s (a lost decade). Ball (2014) is one of few studies to estimate the costs of the Great Recession. He estimates the loss to potential output among 23 countries. These losses average 8.4 per cent in the sample, but are more than 30 per cent in Greece, Hungary, and Ireland; even more ominously, there are considerable hysteresis effects (see Chapter 4 on unemployment): in plain English, the reduction of actual output reduces capacity and therefore potential output (businesses close, infrastructure and physical capital is scrapped or depreciates and is not replaced, individuals retire early or emigrate), while the labour force becomes demotivated and de-skilled; these effects imply that the lost potential is growing over time. Oulton and Sebastiá-Bariel (2013) also find important and very persistent, even permanent, effects of the financial crisis in the UK; for instance, the rate of productivity growth is reduced by about 1 per cent in the long run. Reinhart and Rogoff (2014) present wide-ranging international evidence on systemic banking crises that shows that such crises leave prolonged economic scars as recovery is slow; on average, it takes about seven to eight years to reach the pre-crisis level of income. This was true of the Great Recession: five to six years after the onset of the recent crisis, only Germany and the United States (out of 12 countries) had reached their 2007–8 peaks

---

[30] For a critical discussion of the European sovereign debt crisis with a focus on Greece, the reader could consult the articles in the edited volume: Bournakis et al. (2017).

in real income. In terms of the prolonged nature of the recovery at least, the recent crises in advanced economies stand out and are not comparable to the typical post-war business cycles. For more on the effects of banking crises, the interested reader could start with Dell'Ariccia et al. (2008) and on financial crises more generally with Reinhart and Rogoff (2014).

Secondly, the crisis raises profound questions at all levels. Why did it arise; what are the appropriate policy responses; and, last but not least, the 'Queen's question': why did no one see it coming? (the question that the British monarch famously asked). In truth, a few people had issued warnings, but it is fair to say that the mainstream of both academic economists and public commentators and analysts were caught unawares. An exhaustive treatment of these questions is outside our scope. In particular, we shall attempt no answer at all on the third question, a brief one on the policy responses, and a very partial one on the causes.

On the (big!) question of causes, there is as yet no consensus answer—if there ever will be one. There is little doubt that malpractices (if not worse) on the part of the financial sector have played a major role. The challenge now is to take measures to ensure that those are not repeated again, namely to ban malpractices, to ensure that there is more clarity in the pricing of CDOs and other derivatives, to separate the investment (= riskier) branches of banks from the retail (where the deposits of ordinary people rest and which should be safe) branches, and to ensure that banks are adequately capitalized. These considerations have given rise to a new field, 'macroprudential regulation', a theme further taken up below and in Chapter 7. Measures have already been put in place; critics say that not enough has been done. Some further open questions related to financial architecture are as follows. How to reform regulation and supervision of financial markets both in the UK, across Europe, and the world? How can ratings agencies be appropriately regulated? Are banks adequately capitalized? Can we trust managers to serve the general interest as well that of their institutions (and their own)? What is the appropriate remuneration that optimally combines the need to incentivize the talented people in a globalized world but at the same would appear logical to the rest of society?

In terms of causes, the crisis could be classified as ultimately due to the demand side. Failures in a rather specialized market (sub-prime mortgage sector in the US) led to widespread malaise in the financial markets (keeping in mind the various mechanisms of the 'credit channel') and eventually got transmitted to the 'real' economy; a smallish shock got hugely amplified in the process (see Blanchard, 2009). In an open-economy analysis with data from dozens of episodes from the world economy, Benguria and Taylor (2014) clearly conclude that financial crises are negative demand shocks: they decrease output, imports, and cause a real depreciation. Christiano et al. (2015) find that the ultimate causes were financial frictions interacting with a monetary policy constrained by the zero lower bound. The work of Jorda et al. (2016) on the role of finance in the emergence and propagation of business cycles has been noted. Ireland (2011) provides an early New Keynesian perspective, attributing the crisis to a mixture of AD and AS shocks and putting some blame on the (slow) monetary policy response in prolonging its effects. See Ohanian (2010) for an early neoclassical perspective; Watson (2014) discusses the behaviour of inflation and the NAIRU post-crisis, while Barsky et al. (2014) discuss the (natural) interest rate.

If the shock is classified as an AD one, there is scope for expansionary monetary policy to counter it, particularly one that can encourage banks to expand their lending; this was the express aim of 'Quantitative Easing' in both the US and UK. The open question is to what extent it has worked. There are also questions related to fiscal policy: Is austerity the appropriate path, or should expansion come first and tightening up of the public finances second after recovery is on the way? Has government debt reached an upper limit? If so, how can it be cut? By increasing taxes? By cuts in spending? If so, which public services should face the axe? Are the fiscal stimuli packages justified? We explore some of these issues further in Chapter 8 on fiscal policy.

On the question of causes, Rajan (2012) suggests that the crisis was symptomatic of a deeper malaise than policy, reflecting problems in the supply side; in an effort to pump up growth, governments spent more than they could afford and promoted easy credit to get households to do the same, an unsustainable course of action. In economies featuring sluggish growth, government's aim, it is argued, to generate jobs to offset those lost to technology and foreign competition and to finance the pensions and health care of their ageing populations. This thesis, which this author views with some sympathy, would complicate both the appropriate policy responses (which should therefore be not entirely demand-side but also supply-side) and also the arguments of the Keynesian critics of austerity (e.g. Krugman); if the thesis is correct, trying to achieve growth with public spending on the back of a faltering supply side would both break public finances and result in inflation but no real growth. Other lines of explanation bring in sociological elements: Kumhof and Rancière (2010) attribute the latest crisis to the weak financial markets that arose as those lower down the income ladder got pressured to catch up in housing by unaffordable borrowing.

Obstfeld and Rogoff (2009) have argued that the crisis is closely linked to 'global imbalances' (whose discussion in outside the scope of this book). Global imbalances are chronic and ever-increasing external trade surpluses and deficits (as percentages of GDP), that give rise to perhaps unsustainable borrowing and capital flows across economies. Obstfeld and Rogoff (2009) argue that these imbalances, combined with developments in the financial markets in the US and US policy responses, possibly mistaken, resulted in excessive leverage (over-borrowing) and a housing bubble, which were the proximate cause of the crisis. Global imbalances are also one of the focal points of Eichengreen (2009). He recognizes that they pose important policy challenges at both national and global levels; as does his other major policy theme following from the crisis, which is to ensure that banks and the financial system are more fully capitalized in order to withstand stressful times. Such considerations have led to proposals to increase bank capital, decrease leverage, and generally strengthen bank regulation by the agreed proposals known as Basel III (the third instalment of the Basel Accords), agreed in 2010–11 to be implemented later on in the decade. This 'macroprudential regulation' is based on the recognition that financial market stability has a macroeconomic dimension (i.e. a systemic one) and not only a micro one (focusing only on individual institutions); therefore, regulation should also be carried out at the macro as well as the micro level. Already mentioned, 'macro-pru' will be further discussed in Chapter 7 on monetary policy.

Notes on the Literature

When starting out on business cycles, the reader will find very useful Plosser's (1989) and McCallum's (1989) accounts of the RBC model/theory, Mankiw's (1989) critical review, and

Kydland and Prescott's (1990) overview of the history of business cycles research and discussion of stylized facts. C. Romer (1999) gives a succinct discussion of the historical properties of the business cycle in the US. Anyone interested in modern business cycles research, should begin with the thorough review of the background RBC models, including the analytics of optimization, by King and Rebelo (1999); then see Rebelo (2005) and the early but still useful survey by Stadler (1994). On DSGE, a thorough review is by Christiano et al. (2010).

Guidance for Further Study

Cost of business cycles

Lucas (2003) has persuasively argued that the cost of business cycles is not great. With reference to Figure 6.2, the reasoning is not difficult to see: The cycles (as deviations from trend) appear rather miniscule in comparison with the advances in living standards over time due to trend. This is an argument against stabilization policy: why bother with cycles and not concentrate on improving the trend? Others however take issue with that. What criticisms have been suggested against the Lucas thesis, as reviewed in Barlevy (2004b)? And would the costs be greater if cyclical variations also affect the growth rate of consumption (Barlevy, 2004a)? Why might that be the case? See also Ellison and Sargent (2015) on the costs when there is 'idiosyncratic consumption risk' (risk of illness, injury, death, at least some of which is uninsurable) and the wider ranging review of Heathcote et al. (2009).

Have we stabilized the economy?

There is a wide perception that, post-World War II, the economy has been more stable than before; this is obvious in the data that shows more cyclical variations before rather than after the war. A large part of this improvement must surely be due to the improved institutions of macroeconomic governance (Central Banks as lenders of last resort, sophisticated monetary policy-making, government agencies supported by policy institutes and analysis, not to say much economic analysis and education in higher education institutions). However, in a series of publications, Christina Romer has challenged this popular perception; she has argued that the supposed greater stability post- World War II is an artefact of more sophisticated methods of compiling economic statistics; and if one applied the same methods today, retrospectively, to pre- World War II raw statistics, the resulting GDP and other series would show no more volatility than the post- World War II ones. These findings of course can be quite disconcerting for macroeconomists and have sparked a debate. Read C. Romer (1999) as a portal into this literature. Are you convinced?

Challenges

Did we say that the popular perception is of more sophisticated economic governance and policy institutions that have helped stabilize the economy post- World War II? Well, that view is challenged in two recent papers by Baker et al. (2014) and Taylor (2014). From slightly different perspectives, they argue that policy has become more volatile since the 1960s in line with the growth in the size of government (as per cent of GDP)—the first paper; and that policy has been more discretionary and more prone to volatility in the 2000s—the second paper. Such criticisms have important implications; if they are correct, it is surely better to adopt a policy of 'benign passivity' rather active stabilization. From the US Fed website (or for any other country of your choice), download and examine the post-World War II data on the nominal and real interest rate (you will need to approximately construct that latter as $r = i - \text{inflationrate}$). Do you think that these criticisms of more volatility post-1960 and post-2000 are supported? What conclusions do you draw regarding the conduct of stabilization policy?

Do cycles cast long shadows?

We mentioned early on that the routinely made, clear conceptual distinction between cycles and growth may not be true either in theory or practice. Review the possible reasons and empirical evidence for that from Fatas (2000), Aghion and Saint-Paul (1998), and Saint-Paul (1997). What are the arguments against the neat trend-cycle distinction? Now, proceed to the next question!

The 'medium run'

Comin and Gertler (2006) have argued that the post-World War II time series show that short (but sharp) recessions are often followed by longer, more persistent periods of recovery. They argue that this raises the possibility that fluctuations at different frequencies, particularly short- and medium-term, interact; that cycles may be more persistent phenomena than our conventional measures suggest, involving medium-term components as well as short-term; and that standard de-trending methods that throw away the medium-term component bias our understanding of the cycle. Comin and Gertler (2006) argue therefore that we should identify the cycle in such a way as to include the medium-term, as well as the short-term, frequencies. How do Comin and Gertler explain these possibilities theoretically? What difference do their trend identification methods make to the cyclical properties of various series?

'Business cycles accounting'

Chari et al. (2007) have developed a method of identifying the key shocks that impinge on an economy called 'business cycles accounting', reminiscent of 'growth accounting', see Chapter 9. By applying this methodology, what type of shocks have arguably been quantitatively important during the 'Great Depression' of the 1930s and the 1982 recession?

Earnings inequality and business cycles

There is a popular perception that recessions contribute to increasing inequality. Barlevy and Tsiddon (2006) (partially) challenge this conclusion; they examine the connection between long-run trends and cyclical variation in earnings inequality. What is the connection they find and how does it affect the popular perception argued above?

'Animal spirits'

As discussed in Chapters 2 and 3, recent thinking in 'behavioural macroeconomics' emphasizes cognitive limitations and the adoption of rules of thumb by individuals, as opposed to (fully) rational expectations. As argued above in discussing the Great Recession, recent developments in the financial sector (among other sectors) have given ample reason to think that behaviour develops in this way. De Grauwe (2011) argues that such features give rise to 'animal spirits', which he defines as waves of optimism and pessimism in markets. (Note the implied deviation from the Rational Expectations Hypothesis: the forecast errors will be persistent and serially correlated.) De Grauwe (2011) further explores the implications for stabilization policy; he argues that inflation targeting is not sound as it gives rise to such waves of optimism and pessimism. Are you convinced? If this argument is correct, what modifications to inflation targeting (or the 'Taylor rule') would it suggest?

Big data, forecasting, and 'nowcasting'

Forecasters aim to offer predictions regarding the future evolution of macroeconomic time series that may be of interest to the private sector, government, and the media (see e.g. Diebold, 1998; Chadha, 2017). There has been a long-standing debate as to how useful structural models are for forecasting purposes. See Carriero et al. (2019) for a recent evaluation of alternative forecasting methods and models; they find in favour of a structural (medium-sized DSGE) model. One big obstacle to producing timely forecasts is the fact that key macroeconomic time series (e.g., GDP) are only available with a lag of typically three months, and then are revised a number of times before final numbers appear, sometimes a couple of years later (e.g., the figures for the 2013 GDP may not be finalized until 2015).[31] How can you forecast the GDP of, say, 2015 now (summer of 2014) if you do not even know last year's GDP (let alone this year's)? Some researchers have therefore proposed methods by which any available information is exploited for forecasting purposes at the moment it becomes available—a process that has acquired the fancy name of 'nowcasting'; and that series of different frequencies can be combined for the same purposes, i.e. while you are waiting for the second-quarter 2014 GDP series, which will be available in November 2014 as a first estimate, you can exploit exchange rate information that is available, monthly, daily, even hourly! The interested reader is referred to Anesti et al. (2018), Bok et al. (2017), Andreou et al. (2013), Galvão (2013), and Giannone et al. (2008). The statistical brains out there are invited to take a look at these methods and then explain them to the rest of us!

APPENDIX 6A
Derivation of the Euler-IS Equation (6.23)

Here we derive IS equation (6.23) of Section 5 from intertemporal optimization-related microfoundationa (cf. the Euler equation, 5.11' or 6.17), with the addition to 'habits' in consumption in order to get a richer lag structure. The representative agent's problem is the same as in Section 4, particularly to maximize intertemporal utility subject to an appropriate lifetime budget constraint. The only difference is that period utility is:

$$u(C_t) = \frac{(C_t - \phi C_{t-1})^{1-1/\sigma}}{1 - 1/\sigma}$$

Here, $0 < \phi < 1$ captures 'habits' n consumption, the idea that it is not only the level of your current consumption that matters for utility but also the difference from your consumption last period; we

---

[31] Obviously, this passage was written a few years before publication. As the nature of the argument does not change, there is no reason to change the years.

can see that by re-writing $C_t - \phi C_{t-1} = (1 - \phi)C_t + \phi \Delta C_t$. This is well-established in the literature, and results in more persistence in consumption in the Euler equation, and hence in output. Another difference from earlier is the absence of leisure in this period utility; this is only for ease, and models typically incorporate leisure and include habits in both consumption and leisure (see e.g. Smets and Wouters, 2007).

Expectations (taken at the planning period, which is assumed to t, so they are $E_t(.)$) are suppressed throughout this Appendix. They will be re-instated at the end in front of any variables that are dated $t + 1$ (or later). In other words, the structure of the model is not altered with uncertainty, and future variables are replaced by their expectations. This property is called 'certainty equivalence'. But it is not quite correct, because of the exponential nature of period utility. (Certainty equivalence would have been correct only in the special case of quadratic utility.) Here, certainty equivalence is invoked (or rather, imposed) for simplicity.

In this environment, the Euler equation (6.17) takes the form:

$$\frac{(C_t - \phi C_{t-1})^{-1/\sigma} - \frac{\phi}{1+\rho}(C_{t+1} - \phi C_t)^{-1/\sigma}}{(C_{t+1} - \phi C_t)^{-1/\sigma}} = \frac{1 + r_{t+1}}{1 + \rho}$$

or

$$\frac{(C_t - \phi C_{t-1})^{-1/\sigma}}{(C_{t+1} - \phi C_t)^{-1/\sigma}} - \frac{\phi}{1+\rho} = \left(\frac{C_t}{C_{t+1}}\right)^{-1/\sigma} \frac{(1 + \phi(c_t - c_{t-1}))^{-1/\sigma}}{(1 + \phi(c_{t+1} - c_t))^{-1/\sigma}} - \frac{\phi}{1+\rho} = \frac{1 + r_{t+1}}{1 + \rho},$$

where lower cases indicate logs. Further, approximating $C_t - \phi C_{t-1} \approx C_t(1 - \phi + \phi \Delta c_t)$,

$$\frac{C_t}{C_{t+1}} \frac{1 + \phi \Delta c_t/(1-\phi)}{1 + \phi \Delta c_{t+1}/(1-\phi)} = \left(\frac{1 + r_{t+1} + \phi}{1 + \rho}\right)^{-\sigma}.$$

Using once again an approximation, namely,

$$\frac{C_t}{C_{t+1}} \frac{1 + \phi \Delta c_t/(1-\phi)}{1 + \phi \Delta c_{t+1}/(1-\phi)} \approx \frac{1}{1 + \Delta c_{t+1}} \frac{1 + \phi \Delta c_t/(1-\phi)}{1 + \phi \Delta c_{t+1}/(1-\phi)} \approx 1 + \frac{\phi}{1-\phi} \Delta c_t - \left[1 + \frac{\phi}{1-\phi}\right] \Delta c_{t+1},$$

we get:

$$\frac{1}{1-\phi} \Delta c_{t+1} - \frac{\phi}{1-\phi} \Delta c_t = \sigma(r_{t+1} + \phi - \rho)$$

Or (finally—I promise!)

$$c_t = (1 - \Phi)\Delta c_{t+1} + \Phi c_{t-1} = -\frac{\sigma}{1-\phi}(r_{t+1} + \phi - \rho) \tag{6.A.1}$$

Where $0 < \Phi \equiv \phi/(1 + \phi) < 1$; Φ rises with the importance of habits (ϕ), so that consumption dynamics (6.A.1) becomes more backward-looking; this is translated to output, to which we turn now.

Assuming away investment and an external sector, the National Income Accounting equation $Y_t = C_t + G_t$ is log-linearized (variables in lower cases) as:

$$y_t = c_t + g_t \tag{6.A.2}$$

(6.A.1) and (6.A.2) are consolidated into:

$$y_t = (1-\Phi)y_{t+1} + \Phi y_{t-1} - \sigma(1-\phi)(r_{t+1}+\phi-\rho) + \Gamma_t \tag{6.A.3}$$

where $\Gamma_t \equiv g_t - (1-\Phi)g_{t+1} - \Phi g_{t-1}$. We take this as the exogenous spending shock. With expectations re-instated, (6.A.3) is given as (6.23) in the main text.

APPENDIX 6B
Solution of a Variant of System (6.23), (6.24), and (6.28)

The system as it stands is practically impossible to solve analytically as it involves two second-order difference equations and one first-order one. But we can solve the variant below:

$$g_t = (1-\Phi)E_t g_{t+1} - \sigma(1-\phi)(E_t r_{t+1}+\phi-\rho) + \gamma_t \tag{6.B.1}$$

$$\Delta\pi_t = (1-\Theta)E_t\Delta\pi_{t+1} + \psi(g_t - \bar{g}_t) + v_t \tag{6.B.2}$$

$$r_t = r + (\eta_\pi - 1)\Delta\pi_{t-1} + \eta_y(g_{t-1} - \bar{g}_{t-1}) + \zeta_t \tag{6.B.3}$$

Where $g_t \equiv \Delta y_t \equiv y_t - y_{t-1}$ is the growth rate of real output and Δ is the difference operator as shown (and similarly for the inflation rate). (6.B.1) is essentially (6.23), re-written to take into account of the zero-homogeneity of coefficients (the lead-lag coefficients sum to one); accordingly, the growth rate declines by the real interest rate, increases with impatience (which fuels current spending) and with the spending shock. (6.B.2) is a variant of (6.24), the only difference being that it is the growth rate of output (its deviation from the trend growth rate, $\bar{g}_t$) that fuels inflation; the intuition is obvious. Finally, (6.B.3) is a variant of (6.26') with the growth rate of output (in deviations from trend) and the change in inflation affecting the real interest rate (as a deviation from its long-run level, r); they do so as they both fuel inflation and that raises the nominal and real interests via monetary policy (the Taylor rule). We have three shocks, a spending shock (γ_t), pricing shock (v_t) and a positive productivity shock ($\bar{g}_t$) which increases the trend growth rate.

The long-run solution (variables without subscripts) are:

$$g = \bar{g} \tag{6.B.4}$$

$$\Delta\pi = 0 \tag{6.B.5}$$

$$r = \rho-\phi-(\Phi\bar{g}-\gamma)/\sigma(1-\phi) \tag{6.B.6}$$

Long-run growth is given by the trend; the long-run change in inflation is zero (i.e., we assume that the mean of v_t is zero, of $Ev_t = 0$); the long run interest rate increases with the 'deep fundamentals' of impatience (that requires a reward) and habits, it declines with the trend growth rate (which as trend productivity growth reduces inflation and the nominal and real interest rates) and increases with the spending shock.

We solve the short-run version of this system using the methods of Appendix 5A. Denoting $\hat{g}_t \equiv g_t - \bar{g}_t$ and in a matrix form, the system is:

$$\begin{bmatrix} E_t\hat{g}_{t+1} \\ E_t\Delta\pi_{t+1} \end{bmatrix} = D\begin{bmatrix} \hat{g}_t \\ \Delta\pi_t \end{bmatrix} + \begin{bmatrix} 1-\Phi & 0 \\ 0 & 1-\Theta \end{bmatrix}^{-1}\begin{bmatrix} \sigma(1-\phi)\left(\zeta_t - \eta_y\bar{g}_t\right) - \gamma_t \\ \psi\bar{g}_t - v_t \end{bmatrix}$$

Where

$$D \equiv \begin{bmatrix} 1-\Phi & 0 \\ 0 & 1-\Theta \end{bmatrix}^{-1} \begin{bmatrix} 1+\sigma(1-\phi)\eta_y & \sigma(1-\phi)(\eta_\pi-1) \\ -\psi & 1 \end{bmatrix}$$

$$= \frac{1}{(1-\Phi)(1-\Theta)} \begin{bmatrix} (1-\Theta)\left[1+\sigma(1-\phi)\eta_y\right] & (1-\Theta)\sigma(1-\phi)(\eta_\pi-1) \\ -(1-\Phi)\psi & 1-\Phi \end{bmatrix}$$

The trace and determinant of D are:

$$trD = \frac{\left[1+\sigma(1-\phi)\eta_y\right]}{1-\Phi} + \frac{1}{1-\Theta} > 2$$

The inequality is because of $0 < \Phi, \Theta < 1$. And:

$$detD = 1 + \sigma(1-\phi)\eta_y + \psi\sigma(1-\phi)(\eta_\pi-1) > 0$$

The eigenvalues are given by:

$$\lambda_{1,2} = \frac{trD \pm \sqrt{(trD)^2 - 4detD}}{2}$$

We need to assume that:

$$\sqrt{(trD)^2 - 4detD} = \frac{\left[1+\sigma(1-\phi)\eta_y\right]}{1-\Phi} + \frac{1}{1-\Theta} - 4\left[1+\sigma(1-\phi)\eta_y\right.$$

$$\left. + \psi\sigma(1-\phi)(\eta_\pi-1)\right] > 0$$

For this to happen, appropriate restrictions must be placed on parameters. Essentially, a sufficient condition is that the forward-looking elements in the output and inflation equations (i.e., at least one of each of $0 < \Phi, \Theta < 1$) must be high enough. However, as we have discussed at other instances, the empirical evidence is not always favourable to such assumptions; a higher Φ than Θ may be more realistic in view of the habits in consumption; we return to this point below. Under such assumptions, we get:

$$0 < \sqrt{(trD)^2 - 4detD} < |trD|$$

We therefore have the following eigenvalues:

$$\lambda_{1,2} = \frac{trD \pm \sqrt{(trD)^2 - 4detD}}{2}$$

$$1 < \frac{trD}{2} < \lambda_1 < trD,$$

$$0 < \lambda_2 < \frac{trD}{2}$$

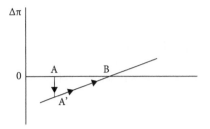

Figure 6B.1. Transition to new long-run equilibria

In view of the evidence as discussed, the forward-looking elements (Θ, Φ) may not be too strong. If so, we may well have $\lambda_2 < 1$, a plausible restriction that we assume from now on. Hence, the two eigenvalues are either side of unity and saddle-point equilibrium results. With this information, exploiting the $_{22}$ element in matrix $D(= 1/(1-\Theta) > 1)$, we conclude (see Appendix 5A) that the slope of the stable arm is positive: g_t and $\Delta\pi_t$ are positively correlated during transition. Furthermore, we can assume that the growth rate is a pre-determined variable, unable to jump instantaneously (due to implicit costs of adjustment), while the change in inflation is a variable free to jump; while price stickiness does not allow the price level to jump instantaneously, $\Delta\pi$ is the change of a change, so free to jump.

Let us first consider the transition to changes in steady-state equilibria. The situation is depicted in Figure 6.B.1. Assume that the old steady state is at A, involving $g = \bar{g}'$ and $\Delta\pi = 0$. Assume that a positive supply-side shock moves the new equilibrium to B $= (\bar{g}'', 0)$, with $\bar{g}'' > \bar{g}'$. (Recall that supply-side shocks are the only possibilities for a permanent change in the growth rate as output is restricted to return to trend in the long run; and that $\Delta\pi = 0$ in the steady state). The upward-sloping stable arm is the thick line. Upon the announcement of the news of the positive shock, we have an instantaneous downward adjustment to $\Delta\pi < 0$ (no jump for growth); during the transition, both the growth rate and $\Delta\pi$ gradually climb up to their values at point B: a permanently higher growth rate and stable inflation. But the fact that $\Delta\pi < 0$ during the transition implies that the inflation rate itself will have fallen to a permanently lower level (as we would expect from the positive supply shock).

It is also instructive to consider the effect of a transitory shock, e.g. a spending shock at time $t = 0$, which raises spending above the steady-state level, $y_0 > y$, for one period only. (The effects of other shocks are left as an exercise to the reader.) This shock will temporarily raise the growth rate; its effect however will die down as t increases. (To gain some intuition on this, consider Appendix 5C.) In fact, the forward-looking nature of the system also raises other interesting possibilities: Future expected shocks (to the extent that can be forecasted with the current information) also have a bearing on current growth (which is linked to the future through its forward-looking dynamics). Hence, growth will be affected by past and future (forecastable) shocks. But here, a crucial difference arises, pointed out by Blanchard and Khan (1980): Non-predetermined ('jump') variables are forward-looking in a stricter sense: They depend on the current state of the system as exemplified in the current predetermined variable (say, g_t) and on future forecastable shocks, only. Past shocks and dynamics do not mater. Because such variables are free to jump (usually, they are asset prices), they are guided by the current state and expectations only: Bygones are bygones, and what matters is where we are now, but not how we have arrived here. This is a property of Rational Expectations. The reader is referred to Blanchard and Khan (1980) for a general (and quite advanced) treatment; see also the discussion around equation (5.38) and Appendix 5A in Chapter 5.

References

Aghion, P., and G. Saint-Paul (1998): Uncovering Some Causal Relationships between Productivity Growth and the Structure of Economic Fluctuations: A Tentative Survey, *Labour*, 12(2), 279–303.

Allen, R.G.D. (1956): *Mathematical Economics*, London: Macmillan.

Altug, S. (1989): Time-to-Build and Aggregate Fluctuations: Some New Evidence, *International Economic Review*, 30(4) (November), 889–920.

Andreopoulos, S. (2009): Oil Matters: Real Input Prices and U.S. Unemployment Revisited, *B.E. Journal of Macroeconomics*, 9(1) (Topics), Article 9.

Andreou, E., E. Ghysels, and A. Kourtellos (2013): Should Macroeconomic Forecasters Use Daily Financial Data and How? *Journal of Business and Economic Statistics*, 31(2), 240–51.

Anesti, N., A.B. Galvao, and S. Miranda-Agrippino (2018): *Uncertain Kingdom: Nowcasting GDP and its Revisions*, Bank of England, mimeo, August.

Azariadis, C. (1993): *Intertemporal Macroeconomics*. Oxford: Blackwell Publishers.

Backus, D.K., P.J. Kehoe, and F.E. Kydland (1995): International Business Cycles: Theory and Evidence, in T.F. Cooley (ed.), *Frontiers of Business Cycle Research*, Princeton: Princeton University Press, chapter 11.

Baker, S.R., N. Bloom, B. Canes-Wrone, S.J. Davis, and J. Rodden (2014): Why has US Policy Uncertainty Risen since 1960? *American Economic Review*, 104(5), 56–60.

Ball, L.M. (1999): Aggregate Demand and Long-Run Unemployment, *Brookings Papers on Economic Activity*, 2, 189–251.

Ball, L.M. (2014): Long-Term Damage from the Great Recession in OECD Countries, NBER WP No. 20185, May.

Barlevy, G. (2004a): The Cost of Business Cycles under Endogenous Growth, *American Economic Review*, 94(4) (September), 964–90.

Barlevy G. (2004b): The Cost of Business Cycles and the Benefits of Stabilization: A Survey, NBER Working Paper No. 10926, November.

Barlevy, G., and D. Tsiddon (2006): Earnings Inequality and the Business Cycle, *European Economic Review*, 50(1) (January), 55–89.

Barnett, W., and Y. He (2002): Bifurcations in Macroeconomic Models, in S. Dowrick, R. Pitchford and S. Turnovsky (eds), *Innovations in Macrodynamics*, Cambridge: Cambridge University Press, 95–112.

Barsky, R., and L. Kilian (2004): Oil and the Macroeconomy since the 1970s, *Journal of Economic Perspectives*, 18, 115–34.

Barsky, R., A. Justiniano, and L. Melosi (2014): The Natural Rate of Interest and Its Usefulness for Monetary Policy, *American Economic Review*, 104(5), 37–43.

Basu, S. (1996): Procyclical Productivity, Increasing Returns or Cyclical Utilization?, *Quarterly Journal of Economics*, 111, 719–51.

Baumol, W., and J. Benhabib (1989): Chaos: Significance, Mechanism, and Economic Applications, *Journal of Economic Perspectives*, 3(1), 77–105.

Baxter, M., and R. King (1999): Measuring Business Cycles Approximate Band-Pass Filters for Economic Time Series, *Review of Economics and Statistics*, 81(4), 575–93.

Beaudry, P., and F. Portier (2006): Stock Prices, News, and Economic Fluctuations, *American Economic Review*, 96(4) (September), 1293–1307.

Beaudry, P., A. Moura, and F. Portier (2015): Reexamining the Cyclical Behavior of the Relative Price of Investment, *Economics Letters*, 135(C), 108–11.

Benassy, J.-P. (1995): Money and Wage Contracts in an Optimising Model of the Business Cycle, *Journal of Monetary Economics*, 35, 303–15.

Benhabib J., R. Rogerson, and R. Wright (1991): Homework in Macroeconomics: Household Production and Aggregate Fluctuations, *Journal of Political Economy*, 99(6) (December), 1166–87.

Benhabib, J. and A. Rustichini (1994): Introduction to the Symposium on Growth, Fluctuations, and Sunspots: Confronting the Data, *Journal of Economic Theory*, 63(1) (June), 1–18.

Bernanke, B.S. (1983): Non-Monetary Effects of the Financial Crisis in the Propagation of the Great Depression, *American Economic Review*, 73(3) (June) 257–76.

Benguria, F., and A.M. Taylor (2014): After the Panic: Are Financial Crises Demand or Supply Shocks? Evidence from International Trade, NBER Working Paper No. 25790, August.

Biddle, J.E. (2014): Retrospectives: The Cyclical Behavior of Labor Productivity and the Emergence of the Labor Hoarding Concept, *Journal of Economic Perspectives*, 28(2) (Spring), 197–212.

Blanchard, O.J. (1981): What is Left of the Multiplier Accelerator? *American Economic Review*, 71(2), 150–4.

Blanchard, O.J. (1984): The Lucas Critique and the Volcker Deflation, *American Economic Review*, 74(2), 211–15.

Blanchard O.J. (1993): Consumption and the Recession of 1990–1991, *American Economic Review*, 83(2) (May), 270–4.

Blanchard, O.J. (2009): The Crisis: Basic Mechanisms and Appropriate Policies, *CESifo Forum* (Ifo Institute for Economic Research at the University of Munich), 10(1) (April), 3–14.

Blanchard, O.J., and J. Gali (2010): The Macroeconomic Effects of Oil Price Shocks: Why are the 2000s so Different from the 1970s?, in J. Gali and M. Gertler (eds), *International Dimensions of Monetary Policy*, Chicago: Chicago University Press, 373–421.

Blanchard, O.J., and C.M. Kahn (1980): The Solution of Linear Difference Models under Rational Expectations, *Econometrica*, 48(5) (July), 1305–12.

Blanchard, O.J., J.-P. L'Huillier, and G. Lorenzoni (2013): News, Noise, and Fluctuations: An Empirical Exploration, *American Economic Review*, 103(7), 3045–70.

Blinder, A.S., and L.J. Maccini (1991): Taking Stock: A Critical Assessment of Recent Research on Inventories, *Journal of Economic Perspectives*, 5(1) (Winter), 73–96.

Bok, B., D. Caratelli, D. Giannone, A. Sbordone, and A. Tambalotti (2017): Macroeconomic Nowcasting and Forecasting with Big Data, Federal Reserve Bank of New York Staff Reports, no. 830, November.

Boldrin, M., and M. Woodford (1990): Equilibrium Models Displaying Endogenous Fluctuations and Chaos: A Survey, *Journal of Monetary Economics*, 25, 189–222.

Bournakis, I., C. Tsoukis, D. Christopoulos, and T. Palivos (eds) (2017): *Political Economy Perspectives on the Greek Crisis: Debt, Austerity and Unemployment*, London: Palgrave Macmillan.

Brock, W., D. Hsieh, and B. Lebaron (1991): *Nonlinear Dynamics Chaos and Instability*, Cambridge, MA.: MIT Press.

Brunnermeier, M.K., and Y. Sannikov (2014): A Macroeconomic Model with a Financial Sector, *American Economic Review*, 104(2) (February), 379–421.

Burns, A., and W.C. Mitchell (1946): *Measuring Business Cycles*, New York: National Bureau of Economic Research (NBER).

Caballero, R.J. (2010): Macroeconomics after the Crisis: Time to Deal with the Pretense-of-Knowledge Syndrome, *Journal of Economic Perspectives*, 24(4) (Fall), 85–102.

Campbell, J.Y. (1994): Inspecting the Mechanism: An Analytical Approach to the Stochastic Growth Model, *Journal of Monetary Economics*, 33(3) (June), 463–506.

Carriero, A., A.B. Galvão, and G. Kapetanios (2019): A Comprehensive Evaluation of Macroeconomic Forecasting Methods, *International Journal of Forecasting*, 35(4) (October–December), 1226–39.

Cecchetti, S., and K. Schoenholtz (2014): *GDP: Seasons and Revisions*, mimeo, 2 July, http://www.moneyandbanking.com/commentary/2014/7/2/gdp-seasons-and-revisions

Cesaroni, T., L. Maccini, and M. Malgarini (2011): Business Cycle Stylized Facts and Inventory Behaviour: New Evidence for the Euro Area, *International Journal of Production Economics*, 133(1) (September), 12–24.

Chadha, B., and E. Prasad (1994): Are Prices Countercyclical? Evidence from the G7, *Journal of Monetary Economics*, 34, 239–57.

Chadha, J.S. (2017): Why Forecast? *National Institute Economic Review*, 239(1) (February), F4–9.

Chari, V.V., P.J. Kehoe, and E.R. McGrattan (2007): Business Cycle Accounting, *Econometrica*, 75(3), 781–836.

Chari, V.V., P.J. Kehoe, and E.R. McGrattan (2008): Are Structural VARs with Long-Run Restrictions Useful in Developing Business Cycle Theory?, *Journal of Monetary Economics*, 55(8) (November), 1337–52.

Christiano, L.J., M. Eichenbaum, and C.L. Evans (2005): Nominal Rigidities and the Dynamic Effects of a Shock to Monetary Policy, *Journal of Political Economy*, 113(1), 1–45.

Christiano L.J., M. Eichenbaum, and R. Vigfusson (2004): The Response of Hours to a Technology Shock: Evidence Based on Direct Measures of Technology, *Journal of the European Economic Association*, 2(2–3), 381–95.

Christiano L.J., M. Eichenbaum, and R. Vigfusson (2007): Assessing Structural VARs, *NBER Macroeconomics Annual 2006*, 21, 1–106.

Christiano L.J., M.S. Eichenbaum, and M. Trabandt (2015): Understanding the Great Recession, *American Economic Journal: Macroeconomics*, 7(1) (January), 110–67.

Christiano, L.J., M. Trabandt, and K. Walentin (2010): DSGE Models for Monetary Policy Analysis, in B.M. Friedman and M. Woodford (eds), *Handbook of Monetary Economics*, Amsterdam: Elsevier, iii. 285–367.

Clarida, R., J. Gali, and M. Gertler (1999): The Science of Monetary Policy: A New Keynesian Perspective, *Journal of Economic Literature*, 37(4), 1661–1707.

Cocherlakota, N. (2010): Modern Macroeconomic Models as Tools for Economic Policy, in Federal Reserve Bank of St. Louis's 2009 Annual Report, 5–22.

Cogan, J.F., T. Cwik, J.B. Taylor, and V. Wieland (2010): New Keynesian versus Old Keynesian Government Spending Multipliers, *Journal of Economic Dynamics and Control*, 34, 281–95.

Cogley, T., and J.M. Nason (1995): Effects of the Hodrick-Prescott Filter on Trend and Difference Stationary Time Series: Implications for Business Cycle Research, *Journal of Economic Dynamics and Control*, 19(1–2), 253–78.

Comin, D., and M. Gertler (2006): Medium-Term Business Cycles, *American Economic Review*, 96(3) (June), 523–51.

Cooley, T.F. (ed.) (1995): *Frontiers of Business Cycle Research*, Princeton: Princeton University Press.

Cooley, T.F., and L.E. Ohanian (1991): The Cyclical Behavior of Prices, *Journal of Monetary Economics*, 28(1), 25–60.

Corrado, C., and J. Mattey (1997): Capacity Utilization, *Journal of Economic Perspectives*, 11(1) (Winter), 151–67.

Danziger, L. (1999): A Dynamic Economy with Costly Price Adjustments, *American Economic Review*, 89(4) (September), 878–901.

De Grauwe, P. (2011): Animal Spirits and Monetary Policy, *Economic Theory*, 47(2–3) (June), 423–57.

Dees, S., P. Karadeloglou, R.K. Kaufmann, and M. Sanchez (2007): Modelling the World Oil Market: Assessment of a Quarterly Econometric Model, *Energy Policy*, 35, 178–91.

Dell'Ariccia G., E. Detragiache, and R. Rajan (2008): The Real Effect of Banking Crises, *Journal of Financial Intermediation*, 17, 89–112.

DeLong, B. (2012): Friends Don't Let Friends Detrend Data Using the Hodrick-Prescott Filter . . . , http://delong.typepad.com/sdj/2012/07/friends-dont-let-friends-detrend-data-using-the-hodrick-prescott-filter.html.July.

Diamond, D.W., and R.G. Rajan (2009): The Credit Crisis: Conjectures about Causes and Remedies, *American Economic Review*, 99(2) (May), 606–10.

Diebold, F.X. (1998): The Past, Present and Future of Macroeconomic Forecasting, *Journal of Economic Perspectives*, 12(2) (Spring), 175–92.

Eichengreen, B. (2009): The Financial Crisis and Global Policy Reforms, Proceedings of the 'Asia and the Global Financial Crisis' Conference Federal, Reserve Bank of San Francisco, October 19–20, 2009; http://www.frbsf.org/economic-research/events/2009/october/asia-global-financial-crisis/Obstfeld_Rogoff.pdf

Ellison, M., and T.J. Sargent (2015): Welfare Cost of Business Cycles with Idiosyncratic Consumption Risk and a Preference for Robustness, *American Economic Journal: Macroeconomics*, 7(2), 40–57.

Erceg, C.J., D.W. Henderson, and A.T. Levin (2000): Optimal Monetary Policy with Staggered Wage and Price Contracts, *Journal of Monetary Economics*, 46(2) (October), 281–313.

Evans, G.W., S. Honkapohja, and P. Romer (1998): Growth Cycles, *American Economic Review*, 88(3) (June), 495–515.

Farmer, R.E.A., and J.-T. Guo (1994): Real Business Cycles and the Animal Spirits Hypothesis, *Journal of Economic Theory*, 63(1) (June), 42–72.

Fatas, A. (2000): Do Business Cycles Cast Long Shadows? Short-Run Persistence and Economic Growth, *Journal of Economic Growth*, 5(2) (June), 147–62.

Feinstein, C.H., P. Temin, and G. Toniolo (1997): *The European Economy between the Wars*, Oxford: Oxford, University Press.

Fernández-Villaverde, J. (2010): The Econometrics of DSGE models, SERIEs: *Journal of the Spanish Economic Association*, 1(1) (March), 3–49.

Fernández-Villaverde, J., J.F. Rubio-Ramírez, T.J. Sargent, and M.W. Watson (2007): ABCs (and Ds) of Understanding VARs, *American Economic Review*, 97(3) (June), 1021–6.

Friedman, M., and A. Swartz (1963): *A Monetary History of the United States, 1867–1960*, Princeton: Princeton University Press.

Galbraith, J.K. (1975): *The Great Crash 1929*, London: Penguin Books (first published in the USA in 1954).

Gali, J. (1999): Technology, Employment and the Business Cycle: Do Technology Shocks Explain Aggregate Fluctuations? *American Economic Review*, 89, 249–71.

Gali, J., F. Smets, and R. Wouters (2012): Unemployment in an Estimated New Keynesian Model, in D. Acemoglu and M. Woodford (eds), *NBER Macroeconomics Annual 2011*, 26(1), 329–60.

Galvão, A.B. (2013): Changes in Predictive Ability with Mixed Frequency Data, *International Journal of Forecasting*, 29(3), 395–410.

Gandolfo, G. (1996): *Economic Dynamics*, New York: Springer.

Gertler, M., and P. Karadi (2011): A Model of Unconventional Monetary Policy, *Journal of Monetary Economics*, 58, 17–34.

Gertler, M., and N. Kiyotaki (2010): Financial Intermediation and Credit Policy in Business Cycle Analysis, in B.M. Friedman and M. Woodford (eds), *Handbook of Monetary Economics*, Amsterdam: Elsevier, vol. 1. 547–99.

Giannone, D., L. Reichlin, and S. Small (2008): Nowcasting: The Real-Time Informational Content of Macroeconomic Data, *Journal of Monetary Economics*, 55(4), 665–76.

Gleick, J. (1998): *Chaos: The Amazing Science of the Unpredictable*, London: Vintage Books.

Goodfriend, M., and R.G. King (1997): The New Neoclassical Synthesis and the Role of Monetary Policy, in B.S. Bernanke and J. Rotemberg (eds), *NBER Macroeconomics Annual 1997*, 12, 231–96.

Goodwin, R.M. (1951): The Nonlinear Accelerator and the Persistence of Business Cycles, *Econometrica*, 19, 1–17.

Goodwin, R.M. (1967): A Growth Cycle, in C.H. Feinstein (ed.), *Socialism, Capitalism and Economic Growth*, Cambridge: Cambridge University Press, 54–8.

Gordon, R.J. (ed.) (1986): *The American Business Cycle: Continuity and Change*, Chicago: Chicago University Press for the NBER.

Greenwood, J., and D Z. Hercowitz (1991): The Allocation of Capital and Time over the Business Cycle, *Journal of Political Economy*, 99(6), 1188–1214.

Greenwood, J., and M. Yorukoglu (1997): 1974, *Carnegie-Rochester Conference Series on Public Policy*, 46, 49–95.

Hamilton, J.D. (1983): Oil and the Macroeconomy since World War II, *Journal of Political Economy*, 91, 228–48.

Hamilton, J.D. (1996): This is What Happened to the Oil Price-Macroeconomy Relationship, *Journal of Monetary Economics*, 38, 215–20.

Hamilton, J.D. (2009): Causes and Consequences of the Oil Shock of 2007–08, *Brookings Papers on Economic Activity* (Spring), 215–61.

Hansen, G.D. (1985): Indivisible Labor and the Business Cycle, *Journal of Monetary Economics*, 16(3) (November), 309–327.

Harvey, A., and T. Trimbur (2008): Trend Estimation and the Hodrick-Prescott Filter, *Journal of the Japanese Statistical Society*, 38(1), 41–9.

Heathcote, J., K. Storesletten, and G.L. Violante (2009): Quantitative Macroeconomics with Heterogeneous Households, *Annual Review of Economics*, 1(1) (May), 319–54.

Hodrick, R.J., and E.C. Prescott (1997): Postwar U.S. Business Cycles: An Empirical Investigation, *Journal of Money, Credit and Banking*, 29(1) (February), 1–16.

Hooker, M.A. (1996): What Happened to the Oil Price-Macroeconomy Relationship? *Journal of Monetary Economics* (October), 195–213.

Hoover, K.D. (1988): The New Classical Macroeconomics, Oxford: Basil Blackwell.

Howitt, P. and R.P. McAfee (1992): Animal Spirits, *American Economic Review*, 82(3) (June), 493–507.

Ireland, P.N. (2011): A New Keynesian Perspective on the Great Recession, *Journal of Money, Credit and Banking*, 43(1) (February), 31–54.

Jaimovich, N. and S. Rebelo (2009): Can News about the Future Drive the Business Cycle? *American Economic Review*, 99, 1097–118.

Jorda, O., M. Schularick, and A.M. Taylor (2016): Macrofinancial History and the New Business Cycle Facts, in M. Eichenbaum and J. Parker (eds), *NBER Macro Annual 2016*, Boston: NBER, chapter 4.

Karnizova, L. (2010): The Spirit of Capitalism and Expectation-Driven Business Cycles, *Journal of Monetary Economics*, 57, 739–52.

Kehoe, P.J., and E.R. McGrattan (2002): Accounting for the Great Depression, *American Economic Review*, 92(2) (May), 22–7.

Khan, H., and J. Tsoukalas (2012): The Quantitative Importance of News Shocks in Estimated DSGE Models, *Journal of Money, Credit and Banking*, 44(8) (December), 1535–61.

Kilian, L. (2014): Oil Price Shocks: Causes and Consequences, CEPR Discussion Paper No. 9823, February.

Kimball, M.S., J.G. Fernald, and S. Basu (2006): Are Technology Improvements Contractionary? *American Economic Review*, 96(5) (December), 1418–48.

Kindleberger, C.P. (1973): *The World in Depression, 1919–1939*, London: Allen Lane.

King, R.G., and C.I. Plosser (1984): Money, Credit, and Prices in a Real Business Cycle, *American Economic Review*, 74 (June), 363–80.

King, R.G., and S.T. Rebelo (1999): Resuscitating Real Business Cycles, in M. Woodford and J. Taylor (eds), *Handbook of Macroeconomics*, Amsterdam: Elsevier, vol 18, 927–1007.

King, R.G., C.I. Plosser, and S.T. Rebelo (1988a): Production, Growth, and Business Cycles: I. The Basic Neoclassical Model, *Journal of Monetary Economics*, 21(2–3), 195–232.

King, R.G., C.I. Plosser, and S.T. Rebelo (1988b): Production, Growth, and Business Cycles: II. New Directions, *Journal of Monetary Economics*, 21(2–3), 309–41.

Krugman, P. (1996): *The Self-Organizing Economy*, Oxford: Blackwell.

Krugman, P. (1998): It's Baaack: Japan's Slump and the Return of the Liquidity Trap, *Brookings Papers on Economic Activity*, 2, 137–87.

Krugman, P. (2013): *End this Depression Now!* New York: W.W. Norton & Co.

Kuttner, K.N., and A.S. Posen (2001): The Great Recession: Lessons for Macroeconomic Policy from Japan, *Brookings Papers on Economic Activity*, 2, 93–160.

Kumhof, M., and R. Rancière (2010): Inequality, Leverage and Crises, IMF Working Paper WP/10/268, November, http://www.imf.org/external/pubs/ft/wp/2010/wp10268.pdf

Kydland, F.E., and E. Prescott (1982): Time to Build and Aggregate Fluctuations, *Econometrica*, 50(6) (November), 1345–70.

Kydland, F.E. and E. Prescott (1990): Business Cycles: Real Facts and a Monetary Myth, *Quarterly Review* (Federal Reserve Bank of Minneapolis), 14(2), 3–18.

Long, J.B., Jr., and C.I. Plosser (1983): Real Business Cycles, *Journal of Political Economy*, 91(1), 39–69.

Lucas, R.E., Jr. (1977): Understanding Business Cycles, *Carnegie Rochester Conference Series on Public Policy*, 5, 7–46.

Lucas, R.E., Jr. (2003): Macroeconomic Priorities, *American Economic Review*, 93(1), 1–14.

McCallum, B.T. (1989): Real Business Cycle Models, in R.J. Barro (ed.), *Modern Business Cycle Theory*, Cambridge, MA: Harvard University Press, 16–50.

McCallum, B. (2003): Japanese Monetary Policy, 1991–2001, *Federal Reserve Bank of Richmond Economic Quarterly*, 89 (Winter), 1–31.

McGrattan, E.R., and E.C. Prescott (2014): A Reassessment of Real Business Cycle Theory, *American Economic Review*, 104(5) (May), 177–82.

Mankiw, N.G. (1989): Real Business Cycles: A New Keynesian Perspective, *Journal of Economic Perspectives* (Summer), 79–90.

Manning A. (1995): Developments in Labour Market Theory and their Implications for Macroeconomic Policy, *Scottish Journal of Political Economy*, 42, 250–66.

Matsuyama, K. (2001): Growing through Cycles in an Infinitely Lived Agent Economy, *Journal of Economic Theory*, 100 (October), 220–34.

Milani, F., and J. Treadwell (2012): The Effects of Monetary Policy 'News' and 'Surprises', *Journal of Money, Credit and Banking*, 44(8) (December), 1667–92.

Mise, E., T.-H. Kim, and P. Newbold (2005): On Suboptimality of the Hodrick–Prescott Filter at Time Series Endpoints, *Journal of Macroeconomics*, 27, 53–67.

Mountford, A., and H. Uhlig (2009): What are the Effects of Fiscal Policy Shocks? *Journal of Applied Econometrics*, 24(6), 960–92.

Nelson, C.R., and C.I. Plosser (1982): Trends and Random Walks in Macroeconmic Time Series: Some Evidence and Implications, *Journal of Monetary Economics*, 10(2) (September), 139–62.

Nickell, S. (1990): Unemployment: A Survey, *Economic Journal*, 100 (June), 391–439.

Obstfeld, M., and K. Rogoff (2009): Global Imbalances and the Financial Crisis: Products of Common Causes, Proceedings of the 'Asia and the Global Financial Crisis' Conference Federal, Reserve Bank of San Francisco, October 19–20, 2009; http://www.frbsf. org/economic-research/events/2009/october/asia-global-financial-crisis/Obstfeld_Rogoff.pdf

Ohanian, L.E. (2010): The Economic Crisis from a Neoclassical Perspective, *Journal of Economic Perspectives*, 24(4), 45–66.

Oulton, N., and M. Sebastiá-Barriel (2013): Long and Short-Term Effects of the Financial Crisis on Labour Productivity, Capital and Output, Bank of England Working Paper No. 470.

Peston, R. (2008): *Who Runs Britain?* London: Hodder & Stoughton.

Plosser, C.I. (1989): Understanding Real Business Cycles, *Journal of Economic Perspectives*, 3(3), 51–77.

Prescott, E.C. (1986): Theory Ahead of Business Cycle Measurement, *Federal Reserve Bank of Minneapolis Quarterly Review*, 10(4), 9–22.

Rajan, R.G. (2012): The True Lessons of the Recession: The West Can't Borrow and Spend its Way to Recovery, *Foreign Affairs* (May/June), http://www.foreignaffairs.com/articles/ 134863/raghuram-g-rajan/the-true-lessons-of-the-recession

Rebelo, S. (2005): Real Business Cycle Models: Past, Present and Future, *Scandinavian Journal of Economics*, 107(2) (June), 217–38.

Reinhart, C.M., and K.S. Rogoff (2014): Recovery from Financial Crises: Evidence from 100 Episodes, *American Economic Review*, 104(5) (May), 50–5.

Romer, C.D. (1999): Changes in Business Cycles: Evidence and Explanations, *Journal of Economic Perspectives*, 13(2) (Spring), 23–44.

Romer, C.D., and D.H. Romer (2013): The Missing Transmission Mechanism in the Monetary Explanation of the Great Depression, *American Economic Review*, 103(3) (May), 66–72.

Romer, D.H. (1993): The New Keynesian Synthesis, *Journal of Economic Perspectives*, 7(1) (Winter), 5–22.

Rotemberg, J.J., and M. Woodford (1997): An Optimization-Based Econometric Framework for the Evaluation of Monetary Policy, *NBER Macroeconomics Annual*, 1997(12), 297–346.

Saint-Paul, G. (1997): Business Cycles and Long-Run Growth, *Oxford Review of Economic Policy*, 13(3) (Autumn), 145–53.

Samuelson, P.A. (1939): Interactions between the Multiplier Analysis and the Principle of Acceleration, *Review of Economic Statistics*, 21(2), 75–8.

Sargent, T.J. (1987): *Macroeconomic Theory*, 2nd ed., Boston: Academic Press

Sargent, T.J., and N. Wallace (1976): Rational Expectations and the Theory of Economic Policy, *Journal of Monetary Economics*, 2(2), 169–83.

Schmitt-Grohé, S., and M. Uribe (2012): What's News in Business Cycles, *Econometrica*, 80, 2733–64.

Shleifer, A. (1986): Implementation Cycles, *Journal of Political Economy*, 94(6), 1163–90.

Smets, F., and R. Wouters (2007): Shocks and Frictions in US Business Cycles: A Bayesian DSGE Approach, *American Economic Review*, 97(3), 586–606.

Solow, R. (1957): Technical Change and the Aggregate Production Function, *Review of Economics and Statistics*, 39, 312–20.

Stadler, G.W. (1994): Real Business Cycles, *Journal of Economic Literature*, 32(4) (December), 1750–83.

Stock, J.H., and M.W. Watson (1989): New Indexes of Coincident and Leading Economic Indicators, in O.J. Blanchard and S. Fischer (eds), *NBER Macroeconomics Annual 1989*, Boston: MIT Press, iv. 351–409.

Stock, J.H., and M.W. Watson (1999): Forecasting Inflation, *Journal of Monetary Economics*, 44, 293–335.

Stock, J.H., and M.W. Watson (2001): Vector Autoregression, *Journal of Economic Perspectives*, 15(4), 101–15.

Summers, L.H. (1986): Some Skeptical Observations on Real Business Cycle Theory, *Federal Reserve Bank of Minneapolis Quarterly Review*, 10(4), 23–7.

Summers, L.H. (2014): U.S. Economic Prospects: Secular Stagnation, Hysteresis, and the Zero Lower Bound, *Business Economics*, 49, 65–73.

Taylor, J.B. (2014): The Role of Policy in the Great Recession and the Weak Recovery, *American Economic Review*, 104(5), 61–6.

Temin, P. (1991): *Lessons from the Great Depression* (The Lionel Robbins Lectures 1989), Cambridge, MA: MIT Press.

Van Robays, I. (2012): *Macroeconomic Uncertainty and the Impact of Oil Price Shocks*, European Central Bank: Working Paper No. 1479.

Wallerstein, I. (2004): *World-Systems Analysis: An Introduction*, Durham, NC: Duke University Press.

Watson, M.W. (2014): Inflation Persistence, the NAIRU, and the Great Recession, *American Economic Review*, 104 (5), 31–6.

Zubairy, S. (2013): On Fiscal Multipliers: Estimates from a Medium-Scale DSGE Model, *International Economic Review*, 55(1) (February), 169–95.

7

Monetary Policy

This chapter reviews the current state of theory in relation to monetary policy. Though it is one continuous narrative, it is structured around two main themes. The early sections will be concerned with the institutional 'architecture' in relation to monetary policy— the current main features of the institutions (mainly, the Central Banks) that determine policy, the underlying justifications for them to have these key features, and the current policy dilemmas. The second theme, in later sections, will be the effects of monetary policy, particularly in the light of our greater understanding of the structure of the banking and wider financial systems. We shall finish by showing how the elementary model of monetary policy, which is centred on the LM Curve, should be modified in the light of all these theoretical and institutional developments.

7.1 Introduction

7.1.1 Recent Developments in the Institutional 'Architecture' of Monetary Policy

Looking at the main features of modern monetary policy-making, we observe a number of key institutional features that are widely shared across countries. Monetary policy is exercised by Central Banks (from now on CB) that are 'independent' in the sense that they enjoy a large degree of autonomy from the government and the rest of the civil service of their countries. The main, though often not only, objective of policy is to maintain a low and stable inflation rate. Policy is determined by unelected specialists ('technocrats'— economists, bankers, etc.), not active politicians. Policy-making is transparent and accountable: CBs have to be open and explain what they do (and admit it when they fail). Though important variations do remain between countries and CBs, on the whole, these features are shared by many, perhaps most, CBs across the world. This setup is about 30 years old; it stands in sharp contrast to the institutional setup of older times. Back then, CBs were more tightly controlled politically by governments; they were in effect the government departments charged with exercising monetary policy. Monetary policy was used for a variety of reasons, for stabilization purposes, to manage the exchange rate, or gain 'seignorage' revenue for government (see Chapter 8 on fiscal policy). Policy relied on surprises and was often secretive.

Why have these institutional arrangements been introduced? The answer to this question is not only of historical interest; it continues to inform the current debates about the appropriate institutional setup of monetary policy; and beyond that, debates about fiscal policy (see Chapter 8 on 'fiscal councils'). Therefore, the underlying analysis will occupy us in the first few sections. The root of the current institutional setup goes back to the 1970s

Theory of Macroeconomic Policy. Christopher Tsoukis, Oxford University Press (2020). © Christopher Tsoukis.
DOI: 10.1093/oso/9780198825371.003.0007

which was a decade of macroeconomic turbulence, at least for the advanced economies (as already discussed on various occasions in this book): high inflation, uncertain exchange rates, erratic policies, etc. The high (and unstable) inflation rate threatens financial stability. Observers then came to a number of conclusions. Chief among them was that inflation was high without any real gain in terms of unemployment; most analysts were leaning to the view that the Phillips Curve is vertical, at least in the long run. Hence, the high and variable inflation was not accompanied by any gain in terms of less unemployment; it was a pure loss.

The high inflation is the result of complex inflationary dynamics. Essentially, every part (employers, workers, government, or CB) pushes for high prices/wages/money supply growth because it expects everyone else to do the same. Analytically, these are the key components of this situation:

- The wage-price spiral: Firms raise prices because workers raise wages, and workers raise wages because firms raise prices.
- The government/CB is in a sharp dilemma:
  o If it answers with expansionary policy ('accommodation'), then we have even higher inflation;
  o If it counters the wage-price spiral with strict monetary policy, there is recession (see the problem with adverse supply shocks in Chapter 6).
- So, everyone is 'chasing' everyone else:
  o Government is forced to follow expansionary policy in order to avoid a painful recession;
  o The private sector raises prices/wages because it does not believe that government will 'disinflate' (reduce the inflation rate by applying restrictive monetary policy).
- A 'Nash equilibrium' of persistent, high inflation follows. Note that there are no gains from that in terms of unemployment, at least in the long run; this is another restatement of the 'vertical long-run Phillips Curve' proposition. This is a crucial point as it implies that inflation persists because we are reluctant to apply the necessary cure, not because of long-term benefits.

Furthermore, attempts by the CB to rectify the situation by announcing and implementing a low-inflation policy face two related problems:

- The 'time inconsistency' of discretionary monetary policy: The policy initiative does not stand the test of time. The policy-maker decides to 'do the right thing' (i.e. disinflate), then changes their mind;
- The lack of 'credibility of anti-inflationary policy': For this reason, no one believes that there will be serious anti-inflation policy and the wage-price spiral continues.

All these conclusions and arguments have prompted a search for the appropriate institutional framework for the conduct of monetary policy. The themes on which the search and ensuing debates have focused are:

- (The appropriate balance between) 'rules' (discipline) versus 'discretion' (flexibility).

This is because too much flexibility in policy-making was seen as underlying many of the above problems. The discretion enjoyed by any CB back then allowed it to reconsider policy at every step of the way, leading to time-inconsistency, lack of policy credibility, and inflation bias as the end outcome. Therefore, a framework was required that would impose discipline via 'rules'. Debate along these lines was so important that much of this literature came to be known as the 'rules vs. discretion' literature. Additionally, the rules-based discipline was instrumental in policy becoming more transparent and accountable.

- The appropriate balance between 'technocratic' versus democratic control of policy.

Underpinning this debate is the realization that policy-making in democracies suffers from 'populist' tendencies. Elected politicians are reluctant to take and implement tough but necessary decisions, particularly near elections, so as not to upset voters. The Phillips Curve analysis highlights a tension between long-term and short-term goals. In the long run, the objective should be low inflation, as there is nothing to be gained by high inflation; but in the short run, we may have a gain in terms of lower unemployment. However, the pursuit of the short-run gain of lower unemployment simply worsens the long-run situation due to the resulting higher inflation. In democracies, governments have a limited horizon as they are up for re-election every few years. Hence, there is a focus on short-term considerations and neglect of long-run goals. This is not to criticize democracy as such, which is the best form of government by far (in the eyes of most people, including this author) but to point out one of its problems. The argument is that entrusting policy to unelected experts ('technocrats') helps refocus policy on longer term objectives.

- The appropriate objective(s) of monetary policy.

Most countries and CBs realized that monetary policy is best placed to focus mainly on the objective of stabilizing inflation ('inflation targeting'). In this way, policy is allowed to do best what it can do and not become overburdened by too many (unattainable) goals.

The search of the appropriate institutional framework for the conduct of monetary policy has been conducted at both the practical policy and theoretical levels. The new institutions were introduced by the pioneering countries in the late 1980s, with the majority following suit in the 1990s. In the UK, these arrangements were introduced by the newly elected Labour government in May 1997. In theory, these and other debates gave rise to the new field of 'political economy' situated at the crossroads between economics and politics. This is one of the areas where practical and theoretical policy searches were most closely aligned.

The new arrangements succeeded in averting many of the highlighted problems; chief of the successes is the permanent reduction in inflation from the mid-1990s onwards (the 'great moderation'), without any permanent increase in unemployment. By the mid-2000s, a new consensus had been reached about the main desirable institutional features of monetary policy. But various features continue to be re-evaluated, particularly after the financial crisis and recession of 2007–9 which drew criticisms towards CBs; they were criticized as not having seen it coming and responding too slowly to recession. Some of the key open questions are:

- What is the appropriate mix of rules and discretion? Rigid discipline is undesirable; some measure of flexibility is needed in order to allow policy to deal with unforeseen shocks.
- What is the appropriate degree of democratic control on policy? While full democratic control may give rise to populist tendencies, should monetary policy be entirely outside democratic control and accountability? Similar considerations apply to fiscal policy and debt (see Chapter 8) and also to other areas of policy (e.g. regulation of utilities and business).
- To what extent should other goals be allowed in addition to inflation targeting?

Our discussion below will examine the problems of discretion, the institutional features that have been proposed and adopted as cures, and will finally examine the current dilemmas and open questions.

7.1.2 Strategic and Political Economy Models of Policy Analysis

Traditional macroeconomic analysis reviews how the macroeconomy works, formalizes this into a model, analyses the effects of policy, and offers policy advice. This policy generally takes the structure of the macroeconomy as invariant to policy, and does not analyse any political or other constraints; so, the processes that led to formation of policy (what was done and how it was decided) are left unexplained. However, the Lucas critique (see Chapters 1 and 2) has taught us that the structure of the economy should not be taken as granted, because it depends (among other things) on the policy regime itself. The public and private sector may be thought of interacting, the former by setting policies, the latter by deciding (macro)economic behaviour. In fact, each part optimally reacts to the other's actions. 'Strategic models' of policy analysis incorporate this strategic interaction between public and private sector and thus lead to a more sound understanding of how policy is actually formed. In this, they often use game theory.

'Political economy' models continue this broad theme; their aim of is to:

- endogenize policy, rather than simply analyse the effects of exogenously determined policies;
- analyse the incentives of government as an agency with its own objectives (e.g. re-election);
- analyse explicitly the interaction between private sector and government via 'strategic' models.

Political economy is a vibrant and very important branch of economics, and is actually situated at the crossroads with politics. Within economics, it interacts with various branches such as macroeconomics, international trade, public economics, etc. Within macroeconomics, political economy models originated in the theory of business cycles ('political business cycle models') and models of monetary policy. Political economy models highlight the fact that the economy often gets locked in 'suboptimal Nash equilibria' or in 'second-best' situations. The models reviewed in this chapter originated in the late 1970s and early 1980s, at a time when inflation was in the double digits in all industrialized economies (and in the double digits as monthly rates in many parts of the less developed world). This persuaded many theorists that inflation could not have been merely the result of more expansionary policies but may have been the outcome of a failure in the design of appropriate institutions to oversee monetary policy. In more technical terms, as we shall see, the high-inflation bias was thought to be a symptom of the prevailing suboptimal Nash equilibrium (intuitively speaking, a kind of trap); the change in the institutional architecture of monetary policy was deemed necessary in order to avoid such a trap.

7.1.3 Time Inconsistency of Optimal Discretionary Policy

American macroeconomists Finn Kydland and Edward Prescott jointly received the 2004 Nobel Prize for Economics for their seminal contribution 'Rules versus Discretion: The Inconsistency of Optimal Plans' (Kydland and Prescott, 1977), which puts the time-inconsistency problem associated with any optimal discretionary policy under sharp focus. The problem of time inconsistency arises in many contexts and has to do with the fact that a policy-maker (in whatever context) may take different decisions concerning the same issue at different times. 'Time inconsistency' is the fact that a policy changes as time goes on; this is not because anything has changed, or because an external new development has occurred, but because it is simply optimal to do so (change policy). Some simple examples may help to illuminate the concept.

Broken promises: Imagine that you propose a business deal to a stranger, the deal requires your business partner to undertake a project by incurring a cost and then you to do something equivalent in return. (Note that this deal can be anything from requesting a simple favour, to be returned by you later, to requesting a loan to be repaid with interest, or something more complex.) You are honest; the deal is beneficial for both parties (including you) and you really mean to fulfil your part. So, *before* your partner does their part, your optimal policy is to fulfil your part. Now, consider what you may be thinking *after* the other party has carried out their bit. Now, you have secured the benefit, so why bother fulfilling your part? Your optimal policy now is to renege on the agreement, effectively breaking your promise.[1]

Exams: Your lecturer has your learning as his main objective; s/he knows that without a bit of pressure this may not happen, so s/he announces an extra (mid-term) exam which aims to force you to study more. The optimal policy *before* the exam occurs (in fact: before the students begin to prepare) is to hold this exam. Now, the pre-set date arrives and the students have (hopefully) prepared for it. The lecturer's main objective has been fulfilled (the students have studied), so why bother hold the exam and have to mark a whole load of scripts? The lecturer's optimal policy *after the students' preparation* is not to hold the exam. The lecturer reneges and on the day of the exam suspends it.

---

[1] You will have noted that the business partner is assumed a stranger—someone you will never see again. If they are not a stranger and you are likely to encounter them again, they will remember that you have broken your promise or reneged on the deal. They are therefore likely to act differently in order to punish you, and this will alter your incentives at the beginning. In the language of game theory, a deal with a stranger is a 'one-shot' game, while with someone you will meet again, it is a 'repeated game'. The equilibria in the two sets of games are quite different.

Taxation of capital: The government aims to promote a high rate of investment of physical capital and growth. To this end, its optimal policy *before investment takes place* is to have a low tax rate for profits. However, after firms invest, the amount of physical capital is now given (if we plausibly assume that physical capital cannot be dismantled easily or costlessly and transformed into another form of wealth, e.g. financial capital—in jargon, investment is irreversible). Therefore, at that point, the government's aim of maximizing growth cannot be furthered any more, and other aims like raising more tax revenue may take precedence. Hence, *after investment,* the optimal policy is to have a higher rate of tax for profits. The government announces a surprise rise in taxation (a 'windfall' tax).

Patents of inventions: The government's objective is dual, to generate and disseminate technological progress. To engage in the costly activity of research and development (R&D), businesses want the prospect of high future returns for it, so they want to have the monopoly in exploiting any technical innovations they may make. The government can guarantee that by patenting their inventions to them, thus excluding any rivals from imitating them and directing all profits to the innovating companies. Thus, *before* the innovations happen, the government's overriding objective is to generate R&D and the optimal policy is to encourage it by granting patents and monopoly profits. *After* R&D has taken place, however, it cannot be reversed, and the government's objective now shifts towards inducing the widest possible dissemination, so at that point abolition of patents is the optimal policy. The government revokes the patents and encourages imitation of the innovations so that they become more widely and cheaply available. Such dilemmas are quite acute in the case of the generation of drugs to fight epidemics and highlight a tension between governments and aid organizations (which want cheap drugs—'generics') and pharmaceutical companies which want patented drugs and associated profits in order to (among other objectives) finance further R&D.

Monetary policy: The discussion here centres on the expectations-augmented Phillips Curve. Let us remember that employment in an economy depends on firms' profitability, which in turn depends on the ratio of prices over marginal costs; the latter may be captured crudely by the wage, so that we can capture profitability by $p - w$ (both in logs). In turn, wages are set at the beginning of the year such as to match the expected price level for the year, $w = p^e$. Now we can state, $U - U^N = -(p - p^e)$: the deviation of the unemployment rate from its long-term, natural rate (U^N) is inversely related to the price surprises within the year. Subtracting p_{-1} (last period's log price) from both terms on the right-hand side, we have the Phillips Curve in its 'accelerationist' form: $U = U^N - (\pi - \pi^e)$, that relates the unemployment rate inversely to inflationary surprises.[2]

Now, the monetary policy-maker knows that $\pi - \pi^e$ and $U = U^N$ in the long run (at least on average), so that from a long-term perspective, the best they can hope to achieve is low inflation. So, *at the beginning of the year* they announce a policy of low inflation, which is their optimal policy at that time. The calculation of course is that this announcement will inform expectations and be embedded into contracts, such that $U = U^N$ but at a low inflation. During the period however, wage contracts have been signed (we can capture this idea in an abstract way by saying that p^e was set at the beginning and is

---

[2] Notation is standard. The log price level is p; inflation is π, and the superscript e denotes expectations formed at the beginning of the period. At the beginning of the current year, the past log-price level, p_{-1}, is known, hence we have $\pi = p - p_{-1}$ and $\pi^e = p^e - p_{-1}$.

fixed during the period). Since this is so, there is the opportunity for the policy-maker to engineer a surprise inflation such that $\pi > \pi^e$ and $U < U^N$. This may be desirable in the short run (particularly if U^N is deemed to be too high from a social point of view) so that *during the year* the optimal policy may shift towards high(er) inflation. In other words, the policy-maker may find it tempting to renege on its earlier pledge of low inflation.

We have now got an idea about the nature of time inconsistency and also of its pervasiveness in the economy (in a very broad sense), so we can elaborate and discuss it a little more. We see first the reaction of the two players (policy-maker against private sector, student, or prospective business partner) to each other. The private sector reacts to the announcement and to the policy-maker's intentions and the latter to the actions of the former. We see in other words two agents with clearly formulated objectives locked in interaction with each other, which is the point made above about the aim of strategic models of policy-making. Formally, this interaction can be formulated like a one-move ('one-shot') game (similar to treliss): the private sector moves first, the policy-maker second, and the game ends. The announcement early on is not a formal move, just an informal statement of intentions—we return to it below.

It is worth emphasizing, as mentioned already, that nothing external has changed that induces the change in optimal policy. The policy-maker is not responding to any changes in the environment; a policy change in response to such a change may have been natural and might warrant little comment. Second, something *has* however changed, and this in fact is the policy action of the private sector (or the friend, or the students) as a response to the policy announcement (or the promise). This is something irreversible so that the announcement cannot affect it; i.e. neither the favour received, nor the students' preparation, nor investment, nor inventions, nor expectations/wage contracts can be undone. So, *ex ante*, before the private sector's action, the optimal policy is one thing, and this is what is announced. *Ex post*, following the private sector's response, however, the optimal policy may be different. Hence, optimal policy is time inconsistent, in other words, it does not stand the test of time: it changes over time following the responses that *it alone* induces.[3] Surprise reversals of policy is the result.

A second main point also needs emphasis. The whole game described above and its logic is pretty transparent; surely, the private sector is not so daft as not to anticipate the temptation to the policy-maker to renege in the various contexts? They do, and therefore these policy announcements are said to lack credibility. The business partner may not sign the deal, students may not prepare, firms not invest, and, finally, the wage setters may not believe the promise of low inflation and therefore may go for higher wages, just in case. More formally, the private sector can anticipate the subsequent move by the policy-maker (like we do in the game of treliss) and act on this basis, rather than on spurious announcements.[4]

---

[3] Kydland and Prescott were in fact not the only ones to have introduced the notion of time inconsistency. At about the same time as K-P's seminal (1977) paper, Calvo (1978) emphasized the tendency of a government to produce surprise inflation in order to reduce the real value of its nominally denominated debt. Another seminal paper in this strand of literature is Barro and Gordon (1983) on 'rules versus discretion'.

[4] We can state the above point slightly differently, highlighting the tension between short-run and long-run objectives. Even if the business partner or private sector believe the announcement, the policy-maker will have secured a short-run benefit (a loan that will not be repaid, or some extra tax revenue, or less unemployment) but which will come at the cost of worsening the long-run situation (loss of trust that will damage future business opportunities, or investment, or inflation).

The outcome of this lack of credibility is invariably bad. To begin with, the business partner will not sign the deal (though it would be beneficial for both—in jargon, Pareto improving); the students will not prepare and will not learn (and this will be a greater cost than the benefit for the lecturer of no marking); investment and technological innovations will not occur; and finally, the monetary authority will have to accommodate the higher wage pressures and inflationary expectations in order not to induce higher unemployment, and will end up with the usual $U = U^N$, albeit at a higher π. In short, real social opportunities will have been missed by simply the structure of incentives, namely the temptation felt by one party not to fulfil their part of the deal. The solution is to impose a discipline mechanism by which the policy is not allowed to change: e.g. to write an 'enforceable contract' between business partners, the lecturer should write the exam into the Module Handbook or syllabus, the patents should be granted by law. In monetary policy, we have the solutions discussed below.

What happens if, as is the case in most real-world contexts, the game is not a one-move one, but were to be repeated in the future? Obviously, the unfulfilled pledge of possible business partner, lecturer, or policy-maker will be remembered in the future, resulting in loss of trust and repetition of the socially worse outcomes as described in periods to come. Thus, the costs to the policy-maker of reneging on the announcement escalate. In these cases, the costs from certain actions rise and act as constraints on the temptations to renege. We *may* not break a promise, if that means we cannot make any business deal in the future (notice the emphasis on 'may': the chances depend on the details of the problem, how many times we play again, how long it takes for trust to be rebuilt, etc.). Instead, if the policy-maker does fulfil their pledges, that will also be remembered and will facilitate such partnerships in the future. In other words, the history of the policy-maker's actions is remembered in future policy games, and they are said to have a certain 'reputation' which matters.

In the next two sections, we analyse in more detail the time-inconsistency problem facing the monetary authority and the resulting persistent high inflation in one-shot games. We then examine reputation in repeated, multi-period games and how things may be affected in this context. Next, we examine possible solutions to such problems, that is, ways of committing the monetary authority to follow courses of action that lead to socially better outcomes.

7.2 Time Inconsistency of (Discretionary) Optimal Monetary Policy and the Problem of Inflationary Bias

7.2.1 Analysis

We now analyse the monetary policy game described above somewhat more formally. The 'accelerationist' Phillips Curve (see Chapter 1) is given by (with the same notation):

$$U = U^N - (\pi - \pi^e) \tag{7.1}$$

At this point, the monetary authority coincides with government (a distinction will be drawn later). Its objective is to minimize the 'bads' of unemployment and inflation, subject to the constraints posed by the macro system (i.e. the Phillips Curve).[5,6] The private sector, on the other hand, is solely interested in getting it right in their wage negotiations, i.e. accurately forecasting inflation for the period. In other words, the policy-maker sets actual inflation (π) through policy, while the private sector sets inflation expectations (π^e) which symbolize the strength of the wage-price spiral; each party observes the other and decides its own best outcome. The situation and the resulting interaction are depicted in Figure 7.1.

The (unmarked) curved lines are effectively the indifference curves of government's utility function. The closer one is to the origin the better (as both inflation and unemployment are bads), so an inner curve represents higher (rather than lower) utility; for the same reason, these indifference curves are concave (as opposed to the indifference curves of standard utility maximization). As is standard, the slope of these indifference curves represents a willingness of the policy-maker to trade one bad for the other; in particular, flatter lines indicate that the monetary authority cares more about inflation, and steeper lines denote more care for unemployment. The thin straight lines are the constraints imposed on government by the macroeconomy (captured by the short-run Phillips Curves—PCs) and, from an analytical point of view, they are the budget constraints. They are conditional on expectations; given the expectations, there is a simple and policy-exploitable trade-off between inflation and unemployment. But rising expectations shift the curves towards more unfavourable outcomes (outwards), as now we need to have higher actual inflation to arrive at the same rate of unemployment as before. Three simple such PCs are shown, with $\pi^e = 0 < \pi^e_1 < \pi^e_2$.

Optimization by government implies that, for each short-run PC, the associated tangency point is selected. The locus of such tangency points is called the 'Government Reaction Function' (GRF) because it represents the optimal response by government to the external constraints it faces. Corresponding to this is the 'Private Reaction Function' (PRF), giving the optimal private actions: These are simpler, as the private sector simply aims to have $\pi^e = \pi$, as stated; if so, the PRF is vertical at the natural rate of unemployment

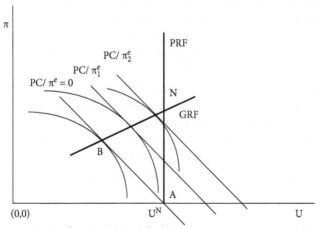

Figure 7.1. The monetary policy game

[5] We need not dwell on the ultimate motives of the government or monetary authority. They may be genuinely interested in society's welfare, or they may be cynical, just seeking re-election. As the saying goes, do governments act because they see the light, or because they feel the heat? This remains an open question! Perhaps the truth is somewhere in the middle.

[6] Society and policy-maker care about inflation for the reasons analysed in Chapter 3. The costs of unemployment are too obvious to mention.

(which is consistent with correct expectations). The two loci represent the best responses of the two parties (government, private sector) given the other party's behaviour. If any party finds that they are outside their respective RF, this means that they are not optimizing, and will act to place themselves on it.[7]

There is only one possible equilibrium for both parties, point N. This is the 'Nash equilibrium' of game theory and represents a situation where the two parties are responding to each other as best they can (optimally), in a way that is both mutually compatible and consistent with the macroeconomy (as represented by the PC). It yields a point where expectations are verified ($\pi^e = \pi$), therefore no more gains on the unemployment front are possible than usual ($U = U^N$), and importantly, inflation is higher than necessary ($\pi > 0$). This generates an 'inflationary bias' which is a pure loss, unaccompanied by any gains in employment. To shed more light on it, we need to connect this framework with the story told in the previous section.

Ex ante, the policy-maker may realize that it will end up with $U = U^N$, anyway, so they might try at least to have some gains on the inflation front. Hence, their optimal policy at that point is $\pi = 0$ and that is what they announce. Next, the private sector makes their (first formal) move by 'forming expectations', which means: they sign wage contracts. At this point, the private sector will ignore the government's zero-inflation announcement. Why? For the simple reason that they are able to predict government's next move. If the private sector locks themselves into wage settlements on the basis $\pi^e = 0$, the left-most PC applies. But since the wage negotiations cannot be undone for a year, a surprise inflation during the period can move the economy from point A to B along the PC/$\pi^e = 0$ that applies. This is a gain for the government, as it will place it on an indifference curve of higher utility;[8] but it unsettles the private sector as they will have signed contracts expecting zero inflation, yet positive inflation actually materializes.[9]

In other words, point A is not on GRF (while B is), and this is something that the private sector will take into account before they move. They thus move to such π^e as is consistent with point N, and the government has no option but to accommodate (match) this rate of inflation, otherwise they will end up with higher unemployment than the natural rate. Thus, the Nash equilibrium N is the only possible one in this game. The initial optimal policy and zero-inflation announcement will be reneged upon after wage commitments have taken place, hence it is time inconsistent.

In plain English, we have two parties interacting: Government pursues high inflation because it anticipates the high inflation expectations (signifying high wages and prices) of the price sector, and the price sector signs high contracts because they expect the high inflation. We can zoom into the wage-price spiral a bit more: wages rise because they expect prices to rise, and prices do because they also expect wages to rise. This is the essence of the situation (and of any Nash equilibrium): neither party has an incentive to

---

[7] Analytically, the GRF is a decision-making process that 'translates' the inflation expectation that the government observes into its optimal policy, i.e. $\pi = \text{GRF}(\pi^e)$. Conversely with PRF: $\pi^e = \text{PRF}(\pi)$.

[8] Why is government interested in deviating from the natural rate of unemployment in the first place? Although it represents the average unemployment rate, U^N may be thought of as too high because it is the product, among other factors, of such inefficiencies and distortions as monopoly power by firms and unions, government taxation that distorts incentives, etc. Hence, government prefers B (which is in fact optimal) to A.

[9] There is a subtle point to be considered here: How can point B give government more utility than point A but the private sector is unsettled by it? Does the government not represent societal welfare? One answer is that here maybe that the government's view of societal welfare may not fully coincide with those of the private sector who is assumed to be behind the PRF; that private sector may be a subset of society (firms, trade unions, etc.).

deviate from the situation on their own; if they do, they lose out. The resulting inflation rate is positive, without delivering in fact any gains in unemployment. That is, this Nash equilibrium is (Pareto) sub-optimal (N): in principle, the economy can do better than that. This is the starting point for the quest for appropriate monetary policy architecture that continues to this day.

The time inconsistency of optimal policy result that Kydland and Prescott (1977) pioneered is a landmark result in macroeconomics and political economy. It may be understood as a dynamic extension of the 'Lucas critique'—see Chapter 2: When the policy-maker plans to intervene, it alters the structure of the macroeconomy, thereby rendering the policy useless (Lucas critique) or even detrimental (due to policy inconsistency and lack of credibility). Alongside the Lucas critique, we list this in Chapter 1 as one of six 'policy ineffectiveness results' as it points out that activist stabilization policy in fact worsens matters. It must be stressed that the result relies crucially on the expectations-augmented or 'accelerationist' Phillips Curve (or equivalently, the 'Lucas supply function' reviewed in Chapter 2); with a Phillips Curve that would give a permanent inflation-unemployment trade-off, the result breaks down. But the time-inconsistency result highlights a broader point, the tension between short- and long-run objectives and the tendency of government (like any agent) to succumb to the former. For a New Classical, the time inconsistency is another nail in the coffin of activist stabilization policy. For anyone that still believes in such policy, like the New Keynesians, the corollary is that policy-making should be exercised with discipline so as to avoid unwanted side-effects.

7.2.2 Credibility-Based Theories of Inflation: An Evaluation

Theories of policy credibility and of time inconsistency of optimal policy leading to inflationary bias provide a forceful explanation on why inflation was so high in the late 1970s and through much of 1980s. But on careful scrutiny, these theories show several gaps—see also the discussion in Romer (2006, chapter 10). First, they rely crucially on forward-looking dynamics in inflation. The private sector anticipates policy actions; this results in the setting of current contracts and current inflation. Therefore, current inflation is determined by expectations of inflation tomorrow, which in turn are influenced by policy actions today. In other words, a forward-looking dynamic is built into inflation. In econometric specifications, these ideas may be captured by an inflation equation like:

$$\pi_t = \alpha \pi_{t+1}^e + x_t, \quad 0 < \alpha < 1 \tag{7.2}$$

Notation is standard, with the addition of explicit time subscripts. x indicates an exogenous fundamental, in our case monetary policy. The parameter $0 < \alpha < 1$ indicates the relevance of the forward-looking behaviour suggested by credibility theory. To see what this equation implies, we can solve it forward by iterated substitution (as in Chapter 2), to obtain:

$$\pi_t = x_t + \alpha x_{t+1}^e + \alpha^2 x_{t+2}^e + \dots \tag{7.2'}$$

Thus, current inflation is influenced by all future fundaments (policy), 'discounted' by α. Nevertheless, as discussed at length in Chapter 3 on the New Keynesian inflation equation, the recent empirical literature on the dynamics of inflation does not speak with one voice on the merits of a specification like (7.2'). In a nutshell, the existence of the expected lead inflation in the equation above has found both strong proponents and opponents.

Secondly, and more importantly, as in the explanation of unemployment and labour market institutions (see Chapter 4), there is a problem of timing in the explanation of inflation with monetary policy institutions. Such institutions were there even in the 1960s and early 1970s, when inflation was low. Additionally, inflation in some countries, notably the UK and US, went down before the introduction of Central Bank independence, suggesting that it was disinflation and restrictive policies that did the trick, and not the precise institutional framework of Central Banks. Moreover, the adverse supply shocks of the 1970s (productivity slowdown, oil price shocks of 1973 and 1979) must have played a role as well in the generation of high inflation of the late 1970s. So, as with unemployment, it is quite possible that it is not the institutions per se but their conjunction with the shocks that produced inflation: The institutions of the old kind inhibited the anti-inflation policies when they were needed. And then inflation got 'locked in'—the inflationary bias. So, these theories are certainly useful in explaining the persistence of inflation, once it sets in. This leads one to agree with Bernanke and Mishkin (1997) that inflation targeting, part of the new arrangements, is a way of 'locking in' the low inflation gains of disinflationary policies. But the deeper issue of whether such ideas can, on their own, provide a convincing theory of inflation is still open.

7.3 A Formal Analysis of Discretion and Commitment

7.3.1 The Basic Model

We now turn to a formal treatment of the ideas developed in the previous section. The aims are to gain a deeper understanding; to extend our results to the case of an external shock (i.e. to develop a *stochastic* environment) and see how the policy-maker deals with this; and finally to prepare the ground for examining some solutions to the inflation bias problem. In this exposition, we draw on the surveys of Persson and Tabellini (2000) and Drazen (2000).

Let us think of the monetary game as a one-move game (for each player). As above, the private sector moves first (to form expectations for the period ahead and sign contracts on that basis, say at the beginning of the year). Then, a supply-side shock occurs during the year; after that, the public sector moves during the year to determine actual inflation (and hence determine (un)employment via the Phillips Curve—PC); and the game ends. (For the moment, a policy announcement commits no one, and is ignored). Figure 7.2a depicts schematically this sequence of moves.

The player that moves last (government) knows the opponent's *action* and incorporates it into their calculation. The player that moves first (private sector) only knows the opponent's *strategy* (i.e. their way of thinking) and incorporate that into their thinking. Government (or monetary authority) chooses its policy stance, out of which inflation is determined; schematically, in this analysis we say that inflation is the policy instrument. Government retains freedom to generate as much inflation as is deemed best, so this setup is said to involve (government's) *discretion*.

Part (a): Without commitment

Step 1: Policy announcement (informal move)

Step 2: Private sector fixes expectations (contracts) (formal move)

Step 3: Shock occurs (PC revealed –not a move)

Step 4: Monetary authority decides actual policy (formal move)

[End of game]

Part (b): With commitment

Step 1: Policy announcement (formal move)

Step 2: Private sector fix expectations (contracts) (formal move)

Step 3: Shock occurs (PC revealed –not a move)

Step 4: Monetary authority carries out the policy announced in Step 1.

[End of game]

Figure 7.2a, b. Sequence of moves in the one-shot monetary game without and with commitment

The Phillips Curve (7.1) now takes the form:

$$n = n^N + \pi - \pi^e - e \tag{7.1'}$$

Employment (percentage of the labour force) is denoted by n and n^N is its 'natural' rate. Equation (7.1') is fully consistent with (7.1), as $U - U^N = n^N - n$, but in addition it incorporates a zero-mean adverse supply shock (e), e.g. a slowdown in productivity, increase in the price of energy or wage/price upsurge, all of which would tend to shift the AS curve to the left and reduce output/employment, given the aggregate demand policy stance.[10]

---

[10] Why do we include only a supply shock and not a demand one in the PC? The PC may well be thought of as a supply-side relation, closely related to the AS curve. By appropriate use of its demand policies, the policy-maker places the economy on their point of choice on the PC. Hence, the demand side is essentially endogenous here (all considered) and is captured by the appropriate choice of π, whereas the supply side is exogenous; developments on that side are captured by the extra term e.

Importantly, this shock is revealed during the year (after wage negotiations have taken place) and is not known to the private sector when they form expectations, but is known to the policy-maker when they decide how much to inflate.

The policy-maker's 'loss' function (the opposite of utility) takes the following form:

$$L^G = (n - \bar{n})^2 + \theta \pi^2 \tag{7.3}$$

This loss function, to be minimized, reflects the government's aversion to the two 'bads' of unemployment and inflation, as mentioned. In fact, the policy-maker has explicit targets for employment and inflation, $\bar{n} > n^N$ and 0, respectively. The former is higher than the natural rate, reflecting the fact that the natural rate is socially considered too low because of the distortions associated with its determination, as discussed. The inflation target could be higher than zero (if the optimal rate of inflation is positive—see Chapter 3), but that would not change the nature of the results; obviously, if the policy-maker aims for a higher inflation rate, inflation will rise. The quadratic terms capture the idea that *any* deviation from the targets (upwards or downwards) is costly. $\theta > 0$ reflects the weight attached to inflation relative to employment deviations in the policy-maker's loss function; $\theta > 1$ is the case of inflation being a worse bad than employment out of target, so that the policy-maker cares more about controlling inflation; $\theta < 1$ characterizes a policy-maker of (broadly speaking) Keynesian persuasion who attaches more importance to employment stabilization.

The analysis begins with the decision made by the *last* player to move (the policy-maker), since for them everything is transparent. They minimize L^G in (7.3), taking account of the Phillips Curve (7.1') as a constraint. The instrument of policy is assumed to be the inflation rate. Using (7.1') into (7.3) to substitute n out, taking both π^e and n^N as given (the former is set by the private sector, the latter is institutionally set), then minimizing with respect to π yields:

$$\pi = (\pi^e + \bar{n} - n^N + e)/(1 + \theta) \tag{7.4}$$

This first order condition (7.4) is the algebraic formulation of the GRF: it gives us the optimal inflation rate for government, given the expectations held by the private sector; the additions are the target employment rate over and above the natural and the supply shock.

To develop the PRF, we note that all the private sector is interested in is to have correct expectations; if so, they will sign the contracts implied by the labour demand and supply functions. So, the private sector aims to have rational expectations:

$$\pi^e = E(\pi) \tag{7.5}$$

(7.5) is in fact the PRF; E(.) is the mathematical expectation of the variable based on the true model of the economy. To get such model-consistent expectations, the private sector takes expectations of (7.4) (recall that the private sector does not know the actual policy action, but can anticipate government's thinking), so it gets:

$$\pi^e = (\bar{n} - n^N)/\theta \tag{7.5'}$$

Combining (7.4) and (7.5'), we get the equilibrium inflation rate,

$$\pi = (\bar{n} - n^N)/\theta + e/(1 + \theta), \tag{7.6a}$$

and employment rate (using 7.1'),

$$n = n^N - \theta e/(1 + \theta). \tag{7.6b}$$

Several comments are in order here. First, we see that the game does not yield any real gain for the government: employment is on average at its natural rate (note that the shock e has a zero mean). Second, average inflation rate is higher than its target (socially optimal) rate of zero (and this, without any gains in employment). In other words, inflation bias is not simply due to a possibly high inflation target (which is zero here, anyway); it is due to policy's futile attempt to stabilize the economy. The bias is due to the target employment rate being higher than the natural rate $(\bar{n} > n^N)$.

We now see how the policy-maker deals with the adverse supply shock, e. Let us remember that an adverse supply shock shifts the AS curve left, thus generating the potential for either a rise in prices, or a drop in output, or a combination of the two; this depends (among other things) on the potential reaction of the government and its use of AD policy. Here, the crucial factor in determining the precise mix of inflation rise and employment fall is the degree to which the policy-maker reacts to it by raising demand and inflation (the degree of 'accommodation', see Chapter 6). This 'degree of accommodation' is captured by $0 < \Theta \equiv 1/(1 + \theta) < 1$ and depends inversely on θ. We see that the shock hits inflation by proportion Θ and by the rest $1 - \Theta(= \theta/(1 + \theta))$, it hits employment. An employment-minded government (low weight on inflation θ, high degree of accommodation Θ) stabilizes employment but lets the shock impact more fully on employment; an inflation-averse government does the opposite.

Next, we can compute the variances of employment and inflation that result from the shock:

$$V(\pi) = \Theta^2 V(e), \quad V(n) = (1 - \Theta)^2 V(e) \tag{7.7}$$

V(.) indicates a variance. We now see that, although there is no Phillips Curve in the long run, there exists a trade-off, a quasi-PC, in the variances of inflation and employment. Given the variability of the exogenous shocks, V(e), the degree of accommodation Θ is critical in deciding whether the economy faces a high variance of inflation and low variance of employment, or the reverse. Table 7.3 in Section 7.7 shows estimates of this inflation-output variability trade-off in the UK.

As far as the average outcome is concerned, this equilibrium describes exactly the Nash equilibrium point N above (to see this, just set $e = 0$ above). It may be asked how this compares with point A. This point might arise if somehow the policy-maker were able to convince the private sector that it will stick to its promise (and if it did so). This is termed the outcome under *commitment*. Formally, this could be represented as a one-move game, with government making a formal announcement first which will be adhered to, and therefore it is a formal move; the private sector setting expectations; the shock occurring; and the game ending there. Figure 7.2b depicts the sequence of moves in this game.

Since the government sets policy before the shock is observed, it cannot react to it; all it does is to set policy in average terms; so its instrument is $E(\pi)$. On the other hand, the private sector observes the actual policy stance and can set $\pi^e = E(\pi)$.[11] Now, the government's loss function (in expected terms) reduces to:[12]

$$L^G = (n^N - \bar{n})^2 + \theta[E(\pi)]^2 \qquad (7.3')$$

Maximizing, we obviously have $E(\pi) = 0$. By $\pi^e = E(\pi)$, it also follows from the Phillips Curve (7.1') that $E(n) = n^N$ (to see this, take expectations of 7.1'). This is the algebraic equivalent of point A and would be attained if a mechanism existed such that it would provide an (effective) commitment. This commitment equilibrium would avoid the inflation bias and hence would be better than N (equilibrium with discretion). Without such a commitment, the temptation to renege and move from A to B exists, and the commitment equilibrium is time inconsistent.

A final important point is in order. Under commitment, the supply shock only hits employment and is not alleviated by accommodating AD (monetary) policy at all—to see this, insert the above information into (7.1'). The variances of inflation and employment are now:

$$V(\pi) = 0, \quad V(n) = V(e) \qquad (7.7')$$

The variance of employment now is higher than under discretion (cf. 7.7). On the other hand, inflation here has no variance at all. The following trade-off then emerges. Under commitment (the game of Figure 7.2b), average inflation and its variance is zero, but the variance of employment is $V(e)$. Under discretion (Figure 7.2a), we have an inflation bias, an employment variance which is a fraction of $V(e)$, and some inflation variance, too. Commitment is a better situation if the variance of the shock is not too high and if inflation aversion (θ) is low; this is because in that case the difference in $V(n)$ is big between the two regimes.

Hence, we see that, in a stochastic environment, the comparison between the two regimes is not an open-and-shut case, and that discretion may be called for in some circumstances. There are models that examine strategies that try to combine the best of both worlds, namely commitment with some degree of discretion when the shock becomes too big. We examine these models in Section 7.6.2 under 'escape clauses'. As we discuss below, such ideas are relevant today, after the experience of the big shock of the 'Great Recession' that followed the financial crisis of 2007–9.

7.3.2 Reputation

We now address the obvious question of what happens if the game is not a one-move one, but if it contains many moves (in the terminology of game theory, it is a 'repeated' game).

---

[11] The assumption that the private sector is atomistic, consisting of agents who cannot affect individually the aggregate outcome, is critical here; it implies that each agent among the private sector has no incentive to cheat and create surprises in order to affect the final outcome.

[12] Disregarding that is a variance term.

In this analysis, we follow the seminal paper of Barro and Gordon (1983). Like in all the strategic situations considered in Section 7.1, government and the private sector interact repeatedly and that changes incentives. The obvious new element in a repeated game is *memory*, past action (history) is remembered by both players; in particular, any reneging on commitments that the policy-maker may have done will be remembered by the private sector. In other words, the government's *reputation* is built on its past policies. This will alter the private sector's expectations in the future, and hence the resulting employment. Any costs to the policy-maker will also be felt in the periods to come. Total expected costs will rise, and thus the temptation to renege on commitments will be smaller.

To elaborate while keeping the framework simple, let us imagine a game of two periods $(t = 1, 2)$—both government and private sector play in both. Two outcomes are initially possible for inflation, either 0 or b/2 (say, low and high—the latter may be the single-period Nash equilibrium outcome of the previous section). The Phillips Curve applies as usual (without any shock) in each of the two periods, so we have:

$$n_t = n^N + \pi_t - \pi_t^e \tag{7.1"}$$

The following now captures the loss function of the government:

$$L = \pi_1^2 - b(n_1 - n^N) + R(\pi_2^2 - b(n_2 - n^N)) \tag{7.3"}$$

$R < 1$ is the discount factor that government applies to the second-period argument. Subscripts refer to the period. Inflation continues to be a pure bad (it increases the loss). The government is a little more 'Keynesian' than before in that it attaches utility to employment gains above the natural rate (n^N) as opposed to employment stabilization (notice that the employment term is not quadratic, in contrast to 7.3); but the results do not depend on this difference. For simplicity, the coefficient indicating the importance of employment is proportional to the inflation rate that government possibly sets; this is an assumption, but its spirit follows from the analysis of the one-shot game (cf. equation 7.5' where average inflation is inversely proportional to the relative importance of inflation). The sequence of moves is again: private sector fixes expectations and contracts first, then government moves, then both move simultaneously in the second period.[13] The private sector's strategy is that it believes the government's announcement in the first period, while in the second it sets low expectations $(\pi^e = 0)$ if the government stuck to its announcement in the first period—whatever that was—or high expectations $(\pi^e = b/2)$ if the government cheated. A highly stylized setup indeed, but rich enough to convey the main ideas.

Following the arguments established above, the government may have an incentive to announce low inflation early on $(\pi = 0)$. It now has two strategies:

- Commitment to the announcement, e.g. by writing $\pi = 0$ into law. In this case, the zero inflationary expectations are validated and zero inflation also follows in the second period;

---

[13] Thus, cheating is precluded in the second period, but the whole point here is to investigate the effects of memory, so we must have one period after cheating.

Table 7.1. Outcomes under alternative government strategies

		1	2	3	4	5
		Commitment to $\pi = 0$ rule	Cheating under discretion	Time-consistent Nash (one-shot game)	Rule of $\pi > 0$	Minimum self-enforceable rule under discretion
π_1		0	$b/2$	$b/2$	π	$b/2$
π^e_1		0	0	$b/2$	π	π
$n_1 - n^N$		0	$b/2$	0	0	$b/2 - \pi$
π_2		0	$b/2$	$b/2$	π	$b/2$
π^e_2		0	$b/2$	$b/2$	π	$b/2$
$n_2 - n^N$		0	0	0	0	0
L		0	$(b/2)^2 - b^2/2 +$ $+ R(b/2)^2$	$(1+R)(b/2)^2$	$(1+R)\pi^2$	$(b/2)^2 - b(b/2 - \pi)$ $+ R(b/2)^2$

- Cheating, by reneging on the announcement; in this case, the government engineers high inflation (b/2), enjoys the employment gains in the first period, but also suffers the inflationary consequences in both periods because expectations in the first period will have been frustrated.

In columns 1 and 2 of Table 7.1, we summarize the outcomes per period under each strategy of the government and calculate the government's loss:[14]

The first two terms of L under cheating are the losses in the first period from cheating; note that this is negative, i.e. the first period on its own presents a temptation to cheat. But the second period is the time of reckoning: The third term is the loss from having to incur high inflation without employment gains in the second period, effectively a punishment for government's broken promise in the first period (Barro and Gordon's 'enforcement').

By collecting terms we find the loss of the cheating strategy to be

$$L(\text{cheating}) = -b^2(1 - R)/4 < 0;$$

the sign follows because of the discount factor R < 1. This is less than the loss from the commitment to zero inflation, which is L(commitment) = 0. Thus, the zero inflation rule requires an external commitment (e.g. a law) to enforce it: without it, the government will cheat, since the gain (negative loss) from cheating now outweighs the cost of punishment

---

[14] This may be a good opportunity to clarify some terminology. A *rule* refers to government actions that are contingent on the current state of the system; e.g. $\pi = \pi(y_{-1})$, i.e. inflation (the instrument of monetary policy) depends on the observable past output (or its deviations from normal, the output gap). Typically, government's maximization of its intertemporal utility (or minimization of loss) subject to the constraints posed by the economic system results in a rule of this kind ('optimal rule'), but such rules may be complicated. To avoid the disadvantages associated with this (imperfect understanding, monitoring, etc.), *simple rules* have been suggested, for instance a 2 per cent inflation rule (which does not depend on the state of the economic system). This requires commitment, otherwise it is time inconsistent and will not be enforced, as we have seen. Column 1 of Table 7.1 lists the outcomes under a zero-inflation rule. *Discretion* refers to government's recalculation of its best strategy (or re-optimization) every period (rather than at the beginning of history once and for all); this is the model underlying Figure 7.2a and the associated analysis. Column 2 of Table 7.1 refers to such a discretionary strategy if the private sector erroneously believes that the zero-inflation policy will be followed. Column 3 assumes that the outcome of the (time-consistent) one-move game is followed throughout—this is there for reference. Finally, column 5 asks what is the minimum π (call it Π) that will be enforced under discretion, when cheating is considered but not chosen by government. $\Pi < b/2$ (the one-shot Nash π) because of *reputation*—memory of past actions.

in subsequent periods.[15] As it is not in the government's interests to adhere to it, the zero-inflation announcement will not be credible. Instead, the private sector will play the time-consistent Nash inflation rate b/2 throughout, followed by government: the one-shot-game outcome (column 3). This means a loss of $L = (1 + R)(b/2)^2 > 0$. In other words, because the government is tempted by the possibility of a negative loss (gain) under cheating, it ends up with the worst-case scenario of a positive loss.

We can obtain a number of additional insights. The more valuable the gains in employment for government and/or the higher the time-consistent Nash inflation rate (that is, the higher b), the higher the overall gains from the cheating strategy, and the more unlikely it is that the commitment will be kept. With respect to the role of future punishment and memory, we find the following: the government's discount factor embodies two elements, its pure discounting of the future (via the real interest rate) and its assessment of the probability that the private sector might forget the current cheating (this may be more relevant in a multi-period setup). Thus, we may write $R = 1/(1 + r + \psi)$, where $\psi > 0$ is the probability of the loss of memory; ψ may also capture the probability of government losing the next election, in which case again the future does not matter. As either of r or ψ rises, the policy-maker cares less about the future and the future punishment becomes less relevant; in which case the temptation to cheat will rise. We see here some of the root causes why short-termism may prevail in policy-making under discretion.

If zero inflation is not enforceable by government, are there positive inflation rates that can be self-policed without commitment? In other words, are there inflation rates in the range $0 < \pi < b/2$ that, if announced, will make cheating NOT worthwhile? The outcomes of sticking to a rule of $\pi > 0$ are given in column 4; the outcomes when the government announces π but generates b/2 instead are given in column 5. We assume again that if government cheats, and if the private sector detects this, their expectations will go to the Nash level (b/2) in the second period, to be followed by the actual inflation rate; π is such that it is not worth cheating, i.e.

$$(1 + R)\pi^2 \le (b/2)^2 - b(b/2 - \pi) + R(b/2)^2,$$

or $(1 + R)\pi^2 - b\pi + b^2(1 - R)/4 \le 0$. Solving the quadratic, we get:

$$0 < (1 - R)b/2(1 + R) \le \pi \le b/2.$$

Let the minimum inflation rate in this range be denoted by Π, we find:

$$\Pi = (1 - R)b/2(1 + R) > 0$$

The significance of Π is that, since $\pi = 0$ is not credible and results in the worse outcome of time-consistent Nash, a self-enforceable $\Pi < b/2$ would improve matters without requiring extra commitment mechanisms. The minimum enforceable inflation rate with memory and reputation thus lies between the time-consistent Nash equilibrium of the single-period game (b/2) and the best possible rule of zero inflation (which however requires extra commitment mechanisms in order to be sustained). Π rises with the gains from inflationary surprises (b)

---

[15] The validity of this particular result, that zero inflation will never be enforced, depends on the exact setup. But the results that follow are more general.

and falls with the discount factor (R): a government more tempted to surprise can credibly maintain only a higher rate of inflation; a government that is far-sighted (because of a higher memory by the private sector and/or more regard for future punishments, lower θ and r, respectively) can credibly maintain a lower rate of inflation.

The upshot of this analysis is that, in a repeated game, the private sector will remember the current cheating by government, and will punish it by not believing any policy announcements. Hence, a lower level of inflation than the Nash equilibrium inflationary bias is believable because the government will find it not worth deviating from it (termed 'minimum self-enforceable inflation rate'). The more far-sighted the private sector is, the lower is this rate. But this lower credible inflation rate is still positive: there is still an inflationary bias that is a net cost to society, as it produces no employment gains. Thus, repeated games and reputation mitigate but do not fundamentally alter the basic conclusions of the analysis based on the one-shot game.

7.4 Solutions to the Problem of Inflationary Bias I: Binding Commitments and Conservative Central Bankers

7.4.1 Binding Commitments—Law and Exchange Rate Arrangements

The zero-inflation commitment cannot be enforced in the model above because the government will find it beneficial to renege on this announcement ('cheating'). However, if somehow an external constraint were to be imposed such that the government could not deviate from zero inflation even if it wanted to, then obviously zero inflation would be a credible strategy. Such an external commitment could in principle come from law: it could be stipulated in the Charter of the Central Bank that it should pursue zero inflation. But, though sound in principle, this strategy encounters impossible practical hurdles. Any, even the slightest, deviation from zero inflation, or whatever else had been stipulated, would be a failure that would wreck the Central Bank's credibility; moreover, there would be no room for manoeuvre if specific shocks occurred that required flexible treatment; and if such flexibility were to be enshrined in the Central Bank's Charter, the latter would become horribly and impracticably complicated. Therefore, such external constraints have not been imposed except in the more limited sense of inflation targeting—reviewed below.[16]

Monetary policy-makers have some times imposed external constraints on themselves in the form of commitments to preserve exchange rates. Exchange rates are closely linked with monetary policy. Simply put, a monetary expansion often leads to exchange rate depreciation, and a monetary contraction to appreciation. So, a commitment on monetary policy might take the form of a constraint on the exchange rate to maintain a certain parity.

---

[16] See Sheffrin (1989) on the attempt made in the US in the 1980s to write into law that the government budget deficit should be balanced (through the Gramm-Rudman Act of 1986). Legal wrangling over the detail ensued until eventually the Act fell into disuse. A famous instance of time-inconsistency and binding external commitment was with Ulysses and the Sirens. The story is familiar: The Sirens' song would be so seductive that anybody who heard it would forever give up the desire to continue the journey home (an instance where the short-run objective overrides the long-run one). Knowing that, Ulysses asked his comrades to tie him on the mast (the external constraint), so that he could hear the song but not forfeit his long-run objective to travel home (his comrades' ears were plugged)! Note the trade-off between short-run and long-run objectives; how individuals resolve this tension is considered when we discuss deviations from (full) rationality, in Chapters 2 and 11.

A prominent example of this arrangement was the European Monetary System (EMS, 1979–93) which required member currencies to limit their fluctuations within specified margins. Analytically, this arrangement was a half-baked monetary union. The informal pivot of the system was (then West) Germany, whose Central Bank had established a reputation of low inflation. For other currencies to limit their fluctuations towards the West German mark, the monetary policies of the other member countries should be such as to maintain low inflation. The hope was that, by entering this arrangement, a strategy of low inflation would be credible to markets, because that was required by the system (Giavazzi and Pagano, 1988). In other words, membership of EMS was an institutional constraint on monetary policy, solving (hopefully) its credibility problem.

As with all external constraints, the gain from this strategy was aimed to be easier disinflation: the transition from N to A of Figure 7.1 would be direct and painless because everybody would believe it. In other words, the private sector would be immediately convinced of the low-inflation commitment of member-country Central Banks and go for low wage increases, thereby avoiding a painful disinflation. (In jargon, it was hoped that Central Banks would 'import' the German Bundesbank's anti-inflation reputation.) Soon, it became clear that credibility was not earned automatically, and disinflation came with an employment cost that many countries found impossible to stomach. Analytically, we went from N to A by first sliding down the short-run Phillips Curve, passing through N and increasing unemployment. The markets sensed the difficulties (economic as well as political) of maintaining the specified parities: the various currency exchange rates came under sustained attack and the system was practically suspended in the summer of 1993. It was thought that the root of the problem lay in the possibility of exit from the system and the associated half-hearted commitment to it by the various countries (other than Germany). This recognition paved the way for the real thing, a full monetary union (from which there is no exit)—European Monetary Union, which came a few years later. A similar strategy is pursued by those countries that have in place a Currency Board arrangement, whereby the exchange rate against a basket of currencies must be kept constant by low-inflation monetary policy. The commitment to the system must be full—to the point that, if the exchange rate comes under attack by speculators selling the currency, the Central Bank in question must be ready (politically and technically) to buy the national currency and withdraw it from circulation, replacing it with the international basket of currencies.

All these episodes reveal the difficulties of achieving the commitment that Figure 7.2b presupposes. Hence, the quest arose for 'softer' mechanisms that aim to reduce the inflation bias but avoid 'hard' constraints.

7.4.2 Conservative Central Bankers and Central Bankers' Contracts

Rogoff (1985) has put forward the suggestion that the Central Banker should be more conservative[17] than the general society, so as to reduce the inflationary bias. It is easy to see

---

[17] Note carefully that by 'conservative' we do not mean politically Conservative; we mean that their aversion to inflation is greater than society's (or government's).

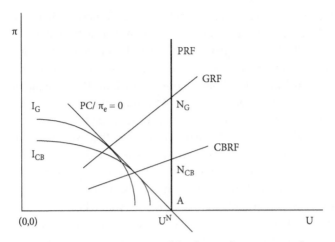

Figure 7.3. Government vs. conservative central banker and monetary policy

how. The general government's and society's preferences are again given by (7.3); but monetary policy is delegated to a Central Banker who has a loss function of:

$$L^{CB} = (n - \bar{n})^2 + (\theta + \varepsilon)\pi^2 \tag{7.8}$$

The parameter $\varepsilon > 0$ gives the extra importance that this policy-maker attaches to inflation control over and above that of government or general society; this may be the case if the central banker attaches more importance to financial stability. This is the meaning of the central banker's conservatism; ε is its index.

Now, the indifference curves based on the central banker's preferences will be flatter (one point of inflation less is now worth more points of unemployment)—see Figure 7.3. Note that $U - U^N = n^N - n$. Let us asume that I_G is a typical society's and government's indifference curve (the one that happens to be tangent on the short-run Philips Curve that passes through U_N) and I_{CB} is the indifference curve of the conservative central banker tangent to the same PC. It is easy to see that the reaction function based on this set of central banker preferences (CBRF) is flatter and below the one based on government's preferences (GRF), while still both emanating from the origin as shown. Thus, the new Nash equilibrium, with the conservative central banker at the helm of monetary policy (N_{CB}), will involve lower inflation than otherwise. This is a powerful argument for delegating monetary policy control from elected politicians, who care more about employment by persuasion or in order to get re-elected, to unelected bureaucrats who will have a more cold-headed aversion to inflation.

It is no surprise that a policy-maker who is more determined to have low inflation can deliver that outcome. The interesting twist in this proposal is that there is an optimal (i.e., NOT unlimited) degree of conservatism for a central banker: when shocks occur, this person will be less inclined to accommodate them and therefore will produce greater unemployment and output variability. So, there is a trade-off between more inflation and lower output variability, and less inflation with more output variability. The government can optimize, i.e. select where to be on this trade-off by selecting an appropriately conservative person as cental banker (effectively, choosing ε). More practically, it does not pay to have as conservative a central banker as possible ($\varepsilon \to \infty$), a moderate degree is optimal.

Proposals in a similar vein have been made by Persson and Tabellini (1993) and Walsh (1995), namely that anti-inflation performance should be written in central bankers' contracts: missing targets would involve financial penalties or even loss of contract, as well as loss of prestige. Such a proposal would aim to make the central banker very anti-inflation-prone. A contract of this type has been implemented by the Bank of New Zealand since 1989.[18] As criticism against it one may say that it would be unfair for a central banker to shoulder the blame entirely at all times; e.g. if inflation rises inescapably because of an oil price shock. Contracts would have to be so sophisticated in distinguishing between an array of possible cases and outcomes as to be impracticable. But central bankers more often than not work with tenures, and governments can deny them reappointment if they underperform.

In conclusion, of the two arrangements considered here, unelected technocrat Central Bankers with a great aversion to inflation (that is is practically the meaning of 'conservatism' employed here) and Central Bankers' contracts, only the first has found application, to some extent; the latter propsal has not been implemented. We offer a few lines of criticism about the outlook of modern central bankers. Before that, we turn to other proposals and arrangements that have found application in modern central banking.

7.5 Solutions to the Problem of Inflationary Bias II: Central Bank Independence and Inflation Targeting

The problems associated with discretionary monetary policy (time inconsistency, lack of credibility, and an inflationary bias) have prompted a search for institutional frameworks which can alleviate these problems. We now review two arrangements that have found institutional support and application—the ones in the previous section are more theoretical investigations and possibilities rather than practical applications. One point to be remembered is that the arrangements reviewed below are not mutually exclusive; rather, they are complementary in nature, and have found joint application, in different mixtures and shades, by all major Central Banks. The one application that comes out of the previous section (Central Banker 'conservatism') is also embedded within the frameworks described in this section.

7.5.1 Central Bank Independence

Until about 1990, a typical Central Bank was just another branch of government, effectively the ministry of monetary policy. It reflected government's policy preferences and often took direct instructions. These policy preferences are the ones that produce the inflationary bias, of which there was plenty in the late 1970s and 1980s. So, making the cental bank independent of government's preferences must be a priority in combating inflation. This proposal has by now been accepted more or less through the OECD economies and beyond.

Many commentators point to a distinction between goal-independence (independence of the Central Bank in choosing its overall objectives), and instrument-independence (independence in deciding what instruments should be used to steer inflation to its target

---

[18] New Zealand's Reserve (Central) Bank appears to be among the first to have applied the new institutional arrangements. Bean (1998) argues that the New Zealand CB is more uncompromisingly anti-inflation than others.

and on other operational matters like when/how often to change interest rates). In terms of goal independence, different Central Banks are characterized by a different degree of independence: for instance, the Bank of England is less independent in this respect, as its main objective is mandated to it by the government.[19] Other Central Banks, like the US Federal Reserve and Germany's Bundesbank (which decided monetary policy before Germany entered the European Monetary Union in 1999), appear to have more autonomy in specifying their precice objectives, as well as their operational procedures and instruments. A related distinction is between independence and conservatism, emphasized by Beger et al. (2001) (the former is instrument-independence, the latter is the strictness of the Central Bank's anti-inflation focus, whether decided by the governor(s) or mandated by government). In principle, one may find different mixtures of these elements, but in practice the two are likely to be rather strongly correlated.

Part and parcel of independence is transparency, accountability, and greater openness. Most Central Banks are required to explain and justify their strategies for achieving their stipulated goals to parliamentary committees. If targets are not achieved, the reasons must be explained, an example being the open letter that the Bank of England needs to write in order to explain why the target inflation is not met and what is being done to ensure that it does. Additionally, the strategies and operations are clearly communicated to the public via newsletters and other publications. Gone are the days when CBs tried to ensure an informational advantage by being secretive; in the spirit of the arguments presented above, the advantage now is gained by informing and guiding the private sector. CB independence is also accompanied by enhanced technical capabilities: not only are the governors and other senior policy-makers experts and 'technocrats'; CBs also contain research departments that provide sophisticated analysis and forecasts (such as the Bank of England inflation forecast) using cutting-edge econometric models. Policy is evidence-based.

Early empirical studies (Grilli et al., 1991; Alesina and Summers, 1993; Cukierman, 1992) found a negative relationship between indices of central bank independence (CBI) and inflation for industrialized economies. It was however less clear whether such a relationship existed for developing countries; and it was even more doubtful whether CBI was correlated with economic growth and other real variables (which might be interpreted as good news in that disinflation did not incur real costs, the interpretation preferred by Grilli et al., 1991), or that, more pessimistically, that there is no real gain from CBI. The early findings have been criticized on the grounds of reliability of CBI indicators, robustness (what happens if more countries/data points are included), and causality (does CBI cause low inflation or the other way round); these are all usual criticisms surrounding any econometric work.

Despite such caveats, by the 1990s, a consensus had emerged that discretionary policy is prone to inflation. Guided by such thinking, in 1997, the newly elected Labour government handed independence over to the Bank of England. In practice, various, more political considerations may have played a role: The Labour government wanted to convince the

---

[19] Currently (May 2019), the inflation target mandated to the Bank England (BoE) by the UK government is to maintain the (CPI-based) annual inflation rate at 2% ± 1%. If the inflation rate happens to deviate from this permissible band, the BoE should write an open letter explaining why there is this deviation and what measures are being taken to eliminate it. One may comment that the value of this open letter is both informational (in line with the transparency objectives) but (one suspects) also moral (to make the BoE and its top people eat a bit of humble pie—containing in effect elements of the Central Banker contracts already discussed, which punish failure). The main instrument of monetary policy is the interest rate at which the BoE lends liquidity to commercial banks, which used to be known as the Bank Rate. The body that takes these decisions is the nine-member Monetary Policy Committee, which meets eight times a year.

City of London (the finance industry) that they were not the tax-and-spend, inflation-prone Labour of old (Glyn, 2007). Additionally, the new Labour government may have wanted to avoid responsibility for monetary policy that could register both successes but also failures. This thinking may have proved far-sighted: while the new arrangements registered early successes (inflation reduction), key Central Banks seem to have been caught off-guard about the onset of the Great Reccesion of 2007–9. As we discuss below, this experience has prompted some re-examination of the optimality of the new institutional arrangements.

7.5.2 Inflation Targeting

Inflation targeting is the requirement that the main and overriding objective of monetary policy should be to maintain price stability; it is currently the mandate given to many Central Banks.[20] As Bernanke and Miskin (1997) point out, inflation targeting should not be understood as an 'ironclad' and rigid operational rule because it does not specify what instruments should be used and when. Rather, it should be understood as a policy *framework*, which gives preponderance to maintaining low inflation and, subject to that, gives some flexibility to Central Banks to achieve other (often loosely specified) short-term policy goals. It is quite possible that, under the overriding objective of price stability, Central Banks can use their policy-making powers to smooth adjustment, and 'correct' anomalies, in exchange rates, external imbalances, and even asset (stock and housing) markets.[21] To put it otherwise, if we think of the polar opposites of full discretion and full discipline, inflation targeting is somewhere between the two, closer to the latter but not identical to it. It is a 'softer' constraint than a rigid policy rule.

In practice, inflation targeting is characterized by the preponderance of inflation stability with a publicly announced inflation target, operational independence with the necessary analytical capability for assessment, a focus on long-term objectives, and clear procedures for an accountable and transparent conduct of monetary policy. It had largely replaced (but not totally eclipsed, see the discussion on the European Central Bank later on) earlier practices of monetary policy, like maintaining the growth rate of money supply at a specified range (the so-called money growth targeting practice).[22] Among those that adopted this institutional framework early were New Zealand, Israel, Finland, the UK, Australia, Canada, and Sweden (Sterne, 2002). It quickly became a global tendency, but with considerable institutional differences among countries in the specifics. Fifty-odd Central Banks had a mandate, stricter or more flexible, to maintain inflation stability in 2000, but less than 20 of them were formally characterized as 'inflation targeting', i.e. as having the institutional apparatus associated with it in place (Mahadeva and Sterne, 2002). Later still, progressively, there was an even greater move towards inflation targeting,

---

[20] Though the objective is commonly stated as 'price stability', in practice, it most often means *inflation* stability. There is a subtle distinction to be made between the two. In a nutshell, if a target is missed under inflation targeting, this has no effect on actions in future periods; on the other hand, as the price level in any period is the result of accumulated past inflation, even a transitory inflation deviation from normal implies price deviations from normal *in all subsequent periods*. So, maintaining a price target involves correcting all past inflationary deviations *ex post*—a much more stringent requirement. See Ambler (2009) for further discussion. Practically, most Central Banks are required to keep inflation low and stable.

[21] See Sutherland (2000) and Svensson (2001) for studies of inflation targeting in open economies.

[22] Rudebusch and Svensson (2002), using US data, compared the relative performance of monetary targeting and inflation targeting. The results show monetary targeting to be quite inefficient, yielding both higher inflation and output variability. See Jensen (2002) for a theoretical comparison of alternative monetary policy strategies.

particularly among advanced rather than emerging economies; see Cobham (2018) for a recent systematic classification of operational regimes of Central Banks. There remains an array of countries whose inflation targeting is characterized as 'loose'; interestingly, that includes the European Central Bank.

While inflation targeting has become popular, various details remain uncertain. First, inflation inertia, due to the complicated structure of staggering of wage contracts and prices, and imperfect information, implies that it is hopeless to aim to control current inflation; rather, it should be the Central Bank's inflation forecast a few periods ahead, the rationale being that this captures the best information about where inflation is heading at any time. (In jargon, the Bank's own inflation forecast is the best target—see Bernanke and Woodford, 1997; Svensson, 1997, 1999.) But there is no consensus on the forecast horizon; and there is an argument that a forward-looking forecast may induce instability for some forecast horizons (see Batini and Pearlman, 2002). Secondly, there remains the open question of whether and when monetary policy should respond to asset price develop-ments, like a stock market crash, or house price developments. The US Fed successfully weathered such crises in 1987 ('Black Monday') and 1997 (South East Asian crises). It seems that some discretion is being called for (providing the inflation goal is not com-promised) and that an established credibility gives more degrees of freedom to respond to any given challenge. Finally, and not less importantly, there is the issue of how to respond to different types of shock. As discussed in Chapter 6, demand-led shocks are rather straightforward to deal with (as inflation and the output gap move in the same direction), but supply-side shocks induce opposite movements in inflation and the output gap; this is where careful judgement, flexibility, and compromises, as well as some luck, are necessary. In any case, various of the above insights (forecast targeting, and the incorporation of other targets to some extent) have been incorporated in some recent proposals on 'flexible' inflation targeting discussed below.

Martin and Milas (2004) estimate a model of monetary policy for the UK, 1963–2000, and find that inflation targeting (introduced in practice in 1992) led to a tightening of monetary policy, with greater emphasis on inflation even prior to the new institutional arrangements that were put in place in May 1997. There are also indications of asymmetry, in that policy-makers respond more to upward deviations of inflation, and non-linearity, in that greater deviations signal a progressive intensification of policy.

As a final remark, let us note that inflation targeting has been criticized broadly along the same lines as Central Bank independence, namely that there is no evidence that disinflation under them has been achieved without pain (see Bernanke and Mishkin, 1997). Time will tell whether this type of institution will deliver 'value for money', i.e. lower inflation/higher growth than otherwise. We may conclude by agreeing with Bernanke and Mishkin that this is an arrangement that helps to 'lock in' the anti-inflation gains made by traditional means, i.e. a tight monetary (and also possibly fiscal) policy.

7.5.3 CB Independence and Inflation Targeting: A Critical Assessment

By the mid-2000s, a wide consensus had developed in support of the new institutional arrangements, primarily Central Bank independence and inflation targeting (Goodfriend, 2007). This consensus was based around the stylized fact of an adverse relationship between CBI and inflation. However, as mentioned, the empirical evidence has never been clear-cut either that Central Bank independence and/or inflation targeting delivered 'disinflation without pain', or (even more) that the lower inflation was accompanied by output gains. These ideas were echoed in the wide-ranging review by Berger et al. (2001) of the enormous early theoretical and empirical literature. In another review, Muscatelli and Trecroci (2000) concluded that 'the emphasis in the political economy literature on institutional design (e.g. central bank independence and inflation targeting) is exaggerated. Formal institutional reform seems neither a necessary nor a sufficient condition for the observation of shifts in monetary policy rules.'

Posen (1995, 1998) has criticized the findings of an inverse CB independence-inflation relationship as not showing any true causal relationship; both CB independence and low inflation may be due to a third, unobserved factor such the general public's aversion to inflation or the economy's strength and high productivity:[23] In countries with high productivity growth or in which anti-inflation feeling runs high, inflation will be low and there will be more political appetite for an independent CB. Thus, the criticism goes, instituting the new arrangements may be both politically difficult and rather pointless. This line of criticism is in accordance with the recent arguments in the literature on the endogeneity of institutions; see also Hayo (1998).

Furthemore, the Great Recession of 2007–9 dealt a further blow to the new institutional arrangements: generally, major Central Banks were slow to respond to the fall in output and the rise in unemployment by cutting interest rates; the rationale was that their mandate was to keep inflation low and since inflation was not falling, there was no scope for easing monetary policy. Thus, the new arrangements came under criticism even from unlikely quarters. Writing in the *Wall Street Journal* (Europe), Mattich (2011) criticized the fact that 'independent central bankers had missed the most egregious private sector debt binge in history, encouraged through moral hazard wholesale financial sector recklessness and fuelled sequential asset bubbles'. The criticism here is more related to the Central Banks' other roles, as financial regulators, rather than their monetary (and anti-inflation) policy.

For all these reasons, in the short space of a few years, the pendulum swung from a near-total consensus in favour of the new arrangements towards a more critical reappraisal of them (though far from a total rejection)—see the text by the Committee on International Economic Policy and Reform (2011). In the next section, we discuss the new elements that this criticism brings, from a more theoretical perspective. But before that, we discuss the lessons and remaining open questions surrounding Central Bank independence and inflation targeting.

It is natural to think that stricter discipline in policy-making and inflation aversion should help maintain a lower inflation. So, there should be no slide back to the old ways of the 1970s. A measure of discipline in monetary policy is the great gain from the new arrangements. Additionally, the longer term perspective and the lack of inflationary surprises for short-term gain are much-needed improvements in policy-making. It seems an inescapable bottomline that central bank independence has put monetary policy above day-to-day politics and its (widely rumoured) populist tendencies. So, we may conclude along with many commentators that the new arrangements are not a 'fix-all' process but do

---

[23] Note that high productivity generally implies lower prices; refer to the price-wage setting framework of Chapter 4.

help in locking in the low-inflation dynamics and expectations that may have been gained by painful disinflation; without this institutional setup, inflation might rise again. An additional clear-cut gain of the new institutional framework is transparency, accountability, evidence-based policy-making in monetary policy-making, and communication between policy-makers and the private sector.

But we probably should take on board some of the critics' points: there is no perfect institutional arrangement; credible disinflation has happened where and when the underlying macroeconomy and the electorate's preferences allowed it; and institutional design will continue to evolve and improve. In this way, we are led to what may be one of the most important open questions. As we have argued, and the experience of 2007–9 shows, discipline helps to avert the inflation bias but also obstructs the necessary response to shocks. So, here is the dilemma: how much technocratic, versus, democratic control of monetary policy should there be? We have argued that conservative, unelected technocrats help maintain discipline in monetary policy and keep it focused on the long-term objectives. But are technocrats and experts truly unbiased? In the UK more specifically, the case could be made that there should be a permanent representative of the TUC (trade unions) and the CBI (confederation of industries) on the Monetary Policy Committee. Additionally, the MPC should convene at a different city in the UK each time.[24] More broadly, should monetary policy keep an eye on wider objectives (such as its effects on inequality, regional imbalances, or deindustrialization) rather than just inflation? Of course, one should bear in mind that monetary policy may not be able to improve matters on these fronts; but it may well be able to worsen them, an outcome which should be avoided (e.g. by raising interest rates and causing an appreciation, it may hurt export-based industry and manufacturing and the regions that rely on these).

More generally there is a debate about the appropriate boundaries of technocratic policy management and a more political/democratically mandated approach to such management. The issue will increase in importance as similar issues to those related to monetary policy arise with respect to fiscal policy and public finances (see Chapter 8 on fiscal councils). Whatever the institutional framework in place, one should always remember Blinder's (1997, 1998) assessment that Central Banking is as much an art as science: while it relies quite heavily on scientific advances, it also requires sound judgement.

7.6 Re-evaluating the Consensus: Flexible Inflation Targeting, Escape Clauses, Forward Guidance, and Nominal Income Targeting

7.6.1 Flexible Inflation Targeting

An important issue is whether the inflation target should be adhered to all the time or whether measured deviations from it are allowed temporarily. The answer in the literature (e.g. Woodford 2013) seems to be that the monetary authority should aim to reach the target only in the medium term—in calendar terms, in, say, two years or so; in the interim, measured deviations are allowed and even required. There are at least two reasons for this.

---

[24] To press this point further, the members of the MPC should travel by train, so as to see the 'brownfield' sites and the industrial dereliction around the country.

First, because of inflation's inherent dynamics and inertia: imagine a shock that brings inflation above target; to bring inflation back to target quickly one may need a heavy dose of monetary contraction, which may harm output too much, and which will need to be at least partially reversed when the target is reached, creating too much fluctuation in interest rates. It may be preferable to apply a mild contraction (rise in interest rates) and let inflation attain its target somewhat more slowly. Secondly, inflation targeting is not incompatible with other objectives of policy, primarily output stabilization (Bernanke and Mishkin, 1997; King, 2005); it only means that an inflation target is the overriding one in the medium term when the level of inflation is thought to be unrelated to real variables (monetary neutrality). It is quite legitimate for the monetary authority to try to stabilize output in the short term, by e.g. slowing down the monetary contraction as above, providing that the medium-term inflation target is not jeopardized. This is all in line with the argument in Bernanke and Mishkin (1997) that inflation targeting is a 'framework', not an 'ironclad rule'; in other words, we want reasonable, but not rigid, discipline.

The idea of flexibility has had some practical relevance following the Great Recession of 2008–9, when the Bank of England was criticized as responding to the recession too little, too late; they kept interest rates too high for too long. The counter-argument was that interest rattes were kept high in order to combat the high inflation that arose as the result of high oil prices (an unfavourable supply shock). Since then, stabilization of employment and output has moved up the scale of importance somewhat for the Bank of England; recent pronouncements in favour of 'flexible inflation targeting' reflect that.

7.6.2 Escape Clauses: A Formal Analysis

Related to the idea of flexibility is the argument that governments should embed some flexibility into their institutional monetary policy design to counter extreme supply shocks (e.g. energy price hikes, natural disasters, strikes, other cost-push shocks). Flood and Isard (1988) and Lohmann (1992) show that this can be done by allowing the central banker to 'escape' their rigid anti-inflation policy and deal with the shock, when the latter is large. The price for this will obviously be *some* inflationary bias, which is of course bad, but better than the risk of not being able to respond to adverse conditions at all. We review this argument here.

Let us recall that equilibrium inflation depends on the deviation between employment at the bliss point and natural rate of employment (which shows the scope for monetary policy activism), θ (a measure of how much the policy-maker cares about inflation), and e (the adverse supply shock). Figure 7.4a graphs inflation against a favourable shock e' (where $e' \equiv -e$) according to this policy regime.

The inclined line is the equation for inflation in (7.6a) with $e' = -e$, repeated below:

$$\pi = (\bar{n} - n^N)/\theta - e'/(1 + \theta) \tag{7.6a'}$$

The idea is that a more favourable supply shock reduces inflation. The intercept in (7.6a') is the pure inflationary bias (i.e. the inflation without any shock), denoted π_0,

$$\pi_0 \equiv (\bar{n} - n^N)/\theta$$

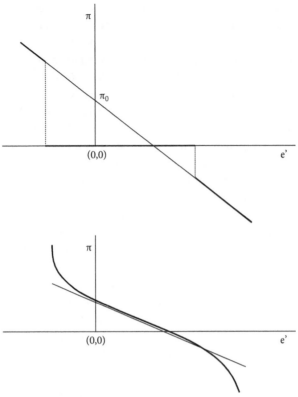

Figure 7.4. (a) Equilibrium inflation with an escape clause; (b) equilibrium inflation with flexible control

Its slope depends negatively on the policy-maker's aversion to inflation (θ); e.g. a policy-maker with little aversion to inflation will wish to stabilize output by incurring the associated inflation cost. It will thus create a steeper line, showing a higher average inflation and a higher variability of it (both intercept and slope actually vary with θ); but less variability for output. The horizontal thick line is the policy rule of a government totally inclined against inflation ($\theta \rightarrow \infty$); implying zero inflation but a lot of output variability. Flood and Isard's (1988) proposal is to let the policy-maker follow normally a policy of zero inflation (thick line), but with an escape clause; if the shock is above a critical size (on either side of 0), the central banker reverts to the rule of the inclined line, allowing some stabilization. Thus, the policy rule in this case is the discontinuous thick segments.

Lohman (1992) generalizes this proposal, by letting the government pick a conservative central banker (with inflation aversion $\theta + \varepsilon$), and letting them follow their normal policy. If, however, big shocks occur and the central banker fails to adequately stabilize them, then the government overrules him/her; for that, they have to apply a fixed cost c (because of the loss of credibility from being seen to intervene, whereas the whole point is to leave monetary management to impartial technocrats; and the central banker will presumably want to avoid the public humiliation of being rebuffed). This results in the policy rule depicted in Figure 7.4b. The thin straight line is the conservative central banker's policy rule, without the posibility of overruling (it is obviously flatter than the policy rule based on government's own preferences, implying less inflation variability). But at shocks of larger sizes, the central banker begins to shift attention increasingly on output stabilization, in order to avoid being overruled by government—and knowing that big losses in employment hurt the government. This arrangement obviously results in more flexibility than even the simple escape clauses described above; it may be described as partial commitment to the conservative central banker, the degree of commitment being captured by c, the cost to government of imposing its will on the central banker.

Lohman (1992) proceeds to endogenize and derive optimal values for ε and c, and shows that this arrangement is better than any other: discretion ($\varepsilon = c = 0$), simple no-inflation rule ($\varepsilon \to \infty, c = 0$), simple escape clause ($\varepsilon \to \infty$ with $0 < c < \infty$), and full commitment to a conservative central banker ($0 < \theta + \varepsilon < 0$ and $c \to \infty$). As an update on the idea of flexibility, Aksoy et al. (2006) evaluate with simulations the effectiveness of an 'opportunistic approach' to disinflation, whereby the policy-maker concentrates on inflation when it is far from its target, but shifts attention to output stabilization when inflation is close to target. They show that this strategy is beneficial in that the cumulative output sacrificed for disinflation is significantly smaller (perhaps one-third) than under a strategy like the inclined straight lines of Figures 7.4a and 7.4b—but disinflation takes longer.

Intuitively, the appeal of the Lohman (1992) proposal over rigid escape clauses (or even tightly specified central bankers' contracts) is that it generates flexibility without having to specify all possible contingencies that monetary policy should respond to, which would be extremely cumbersome. Its appeal against discretion (the situation that gives rise to the inflation bias) is that it allows output considerations only when a supply shock moves the natural rate, not as (short-termist) attempts to reduce unemployment below the natural rate. Such findings should inform the debates around the degree of flexibility of inflation targeting.

7.6.3 Inflation Forecasts and Forward Guidance

The proposition that inflation could or should only reach its target in the medium run but with reasonable deviation in the short run entails some tricky technical considerations. How is the private sector going to be convinced that inflation is on a path that converges to the target in reasonable time? For this reason, it has been suggested, notably by Svensson (1997, 1999; see also Woodford, 2007) that the Central Bank should publish its forecasts of inflation and show that those converge to the target, an idea called 'inflation forecast targeting'. These forecasts should of course be internally consistent, i.e. they should be based on the same model(s) of the economy that the CB uses in its assessments of the macroeconomy, and they should presuppose the same path of interest rates as the CB anticipates following in the near future; in other words, these forecasts should encapsulate all the information that the CB has at the moment it publishes them.

The benefits of such targeting inflation (forecasts) in the medium run is dual. It first allows short-run deviations of inflation from its medium-run target without jeopardizing the CB's credibility, i.e. its ability and willingness to deliver the target in the medium run. Second, it provides valuable information to the private sector about monetary conditions in the medium run, which should inform longer term business decisions (investment, financial structure of firms). Such 'forward guidance' has been embedded into the Bank of England's practice since late 2013; see Miles (2014). Moreover, by announcing medium-run paths of interest rates, the Central Bank influences long-term interest rates, which may be more relevant for borrowing and investment decisions.

The difficulty with such forward guidance is that it should provide information to the private sector that is both truthful and also aids the attainment of the primary target (Woodford, 2013). Consider this scenario: in the middle of a recession, the CB publishes forecasts that say that interest rates need to remain low for some more quarters yet; what conclusions will the private sector get from this? That the recovery is some way off yet; this however will create or enhance the negative psychology and work against the efforts of recovery. The CB, instead, needs to find a way to put the message across to the private sector that 'we are actively working towards a recovery'. This would put a wholly different interpretation on the same situation, creating a positive psychology that will help recovery.

7.6.4 Nominal Income (Growth) Targeting

A proposal floated in the mid-1990s was to target the growth rate of nominal income (GDP), rather than the inflation rate (Hall and Mankiw, 1994; McCallum, 1999; Committee on International Economic Policy and Reform, 2011). Let us recall that nominal GDP may be thought of as $P \times Y$, the price level times real GDP; the nominal income growth rate is $\pi + g$, where g is real output growth. So, the Central Bank could have this target:

$$\text{growth rate of nominal GDP} = \pi + g = k$$

where k (%) would be the target (perhaps with a permissible band around it such as $\pm 1\%$). More generally, the target could be:

$$\gamma\pi + (1 - \gamma)g = k$$

The parameter $0.5 < \gamma \leq 1$ determines the weight placed on inflation relative to real output growth; so, inflation targeting is the special case of $\gamma = 1$. Obviously, this target would give more emphasis to output than otherwise. It would be particularly useful when adverse supply shocks hit the economy: consider, as before, an adverse supply shock of e', with π and g being the pre-shock outcomes; without policy intervention, the shock raises inflation to $\pi + e'$ and reduces output growth to $g - e'$ (say). (Recall, because of the supply shock, inflation and output growth move in opposite directions.) Therefore, the outcome in relation to target becomes:

$$\gamma(\pi + e') + (1 - \gamma)(g - e') = \gamma\pi + (1 - \gamma)g + (2\gamma - 1)e' > k$$

This quantity is less affected by the shock (e') when $\gamma < 1$ (nominal income targeting) than under inflation targeting ($\gamma = 1$) (note that $2\gamma - 1 > 0$). The (modified) nominal income quantity $\gamma\pi + (1 - \gamma)g$ is more stable than inflation on its own, when a supply shock hits. Therefore, targeting nominal income growth would require a smaller interest rate rise than the inflation target, and this would cushion the effect of the adverse supply shock on output and (un)employment.

But this proposal has never been implemented. One problem is that statistics on real GDP are produced with a delay and are frequently revised—typically, they are finalized after a few quarters—therefore they are not available in a timely fashion. More generally, this target may be more difficult to explain to the public. However, the theoretical literature has examined favourably this proposal; see for instance McCallum and Nelson (2010), Woodford (2001, 2013b).

7.7 Monetary Policy-Making in Practice: Taylor Rules

Taylor (1993, 1999) has proposed that the monetary policy of a typical Central Bank is well described by the following interest rate 'policy function':

$$i_t = i^* + a(\pi_t - \pi^*) + \beta(y_t - y^*_t), \quad a, \beta > 0 \tag{7.9}$$

i_t is the nominal interest rate that the Central Bank sets, π_t is as usual the inflation rate and y_t is log real GDP (measured as a deviation from its potential output y^*_t, so it is de-trended output, see Chapter 6). π^* is an inflation target,[25] i^* is a nominal interest rate long-run reference value, and a, β are the sensitivities by which the instrument of policy (interest rate) should be adjusted from its long-run value in order to choke off inflationary pressures (a) and output pressures (β). The rationale is that the nominal interest rate affects aggregate demand adversely, thus reducing output and, gradually, inflation. Thus, both inflationary pressures and output pressures call in principle for an interest rate rise. It should be emphasized from the outset that the Taylor rule is a simple theory of how Central Banks decide policy in practice; but it is not part of any Central Bank's institutional setup and no Central Bank ever admits following a rule like (7.9) explicitly.

Recall the Fisher equation, linking nominal and real interest rates, which in a simplified form is $i_t \approx r_t + \pi_t$. The nominal interest rate (rate of return on nominally denominated assets) is roughly equal to the real rate of return (real interest rate, r) which affects the decisions to spend, save, and invest, plus the loss of purchasing power from inflation. This introduces two restrictions: first, the reference value for the nominal interest rate should be consistent with a long-run real interest rate r* and the central bank's own inflation target, schematically:

$$i^* = r^* + \pi^*$$

Secondly, on the value of a: since it is the real interest rate that really 'bites' for the consumption, investment and other decisions, when inflation rises, the nominal interest rate ought to rise by more, so as to deliver a rise in the real rate. So, the restriction $a > 1$ must be placed on the reaction to inflation. If, instead, we had $a < 1$, the real rate would actually fall after a rise in the nominal rate, increasing aggregate demand, and further increasing inflation; hence, the possibility emerges that inflation spirals upwards (or downwards) out of control. The condition $a > 1$, that interest rates react to inflation sufficiently vigorously, averts this possibility.[26]

---

[25] It is a moot point whether the inflation 'target' (π^*) associated with the Taylor rule is the same as the target rate in inflation targeting (see Svensson, 1999). More generally, an operational interest rule of the Taylor kind is quite compatible with inflation targeting as an institutional regime.

[26] This question of instability is related to another issue, that interest rate-based monetary policy fails to pin down a unique price level (the 'price level indeterminacy' problem), going back to the New Classicals of the 1970s. The idea here is this: if we imagine a simple money demand function $M/P = f(i)$, then a given interest rate i will only fix the ratio M/P, but is not enough to determine the level of either M or P. If for example the function f(i) tells us that $M/P = 2$, that could be accomplished by M = 10, P = 5; or M = 100, P = 50, and so on. Thus, the

Taylor (1993, 1999) argues that values of $i^* = 0.04$, $\alpha = 1.5$, $\beta = 0.5$, and a target $\pi^* = 0.02$ describe quite well the US monetary policy of the last 30 or so years, including the 1990s which have been unusually successful in delivering growth without inflationary pressures. Judd and Rudebusch (1998), in their own description of US monetary policy, generalize the above to incorporate interest rate inertia via the parameter $0 < \rho < 1$:

$$i_t = r^*_t + \pi^* + \rho(i_{t-1} - i^*_{t-1}) + a(\pi_t - \pi^*) + \beta(y_t - y^*_t - \bar{y}), \quad 0 < \rho < 1 \qquad (7.9')$$

Because policy-makers do not want to disrupt financial markets greatly, they may inject a degree of smoothness into their reactions, and this is achieved by letting current interest rates depend partially on past ones (partial persistence of i_t, see the discussion on unemployment persistence). (The other innovation in the Judd-Rudebusch estimated equation is the allowance for a time-varying 'natural real interest rate', 'r^*', the real rate that brings equality of saving and investment.) This induces a degree of gradualism and inertia of policy, at the cost of achieving less stabilization of output and inflation. On the merits of policy inertia, see Woodford (2001); one argument is that the effects of policy depend partially on private sector expectations about future policy itself (recall the forward-looking inflation equation in Chapter 3), and policy inertia helps stabilize those expectations. With post-1980 US data, Clarida et al. (1999, table 1) update the estimates for the Taylor rule to $\alpha = 2.15$, $\beta = 0.93$ but insignificant, and $\rho = 0.79$. The notable features are a big increase in anti-inflation activism (a rise in α) from the pre-1980 period, and a very considerable degree of interest rate inertia and persistence in both (pre- and post-1980) periods.

On the issue of the persistence (coefficient of lagged i) in Taylor rules, Clarida et al. (1999) find 0.79 (table 1). Judd and Rudebusch (1998) find about 0.72–0.75 for the (early) Greenspan period (1987–97), 0.45–0.55 for the Volcker period (1979–87), and 0.4–0.5 for the Burns period (1970–8). Interestingly, the earlier the period, the less was the persistence. Table 7.2 draws on Woodford (2003) in presenting a partial summary of this literature:

Table 7.2. Alternative estimates of US Fed reaction functions (Taylor rules)

	ϕ_π	(s.e.)	ϕ_x	(s.e.)	γ	$\rho1$	(s.e)	$\rho2$	(s.e.)
Taylor (1999c)									
1960–1979	0.81	(.06)	0.25	(.05)					
1987–1997	1.53	(.16)	0.77	(.09)					
Judd-Rudebusch (1998)									
1979–1987	1.46	(.26)	1.53	(.80)	1	0.56	(.12)		
1987–1997	1.54	(.18)	0.99	(.13)	0	0.72	(.05)	0.43	(.10)
Clarida et al. (2000)									
1960–1979	0.83	(.07)	0.27	(.08)		0.68	(.05)	*	
1979–1996	2.15	(.40)	0.93	(.42)		0.79	(.04)	*	
Orphanides (2003)									
1966–1979	1.49	(.38)	0.46	(.13)		0.68	(.07)	0.26	(.14)
1979–1995	1.89	(.64)	0.18	(20)		0.77	(.10)	0.08	(.19)

Source: Woodford (2003, Table 1.1) Asterisks indicated values not reported in the original sources (but not constrained to be zero).

nominal price level P is not pinned down (nor is any other nominal value). See Schmitt-Grohe and Uribe (2000) and Woodford (2001) for further discussion.

The rationale for wanting to stabilize inflation is in order to minimize the distortions in real prices associated with inflation.[27] But why set a $\pi^* = 2\%$ as estimates of (7.9') seem to suggest and not any other inflation target? The question is linked to the question of the optimal rate of inflation, discussed in Chapter 3 (Section 3.8.3). As we saw there, one good argument for suggesting a positive inflation rate ($\pi^* > 0$) is that the Consumer Price Index overstates the true cost of living, primarily because it fails to take into account the quality and technological change in goods; so if we set $\pi^* = 0$, the true inflation rate would be negative. Furthermore, the possibility of more rigidity in nominal wages downwards than upwards requires some inflation as a natural 'lubricant', allowing real wages to fall when necessary (an argument that Keynes put forward; see also Akerlof et al., 1996).[28] Finally, nominal interest rates cannot fall below the floor of zero; this implies a natural downwards limit to the effectiveness of monetary policy. Since the key variable, the real interest rate, can be expressed as $r = i - \pi$, with a target $\pi^* > 0$, it can fall below zero if so required. Instead, with $\pi^* = 0$, $r \geq 0$ as $i \geq 0$, too. In other words, a target of $\pi^* > 0$ gives monetary policy a much-needed margin to help in times of recessions (Summers, 1991).

Any estimated Taylor rule in any form is a positive statement, a description of what has actually been happening. The value of this rule as a normative proposal (i.e. a suggestion of what *should* be happening) is less obvious, and has given rise to some debate. In other words the question is, is the Taylor rule consistent with the idea that the policy-maker minimizes a loss function such as (7.3) subject to the structure of the economic system? Woodford (2001) tackles this question; he concludes that, with a sufficient degree of interest rate inertia, a Taylor rule is optimal in the sense that it can be quite consistent with theoretical priors, and that it is quite robust to uncertainty about the true model of the economy and the nature of shocks. To this, one could add the simulation results of Taylor himself, showing the superiority of this rule over other types of monetary policy, and the favourable simulation results of Jensen's (2002) study of monetary policy rules. So, a simple and robust policy rule—the verdict may be in favour of Taylor rules—which can also be accommodated within a broader policy framework like inflation targeting. The only reservation is that it may not be flexible enough to allow switching emphasis to output stabilization when inflation is under control but there is a recession (in the spirit of the escape clauses and in the light of the experience of 2007–9 discussed above).

With their last gasp of breadth, the reader is now invited to follow a couple of points more specifically on the UK experience of inflation. Following the procedures of Svensson (1997) and Ball (1999), Bean (1998) estimates an efficient frontier of inflation versus output variability (note, it is not a trade-off in levels). His results may be tabulated as in Table 7.3.

θ is the weight on inflation in the loss function (7.3); recall that in the presence of supply shocks, a rising θ implies less variance for inflation and more variance for output (cf. 6a, b). $Std(\pi)$ and $Std(y)$ are the standard deviations of inflation and output, and α, β the Taylor rule coefficients (on inflation and the output gap, respectively) required in order for (7.3) to be minimized. The notable features are that the variability of inflation is not very sensitive to θ except in very low values (so that perhaps not much is lost by switching emphasis to

---

[27] Inflation forces firms to adjust periodically their nominal prices. As discussed in Chapter 3, because of infrequent price adjustment, only a minority of firms will be changing price at any single time, and the *real* price of those firms will at that point be changing.

[28] But Smith (2000) finds little nominal inertia in UK wages, undermining the validity of this argument for Britain, at least.

Table 7.3. Estimated inflation-output variability trade-offs, UK 1950–97

θ	Std(π)	Std(y)	α	β
∞ (pure inflation targeting)	3	3.5	3.4	4
3	3	2.8	2.1	3.25
1	3.1	2.4	1.5	2.9
0.33	3.5	2.1	1	2.5
0	11	1.7	0	1.7

Source: Bean (1998, Figures 1 and 3, and associated discussion)

output stabilization when inflation is generally under control) and that inflation targeting calls for greater Taylor rule coefficients on *both* output and inflation than the empirical work has identified (see Table 7.2 and associated discussion). Thus, the estimated Taylor rule coefficients seem to point in practice to a targeting regime that takes some account of an output target as well. More evidence would be beneficial here in drawing firmer conclusions.

7.8 The Financial System, the 'Credit Channel', and the Monetary Policy 'Transmission Mechanism'

7.8.1 The Traditional Money Market Model

The elementary textbook exposition of the traditional money market model begins with an exogenous, Central Bank-controlled M0,[29] which equals the amount of notes and coins in circulation (i.e. outside the CB). M0 is then 'translated' into broad money (like M4 in the UK) via the 'money multiplier'. This works as follows. Assume:

M0 = C(cash held by the public) + R(cash reserves of commercial banks)
M4 = D(deposits) + C

Assume further that both C(ash) and R(eserves) are in some constant relation to deposits; the former is determined by the behaviour of the public and transactions technology (availability of cash dispensers, usage of credit cards, online banking, as well as habits); while the latter is determined by regulation and commercial banks' experience of what is safe practice:

$$C = c\,D \quad \text{and} \quad R = b\,D, \quad 0 < c, b < 1$$

The fraction b, in particular, depends on the modern practice of 'fractional reserve banking'. Commercial banks keep only a fraction of their deposits in hard cash form (or, what is the same, as a reserve at the CB, immediately withdrawable on demand). The

---

[29] Alternative names are monetary base, high-powered money (often denoted H), outside money, and Central Bank money. There are subtle differences between these terms, which may vary from country to country. Thankfully, the differences in detail do not matter here (and in many other contexts). Practically, all definitions mean the amount of notes and coins in circulation in the economy.

fraction c depends on the public's behaviour, but that is not fundamental for our analysis. Then, the money multiplier is defined as:

$$mm \equiv M4/M0 = (D + cD)/(cD + bD) = (1 + c)/(c + b) > 1 \qquad (7.10)$$

Obviously, $mm > 1$ due to the fact that $b < 1$. This reflects the important fact that deposits are a multiple of deposits. To gain an idea of magnitudes, in the UK, the ratio M4/M0 is of the order of 8, while in the US the ratio M2/MB(ase) is around 3.

The final ingredient of the elementary model is a money demand function for broad money (again, assumed to be M4) with the usual determinants:

$$M4/P = M^d(Y, i)$$

Demand for real money balances is affected by real output (Y) positively as Y raises the need to cover transactions, while the nominal interest rate (i) represents the opportunity cost of holding money (foregoing the interest available to other financial instruments such as bonds) and therefore affects demand negatively. On the left side, we have the supply of broad money in real terms (nominal divided by the price level).

Summing up, money market clearing requires:

$$M0 \times mm/P = M4/P = M^d(Y, i)$$

This equation may be re-expressed as the traditional LM curve:

$$i = LM(Y; M0/P, mm)$$

In terms of policy, when the CB raises (reduces) M0, this reduces (raises) the interest rate, given Y. The elementary macroeconomic model is complemented by an IS curve of the form $Y = IS(i; G, T)$, where G is government spending and T taxes. Putting everything together, a monetary expansion (policy-induced rise in M0) results in an expansion in aggregate demand (Y). Note that the (only) channel by which monetary policy works here is to change the interest rate, investment, and thereby aggregate demand.

One final observation about the basic model: the flip side of deposits held by the public at commercial banks is L(oans) made by the banks to the public; this is how the available liquidity is channelled into the private sector. (The banks' balance sheets, Assets = Liabilities, require that $R + L = D$ in simplified form.) Therefore, the total amount of loans is:

$$L = D - R = D(1 - b),$$

and the loan-deposit ratio is:

$$L/D = 1 - b \equiv \delta$$

This is the amount of credit (loans) generated by the banking system as a constant fraction of deposits.

Modern practices and the very considerable development of the banking/financial system over recent decades have called into question various aspects of this elementary model. First, monetary policy operates directly via the interest rate, rather than influencing it indirectly via the money supply. Secondly, there is more than one interest rate and different ones apply to different instruments; the CB changes the policy rate (the 'base rate' in the UK) and this filters through to the other interest rates. Thirdly, it is now rather generally accepted that the main way by which monetary policy affects the economy is not via the interest rate and the cost of capital and investment; instead, it is the availability of credit. In the modern banking and financial systems, which have expanded enormously in recent decades, the loans are not a fixed multiple of the monetary base. Rather, banks and other financial institutions provide credit whenever that is profitable, considering the demand for loans, the interest rate, as well as the availability of liquidity (reserves) emphasized by the elementary model. In other words, the amount of credit and the broad money supply are both endogenous (not fixed multiples of the monetary base) and determined to a significant degree by the structure and workings of the banking/financial system. To a large extent, monetary policy works by affecting the provision of credit; this is the 'credit channel' of monetary policy. The rest of this section explains the key features of the 'credit channel' and the modifications it brings to the elementary model.

Schematically, the elementary traditional model works as follows:

$$IS : \quad \text{Investment} = \text{Saving} \rightarrow Y = IS(r; G, T)$$

where G and T are government spending and taxes.

$$LM : \quad \text{Broad } M^S = \text{Broad } M^D \quad \rightarrow M0 \times mm/P = M^D(Y, r) \rightarrow r = LM(Y; M0/P, mm)$$

Instead, the model we build below is based on the Central Bank-set 'base rate' (r^{CB}) as the exogenous policy instrument and treats money supply (M0) as endogenous—set at just about the level as to support the chosen policy rate (r^{CB})—so that M0 becomes unimportant.[30] The policy rate is determined by the Taylor rule discussed above. Schematically, the model works as follows:

$$M(\text{odified})IS : \quad Y = IS(r; G, T) \text{ with } r = CC(r^{CB}) \rightarrow Y = MIS(r^{CB}; G, T)$$

where 'CC' stands for the 'credit channel' that translates the policy interest rate (r^{CB}) into a market saving rate (r) (and implicitly a borrowing rate, R); and

$$\text{Taylor Rule}: \quad r^{CB} = TR(Y; \pi)$$

where π is the inflation rate.

---

[30] In this section, we ignore the distinction between nominal and real interest rates; 'r' will denote an interest rate. More broadly, there is no inflation, so all quantities are real.

7.8.2 Further Criticisms of the Traditional Model

In the economy there are three types of markets: goods, money, and credit markets. In traditional analyses (IS-LM), the credit market was assumed homogeneous (all forms of loans, including bonds, were considered perfect substitutes among themselves and with bank loans; correspondingly, all types of asset were perfect substitutes for investors). This logic echoes that of Modigliani and Miller (1958) who argued that the exact structure of the financial system is irrelevant for either borrowers or lenders; see also Fama (1980) specifically on banks. Furthermore, the interest rate (a price variable) moves to clear the credit and money markets. Walras's Law says that if there are n markets in the economy and $n - 1$ of them clear, then this implies that the nth also clears. So, if the goods and money market, so will the credit market. Thus, the credit market was dropped by the IS-LM-credit model and there remained no trace of it in the elementary model. The implication of this analysis is that only money matters among the financial quantity variables, and that its effects are transmitted to the economy only via 'the' interest rate and its effects on investment; the quantity of credit available in the economy is irrelevant.

There are now good reasons to think this type of approach is seriously inadequate. The events surrounding the 'sub-prime' and liquidity crisis of 2007–8 are the obvious practical reason. On the theoretical front, the fundamental reason is that borrowing and lending do not occur in perfectly informed, competitive financial markets. Financial markets are immensely, and increasingly, complex and sophisticated. Lending and borrowing do not occur directly between (ultimate) borrowers and lenders, but it is 'intermediated' by financial institutions who lend to (ultimate) borrowers and borrow from (ultimate) lenders, but also lend to one another. These financial intermediaries often possess significant market power. In addition, there is the issue of asymmetric information that potentially plagues all types of financial transactions: the lender has less information about the chances of success, or bankruptcy, of the borrower, whether this is the ultimate borrower, or the intermediary that borrows in order to lend further down the line. Taking these features on board leads to the conclusion that it is not only one interest rate that matters, but a whole range of them; that other financial market-related quantity variables such as the availability of credit, the quality of firms' balance sheets, and cash flows also matter; and that the financial structure affects the transmission of monetary policy and amplifies its effects over the business cycles. Even broader implications may include such diverse phenomena as more pronounced business cycle dynamics, wealth inequalities, and international development traps (see Matsuyama, 2007).

A voluminous literature has sprung up in the last 25 years examining these ideas and their macroeconomic effects; this is still an active area of research. Though (or because) there is a lot 'out there', the essentials of this literature have not crystallized into a benchmark model as yet, and perhaps as a result, have not found their way into textbook treatments. The aim of this section is to review the basic ideas from this literature. In this, we are guided by the surveys of Bernanke and Gertler (1995), Hubbard (1995), Matsuyama (2007), and Woodford (2010).[31]

---

[31] A precursor literature emphasized some similar ideas based on the notion that the market for credit does not clear, and there is generally an excess demand for credit ('credit rationing') for essentially similar reasons (see e.g. Stiglitz and Weiss, 1981; Blanchard and Fischer, 1989, chapter 9). If so, the availability of credit matters quite

From the literature on asymmetric information (Akerlof, 1970) and agency problems between borrowers and lenders (Diamond, 1984), it is well known that asymmetric information induces two types of problem: moral hazard—as the risky project is partly financed by someone else except its owner, the owner has an incentive to become less risk-averse and undertake riskier projects than if they financed them entirely themselves—and adverse selection—as the interest rate rises, more risk-averse investors prefer to finance the projects by their own means if they possibly can, rather than effectively subsidize the less risk averse by paying a high borrowing rate.

The result of both these problems is that a higher interest rate may imply a lower return on a project (because the risk of bankruptcy increases and the pool of projects that apply for finance is riskier). To counter these difficulties, lenders may require investors to commit part of their own funds in financing the project, may require monitoring the project (which incurs a monitoring or 'state verification' cost, Townsend, 1979), and may be able to charge a monopoly premium for their services. These are the starting points of our analysis.

7.8.3 A Basic Framework of Bank Intermediation, the 'External Finance Premium', and the 'Financial Accelerator'

Consider all the investment projects that require a unit of real resources; due to indivisibilities, the projects cannot be broken down to finer portions. There is a distribution of returns (marginal product of capital, MPK) from these projects; we can indicate this distribution as $I = I(MPK_0)$, where I is the amount of potential projects with $MPK \geq MPK_0$. All those projects whose marginal products are higher or equal to the opportunity cost of investment, i.e. the rate of interest (r), so $MPK \geq r$, will be undertaken.[32] This implies that the total amount of unit-projects that are undertaken is a negative function of the interest rate, $I = I(r)$, with $I'(r) < 0$. The elementary model is closed by the I(nvestment)-S(aving) equality (ignoring government spending and the external sector):

$$S(r, Y) = I(r) \qquad (7.11)$$

$S(r,Y)$ is the saving function, with the usual properties, $\partial S/\partial r > 0$, $\partial S/\partial Y > 0$.[33] (7.11) assumes that the borrowing and lending rate are equal (r) and this presumes a perfectly competitive banking system; an assumption to be reviewed below as banks are big and enjoy therefore monopoly power.

---

independently of its price, an idea echoed in much of the literature on the 'credit channel'. But the starting point of the modern literature is that in general markets clear, hence, no widespread credit rationing occurs, yet the structure of financial markets matters. Gertler (1988) reviews why, as well as providing a bridge between the current and precursor literatures.

[32] To reiterate, in this section, there is no distinction between real and nominal quantities.

[33] The assumed property of the saving function $\partial S/\partial r > 0$ rests on plausible assumptions about the consumer's intertemporal maximization problem; see Chapter 11 for more formal analyses. The discerning reader will notice that while *flow* saving and investment depend on the interest rate, the corresponding *stocks*, i.e. (total) lending and borrowing, are assumed not to depend on r in the elementary money multiplier model. This discrepancy is fixed in the model that follows.

Under monopoly power of lenders and wider credit and financial market imperfections, the lending (R) and borrowing (r) rate will diverge, with $R - r > 0$ called the 'spread'. This is how the spread is determined. In order to reduce moral hazard, the lender (bank or other financial intermediary) requires a down-payment of w per unit-project by the borrower; against that, it contributes one unit of resources, on which a rate of return r is required (thus, the project requires $1 + w$ indivisible units of resources). Moreover, the lender charges a fee $0 < c < 1$ per unit of resources for monitoring costs; this is due to asymmetric information which the lender tries to alleviate. Additionally, the lender charges a profit margin equal to $\mu \geq 0$ which is remuneration for the shareholder capital that is tied in it; this is therefore considered as another element of cost. Thus, the bank will commit total resources equal to $1 + \mu + c$ for this project, whose opportunity cost is $(1 + r)(1 + \mu + c)$ one period later. Additionally, the firm must commit resources of its own (w) whose opportunity cost will be $(1 + r)w$. The project (of size $1 + w$) will have an internal rate of return (return after the capital is replaced) equal to IRR; thus, the project will yield $(1 + w)(1 + IRR)$. The project will be undertaken if its rate of return is greater than the opportunity cost of the resources put together by both the bank and the firm itself:

$$(1 + w)(1 + IRR) \geq (1 + r)(1 + \mu + c) + w(1 + r) \qquad (7.12)$$

The marginal project will have a rate of return R such that (7.12) holds with equality; rearranging that, we find this marginal rate of return to be:

$$1 + R = (1 + r)\frac{1 + w + \mu + c}{1 + w} \qquad (7.12')$$

R is therefore the borrowing rate, which the banks will be able to charge such that they recoup all their operational expenses (c) plus the required rate of profit (μ). All projects that have $IRR > R$ will make a ('super-normal') profit while the project(s) for which $IRR = R$ will just about break even; r is the saving rate—the opportunity cost to the lender of acquiring these funds, as this return is available in alternative financial investments (e.g. in bonds). The borrowing rate (R) is a markup over the rate (r). The markup decreases with the extent of down-payment by the borrower/investor (w), but increases with the monitoring cost (c) and the rate of monopoly profit of the typical financial institution (μ). The markup vanishes when there is zero monopoly power and no asymmetric information (evident in monitoring costs) in the financial markets; in that case, the extent of down-payment (w) has no effect, and the borrower is indifferent between financing the project by own means or obtaining external finance. Given non-zero profits and monitoring costs, the extent of the financial intermediary's involvement increases the borrower-lender interest rate wedge. Parameters μ and c therefore can be interpreted as capturing inversely the availability of credit by lenders, *ceteris paribus*: a rise in μ and/or c indicates a credit squeeze by banks. Parameter w is an index of the ability of borrowers to contribute to their projects; more broadly it can signify the ability/willingness of the borrower to provide a collateral as an insurance to the creditor for the funds that are provided.

Another interpretation of the 'spread' of the borrowing-saving rate $(R - r)$ is as an 'external finance' premium, the cost of raising funds externally by borrowing (R) and the cost of financing investment internally by retained profits (the opportunity cost of savings, r). Summarizing this premium (alternatively: spread) is:

$$R - r = (1 + r)\frac{\mu + c}{1 + w} \tag{7.12''}$$

This depends on parameters in an obvious way.

The next building block is credit provision by the banking sector, which determines endogenously the saving interest rate (r). As deposits are a form of saving, the demand for deposits (D) inherits the properties of the saving function (cf. 7.11):

$$D = D(Y, r), \qquad \partial D(.)/\partial Y > 0, \quad \partial D(.)/\partial r > 0, \tag{7.13}$$

Additionally, Loans depend on output and the borrowing rate (inversely):

$$L = L(Y, R), \qquad \partial L(.)/\partial (Y > 0, \quad \partial D(.)/\partial R < 0 \tag{7.14}$$

We also know from the discussion of the multiplier that the loan-deposit ratio equals $L/D = \delta$. Therefore equilibrium requires $L(Y, R) = \delta D(Y, r)$. The situation is depicted in Figure 7.5. The thick lines show L and D (scaled by δD) as functions of the interest rate.[34]

Under perfect financial markets, point A is the equilibrium where there is no R−r spread. Under market imperfections, there is a borrower-lender spread (alternatively, external finance premium) as required by (7.12"), equal to BC, and equilibrium loans

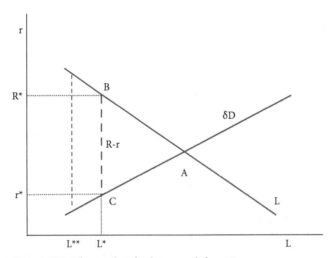

Figure 7.5. The market for loans and deposits

---

[34] It will be noticed that loans and deposits are stock variables, while investment and saving are flows. The two are related by the usual stock-flow relations: $L_t - L_{t-1} = I_t$ and $D_t - D_{t-1} = S_t$. But these relations may not hold under modern banking and financial practices: They will not hold if there are alternative instruments of borrowing and lending, such as bonds. More generally, under modern banking practices, loans and deposits are endogenously determined by the banking system, so that again these stock-flow relationships break down. Hence, they are ignored here.

are L*. It is obvious that the equilibrium loans and deposits are lower the higher the monopoly power and the monitoring costs of banks and the lower ability by the creditor to contribute (lower w); as all these factors require a higher R-r spread. Graphically, a rise in them implies that equilibrium loans fall to L** so that R-r rises. There is also another important consideration to be made, concerning the proportionality term (δ) that arises out of the credit and money multiplier process. A higher δ will shift δD out, resulting in a lower r and higher loans and deposits, *ceteris paribus*. Also, a rising real output (Y) shifts both the deposits and loans out, resulting in a rise of both in equilibrium; the effect on interest rates is ambiguous at this stage and will be discussed more below.

From (7.12' and 7.12"), we also see that both the saving interest rate (r) and the borrowing rate (R) are proportional to the spread (or 'external finance premium', R−r), so when the latter rises, so do the former. Therefore, an intermediate conclusion is that all interest rates and the spread rise (and equilibrium loans and deposits fall) with:

- A 'credit squeeze' due to commercial banks' unwillingness or inability to lend (captured by a rise in c and or μ);
- A fall in firms' financial strength and inability to provide collateral (lower w);
- Additionally, as we shall see below, a number of other factors that affect firms' financial strength (w) will also have a bearing on equilibrium interest rates and deposits/loans.

Associated with the external finance premium are a number of additional mechanisms by which monetary policy affects the real economy, all emphasized by the literature on the 'credit channel'. First, we have assumed that firms are happy to contribute w amount of funds for each project that is funded (or more generally provide collateral). The ability to contribute w, however, may likely vary with the state of the economy: if there is a monetary contraction and the basic interest rate rises, firms may find themselves burdened with higher interest payments, as a result of which their cash flow worsens. This may reduce their ability to contribute own funds (or collateral) to projects (w); this is partly endogenous ($\partial w/\partial r < 0$), but it also is partly exogenous depending on the firms' financial strength. The literature on the credit channel emphasizes the ability of firms to commit funds or provide collateral.

Furthermore, the strength of balance sheets of firms matters (Kiyotaki and Moore, 1997): firms with more liquidity can contribute the required funds and more projects will go ahead. There is also an additional effect via the firm's net worth: a higher interest rate discounts more heavily the firm's future income streams, so that its internal rate of return and the current stock market-based net worth declines. Its ability to provide collateral, which often underpins lending, declines. As a result of all these effects, its borrowing may be seen as riskier by banks and the firm may face a higher cost (premium) for external finance; its ability to get credit may be restricted further. Thus, we have additional channels by which interest rates affect output and the effects of monetary policy are amplified. This is the 'financial accelerator mechanism' (Gertler and Hubbard, 1998; Bernanke et al., 1996), which 'accelerates' the effects of monetary policy on the business cycle.

Analytically, all these effects are also embedded in w, which becomes an inverse index of firms' financial distress; again, partly endogenous (due to the state of the economy) and partly exogenous. Later on, we shall indicate by w_0 the exogenous part of firms' financial strength. Referring to Figure 7.5, and with given L and D schedules, we see that with a stronger financial position (net worth, balance sheets, and liquidity), firms will be able to contribute more (higher w) and the R-r spread and 'external finance premium' fall. Equilibrium loans and deposits rise, the saving rate (r) increases but the borrowing rate (R) falls. In times of distress (low w), the opposite happens.

7.8.4 The Money Multiplier and the Loan-Deposited Ratio Revisited

The next step is to revisit the traditional money multiplier analysis in order to account for the endogenous determination of both broad money and, relatedly, the loan-deposit ratio.[35] In particular, we show the dependence of the market interest rate (r) on the policy interest rate (r^{CB})[36] and the state of the economy. Following Bernanke and Blinder (1988), the fraction of banks' reserves at the CB (b) depends positively on the Central Bank interest rate (r^{CB}), applicable to loans by the Central Bank to commercial banks for very short-term financing:

$$b = b(r^{CB}) \text{ with } \partial b/\partial r^{CB} > 0, \quad 0 < b < 1.$$

Because borrowing short-term from the CB incurs interest at rate r^{CB}, when r^{CB} rises, the commercial banks keep a higher proportion of reserves. Thus, rather than being fixed, both the money multiplier and the loan/deposit ratio now depend on the base rate:

$$mm = (1 + c)/(c + b(r^{CB})) \text{ with } \partial mm/\partial r^{CB} < 0$$

$$L/D = 1 - b(r^{CB}) \equiv \delta(r^{CB}) \text{ with } \partial\delta/\partial r^{CB} < 0$$

Hence, both the money multiplier and the loan-deposit money ratio are endogenous (determined by the behaviour of the banking system) and in particular depend negatively on the interest rate set by the CB.

Furthermore, these ratios may also depend on the state of the economy. Focusing on the loan-deposit ratio in particular, $\delta \equiv L/D$, we may write:

$$L/D = \delta(Y, r^{CB}); \quad 0 < \delta < 1; \quad \partial\delta(.)/\partial Y > 0, \quad \partial\delta(.)/\partial r^{CB} < 0$$

In a good state of the economy, banks may be encouraged to lend on more of their deposits, while in a recession, a greater proportion of their lending may become risky (non-performing loans—loans that are not serviced as the borrowers are in distress) and therefore the banks are more reluctant to lend. The effect of the policy interest rate is inherited from the properties of b(.). Finally, let us recall that δ(.) symbolizes the lending multiplier process (due to 'fractional reserve banking'), whereby any deposits and liquidity are channelled by banks back into the economy in the form of loans/credit, only to come

---

[35] A summary of modern banking practices and their implications for broad money and the provision of loans and deposits by banks is found in McLeay et al. (2014) and Jakab and Kumhof (2015). It is clear from these analyses that the 'money multiplier' is not constant but is considerably affected by the policy and the workings of the financial institutions. This is one of the motivations for this section. Perhaps one should call the multiplier that results the 'flexible money multiplier'.

[36] In the UK, this used to be called the 'Bank Rate'—we read on the Bank of England website (June 2019) that this is no longer the case.

back in the form of deposits and so on and on. This is incorporated in the standard model of the money market; what we are exploring here, let us remember, are the principal reasons why this multiplier is not fixed but depends instead on a number of important macroeconomic and banking structure variables.

Recalling $L/D = \delta(Y, r^{CB})$ and the properties in (7.13, 14, and 12'), the workings of the banking system and credit provision, imply the following relation between loans and deposits:

$$L\left(Y, (1+r)\frac{1+w+\mu+c}{1+w} - 1\right) = \delta(Y, r^{CB})D(Y, r) \tag{7.15}$$

Equation (7.15) summarizes the information we get from Figure 7.5. We can now solve for a saving interest rate as a function of all other variables and parameters; this relation is denoted 'CC'—arising from the credit channel:

$$r = CC\left(Y; r^{CB}; w, \mu, c\right) \tag{7.16}$$

It is instructive to see this more formally; totally differentiating (7.15), we get:

$$dr = \frac{\left(L_Y - L_R\frac{(1+r)(\mu+c)}{(1+w)^2}\frac{\partial w}{\partial Y} - \delta D_Y - \delta_Y D\right)dY - \delta_{r^{CB}}Ddr^{CB} + \frac{L_R(1+r)}{1+w}\left(d\mu + dc - \frac{\mu+c}{1+w}dw_0\right)}{D_r - L_R\frac{1+w+\mu+c}{1+w} + L_R\frac{(1+r)(\mu+c)}{(1+w)^2}\frac{\partial w}{\partial r}}$$

The subscripts indicate partial derivatives. Accordingly, we have the following effects:

$$\partial r/\partial r^{CB} > 0, \tag{7.16a}$$

the saving interest rate increases with the policy interest rate (note $\partial\delta/\partial r^{CB} < 0$);

$$\partial r/\partial x < 0, x = \mu, c, \tag{7.16b}$$

a credit squeeze by banks (higher μ or c) decreases r (note $L_R < 0$);

$$\partial r/\partial w_0 > 0, \tag{7.16c}$$

r increases with the firms' exogenous financial strength;

$$\partial r/\partial Y(>)0; \tag{7.16d}$$

Note that the effect of a rise in output does not have a clear effect on the equilibrium interest rate, as it shifts both the L and D schedules in Figure 7.5 in the same direction. But it is likely that the effect of the state of the economy on interest rates will be positive if anything; so, we put the likely positive sign in parentheses.

The 'financial accelerator' is evident in two terms. In the numerator, we have a term involving $\partial w/\partial Y(>0)$ that increases the ratio on the right; this is due to this sequence:

better state of the economy leads to firms' financial strength (higher w) leads to more demand for loans (L shifts right in Figure 7.5) leads to higher interest rates. Additionally, the numerator shows the effects of policy (r^{CB}) and commercial banks' UNwillingness/INability to provide credit (higher c, μ) and firms' exogenous financial strength (w_0). In the denominator, the fact that $\partial w/\partial r (< 0$—this is the detrimental effect of interest rates on the firms' financial position) works to increase the denominator; this is due to the sequence: a higher interest rate harms firms' financial strength (lower w) so causes the spread to rise and loans to fall, leading to a lower interest rate. So, this effect works to dampen the others. This shows that the 'credit channel' works in rather complicated ways.

Inspection of Figure 7.5 also suggests the following effects on the borrowing interest rate (formal proofs are left to the reader as an exercise):

$$\partial R/\partial r^{CB} > 0; \tag{7.17a}$$

$$\partial R/\partial x > 0, x = \mu, c; \tag{7.17b}$$

$$\partial R/\partial w_0 < 0; \tag{7.17c}$$

$$\partial R/\partial Y > 0. \tag{7.17d}$$

Using this information and (7.14), we can then gauge the properties of L(oans):

$$\partial L/\partial r^{CB} < 0; \tag{7.18a}$$

$$\partial L/\partial x < 0, x = \mu, c; \tag{7.18b}$$

$$\partial L/\partial w_0 > 0; \tag{7.18c}$$

$$\partial L/\partial Y > 0. \tag{7.18d}$$

Properties (a–c) are inherited from $L_R < 0$ and (7.17a–c); the sign in (7.18d) is at first sight ambiguous, but can be gauged safely by looking at the effect of Y on the right hand-side of (7.15).

7.8.5 Further Considerations: Commercial Banks' Capital and Leveraging; Bank Runs, the 'Flight to Quality', and Financial Market Psychology

A newer generation of models has explored in richer detail the institutional features of modern financial intermediation, in particular those factors that affect banks' willingness to provide credit. One such consideration is commercial banks' capital. When banks are better equipped with capital, they need to hold less reserves per pound of deposits (as they can always draw on other assets, e.g. property, to provide themselves with liquidity). In a downturn, banks' capital may decline (for instance, because some borrowers become insolvent and some loans may not be repaid), and this may lead to a rise in the required reserves. If so, the loan provision declines.[37] Conversely, in good times, bank capital is set to rise (a smaller proportion of loans fail, asset and property prices rise), therefore the financial sector may be willing to expand credit. Therefore, we may consider the bank capital-deposit ratio (bc) as a positive determinant of the loan-deposit ratio (δ).

The degree of 'leveraging' (borrowing) by banks played an important role in the financial crisis of 2007–8. As banks became suspicious of each other's liquidity and financial health and even viability, they stopped lending to each other and to the rest of the private sector (a 'credit crunch'); as a result, lending declined, spreads rose, and output took a hit. This is thought to be one of the key steps, if not originators, of the financial crisis of 2007–8. Hence, the extent of leveraging of the wider financial system affects negatively the provision of credit. Thus, the debt-deposit ratio ('leverage') is another, negative, determinant of the loan-deposit ratio (δ).

As discussed in Chapter 6, the financial innovations of the 1980s and 1990s in most of the industrialized world allow banks to draw funds from other sources than simply deposits (see Woodford, 2010). One such method may be borrowing in wholesale money markets. But such borrowing can be risky in the sense that the borrowing is short-term while the assets (loans) are long-term; if the proceeds (interest) from loans are insufficient to cover the interest on short-term borrowing, then a liquidity crisis can engulf the bank, which can be very dangerous. It is widely thought that the non-traditional forms of bank intermediation played an important role in generating and deepening the financial crisis of 2007–9. An example of where non-traditional intermediation can go wrong is the 'bank run' that the UK bank Northern Rock suffered in September 2007. As the hard cash that banks hold is very small in relation to their deposits, a bankruptcy would mean that most depositors lose their deposits. The rational strategy for any depositor is to rush to cash their deposits; and rush to be first, as only the first ones will manage to do so. No bank can cash in all deposits (no matter how financially healthy), and so it goes bankrupt. Thus, any suspicion about any bank's financial health gives rise to a 'bank run' due to the 'flight to quality' of deposits (as cash is safer, hence of higher 'quality', see Hubbard, 1995). As mentioned, this would bring any bank down, causing a decline in the provision of credit not only by this bank but also other banks which had lent to the failed bank. As bank failures are extremely disruptive, not to say dangerous for the entire financial system, the state often steps in and bails out the failed bank with taxpayers' money. Friedman and Swartz (1963) have argued that bank runs and reductions in the money multiplier because of fear about banks' viability precipitated and deepened the Great Depression.

Obviously, bank runs must be avoided at all costs. For this, the financial system must be in good health and must also be seen to be so. Health of financial institutions implies safe practices in terms of reserve ratios, limited leveraging and adequate bank capital, banks meeting certain 'stress tests', provisions that collectively come under the rubric of 'macro-prudential regulation' (elaborated below). The other factor is psychology, investor feelings

---

[37] The requirement that the value of the financial institution's assets should be worth more than a certain fraction of its debt even in the worst-case scenario is called the 'value-at-risk constraint'. The importance of banking capital was highlighted during the financial crisis of 2007/8, which has led to proposals about enhanced regulatory provisions (see later in the chapter on 'macroprudential regulation').

and fear, as even a healthy bank that is seen as risky can be in trouble. For this reason, it is important for policy and the regulatory framework to reassure market participants; as said, the system must also be seen to be healthy. Thus, macroprudential regulation and the various stress tests are publicly visible. Psychology is to a large extent endogenous (psychology is good in a robust financial system, mistrust prevails in a system fraught with risks) but it can play an exogenous role in marginal situations (mood swings can be important in uncertain times).

All these considerations lead us to incorporate the following additional elements into the loan-deposit multiplier (δ):

$$\delta = \delta(Y, r^{CB}; bc, lev, psy); \quad \partial\delta/\partial bc > 0, \quad \partial\delta/\partial lev < 0, \quad \partial\delta/\partial psy > 0$$

where:

- bc: The bank capital-deposit ratio;
- lev: The bank debt-deposit ratio ('leveraging');
- psy: An index of investor psychology and trust in the financial system.

Noting that a rise in δ will shift the δD schedule right in Figure 7.5, we get the following additional effects on interest rates and loans:

$$\partial r/\partial bc < 0; \tag{7.16e}$$

$$\partial r/\partial lev > 0; \tag{7.16f}$$

$$\partial r/\partial psy < 0; \tag{7.16g}$$

and

$$\partial R/\partial bc < 0; \tag{7.17e}$$

$$\partial R/\partial lev > 0; \tag{7.17f}$$

$$\partial R/\partial psy < 0. \tag{7.17g}$$

and

$$\partial L/\partial bc > 0; \tag{7.18e}$$

$$\partial L/\partial lev < 0; \tag{7.18f}$$

$$\partial L/\partial psy > 0. \tag{7.18g}$$

By increasing the loan-deposit ratio, both a higher bank capital ratio and stronger psychology and optimism reduce interest rates (as less deposits need to be raised per unit of loan) while more leverage by banks raises interest rates (effectively, more exposure of banks to debt generates a risk premium). The effects on equilibrium loans are the opposite.

7.8.6 The Modified IS Curve (MIS)

We now revisit the investment-saving relation (7.8.3). Recall that the I(nvestment)-S (aving) equality is another way of expressing the IS curve. With the borrowing rate R, a number $I(R)$ of projects will be profitable. The foregoing analysis of financial intermediation and the 'credit channel' suggests that the availability of loans is a determinant of investment; therefore we should write: $I = I(R, L)$, with $I_L > 0$. Allowing for output to also affect investment, equilibrium requires that:

$$I(R, L, Y) = S(r, Y) \tag{7.11'}$$

Totally differentiating, we get:

$$
dY = \frac{\left(I_R \dfrac{\partial R}{\partial r^{CB}} + I_L \dfrac{\partial L}{\partial r^{CB}} - S_r \dfrac{\partial r}{\partial r^{CB}}\right) dr^{CB} + \left(I_R \dfrac{\partial R}{\partial(\mu+c)} + I_L \dfrac{\partial L}{\partial(\mu+c)} - S_r \dfrac{\partial r}{\partial(\mu+c)}\right) d(\mu+c)}{S_Y - I_Y} +
$$

$$
+ \frac{\left(I_R \dfrac{\partial R}{\partial w_0} + I_L \dfrac{\partial L}{\partial w_0} - S_r \dfrac{\partial r}{\partial w_0}\right) dw_0 + \left(I_R \dfrac{\partial R}{\partial bc} + I_L \dfrac{\partial L}{\partial bc} - S_r \dfrac{\partial r}{\partial bc}\right) dbc}{S_Y - I_Y}
$$

$$
+ \frac{\left(I_R \dfrac{\partial R}{\partial lev} + I_L \dfrac{\partial L}{\partial lev} - S_r \dfrac{\partial r}{\partial lev}\right) dlev + \left(I_R \dfrac{\partial R}{\partial psy} + I_L \dfrac{\partial L}{\partial psy} - S_r \dfrac{\partial r}{\partial psy}\right) dpsy}{S_Y - I_Y}
$$

This may be more compactly written as a M(odified)IS curve:[38]

$$Y = \mathrm{MIS}(r^{CB}; \mu, c, w, bc, lev, psy) \tag{7.19}$$

Noting that in the real data $S_Y - I_Y > 0$ and that $S_r > 0$, $I_R < 0$, and $I_L > 0$, and using the information in (7.16a–f), (7.17a–f), and (7.18a–f), we get the following results:

$$\partial \mathrm{MIS}/\partial r^{CB} < 0, \tag{7.19a}$$

$$\partial \mathrm{MIS}/\partial bc > 0, \tag{7.19b}$$

$$\partial \mathrm{MIS}/\partial lev < 0, \tag{7.19c}$$

$$\partial \mathrm{MIS}/\partial psy > 0. \tag{7.19d}$$

---

[38] This type of IS echoes the analysis of Bernanke and Blinder (1988).

The policy interest rate hurts the real economy; this result parallels the traditional result of policy except that now it is the policy rate that is exogenous, not the money supply. More bank capital, a *lower* bank leverage, and more optimism/stronger market psychology are expected to raise output through the channels we discussed above; these effects are innovations and analytical gains from the consideration of the credit channel.

Additionally, we have the following effects that cannot be a priori signed (can you see why?), but are likely to have the following signs in practice:

$$\partial MIS/\partial \mu < 0, \tag{7.19e}$$

$$\partial MIS/\partial c < 0, \tag{7.19f}$$

$$\partial MIS/\partial w_0 > 0. \tag{7.19g}$$

A greater unwillingness to lend by banks due to a higher monopoly power and/or monitoring costs, exemplified in higher μ and c, hurts output as less loans are provided. In contrast, a stronger financial position by firms (w_0) helps output, as this enables more investment projects to go ahead for various reasons, including the ability to put down collateral.

7.8.7 The Credit Channel and Monetary Policy: The IS-MP Framework

The next question is how monetary policy can be modelled in light of all these considerations. One key point is that these days monetary authorities set (or target) some interest rate, rather than a monetary aggregate; the main reason being that the link between wide monetary aggregates and GDP is not a stable one (see B. Friedman, 1988). Relatedly, as we have mentioned, at the heart of the traditional model is a fixed money multiplier that 'reliably' translates the monetary base into broad money. One key feature of the 'credit channel' is that this multiplier is anything but fixed. So, the traditional mechanism:

CB sets M0 → M0 affects M4 via a stable mm → M4 affects Y via the i.r.

becomes uncertain and unreliable in every step. For this reason, Central Banks have largely abandoned the practice of setting the monetary base and set an interest rate (r^{CB}) in order to affect output more directly and reliably; this is the policy instrument. The money supply is endogenous. The monetary authority simply needs to provide as much narrow money as will be demanded at the going interest rate; they cannot deviate from that otherwise the interest rate they have chosen will not be sustainable in the markets.[39] This invalidates much of the standard IS-LM analysis in which the money supply is the exogenous policy

---

[39] See Clews et al. (2010) on how liquidity is provided by the Bank of England in order to support the chosen policy rate. This study highlights the role of the overnight money market (borrowing and lending between commercial banks) in the provision of short-run liquidity.

instrument. Instead, following Romer (2006) and Woodford (2010) we may proceed as follows.

A second consideration relates to the modified IS relation (MIS) in (7.19). This equation relates real GDP (in particular: output demand) in a negative way with the policy real interest rate, r^{CB}; the negative slope comes from (7.19a). Thus, it is similar to the traditional IS curve with two crucial differences: the relevant interest rate is r^{CB} and not r; and the structure and workings of the financial/banking system affect the slope of *and* shift the MIS. From (7.19b–g), in particular, we have the following shifts:

- A right shift is caused by a rise in bank capitalization (bc), stronger psychology and optimism (all else given—psy), and firms' financial health and ability to contribute to projects (w_0);
- A left shift is caused by higher bank leverage (lev) and reluctance of banks' to lend (higher μ or c).

This MIS (7.19) curve is plotted in Figure 7.6 in (r^{CB}, Y) space.

The upward-sloping M(onetary)P(olicy) line summarizes monetary policy; essentially, it is based on the Taylor rule. The 'policy function' is a simple version of (7.9):

$$r^{CB} = MP(Y; \pi), \quad \partial MP(.)/\partial Y > 0, \quad \partial MP(.)/\partial \pi > 0 \tag{7.20}$$

The policy rate, r^{CB}, features here, as this is what is essentially determined by the Taylor rule (7.9); otherwise, the properties of (7.9) and (7.20) are identical, giving a positive slope to the MP line. Another key property is that a rise in inflation raises the interest rate beyond what the level of output justifies, as the monetary authority now needs to tighten policy to fight inflation.[40] A rise in π shifts the MP line to the broken line in Figure 7.6; equilibrium real output (Y) falls, while the policy interest rate (r^{CB}) rises. From (7.16a, d)

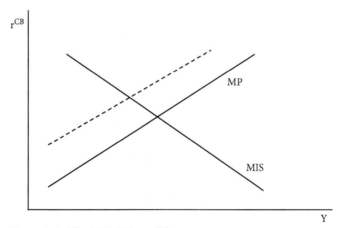

Figure 7.6. The MIS-MP model

---

[40] Recall, that the *real* policy interest rate rises in response to a rise in the inflation rate, π.

and (7.17a, d), we see that both the borrowing (R) and saving (r) rates will follow the policy interest rate upwards.

As the slope of the new MIS and old IS curves are qualitatively the same, so are the slopes of the old LM and the new MP curve, but there is an important difference in interpretation: behind MP there is the Taylor rule, and not a money demand as with the old LM. Another difference is also quite important from a policy point of view. The MP does not shift with a tightening of monetary policy that results from an improvement in the state of the economy (a rise in Y); this change is now endogenous (explained by the Taylor rule) and would be represented by a movement along MP, not a shift. The line shifts only when the monetary stance changes because of a rise in inflation and/or because of any change in the policy regime such as any change in weights on output or inflation in the Taylor rule (i.e. a change in the monetary policy strategy, as opposed to a single action).

7.8.8 A Modified AD-AS Framework

The last step is to obtain the Aggregate Demand curve that incorporates the foregoing analysis—the 'Credit Channel' (CC—i.e. finance and banking structure) and the modern workings of monetary policy (MP):

$$Y = AD^{CC-MP}(\pi; G, t; \mu, c, w, bc, lev, psy), \tag{7.21}$$

G is government spending and -t- the rate of tax. It should be clear from the foregoing discussions that we have the following effects:

$$\partial AD^{CC-MP}/\partial\pi < 0 \text{ (this would give this relation its customary}$$
negative slope in an AD−AS diagram, see below) \hfill (7.21a)

$$\partial AD^{CC-MP}/\partial bc > 0; \tag{7.21b}$$

$$\partial AD^{CC-MP}/\partial lev < 0; \tag{7.21c}$$

$$\partial AD^{CC-MP}/\partial psy > 0; \tag{7.21d}$$

$$\partial AD^{CC-MP}/\partial\mu < 0; \tag{7.21e}$$

$$\partial AD^{CC-MP}/\partial c < 0; \tag{7.21f}$$

$$\partial AD^{CC-MP}/\partial w_0 > 0. \tag{7.21g}$$

Thus, the new AD curve (7.21) shifts because of a number of considerations related to the 'credit channel'.

This curve should be put against a standard Aggregate Supply curve such as:

$$Y = AS(\pi), \quad \partial AS/\partial \pi \geq 0; \tag{7.22}$$

(7.22) would be the analogue of a New-Keynesian Phillips Curve discussed in Chapter 3. We leave aside for the moment the debates as to whether the Phillips Curve is sloping or vertical (therefore, whether $\partial AS/\partial \pi > 0$ or $\partial AS/\partial \pi = 0$).

The system (7.21, 7.22) is a close analogue to the traditional AD-AS model. The differences are that we have inflation (π) instead of the price level (P); and the model is augmented by the credit channel. We will not plot the graph explicitly for economy of space. But the effects of the new elements should be clear:

- Exogenous rises in bc, psy, and w_0 shift $AD^{CC\text{-}MP}$ out, causing rises in both the equilibrium inflation rate and output (if AS is not vertical);
- Exogenous rises in lev, μ, and c shift $AD^{CC\text{-}MP}$ left, causing reductions in both the equilibrium inflation rate and output (if AS is not vertical);

In addition, the customary effects of rises/falls in government spending and taxes as well as the supply-side shocks (via AS) apply in the same way as in the traditional AD-AS model. As an application of this model in relation to the Great Recession of 2007–9, we can see that various factors have played a role, such as worsening psychology (lower psy), a slump in the 'sub-prime' US housing market which worsened both borrowers' ability to repay (here: lower w) and lenders' financial position (bank capital: bc) as mortgage loans were defaulted. In due course, lenders began to be suspicious of one another's financial viability and therefore did not lend to one another (a 'credit squeeze'—here, higher c). In reality, all these are partly causes, partly effects, in a complicated chain, but they are compatible with our framework and show its advantages over the standard model. Woodford (2010) discusses the relevance of this framework in understanding the US financial market experience leading up to and after the credit crisis of 2007–8. For a recent review of the role of 'financial frictions' in the Great Recession, the interested reader is referred to Gertler and Gilchrist (2018).

The literature on the 'credit channel' is ongoing; it continues to offer many new insights about the workings of monetary policy and its 'transmission', based on a more realistic view of the workings of modern financial markets. Incorporation of these features into a basic macro model is important as they have far-reaching effects. For instance, Jakab and Kumhof (2015) compare the effects of identical shocks under standard financial inter-mediation models (i.e. the traditional money multiplier) and financial intermediation models that incorporate the features discussed above (the 'credit channel'). They show that under models of the latter type, changes in bank lending are far larger and faster and have much greater effects on the real economy. The model we have developed incorporates key features of the 'credit channel' (the structure and workings of finance and banking). The various channels analysed are essentially interrelated—balance sheet and net worth effects, spreads and external premia, credit 'crunches', are all interdependent. As such, they enrich the analysis not only in terms of sources of exogenous shocks but also in terms of channels by which monetary policy can have long-lasting, amplified effects. All this while the basic structure of the standard model is not fundamentally altered, making the new structure intuitively clear.

The policy implications are diverse and quite powerful. First and foremost, the monetary authority (and the fiscal one, to the extent that it attempts to stabilize the economy) should take into account the structure of the financial system before determining its stance. Questions—such as, are banks and financial institutions providing liquidity to one another or not because of fear of solvency? are such institutions providing loans to the private sector or are they using any spare liquidity to reduce their debt instead ('de-leveraging')?— all these should be key input in monetary policy decisions. The spreads between various interest rates could be intermediate indicators of this effect, a consideration that has led Taylor (2008) to recommend that the Taylor rule be augmented with such spreads as predictors of Central Bank decision-making.[41]

7.8.9 The 'Transmission Mechanism' of Monetary Policy

The above analysis establishes that the effects of monetary policy are propagated and amplified via the financial structure and the 'credit channel', but tells us little about how these effects are translated into changes in real variables such as output, employment, and inflation (and real wages). In other words, the analysis above tells us that expansionary monetary policy will be manifested in lower interest rates and perhaps greater availability of credit in the economy; the next question is how these will affect the 'real' economy. The subject of this analysis is referred to as the 'transmission mechanism' (from monetary to real effects); its channels are broadly understood and agreed upon, but agreement on details remains elusive.

As Chapter 1 reviewed, traditional analysis assumes that the effects of changes in interest rates work via changes in investment; the evidence, however, shows that this effect is weak if not entirely insignificant (Chirinko, 1993). More significant may be the effects via wealth effects: If interest rates fall, share prices and house prices go up (Case et al., 2005); consumers feel more confident to go out and spend more. Furthermore, businesses may be encouraged to spend because of healthier balance sheets and the availability of 'internal finance', as analysed above. Another important channel is via the exchange rate: there is a close association between that and monetary policy, with a fall in interest rates translated into a depreciation; this provides a boost to net exports sooner or later (allowing for a 'J-curve'). All these factors represent effects of changes in interest rates on real aggregate demand, so these considerations are behind the slope of the IS curve. Finally, the literature on the credit channel has highlighted the effects of credit availability on consumption (particularly on 'credit-constrained' households, see Chapter 11), investment and housing-related spending. It is a moot point whether these factors represent a sloping IS curve (as would be the case if expansions in credit are engineered by reductions in policy interest rates) or whether they represent shifts in IS (as would be the case if such developments

---

[41] You will have noticed that under our assumptions the value of each investment project is $w + 1$, and w seems to have been missed in the $I = S$ equality. The answer is that indeed the true value of investment is $(1 + w)I$, but the wI part comes from retained profits of firms, hence reduced remittances to workers and shareholders, hence reduced consumption. Thus, the National Income Accounting equation becomes $Y = C - wI + I(1 + w) + G + NX$, which reduces to the usual $Y = C + I + G + NX$, or $S + T - G = I + NX$. In the main text, $G = T = NX = 0$.

were engineered from the Central Bank's balance sheet quite independently of interest rates, as the discussion on 'unconventional policy' in the next section suggests).

Christiano et al. (1999, 2005) discuss extensively the existing evidence and the methods available for identifying the policy shocks. Their findings represent more or less the mainstream view of the quantitative effects of monetary policy. Figure 7.7 is reproduced from their (2005) paper.

Effects of an expansionary structural monetary shock are reported; the shock underlying this Figure is equivalent to about a 0.75 per cent reduction in the base interest rate. The vertical axes report percentage deviations from what would prevail without the shock, whereas the horizontal axis is quarters. The '+' are point estimates, the shaded area represents a 95 per cent confidence interval while the solid lines are simulations based on the theoretical model in their (2005) paper.

These estimates suggest that a fall in interest rates by 0.75 per cent for a year or two increases output by about 0.3–0.7 per cent for about two years from what it would otherwise have been (i.e. from trend output). The peak effect on output occurs after

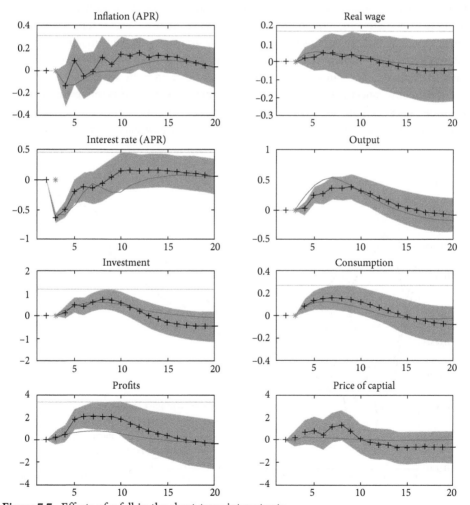

Figure 7.7. Effects of a fall in the short-term interest rate

Source: Christiano, Eichenbaum and Evans (2005, Figure 1). The change in the interest rate is equal to one standard deviation. The numbers on the horizontal axes are quarters (= three months).

about 1.5 years, after which the effect gradually peters out. This 'humped-shaped' response to monetary policy is mirrored in consumption, investment, profits, real wage, productivity, and inflation. Interest rates fall and money supply growth picks up immediately. Similar estimates are reported elsewhere, e.g. in Mankiw (2001) and are therefore close to a consensus. While these may seem like small percentages, monetary policy has by no means a negligible effect. As always, monetary policy is neutral in the long run. However, despite the broad agreement, considerable uncertainty and disagreement remains over the details.

How are the various components of the GDP affected following a monetary policy shock? Bernanke and Gertler (1995) investigate this; Figure 7.8 reproduces one of their key figures. It shows the percentage response of various key variables to an unanticipated, one-standard deviation increase in the 'federal funds rate' (the US policy interest rate), i.e. a monetary policy tightening. Bernanke and Gertler (1995) show that the textbook effect on investment is the weakest one. Consumption is made up of two components, durable and non-durable consumption. Of the two, durable is the one that (theory says) ought to respond mostly to interest rates, yet it is the weakest of the two. The biggest effect is shown in residential investment, i.e. housebuilding. Yet, another puzzle lurks here, in that this ought to respond to long-term interest rates (mortgage interest rates are long term), which however ought not to be affected drastically by transitory movements in short-term interest rates. We see here points of agreement and disagreement with theory. In any case, the main effects occur again about one to two years after the shock.

A final point concerns the delays by which monetary policy affects the real economy—Friedman's (1972) 'long and variable lags'—which are obvious e.g. in Figures 7.7 and 7.8. Recent literature has investigated further these lags with new data spanning a variety of

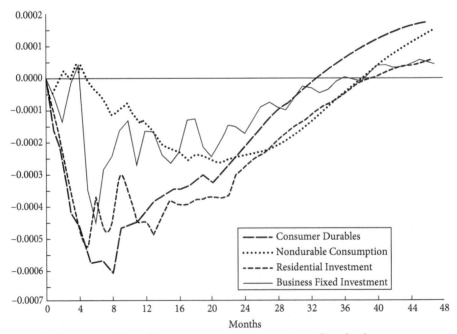

Figure 7.8. Responses of spending components to a monetary policy shock

Source: Bernanke and Gertler (1995), Figure 3.

monetary regimes. Using 30 years of data (therefore spanning a variety of monetary arrangements and policies) from the US and UK, Batini and Nelson (2001) reaffirm Friedman's (1972) conclusion that monetary policy actions take well over a year to have their peak effects on inflation.

7.9 Unconventional Monetary Policy, Macroprudential Regulation, and Optimal Stabilization Policy

7.9.1 'Unconventional' Monetary Policy, the 'Zero Lower Bound', and 'Quantitative Easing'

In this sub-section, we review some unconventional practices in monetary policy that have been put in place in the wake of the Great Recession of 2007–9. It then became clear that one reason behind the credit squeeze experienced by commercial banks was their lack of adequate reserves. Above, we have assumed an endogenous reserve-deposit ratio $R/D = b(r^{CB})$, which depends only on the policy interest rate and the bank's own practices (which we have not modelled). However, this reserve-deposit ratio should be above a certain minimum fixed either by regulation and/or commercial banks' practices. When reserves fall below this minimum, banks will be unable to lend. In this case, the Central Bank can help lending by providing extra liquidity. In order for this extra liquidity not to generate extra inflation, it was provided not in hard cash form, but electronically, by crediting the accounts the commercial banks hold at the Central Bank. The key point is that the increased liquidity should enable commercial banks to extend more credit to the private sector. This is the policy of 'Quantitative Easing' (called 'large-scale asset purchases' by the US Fed). Analytically, this policy will work by shifting the IS right, as more lending is made available which should help spending; in the context of the standard IS-LM, this would be strange, but it is perfectly in line with our discussion above and the M(odified)IS.

Consider a more realistic picture of the balance sheet of commercial banks (compare with the $D = R + L$ we saw in sub-section 7. 8.1):

$$Assets = Res(erves\ held\ at\ the\ CB) + (cash)\ R(eserves) + F(inancial)\ A(ssets) + L(oans)$$
$$= D(eposits) = Liabilities$$

The additional elements to what we have already seen are the electronic Res and FA. The total liquidity is (electronic)Res + (cash)R, and this sum must be a minimum fraction of deposits. The F(inancial) A(ssets) are risky (to varying extents) as they include shares and bonds whose value fluctuates, and therefore cannot serve as reserves. If commercial banks find themselves reserves-constrained (low (Res+R)/D), the Central Bank can alleviate the liquidity shortage by buying FA from banks and paying by crediting their Res accounts.[42] Thus, there is no actual note or coin creation that could engineer inflation, it is

---

[42] Compare Quantitative Easing to the Open Market Operations that underpin the traditional monetary policy: Taking an expansionary policy (the analogue of QE), the CB would buy FA in open markets (not only from banks) and pay by hard cash, so that cash in circulation $(C + R)$ increases.

only accounting entries that change. The assets bought by the CB are good quality: e.g. only government bonds in the UK, government bonds plus good quality private bonds in the US. This is the essence of the 'Quantitative Easing' programme implemented by various major Central Banks in recent years. In addition to providing liquidity, the Central Bank helps restore the quality of the commercial balance sheet. Even though the assets it buys are good quality, they are still risky; the amount of those is reduced, while the Res that increase are free of risk. Apart from the providing financial institutions with more liquidity, QE also means that there is a greater demand for government bonds (and perhaps other quality assets). This increases the price of these bonds and lowers their yields (interest rates). This decreases interest rates in the economy, particularly the long-term ones which are import-ant for investment, and induces a portfolio-rebalancing effect for financial institutions: In their quest for higher returns, such institutions now have an additional incentive to seek funding opportunities by lending to the private sector.

This policy of 'Quantitative Easing' was deemed necessary in recent years when (policy) interest rates are very near the 'zero lower bound'. Note that interest rates cannot go below zero, at least in any practicable sense, hence zero is the 'lower bound' of interest rates and represents the limit of expansionary policy.[43] This limit was reached in the US, UK, and elsewhere in the aftermath of the Great Recession of 2007–8. This posed a great challenge, as monetary authorities were required to help the stagnating economies but policy rates could not go any lower, so there was no possibility for a conventional monetary policy easing. Quantitative Easing to the rescue! The way it works is depicted in Figure 7.9.

For whatever reason, output demand has dropped so low that the policy interest rate prescribed by the Taylor rule (or whatever other decision-making process) is zero.[44] The economy is stuck at an output level that is deemed too low (point A), yet there is nothing that can be done by conventional monetary policy. Unconventional monetary policy that works by asset purchase programmes by Central Banks (such as Quantitative Easing and similar programmes—see the Guidance for Further Study) can help to shift the MIS curve (the modified version we have developed here) as indicated, by providing more liquidity that can prop up loan provision by the financial system. Central Banks have additional tools that can help banks and other financial institutions to restructure their balance sheets; in doing so, they may be able to reduce the spread between borrower-lender interest rates (R-r), reduce the cost of loans and encourage further investment.

Recognition of the limits of conventional monetary policy, particularly at times when interest rates are close to the 'zero lower bound' (ZLB), has led most major Central Banks to engage in massive programmes of 'unconventional' monetary policy (starting with the Bank of Japan in 2001–6, which also coined the term). Many trillions of dollars in the US, hundreds of billions of pounds in the UK and elsewhere, worth of transactions have been conducted in the context of these programmes, truly mind-boggling sums. This is therefore an area of acute practical concern and ongoing theoretical research. The criticism is that

---

[43] Technically, negative interest rates are possible—when accounts require a maintenance fee instead of offering a positive rate of return. But if that is sizeable, the funds will be withdrawn and kept as cash, therefore this possibility is rather theoretical.

[44] This situation is reminiscent of a 'liquidity trap' of the traditional IS-LM framework: a flat section of the LM curve indicating an infinitely elastic money demand, such that any additional liquidity created by the Central Bank (M0) would be absorbed without altering the (already very low) interest rate.

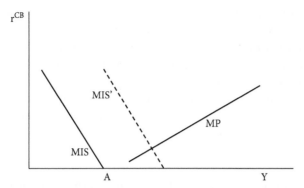

Figure 7.9. The 'zero lower bound' and unconventional monetary policy

these programmes were of a limited effectiveness; and the cynical twist might be that these programmes helped the financial institutions improve their balance sheets at the taxpayer's expense.[45] Theoretical perspectives on monetary policy at the ZLB can be gained by looking at McCallum (2000), Curdia and Woodford (2010), Woodford (2012), and Lenza et al. (2010). Empirical assessments of the effectiveness of these programmes are to be found in Breedon et al. (2012), Joyce et al. (2012), Martin and Milas (2012), Kapetanios et al. (2012), Steeley (2015), and Hamilton (2018) for the US.

7.9.2 Financial 'Fragility' and 'Macroprudential' Regulation

Finally, we highlight some implications of the foregoing analysis for the health (or its opposite, the 'fragility') of the financial system and the set of policies and regulatory framework that these call for. The foregoing analysis suggests important interactions between the state of the financial system and monetary policies; the experience of the last 12 years or so, outlined in Chapter 6, has confirmed such interactions. Monetary policy effects are amplified via channels that depend on the degree of capitalization of financial intermediaries, the health of their balance sheets, and their degree of leveraging. In turn, monetary policy affects financial institutions' decisions on all these fronts; e.g. when monetary policy is lax, financial institutions may be more prone to take risks by pursuing a greater degree of leveraging and lower capitalization. When the wind is favourable, such phenomena may not appear to be problematic; but adverse shocks may tip an economy over the edge when the financial system is in precarious health.

This calls for an oversight of the system and 'macroprudential' regulation, whereby appropriate restrictions (such as minimum capital requirements) are placed on financial institutions structures as to enable them to withstand possible adverse shocks and avoid

---

[45] In assessing the cost of these programmes, we should be careful: The cost to the taxpayer was not all these billions of dollars or pounds, because an equal amount of assets was purchased by the Central Banks. The cost is that the riskiness that the commercial banks offloaded (see above) was transferred to Central Banks, which are public agencies and therefore are ultimately owned by the taxpayer.

instability. Furthermore, as there are important interactions between financial institutions, the oversight must have a systemic element and not just look at individual institutions in isolation; hence the *macro* element of the regulation. The interested reader should consult Hanson et al. (2011) and Shin (2011) for introductions to the topic; and Tucker et al. (2013) specifically on the UK. Furthermore, as Woodford (2010) argues, monetary policy proper should keep an eye on financial structure so as both to help avoid the risk of instability and also to try to avoid situations of fragility that will make the conduct of monetary policy more difficult in the future.

7.9.3 Monetary Policy as Part of the Optimal Stabilization Policy Post-2009

The financial crisis of 2007–9 and the associated Great Recession (that started then and lasted for several years afterwards) has prompted a re-examination of the various aspects of stabilization policy and the role of monetary policy within the overall 'package'. We conclude with some thoughts along these lines, drawing among others on Blanchard and Summers (2017, 2019). This experience has taught us that policy should be more activist (and perhaps proactive); crises and recessions can emerge at any time. Additionally, the point can be made that more emphasis should be placed on output and employment stabilization, as opposed to just on inflation. This is of course not to say that inflation should not be stabilized, or that we should return to discretion and its lack of discipline; the existing rules-based framework should be maintained, but somewhat recalibrated away from an exclusive focus on inflation targeting. The average rate of inflation may rise (it might even be optimal to have an inflation rate of 4 per cent, see Ball, 2014).

Additionally, there now seems scope for having a fuller mix of stabilization policies. Before the crisis of 2007–9, a consensus had emerged that the role of monetary policy was to stabilize inflation (mainly) and output or employment (secondarily), while the role of fiscal policy was to keep public finances (government deficit and debt) in order (see Kirsanova et al., 2009). This effective assignment rule (see Chapter 1) has now been reconsidered. We have seen the limitations of monetary policy, particularly when interest rates are low; and they are expected to continue to be low for a while. Thus, monetary policy, at least in its conventional form, has a limited scope for helping the economy out of a recession.[46] In parallel, macroprudential regulation and other financial policies are necessary in order to minimize the risk of shocks arising from the financial system, or of other shocks (such as the one that emerged in the US housing and 'sub-prime' mortgage markets) getting unduly amplified by the workings of the financial system. All said, monetary policy and the macroprudential framework will remain important in the background, but their role in terms of activist stabilization will be more limited. Inevitably, a greater responsibility for stabilization will now be placed on fiscal policy. Monetary and fiscal policy interactions are therefore important (see Leith and Wren-Lewis, 2000, Sims, 2013). We review fiscal policy in the next chapter.

---

[46] But contractionary monetary policy—a rise in the policy interest rate—has quite some potential in stopping an expansion. A useful analogy here may that of a string: You can use it to pull but not to push.

Notes on the Literature

The path-breaking paper on time inconsistency is widely acknowledged to be Kydland and Prescott (1977), though Calvo (1978) came up with the same notion at about the same time. Barro and Gordon (1983) used the idea to talk explicitly about the inflationary bias and reputation. Good reviews of the literature are the early papers by Blackburn and Christensen (1989) and Rogoff (1989). More wide-ranging are the specialist books on political economy by Persson and Tabellini (2000) and Drazen (2000). On inflation targeting, Bernanke and Miskin (1997) and Svensson (1999) are good places to start. On Taylor rules, let Taylor himself speak first (Taylor, 1993), whereas a good collection of follow-up literature is to be found in his volume of readings Taylor (1999) and in Taylor and Williams (2011). Woodford (2001) provides a good critical survey. Blinder (1997, 1998) are highly readable collections of modern macro-monetary theory and practice. Clarida et al. (1999), Gali and Gertler (2007), and Woodford (2010) are good portals into the modern theory of monetary policy, perhaps with a slight bend towards New Keynesian perspectives. The same is true of the much more substantial volume by Woodford (2003). Cobham (2013) is a good place to start on the experience of modern monetary policy-making in the UK.

Guidance for Further Study

Central Banks

Look at the website of major Central Banks (Bank of England, the US Federal Reserve System, or the European (System of) Central Bank(s)). What is the regime under which they operate, in terms of degree of independence, targets that they are pursuing, and policy-making mechanisms? What unconventional monetary policies have they pursued in recent years, such as Quantitative Easing and related programmes?

Alternatives

What is the experience with alternative monetary regimes according to Ball (2010) and Mishkin (1999)?

Consensus

What was the consensus on monetary policy prior to 2007 as outlined by Goodfriend (2007) and how was it shattered by the events post-2007 according to the Committee on International Economic Policy and Reform (2011)?

Monetary policy

What evidence do Romer and Romer (2013) provide in support of their conclusion that monetary policy matters?

Real economy

Outline the channels by which monetary policy is 'transmitted' to the real (as opposed the financial) economy. In this, you may find Ireland (2010) a useful introduction.

Macroprudential policy

What is 'macroprudential policy' and what is its rationale according to Hanson et al. (2011), Shin (2011), and Yellen (2014)? The last one may be particularly useful (and more recent) as Janet Yellen combines both considerable academic prestige and policy-making experience. What policy reforms are being proposed? What are the 'key steps' in the development of a robust macroprudential framework? Is there a conflict or complementarity between the traditional monetary policy and the more innovative macroprudential regulation? What are the 'key principles' for achieving effective coordination between monetary and macroprudential policies?

The 'natural rate of interest' and its implications for monetary policy

There are some findings (Laubach and Williams, 2003; Barsky et al., 2014; see also Summers, 2014) that the natural real interest rate has fallen to negative values recently. How is the 'natural' real interest rate defined? What may the implications of a negative rate combined with a low inflation rate on the relative effectiveness of monetary and fiscal policy (on this see, in particular, Summers, 2014)?

Central Banks as a twentieth-century institutional innovation

Outline their development, particularly from a policy perspective, following Haldane and Ovigstad (2016). Further information can be gleaned from a special issue on the US Fed in the *Journal of Economic Perspectives* (Fall 2013). See Scheller (2006) for the European Central Bank.

Bitcoin and the other 'cryptocurrencies'

For a review (and a succinct history of money along the way), the reader is invited to read Böhme et al. (2015) and Eichengreen (2019). Is the future 'crypto'?

Monetary policy in a cashless economy

Rapid innovations in transactions technology (automated payments, online banking, credit cards) imply that we live in a world where less and less cash is used (in relation to the volume of transactions). Does this make monetary policy easier or more difficult? Does it have stabilizing or de-stabilizing effects? Thoughts and analyses on these questions are offered by Woodford (2000) and Stiglitz (2017).

Evolution or revolution in policy

As mentioned, various aspects of stabilization policy are being re-examined in the wake of the financial crisis of 2007–9 and the Great Recession. You are invited to read Blanchard and Summers (2017, 2019). What policy revisions do they characterize as evolution and which ones as a more dramatic change of priorities—a 'revolution'?

References

Akerlof, G.A. (1970): The Market for 'Lemons': Quality Uncertainty and the Market Mechanism, *Quarterly Journal of Economics*, 84(3) (August), 488–500.

Akerlof, G.A., W.T. Dickens, and G.L. Perry (1996): The Macroeconomics of Low Inflation, *Brookings Papers on Economic Activity*, 1, 1–59.

Aksoy, Y., A. Orphanides, D. Small, V. Wieland, and D. Wilcox (2006): A Quantitative Exploration of the Opportunistic Approach to Disinflation, *Journal of Monetary Economics*, 53(8) (November), 1877–93.

Alesina, A., and L.H. Summers (1993): Central Bank Independence and Macroeconomic Performance, *Journal of Money, Credit and Banking*, 25 (May), 161–2.

Ambler, S. (2009): Price-Level Targeting and Stabilisation Policy: A Survey, *Journal of Economic Surveys*, 23(5) (December), 974–97.

Ball, L.M. (1999): Efficient Rules for Monetary Policy, *International Finance*, 2(1), 63–83.

Ball, L.M. (2010): The Performance of Alternative Monetary Regimes, in B.M. Friedman and M. Woodford (eds), *Handbook of Monetary Economics*, Amsterdam: Elsevier, iii. 1303–43.

Ball, L.M. (2014): The Case for a Long-Run Inflation Target of Four Percent, IMF Working Papers 14/92, International Monetary Fund.

Barro, R., and D.B. Gordon (1983): Rules, Discretion, and Reputation in a Model of Monetary Policy, *Journal of Monetary Economics*, 12, 101–20.

Barsky, R., A. Justiniano, and L. Melosi (2014): The Natural Rate of Interest and its Usefulness for Monetary Policy, *American Economic Review*, 104(5), 37–43.

Batini, N., and E. Nelson (2001): The Lag from Monetary Policy Actions to Inflation: Friedman Revisited, *International Finance*, 4, 381–400.

Batini, N., and J. Pearlman (2002): Too Much Too Soon: Instability and Indeterminacy with Forward-Looking Rules, Discussion Paper No. 8, Monetary Policy Committee, Bank of England, March.

Bean, C. (1998): The New UK Monetary Arrangements: A View from the Literature, *Economic Journal*, 108, 1795–808.

Berger, H, J. de Haan, and S. Eijffinger (2001): Central Bank Independence: An Update of Theory and Evidence, *Journal of Economic Surveys*, 15, 3–40.

Bernanke, B., and F.S. Mishkin (1997): Inflation Targeting: Anew Framework for Monetary Policy? *Journal of Economic Perspectives*, 11(2) (Spring), 97–116.

Bernanke, B., and M. Woodford (1997): Inflation Forecasts and Monetary Policy, *Journal of Money, Credit and Banking*, 24, 653–84.

Bernanke, B., M. Gertler, and S. Gilchrist (1996): The Financial Accelerator and the Flight to Quality, *Review of Economics and Statistics*, 78(1), 1–15.

Bernanke, B., and A. Blinder (1988): Credit, Money, and Aggregate Demand, *American Economic Review* (May), 435–9.

Bernanke, B., and M. Gertler (1995): Inside the Black Box: The Credit Channel of Monetary Policy Transmission. *Journal of Economic Perspectives*, 9: 27–48.

Blackburn, K., and M. Christensen (1989): Monetary Policy and Policy Credibility, *Journal of Economic Literature*, 27 (March), 1–45.

Blanchard, O.J., and S. Fischer (1989): *Lectures on Macroeconomics*, Cambridge, MA: MIT Press.

Blanchard, O.J., and L.H. Summers (2017): Rethinking Stabilization Policy: Evolution or Revolution? NBER Working Paper No. 24179, December.

Blanchard, O.J., and L.H. Summers (eds) (2019): *Rethinking Macroeconomic Policy after the Great Recession*, Boston: MIT Press.

Blinder, A. (1997): What Central Bankers Could Learn from Academics—and Vice Versa, *Journal of Economic Perspectives*, 11(2) (Spring), 3–19.

Blinder, A. (1998): *Central Banking in Theory and Practice, The Lionel Robbins Lectures*, Cambridge, MA, and London: MIT Press.

Böhme, R., N. Christin, B. Edelman, and T. Moore (2015): Bitcoin: Economics, Technology, and Governance, *Journal of Economic Perspectives*, 29(2) (Spring), 213–38.

Breedon, F., J.S. Chadha, and A. Waters (2012): The Financial Market Impact of UK Quantitative Easing, *Oxford Review of Economic Policy*, 28(4), 702–28.

Calvo, G. (1978): On the Time Inconsistency of Optimal Policy in a Monetary Economy, *Econometrica*, 46, 1411–28.

Case, K., J. Quigley, and R. Shiller (2005): Comparing Wealth Effects: The Stock Market versus the Housing Market, Advances in Macroeconomics, *Berkeley Electronic Press*, 5(1), 1235–5.

Chirinko, R. (1993): Business Fixed Investment Spending: Modeling Strategies, Empirical Results, and Policy Implications, *Journal of Economic Literature*, 31(4), 1875–1911.

Christiano, L.J., M. Eichenbaum, and C. Evans (1999): Monetary Policy Shocks: What have we Learned and to What End? in J.B. Taylor and M. Woodford (eds), *Handbook of Macroeconomics*, Amsterdam: North-Holland, iA. 65–148.

Christiano, L.J., M. Eichenbaum, and C. Evans (2005): Nominal Rigidities and the Dynamic Effects of a Shock to Monetary Policy, *Journal of Political Economy*, 113(1) (February), 1–45.

Clarida, R., J. Gali, and M. Gertler (1999): The Science f Monetary Policy: A New Keynesian Perspective, *Journal of Economic Literature*, 37 (December), 1661–1707.

Clews, R., C. Salmon, and O. Weeken (2010): The Bank's Money Market Framework, *Bank of England Quarterly Bulletin*, 50(4), 292–301.

Cobham, D. (2013): Monetary Policy under the Labour Government 1997–2010: The First 13 Years of the MPC, *Oxford Review of Economic Policy*, 29(1) (June), 47–70.

Cobham, D. (2018): A New Classification of Monetary Policy Frameworks, VOX: CEPR Policy Portal, https://voxeu.org/article/new-classification-monetary-policy-frameworks

Committee on International Economic Policy and Reform (2011): Rethinking Central Banking, http://www.brookings.edu/research/reports/2011/09/ciepr-central-banking

Cukierman, A. (1992): *Central Bank Strategy, Credibility, and Independence: Theory and Evidence*, Cambridge, MA: MIT Press.

Curdia, V., and M. Woodford (2010): Conventional and Unconventional Monetary Policy, *Federal Reserve Bank of St. Louis Review* (May), 229–64.

Currie, D., and P. Levine (1993): *Rules, Reputation and Macroeconomic Policy Coordination*, Cambridge: Cambridge University Press.

Diamond, D.W. (1984): Financial Intermediation and Delegated Monitoring, *Review of Economic Studies*, 51(3) (July), 393–414.

Drazen, A.A. (2000): *Political Economy in Macroeconomics*, Princeton: Princeton University Press.

Eichengreen, B. (2019): From Commodity to Fiat and Now to Crypto: What does History Tell us? NBER Working Paper No. 25426, January.

Fama, E.F. (1980): Agency Problems and the Theory of the Firm, *Journal of Political Economy*, 88(2) (April), 288–307.

Flood, R.P., and P. Isard (1988): *Monetary Policy Strategies*, Cambridge, MA: NBER Working Paper No. 2770, November.

Friedman, B.M. (1988): Lessons on Monetary Policy from the 1980s, *Journal of Economic Perspectives*, 2(3) (Summer), 51–72.

Friedman, M. (1972): Have Monetary Policies Failed?, *American Economic Review*, 62(2) (May), 11–18.

Friedman, M., and A.J. Schwartz (1963): *A Monetary History of the United States, 1867–1960*, Princeton: Princeton University Press.

Gali, J., and M. Gertler (2007): Macroeconomic Modelling for Monetary Policy, *Journal of Economic Perspectives*, 21(4) (Fall), 25–45.

Gertler, M. (1988): Financial Structure and Aggregate Economic Activity: An Overview, *Journal of Money, Credit and Banking*, 20(3) (part 2, August), 559–88.

Gertler, M., and S. Gilchrist (2018): What Happened: Financial Factors in the Great Recession, *Journal of Economic Perspectives*, 32(3) (Summer), 3–30.

Giavazzi, F., and M. Pagano (1988): The Advantage of Tying one's Hands: EMS Discipline and Central Bank Credibility, *European Economic Review*, 32, 1055–82.

Glyn, A. (2007): *Capitalism Unleashed*, Oxford: Oxford University Press.

Goodfriend, M. (2007): How the World Achieved Consensus on Monetary Policy, *Journal of Economic Perspectives*, 21(4) (Fall), 47–68.

Grilli, V., D. Masciandaro, and G. Tabellini (1991): Political and Monetary Institutions and Public Financial Policies in the Industrial Countries, *Economic Policy*, 13 (October), 341–92.

Haldane, A.G., and J.F. Qvigstad (2016): The Evolution of Central Banks, in M. Bordo, Ø Eitrheim, M. Flandreau, and J. Qvigstad (eds), *Central Banks at a Crossroads: What Can We Learn from History?* Studies in Macroeconomic History, Cambridge: Cambridge University Press, 627–72.

Hall, R., and N.G. Mankiw (1994): Nominal Income Targeting, in Mankiw (ed.), *Monetary Policy*, Chicago: University of Chicago Press, 71–94.

Hamilton, J.D. (2018): The Efficacy of Large-Scale Asset Purchases When the Short-Term Interest Rate is at its Effective Lower Bound, *Brookings Papers on Economic Activity*, 2, 1–13.

Hanson, S.G., A.K. Kashyap, and J.C. Stein (2011): A Macroprudential Approach to Financial Regulation, *Journal of Economic Perspectives*, 25(1), 3–28.

Hayo, B. (1998): Inflation Culture, Central Bank Independence and Price Stability, *European Journal of Political Economy*, 14(2), 241–63.

Hubbard, R.G. (1995): Is there a 'Credit Channel' for Monetary Policy? *Federal Reserve Bank of St. Louis Review*, 77 (May/June), 63–77.

Hubbard, R.G. (1998): Capital-Market Imperfections and Investment, *Journal of Economic Literature*, 36 (March), 193–225.

Ireland, P.N. (2010): Monetary Transmission Mechanism, in S.N. Durlauf and L.E. Blume (eds), *The New Palgrave Dictionary of Economics*, London: Palgrave Macmillan, 216–23.

Jakab, Z., and M. Kumhof (2015): Banks are Not Intermediaries of Loanable Funds—and Why This Matters, Bank of England Working Paper No. 529, May.

Jensen, H. (2002): Targeting Nominal Income Growth or Inflation? *American Economic Review*, 92(4), 928–56.

Joyce, M., N. McLaren, and C. Young (2012): Quantitative Easing in the United Kingdom: Evidence from Financial Markets on QE1 and QE2, *Oxford Review of Economic Policy*, 28(4), 671–701.

Judd J.P., and G.D. Rudebusch (1998): Taylor's Rule and the Fed: 1970–97, *Federal Reserve Bank of San Francisco Economic Review*, 3, 3–16.

Kapetanios, G., H. Mumtaz, I. Stevens, and K. Theodoridis (2012): Assessing the Economy-Wide Effects of Quantitative Easing, *Economic Journal*, 122(564) (November), F316–47.

King, M.A. (2005): What has Inflation Targeting Achieved?, in B.S. Bernanke and M. Woodford (eds), *The Inflation-Targeting Debate*, Chicago: University of Chicago Press, 11–16.

Kirsanova, T., C. Leith, and S. Wren-Lewis (2009): Monetary and Fiscal Policy Interaction: The Current Consensus Assignment in the Light of Recent Developments, *Economic Journal*, 119, F482–96.

Kiyotaki, N. and Moore, J. (1997): Credit Cycles, *Journal of Political Economy*, 105(2) (April), 211–48.

Kydland, F., and E. Prescott (1977): Rules Rather than Discretion: The Inconsistency of Optimal Plan, *Journal of Political Economy*, 85(3), 473–92.

Laubach, T., and J.C. Williams (2003): Measuring the Natural Rate of Interest, *Review of Economics and Statistics*, 85(4), 1063–70.

Leith, C., and S. Wren-Lewis (2000): Interactions between Monetary and Fiscal Policy Rules, *Economic Journal*, 110, 93–108.

Lenza, M., H. Pill, and L. Reichlin (2010): Monetary Policy in Exceptional Times, *Economic Policy*, 25, 295–339.

Lohmann, S. (1992): Optimal Commitment in Monetary Policy: Credibility versus Flexibility, *American Economic Review*, 82(1) (March), 273–86.

McCallum, B. (1999): Nominal Income Targeting in an Open-Economy Optimizing Model, *Journal of Monetary Economics*, 43, 3 (June), 553–78.

McCallum, B. (2000): Theoretical Analysis Regarding a Zero Lower Bound on Nominal Interest Rates, *Journal of Money, Credit and Banking*, 32, 870–904.

McCallum, B.T., and E. Nelson (2010): Money and Inflation: Some Critical Issues, in B.M. Friedman and M. Woodford (eds), *Handbook of Monetary Economics*, Amsterdam: Elsevier, vol. 3, 97–153.

McLeay, M., A. Radia, and R. Thomas (2014): Money Creation in the Modern Economy, *Bank of England Quarterly Bulletin*, Q1, 14–27.

Mahadeva, L., and G. Sterne (2002): Inflation Targets as a Stabilisation Device, *Manchester School*, 70, 619–50.

Mankiw, N.G. (1994): *Monetary Policy*, Chicago: University of Chicago Press.

Mankiw, N.G. (2001): The Inexorable and Mysterious Tradeoff between Inflation and Unemployment, *Economic Journal*, 111(471) (April), 45–61.

Martin, C., and C. Milas (2004): Modelling Monetary Policy: Inflation Targeting in Practice, *Economica*, 71 (282), 209–21.

Martin, C., and C. Milas (2012): Quantitative Easing: A Skeptical Survey, *Oxford Review of Economic Policy*, 28(4), 750–64.

Matsuyama, K. (2007): Credit Traps and Credit Cycles, *American Economic Review*, 97(1) (March), 503–16.

Mattich, A. (2011): End of Central Banking's Golden Age, *Wall Street Journal Europe*, 31 January, 2.

Miles, D. (2014): Monetary Policy and Forward Guidance in the UK, *Manchester School*, 82, 44–59.

Mishkin, F.S. (1999): SInternational Experience with Different Monetary Policy Regimes, *Journal of Monetary Economics*, 43(3), 579–605.

Modigliani, F., and M.H. Miller (1958): The Cost of Capital, Corporation Finance and the Theory of Investment, *American Economic Review*, 48(3) (June), 261–97.

Muscatelli, A., and C. Trecroci (2000): Monetary Policy Rules, Policy Preferences, and Uncertainty: Recent Empirical Evidence, *Journal of Economic Surveys*, 14, 597–627.

Orphanides, A., and D. Wilcox (2002): The Opportunistic Approach to Disinflation, *International Finance*, 5(1), 47–71.

Persson, T., and G. Tabellini (1993): Designing Institutions for Monetary Stability, *Carnegie-Rochester Conference Series on Public Policy*, 39 (December), 53–84.

Persson, T., and G. Tabellini (2000): *Political Economics: Explaining Economic Policy*, Boston: MIT Press.

Posen, A. (1995): Declarations are Not Enough: Financial Sector Sources of Central Bank Independence, in B.S. Bernanke and J.J. Rotemberg (eds), NBER Macroeconomics Annual 1995, Boston: NBER, 253–74.

Rogoff, K. (1985): The Optimal Degree of Commitment to an Intermediate Monetary Target, *Quarterly Journal of Economics*, 100, 1169–90.

Rogoff, K. (1989): Reputation, Coordination, and Monetary Policy, in: R.J. Barro (ed.), *Modern Business Cycle Theory*, Boston: Harvard University Press, 236–63.

Romer, D. (2006): *Advanced Macroeconomics*, 3rd ed., Boston: McGraw-Hill Irwin.

Romer, C., and D. Romer (2013): The Most Dangerous Idea in Federal Reserve History: Monetary Policy Doesn't Matter, *American Economic Review*, 103(3) (May), 55–60.

Rudebusch, G., and L.E.O. Svensson (2002): Eurosystem Monetary Targeting: Lessons from U.S. Data, *European Economic Review*, 46 (March), 417–42.

Scheller, H.K (2006): The European Central Bank: History, Role and Functions, https://www.ecb.europa.eu/pub/pdf/other/ecbhistoryrolefunctions2006en.pdf?b06761d1bdc5f8356cdadd d57f5c5135

Schmitt-Grohe, S., and M. Uribe (2000): Price Level Determinacy and Monetary Policy under a Balanced-Budget Requirement, *Journal of Monetary Economics*, 45, 211–46.

Sheffrin, S.M. (1989): *The Making of Economic Policy*, Oxford and Boston: Basil Blackwell.

Shin, H.-S. (2011): Macroprudential Policies beyond Basel III, in Bank for International Settlements (ed.), *Macroprudential Regulation and Policy*, BIS Papers, 60, 5–15.

Sims, C. (2013): Paper Money, *American Economic Review*, 103(2), 563–84.

Steeley, J. (2015): The Side Effects of Quantitative Easing: Evidence from the UK Bond Market, *Journal of International Money and Finance*, 51 (March), 303.

Sterne, G. (2002): Inflation Targets in a Global Context, in N. Loayza and N. Soto (eds), *Inflation Targeting: Design, Performance, Challenges*, Santiago, Chile: Central Bank of Chile, 23–78.

Stiglitz, J.E. (2017): Macro-Economic Management in an Electronic Credit/Financial System, NBER Working Paper No. 23032, January.

Stiglitz J.E., and A. Weiss (1981): Credit Rationing in Markets with Imperfect Information, *American Economic Review*, 71(3) (June), 393–410.

Summers, L. (1991): How Should Long-Term Policy be Determined? *Journal of Money, Credit and Banking*, 23, 625–31.

Sutherland, A.J. (2000): *Inflation Targeting in a Small Open Economy*, Discussion Paper No. 2726, London: Centre for Economic Policy Research.

Svensson, L.E.O. (1997): Inflation Forecast Targeting: Implementing and Monitoring Inflation Targets, *European Economic Review*, 41, 1111–46.

Svensson, L.E.O. (1999): Inflation Targeting as a Monetary Policy Rule, *Journal of Monetary Economics*, 43, 607–54.

Svensson, L.E.O. (2000): Open–Economy Inflation Targeting, *Journal of International Economics*, 50(1) (February), 155–83.

Taylor, J.B. (1993): Discretion versus Policy Rules in Practice, *Carnegie-Rochester Conference Series on Public Policy*, 39 (December), 195–214.

Taylor, J.B. (1999): A Historical Analysis of Monetary Policy Rules, in J.B. Taylor (ed.), *Monetary Policy Rules*, Chicago: University of Chicago Press, 319–48.

Taylor, J.B. (2008): Housing and Monetary Policy, in Proceedings—Economic Policy Symposium, Jackson Hole, KS: Federal Reserve Bank of Kansas City, 463–76.

Taylor, J.B., and J.C. Williams (2011): Simple and Robust Rules for Monetary Policy, in B.B. Friedman and M. Woodford (eds), *Handbook of Monetary Economics*, Amsterdam: Elsevier, iii. 829–59.

Townsend, R.M. (1979): Optimal Contracts and Competitive Markets with Costly State Verification, *Journal of Economic Theory*, 21(2) (October), 265–93.

Tucker, P., S. Hall, and A. Pattani (2013): Macroprudential Policy at the Bank of England, *Bank of England Quarterly Bulletin*, 53(3), 192–200.

Walsh, K. (1995): Optimal Contracts for Central Bankers, *American Economic Review*, 85(1), 150–67.

Woodford, M. (2000): Monetary Policy in a World without Money, *International Finance*, 3(2), 229–60.

Woodford, M. (2001): The Taylor Rule and Optimal Monetary Policy, American Economic Review, 91(2), 232–7.

Woodford, M. (2003): The Return of Monetary Rules, in his *Interest and Prices: Foundations of a Theory of Monetary Policy*, Princeton: Princeton University Press, chapter 1.

Woodford, M. (2007): The Case for Forecast Targeting as a Monetary Policy Strategy, *Journal of Economic Perspectives*, 21(4) (Fall), 3–24.

Woodford, M. (2010): Financial Intermediation and Macroeconomic Analysis, *Journal of Economic Perspectives*, 24(4) (Fall), 21–44.

Woodford, M. (2012): Methods of Policy Accommodation at the Interest-Rate Lower Bound, in Proceedings—Economic Policy Symposium, Jackson Hole, KS: Federal Reserve Bank of Kansas City, 185–28.

Woodford, M. (2013): Inflation Targeting: Fix it, Don't Scrap it, in L. Reichlin and R. Baldwin (eds), *Is Inflation Targeting Dead? Thinking Ahead about Central Banking After the Crisis* (a VoxEU e-Book).

Yellen, J. (2014): Monetary Policy and Financial Stability: Inaugural Michel Camdessus Central Banking Lecture with Janet Yellen, 2 July, http://www.federalreserve.gov/newsevents/speech/yellen20140702a.htm

8

Fiscal Policy and Public Debt

8.1 Introduction

This chapter deals with fiscal policy, particularly its potential as a stabilization policy tool, and the related issues of government budget deficit and public debt. In recent years, interest on all these issues has re-awakened. We ended Chapter 7 by arguing that a new consensus is emerging that the role of fiscal policy in terms of stabilization should increase in comparison both to what it has had in recent decades and to monetary policy (see e.g. Feldstein, 2009; Auerbach, 2012). A further reason, specifically applying to the countries of the Eurozone, is that with monetary policy centralized and responding to average Eurozone conditions only, fiscal policy is the only stabilization policy tool available to national authorities. At the same time, there is a second key reason why interest in fiscal policy and public finances has increased: government debt has shown a tendency to increase across the world. This interest is evident, for instance, in the recent special issues devoted to the matter (alongside the fiscal crisis in the Eurozone) by the *German Economic Review* (February 2014), the *Journal of the European Economic Association* (February 2016), and the International Monetary Fund's *Fiscal Monitor* (various issues). Figure 8.1 shows the evolution of public debt over recent years across two broad groups of countries based on the detailed work by IMF staff (Mbaye et al., 2018b); see their figure 12 for more information. We get additional information from the IMF's *Fiscal Monitor* 2018, particularly figure 1.1). At about 100 per cent, the average debt-GDP ratio of advanced economies is at historically high levels; for the emerging market economies (middle-income countries), it is considerably lower—currently at about 50 per cent, but expected to climb further to also historically high (for them) levels.

The worsening public finances, particularly across the advanced economies, due in part (but only in part) to the financial crisis of 2007–9, point to a contradiction: Fiscal policy is being called upon to play a greater stabilization role at the same time as it faces more severe limitations and constraints. This increases the interest these matters receive. We shall organize the chapter around the two key themes of public finances (debts and deficits) and their implications (Sections 8.2–8.5) and the stabilization potential of fiscal policy (Sections 8.6–8.7).

8.2 Preliminaries: The Budget Deficit, Debt, and the Government Budget Constraint

The budget deficit is measured for two reasons: first, to convey an idea of the fiscal stance (how expansionary/contractionary fiscal policy is), and secondly, as a piece in the government's accounting balance sheet (i.e. in order to measure government's financial

Theory of Macroeconomic Policy. Christopher Tsoukis, Oxford University Press (2020). © Christopher Tsoukis.
DOI: 10.1093/oso/9780198825371.003.0008

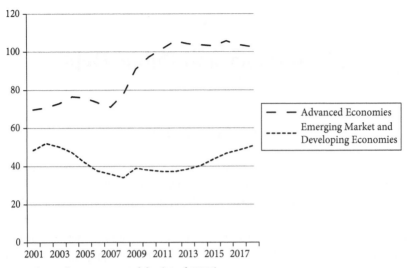

Figure 8.1. General government debt (% of GDP)

Source: IMF Datamapper https://www.imf.org/external/datamapper/GGXWDG_NGDP@WEO/OEMDC/ADVEC/WEOWORLD?year=2019, based on Mbaye, Moreno-Badia and Chae (2018)

obligations). There are two basic definitions of the budget deficit (for short, deficit). The 'primary deficit' is defined as:

$$D_t \equiv G_t + U_t - T_t; \qquad (8.1)$$

it is the sum of all government outlays like expenditures on services, goods and investment (G), and transfers (U) for whatever purpose (including unemployment or welfare benefits and various subsidies, e.g. for investment), minus tax receipts (T). In real life, government accounting books appear a lot more complicated than that, with lots more elaborate categories, but these very broad definitions serve us well here. Occasionally receipts may exceed expenses, in which case $D < 0$ (a negative deficit emerges) and we talk about a (primary) surplus. We shall continue to use the generic term 'deficit' with this point in mind. As is usual, the subscript t indicates the time period.

All the items in (8.1) as well as D itself are in the nature of 'flow variables', i.e. they take place within a time period. In practice, the time periods are specific years, and occasionally the distinction between financial and calendar years may be of great importance. For our argument, however, we do not need to be so specific. Hence, the year (or any other period we may have in mind, e.g. a quarter) is indicated by t which is 'well-defined' insofar as it is very different from $t + 1$! The primary deficit D_t (or any other of the above quantities) is 0 right at the beginning of period t, it gradually builds up, and takes its final value at the end of t. Any items incurred after that will be recorded as D_{t+1} (etc.).

'Government' denotes the public sector (not this or that government). When viewing actual statistics and data (about expenses, revenue, primary deficits, debts, etc.), we need to be careful to see whether those refer to central government, or an extended definition of the public sector ('consolidated government') that encompasses regional/local authorities, or even possibly some of the organizations (banks, pension funds, companies) belonging to the public sector. The question is of increasing relevance in many countries with their increasing sophistication of multi-tiered government (federal, state or regional, and local), and much more for the EU which has developed a higher tier of supranational government and budget. Our framework abstracts from these distinctions; our arguments are general enough and valid under any definition. We may accordingly have any of these definitions in mind, as long as we apply them consistently on all our variables throughout our analysis. Note also that a proper broad definition of government is a consolidated one, in which internal transfers between levels of government (as applicable) cancel out, so that there is no double counting. (In other words: do not take 'central government' and 'local government' accounts and add them up; take the properly 'consolidated government' accounts.) With these points in mind, we can simply talk about 'the government' in what follows.

We now introduce government debt, B_t. It is effectively the amount of outstanding borrowing that government has drawn over the years from the private sector. The latter has lent to government on the understanding that such debt will be properly serviced, i.e. interest will be paid on its outstanding amount, until the debt itself is repaid and ceases to exist at some specified future date. In practice, such debt takes the form of government bonds which vary in various ways, one of which is its 'maturity', i.e. the time horizon between its issue and its eventual repayment and withdrawal. To simplify matters, we shall assume, to begin with, that all government bonds are of maturity of one period. Take the case of a bond issued at the beginning of time t of 'face value' of £1; this bond will pay interest r (per cent, payable at the beginning of $t + 1$) and will also 'mature' at the beginning of time $t + 1$, whereupon the government pays the owner of the bond the face value—£1, the amount outstanding. The amount of funds borrowed at the beginning of $t + 1$ is B_{t+1}, the number of such granular bonds issued at that time. This amount of funds will be used for three reasons: first, to cover any excess of spending over revenue, i.e. the primary deficit of (8.1); second, to pay the interest on the bonds that are just expiring (B_t); and third, to replace ('roll over') bonds now expiring (issued at the beginning of t) that the government does not have funds of its own to pay back. These three uses of the newly borrowed funds at the beginning of $t + 1$ are recorded in equation (8.2). This framework of one-period bonds that are rolled over is the simplest possible, yet allows a number of interesting results to be developed.

The three uses of the new borrowing at $t + 1$ referred to above are recorded in the 'government budget constraint' equation (8.2). An additional item recorded here is 'seignorage', revenue arising from the monetary base (denoted M here) creation; we discuss this shortly.

$$B_{t+1} = B_t(1 + r) + D_t - (M_{t+1} - M_t)/P_t \tag{8.2}$$

This equation effectively shows how debt evolves over time; whether the amount of new bonds will be higher or lower than those outstanding in the previous period. By substituting backwards over time (in a way parallel to the forward substitution we used in Chapter 2 and elsewhere), we can also see that the currently outstanding debt is effectively the amount of past primary deficits (minus seignorage) augmented by interest. It is also informative to rearrange (8.2) as follows:

$$B_{t+1} - B_t = D_t + rB_t - (M_{t+1} - M_t)/P_t \tag{8.2'}$$

In this form, the equation tells us how much revenue the government acquires from *new* borrowing at the beginning of the new period $t + 1$ (hence the difference between the amounts of bonds outstanding during the two periods). On the right, we have the uses of this revenue: primary deficit net of seignorage plus interest payments on existing debt (the real interest rate r times the amount of bonds outstanding at the beginning of period t). On the right, therefore, we have a broader definition of the deficit that includes interest payments. Several comments and further explanation are due.

We mentioned that deficits are in the nature of flow variables. In contrast, debt is in the nature of a 'stock variable'. This is a variable that is measured at a specific point in time, e.g. the beginning or end of period t (and not the entire t as is the case with flow variables); and, between periods, it accumulates according to a scheme like (8.2) above, whereby typically the deficit causes debt to expand. It should be clear, therefore, that the values of flow variables at different time periods are basically unrelated quantities, whereas values of stock variables at different time periods (at the same point in each) are the same variable recorded at different stages.

Everything in (8.2) and (8.2') is in real terms, except the narrow money (M), which is assumed to be nominal, hence deflated in by the price level P. So, each bond is effectively worth one unit of the consumption basket (rather than the nominal £1 we suggested above as a first pass). The interest rate r is assumed to be constant (to simplify the exposition) and is real, i.e. it subtracts the percentage loss in purchasing power resulting from inflation from the nominal return that the bond enjoys. The last term in (8.2) is called seignorage because, as a form of revenue, it is the prerogative of government or sovereign (in French: 'seigneur'). It is based on printing money which is very inexpensive (compared to the nominal amount printed), to the point that it can be assumed zero. But the full nominal amount printed is then available to government to purchase goods and services, hence it is subtracted from the primary deficit. (Here, we are making the simplifying assumption that the Central Bank is part of the consolidated government.) Seignorage is the change in money supply (this is the revenue per period) deflated by the price level.

Equation (8.2) or (8.2') is called the government budget constraint and is fundamental in the theory of fiscal policy.[1] As an accounting identity, it records items of spending and revenue. But it also reveals a fundamental constraint that any government or public sector faces in the conduct of its fiscal, and more widely aggregate demand, policy. To put it in a nutshell, almost any government would like to spend; but there are important limits in financing such spending. Why would governments like to spend? First, in order to provide valuable goods and services (from health and education to defence and justice, from administration to building infrastructure) or subsidies and welfare support. Additionally, spending and taxes are tools of short-run macroeconomic management, i.e. a method to push economies out of slowdowns or recessions. This argument suggests reasons for actively varying spending and taxes, but the business cycles will also have endogenous implications for many elements of the primary deficit, mainly tax receipts and subsidies or welfare payments. The point therefore is that governments would ideally like to spend something extra, particularly

---

[1] As an accounting identity, equation (8.2) applies not only to government but to any financial unit, from a household to any business. The only difference is seignorage, which only applies to government (lawfully). In fact, much of the discussion in this and the next few sections can be readily carried over to another type of debt, that of a country as a whole towards the rest of the world, i.e. what is called external debt. In particular, the budget constraint (8.2) is identical (in this case called a national budget constraint), except that D is the balance of trade of the country in question with others.

during times of hardship. Equation (8.2) shows us the 'dark side of the moon', i.e. the difficulties in paying for such spending. There are three financing options.

One is to print more money. But let us be careful what this implies. It implies that for each additional unit of spending, an extra unit of money must be printed every period. One can see that even for modest increases in spending, the accumulated effect on the money supply after only a few periods is dramatic. And since inflation is generated by 'too much money chasing too few goods' (as the popular saying has it), then obviously this method of finance will no doubt exacerbate inflation. The method of inflationary finance is analysed in some more detail in Section 8.5; it is shown there that it creates one important link between monetary and fiscal policy. Suffice it here to say that for this reason, in the last 40 or so years, it has fallen into disuse in many countries as they sought to bring inflation rates down.

A second method is via more taxation. But there are serious economic and political costs with this method, too. First, particularly at high marginal rates, taxation provides a disincentive to work (for individuals) or invest (for firms). From elementary macroeconomics, we know that the additional taxation dampens the multiplicative expansionary effects of government spending. Second, it is in many countries highly politically undesirable. So, the conclusion is that this method does not provide a free lunch for governments either. In fact, as we shall show, all spending will sooner or later be financed by taxation, and this is the main reason why many people strongly object to government playing an important economic role.

Finally, another option is to raise more debt by issuing and putting in circulation more government bonds. This at first sight appears an innocuous method. After all, the lender (private sector) will get its money back in due course. Close inspection of (8.2) however, reveals an important pitfall. Imagine an increased (for just one period) government spending, to be financed by additional (more than usual) debt issue. This new debt increases the amount of debt outstanding next period and, with it, the interest payments that government must incur. With everything else the same as before, this will enlarge the broad deficit which will necessitate further debt issue, even if spending falls back to its old levels. This will subsequently mean yet more interest payments, new debt issue, etc. Thus, the additional debt issue quickly escalates by its own dynamic, if corrective action is not taken (e.g. by increasing taxes in the future).

At this point, a question arises as to the costs of government indebtedness. Following Buiter et al. (1985), we can argue that there are two types of cost of the debt, distributional and efficiency-related. The debt has distributional implications, as the people who receive interest from it and the people who pay taxes to finance it are not the same. Often, those who own debt (i.e. government bonds) and benefit from it are older and wealthier than the average taxpayer, whereas those who contribute more may be younger. To the extent that the debt holders are foreign, the country's resources are wasted on interest instead of being spent on public services. Furthermore, much of the debt will be repaid by the future generations who are saddled by it without benefiting from the services, and without taking part in the decisions. The efficiency cost arises from the fact that the debt effectively crowds out private investment, as both compete for financing from scarce savings. At the same time, the public debt plays a useful role in allowing government to continue to offer public services even in recessions when tax receipts are low, and even to expand spending and aggregate demand to stimulate the economy. Another useful role of the debt is that it allows spending on items whose benefits will materialize only after some time, such as investment on physical capital (infrastructure) or human capital (education, health). Since the benefits of such spending are long term, it is appropriate that the repayment should also take place gradually, thus giving rise to debt in the meantime. Balancing the benefits and the costs of government debt requires setting some limits on it. We review the associated issues and theory in Sections 8.4 and 8.5. We shall see that there is are no hard and fast rules as to how much indebtedness is allowed or safe to have.

Given that some debt is inevitable or even desirable, the question then arises, how much debt is the government able to raise from the private sector? As debt accumulates, doubts may be raised about the ability of the public sector to raise enough cash to honour its commitments (pay interest and repay the capital later on). As the private sector becomes nervous about the security of its assets, it may demand (through the markets) a 'risk premium' to be added to the interest rate in order to be persuaded to keep the larger amount of debt. This is already bad enough, as higher interest rates act to stifle investment and production through an increased cost of capital but also through the higher interest payments and precarious balance sheets that firms and individuals (e.g. homeowners) face. But importantly, it will also exacerbate the problem by adding to the interest payments. The worst-case scenario then is that the government becomes 'insolvent', i.e. unable to pay, and defaults. Thinking only of the loss of assets to individuals, this is a disruption of catastrophic proportions for the economy. While there have been a few episodes of public-sector default in modern economic history, due to the severity of such a contingency, advanced industrial economies (at least) have developed mechanisms (institutional and market-related) that avert this contingency, so it very rarely happens today. In other words, the solvency of governments is quite closely watched. The next section develops the notion of solvency more formally and shows ways in which it can be practically monitored.

The bottomline is, all methods of finance of deficits involve costs; there is 'no free lunch'. Equation (8.2) or (8.2') is a government budget 'constraint' exactly because it constrains the government's ability to provide spending on goods and services or welfare. Ultimately, government pays for the services it provides by raising taxes, which are economically and politically costly. Therefore, government (the public sector) is subject to resource constraints in the same way that any individual or private business is.

8.3 Measurement Issues, Inflation, and Variable Maturities

The above budget equation, or identity (8.2), sweeps under the carpet a number of measurement and other issues that merit a brief review; in this, we follow quite closely Buiter et al. (1985) and Elmendorf and Mankiw (1998). For more details and further references, the interested reader should consult these articles and Bohn (1992) and US Congressional Budget Office (2009).

8.3.1 Inflation

The budget equation is expressed in nominal terms in government accounts. Thus, instead of (8.2'), it takes the form, with superscript n on quantities:

$$B_{t+1}^n - B_t^n = D_t^n + i_t B_t^n - (M_{t+1} - M_t) \tag{8.2''}$$

where i_t is the nominal interest rate that prevails during period t. Now, the 'Fisher hypothesis' links the nominal and real interest rates via inflation, expected at the beginning of the period, π_t^e, as follows:

$$r_t = i_t - \pi_t^e \tag{8.3}$$

Dividing everywhere by the price level at t, we have:

$$B_{t+1}^n/P_t - B_t^n/P_t = D_t^n/P_t + i_t B_t^n/P_t - (M_{t+1} - M_t)/P_t \tag{8.4}$$

Or, using real quantities (without superscript n so that $B_t \equiv B_t^n/P_t$):

$$B_{t+1}(P_{t+1}/P_t) - B_t = D_t + i_t B_t - (M_{t+1} - M_t)/P_t \tag{8.4'}$$

We then use the definition of inflation:

$$\pi_t \equiv (P_{t+1} - P_t)/P_t \tag{8.5}$$

(Note: This exact definition assumes that the price level is measured at the beginning of the period.) We can rearrange the left side to get:

$$B_{t+1}(1 + \pi_t) - B_t = \Delta B_{t+1} + B_t(1 + \Delta B_{t+1}/B_t)(1 + \pi_t) = D_t + i_t B_t - (M_{t+1} - M_t)/P_t$$

where Δ is the 'difference operator', i.e. $\Delta B_{t+1} \equiv B_{t+1} - B_t$. Ignoring the second-order product above, $(\Delta B_{t+1}/B_t)\pi_t$ (change in debt times % change in prices), and utilizing the 'Fisher equation' (8.3), we finally get:

$$\Delta B_{t+1} = D_t + (r_t + \pi_t^e - \pi_t)B_t - (M_{t+1} - M_t)/P_t \tag{8.6}$$

As long as inflationary expectations coincide with actual inflation, the budget equation (8.6) takes exactly the same as the version (8.2), where everything is expressed in real terms. If, however, expectations diverge from actual, the two forms of the budget equation also diverge. In particular, an actual inflation rate above the expected reduces the effective interest rate by which government borrows. This may cause tendencies for government to engineer, or at least allow, surprise inflation. As we noted in Chapter 7, this fact may have been one of the reasons for the inflation bias prevalent in former decades. To limit this tendency, and its perception by markets, governments may use index-linked government bonds, whose value rises with the price level, therefore the 'real equation' (8.2) applies straight away. We return to this point below.

The key point in (8.6) is that, if the debt is considered in real terms, one should apply the real and not the nominal interest rate. The difference of course produces the item $\pi B/P$, inflation times the real debt; this is the erosion in the real value of debt due to inflation. This can be high, particularly in times of high inflation and/or high indebtedness. As Buiter et al. (1985, figure 3) show for UK finances 1967–83, applying the real interest rate instead of the nominal one in (8.6) can turn a heavy overall deficit inclusive of interest payments into a moderate one.

8.3.2 Different Maturities of Government Debt

In practice, governments use a variety of securities to raise funds, whose main differences may be in terms of maturity, but also in terms of the structure (some pay interest—a 'coupon'—explicitly, others do not pay any coupon but rely on capital gains in the price of bonds to deliver a return), or even currency of denomination. The question then is whether the simplified budget equation above is general enough to encompass a variety of bonds, particularly of different maturities. For concreteness, we assume two bonds that differ only in terms of the maturity, being otherwise identical. Further, one bond is a one-period bond as before, which is issued and redeemed at its face value (assumed unity in real terms) and pays a real interest rate r at its maturity. There is also a longer-period bond (its exact maturity does not matter), which is redeemed at its face value (also assumed unity in real terms) but at its issue, and during its life, it is traded at the secondary bond market; its price there is P_t^b (again in real terms). If so, the valuation of existing debt is $P_t^b B_t$, the number of bonds times their price. These bonds pay a real rate of return R_t. Thus, if only such bonds are used, the budget constraint takes the form (8.2'''):

$$P_t^b B_{t+1} - P_t^b B_t = D_t + R_t P_t^b B_t - (M_{t+1} - M_t)/P_t \qquad (8.2''')$$

At the beginning of each period, the policy-maker takes the second-hand bond prices as given and calculates how many new bonds to issue at those prices; this is the left side above. The needs to be financed are those on the right, that is, the primary deficit (D), the need to pay the appropriate rate of return on existing debt valued at market prices, minus seignorage.

Financial markets are assumed to be 'efficient', utilizing all available information valuing assets, and agents' attitude towards risk is risk neutrality. Under these crucial assumptions, agents equalize, through costless and riskless arbitrage, the rates of return over the two types of bond; this gives rise to the 'expectations hypothesis of the term structure of interest rates'. In particular, we have:

$$r_t = \frac{\bar{r} + P_{t+1}^b - P_t^b}{P_t^b} \qquad (8.7)$$

The future price should be the expected one, but expectations have been dropped. Note also that our assumptions imply that there is no risk premium associated with holding the long bond even though this is risky (under the existence of risk or uncertainty). According to the 'expectations hypothesis' (8.7), the rate of return on the 'short' bond (r_t) equals the overall rate of return on the 'long bond' on the right; this consists of the 'coupon' $\bar{r}$, i.e. a fixed payment on the long bond, as a percentage on the capital tied up in the bond—its trading price, and the percentage capital gains that may be realized as the bond price goes up (or loss if the bond price goes down). A number of observations here: first, as the bond reaches maturity, its price should tend to unity. (If it is redeemed at the fixed price of 1, why should anyone buy or sell it at a significantly different price one instant before maturity?) If so, then the 'short' real interest rate should equal the exogenous coupon rate. Secondly, defining the rate of (simple—without capital gains) rate of return on long bonds as $R_t = \frac{\bar{r}}{P_t^b}$, we see that in the long run, when long bond prices tend to unity, long and short rates are equal to each other. With this definition, we also have from (8.7),

$$r_t = R_t - \frac{R_{t+1} - R_t}{R_t} \tag{8.7'}$$

We finally see that the market rate of return on existing debt is none other than the coupon payments on existing bonds, $R_t P_t^b B_t = \bar{r} B_t$. Utilizing this information, and following the same steps as with the analysis on inflation, we can rewrite (8.2''') as:

$$B_{t+1}^m - B_t^m \approx D_t + (R_t + 1 - P_t^b/P_{t+1}^b)B_t^m - (M_{t+1} - M_t)/P_t$$

Where $B_t^m \equiv P_t^b B_t$ is the market value of existing debt (in real terms, but valued in the second-hand bond market). But from the previous formula,

$$R_t + 1 - P_t^b/P_{t+1}^b = R_t - \frac{R_{t+1} - R_t}{R_t} = r_t.$$

Thus, the budget constraint finally becomes:

$$B_{t+1}^m - B_t^m \approx D_t + r_t B_t^m - (M_{t+1} - M_t)/P_t \tag{8.8}$$

(8.8) is of the same form as the initial equation (8.2), therefore the latter may be used, with the understanding that B_t should be the total amount of existing debt as valued by the market. Therefore, under the assumptions underlying the 'expectational hypothesis of the term structure', the term structure of debt does not matter.[2]

8.3.3 Digression on the 'Term Structure of Interest Rates'

There is an interesting digression that may be developed from this analysis, related to the 'term structure of interest rates', i.e. the relation between 'short' and 'long' rates of return.

---

[2] Even though the economically meaningful B_t is the one that weighs each bond by its value in second-hand trading markets, typically, the published statistics give debt as the sum of the face value of the bonds. In this way, say, two governments that have the same debt-GDP ratio, one of which predominantly has bonds that expire in a short time while the other has long bonds, appear to be in exactly the same shape, which is obviously not true. In order to avoid this ambiguity, the IMF now monitors the 'Gross Financing Needs' of each country, which is payments of principal (expiring bonds), plus interest as well as the primary deficit; this is the amount that needs to be covered with new bonds. The point here is that a government can only issue a small amount of new bonds each year even if their overall indebtedness is not high. See Ellison and Scott (2017) for a measurement of UK debt and its sustainability based on market value; and Schumacher and Weder di Mauro (2015) for a measurement of Greece's debt, which is a lot but made up mostly of bonds of long maturities (so that the above arguments are particularly relevant).

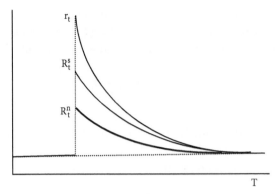

Figure 8.2. The term structure of interest rates following an unanticipated, temporary rise in the short rate

Starting from the equation on the short rate of return and long bond prices (8.7), we can solve for the long bond price as follows:

$$P_t^b r_t = \bar{r} + P_{t+1}^b - P_t^b$$

Solving forward by 'iterated substitution' as we have already seen, we get:

$$P_t^b = \bar{r}\{(1+r_t)^{-1} + (1+r_t)^{-1}(1+r_{t+1})^{-1} + \dots + (1+r_t)^{-1}(1+r_{t+1})^{-1}\dots(1+r_{t+n})^{-1}\},$$

where n is the periods to maturity. Or, using the definition of the 'long' rate of return R_t:

$$R_t = \frac{1}{(1+r_t)^{-1} + (1+r_t)^{-1}(1+r_{t+1})^{-1} + \dots + (1+r_t)^{-1}(1+r_{t+1})^{-1}\dots(1+r_{t+n})^{-1}}$$

$$(8.9)$$

This is a more extensive form of the same 'expectational hypothesis' embodied in (8.7). The long rate becomes a quasi-average of the short rates from now all the way to maturity. The long rate rises as the short ones do; it is also easy to check that in the steady state (when r is constant), R = r. Figure 8.2 illustrates the behaviour of the interest rates on two bonds, of maturities s and n with $1 < s < n$, when the one-period rate (r_t) rises unexpectedly from its long-run equilibrium value and then gradually returns to it.

Being an average of future one-period rates, and with the latter returning gradually to base, the long rate is always lower than the short rate, and gradually tends to it. In fact, the longer the maturity (the thicker the line above, and with $n > s$), the lower will be the long rate as the short rate is expected to fall. So, this 'term structure' implies that shorter rates are higher than the longer ones when they are temporarily high and expected to fall. But this term structure may be inverted when future short rates are expected to rise: in this case, the long(er) rates will be higher than the short(er). Finally, note that the above (exogenous) change in the short rate is sudden and unexpected. If it is expected to happen in the future, the long rate, being the average of future short ones, may jump before the short rate. The dynamics of change will be dictated by the arbitrage formula that equalizes their overall rates of return.

Note that (8.9) and the graph above embody only the 'expectations hypothesis on the term structure' (8.7) and no information about the deficit or the budget constraint, but they are perfectly consistent with those. In particular, the movement of the short rate exhibited above may be due to an expansionary fiscal policy. Blanchard (1981, 1984) and Turnovsky and Miller (1984) analyse further the effects of fiscal policy on interest rates in the presence of different maturities of government bonds, and develop graphs like the one above.

8.3.4 Adjustment of the Deficit for the Economic (Business) Cycle

The budget deficit is often used as a measure of the government's fiscal stance, i.e. how expansionary or contractionary it is. The problem with this idea is that the deficit varies endogenously with the economic cycle because tax receipts vary positively with output and incomes, and expenditures (unemployment benefits and other transfers) vary inversely with the cycle. Thus, the endogenous movement of the deficit will give misleading information about the fiscal stance; the deficit will take different values along the different phases of the cycle without any change in the fiscal stance and policies in place. An objective measure of fiscal stance therefore would disentangle the effects of policy itself (on expenditures, taxes, or transfers) and the endogenous ones due to the state of the economy on the deficit. To this end, the US constructs a 'standardized employment deficit' which is based on estimates of expenditures and tax receipts that would be incurred if the economy were operating at 'normal' levels of unemployment and 'trend output' capacity utilization (Elmendorf and Mankiw, 1999). The OECD constructs a 'cyclically-adjusted budget deficit' that estimates the deficit that would obtain under current policies in mid-cycle. The problem with all these measures, however important, is that they need to grapple with difficult and controversial issues such as the (expected) length of the cycle, the trend and normal output levels, etc.; see Blanchard (1990) for a thorough discussion of these issues, and his proposed 'indicator of discretionary change in fiscal policy' (IDCFP):

$$IDCFP_t = \left.\frac{PS_t}{GNP_t}\right|_{u_{t-1}} - \frac{PS_{t-1}}{GNP_{t-1}}$$

This is the primary surplus-GNP ratio at time t but calculated as if unemployment were at its $t-1$ rate, and taken as the change over the $t-1$ level. If policy changes between $t-1$ and t, this will change even at constant rates of unemployment; if the unemployment rate alone changes without any policy change, this index will be zero.

8.3.5 Government Assets and Liabilities, and the Deficit

Private sector firms' balance sheets equate their assets and liabilities, so a natural question is whether this applies to the public sector, and what is the relation of the public sector's assets and liabilities to the deficit. Government assets include financial assets (shares in private sector firms plus mortgages and loans extended to the private sector), physical capital, of which defence capital is a big item, and other assets such as land, ownership of mineral deposits, and other such resources. On the liability side, debt held by the public (B above) is the most obvious item, but also future claims on government because of commitments on social security (pensions) and the health system may be included. As the US Congressional Budget Office (2009, chapter 13) makes clear, unlike for private enterprises, assets need not equal liabilities in the case of government or state. This is because government can adjust unilaterally those items by law or decree—it is in fact the only entity on the land that has the authority to do so. Government can alter unilaterally its liabilities (e.g. future commitments on pensions or health care) and the resources it can muster to cover them (taxation). Another difficulty arising in the comparison between assets and liabilities is that many of the assets do not have an obvious valuation, certainly not from the market; e.g. the capital (defence, but also infrastructure), land, energy and mineral resources, etc. See Auerbach (2004) on the measurement of government equity.

How do the overall assets and liabilities relate to the deficit? Assets and liabilities are stock variables, whereas the deficit is a flow variable. As such, they are conceptually related by an equation of the same form as (8.2):

$$(L - A)_{t+1} - (L - A)_t = D_t + rL_t + (\theta - \delta)A_t - (M_{t+1} - M_t)/P_t$$

Here, instead of bonds, we have the difference between total public-sector liabilities and assets, $L - A$ (where L includes the debt held by the public B). Furthermore, we have the rate of return θ on assets (often a social rate of return, as it applies to infrastructure, capital such as education, and land) net of their depreciation and maintenance rate, δ. Furthermore, the financial deficit includes the investment expenditure on public capital, as is standard practice. Such an equation would link 'capital budgeting' (a public-sector balance sheet accounting for assets and liabilities) to 'operational budgeting' (the standard deficit that accounts for flow expenditures and receipts). The merit of such an approach would be that it would highlight all the connections between the two. For instance, government may undertake investment or maintenance expenditures on public capital of all kinds. In accounting terms, the financial expenditure on capital should be matched by the higher/better capital (assuming that no expenditures are wasted, e.g. via corruption). In the absence of capital budgeting, the investment/maintenance expenditures show up in the deficit, but the social benefit from better public capital does not show up anywhere. Similarly, if the government plugs a hole in its financial position by selling some of its assets, e.g. through privatization of public enterprises, the (one-off) proceeds from the sale decrease the deficit but the decline in public resources does not show up. (This is of course straightforward to amend, and is done by showing separately the one-off receipts from the main deficit.) But the point remains that capital budgeting would give a fuller picture of the state's net worth and future ability to meet its obligations. But it is not undertaken in any considerable degree due largely to the informational difficulties mentioned above.

8.4 Fiscal Solvency

8.4.1 The Meaning of Fiscal Solvency

A key question is, how much debt can a government raise without jeopardizing its ability to service it properly and repay it eventually? To gain intuition, consider a government that has inherited debt B_t at time t, and from then on runs a balanced budget—there are no primary surpluses, nor deficits (inclusive of seignorage), so $D_t = 0$. Their strategy is to finance the interest on existing debt and any bonds that are about to expire and their capital needs to be repaid by issuing yet more bonds. This government's budget constraint is:

$$B_{t+1} = (1+r)B_t$$

It is easy to see that, in this case, government debt will grow at exactly rate r. This is a strategy of indefinitely 'rolling over' government debt, financing any obligations that arise with yet more issue of debt. The question is, will the private sector be happy with this strategy? Obviously not, as there is no hope for the lenders to the government to recoup any of their money ever. So, the private sector will not allow this to happen except temporarily; as soon as they realize that this is a regular strategy, they will simply refuse to hold any more of this debt, and government will fail to finance its obligations by this method. A default will ensue. If the government ran deficits, it is obvious that the debt would grow at even higher rate than r, making the private sector even unhappier.

The only admissible strategy is for government to let debt grow at rate less than r. This will be possible only when there is a surplus (inclusive of seignorage), so $D_t < 0$. In this case, the government does not finance all its obligations (interest and capital repayment) by issuing more debt, but will start gradually repaying some of that by own means, i.e. by amassing a surplus. This need not happen every single period, but it should be the long-run strategy.

More formally, at the end of history, the government must have paid back all its debt; any remaining at that time will represent a net transfer of resources from private to public sector (a 'free lunch' for government) and the private sector will not allow that. Equally, the government will not allow any remaining debt of the private sector towards itself, so it cannot die with negative debt, either. These ideas are formalized as follows:

$$\lim_{t \to \infty} \frac{B_t}{(1+r)^t} = 0 \tag{8.10}$$

This equation is called a 'transversality condition' because it applies at the far-end boundary of history (as t approaches the limit of infinity). We have seen a similar equation in the dynamic analysis of Chapter 5. Accordingly, *discounted* debt at the far future equals 0 because, as analysed, if positive it would have been a free lunch for government, if negative for the private sector; both are excluded if each sector is to honour their commitments. One important feature is the presence of the discount factor applying to debt; this is so because one makes calculations now about the future. Finally, a point of terminology: if a government is solvent, its debt is said to be sustainable; the two terms are used interchangeably.

8.4.2 Implications of Fiscal Solvency

Thus, the transversality condition (8.10) stipulates that, for a government to remain solvent, discounted debt must vanish asymptotically. Repaying the principal in due course essentially requires that debt should not be rolled over indefinitely; in other words, that interest payments on existing debt should not be possible through the issuing of yet more debt. Instead, at least some interest payments (and/or repayment of the principal) should be made by own resources. In turn, this implies that debt should grow more slowly than the rate of interest (both considered in real terms). The effect therefore of the ratio is to measure the level of debt against the discounting factor in the denominator: Since the growth rate in the numerator is the growth rate of debt while the growth rate in the denominator is the real interest rate, equality to 0 implies that the latter should exceed the former.

Schemes whereby payment of interest occurs entirely through raising new debt have existed in history and continue to occur occasionally. They are commonly known as pyramid schemes (or Ponzi games, from a Boston esquire who pioneered them in the inter-war years) and attract subscribers on the back of promises of exorbitant returns that are to be made by attracting yet more subscribers. Eventually the pool dries up and everybody loses their money (except the scoundrels who however risk losing their freedom). Such schemes violate the transversality condition because no interest or capital payment occurs through the scheme's productively earned resources (as would have been the case with a healthy loan to a firm or individual). For this reason, such schemes are illegal.

Let us now explore condition (8.10) further. In order to do so, we are going to use the forward-substitution technique we have seen already. It goes like this: equation (8.2) holds for all periods, therefore it also holds for period $t + 2$:

$$B_{t+2} - B_{t+1} = \bar{D}_{t+1} + rB_{t+1} \tag{8.11}$$

where $\bar{D}_t \equiv D_t - (M_{t+1} - M_t)/P_t$ indicates the primary deficit net of money creation. We can solve for B_{t+1},

$$B_{t+1} = \frac{B_{t+2} - \bar{D}_{t+1}}{1 + r}, \tag{8.11'}$$

and insert into (8.2) to substitute B_{t+1} out:

$$\frac{B_{t+2} - \bar{D}_{t+1}}{1 + r} = \bar{D}_t + (1 + r)B_t \tag{8.11''}$$

We can do the same with employing the budget constraint yet one period ahead and using it to substitute B_{t+2} out; and continue repeatedly ('repeated iterations') until we obtain:

$$B_t = -\sum_{i=0}^{\infty} (1 + r)^{-i-1} \bar{D}_{t+i} + \lim_{s \to \infty} \frac{B_{t+s}}{(1 + r)^{s+1}}$$

By the transversality condition (8.10), the last term on the right side vanishes, so we are left with current debt equalling the present value of the (discounted) future negative primary budget deficits net of money creation:

$$B_t = -\sum_{i=0}^{\infty} (1 + r)^{-i-1} \bar{D}_{t+i} \tag{8.12}$$

Equation (8.12) contains a key implication of fiscal solvency. The important point is this: since $B > 0$ (all public sectors have debts and none is a net creditor), the quantity on the right must also be positive; because of the negative sign, at least some of the deficits must be negative (surpluses). Current debt must be matched (in order to be repaid) by future primary surpluses. These may arise from the excess of tax revenues over expenditures (ignoring money creation which is not being used as a method of finance any longer). Ultimately, all spending must be financed by taxation, now or sometime in the future; borrowing is simply a method of reallocating this burden of taxation across time. Note, however, that not all future deficits ought to be negative; just enough of them and in enough quantities to make their discounted sum equal to B_t.

Note that (8.12) and the analysis that led to it does not tell us how this debt has arisen. Rather, it tells us how it should be repaid in the future. To see how the debt arose as a result of past deficits, one should substitute backwards: Rewrite (8.2) as

$$B_{t+1} = \bar{D}_t + (1+r)B_t;$$

notice the root of $1 + r > 1$ in this autoregressive series; back-shift one period to get,

$$B_t = \bar{D}_{t-1} + (1+r)B_{t-1}.$$

Using this to substitute out B_t in the previous, we get:

$$B_{t+1} = \bar{D}_t + (1+r)\bar{D}_{t-1} + (1+r)^2 B_{t-1}$$

Carrying on in the same way, we get:

$$B_t = \sum_{i=0}^{\infty} (1+r)^{i-1}\bar{D}_{t-i}$$

Here, we have substituted backwards. This equation does tell us how debt has been generated: it is the result of past deficits augmented by interest. The interest is evident in the coefficient $1 + r > 1$, which will result in an explosive series (the coefficient of any given past deficit will increase geometrically as t grows, because of accumulated interest payments). Because such an explosive series makes little empirical sense, whenever roots greater than unity are encountered, those are 'solved forward' as in (8.12). Backward substitution is preferred, however, for roots less than unity. For more discussion, see Sargent (1987, chapter 9) and Blanchard (1979).

Forward-looking solutions and sums play an important role in macroeconomic theory. They are often used to represent financial relationships like the one between share prices and future dividends, and they are often called present value relations in that context. Present-value relations have a natural statistical parallel in co-integration (Campbell and Shiller, 1987).

8.4.3 Theory-Based Conditions of Fiscal Solvency

Intuitive approaches
The difficulty with both the transversality condition (8.10) and the present value formula (8.12) is that they are not readily operational. It is very difficult to make predictions about

debt or the fiscal plans of government beyond just a few periods, let alone at the end of history! Commentators therefore often take the more intuitive approach of monitoring the debt-to-income ratio, B/Y. Alarm bells sound when that ratio approaches excessive levels. This approach is intuitive and practical, yet theory does not give any guidance as to what is 'excessive' and leaves the door open to contrasting interpretations. Yet, this approach is sometimes adopted at high-profile fora, such as the Maastricht Treaty (1992) conditions for admission into the Economic and Monetary Union in Europe which stipulated a maximum permissible debt-to-income ratio of 60 per cent. Quite often, because of the arbitrariness of determining such a threshold, commentators monitor the evolution over time of B/Y and try to ascertain whether it increases or not; if it does, this is evidence of growing indebtedness, though nobody can say exactly when this becomes excessive. This approach also lends itself to econometric implementation, as one can apply stationarity tests on B/Y. Under an oft-made assumption, namely that the real interest rate exceeds the rate of growth of real GDP, r > g,[3] keeping B/Y constant is sufficient for satisfying the transversality condition (8.10); this is because B should be growing at the rate of growth of real GDP, g (so as to keep B/Y constant) which is less than the real rate of interest, r. On these grounds, the approach of focusing on the B/Y ratio can be a given a better theoretical justification.

Time-series properties of debt series as conditions for sustainability

A body of literature has sought to establish more rigorous, yet empirically testable criteria that are equivalent to or sufficient to ensure that the transversality condition (8.10) or, equivalently, the present value formula (8.12) should hold. The following results have been suggested about sufficient conditions of sustainability:

- Hamilton–Flavin (1986): Stationarity of debt (B_t should be an I(0) variable);
- McCallum (1984), Trehan and Walsh (1988): Stationarity of the deficit inclusive of interest (ΔB_t should be I(0));
- Quintos (1995) and Bohn (2007) have proposed that the first or m^{th} difference of debt should be an I(1) variable (where $m + 1$ should be a finite number). However, it is difficult to follow the intuition of such arguments. Logic suggests the second condition as most plausible, while the first seems too restrictive and the third unduly relaxed.

The reason why interest-inclusive deficit stationarity is sufficient for debt sustainability may be best understood with reference to Figure 8.3. A constant broad budget deficit

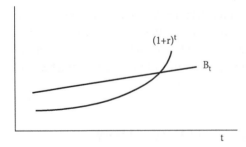

Figure 8.3. Time profiles of debt and the discount factor

---

[3] The assumption of r > g is valid if the economy is 'dynamically efficient', see Chapter 5.

(inclusive of interest payments) would raise the debt in such a way that the latter's time profile is a straight line. A higher (constant) deficit would raise the slope of the B line, while random fluctuations in the deficit would not alter significantly its outlook. The important point is to compare the time profile of B_t with the time profile of the discount factor $(1 + r)^t$. Since the latter has a constant growth rate (r), its time profile is exponential as shown in the Figure; the level of the real interest rate determines its slope. Whatever the level of the deficit and whatever the level of the real interest rate, the two lines will cross by virtue of the fact that the B line is a straight one, while the discount factor line is exponential. At the intersection, $B_t/(1 + r)^t = 1$. Allowing for sufficient time after that (as time grows to infinity), the ratio will tend to 0 and therefore (8.10) will be satisfied. The above discussion therefore calls for testing for the stationarity of the change in government debt, or else the broad budget deficit, which is a test that can be applied econometrically.

Furthermore, broad deficit stationarity implies co-integration between expenditures, taxes, and interest payments (rB). A practical problem is that the co-integrating vector should have specific coefficients $(1, -1, 1)$, something that cannot be easily ascertained, as co-integration tests have low power. An interesting approach is that of Trehan and Walsh (1991) who assume an arbitrary co-integrating coefficient $\alpha > 0$, namely that $D_t + \alpha B_t = $ constant; they show that sustainability follows (sufficient condition) if the above is of order I(0), and if in addition $D_t - \lambda D_{t-1}$ is also I(0) for any constant λ such that $0 < \lambda < 1 + r$. The interesting case here is $1 < \lambda < 1 + r$, as in this case the deficit will be I(1). To see why this is sufficient, note that under the assumptions, $B_t - \lambda B_{t-1}$ is also I(0) (as proportional to D_t), in other words the debt will be of order greater than I(1) but not quite I(2). In fact, its rate of growth will be $\lambda < 1 + r$, guaranteeing stationarity by the above arguments (see Bohn, 2007). We come back to these assumptions shortly, in the context of error corrections for the deficit and 'fiscal policy reaction functions'.

Debt, deficit, and output growth

The difficulties of both establishing clear-cut theoretical prescriptions but also empirically distinguishing orders of integration and co-integration has led some researchers to investigate more structural approaches. Consider again (8.12) with a constant deficit-GDP ratio:

$$B_t = -\sum_{i=0}^{\infty} (1 + r)^{-i-1} \bar{D}_{t+i} \rightarrow B_t/Y_t = -\sum_{i=0}^{\infty} (1 + r)^{-i-1} (\bar{D}_{t+i}/Y_t) \qquad (8.13)$$

Assuming a constant growth rate of g for Y_t, we can recast (8.13) in terms of ratios, $b_t \equiv B_t/Y_t$ and $\bar{d}_t \equiv \bar{D}_t/Y_t$ as follows:

$$b_t = -\frac{1}{1 + r} \sum_{i=0}^{\infty} \left(\frac{1+g}{1+r} \right)^i \bar{d}_{t+i} \qquad (8.13')$$

At the steady state when all ratios are constant ($b_t = b$ and $\bar{d}_t = \bar{d}$ for all t), we can solve out to get:

$$-\bar{d} = (r - g)b \qquad (8.13'')$$

(8.13") is sufficient for sustainability, as (8.12) is satisfied. The policy rule (8.13") ensures that debt-GDP returns to its original value after some time. Note that D < 0, i.e. a surplus is required to ensure that the initial debt is serviced and ultimately repaid. One key lesson of (8.13") is the important role of real GDP growth: it effectively decreases the real interest rate payable on existing debt and therefore decreases the required surpluses. This is important, as post-2009 we seem to have entered a phase of more sluggish growth (see Chapter 9 on 'secular stagnation'); we revisit the link between growth and indebtedness below. Note also that now the (growth-adjusted) overall deficit should be zero: $D/Y + (r - g)B/Y = 0$. This represents a strengthening and weakening of the condition we met earlier, when we said that the overall deficit should be constant or stationary, but not necessarily zero: strengthening in so far as now the interest-inclusive deficit must be 0; weakening, as the interest rate is reduced by the growth rate.

Partial summary: the relation between output and debt growth rates, and the real interest rate

In this sub-section, we explore the relation between the real output growth rate (g_Y), real debt growth rate (g_B), and the real interest rate, and their implications for fiscal (in-)solvency, as a way of partially summarizing our findings so far. Let us provide a typology of the various cases:

- $g_Y = g_B < r$: Fiscal solvency. The equality at the front implies a constant B/Y, while the inequality satisfies the transversality condition (8.10), ensuring fiscal solvency. This is the healthiest case that can realistically be expected.
- $g_B < g_Y < r$: This again satisfies the transversality condition but also ensures a falling B/Y ratio. No government will maintain this kind of discipline for long, unless they are required to tidy up their finances (and it will be difficult to maintain for the reasons explained in the next section).
- $g_B < r < g_Y$: Here, solvency is maintained in that (8.10) is satisfied, and B/Y is falling. But this case presents the logical problem that any discounted sum like the one on the right side of (8.13') above will not converge (i.e. they will sum up to infinity). As we discussed in Chapter 5, this is a case of 'dynamic inefficiency', which is both an anomaly and the available empirical evidence shows as being unlikely; for these reasons, it is not considered much in dynamic macroeconomics.
- $r < g_Y = g_B$: Here, a constant B/Y is maintained, but the discounted growth does not approach zero asymptotically: Apart from the insolvency implied here by the failure of (8.10), this case, too, shows dynamic inefficiency.
- $g_Y < r \leq g_B$: Plain fiscal insolvency: (8.10) fails and B/Y is growing perpetually. This government is either paying for interest payments by issuing yet more debt ('rolling over of debt'), or even adding yet more deficits.

Error corrections and fiscal policy reaction functions: stabilization and indebtedness

The Trehan and Walsh (1991) setup mentioned above generates an error-correction mechanism for the deficit, of the form:

$$\bar{D}_t = -\alpha B_t \tag{8.14}$$

According to this 'fiscal policy reaction function', the deficit adjusts negatively to the debt, in order to stabilize it; when the debt rises, a surplus emerges which checks the growth of the debt. It can be stochastic, but we ignore this possibility here. Its implications for sustainability are seen if (8.14) is combined with the period budget constraint (8.2), to yield:

$$B_{t+1} = (1+r)B_t + \bar{D}_t = (1+r-\alpha)B_t \qquad (8.14')$$

We thus have the following cases (see Bohn, 2007):

- Reaction functions with $\alpha > r$ imply stationary debts and deficits;
- Reaction functions with $\alpha < r$ imply mildly explosive paths for debts and deficits, but growing slowly enough to be consistent with sustainability (this is because in this case the debt will be growing at rate $r - \alpha$, while the discount rate is at r);
- The special case of $\alpha = r$ implies a stationary debt-difference and interest-inclusive deficit, and fits exactly the unit root and co-integration conditions discussed above.

However, (8.14) is a very restrictive fiscal policy reaction function. The 'model based sustainability' analysis of Bohn (2005) and Mendoza and Ostry (2008) consider both the repercussions of the deficit onto the rest of the economy as well as more general reaction functions. In that respect, with u_t being an error term, the following stochastic reaction function provides a sufficient condition for sustainability:

$$\bar{D}_t/Y_t = \delta_0 - \delta_1 y_{t-1} - \delta_2 B_{t-1}/Y_{t-1} + u_t \qquad (8.15)$$

The deficit-GDP ratio is expected to vary inversely with de-trended output, y_t, because of the endogenous behaviour of tax receipts and spending over the cycle, but also because of explicit stabilization policy. The key, sufficient though not necessary, condition for sustainability is that it should also decline as indebtedness increases, $\delta_2 > 0$. If so, more net revenues will be raised as the level of the debt rises, so the debt will be rising at less than the real rate of interest, and sustainability will be ensured. To see what this implies for the debt-GDP ratio, we again combine it with (8.2) to get:

$$\bar{D}_t/Y_t = \delta_0 - \delta_1 y_{t-1} - \delta_2(B_{t-1}/Y_{t-1}) + u_t = B_{t+1}/Y_t - (1+r)B_t/Y_t \qquad (8.15')$$

Assuming a constant growth rate of output (g), we can see that the debt-GDP stabilizes at the following mean level (for a sufficiently high δ_2 such that the denominator be positive):

$$E(b_t) = \frac{\delta_0}{\delta_2 - (r - g)} \qquad (8.16)$$

This is a powerful as well as intuitive formula. Accordingly, the debt-GDP is fuelled by the 'autonomous' deficit' δ_0. The degree to which the deficit responds (negatively) to the debt helps reduce the average debt ratio, as well as ensuring sustainability. The growth rate g also decreases this ratio. Mendoza and Ostry (2008) report a δ_2 mostly in the region of 0.02 to 0.04 in a panel of industrialized and emerging economies. Sustainability on the whole seems to be confirmed, but high-debt economies show little or no responsiveness in the primary deficit to increasing indebtedness (insignificant δ_2).

This argument may be extended by incorporating the stabilization role played by the deficit. Consider again the deficit reaction function (Z) above, but now let the state of the economy respond to the fiscal stance via a simple 'multiplier' (Keynesian or otherwise), $m > 0$, so that:

$$y_t = md_t$$

Incorporating this in the fiscal rule (8.15), the deficit (ignoring seignorage) is:

$$d_t = \delta_0 - \delta_1 d_{t-1}/m - \delta_2 B_{t-1}/Y_{t-1} + u_t$$

In the steady state, the mean debt-GDP ratio becomes:

$$E(b_t) = \frac{\delta_0/(1 + \delta_1/m)}{\delta_2/(1 + \delta_1/m) - (r - g)} = \frac{\delta_0}{\delta_2 - (r - g)(1 + \delta_1/m)}$$

Here, the responsiveness of the deficit to past output (δ_1) increases the debt, whilst the fiscal multiplier (m) decreases it, as it increases the response of output to deficits, therefore requires less deficit variability in the future. Differentiating with respect to δ_1/m, we can establish (left as an exercise) that the mean debt-GDP ratio increases with the stabilization role of the deficit (as more deficits are thus generated), but it declines with the multiplier, as with a higher multiplier the stabilization role of deficit is made easier. These points at the interface between the stabilization role of fiscal policy and the need to keep public finances in order are worth keeping in mind as governments increasing grapple with both issues, as we stated at the beginning. These issues merit more attention than they seem to have received so far in the literature.

8.4.4 Institutional Implications and Fiscal Rules

As theory does not seem to provide a clear-cut criterion of fiscal solvency and debt sustainability, many commentators look at the debt-GDP ratio, B/Y. For instance, the 'Maastricht Treaty' of 1992 that provided the cornerstone for the foundation of European Monetary Union established the following 'criteria': a debt ratio ceiling of B/Y < 60 per cent and deficit ratio of D/Y < 3 per cent. Though these requirements were never rigorously enforced, they were subsequently enshrined in the EU's 'Stability and Growth Pact'. However, as mentioned, the main problem with such restrictions is that they are reasonable but arbitrary: theory does not provide any reason to think that a specific debt-GDP ratio is a threshold beyond which the debt-GDP becomes really too much. Nor does theory provide any indication that any level of debt is optimal. Reinhart and Rogoff (2010) have argued that a threshold of B/Y = 90 per cent is critical, after which interest rates rise and growth is hampered; but the validity of this conclusion has been contested. See Panizza and Presbitero (2014) and Lee et al. (2017) for follow-up work on the link between debt and growth.

So, this author would suggest 100 per cent as a critical threshold, beyond which indebtedness becomes dangerously high. On what grounds? Behavioural and psychological, as much as anything else. You must put the marker down somewhere and 100 seems a natural threshold. A debt-GDP in excess of that is obvious to all; whereupon not only are the owners of the debt (bondholders) unwilling to keep them and try to sell, but also 'behaviouristic' effects set in such as contagion, herd behaviour, and panic. So, when $B/Y > 100$ per cent, one may be unwilling to hold a government bond not only because of one's own doubts about the solvency of this government bond but also because one can see the others selling. Such panic-driven selling of government bonds is the preamble to a 'sovereign' (government) debt crisis. Interest rates applicable to the bonds of the affected government rise sharply; a 'spread' develops between the interest rates of these bonds and of bonds of financially viable governments. See later in this chapter about the effect of indebtedness on interest rates.

In view of the rising indebtedness, various countries have tried to put in place various limits on either deficits or debt to ensure that public finances be kept on a sustainable footing—and are seen to be so. The overall objective is to ensure solvency while allowing the deficit and debt to vary over the cycle so as to perform two functions: a 'cushioning' function, where the variable elements of the deficit (taxes and transfer payments that are affected by the state of the economy) are allowed to vary without affecting public services; and a stabilization function, where spending and taxes vary across the cycle to provide the necessary fiscal stimulus. At the same time, there is a need to allow public investment, whose benefits will spread over time but the costs are upfront. Famously, the Gramm–Rudman–Hollings Acts of 1985 and 1987 in the US attempted to write into law the requirement to balance the budget; it did not work. In the UK in 1997, the new government (Labour) set out a twin rule: first, the 'golden rule': the deficit net of investment should be balanced over the business cycle; and secondly, the 'sustainable investment rule': investment should be such that debt should be kept less 40 per cent of GDP. These rules were in line with the objectives set out above but were later abandoned. However, the quest for appropriate rules and fiscal framework continued: The Budget Responsibility and National Audit Act of 2011 requires transparency of fiscal policy (clear targets and plans) and established the Office for Budget Responsibility to evaluate government plans and assess the long-term sustainability of the public finances. There have also been calls (Blanchard and Giavazzi, 2004) for the EU's Stability and Growth Pact to be amended along the lines of the UK's (former) 'golden rule'. See the Guidance for Further Study for more on fiscal rules and 'fiscal councils'.

8.5 'Fiscal Consolidation', Growth, and Inflation

8.5.1 Fiscal Solvency and 'Fiscal Consolidation'

If indebtedness in many countries is at very high levels, what does it take for it to come down? Typically, highly indebted countries embark on programmes of 'fiscal consolidation', commonly known as 'austerity': these aim to provide the required surpluses that will allow repaying the debt, as required by the sustainability condition (8.12). The catch is that these programmes are painful in their own right (they are fiscal contractions, by definition) and therefore they hurt growth. But we have seen various arguments why low growth in fact worsens the public finances, i.e. it worsens the task that the fiscal consolidation sets about to accomplish in the first place.

The April 2013 issue of the IMF's *Fiscal Monitor* (Statistical Table SA13a) calculated the cyclically adjusted primary surpluses required over the 2020–30 horizon in order for debt to fall to sustainable levels (< 60 per cent in advanced economies, < 40 per cent in 'emerging economies') by 2030. The average over the G-20 biggest group of economies is (in per cent) 3.8, with a number of countries required to produce larger surpluses than that: 5.6 per cent for Ireland, 6.6 per cent for Italy, 5.9 per cent for Portugal, 4.0 per cent for Spain, 4.2 for the UK, 4.1 for the US, and 7.2 per cent for Greece. These are large surpluses and they are required to be produced for prolonged periods of time, putting the respective countries under tough 'austerity' regimes for long. Eichengreen and Panizza (2016) have criticized the political and economic feasibility of such large and sustained surpluses, and show that, historically, they are rare. The German think-tank the Kiel Institute for the World Economy publishes a regular assessment of indebtedness among European countries (the 'Eurobarometer'); its February 2015 issue (Kiel Institute, 2015) is more optimistic about the required surpluses (the magnitudes of the required surpluses are smaller than those calculated by the IMF), but is equally pessimistic as Eichengreen and Panizza are about their feasibility.

In this section, we examine some more formal arguments linking fiscal consolidations to growth and explore the limits to 'austerity'. We also explore some related themes such as the costs of delaying the necessary consolidations and the (possible) link between the fiscal solvency and inflation.

8.5.2 Debt, Deficit, and Growth (Again): The Debate on Austerity vs. Growth

Growth plays an important role in the debt sustainability considerations—we saw that in the context of equation (8.13"), where the growth rate reduces the effective interest payments that government has to make. But the role of the growth rate can be emphasized more. Use the fundamental equation (8.2—with a variable interest rate and ignoring seignorage) and divide across by real GDP (Y_t) to obtain in ratios ($b_t \equiv B_t/Y_t$ and $d_t \equiv D_t/Y_t$):

$$\Delta b_{t+1} = d_t + (r_t - g_t)b_t \tag{8.17}$$

Imagine that there is an austerity policy in place whereby the d_t declines by about 5 per cent a year, but also real GDP and its growth rate decline by 5 per cent per year; this is due to the fiscal multiplier, discussed later on, and assumed to be around 1—a consensus figure. Imagine that the real interest rate remains constant, and the debt-GDP ratio (b_t) is 1.5. (All these numbers draw from the Greek experience, 2010–13.) Feeding the numbers into the above implies that the austerity policy will actually result in increasing the debt-GDP ratio by 2.5 per cent (= 0.5 × 5 per cent) a year! Then, more austerity may be required, with yet more similar results. Tsoukis (2017) pushes this argument one step further: a country with an already big debt may find it impossible to decrease debt via fiscal consolidation, as the austerity kills growth, requiring further austerity, leading eventually to a debt spiral. In this argument, the size of the fiscal multiplier is critical.[4] For example, in the above example, a debt-GDP ratio greater than one implies that fiscal consolidation will in fact lead to a rise of b_t, which spirals out of control.[5] A prime current example may be Greece, whose debt persists at 180 per cent of GDP, after years of crushing austerity (and a debt forgiveness initiative in 2012 which wrote off about half of the then debt).[6]

In any case, the results of the fiscal consolidation, whether it will reduce debt and over what horizon, become rather questionable. An example may be the UK where fiscal consolidation has been pursued for the best part of the decade, yet the debt-GDP persists around the 90 per cent mark and the date when the deficit will be eliminated keeps being pushed back. See Denes et al. (2013), De Grauwe and Ji (2013), Eyraud and Weber (2013), and Krugman (2012) for criticisms of austerity along these lines. These lines of arguments have led eminent commentators, e.g. Reinhart et al. (2015), to suggest that excessive indebtedness must be resolved by a mixture of measures, including fiscal consolidation but also debt forgiveness and perhaps some inflation (to reduce the real value of the debt); the exact mix and relevance of each of these elements remains to be determined. Additionally, as Denes et al. (2013) emphasize, any consolidation must be carefully designed so as to maximize the benefits and avoid the detrimental effects as much as possible.

8.5.3 Can Fiscal Consolidations be Expansionary?

A while ago, a number of important papers argued that far from being harmful for growth, fiscal consolidations can actually be expansionary even in the short run (Giavazzi and Pagano, 1990; Alesina and Perotti, 1995; Alesina and Ardagna, 1998). (This literature defined 'consolidation' as any episode during which the cyclically adjusted deficit-GDP ratio fell by more than 1.5 per cent within a year.) The reason for this strongly counter-intuitive effect is that, with such consolidations, a forward-looking sector foresees less government debt in the future therefore possibly lower interest rates, lower wage pressure and inflation, and increased profitability. A lot depends on the specifics, but typically such studies regressed growth on a constant and a dummy which takes the value of one in country-years when there was a consolidation; the estimated coefficient of this dummy turns out to be positive. A rejoinder is by Alesina et al. (2017), which looks at the effects of various types of fiscal measures in detail and argues that there are recessionary effects of fiscal consolidations, but mild and temporary.

---

[4] The role of the fiscal multiplier in this argument has been emphasized by Keynes. See Crafts and Mills (2015) who refute the suggestion of 'self-defeating austerity' for 1930s Britain.

[5] In other words, there is a 'debt Laffer curve', whereby a maximum amount of debt (as a per cent of GDP) is repayable by producing surpluses; beyond that, further fiscal consolidation produces more debt. This situation is related to 'debt overhang': so much indebtedness that even good projects will not be financed by the market; see the Guidance for Further Study.

[6] The flip side of this argument is that, if a government is on the good side of the Laffer curve, then there is the possibility of a fiscal free lunch: a fiscal expansion can pay for itself by in fact decreasing the debt-GDP ratio and the interest payments on it. This is essentially what is being suggested by DeLong and Summers (2012) and is at the heart of the 'Green New Deal' currently being proposed in the US and elsewhere. See Section 8.6.5 below.

These findings have recently been re-examined by Hernandez de Cos and Moral-Benito (2013) and Perotti (2013). The former paper argues that fiscal consolidations are not exogenous to economic growth as assumed in this literature; they are more likely to go ahead when times are good, and they are likely to stop (even temporarily) when there is a recession. Accounting for this endogeneity and reverse causality (from growth to consolidation episodes) reverses the earlier result: fiscal consolidations are shown to have contractionary effects on output, investment, and employment. The latter paper (Perotti, 2013) reviews in detail four major fiscal consolidation episodes in Europe in the 1980s and 1990s and records the details—composition of the fiscal contraction, exchange rate policy, and incomes policy for wage restraint, among other features. He finds that most of the consolidations were modest and not spending-based. The (modest) real output expansions were export driven. So, the consolidations were not expansionary as envisaged in the aforementioned literature; they are not caused by the private sector thinking that 'there are better days ahead'. They were demand driven, by the export sector. Incomes policies were key and there were serious distributional effects (widening inequality, poverty). Cugnasca and Rother (2015) examine the fiscal consolidations following the European debt crisis; on the whole, the multipliers are negative (and asymmetric—see below), with expansionary effects arising out of improved confidence in only a few cases.

Ball et al. (2011) also argue that fiscal consolidations do induce employment and output loss in the short run; they conclude that such programmes have the best chances of succeeding when they allow some short-term flexibility around their medium-term objectives. In follow-up work, Ball et al. (2013) find that fiscal consolidations have significant distributional effects by raising inequality, decreasing wage income shares, and increasing long-term unemployment.

8.5.4 The Cost of Delayed Stabilization

As consolidation is costly, as at least is suggested by everyday experience if not always by formal evidence, governments find themselves politically constrained to embark on it. We close this section by looking at what happens if a necessary consolidation is postponed due to political pressures; in this, we ignore the question of whether consolidation affects output and how, and simply assume that it is politically difficult (as suggested by Eichengreen and Panizza, 2016). In this analysis, we draw on Blanchard (1990).

We begin from the solvency requirement expressed as ratios over GDP (8.13') (ignoring seigniorage). We assume that the debt at time t is b_t and the spending-GDP ratio from t on (including transfers) is y_{t+i}, for $i \geq 0$. (with the expectation sign ignored). Let us assume that, with this debt and spending profile, the constant tax rate that satisfies (8.13') if applied from t onwards is denoted τ^{*t}; i.e. this is such as to satisfy:

$$b_t = -\frac{1}{1+r}\sum_{i=0}^{\infty}\left(\frac{1+g}{1+r}\right)^i (y_{t+i} - \tau^{*t})$$

Therefore:

$$\tau^{*t} = (r-g)\left[\frac{1}{1+r}\sum_{i=0}^{\infty}\left(\frac{1+g}{1+r}\right)^i y_{t+i} + b_t\right]$$

The sustainable tax rate equals an intertemporal average of the spending-GDP ratio, plus (growth-adjusted) interest payments on existing debt. This is informative in its own right, but it can also tell us something about the cost of delaying a stabilization programme. If we replace b_t with recourse to basics, we then get:

$$\tau^{*t} = (r - g)\left[\frac{1}{1+r}\sum_{i=0}^{\infty}\left(\frac{1+g}{1+r}\right)^i y_{t+i} + \frac{1+r}{1+g}b_{t-1} + \frac{y_{t-1} - \tau_{t-1}}{1+g}\right] = \frac{1+r}{1+g}\tau^{*t-1} - \frac{r-g}{1+g}\tau_{t-1}$$

where τ_{t-1} is the actual tax rate that applied in $t-1$ and τ^{*t-1} is the tax rate that would have balanced the books if it had been applied from $t-1$ onwards (in analogy to the previous). We can then rewrite this formula as:

$$\tau^{*t} = \tau^{*t-1} + \frac{r-g}{1+g}(\tau^{*t-1} - \tau_{t-1}).$$

This equation links the constant tax rates that would have applied if sustainable fiscal policies had been initiated at times t and $t-1$. The quantity in parentheses is the shortfall between the sustainable and actual tax rates at time $t-1$—this will be positive if the actual tax rate at $t-1$ is less than the one required for sound public finances (stabilization is delayed). The formula tells us how much this costs next period, in the sense of how higher the sustainable tax rate will be if stabilization is initiated at t instead of $t-1$. In other words, this tells us that for every 1 per cent that the tax rate is less than the sustainable level and for every period that the stabilization is delayed, the required rate next period increases by $(r-g)/(1+g)$ per cent. For instance, with $r-g=2$ per cent, a tax shortfall of 5 per cent implies a 0.1 per cent tax rate higher next period, and a permanently higher tax rate by 1 per cent if stabilization is delayed by 10 years (the example of Blanchard, 1990). Again, we see the critical role played by the output growth rate in such calculations.

8.5.5 Fiscal Policy, Seignorage, and Inflation

As mentioned, seignorage revenue has greatly decreased by now in industrialized economies as the inflation rate has decreased dramatically. However, as public finances have worsened, it is conceivable that inflation may arise again in the future as a partial solution (see Ball, 2014; Blanchard and Summers, 2017; Rogoff, 2014). The purpose of this section is therefore to investigate the links between deficits, debt, and inflation.

We have called 'seignorage' the nominal quantity of monetary base (M0) created every period deflated by the price level—let us now denote it by S_t:

$$S_t = (M_{t+1} - M_t)/P_t \tag{8.17}$$

Now, we can divide and multiply by M_t to obtain:

$$S_t = ((M_{t+1} - M_t)/M_t)(M_t/P_t) \tag{8.17'}$$

In other words, seignorage is the percentage growth rate of monetary base times its real quantity. The latter is determined by the public's willingness to hold real money balances (the real money demand), whereas the former is decided by the government. We can analyse the rate of growth of M in a useful way. Let us assume for the moment that real money demand is given by a simple quantity-theory-type equation:

$$\frac{M_t}{P_t} = mY_t, \quad m > 0 \tag{8.18}$$

where m > 0 is a constant (*not* the fiscal multiplier as above). Then, for the equality between the two sides of (8.18) to be maintained, the rates of growth must be related as:

$$(M_{t+1} - M_t)/M_t = (Y_{t+1} - Y_t)/Y_t + (P_{t+1} - P_t)/P_t \tag{8.19}$$

The rate of growth of monetary base must equal the rate of growth of GDP plus the inflation rate. In other words, the monetary authority must supply enough extra cash to cover the growing transactions need due to the growing output, while the rest of the money growth will fuel inflation. Indicating the real GDP rate of growth by g and inflation by π and substituting in (8.15) above, we have:

$$S_t \equiv (M_{t+1} - M_t)/P_t = (g_t + \pi_t)(M_t/P_t) \tag{8.19'}$$

The first part of seignorage due to the growth in real GDP is called real seignorage and represents a free lunch for government, insofar as the marketplace needs to be furnished with enough cash for its needs, cash that the monetary authority supplies almost costlessly. The latter part, linked more directly to inflation, is called an inflation tax, because, by eroding real balances through inflation, it acts as a tax on the private sector. Financial liberalization and innovation have reduced the demand for real balances by the private sector (M/P) and this provides another reason why seignorage has by now practically vanished.

One lesson we can glean from (8.19') brings us back to Friedman's 'k per cent' rule we discussed in Chapter 1. The point is that government can create enough seignorage to cover the economy's new transactions needs without generating inflation; this is k per cent, equal to $g_t M_t/P_t$ in our context. Any seignorage in excess of that will generate inflation. This brings us to the relation between fiscal and monetary policy, or else between deficits and inflation. The link arises as a way of financing the deficit; as all methods of finance are costly, a government may resort to creating seignorage revenue, in effect monetizing the deficit. Furthermore, equation (8.6) suggests that it is unexpected inflation that really reduces the deficit, as the expected inflation will be incorporated into a higher interest rate (recall the Fisher equation $i = r + \pi^e$). This provides a temptation for governments to produce unexpected inflation, which may have been one of the driving forces behind the problems of discretionary policy that we saw in Chapter 7.

The 'unpleasant monetarist arithmetic' of Sargent and Wallace (1981) brings this analysis to its logical conclusion by suggesting that any unsustainable spending and taxing plans will necessarily lead to inflation. This is because the government will have to resort to seignorage in order not to violate the transversality condition (8.12). This will cause inflation in the future. But any future inflation will manifest itself in inflation *now* as well. It is not difficult to imagine why, particularly if we consider the wage-price spiral:

wage contracts that are signed now and will be valid for some time will have to consider future inflation and will therefore stipulate higher wages. Firms' costs rise now, and they pass this on to higher prices now, so inflation rises straight away when unsustainable fiscal plans emerge.

8.5.6 The 'Fiscal Theory of the Price Level'

A direct link between (excessive) debt and inflation was boldly proposed by a literature known as the 'fiscal theory of the price level'. The starting point here is the sustainability condition (8.10), which may be rewritten as:

$$B_t^n / P_t = -\sum_{i=0}^{\infty} (1+r)^{-i-1} \bar{D}_{t+i}, \tag{8.20}$$

where we have made use of the real and nominal debt link, $B_t \equiv B_t^n / P_t$. Now, nominal debt divided by the price level equals the future surpluses (in real terms). At any time, the debt is given by the past history of deficits. What happens if the projected fiscal plans of government (the future surpluses on the right) do not ensure that the above equation holds? The FTPL asserts that the price level (P_t) will do the adjustment: If debt is higher than the expected future surpluses, the price level will rise to ensure equality.

The theory did attract some attention a few years back, but it somehow failed to catch. A very indicative list of contributions would include early ones by Leeper (1991), Sims (1994); exponents like Woodford (1995, 2001), Cochrane (2001), and Schmitt-Grohe and Uribe (2000); critics include Buiter (2002), and McCallum and Nelson (2005). Canzoneri et al. (2001) evaluate the theory on empirical grounds and argue that post-war US data are not consistent with it.

What happens in the case when (8.20) is not satisfied? One possibility is default by the government. The 'fiscal theory of the price level' gives another answer: the market mechanism has a way of averting this outcome by the rise of the price level such that, given the value of nominal debt, real debt declines and (8.20) holds. The mechanism how this may happen is via excess demand: if (8.20) is not satisfied, markets will think of government bonds as worthless as there are not sufficient funds for them to be repaid in due course. Bondholders will start selling those; some of the proceeds will go to other assets but some will be used to buy goods and services, creating excess demand and inflation. A criticism that can be made here (though I have not seen it in the literature) is that the price level is unable generally to adjust in discrete jumps as might be required, because of price stickiness. What can adjust as fast as required is the rate of growth rate of prices, inflation (π). The theory is in fact flexible enough to incorporate this possibility. Take equation (8.13") again and re-express it as:

$$b = \frac{-\bar{d}}{i - \pi - g} \tag{8.13'''}$$

Since both debt and the price level are given at any time t, there is no harm writing real debt on the left as a given. The real interest rate is written as nominal minus inflation (disregarding inflation expectations). We see that, if the nominal interest rate is kept constant by monetary policy in the background, a rise in inflation will raise the discounted value of future surpluses (assumed constant at d per cent of GDP). This is where the potential for inflation arises. As mentioned, eminent commentators do not exclude the possibility that inflation might rise again. And the idea that inflation is a joint fiscal-monetary phenomenon (and not simply monetary) is gaining ground; see Leeper and Leith (2016) and Cochrane (2019).

Buiter (1985, table 2) provides information on how the large post-war debt in the UK (of the order of 250 per cent of GDP in the end of 1940s) was gradually decreased between 1949 and 1984. This information can be examined with equation (8.13''') in mind. The debt-GDP declined by 194 per cent; on average, there were deficits (not surpluses as the theory requires) that in fact created another 106 per cent of debt over time. The effect of inflation (πb) was to reduce debt by 195 per cent and of growth (gb) by another 98 per cent. In other words, the (very considerable) war indebtedness was reduced in relative terms by inflation and the growth of the economy; it was not actually repaid. Interestingly, interest payments do not seem to have had much of an effect, presumably because they were kept at low levels by administrative control throughout that period.[7] But see Hilscher et al. (2014) for a sceptical examination as to whether such a strategy may significantly reduce the US debt.

8.5.7 The Fiscal Theory of Interest Rates?

In the spirit of the 'fiscal theory', one may show the effect of indebtedness on interest rates; we finish by showing this. To see this, take again (8.13''') and write $b = P^b B/Y$, i.e. debt valued at market prices as a per cent of GDP, as we discussed in Section 8.2. B is the number of bonds (of long maturity outstanding at t) and P^b is their market price in real terms. Now, if the surpluses on the right are lower than the debt on the left, the markets will perceive insolvency and try to get rid of these government bonds. Their price will drop, bringing about the required equality. As the bond price is inversely related to their real interest rate, the observable symptom here will be a rise in long interest rates. This is straightforward extension of the theory but seems to have received little attention.

Hubbard and Engen (2005), Faini (2006), and Laubach (2009) have looked empirically at the relation between government bonds and interest rates; the finding seems to be a modest relation; in the words of Hubbard et al. (2005), 'an increase in government debt equivalent to 1 per cent of GDP would likely increase the real interest rate by about two to three basis points' (= 0.02 or 0.03 per cent). The experience of sovereign debt crisis in the Eurozone from 2010 onwards may prompt an upward revision of this finding. This experience has brought the relation between debt and interest rates into sharp relief, with the 'spreads' between the interest rates of the vulnerable bonds and the German bond rate (safe bond) rising. One factor that confuses things is the possible non-linearity

---

[7] The administrative control of monetary and financial matters (e.g. fixing interest rates or maturities of government bonds) is referred to as 'financial repression'.

involved: interest rates may rise faster after debt reaches a certain threshold. This may be due to limited information and the bounded rationality of market participants: e.g. no one took seriously the possibility that a Eurozone country, such as Greece in 2009, could practically default. But once the possibility dawned on market participants, no one wanted to be left holding bonds whose price would decline over time. So, selling of bonds accelerated, and Greek bond interest rates escalated. This is the 'herding behaviour' and 'contagion' we mentioned above, evident in all financial crises.

8.6 On the Effects of Government Spending on Economic Activity: A Toolkit of Static Multipliers

Having examined debts and deficits, the rest of this chapter turns to more traditional themes, predominantly the stabilization role of fiscal policy. Can fiscal policy play a stabilization role? What are its effects on output? Will a 'stimulus package' like that enacted by President Obama in 2009 work? We begin in this section by reviewing the theory and evidence around the fiscal multipliers.

8.6.1 The Demand-Based ('Keynesian') Multipliers

We begin with the standard textbook multipliers that go all the way back to the followers of Keynes. They may be called 'Keynesian' in the sense that they focus entirely on aggregate demand. Denoting the output by y and government spending by g (all real) and by MPC the constant marginal propensity to consume, the spending multiplier with given lump-sum taxes is:

$$\frac{dy}{dg} = \frac{1}{1 - MPC} > 1 \qquad (8.21a)$$

As spending rises (falls) but taxes stay the same, the deficit also rises (falls) in the background, financed by issuing more (less) bonds. Numerical illustration: with $MPC = 0.6$, this is of the order of 2.5. Note that real consumption is $dc/dg > 1 (= 1.5)$. This is in fact what makes it a 'multiplier'. The implication of this is that the consumer is better off with the fiscal expansion, the fiscal expansion is not 'eating into' private consumption but actually increasing it. This crucially depends on the multiplier being higher than one; therefore, as we shall see, this becomes a focal question in the literature.

The tax multiplier (tax being always lump-sum, τ):

$$\frac{dy}{d} = -\frac{MPC}{1 - MPC} \qquad (8.21b)$$

Again, the background assumption is that any tax change will have an impact on the deficit and debt issue. As (8.21b) is less than the spending multiplier (8.21a), the implication is that for each pound of worsening of the deficit, one gets more stimulus (bigger 'bang for the buck') by increasing spending than by cutting taxes.

The balanced-budget multiplier (i.e. with $dg = d\tau$):

$$\frac{dy}{dg}\bigg|_{dg=d\tau} = 1 \tag{8.21c}$$

The serious implication here is that you can expand government spending to get the economy out of a recession without hurting public finances.

These are powerful results but also subject to powerful criticisms, so that almost no one takes them seriously today beyond elementary textbook level.

- As these multipliers are entirely demand-based, the implicit assumption is that the economy is not subject to any supply-side restrictions. Roughly speaking, this only applies under conditions of a lot of unemployment, spare capacity, and slackness, a deep recession. In the real world, there will be at least partial crowding out of the extra expenditure by either higher interest rates and/or higher prices (cf. IS-LM and AD-AS models). The crowding out will be stronger the closer we are to 'full employment' and 'full capacity'—in other words, closer to the point where supply-side constraints begin to 'bite'. This motivates the supply-side multipliers below.
- The MPC is assumed constant, irrespective of whether we are in a good or bad year, whether we are savers or borrowers, young or old, and whatever the method of finance of government spending. The 'intertemporal approach' to fiscal policy, reviewed below, rectifies many of these weaknesses. A specific result arising from that model is the 'Ricardian equivalence' proposition, which suggests that the tax multiplier in particular is zero.

8.6.2 The 'Neoclassical' (Supply-Based) Approach

As we approach full employment, supply constraints begin to emerge: there will be shortages of labour, so that higher wages must be paid to motivate more supply or materials. In some cases, capacity constraints may be reached. Firms and workers may be encouraged to raise prices and wages rather than supply more (output or labour). The 'neoclassical multiplier' takes these considerations into account: it focuses entirely on the supply side, and in particular on labour supply and (implicitly) assumes that the economy is at its 'normal' state with unemployment at its 'natural' rate (this is 'full employment'). The overall question that this model addresses is as follows. For the extra output demanded by government, supply must increase and this needs extra work. If I am working my 'normal' hours, will I wish to work the overtime required, getting more tired, and foregoing leisure time? (Note, leisure does not mean idle, it means quality time with family or hobbies.) Will the housewife or househusband be tempted to work more? They will need extra childcare for that. In all cases, to induce the extra work, the real wage needs to go up. This argument is at the heart of this multiplier. See Hall (2009), Mulligan (2011), Woodford (2011).

The argument focuses on the individual's and firm's decisions. It may be useful to refer to Chapters 3 and 5 for a better understanding. Utility takes the additively separable form (sub-utility of consumption, $u(c)$, minus sub-utility of work, $v(h)$):

$$\text{Max}_h \quad u(c) - v(h)$$

where c is real consumption, h is hours, with u' > 0, u" < 0 (diminishing marginal utility of consumption), v' > 0, v" > 0 (increasing disutility of work). This maximization is subject to the budget constraint:

$$y = wh + \pi = c + \tau$$

Income (equal to output or GDP) is equal to labour income, wh, with a real wage w, and profits ($\pi \geq$, positive if there is imperfect competition). All income is used for consumption and for paying lump-sum taxes. In this model, there is no saving or investment, as there is no growth. The economy is closed. As profits are exogenous to the individual, this results in the standard optimality condition:

$$\frac{v'(h)}{u'(c)} = w$$

The marginal disutility of labour, normalized by the marginal utility of consumption, equals the marginal benefit from work (real wage). Rewriting this as:

$$v'(h) = wu'(c), \tag{8.22a}$$

we see that marginal cost equals marginal benefit—from work. This equation is effectively a labour supply function, as v'(h) varies inversely with h.

Firms maximize profits:

$$y = f(h) - wh$$

Where f(h) is a standard production function without capital, with the usual properties of f'(.) > 0, f"(.) < 0 (positive but diminishing marginal product). This results in:

$$f'(h) = w$$

The marginal benefit from an extra hour of employment is equalized to its marginal cost for the firm, i.e. the real wage. This equation is essentially labour demand. This needs to be generalized to take into account imperfect competition, when prices are set with a markup $\mu > 1$ over marginal cost (w/f'(h)), resulting in:

$$f'(h) = (1 + \mu)w \tag{8.22b}$$

In this case, the real wage equals the marginal revenue product of labour (f'/(1 + μ), which is less than the marginal product. As we saw in Chapters 3 and 4, the monopoly markup reduces the real wage, equilibrium hours, and output of the model. If it varies, it possibly affects the multiplier over the business cycle.

Government is initially assumed to run no deficit, $g = \tau$. From national Income Accounting, we also have:

$$y = c + g.$$

With $u'(c) = u''(y - g) = u'(f(h) - g)$, the two optimality conditions yield:

$$\frac{v'(h)}{u'(f(h) - g)} = f'(h)/(1 + \mu)$$

Totally differentiating, we get:

$$\frac{v''(.)dh}{u'(.)} - \frac{v'(.)}{(u'(.))^2} u''(.)(f'(.)dh - dg) = f''(.)dh/(1 + \mu)$$

Dividing by the previous:

$$\frac{v''(.)dh}{v'(.)} - \frac{u''(.)}{u'(.)}(f'(.)dh - dg) = \frac{f''(.)dh}{f'(.)}$$

It is useful to express the above in terms of the following elasticities:

$$\eta_{uu} \equiv \frac{u''c}{u'} < 0 \quad \omega_{vv} \equiv \frac{v''h}{v'} > 0, \quad \phi_h \equiv \frac{f'h}{f} > 0, \quad \phi_{hh} \equiv \frac{f''h}{f'} < 0$$

The signs follow from the fact that all first derivatives are positive, while second derivatives of convex functions are positive but of concave functions negative. Hence, we get:

$$\omega_{vv}\frac{dh}{h} - (\eta_{uu}/c)(\phi_h ydh/h - dg) = \phi_{hh}\frac{dh}{h}$$

where of course $f(h) = y$. Sorting things out:

$$\frac{dh/h}{dg/g} = \frac{-\eta_{uu}\left(\frac{g}{c}\right)}{-\eta_{uu}\left(\frac{y}{c}\right)\phi_h + \omega_{vv} - \phi_{hh}}$$

And in a straightforward manner:

$$\frac{dy/y}{dg/g} = \frac{-\eta_{uu}\left(\frac{g}{c}\right)\phi_h}{-\eta_{uu}\left(\frac{y}{c}\right)\phi_h + \omega_{vv} - \phi_{hh}}$$

Thus, with the signs of the elasticities shown above, we have the following key result about the multipliers:

$$0 < \frac{dh/h}{dg/g}, \quad 0 < \frac{dy/y}{dg/g} < 1 \tag{8.23a}$$

Hours of work rise in response to the spending stimulus (dg > 0) and output rises but less, in percentage terms, than the rise in spending. The intuition for this result is the following: as government spending rises, with a given output, consumption is crowded out. As u'(c) rises (why?), the marginal disutility of work falls, and the individual supplies more hours of employment. This allows extra output to be produced to accommodate the extra output. But consumption must fall: this is what motivates the individual to work harder (as just argued). This argument is at the heart of the result that output rises but proportionally less than government spending.

We also want a multiplier in terms of pound change in output for pound change in government spending (not in percentage changes). Multiplying both sides by y/g, we get:

$$\frac{dy}{dg} = \frac{-\eta_{uu}\left(\frac{y}{c}\right)\phi_h}{-\eta_{uu}\left(\frac{y}{c}\right)\phi_h + \omega_{vv} - \phi_{hh}}$$

We immediately have:

$$0 < \frac{dy}{dg} < 1 \tag{8.23b}$$

Output rises but by less than the increase in government spending. This is a key result of the neoclassical multiplier (see Hall, 2009; Woodford, 2011; and Mulligan, 2011). The intuition is essentially as given above.

Let us give a numerical illustration based on Hall (2009). With output $y = h^a$ and the following utility function:

$$u(c) - v(h) \equiv \frac{c^{1-\frac{1}{\sigma}}}{1 - \frac{1}{\sigma}} - \beta\frac{h^{1+\varphi}}{1 + \varphi}$$

σ would be the elasticity of intertemporal substitution in consumption in an intertemporal setup; as discussed in Chapter 5, the evidence shows $0 < \sigma < 1$. $\varphi > 0$ determines the convexity of the disutility of work; because $\frac{\beta h^\varphi}{u'(c)} = w$, $1/\varphi$ tells us how hours (h) respond to changes in the real wage, therefore φ is an inverse index of the elasticity of labour supply. $\beta > 0$ generally determines the importance of the disutility of work. With these, $-\eta_{uu} = \frac{1}{\sigma}$, $\phi_h = \alpha$, $-\phi_{hh} = 1 - \alpha$, $\omega_{vv} = \varphi$, so that we get:

$$\frac{dy}{dg} = \frac{\frac{1}{\sigma}\left(\frac{y}{c}\right)\alpha}{\frac{1}{\sigma}\left(\frac{y}{c}\right)\alpha + \varphi + 1 - \alpha} = \frac{\alpha}{\alpha + \sigma(1 - g/y)(\varphi + 1 - \alpha)}$$

This is positive as $0 < \alpha < 1$ (diminishing marginal product of labour). The output multiplier is a decreasing function of the inverse labour supply elasticity φ, an increasing function of the labour elasticity of production α, and a decreasing function of the consumption curvature parameter σ. Hall (2009, p. 199) gives the following likely magnitudes for theses parameters: $\alpha = 0.7$; $0.2 < 1/\varphi < 1$; $\sigma = 0.5$; $g/y = 0.2$. With these, the multiplier takes a value of the order of 0.4, at the lower end of empirical estimates (see below).

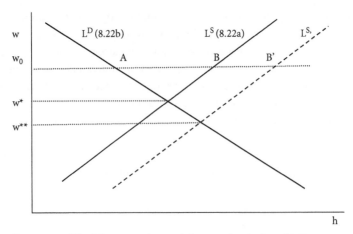

Figure 8.4. The labour market and the neoclassical multiplier

Leaving aside its foundational assumption of 'full' employment and abstraction from demand, this multiplier may be criticized on a couple of points. First, it depends crucially on the marginal utility of consumption. But how likely is that to change when government changes its spending incrementally? The multiplier would have been zero if the marginal utility of consumption stayed constant. Secondly, the real wage appears counter-cyclical, at least when the output fluctuation is caused by government spending. But as we have seen, this is in contrast to empirical evidence. Even more intriguingly, there seems a logical difficulty with this line of argument, exemplified in Figure 8.4.

This Figure casts this multiplier into the labour supply-demand framework, which is its natural context as it focuses on employment. Demand comes from the firm's optimality condition (8.22b) and supply from the individual's (8.22a). The argument is that a government spending rise effectively shifts the labour supply L^S to $L^{S'}$. The real wage declines (w^* to w^{**}) and hours worked expand. But this crucially depends on market clearing. If the real wage is stuck at w_0 (say) due to wage stickiness, then there is involuntary unemployment of AB; the expansion will raise this unemployment to AB'. This result of rising involuntary unemployment in the face of a rise in government spending is strongly counter-intuitive and casts some doubt on the validity of this multiplier. More research in this area would seem to be warranted.

As an extension of the basic model, Hall (2009) considers a variant of this multiplier with sticky prices, in order to bring the magnitude of the theory-based multiplier closer to empirical estimates; see also Woodford (2011). This extension relies on variations of the markup over the cycle. If the markup varies, then the total differentiation above should be modified to:

$$\frac{v''(.)dh}{u'(.)} - \frac{v'(.)}{(u'(.))^2}u''(.)(f'(.)dh - dg) = \left(f''(.)dh - \frac{d\mu}{1+\mu}\right)/(1+\mu)$$

If the markup is inversely related to output and hours (counter-cyclical), this can be captured schematically by $d\mu/(1+\mu) = -\theta dh/h$, with $\theta > 0$ indicating the variability of the markup relative to output. Incorporating this, and retracing the previous steps, we get:

$$\frac{dy}{dg} = \frac{-\eta_{uu}\left(\frac{y}{c}\right)\phi_h}{-\eta_{uu}\left(\frac{y}{c}\right)\phi_h + \omega_{vv} - \phi_{hh} - \theta}$$

Thus, the multiplier increases (note how the θ term works). To see the intuition, recall the labour demand relation (8.22b). As the real wage falls due to the fiscal expansion, a counter-cyclical markup implies that the effective wage $(1 + \mu)w$ falls more; it is like a right shift of the labour demand during times of expansion.[8] Hall (2009) argues that this effect may render this multiplier even greater than 1.

8.6.3 The New Keynesian Multiplier

The New Classical thinking cast grave doubt on the rules-of-thumb-based Keynesian thought; it was questioned why individuals should adhere to patterns of behaviour, like the constant-propensity consumption function, that may in general not be optimal. New Keynesians have sought to establish whether the Keynesian multiplier holds when agents are optimizers (there is no naïve Keynesian consumption function) and when the economic environments are more realistic (imperfect competition, price setting); see Chapter 3. The multiplier of this sub-section was developed more or less independently by Dixon (1987), Mankiw (1988), and Starz (1989), and further elaborated on by Sylvestre (1993), Dixon and Lawler (1996), Coto-Martinez and Dixon (2003).

Individuals optimize utility and firms maximize profits. The environment is static. In the New Keynesian multiplier, consumption is built from the individual's (static) optimization problem. The balanced-budget multiplier emerges in the short run because of the virtuous circle of higher spending generating higher company profits, which then feed on to higher spending through consumption. The core idea of the Keynesian multiplier is preserved here. The focus is mostly on the demand side, but optimization and labour supply considerations are also present. Thus, this multiplier may be thought of as a hybrid between the naïve Keynesian and the neoclassical ones.

Beginning with firms first, the representative firm (i) maximizes profits, in obvious notation:

$$\max \quad P_i Y_i - W L_i,$$

subject to the individual output demand function,

$$Y_i^D = (P/P_i)^{-\theta} Y,$$

with constant elasticity $\theta > 1$. $\theta \to \infty$ for perfect competition (giving the familiar horizontal demand curve), and θ declines with monopoly power. P_i and W are the individual price and market wage, respectively, both nominal. The markup is defined as: $\mu \equiv \frac{\theta}{\theta-1} - 1 > 0$ (note $\theta > 1$). It tends to zero as monopoly power decreases.

---

[8] See Chapter 6 for the cyclical properties of the markup.

We assume (here) that the marginal product of labour is constant; the inverse of MPL, $K \equiv 1/\text{MPL}$, gives the (constant) labour requirement for the production of one unit of good. So, KW is the marginal cost of an additional unit of good. Letting $w \equiv W/P$, the optimality condition is:

$$P_i/P = K(1 + \mu)w$$

Next, we observe the production function; assume that it takes the form, with $F_i > 0$:

$$Y_i = \begin{cases} 0 \\ (L_i - F_i)/K \end{cases} \quad \text{for} \quad \begin{cases} L_i \leq F_i \\ L_i > F_i \end{cases}$$

The quantity $F_i > 0$, specific to each firm, gives the units of labour that must be expended as a fixed cost before production begins (one can think of it as the resources required to have a building or piece of machinery set up). Beyond those F units, every K units of labour produce one unit of good, so that $\text{MPL} = 1/K$. In this way, we assume a constant MPL and marginal cost of goods, but increasing returns to scale (declining average cost).

For the individual firm i, the profit (Π_i) is:

$$\Pi_i = P_i Y_i/P - wL_i = P_i Y_i/P - w[KY_i + F_i]$$

Inserting here the pricing rule derived above and the demand for the individual product, we get:

$$\Pi_i = \frac{Y_i}{\theta} - wF_i$$

Profits depend on output minus the fixed cost F that firms need to spend before getting production going.

This simple structure allows us to aggregate over firms. Denoting aggregates as $Y = \sum_i Y_i$, where N is the number of firms, and similarly for Π and F, with a constant elasticity of demand (θ) across firms, and using $\theta = (1 + \mu)/\mu$, aggregate profits are:

$$\Pi = \frac{\mu Y}{1 + \mu} - wF \tag{8.24a}$$

The analysis that follows below depends on how the rate of profit behaves in the short and the long run. In the short run, the number of firms (N) and the total fixed costs (F) is given so that short-run profits are as in (8.24) above. Short-run profit as a percentage of GDP (i.e. with a given real wage and F) is pro-cyclical (note how Π/Y behaves as Y rises), which is in line with evidence (see Hall, 2009).

In the long run, a non-zero rate of profit will attract more firms into the market. If so, the number of firms will rise until profits are completely dissipated (think of standard microeconomics). In this case, as Starz (1989) emphasizes, long-run profits are zero.[9] This textbook

---

[9] This is because more firms will be operating at a lower scale, all having to pay the fixed cost.

prediction goes however against both casual observation and empirical evidence.[10] To rectify it, we can generate a more general formula to describe long-run profits. To this end, let us call $\pi > 0$ the long-run profit rate expressed in terms of the capital that needs to be expended before production, wF, so that $\pi \equiv \Pi/(wF)$.[11]

Inverting this to write $wF = \Pi/\pi$, inserting above and rearranging, we have:

$$\Pi = \frac{\mu Y}{1 + \mu} \frac{\pi}{1 + \pi}. \qquad (8.24b)$$

(8.24b) gives long-run profits given the profit rate π. As a fraction over total output (Y), long-run profits depend on market structure and the profit rate (positively in both cases). In the polar textbook case of free entry of firms in the long run, profits disappear in the long run ($\pi = \Pi = 0$). But more realistically, we may state that in the long run, there are two countervailing processes on aggregate profits, a positive effect since the number of firms increases, and one via the falling scale of operations for each firm due to entry of new players in the market. Let us take the resulting long-run rate of profit (π) as somehow institutionally and exogenously given.

Next, we turn to the representative individual. As we do not need to distinguish between individuals, we drop subscripts. S/he maximizes utility which is made up of consumption and leisure in a simple Cobb-Douglas specification:

$$U = C^{\alpha}(1 - L)^{1-\alpha}, \quad 0 < \alpha < 1,$$

subject to their budget constraint,

$$C = wL + \Pi - T,$$

where C is consumption, L labour, and $1 - L$ leisure, w the real wage, Π are profits, e.g. dividend payments, and T are lump-sum taxes. Every household earns a salary and also owns an equal amount of shares.[12] $0 < \alpha < 1$ is the share of consumption in the utility function, and $(1 - \alpha)$ that of leisure. This Cobb-Douglas utility function allows substitution between consumption and leisure with an elasticity of substitution fixed at unity. It also allows a simple closed-form solution of consumption, which is a fraction of total available income:

$$C = \alpha[w + \Pi - T] \qquad (8.25)$$

On the right side, we have what can be called 'total income', made up of the wage times the total time endowment of 1 (so that we do not only have wL) plus the profit minus taxes. In

---

[10]   The share of capital in output (what we call here the profit rate) in industrialized economies is around 35 per cent (see Chapter 10), showing some signs of increasing recently—it certainly does not tend to zero. The textbook prediction of zero profits in the long run is an exaggeration to make the point that the number of firms in the long run is endogenous, because of new entrants into the market.

[11]   A situation of a positive long-run rate of profit is characteristic of oligopoly.

[12]   A subtle assumption is that the 'unit mass' of individual is one, so that aggregate profits and the individual share in them are equal; this is a very convenient but also puzzling (at first sight) assumption. Think that there are 1,000 individuals, so that aggregate and individual profits are the same (except the zeros!).

most versions of this model, the real wage is fixed. The idea is that there are two goods, consumption and leisure, and each take up proportion of total income equal to their weight in utility, so that C is as above and $1 - L = (1 - \alpha)(w + \Pi - T)$. (Can you explain why?)

Finally, the model is closed by the National Income Accounting identity, equating output to its total demand:

$$Y = C + G \tag{8.26}$$

There is no investment or external sector in this model.

A fiscal expansion in this setup causes a similar circular process as in the textbook multiplier: the rise in spending raises GDP, then profits, consumption, output, profits, consumption, and so on. Here, the mechanism goes via profits, in other words it is more sharply specified than in the traditional multiplier. There are two leakages, as profits are only a fraction of income (depending on market structure, which is another extra feature); so is consumption which only takes a fraction of resources, the rest of total income going into leisure. This setup delivers a multiplier reminiscent of the old one, but which would leave some Keynesians somewhat uneasy.

More formally, a rise in government expenditure causes an increase in the first instance to output by 1 (cf. 8.26) and short-run profits by $\mu/(\mu + 1)$ (cf. 8.24); in the second round, consumption rises by $\alpha\mu/(\mu + 1)$ (cf. 8.25) and so does output; profits then rise by $\alpha\mu^2/(\mu + 1)^2$; in the third round, consumption and output rise by $\alpha^2\mu^2/(\mu + 1)^2$; etc.; much like in the Keynesian multiplier (8.21a), with $\alpha\mu/(1 + \mu)$ instead of the marginal propensity to consume (MPC). The key mechanism is the generation of profits and the concomitant increase of available resources and consumption.

As a first experiment, let the government increase its expenditures G, again to be financed by issuing government bonds (so that taxes stay the same).[13] It is easy to calculate that:

$$\frac{dY}{dG} = \frac{1}{1 - \alpha\mu/(1 + \mu)} > 1 \tag{8.27a}$$

This is a short-run multiplier. In the long run, profits are given by (8.25b), in which case the multiplier becomes:

$$\frac{dY}{dG} = \frac{1}{1 - \alpha\mu\pi/(1 + \mu)(1 + \pi)} > 1 \tag{8.27a'}$$

The long-run rate of profit captures the complex interactions between a greater number of firms and smaller size per firm in the long run and therefore plays a crucial role in the determination of the multiplier. We can see that the long-run multiplier rises with the rate of profit, as this fuels the virtuous circle described above.

---

[13] Some of the models in that strand of the literature assumed that the bonds end up in the portfolio of the private sector and thus augment its net available resources, so consumption rises further. However, the 'Ricardian Equivalence Proposition' (see the next section), which is in the spirit of this model, argues that governments bonds are not net wealth, therefore they are not assumed to be part of individuals' wealth and have been omitted from the analysis and the multiplier.

Three obvious results emerge now. First, both short- and long-run versions are greater than unity. Second, the short-run multiplier is greater than the long-run one since $0 < \pi$; this is emphasized by Starz (1989). Essentially, the profit rate is smaller in the long run because, though the number of firms increases, each operates at a lower scale as this is happening and production economy-wide is more inefficient: More fixed costs are to be paid. Because of the lower rate of profit, the virtuous circle of more consumption–more profits–more consumption is weakened. In the limiting case of zero long-run profits, the multiplier obviously attains it lowest possible value of 1 (but notice that it does not disappear). Finally, the multiplier increases with higher monopoly power in the product market (Dixon, 1987). Thus, monopolistic or oligopolistic competition is responsible for generating profits in the first place, and enhances the multiplier as well.

Furthermore, two more policy experiments can be conducted, first a change in lump-sum taxation (with an opposite change in the amount of government bonds in private-sector hands); and second, a balanced-budget change in government spending ($dG = dT > 0$). We shall show only the short-run multipliers and the interested reader can work out the long-term versions. In the first case, we have:

$$\frac{dY}{dT} = -\frac{\alpha}{1 - \alpha\mu/(1+\mu)} \tag{8.27b}$$

Finally, a balanced-budget fiscal expansion is easily seen as a straightforward combination of the above policies:

$$0 < \left.\frac{dY}{dG}\right|_{dG=dT} = \frac{1-\alpha}{1 - \alpha\mu/(1+\mu)} < 1$$

While raising total output, such an increase in government expenditure partially crowds out private consumption (this is the effect of taxation on total income). As a result, the multiplier is less than one—this is a result emphasized by all the relevant literature, and is in sharp contrast with textbook analysis.

These multipliers preserve the key idea of multiple rounds of spending. They also provide valuable insights about the role of market structure (monopolistic completion) and the profit rate. But people of Keynesian persuasion would feel uncomfortable with a number of aspects of these New Keynesian multipliers:

- Both a 'bond-financed' increase in spending and a tax cut (8.27a, b) increase welfare (the former because it expands output more than the expansion in spending, therefore private consumption also increases, the latter because it frees up private resources for spending). But a balanced-budget fiscal expansion in fact lowers individual welfare (Mankiw, 1988). The latter is a rather 'un-Keynesian' result and emerges because private resources diminish, and together with them consumption and leisure.[14]

---

[14] Note that government spending is entirely wasteful here and does not appear on the utility function. Thus, welfare falls simply because private consumption falls. It may be argued, though, that government spending in such areas as health and education enhances private utility, therefore utility might under some circumstances

- In this model, the labour market clears. There is therefore no possibility of unemployment, much like under the neoclassical multiplier. Any change in output is done by voluntarily increasing the work hours by workers.
- More generally, the above analysis has been criticized (notably by Dixon, 1987) as more Walrasian than Keynesian; meaning that behind it there is continuous market clearing, both in the labour and product markets. Thus, there is no possibility here of excess supply in any of these markets, an outcome that was so abundantly evident in the inter-war years of the Great Depression that prompted John Maynard Keynes to write the *General Theory*. Thus, such a fiscal expansion does not correct any evident market failure like (involuntary) unemployment or unused (excess) output capacity. There is simply no possibility of such failures in these models; true, labour (and output) may increase or decrease, but in a voluntary manner, based on individuals' calculations of resources and relative prices (the opportunity cost of leisure, real wage).
- One could also criticize the specific mechanism by which the multiplier arises, namely by the circular link of expansion-profits-further expansion. Not all profits are disseminated; a proportion is withheld to finance investment or otherwise buttress the financial health of the firm. In either case, the link seems to weaken. Moreover, dissemination of profits is not even, as financial asset ownership is not even. The additional profits are likely to go in greater proportion to those with a greater financial wealth, but these individuals may have a lower average propensity to consume. This is an idea that has surfaced in various guises at various times: The older Post-Keynesian School has maintained that the marginal propensity to consume out of profits is less than that out of wages. The same point is reiterated by Galor and Zeira (1993), and is implied by Mankiw (2000) who draws a sharp distinction between those households that are able to save and those that are not. All these arguments imply that the multiplier arising out of the propensity to consume profits may not be as strong as this literature assumes. But ultimately the strength of this effect must be gauged empirically.

8.6.4 Discussion

The multipliers we have derived fall under three under categories: The demand-based ones (sub-section 8.6.1), the neoclassical (supply-based) ones (8.6.2) and the New Keynesian ones (8.6.3) that are hybrid, combining features of either. The predictions of the demand-based multipliers are a bond-financed (leaving taxes unchanged) spending multiplier (8.21a) of greater than one, while the neoclassical counterpart (8.23b) is clearly less than unity; strictly speaking, the neoclassical multiplier (8.23b) is a balanced-budget one, so comparable to (8.21b), which is higher anyway (at unity). The New Keynesian bond-financed multiplier (8.27a) is also greater than unity, but the balanced-budget version (8.27c) is less than unity. A rough conclusion that may be gleaned is that the demand-

---

actually rise with government spending, and that might make this multiplier welfare-enhancing and therefore more 'Keynesian'.

based multipliers are generally higher than the neoclassical and even the New Keynesian ones (comparing like for like).

More broadly, what do these analyses suggest? The demand-based multipliers assume away any supply constraints and focus entirely on demand. In a sense, the neoclassical multipliers are the mirror image of that. New Keynesian multipliers are in-between. So, in situations when output is demand-constrained and supply or capacity constraints are absent, the demand multipliers are more relevant; this is the case, as mentioned, of an economy in recession with a lot of unemployment. When, instead, demand is no problem but supply constraints 'bite', then the neoclassical multipliers are more relevant; this is the case of an economy at full employment, with unemployment at its natural rate or below. Hence, one big conclusion is that multipliers are expected to depend on the state of the economy; the multipliers during a recession should be higher than those in a boom. This theoretical prediction accords with empirical evidence (see Auerbach and Gorodnichenko, 2012).

There is another implication of this analysis that has received less attention: Multipliers may well be asymmetric. The common presumption is that all the multipliers we have derived are symmetric, they apply equally to fiscal expansions ($dG > 0$ and/or $dT < 0$) and contractions ($dG < 0$ and/or $dT > 0$). The signs and numerical magnitudes should be the same in both cases. But it can be strongly argued that a fiscal contraction encounters less capacity side constraints than an expansion (with capacity constraints more broadly interpreted than the labour supply decisions of sub-section 8.6.2): It is easier to lay off employees, wrap up equipment, even shut down a business, than hire, invest, or set up a business. Therefore, the effects of fiscal contractions should be more accurately described by demand multipliers, while expansions should have 'more of' the neoclassical multipliers in them; if so, fiscal contractions should have stronger effects than expansions. Hence, the presumption of symmetry would lead us to wrong predictions. Typically, multipliers are estimated using data on expansions (as fiscal consolidations are rarer episodes); but then using those to predict the effects of contractions would lead us to seriously underestimate the latter, as has been found by Blanchard and Leigh (2013); see also Cugnasca and Rother (2015).

As mentioned already, one focal question surrounding the spending multipliers in particular is whether they are higher or lower than unity. This is because, from the national income accounting equation of $Y = C + G$ (keeping constant and suppressing the other elements), a spending multiplier of $dY/dG > (<)1$ implies $dC/dG > (<) 0$. In words, a multiplier greater than one implies that private consumption rises following the fiscal expansion. In that case, a fiscal expansion unambiguously increases welfare and is politically more feasible. If, instead, the multiplier is less than unity and consumption falls, then the expansion may or may not increase welfare, depending on whether the government spending is welfare-enhancing or not; in any case, a much more careful case should be made in favour of the expansion, which will be politically more controversial. Hence, we shall find that the empirical literature has been preoccupied with this question; to pre-amble, there are no clear-cut answers.

8.6.5 Econometric Evidence and Broader Discussion

Ramey (2012) presents a wide-ranging review of empirical work associated with the fiscal multipliers, particularly the spending one. She notes that theory gives a wide range of possible values of this multiplier, depending of course on the sample and estimation method, but also on the type of model, the monetary policy operating in the background, the nature of spending (is it on infrastructure, health, or services?) and its persistence (how long is it expected to last?), and method of finance. Her table 1 (p. 679) is a good summary of evidence. Despite their diversity, the bulk of studies estimate multipliers ranging from around 0.6 to 1.8. She then (p. 680) further narrows down the plausible range to 0.8 to 1.5. But there is considerable variation both across and within studies, and the estimates are not very precise (large standard errors), so 'reasonable people might argue that the multiplier could be from 0.5. to 2.0'. Finally, Ramey (2012) offers evidence from US cross-state fiscal policy, concluding more optimistically: 'These findings suggest that some types of stimulus spending that redistribute resources from low unemployment states to high unemployment states could result in sizable aggregate multipliers. More research is needed, however, to understand how these local multipliers translate to aggregate multipliers.' (Ramey, 2012, p. 683). These findings may be relevant to the European Union to the (very limited) extent that it involves fiscal transfers between member states and regions.

A leading neoclassical, Hall (2009) suggests that the plausible range for the multiplier is between 0.5 and 1. The dynamic New Keynesian model of Cogan et al. (2010) predicts that a permanent rise in fiscal expenditures equal to 1 per cent of GDP, even under situations of a zero lower bound of interest rates (see below), leads to a 1 per cent rise in GDP in the first quarter, falling to 0.6 per cent at the eighth quarter and to 0.4 per cent rise after four years. Eggertsson (2010) and Woodford (2011), however, show significantly stronger effects.

A voluminous literature uses the Structural VAR methodology (see Chapter 6) to identify various fiscal shocks and estimate their effects. In this vein, Blanchard and Perotti (2002) find that a deficit-financed government spending increase that persists for four quarters raises output less than one-to-one but persistently (for up to 20 quarters ahead); so the cumulative multiplier is well above unity. In contrast, Mountford and Uhlig (2009) do not find encouraging results for a deficit-financed spending expansion; they argue that the multiplier is below unity, and when one factors in the tax rise that will inevitably arrive later on in order to repay the debt, there is an output loss (in present-value terms). Instead, they find very encouraging results for a deficit-financed tax cut: The cumulative, appropriately discounted multiplier is close to 5. Using historical US data covering multiple large wars and deep recessions, Ramey and Zubairy (2018) find that the multiplier is lower than unity even in conditions of slackness and recession; the only condition that might push multipliers above unity seems to be interest rates stuck at the zero lower bound.

Ramey (2012) and DeLong and Tyson (2013) discuss various differences (apart from differences in methodology of estimation) that could account for the differences in estimates. Drawing on them, we now discuss various factors affecting the multipliers:

- We have already commented on the effects of financing regimes (deficit or tax finance, and what type of tax, lump-sum or distortionary?). The Ricardian Equivalence Proposition, reviewed below, suggests that under some, quite stringent, conditions, the tax multipliers may be zero. Generally, the models lead us to think that the spending multipliers are higher than the tax multipliers, but the evidence does not seem clear on this point (e.g. see Mountford and Uhlig, 2009, for a strong exception).

- We have also commented on the effect of the underlying state of the economy (excess capacity and unemployment?—is the fiscal stimulus exercised during the expansionary or contractionary phase of the cycle?). Auerbach and Gorodnichenko (2012, see in particular figure 5) find that multipliers are indeed 'state-dependent': stronger (and possibly higher than unity) in a recession, weaker (less than unity) in a boom. Ramey and Zubairy (2018) would not agree.

- As we have discussed, there is reason to think that multipliers are asymmetric; stronger for fiscal contractions than for expansions (Blanchard and Leigh, 2013).

- Other factors are the type of monetary policy that operates in the background and the response of the interest rates to the fiscal expansion. Recalling elementary macroeconomics, this determines the degree of crowding out, namely how much reversal there is of the expansion due to the rise of interest rates. On this point, all advanced literature is in agreement. Woodford (2011) provides an informative analysis. If monetary policy maintains a strict inflation target (not necessarily zero), then the multiplier will be the neoclassical one, essentially because a constant inflation implies a constant output gap, which cannot be changed by fiscal policy. In other words, we are in the domain of the neoclassical model of full price and wage flexibility and only supply constraints, and no 'slackness' (idle output capacity) that can be eliminated by fiscal policy. The multiplier will be greater in the case of a monetary policy that operates an interest rate Taylor rule, which allows a degree of monetary accommodation, namely, it allows a fiscal expansion to impact to an extent on inflation. This implies that the output slackness should narrow (which would cause inflation to rise), therefore the fiscal expansion causes output to increase more than under strict inflation targeting. It is shown that the multiplier rises with the degree of 'monetary accommodation': even though monetary policy partly 'accommodates' the fiscal expansion, it does raise the real interest rate so that it partly crowds it out. The multiplier takes its extreme value if 'monetary accommodation' is full, i.e. if the real interest rate maintained by monetary policy is constant, so that it does not work against the fiscal expansion at all.

- A related, but distinct situation arises when nominal interest rates remain stuck at the 'zero lower bound', as often happens in recessions (and is still largely the case following the crisis of 2007–9). As a fiscal expansion is likely to raise inflation, the real interest rate will fall. In this case, and if the nominal interest rate remains stuck at zero, monetary policy is such that it will in fact help fiscal policy further (by letting real interest rates become lower)—the opposite of the crowding out that would normally be expected. In this case, the fiscal multiplier may well be greater than unity (Woodford, 2011; Eggertsson, 2010; Ramey and Zubairy, 2018).

- When a government faces borrowing constraints as a result of high public debt, multipliers are smaller—as in that case, the costs of servicing the debt are high. We commented at the beginning about the need for fiscal policy to become more active as a stabilization policy tool, right at the time that many governments find themselves more constrained than ever due to their worsened public finances.

- However, an interesting possibility arises from the combination of depressed economies and low costs of borrowing by government, as interest rates are stuck at low levels: DeLong and Summers (2012) have put forward a strong argument that a fiscal expansion financed by borrowing can pay for itself, in the sense that the output expansion may be so strong that the tax receipts will repay the borrowing in due course. The case is stronger if there is 'hysteresis', where temporary unemployment has long-lasting, even permanent, effects because the long-term unemployed are becoming de-skilled and demoralized or because they possibly retire; see Chapter 4. In other words, the underlying trend of GDP is not constant but is affected by the output gap itself. In this case, a fiscal expansion-led recovery should happen sooner rather than later, as the effects of recessions are not temporary but persist into the future. Additionally, it is argued (DeLong and Tyson, 2013) that the costs of government borrowing will remain very low for key economies, as there is a glut of savings world-wide that is looking for safe assets; yet, there are not many of those after the crisis of 2007–9, when a lot of private financial assets turned out to be toxic, and after the sovereign debt crisis in Europe. So, there is precious little supply of assets while there is a lot of demand for safe government bonds—implying that the price of the latter will remain high and interest rates low for some time to come. This point strengthens DeLong and Summer's (2012) argument.

- Following on from the above point, Summers (2014) and Sachs (2014) propose smart government investment: a fiscal expansion that renovates the ageing infrastructure, installs the smart investment that addresses climate change, and pushes the economy out of stagnation with job creation; see also Basu (2014) on how government guarantees can promote infrastructure investment. Under the previous argument, such a strategy will pay for itself. The proposals for a 'Green New Deal' that have been tabled in the US, also under discussion in the UK, do exactly that. It is a win-win-win strategy. Similar proposals have been tabled by the European Commission in recent years, but the sums are paltry as the central EU budget is miniscule in relation to EU GDP. At the core of the Green New Deal is the necessary investment to turn the economy green so as to counter environmental change, and this gives this strategy a strong sense of urgency. The question is not whether it will work; the question is how to make it work.

- Multipliers are smaller in small, open economies than in large economies; this is an elementary result. Furthermore, cross-border multiplier effects can be significant: fiscal stimulus in one country is likely to have economically and statistically significant effects on output in other countries, with the effects depending on the intensity of trade between the countries and their overall openness to trade. The strength of the spillovers also depends on the conditions in the recipient country and the source country, with large multipliers when both economies are in recessionary conditions. This all suggests that fiscal expansions have best chances when they happen in a coordinated way across countries.

- Continuing on the theme of open economies, countries operating fixed exchange rate systems have larger multipliers than countries with flexible exchange rate systems. This is a standard point made by the Mundell-Fleming model of Open Economy Macroeconomics (not discussed in this book). The intuition is that, under flexible exchange rates, a fiscal expansion causes an exchange rate appreciation which crowds out that expansion. The extent of crowding out varies, depending among other factors on the degree of capital mobility across borders. So, in a zone of permanently fixed exchange rates (currency union) such as the Eurozone, fiscal multipliers should be high. This argument also points to the need for fiscal policy coordination.

- Virtually all the literature agrees that the multipliers are larger when agents are credit-constrained, i.e. unable to borrow against future resources or incomes (see Mankiw, 2000; Galí et al., 2007). The reasons for these constraints are the financial market imperfections that we highlighted in Chapter 7. Under these circumstances, consumption and investment depend more on current income or profits than on intertemporal income or profits (see Chapter 11); in this case, we are closer to the static demand multipliers than under the case of freely intertemporally optimizing agents who are able to save a greater part of the rise in income. Estimates of multipliers with credit-constrained 'hand-to-mouth' consumers ('spenders', in the terminology of Mankiw, 2000) are 50 per cent larger than estimates under normal credit conditions—these people do not save the tax cuts.
- The previous point suggests that tax cuts and transfer payments are most effective when aimed at households that have the highest marginal propensity to consume. 'Progressive' discretionary fiscal policies that are targeted toward lower-income groups not only have larger multipliers but also address the growing problem of income inequality. Instead, tax cuts for the rich will have a lower impact on output, as a larger part will be saved, as well as worsening income inequality.
- Tax cuts aimed at businesses should focus on investment incentives. Changes in corporate taxes that affect after-tax profits—like a cut in the corporate tax rate—have smaller multipliers than targeted changes in corporate taxes that affect after-tax returns to new investment—like a temporary investment tax credit.
- Finally, one should bear in mind the difficulties with using fiscal policy as a stabilization policy tool. It often requires protracted parliamentary deliberation and approval, and a lengthy implementation because of administrative delays. So, fiscal policy is more difficult to operate than monetary policy (requiring just the decision-making of a Central Bank and with instant implementation on interest rates). There is also uncertainty about its effects regarding both the magnitude and the timing; on this score, fiscal policy is not much different from monetary policy and the 'long and variable lags' by which it affects output. All these are real challenges, but they should not distract us from the stabilization role that fiscal policy should play.

8.6.6 The 'Obama Stimulus Plan'

The American Recovery and Reinvestment Act (ARRA) of 2009, a.k.a. 'Obama stimulus plan', provides a unique real-world experiment for the evaluation of fiscal policy. It is worth discussing it at some length—even if there seems to be no consensus assessment (or perhaps, because of that!). Taylor (2011) provides a sceptical account of the effects of the stimulus plans of the 2000s: 2001, 2008, and the ARRA of 2009. In the first two, the stimulus was intended only via transfers and tax rebates, while these were also a sizeable proportion of the ARRA plan. Taylor shows that the real output effects of these were statistically insignificant, providing evidence in favour of the Ricardian Equivalence (see below), and also in line with the Permanent Income and Lifetime Hypotheses of Consumption (see Chapter 11). Another sizeable component of ARRA was transfers to state and local authorities, which however were largely saved rather than used to stimulate expenditures, as was intended. Finally, the direct purchase of goods and services by federal government component of ARRA was negligible. Thus, through a combination of the above, according to Taylor, ARRA did not have any palpable effect on stimulating the US economy.

This sceptical account is vigorously disputed by C. Romer (2011, 2012), the Chair of the US President's Council of Economic Advisers at the time. Her basic argument is that Taylor's (2011) argument suffers from an 'omitted variable bias', i.e. it does not take into account other factors that were in force and would have meant that without the stimulus plan the economic situation would have been worse. Such an important factor was the private sector's net wealth which was declining due to the dramatic deterioration in the US housing market at that time. Romer's argument is that, without the stimulus, the state of the US economy would have been a lot worse for that reason. Citing a number of careful studies that evaluate the effects of ARRA, she concludes that the stimulus plan created or saved three million jobs by 2010 that would not be there without it, and that fiscal policy in general matters—big time (in her words). Further discussion of the Obama stimulus plans is provided by Aizenman and Pasricha (2011) which argues, somewhat provocatively, that the net aggregate fiscal expenditure stimulus, accounting for both federal and the declining state government spending, was in fact close to zero in 2009.

8.7 The Intertemporal Approach to Fiscal Policy

The static multipliers reviewed in the previous section are not in a position to analyse changes in policy between now and the future, nor distinctions between temporary and permanent policies, as they do not take into account time. Additionally, the Keynesian multipliers of sub-section 8.6.1 are not able to consider any micro-founded behaviour of households along the lines suggested by the New Classicals; in them, households only follow 'rules of thumb' (e.g. a constant marginal propensity to consume out of disposable income), without regard to whether current resources are lower than future resources (as is the case of students) or the reverse (as is the case of someone who is about to retire). Yet, such changes in circumstances are important in order to understand the response of households to fiscal policy changes. To explore these issues, following Aschauer (1985, 1988) and Barro (1989b) and others, we examine fiscal policy in the context of the intertemporal macro model of Chapter 5.

8.7.1 The Model

To simplify, the model is based on a single representative consumer (there is no population growth) who optimizes intertemporally, that is s/he maximizes utility subject to resources available over his (infinite) lifetime. At the beginning of the planning period (t), intertemporal utility ($\bar{U}_t$), based on information available then (suppressing the expectations operator) is:

$$\bar{U}_t = \sum_{s=0}^{\infty} (1+\rho)^{-s} U(C_{t+s}, 1 - L_{t+s}), \tag{8.28}$$

where ρ is the subjective discount rate, and where utility in each period is made up of two components: private consumption C and leisure $1 - L$. The units of time have been chosen such that the individual's total labour endowment is one (say, one year), and this is allocated between labour L and leisure $1 - L$.[15] Everything is real in this model; the price level does not appear at all.

The economy's production function is characterized by constant returns to scale:

$$Y_t = F(L_t, K_t) \qquad (8.29)$$

Y is real output and K is physical capital.[16] The typical representative firm will hire capital and labour up to the point that the marginal products equal the factor returns:

$$F_L(L_t, K_t) = w_t, \quad F_K(L_t, K_t) = r_t$$

The real wage and real interest rate (both gross: before tax) are denoted by w and r, respectively. With these optimality conditions, Euler's theorem allows us to express output as:[17]

$$Y_t = w_t L_t + r_t K_t \qquad (8.29')$$

The individual faces a period-by-period budget constraint as follows:

$$
\begin{aligned}
&C_t + B_{t+1} - B_t + K_{t+1} - K_t = w_t L_t + r_t(B_t + K_t) - T_t, \\
&T_t = \bar{T}_t + \tau_t(w_t L_t + r_t(B_t + K_t))
\end{aligned}
\qquad (8.30a)
$$

B is government bonds, which is the only form of financial wealth; arbitrage in financial markets ensures that the rate of return on physical capital and bonds is equalized (to r_t). The total tax paid by the household (T_t) is made up of lump-sum taxes ($\bar{T}_t$) and income tax from a rate (τ_t) applied flatly across labour income and asset income. The right side of (8.30a) gives the sources of income (labour earnings and interest income minus taxes), while the left side gives the uses of these resources, namely consumption and saving (accumulation of the various types of assets). For simplicity, there is no depreciation; this can be easily incorporated but will not offer any important insights.

Consolidation of these two equations, gives:

$$C_t + B_{t+1} - B_t + K_{t+1} - K_t = (1 - \tau_t)w_t L_t + (1 - \tau_t)r_t(B_t + K_t) - \bar{T}_t \qquad (8.30a')$$

---

[15] We ignore here the possibility that government spending features in the utility function, as it sustains public services such as education, health, and even justice and security, which enhance welfare; the interested reader can consult the literature mentioned above. Government spending in utility would affect the optimality conditions as it would affect the marginal utility of consumption and leisure. But it is difficult to know how. It depends on whether government services are substitutes with private consumption, as they would be with private health and education; or whether they are complements, as they would be with most of the other items of consumption.

[16] For simplicity, we ignore the productive role of public spending, through infrastructure and such services as administration or justice, police, and defence; see Aschauer (1988) and the review by Irmen and Kuehnel (2009) on these.

[17] Euler's theorem allows us to write a linearly homogeneous (i.e. with constant returns to scale) production function as the sum of the arguments times their marginal products.

Using the methods of Chapter 5, and assuming implicitly appropriate transversality conditions, the period constraint (8.30a') can be consolidated into an intertemporal resource constraint (cf. equation 5.7 of Chapter 5):

$$\sum_{t=0}^{\infty} R_t^{-1} C_t = [1 + r_0(1 - \tau_0)](K_0 + B_0) + \sum_{t=0}^{\infty} R_t^{-1}((1 - \tau_t)w_t L_t - \bar{T}_t), \qquad (8.30b)$$

where $R_{t+1} \equiv (1 + (1 - \tau_{t+1})r_{t+1})R_t$ is the inverse discount factor that takes into account the tax-adjusted real interest rate. Apart from cumulating over the lifetime, the difference between (8.30a) and (8.30b) is that the latter emphasizes the ultimate sources and uses of funds. On the right side, we have the resources over the economy's lifetime: assets (K_0 and B_0) that existed at the beginning of history, plus accumulated net-of-tax labour earnings minus lump-sum taxes; the tax on asset income, i.e. $r(B + K)$, is netted out of the discount factor. The left side records the ultimate use of the resources, which is consumption. Interest income from assets has been dropped out, as assets are merely the vehicles for shifting incomes between periods.

Maximization of (8.28) subject to (8.30b) takes place by appropriate choice of the sequence of assets $A_t \equiv B_t + K_t$ (which can be aggregated as they offer the same rate of return) and C_t, for all $t = 1, 2, ..., \infty$, taking the sequence of government spending G_t and tax rates τ_t as given. As analysed in Chapter 5, the first-order conditions are:

$$\frac{\partial U_t / \partial C_t}{\partial U_{t+1} / \partial C_{t+1}} = \frac{1 + (1 - \tau_{t+1})r_{t+1}}{1 + \rho} \qquad (8.31a)$$

$$\frac{\partial U_t / \partial (1 - L_t)}{\partial U_t / \partial C_t} = (1 - \tau_t)w_t \qquad (8.31b)$$

It will be noticed that lump-sum taxes have no effect on these conditions; this is because they are determined by government irrespective of the individual's actions and therefore they do not impinge on it. What they do is alter the total amount of lifetime wealth and therefore the level (but not rate of growth) of consumption and leisure or work effort. The income tax rate τ, on the other hand, does alter the net rate of return on saving (the interest rate is net of tax) and on the work effort (likewise for the wage), so incentives for saving and work, and therefore economic outcomes, are altered. For this reason, all taxes except lump-sum ones (i.e. on income, wealth, consumption, etc.) are *distortionary*: They distort the outcomes that the market mechanism would furnish without them.

Government faces the period budget constraint (8.2'), which without transfer income and seignorage takes the form:

$$B_{t+1} - B_t = G_t - T_t + r_t B_t \qquad (8.32a)$$

Using the information on the composition of taxation, we can write this as:

$$B_{t+1} - B_t = G_t - \bar{T}_t - \tau_t(w_t L_t + r_t K_t) + (1 - \tau_t)r_t B_t = G_t - \bar{T}_t - \tau_t Y_t + (1 - \tau_t)r_t B_t \qquad (8.32a')$$

Consolidating over time and imposing solvency via the transversality condition (8.10), we get:

$$B_0 = \frac{1}{1 + (1 - \tau_0)r_0} \sum_{t=0}^{\infty} R_t^{-1}(\bar{T}_t + \tau_t Y_t - G_t) \qquad (8.32b)$$

This is parallel to the solvency condition (8.12), as it states that any debt at the beginning of history will be matched (repaid) by future primary surpluses; the net-of-tax interest rate incorporates the fact that future interest payments are taxable.

Finally, let us note that the individuals' period-by-period budget constraint (8.30a) and that of the government (8.32a) can be consolidated into the national budget constraint:

$$C_t + G_t + K_{t+1} - K_t = Y_t \qquad (8.33)$$

The real income of the economy (GDP) on the right must be used for three purposes, consumption by the private sector and government, and physical capital accumulation.

8.7.2 The 'Ricardian Equivalence Proposition'

We are now in a good position to summarize the 'Ricardian Equivalence Proposition' (REP) due in its present form to Barro (1974); it is one of the landmark results of modern macroeconomics and one of the six 'policy ineffectiveness results' we outlined in Chapter 1. Simply put, the REP states that, with a given stream of government expenditures over history, under some conditions, changes in taxation will fail to have any real effects.

Consider two alternative assumptions:

- Assumption 1 (most restrictive): There is no income taxation ($\tau_t = 0$ in all t), only lump-sum taxes exist;
- Assumption 2 (less restrictive): There exists income taxation ($\tau_t \geq 0$) but income is exogenous—in particular, w, L, r, K all are exogenously given to the policy-maker (i.e. unaffected by the tax rate τ).

Under either of these two assumptions, we get the Ricardian Equivalence Proposition, which comes in two parts:

- Given the government's intertemporal spending plans, a tax change today (or any other time) will have no impact on the economy (output, labour supply, real wage, or interest); in particular, a tax cut will fail to elicit any increase in output.
- Government bonds are not net wealth for the private sector.

To see how REP arises, use the intertemporal government budget constraint (8.32b) into its private equivalent (8.30b), to get:

$$\sum_{t=0}^{\infty} R_t^{-1} C_t = [1 + r_0(1 - \tau_0)]K_0 + \sum_{t=0}^{\infty} R_t^{-1}(w_t L_t + \tau_t r_t K_t - G_t) \qquad (8.34)$$

This is the effective intertemporal budget constraint that the private sector faces after we have taken into account the government's behaviour. The private sector's optimization problem can now be restated as: the private sector maximizes (8.28) subject to (8.34).

The second part of the proposition is immediately obvious: government bonds (B), which could have been thought of as a part of private sector's wealth, do not feature on the asset side of their budget constraint (8.34). The reason is that such bonds will require future taxation in order to be repaid as required by (8.32b), taxation that will be raised from the private sector itself. The forward-looking private sector will factor that into their calculations. Hence, bonds have been netted out against the future tax liability. Let us next examine the first part of the proposition. Under either of the stated assumptions, all variables are exogenously given and unaffected by taxation.[18] In this case, the intertemporal profile of taxation is fixed by the government's intertemporal spending plans, as required by (8.32b). So, consider a policy experiment whereby government now reduces either its lump-sum taxes ($\bar{T}_t$) or the tax rate (τ_t). This is going to be financed by a deficit now and new debt issue; but fiscal solvency requires that future extra tax revenues must be raised, of an equal present value, so as to repay the current extra debt. Again, a forward-looking private sector will realize this and will not consider these tax cuts a real bonus; they come with an equal amount of future liabilities, in a present-value sense. Hence, consumption spending will not rise; instead, these tax cuts will be saved to enable the private sector to repay the future tax liabilities. The situation would be symmetrically opposite with a current tax increase; but the net result will be the same, namely that the tax change will not have any effect, now or in the future.

Note carefully that the REP considers tax changes keeping the intertemporal profile of government spending constant. Any changes in spending plans will have real effects; government spending does feature in the effective private-sector budget constraint (8.32b). This is because government spending withdraws resources from the economy and does affect the private sector's net resources. Therefore, any tax changes that accompany (are equal in a present-value sense to) real government spending will have real effects. One corollary of this proposition is that the size of the government budget deficit is not important, since, with given expenditures, a change in tax is tantamount to a change in the deficit, repayable later with future surpluses.

The proposition is in sharp contrast to the teaching of the basic textbook model (which we may term 'IS-LM'). To appreciate the differences, consider the individual's budget constraint (in obvious notation):

$$Y_t - T_t = C_t + S_t^P$$

Disposable income is allocated between consumption and private saving, all in period t. Next, consider the primary budget surplus (denoted as 'government saving'):

$$S^G = T - G$$

---

[18]   A subtle point: Assumption 2 implies that the optimality conditions (8.31a, b) do not apply. Viewed from this angle, it is in fact more restrictive than Assumption 1.

Finally, national saving is the sum of private and government saving:

$$S = S^P + S^G$$

Next, consider the current account (CA, the net exports of goods and services plus net movement of profits and interest income across borders—a key measure of openness). From national income accounting, this is given as the difference between national saving and investment:

$$CA = S - I$$

This will of course be zero in a closed economy, but we can relax this here to see the effects of a tax change.

Let us consider a tax change in two different economies, the IS-LM and the REP one, under the assumption that investment (I) and exports remain unchanged. In the textbook IS-LM model, the tax cut will be partly saved and partly consumed; the multiplier analysis of Section 8.6.1 will guide us here. In order to accommodate the possibility of an open economy, we must allow for a marginal propensity to consume domestic goods (MPC') being less than the overall marginal propensity to consume (MPC), as some of the rise in disposable income will go to imports; hence, $0 < MCP' < MPC < 1$. (Can you recall why?) In this case, the output-tax multiplier is $\Delta Y/\Delta T = -MPC'/(1 - MPC')$. Under the REP, all the tax cuts will be saved, without any extra consumption and no output effects. Let us trace the steps side by side—see Table 8.1:

Table 8.1. Effects of a tax cut

Variable	IS-LM world	REP world
Y	$\Delta Y_t/\Delta T_t = -MPC'/(1 - MPC') < 0$	0
C	$\Delta C_t/\Delta T_t = MPC(\Delta Y_t - \Delta T_t)/\Delta T_t = -MPC/(1 - MPC') < 0$	0
S^P	$-1 < \Delta S_t^P/\Delta T = -(1 - MPC)/(1 - MPC') < 0$	$\Delta S_t^P/\Delta T = -1 < 0$
S^G	$\Delta S_t^G/\Delta T = 1 > 0$	$\Delta S_t^G/\Delta T = 1 > 0$
S	$\Delta S_t/\Delta T = (MPC - MPC')/(1 - MPC') > 0$	0
CA	$\Delta CA_t/\Delta T = (MPC - MPC')/(1 - MPC') > 0$	0

A major result under the textbook ('IS-LM') model is that the domestic budget deficit due to tax cuts ($\Delta T < 0$) will be mirrored in an external deficit—the 'twin deficits hypothesis'.[19] This is because the tax cut fuels consumption spending; it also increases output, but less so than consumption, as part of consumption is channelled to imports. The REP overturns all this: private and government saving move in exactly opposite directions, hence national saving and the current account remain unaffected. The domestic budget deficit is all absorbed domestically by a rise in private saving. This sharp contrast of results, particularly in the relation between domestic and external deficits, has been used as the basis of tests of the REP, as will be reviewed shortly. We first explain the (many) instances when the REP fails.

---

[19] Similar results apply to the trade balance (TB) as well as the Current Account.

8.7.3 Violations of the REP

- 'Fiscal illusion' and myopia: The REP relies crucially on forward-looking behaviour of the private sector; in particular, their ability to understand the government's solvency requirement (8.12) or (8.32b) and to incorporate it into their calculations. Failure of that ('fiscal illusion') implies that they do not foresee that the tax cuts now (say) will be followed by equal future tax liabilities. Even more fundamentally, REP relies on the private sector's ability to engage in intertemporal optimization. Failure of that (myopia) means that the household lives 'like there is no tomorrow' and the tax cut will be spent.
- Perfectly competitive financial markets: Not only are consumers aware of the government's constraint (8.32b) according to REP, but their own budget constraint (8.30b) is built on the same discount rate as government's. For this to happen, the interest rate that applies to the private and government sectors must be equal. As we have seen, financial market imperfections that affect interest rates also imply that they are not equalized across the two sectors. Other considerations, such as indebtedness, may imply that interest rates are not uniform. In all these cases, REP fails.
- Credit constraints: In particular, a high interest rate is a sign of 'credit constraints': inability to borrow against future income (which exists). Financial market imperfections (due to asymmetric information and monitoring costs, or risk aversion of lenders and unwillingness to lend without collateral) imply that. In that case, saving is possible and will take place when optimization dictates that, but borrowing may be impossible when required. If so, tax cuts and tax rises will have different effects, and each type of policy will have different effects in different sections of the population.

A good illustration is provided by the behaviour of the young (borrowers) versus the old (savers). The young have low incomes now and higher incomes in the future. They decide their current (as well as future) consumption on the basis of lifetime resources, so that they may wish to maintain a current consumption level above their current means by borrowing and repaying later. They may however not be able to do that (as much as optimal) if their bank refuses credit above a certain level—even though they anticipate the future income. One implication of this situation is that the individual or household will consume all their disposable income. In reviewing the empirical evidence, Mankiw (2000) terms them 'spenders' and argues that they are a sizeable part of the population.

In that case, a current tax cut enables the young to go closer to their chosen level of consumption. It is as if the government borrows on their behalf, passes the proceeds on via a cut in taxation, then taxes them more later; the young are thus able to get extra funds to what the bank would have lent them. Their consumption rises and this raises current output. But note that this line of argument does not apply to savers, who face no external constraints in approaching their optimal behaviour; and they therefore may be more inclined to save the tax cut, as REP suggests. They are 'savers', in Mankiw's (2000) terminology. We have discussed at various places in this book, notably in relation to business cycles research in Chapter 6 and the multiplier (Section 8.6) that credit (or 'liquidity') constraints are among the key factors that affect the behaviour of households and their responses to tax cuts; see also Chapter 11.

- Distortionary taxation: Neither of Assumptions 1 or 2 holds in practice; there is both income taxation ($\tau > 0$) and income is not exogenous as the optimality conditions (8.30a, b) are affected by it. This implies that even given the total amount of resources the government appropriates, altering the timing of distortionary taxes has real effects. A lower income tax rate now e.g. may induce a higher work effort and more consumption and output: REP fails.
- Finite lifetimes and overlapping generations: The above setup is made up of infinitely lived individuals. But if we allow finite lives and 'overlapping' generations (see Chapter 5), a tax cut now (and associated increased debt) will be repaid by new generations in the future. This is a free lunch for currently existing generations, so that current consumption may rise; REP breaks down. However, there is an objection here. If current generations are altruistic about future generations (the Utility function of children enter the Utility function of parents, in a chain) and if parents leave positive ('operative') bequests, then the situation is formally like optimization over two periods, one being the current life, the other the child's life. A tax cut now with debt to be repaid next period will not alter consumption, it will only increase the bequest (out of saving now) that will just enable the child to meet future increased tax payments. Thus, the tax cut now will not alter anybody's behaviour, either in the current or future generation. In this case, REP is reinstated.
- Labour income uncertainty (Barsky et al., 1986): If there is uncertainty about future income, lower income taxation now against higher in the future operates as a form of insurance (the uncertain future income is taxed more heavily and the certain current income increases); a tax cut now would increase consumption.

8.7.4 REP: An Evaluation

We have emphasized that REP is a landmark result in macroeconomics. At the same time, the underlying assumptions are so stringent that they make it unlikely that the Proposition holds in a pure form. Therefore, we turn to empirical evidence, reviewed in Bernheim (1987), Barro (1989a), Seater (1993) and Mankiw (2000). One line of results finds that the behaviour of private and national saving following tax cuts is more in line with the 'IS-LM' model of Table 8.1 rather than the REP. This has been shown in relation in particular to the fiscal deficits of the 1980s in the US ('Reaganomics'). Also, the empirical evidence of later years, reviewed in Chapter 11, suggests that about a half of the tax cuts are saved and half consumed.

Thus, neither theory nor empirical evidence give us grounds to think that REP holds in a pure form. But it continues to be an important benchmark, in juxtaposition to the 'IS-LM' world and warning us of the limited nature of the latter. The real world is likely to be a hybrid of the two. The real contribution of REP is that it sharpens our thinking about household behaviour and the effects of policy; in designing policy, the policy-maker should take careful account of REP and have as clear an idea of the assumptions that may invalidate it.

8.7.5 Effects of Government Purchases on
Output, Consumption, and Interest Rates

We now proceed to discuss the effects of temporary and permanent government purchases on output, consumption, and interest rates in the setup of sub-section 8.7.1. We are interested in particular to compare the contemporaneous and long-run effects of a permanent change in government spending. Furthermore, we want also to contrast the effects of a permanent to that of a temporary rise in such spending. For simplicity, we shall make invoke the government's intertemporal budget constraint and solvency condition (8.32b): taxes are just about enough to pay for future spending and repay the current debt. Therefore, our effort is to analyse the effects of spending without being concerned how it is financed (by current taxation or debt and future taxation). The discussion will begin from the simplest of setups, namely with Ricardian Equivalence and without a labour/leisure choice or physical capital; it will then introduce the former; and finally will also introduce physical capital and investment. Thus, the discussion aims to give a flavour of the results derived from the intertemporal approach to fiscal policy.[20]

A toy economy: no labour/leisure choice or physical capital or growth
Let us begin with the simplest case of fixed capital and no leisure in the utility function. These all imply that output is exogenously set; Ricardian Equivalence holds. As a further assumption, this economy is not growing over time; trend growth will be introduced later. As a result, the baseline consumption profile is flat over time. From (8.30a), this implies that the real interest rate simply equals the rate of time preference, $r = \rho$. Despite the patently unrealistic assumptions, this case is instructive. Furthermore, we need to specify the horizon over which a change in government spending is to take effect. We distinguish between a permanent (and unanticipated) rise in government spending, $dG > 0$ (i.e. for all periods t),[21] in which case the government takes hold of a total of $\Sigma R_t^{-1} dG$ of resources over the course of history; and a temporary rise, $dG_t > 0$, for only a certain $t = t_0$ and $dG_t = 0$ for $t \neq t_0$. The latter has the interesting property that the present value of the extra resources that government commands is negligible compared to the baseline total $(\Sigma R_t^{-1} G)$, whereas in the former case the extra resources are sizeable. This distinction practically means that the private sector feels poorer out of a permanent rise in government spending, whereas it does not do so under temporary changes; in the former instance, it will therefore adjust permanently the level of consumption, whereas in the latter it will not.

A permanent and unanticipated increase in G, $dG > 0$
As the resources that government claims intertemporally are non-negligible, the private sector feels poorer, as evident from the reduction on the right side of (8.34). Permanent changes in available resources will change permanently the level of consumption but will otherwise leave its time profile flat—as stipulated by (8.31a) with $r = \rho$. In other words, in

---

[20] Written in the 1980s and early 1990s, much of the associated literature abstracted from issues of endogenous growth (see Chapter 9). Thus, the effects on output of government spending under this analysis should be interpreted as being percentage deviations from an exogenous path of output.

[21] A notational point: the symbol d indicates a deviation from a given baseline path.

the case of a permanent increase in government spending, private consumption will be crowded out one-for-one, and permanently, with no other changes. This information is plotted in the upper part of Figure 8.5, inspired by Barro (1989b).

A temporary increase in G, $dG_t > 0$ for $t = t_0$

In contrast, temporary changes in G will in general induce temporary changes in the real rate of interest, the consumption growth rate and therefore the time profile of consumption. This is because consumption will not change permanently, as the reduction in intertemporal resources (on the right of 8.34) is negligible. On the other hand, with a given output, private consumption will be crowded out at t_0 (only), hence $dC_{t_0} = -dG_{t_0} < 0$. But $dC_t = 0$ at any other time, in particular $dC_{t_0+1} = 0$. Thus, consumption rises from $t = t_0$ to $t_0 + 1$. From the Euler equation (8.31a), r_{t+1} must rise in order to facilitate this. (Note that the fall in consumption at t_0 from its level at $t_0 - 1$ is unexpected, therefore it does not elicit any fall in the interest rate as 8.31a holds in an expected sense.) In other words, after the unanticipated fall in consumption, there is an expected rise (back to normal) and this raises the interest rate. Hence, we get that the temporary increase in government spending raises the real interest rate, also temporarily. As Barro (1989b) suggests, war expenses fit this description quite well.[22] This information is plotted in the lower part of Figure 8.5.

Thus, the main point here is crowding out of private consumption by government spending, permanently or temporarily, in sharp contrast to the simple Keynesian model. This is purely a consequence of the economy-wide budget constraint, with fixed output.

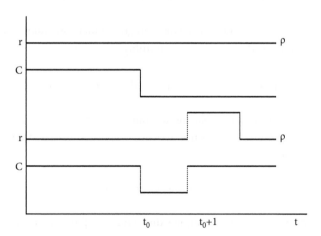

Figure 8.5. Effects of permanent and temporary increases in government purchases in a toy economy

---

[22] What would be the change if the change at t_0 were anticipated? An important feature of Rational Expectations (see Chapter 2) is that agents take action when the news breaks, not when changes take effect. In other words, it is not profitable simply to wait for things to happen, one should act in advance if the information is available. This would lead to a gradual decline in C before even t_0, with any abrupt change occurring only at the time of the announcement or news, and not afterwards—that is, before the actual policy takes effect at t_0. See Chapter 2 on the effect of 'news'.

One could think that too much spending 'chases' a fixed amount of output, prices rise, and when all dust is settled, G has crowded out C in real terms. Think of a shift in textbook AD curve with a vertical AS.[23] We have:

Result 1: In the case of no labour-leisure choice and no physical capital (in effect, exogenous output):

(a) In both the cases of permanent and temporary increases in government spending, the multiplier is zero. This is because, while in place, the increased government spending (net of its productive contribution) crowds out private consumption one-for-one.

(b) The real interest rate rises with a (temporary) budget deficit.

Labour/leisure choice but no physical capital

Next, we introduce the leisure/labour choice (cf. 8.31b) but still without capital. In this case, the intertemporal budget constraint (8.34) is usefully rewritten as:

$$\sum_{t=0}^{\infty} R_t^{-1}[C_t + (1 - L_t)w_t] = \sum_{t=0}^{\infty} R_t^{-1}(w_t - G_t) \tag{8.35}$$

Equation (8.35) gives total lifetime revenues on the right, valuing the total time available (which is 1), rather than only the hours worked, minus the requirement that government spending should be financed. On the left, we have the two possible uses of resources, which are consumption and leisure (valued by its opportunity cost, the real wage). In other words, the main difference of (8.35) from (8.34) is that it adds the value of leisure on both sides.

To see how leisure is affected by the changes in government spending, let us postulate a simple Cobb-Douglas specification for period utility in (8.28):

$$U(C_t, 1 - L_t) = C_t^{\beta}(1 - L_t)^{1-\beta}, \quad 0 < \beta < 1.$$

For simplicity, we also assume that the tax rate is constant, $\tau_t = \tau$ for all t. With this utility function, the consumption-leisure first-order condition (8.31b) results in a simple proportionality relation:

$$(1 - \tau)w_t(1 - L_t) = (1 - \beta)C_t/\beta.$$

It is also instructive to note that this implies that a fraction β of total resources should buy consumption and $1 - \beta$ should 'buy' leisure, weighted by its relative price, which is the opportunity cost of not working—the (tax-adjusted) real wage. With a given marginal

---

[23] The perceptive reader might ask, what if government spending is productive, as briefly mentioned above? Then, the rise in G will raise output (permanently or temporarily, as the case is). Thus, the crowding out of consumption will be partial, less than one-for-one. Hence, the effects we have described will be qualitatively the same but quantitatively less strong.

product of labour and real wage, this suggests that leisure follows the same patterns as consumption. With this information, (8.35) becomes:

$$B(\tau)\sum_{t=0}^{\infty}R_t^{-1}C_t = \sum_{t=0}^{\infty}R_t^{-1}(w_t - G_t) \equiv \Upsilon_0 - \Gamma_0,$$

$$B(\tau) \equiv \frac{1 - \beta\tau}{\beta(1 - \tau)} > 1, \quad dB(\tau)/d\tau > 0 \tag{8.35'}$$

(8.35') suggests that a rise in government spending exerts a direct, resources effect: The rise in government spending (financed by taxation in the background) means that intertemporal net resources available to the individual (on the right) fall. As a result, both consumption and leisure fall; labour supply rises. There is also a combination of the income and substitution effects induced by the tax rate (τ). The effect of the real wage is evident on the resources on the right.

It is useful to write total lifetime labour income (for the entire time endowment of 1) as:

$$\Upsilon_0 \equiv \sum_{t=0}^{\infty}R_t^{-1}w_t$$

And likewise intertemporal government spending:

$$\Gamma_0 \equiv \sum_{t=0}^{\infty}R_t^{-1}G_t$$

With this notation, (8.35') may be re-expressed in compact notation as:

$$C_t = C(\Upsilon_0 - \Gamma_0)/B(\tau), \quad \partial C_t/\partial(\Upsilon_0 - \Gamma_0) > 0, \quad \partial C_t/\partial\tau < 0 \tag{8.36}$$

Therefore, demand for output in obvious notation ($C_t + I_t + G_t$ in a closed economy) is:

$$Y_t = C(\Upsilon_0 - \Gamma_0)/B(\tau) + I_t + G_t \tag{8.37}$$

Equation (8.37) is a Modified Aggregate Demand relation, showing a positive relation between intertemporal labour income (Y_0) and current output (Y). We show this as the upward-sloping y^D in a Modified AD-AS diagram, 8.6 below.[24]

There is also a Modified Aggregate Supply relation (y^S), which is downward sloping. As mentioned, the above implies that a fraction of intertemporal resources should be used to 'buy' leisure, i.e.:

$$(1 - \tau)w_t(1 - L_t) = (1 - \beta)(\Upsilon_0 - \Gamma_0)$$

---

[24] Ideally, one ought to use another name in order to emphasize the important differences from the standard AD-AS diagram. As should be clear, in this framework, AS is downward-sloping curve and AD upward-sloping; also, the variables on the axes are different from the standard framework. This 'Modified AD-AS' framework is an innovation of this book.

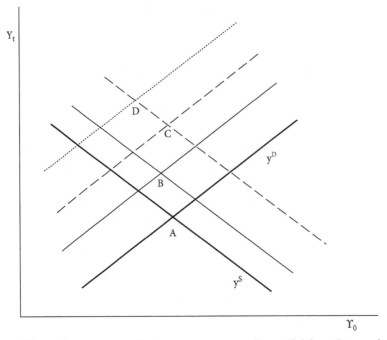

Figure 8.6. Effects of a permanent rise in government spending with labour/leisure choice and capital accumulation

This implies that a rise in intertemporal resources causes leisure to rise. Note also that leisure $(1 - L_t)$ is proportional to the real wage, as labour is inversely proportional to its marginal product and the real wage. Hence, a rise in Υ_0 will elicit a rise in leisure and the wage and a fall in labour supply (L_t). This relation is written as, $L_t = L(\Upsilon_0 - \Gamma_0)$, with $L'(.) < 0$. From the production function, aggregate output (Y_t) will also fall. So, with the production function $Y_t = F(.)$ introduced above and constant capital, we have the Modified AS (y^S):

$$Y_t = F(L(\Upsilon_0 - \Gamma_0)), \quad dY_t/d\Upsilon_0 < 0 \tag{8.38}$$

With this apparatus, we analyse the effects of a rise in government spending. For simplicity, we limit ourselves to the case of an unanticipated, permanent rise in G at time $t = 0$, i.e. a constant dG > 0 for all t.[25]

With reference to Figure 8.6., the initial setup is the thick lines; initial equilibrium is at A. Comparison of (8.37), (8.36), and (8.35') shows that the y^D is affected as follows:

$$Y_t = [C(\Upsilon_0 - \Gamma_0) - dG]/B(\tau) + I_t + G_t + dG \tag{8.37'}$$

[25] We also assume that the real interest rate is constant, unaffected by the change in labour.

With $B(\tau) > 1$, this means that, on balance, the y^D shifts right in Figure 8.6 to the thin line. The y^S curve is modified to:

$$Y_t = F(L(\Upsilon_0 - \Gamma_0 - \Sigma(R_t)^{-1}dG)) \tag{8.38'}$$

Clearly, intertemporal resources have gone down and labour supply and current output have increased; the line also shifts right to the thinner version. Equilibrium shifts to point B. As can be easily read off the graph, equilibrium current output rises. In principle, intertemporal labour resources Υ_0 may go either way, but intuition suggests they will fall. To see the intuition, the fall in $\Upsilon_0 - \Gamma_0$ has induced a fall in leisure and rise in labour, enabling output supply to rise to meet demand. There is a secondary effect, too. As labour supply increases, more hours are put to work with the same amount of capital, and the marginal product of labour (real wage) falls; this reduces intertemporal resources further. A Keynesian might feel uneasy about this last result, which is due to the fact that labour is entirely supply-driven in this model.

The end result essentially shows the static neoclassical multiplier that we analysed in Section 8.6.2. Private consumption will have fallen in the new equilibrium; this induces the rise in labour that supports the rise in equilibrium output.[26] Since $Y = C + I + G$, and I is unaffected, we obtain a multiplier of $0 < dY/dG < 1$. So, a key result of the intertemporal framework is:

Result 2: In the case of a permanent change in government spending, under a labour-leisure choice but no physical capital, the steady-state spending multiplier is the neoclassical one: positive but less than unity. Following a rise in government spending, labour supply rises and the real wage falls.

Aschauer (1988) and Baxter and King (1993) derive the general formulae. But Aiyagari and Christiano (1992) question whether the long-run multiplier should be bounded by 1.

Labour-leisure choice with physical capital and investment

Introducing physical capital and investment makes things slightly more complicated—and interesting. Here, we shall be concerned with the steady-state and short-run effects of a permanent and rise in government spending. At B (the steady state in the previous case) there is a rise in labour supply compared to A. This will increase the marginal product of capital and the real interest rate. With the rise in the interest rate, consumption growth will rise (temporarily). Inserting this information into (8.35'), we see that (8.36) and (8.37) will temporarily rise as consumption is now higher; y^D shifts right to the broken line. At the same time, the rise in the marginal product of capital implies that it is profitable to hire more capital; this will increase current output; the thin y^S curve now shifts up to its broken-line version.[27] Equilibrium is at point C. Clearly, current output will have risen compared to B.

---

[26] Diagrammatically, dG is the vertical distance between the thick and the thin versions of y^d. Obviously, from point A to B, current output (Y) will not have risen as much $(0 < dY < dG)$.

[27] There is a second reason why y^S shifts up temporarily: the rise in the interest rate will induce a heavier discounting of future resources, which fall, inducing a further rise in labour supply. This implies a temporary shift of the y^S curve beyond the broken line. We do not show that.

In the steady state, we have no growth. Therefore, noting the consumption Euler equation (8.31a) and the marginal product-interest rate equality, in the steady state we get:

$$F_K(L, K) = r = \rho$$

Therefore, the rise in labour supply induces such a rise in capital that the equality MPK = ρ is eventually restored. In the new steady state (C), all variables will have risen such that the above equality is restored. There will be no more growth, but consumption, output, and capital will have settled at higher levels. We get:

Result 3: If one introduces the possibility of capital accumulation, the steady-state output multiplier will be higher than under Result 2, and may even be above unity.

In the short run, the rise in capital will induce a rise in investment (I_t); this will be an extra item of demand which will shift the y^D curve temporarily upwards to the dotted line. Thus, the short-run equilibrium is at D; output will have risen even more, falling back to C in the steady state when investment returns to normal.[28] Thus, we observe the result derived in much of this literature:

Result 4: Under a labour-leisure choice and capital accumulation, the short-run effect on output of a permanent rise in government spending is higher than the long-run (steady-state) effect.

Thus, the intertemporal approach embodies essentially the static neoclassical multiplier. However, the addition of capital accumulation implies that this multiplier is not necessarily bounded by one, as often presumed in this literature, Furthermore, it is easy to see intuitively that, if government spending supports productive public services, then the expansionary potential of government spending rises, as it will affect supply further (the y^S will shift up more).

Notes on the Literature

While fiscal policy is covered in all macroeconomic texts, the vastness of the topic makes is difficult to suggest a few papers that are representative portals into the literature, particularly now that the focus seems to be shifting somewhat from the traditional question of the stabilization potential of fiscal policy (which we covered in Sections 8.6–8.7) to debts, deficits, and fiscal solvency (Sections 8.1–8.5). Good places to start on the traditional themes of Ricardian Equivalence and the intertemporal approach are Barro (1989a, b) and Mankiw (2000). DeLong and Tyson (2013), Ramey (2012), and Ramey and Zubairy (2018) are good summaries of debates and findings on the fiscal multipliers. C. Romer discusses the role of fiscal policy in ameliorating the crisis of 2007–9. Blanchard et al. (2016) analyse whether and how expansionary fiscal policy can 'jump-start' the Eurozone recovery. About fiscal solvency and public finances, a good place to start is—well, this book! Reinhart and

---

[28] We assume that there are no adjustment costs in capital or labour; if there are, these variables will adjust more sluggishly than suggested here.

Rogoff (2009) and Reinhart et al. (2012) are good histories of financial crises, including sovereign debt crises. Bournakis et al. (2017) is an overview of the European sovereign debt crisis with an emphasis on the Greek experience.

Guidance for Further Study

Government debt maturity and structure

We have argued that, under some assumptions, the maturity of government debt does not matter. But this is only an approximation that allows us to review the issues without getting too bogged down in 'details'. In practice, however, the maturity of government debt often matters a lot and the government agencies that manage this debt attempt to maintain an optimal profile in terms of maturities of bonds. There is a sizeable literature that approaches these issues from different perspectives; see Missale and Blanchard (1994), Missale (1997), Angeletos (2002), Nosbusch (2008), and Greenwood et al. (2015). See Cochrane (2015) on a proposal on how government debt should be optimally structured.

History of debt

For meticulous historical reconstructions of US debt, including comparisons between face ('par') and market value and limits on debt imposed by the Congress, see Hall and Sargent (2018); for the UK, see Ellison and Scott (2017).

On private debt

Although not much discussed in public discourse or indeed in the literature, private debt is rising as well, and is in many countries much higher than public debt. The same team that has carefully measured public debt has also measured private debt across the world (Mbaye et al., 2018b); see also Buttiglione et al. (2014). A number of papers have shown that private debt and public debt are communicating vessels, as the former tends sooner or later to morph into the latter—i.e. the private debt is eventually socialized; see Jordà et al. (2013), Mbaye et al. (2018a). Gourinchas and Obstfeld (2012) argue that private debt accumulation causes financial crises; Bernardini and Forni (2017) argue that the opposite line of causation holds. One thing is for sure: this area of research is going to develop fast.

Debt in overlapping-generations models

One implication of Ricardian Equivalence is that debt is neutral in infinite-horizons (the 'Ramsey model' we analysed in Chapter 5); intuitively speaking, the same private sector who holds the debt will also need to repay it later on. But as we have noted, things change with overlapping generations, as the generations who own the debt and who pay the tax liability are different. Starting with Diamond (1965), the effects of government debt have been investigated in that context. One strand uses the model by Blanchard (1985); the interested reader can start from Buiter (1988) and Weil (1989).

'Tax smoothing'

We have not touched much on the question why deficits appear in the first place. One line of explanation (see Barro, 1979) is that, because of convex costs of taxation, a government has an incentive to 'smooth' taxation (roughly speaking, to keep it constant). If government spending varies over the cycle (counter-cyclically), then deficits and debts will also be counter-cyclical. See Aiyagari et al. (2002) and the references therein for elaborations of this insight.

More on the political economy of government debt

Like in monetary policy, the accumulation of public debt may be due to strategic interactions between the government and private sectors, evident in elections, political business cycles, bargaining in legislatures, etc. See the wide-ranging review by Alesina and Passalacqua (2016) as a portal to this literature.

Fiscal councils

The recognition that discretion in fiscal policy has led to suboptimal outcomes such as deficits and debts—much as monetary policy discretion once led to problems—has led to calls for fiscal policy being less subject to the control of democratic politicians and more under technocratic oversight—again, as with monetary policy (although the extent of technocratic control in fiscal policy's case is a lot less). This has led to the establishment of independent budgetary agencies like Sweden's Fiscal Policy Council and the UK's Office of Budget Responsibility. What do these agencies do? How much control do they exercise over the conduct of fiscal policy? What is the optimal balance between democratic and technocratic control? On these issues, see Calmfors and Wren-Lewis (2011), Leith and Wren-Lewis (2006), and Wyplosz (2005).

Fiscal activism and rules versus discretion in fiscal policy

We have noted the emerging consensus that more emphasis should be placed on fiscal policy-led stabilization (despite the legislative and administrative delays involved). But should fiscal policy be discretionary or follow rules such as the Taylor rule of monetary policy? On these issues, see Taylor (2000—who disagrees with fiscal activism) and Auerbach (2012). Furthermore, how should such rules combine the aims of stabilization of the cycle and of stabilization of the debt? On this, see Auerbach (2014).

How effectively does the government control its spending?

We generally assume that 'G' (government spending) is entirely under government's control. But government makes policies (i.e. plans), enacts them through parliament, and carries them out administratively. 'G' is only the outcome of this process, and under imperfect control. Crawford et al. (2018) elaborate for the UK.

On the composition of government expenditures

Another issue is that 'G' is not a homogeneous quantity: see Shelton (2007) on this.

Automatic stabilizers

Elementary macroeconomics teaches that an income tax rate is an 'automatic stabilizer'. (Can you explain why?) How effective is such an automatic stabilizer? Does stabilization of disposable income over time stabilize cycles more than (say) tax-and-transfer programmes that address poverty and inequality? For updates on this front, see Auerbach and Feenberg (2000), Fatas and Mihov (2001), and McKay and Reis (2016).

Optimal fiscal policy

Perhaps under the influence of the Ricardian Equivalence Proposition, the analysis of fiscal taxation policy has focused more on government spending and less on taxation. There is, however, a literature that analyses optimal taxation, borrowing from public policy. For an overview of this literature, and its implications for monetary policy, see Chari and Kehoe (1999). On fiscal-monetary policy interactions, in particular, see Kirsanova et al. (2009).

Fiscal policy and inequality

In talking about the fiscal multipliers, i.e. the effects of 'G' on aggregate output, we forget the important effects of fiscal policy on income inequality, first by redistributive taxes and transfers and, second, because fiscal consolidations and austerity are not distribution-neutral; they do cause a rise in inequality. A study by the International Monetary Fund (2014) explores these issues.

'Dynamic scoring'

This is a methodology for calculating the effects of tax cuts allowing for a dynamic adaptation of the private sector to them. Some critics say it is a clever approach but requires a lot of contestable assumptions in order to become operational. The approach is also controversial because it is generally associated with the view that tax cuts pay for themselves by generating vigorous growth. See Auerbach (2005) for an introduction and Mankiw and Weinzierl (2006) for an application in that spirit.

The size of government

A literature has investigated the size of the public sector, measured as either spending over GDP or tax revenues over GDP, and its dramatic rise during the twentieth century. See Tanzi and Schuknecht (1997, 2000) for the facts and Alesina and Wacziarg (1998) and Rodrik (2000) for various lines of explanation. See also Chapter 9 on growth on the question of the optimal size of government.

References

Aiyagari, S.R., and L.J. Christiano (1992): The Output, Employment, and Interest Rate Effects of Government Consumption, *Journal of Monetary Economics*, 30, 73–86.

Aiyagari, R.S., A. Marcet, T.J. Sargent, and J. Seppala (2002): Optimal Taxation without State-Contingent Debt, *Journal of Political Economy*, 110(6), 1220–54.

Aizenman, J., and G.K. Pasricha (2011): The Net Fiscal Expenditure Stimulus in the US, 2008–9: Less than What You Might Think, and Less than the Fiscal Stimuli of Most OECD Countries, *The Economists' Voice*, Berkeley Electronic Press, 8(2) (June), 1–6.

Alesina, A., and S. Ardagna (1998): Tales of Fiscal Adjustment, *Economic Policy*, 27, 487–545.

Alesina, A., and A. Passalacqua (2016): The Political Economy of Government Debt, in J.B. Taylor and H. Uhlig (eds), *Handbook of Macroeconomics*, Amsterdam: Elsevier, ii. 2599–2651.

Alesina, A., and R. Perotti (1995): Fiscal Expansions and Adjustments in OECD Countries, *Economic Policy*, 10, 205–8.

Alesina, A., and R. Wacziarg (1998): Openness, Country Size and Government, *Journal of Public Economics*, 69(3) (September), 305–21.

Alesina, A., O. Barbiero, C. Favero, F. Giavazzi, and M. Paradisi (2017): The Effects of Fiscal Consolidations: Theory and Evidence, NBER Working Paper No. 23385, revised November.

Angeletos, G.-M. (2002): Fiscal Policy with Non-Contingent Debt and the Optimal Maturity Structure, *Quarterly Journal of Economics*, 117, 1105–31.

Aschauer, D.A. (1985): Fiscal Policy and Aggregate Demand, *American Economic Review*, 75(1) (March), 117–27.

Aschauer, D.A. (1988): The Equilibrium Approach to Fiscal Policy, *Journal of Money, Credit and Banking*, 20(1) (February), 41–62.

Auerbach, A.J. (2004): How Much Equity Does the Government Hold? *American Economic Review*, 94(2) (May), 155–60.

Auerbach, A.J. (2005): Dynamic Scoring: An Introduction to the Issues, *American Economic Review*, 95(2), 421–5.

Auerbach, A.J. (2012): The Fall and Rise of Keynesian Fiscal Policy, *Asian Economic Policy Review* (December), 157–75.

Auerbach, A.J. (2014): Budget Rules and Fiscal Policy: Ten Lessons from Theory and Evidence, *German Economic Review*, 15(1) (February), 84–99.

Auerbach, A.J., and D. Feenberg (2000): The Significance of Federal Taxes as Automatic Stabilisers, *Journal of Economic Perspectives*, 14(3) (Summer), 37–56.

Auerbach, A.J., and Y. Gorodnichenko (2012): Measuring the Output Responses to Fiscal Policy, *American Economic Journal: Economic Policy*, 4(2) (May), 1–27.

Ball, L.M. (2014): The Case for a Long-Run Inflation Target of Four Per Cent, IMF Working Paper 14/92, International Monetary Fund.

Ball, L.M., D. Furceri, D. Leigh, and P. Loungani (2013): The Distributional Effects of Fiscal Consolidation, IMF Working Paper 13/151, International Monetary Fund.

Ball, L.M., D. Leigh, and P. Loungani (2011): Painful Medicine, Finance and Development, IMF e-journal (September), https://www.imf.org/external/pubs/ft/fandd/2011/09/PDF/ball.pdf

Barro, R.J. (1974): Are Government Bonds Net Wealth? *Journal of Political Economy*, 82(6), 1095–1117.

Barro, R.J. (1979): On the Determination of Public Debt, *Journal of Political Economy*, 87(5), 940–71.

Barro, R.J. (1989a): The Ricardian Approach to Budget Deficits, *Journal of Economic Perspectives*, 3(2) (Spring), 37–54.

Barro, R.J. (1989b): The Neoclassical Approach to Fiscal Policy, in Barro *Modern Business Cycle Theory*, Oxford: Basil Blackwell, chapter 5.

Barsky, R.B., N.G. Mankiw, and S.P. Zeldes (1986): Ricardian Consumers with Keynesian Propensities, *American Economic Review*, 76(4) (September), 676–91.

Basu, K. (2014): Fiscal Policy as an Instrument of Investment and Growth, The World Bank Policy Research Working Paper No. S6850, May.

Baxter, M., and R. King (1993): Fiscal Policy in General Equilibrium, *American Economic Review*, 83(2) (June), 315–34.

Bernardini, M., and L. Forni (2017): Private and Public Debt: Are Emerging Markets at Risk? International Monetary Fund Working Paper 17/61, March.

Bernheim D.B. (1987): Ricardian Equivalence: An Evaluation of Theory and Evidence, in S. Fischer (ed.), *NBER Macroeconomics Annual 1987*, Cambridge, MA: MIT Press, ii. 263–316.

Blanchard, O.J. (1979): Backward and Forward Solutions for Economies with Rational Expectations, *American Economic Review*, 69(2) (May), 114–18.

Blanchard, O.J. (1981): Output, the Stock Market, and Interest Rates, *American Economic Review*, 71(1) (March), 132–43.

Blanchard, O.J. (1984): Current and Anticipated Deficits, Interest Rates and Economic Activity, *European Economic Review*, 25(1) (June), 7–27.

Blanchard, O.J. (1985): Debt, Deficits, and Finite Horizons, *Journal of Political Economy*, 93(2), 223–47.

Blanchard, O.J. (1990): Suggestions for a New Set of Fiscal Indicators, OECD Economics Department Working Paper 79.

Blanchard, O.J., and F. Giavazzi (2003): Macroeconomic Effects of Regulation and Deregulation in Goods and Labor Markets, *Quarterly Journal of Economics*, 118(3), 879–907.

Blanchard, O.J., and D. Leigh (2013): Growth Forecast Errors and Fiscal Multipliers, *American Economic Review Papers and Proceedings*, 103(3) (May), 117–20.

Blanchard, O.J., and R. Perotti (2002): An Empirical Characterization of the Dynamic Effects of Changes in Government Spending and Taxes on Output, *Quarterly Journal of Economics*, 117(4), 1329–68.

Blanchard, O.J. and L.H. Summers (2017): *Rethinking Stabilization Policy: Evolution or Revolution?*, NBER Working Paper No. 24179, Cambridge, MA: National Bureau of Economic Research (NBER).

Blanchard, O.J., C. Erceg, and J. Lindé (2016): Jump-Starting the Euro Area Recovery: Would a Rise in Core Fiscal Spending Help the Periphery? in M. Eichenbaum and J. Parker (eds), *NBER Macroeconomics Annual 2016*, Cambridge, MA: MIT Press, 31(1), 103–82.

Bohn, H. (1992): Budget Deficits and Government Accounting, *Carnegie-Rochester Conference Series on Public Policy*, 37(1) (December), 1–83.

Bohn, H. (2005): *The Sustainability of Fiscal Policy in the United States*, CESifo Working Paper No.1446, Munich: CESifo Group.

Bohn, H. (2007): Are Stationarity and Cointegration Restrictions Really Necessary for the Intertemporal Budget Constraint? Journal of Monetary Economics, 54(7) (October), 1837–47.

Bournakis, I., C. Tsoukis, D. Christopoulos, and T. Palivos (eds) (2017): *Political Economy Perspectives on the Greek Crisis: Debt, Austerity and Unemployment*, London: Palgrave Macmillan.

Buiter, W.H. (1988): Death, Birth, Productivity Growth and Debt Neutrality, *Economic Journal*, 98(391), 279–93.

Buiter, W.H. (2002): The Fiscal Theory of the Price Level: A Critique, *Economic Journal*, 112(481) (July), 459–80.

Buiter, W.H., T. Persson, and P. Minford (1985): A Guide to Public Sector Debt and Deficits, *Economic Policy*, 1(1) (November), 13–79.

Buttiglione, L., P. Lane, L. Reichlin, and V.R. Reinhart (2014): *Deleveraging, What Deleveraging?* The 16th Geneva Report on the World Economy, CEPR Policy Portal, September, https://voxeu.org/content/deleveraging-what-deleveraging-16th-geneva-report-world-economy

Calmfors, L., and S. Wren-Lewis (2011): What Should Fiscal Councils Do? *Economic Policy*, 26 (October), 649–95.

Campbell, J.Y., and R.J. Shiller (1987): Cointegration and Tests of Present Value Models, *Journal of Political Economy*, 95(5), 1062–88.

Canzoneri, M.B., R.E. Cumby, and B.T. Diba (2001): Is the Price Level Determined by the Needs of Fiscal Solvency? *American Economic Review*, 91, 1221–38.

Chari, V.V., and P.J. Kehoe (1999): Optimal Fiscal and Monetary Policy, in J.B. Taylor and M. Woodford (eds), *Handbook of Macroeconomics*, Amsterdam: Elsevier, i. 1671–1745.

Cochrane, J.H. (2001): Long Term Debt and Optimal Policy in the Fiscal Theory of the Price Level, *Econometrica*, 69, 69–116.

Cochrane, J.H. (2015): A New Structure for U.S. Federal Debt, Economics Working Paper 15108, Hoover Institution, Stanford University.

Cochrane, J.H. (2019): The Fiscal Roots of Inflation, NBER Working Paper 25811.

Cogan, J.F., T. Cwik, J.B. Taylor, and V. Wieland (2010): New Keynesian versus Old Keynesian Government Spending Multipliers, *Journal of Economic Dynamics and Control*, 34, 281–95.

Coto-Martinez, J., and H.D. Dixon (2003): Profits, Markups and Entry: Fiscal Policy in an Open Economy, *Journal of Economic Dynamics and Control*, 27(4), 573–97.

Crafts, N., and T.C. Mills (2015): Self-Defeating Austerity? Evidence from 1930s' Britain, *European Review of Economic History*, 19(2) (May), 109–27.

Crawford, R., P. Johnson, and B. Zaranko (2018): The Planning and Control of UK Public Expenditure, 1993–2015, IFS Report 147, July, https://www.ifs.org.uk/publications/13155

Cugnasca, A., and P. Rother (2015): Fiscal Multipliers during Consolidation: Evidence from the European Union, European Central Bank Working Paper No. 1863, October.

DeGrauwe, P., and Y. Ji (2013): Self-Fulfilling Crises in the Eurozone: An Empirical Test, *Journal of International Money and Finance*, 34(C), 15–36.

DeLong, J.B., and L. D'Andrea Tyson (2013): Discretionary Fiscal Policy as a Stabilization Policy Tool: What do we Think Now that we did Not Think in 2007? http://www.imf.org/external/np/seminars/eng/2013/fiscal/pdf/tyson.pdf

DeLong, J.B., and L.H. Summers (2012): Fiscal Policy in a Depressed Economy, *Brookings Papers on Economic Activity* (Spring), 233–74.

Denes, M., G.B. Eggertsson, and S. Gilbukh (2013): Deficits, Public Debt Dynamics, and Tax and Spending Multipliers, *Economic Journal*, 123(566) (February), F133–63.

Diamond, P.A. (1965): National Debt in a Neoclassical Growth Model, *American Economic Review*, 55(5), 1126–50.

Dixon, H.D. (1987): A Simple Model of Imperfect Competition with Walrasian Features, *Oxford Economic Papers*, 39(1) (March), 134–60.

Dixon, H.D., and P. Lawler (1996): Imperfect Competition and the Fiscal Multiplier, *Scandinavian Journal of Economics*, 98(2) (June), 219–31.

Eggertsson, G.B. (2010): What Fiscal Policy is Effective at Zero Interest Rates? in D. Acemoglu and M. Woodford (eds), *NBER Macroeconomics Annual 2010*, Cambridge, MA: MIT Press, 25, 59–112.

Eichengreen, B., and U. Panizza (2016): A Surplus of Ambition: Can Europe Rely on Large Primary Surpluses to Solve its Debt Problem? *Economic Policy*, 31(85), 5–49.

Ellison, M., and A. Scott (2017): *Managing the UK National Debt 1694-2017*, CEPR Discussion Paper No. DP12304, London: Centre for Economic Policy Performance (CEPR), September.

Elmendorf, D.W., and G.N. Mankiw (1999): Government Debt, in J.B. Taylor and M. Woodford (eds), *Handbook of Macroeconomics*, Amsterdam: Elsevier, i/3. 1615–69.

Eyraud, L., and A. Weber (2013): *The Challenge of Debt Reduction During Fiscal Consolidation*, IMF Working Paper No. 13/67, Washington, DC: International Monetary Fund (IMF), March.

Faini, R. (2006): Fiscal Policy and Interest Rates in Europe, *Economic Policy*, 21(47), 443–89.

Fatas, A., and I. Mihov (2001): Government Size and Automatic Stabilisers: International and Intranational Evidence, *Journal of International Economics*, 55(1) (October), 3–28.

Feldstein, M. (2009): Rethinking the Role of Fiscal Policy, *American Economic Review*, 99(2) (May), 556–9.

Galí, J., J.D. López-Salido, and J. Vallés (2007): Understanding the Effects of Government Spending on Consumption, *Journal of the European Economic Association*, 5(1) (March), 227–70.

Galor, O., and J. Zeira (2003): Income Distribution and Macroeconomics, *Review of Economic Studies*, 60(1), 35–52.

Giavazzi, F., and M. Pagano (1990): Can Severe Fiscal Contractions be Expansionary? Tales of Two Small European Countries, in O.J Blanchard and S. Fischer (eds), *NBER Macroeconomics Annual*, Cambridge, MA: MIT Press, 75–122.

Gourinchas, P.O., and M. Obstfeld (2012): Stories of the Twentieth Century for the Twenty-First, *American Economic Journal: Macroeconomics*, 4(1) (January), 226–65.

Greenwood, R., S.G. Hanson, and J.C. Stein (2015): A Comparative-Advantage Approach to Government Debt Maturity, *Journal of Finance*, 70, 1683–1722.

Hall, G.J., and T.J. Sargent (2018): Brief History of US Debt Limits Before 1939, *Proceedings of the National Academy of Sciences*, 115(12) (March), 2942–5.

Hall, R.E. (2009): By How Much does GDP Rise If the Government Buys More Output? *Brookings Papers on Economic Activity*, 40(2) (Fall), 183–249.

Hamilton, J., and M. Flavin (1986): On the Limitations of Government Borrowing: A Framework for Empirical Testing, *American Economic Review*, 76, 808–19.

Hernandez de Cos, P., and E. Moral-Benito (2013): Fiscal Consolidations and Economic Growth, *Fiscal Studies*, 34(4) (December), 491–515.

Hilscher, J., A. Raviv, and R. Reis (2014): Inflating Away the Public Debt? An Empirical Assessment, NBER Working Paper No. 20339, July.

Hubbard, R.G., and E. Engen (2005): Federal Government Debt and Interest Rates, in M. Gertler and K. Rogoff (eds), *NBER Macroeconomics Annual 2004*, Cambridge, MA: MIT Press, vol. 19, 83–138.

IMF (2014): Fiscal Policy and Income Inequality, International Monetary Fund Policy Paper, January, http://www.imf.org/external/pp/ppindex.aspx

Irmen, A., and J. Kuehnel (2009): Productive Government Expenditure and Economic Growth, Journal of Economic Surveys, 23(4), 692–733.

Jordà, Ò., M. Schularick, and A.M. Taylor (2013): When Credit Bites Back, *Journal of Money, Credit and Banking*, 45 (November), 3–28.

Kiel Institute (2015): Eurobarometer, February; https://www.ifw-kiel.de/think-tank/economic-policy-center/the-kiel-institute-barometer-of-public-debt/?searchterm=barometer%20of%20public%20debt

Kirsanova, T., C. Leith, and S. Wren-Lewis (2009): Monetary and Fiscal Policy Interaction: The Current Consensus Assignment in the Light of Recent Developments, *Economic Journal*, 119, F482–96.

Krugman, P. (2012): End This Depression Now!, New York: W.W. Norton & Co.

Laubach, T. (2009): New Evidence on Interest Rate Effects of Budget Deficits and Debt, *Journal of the European Economic Association*, 7(4), 858–85.

Lee, S., H. Park, M.H. Seo, and Y. Shin (2017): Testing for a Debt-Threshold Effect on Output Growth, Fiscal Studies, 38(4) (December), 701–17.

Leeper, E.M. (1991): Equilibria under 'Active' and 'Passive' Monetary and Fiscal Policies, *Journal of Monetary Economics*, 27(1), 129–47.

Leeper, E.M., and C. Leith (2016): Understanding Inflation as a Joint Monetary–Fiscal Phenomenon, in J.B. Taylor and H. Uhlig (eds), *Handbook of Macroeconomics*, Amsterdam: Elsevier, ii. 2305–2415.

Leith, C., and S. Wren-Lewis (2006): Fiscal Stabilisation Policy and Fiscal Institutions, *Oxford Review of Economic Policy*, 21(4) (Winter), 584–97.

McCallum, B. (1984): Are Bond-Financed Deficits Inflationary? A Ricardian Analysis, *Journal of Political Economy*, 92, 123–35.

McCallum, B.T. and E. Nelson (2005): Monetary and Fiscal Theories of the Price Level: The Irreconcilable Differences, *Oxford Review of Economic Policy*, 21(4) (Winter), 565–83.

McKay, A., and R. Reis (2016): The Role of Automatic Stabilizers in the U.S. Business Cycle, *Econometrica*, 84(1), 141–94.

Mankiw, N.G. (1988): Imperfect Competition and the Keynesian Cross, *Economics Letters*, 26(1), 7–13.

Mankiw, N.G. (2000): The Savers-Spenders Theory of Fiscal Policy, *American Economic Review*, 90(2) (May), 120–5.

Mankiw, N.G., and M. Weinzierl (2006): Dynamic Scoring: A Back-of-the-Envelope Guide, *Journal of Public Economics*, 90(8–9) (September), 1415–33.

Mbaye, S., M. Moreno-Badia, and K. Chae (2018a): Bailing out the People? When Private Debt Becomes Public, International Monetary Fund Working Paper 18/141.

Mbaye, S., M. Moreno-Badia, and K. Chae (2018b): Global Debt Database: Methodology and Sources, International Monetary Fund Working Paper 18/111.

Mendoza, E.G., and J.D. Ostry (2008): International Evidence on Fiscal Solvency: Is Fiscal Policy 'Responsible'? *Journal of Monetary Economics*, 55(6) (September), 1081–93.

Missale, A. (1997): Managing the Public Debt: The Optimal Taxation Approach, *Journal of Economic Surveys*, 11(3), 235–65.

Missale, A., and O.J. Blanchard (1994): The Debt Burden and Debt Maturity, *American Economic Review, American Economic Association*, 84(1), 309–19.

Mountford, A., and H. Uhlig (2009): What are the Effects of Fiscal Policy Shocks? *Journal of Applied Econometrics*, 24, 960–92.

Mulligan, C.B. (2011): Simple Analytics and Empirics of the Government Spending Multiplier and Other 'Keynesian' Paradoxes, *B.E. Journal of Macroeconomics, Berkeley Electronic Press*, 11(1) (June), Article 19.

Nosbusch, Y. (2008): Interest Costs and the Optimal Maturity Structure of Government Debt, *Economic Journal*, 118, 477–98.

Panizza, U., and A. Presbitero (2014): Public Debt and Economic Growth: Is there a Causal Effect? *Journal of Macroeconomics*, 41, 21–41.

Perotti, R. (2013): The 'Austerity Myth': Gain without Pain? in A. Alesina and F. Giavazzi (eds), *Fiscal Policy after the Financial Crisis*, Chicago: NBER and Chicago University Press, 307–54.

Quintos, C.E. (1995): Sustainability of the Deficit Process with Structural Shifts, *Journal of Business and Economic Statistics*, 13(4), 409–17.

Ramey, V.A. (2012): Can Government Purchases Stimulate the Economy? *Journal of Economic Literature*, 49(3), 673–85.

Ramey, V.A., and S. Zubairy (2018): Government Spending Multipliers in Good Times and in Bad: Evidence from US Historical Data, *Journal of Political Economy*, 126(2), 850–901.

Reinhart, C.M., and K.S. Rogoff (2009): *This Time is Different: Eight Centuries of Financial Folly*, Princeton: Princeton University Press.

Reinhart, C.M., and K.S. Rogoff (2010): Growth in a Time of Debt, *American Economic Review*, 100(2) (May), 573–8.

Reinhart, C.M., V.R. Reinhart, and K.S. Rogoff (2012): Public Debt Overhangs: Advanced Economy Episodes since 1800, *Journal of Economic Perspectives*, 26(3) (Summer), 69–86.

Reinhart, C.M., V. Reinhart and K.S. Rogoff (2015): Dealing with Debt, *Journal of International Economics*, 96(S1), 43–55.

Rodrik, D. (2000): What Drives Public Employment in Developing Countries? *Review of Development Economics*, 4(3) (October), 229–43.

Romer, C. (2011): What do we Know about the Effects of Fiscal Policy? Separating Evidence from Ideology, Lecture at Hamilton College, available at: http://elsa.berkeley.edu/~cromer/Written%20Version%20of%20Effects%20of%20Fiscal%20Policy.pdf

Romer, C. (2012): Fiscal Policy in the Crisis: Lessons and Policy Implications, IMF Fiscal Forum, 18 April, https://eml.berkeley.edu/~cromer/Lectures/Lessons%20for%20Fiscal%20Policy.pdf

Sachs, J.D. (2014): *A New Macroeconomic Strategy*, Project Syndicate, October; https://www.earth.columbia.edu/sitefiles/file/Sachs%20Writing/2014/A%20New%20Macroeconomic%20Strategy%20by%20Jeffrey%20D_%20Sachs%20-%20Project%20Syndicate_2014.pdf.

Sargent, T.J. (1987): *Macroeconomic Theory*, 2nd ed., Bingley, UK: Emerald.

Sargent, T., and N. Wallace (1981): Some Unpleasant Monetarist Arithmetic, *Federal Reserve Bank of Minneapolis Quarterly Review*, 1981(5) (Fall), 1–17.

Schmitt-Groh, S., and M. Uribe (2000): Price Level Determinacy and Monetary Policy under a Balanced Budget Requirement, *Journal of Monetary Economics*, 45, 211–46.

Schumacher, J., and B. Weder di Mauro (2015): Diagnosing Greek Debt Sustainability: Why is it so Hard? *Brookings Papers on Economic Activity* (Fall), 279–305.

Seater, J.J. (1993): Ricardian Equivalence, *Journal of Economic Literature*, 31(1), 142–90.

Shelton, C.A. (2007): The Size and Composition of Government Expenditure, *Journal of Public Economics*, 91(11), 2230–60.

Silvestre, J. (1993): The Market-Power Foundations of Macroeconomic Policy, *Journal of Economic Literature*, 31(1) (March), 105–41.

Sims, C.A. (1994): A Simple Model for Study of the Determination of the Price Level and the Interaction of Monetary and Fiscal Policy, *Economic Theory*, 4(3), 381–99.

Starz, R. (1989): Monopolistic Competition as a Foundation for Keynesian Macroeconomic Models, *Quarterly Journal of Economics*, 104(4) (November), 737–52.

Summers, L. (2014): Why Public Investment Really is a Free Lunch, blog, http://larrysummers.com/2014/10/07/why-public-investment-really-is-a-free-lunch/

Tanzi, V., and L. Schuknecht (1997): Reconsidering the Fiscal Role of Government: The International Perspective, *American Economic Review Papers and Proceedings*, 87(2) (May), 164–8.

Tanzi, V., and L. Schuknecht (2000): *Public Spending in the 20th Century: A Global Perspective*, Cambridge: Cambridge University Press.

Taylor, J.B. (2000): Reassessing Discretionary Fiscal Policy, *Journal of Economic Perspectives*, 14(3), 21–36.

Taylor, J.B. (2011): An Empirical Analysis of the Revival of Fiscal Activism in the 2000s, *Journal of Economic Literature*, 49(3), 686–702.

Trehan, B., and C. Walsh (1988): Common Trends, the Government's Budget Constraint, and Revenue Smoothing, *Journal of Economic Dynamics and Control*, 12(2–3), 425–44.

Trehan, B., and C. Walsh (1991): Testing Intertemporal Budget Constraints: Theory and Applications to U.S. Federal Budget and Current Account Deficits, *Journal of Money, Credit and Banking*, 23(2), 206–23.

Tsoukis, C. (2017): The Limits to Austerity: The Fiscal Multiplier and the 'Debt Laffer Curve', in I. Bournakis, C. Tsoukis, D. Christopoulos, and T. Palivos (eds), *Political Economy Perspectives on the Greek Crisis: Debt, Austerity and Unemployment*, London: Palgrave Macmillan, 223–47.

Turnovsky, S.J., and M.H. Miller (1984): The Effects of Government Expenditure on the Term Structure of Interest Rates, *Journal of Money, Credit and Banking*, 16(1) (February), 16–33.

US Congressional Budget Office (2009): Stewardship, in *US Budget, Analytical Perspectives*, ch.13), Washington, DC: GPO, 179–96, http://www.gpoaccess.gov/usbudget/fy09/pdf/spec.pdf

Weil, P. (1989): Overlapping Families of Infinitely-Lived Agents, *Journal of Public Economics*, 38(2), 183–98.

Woodford, M.D. (1995): Price Level Determinacy without Control of a Monetary Aggregate, *Carnegie-Rochester Conference Series on Public Policy*, 43, 1–46.

Woodford, M.D. (2001): Fiscal Requirements for Price Stability, *Journal of Money, Credit and Banking*, 33, 669–728.

Woodford, M.D. (2011): Simple Analytics of the Government Expenditure Multiplier, *American Economic Journal: Macroeconomics*, 3(1) (January), 1–35.

Wyplosz, C. (2005): Fiscal Policy: Institutions versus Rules, *National Institute Economic Review*, 191, 64–78.

9

The Theory of Growth

9.1 Introduction: The Questions and Facts of Growth

9.1.1 The Questions of Growth

In 2005, the real (in terms of 2005 dollars) per capita GDP in the US was about $38,000. It had grown about 12 times (= 1200 per cent) from about £3,000 in 1870 (again in terms of 2005 dollars, i.e. as if prices were at their 2005 levels) and about £5,000 in 1905, i.e. more than seven-fold within the preceding century. The overall US prosperity is shared by a small group of 'advanced industrialized economies' but is by no means shared by all the seven-plus billion inhabitants of this planet. To emphasize the diverse experiences, Table 9.1 looks at the living standards (real per capita GDP) for a small set of countries, based on information provided by Barro and Sala-i-Martin (1995). In about 1910, in terms of 1985 US$ (i.e. evaluated at 1985 prices and translated into dollars), the US and Japanese GDP per capita was 4,538 and 1,084 dollars, respectively. Their 1990 figures were 18,258 and 16,144. Compare those with the nearly corresponding figures for India ($399 in 1913 and $662 in 1987), Philippines ($985 in 1913 and $1,519 in 1987), and Argentina ($1,770 in 1913 and $3,302 in 1987); all in 1985 US$, i.e. directly comparable. The differences they reveal are astonishing, both across countries and across time. India for instance registered a very small rate of growth; an experience shared by other countries (not shown) with no, or even negative (i.e. reversal), growth for long periods of time. In about 1910, Japan was comparably affluent (or poor) to the Philippines, while Argentina was more affluent. Yet, two generations later, Japanese affluence bears no comparison with that in either country. (Since then, however, Japanese growth seems to have stalled to a large extent.) The Japanese experience of development was mirrored to a large extent by a number of other South-East Asian countries ('tigers') which registered a sudden growth spurt from about 1970 or so. The list of such amazing facts and comparisons could go on. Not to forget of course the emergence of China in the last 30 years or so, but also of the other 'BRICs') (Brazil, Russia, India, China), and others besides (e.g., Turkey, Chile), each with its own individual experience but all on the (long) course of catching up with living standards of the developed world.

These facts set the scene for the theory of growth. In particular, they pose a number of questions that motivate this theory. What determines a country's evolution of prosperity? Why did countries that were prosperous at a different age stagnate while others grew? What determines these growth spurts, the rather sudden 'reawakening' of countries and their subsequent joining into the developmental 'race'? What determines the cross-country distribution of living standards? Is there a prospect of countries' converging to common

Theory of Macroeconomic Policy. Christopher Tsoukis, Oxford University Press (2020). © Christopher Tsoukis.
DOI: 10.1093/oso/9780198825371.003.0009

Table 9.1. Evolution of GDP per capita (1985 US$) for selected countries

	US	Japan	India	Argentina	Philippines
1910/13	4538	1084	399	1770	985
1990/87	18258	16144	662	3302	1519

Source: Based on information provided in Tables 10.1 and 10.2 of Barro and Sala-i-Martin (1995)

such standards any time in the future? What are the appropriate policies the countries that lag behind should put in place if they hope to maintain vigorous growth and catch up?[1]

One cannot but agree with Lucas (1988) that '[T]he consequences for human welfare involved in questions like these are simply staggering: Once one starts to think about them, it is hard to think about anything else.' (Lucas, 1988, p. 5). Such questions gave rise to growth theory. This has come in two waves. An early generation of theories and models was built around the idea that capital accumulation is central in the process of growth. Many of the insights of those early theories are still valuable today, but what is mostly remembered from this very rich literature is the Solow Growth Model, which we review in Section 9.2. The literature then lay dormant for some time, until it was rekindled in the mid-1980s, partly by the emergence of the 'Asian tigers'. This second wave, developed in the following 20 years, has been termed 'Endogenous Growth Theory' and explored the importance of productivity, technology, and human capital. We shall review it in Section 9.4. In the remainder of this section, we further explore various facts related to growth as a way of setting the scene for the theories that follow.

9.1.2 Small Numbers with a Big Effect

If the US had $4,538 and $18,258 of per capita GDP in 1910 and 1990, respectively, what was its growth rate? This is worked out from the basic equation

$$18528 = 4538(1 + g)^{80}.$$

Taking (natural) logs, noting that $\log(1 + g) \approx g$ is a good approximation if $g < 0.1$, then we have:

$$\log(18528) = \log(4538) + 80g$$

Therefore $9.83 = 8.42 + 80g$, so $g = 1.8$ per cent (approximately). This has been the average per capita growth rate in the US over this period. The average masks of course the fact that there have been slower and faster years of growth. Now, a number like 0.02 (= 2 per cent) does not make a big impression! People may wonder why strive (study, put the policy apparatus and measures in place) to raise a growth rate of, say,

---

[1] In much this chapter, and indeed elsewhere in the book, we use 'living standards' to be more or less equivalent to 'real GDP per capita'. However, the former term is much broader: it encompasses many other considerations such as quality of life (including environmental quality, stress, overall happiness), institutions, educational and health standards, even human rights and freedoms, as well as the material resources that real GDP per capita records. There are currently calls for these wider considerations to be included in the measurement of output (whereas now they are excluded). See the Guidance for Further Study.

Table 9.2. Numerical illustrations of growth

Annual growth rate of real GDP		How long it takes for real GDP to double
g = 0.005 (=0.5%) (India 1913–1987)		138 years
g = 0.01 (=1%)		69 years
g = 0.02		35 years
g = 0.03	(US in the 20th century)	23 years
g = 0.1	(China 1980–2015)	7 years

With an annual growth rate of real GDP per capita equal to g, what will living standards be (% of the original) after certain years?

		20 years	40 years
g = 0.02	(US now)	150%	220%
g = 0.06	(China now)	320%	1000%

Source: Author's calculations

0.02 to 0.03. But as Romer (2007) forcefully reminds us, multiplicative calculations are very different from additive ones.[2] Table 9.2 provides some numerical illustrations of this broad point. For instance, we can ask the question of how long it takes for a country to double its real GDP if the growth rate of that is g. With an annual real GDP growth rate of g = 0.005 (= 0.5 per cent, close to the case of India 1913–87) the answer is 138 years, 35 years if g = 0.02 (close to the US case), 14 years if g = 0.05, and finally 7 years if g = 0.1, the growth rate experienced by China in much of the last 30 years.[3] Furthermore, a country whose real GDP per capita is growing by the (historically 'healthy') rate of 2 per cent per annum will see its living standards rise by a factor of 1.5 after 20 years and 2.2 after 40 years; if it is growing like China, with a per capita growth rate of 6 per cent or so, its living standards will have risen by a factor of 3.2 (more than trebled) after 20 years and ten-fold after 40 years. Obviously, these humble numbers have tremendous, indeed dramatic, implications for the relative economic fortunes of countries, the living standards and welfare of their citizens, not only over the course of centuries, but even over the space of two or three generations. These numbers are to be taken seriously, and policy formulation should follow accordingly.

9.1.3 Growth Experiences and Facts

Durlauf et al. (2005) provide a panorama of empirical research related to growth, and we follow them here. The first fact is the unprecedented, in the history of mankind, rise in

---

[2] Romer (2007) gives the following example. If we put one penny (note: one penny) on the first square of a board of chess and double this amount (notionally) on every square, then if we use only black squares, we shall end up with $21.5 million at the end of the board, while if we used all the squares, we would have ended up with $92,000,000 billion (a number with 15 zeros)! These numbers are almost barely comprehensible, making the point how seriously wrong we can go if we use the 'additive' intuition when making multiplicative calculations. The experience of growth never witnesses doubling every year (growing at an annual rate of 200 per cent), but the point remains that compounding has serious numerical implications.

[3] $2 = (1 + g)^x$, with $log2 \approx 0.69$, so $x = 0.69/g$. If the growth rate is expressed as $g = G\%$, the rule of thumb is: $x = 70/G$; e.g. if the growth rate is 5 per cent, it takes $70/5 = 20$ years. Note that in economics we almost never use anything other than natural logarithms, so the symbols 'log' and (the more correct) 'ln' are often used interchangeably.

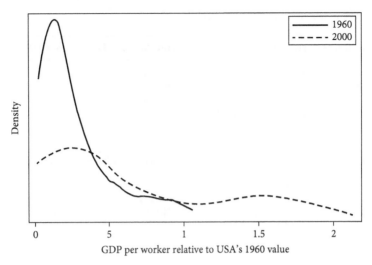

Figure 9.1. Distribution of GDP per worker, 1960 and 2000
Source: Replicated from Durlauf, Johnson and Temple (2005), Figure 1.

living standards that has taken place in the last two centuries in most parts of the planet, following the industrial revolution. After a period (a century or so) of what is called 'Smithian' growth, the UK was the first country to embark on the industrial revolution, commonly thought to have started in the last quarter of the eighteenth century.[4] Since then, living standards have increased many-fold, probably by an order of 15 (fifteen-fold). Between 1870 (when more reliable data begin to be assembled) and 2005, the US GDP per capita rose by a factor of 12.5; during the twentieth century, it rose by a factor of 7. The US was at the forefront of development for most of this period; but other industrialized country experiences were similar (notably in the UK, Germany, France). Japan joined the group of industrial economies only post-World War II. Its average growth rate between 1950 and 1990 was 5.9 per cent (against 2.1 in the US), but it seems to have stalled after that.

The second broad fact is that the growth and development experience has not been shared equally among countries. To make this point, Figure 9.1 reproduces figure 1 of Durlauf et al. (2005), and shows the world income distribution of GDP per worker in 1960 and 2000. Specifically, it plots the frequency ('density') distribution of GDP per worker relative to that of the US in 1960.[5] We note that a large number of countries lagged behind the US in 1960 (most of the mass was below 1), that some continued to have the same roughly living standards in 2000 as in 1960, and that the living standards in 2000 are more

---

[4] 'Smithian' growth was the mild growth experienced particularly during the eighteenth century in the UK as a result of greater specialization in production in primitive factories (as argued by Adam Smith), better transportation (with the improvement of roads and canals), more efficient bureaucracies, and the development of domestic markets. But 'Smithian growth' did not feature the processes highlighted in the growth literature, namely capital accumulation, and sustained productivity improvement due to technical progress. If we plot living standards of the industrialized countries on a graph against historical time (across centuries), the graph will look like a 'step function': flat until about 1800, and rising steeply thereafter. But that is not quite accurate. Living standards had been rising over many centuries before 1800. The growth was very slow, but the effect cumulatively over centuries was very important; the living standard in the eighteenth century was very different from earlier centuries. Jones (2016, table 2) suggests the world real GDP per capita at about 1800 was about double that of imperial Roman times; but one should be aware of the difficulties involved in such comparisons. The reasons include improvements in agriculture, the arrival of internal peace and security, as well as the 'Smithian growth' just mentioned.
[5] Note the difference with 'GDP per capita'. The measure used in the graph is not affected by the size of the labour force in relation to population, and is a more accurate measure of (average) productivity.

unevenly distributed across countries than in 1960. Also notable is a tendency for the distribution to become bi-modal, while the middle of the distribution is getting thinner. This is a phenomenon that has been described as 'Twin Peaks'; see Section 9.3 on convergence. At the same, there has been clear economic progress, as the 2000 distributions shows a lot of mass higher up the scale than the 1960 one.

More information is conveyed by Figure 9.2 (Durlauf et al. 2005, figure 6), which shows that the growth rates between 1980 and 2000 were more diverse than between 1960 and 1980; additionally, the Figure shows that the average growth rate across countries fell in the latter period compared to the former. Finally Table 9.3, also from Durlauf et al. (2005, table 7) gives an idea of actual growth rates of real GDP per worker for the various regions and groups of countries (averages for 1960–2000). Notable are the disparities, the 'miracles' particularly in East and South East Asia, the 'disasters' (negative average growth across the time period, mainly in Sub-Saharan Africa), and the 'normal' growth rates of about 2–3 per cent experienced by industrialized economies.[6]

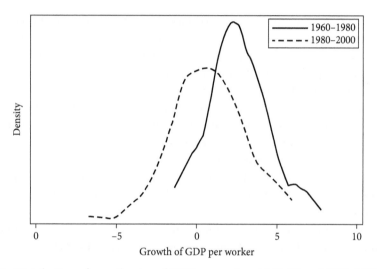

Figure 9.2. Distribution of growth rates of GDP per worker, 1960–80 and 1980–2000
Source: Replicated from Durlauf, Johnson and Temple (2005), Figure 6.

Table 9.3. Growth rates of real GDP per worker, 1960–2000, by country group

Group	N	25th	Median	75th
Sub-Saharan Africa	36	−0.5	0.7	1.3
South and Central America	21	0.4	0.9	1.5
East and Southeast Asia	10	3.8	4.3	5.4
South Asia	7	1.9	2.2	2.9
Industrialized countries	19	1.7	2.4	3.0

Notes: The Table shows the 25th, 50th and 75th percentiles of the distribution of growth rates of real GDP per worker for various groups of countries. Replicated from Durlauf, Johnson and Temple (2005), Table 7.

[6] With reference to Figure 9.2 (see Durlauf et al., 2005, section II.ii), it is important to note that the unit of observation is the country unweighted by its population. For example, China and Malta count as equally important observations. If we weighted countries by their populations, then the 1980–2000 period, with the rise of China and to some extent India, would have lifted the average growth rate in that period; conversely, the

9.1.4 The 'Kaldor Stylized Facts'

Many expositions of growth begin by recalling six 'stylized' empirical observations that are thought to characterize the growth process, due to Kaldor (1963). Barro and Sala-i-Martin (1995, chapter 1) summarize them thus:

i. Per capita output grows over time, and its growth rate does not tend to diminish over the long run;
ii. Physical capital per worker grows over time;
iii. The rate of return to capital is approximately constant;
iv. The ratio of physical capital to output is approximately constant;
v. The shares of labour and physical capital in national income are approximately constant;
vi. The growth rate of output per worker differs substantially across countries.

These empirical regularities were once thought to be quite solid, hence given the characterization as 'stylized facts'.[7] More recent research however casts a more critical light on these 'facts'. As discussed above, growth rates (fact i) vary quite a lot between countries and time periods. At the same time, Jones (2016, figure 1 and table 1) shows that the growth rate of the US real GDP per capita has remained rather stable (with only temporary deviations) around the 2 per cent mark for the entire twentieth century and more.

The US non-residential capital-output ratio (fact iv) seems to have been stable for the entire post-war period (Jones, 2016, figure 3); while it hovers around 2 to 2.5, it seems stationary. The real interest rate, equal to the rate of return to capital (fact iii) in competitive equilibrium, has changed considerably across time (Barro and Sala-i-Martin, 1990). As argued in Chapter 10 on inequality, factor shares have been changing recently in favour of capital income (and against labour income). And more recent work, reviewed next, has made new observations arising from more recent experience. However, even though the Kaldor 'facts' may now appear dated and even contestable, they have been

---

average growth of 1960–80 is relatively high partly because Sub-Saharan Africa, with its many small countries, was doing relatively well during that period.

[7] Kaldor was of course not alone in blending history-minded empirical and theoretical research on growth. Growth has featured high on the research agenda of (what one might term) macro-economic historians. Kuznets (1971, 1973) has highlighted the structural transformation associated with growth (from agriculture to industry and then on to services, urbanization). In a similar vein, Rostow (1960), Maddison (2007), Abramovitz (1989, containing the evocatively titled essay 'Catching Up, Forging Ahead, and Falling Behind') highlight the phases of growth from a historical perspective. Temin (1999) discusses the Great Depression while Feinstein et al. (1997) reviews the European inter-war experience. See Crafts and Toniolo (1996) on post-World War II European growth. Good interfaces between macroeconomic theory and history are by Crafts (1996a, 2018, 2019), David (1977), and Kindleberger (1989). See Landes (2003) and Mokyr (2010) on the history of technological innovation. Recent work has focused on the origins of the industrial revolution (e.g. Crafts, 2011). Then, for the more econometrically minded historian, there is 'cliometrics' (or quantitative economic history); see e.g. among many others, Clark et al. (2008) on trade and the industrial revolution. Such work is facilitated by advances in data collection and statistical analysis that allow long, historical data series to be constructed. Sources of such data will be discussed below. These advances enable a fascinating fusion of macro/growth theory, history, and econometrics. The reader interested in cliometrics can consult the collection of readings in Diebolt and Haupert (2019) for a wide-ranging review.

embedded in practically all the models that we review below. Hence, they are central, even if as benchmarks and not immutable facts.

9.1.5 Structural Change, the 'New Economy', and New Facts (?)

Over recent years, there has been much talk of the 'new economy', which is commonly taken to mean the rise of the services sector and the prevalence of information technology (IT). Jorgenson and Timmer (2011) investigate these themes, using detailed data from the European Union, Japan, and the United States. They document patterns of structural change in economic activity in advanced economies. Since 1980, the services sector has overwhelmingly predominated in the economic activity of these countries, and it has grown since in terms of both shares of value added and employment (now accounting for three-quarters of value added and employment). Correspondingly, the share of manufacturing has declined, a phenomenon known as de-industrialization (see the Guidance for Further Study). In many ways, they argue, the age-old 'trichotomy' of economic activity into agriculture, manufacturing, and services, is now obsolete. There is substantial heterogeneity among sectors in terms of productivity growth, especially among information technology, communications, and electrical equipment manufacturing, accompanied by a decline in relative prices and shares in output and employment in these sectors. Personal services (hotels, catering, etc.), finance, and business services have low productivity growth and increasing shares in total employment and GDP. By contrast, the shares of distribution services are constant, and productivity growth is fast. To emphasize the decline of physical goods production (de-industrialization) and the rise of sectors such as specialized service provision (information technology, research and development (R&D), banking and finance, law, management), the term 'knowledge economy' is often used in public discourse, but this is rather fuzzy as there is substantial heterogeneity between these sectors.

   Jorgenson and Timmer (2011) also find that the labour share in value-added has been declining almost everywhere (countries and sectors); this decline was 5 to 10 percentage points in many sectors and most of it occurred in the period 1980–95. This finding should be compared with Kaldor's fact (v) above; it will be further discussed in Chapter 10 on inequality. The intensity in the use of the information technology (IT), broadly construed, is increasing over time in all sectors and regions, as is that of skilled labour. This is fascinating work. One of its messages seems to be that growth models with sectoral imbalances or asymmetries and changing factor shares are urgently needed. Herrendorf et al. (2015) investigate the sources of structural change in post-war US and find that the main driver is sectoral differences in labour-augmenting technological progress (see Chapter 1). Ngai and Pissarides (2007) investigate the implications of different productive growth rates across sectors in a multi-sector growth model; they argue that a balanced path of some kind still holds.

   Structural change is related to another finding associated with Baumol (1967)—the 'Baumol effect'. Imagine an economy with two sectors, e.g. services and manufacturing, in which productivity (due to technical progress, say) grows at an even pace; this is plausible, as productivity rises faster in manufacturing (due to IT, robotics, etc.) than parts of the service sector such as hospitality and catering. The faster productivity growth raises wages in manufacturing, but because of labour mobility between the sectors, wages rise everywhere. For the less productive sector, however, the rising wages cannot be absorbed by the higher productivity, and therefore unit labour costs rise. This differential growth in the rise of costs will drive sectoral reallocations. See Nordhaus (2008) for further discussion.

The rise of IT and the internet has generated a fair amount of change and debate. One striking finding, first made by Gordon (1990), is that the second-hand prices of computers decline very fast (we need to be careful: comparing like with like, i.e. computers of a given specification and capability at different times). Jones (2016, figure 5) shows that this is even true of investment goods more generally: For instance, the price of equipment investment, relative to the GDP deflator has fallen by more than a factor of 3 since 1960 in the US, while the relative price of structures has risen since 1929 by a factor of 2 (for residential building investment) or 3 (for non-residential building investment). For computer-related goods, the fall has been even sharper.

One topic that has been receiving a lot of attention lately is the effect of IT on business and work practices. IT enables businesses to deal with customers directly via the internet without the help of intermediaries such as retailers, and/or to employ labour flexibly (or perhaps 'facilitate work' may be a better description) often via online platforms such as Uber and Deliveroo. Aside from long-established firms (e.g. Amazon), many of the businesses are startups. The internet also allows many people to find freelance work directly without belonging to any business; this can be true of architects or interpreters, IT analysts or accountants. This segment of the private sector (it should not be called a sector as such as it spans many sectors such as hospitality and catering, transport and other sectors) has been variably called the 'new economy', or the 'gig economy' (mainly the work via online platforms) or the 'sharing economy'; these terms overlap to a great extent even if they are not exactly the same. Estimates (as well as the definitions) vary, but this segment of business and employment is rapidly expanding and attention to it will increase. Measurement is quite difficult, but a start has been made (see ONS, 2017). This topic is related to structural change but also to income inequality (as often the conditions of work and pay in the 'gig economy' are not great) and the future of work itself.

No doubt, observations will continue to be accumulated as time goes on. So far, the finding that most contradicts the 'Kaldor facts' is perhaps the falling labour share. A further two findings are not accounted for by the 'Kaldor facts', namely structural change and the falling relative price of investment goods. As yet, however, these findings do not lead to any clear alternative 'stylized facts' that can replace the Kaldor facts, even as the latter continue to be re-examined.

9.1.6 Data Sources

Before we leave this section, we should comment on the sources of data useful in the analysis of growth. Many analysts use the World Development Indicators of the World Bank which is the most complete dataset of international statistics on global development. Apart from information on national accounts (macro statistics), it includes information on indicators of human development (health education, poverty and inequality, demographics, environment, and more). The Penn World Tables, originally developed by analysts at the University of Pennsylvania (Robert Summers, Irving Kravis, and Alan Heston), offer macro data (output, employment, capital, productivity, population) and are very useful in cross-country comparisons that are done on the basis of detailed purchasing power parity (PPP) comparisons. Another dataset was initiated by the economic historian Angus Maddison (the 'Maddison Historical Statistics Project', see Maddison, 2010) and is now further developed and maintained at the University of Groeningen, as are the Penn World Tables. The advantage of the Maddison dataset is that it is very useful for information on long historical time (representing our best estimates for output and living standards over centuries).

Much of the work on structural change is facilitated by the 'KLEMS' initiative which gives detailed production accounts across industries and across several countries. Alongside output, these accounts measure five inputs, capital (K), labor (L), energy (E), materials (M) and services (S)—hence the name. This work follows the methodology of Dale Jorgenson and his associates (see Jorgenson et al., 2008) and has been extended to the EU and other countries by O'Mahony and Timmer (2009) and Timmer et al. (2010). Finally, on macro-financial history in particular, very useful will be the recent 'Jordà-Schularick-Taylor Macrohistory Database', a product of the work of these economic historians and their teams.

9.1.7 The 'Balanced Growth Path' (BGP)

The Kaldor (1963) 'stylized facts' reviewed above simultaneously constrain and help the analytical work on growth. They imply that in the 'steady state' of growth models (i.e. in the long run, or 'when the dust settles'), three basic properties should hold:

Property 1 (common stochastic trends among variables)
Levels variables (variables such as output, physical capital and investment, consumption and similar, all in real terms, also population) must grow at a constant rate. In econometric terminology, these variables (in logs) should be cointegrated and driven by a common exogenous stochastic process.

Property 2 (constant 'grand ratios')
At the same time, the so-called 'grand ratios' should stay constant (variables such as the capital-output, consumption-output, and investment-capital ratios). From the Cobb-Douglas production function, the constant Y/K ratio also implies that the marginal product of capital and the real interest rate are also constant, as required.

Property 3 (BGP)
A corollary of properties 1 and 2 is the property of the 'Balanced Growth Path' (BGP). Starting from the National Income Accounting equation, we have, in usual notation, $Y = C + I$ (with no government or external links). Then, since $I/K = g$ (where g is the growth rate of capital), dividing by K we have: $Y/K = C/K + g$. The ratio Y/K is constant so Y and K should grow at the same rate, g. If the Y/K and g are constant quantities, it follows that C/K should also be constant, therefore C also grows at the constant rate g.

The BGP characterizes the steady state in virtually all growth models. Transitional dynamics are generally allowed in the short run, after an equilibrium has been upset by an exogenous change.[8] Stationary deviations from properties 1 and 2 may also occur. However, in the long run, all models lead to steady states that embody all three properties. King et al. (1991) for the US and Attfield and Temple (2010) for the US and UK investigate and generally confirm property 1 by finding stationarity of the great ratios (the latter article after allowing for structural breaks). As noted, this stationarity implies that consumption and investment should be co-integrated with output (in logs). This process allows these articles to extract the common stochastic trend that drives all the variables.

In order for BGP to obtain in growth models, any assumed technical progress must be restricted to be of a certain form. In particular, it must be labour-augmenting (see Chapter 1), otherwise BGP will fail to obtain. This important result is known as the Uzawa theorem (Uzawa, 1961; Jones and Scrimgeour, 2008). See Grossman et al. (2017) on what modifications are required in order for growth models to accommodate the new finding of the decline in the relative price of new investment goods, especially IT-related, mentioned above.

As mentioned, the 'Kaldor facts' are being re-examined in the light of the structural change of recent decades. However, it is as yet unclear whether any new findings represent 'statistically significant' deviations from those facts (note the word 'approximately' in (iii–v) above). Also, if the Kaldor facts are to be abandoned, it is unclear what should replace them. Correspondingly, it is unclear what properties growth models should embody; and any models that allow for asymmetric growth of sectors (for instance) will be much harder to construct, both conceptually and technically. The interested reader may begin with Herrendorf et al. (2014). The bottomline is, most growth models continue to embody the 'Kaldor facts' and BGP as steady-state properties.

9.2 The Solow Growth Model

This section reviews the vintage Solow (1956) Growth Model (SGM), one of the highlights of the first-wave growth literature of the 1950s and 1960s; see also Swan (1956). It is a workhorse model in growth and development and studied in most macro textbooks. On its origins and precursors, the paper by Solow (1994) is very useful.

9.2.1 Overview

The model is underpinned by four basic assumptions:

- The long-run rate of growth is exogenous—it might be thought of as the exogenous world growth rate in the case of an economy that joins the development process late for whatever reason, or for an economy that has suffered a setback (e.g.) and is developing again, or the long-run growth rate determined by exogenous productivity growth and/or technical progress in the case of the global economy;

---

[8] There are important exceptions, notably the 'AK' model, where there are no short-run dynamics; an exogenous change leads immediately to a new steady state.

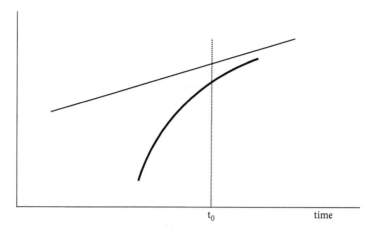

Figure 9.3. A hypothetical time profile of the (log) output per capita according to SGM

- The main 'engine' or driver of growth is factor accumulation, in particular capital accumulation; hence, there is a lot of emphasis on investment (in physical capital) and saving that underpins investment;
- Diminishing marginal products apply to each factor, most importantly capital;
- And, from the last assumption, convergence (roughly speaking: 'catching up') follows.

These assumptions will be discussed further as the need arises.

Now, consider Figure 9.3 which shows the hypothetical time profile of a key variable of an economy of interest. The vertical axis shows the log of output per capita, $\log(Y/L)$, so that a straight line would imply a constant growth rate; the horizontal axis shows time. The thick, curving line shows the hypothetical path of $\log(Y/L)$ of this economy; the thin, straight line shows an exogenous benchmark path that is either followed by the world economy or represents the productivity and technological frontier. Assume that this economy (on the curvy line) begins its growth path at a low level as shown, either because it is a late developer, or because it suffered some considerable destruction (obvious example is a war). The model predicts that it will *to some* extent catch up, or 'converge', to the living standards of the world economy in due course ('in the long run'). After the process of (perhaps partial) convergence is complete, the economy's living standards (per capita income) will grow at the same rate as that of the leader's or world economy's (but at a possibly different level). The SGM analyses the determinants (position, slope, etc.) of the curvy line that represents the path of our economy. The model is not suitable for the analysis of what determines the exogenous path underlying the thin line; this is taken as exogenous, as mentioned, either from the world economy or from exogenous productivity growth and/ or technical innovation, which is not amenable to economic analysis. The 'Endogenous Growth Theory', developed later, takes the view that productivity or technical growth is amenable to economic modelling and is concerned with an analysis of its determinants.

So, the model is built on two key hypotheses, exogenous long-run growth, and convergence. You might say that two questions are not even asked:

- what determines this long-run rate (this is not investigated);
- and whether convergence actually happens or not (it is assumed so by construction).

But the model is suitable to answer the following three, somewhat more limited, but very important questions:

- To what extent will converge happen? The new economy may manage only a partial convergence to the leader, or a full one, or it may even manage to develop higher living standards than the leader. What determines then the living standards of an economy, in particular in relation to world average? (Note that, in the long run, the ratio of living standards of both new and old will be constant—they grow at the same rate.)
- What determines the speed of adjustment, or convergence?
- Taking a snapshot of countries at time t_0 (as indicated by the dotted line), what determines the world income distribution? The answer here follows from the answers to the previous two questions. That is, it depends on how far the new economies have progressed in their convergence, and to what extent they converge on the leader's living standards eventually.

So, this is the genius of this model. It discards the questions that are 'too big to answer' and limits itself to those questions that are both important and manageable.

9.2.2 The Basic Model

The model assumes a closed economy, without any exports or imports, and no government. Furthermore, aggregate demand equals supply at all times. Physical capital accumulation is the sole driver of growth. (This is true in the basic model; in the 'Augmented' Solow model to follow below, it will also be human capital.) In its basic setup, the model has some close parallels with the Ramsey model, discussed in Chapter 5; so, recourse to that chapter in order to refresh memory will be useful. However, there is an important difference with the Ramsey model, which is that the SGM does not assume optimization on either the consumption/saving or the production side (in contrast to Ramsey). Saving is assumed a fraction of income and not decided by the intertemporal production of the individual; and production is not based on optimal use of the factors of production—firms just use all the capital and labour that is available.

As in Ramsey, aggregate production is characterized by a function of the form:

$$Y_t = F(K_t, L_t, A_t) \tag{9.1}$$

The notation is as follows:

Y: Aggregate output (in real terms);
K: Aggregate capital (also in real terms);
L: Employment;
A: An index of exogenous productivity (arising out of the state of technology, organization, human capital and skills, provision of public services).

This production function has the properties described in Chapters 1 and 5. Employment (L) coincides with total population of working age and there is no possibility of unemployment in this model; so, output per capita coincides with output per worker (Y/L). Virtually all variables in growth theory are in real terms; there is no place for nominal variables, prices, or inflation in the context of this theory.[9]

Often, (9.1) is assumed to take the 'Cobb-Douglas' form:[10]

$$Y_t = K_t^a (A_t L_t)^{1-\alpha}, \quad 0 < a < 1 \tag{9.1'}$$

There are two properties that should be noted here. First, diminishing returns to capital (the marginal product of capital declines with K);[11] this is indispensable for the properties of the model—see below. Second, constant returns to the two factors taken together; this is not instrumental, but merely a simplification, allowing the model to be expressed in the form of ratios (see Solow, 1994).

Again as in Ramsey, the model proceeds by defining ratios $k_t \equiv K_t/(A_t L_t)$ and $y_t \equiv Y_t/(A_t L_t)$ (see equations 5.22a, b of Chapter 5—they are in hatted variables there). These are, respectively, capital and output over productivity-adjusted labour. We can think of AL as quality-adjusted labour,[12] k as a capitalization ratio (per unit of quality-adjusted labour), and y as output per quality-adjusted hour of work.[13] These ratios play a key role in the analysis. Dividing (9.1') across by AL, we obtain the 'intensive form' of the production function:

$$y_t = k_t^\alpha \tag{9.1''}$$

The National Income Accounting (NIA) fundamental equation can be written as,

$$Y_t - C_t = I_t = sY_t, \tag{9.2}$$

where saving (on the left) equals investment (on the right). The model makes the assumption that all saving is channelled to investment; as there are not external or government sectors, there are no leakages. Let saving be a fraction $0 < s < 1$ of income; we then have: $Y - C = S = sY = I$.

Furthermore, indicating by Δ the difference operator,[14] investment is linked to capital accumulation, by the equation:

$$\Delta K_{t+1} = I_t - \delta K_t \tag{9.3}$$

$0 < \delta < 1$ is the depreciation rate of existing capital;[15] gross investment is used first to fix the wear and tear, so as to replace/maintain the depreciating capital at its existing standard, and secondly, to add to the capital stock.

With these definitions, dividing (9.3) across by $A_t L_t$ and using the NIA equation (9.2), we get an intermediate expression:

---

[9] The (related) assumptions of full employment and equality between aggregate demand and supply (equivalently: between saving and investment) are manifestations of the fact that this model is entirely a supply-side one, and with a long-term focus. In fact, virtually the whole of growth theory focuses on the supply side and leaves essentially no role for demand.

[10] The Cobb-Douglas production function has been discussed in Chapter 1.

[11] The marginal product of capital is $\alpha K^{\alpha-1} L^{1-\alpha}$, this quantity falls as K rises (keeping L constant).

[12] This makes more sense if we specifically interpret A to indicate human capital and skills.

[13] Note the difference with per capita output, which is Y/L (assuming that the labour force, L, and population coincide, and all workers provide one unit of labour each).

[14] That is, for any variable x, $\Delta x_t \equiv x_t - x_{t-1}$.   [15] See (Section 11.3) for a discussion on depreciation.

$$\Delta K_{t+1}/(A_t L_t) = s y_t - \delta k_t \tag{9.3'}$$

The next step is to time-differentiate k:[16]

$$\Delta k_{t+1} = \Delta K_{t+1}/(A_t L_t) - (\Delta A_{t+1}/A_t + \Delta L_{t+1}/L_t) K_t/(A_t L_t) \tag{9.4}$$

Next, we insert the intermediate expression (9.3') combined with production (9.1") into (9.4), to get:

$$\Delta k_{t+1} = s y_t - \delta k_t - (\Delta A_{t+1}/A_t + \Delta L_{t+1}/L_t) K_t/(A_t L_t)$$

Let productivity and labour grow at rates $g_A \equiv \Delta A_{t+1}/A_t$ and $g_L \equiv \Delta L_{t+1}/L_t$, respectively, both assumed constant (as well as exogenous). Dividing by k, we finally obtain:

$$\Delta k_{t+1} = s k_t^{\alpha} - (\delta + g_A + g_L) k_t \tag{9.5}$$

This is the fundamental equation of the model; see the similar equation (5.24) and the associated discussion in Chapter 5. The left side shows capital accumulation. The right side shows the resources available for that, which is injections (saving) minus three leakages; these leakages are the expenditures required to preserve the existing level and standard of capital (per unit of quality-adjusted labour), i.e. maintenance (equal to physical depreciation, δk), adjustment of capital in line with the growth of quality of labour so as to maintain the same level of capital per quality-adjusted unit labour is increasing (equal to $g_A k$, which can be interpreted as economic depreciation), and endowment of each new member of population and labour force with the same level of capital (equal to $g_L k$). The implication of (9.5) is that capital (per unit of quality-adjusted labour) will be growing for as long as injections are higher than leakages; inversely, it will be falling when leakages are higher. The steady state involves constant capital, k*, and is arrived at when injections and leakages are equal.[17]

The model is now complete; as mentioned, unlike in the Ramsey model, there is no optimization. The key equation (9.5) is given in graphical form in Figure 9.4, which is the key graph of the SGM. Time subscripts are dropped as they all refer to time t. The injections (saving, $sy = sk^a$) are represented by the line whose declining slope reflects diminishing returns to capital; withdrawals are indicated by the straight line whose slope is $g \equiv \delta + g_A + g_L$. The steady-state level of capital, k*, is also shown; clearly, for any $k < k^*$, injection of resources outweighs leakages, so k rises and will approach k* from below. For any $k > k^*$, the opposite is true. Thus, k is said to converge over time to k*. Let us point out the importance of the diminishing returns to capital (alone) for this result: graphically, this makes the sy line decline in slope. It is easy to see that this property is crucial for the sy and

---

[16] This is another instance of rather loose talk. We can only time-differentiate variables that are functions of *continuous* time, whereas time has been assumed *discrete* here—hence the use of differences. But it is more intuitive to think how k would be differentiated with respect to time if time were continuous and to replace time-derivatives with differences.

[17] The 'steady state' is often used interchangeably with the 'long run'; but the former term is more mathematical while the latter depends more on economic context. In intermediate macroeconomics, we often distinguish between three horizons, the short run, the medium run (when prices, wages, and unemployment have had time to adjust), and the long run (when capital adjusts). The steady state of the SGM (or any other growth model) obtains over the long run. In business cycles analysis, sometimes a different terminology is used. The same horizons might be called short run, long run, and very long run; clearly, in that terminology, the steady state of any growth model arrives at the very long run.

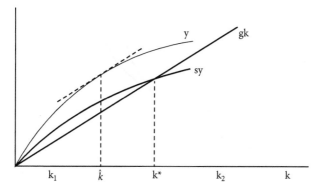

Figure 9.4. The Solow Growth Model

gk lines to cross, i.e. for the existence of equilibrium; and for the convergence property to hold. (The interested reader could check to see that if sy crossed gk from below, there would be divergence, not convergence.)

It is informative to solve for k* explicitly. Setting $\Delta k = 0$ in (9.5) and solving, we obtain:

$$k^* = (s/(\delta + g_A + g_L))^{1/(1-a)} \qquad (9.6)$$

We immediately have the following results. The steady-state capitalization ratio (capital per unit of quality-adjusted labour) k*:

- increases with a higher saving rate (as more resources are made available),
- decreases with the leakages that tend to absorb resources; a higher rate of depreciation, higher rate of population growth, and a higher rate of productivity growth (determining 'economic depreciation') decrease the steady-state capitalization ratio.[18]

Finally, since k and y are related by (9.1"), there is a corresponding steady-state output per unit of quality adjusted labour:

$$y^* = (s/(\delta + g_A + g_L))^{a/(1-a)} \qquad (9.7)$$

The same factors determine y* as do k* and in the same way. Anything that in/decreases k* also in/decreases y*.

9.2.3 Output Per Capita and Consumption: Level vs. Growth Effects

We now turn to a discussion of what this model says about living standards. Strictly speaking, living standards are captured by per capita output (Y/L), which is related to y

---

[18] Population control measures, as the one formerly in place in China whereby families were allowed only one child, must be understood in this light. Various developing countries try to stem population growth, perhaps in not quite so drastic ways. But population growth controls distort the demographic pyramid (increase the proportion of the old compared to the young) and, as the overlapping-generations models reviewed in Chapter 5 warn us, this is bad in a number of respects, primarily for social insurance (pensions). Such considerations explain China's recent reversal of the one-child policy. A branch of endogenous growth theory attempts to endogenize the population growth rate (assumed exogenous in SGM).

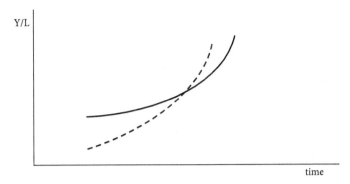

Figure 9.5. Level vs. growth effects on living standards in the Solow Growth Model

with $Y/L = Ay$. In the steady state, $y = y^*$ as given above, but A keeps growing at rate g_A. Hence, there are two effects of exogenous technical progress (g_A) on living standards (per capita output, $Y/L = Ay$) in this model: A *levels effect* via y^*, on the determinants of which the model is informative via (9.7); there is also a *growth* effect via the growth rate of A. The two effects are depicted in Figure 9.5.

This Figure shows the time profile of Y/L; both curves are exponential, showing a constant growth rate (g_A). The steady state (y^*) is assumed to apply throughout. The initial benchmark is the solid line. A rise in g_A decreases Y/L via the levels effect (a fall in y^* from 9.7); this shifts Y/L downwards to the dashed line. At the same time, the slope and growth rate of the new line rise; the dashed line is tilted upwards. It is easy to realize that the growth effect is more important, no matter how important the levels decline in y^* is, as eventually the dashed line will overcome the solid one, no matter how much the original shift is. In other words, growth is more important for living standards in due course rather than the once-and-for-all shift. Thus, the model seems to have left the most interesting issue untackled. This has prompted the emergence of the new generation 'endogenous growth models', which purport to endogenize (= explain) the growth rate of A and of the economy more broadly.

How about consumption? Since consumption and saving make up GDP exactly in this model ($C = (1-s)Y$), and since $1-s$ is a constant, C grows at exactly the same rate of Y; which brings us to the question of what the growth rate of aggregate GDP (Y) itself is. Let us limit the discussion to the steady state. Since $Y/L = Ay^*$ grows at rate g_A and $Y = LAy^*$, aggregate GDP grows at rate $g_A + g_L$ in the steady state. Thus, the growth rate of aggregate output can be decomposed into the growth rate of per capita GDP (g_A), plus the growth rate of population.[19] And so, as above, the influences on Y go again via levels (y^*) and exogenous growth rates ($g_A + g_L$). Summarizing, we see that ratios like k, y and C/Y are constant in the steady state, while levels variables like Y, C, and K grow at constant, and common, growth rates ($= g_A + g_L$). In other words, the model satisfies the BGP property.

---

[19] This decomposition of aggregate output growth rates is in fact more general than the SGM; it is simply derived from the definition of per capita GDP.

9.2.4 The 'Golden Rule of Capital Accumulation'

The model can be used to answer the question whether, in the steady state, the economy has over-accumulated capital. Rephrased, this question is whether the individual can increase consumption by reducing capital.[20] Normally, an increase in capital is expected to increase consumption as it increases output and income. However, if capital has increased too much, the costs of maintaining it may be so high that one may actually be better off by reducing it.

To follow this argument, take the basic equation for consumption in the steady state (variables in quality-adjusted labour units)—a combination of (9.2) and (9.5):

$$c^* = (k^*)^\alpha - (\delta + g_A + g_L)k^*$$

At what level of capital does steady-state consumption become maximal? Differentiating with respect to level of capital, we get:

$$\partial c^*/\partial k^* = \alpha(k^*)^{\alpha-1} - (\delta + g_A + g_L) = 0 \tag{9.8}$$

Solving, we find the level of capital that maximizes consumption:

$$\hat{k} = \left(\frac{\alpha}{\delta + g_A + g_L}\right)^{1/(1-\alpha)} \tag{9.9}$$

This level of capital is said to obey 'the golden rule of capital accumulation'; this maximizes consumption per capita (in terms of quality-adjusted units) not only for the current but also for the future (as yet unborn) generations. For k^* different than that level, consumption will not be maximized: if $k^* < \hat{k}$, consumption will increase if there is more capital accumulation, thus raising output. If $k^* > \hat{k}$, then capital has grown too much: As a result, the capital stock needs so much maintenance (to fix physical depreciation but also to provide the same standard for the newborn and allow for economic depreciation and obsolescence) that we can actually increase consumption by scaling down the economy.[21] This is the case of dynamic inefficiency. Comparing steady-state capital (9.7) with the golden-rule level (9.9), we see that $k^* > \hat{k}$ if $s > \alpha$. The implication is that, unlike in the Ramsey model of Chapter 5, dynamic inefficiency can arise in the SGM.[22]

9.2.5 Empirical Evidence and the 'Augmented' SGM

In a seminal paper, Mankiw et al. (1992) tested the main predictions of SGM. They introduce steady-state capital (9.6) into the production function (9.1') and take logs to get a long-run relationship:

---

[20] As we have seen in Chapter 5, this is the question of 'dynamic (in)efficiency'. The reader is referred back to that chapter for more information and a discussion of the empirical evidence.

[21] From (9.8), it is easy to check that, geometrically, $\hat{k}$ occurs where the production function has a slope of $g \equiv \delta + g_A + g_L$, i.e. it is parallel to the 'leakages' line. As shown in in Figure 9.4, $k^* > \hat{k}$, but this does not have to be the case, as we discuss next.

[22] See in particular Result 5 in Section 5.2.3. The 'golden-rule' capital stock is the same, see equation (5.34); but the steady-state capital stock is not. Note that in Chapter 5, we denoted the population growth rate by η.

$$\ln(Y_{it}/L_{it}) = A_t + \frac{\alpha}{1-\alpha}(\ln s_i - \ln(\delta_i + g_{Ai} + g_{Li})) + error_{it}$$

This equation is then tested across countries (denoted by i). Under appropriate assumptions, the state of technology or productivity, A_t, is common across countries (notice the absence of subscript i). So, this gives a relationship between per capita output and the parameters of interest in the SGM across countries. An important assumption is that the error term is not correlated with the country-specific parameters on the right side. This estimation yields an estimate of α, the elasticity of capital in production.[23] Mankiw et al. (1992) find that the data support the predictions on the coefficients of the saving rate and leakages (equal and of opposite signs) and that the model explains about 60 per cent of the variation of Y/L across countries in a large data sample (but much less, only about 6 per cent, of the variation among OECD economies). The estimated α is about 0.6 (in the large sample), a lot higher than capital's share of about one-third. Thus, they conclude that the simple textbook model has a lot of qualitative lessons to offer but needs refinement.

Taking the lead from a variety of studies pointing out the importance of human capital, Mankiw et al. (1992) augment the production function (9.1') with human capital H, to get:

$$Y_t = K_t^a H_t^\beta (A_t L_t)^{1-\alpha-\beta}$$

Thus, human capital is another driver of growth in addition to physical capital. In production, it has elasticity $0 < \beta < 1$. We now differentiate between saving for physical and human capital, s_k and s_h, respectively; they are the fractions of GDP that goes to physical investment and education. Following the same steps as above, the steady-state capital ratio, the counterpart to (9.6) is given by:

$$k^* = \left(\frac{s_k^{1-\beta} s_h^\beta}{\delta + g_A + g_L} \right)^{1/(1-a)}$$

Now, per capita output (Y/L) ratio is given by:

$$\ln(Y_{it}/L_{it}) = A_t + \frac{\alpha \ln s_{ki} + \beta \ln s_{hi} - (\alpha + \beta)\ln(\delta_i + g_{Ai} + g_{Li})}{1 - \alpha - \beta} + error_{it}$$

A proxy for human capital-related saving (s_h) is given by school enrolment rates.[24] A regression of this form explains about 80 per cent of the variation in Y/L in the big sample (about 30 per cent in OECD countries). The other restrictions of the model are also supported. The estimates of α and β are both of the order of 0.3, so plausible.

Thus, this paper affirms the role of an augmented version of SGM as a vehicle of explanation of cross-country differences in living standards, emphasizing the role of human capital in the process. A panel (pooled time-series and cross-section) follow-up

---

[23] If capital is paid its marginal product (as would be the case in perfectly competitive markets) so that MPK = αY/K, then capital's share in GDP is MPK × K/Y = α. Capital's share in GDP is given in National Income Account statistics. Thus, the estimated α from the model can be checked against the data from the national accounts.

[24] Much empirical work on human capital uses the dataset described in Barro and Lee (2013), who have computed internationally comparable indices of educational attainment for various countries. The dataset is now maintained and updated by the World Bank.

study by Islam (1995) improved the fit of the model, but raised the estimate of α to about 0.5 and lowered that of β to insignificance.

9.3 Convergence (?), the World Income Distribution, and Growth Accounting

9.3.1 Transition to the Steady State and Convergence in the SGM: A Recap

What happens if a country was to find itself away from its potential equilibrium capital k^* and associated living standards? The SGM predicts a simple pattern of transition to k^*. If the country found itself below equilibrium, say at $k_1 < k^*$ in Figure 9.4, then saving and investment would exceed leakages $(sy(k_1) > gk_1)$, and the capital stock would begin to rise. If, on the other hand, the starting point were above k^*, like at k_2, then the opposite would happen, and the capital stock would begin to shrink. Why might we be outside equilibrium k^*? For a variety of reasons: either because a country began the process of growth late, starting at k_1; or because a war destroyed capital and moved us from k^* to k_1; or we may start at k_2 as that used to be an old equilibrium that has now changed to k^* because the saving rate decreased.

These adjustments cease obviously only when $k = k^*$, which is the steady-state level. The bottomline is, the SGM predicts convergence of the capital ratio (in quality-adjusted labour units, k) to its steady-state level k^* within *a given country over time*. As argued, this is a straightforward result of the diminishing marginal product of capital. But will countries' living standards converge to one another over time? We turn to this question next.

9.3.2 Convergence: Key Concepts

An important question concerns the distribution of output per capita *across countries*. Following Galor (1996) and Sala-i-Martin (1996), we may distinguish two cases. If the various countries share the same parameters in terms of depreciation and productivity and labour growth rates, all their k's will converge to the same common k^* in the long run, and convergence is said to be *absolute*. In other words, per capita incomes will converge to one another in the long run, independent of their starting points or initial conditions. If the k^* is country-specific (i.e. the said parameters differ across countries), then convergence is *conditional* (countries do converge but to country-specific potentials). In this case, per capita incomes will converge to constant ratios in the long run, again independently of initial conditions. The per capita incomes will be equalized in the special case of all structural parameters being the same across countries, in which case conditional convergence reduces to absolute convergence.

Finally, both absolute and conditional convergence are collectively called 'β (beta)-convergence' and are to be contrasted with 'σ (sigma)-convergence'. The latter holds when the dispersion of per capita incomes across a group of countries diminishes over time. Theoretically speaking, β-convergence is necessary but not sufficient for

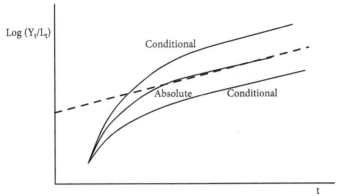

Figure 9.6. β-convergence

σ-convergence (see the discussion in Sala-i-Martin, 1996). In the work reviewed below, σ-convergence is found when there is also strong evidence of (absolute) β-convergence. The graph (Figure 9.6) illustrates the concepts of absolute and conditional β-convergence. The thick line represents the time path of output per capita of the leader or country that started growth early, whereas the thin lines illustrate a variety of paths of countries that catch up. All variables are logged, so constant growth rates are indicated by straight lines.

As evident in the graph, and discussed further below, conditional convergence implies that a country's per capita GDP grows faster the further away it is from its steady state. Note, this only depends on the distance from the steady state, not current level, so (for instance), a poor country may grow slowly if it is not far from its steady state. As the special case of conditional convergence when the steady state is common, absolute convergence then implies that poorer (richer) countries grow faster (more slowly). To take one example, not entirely hypothetical, consider countries A (Argentina?) and G (Germany?) in 1945. Both are poor, but A is chronically so, so it is not too far away from its potential, while G is poor because of war devastation but with a high potential. Absolute converge would imply that they both grow equally fast in the years after 1945, while conditional convergence would imply that G does grow fast but A less so.

9.3.3 The SGM and Cross-Country Convergence

What does the Solow model imply about convergence in living standards *between countries* over time? Intuitively, if we take two snapshots of all countries' living standards at two different times, at an initial date (0) and now (t), would we observe the gaps potentially present at 0 to have been closed at t, or not? To see whether this is the case for living standards (Y/L), take a linear approximation of (9.5) around $k_t = k^*$, using (9.6), to rewrite it as:[25]

$$\Delta k_{t+1}/k_t = -\lambda(\ln k_t - \ln k^*), \tag{9.10}$$

[25] First, take a first-order Taylor expansion: $\Delta k_{t+1} = \alpha s(k^*)^{\alpha-1}(k_t - k^*) - (\delta + g_A + g_L)(k_t - k^*)$ and use (9.6) to substitute out k^*. Then, divide by k_t and write $(k - k^*)/k \approx \ln k - \ln k^*$.

where:

$$\lambda \equiv (1 - \alpha)(\delta + g_A + g_L) > 0$$

The parameter $0 < \lambda < 1$, linked to structural model parameters as shown above, encapsulates the convergence property: the capital ratio k tends to close any gap between its actual value and that of the steady state by λ per cent every period. Thus, λ is closely related to the 'speed of convergence', the speed at which the current—steady-state gap is closing.[26]

Furthermore, since $\Delta k_{t+1}/k_t = \Delta \ln k_{t+1}$ to a very good approximation, and since by definition $\ln k_t \equiv \ln(Y/L)_t - \ln A_t$, we get:

$$\Delta \ln(Y/L)_{t+1} = -\lambda \left(\ln(Y/L)_t - \ln k^* \right) + \ln A_{1+t} - (1 - \lambda) \ln A_t \qquad (9.11)$$

The right side now involves a gap in living standards, to be closed by a fraction λ every period, plus a process depending on the evolution of productivity.

This equation is testable. It may be used either to test whether per capita output (therefore, living standards) converge to a certain level over time within each country (i.e. to test convergence in a time-series sense); or to ask the real question, posed at the beginning, whether convergence occurs between countries (in a cross-sectional sense, i.e. test for 'β (beta)-convergence'); if that is the case, countries may be expected to share the same standard of living at an unspecified point in the future. The issue of convergence in a time-series sense is not so interesting because casual observation suggests that it does not happen (most countries tend to get richer over time). The cross-section convergence question is however of central importance in growth theory. It may be tested by running a panel data regression of the form:

$$[\ln(Y_{i,t}/L_{i,t}) - \ln(Y_{i,t-\tau}/L_{i,t-\tau}) = a_{i,0} + b \ln(Y_{i,t+\tau}/L_{i,t-\tau}) + u_{i,t} \qquad (9.11')$$

Equation (9.11') is the empirical analogue of (9.11), for individual country i and time t (current) and $t - \tau$ (initial point). Intuitively, this equation relates the growth rate of a country's per capita output to its earlier level. Often, this regression averages the growth rate over $\tau > 1$ periods for each country. This is done in order to avoid measurement error (any over- or under-estimates of the per capita output growth rate are averaged over τ, yielding perhaps a more accurate dependent variable). Another reason is that early empirical work relied a lot on the 'Penn World Tables' data, which initially gave only five-year averages ($\tau = 5$). The downside of course of averaging data across time periods is that one reduces the number of useful observations and therefore the available information. One possibility is to have $\tau = t$, in which case we get only one observation per country (i.e. to have a cross-section as opposed to a panel-data regression). The error term ($u_{i,t}$)

---

[26] (9.10) implies that the per capita growth closes λ per cent of the gap between actual and steady-state capital ratio every period, a fact reminiscent of the adaptive expectations mechanism. This implies that the actual growth rate of k is not constant but will decline as k approaches its steady state. This property forms the basis for a test of convergence, as we discuss below. We can rewrite this equation as: $\ln k_{t+1} - \ln k_t = -\lambda(\ln k_{t-1} - \ln k^*)$. The solution is: $\ln k_t = (1 - \lambda)^t \ln k_0 + [1 - (1 - \lambda)^t] \ln k^*$. Intuitively, the equation expresses current capital as a combination of history (k_0) and its steady state (which can be interpreted as its future potential, k*). As $1 - \lambda < 1$, the weights gradually change so that the steady state gets a greater weight in determining current capital. This formula applies more widely, and not just in the context of SGM or for capital.

involves unknown shocks plus the country-specific deviations of productivity growth from its common growth rate; these are not modelled or estimated, and are left as residuals.

The coefficient of interest is b, identical or closely related to the negative of the speed of adjustment, $-\lambda$. Convergence is found if b < 0, implying an inverse relationship between the initial per capita and its subsequent growth rate. Intuitively, this is because an implication of (9.10) is that the growth rate declines as we get closer to the steady state. Formally, this requires two conditions: first, diminishing marginal product of capital indicated by $\alpha < 1$ (see the definition of λ); second, the country-specific growth rate of A (captured by $u_{i,t}$) should not be positively related to the living standards in the initial period (t = 0), that is, countries that happened to start 'the growth race' first should not have a lead in terms of subsequent technological growth; if that were the case, the influence of the country-specific error term would blur the negative effect exerted by the initial Y/L. If either of the diminishing returns and 'no systematic technological lead' assumptions fail, the subsequent growth in living standards $\ln(Y/L)_t - \ln(Y/L)_{t-\tau}$ will not decrease as we move from poorer to richer countries, and therefore convergence will not hold in any form.

Provided that convergence has been found, it may be characterized as absolute if $a_{i,0} = a$ (common across all countries i), and conditional if $a_{i,0} \neq a_{j,0}$ for any two countries i and j, so that each country converges to its own steady state. Typically, in cross-section or panel regressions, which are used in this type of work, the econometrician will start with a common intercept. If s/he then finds b < 0, this is a clear indication of absolute convergence. If the regression coefficient has the wrong sign, s/he then proceeds to test for conditional convergence by entering on the right-hand side a number of extraneous regressors such as country-specific dummies (or 'country effects') and exogenous variables including human capital, population growth, or fertility rates and other demographic variables, political/geographical variables, etc., as determinants of country-specific steady-state per capita GDP. If such country-specific dummies or extraneous variables are significant, and if the coefficient b changes to negative and significant, then conditional convergence holds. If not, then convergence is not there in any form—but the possibility that we have not captured adequately the determinants of the steady-state living standards cannot be precluded, so the quest continues!

Mankiw et al. (1992) find convergence only when human capital is included; they estimate the speed to be $\lambda = 1.5$ per cent, i.e. very slow: The estimated 'half-life' (the time it takes for half of the initial discrepancy between actual-steady-state Y/L to be eliminated) is 46 years.[27] If so, practically, 40 per cent of the damage that World War II made in terms of deviation of actual from potential living standards would still remain more than 50 years later! This is implausibly slow, particularly given the experiences the South East Asian countries who shot to the top league within a generation or so. Islam (1995) estimates λ to be of the order of 5 per cent or even higher, implying a half-life of 12 years. He interprets this to be the result of his estimation, which allows more precise estimation of the country-specific steady states, through the inclusion and estimation of the 'country-specific effects'.

---

[27] Recall that half-life is the time period required for the initial discrepancy $k_0 - k^*$ to be eliminated. Using the solution in n. 26, where $\ln k_t - \ln k_0 = [1 - (1 - \lambda)^t][\ln k^* - \ln k_0]$, half-life is the t for which $(1 - \lambda)^t = 0.5$.

9.3.4 The Question of Convergence, Growth Experiences, and the World Income Distribution

In general, empirical evidence on convergence is very mixed at best. On the positive side, Baumol (1986) has shown convergence among industrialized economies; Dowrick and Nguyen (1989) have also shown productivity to converge among the OECD. But DeLong (1988) showed that this may not be shared across the world as a whole. Sala-i-Martin (1996) offers a brief survey of early work to this effect. This paper and Barro and Sala-i-Martin (1995, chapters 11–12) offer some evidence representative of work in this area. They find evidence of absolute convergence among homogeneous groups of regions such as US states (1880–1990), Japanese prefectures (1930–90), and European regions (1950–90), with a speed of adjustment of the order of 2–3 per cent per annum. However, things change when a larger sample of about 100 world economies is considered, with a more limited dataset time-wise. In this case, absolute convergence does not hold, but conditional does, with a speed of adjustment of about 3 per cent. There are some open issues about the stability of the key coefficient (on lagged per capita GDP) across time periods, while the coefficient seems to be common when the large group of countries is split into rich and poor sub-groups. Another relevant piece of information is about σ-convergence, which holds among the homogeneous groups but not in the world economy at large. There is also evidence of persistence of growth rates (*contra* convergence): McGrattan and Schmitz's (1999) figure 27 shows that average growth rates in 1961–72 mostly positively affect the average rates for 1973–85, with a correlation of 0.78.

In general, it seems that as one moves from more to less homogenized groups of countries or regions, the evidence for convergence weakens (in highly homogenized groups or regions absolute convergence holds, in less homogeneous groups only conditional convergence holds), and the speed of convergence seems to fall too (see e.g. Sala-i-Martin, 1996, table 1). But Pritchett (1997) is even more forcefully critical of the idea of convergence based on historical evidence: He argues that a small (dozen or so) group of advanced industrialized economies have grown vigorously since 1870 (by a factor of about 10 between 1870 and 2000 in the case of the US), but that experience has not been shared by the 'others' (and may not even be uniform across time periods or across countries even in that small group). On that basis, he even argues that there has been divergence of world living standards over the last century or so, not convergence.

Such scepticism, often voiced by economic historians, has given rise to the idea of 'club convergence' (Pritchett, 1997), the idea that economies tend to converge (conditionally) to the living standards of 'their group', the group being similar countries in terms of geography, politics, culture, or history, but little or no convergence across groups of countries. This idea seems to be corroborated with more recent data by Jones (2016): Comparison of his figures 25 and 26 shows convergence among West European countries (a clear negative relation between growth rates and initial per capita GDP) and absence of convergence in the world economy at large. This is related to the 'Twin Peaks' phenomenon, noted by Quah (1993, 1996, 1997) and evident in Figure 9.1: the thinning of the middle ground of the distribution of world per capita incomes from 1960 to 2000 and the emergence of two groups or clusters (or 'clubs'). As Jones (1997, p. 22) notes, this shows that 'there has been some convergence or "catch-up" at the top of the income distribution and some divergence at the bottom'.

A similar idea is that of 'poverty traps', whereby a country or countries is unable to break out of the vicious circle of poverty, either because it saves and invests little (as it lives close to subsistence) or because of faulty policies, or because of violence (and often all of these factors can be linked) or other reasons. We may distinguish between a relative poverty trap, whereby all countries grow but at unequal rates so that their relative standards of living diverge over time, and an absolute poverty trap, of plain stagnation or even regression. While a number of potentially fruitful avenues have been explored, there is apparently no consensus in the literature about the causes of poverty traps; nor is it obvious whether the models can account simultaneously for both relative and absolute poverty traps; see Azariadis and Stachurski (2005) for a review of this literature.

There is a variety of possible reasons why 'club convergence' (or related phenomena) can arise. First, those countries with higher incomes at the starting point may retain a technological or other productivity advantage; see Jones (2016, figure 29) for evidence of that. (Technically, one of the conditions of convergence fails, namely the error term in regression 9.11' may be correlated with some of the regressors.) Another plausible possibility is that poor (rich) countries save a lower (higher) proportion of their incomes. If so, then we shall have two equilibria in the basic Solow Growth Model graph, one for poor and one for rich, and systematically different levels of living standards even in the long run (though the growth rates are equalized in the long run). See Edwards (1996) for evidence that saving rates indeed differ across countries, with some evidence that richer economies save more, thus creating the potential for multiple equilibria in the SGM. However, saving rates are not (entirely) exogenous, as the SGM assumes; one of its determinants may be the growth rate and there is evidence of bi-directional causality between growth and saving rates (Carroll and Weil, 1994). See Chapter 11 for more on saving.

Human capital may also give rise to permanent divergence if it causes increasing (as opposed to the usually assumed constant) returns to scale in production; in this case, higher initial levels of income or human capital will lead to higher growth rates (see Galor, 1996). Other reasons for club convergence may include differences in capital mobility (though now these have disappeared due to globalization), income distribution within countries, and fertility. Galor (1996) discusses how these may give rise to multiple equilibria in a variety of growth models, and how countries may end up with different steady states even if their 'deeper structures' are the same, simply because they happen to begin from different starting points. Note that this possibility is absent in the simple version of Solow, in which where you end up depends only on structure, the parameters of the production function, depreciation, and population growth rates, etc.—history does not matter for your endpoint. The idea that history matters in the sense that your steady state depends not only on your structure but also on your history and actual path that you have travelled so far has been explored in natural sciences where it is called 'path dependence' (see Chapters 3 and 5 and Krugman, 1991). It surely is relevant for growth, but it is not a standard feature in the main growth models.

The question of convergence is linked to the distribution of per capita incomes or GDP across the world. Do countries' living standards converge over time? This is one key motivating question for the theory of growth, as we have noted. On the other hand, over the last 50 years, alongside the growth of the OECD (most advanced) economies, we have also witnessed 'growth miracles' in South East Asia (the 'Asian Tigers'—Hong Kong, Singapore, South Korea, and Taiwan, and to a lesser extent Thailand and Malaysia), in

Latin America, Eastern Europe, and elsewhere. Pockets of Africa, which have fallen behind quite a lot since the 1970s, and been ravaged by war, disease, and famine, are now stabilizing and even picking up. If anyone had predicted the emergence of the (big!) BRICs (Brazil, Russia, India, and China) in 1995, they would have been thought a fool. Yesterday's (1970s) impoverished sub-continent (China) is today's economic superpower. There have also been 'growth disasters'. Jones (1997) highlights the absolute stagnation experienced by 11 per cent of the economies, whose GDP per worker actually fell over the last third of the twentieth century; several of those are in Sub-Saharan Africa (see also Rodrik, 1999, p. 106). McGrattan and Schmitz (1999) summarize thus:

> [The] data show that the disparity in incomes is large and has grown over time [Note: directly refuting convergence], that there is no correlation between income levels and subsequent growth rates [Note: refuting the basic test of convergence], that growth rate differences are large across countries and across time, and that the highest growth rates are now much higher than those 100 years ago.   McGrattan and Schmitz (1999, p. 5)

In a more recent contribution, Sala-i-Martin (2006) investigates the world income distribution. This paper combines micro (survey) and macro data to estimate the world distribution of income. More specifically, it uses survey-based information from individual countries to estimate the income distribution within each of 138 countries for each year between 1970 and 2000 and population-weighted PPP-adjusted national accounts GDP per capita data to pin down the mean of each of these distributions. In this way, the paper estimates a world income distribution. The rather striking and optimistic results that emerge is that both poverty (defined as the number of people and percentage of world population with income below a certain level of income, $1/per day or $2/per day, etc.) and inequality (Gini coefficient) are falling.

An interesting rejoinder in the world income distribution and convergence debate is provided by Milanovic (2018, see also 2016). On the basis of recent data, he shows that over the past 25 years we have had a number of contradictory developments. On the positive side, the mean global income in 2013 was almost 40 per cent higher than in 1988. Additionally, the global median income has risen strongly and faster than the mean (resulting in the emergence of the 'global middle class', generated to a large extent by the rise of large numbers of Chinese people out of poverty), thus reducing global inequality. On the other hand, we have two developments that increase inequality: first, the rising share of the global top 1 per cent of incomes and, secondly, an increasing number of people in relative poverty (those below half the median income, mostly in Africa). The last point leads back to the vexed issue of lack of convergence of Africa and its growing falling behind Asia and the rest of the world. So, a mixture of good news (growing prosperity and the emergence of the global middle class) and bad news (an increase in world-wide polarization).

9.3.5 Growth Accounting

Often associated with Solow (1957), but with other important contributors before or since (see Hulten, 2010), 'growth accounting' is a method by which we can measure the contribution of the factors of production, typically capital and labour, as well as of productivity, to growth. The starting point is a slightly restricted version of the production function (9.1):

$$Y_t = A_t F(K_t, L_t) \tag{9.12}$$

Taking changes over time (denoted as usual by Δ) and dividing by Y_t, we have:[28]

$$\frac{\Delta Y_{t+1}}{Y_t} = \frac{\Delta A_{t+1}}{A_t} + \frac{F_K(K_t, L_t)K_t}{F(K_t, L_t)}\frac{\Delta K_{t+1}}{K_t} + \frac{F_L(K_t, L_t)L_t}{F(K_t, L_t)}\frac{\Delta L_{t+1}}{L_t} \tag{9.12'}$$

$F_K(.)$ and $F_L(.)$ are the marginal products of capital and labour, respectively. Furthermore, we assume, as in Chapter 5, that factors are paid their marginal products, so that $F_K(.) = r$, $F_L(.) = w$ (interest rate and the wage, both real) and $F_K(.)K/Y = rK/Y$ and $F_L(.)L/Y = wL/Y$ are the shares of labour and capital in national income.[29] These shares, rK/Y and wL/Y, can be obtained from national statistics. Assuming that $rK/Y = \beta$ and $wL/Y = 1 - \beta$, where $0 < \beta < 1$ is obtained from the data, (9.12') may be rewritten as:

$$\frac{\Delta Y_{t+1}}{Y_t} = \frac{\Delta A_{t+1}}{A_t} + \beta\frac{\Delta K_{t+1}}{K_t} + (1 - \beta)\frac{\Delta L_{t+1}}{L_t} \tag{9.13}$$

Equation (9.13) is the fundamental equation of growth accounting. It relates the growth rates of productivity (A), capital (K), and labour (L), the latter two appropriately weighted by their shares in income, to real output growth on the right. It is not a regression: all the elements in it, with the exception of $\Delta A/A$, can be calculated (not estimated) from the data. This equation can be used in two types of measurement: first, to calculate the growth rate of productivity, which is a multi-faceted 'factor' that cannot be directly measured. Its growth rate can be indirectly measured by rewriting (9.13) as:

$$\frac{\Delta A_{t+1}}{A_t} = \frac{\Delta Y_{t+1}}{Y_t} - \beta\frac{\Delta K_{t+1}}{K_t} - (1 - \beta)\frac{\Delta L_{t+1}}{L_t} \tag{9.13'}$$

In this way, the growth rate productivity/technology is written as a 'residual', termed the 'Solow residual' in honour of Solow (1957); in other words, this is the residual from growth once the contributions of capital and labour have been netted out.[30] It is commonly called 'Total Factor Productivity (TFP)' or 'Multi-Factor Productivity (MFP)' growth (the two terms are more or less interchangeable, the latter being the one preferred recently) and it reflects the accumulation of knowledge and the propensity to innovate.

Once the analyst has collected all the data, the right side of (9.13') is constructed and this is a measure of productivity growth; this is the first use of growth accounting. Secondly, (9.13), once $\Delta A/A$ has been measured from (9.13'), this can be taken back to (9.13) to measure the percentage contribution of each factor to growth, including that of productivity,

---

[28] Formally, this is correct for continuous time, in which case (9.12') is obtained by time-differentiating (9.12) and dividing by Y_t. In discrete time, taking time changes works in analogy and approximation to time-differentiation.

[29] As discussed in Chapter 1 and will be reviewed again in Chapter 10, in the case of the Cobb-Douglas production function (9.1'), these factor shares are closely linked to parameter β: $F_K(.)K/Y = \beta$ and $F_L(.)L/Y = 1 - \beta$.

[30] Because productivity is so multi-faceted and fuzzy, therefore difficult to measure directly, the Solow residual has also been dubbed 'a measure of our ignorance' (about productivity).

to output growth. This exercise can identify the main drivers of growth, essentially whether it was factor growth (as the SGM would have us believe) or productivity growth (as endogenous growth theory argues) that is the ultimate cause for growth. Before we elaborate on the results, we turn towards the difficulties with this approach.

One strong and implausible assumption is that factor returns (interest rate, wage rate) have been equalized to the respective marginal products; this presumes competitive markets. Subsequent work has strived to calculate the factor contributions when factor shares do not reflect competitive factor pricing due to monopoly markups. Secondly, the weight β is generally not constant but time-varying; this can be easily incorporated into (9.13') where β_t should appear. (Recall that β and $1 - \beta$ are not estimated coefficients but taken from the data.) Additionally, factor inputs should incorporate factor quality as well as physical quantity and this creates a whole raft of measurement issues: education and human capital and their quality should accompany the labour input; depreciation, rates of utilization, 'intangibles' (see below), and state-of-the-art technology embodied in different vintages, are some of the measurement issues related to capital. The literature post-Solow has tried to find the best solutions to these issues. As Solow himself (quoted in Hulten, 2010) and many others note, all these difficulties mean that the findings should be taken as approximate rather than precise; but this is not very different from the state of knowledge in many other areas of (macro)economics.

It is beyond the scope of this chapter to review the voluminous literature on growth accounting. The interested reader can consult Barro and Sala-i-Martin (1995, chapter 10) and for more advanced reviews, Hulten (2010), Jorgenson (2005), and Griliches (1996), the latter two being among the top contributors to this literature and associated with the measurement of productivity and innovation as well as the theory of capital. What have we learnt? Following the review by Hulten (2010), some of the key findings that can be gleaned are: as follows.In the US, output per unit of labour has grown at an average annual rate of 2.5 per cent per year over the period 1948 to 2007. According to estimates by the US Bureau of Labor Statistics (BLS), about 58 per cent of the increase of output during this period happened because of the growth in MFP and the rest was due to the growth of inputs. Among the latter, there has been a progressive shift in the composition of capital toward information and communication technology (IT) equipment; on which more below. Another key finding is that, at about 1.5 per cent per year, the growth rate of output per labour-hour in Europe over recent years (1995 to 2005) has only been half that of the US (about 3 per cent). Moreover, the drivers of growth were quite different: MFP explained about one-half of the US growth rate, but only one-fifth of the EU rate. EU growth relied more heavily on the growth of capital per hour worked, and within capital, more heavily on non-IT capital. The precise picture of course differs across countries.

But there is no consensus on the high contribution of TFP/MFP reported by Hulten (2010). The studies quoted in Barro and Sala-i-Martin (1995, table 10.8) find that for the advanced economies in the post-World War II era, each of the two has contributed a roughly equal proportion to output growth (with physical capital accumulation more important, if anything) and labour growth a distant third. A recent rejoinder to the debates is by Jorgenson et al. (2008), who incorporate human capital as a separate factor into growth accounting, alongside physical capital, labour, and general productivity. Interestingly, they found that input growth, due to investments in human and physical capital, accounted for more than 80 per cent of US economic growth after World War II, while growth in total factor productivity accounted for only 20 per cent. All this is important, as much of the Endogenous Growth Theory is motivated by and premised on the fact that the ultimate driver of growth is productivity growth.

A key property of capital is that it often includes intangible aspects like technological sophistication, brand equity, and organizational capital; all are subject to serious measurement difficulties. Hence, Research and Development activity (R&D) and investment in organization and brand name should be included in a broad definition of capital accumulation ($\Delta K/K$). Accounting for such intangible investment (as best as possible) is a recent endeavour in growth accounting. According to Hulten (2010), in the US, the inclusion of intangibles results in the role of MFP as a driver of growth diminishing significantly: from 50 per cent without intangibles to 35 per cent when they are included. The role of IT capital is also diminished, and intangible capital is found to account for more than a quarter of growth.

The argument about the importance of intangibles in capital leads us to the idea of 'embodied technical progress' that is built into new capital; e.g. (some) better computer software may be built into newer hardware. If so, installation of new capital is required in order for technical progress to be materialized; the flip side of this argument is that physical investment may carry with it the intangible property of higher sophistication. Testing for embodied technical progress is difficult as it implies that capital is divided into 'vintages' (time of its production) of different sophistication that are not perfect substitutes of one another; the measurement issues required to substantiate this plausible idea are considerable. An indication however of embodied technical progress is the inclusion of R&D in intangible investment as a measure of the (growth in) the technical sophistication of capital. As reported above, this alters the findings of growth accounting. See Zeira (1998) for a model where machines are key to the process of growth, something de-emphasized by EGT; in the mind of this author, this set of ideas merits more attention than they have received so far.

Embodied technical progress may lead to more emphasis on capital and investment as a driver of growth as this is the vehicle by which technical sophistication is achieved. 'Capital fundamentalism' is the idea that physical capital is central for growth. To be sure, both physical capital accumulation and productivity growth matter, although we cannot be too precise as argued. But the real question is which of the two is more fundamental; in econometric terms, which is the exogenous factor? King and Levine (1994) report a couple of findings in favour of capital fundamentalism. Differences in physical capital accumulation can explain a lot of the differences in levels of output across countries; and increases in national investment rates can produce major increases in rates of economic growth. But against capital fundamentalism, they find: differences in capital-per-person explain few of the differences in output-per-person across countries; there is more reason to believe that economic growth causes investment and savings than investment and savings cause economic growth. The latter finding, in particular, is a refutation of capital fundamentalism.

Apart from being a differentiating point between the SMG and Endogenous Growth Theory, 'capital fundamentalism' also has important policy implications: For instance, many policy-makers (and analysts) put a lot of emphasis on attracting Foreign Direct Investment (FDI) as a spur to growth. If you are a capital fundamentalist you would agree; if not, however, you would tend to think of this emphasis as misplaced. You would think that productivity rises first and foremost and, if that happens, demand for capital investment (internal or external) follows due to higher profitability. Furthermore, there is concern in some policy circles about 'de-industrialization' in developed countries; the process by which the share of industry and (more narrowly) manufacturing in the value added or the employment of a country is progressively declining. We will not go into these debates here; the point is only to note that one would be concerned about de-industrialization if a concept of capital fundamentalism is adhered to, i.e. the notion that capital (therefore industry/manufacturing) is somehow central for development and prosperity.

Another debate a few years back concerned the growth of the South East Asian 'Tigers' mentioned above—Singapore, Taiwan, Hong Kong, and South Korea. The question was whether their growth was fuelled mainly by physical factor accumulation or by productivity growth. Looking at Barro and Sala-i-Martin's (1995) table 10.8 which reports the findings of Young (1995), we see that the very considerable growth rate of real GDP in these countries between 1966 and 1990 (7–10 per cent per annum) was due to about 40–70 per cent to capital accumulation (i.e. capital contributed, say, $0.4 \times 0.1 = 0.04$ of the 0.1 growth rate), about 30–40 per cent to growth in hours of work, and only the remainder (0–30 per cent) to productivity growth. The implication of this debate is that, if growth is mainly due to the growth of physical inputs, this will sooner or later dry up as limits to these resources will be reached (all population of working age will be put to work and immigration will dry up; capital will reach natural resource constraints); whilst if growth is driven by productivity, this can keep going for longer. This debate has now subsided partly because South East Asia, following Japan, seems now to be growing more slowly. Given the findings just reported, this should not be surprising.

A final issue, that will stay with us for the foreseeable future, is the impact of investment in information technology (IT) on growth. Though IT has been a part of our everyday lives for nearly 30 years now, its impact on statistics has been slow to show up. Eminent commentators used to remark until a few years ago that IT did not have quantitative significance; but now the picture seems to be unanimously shared. Oliner et al. (2007) analyses the sources of US productivity growth during the 1990s and early 2000s. It confirms the central role of IT in the productivity revival during 1995–2000 and shows that it played a significant, although smaller, role after 2000. Furthermore, after 2000, there has been industry restructuring and cost cutting in response to profit pressures. Jorgenson (2007) provides detailed information on the effect of IT on the G7 economies during 1980–2001, accounting carefully for the changing price of IT equipment. He finds that, post-1995, investment in IT and related equipment increases significantly across all G7 economies. This contributed by a large portion to the resurgence in growth in all economies (see his Table 11.15). Importantly as well, the increase in the G7 growth after 1995 is due to a rise in productivity growth in IT-producing industries.

9.3.6 Development Accounting

Finally, we turn to development accounting. This is an exercise parallel to growth accounting that aims to shed light to the sources of income differences across countries (rather than across time as does growth accounting). It purports to answer one of the fundamental questions of growth, namely what makes some countries richer than others? It starts from the production function (9.12) and proceeds in the same way as growth accounting; the change is that the differencing is taken not across time but across countries. Skipping the details, this results in an equation of the form:

$$\frac{\Delta Y_i}{Y_i} = \frac{\Delta A_i}{A_i} + \beta \frac{\Delta K_i}{K_i} + (1 - \beta) \frac{\Delta L_i}{L_i} \tag{9.14}$$

An equation like (9.14) applies to country i (at a certain point in time or using averages over a time period). Now, 'Δ' signifies differences from an average across countries, so (9.14) relates country i's percentage income difference from the average to its percentage difference in productivity and the capital and labour inputs (appropriately weighted). This equation can be used in a similar manner as equation (9.13), namely to calculate (as a residual) the percentage difference of this country's productivity and then to work out the percentage contribution of each factor, including productivity, to this country's income difference from the mean.

Development accounting grapples with the same sort of issues as growth accounting: primarily, the many difficulties in the measurements of the inputs and their quality. Additionally, one must remember that this is an exercise across countries, many of which do not have the same statistical capabilities and advanced data collection bureaus as the developed countries (on which the most advanced growth accounting studies typically focus). So, the quality of data is more of an issue here. As development accounting touches on the issue of cross-country income distribution, which we have discussed at length, we are not going to dwell a lot more here; the interested reader is referred to Caselli (2005) for more.

One use of development accounting is the following. One can take variances of (9.14) across countries:

$$Var\left(\frac{\Delta Y_i}{Y_i}\right) = Var\left(\frac{\Delta A_i}{A_i}\right) + Var\left(\beta \frac{\Delta K_i}{K_i} + (1 - \beta) \frac{\Delta L_i}{L_i}\right)$$
$$+ Cov\left(\frac{\Delta A_i}{A_i}, \beta \frac{\Delta K_i}{K_i} + (1 - \beta) \frac{\Delta L_i}{L_i}\right)$$

Then, one can measure the extent to which physical factor accumulation (including their quality) can explain the variation in income; this is done by computing the ratio:

$$\frac{Var\left(\beta \frac{\Delta K_i}{K_i} + (1 - \beta) \frac{\Delta L_i}{L_i}\right)}{Var\left(\frac{\Delta Y_i}{Y_i}\right)}$$

Caselli (2005, table 1) finds this ratio to be 0.4: about 40 per cent of cross-country income variation is explained by physical factors and their quality while the rest is explained by differences in productivity. While there are some variations across groups of countries, he shows that his estimates are robust to more refined measurements and are in line with other literature. So, the bottomline is, while there is no perfect knowledge or agreement, variation in productivity seems to account for a large part of both the growth experiences of individual countries or income variation across countries. This is then enough motivation for the Endogenous Growth Theory, to which we now turn.

9.4 Models of Endogenous Growth

9.4.1 What is Wrong with the Solow Growth Model? The Origins of Endogenous Growth Theory

Let us begin by pointing that endogenous growth theory (EGT) is a large family of theories and models, busily developed from the mid-1980s on and throughout the 1990s in successive waves. Hence, there is a lot of diversity within it. It is fair to say that four considerations gave rise to EGT: (a) the aim to provide an economic theory of technological growth, assumed exogenous under SGM; (b) the empirical failure of the convergence hypothesis, a key premise of SGM; (c) the implication that rates of return to capital are higher in (capital) poorer countries and lower in advanced countries; and lastly (d) the need to enrich the menu of explanatory factors in cross-country growth regressions and the associated policy prescriptions.

The Solow growth model (SGM) does not explain what drives growth in the long term. The nature of the catch-all productivity variable A is not explained—it is just assumed to grow at an exogenous rate. Yet, technological growth is driven by the research and development activities (R&D) of firms, which are motivated by profits from using the discoveries to enhance their products. Researchers are into research because they see the potential financial incentives in terms of a greater salary in research than elsewhere. In turn, the profits of the firms (and the salaries of workers) are determined by the chances of success of research, the chances and probability that their invention will be surpassed by a newer, rival invention any time soon, and the prices of the goods produced on the basis of a new invention (state-of-the-art technology). Thus, the decisions on whether research should be undertaken and of what type, are economic decisions, amenable to modelling. Sure enough, as Solow (1994) notes, much of this is truly exogenous or even erratic (who knows what twists technology will take, there is so much unquantifiable, 'Knightian' uncertainty) as to make this process not smooth or accurately predictable. But equally surely, pushing the whole issue under the carpet (as SGM does) is not satisfactory, and much can be learnt by careful formal modelling.

By the late 1980s, it was becoming increasingly evident that convergence across countries to some reasonably comparable living standards was becoming elusive. The earlier optimism had been shattered by the experience of several countries in the 1980s which showed even negative rates of growth. At the same time, other clusters of countries, notably in South East Asia but also in southern Europe, showed very rapid rates of industrialization and growth. Thus, the idea of a convergence process shared more or less universally was replaced by selective, or 'club', convergence. More generally, it was now clear that different countries could settle for different growth rates for considerable periods of time, or what the modeller calls 'the long run'. This empirical fact was a major challenge to the SGM.

The SGM was characterized by diminishing returns to each factor separately. With respect to capital in particular, this means that capital poor countries have a high marginal product of capital, while the opposite occurs for rich countries. Since the marginal product of capital is equalized to the real interest rate (optimizing firms will accumulate so much that the last unit of capital yields a marginal return equal to its cost, no more and no less), this means that rich countries must have low real interest rates and poor countries high real interest rates. Furthermore, capital should flow from rich to poor countries. This is not true

(Lucas, 1990): capital flows to a large extent between developed countries, as happens e.g. with Foreign Direct Investment (FDI).

Furthermore, while empirical models guided by SGM have had some success in identifying the factors guiding growth, with emphasis on the saving/investment rate and education, they fail to account for much of the cross-country differences in living standards. For instance, Romer (1994) also points out that in a cross-country regression of the rate of growth against the (gross) investment ratio (see his figure 2), the correlation has the same sign as that predicted by the SGM (positive), but it is much too low to provide a meaningful theory of the variation in growth experiences between countries. To take an example, the share of investment in output in the United States is at most, twice as large as the share in the Philippines. With plausible parameter values (i.e. an elasticity of capital in the aggregate production function), this difference is inadequate to explain why the Philippines had output per worker in 1960 that was equal to about 10 per cent of output per worker in the United States. More generally, as we concluded in the previous section, much of the growth experience and income differences across countries are explained by factors other than the availability of capital and labour (even accounting for their quality), on which the SGM puts the emphasis. EGT attempts to answer these questions by placing more emphasis on intangible factors like human capital, R&D, and government services, and much less on physical capital accumulation (though with a lot of difference in emphasis across models, as we shall see).

Let us therefore take stock. As mentioned in sub-section 9.2.1, the SGM makes four assumptions (with an additional fifth one we mention now):

- Exogenous technical progress and long-run growth;
- Exclusive focus on physical capital (and exogenous human capital in the case of the augmented SGM);
- Diminishing marginal products, particularly that of capital, of which two implications are
- Convergence;
- Capital flows from capital-rich to capital-poor countries.

As almost all these assumptions and predictions are against empirical evidence or are otherwise limiting, EGT departs from all of these. It first purports to explain the determinants of technical progress (which comes as the result of conscious and purposeful activity with the aim of securing an advantage and profits). In other words, it explains ('endogenizes') the determinants of long-run growth. Second, it assumes constant returns on aggregate—therefore, it presumes no convergence or clear-cut pattern of capital flows. Thirdly, other elements apart from physical capital also play a role. In fact, all the other elements (productivity and its various components like technology, human capital, institutional structures, etc.) are considered more fundamental, so that physical capital is only relegated to a subsidiary role in the growth process.

9.4.2 The Nature of the Aggregate Production Function under EGT

EGT begins with a production function like (9.1):

$$Y_i = F(A_i, K_i, L_i) \tag{9.15}$$

The main difference from (9.1) is that this is not aggregate but applies to the individual firm; it may also be time-varying but time-subscripts are suppressed. Productivity (A_i), which is to be endogenized, may or may not be a privately purchased factor. This production function F(.) is characterized by the standard 'Inada conditions' for the physical inputs K and L (see Chapter 1). The key assumption is that each physical factor or input (K, L) on its own (everything else kept constant) is subject to diminishing marginal product; it is very valuable if in short supply, and will contribute to some extent even if it is abundant.

But note that there is no presumption as to what will happen if other factors (particularly productivity) increase simultaneously: e.g. increasing the amount of capital with a given amount of workers may not reduce its marginal product if technology rises as well. The same might happen with any other general increases in productivity, due, say to better skills or organization. So, though there are diminishing returns to each factor alone, this may not be the case if productivity A rises, too.

For concrete, let the production function be Cobb-Douglas as in (9.1'), except across countries rather than across time:

$$Y_i = AK_i^\alpha L_i^{1-\alpha} \tag{9.15'}$$

As before, there are diminishing marginal products to the physical inputs (separately). But now, imagine that productivity (A), common across all firms, is proportional to output in some way. Let's take a minute to explain why this may be so. There may be three reasons in particular. If A is mostly made up of human capital, and if human capital depends on aggregate output, then A is proportional to aggregate Y. Likewise, if A depends heavily on government services (administration, justice, security, health, education), then we have the same dependence. Finally, a slightly more involved reason: imagine that A is made up of technology, and imagine that technology grows over the long run at the same rate as output. Then again, A and output are proportional.

In particular, let there be a proportional relation like:[31]

$$A = Y^{1-\alpha}$$

Note that both A (common across firms) and Y (aggregate) are without firm-specific subscript. If so, the production function for firm i becomes:

$$Y_i = Y^{1-\alpha} K_i^\alpha L_i^{1-\alpha}$$

(Note: K_i is still subject to a diminishing marginal product.) Aggregating over firms by taking the mean over i, we get:[32]

$$Y = Y^{1-\alpha} K^\alpha L^{1-\alpha} \Rightarrow Y = KL^{(1-\alpha)/\alpha}$$

Now, at the aggregate level, the marginal product of capital (MPK) is $L^{(1-\alpha)/\alpha}$, which is constant (at least in the steady state). (Population growth has not been considered so intensively in the context of EGT; indeed, it may raise special problems if it is allowed. Let

---

[31] It would be practically equivalent to assume a proportionality between A and aggregate capital (K): $A = K^{1-\alpha}$.

[32] Strictly speaking, we should first log the expression and then take the mean. The mean should therefore be a geometric one (mean over logs) rather than the common arithmetic mean.

us leave this for now.) So, returning to our main theme, the MPK is a constant: diminishing MPK, the hallmark of the SGM, does not apply here on aggregate. Why is this so? Well, any rise in private capital elicits two effects on (private) output. First, there is the direct effect, to which a diminishing MPK still applies (K_i receives an exponent of $\alpha < 1$.) Secondly, as private output rises, so does the shared productivity, A (from the $A = Y^{(1-\alpha)/\alpha}$ element of the production function, due to any of the three channels identified above). This helps raise individual output further. This is a secondary effect. This effect however is not considered by the individual firm, because its individual effect on the aggregate output is too small to take into account—we call this an external (to the firm) effect, or an externality. This externality complements the direct effect of K_i on Y_i (on which a diminishing return applies), with the effect that, at the aggregate level, the diminishing return vanishes. We say that there are constant returns to scale on both the private factors taken together (the exponents of K_i and L_i sum to one) and to physical capital on its own if both its private and external effects are taken together. As a result, aggregate output (Y) is proportional to aggregate capital (K). From these properties, a number of important implications result, namely perpetual growth, no convergence, and no declining pattern to MPK as development proceeds. The externalities that complement private capital in production and the associated constant returns to scale to capital are key features of the EGT, present particularly in the early strands of the literature. A later strand of the literature emphasizes the effects of technological growth: if the state of technology rises with the rise in output, so the rise in private capital is complemented by growing productivity. Thus, the diminishing returns to capital are outweighed by this process, and growth never stalls.

However, while EGT has the potential to overcome many of the defects of SGM, note some difficulties that arise. First, we noted that these models do not easily admit population growth. It is easy to see why. From above, $MPK = L^{(1-\alpha)/\alpha}$; population growth would make this, and growth that depends on it MPK (see below) infinite in due course—an absurd property for any model to have. Secondly, note the rather specific nature of the proportionality above, $A = Y^{1-\alpha}$: what would happen if the proportionality did not follow this knife-edge condition (very special, like walking on a knife's edge)? The arguments above would not apply. In fact, these two difficulties are interrelated. A number of papers (Mulligan and Sala-i-Martin, 1993; Eicher and Turnovsky, 1999) investigate the general conditions between such and other relations that allow endogenous growth to emerge. We shall not dwell on those any more. In what follows, we shall take the above assumptions as given, and refer interested readers to these special papers.

9.4.3 The Setup I—Individual Optimization

The setup is one of intertemporal optimization with micro-foundations as developed in Chapter 5. The key points are the following. Constant population is assumed throughout—things would change only slightly with an exogenously increasing population. Labour is inelastic (fixed at unity per person), so there is no labour-leisure choice. The individual household/agent is assumed to maximize intertemporal welfare V:

$$\text{Max (w.r.t. } C_t) \quad V = \sum_{t=0}^{\infty} (1+\rho)^{-t} U(C_t)$$

$\rho > 0$ is the subjective discount rate; it is used to discount future sums (in a utility sense). Intuitively, it tells us how much we disregard the future relative to the present and is a measure of impatience. For simplicity, period utility is assumed to be of the isoelastic form:

$$U(C_t) \equiv \frac{C_t^{1-1/\sigma}}{1 - 1/\sigma}$$

$\sigma > 0$ is an important parameter: It gives the intertemporal elasticity of substitution in consumption (how much the intertemporal profile of consumption can vary in response to incentives—see below).

The individual's intertemporal budget constraint is the analogue of equation (5.5) of Chapter 5:

$$\sum_{t=0}^{\infty} R^{-t} C_t \leq A_o + \sum_{t=0}^{\infty} R^{-t} W_t$$

R is the gross real interest rate ($R \equiv 1 + r$); this may vary from period to period, but to save notation this is not shown—similar but more complicated formulae can be derived in the general case of variable r. Therefore $R^{-1} \equiv 1/(1+r) < 1$ is the discount factor. W_t: Exogenous labour income (exogenous wage for the fixed unit of work each individual contributes). A_t (in this sub-section only) is financial wealth (money, shares, housing), so A_o is the wealth at the beginning of the planning period. Equality will result if households are assumed to exhaust all consumption opportunities (it will be implausible to assume otherwise).

The individual chooses all future consumption levels (C_t for all t) so as to maximize intertemporal utility, subject to their budget constraint. Form the 'Hamiltonian' (dynamic Langangean):

$$\text{Max (w.r.t. } C_t) \quad \pounds \equiv \sum (1+\rho)^{-t} \left(\frac{C_t^{1-1/\sigma}}{1 - 1/\sigma} + \lambda \left[A_o + \Sigma R^{-t} W_t - \Sigma R^{-t} C_t \right] \right)$$

A 'no-Ponzi-game condition' is assumed: individuals cannot/will not die either with debt or with unspent wealth at the end of history:

$$\text{Lim}_{t \to \infty} \quad \Sigma R^{-t} A_t = 0$$

The first-order conditions for t and $t + 1$ are (just differentiate the Hamiltonian with respect to C_t and C_{t+1}, respectively—the same applies to all periods, in other words, any t):

$$(1 - 1/\sigma)(1+\rho)^{-t} C_t^{-1/\sigma} = \lambda R^{-t}$$

and

$$(1 - 1/\sigma)(1+\rho)^{-t-1} C_{t+1}^{-1/\sigma} = \lambda R^{-t-1}$$

Dividing by parts, we get the 'Euler equation' for consumption, the analogue of equation (5.11') of Chapter 5:

$$\left(\frac{C_{t+1}}{C_t} \right)^{1/\sigma} = R/(1+\rho) \tag{9.16}$$

Taking logs, we get:[33]

$$\Delta c_{t+1} = \sigma(r - \rho) \tag{9.16'}$$

A lower-case letter indicates a log, $c = \log C$. According to this, consumption growth is essentially determined by the difference between the real interest rate of the period minus the discount rate. Why is this so? Let us think about the benefits and costs of postponing consumption (i.e. saving) in period t. The benefit of saving now is the interest rate; we will consume the proceeds later, but due to impatience, we discount the future utility so obtained by ρ—the cost. Thus, if the difference $r - \rho$ is positive, it pays to save now (reduce C_t) and increase C_{t+1}; i.e., increase the growth rate of consumption between periods t and t + 1. The parameter that tells us how responsive consumption is to a change in $r - \rho$ (by altering its intertemporal profile) is the elasticity of intertemporal substitution, σ.

(9.16') is an equation for consumption growth, but we are of course interested in building a theory of general output (GDP). To go to a general growth theory, we make use of the arguments in sub-section 9.1.7 on the 'Balanced Growth Path' (BGP). The basic national income accounting equation is:

$$Y = C + I + G$$

This is in familiar notation and applies to every period. In the steady state, on which most of the EGT focuses, GDP (Y) grows at a constant rate; with output proportional to capital as argued above, private capital also grows at the same rate. Hence, the investment share in GDP($I/Y = (I/K) \times (K/Y)$) is also constant. So is assumed to be the government spending-to-GDP ratio (on empirical grounds). So, C/Y must be constant as well (division by Y above establishes that). Thus, consumption and GDP grow at the common rate, to be indicated by g. In other words, in the steady state, a BGP holds whereby all Y, C, I, G are growing at a common rate. Such balanced growth will also obtain even if the leisure-labour choice is endogenous (unlike here), but these implications will not hold outside the steady state if labour supply is endogenous.

Limiting attention to the steady state (and forgetting what happens in the transition to it) is a legitimate simplification, as the theory of growth is mostly concerned with the long run. So, we may write,

$$g = \sigma(r - \rho) \tag{9.17}$$

9.4.4 The Setup II—Optimization by Firms

The firm is assumed to maximize profits subject to its production function and exogenously taken factor prices, W (real wage) and r (return to capital: the real interest rate). The firm is assumed to rent (or lease) its capital from suppliers of capital, hence its rental cost is the return to capital (r) plus maintenance (the depreciation rate, δ, assumed constant).[34]

---

[33] Note that, since $R = 1 + r$, $\log R \approx r$ and that $\ln C_{t+1} - \ln C_t \approx C_{t+1} - C_t)/C_t$. Equation (9.16') is also called the 'Keynes-Ramsey' rule of consumption growth.

[34] One could alternatively assume more naturally that the firm owns its physical capital K; the same results would be derived in that case. Our assumptions here result in a simpler exposition.

As in Chapter 5 which has more details, this results in the following first-order condition with respect to K:

$$F_K = r + \delta$$

Where F_k is the marginal product of capital.[35] Inserting into (9.7), we get:

$$g = \sigma(F_k - \delta - \rho) \tag{9.17'}$$

Equations (9.17) or (9.17'), which are alternatives, are fundamental for EGT in all its versions. But note: we have not yet established what the value of the growth rate (g) is. We do not even know whether perhaps it settles to zero—no growth—in the long run. We discuss this next.

9.4.5 What Delivers Ongoing Growth?

We now want to see the mechanism at the heart of endogenous growth models that results in ongoing growth. Consider Figure 9.7 which plots the growth rate (g) against capital, K.

Each of the lines plots the marginal product of capital given a certain level of productivity A. Consider what happens if there is growth without any increase in productivity—let us take the lower line. When capital is scarce, low K, its marginal product is very high, therefore $F_k - \delta - \rho > 0$ and the economy grows by equation (9.17'); we are moving towards the right-hand side of the graph. Under the assumption of diminishing marginal product, MPK declines as K grows. As long as the marginal product of capital is above the subjective discount rate plus depreciation rate, growth continues. If it falls enough, so that $F_k = \delta + \rho$ at some K*, the economy stalls. This is essentially the SGM (though, strictly speaking, even the SGM allowed K to grow, albeit at an exogenous rate).

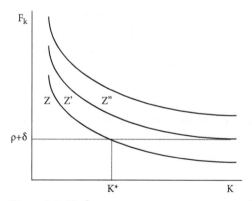

Figure 9.7. Endogenous versus exogenous growth

---

[35] A counterpart condition applies to the choice of how much labour to hire, but it is not so interesting here. For information, it would equate labour's marginal product to the real wage, in a standard way.

Things change, however, if productivity (A) increases as the economy grows. If that is the case, the curve shifts up and right—each level of capital yields a higher MPK. So, as K accumulates, MPK may remain constant—say, from Z, to Z', to Z''. In other words, if the marginal product somehow manages to stay at a high enough level for ever, growth is perpetual. Endogenous growth theory can be seen as essentially searching for the mechanisms that keep the marginal product of capital from falling, despite the technical tendency to do so (the diminishing MPK).

Our previous discussion suggests how this may happen. The crucial factors may be the external effects of capital (that in turn come from various sources), and technological improvements. We may then classify endogenous growth models into two broad classes, one that investigates how constant returns to a broad definition of capital may emerge, and another that investigates the nature of technical innovation. There is also a third, in-between class, the two-sector models. We take them up in turn.

9.5 Early Models of Endogenous Growth

9.5.1 Externalities from Private Capital and the AK Model: Learning-by-Doing, Government Services, Human Capital

The first class of models assumes that productivity A complements private capital. This class of models essentially formalizes the arguments presented above, that the external effects of capital (or output) complement the effects of private capital, such that eventually the total effect of capital on output shows no tendency to diminish. We use the following Cobb-Douglas version of the production function (9.15):

$$Y_t = K_t^\alpha (A_t L_t)^{1-\alpha} \qquad (9.18a)$$

In an important early model, productivity A_t depends on K_t (equivalently, it could be Y_t) via 'learning by doing' (Romer, 1986). The idea here is that a higher level of capitalization enables the workforce to be more familiar with technology and more productive; e.g. in an economy with many computers, workers will in general be more computer-savvy. Quite simply, using the scaling factor $\omega > 0$, we assume:

$$A_t = \omega K_t \qquad (9.18b)$$

More broadly, skills and productivity improve if there is a lot of activity in the economy and workers learn by simply emulating (freely) what is going on around them. Then, the production function becomes:

$$Y_t = \omega^{1-\alpha} K_t L_t^{1-\alpha}$$

In the steady state labour is constant, and in any case unimportant for our purposes. If we set $L = 1$, we can write more generically the following production function:

$$Y_t = AK_t, \qquad (9.19)$$

where $A \equiv \omega^{1-\alpha}$. This is the 'AK' production function, positing a simple linear relationship between output and capital on aggregate. This is not so much a theory as a formulation, as it presupposes one or more theories that generate it. Furthermore, since now in the aggregate the marginal product of capital is $F_K = A$, growth (9.17') becomes:

$$g = \sigma(A - \rho - \delta) \qquad (9.20)$$

Production (5.19) and growth (5.20) together make the 'AK' model of growth (analysed by Rebelo, 1991).

Another theory supporting the AK formulation is that of productive government services (Barro, 1990; Turnovsky, 1996). The idea here is that government provides a range of services (that mostly cannot be produced by the private sector as they are public goods, like justice and security, administration, but also health, education, infrastructure); all these complement private capital in production as a productive economy also requires the rule of law to be respected and the workforce to be healthy and productive.[36] Such services are again assumed to be proportional to output or private capital,

$$A_t = AG_t = A\tau Y_t,$$

where τ is the tax rate; the idea being the government spending (G) equals tax receipts (thus there is no budget deficit). In this case, the aggregate production function becomes,

$$Y_t = (A\tau)^{(1-\alpha)/\alpha} K_t L_t^{(1-\alpha)/\alpha}. \qquad (9.18')$$

With fixed labour ($L = 1$), the production function is again of the 'AK' type (5.18). In this way, the same formulation and much of the same discussion as above is valid. We explore the implication of this for the question of optimal provision of productive public services in sub-section 9.6.5, in talking about the policy implications of EGT. Finally, the same formulation would result if productivity resulted from human capital which might also be proportional to output; e.g. for simplicity, $A_t = H_t = AY_t$. Then again, an 'AK' aggregate production function results.

Human capital has played a prominent part in the research on growth in its various phases. We saw above how human capital complements physical capital in the augmented Solow model (Mankiw et al., 1992). In the context of EGT, some of the initial papers of the newer, endogenous growth literature were focused on human capital (Lucas, 1988; Barro and Lee, 1993) and there has been a lot of follow-up. We shall return to human capital in the context of two-sector models below and when discussing the empirical evidence in Section 9.7.

9.5.2 Properties of the AK Model: (Sub)Optimality, (Lack of) Dynamics, and (Possible) Scale Effects

We now turn to some key properties of the AK model. We shall in particular review the properties of the model for the optimal growth rate, for dynamics, scale effects, and investment. First, we need to distinguish between the private and social marginal products of capital (PMPK and SMPK). PMKP takes into account only the private effect of capital; it

---

[36] Both health and education feature prominently in growth/development accounting and the empirical work on growth.

is obtained by differentiating (9.18a) with respect to K_t, taking A_t as given and then replacing it via (9.18b). SMPK takes into account all the external effects via learning-by-doing, productive public services, human capital, therefore it adjusts A_t as K_t changes; it is obtained by first inserting (9.18b) into (9.18a) and then differentiating by K_t:

$$PMPK = \alpha A_t^{1-\alpha} K_t^{\alpha-1} L_t^{1-\alpha} = \alpha A L_t^{1-\alpha},$$
$$SMPK = A L_t^{1-\alpha}.$$

It is easy to see from this and from the foregoing reasoning, that the social MPK is greater than the private one:

$$SMPK > PMPK$$

What matters for the individual firm in selecting its capital level is the PMPK (in earlier notation, $F_K = PMPK$) because only that confers benefit to it, the rest of the benefit is external to it. The PMPK is what is considered in the growth equation (9.20) (with a constant labour force, $L = 1$); and this is what the 'decentralized' market economy without government intervention will deliver. We may write:

$$g^{\text{decentralized}} = \sigma(PMPK - \rho - \delta) \tag{9.21a}$$

A question that arises here is whether this growth rate is optimal from a social point of view. As in Chapter 5, we may judge this by asking what growth rate a 'benevolent dictator' or central planner caring about the whole of society would have chosen. The central planner optimizes exactly as the individual and the firm, with the only exception that s/he is aware of the external effects and takes them into account in the optimization. Thus, the central planner would have decided in exactly the same way about everything, except that they would have valued the marginal product of capital at SMKP. So, they would have chosen such a capital level that its cost equals the SMPK, i.e. $SMPK = r + \delta$. From the growth (9.17), the resulting socially optimal growth rate would be:

$$g^{\text{socially optimal}} = \sigma(SMPK - \rho - \delta) \tag{9.21b}$$

Thus, the socially optimal growth rate, chosen by the central planner, is higher than the privately chosen one via the market mechanism. The reason is that the central planner recognizes the positive externalities of private capital. By taking into account fully the effects of private capital, the central planner commits more resources to investment and growth, less to private consumption, and achieves a higher growth rate. Thus, the conclusion is that to the extent that there are positive externalities from private capital, the 'decentralized' market economy (where individuals and firms act independently from one another) achieves a socially suboptimal growth rate:

$$g^{\text{decentralized}} < g^{\text{socially optimal}}$$

In a similar fashion, there is underinvestment by the private economy on R&D, as this also exerts positive externalities that are not all captured by the entrepreneur who carries out the (costly) R&D activity. For instance, Jones and Williams (1998) use a conservative estimate for the rate of return on investment in R&D of about 30 per cent; on this basis, they find that the socially optimal rate of R&D investment is about four times the actual rate, an astonishing result. Correspondingly, the decentralized market economy invests too little in R&D and therefore grows too slowly.

On the other hand, there are well-known negative externalities associated with capital and economic activity more generally. The obvious one is the low quality of life due to pollution and over-crowding of cities, but also stress from trying to keep up, as the theories of 'keeping up' and 'status' suggest (see Chapters 2 and 11). These insights are well known, but do not seem to be integrated into the theory of growth. They suggest reasons why in fact the market economy grows too fast, more than the socially optimal rate. Perhaps the wider point is that, without government intervention, there is no guarantee that market economy will achieve a socially optimal rate of growth (whatever that might be).

A second key property of the AK model is related to dynamics. Note that, from equation (9.20), the growth rate is constant at all times. There are no dynamics; following a possible change in any of the parameters, the growth rate 'jumps' to the value dictated by the productivity of capital and all the other considerations we saw above. In terms of Figure 9.7, the marginal product is a flat line.[37]

In terms of cross-country comparisons, there will generally be no convergence, either in terms of living standards, or even in terms of growth rates. Growth rates will be dictated by separate country characteristics, essentially determined by the parameters of equation (9.20), which will not be the same except in very special cases. In terms of living standards, there is no presupposition of convergence except in the very fortunate (and special) case whereby poorer countries happen to have higher growth rates. But there is no compelling reason to think that this is the case. The lack of dynamics is therefore a great simplifying device but very unlikely to be useful in the investigation of real world-related questions. There is a question what happens when endogenous labour supply is grafted on to it. In this way, the model acquires transitional dynamics but it is unclear how realistic it is. King and Rebelo (1993) undertake a general investigation of the dynamic properties of the AK model, under an endogenous labour supply but exogenous productivity growth. Their overall result in the transitional dynamics of the model does not match the US growth experience; this points to the necessity of building models of endogenous technical change.

Finally, we turn attention to the issue of scale effects, a tricky little corner of growth theory: quite simply, the MPK and the growth rate depend on labour, which has been assumed constant in each country's steady state. However, L will vary from country to country, and the implication is that larger economies have a higher (private and social) MPK, all other things equal, and as a result, they grow faster. This is a strong implication: bigger economies grow (forever) faster, all else the same. The question of scale effects is of some importance given the process of globalization: Is the formation of larger economic entities (larger countries over the course of history, regional formations like the European Union and others) motivated by such scale effects (among other things), and does it imply them? The consensus is that there may be some scale effects, but very weak (e.g. Jones, 1997, refutes the link). There is some evidence that in the global economy over the long history, the growth rate (of the economy and population) has increased together with the scale (see Kremer, 1991). While the issue is far from settled, it is probably fair to say that various theorists regard the existence of scale effects in their models as an embarrassment,

---

[37] In an extended AK model with endogenous labour supply, where the production function (9.19) is modified to $Y = AKL^{1-\alpha}$ with L flexible, Turnovsky (2000) shows that in that case, too, there are no transitional (short-run) dynamics. The reason is somewhat different. There are in fact unstable dynamics, which lead to unbounded outcomes. Thus, the only sensible solution is to rule these dynamics and outcomes out and impose the condition that the growth rate should be constant at all times.

and have devoted some effort to get rid of them. Some formulations, in alleviating scale effects, end up relating the economy's growth rate to population growth rate only—which is exogenous, hence 'semi-endogenous' growth arises, which only ties growth to a few exogenous variables like the population growth rate, without any role for policy; other models however manage to overcome this uncomfortable property (see Jones, 1995b, 1999).

Scale effects are a manifestation of the deeper fact that the aggregate production function $Y_t = K_t^\alpha (A_t L_t)^{1-\alpha}$ embodying all external effects mentioned above exhibits homogeneity of a degree higher than one (increasing returns to scale); e.g. the sum of elasticities to A_t (the external effects) as well as capital and labour is here $2 - \alpha > 1$. (A reminder that constant returns implies a sum of elasticities equal to 1.) Constant returns to private capital and labour alone are generally assumed on the basis of a 'replication argument'. Imagine that you have a factory, or economy, with capital K and labour L, producing output Y. You can always construct (or imagine that you can) another factory or economy with exactly the same characteristics, so in total you will have 2K, 2L, and 2Y: constant returns to scale. But this argument does not apply when growth is generated by new technological inventions and designs ('blueprints', or 'ideas' or simply knowledge) that some other models, reviewed below, emphasize. The key point is that such knowledge (captured by A above) is non-rivalrous. It costs a lot to develop a new 'idea' or design for a product, but once this is developed, then it can be used across many factories at zero marginal cost; given the fixed cost of producing the design, higher production implies lower per-unit costs, a sign of increasing returns to scale. So, if you double all factors, including the stock of 'knowledge' (A), you get more than 2Y—increasing returns to scale. Jones (2005) reviews this line of argument and its implications.

Now, the designs can be used at zero marginal cost once they have been invented, but they do cost (and often quite a lot) to be invented in the first place. How are the R&D entrepreneurs going to recoup their costs of invention? To do so, the tangible factors (K and L) must not be offered their marginal products as remuneration, as would be standard if assumed perfect competition. Why?—because if W = MPL, r = MPK, from the Euler theorem applied to functions of homogeneity of degree one (i.e. constant returns to scale, that still apply to the tangible factors), output would be just exhausted,

$$Y = \text{MPK K} + \text{MPL L}$$

In this way, there would be no payment left to compensate the R&D activity. Hence, we must assume a monopolistic power of the firm, so that the tangible factors are paid below their marginal products, and profits arise. These profits provide a return for the inventions and the R&D activities. These profits also give rise to 'rent-seeking activities' (e.g. copying, crime, and even bureaucratic harassment, all of which aim to get a share of the profits by non-productive means) so that you need to spend resources to defend your business against them.

The bottomline is that the existence of scale effects is an uncomfortable property, as it implies that the growth rate of an economy depends on its size. Various models attempt to 'explain away' scale effects by arguing that even if you double all, K, L, and A, output would only double (not more than that), because of the above mechanisms. Inventions require purposeful activity and cost, rent-seeking activity and counter-activity wastes some of the extra product, and costly learning is also required (you need to spend resources familiarizing yourself with the new products/process). Thus, the more-than-linear homogeneity effect is 'dissipated', scattered away.

Finally, we review some empirical evidence related to the AK model. We saw above that Baxter and King (1993) do not find in its favour. Jones (1995a) notes one important implication of the AK model: the output growth rate is closely linked to the investment/ GDP ratio. Time-differentiate both sides of (9.19) and divide by Y to get:

$$g = Ai, \quad i \equiv I/Y$$

Jones (1995a) points out that historically there has been a lot of variation of the investment ratio but little in the growth rate; thus, the two cannot be related (we return to the wider points that Jones raises later on). But using data from 1870 to 1989, McGrattan (1998) answers this critique by pointing out that this is so if L is kept fixed; if however, L varies in response to exogenous developments like policies, then the growth-investment relationship will be more complicated. She presents evidence from a longer/wider dataset showing a clear relationship between g and i. We also saw above the evidence in Romer (1994) which suggests that growth rates are positively related to investment rates internationally, but the latter do not quite explain all the variation in the former. Further supporting evidence has been offered by Li (2001) who conducts several time series and panel data tests to demonstrate that the implications of the AK model fit with the observations for a large number of European countries, Australia, Canada, Japan, and US. Bond et al. (2010) use annual data in 98 countries from 1960 to 1998 to show that an increase in the share of investments predicts a higher growth rate both in the short and the long run. In conclusion, the balance of evidence seems to be in line with the conclusion that growth rates and investment rates are closely correlated, which is one of the key facts of growth empirics, as we shall see.

Let us conclude here by saying that the AK model and theories behind it offer us valuable insights about the social returns to capital and their effects on growth. But there is an important drawback, noted by Solow (1994) among others: This is that the (social) returns to capital must be exactly constant, otherwise we return to the SGM (if diminishing), or growth accelerates out of control (if higher than one—as K increases, so does it its growth rate, an unstable process). As we argued above, various endogenous growth models are fraught with the difficulty that some parameter or other must take an exact value (a 'knife-edge' condition) for the model not to break down. This difficulty is especially acute with the models of this section. There are often no compelling economic arguments why such conditions must hold exactly.

9.5.3 Two-Sector Models and Human Capital (Again)

Two-sector models are a way of building more realistic, yet tractable, frameworks of growth. The following simple model in the spirit of Rebelo (1991) conveys the flavour of such models with a specific application to human capital and education; but the setup may be applied more generally. This economy has two sectors, one producing general output and the other human capital (the education sector). This is because human capital is formed by conscious training, a process that is modelled as a separate sector. General output may be used for consumption, physical capital accumulation, while a fraction of it is spent in the education sector. Let the production function of general output be

$$Y_t = K_t^\alpha (H_t L_t)^{1-\alpha} \tag{9.22a}$$

as before, except that human capital, H, now replaces A. Again, let us fix $L = 1$. Individual optimization results in a similar growth equation as (9.17') without depreciation and with an appropriate expression for the PMPK:

$$g = \sigma(\alpha K_t^{\alpha-1} H_t^{1-\alpha} - \rho) \tag{9.23}$$

As we shall focus on the BGP, g is constant, therefore without time subscript; in contrast, K and H will be growing perpetually. In turn, human capital is produced by a simple production function in the second sector (education):

$$\Delta H_{t+1} = \phi H_t^{1-b}(\lambda_t Y_t)^b \tag{9.22b}$$

New human capital $(\Delta H_{t+1} \equiv H_{t+1} - H_t)$ is produced from a combination of human capital and output Y_t, with geometric weights $1 - b$ and $0 < b < 1$. Note that human capital can be employed in both the production of general output and human capital without restrictions, but only a fraction $0 < \lambda_t < 1$ of general output is employed in the education sector. This share of output resources employed in education (λ_t) is an endogenous parameter. The exogenous parameter ϕ is an index of the effectiveness of the education process; the polar case $\phi = 0$ brings us back essentially to SGM.

The National Income Accounting equation sums up the expenditures on consumption, physical capital accumulation, and in the education sector, and equates them to output:

$$Y_t = C_t + \Delta K_{t+1} + \lambda Y_t \tag{9.24}$$

Note that both physical and human capital are assumed not to depreciate at all (for simplicity). Furthermore, by log-linearizing and time-differentiating the production function (9.22a), the various growth rates are linked by $g_Y = \alpha g_K + (1 - \alpha)g_H$. Under the BGP, on which we focus, all key variables grow at the same rates, $g_Y = g_K = g_H = g$. At that state, the fraction of resources devoted to the education sector is also constant (λ).

The solution strategy here involves setting a ratio $k \equiv K_t/H_t$, which will be constant in the BGP. With this, rewrite the growth and the education equations as:

$$g = \sigma(\alpha k^{\alpha-1} - \rho), \tag{9.23'}$$

and

$$g_H = \phi \lambda^b k^\beta, \quad \beta \equiv ab, \tag{9.22b'}$$

where we have dropped the time-subscripts of the ratios (λ, k) and growth rates as they will be constant under the BGP, and where $g_H \equiv H_{t+1}/H_t$ is the growth rate of education. For the education equation, we have used the general output production function to substitute Y out.

Apart from the Euler equation that determines the consumption profile, there are three other sets of optimality conditions. One determines how much output to allocate to consumption and physical capital production, which are essentially of the same nature, and how much to devote to the education sector. Moving general output across sectors essentially implies moving physical capital, since human capital can be employed in both sectors fully (in a non-rivalrous way). Thus, agents will move general resources between sectors until the marginal returns obtainable from physical capital across them are equalized. Thus, the marginal product of physical capital is equalized across the two sectors, and that will essentially determine λ. To see the implications, insert (9.22a) into (9.22b) and differentiate with respect to K_t to get its marginal product in the educational sector. Then, equalize that with the standard MPK from (9.22a):

$$\alpha k_t^{\alpha-1} = p_t \phi \beta \lambda^b k_t^{\beta-1}$$

p_t is the relative price of human capital in terms of the general good. From this, we get in the steady state:

$$k^{\alpha-\beta} = p\phi\beta\lambda^b/\alpha \tag{9.25}$$

A second set of equations then determines how much physical and human capital agents will accumulate. The answer is, until their marginal products in the general output sector are equated to the opportunity cost of investment, the real interest rate (which is the return on a pound invested in financial markets):

$$r_t = \alpha k_t^{\alpha-1}$$
$$r_t = (1-\alpha)\lambda_t^b k_t^\alpha + \Delta p_{t+1}/p_t$$

An alternative to investing in physical capital is to use £1, buy $1/p_t$ of human capital, keep it for a period and sell it back into general output next period at price p_{t+1}. In this process, one will have gained the marginal product of human capital plus the capital gain—the last term on the right side. In the steady state, this is assumed to be zero, so, equating the last two equations by parts and eliminating the real interest rate, and noting that the relative price of education is constant in the BGP ($\Delta p = 0$), we get:

$$k = \alpha/((1-\alpha)\lambda^b) \tag{9.26}$$

Schematically, these conditions may be tabulated as follows. Let the two sectors be the general sector (output Y) and the educational sector (output E), with the marginal products of physical and human capital as shown in Table 9.4. The condition leading to (9.25) is the horizontal equality, the condition leading to (9.26) is the vertical one.

So, we have a system of four non-linear equations, (9.23', 9.22b', 9.25, and 9.26), in four unknowns, k, p, g($= g_H$), and λ. The price of education (p), however, only appears in (9.25), which we solve last for p—the system is said to be 'block recursive'. Combining (9.22b') with (9.26) we get:

$$g = \alpha\phi k^{\beta-1}/(1-\alpha)$$

Furthermore, (9.23') is rewritten as:

$$k = ((g+\sigma p)/(\sigma\alpha))^{-1/(1-\alpha)}$$

Table 9.4. Optimality conditions in a two-sector model

General sector	Education
$\partial Y/\partial K \rightarrow$	$\leftarrow$ (p) $\partial E/\partial K$
$\downarrow$	
r	
$\uparrow$	
$\partial Y/\partial H$ (+ 'capital gains' $\Delta p/p$)	$\partial E/\partial H$

Finally, combining the last two equations, we have the solution for growth:

$$g = \alpha\phi((g + \sigma\rho)/(\sigma\alpha)^{(1-\beta)/(1-\alpha)}/(1 - \alpha)$$

or

$$g(g/\sigma + \rho)^{-(1-\beta)/(1-\alpha)} = \alpha^{(\alpha-\beta)(1-\alpha)}\phi/(1 - \alpha)$$

The left side is a non-linear equation of g. The derivative with respect to g is proportional to $g/\sigma + \rho - A(g/\sigma)$, where $A \equiv (1 - \beta)/(1 - \alpha)$. Now, from definitions, $\beta \equiv ab < \alpha$, with $0 < b < 1$, so that $A > 1$, and the sign of the above expression is not clear. To sign it, we can reason as follows: real quantities including consumption will be growing at rate g in the BGP in this economy, while they will be discounted at rate ρ. For utility to converge, we require $\rho > g$. So, the above becomes $g/\sigma + \rho - A(g/\sigma) > g/\sigma[1 + \sigma - A](> 0)$, where the restriction in parentheses is satisfied when $A < 1 + \sigma$. Recall that σ is the rate of inter-temporal substitution, found by Hall (1988) and others to be lower than unity, perhaps as low as 0.1. So, we are happy to make the assumption above. This allows us then to conclude that the steady-state growth rate increases with the efficiency for the education sector (ϕ), while it falls with the rate of impatience (ρ) that works for current consumption and against capital accumulation. From $g = \alpha\phi k^{\beta-1}/(1 - \alpha)$, we can then solve for the equi-librium physical-human capital ratio; from $k = \alpha/((1 - \alpha)\lambda^b)$ we see that the fraction of output spent in education is inversely proportional to the abundance of physical capital in relation to human (less proportional resources will be spent in education in a capital-rich country, because that capital will be less productive there due to diminishing returns). Finally, from (9.25), we may solve for the relative price of education (p). But this relation is not easy to summarize intuitively.

Many variants of two-sector models are possible in general. Mulligan and Sala-i-Martin (1993) investigate the dynamics of general two-sector growth models and Eicher and Turnovsky (1999) do the same in an optimizing model. The snag in all of this is (once again!) the knife-edge conditions involved (note the exactly constant returns to scale applicable to the accumulable factors—K and H—in both production functions). The above two papers, particularly the one by Eicher and Turnovsky (1999) investigate their nature more fully.

9.6 Models of Endogenous Growth Based on Technological Innovation

A second generation of models took up the theme of technological innovation. In this family of models, the marginal product of capital does not show diminishing returns because of technological innovation and increasing sophistication. Advances in technology derive from (industrial) research and innovation, which is a purposeful activity, motivated by the profits from the marketing of the new industrial designs and blueprints. All models in this area analyse these issues. There are two notable strands in the literature, one that emphasizes the addition of new products and varieties as a manifestation of new technology ('horizontal innovation'), and the other the replacement of old products and processes by new ones ('vertical innovation'). Of course, the process of growth probably contains elements of both, but the two may be thought of as distinct conceptually. We present a model of each in turn.

9.6.1 Horizontal Innovation and Expanding Number of Products ('Product Variety')

New products or varieties of existing ones appear in the market all the time. This self-evident truism may be lost momentarily in our information-laden lives, but let us take a second to wonder how many of the new consumer electronics and gadgets (or 'gizmos') existed 10, 20, or 30 years ago (for those of us that can remember that far back, that is).[38] This is just an example; the principle applies to all areas of production.

One wave of models of endogenous growth (Romer, 1987, 1990, and others) has explored the idea that the 'A' in the production function is made up by ever more sophisticated goods emerging from ongoing technological progress and inventions. In this model, any new products add to the existing stock of products; each addition however embodies better technology than the previous ones. Hence, this process is called 'horizontal innovation', as the new inventions sit side by side with older ones. The researchers who make these new inventions can restrict access to these new products through patents. Thus, the new designs are potentially available to everybody to use simultaneously (they are 'non-rival') but access to them can be restricted in practice to those that pay for them (they are 'excludable'). So, though the marginal cost of using the designs is zero, once they have been discovered, the patent-holder can charge a price for it. Thus, the link between marginal cost and price is broken. The researcher (or research firm) that also produces the new design earns a monopoly profit, which is what motivates them to pay a research cost and invent the new design in the first place. To account for these interactions, these models assume that there is a monopolistically intermediate goods sector that researches, invents the new designs, and produces them, while a perfectly competitive final goods sector assembles all the intermediate (technological) goods into the final consumption good (which is not directly subject to innovation but uses the intermediates).

More formally, there is (a fixed number) I of perfectly competitive firms producing the final good by assembling intermediate goods. There are N_t intermediates, but their number is ever expanding with the addition of new varieties. Such intermediate goods are based on designs made by their inventors. These inventors establish the monopoly rights over the production of these designs (they establish them as patents) and begin their production as monopoly producers. In fact, their monopoly power is tempered by the fact that there are various other similar patents in existence. They are therefore monopolistically competitive and make monopolistic profits that allow them to make the expenditures required in order to make the inventions. (No inventions would be made under perfect competition, as there would be no profits to cover the costs of invention.)

---

[38] To add a little personal anecdote, I say that my parents grew up with radio, I grew up with TV, and my daughter is growing up with the computer. Surely this experience is typical of my generation.

Let the production function of the typical final-good producer $i \in [1, I]$ be:

$$Y_{it} = \sum_{j=0}^{N_t} X_{jit}^{\alpha}, \quad 0 < \alpha \le 1.$$

Y_i is final output production by firm i, X_{ji} is the quantity of intermediate good $j \in [1, N_t]$ used by i. To repeat, we make a distinction between a final output and consumption good Y, of which there are i producers, and the existence of the intermediate goods that are the only physical inputs to production—there is no physical capital or labour. The equation above aggregates the intermediates purchased by firm i into a single final good according to a Dixit-Stiglitz aggregator function as discussed in Chapter 3. The degree of substitutability of intermediates in the production of final good is given by α, so $1/\alpha$ is an index of the monopoly power enjoyed by the producer of each j. The polar case of $\alpha = 1$ implies infinite substitutability between individual goods, and no monopoly power: perfect competition.

There is a dual role of N_t in this model. First, the expansion of the number of products is what drives growth; with a constant quantity of each X_j (see below), it is easy to see that the growth rate of Y coincides with the growth rate of N. Secondly, intermediates range from the least sophisticated ($j = 1$) to the most sophisticated ($j = N_t$) so that N_t may be thought as an index of technology, as well.

Patents are permanent, but the physical intermediate goods last only one period (consumables). The price of the final good is unity (it is the numeraire, i.e. the unit of account), whereas the intermediates all have their own individual prices P_{jt} (they are each worth P_{jt} units of Y).

To solve the model, let us begin by asking, how much of each intermediate does the typical final good producer buy every period? Obviously up to the point where marginal cost (MC) equals marginal revenue (MR). We have

$$MC = P_{jt}$$

i.e the MC is equal to the price of each unit of intermediate purchased; and

$$MR = \alpha X_{jit}^{\alpha-1}$$

which is simply the marginal product of intermediate j, valued at 1, the price of the consumption good. Equating:

$$X_{jit} = (\alpha/P_{jt})^{1/(1-\alpha)}$$

Hence, the inventor-patent holder of product j and monopolistic producer of this good faces a demand curve which is the sum of the demands of all final producers i:

$$X_{jt} = \sum_i X_{jit} = I(\alpha/P_{jt})^{1/(1-\alpha)}$$

In a 'symmetric equilibrium', all final producers are identical; we limit ourselves to that situation as we are not interested in differences between firms. Furthermore, by an appropriate normalization of the number of final good firms ('unit mass') we need not worry about their number I any longer, and equate the quantities of a typical such firm to those in the aggregate. Profit within period t for each inventor j depends on the sales they s/he makes and the price s/he sets on them. In particular, inventors maximize period profits as follows (ignoring I):

$$\text{Max } _{Pjt}(P_{jt} - 1)X_{jt} = (P_{jt} - 1)(\alpha/P_{jt})^{1/(1-\alpha)}$$

Another assumption is that the marginal cost of manufacturing the intermediate good (after it has been invented) is 1; each takes up one unit of final good. Utilizing all the information, we find that the first-order condition is:

$$\alpha^{\frac{1}{1-\alpha}}P_{jt}^{-\frac{1}{1-\alpha}} - \frac{1}{1-\alpha}\alpha^{\frac{1}{1-\alpha}} P_{jt}^{-\frac{2-\alpha}{1-\alpha}}(P_t - 1) = 0$$

Simplifying, this gives optimal price as follows,

$$P_{jt} = \frac{1}{1-\alpha}(P_{jt} - 1) \Rightarrow P_{jt} = \frac{1}{\alpha}.$$

The noteworthy feature is that the intermediate good price is constant, and depends simply on the monopoly power enjoyed by the intermediate goods inventors, $1/\alpha$: a higher monopoly power implies a higher price, or higher markup over the unitary marginal cost. The demand for good j therefore is:

$$X_{jt} = \alpha^{2}/(1-\alpha)$$

In the limiting case of perfect competition we have $\alpha = 1$, in which case $P_j = 1$ (i.e. the price equals the marginal cost of the good after its invention) and $X_j = 1$. In monopolistic competition $(\alpha < 1)$, like all monopolists, the inventor sets a higher price and lower quantity than a perfectly competitive producer. Thus, there emerges a fundamental tension here: Monopoly power (by innovating firms) is good because the corresponding profits encourage innovation, but bad because it raises prices and reduces the produced quantities.

Hence, period t profits for inventor-producer j are:

$$(P_{jt} - 1)X_{jt} = \frac{1-\alpha}{\alpha}\alpha^{\frac{2}{1-\alpha}} = (1-\alpha)\alpha^{(1+\alpha)/(1-\alpha)}$$

The profits made over time are therefore:

$$V_o = \sum_{t=0}^{\infty} A(1+r)^{-(t+1)} = A/r, \qquad A \equiv (1-\alpha)\alpha^{\frac{1+\alpha}{1-\alpha}}$$

(A here is a symbol, not the productivity term at the beginning of this section.) It turns out that $dA/d\alpha < 0$ (most likely), so A is a modified index of monopoly power—it rises with it, together with intertemporal profits.

Next, we determine the number of inventors/intermediate producers. Research is assumed to be predictable. It yields a constant rate of inventions per unit of effort, so the cost of each invention is assumed to be C—a constant. Free entry of inventors is assumed, and this lowers intertemporal profits to the point where the cost of invention is just covered, leaving no net profit:

$$C = V_o = A/r,$$

Analytically, what this does is to effectively pin down the real interest rate, which is positively related to the (modified) index of monopoly power (A) and inversely to the cost of producing an invention. More intuitively, note that the real interest rate is an (inverse) index of an inventor's effective horizon. (Why? Because if r is higher, their future profits are more heavily discounted, so their effective horizon shortens. So, r may be thought of as the inverse length of the horizon required by an inventor in order to recoup their expenditures from inventing and break even.) The greater the monopoly power (higher A), the greater their profits every period, so the lower the required horizon (higher r). The greater the cost of invention C, the greater the necessary horizon (lower r).

What happens if by any chance the equality does not hold—say, if $A/r > C$? In that case, the monopolist's profits are greater than the sunk (research) costs required in order to start the business. More potential innovators will be attracted, with the result that the pace of technological innovation will be quickened and growth increased. From the Euler equation (below), for this to happen, the interest rate must increase. (We may think that the consumers will need to have an incentive to save and postpone consumption, which will also give space in the economy for more sunk costs C to be made.) So, r will rise to restore the equality.

We can then substitute this information on the real interest rate into the growth equation (9.17), to get:

$$g = \sigma(r - \rho) = \sigma(A/C - \rho).$$

So, the cost of research influences inversely the growth rate, but monopoly profits raise it. The rate of time preference (rate of impatience) reduces the growth rate, as is standard. This growth rate is the rate at which new designs are produced, i.e. $g = (N_{t+1} - N_t)/N_t$.

In conclusion, the model involves a number of assumptions, whose role is to describe in a stylized way the dynamics of invention and technological innovation. It works brilliantly. The rate of profit (A/C) determines the interest rate in this economy. The interest rate, in turn, determines (via the Euler equation) how many new products per period this economy wants. Monopolistic competition in the production of intermediate goods generates profits that are instrumental for research and development of new products, but at the same time implies that the price of such products is suboptimally high, their quantity suboptimally low (in comparison to perfect competition where pricing reflect marginal cost). A benevolent social planner would have chosen a price for individual intermediates equal to $P_j = 1$, i.e. the price obtained in perfect competition; the quantities X_j would also be higher. In other words, there is a static inefficiency (too few Xs and Y, i.e. the level of final output is too low). There is also a dynamic inefficiency (too little growth) in so far as the socially, as well as privately, productive activity of invention is borne entirely by private investors, and this lowers the rates of interest and growth. Appropriate subsidies to intermediate producers can rectify both inefficiencies, while subsidies to research will rectify the dynamic inefficiency but not the static one.

9.6.2 Vertical Innovation, Product Replacement, and 'Schumpeterian' Growth

Another strand of literature recognizes that new patents create new generations of goods/ processes that render obsolete and replace older vintages. Innovation here is 'vertical' in the sense that the new innovation completely supersedes the old. Vinyl discs were replaced by

CDs, which were replaced by MP3s, which were in turn eclipsed by smartphones. Thus, invention is a process of 'creative destruction', to use a phrase coined by the great Austrian economist Joseph Schumpeter: products (and sectors) become obsolete ('destruction') but new opportunities arise elsewhere ('creation'). The most often quoted modern references are Grossman and Helpman (1991a), and Aghion and Howitt (1992); see also Segerstrom et al. (1991) for another early paper, and Aghion and Howitt (1997)—virtually this entire book is devoted to the study of this approach. Here, we follow Aghion and Howitt (1992, 1997, chapter 2) to give an exposition of the basic model.

This approach uses a cost-benefit calculus similar to the horizontal-innovation model, taking into consideration the cost of innovation (research) and the benefit from the monopoly profits from exploiting the new invention. In doing so, it recognizes the probability that an improved idea will appear at some time, driving the patent-holder of the obsolete design out of business. This approach provides a richer framework to investigate further the role of product market structure and R&D, the technology of inventions and the role of patents, as well as the role of rent-seeking and scale effects.

As before, there is a final goods sector that employs the only existing intermediate good to produce the final, consumption good (recall, all other intermediates are obsolete and their production has ceased). The intermediate good is the subject of technological innovation, so its quality increases over time. Thus, the total good can be 'unbundled' into a quality component, to be indicated by A_t, and a quantity component, x_t.[39] The former component increases secularly (though at an irregular pace) with the technological innovations, whereas the latter is constant in the steady state. The production function of the consumption good is:

$$c_t = A_t x_t^\alpha$$

The quantity of intermediate good, x, is subject to a diminishing marginal product, as it is assumed implicitly to be worked by the same constant amount of labour; this is determined by the value of $0 < \alpha < 1$. But the quality (A) is not subject to a diminishing marginal product. With p_t being the relative price of the intermediate good in terms of the consumption good, the final good producer decides the quantity of the intermediate good to be employed (x) by maximizing profits:

$$\text{Max}(x_t) \qquad c_t - p_t x_t = A_t x_t^\alpha - p_t x_t$$

Straightforward maximization with respect to x yields the demand curve for the quantity of the intermediate good:

$$x_t = p_t^{-1/(1-\alpha)} (aA_t)^{1/(1-\alpha)}$$

The quantity of the intermediate good depends inversely on its price, but positively on its level of technology (as this increases its productivity). As before, the intermediate is a non-durable good that needs to be produced anew every period. (We may think of this as consumables or energy.)[40]

---

[39] Technology is said to be 'embodied', built into the newer-vintage good.

[40] Alternatively, at the cost of some extra complexity, we could assume that intermediates are durables that are produced only once, when the new successful researcher-monopolist starts business. But the main insights of the model do not change (see Aghion and Howitt, 1997, chapter 2).

There is a fixed amount of workers in this economy, who can provide a maximum flow of L hours of labour supply per period. This is allocated between the production of the intermediate good and research (the final good requires no labour). The production of the intermediate good is a very simple one, requiring one hour of work per unit of x, so that x_t also indicates the labour hours spent in the production of the intermediates—let us call this 'industry'. The other portion of labour is spent in research—the amount of hours here is denoted by n_t so that we have:

$$L = x_t + n_t$$

This is a condition for the labour market to clear.

The workers will pursue the activity (industry or research) that yields the greater return (real wage). In doing so, they bring about equality of the two returns. This requires us to specify the return from research. Research does not pay any wage, strictly speaking, but enables the researcher to exploit the new invention, if and when they make it, to produce the next generation of intermediate goods. In other words, by establishing the invention to their name by way of a patent, the lucky researcher becomes the new monopoly producer of the intermediate good—until this is superseded by the next invention. Thus, the model proceeds here by incorporating insights form the literature on patents and technological races (see Aghion and Howitt, 1997, chapter 2).

'Hitting' a new invention is an irregular, random process. The model postulates that if you work for a unit of time in research (say: an hour), you have a probability $0 < \lambda < 1$ of making a new invention. The technology embodied in the latest invention is simply A_t. The new invention is an improvement on previous technology, and is in turn freely available to all potential researchers to improve upon.[41] If you are successful in research and establish a patent, you begin production as a monopoly producer of the intermediate good next period and you get the present value of the profits from its production until superseded by a better product. Let us indicate this present value of profits as V_t. A researcher has a probability λ of making an invention and getting monopoly profits from the commercial exploitation of the patent; and probability $1 - \lambda$ of working in vain (getting nothing). Therefore, in expected terms, the return from research is λV_t.

On the other hand, a worker in industry gets the wage rate, w_t. Labour mobility between sectors (industry or research-invention-production) results in equalization of the respective returns:

$$w_t = \lambda V_t$$

Furthermore, the present value of profits from monopoly production of the intermediate good is the discounted sum:

$$V_t = \sum_{s=1}^{\infty} \pi_{t+s}(1 + r + n\lambda)^{-s}$$

---

[41] The technology embodied in the latest research is available to all researchers to improve upon, but it is only available to the patent-holder for commercial production. Thus, technology is 'non-rivalrous' (the idea or knowledge can be used by many people simultaneously—see Jones, 2005) but 'excludable' (its commercial use is restricted).

The period profits (π_{t+s}) are discounted by the real interest rate (assumed constant for the moment) and the probability of a better product arising during the period, in which case the monopoly position is lost.[42] This probability is the product of the probability of a new invention arriving out of an hour of research (λ) times the amount of hours in research per period (number of researchers—n—that is also assumed constant). Both the constancy of the real interest rate (r) and amount of hours in research will be guaranteed in the steady state and BGP, upon which we shall focus. The monopolist producer's profits come from their sales according to their demand curve:

$$\pi_t = p_t x_t - w_t x_t = \alpha A_t x_t^\alpha - w_t x_t$$

(This comes from rearranging the demand curve to get $p_t = x_t^{-(1-\alpha)} \alpha A_t$.) Maximizing with respect to x (sales of the intermediate good), the monopolist sells an amount:

$$x_t = \left(\alpha^2 A_t / w_t\right)^{1/(1-\alpha)}$$

Obviously, sales are higher the higher is the marginal product of this intermediate (a higher α), the higher is productivity (which fuels the demand by the final producer), and the lower is the wage of the workers who are employed in its production. Note also that, because of the very simple production function of intermediates (they only require labour one-for-one), this also gives the amount of labour demand from industry. The resulting profits are:

$$\pi_t = \alpha A_t x_t^\alpha - w_t x_t = A_t (w_t/A_t)^{-\alpha/(1-\alpha)} A, \qquad A \equiv (1-\alpha)\alpha^{2/(1-\alpha)}$$

Profits increase with the state of technology but fall with the productivity-adjusted real wage ($\omega \equiv w/A$). Inserting into the present value of profits and focusing on the steady state (where r and n in particular are constant), we obtain:

$$V_t = \frac{1 + r + n\lambda}{r + n\lambda} A_t (\omega_t)^{-\alpha/(1-\alpha)} A$$

The equality of returns in the two activities (industry-research) can then be expressed as:

$$\omega^{1/(1-\alpha)} = A\lambda \frac{1 + r + n\lambda}{r + n\lambda} \tag{9.27}$$

Equation (9.27) in the productivity-adjusted real wage (ω) and the hour of work in industry (n) form the first of two key equations in this model. To recap, this embodies the expected rate of return from invention and its equality with the wage.

The other equation is the labour marketing clearing condition ($L = x + n$), which, from the demand for intermediates and associated labour, is:

$$L = \left(\omega/\alpha^2\right)^{-1/(1-\alpha)} + n \tag{9.28}$$

---

[42] That the probability of obsolescence effectively augments the discount rate is a standard result that we have seen in various contexts. For example, in Chapter 3, when discussing price adjustment by firms and inflation, we argued that the probability that a currently set price is changed makes a firm consider more the costs of deviation of actual price from optimal in the near future, and less so those of the far future. In discussing the equilibrium, flow approach to unemployment in Chapter 4, the probability of losing a job reduces the worker's (present) value derived from that job. A common theme in all cases is that the probability of obsolescence makes us more focused on the short term than without it. It effectively reduces the planning horizon.

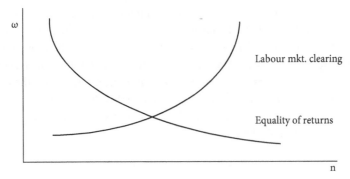

Figure 9.8. Real wage in industry and intensity of research in vertical innovation

Equations (9.27) and (9.28) are graphed in Figure 9.8 in (ω, n) space. Note that, for the moment, we are taking the real interest rate as exogenous. This assumption will be relaxed below. The 'equality of returns' condition (9.27) implies a negative relation between ω and n; the intuition is that, as work in research (n) increases, the probability of new inventions also increases, and this means that profits from production of the intermediate good will be reduced as it is likely to become obsolete sooner. Because of equality of returns across the two sectors, the lower monopoly benefits from research also imply a lower rate of pay economy-wide—in industry, too. In contrast, the 'labour market clearing' condition (9.28) implies a positive relation between ω and n: a higher real wage reduces industry and attracts more people in research.

With the help of the graph, we are able now to derive a few intermediate results, namely on the effects of the probability (or effectiveness) of research (λ), the real interest rate (r), the monopoly power of the intermediate goods producer, and the size, or scale, of the economy (L). The first of these is the most interesting. λ has two key effects. More successful research increases the effective pay from research *ceteris paribus*—you are more likely to become a monopolist with an invention. At the same time, it also increases the probability that a replacement will arrive and the monopoly profit will be lost sooner. In fact, the first effect dominates, so that the reward in both research and industry rises— the 'pay equality' curve (9.27) shifts up, and equilibrium pay and hours in industry rise. A rise in the real interest rate is simpler—it discounts future monopoly profits more heavily so that the present value of the monopolist (V) declines, and rates of pay both decrease— (9.27) shifts down, and there is a lower wage, more hours in industry, and less intensive research. Furthermore, the intermediate goods producer faces an elasticity in the demand for their product that increases (in absolute value) with α, the elasticity of the intermediate good in the final goods production. Now, a greater elasticity of demand weakens the monopoly power of the intermediate goods producer and their profits. Hence, the value of research drops. This works its way through various channels here, but the result is unambiguous: the intensity of research (n) drops. Monopoly power is unambiguously good for research activity (and growth) in this basic model. Finally, an increase in the (population) size of the economy (L) means that there is more labour supply available, so both sectors potentially see an influx of hours. Given the real wage, this increases n and shifts the labour market clearing locus (9.28) right. There are more hours in research, but the more intensive research implies a greater rate of obsolescence and less value in research, hence a lower wage in industry too. As will be seen later, a more intensive research effort will increase the rate of growth in the economy: This is another manifestation of the scale effects issue that was discussed above. It is due to the non-rivalrous nature of research. Any advancement will be made available to all researchers who can potentially improve on that. Hence, more labour in research implies a higher rate of inventions and growth.

Our next task is to relate this discussion to the economy-wide growth rate. Note that the probability of innovation per period is $n\lambda$, the probability of innovation per hour times the flow of hours of research in the period. As it turns out, the probability of innovation $n\lambda$ also gives the average amount of innovations during the period.[43] If each new innovation is assumed to improve the technology embodied in the previous one by a fixed factor γ (%), then technology shows an expected growth rate of $g = n\lambda\gamma$ per period—the expected amount of innovations times the fixed size of each. Since in the steady state the amount of hours in industry (and therefore the size of the intermediate good—x) is given, from the production function of the final good, that good grows in the steady state at the same rate as technology A_t.

Thus, both technology A_t and the real final good (c_t) both grow at an expected rate of $g = n\lambda\gamma$ each period. In principle, we can use (9.27) and (9.28) to get a closed-form solution of n (and ω) but their non-linear nature forbids that. Instead, we use them to substitute ω out, to get:

$$g = \lambda\gamma\left(L - \frac{\alpha^2(r+n\lambda)}{A\lambda(1+r+n\lambda)}\right) \tag{9.29}$$

We shall use (9.29) as an equation relating g and r, keeping in mind the results shown in Figure 9.8 and the associated discussion about n. The growth rate increases with the probability of success in research (λ) for two reasons now, both because that directly increases expected growth, and because more labour flows into research.

Time now to relax the assumption of an exogenous real interest rate; analytically, this is done by linking it to growth via the growth equation (9.17). Setting $\sigma = 1$ (log utility) for simplicity (the model is complex enough), we have:

$$g = r - \rho \tag{9.30}$$

Equations (9.29) and (9.30) in g and r are graphed in Figure 9.9. The former (termed the 'research equation') shows the growth rate to decrease with the real interest rate (because that reduces the present value of monopoly profits, the wage in industry, and the intensity of research), while the 'growth equation' (9.30) relates the two positively.

The probability of success in research (λ) increases the growth rate, therefore it shifts the 'research equation' up. The result is both higher growth and real interest rates. Monopoly profits, that are good for research, will also have the same effect. Finally, the rate of time preference will provide an incentive for consumers to consume now rather than wait—the 'growth equation' shifts right/down, yielding a higher real interest rate but lower growth. It may be useful to think of all these effects on the real interest rate as coming via the supply

---

[43] Formally, the number of new 'arrivals' of innovations is governed by a Poisson density function, whose mean is simply $n\lambda$ (for a unit-long period of time).

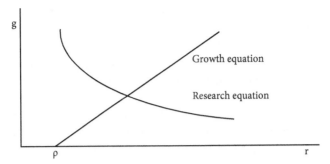

Figure 9.9. The growth and real interest rates in vertical innovation

and demand for financial funds. When the consumer decides not to consume now and saves instead, the supply of funds (in the form of financial assets) increases. The demand by intermediate goods firms to set up business and produce gives the demand in the funds market (implicitly: for loans). Hence, more success in research and a greater monopoly power imply more business and demand for funds; they both increase the real rate. On the other hand, a more impatient and less saving-prone consumer reduces the supply of such funds, with a similar effect on their price.

Thus, with a degree of manageable complexity, the model succeeds in capturing the macroeconomics of technological innovation and growth under vertical innovation and Schumpeterian 'creative destruction'. Of course, as Solow (1994) reminds us, technological innovation cannot fit neatly into a formal model: there is too much uncertainty and unpredictability. At the end of the day, it also depends on science and engineering, not just economics. That probably means that we cannot use the model to predict (say) how the IT revolution and AI (Artificial Intelligence) are going to develop in the future. But we can use the model to shed light on some important aspects of the dynamics of market economies.

Nordhaus (2004) has undertaken an empirical investigation of the effects of innovation on profits and the wider economy: he found that the profits of innovators were 2.2 per cent of the total benefits generated by innovation. The (startling) remaining 97.8 per cent was passed on to the consumer in the form of lower prices, more quantities, more variety, and better quality. See also Jones and Williams (1998) on the measurement of the social returns to R&D.

9.6.3 Evidence on EGT

Reflecting the process of growth itself, growth theory is also multi-faceted. The empirical work that attempts to quantify and test the various sub-processes and factors that give rise to the totality of growth has therefore highlighted a large range of determinants; Temple (1999) and Durlauf et al. (2005) mention about 150 variables that have been used as regressors. A problem however that was noticed early by Levine and Renelt (1992) was that cross-country growth regressions were 'fragile': with a small change in the specification, e.g. adding or changing one regressor, rather radical changes ensued, e.g. the sign of coefficients changed or one or more coefficients might turn from significant to insignificant. This inspired little confidence in the estimates.

The way forward was to investigate 'robustness', i.e. the survival of coefficients when the specification of a growth regression changed many times. Brushing a lot of the details under the carpet, the main idea is the following. Imagine that we are testing the relevance of N regressors as determinants of growth. Perhaps there are $M < N$ variables that are treated as standard ('core') explanatory variables that are included in every single regression (in addition to a constant). Of the rest $N - M$ variables, one (at a time and each in turn) becomes the variable of interest; of the remaining $N - M - 1$ variables, three are selected to enter as regressors; the rest $(N - M - 1 - 3)$ are discarded. The regression is then repeated as before, the only difference being that a different triad of variables is selected; and again with a different triad, until all the possible triad-combinations of the $N - M - 1$ variables have entered as regressors (in separate regressions). The variable of interest is then deemed to be 'robust' if it is significant with the same (and presumably theory-consistent) sign 'most' (often, 95 per cent) of the time. Following this methodology, Levine and Renelt (1992) highlighted the following robust determinants: Initial income (negatively—indicating convergence), investment share, educational variable (often: secondary school enrolment), and rate of population growth. These are essentially the variables suggested by the Solow model; their importance has recently been reaffirmed by Durlauf et al. (2008) who term them the 'neoclassical theory'.

Obviously, this methodology involves large computational power ('I just ran two million regressions', proclaimed one of the pioneers of the method, Sala-i-Martin, 1997), something not available before the mid- or late 1990s. Among the 50 or so variables that this study considers as regressors, 22 are 'robust'. Those include geographical (see Sachs, 2003), political (Papaioannou and Siourounis, 2008), cultural (religion) and historical (colonial status) variables; the only ones that can be interpreted as related to policy are equipment and non-equipment investment (following the suggestion of De Long and Summers, 1991—though the coefficient of the latter is about one-fourth the coefficient of the former), the rule of law, openness to trade, and a floating exchange-rate policy. Again, the significance of investment is more in line with the Solow model that emphasizes capital accumulation, rather than EGT that de-emphasizes 'capital fundamentalism', as discussed.

We have already discussed the findings of Jones (1995a, 2016), which are worth recalling; he points out that investment rates have trended upwards in many OECD countries, with no corresponding increase in growth rates, which have actually remained fairly stable over long periods of time at least in the US. In addition to casting a sceptical note on the role of investment, this finding casts a sceptical note on policy in general, as policies have changed over the same time period and country sample in which growth appears largely constant. Hence, such a finding may be interpreted as a 'Policy Ineffectiveness Result', the sixth (and last) among those we listed in Chapter 1.

In their review of robustness studies, Durlauf et al. (2008, section 4.1) find that the robust growth theories include the four 'neoclassical' variables of the Solow model (see above), macroeconomic policy, and religion. With regards to macroeconomic policy, government consumption (indicating a bigger government, therefore taxation), and inflation (indicating financial instability) are harmful for growth. With respect to religion, there has been an age-old controversy; an oft-repeated argument is that Protestantism has been in line with the 'spirit of capitalism' as it emphasizes the individual's contribution to their own salvation via personal effort. Echoing Sala-i-Martin's (1997) findings, Durlauf et al. (2008) found that Eastern religion (Buddhism and Comfucianism) had a positive correlation with growth while the incidence of Protestantism had a negative one. With respect to institutions, their results are consistent with the idea that good institutions influence growth through the promotion of better macroeconomic policies; nevertheless, the evidence on direct importance of institutions to growth is fragile. A partial summary of these findings might be that many of the determinants of growth according to EGT, particularly measures of R&D and innovation, do not feature robustly in empirical work.

As concluding thoughts, and as Durlauf et al. (2008) emphasize, empirical work on growth is hampered by the fact that the theory of growth is open-ended in the sense that none of the models precludes any of the others from being valid. In other words, the models are complementary rather than mutually exclusive. As a result, empirical work is only vaguely guided by theoretical models and almost never tests for a specific model against well-specified alternatives. If so, then this poses a problem for empirical work in the sense that the researcher cannot specify well-defined alternatives, and that in any estimation there are bound to be missing relevant variables, with all the problems that that might imply about the validity of the estimators. In defence of this work, it must be pointed out that all this is in line with empirical work elsewhere in macroeconomics and it may be the consequence of theory having developed so much that there are connections and overlaps between all the various models. Hence, far from discrediting the empirical work, these observations suggest that we must interpret the findings with some caution. No result is as watertight as we would like it to be.

Equally, it is conceivable that the elusive robustness of some possible determinants may not truly reflect insignificance, but rather our inability to estimate precisely their effects. The 'prime suspect' here is human capital, whose surely important contribution to growth is often hard to pin down. The reader should consult Krueger and Lindahl (2001), Galor and Moav (2006), Barro and Lee (2013), and Manuelli and Seshadri (2014) for recent work on the role of education and human capital in growth.

9.6.4 Policy Implications of EGT

We finish this section with the policy implications of growth theories in general, including Endogenous Growth Theories. At the most general level, the growth theories we have reviewed here (Solow and EGT) are all supply-side based; so there is no scope in them for aggregate demand (AD) policies. As emphasized throughout this book, AD policies are a tool for short-run macroeconomic management; for long-run growth, for prosperity to rise over decades and generations, supply-side policies are called for, on which we elaborate below.

Before that, let us spell out one concrete policy implication of the Solow model:[44] This model emphasizes the importance of saving and investment (which in a closed economy are identical); and we saw that the saving rate is one among the few robustly significant determinants of growth in growth regressions. As we shall see in Chapter 11, there is some cause for concern in this respect, in the sense that the saving rates have been dropping in recent years in advanced industrialized economies. Therefore, one important policy

---

[44] The model also emphasizes the relevance of the population growth rate, on which China's former one-child policy was (possibly) based; but we would not call this aspect of the model a concrete guidance for policy.

recommendation stemming from the SGM is to enhance the saving and investment rates; this objective is to be achieved by appropriately tailored tax reductions and subsidies on saving (like tax-free deposits, incentives for entering saving and pension plans, etc.) and investment (like tax exemptions on profits that are invested, subsidies, etc.). Against all this, it should be remembered that the 'paradox of thrift' warns us that the effects of saving may not be the ones planned, if a rise in saving reduces spending and GDP; more generally, there may be a 'dilemma of saving': more consumer spending is required in the short run, while more saving is called for in order for longer run growth to be promoted.

Finally, in view of the importance of investment, in open economies, policy-makers are often keen to encourage foreign direct investment (FDI)—investment by foreign businesses—which, apart from alleviating domestic capital shortages, may also bring in foreign technology, know-how ('ideas', see Jones, 2005), and ability to access international markets. Hence, as mentioned in the Guidance for Further Study of Chapter 11, FDI has attracted considerable attention among policy-makers (even if not so much among researchers). The empirical analysis of FDI encounters the same problems as the deter-minants of growth, namely the (non-)robustness of many of its determinants. It is also possible that two-way causality exists between growth and FDI.

Turning now to EGT, the BGP growth rate is given by the Euler equation:

$$g = \sigma(F_k - \delta - \rho)$$

where F_K is the marginal product of capital (on which see the Guidance for Further Study). As mentioned, much of EGT analyses the reasons why this marginal product of capital does not fall to zero (or too low) as output rises, so growth is perpetual. These include all the factors that enhance the productivity of capital (technology, research and development; education and human capital; organization, governance, and institutions; productive public services), so the government's role is to enhance all these. Let us comment briefly on each.

Technology should be promoted by granting of patents for commercial exploitation, tax exemptions, and subsidies on R&D. The importance of respecting patents and broader 'property rights' will be discussed below. We reviewed some evidence that R&D activity is seriously sub-optimal, therefore there is scope for government policy to reduce the 'ideas gap' by supporting innovation and technology transfer (often facilitated by FDI). By all accounts, education is a key process underpinning growth, yet (as we saw) the empirical evidence remains rather elusive; the quest for an efficient educational system (funding, structure, content) continues, considering its contribution to growth education but also the fact that education is a wider social good.

Externalities and 'spillovers' are important for growth, including 'learning-by-doing' externalities and technological spillovers. We saw that, to the extent that such positive externalities exist, the growth rate generated by a market system will be sub-optimal, and there is an important role for government policy to promote growth via tax policy and subsidies; e.g. to support education and technological innovation that are the main processes that generate externalities. Conversely, there is a role for government to correct negative externalities by taxation (called 'Pigouvian taxation').

Important externalities are of course related to the environment, gaining increasing attention at the time of global warming and climate change; see Sachs and Warner (1997, 1999) for an analysis of the importance of natural resources and environmental factors. More broadly, the limits imposed on growth by the environment and a finite planet are as yet unclear; but it is clear that all conventional inputs (carbon fuel, fresh water) are being depleted, while all outputs (greenhouse gases, plastic) are in over-supply (to put it politely). Some commentators (mainly non-economists) advocate 'de-growth', scaling growth down or even getting it to negative rates, so to as to limit its environmental consequences. This author is sceptical about 'de-growth', essentially because of its social repercussions; but that is a story for another day. What is clear is that the quest for 'sustainable growth', growth that respects the 'budget constraints' that mothers earth and nature place upon us, continues.

Furthermore, growth is underpinned by efficient institutions, good governance, rule of law, and respect of property rights, so that individual entrepreneurs reap the benefits of their efforts and innovations. Apart from their value as attributes of the good society, these features are crucial for growth as their absence reduces the incentive to produce. Just imagine a society in which a business person or innovator sees the fruit of their efforts squandered by crime, corruption, or simply illegal copying. In line with tendencies in other social sciences, economics has paid increasing attention in the last 20 years on institutions, giving rise to the field of 'institutional economics'. Following that, an expanding literature has explored the relevance of 'institutions' for growth. What may be relevant here is a vast array of concepts, to include the 'rules of the game' such as laws and constitutions, democracy and political regimes, policies and regulation, market structure (such as the labour market which we analysed in Chapter 4), organizational structures in businesses and the public sector, norms of behaviour (including corruption, tax evasion, crime), and actors within these structures such as governments, businesses (again), trade unions, even political parties. The bewildering range of concepts involved here makes one wonder whether an umbrella concept such as 'institutions' can be useful at all. In any case, review of this literature is beyond our scope; the interested reader is directed to Sokoloff and Engerman (2000); Persson and Tabellini (2003); Glaeser et al. (2004); Rodrik et al. (2004); and Robinson et al. (2005) in the first instance, with the reminder that there is a lot more before and after these contributions. Crafts (1996b) and Li (2001) further discuss the policy implications of EGT and technological progress.

9.6.5 Productive Public Services, the Size of 'Government', and Growth

Finally, we turn attention to the role of productive public services that are one of the reasons why the marginal product of capital is supported at a permanently high level. Such services (education, health, but also administration, police and justice, provision of infra-structure) underpin many of the effects discussed above, such as human capital and externalities, rule of law, and property rights. The downside is that such service provision must be financed by taxation, which reduces the net return to capital and the rate of growth (Rebelo, 1991). Hence, there are two effects of a greater public sector ('government'), a productivity-enhancing effect (through service provision) and a return-reducing effect (through the necessary taxation). The balance of these effects gives a hump-shaped curve of growth against the size of government; this analysis, originally due to Barro (1990), suggests that there is a well-defined size of 'government' that maximizes growth. The model is not difficult to sketch formally; it follows the growth equations (9.18a, b), where the external effect is produced by public services.

Production is described by equation (9.18'), briefly redeveloped here. Original production is: $Y_t = K_t^\alpha (A_t L_t)^{1-\alpha}$, where labour-augmenting productivity (A_t) is underpinned by productive public services; those are proportional to output with the factor of proportionality being a constant, flat rate of tax ($\tau > 0$) that is applied homogeneously to all sources of income. Therefore: $A_t = AG_t = A\tau Y_t$.

This gives rise to (9.18'), which with fixed labour ($L = 1$) takes the form:

$$Y_t = (A\tau Y_t)^{1-\alpha} K_t^\alpha = (A\tau)^{(1-\alpha)/\alpha} K_t \tag{9.18''}$$

The net-of-tax (private) marginal product of capital equals: $(1 - \tau)\alpha A\tau^{(1-\alpha)/\alpha}$. Hence, growth (9.20) becomes:

$$g = \sigma((1 - \tau)\alpha A\tau^{(1-\alpha)/\alpha} - \rho - \delta) \tag{9.20'}$$

Maximization of g subject to τ yields the first-order condition:

$$dg/d\tau = -\sigma\alpha A\tau^{(1-\alpha)/\alpha} + \sigma(1 - \tau)(1 - \alpha)A\tau^{(1-\alpha)/\alpha - 1} = 0$$

The first term on the right is the negative private return-reducing effect of taxation, while the second one is the productivity-enhancing effect of public services. At the optimum, these two marginal effects are equal, yielding the following:

$$\tau^* = 1 - \alpha$$

In this strikingly simple and equally intuitive result, the optimal tax rate (τ^*—here acting as a proxy for the overall size of the public sector in GDP) should be equal to the contribution that public services make in production; recall that they underpin the labour-augmenting productivity, hence their elasticity in production is $0 < 1 - \alpha < 1$. In other words, the government should command as many resources as the importance of its services in supporting productivity. Both Barro (1990) and a sizeable follow-up literature have been busy exploring under what circumstances such a tax rate will also be welfare-maximizing as well as growth-maximizing. The significance of Barro's insight and these results is dual, both normative and positive. In normative analysis, these results can inform us about the optimal size of the government sector, a question of great importance in the public discourse and politics, about which an answer remains elusive. For this, one needs estimates of the elasticity of public services in production (here, $1 - \alpha$). Unfortunately, this analysis has not been pursued much (but see Tsoukis and Miller, 2003, for a start). Positive analysis could help shed light on the fact that the public sector has risen over much of the twentieth century. Various political-economy explanations have been offered for this development but without having nailed the issue conclusively. Assuming that it became gradually understood that public services are productive but not in an immediately obvious way, this may have generated a tendency for the government size to rise; but again, this line of investigation has not been taken up.

Finally, the public sector is also a key provider of infrastructure (related to transport, power, telecoms, utilities) through public capital. In contrast to public services, which is a flow variable, public capital is a stock variable that gets accumulated over time; its analysis requires a simple extension of the above framework. For an analysis of the growth effects of public capital, the interested reader is directed to Demetriades and Mamuneas (2000); they find that such infrastructure provision by government has a beneficial effect on output, employment, and even crowding-in private capital, the more so in the long run than in the short run.

Notes on the Literature

A vast area, growth theory is well summarized in a few contributions: Barro and Sala-i-Martin (1995) remains a very good, single-volume introduction to the field. Aghion and Howitt (1997) is equally impressive (and more expansive), invaluable as a portal into the industrial organization-end of the field (innovations, R&D, patents, etc.). Their more recent text (Aghion and Howitt, 2008) offers an all-round coverage with good policy discussions. The textbook by Weil (2012) de-emphasizes the analytics in favour of the wider issues such as population, human capital, and geography (among others) that are interconnected with growth. In an in-depth way, the two-volume *Handbook of Economic Growth* (vols. 1A and 1B) edited by Aghion and Durlauf (2005) summarizes much of the state-of-the-art of the subject, drawing on the immense amount of theoretical and empirical work that had taken place in the preceding 30 years. The second part of the same collection (Aghion and Durlauf, 2014) widens the scope by connecting growth to demographics, institutions, geography, and many other issues, as well as reviewing more recent work. The collection by Durlauf and Blume (2010), part of the Palgrave Dictionary of Economics series, gives useful and succinct overviews of many topics in growth theory. Finally, (some of) the pioneers deserve a special mention: Romer (1986, 1987, 1990), for which he got the Nobel Prize in Economics in 2018, Grossman and Helpman (1991a), and Aghion and Howitt (1992).

Guidance for Further Study

The 'headwinds' and 'secular stagnation'

Macroeconomist and economic historian Robert Gordon (2010, 2016) has put forward a powerful proposition, based on history and long and carefully constructed data, that growth in per capita GDP in the foreseeable future will not be as high as in the past; in fact, it is forecasted to be at historically low levels. In effect, the golden age of growth is over. This is because, the major technological breakthroughs (the steam engine of the industrial revolution, the internal combustion engine and electrification at the turn of the twentieth century, and computers and information technology at the end of it) have all run their basic courses; well, diminishing returns will set in at some stage. The effects of slowing technological progress will be reinforced by a set of 'headwinds': rising inequality, steady-state in education levels, an ageing population. To this, one must surely add the constraints that the environment will place on economic activity and the effects of structural change (information technology and automation, financialization).

A parallel thesis is that of 'secular stagnation', advanced in the inter-war years by the (Keynesian) economist Alvin Hansen and revived recently by Lawrence Summers (e.g. Summers, 2018). This proposition holds that, left to its own devices, the private economy may not find its way back to full employment following a sharp contraction, such as the 2007–9 crisis and its aftermath (the 'Great Recession'). Active macroeconomic policy, particularly fiscal policy, is essential in order for growth to be restored; as we saw in Chapter 8, Summers and Brad DeLong have made a powerful argument that a big fiscal expansion is called for, with spending on infrastructure in particular, and this could pay for itself. The reasons that have led Summers and others to argue that secular stagnation is looming is the experience post-2009, with sluggish growth despite the low interest rates and quantitative easing, and high public deficits and debts. Add to all that the 'headwinds', and the picture is not rosy. The Eurozone experience, whatever the ultimate causes, surely does not offer grounds for optimism. See also what Charles Jones, one of the top growth researchers, has to say on the issue in Jones and Fernald (2014).

An additional reason for concern is inequality; this implies that there is a savings glut worldwide. (As we discuss in Chapter 10, high incomes have a higher propensity to be saved, and the rising inequality creates many very large incomes.) This creates a shortfall of investment in relation to saving, and this reduces output to a low level. In theory, the interest rate can always drop to equalize saving and investment; but with interest rates close to the 'zero lower bound', this is not possible. In other words, we have a situation here reminiscent of Keynes's 'liquidity trap', who also advocated (let us remember) fiscal policy. In fact, as many Keynesians, old (Keynes, James Tobin) and modern (including Summers) have emphasized, wage and price flexibility may well exacerbate the problem. The more flexible wages and prices are, the more they will be expected to fall during an output slowdown, leading to an increase in real interest rates. Indeed, there is the possibility of destabilizing deflation, with falling prices leading to higher real interest rates leading to greater output shortfalls leading to more rapidly falling prices and onwards in a vicious circle. Secular stagnation is a powerful and intuitive thesis but only time will tell how true it is. Of course, it is possible that policy could change (as the thesis itself proposes) so as to avert the gloomy scenario; if so, the thesis may be true but its forecast will turn out to be wrong. For more discussion, see the recent e-book edited by Teulings and Baldwin (2014) with contributions from many leading commentators.

Finance and growth

The size of the financial sector has grown inexorably over recent decades, a process known as 'financialization' (see Chapter 11). The relationship between finance and growth has sparked a long-standing debate. On the one side, there is a powerful argument that financial development and the depth of the financial system promotes growth. The main mechanisms may be that the financial system pools scattered savings; facilitates transactions and exchange; collects and processes information about the quality of investment projects and thereby achieves an efficient capital allocation; and enforces the implementation of contracts by monitoring the delivery of the projects. On the other hand, there are equally powerful critical voices of finance. One argument is that an oversized financial system tends to create volatility (Loayza and Ranciere, 2006). This thesis received big support with the banking crisis and recession of 2007–9, when the complexity of the system and the lack of transparency of financial instruments suddenly became obvious. No one could see exactly how these worked and what would be a fair price for them. An obscure system cannot possibly promote efficiency. Furthermore, an oversized financial system may become simply a rent-seeking mechanism (Zingales, 2015). Another powerful criticism pursued by Tobin (1984) is that a well-developed financial system drains the rest of the economy of its human capital as it draws the best talent through the high rewards it offers. Continuing the same argument, one may argue that developed finance diverts resources away from purely productive uses. For instance, housing bubbles may be created that raise the cost of living and prices and reduce the economy's competitiveness. Also, with the cost of land going up, land use may be diverted away from agricultural or manufacturing use to commercial use (shopping areas, luxury housing). The net effect is again the diversion of resources away from production. At the extreme, there can be purely speculative and harmful finance. To stem these effects, Tobin (1984) proposed the introduction of a financial transactions tax (the 'Tobin' tax) aimed at limiting the incentives to use financial instruments for pure speculative purposes.

A voluminous modern literature has undertaken to assess empirically the effect of finance on growth. Among the first in this literature was King and Levine (1993), which showed that the size of the financial sector was a good predictor of key measures of economic performance: economic growth, investment, and productivity growth, even after controlling for the key determinants of growth such as those suggested by the Solow model and similar variables. Various follow-up studies (including Levine and Zervos, 1998; Levine et al., 2000) also suggested a positive effect of financial development (as measured e.g. by the amount of credit in an economy over GDP) on growth. For a while, this appeared a well-established conclusion.

More recent studies, however, critically revisit this thesis (Arcand et al., 2015; Cecchetti and Kharroubi, 2015), finding that the relation is not linear. While there is a positive correlation for 'reasonable' levels of financial development, when this becomes 'excessive' (in the sense that credit to the private sector is more than 100 per cent of GDP—the exact threshold varies between estimations) the correlation becomes negative. At that point, further financial development hinders growth. Thus, no doubt spurred on by the 2007–9 crisis, the idea is getting established that there is a level of financial development which may be considered optimal, beyond which we may say that we have 'too much finance'. See Panizza (2017) for a review of this debate and Levine (2005) for the econometrics associated with it, particularly of the earlier phase which unambiguously found a positive effect of finance on growth.

De-industrialization

We have mentioned above that 'industry' (= manufacturing, energy, and mining) has declined in recent decades in terms of both employment and output shares. Rodrik (2016) shows that the phenomenon goes considerably beyond the advanced, post-industrial economies and encompasses countries that embarked on industrialization and development late. In fact, such countries are running out of industrialization opportunities sooner and at much lower levels of income compared to the experience of early industrializers. Rodrik (2016) shows that globalization and labour-saving technological progress in manufacturing have been behind these developments. See Nickell et al. (2008) for further evidence on de-industrialization among OECD economies. But although de-industrialization may be an inevitable consequence of technical progress and structural change, concerns have arisen about its consequences. Commentators have asked whether de-industrialization may be related to unemployment (Kollmeyer and Pichler, 2013), external imbalances such as balance-of-payments deficits (Rowthorn and Coutts, 2004), or whether it will hamper international convergence (Rodrik, 2016). Additionally, regional imbalances may be exacerbated if industry is geographically unevenly spread across regions. Crafts (1996a) discusses the UK experience of structural change and de-industrialization in the Thatcher years (1980s) in terms of productivity growth. The issues remain open and merit more attention.

Trade and growth

We have seen above evidence that trade openness has a positive effect on growth, but we did not dwell much. There are obvious reasons why trade may have beneficial effects, including competition that enhances productivity and technology adoption—important in the 'knowledge economy', as emphasized by one of the salient early contributions, Grossman and Helpman (1991b). On the other hand, the businesses or countries that lag behind on the 'ideas frontier' or are not price-competitive may stand to lose. All these effects are analysed in the specialist branch of trade theory. From a policy perspective, the overarching question is whether trade liberalization (opening up to trade via a reduction of tariffs and quotas on imports) is conducive to growth. In the growth literature, there is a voluminous literature on this question; Frankel and Romer (1999), Rodriguez and Rodrik (2001), Dollar and Kraay (2003), Yannikaya (2003), and Baldwin (2004) give a flavour and offer some contrasting views.

Macroeconomic 'volatility' and growth

A number of empirical studies ask whether the 'volatility' of output, or of other key macroeconomic variables like investment or inflation, is related in any way to the growth rate. Typically, such studies employ cross-country growth regressions in which average-across-time country growth rates are the endogenous variable, while volatility (of the growth rate or other variables across a time period) is included among the explanatory variables. One would expect that if volatility stems from or captures the randomness of innovations and productivity shocks, then it might be positively related to growth; this would be a verification of the Schumpeterian model in particular. If on the other hand volatility stems from erratic policies or other exogenous shocks, then it might be negatively related to growth as it hampers planning. Unfortunately, the empirical literature does not speak with one voice; the results vary across studies and lack robustness. A good place to visit this literature is Jones et al. (2005).

Hours worked over the very long run

A standard assumption in many growth models is that, in the steady state, labour remains constant. Yet, recent findings show that over the long twentieth century, hours worked per capita have steadily declined; individuals tend to benefit from the higher wages by enjoying more leisure (to some extent) as well as having more consumption. This is not inconsistent with the labour-leisure choice. The income effect of the wage rise, which 'buys' more of both goods, outweighs the substitution effect, which would have implied that leisure falls as its opportunity cost rises. Another possibility is that consumption and leisure are not separable, namely the former requires the latter in order to be enjoyed. See Boppart and Krusell (2016), Ramey and Francis (2009), and Rogerson (2006) for recent analyses. Questions galore arise of course from such findings. Are these gains in living standards shared equally across workers, or do the more affluent ones benefit more? What will technological innovation (automation, artificial intelligence) that encourages capital-labour substitution bring? What will be the effects of the 'secular stagnation' we discussed above—if it occurs?

Growth accelerations, strategies, diagnostics

Dani Rodrik has been more closely associated than most with (in my terminology) a 'critically engaged' study of the international economy, growth, and development. One of the themes that he has studied is the incidence of growth 'spurts' and accelerations, episodes when there has been a change from stagnation to sustained growth; in particular, the emphasis has been on the strategies and policy reforms that gave rise to such accelerations (Rodrik, 2005). Another question that has preoccupied him and his associates is to diagnose ('growth diagnostics') the bottlenecks, the sticky points (institutional impediments?, wrong policies?) that block growth; see Hausmann et al. (2008) and Rodrik (2010). The overarching question is to identify the appropriate policy reforms and strategies that are conducive to growth; and here his overall answer is that there is no single template, the effectiveness of various policies and 'recipes' must be evaluated in context, in relation to the totality of institutions in a country.[45] Some of the successful policies and reforms have been 'unorthodox'; full-scale market liberalization (an umbrella term that encompasses liberalization in labour markets, trade, and capital markets, as well as privatizations) may not always be the best strategy. Several of his contributions are collected in the evocatively titled 'One Economics, Many Recipes' volume (Rodrik, 2007). The reader is encouraged to take a look—fascinating stuff. But of course, before leaving the topic of policies and strategies, one should also mention Easterly (2001), a critic of formulaic policies with disastrous effects on the ground.

Population and growth

Here is a good place to draw together all the threads that we have seen link population growth to economic growth—with population growth taken as exogenous, an important assumption. The Solow model tells us that population growth is bad for prosperity—crudely putting the argument, the more mouths you have to feed, the lower the living standard. But the 'semi-endogenous' growth models (Jones, 1995b, 1999) imply that growth may be positively related to population growth; as we have seen, these models are an effort to by-pass the empirically unappealing scale effects that arise out of the non-rivalrous nature of 'ideas'. Even more broadly, as we saw in Chapter 5, population growth may be good for growth as it implies healthier demographics and younger societies; instead ageing societies face problems such as unsustainable social insurance systems and public deficits, too high saving rates (as in Japan), etc. Confusing? Well, wait until we relax the exogeneity assumption: population growth is endogenous, linked to prosperity, development, and growth. Allowing for that brings in a whole range of new possibilities, reviewed next.

'Malthusian traps' and 'unified growth theory'

Biologically, procreation is dictated by the need of individuals to ensure that their genes survive. With that as background, child-rearing is (partly of course) an economic decision (Becker et al., 1990): children require resources but also generate emotional fulfilment (because of gene survival) and may support parents in their old age; a family weighs all these in deciding (often unconsciously) its fertility. A theory associated with Thomas Malthus highlights the possibility that the rate of population growth may be so high that all resources are depleted and the standard of living remains at a subsistence level—a 'Malthusian state' or trap. On the other hand, it is well known that if or when incomes rise (and this applies to individuals as well as whole societies), the optimal gene survival strategy changes. Instead of large numbers of offspring, survival now requires heavier investment (nutrition, health, education, but also spending quality time with them) in smaller numbers of children. But lower population growth facilitates economic growth, as we have seen. Thus, when we allow for an endogenous population growth, two possible equilibria emerge: the 'Malthusian' one, with stagnating income at a subsistence level but a high population growth; and 'development', a state of sustained economic growth with low population growth. Less developed countries have high fertility rates, while developed ones have low, sometimes negative, population growth rates and ageing societies (see Spolaore and Wacziarg, 2019). So, these two equilibria are real-world possibilities, not theoretical curiosities. See Foreman-Peck (2019) for a historical analysis of the interplay

---

[45] Here, one can invoke the 'theorem of the second-best' which states that the effectiveness of a policy change must be judged keeping in mind that the economy in question is imperfect, 'second-best'. Application of policies that might work well in a first-best world to second-best situations may in fact produce third-best outcomes.

between economics and demographics, with emphasis on the transition of Europe from the Malthusian/stagnation to the growth states during the nineteenth century.

What determines when a society might break away from a 'Malthusian' state or poverty trap? 'Unified growth theory' (UGT) blends growth economics and economic history in order to shed light on this question. It analyses if and when a transition from one equilibrium to the other takes place; in so doing, it is informative about international income distribution and the question of convergence—in particular the emergence of convergence clubs. It is mostly associated with Oded Galor; see in particular Galor (2005, 2010), Galor and Weil (2000), and Ashraf and Galor (2011).

New directions—biology, evolution, and development

The new field of 'macrogenoeconomics' comes in the wake of UGT and considers migration as well as endogenous population growth. The survey paper by Ashraf and Galor (2018) reviews the evidence on biological evolution, population migration, and dynamics of development over the very long horizon (from the dawn of civilization to today). What do you make of it?

Socio-behavioural influences on growth

The behavioural macroeconomics literature has highlighted the influence of behavioural factors such as 'keeping up with the Joneses' or status on growth (and inequality). The idea is simple at its essentials: trying to keep up with the others (as relative consumption matters for status) makes me work harder and consume more than I would have decided on my own; therefore growth is higher, but this may be suboptimal. There is a voluminous literature here; the interested reader can consult Tsoukis and Tournemaine (2013) as a partial review. Additionally, the structure of discounting, which may not be exponential or geometric, matters; it may be more short-termist or 'presently biased' than is implied by exponential/geometric and therefore less favourable to saving and growth; see Barro (1999). We saw these effects briefly in Chapter 2 and will meet them again in Chapter 11 in our discussion of consumption; they are important themes in the emergent sub-field of behavioural (and social, in my view) macroeconomics.

Last, but by no means least—inequality and growth

The relationship will be reviewed more closely in Chapter 10. But here, let us point out one implication of the 'Schumpeterian' model of innovation-driven growth highlighted by Jones and Kim (2018). Entrepreneurs who generate path-breaking innovations earn high returns; this potentially explains the rising shares of national incomes that the 'top incomes' earn and the 'Pareto' distributions that wealth distribution in particular obeys. This gives rise to a 'growth-equality trade-off'; we shall visit all these themes in Chapter 10. One policy implication, highlighted by C. Jones in a very recent (as yet unpublished) contribution, is that taxing heavily the top incomes will stall innovation and growth and hurt all, not just the top incomes. Of course, as Jones himself acknowledges, not all incomes are the product of innovation; many are the product of 'rent-seeking', grabbing a (large) slice of the pie without contributing to its growth. Furthermore, the evidence about the growth-equality trade-off is not clear, as we shall see. The reader is invited to make up their own mind.

References

Abramovitz, M. (1989): *Thinking about Growth; and Other Essays on Economic Growth and Welfare*, Cambridge: Cambridge University Press.

Aghion, P., and P.W. Howitt (1992): A Model of Growth through Creative Destruction, *Econometrica*, 60(2), 323–52.

Aghion, P., and P.W. Howitt (1997): *Endogenous Growth Theory*, Cambridge, MA: MIT Press.

Aghion, P., and S.N. Durlauf (eds) (2005): *Handbook of Economic Growth*, Amsterdam: Elsevier North Holland, 1A.

Aghion, P., and S.N. Durlauf (eds) (2014): *Handbook of Economic Growth*, Amsterdam: Elsevier North Holland, 1B.

Aghion, P., and P.W. Howitt (2008): *The Economics of Growth*, Cambridge, MA: MIT Press.

Arcand, J.-L., E. Berkes, and U. Panizza (2015): Too Much Finance? *Journal of Economic Growth*, 20, 105–48.

Ashraf, Q.H., and O. Galor (2011): Dynamics and Stagnation in the Malthusian Epoch, *American Economic Review*, 101(5), 2003–41.

Ashraf, Q.H., and O. Galor (2018): The Macrogenoeconomics of Comparative Development, *Journal of Economic Literature*, 56(3), 1119–55.

Attfield, C., and J.R.W. Temple (2010): Balanced Growth and the Great Ratios: New Evidence for the US and UK, *Journal of Macroeconomics*, 32(4) (December), 937–56.

Azariadis, C., and J. Stachurski (2005): Poverty Traps, in P. Aghion and S.N. Durlauf (eds), *Handbook of Economic Growth*, Amsterdam: Elsevier North Holland, 1A, chapter 5.

Baldwin, R.E. (2004): Openness and Growth: What's the Empirical Relationship?, in R.E. Baldwin and L.A. Winters (eds), *Challenges to Globalization: Analyzing the Economics*. Chicago: National Bureau of Economic Research-University of Chicago Press, 499–526.

Barro, R.J. (1990): Government Spending in a Simple Model of Endogenous Growth, *Journal of Political Economy*, 98(5), S103–26.

Barro, R.J. (1999): Ramsey Meets Laibson in the Neoclassical Growth Model, *Quarterly Journal of Economics*, 114(4) (November), 1125–52.

Barro, R.J., and J.-W. Lee (1993): International Comparisons of Educational Attainment, *Journal of Monetary Economics*, 32(3), 363–94.

Barro, R.J., and J.-W. Lee (2013): A New Data Set of Educational Attainment in the World, 1950–2010, *Journal of Development Economics*, 104 (September), 184–98.

Barro, R.J. and X. Sala-i-Martin (1990): World Real Interest Rates, in O.J. Blanchard and S. Fischer (eds), *NBER Macroeconomics Annual 1990*, Cambridge, MA: NBER, vol. 5, 15–61.

Barro, R.J., and X. Sala-i-Martin (1995): *Economic Growth*, New York: McGraw-Hill.

Baumol, W.J. (1967): Macroeconomics of Unbalanced Growth: The Anatomy of the Urban Crisis, *American Economic Review*, 57, 415–26.

Baumol, W (1986): Productivity Growth, Convergence, and Welfare: What the Long-Run Data Show, *American Economic Review*, 76(5), 1072–85.

Baxter, M., and R.G. King (1993): Fiscal Policy in General Equilibrium, *American Economic Review*, 83(3) (June), 315–34.

Becker, G.S., K.M. Murphy, and R. Tamura (1990): Human Capital, Fertility, and Economic Growth, *Journal of Political Economy*, 98(5) (October), S12–37.

Bond, S., S. Leblebicioglu, and F. Schiantarelli (2010): Capital Accumulation and Growth: A New Look at the Empirical Evidence, *Journal of Applied Econometrics*, 25, 1073–99.

Boppart, T., and P. Krusell (2016): Labor Supply in the Past, Present, and Future: A Balanced-Growth Perspective, CEPR Discussion Paper No. 11235.

Carroll, C.D., and D.N. Weil (1994): Saving and Growth: A Reinterpretation, *Carnegie-Rochester Conference Series on Public Policy*, 40(1) (June), 133–92.

Caselli, F. (2005): Accounting for Cross-Country Income Differences, in P. Aghion and S.N. Durlauf (eds), *Handbook of Economic Growth*, Amsterdam: Elsevier North Holland, 1A. 679–741.

Cecchetti, S., and E. Kharroubi (2015): *Why does Financial Sector Growth Crowd out Real Economic Growth?* Basel: Bank for International Settlements, Working Paper No. 490.

Clark, G., K.H. O'Rourke, and A.M. Taylor (2008): Made in America? The New World, the Old, and the Industrial Revolution, *American Economic Review*, 98(2) (May), 523–28.

Crafts, N.F.R. (1996a): Deindustrialisation and Economic Growth, *Economic Journal*, 106(434) (January), 172–83.

Crafts, N.F.R. (1996b): Post-Neoclassical Endogenous Growth Theory: What are its Policy Implications? *Oxford Review of Economic Policy*, 12(2) (June), 30–47.

Crafts, N.F.R. (2011): Explaining the First Industrial Revolution: Two Views, *European Review of Economic History*, 15(1), 153–68.

Crafts, N.F.R. (2018): The Golden Age of European Economic Growth, in C. Diebolt and M. Haupert (eds), *Handbook of Cliometrics*, Berlin and Heidelberg: Springer, 1–33.

Crafts, N.F.R. (2019): The Sources of British Economic Growth since the Industrial Revolution: Not the Same Old Story, University of Warwick Department of Economics Working Paper No. 430, July.

Crafts, N. F. R., and G. Toniolo (eds) (1996): *Economic Growth in Europe since 1945*, Cambridge: Cambridge University Press.

David, P.A. (1977): Accumulation in America's Economic Growth: A Nineteenth Century Parable, *Carnegie-Rochester Conference Series on Public Policy (Supplement of the Journal of Monetary Economics)*, 6, 179–228.

DeLong, J.B. (1988): Productivity Growth, Convergence, and Welfare: Comment, *American Economic Review*, 78(5) (December), 1138–54.

DeLong, J.B., and L.H. Summers (1991): Equipment Investment and Economic Growth, *Quarterly Journal of Economics*, 106(2) (May), 445–502.

Demetriades, P., and T. Mamuneas (2000): Intertemporal Output and Employment Effects of Public Infrastructure Capital: Evidence from 12 OECD Economics, *Economic Journal*, 11046 (5), 687–712.

Diebolt, C., and M. Haupert (eds) (2019): *Handbook of Cliometrics*, Berlin and Heidelberg: Springer.

Dollar, D., and A. Kraay (2003): Institutions, Trade and Growth, *Journal of Monetary Economics*, 50(1) (January), 133–62.

Dowrick, S., and D.-T. Nguyen (1989): ECD Comparative Economic Growth 1950–85: Catch-Up and Convergence, *American Economic Review*, 79(5), 1010–30.

Durlauf, S.N. and L.E. Blume (2010): *Economic Growth* (part of the New Palgrave Dictionary of Economics series), 2nd ed., London: Palgrave Macmillan.

Durlauf, S.N., P.A. Johnson, and J.R.W. Temple (2005): Growth Econometrics, in P. Aghion and S.N. Durlauf (eds), *Handbook of Economic Growth*, Amsterdam: Elsevier North Holland, 1A. 555–667.

Durlauf, S.N., A. Kourtellos, and C.M. Tan (2008): Are any Growth Theories Robust? *Economic Journal*, 118, 329–46.

Easterly, W. (2001): *The Elusive Quest for Growth: Economist's Adventures and Misadventures in the Tropics*, Cambridge, MA: MIT Press.

Edwards, S. (1996): Why are Latin America's Savings Rates So Low? An International Comparative Analysis, *Journal of Development Economics*, 51(1), 5–44.

Eicher, T.S., and S.J. Turnovsky (1999): Non-Scale Models of Economic Growth, *Economic Journal*, 109(457) (July), 394–415.

Feinstein, C.H, P. Temin, and G. Toniolo (1997): *The European Economy between the Wars*, Oxford: Oxford University Press.

Foreman-Peck, J. (2019): Economic-Demographic Interactions in the European Long Run Growth, in C. Diebolt and M. Haupert (eds), *Handbook of Cliometrics*, Berlin and Heidelberg: Springer, 1–25.

Frankel, J.A., and D. Romer (1999): Does Trade Cause Growth, *American Economic Review*, 89 (3) (June), 379–99.

Galor, O. (1996): Convergence? Inferences from Theoretical Models, *Economic Journal*, 106 (437) (July), 1056–69.

Galor, O. (2005): From Stagnation to Growth: Unified Growth Theory, in P. Aghion and S.N. Durlauf (eds), *Handbook of Economic Growth*, Amsterdam: Elsevier North Holland, 1A. 171–293.

Galor, O. (2010): The 2008 Lawrence R. Klein Lecture—Comparative Economic Development: Insights from Unified Growth Theory, *International Economic Review*, 51(1), 1–44.

Galor, O., and O. Moav (2006): Das Human-Kapital: A Theory of the Demise of the Class Structure, *Review of Economic Studies*, 73(1) (January), 85–117.

Galor, O., and D.N. Weil (2000): Population, Technology, and Growth: From Malthusian Stagnation to the Demographic Transition and Beyond, *American Economic Review*, 90(4), 806–28.

Glaeser, E.L., R. LaPorta, F. Lopez-de-Silanes, and A. Shleifer (2004): Do Institutions Cause Growth? *Journal of Economic Growth*, 9(3), 271–303.

Gordon, R.J. (1990): The Measurement of Durable Goods Prices, Chicago: University of Chicago Press.

Gordon, R.J. (2010): Revisiting U. S. Productivity Growth over the Past Century with a View of the Future, NBER Working Paper No. 15834, March.

Gordon, R.J. (2016): *The Rise and Fall of American Growth: The U.S. Standard of Living since the Civil War*, Princeton: Princeton University Press.

Griliches, Z. (1996): The Discovery of the Residual: A Historical Note, *Journal of Economic Literature*, 34 (September), 1324–30.

Grossman, G.M., and E. Helpman (1991a): *Innovation and Growth in the Global Economy*, Boston: MIT Press.

Grossman, G.M., and E. Helpman (1991b): Trade, Knowledge Spillovers, and Growth, *European Economic Review*, 35, 517–26.

Grossman, G.M., E. Helpman, E. Oberfield, and T. Sampson (2017): Balanced Growth despite Uzawa, *American Economic Review*, 107(4), 1293–1312.

Hall, R.E. (1988): Intertemporal Substitution in Consumption, *Journal of Political Economy*, 96(2), 339–57.

Hall, B.H., and N. Rosenberg (eds) (2010): *Handbook of the Economics of Innovation*, Amsterdam: Elsevier-North Holland.

Hall, R., and C. Jones (1999): Why do Some Countries Produce So Much More Output Per Worker than Others, *Quarterly Journal of Economics*, 114(1) (February), 83–116.

Hausmann, R., D. Rodrik, and A. Velasco (2008): Growth Diagnostics, Chapter 15 in: Narcís Serra and Joseph E. Stiglitz (eds), *The Washington Consensus Reconsidered: Towards a New Global Governance*, Oxford: Oxford University Press, 324–55.

Herrendorf, B., R. Rogerson, and A. Valentinyi (2014): Growth and Structural Transformation, in P. Aghion and S.N. Durlauf (eds), *Handbook of Economic Growth*, Amsterdam: Elsevier North Holland, 1B. 855–941.

Herrendorf, B., C. Herrington, and Á. Valentinyi (2015): Sectoral Technology and Structural Transformation, *American Economic Journal: Macroeconomics*, 7(4) (October), 104–33.

Hulten, C.R. (2010): Growth Accounting, in B.H. Hall and N. Rosenberg (eds), *Handbook of the Economics of Innovation*, Amsterdam: Elsevier-North Holland, 987–1031.

Islam, N. (1995): Growth Empirics: A Panel Data Approach, *Quarterly Journal of Economics*, 110(4) (November), 1127–70.

Jones, C.I. (1995a): Time Series Tests of Endogenous Growth Models, *Quarterly Journal of Economics*, 110 (May), 495–525.

Jones, C.I. (1995b): R&D-Based Models of Economic Growth, *Journal of Political Economy*, 103(4) (August), 759–84.

Jones, C.I. (1997): On the Evolution of the World Income Distribution, *Journal of Economic Perspectives*, 11 (Summer), 19–36.

Jones, C.I. (1999): Growth: With or without Scale Effects? *American Economic Review Papers and Proceedings*, 89 (May), 139–44.

Jones, C.I. (2005): Growth and Ideas, in P. Aghion and S.N. Durlauf (eds), *Handbook of Economic Growth*, Amsterdam: Elsevier North Holland, 1A. 1063–1111.

Jones, C.I. (2016): The Facts of Economic Growth, in J.B. Taylor and H. Uhlig (eds), *Handbook of Macroeconomics*, Amsterdam: Elsevier, ii. 3–69.

Jones, C.I., and J. Fernald (2014): The Future of U.S. Economic Growth, *American Economic Review Papers and Proceedings*, 104(5) (May), 44–9.

Jones, C.I., and J. Kim (2018): A Schumpeterian Model of Top Income Inequality, *Journal of Political Economy*, 126(5) (October), 1785–1826.

Jones, C.I., and D. Scrimgeour (2008): A New Proof of Uzawa's Steady-State Growth Theorem, *Review of Economics and Statistics*, 90(1), 180–2.

Jones, C.I., and J. Williams (1998): Measuring the Social Return to R&D, *Quarterly Journal of Economics*, 113 (November), 1119–35.

Jones, L.E., R.E. Manuelli, H.E. Siu, and E. Stacchetti (2005): Fluctuations in Convex Models of Endogenous Growth I: Growth Effects, *Review of Economic Dynamics*, 8(4) (October), 780–804.

Jorgenson, D.W. (2005): Accounting for Growth in the Information Age, in P. Aghion and S.N. Durlauf (eds), *Handbook of Economic Growth*, Amsterdam: Elsevier North Holland, 1A. 743–815.

Jorgenson, D.W. (2007): Information Technology and the G7 Economies, in E.R. Berndt and C.R. Hulten (eds), *Hard-to-Measure Goods and Services: Essays in Honor of Zvi Griliches*, Chicago: University of Chicago Press, 325–50.

Jorgenson, D.W., M. Ho, and K.J. Stiroh (2008): A Retrospective Look at the US Productivity Growth Resurgence, *Journal of Economic Perspectives*, 22(1) (Winter), 3–24.

Jorgenson, D.W., and M.P. Timmer (2011): Structural Change in Advanced Nations: A New Set of Stylised Facts, *Scandinavian Journal of Economics*, 113(1) (March), 1–29.

Kaldor, N. (1963): Capital Accumulation and Economic Growth, in F. A. Lutz and D. C. Hague (eds), *Proceedings of a Conference Held by the International Economics Association*, London: Macmillan, 177–222.

Kindleberger, C.P. (1989): *Economic Laws and Economic History: Rafaelle Matioli Lectures*, Cambridge: Cambridge University Press.

King, R.G., and R. Levine (1993): Finance and Growth: Schumpeter Might Be Right, *Quarterly Journal of Economics*, 108(3), 717–37.

King, R.G., and R. Levine (1994): Capital Fundamentalism, Economic Development, and Economic Growth, *Carnegie-Rochester Conference Series on Public Policy*, 40(1) (June), 259–92.

King, R.G., and S. Rebelo (1993): Transitional Dynamics and Economic Growth in the Neoclassical Model, *American Economic Review*, 83(4), 908–31.

King, R.G., C. Plosser, J. Stock, and M. Watson (1991): Stochastic Trends and Economic Fluctuations, *American Economic Review*, 81(4), 819–40.

Kremer, M. (1991): Population Growth and Technological Change: One Million B.C. to 1990, *Quarterly Journal of Economics*, 108(3) (August), 681–716.

Kollmeyer, C., and F. Pichler (2013): Is Deindustrialization Causing High Unemployment in Affluent Countries? Evidence from 16 OECD Countries, 1970–2003, *Social Forces*, 91(3) (March), 785–812.

Krueger, A., and M. Lindahl (2001): Education for Growth: Why and for Whom? *Journal of Economic Literature*, 34(4), 1101–36.

Krugman, P. (1991): History versus Expectations, *Quarterly Journal of Economics*, 106(2), 651–67.

Kuznets, S. (1971): *Economic Growth of Nations: Total Output and Production Structure*, Cambridge, MA: Harvard University Press.

Kuznets, S. (1973): Modern Economic Growth: Findings and Reflections, *American Economic Review*, 63(3) (June), 247–58.

Landes, D.S. (2003): *The Unbound Prometheus: Technological Change and Industrial Development in Western Europe from 1750 to the Present*, Cambridge: Cambridge University Press.

Levine, R. (2005): Finance and Growth: Theory and Evidence, in P. Aghion and S.N. Durlauf (eds), *Handbook of Economic Growth*, Amsterdam: Elsevier North Holland, 1A. 865–934.

Levine, R., and D. Renelt (1992): A Sensitivity Analysis of Cross-Country Growth Regressions, *American Economic Review*, 82(4) (September), 942–63.

Levine, R., and S. Zervos (1998): Stock Markets, Banks, and Economic Growth, *American Economic Review*, 88(3) (June), 537–58.

Levine, R., N. Loayza, and T. Beck (2000): Financial Intermediation and Growth: Causality and Causes, *Journal of Monetary Economics*, 46, 31–77.

Li, C.-W. (2001): On the Policy Implications of Endogenous Technological Progress, *Economic Journal*, 111(471) (May), 164–79.

Loayza, N., and R. Ranciere (2006): Financial Development, Financial Fragility, and Growth, *Journal of Money, Credit and Banking*, 38, 1051–76.

Lucas, R.E., Jr. (1988): On the Mechanics of Economic Development, *Journal of Monetary Economics*, 22, 3–42.

Lucas, R.E., Jr. (1990): Why doesn't Capital Flow from Rich to Poor Countries? *American Economic Review*, 80, 92–6.

McGrattan, E.R. (1998): A Defense of AK Growth Models, *Federal Reserve Bank of Minneapolis Quarterly Review*, 22, 13–27.

McGrattan, E.R., and J.A. Schmitz (1999): Explaining Cross-Country Income Differences, in: J.B. Taylor and M. Woodford (eds), *Handbook of Macroeconomics*, Amsterdam: Elsevier, i. 669–737.

Maddison, A. (2007): *Contours of the World Economy, 1–2030 AD: Essays in Macroeconomic History*, Oxford: Oxford University Press.

Maddison, A. (2010): *The World Economy* (Development Centre Seminars), Paris: OECD Publishing.

Mankiw, N.G., D. Romer, and D.N. Weil (1992): A Contribution to the Empirics of Economic Growth, *Quarterly Journal of Economics*, 107(2) (May 1992), 407–37.

Manuelli, R.E., and A. Seshadri (2014): Human Capital and the Wealth of Nations, *American Economic Review*, 104(9) (September), 2736–62.

Milanovic, B. (2018): What is Happening with Global Inequality? posted on Vox—CEPR Policy Portal, 20 November, https://voxeu.org/content/what-happening-global-inequality

Mokyr, J. (2010): The Contribution of Economic History to the Study of Innovation and Technical Change: 1750–1914, in B.H. Hall and N. Rosenberg (eds), *Handbook of the Economics of Innovation*, Amsterdam: Elsevier-North Holland, 11–50.

Mulligan, C., and X. Sala-i-Martin (1993): Transitional Dynamics in Two-Sector Models of Endogenous Growth, *Quarterly Journal of Economics*, 108(3), 739–73.

Ngai, L.R., and Pissarides, C. A. (2007): Structural Change in a Multisector Model of Growth, *American Economic Review*, 97, 429–43.

Nickell, S., S. Redding, and J. Swaffield (2008): The Uneven Pace of Deindustrialisation in the OECD, *World Economy*, 31, 1154–84.

Nordhaus, W.D. (2004): Schumpeterian Profits in the American Economy: Theory and Measurement, NBER Working Paper No. 10433, April.

Nordhaus, W.D. (2008): Baumol's Disease: A Macroeconomic Perspective, *B.E. Journal of Macroeconomics* (Contributions), 8(1).

O'Mahony, M., and M.P. Timmer (2009): Output, Input and Productivity Measures at the Industry Level: The EU KLEMS Database, *Economic Journal*, 119(538), F374–403.

Oliner, S.D., D.E. Sichel, and K.J. Stiroh (2007): Explaining a Productive Decade, *Brookings Papers on Economic Activity*, 38(1), 81–152.

ONS (Office for National Statistics, 2017): The Feasibility of Measuring the Sharing Economy: November 2017 Progress Update, https://www.ons.gov.uk/economy/economicoutput-andproductivity/output/articles/thefeasibilityofmeasuringthesharingeconomy/november2017-progressupdate

Panizza, U. (2017): Nonlinearities in the Relationship between Finance and Growth, *Comparative Economic Studies*, 60(1) (March), 44–53.

Papaioannou, E., and G. Siourounis (2008): Democratisation and Growth, *Economic Journal*, 118(532), 1520–51.

Persson, T., and G. Tabellini (2003): *The Economic Effects of Constitutions: What do the Data Say?* Cambridge, MA: MIT Press.

Pritchett, L. (1997): Divergence, Big Time, *Journal of Economic Perspectives*, 11(3) (Summer), 3–17.

Quah, D. (1993): Galton's Fallacy and Tests of the Convergence Hypothesis, *Scandinavian Journal of Economics*, 95, 427–43.

Quah, D. (1996): Twin Peaks: Growth and Convergence in Models of Distribution Dynamics, *Economic Journal*, 106(437), 1045–55.

Quah, D. (1997): Empirics for Growth and Distribution: Stratification, Polarization, and Convergence Clubs, *Journal of Economic Growth*, 2(1), 27–59.

Ramey, V.A., and N. Francis (2009): A Century of Work and Leisure, *American Economic Journal: Macroeconomics*, 1(2), 189–224.

Rebelo, S. (1991): Long-Run Policy Analysis and Long-Run Growth, *Journal of Political Economy*, 99(3) (June), 500–21.

Robinson, J.A., D. Acemoglu, and S. Johnson (2005): Institutions as a Fundamental Cause of Long-Run Growth, in P. Aghion and S.N. Durlauf (eds), *Handbook of Economic Growth*, Amsterdam: Elsevier North Holland, 1A. 386–472.

Rodriguez, F., and D. Rodrik (2001): Trade Policy and Economic Growth: A Skeptic's Guide to the Cross-National Evidence, in B.S. Bernanke and K. Rogoff (eds), *NBER Macroeconomics Annual 2000*, Cambridge, MA: MIT Press, 15, 261–338.

Rodrik, D. (1999): Where did All the Growth Go? External Shocks, Social Conflict, and Growth Collapses, *Journal of Economic Growth*, 4 (December), 385–412.

Rodrik, D. (2005): Growth Strategies, in P. Aghion and S.N. Durlauf (eds), *Handbook of Economic Growth*, Amsterdam: Elsevier North Holland, 1A. 967–1014.

Rodrik, D. (2007): *One Economics, Many Recipes: Globalization, Institutions and Economic Growth*, Princeton: Princeton University Press.

Rodrik, D. (2010): Diagnostics Before Prescription, *Journal of Economic Perspectives*, 24(3), 33–44.

Rodrik, D. (2016): Premature Deindustrialization, *Journal of Economic Growth*, 21, 1–33.

Rodrik, D., A. Subramanian, and F. Trebbi (2004): Institutions Rule: The Primacy of Institutions over Geography and Integration in Economic Development, *Journal of Economic Growth*, 9(2) (June), 131–65.

Rogerson, R. (2006): Understanding Differences in Hours Worked, *Review of Economic Dynamics*, 9(3), 365–409.

Romer, P.M. (1986): Increasing Returns and Long-Run Growth, *Journal of Political Economy*, 94(5) (October), 1002–37.

Romer, P.M. (1987): Growth Based on Increasing Returns Due to Specialization, *American Economic Review*, 77(2) (May), 56–62.

Romer, P.M. (1990): Endogenous Technological Change, *Journal of Political Economy*, 98(5) (October), 71–102.

Romer, P.M. (1994): The Origins of Endogenous Growth, *Journal of Economic Perspectives*, 8(1) (Winter), 3–22.

Romer, P.M. (2007): Economic Growth, The Library of Economics and Liberty, https://www.econlib.org/library/Enc/EconomicGrowth.html

Rostow, W.W. (1960): *The Stages of Economic Growth: A Non-Communist Manifesto*, Cambridge: Cambridge University Press.

Rowthorn, R., and K. Coutts (2004): De-industrialisation and the Balance of Payments in Advanced Economies, *Cambridge Journal of Economics*, 28(5), 767–90.

Sachs, J.D. (2003): Institutions Don't Rule: Direct Effects of Geography on Per Capita Income, NBER Working Paper No. 9490.

Sachs, J.D., and A.M. Warner (1999): The Big Rush, Natural Resource Booms and Growth, *Journal of Development Economics*, 59(1) (June), 43–76.

Sala-i-Martin, X. (1996): The Classical Approach to Convergence Analysis, *Economic Journal*, 106(437) (July), 1019–36.

Sala-i-Martin, X. (1997): I Just Ran Two Million Regressions, *American Economic Review, Papers and Proceedings*, 87(2) (May), 178–83.

Sala-i-Martin, X. (2006): The World Distribution of Income: Falling Poverty and… Convergence, Period, *Quarterly Journal of Economics*, 121(2) (May), 351–97.

Segerstrom, P., T.C.A. Anant, and E. Dinopoulos (1991): A Schumpeterian Model of the Product Life Cycle, *American Economic Review*, 80(5), 1077–91.

Sokoloff, K., and S. Engerman (2000): Institutions, Factor Endowments, and Paths of Development in the New World, *Journal of Economic Perspectives*, 14(3) (Summer), 217–32.

Solow, R.M. (1956): A Contribution to the Theory of Economic Growth, *Quarterly Journal of Economics*, 70(1) (February), 65–94.

Solow, R.M. (1957): Technical Change and the Aggregate Production Function, *Review of Economics and Statistics*, 39(3) (August), 312–20.

Solow, R. (1994): Perspectives on Growth Theory, *Journal of Economic Perspectives*, 8(1) (Winter), 45–54.

Spolaore, E., and R. Wacziarg (2019): Fertility and Modernity, NBER Working Paper No. 25957, June.

Summers, L.H. (2018): The Threat of Secular Stagnation has Not Gone Away, http://larrysummers.com/2018/05/06/the-threat-of-secular-stagnation-has-not-gone-away/

Temin, P. (1999): *Lesson from the Great Depression*. Cambridge, MA: MIT Press.

Temple, J.R.W. (1999): The New Growth Evidence, *Journal of Economic Literature*, 37(1), 112–56.

Teulings, C., and R. Baldwin (2014): Secular Stagnation: Facts, Causes and Cures, Vox e-Book, 10 September; http://voxeu.org/article/secular-stagnation-facts-causes-and-cures-new-vox-ebook

Timmer, M.P., R. Inklaar, M. O'Mahony, and B. van Ark (2010): *Economic Growth in Europe*, Cambridge: Cambridge University Press.

Tobin, J. (1984): On the Efficiency of the Financial System, *Lloyds Bank Review*, 153, 1–15.

Tsoukis, C., and N.J. Miller (2003): Public Services and Endogenous Growth, *Journal of Policy Modelling*, 25(3), 297–307.

Tsoukis, C., and F. Tournemaine (2013): Status in a Canonical Macro Model: Status, Growth, and Inequality, Manchester School, 81(S2) (October), 65–92.

Turnovsky, S.J. (1996): Fiscal Policy, Growth, and Macroeconomic Performance in a Small Open Economy, *Journal of International Economics*, 40(1–2), 41–66.

Turnovsky, S.J. (2000): Fiscal Policy, Elastic Labor Supply, and Endogenous Growth: 'Dynamic Scoring' of the Long-Run Government Budget', *Journal of Monetary Economics*, 45(1) (January), 185–210.

Uzawa, H. (1961): Neutral Inventions and the Stability of Growth Equilibrium, *Review of Economic Studies*, 28 (Summer), 117–24.

Weil, D.N. (2012): *Economic Growth*, 3rd ed., London: Routledge.

Weil, D.N., and O. Galor (1999): From Malthusian Stagnation to Modern Growth, *American Economic Review*, 89(2) (May), 150–4.

Yannikaya, H. (2003): Trade Openness and Economic Growth: A Cross-Country Empirical Investigation, *Journal of Development Economics*, 72(1) (October), 57–89.

Young, A. (1995): The Tyranny of Numbers: Confronting the Statistical Realities of the East Asian Growth Experience, *Quarterly Journal of Economics*, 110(3), 641–80.

Zeira, J. (1998): Workers, Machines and Economic Growth, *Quarterly Journal of Economics*, 113, 1091–1113.

Zingales, L. (2015): Presidential Address: Does Finance Benefit Society? *Journal of Finance*, 70, 1327–63.

10

Inequality

10.1 Introduction

If anyone wonders why bother with inequality, a look at the book *The Spirit Level* (Wilkinson and Pickett 2009) will convince them that it is the mother of all social ills. A wealth of empirical information from across developed economies and from US states is contained in it, showing that a range of indicators of social welfare are correlated with inequality and not (so much) on the level of development or average income of an economy: from a composite index of health and social problems, to child well-being to social trust to women's status to mental illness to drug use to life expectancy to infant mortality to obesity to literacy scores and school attainment to teenage pregnancy to homicides to imprisonment to social mobility and more: all these indices are correlated with inequality. How? Invariably in the bad and dysfunctional way: 'goods' (such as life expectancy, literacy, or social trust) decline with inequality while 'bads' (homicides, mental illness, drugs) rise with it.

Although inequality is traditionally not considered as a macro topic, there is now a growing body of macroeconomics related to it. The traditional line of thinking is that macroeconomics is concerned with an analysis of the size of the aggregate 'pie' (or GDP), leaving it to other branches of economics (microeconomics, labour economics, public economics) and other disciplines (political economy, politics) to analyse how this pie is shared. Lately, however, the thinking is that the size and the distribution of the pie interact with each other. Hence, inequality is a topic worth analysing both in its own right, as it affects the welfare of many, but also as a factor affecting the aggregate income and wealth. This chapter will present some of the, still rather disparate, contributions to the macro-economics of inequality.

10.1.1 Inequality: Measurement Issues

We may be interested in the inequality present in various economic variables; primarily, we are interested in inequality of income and wealth, as both impact economic welfare directly (the latter because income can be derived from wealth both now and in the future). Less commonly, we may also be interested in the inequality of consumption. We abstract here from the question, discussed in Chapter 1, of whether the usual income statistics (GDP and the like) capture adequately all the information required to have an idea of economic welfare; we take it as a given starting point that economic welfare is measured by metrics such as real GDP per capita that statistical offices routinely compile. The question that preoccupies us in this chapter then is, how unequal are the distributions of GDP per capita

Theory of Macroeconomic Policy. Christopher Tsoukis, Oxford University Press (2020). © Christopher Tsoukis.
DOI: 10.1093/oso/9780198825371.003.0010

or wealth across the individuals of a country? There exist various measures of inequality (see Sen with Foster, 1997), none of which is perfect. The following are often used:

- The income or wealth share of the richest 1 per cent or 10 per cent of the population: The higher those are, the greater is inequality; we can compare these shares across countries at a point in time, or within a country across time.
- The income or wealth of the top 20 per cent as a ratio over the income or wealth of the bottom 20 per cent: the fifth (top) and first (lowest)—quintiles.

These measures are intuitive and often tell a story that captures attention (e.g. in the US, the top 1 per cent earns about 20 per cent of income while they own about 40 per cent of national wealth; and similarly in the UK and elsewhere). The downside is that such numbers only focus on what happens at narrow segments of the distribution. For this reason, a more synthetic measure is required that can capture in a single number as much information as possible from the entire distribution. The most widely used such measure is the Gini coefficient. Its maths is somewhat involved, but the idea behind is very simple and intuitive. It is best explained by considering the 'Lorenz Curve', which is depicted in Figure 10.1.

The horizontal axis shows all individuals from P(oorest) to R(ichest). The vertical axis shows the cumulative income of all individuals below a certain individual. For example, consider point B; it shows individual β on the horizontal axis, where $P < \beta < R$, i.e. β is somewhere between the poorest and richest individual. On the vertical axis, point B is projected onto CI_B, the cumulative income (as a percentage of the total) owned by the $P\beta$ segment of the population.

The curvy line PBD is the 'Lorenz Curve' (LC), showing the same information about all individuals between PR as for individual β; it is constructed from the data on the distribution of income. Its convexity indicates income inequality: the percentage income share of any segment of the population rises as the segment is higher up the distribution.

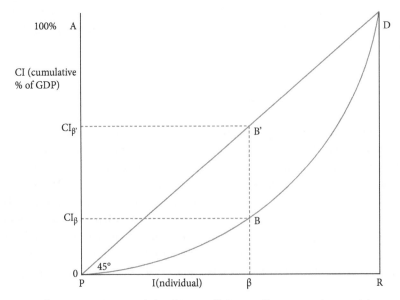

Figure 10.1. The Lorenz Curve and the Gini coefficient: a diagrammatic exposition

For example, the bottom fraction of the population equal to Pβ /PR has 0CIβ/0A share of income; it should be clear from the geometry that 0CIβ/0A < Pβ/PR. This means that the fraction of income owned by the Pβ segment is less than the fraction of this segment in the population (they are equal—both 1—when β = R): The LC is below the 45° line. Furthermore, the further away LC is from the 45° line the greater the inequality, as the lower will be the fraction of incomes owned by those lower down the distribution.

The straight line is a line that would result if, hypothetically, all individuals had equal incomes; then, the lowest Pβ /PR fraction of the population would have 0CIβ/0A = Pβ/PR. In other words, every fraction of the population would have an equal fraction of income. Another hypothetical line is the line of full inequality: PRD. In that case, the 99.999...per cent of population would have no income at all and only one person would earn all of national income. The LC is located in-between the two extremes. The Gini coefficient (G) tells us how close the LC is to the line of total inequality (PRD). It is defined as the ratio of the area between the LC and the line of full equality as a ratio over the entire region below the line of full equality:

$$G \equiv PBDB'0/PRD0$$

Obviously, the coefficient is bounded by $0 \le G \le 1$. Note that as Gini rises, INequality rises: $G = 0$ is full equality (the LC coincides with the 45° line), while $G = 1$ is total inequality (the LC is the angular line PRD of full inequality). The algebraic formulation of the Lorenz Curve and the Gini coefficient are less straightforward; the interested reader is referred to Sen with Foster (1997) and Aaberge (2007).

At this point it is worth mentioning the 'Pareto' statistical distribution which has been found useful in the empirical modelling of income distribution (see Piketty, 2014, 2015). Under the Pareto distribution, the 'density function' is:

$$f(x) = \frac{\beta - 1}{x_m} \left(\frac{x_m}{x}\right)^{\beta}, \quad x > x_m, \quad \beta > 2$$

Where x is the variable of interest (typically, income or wealth) and f(x) is the fraction of the population with income/wealth level x. The mean is:

$$E(x) = \frac{(\beta - 1)x_m}{\beta - 2}$$

Aaberge (2007) shows that under Pareto, the Gini coefficient is:

$$G = \frac{1}{2\beta - 3}$$

Note the inverse relation between β and G: with higher β, there is more equality.

Associated with the name of Wilfredo Pareto is also the 'Pareto principle',[1] whereby 20 per cent of society owns 80 per cent of the variable in question; and within each of these

---

[1] As is of course the concept of 'Pareto efficiency'.

Table 10.1. Quintile wealth shares and income Gini for selected countries

Country (unit:household except USA)	Wealth share of 1st quintile	Wealth share of 5th quintile	Wealth Gini	Gross income Gini 2014
Australia	0.002	0.63	0.62	0.39
Finland	−0.009	0.61		0.304
Germany	−0.002	0.66	0.67	0.344
India	0.01	0.7	0.67	0.495 (2011)
Japan	0.02	0.58	0.55	0.352(2012)
Sweden	−0.07	0.8		0.303
US (family)	−0.001	0.83	0.8	0.433

Notes: Quintile wealth shares (T7) and Wealth Ginis (T9) from Davies, Sandström, Shorrocks and Wolff (2011); the time is around 2000. The gross (before-tax) income income Gini is from the OECD (year: 2014).

segments, we have the same (i.e. the top 20 per cent of the 20 per cent owns the 80 per cent of the 80 per cent, i.e. the top 4 per cent owns 64 per cent). The Pareto principle has been shown to apply in many walks of life, both economic but also social and even biological. It begins to appear that the Pareto principle (or 80-20 'law' or rule) is an expression of a deeper principle at work, but we leave the investigation of this conjecture to the interested reader. The key point for us is that, as a ball-park estimate, the Pareto principle seems to describe wealth distribution well for some countries like the US (see Table 10.1), as was also originally noticed by Pareto in the case of nineteenth-century Italy. The β that gives the Pareto 80–20 principle is $\beta \approx 2.16$. The associated Gini is $G \approx 0.76$, which is reasonably close to the wealth Gini of the US (of about 0.83). This is an indication that indeed the US wealth distribution is described fairly well by the Pareto distribution.

10.1.2 Evidence on Inequality

In the UK, the income Gini is of the order of 0.35. More data on wealth and income inequality for selected countries are given in Table 10.1. It should be emphasized that these are measures of within-country inequality; each country's inequality is measured as if there is no other country in the world. In other words, there is no attempt to gauge the extent of between-country inequality.

From the US Congressional Budget Office (CBO, 2011), we learn that, in the US in 2007, the first (bottom) quintile earned about 5 per cent of national income, whilst the fifth (richest) more than 50 per cent. From Table 10.1, we see that the gap is even more pronounced in terms of wealth inequality.

Led by Thomas Piketty, a large international team of researchers has recently compiled a rich international database on inequality, the World Inequality Database. It is fast becoming one of key data sources on inequality. Apart from its wide coverage of countries, this database also makes cross-country comparisons of living standards; by merging information on within-country and between-country inequality, the database can now offer estimates of global inequality, as if all people on the planet were citizens of a single country. Though we shall not be concerned about global inequality so much, as we covered cross-country income differences in Chapter 9, it is worth reporting some findings from their World Inequality Report (see Alvaredo et al., 2018).

The main finding is that global inequality is wide and rising. Inequality was at historically lowest levels in the advanced world in about 30 years following World War II; but it has been rising since then. Between 1980 and 2016, the richest 0.1 per cent (one-thousandth) of the world's adult population have increased their combined wealth by as much as the poorest 50 per cent. As a result, the middle 40 per cent (50th to 90th percentile) experienced little or even no income growth at all in the same period. And whatever income growth there has been, has been due to a rise in work effort. Moreover, the rise in wealth is greater the richer the segment of the population in question. The richest 1 per cent of the global population gained 27 per cent of the world's income growth between 1980 and 2016 (WIR, 2018, table E4). Obviously, the wealth increases (i.e. cumulative income rises) have been disproportionately high at the higher end, and this is even more pronounced the higher one looks at. The bottom 50 per cent captured 12 per cent of income growth during the same period. See also ILO (2019, figure 5) on labour income inequality that tells a similar story. So, part and parcel of the story of rising inequality is the dramatic rise in top incomes (see Alvaredo et al., 2013; Atkinson et al., 2011).

There is a lot of variation in (within-country) inequality across countries and regions. As an indicative measure, one can look at the percentage share of the national income of the top 10 per cent of the population (10th decile). From Table E1 of the World Inequality Report (Alvaredo et al., 2018), in 2016, this was 37 per cent in Europe, 41 per cent in China, 46 per cent in Russia, 47 per cent in US-Canada, and around 55 per cent in sub-Saharan Africa, Brazil, and India. In the Middle East, the world's apparently most unequal region, it was a whopping 61 per cent of national income.

Income inequality is rising; there is a lot of variation across countries but the main picture is clear: inequality has been rising in the last 40 years, as evident from both table E2a (shares of the top 10 per cent of income earners) which have been rising and table E3 which shows the income share of the top 1 per cent in the US (rising, about 11 per cent in 1980 and 20 per cent now) and of the bottom 50 per cent (about 21 per cent in 1980 and 13 per cent now). However, these tendencies may be less pronounced in western Europe, where the share of the top 1 per cent seems to be hovering around the 12 per cent mark and of the bottom 50 per cent around 22 per cent. For the reader interested in more detailed information for the UK, the Institute of Fiscal Studies (IFS) produces annual Inequality and Poverty Reports; we skip details here.

The charity organization Oxfam compiles additional data on global income inequality and produces annual reports with the key findings. Its emphasis is on the huge contrasts between bewildering affluence and abject poverty. Although not a statistical agency and therefore (perhaps) its data is not compiled with as rigorous a methodology, it does highlight the trends. Its reports make compelling reading and send chills down the spine. Among the findings highlighted in its latest report (Oxfam, 2019) are: billionaire wealth increased by $900bn in 2018, or $2.5bn a day, while the 3.8 billion poorest people saw their wealth decline by 11 per cent a day. In 2018, 26 people owned the same as the 3.8 billion people who make up the poorest half of the world, down from 43 people the year before. The income of the richest person on the planet (can you name him?) is about 100 times the health budget of Ethiopia, a country of 105 million. The report goes on to highlight some of the implications of such contrasts, in terms of lack of healthcare, opportunity, and life chances for the world's poor; the under-taxation of rich individuals and rich corporations; the wider social implications of such inequalities (e.g. huge wealth is mostly male, implying gender inequality on top of everything else); the huge policy challenges; and many other issues.

Finally, let us note that these are essentially findings about cumulative income gains and wealth, which is more unequally distributed than income. However, there is also bewildering inequality in labour income across the world: The International Labour Organization, which combines such data, reports that in 2017, across the world, the top 10 per cent received 48.9 per cent of total pay, the next decile received 20.1 per cent, whereas the remaining 80 per cent of workers received just 31.0 per cent; the lowest-paid 50 per cent of workers received just 6.4 per cent (ILO, 2019).

10.1.3 The 'Kuznets Curve' and the 'Elephant Curve'

All this raises the question whether there is a steady-state income or wealth distribution to which countries tend to. In this respect, an early optimistic result was proposed by Kuznets (1955) and has been known as the 'Kuznets Curve' (after Nobel laureate Simon Kuznets, whom we encountered in Chapter 6 on fluctuations and in Chapter 9 on growth). The Kuznets Curve is a statistical finding: a hump-shaped curve in a plot of inequality against the level of development: It was shown that in early modern societies inequality was relatively low; it increased with the industrial revolution and urbanization, while developed societies saw inequality decrease in the twentieth century, thanks to a variety of mechanisms related to the welfare state (tax-related redistribution, social security, public employment). Shifts in demographics may have also played a role (see Anand and Kanbur, 1993): when societies reach a certain level of income, their population growth drops, allowing greater segments of the population to share the prosperity.

Empirical support for a Kuznets Curve, particularly its right side that shows declining inequality as development proceeds, comes from findings such as ILO (2019, figure 4); this shows a negative correlation between inequality and per capita income across countries. However, the negative correlation seems to be driven by a few very low-income countries; for two-thirds of the countries (the middle and upper-level ones, where there is still a fair amount of income variation), there seems to be little or no correlation.

The Kuznets Curve is an optimistic finding, in the sense that with development, in due course, countries will see their levels of inequality decline. Though well known, it is however now being critically re-examined. Piketty (2014) documents how various ambiguities, present in the data from the start, were swept under the carpet in the original showcasing of the curve in Kuznets (1955); these ambiguities meant that the finding was less statistically secure than its presentation implied. Recent work, associated with both Lakner and Milanovic (2016) and the World Inequality Database, highlights instead an 'elephant curve' (see Alvaredo et al., 2018, table E4; ILO, 2019, figure 3). It is a statistical finding of the share of global income growth gained by various segments of the world population (of which various pieces of information were presented above) plotted against their income levels. The lower part, which features a hump-shaped curve (the 'main body' of the elephant) shows that the bottom 50 per cent of the world population has captured some of the income growth and has improved its position in the last 40 years; this is due to the fact that various economies emerged to partially close the gap in incomes with the advanced countries, while within-country inequalities rose all along. The middle section got 'squeezed' and the various segments of the top 10 per cent has captured ever higher shares of income growth the richer they are; this part is the elephant's 'trunk'. Thus, in place of the optimism of the Kuznets Curve, we now have a much more limited optimism offered by the fact that some of the poorest populations in the world did manage to break out of (utter) poverty; but we also have the fact of the squeezed middle class and the spectacle of a tiny fraction of the global population getting bewildering shares of global income.

Thus, from the discussion of all this evidence, one may perhaps collect the following 'stylized facts' related to inequality.

10.1.4 Stylized Facts of Inequality

- Wealth inequality is higher than income inequality.
- Though there are differences across countries, inequality of both income and wealth has been increasing in recent decades (over the last 40 years or so) in many parts of the world.
- This followed a period (around the 1950s and 1960s) of historically low inequality in the industrialized economies in particular.
- A 'concertina effect': The increases in the income and wealth shares of the rich, over the last 40 years, are greater the higher up the distribution one looks at.
- As a corollary of the preceding point, incomes at the very top of the distribution have risen quite dramatically in recent years.
- There is a question mark over the 'Kuznets Curve', whereby inequality rises at the middle level of development but declines at an advanced stage.
- The 'elephant curve': Across the world economy, taking into account cross-country comparisons of living standards as well as within-country inequality, again over the last 40 years, we have seen some important gains at the lower end of the income distribution as various countries have broken out of poverty, important increases in income shares of the (very) rich, but a squeeze of the middle which seems to have stagnated or even lost ground.

10.1.5 Determinants of Inequality: A Primer

Though there is no consensus, it is worth reviewing here some of the reasons that have been suggested in the literature as the main determinants of inequality. The emphasis will be to pinpoint the factors that may be useful in explaining the observed changes. At the most basic level, there is of course the uncertainty in personal fortunes (positive or negative, winning the lottery or falling ill), particularly those that are not/cannot be insured (e.g. by having health insurance). The key question of course is how quantitatively important the inequality that is due to such personal uncertainty is, as opposed to total inequality. Aiyagari (1994)—and a large follow-up literature—has taken up this theme. He investigates in particular how significant 'precautionary saving' is (the saving that guards against unforeseeable accidents—see Chapter 11) as a share of the total; the answer is that it is not significant, which may be due to the fact that this source of inequality is not great or that individuals take inadequate precaution against it. But the Aiyagari (1994) model is successful in explaining the positive skewness (i.e. the right tail) of the income and wealth distributions and the higher wealth inequality compared to the income one. Additionally, Castañeda et al. (2003) find that a model of the lifecycle (see Chapter 11), where individuals are identical but face uninsured idiosyncratic shocks, accounts very well for the US earnings and wealth inequality.

Individuals may also differ in terms of motivation and preferences towards labour or leisure (e.g. some are more motivated to work than others—technically, their disutility of labour is lower) and this of course implies differences in labour supply and earnings; but it is questionable whether these preferences are changing in any way, so as to explain the observed rise in inequality. Differences also arise in terms of productivity and skills, but one here should be careful to distinguish between genuinely exogenous personal differences (e.g. in innate talent) and differences that arise because of educational choices and training; there may be a large endogenous element in the latter, as individuals from higher socio-economic backgrounds may be more prone or able to receive a better education. In any case, better education and training implies higher wages (the 'college premium' that we discussed in Chapter 4, or more generally a skills premium). Often, the educational choices interact with other aspects of the economy, such as credit constraints, as some individuals that might be in a position to benefit from loans for education are unable to receive them. The model of Galor and Zeira (1993) discussed below emphasizes this interaction.

Another source of heterogeneity between individuals is wealth ownership, including capital. Although this is endogenous to society, as wealth distribution evolves over time and across generations, it is more of a given for an individual (although individuals can also amass or lose wealth). We saw in Chapter 5, in the discussion of generational accounting, that most of wealth in the US is amassed across generations and not within a lifetime; it is then passed on from one generation to the next in the form of bequests. This finding has prompted some to model capital endowment as exogenous. We review such a model in Section 10.2. Other forms of wealth such as housing can be treated in a similar way.

National income is divided between labour income (wages, salaries, and related earnings, inclusive of premia for education, skills, and talent) and capital income (payments to shares, interest on bonds and deposits, and land rents). Recently, Piketty (2014) has highlighted the fact that the balance between labour and capital shares has been shifting in favour of capital. This is important as labour income is distributed unequally yet much more equally than capital income; hence, a shifting balance in favour of capital implies a more unequal overall income distribution. Moreover, as capital income is distributed more among the more affluent segments of the population, and the rich save more (see Section 10.2), the capital income tends to be saved more; hence, it tends to rise further, and income inequality acquires a self-perpetuating dynamic. In this regard, Piketty (2014) is associated with another finding: that the capital share tends to grow at a faster rate than the labour share (the 'r > g' issue). This finding, which is corroborated by newer work, implies that the balance between labour and capital income will be shifting for some time to come. We discuss the labour share and 'r > g' in Section 10.3.

Education and training offer a potential to explain the rising inequality because of the 'skills-biased technical progress' discussed in various chapters. Briefly, much technical progress requires skilled labour to use it, therefore this type of labour is in greater demand. In contrast, unskilled labour is in lower demand. The result is that the skills (or 'college') premium has been rising in recent years, increasing inequality. This is important because, as we discussed in Chapter 9, the pace of such technical progress is set to intensify due to information technology and artificial intelligence. Demand for unskilled labour, or even moderately skilled but routine, is set to decline to the point of total replacement (see Autor, 2019). If it is realized as currently forecast, this development will pose profound questions related to income inequality.

Even though differences in education-related productivity are important for wage and income inequality, it is doubtful whether they explain the totality of inequality. For instance, it is well documented that CEOs (chief executives) of many business and corporations in countries like the US and the UK earn hundreds of times in total remuneration (including salaries, bonuses, shares, etc.) the salaries of the average factory-floor employees; moreover, the tendencies is for these ratios to rise. CEOs may (on average) have more education and be harder working than shop-floor assistants, but does the product of more intelligence times harder work amount to the 200 times that may be the ratio sometimes? The answer is obviously not; something else is at work, not just the more productivity or education or hard work, or even the combination of all these.

What may be at work is the nature of prestige work as a 'tournament contest'. The work of top talent and 'stars' (footballers and other athletes, singers, novelists, or star professors) can be enjoyed by millions at once. This gears the demand towards the top talent; hence, there is a 'winner takes all' structure of pay.[2] Of course, a CEO is not a 'star' who can reach millions, but a top firm may be a star and its CEO may receive some of the super-profits of this firm in the form of remuneration. This line of reasoning is gaining ground as an explanation of inequality at the top end of incomes; see Kaplan and Rauh (2013), Dew-Becker and Gordon (2008), Autor et al. (2017), and Gabaix et al. (2016).

Benhabib et al. (2019) examine various factors as explanations of wealth inequality; in particular, they aim to reconcile the observed dual facts of high wealth inequality and high social mobility in the US. (Formally, social mobility is defined as the probability that an individual will move over the lifetime to a different economic class from the one in which they were born; crudely speaking, there are many 'self-made' people in the US, and correspondingly others that fall down the ladder.) Obviously, these two facts are generally contradictory, as wealth accumulation happens mostly across generations rather than within lifetimes (see Chapter 5) and more social mobility implies less chance for that to happen. The first potential explanation is the inequality in incomes and the associated uncertainty. The second is differential saving rates as the rich save proportionately more; higher saving rate may occur both within lifetimes and across generations in the form of higher bequests as a fraction of wealth (Cagetti and De Nardi, 2006; Piketty, 2014). Finally, there is uncertainty in the returns on wealth, or capital income risk; this also creates wealth inequality, as some business projects are successful and increase wealth while others fail and the capital is lost. Benhabib et al. (2019) analyse the contributions of these three factors in driving wealth accumulation; each of them is shown to have a distinct role. In particular, unequal and uncertain earnings allow for upward mobility at low incomes. Saving rate differentials are important as they allow (indeed) the rich to get richer by accumulating at

---

[2] E.g. in the structure of pay in a top tennis tournament it may be that the second-best (who is only a tiny fraction worse than the champion) may receive something like half the pay, the third-best an even smaller fraction, etc. And, by the way, the woman champion receives less than the man champion.

higher rates. Finally, capital income risk also contributes to wealth inequality but also allows for downward social mobility (for the unsuccessful entrepreneurs).

One factor that may have impacted on inequality is globalization. This development is multi-faceted and the effects may work via various channels. One is the effect of greater international trade on businesses: Those firms that are able to benefit from globalization by exporting and gaining new markets will see their profits rise and their demand and pay of labour also rise; conversely, those firms that find stiff competition from imports will do the opposite. Hence, inequality will increase. One (inverse) measure of globalization is the extent of tariffs, as they impede cross-country trade. Milanovic and Squire (2007) find mixed evidence concerning this hypothesis: They find that tariff reduction (i.e. a boost to globalization) is associated with higher inter-occupational and inter-industry wage inequality in poorer countries and the reverse in richer countries.

Another aspect of globalization is immigration. There is both theory and evidence that immigration is good for a high-productivity country facing labour shortages. The question for inequality is whether immigration benefits a segment of the population and business, by providing cheaper and/or more skilled labour, while it antagonizes some other segment of the labour force. Card and Shleifer (2009) addresses these issues; they account carefully for the skills of immigrants into the US. One thing to note, and this is probably true of other countries as well, is that immigrants have lower skills than the natives. Card and Shleifer (2009) find that the impact of immigrant inflows on the relative wages of US natives are small, but the effect on overall wage inequality (including natives and immigrants) is larger, but still not dramatic. In their estimates, immigration accounts for only 5 per cent of the increase in US wage inequality between 1980 and 2000.

Finally, we should not forget the institutional and political factors, including taxation. In this respect, it is worth quoting the findings of Piketty and Saez (2007) on the effects of taxation in the US and UK. They find that taxation has become dramatically less progressive in the US and the UK since the 1960s, while it has become more progressive in France. One could therefore put forward the conjecture, in need of empirical investigation, that at least part of the rise in inequality in the US and UK is due to the fall in the progressivity of their tax systems. Of course, an argument against tax-led redistribution is that a greater taxation provides a disincentive for labour supply; we discuss this below. More generally, taxation is harmful for growth. There is a long-run argument that there is a 'growth-equality trade-off'; society and policy-makers need to make a choice between these two objectives. We review this debate and the evidence in Section 10.2; see also the Guidance for Further Study for more discussion of the Piketty-Saez findings.

Other relevant considerations may be the labour market institutions that we discussed in Chapter 4 and the nature of the political systems. But these issues do not seem to have received much attention in a macro context. There is no consensus and the above review is by no means exhaustive. One thing is sure, the issue of inequality will gain further attention in the foreseeable future.

10.1.6 Poverty and Further Issues

One reason why one may be interested in inequality is because it is related to (but distinct from) poverty. Poverty is the fact that some sections of the population live without adequate (in a sense to be defined) means or income. Poverty looks at the low end of the income distribution, so in a sense inequality is a wider issue, but poverty is the more acute issue. To put it schematically, an economy with poverty will also be unequal, but the converse may not be true: you may have inequality (at the upper end) without (much) poverty. But in practice high inequality and the incidence of poverty are highly correlated. Poverty is under scrutiny and policy discussion because of the hardship it entails, the ugly irony that some individuals live with so little amid the plenty, and because of the policy challenges it poses. Poverty affects families and children, depriving them of basic material comfort, dignity, and a fair chance in life. Hence, it is worth digressing briefly into the issue.

Similar measurement issues arise with poverty as with inequality. There is also an additional issue related to the fact that there are increasing returns to scale (so to speak) in producing household welfare and therefore the marginal cost of maintaining a given level of living standards falls with each additional member of a household. This implies that income per capita (i.e. division of a household or family income by its members) is inadequate as a measure of living standards or economic welfare. For this reason, statistical agencies generate 'equivalence scales': if the first adult costs an amount x in order to maintain a given living standard, the second adult costs x/2, and each child costs 0.3x. Thus, to gauge living standards properly, the total income of the household must be divided by 1 in the case of a one-member household, 1.5 in the case of two adults, and $2.1 (= 1 + 0.5 + 0.3 + 0.3)$ in the case of a two-adult, two-children family. Put otherwise, this implies that the same living standard is maintained by a single-member household earning £20k, or a two-adult one earning £30k, or a $2 + 2$ family with £42k. A plain income per capita, which would divide family income by 2 in the two-adult case, would give a misleading picture of living standards; the correct approach is division of family income by 1.5.

We may distinguish between absolute and relative poverty. Starting with relative first, it considers 'poor' every household or individual below a 'poverty line', which is based on a per capita income equal to 60 per cent (or thereabout) of the median per capita income.[3] In the case of absolute poverty, in contrast, the poverty line is defined in terms of the income required to buy a 'subsistence' level of goods and services. Of course, the difficulty with absolute measures is to determine the set of goods that define a minimum acceptable living standard (or 'subsistence' level). In this respect, one approach is based on wider 'capabilities': minimum 'functions' such as shelter, nutrition, clothing but also health, education, freedom, choice, as well as private consumption. Thus, even absolute measures are not free from relative considerations (what is an acceptable standard or 'subsistence' is defined in a social context). Relative and absolute measures can give different results across countries and across time. It is fair to say that, as with inequality, no measure of poverty is perfect.

Why should we care about inequality and poverty? We have discussed brief answers in relation to both. Concerning inequality, one additional important reason is that inequality has been rising in the last 40 years, as already discussed. As Piketty (2014) remarks, complete equality is not desirable (nor feasible), because not everyone is the same; people

---

[3] Since 2015, the poverty line in the UK has been officially defined by the 'Social Metrics Commission' to be at 55 per cent of the median of 'Total Resources Available' (TRA), which measures income plus net assets minus living costs and is adjusted for family size. More formally, TRA = Net Earnings + Benefit Income + 1/12 Liquid savings — 1/12 Debts owed — costs for Housing, Disability and Childcare; all adjusted for family size and number of bedrooms. The rationale for the adoption of this approach is that TRA is a more comprehensive measure of the financial position of a family or household than income (which it encompasses under Net Earnings).

differ in terms of talent, skills, and motivation, and need to be rewarded and incentivized for their effort; however, the levels of inequality that we see today, as described above, are beyond any sense of fairness. Furthermore, inequality generates negative externalities (low trust, cynicism, crime, corruption).

Moreover, the inequality of innate skills and human capital that we take as exogenous in public policy discussions (and in our models in Section 10.2) is surely partly endogenous; not only by the educational choices and human capital investment of the individual and their family but by the social conditioning that all social animals receive. A good perform-ance is not only due to natural aptitude but also good schooling, which may itself be the result of inequality. So, apart from fairness considerations, there are various mechanisms by which inequality, and a fortiori poverty, can become entrenched and self-perpetuating. As we saw in Chapter 5 on generational accounting, the vast majority of wealth in the US is due to inheritance rather than accumulation within a lifetime. We call 'social mobility' the ability of individuals to break out of the position in which their accident of birth has put them and move towards a position dictated by their abilities and talents. Statistical offices measure both within-lifetime and intergenerational social mobility, which more practically shows the extent to which individuals can break out of poverty if their personal abilities allow it; this is obviously an objective of public policy.

Inequality and poverty, and the questions and challenges they pose, are among the defining issues of our time. At core, they raise questions about social and distributive justice. What is fair? A number of approaches to fairness have been suggested. A 'minimum standards' approach postulates that, providing everyone enjoys an acceptable standard of living, we should not be concerned about wider inequality. It justifies attention to poverty and deprivation indices (whether absolute or relative or 'capabilities'-based), more than inequality, and in terms of policy assigns a role to government in providing such key services and goods as healthcare, education, and social insurance against unemploy-ment and old age. It may well also suggest a 'basic income', which has gained some attention lately. It is a minimum universal income which will be paid to all regardless of employment status or income and will be financed by general taxation. The main advan-tages of basic income will be administrative simplicity and the fact that it will not provide a disincentive to work effort: it will not be lost no matter how high the privately earned income is. The main disadvantage of basic income is that, for it to support a standard of living that is in any sense acceptable, the required taxation will have to be way higher than the currently accepted norms. For an introduction to basic income, one could consult Atkinson (2011); see also the Guidance for Further Study.

Another approach to fairness and social justice is 'equality of opportunity'; in a nutshell, it suggests that, if we cannot have a 'just' economy, at least do let us ensure that individuals will tend to personal steady states that are guided more by their ability and personal characteristics rather than their accident of birth. The most ambitious approach to fairness is, of course, one that emphasizes (the need for) 'equality of outcomes'. At the core of this approach is the twin idea that (a) the existing income and wealth distribution are not in any way egalitarian, and likely not fair; and (b) that the market mechanism does not have any self-corrective mechanisms. Once, a theory of 'trickle-down prosperity' was put forward (see Aghion and Bolton, 1997), namely that as the fortunes of the well-off improve, so will gradually those of the rest of society, as the rich will demand services and goods from the poor and prosperity will 'trickle down'. But, with the newer evidence, not many people would now seriously defend this over-optimistic argument. So, equality of outcomes will not arise by itself in any sense. The question then is what course of action might get us closer to the principle of 'equality of outcomes'.

No one would probably suggest absolute equality as a model of fairness and justice; rather, any reasonable proposal would envisage an income or pay that would 'appropriately' and 'fairly' reward ability and effort. The difficulty is in defining 'fairly'; there are no easy answers here. Any attempts for a definition are inevitably based on 'value judgments'; the room for objective analysis and agreement may be limited. Perhaps a pragmatic criterion is that, whatever is a 'fair' and 'just' society, the levels of inequality we are currently seeing cannot be in any sense fair or just. Thus, this approach leads to corrective measures in terms of progressive taxation and tax-led redistribution. Redistribution can be direct and indirect, first by providing support and benefits to the economically weak, but also by providing welfare-state services (education, healthcare, etc.), social security (pensions), and even infrastructure (housing). As inequality is worsening, so such efforts should be intensified. In sum, many of these points and proposals are in need of further development, and there is certainly no consensus. But as inequality and poverty are rising, the issues and proposals will stay with us.

10.2 Models of Inequality

10.2.1 Saving and Income Distribution in Early Models

It is convenient to begin from some distributional insights of early models, following Bertola et al. (2006). As we have reviewed similar arguments in both Chapters 5 and 9, only a sketch will be given. The approach assumes that in the long run we follow a Balanced Growth Path (BGP), whereby injections to capital (investment) equal leakages. All variables are defined as ratios over labour in efficiency units, e.g. in the case of capital we have $k_t \equiv \frac{K_t}{A_t L_t}$, where K is physical capital, L is labour (identical to population), and A is productivity (or quality of labour).[4] As in Chapters 5 and 9, we can roughly speaking call k the 'capitalization rate' of the economy. The growth rate of labour in efficiency units is, in balanced growth, equal to the population growth (g_L) plus the rate of growth of productivity (g_A). In the BGP, where k is constant, this is all equal to the growth rate of capital (g_K). From National Income Accounting, this in turn is equal to saving: $g_K K = sY$, where s is the saving rate. Note the assumptions we make of no depreciation and a closed economy. Thus, we have the following relationship:

$$g_L + g_A = g_K = sY/K \tag{10.1}$$

We assume that the economy is made up of two groups, 'workers' and 'capitalists'. In both groups, each individual offers inelastically one unit of labour, for which they receive the economy-wide wage rate w. Groups differ in their holdings of capital. Capitalists own more capital; more about this later on. Each individual earns an amount of dividend income

---

[4] Note a couple of notational changes from Chapter 5. There, we had hatted variables, e.g. $\hat{k}_t \equiv \frac{K_t}{A_t L_t}$, while we dispense with hats here. The population growth rate was η (g_L here). Also, here, there is no depreciation ($\delta = 0$).

equal to their ownership of capital times the real interest rate, which reflects the rate of return to capital across the economy. The bottomline is that both classes earn the same labour income but capitalists earn more capital income. The two classes also differ in their saving rates. The 'capitalists' save more in proportion to their total income; this is line with empirical evidence: Dynan et al. (2004, table 3) estimates that the saving rate of the first quintile (20 per cent of the population with the lowest income) is zero while that of the fifth (20 per cent with highest income) about 0.46; see also Mankiw (2000) for further discussion.

Rather than postulating saving rates for each class, we shall distinguish between sources of income (labour income from wages, capital income from dividends) and we shall say that different saving rates apply to each: the saving rates applying to labour and capital income are, respectively, $s^w \geq 0$ and $s^k > 0$; the former is lower, i.e. $s^w < s^k$. We indicate the share of national income (GDP) that goes to remuneration of labour as $0 < \gamma$ and the share going to capital to be the remaining $1 - \gamma$. To preamble, we used to think that $\gamma/(1 - \gamma) \approx 2$; it has been traditionally assumed that two-thirds of GDP went as remuneration to labour. But now the evidence shows that the balance is shifting in favour of capital and this has important implications for overall income inequality. We review these issues in Section 10.3.

The aggregate saving rate s may therefore be decomposed as:

$$s = s^w \gamma + s^k (1 - \gamma) \tag{10.2}$$

Combining (10.1) and (10.2), we have:

$$g_L + g_A = \left(s^w \gamma + s^k (1 - \gamma) \right) Y/K \tag{10.3}$$

On the basis of (10.3), Bertola et al. (2006) offer a nice typology of the early growth models. The early 'Harrod-Domar' growth model takes all the parameters as given, in which case (10.3) becomes a knife-edge condition: the economy runs into trouble unless by a happy coincidence (10.3) holds. According to Harrod-Domar, the output-capital ratio (Y/K) is given by technology and an assumed non-substitutability between the factors of production (the 'Leontieff' fixed-factor-proportions technology of Chapter 1). Thus, the chances of the above equation holding, and balanced growth, are quite slim. If the left side is greater than the right (LHS > RHS), then labour in efficiency units is growing faster than capital, and because of fixed proportions in which they are required to be used, a growing proportion of labour will be left unemployed. At the opposite end, if RHS > LHS, then capital will be growing faster than the available labour in efficiency units and that will be lying unemployed (there will be a labour shortage).

The Solow Growth Model (SGM) is a neoclassical theory in the sense that the technology has all the nice properties described by the Inada conditions and, key among them, substitutability between factors. Thus, any given level of output may be produced by many different combinations of labour and capital. The SGM therefore lets Y/K adjust because of the properties of the production function, so that the equality in (10.3) is satisfied at all times (see Solow, 1994). The SGM assumes no optimization. The neoclassical theory with optimization (the Ramsey model of Chapter 5) lets the saving rate (as well as Y/K) be endogenously determined. Finally, the post-Keynesian school associated with Cambridge,

England (a review of which is outside our scope), lets the factor shares $(\gamma, 1 - \gamma)$ adjust, thus enabling the equation to be satisfied.

Labour and capital income are unequally distributed across individuals. Moreover, these two categories of income are not distributed in the same way. While labour income is unequal (the skilled individuals and those who work harder generally get higher wages), capital income is even more unequally distributed across individuals. Therefore, not only are those with higher capital ownership richer; they also save at a higher rate, therefore they accumulate assets at a higher rate and become ever richer. So, one implication of equation (10.3) is that the more unequal the wealth (capital) distribution and income in relation to the labour income, the higher the capital share (remuneration of capital) and the higher the saving rate of the rich (in relation to the poor), then the more unequal the current income distribution will be and the higher the tendency for the inequality to rise further. We shall revisit similar arguments in Section 10.3 when we discuss the 'r > g' relation.

10.2.2 Income Distribution in an Endogenous-Growth Model: Fixed Labour

We now follow a model by Garcia-Penalosa and Turnovsky (2006), which is a variant of the neoclassical optimization model that allows for endogenous long-run growth. The model is more fruitful than either SGM or Ramsey for our purposes. We will review how the parameters of equation (10.3) are determined in the model and we will use that model to shed light on income distribution. Section 5.2 (Ramsey model) and Section 9.5 have the essentials so we shall only sketch the model here; we also drop time subscripts. The economy is made up of a 'unit mass' of identical firms (therefore, the typical firm essentially is a replica of the aggregate economy). Each firm (and the aggregate economy) has access to a production function (9.18a), in which capital is a proxy for productivity; this is due either to 'learning-by-doing' externalities, or to growth-enhancing public services being proportional to the scale of the economy. We also set the unimportant proportionality parameter $\omega = 1$.

As in (9.18a), the production therefore takes the Cobb-Douglas form:

$$Y = AK^{\alpha}(KL)^{1-\alpha}, \quad 0 < \alpha < 1 \tag{10.4}$$

Determined in competitive markets, the factor (capital-labour) rates of return (real interest rate and wage, respectively), are:

$$r = \frac{\partial Y}{\partial K} = \alpha \frac{Y}{K} = \alpha AL^{1-\alpha}, \tag{10.5a}$$

$$w = \frac{\partial Y}{\partial L} = (1 - \alpha)\frac{Y}{L} = (1 - \alpha)AKL^{-\alpha} \tag{10.5b}$$

Both are common across the economy.

There is also a unit mass of individuals; here, because we want to delve more deeply, we index them by i. Each individual is endowed with K_i units of capital (the only form of wealth), which is the only source of heterogeneity; otherwise, the individuals are identical.

There is thus a distribution of capital across individuals i; as we shall see, the properties of the model imply that the initial distribution remains unchanged for ever. Because of the unit mass, the aggregate capital is the mean of the individuals, $K = E(K_i)$; and similarly with income (Y) and labour (L). Individuals own the shares of the firms in proportion to their capital ownership. Next, we are going to develop the sources of income in two versions, for the individual i and for the aggregate economy:

$$Y_i = rK_i + wL_i \tag{10.6a}$$

$$Y = rK + wL \tag{10.6b}$$

The individual maximizes intertemporal utility subject to the appropriate intertemporal budget constraint; as in Chapter 9 (equation 9.17), this results in the Euler growth equation (valid in the BGP):

$$g = \sigma(r - \rho) = \sigma\left(\alpha A L^{1-\alpha} - \rho\right) \tag{10.7}$$

The second equality uses the interest rate (10.5a).

As Garcia-Penalosa and Turnovsky (2006) show, the BGP holds at all times in this model, and there are no transitory dynamics. Thus, the initial distribution of capital and anything that depends on it are preserved unaltered; all variables, aggregate and individual, grow at the common rate g at all times (except of course labour supply, the interest and the wage rates).

Additionally, the budget constraint is presented in the individual and aggregate versions:

$$Y_i = C_i + gK_i \tag{10.8a}$$

$$Y = C + gK \tag{10.8b}$$

Income is used for consumption and for investment (growth of capital which is reflected also in the shares that individuals hold).

Combination of (10.6), (10.7), and (10.9) then gives:

$$rK_i + wL_i = C_i + \sigma(r - \rho)K_i$$

$$rK + wL = C + \sigma(r - \rho)K$$

Or

$$C_i = [r(1 - \sigma) + \sigma\rho]K_i + wL_i \tag{10.9a}$$

$$C = [r(1 - \sigma) + \sigma\rho]K + wL \tag{10.9b}$$

The simplest version of the model assumes fixed labour supply, in which case we set $L_i = L = 1$. For a moment, let us also assume log utility ($\sigma = 1$). In this case, we have:

$$C_i = \rho K_i + w \tag{10.9a'}$$

$$C = \rho K + w \tag{10.9b'}$$

Individuals and the aggregate economy consume all their labour income, w (recall $L = 1$), plus a fraction (ρ) of their capital endowment every period (Bertola, 1993; Alesina and Rodrik, 1994). In other words, there is no saving out of labour income; in the notation above, $s^w = 0$; out of capital income (rK), a portion gK is saved and invested, therefore $s^k = g/r = (\alpha A - \rho)/(\alpha A) > s^w = 0$. These are interesting results in their own right. However, even though part of capital income is saved while labour income is not, the relative capital assets (K_i/K) do not change in this model. So, both income and wealth (capital) inequality remain unchanged over time.

From (10.5a, b) and (10.6a, b), income is:

$$Y_i = \alpha A K_i + (1 - \alpha) A K \tag{10.10a}$$

$$Y = \alpha A K + (1 - \alpha) A K \tag{10.10b}$$

It is instructive to see relative income and wealth (capital) as deviations from the mean (=1); dividing by $Y = AK$, we have:

$$\frac{Y_i}{Y} - 1 = \alpha \left(\frac{K_i}{K} - 1 \right) \tag{10.10c}$$

With $0 < \alpha < 1$, we a major result of this model:

$$Var(Y_i/Y) = \alpha^2 Var(K_i/K) < Var(K_i/K) \tag{10.11}$$

The variance of relative income, a measure of income inequality, is less than the variance of relative capital. Thus, income inequality is less than wealth inequality, which is in line with empirical evidence (Davies et al., 2011; Kennickell, 2009). This result is independent of the value of the intertemporal elasticity of substitution (σ).

The factor shares in this model are $\gamma = wL/Y = (1 - \alpha)$ (labour share) and $1 - \gamma = rK/Y = \alpha$ (capital share). The noteworthy feature is that factor shares depend only on the technical parameter (α), which determines the real interest rate and capital income; this is the result of the Cobb-Douglas production function. In the next section, we shall relax this restrictive feature by considering the more general CES production function. The same parameter determines the ratio of income inequality/wealth inequality. Things are more interesting (and slightly more complicated) with endogenous labour supply; we do that next.

10.2.3 Income Distribution in an Endogenous-Growth Model: Endogenous Labour

In the spirit of Section 5.1, but following Garcia-Penalosa and Turnovsky (2006) more closely, the period utility function (cf. equation 5.9 of Chapter 5) is:

$$u(C_{it}, l_{it}) = (C_{it} l_{it}^\theta)^{1/\sigma}$$

where $l_i \equiv 1 - L_i$ is leisure; $\theta \geq 0$ is the elasticity of leisure in utility and $\sigma < 1$ is the intertemporal elasticity of substitution (the numerical restriction follows the empirical evidence).

The intra-temporal first-order condition (5.14) takes the form:

$$\theta l_{it}^{-1} = w_t C_{it}^{-1} \tag{10.12}$$

Using $l_i \equiv 1 - L_i$, this can be used to solve for individual labour supply (given the wage):

$$\theta C_i = w(1 - L_i) \tag{10.13a}$$

Aggregating:

$$\theta C = w(1 - L) \tag{10.13b}$$

We see immediately that the case where leisure does not matter in utility ($\theta = 0$) implies a fixed labour supply ($L_i = L = 1$). Thus, the case of fixed labour is a special case of the more general framework.

Although it is not central to our argument, as a digression, let us now solve for the aggregate labour supply—or alternatively for the wage. With the wage (10.5b) and (10.13b), we can write:

$$\theta C = (1 - \alpha)AKL^{-\alpha}(1 - L) = w - (1 - \alpha)Y$$

Or

$$w = \theta C + (1 - \alpha)Y \tag{10.14}$$

The consumption equation (10.9b) and (10.14) allow us to solve for the wage:

$$w = (1 + \theta)(1 - \alpha)Y + \theta[(1 - \sigma)r + \sigma\rho]K$$

The production function (10.4) and wage (10.5b) imply:

$$(1 - \alpha)AL^{-\alpha} = [(1 + \theta)(1 - \alpha) + \theta(1 - \sigma)\alpha]AL^{1-\alpha} + \theta\sigma\rho \tag{10.15}$$

Theoretically, (10.15) allows us to solve for L; in practice, it is difficult to solve due to the non-linearity. Figure 10.1 graphs the left (LHS) and right (RHS) sides of (10.15). With this

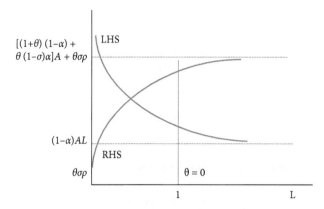

$[(1+\theta)(1-\alpha) + \theta(1-\sigma)\alpha]A + \theta\sigma\rho$ — LHS

$(1-\alpha)AL$ — RHS

$\theta\sigma\rho$

$\theta = 0$

1

L

Figure 10.2. Endogenous labour supply determination according to (10.15)

aid, we discuss existence and uniqueness of equilibrium and comparative statics. Once L is determined, one will obtain growth from (10.7), output from (10.4) (assuming an exogenous initial level of capital for $t = 0$ and using growth 10.7 to obtain the subsequent time-profile of capital), real wage and interest rate from (10.5a, b), and consumption from (10.9).

The geometry in Figure 10.1 suggests the existence and uniqueness of equilibrium; for more details, one can consult Garcia-Penalosa and Turnovsky (2006). For completeness, we note that equation (10.15) reduces to fixed labour ($L = 1$) in the special case of $\theta = 0$, which is shown as a vertical line. Looking at the coefficients of L on the left and right sides of (10.15), we can get the following results:

- A rise in the discount rate (ρ) shifts the RHS up and decreases labour supply. This is essentially because a rise in impatience decreases saving and growth; this raises current consumption and leisure (which, by 10.12a, b, are proportional to each other given the wage) and decreases labour supply.
- A rise in the elasticity of leisure in utility (θ) both shifts and tilts the RHS upwards and again decreases labour; this is intuitive, as leisure is more valuable;
- A higher productivity shifts the RHS down/right (to see this, divide across 10.14 by A) and increases labour supply; this is essentially because the marginal product of labour, the wage, and thus the opportunity cost of leisure all rise.
- The effect of the intertemporal elasticity of substitution (σ) is unclear.

We now return to our main line of argument on income distribution. With (10.13a, b), (10.9a, b), consumption now takes the form:

$$C_i = \frac{[(1-\sigma)r + \sigma\rho]K_i + w}{1+\theta} \tag{10.16a}$$

$$C = \frac{[(1-\sigma)r + \sigma\rho]K + w}{1+\theta} \tag{10.16b}$$

Finally, from (10.7a, b), incomes are:

$$Y_i = \frac{[r + \theta\sigma(r - \rho)]K_i + w}{1 + \theta} \tag{10.17a}$$

$$Y = \frac{[r + \theta\sigma(r - \rho)]K + w}{1 + \theta} \tag{10.17b}$$

Dividing by Y and noting (10.5a), relative income is:

$$\frac{Y_i}{Y} - 1 = \left[\frac{\alpha + \theta\sigma(\alpha - \rho K/Y)}{1 + \theta}\right]\left(\frac{K_i}{K} - 1\right) \tag{10.17c}$$

We now have the following variance of relative income:

$$Var(Y_i/Y) = \left[\frac{\alpha + \theta\sigma(\alpha - \rho K/Y)}{1 + \theta}\right]^2 Var(K_i/K) < \alpha^2 Var(K_i/K) \tag{10.11'}$$

We see here another result, namely that the endogenous labour supply decreases the variance of relative income relative to the fixed labour case (10.11). Formally, this is because:

$$\frac{\alpha + \theta\sigma(\alpha - \rho K/Y)}{1 + \theta} = \alpha \frac{1 + \theta\sigma(1 - \rho K/\alpha Y)}{1 + \theta} \leq \alpha$$

The equality holds in the special case of $\theta = 0$. Intuitively, the lower relative income variance in the flexible labour case is due to the fact that the richer individuals (endowed with more capital) also choose higher leisure (cf. again the proportionality relation 10.11), therefore their higher capital income is partially offset by a lower labour income. Hence, the income distribution is less unequal now. But note, the higher leisure only partially offsets the higher capital income, therefore the individual with higher capital still has a higher overall income.

Furthermore, from production (10.4), we have that $K/Y = A^{-1}L^{-1+\alpha}$. Hence, by the results derived in Figure 10.1 and the associated discussion, K/L rises with ρ and θ (while the effect of σ is unclear). It also falls with higher productivity, A. The results we can therefore glean from (10.11') are the following. Given the exogenous distribution of capital endowment, the income inequality rises with:

- A higher elasticity of capital in production (α), as this implies a higher share of capital income in national income;
- A lower discount rate (ρ), as a higher ρ decreases the labour supply of the rich; it also reduces the rate of return from capital;
- A higher productivity (A), as this decreases the capital-output ratio (K/Y) and ultimately raises the rate of return from the (unequally distributed) capital endowment.

The interested reader is invited to derive and explain other, less straightforward results, in particular, in relation to θ and σ.

10.2.4 The 'Representative-Agent' Assumption and Distributive Considerations

In order to deal with aggregation (i.e. how to go from individual optimization and behaviour to the behaviour of aggregate variables), much of dynamic macroeconomics postulates a 'representative agent' (RA): a fictitious individual who is a scaled-down replica of the aggregate economy. This 'person' faces the constraints of the aggregate economy, optimizes and decides optimal behaviour (goods demands, labour supply, etc.). Such models take the individual optimal behaviour of the RA and turn it into aggregate: e.g. they take the individual optimal consumption and they assume that this is what aggregate consumption looks like. In many models, the economy is assumed to be made up of identical individuals, in which case the RA is one of these. In such cases, the models inform us about the behaviour of the aggregate economy; however, by assumption, they cannot tell us anything about the distribution of either income or wealth. The really interesting question is whether there can be models which can be based on an RA (so that they can tell us about the aggregate economy in a tractable way), while allowing agent heterogeneity such that income and wealth distribution are not trivial. For this to happen, heterogeneity must be in some ways limited, it must have some 'structure'. What is the heterogeneity that is permitted in order for the RA property to hold? In what way is the RA 'typical' of the heterogeneous population in such economies? Caselli and Ventura (2000) deal with these questions.

Caselli and Ventura (2000) show that, in order for the RA property to obtain, there must be a common marginal propensity to consume out of intertemporal resources; this implies a common elasticity of intertemporal substitution, common discount rate, and common interest rate (i.e. not depending on wealth endowments or skills). Providing this, a wide variety of distributions of consumption, income, or wealth can be accommodated and analysed, which do not affect the aggregate quantities; Caselli and Ventura (2000) investigate the nature of these distributions. Absence of a government sector, moreover, implies that relative consumption remains constant (unaltered consumption distribution). Note that in the 'learning-by-doing' AK model of Garcia-Penalosa and Turnovsky (2006), all distributions (capital, income, consumption) remain unaltered at all times (see also Caselli and Ventura, 2000, Section IIB).

The assumption of a RA is a major convenience, as it implies that we do not need to consider how the various resources (e.g. capital or wealth endowments, skills and productivity) and preferences (e.g. disutility of labour and motivation) are distributed in order to determine aggregate outcomes; knowledge of just average capital, skills, or motivation is enough in order to model aggregate consumption or labour supply. In other words, the aggregate system is exogenous to the distributional considerations: while distributions do not matter for the averages, the converse is not true. Hence, one should solve the model for the aggregate variables, then, conditional on those and the postulated exogenous distributions (as applicable), one will obtain predictions about distributional considerations for variables of interest (consumption, income, wealth). In our previous sub-section, equations (b), the aggregate ones, must be solved first together with factor returns (10.5a, b) and the aggregate labour supply (10.14), which are all aggregate relations; after L, r, and w have been determined, one then proceeds to solve the (a) versions of the equations (individual variables). Thus, the RA property holds in the model of sub-section 10.2.4.

10.2.5 Discussion

The model sketched above relies on only one source of heterogeneity, namely heterogeneity in capital endowments; some individuals are born with more wealth inheritance than others. As Garcia-Penalosa and Turnovsky (2006) argue, this is an important source of heterogeneity, as it is related to the heterogeneity of capital income, which is showing signs of widening inequality, as we discuss in the next section. However, there can be important heterogeneity in other respects, such as in skills and productivity, in tastes and preferences (disutility of labour and motivation), or human capital and education. But care should be taken, as heterogeneity in human capital is endogenous, the result of more fundamental (exogenous) differences in other respects (endowments or preferences), possibly amplified by the effects of imperfect capital markets that do not allow some individuals to reach their true potential. See Turnovsky (2013) for a more general discussion on the distributive implications of theoretical models with multiple sources of heterogeneity.

In an important early contribution, Galor and Zeira (1993) presented an overlapping-generations model with human capital. Capital market imperfections, of the type we discussed in Chapter 7, imply that borrowing interest rates are higher than lending rates, thus restricting borrowing. Individuals make a choice as to work as unskilled workers and earn a low wage; or borrow, invest in education, and earn a higher wage at a later stage. For this decision, the inheritance each individual receives from their parent is crucial: individuals who receive a low inheritance prefer not to invest in human capital but work as unskilled labour. Education is, therefore, limited to individuals with high enough initial wealth, due to a higher interest rate for borrowers. The wider point here is that growth and inequality are interdependent: the distribution of incomes of the earlier generation, and therefore the bequests they leave to their young, determine the amount of human capital investment that the younger generation undertakes, which in turn determines growth but also the distribution of future incomes. In general, a variety of possible outcomes emerges. There are multiple equilibria and a possible explanation of the Kuznets (1955) Curve arises, as an economy on a high equilibrium (a developed economy) has a lower income inequality than a less developed economy (one on a lower equilibrium).

Heathcote et al. (2010) present an overlapping-generations model where exogenous factors that drive changes in the wage structure interact with the choices of individuals about labour supply, education, and saving. Appropriately calibrated, the model can arguably account for the key trends in cross-sectional US data on these variables. As we discussed in the Guidance for Further Study of Chapter 9, Jones (2015) and Jones and Kim (2018) present a model of 'Schumpeterian growth' through creative destruction, where entrepreneurs who generate path-breaking innovations earn very high returns and top incomes; the model predicts a Pareto distribution of top incomes, in line with the data. As we discussed, there are some strong (and possibly controversial) policy implications stemming from these analyses.

Garcia-Penalosa and Turnovsky (2011) analyse distributional dynamics in a Ramsey model with endogenous labour supply and heterogeneity derived from differences in initial capital endowments; thus, this paper is similar to their 2006 paper, the innovation being an analysis of how tax policies affect the dynamics of the distributions of wealth and income. Taxes affect the optimal hours of work and this will affect the distribution of wealth and income in addition to the direct redistributive impact. They find a trade-off: tax policies that are associated with a more equal distribution of after-tax income also result in lower output; the effect on labour supply is crucial here. These findings have profound policy implications. They lead us to the wider issue of a possible trade-off between two legitimate objectives of policy, namely equality and growth (or high output); we examine this issue next.

10.2.6 The Growth-Equality Trade-off (?)

Following Okun (1975), there has been an argument that there is a trade-off between growth and equality. Tax-led redistribution, which is required for equality, provides a disincentive to labour supply, investment, and even innovation. Thus, equality and growth are antithetical and society and its policy-makers must make a choice as to which one they should prioritize among the two objectives. This suggestion has given rise to a lively debate of a great policy relevance; however, not everyone shares the view that growth and equality undermine each other. Before we go to specifics, we should first note some methodological points. If there is a trade-off, it is conditional on a myriad of other, often country-specific, factors and considerations that may drive the relationship in any direction. The policy-relevant question is how redistribution affects the growth-equality relationship that may exist due to these other factors. Another issue is causality: a correlation, of whatever sign, would not establish causality. In fact, there may be more than one causal mechanisms that may induce different partial correlations (see Bénabou, 1996, 2000), which may be conflated in cross-country regressions. Even more broadly, both growth and (in)equality may be the outcomes of a number of other factors, including policies, and cross-country regressions should take this into consideration. Barro (2002) and Lundberg and Squire (2003) explore the relation between inequality and growth.

However, the presumed trade-off was never universally accepted. For instance, Persson and Tabellini (1994) argue that inequality gives rise to redistributive policies that reduce growth; therefore, inequality is correlated with low growth. Furthermore, recent studies continue to re-evaluate the relationship and tend to show that equality is good for growth; see Andersen and Maibom (2019) and references therein. Although there is no consensus, one may argue that greater equality may be conducive to growth as it promotes more societal trust, social capital, and cooperation, among other characteristics. Additionally, it alleviates all the social ills that Wilkinson and Pickett (2009) highlight. In a recent contribution, Ostry et al. (2014) boldly reconsider the growth-inequality trade-off thesis. They consider carefully the impact of redistribution on any trade-off that is due to other factors by distinguishing net (post-tax and transfers) inequality from market (pre-tax and transfers) inequality. This allows them to calculate redistributive transfers for a large number of countries over time—covering both advanced and developing countries. They then analyse the effect of this redistribution on growth and come up with some striking results that challenge the received wisdom about a growth-equality trade-off. First, inequality is a negative, robust, and powerful determinant both of growth and its duration. Inequality and unsustainable growth may be two sides of the same coin. Second, there is remarkably little evidence in the historical data of adverse effects of fiscal redistribution on growth. Instead, the average redistribution, and the associated reduction in inequality, are robustly associated with higher and more durable growth. It is only very large redistributions that may have direct negative effects on the duration of growth.

10.3 Factor Shares

10.3.1 Factor (Labour and Capital) Shares

Factor shares are the proportion of national income that is awarded as remuneration to the main factors of production, capital, and labour. They depend on the wage and the interest rate, of course, but those in turn depend on deeper fundamentals like the structure of production and markets, institutions of various types (labour market, laws, taxation, etc.); we discuss them later. It is important to study factor shares for a dual reason: first they seem to be changing in recent years for reasons that are unclear, and second, they are important for income distribution; more on both these points below. As we saw in Chapter 9, one of the 'Kaldor facts' concerns factor shares, which are supposed to stay constant; but we found grounds to doubt this 'fact'. Table 10.2a, b contains information on the labour shares from various regions, countries, and times. Only the labour share is shown, as the two factor shares sum to unity, therefore the capital share is the mirror image of the labour share.

A couple of tentative observations pointing towards some 'stylized facts' related to factor shares:

- There is a lot of variation across countries and regions (Table 10.2a). But a simple correlation seems to suggest itself: more developed countries or regions have a higher labour share. This does not seem to have been noted in the literature.
- Again there are country variations, but there seems to be a tendency in recent years for the labour share to fall. The change appears to be marginal in the years covered in Table 10.2.b, but we should keep in mind that, as with growth in Chapter 9, these are 'small numbers with a great significance'. The tendency of the labour share to fall is noted by numerous studies, e.g. Autor et al. (2017) and references therein. As the same study notes, the reasons are poorly understood.

Estimating precisely the labour share (and its mirror image, the capital share) is fraught with measurement problems: among other issues, one needs to carefully treat the incomes of the self-employed, small—unincorporated—businesses and income from renting housing; see Gollin, (2002), Karabarbounis and Neiman (2014), and Ronglie (2015). But the falling tendency seems beyond question. The reason why the evolution of the factor shares is important is that labour income is more equitably distributed across workers than capital income (though with far from full equality); therefore, the higher the share of national

Table 10.2. Labour shares for selected countries/regions and years

Part (a): Labour shares in the international economy in 2017

	%	Region	%	Region	%	Region	%
	52	Northern Europe	55.4	North Africa	39.7	Central America	36.2
Asia	40.1	Southern Europe	57.8	Sub-Saharan Africa	52.4	Carribean	50.2
	46.1	Western Europe	61.6	Central Africa	43.7	South America	56.8
Central Asia	41.3	Eastern Europe	50.1	Eastern Africa	44.6	North America	58.8
	39.5	European Union	57.6	Southern Africa	53.5	BRICs	51.6
Arab countries	32.2	World average	51.4	West Africa	59.1		

Part (b): Evolution of the labour shares (%) over time for selected countries

	UK	US	Japan	Germany	France	Australia
2004	59,9	61,7	54,6	61,8	59,9	59,9
2005	59,2	60,7	54,7	61,1	61,1	59,5
2006	59,8	60,7	54,9	59,7	61,6	59,2
2007	60,3	60,9	54,6	58,4	63,7	59,0
2008	59,7	61,1	56,1	59,0	61,5	57,4
2009	61,3	60,2	56,8	61,7	62,5	57,7
2010	61,2	59,2	55,6	60,4	63,2	57,9
2011	59,6	59,1	56,8	60,1	63,0	58,0
2012	59,4	59,0	56,1	61,1	62,3	58,2
2013	58,9	58,6	55,3	60,9	61,6	57,7
2014	58,5	58,6	55,0	60,7	63,5	58,6
2015	57,7	59,0	53,8	60,6	62,2	59,0
2016	57,9	59,0	54,5	60,5	61,8	57,0
2017	58,0	58,6	54,2	60,3	61,0	57,2

Notes: Labour share comprising wages and social protection transfers (% of GDP); source: International Labour Organization – ILO (ILOSTAT, Table 10.4.1).

income that is awarded as labour income, the lower will be income inequality. It helps to see this with a simple equation. Income of individual i is:

$$Y_i = w_i L_i + r K_i$$

(We assume a constant real interest rate r.) And average income:

$$Y = wL + rK$$

Defining the labour and capital shares as: $\gamma \equiv wL/Y$ and $(1 - \gamma) \equiv rK/Y$, we may trivially write:

$$Y_i/Y = \gamma w_i L_i/wL + (1 - \gamma)K_i/K$$

In this formulation, relative income is a weighted average of relative wage and relative capital holdings, the weights determined by the labour and capital shares in the aggregate economy (i.e. what proportion of national income is awarded to each factor). Assuming that the labour income and capital ownership distributions are independent of each other,[5] then we have:

$$Var\left(\frac{Y_i}{Y}\right) = \gamma^2 Var\left(\frac{w_i L_i}{wL}\right) + (1-\gamma)^2 Var\left(\frac{K_i}{K}\right) \qquad (10.18)$$

Considering that $Var\left(\frac{w_i L_i}{wL}\right) < Var\left(\frac{K_i}{K}\right)$, i.e. that labour income is more equally distributed than wealth, in line with the evidence, taking the variances of labour income and capital as given, then we see that $\frac{\partial Var\left(\frac{Y_i}{Y}\right)}{\partial \gamma} < 0$: overall income inequality decreases when the labour share rises. The decline in the labour share is closely associated with the well-documented rise in economic inequality in recent decades. Piketty (2014), moreover, argues that the odds are that the labour share will further decline into the twenty-first century.

10.3.2 CES Production and Factor Shares

Factor shares can be analysed with the CES production function (1.2) of Chapter 1:

$$Y = \left(aK^b + (1-a)L^b\right)^{1/b}, \qquad 0 < a < 1, \quad b < 1 \qquad (10.19)$$

The constant 'elasticity of substitution' between factors is:

$$\varepsilon \equiv -\frac{d\log(K/L)}{d\log(r/w)} = \frac{1}{1-b} \qquad (10.20)$$

The Cobb-Douglas production function is the special case of unitary elasticity of substitution, $\varepsilon = 1$, therefore $b = 0$. The marginal products of capital and labour are given by:

$$\frac{\partial Y}{\partial L} = (1-a)\left(\frac{Y}{L}\right)^{1-b} \qquad (10.21a)$$

$$\frac{\partial Y}{\partial K} = a\left(\frac{Y}{K}\right)^{1-b} \qquad (10.21b)$$

Therefore the factor shares (labour, $0 < \gamma < 1$, and capital, $1 - \gamma$) are:

$$\gamma = w\frac{L}{Y} = \frac{\partial Y}{\partial L}\frac{L}{Y} = (1-a)\left(\frac{Y}{L}\right)^{-b} \qquad (10.22a)$$

---

[5] This is a convenient but rather unrealistic assumption, as the well-off in capital may receive better education and therefore higher wages as well.

$$1 - \gamma = r\frac{K}{Y} = \frac{\partial Y}{\partial K}\frac{K}{Y} = a\left(\frac{Y}{K}\right)^{-b} \tag{10.22b}$$

As we discussed in Chapter 1, the commonly employed Cobb-Douglas production function ($b = 0$) implies that factor shares are determined by a single parameter that determines the relative weights of capital and labour in production; indeed, $\gamma = wL/Y = 1 - \alpha$ and $1 - \gamma = rK/Y = \alpha$. The first difficulty is that this parameter (α) is technical in nature and difficult to measure. Secondly, there is no role for policies, taxation, 'institutions' like trade unions, the welfare state, nature of markets, technology, etc. Furthermore, such simple relations cannot account for changes in factor shares; there is no compelling reason to think that the relative weights of capital and labour in production are changing. In sum, a distributional theory that depends on a fixed technical parameter will be uninformative about the issues that concern us here. Another implication of Cobb-Douglas is that the marginal product of capital (MPK) will be proportional to Y/K : MPK $= \alpha Y/K$, which is particularly useful in the 'AK' growth model.

Using the general CES case ($b \neq 0$), we can get a more fruitful framework, as Y/L and Y/K in (10.22a, b) are variable. Firms can alter the capital-output ratio by changing the capital-labour ratio (it is easy to see that K/Y is related to K/L: just divide across equation (10.19) by K and L). Individual firms will respond to factor prices (w, r) by adjusting the capital/labour ratios (equivalently: Y/K and Y/L). To get a flavour of what this implies, the marginal product of capital will be equated to the real interest rate (r); equating and rearranging yields this capital/output ratio:

$$K/Y = (r/a)^{-1/(1-b)}$$

Capital intensity depends inversely on the price of capital (r). Correspondingly, the labour-output ratio will be:

$$L/Y = (w/(1-a))^{-1/(1-b)}$$

Combining the two, we get the capital-labour ratio:

$$K/L = (r(1-\alpha)/w\alpha)^{-1/(1-b)} \tag{10.23}$$

The capital-labour will be inversely proportional to the ratio of interest-to-wage rate; when the latter rises, firms will substitute away from capital and towards labour. The factor shares can be solved by relating (10.22a, b) and (10.21a, b), to have:

$$\frac{1-\gamma}{\gamma} = \frac{rK/Y}{wL/Y} = \frac{a^{1/(1-b)}r^{-b/(1-b)}}{(1-a)^{1/(1-b)}w^{-b/(1-b)}} = \left(\frac{a}{1-\alpha}\right)^{\varepsilon}\left(\frac{r}{w}\right)^{1-\varepsilon} \tag{10.24}$$

Equation (10.24) neatly summarizes the relation between factor shares on the left and factor prices (r and w) and technology (a, ε). Note in particular the role of the elasticity of substitution between factors (ε). As the r-w ratio rises and capital becomes relatively more expensive, firms will switch away from capital towards labour. If the switch is strong (due to a high elasticity of substitution, $\varepsilon > 1$), then firms will manage to reduce the payment to capital in comparison to labour and the ratio of factor shares will change in favour to labour: $(1 - \gamma)/\gamma$ falls. If, on the other hand, the factor proportions are rather inelastic ($0 < \varepsilon < 1$) and the switch weak, as the balance of the evidence shows, the ratio of the factor shares will in fact rise as the price ratio rises, simply because firms pay relatively more for capital without being able to significantly replace. Of course, though r and w are exogenous to an individual firm, they are endogenous to the economy as a whole. Other fundamentals, such as the economy's productivity, market structure, institutions (labour markets, organization, laws, taxation) will influence factor shares via r and w.

10.3.3 Factor Shares in a Full Model

As alluded to above, it should be clear that neither (10.22a, b) nor (10.24) are a complete model of factor shares; instead, these equations should be part of a full model (which will include also a labour/leisure choice, a consumption Euler equation, etc.), therefore factor shares will in general be determined in a wider context. (Also, note that 10.24 is the ratio of 10.22a, b, therefore redundant.) To illustrate this point, let us briefly embed the marginal products (10.21a, b) and the factor shares (10.22a, b) into the model of Section 10.2. Only the aggregate equations will be shown; also, only the relevant equations will be shown.

Growth consumption and the consumption/leisure proportionality are as before:

$$g = \sigma(r - \rho) \tag{10.7}$$

$$C = [r(1 - \sigma) + \sigma\rho]K + wL \tag{10.9b}$$

$$\theta C = w(1 - L) \tag{10.13b}$$

Using the above, we can combine in a way analogous to (10.9b) but replacing consumption by the labour share:

$$\frac{w(1 - L)}{\theta} = [r(1 - \sigma) + \sigma\rho]K + wL \tag{10.25}$$

Using the marginal products (10.21a, b), we then get:

$$\frac{(1 - \alpha)\left(\frac{Y}{L}\right)^{1-b}}{\theta} = (1 - \gamma)(1 - \sigma) + \sigma\rho\frac{K}{Y} + \gamma\frac{\theta + 1}{\theta} \tag{10.25'}$$

Using (10.22a, b), we can replace the marginal products by the factor shares:

$$\frac{(1 - \alpha)\left(\frac{\gamma}{1-\alpha}\right)^{-(1-b)/b}}{\theta} = (1 - \gamma)(1 - \sigma) + \sigma\rho\left(\frac{1 - \gamma}{\alpha}\right)^{1/b} + \gamma\frac{\theta + 1}{\theta} \tag{10.26}$$

This is an equation expressed entirely in terms of the labour share (γ), so can be used in principle to solve for it. The considerable practical difficulty is its non-linearity. One may use the result that much (though not all) of the empirical literature suggests that the elasticity of substitution between factors (10.20) is not high, i.e. $0 < \varepsilon < 1$ (see Chapter 1); this implies $b < 0$ therefore the left-hand side will be upward-sloping in a graph against γ. Another useful result that may be used is $\sigma < 1$. Even so, an analytical solution seems too difficult to obtain and numerical simulations may be useful. Analysis of this equation and the effects of the various parameters of interest (σ, b, ρ, α, θ) on the labour share (γ) are left as an exercise to the interested reader. See Grossman et al. (2017) for a fuller model in this spirit that also incorporates education and human capital.

10.3.4 Determinants of Factor Shares and the Possible Drivers of Change

We now review various determinants of labour shares and the reasons why the balance between capital and labour shares may have changed recently. It is useful to remember the starting point that the labour share declines when wages grow more slowly than productivity, or the amount of output per hour of work. As a result, a growing fraction of productivity gains goes to capital. The question is why wages may be growing less than productivity. Various studies attribute that to different factors.

- Technological progress, capital-labour substitution, and automation: Karabarbounis and Neiman (2014) attribute the fall in the labour share to investment-specific technical progress (Greenwood et al., 1997) and the resulting, well-documented, long-term downward trend in the price of investment goods. As discussed in Chapter 9, the price of *the same* car, computer, etc., declines quite dramatically over time; the price of the average or even cutting-edge car or computer may remain the same, but this good is a lot better compared to its counterpart even a decade ago (and much more if comparisons are made over longer periods). Combined with a high elasticity of substitution between factors ($\varepsilon > 1$), as they estimate, the story is as follows. The decline in the price of investment goods brings a corresponding decline in the (competitive) rental price of capital (the interest rate adjusted for depreciation and capital gains—see Chapters 5 and 11), so the firms substitute away from labour and towards capital. As equation (10.24) shows, with $\varepsilon > 1$, the capital share rises and the labour share drops. In the same vein, Acemoglu and Restrepo (2018) suggest that automation of tasks previously performed by labour can cause a permanent reduction in the labour share. In a slight twist on the theme of technology, Krusell et al. (2000) argue that there are different rates of complementarity between capital and skilled/unskilled labour, and the documented rise in the premium of the skilled over the unskilled labour wages due to skills-biased technical progress encourages firms to substitute away from labour altogether. In yet a further twist, the theoretical growth model with human capital of Grossman et al. (2017) suggests that the decline in labour share is due to the productivity slowdown post-1975 and all that is hidden behind it. The model shows that the declines in the labour share and the rate of productivity growth are correlated.

- Technology and global integration: Dao, Das, Koczan and Lian (2017) investigate the role of technology and global integration (and their interaction). In advanced economies, they find that about half of the decline in labour shares can be attributed to technology. The decline was driven by a combination of rapid progress in information and telecommunication technology, and a high share of occupations that could easily be automated. On the other hand, global integration—increasing final goods trade, creation of global supply chains, foreign direct investment—contributed about half that of technology. For instance, participation in global supply chains implies offshoring of labour-intensive tasks and this results in lower labour shares in tradable sectors. Taken together, technology and global integration explain close to 75 per cent of the decline in labour shares in Germany and Italy, and close to 50 per cent in the United States. Regarding developing and emerging economies, participation in global supply chains was the key driver of declines in labour shares, by shifting production towards more capital-intensive activities. It is difficult to separate the impact of technology from global integration, as there are important interactions between them. One area where this is evident is the 'hollowing-out' phenomenon of labour in advanced economies: Dao et al. (2017) find that in these economies, the decline in labour shares has been particularly sharp for middle-skilled labour. Routine-biased technology has taken over many of the tasks performed by these workers, contributing to job polarization toward high-skilled and low-skilled occupations. This has been reinforced by global integration, as firms increasingly have access to lower-cost global labour supply through cross-border supply chains. An earlier contribution on the same theme of integration-technology interactions is Bentolila and Saint-Paul (2003); it emphasizes the role of the declining price of imported materials and of the nature of technological progress (particularly the existence of capital-augmenting technical progress that may bias production in favour of capital).
- Capital-augmenting technical progress: Summarizing the discussion so far, the nature of technological progress and an inherent capital-augmenting bias in it seems to be a common thread running through all these contributions: This technical progress enables firms to substitute away from labour and towards capital, causing the labour share to fall. The other factors, such as the falling price of investment goods and global integration, seem to either facilitate or further enhance the effects of technological progress.
- 'Superstar firms': A recent paper by Autor et al. (2017) advances a line of investigation based on 'superstar firms'. Industries are increasingly characterized by 'winner take most' competition, leading a small number of highly profitable (and low labour-share) firms to acquire a growing market share. As these low labour-share superstars gain ground, so the labour share falls on average. There are two key components of the superstar firm hypothesis: a general tendency for rising concentration of sales among firms within individual industrial sectors; and larger declines in the labour share in industries with a greater concentration. Autor et al. (2017) empirically confirm both these propositions.
- Structure of labour and product markets: Blanchard and Giavazzi (2003) relate the labour share to labour and product market regulation. Azmat et al. (2012) relate it to privatization which leads to loss of jobs; they find that, privatization accounts for a fifth of the fall of the labour share on average across OECD economies and over half in Britain and France. Labour market institutional features, such as trade unions,

employment protection, minimum wages, and other features reviewed in Chapter 4 and arguably related to unemployment, are likely to have a bearing on the labour share as they affect labour supply and the wage. The interesting observation here is that these institutional features have weakened over the last 40 years in developed economies, the same period where the fall in the labour share has occurred. See Bentolila and Saint-Paul (2003) for an analysis along these lines. However, all these points do not seem to have attracted the attention they deserve.

- Taxation: Taxation is a potentially important determinant of factor shares, as well as of wider income inequality. The structure of taxation, in particular the division between income, capital, and commodity taxation, as well as its progressivity, matter; see the Guidance for Further Study. We saw in Chapter 4 that taxation can explain a (modest) part of European unemployment. However, to the knowledge of this author, its role as a potential determinant of the labour share and explanation for its decline has not been investigated.

- Politics: Politics may also be important, as it possibly affects factor shares through policies, regulation, and taxation. In the same way that labour market institutions have changed over the last 40 years, the political climate has also changed away from egalitarianism as a key social objective, and this may hold the potential for a (perhaps partial) explanation of the falling labour share. See Stiglitz (2012) for an account of the role of politics in inequality, particularly as a self-perpetuating force. More inequality allows certain individuals to buy more influence through lobbying, and donations to parties, and shape policy closer to their interests, thus further enhancing inequality. But more formal analysis of these issues is also required.

10.3.5 The '$r > g$' Debate

Piketty (2014) has presented a simple, and possibly powerful, argument related to the intertemporal evolution of wealth inequality and the labour share. It has to do with '$r > g$', i.e. the historical tendency of the real interest rate (r) to be greater than the rate of growth of real GDP. The significance of this is that the former is the rate of return of real wealth (on average, considering that the various forms—capital, liquid wealth, housing—may be offering different rates of return). Now, if a constant fraction of the proceeds from wealth are consumed, a constant fraction of this rate of return will also be the rate of growth of wealth. For example, if interest from wealth is rW (W is wealth), and a fraction $0 < c < 1$ of that is consumed (in earlier notation, $s^K = 1 - c$), then wealth will be growing at rate equal to $r(1 - c)$. (Can you see why?) Additionally, as discussed above, there is plenty of evidence that wealth is highly unequally distributed and that the rich save a lot. All this implies that the 'c' above is likely to be very small: little is consumed out of capital income. On the other hand, g is the real growth rate of the general economy. Hence, $r > g$ implies (assuming $c \approx 0$) that wealth grows faster than the general economy. Thus, wealth and income from wealth have a tendency to rise over time as a proportion of GDP. All this further implies that the capital (labour) share will be rising (falling) over time and that overall income inequality will keep rising—for as long as $r > g$.

To cap it all, Jordà et al. (2019) have recently confirmed that all forms of wealth have historically offered a higher rate of return than the rate of growth of the general economy—and for more countries, more years, and more dramatically than Piketty (2014) himself reported. The only exceptions to 'r > > g' (note '>>': much higher) happen in very special periods: the years in or close to war-time. In effect, r > g must be a stylized fact.

A key point, acknowledged by Piketty (2015), is that r > g is built into all modern macro models. For instance, our growth equation (10.7) above implies $g - r = r(1 - \sigma) + \sigma\rho$; this is positive at least for $\sigma < 1$, which is the empirically relevant case. As we saw in Chapter 5, r > g is a precondition for dynamic efficiency, which receives empirical confirmation (on balance). Additionally, if we assumed that r < g, we would have GDP (and other variables in a Balanced Growth Path) growing at a common rate (g) higher than the discount rate (r); thus, discounting future sums (say, incomes) would not produce a finite number. Thus, 'r < g' both is a sound analytical proposition and receives robust empirical support; the question is not whether it could be otherwise but what it really implies.

Predictably, Piketty's (2014) gloomy prediction has caused quite a stir. The *Journal of Economic Perspectives* devoted a special issue (Spring 2015) to the discussion of r > g. Mankiw (2015) raises three objections: first, part of the income from wealth is consumed (in effect, that c > 0 above); secondly, part of same must be used for maintenance of wealth (to correct physical depreciation); and thirdly, one needs to account for the population growth rate in order to translate any form of income into per capita income. The first of these two points is correct, implying that the rate of growth of wealth is not r but $r(1 - c - \delta)$, where $\delta > 0$ is the depreciation rate. But it is doubtful whether empirically relevant magnitudes can alter the argument substantially. Indicatively, $\delta \approx 0.025$, see Chapter 11; with an r = 0.03, g = 0.01, and c = 0.3, then $r(1 - c - \delta) \approx 0.02$ and the differential between the wealth and GDP growth rates will be $r(1 - c - \delta) - g \approx 0.01 > 0$; this is less than r − g = 0.02, but the essence of Piketty's argument does not change (particularly in view of the findings of Jordà et al., 2019, that r > > g). As regards population growth, this does not seem relevant to wealth or income inequality, because the same adjustment must be done to all sources of income (wealth or labour) in order to obtain per capita incomes. Weil (2015) clarifies various issues related to the measurement of productive capital (the notion of capital employed in much of this book), human capital, and other forms of capital, which are indeed important before one arrives at any definitive conclusions about the dynamics of income and wealth inequality.

In his response, Piketty (2015) acknowledges all these points. He clarifies that a higher r-g gap will tend to amplify more the steady-state wealth inequality that arises out of various types of shocks (including labour income shocks); relatively small changes in r-g can generate large changes in steady-state wealth inequality. In other words, in this later restatement, it is not the inequality as such (r > g) that is the problem, but its magnitude; and a given r-g differential does not imply that wealth keeps rising forever as a proportion of GDP, but determines the steady-state wealth distribution. Piketty (2015) reports simple simulations suggesting that going from r − g = 2 per cent (the number we used above) to r − g = 3 per cent is sufficient to move us from a moderate wealth inequality—say, with a top 1 per cent wealth share around 20–30 per cent, such as in present-day Europe or the US—to a very high wealth inequality with a top 1 per cent wealth share around 50–60 per cent, such as in pre-World War I Europe. These observations lead Piketty (2014) and his co-authors to recommend various forms of progressive taxation, including income taxes, capital taxation, and wealth and inheritance taxation (see the Guidance for Further Study); as well as a more generous welfare state.

In conclusion, there is no doubt that income and wealth inequality and the division of income into 'factor shares' are issues of increasing importance. Research on them is picking up, but many issues remain poorly understood; nothing will ever be perfectly clear, but this area remains relatively underdeveloped as a branch of macroeconomics. Greater effort must be made to investigate empirically various issues, to incorporate inequality and factor shares into mainstream models, and to integrate inequality into the standard macro curriculum (and this book is a modest effort towards the last goal!). In terms of policy, issues like bolder taxation (along the lines suggested by Atkinson, Piketty, Saez, and many others) and a more generous welfare system (e.g. proposals about 'basic income') deserve a more prominent place in the public discourse.

Notes on the Literature

As a background to inequality and poverty, measurement issues, indices, etc., particularly from a welfare-economics perspective, Sen with Foster (1997) remains very valuable. From a wider social policy perspective, Wilkinson and Pickett (2009) contain compelling empirical information as to why inequality matters for societal well-being. Similarly, Stiglitz (2012) discusses the costs of inequality, including macroeconomic risks. The recent monograph by the late Tony Atkinson (2015), who spent a lifetime studying inequality, contains a wide discussion and bold policy proposals. Piketty (2014) contains a treasure-trove of historical information on the evolution of wealth, the labour share, and 'r < g'. The resulting debates have been discussed in the special May 2015 issue of the *Journal of Economic Perspectives* (and reviewed above). The work of Piketty and his associates is summarized in Alvaredo et al. (2013), Atkinson et al. (2011) and more recently Saez and Zucman (2016) and Alvaredo et al. (2017). The early work on the US (Piketty and Saez, 2003) also deserves a mention. Detailed information about the UK is contained in the annual publications of the Institute of Fiscal Studies (IFS): *Living Standards, Poverty and Inequality in the UK*; e.g. I am holding the 2017 edition right now—really worth a look. Dew-Becker and Gordon (2008) contains a wide survey of the issues related to US inequality and discusses the unresolved questions. Aghion et al. (1999) review inequality from the perspective of new growth theories, while Bowles (2012) takes a more political-economy perspective. Alacevich and Soci (2018) is an all-round, concise introduction to the field. On poverty, particularly from a global perspective, we should mention Banerjee and Duflo (2011). At a more advanced level, the twin volumes of Atkinson and Bourguignon (2015) are invaluable. The literature is developing fast, perhaps more so than in other areas, so the interested reader should make their own searches.

Guidance for Further Study

Income inequality and regional inequality

Income inequality may be correlated with geographical inequality, creating further social and political implications. For instance, quoting the IFS, the *Guardian* (2019) reports that the proportion of top 1 per cent highest income tax payers who live in London increased to 35 per cent in 2014–15 from 29 per cent in 2000–1. More than half of the country's top 1 per cent live in London and the south-east of the UK, clustering together in as few as 65 parliamentary constituencies, compared with 78 at the start of the 2000s (out of a total 650). It is not difficult to imagine that this may generate a feeling of regional inequality and discontent alongside the income inequality; some commentators would argue that such feelings may have influenced (the so-called) anti-systemic vote such as (again, in some people's view) the Brexit vote and the rise of President Trump.

Politics

As we have mentioned in the context of factor shares, democratic politics is important for inequality, as it determines policies, redistributive and other taxation, welfare state provisions, regulation, etc. But all this discussion belongs more to the field of political economy than macroeconomics, so we have left it out. The interested reader should consult Acemoglu et al. (2015) as an introduction to the topic and portal into the relevant literature.

Macroeconomic effects of inequality

We have touched on the social implications of inequality (Wilkinson and Pickett, 2009) but less on its macroeconomic implications. We briefly discuss two lines of argument: one emphasizes the inequality–credit boom–crisis nexus. Inequality generated demand for lending and a credit boom, leading to a financial crisis in the US in the first decade of the twenty-first century as it did in the 1920s (Rajan, 2010; Kumhof and Rancière, 2011); but this line of argument is disputed by Bordo and Meissner (2012). Another high-profile contribution argues that political-economy factors—especially the influence of the rich—allowed financial excess to balloon ahead of the crisis (Stiglitz 2012). Obviously, we are in a rather uncertain territory here, with tentative arguments. The reader is invited to make up their own mind.

Taxation and income inequality

As mentioned, if one thinks that there is too much inequality, the obvious policy implication is to employ redistributive taxation. Here, the notion of the progressivity of taxation is important: taxation is progressive (regressive) if the tax burden-income ratio rises (falls) as we move up the income distribution. More broadly, one may argue that taxation is progressive (regressive) if after-tax income is more (less) equally distributed than before-tax income (Piketty and Saez, 2007). This is determined by the entire structure of taxation, including income taxes but also corporate taxes, wealth and inheritance taxes. Piketty and Saez (2007) analyse the progressivity of the US and French tax systems taking all these considerations into account. They show that the US federal tax system at the top of the income distribution has declined dramatically since the 1960s; a similar picture emerges for the UK. In contrast, France had less progressive taxes than the US or UK in 1970 but has experienced an increase in tax progressivity and now has a more progressive tax system than either the US or the UK. As mentioned, these developments may have affected the evolution of factor shares and inequality; but this line of investigation has not been pursued in the literature. Recommendations about the taxation required to deal with inequality can be found in Piketty and Saez (2013) and Piketty et al. (2014).

'Basic' and 'participation' income

Associated with Van Parijs (1995) and Atkinson (2010, 2011) the proposals on 'basic income' (BI) advocate a fixed income for all financed by proportional taxation. The idea was briefly discussed above. The idea is to guarantee an acceptable standard of living to everyone, with little administrative burden. One of the criticisms is its non-reciprocity: everyone takes something without necessarily contributing. This has led to the proposal for a 'participation income' (PI), i.e. a BI that would be awarded if one participated in good citizenship by either working, or contributing to volunteer work (unless one were in education or were incapacitated, in which case they could claim the income anyway). Apart from the above sources, see the symposium introduced by Stirton (2018) on PI and a critical review of BI by Ghatak and Maniquet (2019).

Austerity and income distribution

Furceri et al. (2018) find that unanticipated fiscal consolidations lead to a long-lasting increase in income inequality, while fiscal expansions lower inequality. They define an 'inequality multiplier' and show that it is about 1 in the medium term, namely a cumulative decrease in government spending of 1 per cent of GDP over five years is associated with a cumulative increase in the Gini coefficient over the same period of about 1 percentage point. Finally, it is shown that (unanticipated) fiscal consolidations lead to an increase in poverty. All these results are related to the effects of fiscal consolidations discussed in Chapter 8.

Inclusive prosperity

The ugly irony (as we it called above) of poverty amid the plenty is leading to increasing research and policy proposals for creating more equitable and fair societies and economies. Among academic fora, see the 'Economics for Inclusive Prosperity' (https://econfip.org/) created by Dani Rodrik and his associates and the policy advice provided by IMF researchers (Duttagupta et al., 2017; Gaspar and Garcia-Escribano, 2017).

References

Aaberge, R. (2007): Gini's Nuclear Family. *Journal of Economic Inequality*, 5(3) (December), 305–22.

Acemoglu, D., S. Naidu, P. Restrepo, and J.A. Robinson (2015): Democracy, Redistribution, and Inequality, in A.B. Atkinson and F. Bourguignon (eds), *Handbook of Income Distribution*, Amsterdam: Elsevier, ii. 1885–1966.

Acemoglu, D., and P. Restrepo (2018): The Race between Man and Machine: Implications of Technology for Growth, Factor Shares, and Employment, *American Economic Review*, 108(6), 1488–1542.

Aghion, P., and P. Bolton (1997): A Trickle-Down Theory of Growth and Development with Debt Overhang, *Review of Economic Studies*, 64, 151–72.

Aghion, P., E. Caroli, and C. García-Peñalosa (1999): Inequality and Economic Growth: The Perspective of the New Growth Theories, *Journal of Economic Literature*, 37, 1615–60.

Aiyagari, S.R. (1994): Uninsured Idiosyncratic Risk and Aggregate Saving, *Quarterly Journal of Economics*, 109(3) (August), 659–84.

Alacevich, M., and A. Soci (2018): *A Short History of Inequality*, Washington, DC: Brookings Institution.

Alesina, A., and D. Rodrik (1994): Distributive Politics and Economic Growth, *Quarterly Journal of Economics*, 109, 465–90.

Alvaredo, F., A.B. Atkinson, T. Piketty, and E. Saez (2013): The Top 1 Percent in International and Historical Perspective, *Journal of Economic Perspectives*, 27(3) (Summer), 3–20.

Alvaredo, F., L. Chancel, T. Piketty, E. Saez, and G. Zucman (2017): Global Inequality Dynamics: New Findings from WID.world, *American Economic Review*, 107(5), 404–9.

Alvaredo, F., L. Chancel, T. Piketty, E. Saez, and G. Zucman (eds) (2018): *World Inequality Report*, Paris: World Inequality Lab, https://wir2018.wid.world/files/download/wir2018-full-report-english.pdf.

Anand, S., and R. Kanbur (1993): The Kuznets Process and the Inequality-Development Relationship, *Journal of Development Economics*, 40, 25–52.

Andersen, T.M., and J. Maibom (2019): The Big Trade-off between Efficiency and Equity—is it There? *Oxford Economic Papers*, forthcoming.

Atkinson, A.B. (2010): Progressive Social Justice and Responding to the Crisis, *Journal of Poverty and Social Justice*, 18, 221–8.

Atkinson, A.B. (2011): Basic Income: Ethics, Statistics and Economics, http://www.nuff.ox.ac.uk/users/atkinson/Basic_Income%20Luxembourg%20April%202011.pdf

Atkinson, A.B. (2015): *Inequality: What can be Done?* Cambridge, MA: Harvard University Press.

Atkinson, A.B., and F. Bourguignon (eds.) (2015): *Handbook of Income Distribution*, Amsterdam: Elsevier.

Atkinson, A.B., T. Piketty, and E. Saez (2011): Top Incomes in the Long Run of History, *Journal of Economic Literature*, 49(1), 3–71.

Autor, D.H. (2019): Work of the Past, Work of the Future, *American Economic Review, Papers and Proceedings*, 109, 1–32.

Autor, D.H., D. Dorn, L.F. Katz, C. Patterson, and J. Van Reenen (2017): Concentrating on the Fall of the Labor Share, *American Economic Review*, 107(5), 180–5.

Azmat, G., A. Manning, and J. Van Reenen (2012): Privatization and the Decline of Labour's Share: International Evidence from Network Industries, *Economica*, 79, 470–92.

Banerjee, A.V., and E. Duflo (2011): *Poor Economics: A Radical Rethinking of the Way to Fight Global Poverty*, New York: Public Affairs.

Barro, R.J. (2002): Inequality and Growth in a Panel of Countries, *Journal of Economic Growth*, 5, 5–32.

Bénabou, R. (1996): Inequality and Growth, in B. Bernanke and J.J. Rotemberg (eds), *NBER Macroeconomics Annual 1996*, Cambridge, MA: MIT Press, xi. 11–74.

Bénabou, R. (2000): Unequal Societies: Income Distribution and the Social Contract, *American Economic Review*, 90(1), 96–129.

Benhabib, J., A. Bisin, and M. Luo (2019): Wealth Distribution and Social Mobility in the U.S.: A Quantitative Approach, *American Economic Review*, 109(5), 1623–47.

Bentolila, S., and G. Saint-Paul (2003): Explaining Movements in the Labor Share, *The B.E. Journal of Macroeconomics*, 3(1) (October), 1–33.

Bertola, G. (1993): Factor Shares and Savings in Endogenous Growth, *American Economic Review*, 83(5) (December), 1184–98.

Bertola, G., R. Foellmi, and J. Zweimuller (2006): *Income Distribution in Macroeconomic Models*, Princeton: Princeton University Press.

Bordo, M.D., and C.M. Meissner (2012): Does Inequality Lead to a Financial Crisis? *Journal of International Money and Finance*, 31(8), 2147–61.

Bowles, S. (2012): *The New Economics of Inequality and Redistribution*, Cambridge: Cambridge University Press.

Cagetti, M., and M. De Nardi (2006): Entrepreneurship, Frictions, and Wealth, *Journal of Political Economy*, 114(5) (October), 835–70.

Card, D., and A. Shleifer (2009): Immigration and Inequality, *American Economic Review*, 99(2), 1–21.

Caselli, F., and J. Ventura (2000): A Representative Consumer Theory of Distribution, *American Economic Review*, 90(4), 909–26.

Castañeda, A., J. Díaz-Giménez, and J.-V. Ríos-Rull (2003): Accounting for U.S. Earnings and Wealth Inequality, *Journal of Political Economy*, 3(4), 818–57.

CBO (2011): *Trends in the Distribution of Household Income between 1979 and 2007*, Washington, DC: Congressional Budget Office, October, https://www.cbo.gov/sites/default/files/112th-congress-2011-2012/reports/10-25-householdincome0.pdf.

Dao, M.C., M. Das, Z. Koczan, and W. Lian (2017): Understanding the Downward Trend In Labor Income Shares, in *IMF World Economic Outlook*, April, chapter 3, https://blogs.imf.org/2017/04/12/drivers-of-declining-labor-share-of-income/.

Davies, J.B., S. Sandström, A. Shorrocks, and E.N. Wolff (2011): The Level and Distribution of Global Household Wealth, *Economic Journal*, 121(551), 223–54.

Dew-Becker, I., and R.J. Gordon (2008): Controversies about the Rise of American Inequality: A Survey, NBER Working Paper No. 13982, May.

Duttagupta, R., S. Fabrizio, D. Furceri, and S. Saxena (2017): Growth that Reaches Everyone: Facts, Factors, Tools, IMF Blog, 20 September; https://blogs.imf.org/2017/09/20/growth-that-reaches-everyone-facts-factors-tools/

Dynan, K.E., J. Skinner, and S.P. Zeldes (2004): Do the Rich Save More? *Journal of Political Economy*, 112(2), 397–444.

Furceri, D., J. Ge, P. Loungani, and G. Melina (2018): The Distributional Effects of Government Spending Shocks in Developing Economies, IMF Working Paper 18/57, March.

Gabaix, X., J. Lasry, P. Lions, and B. Moll (2016): The Dynamics of Inequality, *Econometrica*, 84(6), 2071–2111.

Galor, O., and J. Zeira (1993): Income Distribution and Macroeconomics, *Review of Economic Studies*, 601 (January), 35–52.

García-Peñalosa, C., and S.J. Turnovsky (2006): Growth and Income Inequality: A Canonical Model, *Economic Theory*, 28, 25–49.

García-Peñalosa, C., and S.J. Turnovsky (2011): Taxation and Income Distribution Dynamics in a Neoclassical Growth Model, *Journal of Money, Credit and Banking*, 43, 1543–77.

Gaspar, V., and M. Garcia-Escribano (2017): Inequality: Fiscal Policy Can Make the Difference, IMF Blog, 11 October1; https://blogs.imf.org/2017/10/11/inequality-fiscal-policy-can-make-the-difference/.

Ghatak, M., and F. Maniquet (2019): Universal Basic Income: Some Theoretical Aspects, CEPR Discussion Paper No. 13635.

Gollin, D. (2002): Getting Income Shares Right, *Journal of Political Economy*, 110(2) (April), 458–74.

Greenwood, J., Z. Hercovitz, and P. Krusell (1997): Long-Run Implications of Investment-Specific Technological Change, *American Economic Review*, 87(3), 342–62.

Grossman, G.M., E. Helpman, E. Oberfield, and T. Sampson (2017): The Productivity Slowdown and the Declining Labor Share: A Neoclassical Exploration, NBER Working Paper No. 23853, September.

Guardian (2019): London is increasingly home to the top 1% by income, study finds; highest earners in the country overwhelmingly middle-aged men living in the south-east, 6 August, https://www.theguardian.com/business/2019/aug/06/london-is-increasingly-home-to-the-top-1-by-income-study-finds?CMP=Share_AndroidApp_Gmail.

Heathcote, J., K. Storesletten, and G.L. Violante (2010): The Macroeconomic Implications of Rising Wage Inequality in the United States, *Journal of Political Economy*, 118(4) (August), 681–722.

ILO (International Labour Organization) (2019): The Global Labour Income Share and Distribution: Key Findings, Data Production and Analysis Unit, Department of Statistics, July, https://www.ilo.org/wcmsp5/groups/public/—dgreports/—stat/documents/publication/wcms_712232.pdf

Jones, C.I. (2015): Pareto and Piketty: The Macroeconomics of Top Income and Wealth Inequality, *Journal of Economic Perspectives*, 29(1) (Winter), 29–46.

Jones, C.I., and J. Kim (2018): A Schumpeterian Model of Top Income Inequality, *Journal of Political Economy*, 1265 (October), 1785–1826.

Jordà, Ò., K. Knoll, D. Kuvshinov, M. Schularick, and A.M. Taylor (2019): The Rate of Return on Everything, 1870–2015, *Quarterly Journal of Economics*, 134(3) (August), 1225–98.

Kaplan, S.N., and J. Rauh (2013): It's the Market: The Broad-Based Rise in the Return to Top Talent, *Journal of Economic Perspectives*, 27(3) (Summer), 35–56.

Karabarbounis, L. and B. Neiman (2014): The Global Decline of the Labor Share, *Quarterly Journal of Economics*, 129(1), 61–103.

Kennickell, A.B. (2009): Ponds and Streams: Wealth and Income in the U.S., 1989 to 2007, Finance and Economics DP 2009–13, Board of Governors of the Federal Reserve System.

Krusell, P., L.E. Ohanian, J.-V. Ríos-Rull, and G.L. Violante (2000): Capital-Skill Complementarity and Inequality: A Macroeconomic Analysis, *Econometrica*, 68(5) (September), 1029–53.

Kumhof, M., and R. Rancière (2011): Inequality, Leverage and Crises, IMF Working Paper 10/268.

Kuznets, S. (1955): Economic Growth and Income Inequality, *American Economic Review*, 45, 1–28.

Lakner, C., and B. Milanovic (2016): Global Income Distribution: From the Fall of the Berlin Wall to the Great Recession, *World Bank Economic Review*, 30(2), 203–32.

Lundberg, M., and L. Squire (2003): The Simultaneous Evolution of Growth and Inequality, *Economic Journal*, 113, 326–44.

Mankiw, N.G. (2000): The Savers-Spenders Theory of Fiscal Policy, *American Economic Review*, 90(2), 120–5.

Mankiw, N.G. (2015): Yes, r>g. So What? *American Economic Review*, 105(5) (May), 43–7.

Milanovic, B., and L. Squire (2007): Does Tariff Liberalization Increase Wage Inequality? Some Empirical Evidence, in A. Harrison (ed.), *Globalization and Poverty*, Chicago: University of Chicago Press, 143–82.

Okun, A.M. (1975): *Equality and Efficiency: The Big Trade-Off*, Washington, DC: Brookings Institution Press.

Ostry, J.D., A. Berg, and C.G. Tsangarides (2014): Redistribution, Inequality, and Growth, IMF Staff Discussion Note 14/02.

Oxfam (2019): *Public Good or Private Wealth?*: Oxfam Inequality Report 2019, January 2019 bp-public-good-private-wealth-210119-full report-english_EMBARGOED.pdf.

Persson, T., and G. Tabellini (1994): Is Inequality Harmful for Growth? Theory and Evidence, *American Economic Review*, 84(3) (June), 600–21.

Piketty, T. (2014): *Capital in the Twenty-First Century*, Boston, Harvard University Press.

Piketty, T. (2015): About Capital in the Twenty-First Century, *American Economic Review*, (May), 48–53.

Piketty, T., and E. Saez (2003): Income inequality in the United States, 1913–1998, *Quarterly Jounral of Economics*, 118(1) (February), 1–39.

Piketty, T., and E. Saez (2007): How Progressive is the U.S. Federal Tax System? A Historical and International Perspective, *Journal of Economic Perspectives*, 21(1) (Winter), 3–24.

Piketty, T., and E. Saez (2013): A Theory of Optimal Inheritance Taxation, *Econometrica*, 81(5), 1851–86.

Piketty, T., E. Saez, and S. Stantcheva (2014): Optimal Taxation of Top Labor Incomes: A Tale of Three Elasticities, *American Economic Journal: Economic Policy*, 6 (1), 230–71.

Rajan, R. (2010): *Fault Lines*, Princeton: Princeton University Press.

Rognlie, M. (2015): Deciphering the Fall and Rise in the Net Capital Share, *Brookings Papers on Economic Activity* (Spring), 1–54.

Saez, E., and G. Zucman (2016): Wealth Inequality in the United States since 1913: Evidence from Capitalized Income Tax Data, *Quarterly Journal of Economics*, 131(2), 519–78.

Sen, A., with J.E. Foster (1997): *On Economic Inequality*, Oxford: Clarendon Press.

Solow, R. (1994): Perspectives on Growth Theory, *Journal of Economic Perspectives*, 8(1) (Winter), 45–54.

Stiglitz, J. (2012): *The Price of Inequality: How Today's Divided Society Endangers Our Future*, New York; W.W. Norton & Co.

Stirton, L. (2018): Symposium Introduction: Anthony Atkinson's 'The Case for a Participation Income', *Political Quarterly*, 89, 254–5.

Turnovsky, S.J. (2013): The Relationship between Economic Growth and Inequality, *New Zealand Economic Papers*, 47(2), 113–39.

Van Parijs, P. (1995): *Real Freedom for All*, Oxford: Clarendon Press.

Weil, D.N. (2015): Capital and Wealth in the Twenty-First Century, *American Economic Review*, 105(5) (May), 34–7.

Wilkinson, R., and K. Pickett (2009): *The Spirit Level: Why Equality is Better for Everyone*, London: Allen Lane.

11

Sectoral Analyses

Consumption, Saving, Investment, Housing, and the Stock Market

Building on Chapter 5, this chapter looks at the determinants of consumption, saving, and investment in more detail. Sometimes called 'sectoral' analyses, these analyses provide essential background information for any aggregative model, from the simple IS-M type of analysis to more sophisticated micro-founded, dynamic models of the business cycle or growth. Around the main themes, we shall also deal with topics that are of equal importance but less often dealt with, such as housing and inventories. Finally, our analyses will lead us towards a brief introduction to the macroeconomics of financial markets, particularly stock (equity) markets.

11.1 Consumption

Consumption (of new, final goods and services) is the biggest spending component of GDP in modern developed economies, typically about two-thirds. In addition, consumption is the main item (together perhaps with public services) on which private utility and welfare depends. These two observations alone are enough to convince us of consumption's importance. Additionally, as a major component of demand, the behaviour of consumption is an important determinant of the fiscal multiplier. The flip side of consumption, saving, is important for growth. For these reasons, macroeconomics has researched the topic quite intensively. This section reviews the theory of consumption, setting thus the scene for more work on saving in the next section and on asset pricing in Section 11.5.

11.1.1 Stylized Facts

Figure 11.1 gives the private consumption expenditure as a percentage over GDP. Panel (a) is a time-series plot of the ratio for the UK, USA, and the Euro area (EU-19), whereas panel (b) gives the cross-section in 2016. Data are from the OECD.

There is a great cross-country variation, with the typical value being around 55–60 per cent (60 per cent is the average for OECD). Regarding time, the ratio seems on the whole stationary for the UK and EU-19 but not for the USA. In general, the following are considered to be the 'stylized facts' of private consumption (Attanasio, 1999; Attanasio and Weber, 2010); they can be grouped into two sets according to whether they related to

Theory of Macroeconomic Policy. Christopher Tsoukis, Oxford University Press (2020). © Christopher Tsoukis.
DOI: 10.1093/oso/9780198825371.003.0011

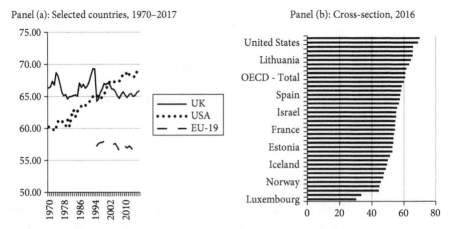

Figure 11.1. Household final consumption expenditure-to-GDP ratio (%): panel (a) Selected countries, 1970–2017; panel (b) cross-section, 2016

Source: OECD *National Accounts at a Glance*. Not all 38 countries of the sample are named on the cross-sectional bar panel.

the dynamics of consumption over time or to the behaviour of consumption across the individual's lifetime (or 'life-cycle'):

Over time

- Consumption rises in line with disposable income (in time-series econometrics terminology, the two series seem co-integrated—this makes the consumption-income ratio constant, an observation going back to Kuznets, 1955); but,
- *Non-durable* consumption is smoother than the income series;
- *Durable* consumer expenditure (the expenditure made to upgrade the stock of durables, such as appliances, furniture, cars, etc.) is much more volatile than both the income and the non-durables series.

Over the life-cycle

- *The age-profile* of consumption (consumption graphed against the age of families/ cohorts) appears to be quite strongly hump-shaped, with the hump almost as pronounced as that of disposable income (Carroll and Summers, 1991). That income is hump-shaped is obvious (individuals earn little early on, more in middle life, then earnings again drop in retirement). But most theories of consumption suggest that individuals smooth their consumption over the lifetime, so this finding appears to be a puzzle. But Attanasio (1999) shows that, if non-durable consumption is scaled down by the number of individuals in each household, most of the hump in it goes away.
- The age-profile of durable consumption has a considerably more pronounced hump than that of non-durable consumption.
- There is also some evidence that there are differences in the humps of both the income and consumption age-profiles across different educational/economic groups: the humps in both income and consumption of better educated individuals are steeper and with a steeper 'ascent' in the earlier part of life (Attanasio, 1999, p. 759).

11.1.2 Early Theories: The 'Keynesian' Consumption Function, the 'Permanent Income Hypothesis' (PIH), and the 'Life-Cycle Model' (LCM)

Keynes (1936) suggested that there is an aggregate consumption of the form:

$$C_t = \bar{C} + cY_t^d, \quad \bar{C} > 0, \quad 0 < c < 1 \tag{11.1}$$

Y^d is disposable income, $\bar{C} > 0$ is 'autonomous' consumption, somehow fixed perhaps by subsistence needs or depending on psychology ('consumer sentiment' and the 'feelgood factor'). $0 < c < 1$ is the marginal propensity to consume out of current disposable income. Still used today at elementary level (notably in the fiscal multiplier in Chapter 8), this view of consumption is remarkably simple—and remarkable for the factors that it excludes: there is no role at all for future income in influencing current consumption, the marginal propensity to consume is constant, irrespective of whether current disposable income is normal or high or low, and irrespective of whether the individual is a borrower or saver, what the interest rate (= cost of borrowing) is, etc. Modern theories aim to rectify such weaknesses. Furthermore, (11.1) implies an average consumption of $\frac{C_t}{Y_t^d} = \frac{\bar{C}}{Y_t^d} + c$, which is falling as disposable income rises. Kuznets (1955) however, observed that the consumption-to-GDP ratio remains roughly constant. Disagreement with this stylized fact is an empirical weakness of (1) that has motivated subsequent developments.

Friedman's (1957) Permanent Income Hypothesis (PIH) may be summarized with the aid of a graph (Figure 11.2). The bullets represent actual income over time. Individuals are motivated to 'smooth' consumption over time, implicitly because of risk aversion. The broken line is the level of income that is permanently sustained, effectively an average over income over time; it is 'permanent income'. The deviations of actual income from this permanent level are called transitory income. The key premise of the theory is that consumption equals permanent income; transitory income deviations will be smoothed away by saving and borrowing: saving the positive deviations and borrowing when income is not so good against lifetime resources. Note that, with 'permanent income' being an average of actual income, consumption is influenced not only by current but also future income. And what is true of the representative individual is true of societies as a whole, so Figure 11.2 refers to aggregate magnitudes, and time goes on forever.[1] This theory, almost by construction, accounts well for the close relationship between

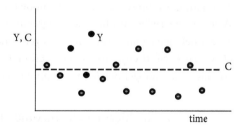

Figure 11.2. The Permanent Income
Hypothesis

---

[1] For simplicity, income, and therefore consumption, has no long-run tendency to increase.

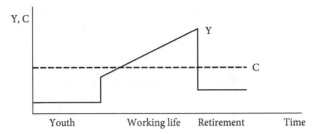

Figure 11.3. The Life-Cycle Model

consumption and income, but cannot account for the hump-shaped consumption over the lifetime.

The vintage Life-Cycle Model (LCM) developed by Modigliani and associates (Ando and Modigliani, 1965; Modigliani and Brumberg, 1954) starts from the same premise as the PIH, namely that individuals wish to smooth consumption over time, but focuses more on an individual lifetime rather than society as a whole. It takes into account the profile of income which exhibits a 'hump' over the lifetime—low early on, high in middle age, and low again in retirement. In order to maintain a constant consumption according to the smoothing motive, individuals borrow early on (the result of low income and higher consumption), save in the middle and dis-save (consume their accumulated assets) in retirement. Figure 11.3 tells the story.

The difference between income (Y) and consumption (C) is either saved and involves accumulation of assets, if positive; or, if negative, it requires borrowing and building up debt against future income and/or dis-saving (consumption financed by accumulated assets). Over the lifetime, a basic budget constraint is satisfied whereby:

any inheritance received at birth + income over the lifetime =
= consumption over the lifetime + bequests left at the end of life

The theory is good in accounting for the profile of individual behaviour (i.e. in analyzing such issues as pensions) and the effect of demographics, but it does not do a good job at explaining why consumption tracks income.

Modern theories of consumption start from Irving Fisher's intertemporal optimization approach expounded in Section 5.1 of and then borrow various elements from both PIH and LCM. Analyses of the 1970s and 1980s proceeded more along the lines of PIH whereby they aimed at understanding the dynamics of aggregate consumption over time by postulating a representative agent; models in this spirit will be most of the ones below. Work in the 1990s and beyond progressively became more micro in nature, focusing on individual behaviour over the life-cycle and thus progressively adopted the spirit of LCM. This will occupy us in sub-section 11.1.16 where we examine the roles of demographics and endogenous labour supply in consumption.

11.1.3 The 'Permanent Income Hypothesis': Deterministic Income

The setup of the PIH is practically that of Section 5.1, so it will not be repeated here. There is no population growth. The household is of fixed size 1. We also assume away depreciation, so $\delta = \eta = 0$. Instead of only physical capital, agents may have any net assets $A_t > 0$

(including physical capital, housing, or government bonds). A further assumption is that the rate of time preference equals the fixed rate of interest, $r = \rho$; this implies that consumption is constant across time ($g = 0$). Thus, the decision-making agent/household selects the constant maximum sustainable level of consumption that exhausts its lifetime resources; this is 'permanent income'. The analysis of Chapter 5 applies; in particular, in view of (5.7'), we have:[2]

$$C_t = C_{t+1} = \cdots = r[A_t + H_t], \quad \text{for all } t = 0, 1, 2, \cdots, \infty, \tag{11.2}$$

$$H_t \equiv \frac{1}{(1+r)} \Sigma_{s=0}^{\infty} (1+r)^{-s} Y_{t+s}^L \tag{11.3}$$

H_t is human wealth, the present value of all future labour income, denoted by Y^L_t. The level of consumption shown in (11.2) is the maximum that is permanently sustainable given the lifetime resources, called 'permanent income' by Friedman (1957). If actual income at a certain time is (temporarily) higher/lower than this 'permanent' level, then the extra/deficit will be saved/made up by borrowing. The level of consumption will not change.[3] As such, the PIH asserts that individuals smooth out all temporary deviations of income in determining consumption.

11.1.4 The PIH, Stochastic Income, and the 'Random Walk' Model

The above analysis assumes deterministic (certain) labour income. This sub-section shows how uncertain labour income can be considered. The analysis here cannot follow the exact same path as those that led to (5.7') and (11.2). In particular, under stochastic income, the assumption of iso-elastic utility as in (5.1') does not deliver (5.7') even under the assumption of $r = \rho$. To get equality of consumption (in an expected sense), one needs to assume a period utility of a quadratic form:

$$u(c_t, l_t) = \left(c_t - \frac{bc_t^2}{2} \right) - l_t^{\theta}$$

Tracing the same steps as in Section 5.1, we arrive at the following Euler equation:

$$E_t(1 - bc_{t+1}) = \frac{1+\rho}{1+r}(1 - bc_t)$$

Assuming $r = \rho$, we then get $C_t = E_t(C_{t+1})$. (Recall that with household of size 1, we have $c_t = C_t$.) We can then relate period-t consumption to period-$t+2$ and thereafter as follows:

$$C_t = E_t C_{t+1} = E_t(E_{t+1} C_{t+2}) = E_t C_{t+2} = \cdots = E_t C_{t+s}, \quad \text{for all } s > t \tag{11.4}$$

---

[2] In this and subsequent Sections, we draw on Abel (1990a).
[3] Strictly speaking, permanent income is defined over a lifetime of any duration $T \leq \infty$: the maximum sustainable level of income/consumption over the (possibly finite) lifetime. But it is easier to work with infinite lives.

Because of the 'law of iterated expectations',[4] we get (11.4): current consumption is the best predictor ('conditional forecast') not only of next period's consumption, but also of all other future consumption. Empirically, (11.4) translates into the 'random walk' model of consumption:

$$C_t = E_{t-1}C_t = C_{t-1} + e_t, \qquad (11.4')$$

where e_t is a 'white-noise' (mean-zero, unitary variance) error term.

A side point is that a quadratic objective function with linear constraints often delivers 'certainty equivalence': the resulting behavioural equations involve expected values but other moments (e.g. variance) do not matter. But quadratic utility has other counter-intuitive properties. (Can you think of any in relation to the marginal utility of consumption? See also Attanasio and Weber, 2010, section 3.) We review some implications of non-quadratic utility later.

The key point here is equation (11.4'). Consumption follows a 'random walk' whereby its expectation of the future equals the current level (Hall, 1978). Thus, *all* the information required in order to best forecast future consumption is contained in current consumption *only*; *no other* variable, in the history of consumption or any other variable, conveys any useful *additional* information. Several implications follow from this, shown below.

11.1.5 Tests of the 'Random Walk' Model and 'Excess Sensitivity'

The 'random walk' model of consumption (11.4') can be tested by regressing C_t on lagged consumption and other variables, as in the following equation:

$$C_t = C_{t-1} + b\Delta Y_t + e_t \qquad (11.4'')$$

Theory suggests that the change in consumption is white noise, therefore uncorrelated with other variables. A rejection of the null hypothesis that the change in GDP (ΔY_t) or other variables is insignificant would provide evidence against the theory. Hall (1978) and subsequent studies repeatedly rejected the null. However, this rejection is not necessarily a wholesale rejection of the theory; it may just be a rejection of the specific assumptions implicit in (11.4'), namely quadratic utility and $r = \rho$. So, a sharper test is required than simply a test of whether $b = 0$ or not in (11.4'').

Closer scrutiny of (11.4'') suggests that ΔY_t is made up of a mixture of developments some of which may be anticipated at $t - 1$ and some which may be truly unanticipated 'news' or 'surprises' (see below). Even if it entered significantly in (11.4'), any *un*anticipated component of ΔY_t would not constitute a rejection of the theory as news and unexpected developments do affect consumption (again, see below). It is only the presence of anticipated, forecastable component of ΔY_t that would reject the theory, if significant in (11.4'). To

---

[4] The law of iterated expectations says that the current expectation of the future expectation of a variable equals the current expectation of that variable: $E_t(E_{t+1}c_{t+2}) = E_t c_{t+2}$. What is my best view today of the view that I will hold tomorrow about c_{t+2}? It is my current view; if I expected today to have a different, more informed view tomorrow, I might as well have that view of c_{t+2} right now.

distinguish between the two components of ΔY_t, Flavin (1981) in a seminal early study assumes an AR(1) GDP process:

$$Y_t = \theta Y_{t-1} + v_t, \quad 0 < \theta < 1, \tag{11.5}$$

where v_t is white noise ($E_t v_t = 0, \mathrm{Var} v_t = 1$). Equivalently:

$$\Delta Y_t = (\theta - 1) Y_{t-1} + v_t \tag{11.5'}$$

(11.5') into (11.4") becomes:

$$\Delta C_t = -b(1 - \theta) Y_{t-1} + bv_t + e_t \tag{11.6}$$

Now, the change in GDP is decomposed into an anticipated component ($b(1 - \theta) Y_{t-1}$) and an unanticipated error term which is indistinguishable from e_t. On the basis of this approach, Flavin (1981) finds against the theory ($b \neq 0$). This result has been termed 'excess sensitivity' of consumption to current income, or anticipated income changes: the data show that consumption responds to these, against the prediction of the theory. It is consistent with the visual impression from graphs that consumption tracks income closely, against the predictions of the smoothing motive. The finding of 'excess sensitivity' has been a puzzle that occupied the literature during the 1980s and 1990s.

11.1.6 The 'Random Walk' Model and Current Income

Here, we develop further implications of the random walk nature of consumption. The departure point is that consumption is constant in an expected sense as shown in (11.4). In practice, consumption will vary as new information is revealed about future labour income. In analogy to (11.2), consumption will be:

$$C_t = E_t(C_{t+1}) = \cdots = r[A_t + E_t(H_t)] \tag{11.2'}$$

Thus, consumption depends on expected human wealth. The variance of H_t does not matter: this is a manifestation of 'certainty equivalence'.

Let us first examine expected human wealth. To this end, assume an autoregressive process of labour income:

$$Y_t^L = (1 - \theta)\bar{Y}^L + \theta Y_{t-1}^L + v_t, \quad 0 < \theta < 1 \tag{11.7}$$

Labour income is a weighted average of a constant ($\bar{Y}^L > 0$) and of past income, which can temporarily deviate from the constant. The cause of the deviation is the 'white-noise' error term v_t. We can rewrite (11.7) as:

$$Y_t^L = \bar{Y}^L + v_t + \theta v_{t-1} + \theta^2 v_{t-2} + \theta^3 v_{t-3} + \cdots \tag{11.7'}$$

Thus, the influence of any particular shock declines the further back the shock occurred (note $\theta < 1$). So, following a shock at a certain time, labour income gradually regresses to its constant.[5] Note that adjustment takes more than one period even if the shock happens only once. θ is a measure of the 'persistence' of shocks; conversely, the speed of adjustment is inversely related to θ. Finally, an intermediate expression between (11.7) and (11.7') is (can you see why?):

$$Y^L_{t+s} = (1 - \theta^s)\bar{Y}^L + \theta^s Y^L_t + v_{t+s} + \theta v_{t+s-1} + \theta^2 v_{t+s-2} \cdots + \theta^s v_t \qquad (11.7")$$

Income at $t + s$ is a weighted average of the constant and past income (t) plus the shocks between t and $t + s$.

With these preliminaries, we can now develop the expected human wealth in (11.3):

$$E_t(H_t) \equiv \frac{1}{(1+r)}\sum_{s=0}^{\infty}(1+r)^{-s}E_t(Y^L_{t+s}) \qquad (11.3')$$

With (11.7"), noting that the expectation of shocks from t on is zero, this turns out to be:

$$E_t(H_t) \equiv \frac{1}{(1+r)}\sum_{s=0}^{\infty}(1+r)^{-s}[(1-\theta^s)\bar{Y}^L + \theta^s Y^L_t] = \frac{1}{r}\frac{(1-\theta)\bar{Y}^L + rY^L_t}{1+r-\theta} \qquad (11.3')$$

With this, consumption (11.2') becomes:

$$C_t = r[A_t + E_t(H_t)] = rA_t + \frac{(1-\theta)\bar{Y}^L + rY^L_t}{1+r-\theta} \qquad (11.8)$$

Consumption depends on the interest on assets plus a weighted average of the long-term fixed and current incomes. Note that although consumption is constant *ex ante* (in expected terms), actual consumption varies because of the realization of the shocks. The history of these shocks is embedded in the current income. Note further that consumption is smoother than current income. Ignoring non-human wealth (A) and taking variances:

$$Var(C_t) = \left(\frac{r}{1+r-\theta}\right)^2 Var(Y^L_t) < Var(Y^L_t) \qquad (11.8')$$

The inequality follows from $r/(1+r-\theta) < 1$. Because consumption is determined by permanent income, which is an intertemporal average, any temporary fluctuations in current income are partially smoothed out. This seems in line with the stylized fact that consumption, at least its non-durable part, is smoother than income.

---

[5] (11.7) can also be written in an adaptive pattern: $Y^L_t - \bar{Y}^L = \theta(Y^L_{t-1} - \bar{Y}^L) + v_t$. The deviation from the fixed, long-run level is a fraction θ of last period's deviation; this brings out the similarity with Adaptive Expectations, considered in Chapter 2. If we thought that Y^L_t is the expectation of labour income, then we would have 'regressive expectations' (regressing to $\bar{Y}^L$ after a temporary deviation).

11.1.7 'News' and 'Surprises' in Consumption

As suggested above, the theory is consistent with the idea that the change in consumption depends on unanticipated 'news', particularly those related to the evolution of income. Following Deaton (1992), we now develop this theme further. Start again with the PIH in a stochastic setup, (11.2'):

$$C_t = r[A_t + E_t(H_t)] \qquad (11.2')$$

Combine this with the individual's period budget constraint,

$$A_{t+1} = Y_t^L + (1+r)A_t - C_t,$$

and shift forward once to get:

$$C_{t+1} = r[A_{t+1} + E_{t+1}(H_{t+1})] = r[Y_t^L + (1+r)A_t - C_t + E_{t+1}(H_{t+1})]$$

We also have trivially:

$$(1+r)C_t = r(1+r)(A_t + E_t(H_t))$$

Subtract from the previous:

$$C_{t+1} - C_t = r[Y_t^L + E_{t+1}(H_{t+1}) - (1+r)E_t(H_t)]$$

From the definition of human wealth (11.3), we also have that:

$$(1+r)E_t(H_t) - Y_t^L = E_t \sum_{s=0}^{\infty} (1+r)^{-s} Y_{t+s}^L - Y_t^L = E_t \sum_{s=1}^{\infty} (1+r)^{-s} Y_{t+s}^L = E_t(H_{t+1})$$

Substitute into the previous to get a relation between consumption dynamics and 'news':

$$C_{t+1} - C_t = r[E_{t+1}(H_{t+1}) - E_t(H_{t+1})] \qquad (11.9)$$

The RHS of (11.9) involves the same human wealth, H_{t+1}, expected at two different times, $t+1$ and t. It represents an update in expectations of the same variables which is due to developments that occur between t and $t+1$ and are unanticipated at t; such updates are called 'news'. Consumption changes between t and $t+1$ depend on this. As future consumption is expected to remain at current levels, any actual consumption changes must be only due to developments that were not anticipated at t. Such are the re-evaluation of future labour incomes using more updated information; but in principle, any news that is relevant to human wealth is admissible in (11.9).

From here, we can get valuable insights on the relation between the evolution of consumption and the innovations in labour income—what Muellbauer (1983) has termed 'surprises'. In other words, this is an analysis of the marginal propensity to consume out of shocks ('surprises') in income, a very important issue. To this end, consider again the income process (11.7'). This implies for future incomes:

$$Y^L_{t+1+s} = \bar{Y}^L + v_{t+1+s} + \theta v_{t+s} + \cdots + \theta^s v_{t+1} + \theta^{s+1} v_t + \theta^{s+2} v_{t-1} + \cdots$$

Therefore:

$$E_{t+1} Y^L_{t+1+s} - E_t Y^L_{t+1+s} = \theta^s v_{t+1}$$

This update of expectations reflects the information available at the different dates.[6] With the use of (11.3') and the above, the 'news' equation (11.9) becomes:

$$C_{t+1} - C_t = \frac{r}{1+r} \sum_{s=0}^{\infty} (1+r)^{-s} \left[E_{t+1} Y^L_{t+1+s} - E_t Y^L_{t+1+s} \right] =$$

$$= \frac{r}{1+r} \sum_{s=0}^{\infty} (1+r)^{-s} \theta^s v_{t+1} = \frac{r}{1+r-\theta} v_{t+1} \tag{11.10}$$

Accordingly, following a shock v_{t+1} (unexpected at the end of t), consumption will change by the ratio $r/(1+r-\theta)$, which can be therefore called the 'marginal propensity to consume' (MPC). This rises with the persistence of the shock: in the polar cases of no persistence ($\theta = 0$), the MPC is of the order of the interest rate, whereas under full persistence ($\theta = 1$), MPC $= 1$. In the intermediate case, the more persistent the shock, the more sizeably it will affect intertemporal resources and therefore consumption.

11.1.8 'Excess Smoothness'

Various key results above, such as those related to the variance of consumption (11.8') or consumption dynamics and 'news' (11.10), have been based on a stochastic AR(1) process for income such as (11.7). The key property of this is the absence of a unit root. However, a voluminous literature starting from Nelson and Plosser (1982) has confirmed the existence of a unit root in many macroeconomic time series, including labour income. Based on this evidence, the income process should be written as:

$$\Delta Y^L_t = \theta \Delta Y^L_t + v_t \tag{11.11}$$

instead of (11.7). This change has serious implications; to see those, unravel (11.11):

$$\Delta Y^L_{t+1+s} = v_{t+1+s} + \theta v_{t+s} + \theta^2 v_{t+s-1} + \cdots$$

---

[6] As before, we assume that $E_t v_t = v_t$: The shock that occurs during period t is known at the end of the period, when expectations $E_t(.)$ are taken (technically, it is 'in the information set' that underpins E_t; but note that this depends on the setup that can vary but needs to be applied consistently). Therefore, the only new element between expectations taken at t and t + 1 is v_{t+1} (appropriately weighted because it relates to a future labour income).

This leads to:

$$Y^L_{t+s+1} = v_{t+s} + \theta v_{t+s-1} + \theta^2 v_{t+s-2} + \cdots +$$
$$+ v_{t+s-1} + \theta v_{t+s-2} + \theta^2 v_{t+s-3} + \cdots +$$
$$+ v_{t+s-2} + \theta v_{t+s-3} + \theta^2 v_{t+s-4} + \cdots +$$
$$+ \cdots$$

Rearranging:

$$Y^L_{t+s+1} = v_{t+s+1} + v_{t+s} + \cdots +$$
$$+ \theta(v_{t+s} + v_{t+s-1} + \cdots) +$$
$$+ \theta^2(v_{t+s-1} + v_{t+s-2} + \cdots) +$$
$$+ \cdots$$

Then, following the same reasoning as the one leading to (11.10), we get:

$$E_{t+1}Y^L_{t+1+s} - E_t Y^L_{t+1+s} = v_{t+1}(1 + \theta + \theta^2 + \cdots + \theta^s)$$

Note that the brackets increase with s. Therefore,

$$C_{t+1} - C_t = \frac{r}{1+r}\sum_{s=0}^{\infty}(1+r)^{-s}[E_{t+1}Y^L_{t+1+s} - E_t Y^L_{t+1+s}] =$$

$$= v_{t+1}\frac{r}{1+r}\left[\sum_{s=0}^{\infty}(1+r)^{-s} - \sum_{s=0}^{\infty}(1+r)^{-s}\theta^{s+1}\right] = \frac{1+r}{1+r-\theta}v_{t+1}$$

The MPC out of an unexpected change in income is now greater than unity. For instance, Campbell and Deaton (1989) estimate $\theta \approx 0.44$ in (11.11), so that the MPC is now of the order 1.75–1.8, depending on the value of the interest rate.

Another implication of the unit root process in (11.11) is that:

$$Var(\Delta C_{t+1}) = \left(\frac{1+r}{1+r-\theta}\right)^2 Var(v_t) > Var(v_t) \tag{11.12}$$

The increase in consumption is now predicted to be greater in variance than the innovation in income. Though not directly comparable, one can see that the inequality in (11.12) contradicts in spirit the inequality in (11.8'); the difference arises from the fact that the former assumes a unit root while the later assumes a stationary income process. Because the unit root in such variables as income is confirmed, however, (11.12) is taken to reflect better the spirit of the theory. In that regard, we have a puzzle: the data show consumption to be smoother than the estimated innovation of income (the ratio of standard deviations is about 0.6—Campbell and Deaton, 1989). This is actually one of the observations that started the theory of consumption, but it is incompatible with (11.12). This is the 'excess smoothness' puzzle—consumption seems smoother than unforecastable income, in contrast to theoretical predictions; see also Deaton (1992).[7]

11.1.9 The PIH and 'Saving for a Rainy Day'

Further insights can be gained from the relation between saving and labour income dynamics. The definition of saving is income in excess of consumption:

$$S \equiv rA_t + Y_t^L - C_t$$

Using the budget constraint $A_{t+1} = Y_t^L + (1+r)A_t - C_t$, it is obvious that saving equals asset accumulation:

$$S_t = A_{t+1} - A_t$$

From the basic PIH model of consumption (11.2'):

$$S_t = rA_t + Y_t^L - r[A_t + E_t(H_t)] = Y_t^L - \frac{r}{1+r}E_t\sum_{s=0}^{\infty}(1+r)^{-s}Y_{t+s}^L$$

Rearranging the labour income quasi-difference on the right, we arrive at an expression linking saving and labour income dynamics:[8]

$$S_t = -\frac{r}{1+r}E_t\sum_{s=0}^{\infty}(1+r)^{-s}\Delta Y_{t+s+1}^L \tag{11.13}$$

This is the 'saving for a rainy day' equation, first derived by Campbell (1987).[9] Saving anticipates future labour income changes; in particular, we have positive saving when such income is on the whole expected to fall in the future (i.e. it is high now), and dissaving when labour income is expected to grow (currently low). At the heart of this equation is the smoothing motive of consumption: if income happens to be high now, and therefore is expected to fall in the future (the 'rainy day'), the extra income will be saved; if income is low and expected to rise, we consume against future resources by borrowing and dissaving.

Equation (11.13) presents a testable version of PIH; a testable hypothesis of the basic model is that consumption and labour income should be co-integrated. Campbell (1987) shows that co-integration is a weak implication of all present value models, and is indeed verified for (11.13). But it is unclear whether this produces a one-to-one movement;[10] for

---

[7] Campbell and Deaton (1989) propose a reconciliation between the 'excess sensitivity' (to predictable income changes) and the 'excess smoothness' (to unexpected income 'news') puzzles of consumption: Given the intertemporal resources, if consumption overreacts to predictable income changes, it should under-react to the unpredictable such changes, and the two puzzles are said to be really two sides of the same coin.

[8] This can be most easily done by the 'lag operator'; see Sargent (1987, chapter 2).

[9] Campbell and Deaton (1989) derive an alternative, very similar, version in which the saving rate (as a percentage of labour income) is the present value of future labour income growth.

[10] This is so because $\frac{r}{1+r}\sum_{s=0}^{\infty}(1+r)^{-s} = 1$, therefore a once-and-for-all, unanticipated rise in labour income should produce an equal increase in consumption (permanently).

that, estimation of a co-integrating coefficient would be required, something that it is not easy to test as co-integration tests have low power. A different, more reliable test uses the fact that the 'saving for a rainy day' equation (11.13) implies restrictions on the parameters of a joint statistical process (Vector Autoregression—VAR) that governs the statistical evolution of saving and labour income; Campbell and Deaton (1989) reject the theory on the basis of such tests.[11]

Taking stock, on the basis of a number of tests such as: of the random walk model by Hall (1978) and Flavin (1981), of the 'excess sensitivity' and 'excess smoothness' puzzles, and of the saving-labour income equation by Campbell and Deaton (1989), the simple version of the PIH of consumption seems to be rejected by the data. Something is amiss. Campbell and Deaton (1989) included in the list of possibilities liquidity constraints, durable consumption, or other missing variables in the utility function. These were the issues that the next phase of the literature explored, and to which we shall shortly turn. Before that, we take a brief look at the effects of uncertainty under an iso-elastic utility and precautionary saving.

11.1.10 Uncertainty, the Euler Equation, and Precautionary Saving

It is natural to think that saving occurs not only when income is expected to fall (as the 'saving for a rainy day' model argues) but because of general uncertainty; whether future income might fall or rise, we would like to have a cushion to deal with all eventualities. But the above approach misses that. Under quadratic utility, we have certainty equivalence, and the random walk model uncertainty per se does not matter. However, with a utility function other than quadratic, certainly equivalence disappears: the variance of income or consumption matters. We then get 'precautionary saving': uncertainty induces a reduction in the level of consumption in order to build a cushion (or 'buffer stock' saving). This is an idea with a long history, more recently associated with Carroll (1992), Kimball (1992), and others.

To see this, consider the consumption Euler equation (5.11) which, with the assumptions of the present context (no population growth, fixed labour, fixed interest rate), takes the form:

$$E_t u'(C_{t+1}) = \frac{1+\rho}{1+r} u'(C_t) \tag{11.14}$$

Importantly, uncertainty is present here, making it necessary to take expectations at the beginning of the planning period (t). Thus, the expected marginal utility at $t+1$ is proportional to the current marginal utility. Now, here is the point: By Jensen's

---

[11] That PIH implies restrictions on the joint statistical process (VAR) that generates consumption and income had been noticed earlier by Sargent (1978) and Flavin (1981). The advantage of the approach that relies on saving (instead of consumption) and income, proposed by Campbell (1987), is that saving reflects the individual's perception of future labour income growth (via the 'rainy day' equation 11.13), hence it may carry more information about future income growth than is directly available to the econometrician.

inequality,[12] if the marginal utility is convex (i.e., $u'''(C) > 0$), a rise in uncertainty will induce a reduction in current consumption (C_t)—a rise in precautionary saving.[13]

Imagine an initial situation where there is no uncertainty; in that case, we have $E_t u'(C_{t+1}) = u'(E_t C_{t+1}) = u'(C_{t+1})$. And, the equality in (11.14) would hold if current consumption were set at such a level (C^0) that by definition obeys:

$$u'(E_t C_{t+1}) = \frac{1+\rho}{1+r} u'(C_t^0)$$

Consider now the emergence of uncertainty about future income. Given $E_t C_{t+1}$, uncertainty will raise the expected marginal utility: Now, we shall have $E_t u'(C_{t+1}) > u'(E_t C_{t+1})$. The equality (11.14) will now be satisfied by another current consumption level (C^1) such that:

$$E_t u'(C_{t+1}) = \frac{1+\rho}{1+r} u'(C_t^1)$$

But because $E_t u'(C_{t+1}) > u'(E_t C_{t+1})$, current consumption must fall: $C_t^1 < C_t^0$. (Note that $u'(.) < 0$.) In other words, the emergence of uncertainty induces a fall in current consumption—the emergence of precautionary saving.[14] The implication of precautionary saving for consumption dynamics is that optimal consumption should increase over time as it should be lower early on.

The empirics around this intuitive idea are however rather confused. In practice precautionary saving does not appear to be all that important: with US data from 1980s and 1990s, Hurst et al. (2010) estimate the amount of precautionary saving with respect to labour income risk to be less than 10 per cent of total household wealth. Importantly, precautionary saving varies across different segments of the population. The same authors show that it is more predominant among business-owning households than others (as perhaps those are accustomed to risk and develop more prudent strategies in dealing with it). It may also be more prominent among older individuals. With Italian data, Ventura and Eisenhauer (2005) estimate that 20 per cent of total saving is driven by precautionary reasons.

The Euler equation under uncertainty has given rise to another test of the PIH by Hansen and Singleton (1983). The starting point is that, under uncertainty, the interest rate is also uncertain; under iso-elastic preferences $(u(C_t) = \frac{C_t^{1-1/\sigma}}{1-1/\sigma})$, the Euler equation (11.14) takes the form:

$$E_t \left\{ \left(\frac{C_{t+1}}{C_t} \right)^{-\frac{1}{\sigma}} (1 + r_{t+1})/(1+\rho) \right\} = 0 \tag{11.14'}$$

---

[12] Jensen's inequality: for any convex function f(x), we have $Ef(x) > f(Ex)$. Try drawing this on a graph (a convex f(x) against x) to convince yourself!

[13] The assumption of $u'''(C) > 0$ is critical. (Note: this is the third derivative.) It is guaranteed by the iso-elastic utility $u(C_t) = \frac{C_t^{1-1/\sigma}}{1-1/\sigma}$, whereas quadratic utility implies $u'''(C) = 0$ (Can you verify these?); hence quadratic utility delivers certainty equivalence. It is said that the size of $u'''(C)$ captures the property of 'prudence' and determines the size of precautionary saving (Carroll and Kimball, 1996).

[14] This argument takes $E_t C_{t+1}$ as given, but this will also fall in general equilibrium, mitigating the fall in C_t. But the point remains that uncertainty reduces the level of consumption.

This equation is estimated by the 'Generalized Method of Moments' (GMM); instrumental variables are used to account for the endogeneity of the interest rate. In fact, there is more than one interest rate, and the equation should hold with respect to each of them. The GMM method presents a number of 'over-identifying' restrictions across the equations (11.14') that apply to different interest rates; these must be satisfied if the approach is valid. Hansen and Singleton (1983) find that these cross-equation restrictions are rejected. On the other hand, when (11.14') is estimated with respect to one interest rate only, the parameter estimates are rather implausible. These results represent yet another vote of no-confidence on PIH.

11.1.11 Durable Consumption

The analysis so far assumes homogeneous consumption. In practice, we may distinguish between consumption of services (catering, hairdresser's, lawyer's), non-durable consumption (of perishable goods such as food, cigarettes, office consumables) and durable goods consumption (of goods that last a long time, such as cars, furniture, electric, and other appliances).[15] While the distinction between services and non-durables may not be so important, the distinction of durables from the other categories is more important for a number of reasons. First, even though durables purchases are not so sizeable (10–15 per cent of total consumption in an economy like the US), they are important as they are more volatile (see Section 11.1). Second, though this is not a defining property, in practice many durables are sizeable items; as a result, their purchases are infrequent (and this may account for the volatility). Relatedly, durables purchases may lead the cycle (see Chapter 6), so they provide information on what comes next; this may be due to the fact that, because these are sizeable purchases, households gather more information about future incomes before committing themselves. Finally, for all these reasons, durables purchases may help explain one of the key puzzles in the theory of consumption, that of 'excess sensitivity'—the correlation of consumption with anticipated income.

It has been noticed since at least Mankiw (1982) that durables consumption requires a different approach to modelling that of non-durables. Due to their durability, these goods should be modelled in a way akin to investment—see Section 11.5. In particular, as durable consumption lasts more than one period (by definition), the relevant cost item is a 'user cost' (of the car, appliance, etc.). This will take account of the purchase price, the opportunity cost of the committed funds (interest rate), the depreciation rate (δ—see Section 11.3) and the resale price (if applicable). Let us follow Abel (1990a) in ignoring the resale price and assume a fixed purchase price (price of durables in terms of non-durables, p).[16] If so, the durables' user cost (UCD) is:

$$UCD = p(r + \delta) \tag{11.15}$$

---

[15] The durable/non-durable distinction may not be so sharp; there may be goods of intermediate durability, such as clothing. Moreover, the durability itself may not be the same across durables, e.g. furniture lasts longer than cars.

[16] This may not be appropriate for a limited category of durables such as cars and (even more importantly) works of art where there is the possibility of capital gains.

This would be the rental price if durables were rented on a period-by-period basis; this is possible in only a few of them (e.g. leasing cars).

The individual's problem is as set out in Chapter 5; the only difference is that utility also depends on the available stock of durables, D_t (mind: the stock that is always there, not the expenditure which is made infrequently). Thus, the problem is to maximize:

$$U_0 = \sum_{t=0}^{\infty} (1+\rho)^{-t} u(C_t, D_t) \tag{11.16}$$

subject to the standard budget constraint:

$$C_t + I_t + A_{t+1} - A_t = Y_t^L + rA_t \tag{11.17a}$$

This states that non-durable consumption (C) plus durables purchases during the period (I) plus asset (A) accumulation should equal disposable income: labour income plus interest income from assets. In turn, the expenditure on durables is linked to their stock in an equation familiar from investment:

$$D_{t+1} = (1-\delta)D_t + I_t \tag{11.17b}$$

The stock of durables is as inherited from last period, allowing for depreciation (at rate $0 < \delta < 1$), plus any new expenditure on them.

There are two sets of first-order conditions related to C_t and D_t. The dynamic evolution of durables (11.17b), after consolidation into (11.17b), induces a dynamic condition that is reflected in the presence of the future resale price in the UCD. But if we ignore that, then the presence of durables involves only an additional intra-temporal (i.e. non-dynamic) condition that relates the durables' stock to non-durable consumption:

$$\frac{u_D(C_t, D_t)}{u_C(C_t, D_t)} = p(r + \delta) \tag{11.18}$$

The marginal rate of substitution between durables and non-durables equals the marginal rate of transformation (the UCD). We assume an iso-elastic utility,

$$u(C_t, D_t) = \frac{(C_t^\beta D_t^{1-\beta})^{1-1/\sigma}}{1 - 1/\sigma}, \qquad 0 < \beta < 1$$

where $0 < 1 - \beta < 1$ reflects the relative importance of durables in utility. Then, (11.18) delivers a proportional relation between non-durables and the durables' stock:

$$C_t = \frac{\beta p(r+\delta)}{1-\beta} D_t, \qquad 0 < \delta < 1 \tag{11.19}$$

Accordingly, a rise in the user cost will induce a fall in the stock of durables; preferences (β) also matter. As such, the *stock* of durables as a macroeconomic series inherits all the properties of the durables consumption variable (C_t). The question of more interest to us is how the durables *purchase* (I_t) is related to consumption and thereby to income.

To proceed, rewrite (11.17b) as:

$$I_t = D_{t+1} - (1 - \delta)D_t = \frac{1 - \beta}{\beta p(r + \delta)}[C_{t+1} - (1 - \delta)C_t] \qquad (11.20)$$

Durability, i.e. $\delta < 1$, gives rise to new possibilities. First, we now have richer dynamics for I_t, inherited from the lag structure on the right. This is significant, as durables purchases are more serially correlated than general consumption (see Attanasio, 1999). Furthermore, the unconditional variance of durable purchases is:

$$Var(I) = \left(\delta \frac{1 - \beta}{\beta p(r + \delta)}\right)^2 Var(C) \qquad (11.20')$$

Depending on the value of parameters, we now have the potential to explain the greater volatility of durables purchases in relation to general consumption if $\delta \frac{1-\beta}{\beta p(r+\delta)} > 1$; this quantity rises with the importance of durables in utility, i.e. $1 - \beta$. See Bernanke (1985) and Abel (1990a) for details.

One final point concerns the fact that some durables such as cars do have a resale value, as mentioned. If so, their modelling can be done along the lines of investment. One approach in investment, as will be reviewed below, is to consider an (S, s) rule—a rule that says that the quantity of a durable good (or capital) should be adjusted when it reaches a lower threshold (s > 0) and will then be replenished to a ceiling (S > s). The individual decides their own optimal S and s. For example, for cars, an (S, s) rule may be to keep a car until its value declines to a low level s that I determine (e.g. keep it for a few years till it depreciates to my optimal level, which is generally above zero—i.e. I sell the car while it is still operational) and then buy more 'car' to have my stock adjusted to S—which may be a car of a certain level (low, medium, high class) and of a certain condition (new, second-hand) that is optimal for me; then I keep this car till it depreciates gradually to my -s- level and then buy again. In an early contribution, Eberly (1994) found that about half of households purchase cars according to this rule.[17]

The key point of the (S, s) rule is that purchases are infrequent due to transactions costs—I do not buy 'car' every day in the same way that I buy 'food'. Hence, behaviour at the individual level is inertial (the need for a car upgrade will generally emerge gradually but I only buy when the need has accumulated to a high level); but this inertia generally is likely to 'wash out' in the aggregate as the individual projects (each car purchase) are generally of a small value compared to the aggregate. As a result, the aggregate durables purchase series will be smooth. But this may not be true in capital investment. As we shall see, the spending on each individual investment project is so large that the individual inertia (infrequent investment spending) still shows in aggregate investment spending, which is 'spiky'.

---

[17] A general (S, s) rule is worked out and estimated by Attanasio (2000). A general point is that aggregation over the individual optimal rules is quite hard, a feature that has prevented more general use of this approach.

11.1.12 Liquidity Constraints

The PIH is based on the idea that individuals are able to smooth their consumption intertemporally by engaging in unlimited borrowing and/or saving. Borrowing should be limited only by lifetime income; to take an extreme example, *if* I wanted to consume all my lifetime's worth (in a present value sense) in one period (if my preferences dictated so), my bank would have no objection in giving me a loan equal to that amount. Obviously, this will not happen (even if I wanted it); realistically, any bank will place a limit on the amount of borrowing they allow, much less than the expected future resources. This is due to such (real-world) 'imperfections' as monitoring costs by banks, unwillingness to take too much risk, etc. Analytically, it is said that some households face 'liquidity constraints' (or borrowing, or credit restrictions): if so, they may not have the necessary liquidity that would allow them to smooth consumption. In practice, such restrictions can take several forms (see Hayashi, 1987): the simplest may be to disallow any borrowing at all for some households; or to require collateral for borrowing; or finally, to let the interest rate vary with the net asset position of the household (and thus in particular, to vary between borrowers and lenders).

There is ample evidence that seems to be consistent with the existence of liquidity constraints of some kind that affect mainly the young and those with low assets, e.g. Zeldes (1989). There are also findings that the immediate effects of once-only, predictable tax changes (e.g. rebates) on consumption are not in line with the predictions of the PIH. They tend to be sizeable, whereas the smoothing motive suggests that they would be spread over a long time, hence indistinguishable from zero. For instance, Johnson et al. (2006) found that households spent 20 to 40 per cent of the amount of the 2001 federal income tax rebates in the US in the next three months and two-thirds over the sixth-month horizon. Interestingly, responses are larger for households with low liquid wealth or low income, which is a strong indication of liquidity constraints. Obviously, such findings have a tremendous importance for the demand effects of tax cuts (e.g. they cause Ricardian Equivalence as discussed in Chapter 8). More evidence on liquidity constraints will be discussed in relation to consumer borrowing and saving shortly.

Not only are some households unable to borrow but, in a kind of symmetrical way, many are unable or unwilling to engage in serious saving. This may be due to a number of reasons, one set of reasons being subjective (lack of confidence, financial 'literacy', or expertise). Another reason is the lack of assets and net worth that would allow the flexibility to readjust the consumption intertemporal profile as theory suggests. There is indeed strong evidence that saving rates are strongly correlated with lifetime incomes; the rich save proportionately more (Dynan et al., 2004), as we discuss below. This is in line with the considerable inequality in wealth among US households, particularly in terms of equity wealth (see e.g. Poterba, 2000, T2, for 1998, which is further discussed in Section 11.5 on the stock market). As a result of inability to either borrow or save, many households live 'paycheck to paycheck'. They lack the 'financial wherewithal' to engage in intertemporal optimization and as a result they are 'spenders', not 'savers', as Mankiw (2000) puts it. Their consumption as a 'rule of thumb' follows the ups and downs of current income, without being smoothed intertemporally as the PIH assumes.

Let us explore the implications of this insight. We follow Campbell and Mankiw (1989) in assuming that a fraction $0 < \lambda < 1$ of households follow such a 'rule of thumb' whereby their consumption closely tracks disposable income. The rest, $1 - \lambda$, of households follow the behaviour described by PIH, namely the random walk model of consumption. This would suggest modifying equation (11.4") to:

$$C_t = C_{t-1} + \lambda \Delta Y_t + (1 - \lambda)e_t$$

If this equation were the 'true' one, this would explain the rejection of the restriction of $b = 0$ in (11.4"). This has been the approach that many researchers have taken to explain the rejection of the random walk model and the related finding of 'excess sensitivity' (of consumption to anticipated income). With data from Canada, France, Germany, Italy, Japan, and the United States, Campbell and Mankiw (1989) estimated a coefficient $b = \lambda \approx 0.5$ and interpret that as the proportion of income that goes to the liquidity constrained households; which implies, considering that such households are the poorer ones, that more than half the households are liquidity constrained. This way of modelling liquidity constraints is now routinely incorporated in dynamic macro models such as those used in business cycles research.

But despite being influential, this approach remains open to debate (see Attanasio, 1999, and Attanasio and Weber, 2010 for discussion and other estimates): Is λ constant across time? Secondly, the estimated λ may overstate the prevalence of liquidity constraints: it indicates the extent of 'tracking' (of current income by consumption) which is done not only by the liquidity constrained households but also by those unable or unwilling to save.[18] But equally, constraints may be more than the extent of tracking if some demand for borrowing will have been endogenously absorbed (decreased) by the equilibrium interest rates. If so, we have the opposite effect: constraints do not necessarily imply tracking and the estimated λ will understate them. In any case, understanding the exact nature of liquidity constraints is important for public policy in a number of respects (saving and borrowing, pensions, tax multipliers) but remains a challenge.

11.1.13 Variations on Preferences and Utility I: Hyperbolic Discounting

Recently, attention has been given in the literature to some aspects of behaviour traits emphasized by cognitive psychology, behavioural, and experimental economics; features that may or may not be consistent with full rationality. Some of these ideas build on insights reviewed in Chapter 2. As explained by Attanasio and Weber (2010), these may help to account for the empirical failure of the Euler equation and the empirical puzzles related to consumption (discussed) and saving.

We begin with hyperbolic discounting (HD). This suggests that we may be more short-termist and less consistent in our attitudes to time than the standard geometric/exponential discounting implies. Evidence from psychology and experimental economics suggests that individuals exhibit short-termism ('present-bias') in the following sense: individuals are more impatient if the same dilemma involving intertemporal choices

---

[18] Someone may be a 'rule of thumb' person (no borrowing) without necessarily facing liquidity constraints. This may reflect myopia or lack of 'financial literacy' and confidence.

emerged in the near and in the far future (but both were to be decided now). Consider the following thought experiment: I plan to buy a TV, about which I have two options: either I can buy it outright at time $t + 1$ or I can buy it at time t by borrowing funds for a period with interest rate r; the price of TV will be the same at both $t + 1$ and t. What interest rate am I prepared to pay in order to borrow and buy the TV one period earlier? The answer depends on my rate of time preference, i.e. how impatient I am to enjoy this item sooner rather than later. For any $r < \rho$ my utility and financial arithmetic suggests borrowing and buying earlier, for $r > \rho$ I would rather wait, while $r = \rho$ makes me indifferent between the two options. Suppose now that at the planning period $t = 0$, I am asked what would my cut-off interest rates be (that would make me indifferent) if the dilemma arose now but were to be implemented at two different dates in the future, $t = t1 > 0$ (the near future) and at $t = t2 > t1$ (the far future). The price of the TV is always the same. The evidence is that $r1 > r2$, suggesting that the rate of time preference is higher in the near future and lower further away: I am more impatient as far as the dilemma of the near future is concerned while I am more 'cool-headed' if the same dilemma were to take effect in the more distant future; roughly speaking, I can wait from t2 till $t2 + 1$ but not from t1 till $t1 + 1$. This suggests a rate of time preference (discount rate) that declines with time, resembling a hyperbola. This is in contrast to the standard geometric discounting (or exponential in continuous time) that assumes a constant rate.[19] There is ample evidence in favour of hyperbolically discounting behaviour (see Frederick et al., 2002; Angeletos et al., 2001). Laibson et al. (2007) find considerable divergence between discount rates within lifetimes: in one of their estimates, the short-term discount rate is 15 per cent and the long-term discount rate is 3.8 per cent.

Appealing though it is, this insight is quite hard to model. The main reason is that it fundamentally alters the way we view intertemporal decision-making. As mentioned in Chapter 5, under geometric (or exponential) discounting, the same intertemporal plan is optimal no matter when the planning period is; every time we optimize, we decide on the same course of action: geometric/exponential discounting is said to be 'time consistent'. As a result, the optimization calculation takes place only once and we do not need to worry when. But under HD, decision-making is time-inconsistent: The plan that I decide today will no longer be optimal tomorrow—just because of the passage of time. We do not need to look hard to find evidence of this: I know (today) that it is good for me to start jogging, but when tomorrow comes (when jogging should occur), the plan changes! Thus, generally speaking, HD has the potential to explain prevarication (I keep postponing to implement hard decisions), regret (I will regret tomorrow the TV that I buy impulsively with a loan today), etc.; all features of real life, yet that geometric/exponential discounting (and full rationality) do not allow.

The question for the modeller is how to deal with this time inconsistency. One approach is to assume (full) commitment: we enrol at the gym so as to force ourselves to do exercise, we ask professors to give us deadlines spread over the entire semester rather than allowing us flexibility as in this case we end up writing everything at the last minute, we commit to

---

[19] To be clear, both HD and geometric discounting (GD) accept that there is impatience towards the future; I would always rather have the TV earlier rather than later, if I can help it. The difference lies in the fact that GD assumes a constant period-to-period impatience, where under HD this is higher in the near future than in the far future.

pension schemes so as not to enter retirement penniless. Evidence for commitment is ample, from enrolment at the gym to pensions and other saving products (see Attanasio and Weber, 2010). In other words, individuals find it optimal to 'tie their hands' in relation to saving decisions, so, as a result, they save more.[20] In the presence of full commitment, the modeller need only consider optimization once; the plan will be adhered to even though it will not look optimal later on.

But commitment is not, cannot be, full. In its absence, there are various approaches to dealing with time inconsistency. Laibson (1997) and a follow-up literature consider the discrete-time case. Their main approach, following insights from psychology, is to assume the 'game' between two 'selves' within each of us: the longer thinking 'self' thinks of the long-term benefit (e.g. knows that exercise is good), while the short-term 'self' seeks immediate gratification (why bother with exercise, s/he asks lazily). The course of action we decide on is represented by the Nash equilibrium in this game. One advantage of this approach is that it introduces mechanisms of psychological self-control in real-world economic behaviour. In continuous time, however, this modelling strategy is not available. One alternative is to assume a 'naïve short-termist': someone who will re-optimize tomorrow and alter the plan devised today but does not know that today. Yet another, more satisfactory, approach is to assume a 'sophisticated short-termist': someone who knows today that they will alter the plan tomorrow and they incorporate that in today's thinking.[21] Barro (1999) follows this approach and incorporates it into a dynamic macro model; see Tsoukis et al. (2017) for subsequent work. Though it is too early to see how HD will be incorporated into standard macro theory, its importance is beyond doubt.

11.1.14 Variations on Preferences and Utility II: 'Keeping up with the Joneses', Status and Relative Income

Next, we turn attention to extensions that go under the names of 'keeping up with the Joneses', the status motive, or simply social comparisons that emphasize the importance of peer pressure in utility, based on relative income and consumption. The following period utility for individual i considers these effects:

$$u_t^i = u\left(c_t^i, \frac{c_t^i}{c_t}, l_t^i\right) \tag{11.21}$$

Apart from individual consumption and labour (both superscripted i), we also have individual consumption relative to aggregate (no superscript). Apart from individual consumption and labour, we also care about what others ('the Joneses') do as captured

---

[20] The potential advantage of 'tying one's hand' (i.e. denying oneself flexibility) was discussed in relation to discretionary monetary policy in Chapter 7. Time inconsistency is key there, too.

[21] Schematically, a naïve person will decide on Monday to go jogging on Tuesday but will not do it (will alter the plan); and will again decide on Tuesday to go on Wednesday and again will not go, and so on. A sophisticate will know that they will not carry out the plan and incorporate that into their thinking; they may instead decide to do milder exercise (e.g.) that will in fact be carried out.

by aggregate consumption. There is growing evidence that individual consumption in relation to 'the Joneses' (i.e. aggregate consumption) matters (see Frey and Stutzer, 2002; Clark et al., 2008, for evidence and reviews).[22] The existence of relative consumption represents a negative externality: as others try to improve their position, this represents a loss for me. As is standard with externalities, this leads to a suboptimal outcome, see below.

To see what is involved, consider an oft-used tractable specification (ignoring habits for the moment):

$$u_t^i = \log[c_t^i - \beta c_t] - \theta l_t^i \tag{11.21'}$$

$0 < \beta < 1$ embodies the 'Joneses effect'; the standard case is recovered when $\beta = 0$. Appropriate restrictions ensure that the quantity in brackets is not negative. With this, the Euler equation (5.11) becomes:

$$\frac{\frac{du_{t+1}^i}{dc_{t+1}^i}}{\frac{du_t^i}{dc_t^i}} = \frac{c_t^i - \beta c_t}{c_{t+1}^i - \beta c_{t+1}} = \frac{c_t}{c_{t+1}} \frac{c_t^i/c_t - \beta}{c_{t+1}^i/c_{t+1} - \beta} = \frac{1+\rho}{1+r} \tag{11.22}$$

Now, if the cross-sectional distribution of consumption stays invariant so that c_t^i/c_t is constant over time, we recover the original Euler equation (with log utility),

$$\frac{c_t}{c_{t+1}} = \frac{1+\rho}{1+r}$$

Of course, this invariance is a standard assumption used in some work but may not be realistic; in its absence, (11.21') implies that individual consumption growth is affected by aggregate consumption growth as well the interest rate. For example, Maurer and Meier (2008) estimate a consumption growth equation of the form:[23]

$$\Delta \log c_t^i = \alpha + \beta X_t^i + \gamma \Delta \log C_t^i + u_t$$

where C_t^i is the consumption of the 'household i's peer group, i.e., among households that share some common socio-demographic characteristics' (and X is a vector of other controlling variables). They estimate $\gamma = 0.3 - 0.4$. This is indicative of strong relative consumption effects in utility; but note that the peer (comparison) group is 'local', with similar characteristics, not society at large. This is theme echoed in some other literature, e.g. Clark and Senik (2010).

---

[22] Apart from 'keeping up with the Joneses', this effect also goes by the names of 'external habits', 'rat races', and the status motive; but the key point is clear: relative consumption matters. It is not clear whether this is consistent with full rationality. On the one hand, relative consumption may well be a legitimate argument in utility if the 'sovereign consumer' thinks so; on the other hand, what is the motive for relative consumption? In the mind of this author, one motive is to self-check: Have I done OK in my optimization? Have I found the optimal plan, have I followed it up consistently? One way to check is by looking over my shoulder at what others are doing. These effects are not allowed by full rationality which assumes clarity of objectives, full cognitive ability to work out the optimal plan, and self-discipline to carry it out; therefore no need to check by looking at relative consumption.

[23] Note that it is not clear what period utility specification will deliver an Euler equation of this form.

Furthermore, consider the first-order condition that determines the labour-leisure choice (see equation 5.14):

$$\frac{\partial u(c_t, l_t)}{\partial l_t} = w_t \frac{\partial u(c_t, l_t)}{\partial c_t}$$

With the period utility (11.21), we have:

$$\theta = w_t \frac{1}{c_t^i - \beta c_t}$$

or

$$c_t^i = \frac{w_t}{\theta\left(1 - \frac{\beta c_t}{c_t}\right)}$$

Now the presence of relative consumption in utility ($\beta > 0$) implies that consumption is higher than what it would have been otherwise. In order to gain utility by improving my relative consumption, I increase my individual consumption; since everyone does the same, aggregate consumption increases. The willingness to keep up with others motivates individuals to work harder (Goerke and Pannenberg, 2015). Thus, cultural factors may hold the potential to explain the difference in labour supply between the US and Europe (Prescott, 2004); unlike a generation ago, Europeans seem currently to work less than Americans, who may be more motivated to work in pursuit of the 'American dream'. But these effects are generally suboptimal and reduce welfare: This is the implication of the negative externality mentioned above.[24] Note also the implications for long-term growth: since labour supply increases, so does the marginal product of capital and the real interest rate. Thus, although in the long run the standard Euler equation is recovered, as mentioned, the rate of growth will be permanently higher. Additionally, Clark and Senik (2010) find that income comparisons are associated with both lower levels of subjective well-being and a greater demand for income redistribution. Using subjective data on well-being ('happiness'), Clark and Senik (2010) find support for consumption comparisons, but they are localized (one compares oneself with one's social milieu); Goerke and Pannenberg (2015) also find localized effects. But despite the ambiguity in the details, the near-consensus is that such comparisons are important. Their macroeconomic implications have been investigated in a voluminous literature; see e.g. Tsoukis and Tournemaine (2013) for references.

11.1.15 Variations on Preferences and Utility III: Habit Formation

Now let us turn to 'habits', sometimes referred to as 'internal habits', which introduces consumption comparisons to the individual's own past consumption as a kind of established norm; utility is derived from improvement over this norm as well as the level

---

[24] The analogy often used is with the spectators in the stadium: in order to see better (relative consumption), they stand up; since everyone does the same, on average the view is not better, but we get sore feet—welfare declines.

of consumption itself. In this case, a tractable specification of utility (ignoring labour supply) is:

$$u_t^i = u\left(c_t^i, \frac{c_t^i}{c_{t-1}^i}\right) = \log[c_t^i - \varphi c_{t-1}^i] \tag{11.23}$$

'Habits' is introduced by $0 < \varphi < 1$; the standard formulation is recovered by setting $\varphi = 0$. The justification for the individual consumption growth in utility is that, to some extent, it is the improvement in consumption that gives us utility, not just the level. (E.g. part of the fun of exercise is to do better than last time.) Conversely, given current consumption, the higher was last period's consumption, the lower is my current utility.[25] Now equation (5.10) takes the form:

$$\frac{(1+\rho)^{-t}}{c_t^i - \varphi c_{t-1}^i} - \varphi \frac{(1+\rho)^{-t-1}}{c_{t+1}^i - \varphi c_t^i} - \lambda R_t^{-1}(1+\eta)^t = 0$$

Therefore, the Euler equation becomes:

$$\frac{\frac{1}{c_{t+1}^i - \varphi c_t^i} - \varphi \frac{(1+\rho)^{-1}}{c_{t+2}^i - \varphi c_{t+1}^i}}{\frac{1}{c_t^i - \varphi c_{t-1}^i} - \varphi \frac{(1+\rho)^{-1}}{c_{t+1}^i - \varphi c_t^i}} = \frac{1+\rho}{1+r} \tag{11.24}$$

The effect of this extension is that the Euler equation now involves more interesting dynamics. (Note the unitary elasticity of substitution due to log utility.) If we linearize (11.24) around $\varphi = 0$ through a Taylor expansion, we get a linearized Euler equation:

$$\Delta \log c_{t+1}^i = \frac{\varphi}{\Phi} \Delta \log c_t^i + \frac{\varphi}{(1+\rho)\Phi} \Delta \log c_{t+2}^i + \frac{r-\rho}{\Phi}$$
$$\Phi \equiv 1 + \varphi + \frac{\varphi}{(1+\rho)} \tag{11.24'}$$

(The deterministic setup greatly simplifies things.) There is now more complex dynamics, with consumption growth lags and leads as well as the current growth (c_{t+1}^i/c_t^i); there is also a homogeneity restriction (the coefficients of the consumption growth terms equal one) that ensures that in the long-run steady state (when $\Delta \log c_{t+1}^i = \Delta \log c_t^i = \Delta \log c_{t+2}^i = \Delta \log c$) we get $\Delta \log c = r - \rho$, i.e. we recover the standard consumption Euler equation with $\sigma = 1$. As a result of the richer transitional dynamics, consumption can capture the humps in income and the gradual hump-shaped response of real spending to various shocks. On this basis, Fuhrer (2000) offers strong support to the habits hypothesis and analyses its implications for monetary policy.

11.1.16 Variations on Preferences and Utility IV: Recursive Preferences

Finally, another variation of utility, due to Epstein and Zin (1989) and others, is based on recursive preferences and has proved quite fruitful in many fields of macroeconomics and

---

[25] This is all not good news at a time when living standards may be stagnating (see Chapter 9).

finance. In a nutshell, this disentangles the rate of intertemporal substitution and the degree of relative risk aversion from one another. Consider the standard utility maximization problem. It starts from maximizing intertemporal utility in the following form (ignoring anything else other than consumption):

$$U_0 \equiv \sum_{t=0}^{\infty} (1+\rho)^{-t} E_0 u(c_t) \tag{11.25}$$

Allowance is made for uncertainty via expectations taken at the planning time $(t=0)$. The standard approach would be to specify a period utility u(c) and insert into the above. The specification could be a quadratic, or more commonly iso-elastic as above:

$$u(c_t) = \frac{c_t^{1-1/\sigma}}{1-1/\sigma}$$

The problem with this approach is that it conflates two processes, the processes of aggregating (bundling up in utility) uncertain outcomes within each period (i.e. risk) and of aggregating utilities across time. The parameters that regulate behaviour in these respects are the coefficient of relative risk aversion (CRRA, capturing attitudes to risk, hence how utility weighs two uncertain outcomes) and the intertemporal elasticity of substitution (IES, familiar). In fact, the two become inextricably linked in this specification: IES $= \sigma = 1/\text{CRRA}$. Yet there is no reason why the two should be tied up in this way except convenience; Epstein and Zin (1989) propose a formulation that disentangles the two.

To see how this works, start again from (11.25) and write for period 1:

$$U_1 \equiv \sum_{t=1}^{\infty} (1+\rho)^{-t+1} E_1 u(c_t) \tag{11.25'}$$

Inserting into (25), we get:

$$U_0 = u(c_0) + \frac{1}{1+\rho} E_0 U_1 \tag{11.25''}$$

Note that c_0 is known with certainty (so that $Eu(c_0) = u(c_0)$) and that, because of the law of iterated expectations,

$$E_0 U_1 = \sum_{t=1}^{\infty} (1+\rho)^{-t+1} E_0 u(c_t).$$

Now rather than positing a period utility u(c), Epstein and Zin (1989) posit a CES function of the elements on the right-hand side of (11.25''):

$$U_0 \equiv \left(\frac{\rho}{1+\rho} c_0^{\psi} + \frac{1}{1+\rho} [(E_0 U_1^{\alpha})^{1/\alpha}]^{\psi} \right)^{1/\psi}, \quad \psi \equiv (\sigma-1)/\sigma \tag{11.26}$$

This 'bundles up' current consumption and future utility in making total current utility. There are three independent parameters: $\rho > 0$ is the rate of time preference (subjective discount rate), IES = σ and 0 < CRRA = α < 1. The first two are familiar, the third one is an innovation. The restriction 0 < α < 1 embodies risk aversion because $EU^\alpha < (EU)^\alpha$: The utility of a fair lottery (a win and a loss of one pound with equal probability) is less than the utility of the 'sure thing' (£0) as we dislike risk. The greater the risk aversion (α), the greater is the difference. Hence, IES and CRRA are separated. The approach then works directly without the need to specify a functional form for period utility. It is in fact more general than the standard approach that it encompasses as a special case: if we set $\alpha = \psi \equiv (\sigma - 1)/\sigma$, it turns out that we recover (11.25). As mentioned, the recursive preferences approach has found widespread application in many areas of macroeconomics and finance; see Weil (1990).

11.1.17 The LCM: Finite Lifetimes, Demographics, and Other Issues

The vintage Life-Cycle Model (LCM) starts from the same premise as the PIH, namely that individuals wish to smooth consumption over time, but adds the realistic features of finite lives and an income 'hump' over the lifetime—low early on, high in middle age, and low again in retirement. Hence, individuals borrow early on (the result of low income and higher consumption), save in the middle, and dis-save (consume their accumulated assets) in retirement. Additionally, account is taken of the desire to leave bequests to offspring. Analytically, the overlapping-generations model of Chapter 5 may be closer to this model than the infinite-horizon Ramsey model.[26]

As we saw in the beginning, consumption over life is not entirely flat as the smoothing motive would dictate; rather, it itself exhibits a hump that tracks that of income. But if consumption of the household is adjusted by its size, almost all the hump goes away; so the higher consumption in middle life seems to be the result of the larger family/household size. Hence, so far, the core logic of the model is in line with basic facts. But then we have the 'retirement savings puzzle': against the predictions of the smoothing motive, apparently households do not save enough to maintain the same consumption level over retirement. As a result, consumption drops sharply at retirement. Total consumption at age 70 is roughly 35 per cent of the peak in the UK and just above 50 per cent in the USA (Attanasio, 1999). Bernheim et al. (2001) calculate that '31 percent of the [households in the US] sample reduce their consumption by at least 35 percent' at retirement. This drop varies across income groups, with those with low wealth dropping the most (see Attanasio and Weber, 2010). There are suggestions that accounting carefully for family size (which drops at retirement) also explains this finding. In any case, modern work strives to explain this apparent puzzle and other salient empirical findings by enriching the analysis with demographics, endogenous labour supply, and other considerations.

An interplay of demographics and precautionary saving may explain the hump in the age-profile of consumption that matches that of income (Attanasio et al., 1999); demographics 'pushes' for an early hump in consumption, precautionary saving for a late one, with the result that the hump occurs in middle life at the same time as income. Gourinchas

---

[26] Hybrid PIH/LCM models are presented by Gali (1990) and Clarida (1991). They explore the extent to which individual LCM models aggregated over cohorts can replicate the main features of aggregate consumption such as the tracking of income.

and Parker (2002) construct and compare age-profiles of consumption and income over the working lives of typical households. They are thus able to analyse saving and wealth according to precautionary and life-cycle motives. They find that, in early life, households save for precautionary purposes; more serious saving starts at around age 40, when the typical household starts accumulating liquid assets for retirement.

In recent years, the literature has increasingly exploited microeconomic (related to individual households) rather than aggregate data. Other issues that have been explored with such data include endogenous labour supply and the insurability of individual earnings shocks. It is argued that incorporation of leisure in consumption models can resolve various empirical puzzles (Attanasio and Weber, 2010, section. 3). The first-order condition that relates leisure to consumption has the form:

$$U_l/U_C = w$$

The ratio of the marginal utilities of consumption and (disutility) of work equals the real wage. To fix ideas, consider a CES period utility,

$$u = (c^{(\theta-1)/\theta} + (1-l)^{(\theta-1)/\theta})^{\frac{\theta}{\theta-1}},$$

where θ is the elasticity of substitution between consumption and leisure. The first-order condition then becomes:

$$\left(\frac{c}{1-l}\right)^{1/\theta} = w$$

If leisure and consumption are (gross) substitutes ($\theta > 0$), then a rise in the real wage, as happens in middle life, will imply that consumption rises and/or leisure falls so work rises; conversely, in retirement, we have a low wage, consumption, and high leisure. Intuitively, in retirement we have lots of free time therefore we do not need so much consumption; in middle life, we make up for scarce leisure by more plentiful consumption. Thus, the hump in both consumption and earnings coincide. The effect is more pronounced with a higher elasticity of substitution.

Another strand of literature has explored the existence of idiosyncratic shocks (illness, unemployment, etc.) among heterogeneous agents in addition to aggregate risk. In perfect financial markets, full insurance should be available and thus all idiosyncratic risk should be diversified away.[27] There is strong evidence that such perfect or complete markets do not exist; in fact, their limitations are related to liquidity constraints. More transitory shocks (e.g. temporary unemployment) can be more easily insured away, but the possibility of more permanent shocks (e.g. illness) will imply earnings uncertainty. In this way, consumption will be more severely affected. The interested reader can consult Attanasio and Weber (2010) and Meghir and Pistaferri (2011) as recent portals to this large and expanding literature.

---

[27] E.g., suppose that I am subject to an aggregate risk (a rise/fall in the market wage) and I face extra idiosyncratic risk (e.g. because I live in an unsafe neighbourhood). Insurance markets would allow me to get rid of the idiocyncratic risk at the cost of a premium; my average consumption falls but it is less risky. In this case, it is said that there is 'risk sharing' across society.

11.2 Saving

11.2.1 Theoretical Considerations

Saving is defined as consuming less out of a given amount of resources at present in order to consume more in the future. In other words, saving is the decision to defer consumption. As this deferred consumption must be stored in some form of asset, it gives rise to the popular notions of saving as putting money in the bank or into a pension scheme or buying bonds or shares. But we must not confuse the act itself with the media that facilitate it. Applying the definition to national income accounting, we get that saving is the difference between national income (the available resources) and (current) consumption, private and public. If the difference is positive, current resources are transferred to the future, while if it is negative, future resources are transferred for present consumption (via borrowing). Care should be taken to distinguish between the flow concept (saving in each year) and the stock concept (accumulated saving), which we shall call saving$S$ here.[28]

Saving is very important for a number of reasons. First, saving is key for growth: the accumulated savings (net of borrowing) are channelled by the financial system back into the production-spending cycle via loans; as such, saving maintains spending but, when it finances investment, it also supports the expansion of fixed capital and growth. Secondly, saving is key for the external finances of a country: From national income accounting, we have that the external current account equals national saving (private plus public) minus investment, $CA = S - I$. Hence, vigorous saving is part and parcel, part cause and part effect, of a positive external position. A country with low saving and a negative current account will be accumulating external debt. Thirdly, saving will have implications for inequality (see Chapter 10): as the rich generally save more, they accumulate yet more wealth. Promoting social mobility (giving a chance to those born poor to advance if they have the skills and motivation) requires encouraging saving among all the sections of society; this remains a public policy objective.

The household saving rate shows considerable variation both across time and countries, as Figure 11.4(a, b) shows.[29] It ranged in 2015 from Switzerland's 18 per cent all the way down to Latvia's −8 per cent dissaving; intermediate values range from 0 per cent (e.g. the UK) to Italy-France-US-Japan and many others in the range 0–5 per cent to Germany (about 10 per cent) to Sweden-Switzerland-Korea (10–15 per cent). While differences between countries are important, there is a clear tendency for the rates to fall, from the range of 10–20 per cent in 1970 to 0–10 per cent currently (there is some indication of stabilization recently). The cause of this decline is not well understood. The EU-19 average currently stands at nearly 6 per cent. As in many other areas of macroeconomics, the analyst has a lot of work to do in order to explain why countries with rather similar socio-economic characteristics display such dissimilar behaviour. Thus, both the importance of

---

[28] We can distinguish between private and government saving; the sum of the two is national saving. This section deals with private saving.

[29] The series in Figure 11.4 (a, b) is formally called 'net household saving as percentage of the household's net disposable income'. The series is the ratio of household saving (plus NEP = the change in net equity of households in pension funds) to household disposable income (plus NEP). Household saving is given by subtracting household consumption from household disposable income plus NEP. Consumption includes 'imputed rent' that owner-occupiers of dwellings 'pay', as occupiers, to themselves as owners. Household disposable income is all income including net interest and benefits minus taxes. It also includes income from 'imputed rent'.

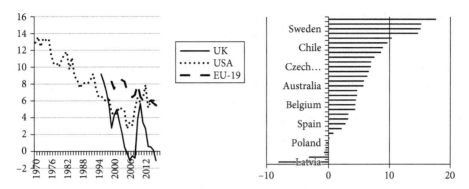

Figure 11.4. Household saving rates (%): panel (a) selected countries, 1970–2017; panel (b) cross-section, 2015

Source: OECD *National Accounts at a Glance*. Not all 32 countries of the sample are named on the cross-sectional bar panel.

saving and the real-world developments such as large variations across countries and decreases over time, motivate the study of saving. Despite its importance, it is perhaps fair to say that saving has not received a lot of attention; the literature seems to treat it as the flip side of consumption and derive implications from there.

There are various motives for the intertemporal transfer of resources implied by saving. First, we save for precautionary reasons and in order to smooth consumption over 'the rainy day' (sub-section 11.1.8): if I expect future income to be low, I save today in order to maintain a smooth profile of consumption. (Conversely, borrowing or dis-saving exists when current income is low and expected to rise, when we maintain a relatively high consumption against future resources.) More generally, I save in order to cover against unexpected contingencies (precautionary or 'buffer-stock' saving). These theories imply that saving is higher when national income is more variable and unpredictable; but it is unclear whether this is enough to explain the large cross-sectional variance of saving (is income in the countries that save less more stable?) and the drop in saving in recent decades (has income become more stable?). A special case of reasoning, emphasized more by the Life-Cycle model, applies to retirement when income is zero: A powerful saving motive arises from the need to secure enough means for retirement via either social security and a pension, or via the accumulation of private assets. Finally, another motive is the desire to leave resources to our offspring by leaving them bequests. A seminal paper by Kotlikoff and Summer (1981) calculated that most of US saving occurred because of the bequest motive. As we saw in Chapter 5, this implies that the majority of the assets of the economy (capital, housing) were built over generations through bequests, rather than through saving within a lifetime (which is liquidated by the end of the life).

It may be useful to start by recalling the result of Section 5.2 that in a basic overlapping-generations model, the saving rate increases with the population growth rate and the growth rate of the economy. But we should also recall that the OLG model of that section is built on two generations, young-productive and the old-retired; so, saving rises as more people are anticipated to go into retirement and save now. But there may be more than one generations, including unproductive young. The very young are in education or may be unemployed in greater proportion; if they are more numerous, then a higher population growth rate implies more young dependants, therefore less saving. Thus, in more realistic setups, the effect of the 'dependency ratio' (number of inactive dependants per currently active individual) has an ambiguous relationship with the saving rate. The effects of the rising dependency ratio are very important considering the fact that the populations of developed economies age fast.

Similarly ambiguous results emerge in a richer setup in relation to income growth. A higher income growth rate may imply *borrowing* against higher future resources (something not allowed in the basic OLG model of Chapter 5 where the growth rate made available more resources for both consumption *and* saving), therefore again the relationship between the growth and saving rates is ambiguous (see Jappelli and Pagano, 1994).

11.2.2 Empirical Evidence

The wide-ranging and careful study of Loayza et al. (2000) on the determinants of saving (both national and private) across countries has highlighted a number of factors. First, saving rates display considerable serial correlation, therefore change only sluggishly, whatever policies are put in place. Secondly, both the level and growth rate of income are positively related to saving rates; the effect of the growth rate is in accordance with the basic model discussed above; the effect of the level is in line with findings that the rich save proportionately more (see below); this finding may have pessimistic implications about the world income distribution, insofar as richer countries are able to save proportionately more, therefore invest and grow even more. Next, there is some indication that instability causes saving to rise, in line with the precautionary motive. Finally, public saving (the budget surplus) tends to raise national saving, but less than one-to-one. As was discussed in Chapter 8, such a finding does not lend support to either the polar Keynesian view of the effects of fiscal policy (government budget deficits) or to the polar opposite of Ricardian Equivalence.

Loayza et al. (2000) find that the dependency ratio has a negative effect on growth; interestingly, it is the old-dependency ratio that has a stronger (negative) effect than the young-dependency ratio (recall that in the basic model, the old-dependency affected positively growth as the young save for retirement). The implications of the dependency ratio for Japan in particular, which is renowned for its aged population and has a low saving rate (at about 5 per cent) are discussed by Horioka (2010). Modigliani and Cao (2004) consider the strikingly high saving rate in China (> 45 per cent), which may be due to a combination of:

- the high growth rate of the economy as concluded in Chapter 5;
- the lack of generalized social insurance and the need for the middle-aged to build assets for their old age;
- the low population growth rate due to the one-child policy the country has had for several decades (recently abandoned). This implies that the old cannot rely on extended families for support, which again was not considered in Chapter 5.

Finally, to the mind of this author, cultural/behavioural factors such as the 'keeping up with the Joneses', status-seeking, and 'habits' highlighted above may have something to do with the decline of saving rates evident in Figure 11.4a; but the issue has not received formal attention in the literature.

11.2.3 Credit/Liquidity Constraints and Financial Market Reforms

Considerable attention has been paid to the important issue of credit/liquidity constraints and the financial sector reforms that have taken place since the 1980s across the world. By relaxing the requirements for collateral and loan-to-value ratios, the general thrust of these reforms have been to allow more borrowing against *the same* amount of future (expected) lifetime resources. Simple reasoning suggests that this will reduce saving, and this is indeed borne out by the data, as found by both Loayza et al. (2000) and Jappelli and Pagano (1994).

Micro-based studies have corroborated these findings (see Deaton, 1991, for an interface between aggregative and micro studies). Using a questionnaire methodology, Shapiro and Slemrod (2003) analyse the responses of US households to the tax rebates that US households received in the early 2000s: about 20 per cent of households would consume the extra income, 40 per cent would save it, of whom 60 per cent would use it to repay existing debt (repaying debt is a form of saving from a National Income Accounting point of view—though of course it offsets the dis-saving/higher consumption that occurred earlier when the debts were built up).

The issue of credit card debt has received some attention, as this type of debt shows a tendency to increase. As mentioned, debt is essentially negative savings (i.e. accumulated dis-saving). Gross and Souleles (2002) point out that many households have credit card debt and no savings; in other words, except housing, their net worth is negative. But credit card debt does not seem to be concentrated only among the poorer households as one might think from the above study. Laibson et al. (2003) conclude that 'the typical American household accumulates wealth in the years leading up to retirement and simultaneously borrows on their credit cards'. For instance, over 80 per cent of households whose head is in their thirties and are median in terms of wealth had credit card debt; among households with a head between ages 50–59 and in the third wealth quartile, 56 per cent had credit card debt. The rise of credit card debt seems to be related to social pressures to catch up or show off, as the theories on the status and 'keeping up with the Joneses' discussed above suggest. For instance, using data from a Dutch household survey, Georgarakos et al. (2014) find that peer pressure related to perceived income differentials contributes to debt and the likelihood of financial distress among those who consider themselves poorer than their peers. Attanasio et al. (2008) consider dis-saving arising from loans in the US car ('auto') market and find evidence of binding credit constraints.

11.3 Investment

11.3.1 Introduction

The theory of investment is concerned with society's use of current resources for the augmentation of capital, so that better production opportunities arise in the future. So, investment implies reducing the current resources readily available for consumption, in order to have greater consumption opportunities in the future. In many ways, this parallels the individuals' process of saving. Thus, investment is very important from the point of view of growth. But investment is also important for another reason: it is the most volatile element of aggregate demand; so, understanding it is crucial for understanding a range of

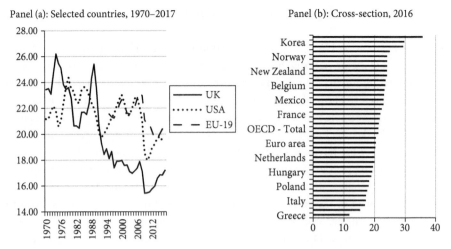

Figure 11.5. Gross fixed capital formation-to-GDP ratio (%): panel (a) selected countries, 1970–2017; panel (b) cross-section, 2016

Source: OECD *National Accounts at a Glance*. Not all 38 countries of the sample are named on the cross-sectional bar panel. See the text for the definition of Gross Fixed Capital formation.

issues related to the fiscal multipliers, business cycles, and the optimal design of stabilization policy.

What we commonly call 'investment' is formally called 'Gross Fixed Capital Formation' (GFCF) and is defined as the spending on produced fixed assets (goods) that help produce other goods and services; as such, it involves expenditure on physical capital by businesses (on equipment, buildings, and vehicles), expenditure on dwellings (housing) by households and expenditure by government on infrastructure (transport, communications, schools, hospitals), expenditure by government on R&D and expenditure on military assets and weapons systems. The data include all transport and installation charges. This section refers to business investment; housing investment will be dealt with in the next section.[30] Figure 11.5(a, b) gives data from the OECD on GFCF as a percentage over GDP: panel (a) is a time-series plot of the ratio for the UK, USA, and the Euro area (EU-19), whereas panel (b) gives the cross-section in 2016.

Most observations in the cross-country panel fall in the 15–25 per cent range, with the OECD average being about 21 per cent. Regarding time, the ratio seems to be declining since the 1970s and is quite volatile; not surprisingly, in both aspects, it shows similarities with the saving ratio of Figure 11.4(a and b).

11.3.2 A Digression on Decay and Depreciation

An important distinction is to be made between Gross Fixed Capital Formation (GFCF) and Net Fixed Capital Formation (NFCF). The difference is the expenditure made in order to fix the wear and tear (depreciation) of existing capital; as we have discussed in Chapters 5 and 9, the simple equation that links these concepts is:

---

[30] There is a broader definition of investment as all goods that are produced but not consumed in this period. Under this definition, apart from GFCF, investment also includes inventory investment: changes in inventories (stocks of goods); this will be discussed later on in this section.

$$GFCF = NFCF + depreciation$$

The distinction between gross and net is then carried over to Gross Domestic Product (GDP) and NDP and between Gross National Product (GNP) and NNP; the gross measures include GFCF and the net ones NFCF.

The term 'depreciation' as used throughout this book, in common with macroeconomic theory, means a decline in the services derived from the asset (physical capital or durable goods) due to the wear and tear of the asset as it ages. Used in this way, the term corresponds to physical 'decay'; but in many contexts (finance, accountancy), the term is used to signify financial depreciation: the loss of price in second-hand markets as the asset ages. The two (physical decay and financial depreciation) do not coincide. The most obvious example is the pattern of depreciation of the 'light-bulb' type, whereby the asset delivers the same service until it dies. In this case, the rate of decay is zero throughout the asset's life and 100 per cent at its death; but financial depreciation will have started earlier, as the second-hand price is the present value of all future services from the asset, and this will decline as the horizon shortens. As another example, the second-hand price of a car declines faster than its physical roadworthiness. With this in mind, as mentioned, we use the term 'depreciation' to imply physical depreciation or decay.[31]

In our models of Chapter 5 and 9, we assume that if an expenditure is made equal to the asset's depreciation, the latter can be entirely reversed and the asset's ability to yield services is forever maintained; e.g. if we spend an amount fixing the leak in the roof, or service the car or an engine, the house/car/factory will be forever as good as new. Obviously, this is a convenient, if not realistic, assumption: Capital assets, whether buildings, vehicle, or machinery and mechanical equipment, do age however well they may be maintained. At some point, the assets decay to the point of not being in working condition and are scrapped or retired. Often, the assets that are retired are replaced by new ones of an improved quality or 'vintage'; we talk about vintages of capital at the end of this section. Furthermore, the rates of decay may not be constant but age-related; an asset may decay faster towards the end of its useful life. Another real-life issue is how to aggregate over the many different types of capital; this is where financial value (price) is very useful. Relatedly, the rates of depreciation (in either physical or financial sense) differ across the many different types of capital; generally, equipment depreciates faster than buildings, and there are differences among the various types of equipment. In our models, we have abstracted from all these issues in order to maintain tractability. But one consideration we have incorporated in Chapters 5 and 9 is that an asset may be retired, even if it is still in workable condition, if it cannot be profitably maintained or if it is profitable to replace it with one of a better vintage (e.g. a more powerful computer or engine). We have called this 'economic depreciation' (it is also called 'obsolescence') and, though not unrelated, it is not the same as the financial depreciation (loss of second-hand price) that we talked about above.

Depreciation is assumed to be of a few generic types: we have mentioned the 'light-bulb' (or 'one-hoss shay') type; another one is the 'straight-line' type, whereby an asset depreciates (in either physical or financial terms, which will not be equal) linearly, by a fixed

---

[31] A subtle point: 'depreciation' in the national statistics ($= GFCF - NFCF$) is financial depreciation, also called 'capital consumption' by national income statisticians. It does not generally equal the expenditure required for replacement and to reverse decay. As Oulton and Srinivasan (2003, section 3) shows, the two are equal in the special case of geometric depreciation.

amount each year. The most commonly used type, which is also analytically very convenient, is 'geometric depreciation', whereby an asset loses value (again, in either a physical or financial sense) at a constant rate.[32] The US statistical agencies use geometric depreciation and calculate an annual depreciation rate for plant and machinery (excluding computers and software) of about 13 per cent; this yields a 'half-life' is about 5 years and 'mean life' about 6.5. In the United Kingdom, the ONS assumes that plant and machinery has a life of 25–30 years in most industries, a much higher life expectancy and a lower depreciation rate (equivalent to a 5–7 per cent geometric rate) than that implied by the US calculations (Oulton and Srinivasan, 2003, section 3).

Empirical studies (Oulton and Srinivasan, 2003; Fraumeni, 1997) tend to agree that the pattern of geometric depreciation fits the data well. On this basis, Oulton and Srinivasan (2003, table F) finds that for plant and machinery the estimated annual depreciation rate varies between 5 and 13 per cent; for buildings (offices) it is typically around 2.5 per cent (implying a half-life of about 30 years), while for vehicles it is 20–5 per cent (half-life of about two to three years). The depreciation rate is much higher for computers and related equipment (>30 per cent), which is related more to economic depreciation and obsolescence than to physical decay. This is in turn related to the finding, mentioned in Chapter 9, that the second-hand prices of computers (of given specifications) tend to fall in real terms over time.

11.3.3 The 'Flexible Accelerator' Model

Early attempts to model investment posited that investment responds to past changes in optimal capital:

$$I_t = \sum_{i=0}^{\infty} \alpha_i (K_{t+i}^* - K_{t+i-1}^*) + \delta K_t, \quad \alpha_i > 0 \tag{11.27}$$

where K* is the desired capital level and $\delta > 0$ the depreciation rate. The coefficients $\alpha_i > 0$ tell us that investment responds with a lag to changes in the desired capital stock. The rationale is that investment projects take time to complete, in line with the 'time-to-build' insight of the early Real Business Cycle literature, see Chapter 6.

The next question is how optimal capital is determined. The early approach was simple. Imagine that there is a proportional relation between the two:[33]

$$Y_t = AK_t$$

Labour may be involved, but it is in fixed proportions to capital. This would imply that optimal capital is in proportion to output:

---

[32] A problem that arises is that with geometric depreciation, there is always some value left; if an asset loses value by x per cent a year, its value only goes to zero asymptotically, i.e. after an infinite amount of periods. For this reason, a useful concept is 'half-life' (or 'median life'), i.e. the amount of years it takes for the value to decrease by 50 per cent. In other words, half-life is the t such that $(1 - d)^t = 0.5$, where $0 < d < 1$ is the depreciation rate. Another relevant concept, useful if we assume that d is the percentage of capital items replaced every period, is 'mean life', the expected life of a capital item at its installation. The probability that an item will be replaced in t years is $(1 - d)^t d$; therefore, mean life (n) is $n = (1 - d)/d$.

[33] This is the 'AK' production function of growth theory, see Chapter 9.

$$K_t^* = Y_t/A$$

Taking differences of this and inserting into (11.27), we have:

$$I_t = \sum_{i=0}^{\infty} \beta_i (Y_{t+i} - Y_{t+i-1}) + \delta K_t, \quad \beta_i \equiv \alpha_i/A \tag{11.28}$$

This is the 'flexible accelerator' model of investment; investment responds with lags to everything captured by Y: output and (implicitly) market size, sales, etc. As we have seen, it formed the basis of some early, demand-driven models of the business cycle. Naturally, this approach is too basic. There is no optimization by the firm (e.g. in setting the optimal capital-labour ratio), no cost elements (interest or wage rates, taxes), other any elements of cost, prices, even profits; all are absent. And, in the aggregate picture, output is endogenous, requiring explanation from some deeper fundamentals. So, despite some early empirical successes, the model was abandoned in this form.

11.3.4 The Early Neoclassical Approach and the Cost of Capital

The early neoclassical approach (Jorgenson, 1963; Eisner and Strotz, 1963) retained the above structure but attempted to derive optimal capital (K*) from the firm's optimization; in so doing, it rectified various weaknesses identified above. Consider the firm's static maximization problem with a Cobb-Douglas production function ($Y_t = AK_t^\gamma L_t^{1-\gamma}$):

$$\text{Max}_{k,L} \quad AK_t^\gamma L_t^{1-\gamma} - w_t L_t - c_t K_t$$

where w and c are the wage rate and cost of capital; the latter is essentially the 'user cost of capital' defined in Chapter 5 and below. From the optimality condition in relation to capital (MPK = c), we have $\gamma Y_t/K_t = c_t$, therefore the demand for capital is:

$$K_t^* = \gamma Y_t/c_t \tag{11.29}$$

This is used to replace optimal capital in the flexible accelerator model (11.27).

Though this model rectifies many of the problems highlighted above, there was unease that the empirical performance of the cost-of-capital variable was not that strong, or that, wherever it was, its strength was an artefact of its coefficient constrained to be one; see Chirinko (1993) and Caballero (1999) for discussions. Caballero (1999), in particular, takes logs of the above (lower cases) and rewrites it more flexibly to get:

$$k_t^* - y_t = log\gamma + blogc_t + u_t \tag{11.29'}$$

u_t is an error term. Using US data for 1957–87, he estimates b = −0.4 with the OLS procedure for co-integration (thus, a long-run finding); an estimate significantly different from 0, and statistically indistinguishable from -1 (the neoclassical benchmark) if one takes into account the small sample bias which is particularly damaging in co-integration procedures. Whether it is -1 or not, its statistical significance confirms the role of the cost of capital.

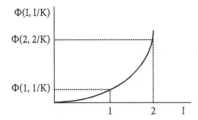

Figure 11.6. Installation costs

Note that γ should equal the elasticity of substitution between capital and labour in production—unitary in Cobb-Douglas but more flexible under a CES production function. Despite this significant finding, the problem remains that in a general equilibrium model, output is endogenous. The next-generation neoclassical models dispense with it altogether.

11.3.5 Digression: Capital Adjustment (Installation) Costs

Before proceeding, we discuss capital adjustment costs as they will be used as an element in the analysis that follows. As discussed in Chapter 5, the idea is that investment expenditure is made up of two components: the investment itself (think of this as the materials) and the expenses required in order to install this new capital. Thus, the total expenditure required for investment is:

$$\text{Total expenditure required for } I_t = \Phi\left(I_t, \frac{I_t}{K_t}\right)$$

The function $\Phi(.)$, with $\Phi_I > 0$, $\Phi_{I/K} > 0$, depends on both the level of investment and its ratio to existing capital. A common assumption is that $\Phi(.)$ is convex in I as plotted in Figure 11.6, i.e. the installation costs rise more than proportionately with the amount of investment itself. The underlying idea is that a very small rate of investment requires little labour cost for installation, and these installation costs *per unit of investment* rise as investment becomes more sizeable in relation to existing capital stock.

The implication of this type of costs is that it pays to undertake investment piecemeal (in small doses) rather than in big chunks. Imagine that a firm needs to install two additional units of capital. The cost is $\Phi(2, 2/K)$, which, by the convexity of the $\Phi(.)$ function, is higher than $2\Phi(1, 1/K)$ as shown above. It is not hard to think why. Imagine that a university needs to upgrade its computer stock. This is more easily done piecemeal, when existing staff can undertake the task without major disruptions, etc. If it were to happen in a 'big bang' sort of way, extra staff might be needed, alongside room closures and system shut-downs, etc.[34] If capital adjustment costs are mainly of this type, then we should see a smooth aggregate investment series made up of frequent but small investment 'episodes'. To sum up, convex costs are intuitive and appealing because they deliver a particularly

---

[34] Another example may be big sports infrastructures for events such as the Olympics, World Cups, etc, which frequently go over budget as much of the infrastructure is constructed in a very short period of time (requiring overtime) and not spaced out over a longer period. (There may be of course other reasons for these costs to be excessive which are not related to the present discussion.)

simple relation between investment and its determinants.[35] As in Chapter 5, in what follows we use the simple form:[36]

$$\Phi\left(I_t, \frac{I_t}{K_t}\right) = I_t\left(1 + \varphi\frac{I_t}{K_t}\right)$$

However, empirical work does not (fully) support convex adjustment costs and their implications for smooth investment. In a widely quoted study, Doms and Dunne (1998) present evidence from US firms showing that investment projects are often lumpy: over a 17-year period, the largest investment episode (within a single year) provides on average more than 25 per cent of the total investment for the period. Moreover, quite often, years of high investment sit next to one another, suggesting that a given investment project took more than one year to complete (similar to the 'time-to-build' insight).[37] See Disney et al. (2020) for a recent study affirming the 'lumpiness' of investment with UK data. Cooper and Haltiwanger (2006) estimate that adjustment costs incorporate both convex and non-convex elements. The implications of this for the relation of investment to q are subject to debate.

11.3.6 The Mature Neoclassical Model: The (Marginal) 'q' and the User Cost of Capital

The mature neoclassical approach starts from deeper micro-foundations, along the lines of Chapter 5. Consider the maximand:

$$\text{Max}_{i(t), l(t), k(t)}$$

$$V \equiv \sum_{t=1}^{\infty} R_t^{-1}\left[F(K_t, L_t) - w_t L_t - I_t\left(p_t^I + \varphi\frac{I_t}{K_t}\right) + q_t(I_t - K_{t+1} + (1 - \delta)K_t)\right]$$

This is the same as in Chapter 5 with the exception that the price of investment goods is now p^I, not restricted to one. As before, q_t is the dynamic Langrange multiplier or shadow price of capital, measuring the contribution to intertemporal profitability (net of adjustment costs) of an extra unit of installed capital, and is known as the 'marginal q' (or simply 'q'—to be contrasted with the 'average q' below). Proceeding exactly as in Chapter 5, we get:

$$q_t = p_t^I + 2\varphi\frac{I_t}{K_t} \tag{11.30}$$

---

[35] Convex adjustment costs are also convenient and popular in a growth context, as they give rise to endogenous growth with transitional dynamics.

[36] An objection here may be that the recorded investment (GFCF) already contains the installation element. Thus, we should more properly write: $I_t = (K_{t+1} - K_t)\left(1 + \varphi\frac{K_{t+1} - K_t}{K_t}\right)$. This would suggest a concave specification $\frac{K_{t+1} - K_t}{K_t} = \Omega\left(\frac{I_t}{K_t}\right)$ with $\Omega'(.) > 0$ and $\Omega''(.) < 0$, so that more investment translates into more installed capital but less so as the rate of investment rises.

[37] Caballero (1999, footnote 15) suggests that 'time-to-build' and convex adjustment costs are separate ideas. One may argue, however, that time-to-build results from convex adjustment costs *within a certain project*, i.e. it is less costly to finish a project in small chunks.

The shadow price of capital turns out to be the real price of investment goods with the addition of the adjustment cost element.

Furthermore, the marginal revenue product of capital (MRPK) should equal the user cost of capital (UCK), or:

$$\Pi_k(K_t, L_t) = q_{t-1}[r + \delta - (q_t - q_{t-1})/q_{t-1}] \tag{11.31}$$

Included on the left is the MRPK and all that affects it: technology (the marginal product of capital), market structure (monopoly markup), taxation, and other elements of profitability (e.g. raw materials). On the right, we have the UCK: interest rate, depreciation, the price of investment goods, and adjustment goods (implicit in q).

Solving (11.31) forward by repeated iterations, we get:

$$q_t = \sum_{s=1}^{\infty} \frac{\Pi_k(K_{t+s}, L_{t+s})}{(1 + r + \delta)^s} \tag{11.32}$$

So, (marginal) 'q' embodies all the intertemporal marginal profitability arising from an extra unit of installed capital. Combining with (11.30), we now get:

$$\frac{I_t}{K_t} = \frac{q_t - p_t^I}{2\varphi} = \frac{\sum_{s=1}^{\infty} \frac{\Pi_k(K_{t+s}, L_{t+s})}{(1+r+\delta)^s} - p_t^I}{2\varphi} \tag{11.33}$$

Investment arises from a difference between the 'shadow price' of capital (q, the profit to be had from the marginal project) and the price of investment goods.

Equation (11.33) suggests that investment depends on profitability and cost elements, but should not respond to output and related measures that have essentially been solved out through the deep micro-foundations. Empirically, however, almost the opposite happens: Profitability, cost-of-capital and interest rates generally show up very weakly, while scale variables such as output or sales and financial variables such as cash flow feature strongly; see the surveys by Chirinko (1993) and Caballero (1999). For an indication, consider the information in Caballero (1999, figure 2.1) reproduced from Hassett and Hubbard (1997); it shows the co-movement of investment (in percentage changes) with various variables: the correlation with the acceleration (per cent change) of business output is 0.7, whereas with 'real domestic corporate cash flow' (an index of liquidity in the sector) it is 0.64. Neither of these variables is in the model. In contrast, the correlation of investment with the user cost is 0.11; this is the (only) variable that theory tells us that matters.

Before leaving this sub-section, it is worth clarifying the relation between the user cost of capital and its rental price which is useful in some contexts, e.g. in housing. Imagine a firm that owns a unit of capital that it then rents or leases in the market (think of a car or house). The firm charges a rental price of h_t (from hire) per period per unit. Doing the usual marginal cost-benefit analysis, the firm is going to own an amount of capital such that its receipts just about equal the costs:

$$h_t = q_t[r + \delta - (q_{t+1} - q_t)/q_t] \tag{11.34}$$

The real interest rate is the cost of borrowing in financial markets or the return available to other financial investments; in any case, it is the opportunity cost of tying capital in the firm. The landlord/leasing firm will charge more the more valuable the unit (q), the higher the interest and depreciation costs and the less the capital gains. An alternative way to understand (11.34) is by rewriting it as:

$$r = \frac{h_t}{q_t} - \delta + \frac{q_{t+1} - q_t}{q_t} \qquad (11.34')$$

Equilibrium in markets, financial and others, is reached when the composite rate of return to the landlord on the right-hand side (including the rental per pound of value, depreciation, and capital gains) equals the real market return (r).

11.3.7 'Tobin's (Average) q' and the Stock Market Price of the Firm

A parallel development occurred with Tobin's (1969) intuitive idea that investment should be a positive function of the stock market valuation of the firm, something missing from the analyses above. 'Tobin's q' or 'average q' is defined as,[38]

$$Q_t \equiv \frac{V_t}{p_t^K K_t}. \qquad (11.35)$$

V_t is the stock market valuation of the firm, p^K_t is the replacement cost of every unit of capital (the resale value of the firm's assets, land, buildings, and equipment).
   Tobin's (1969) insight is that

$$I_t >, = \text{or} < 0 \quad \text{if} \quad Q_t >, = \text{or} < 1.$$

In words, investment takes place when $Q > 1$, i.e. if the stock market valuation is above the replacement cost. There is also an additional possibility, which is that there can be disinvestment (scaling down) if $Q < 1$. The rationale is simple: the stock market/equity price reflects the market value of the firm, so if this is above/below the value of the assets it has, the firm creates/destroys value, so there is positive/negative investment. Furthermore, a firm with a higher equity is better able to finance investment from own means rather than borrowing, hence avoiding the 'external finance premium' (see Chapter 7), so is more likely to undertake the investment. This simple but appealing theory has the additional advantage that it brings the stock market/equity price of the firm as a determinant of investment, something missing from the neoclassical approach. At the same time, the other determinants highlighted above, profitability, user cost, and the like, are absent. In response to this, Abel (1979) and Hayashi (1982) integrated the marginal and average q approaches.
   Before proceeding, let us highlight some implications of this theory. A firm expands if it produces *enough* profits to cover its replacement value, *not simply* positive profits. Take an example. Imagine a firm that has valuable assets (often this is the case when the firm is

---

[38] Both Tobin and the literature use lower-case q, but we shall use Q to distinguish it from the marginal q.

sitting on valuable land, which may thought of as part of its capital) but mediocre (though positive) profitability. Then the assets (mainly land) may be sold at such a price that shareholders may be compensated and a surplus left; in other words, this firm will be dissolved.[39] This is relevant where the price of land is high, which might make it optimal for the firm to be scrapped (even though it might make positive but insufficient profits), the land to be sold, with the proceeds to compensate the shareholders—and make a hefty profit for the smart financial advisers who facilitate the whole process. This theoretical result is surely relevant for de-industrialization, prevalent in all (formerly) 'industrialized' countries, and for all the formerly industrial land that has been sold off for redevelopment in retail or housing.

Hayashi (1982) has shown that marginal and average q will be equal under some conditions. The firm must have a technology of constant returns to scale in both its production function and in its investment cost function (the former in terms of capital and labour, the latter in terms of investment and capital)—observe that our specification of investment costs as $I(1 + \varphi I/K)$ satisfies this requirement. But most stringent of all is the requirement that the firm ought to be perfectly competitive.[40]

The final piece in the jigsaw emerges when we connect the stock market price of the firm to its intertemporal profitability. In equilibrium, the stock market value of a firm should be equal to the present value of its future profits:[41]

$$V_t = \sum_{s=1}^{\infty} \frac{\Pi(K_{t+s}, L_{t+s})}{(1 + r + \delta)^s} \tag{11.36}$$

Using (11.32), (11.35), (11.36) and the average-marginal q equality, we are now able to connect all the dots:

$$\sum_{s=1}^{\infty} \frac{\Pi_k(K_{t+s}, L_{t+s})}{(1 + r + \delta)^s} = q_t = \frac{V_t}{p_t^K K_t} = Q_t = \frac{\sum_{s=1}^{\infty} \frac{\Pi(K_{t+s}, L_{t+s})}{(1+r+\delta)^s}}{p_t^K K_t} \tag{11.37}$$

The marginal profitability of a unit of capital (observable with difficulty) equals its shadow price (non-observable) equals its average stock price (observable) equals the average profitability per pound of installed capital (observable under some assumptions about the future). From (11.33), investment now equals:

---

[39] This is essentially the plot of the film *Trading Places*, starring Danny DeVito and others. The firm was making some mediocre profits (note: it was not making losses) but was sitting on valuable land. As is often the case in real life, it was dissolved by the hostile action of a financier/corporate raider, against the management's wishes. The shareholders were compensated by the proceeds from land sale and the financier made a hefty profit for himself.

[40] See Schiantarelli and Georgoutsos (1990) for the link between marginal and average q when the firm possesses some monopoly power.

[41] This equality follows from a simple arbitrage argument. How much are shareholders prepared to pay to buy a certain firm? No more than the profits they expect to derive from it over time; and no less than that either, because there will always be someone prepared to pay more, as long as the share value is below the present value of profits. (Note that we are assuming away uncertainty here.) Note the feature of forward-lookingness inherent in Rational Expectations: only future profits matter for the prospective buyer, not past profits from which a potential shareholder will not benefit. If the firm has debt (B), then the numerator of the Q ratio should be total liabilities, i.e. equity and debt (V + B). The intuition is that the prospective borrower expects to earn future profits minus the debts they undertake ($\sum_{s=1}^{\infty} \frac{\Pi(K_{t+s}, L_{t+s})}{(1+r+\delta)^s} - B_t$) and that should equal how much they are prepared to pay for the firm and its stock market price (V_t).

$$\frac{I_t}{K_t} = \frac{\frac{V_t}{p_t^K K_t} - p_t^I}{2\varphi} = \frac{\frac{\sum_{s=1}^{\infty} \frac{\Pi(K_{t+s}, L_{t+s})}{(1+r+\delta)^s}}{p_t^K K_t} - p_t^I}{2\varphi} \tag{11.38}$$

Thus, the investment-capital ratio is a positive function of the ratio of the present value of future profits over replacement cost. This integrates stock market considerations into the theory of investment and the econometrician is greatly helped by having to consider observable determinants. Note however that we still do not have any scale variables (output market size and the like) or financial variables (cash flows, etc.) of the type that we saw are important in empirical work.

Empirically, all the equalities involved in (11.38) are contestable. More specifically, the evidence on the role of average q and stock market price in determining investment is rather mixed; see Price and Schleicher (2005). This study explores empirically the relevance of average q in predicting the terms involved in the present value of future profits (profitability itself, indebtedness, but also the interest rates that discount) as well as investment; it finds that q itself does indeed help forecast investment as well as the other variables in the UK. See Lin et al. (2018) for more recent related work. Moreover, Cummins et al, (1994) consider the *exogenous* effects to the user cost by US tax reform and find significant and plausible coefficients of q.

11.3.8 Further Themes: Financial Imperfections, Uncertainty, and Irreversibility

So far, the model implies that it does not matter whether you invest from own accumulated profits, or you borrow to invest (and from where—stock market or money markets). As discussed in Chapter 7, however, there is a large body of literature suggesting that the cost from 'external finance' is higher than from finance from own funds. This is probably due to asymmetric information on the part of firm and (financial) investor on the real chances of a project, and on 'costly state verification' and 'external monitoring costs'. This means that the rate of return the external financial investor may require in order to lend to finance a project may be above the riskless money-market rate (the 'external finance premium'). Hence, investment will be lower. The implication is that firms with a greater cash flow (available cash) will have more investment, *ceteris paribus* (as they will need to rely less on costly external borrowing). The problem is that the cash flow is correlated with profits, so unlikely to differentiate reliably between the traditional (q) and 'financial imperfections' theories (see Fazzari et al, 1988). Overall, there is overwhelming evidence that financial imperfections matter.

Another theme in empirical work concerns uncertainty, the irreversibility of investment and the 'value of waiting'. In any reasonably realistic model uncertainty will be important, particularly if it manifests itself via more than one sources; e.g. profit uncertainty combined with interest rate uncertainty. Consider a simple model of q whereby $q_t = E_t\{(1/(1 + r_{t+1})) \times \text{Profits}_{t+1}\}$ (an investment with an horizon of one year). Unravelling the expectations, we have $q_t = E_t(1/(1 + r_{t+1})) \times E_t \text{Profits}_{t+1} + \text{Cov}\{(1/(1 + r_{t+1})), \text{Profits}_{t+1}\}$. Given the expected values, if profits and the real interest rate (r) are both pro-cyclical, so $\text{Cov}\{(1/(1 + r_{t+1})), \text{Profits}_{t+1}\} < 0$, then q_t falls as macroeconomic uncertainty rises, and so does investment. The intuition is that capital (K) does not hedge (insure) against aggregate risk but is subject to it, therefore we keep less of it—we would keep more if its correlation with r were negative, so it would hedge us against aggregate risk.

Uncertainty is particularly important if combined with the 'irreversibility' property of investment, i.e. the fact that it represents a 'sunk cost': uninstalling capital often gives very little back, disinstallation often means 'scrapping'. In other words, the irreversibility argument suggests that the costs of disinvesting are much higher than investing, to the point perhaps that, after disinvestment, one may get very little back. To see the implications, consider the uncertainty surrounding a favourable tax proposal which may pass or not with some probability (say, 50–50). With reversible investment, we might follow the logic of expected utility, which says that $E(\text{Profits}) = 0.5 \times \text{Status Quo} + 0.5 \times \text{Higher}$ Profits with the favourable proposal. Consequently, we might do 50 per cent of the investment we would do if we knew that the favourable tax proposal had passed with certainty. This is because, if the proposal does not eventually pass, we can always reduce the capital stock and go back to the level we had before. But with *IR*reversible investment, once installed, the investment is non-recoverable. Therefore, we should wait and see before committing ourselves (the 'value of waiting'—Abel et al., 1996), hence aggregate investment will be lower. See Abel (1999) and Abel and Eberly (1994) for analyses of the effects of uncertainty and irreversibility.

11.3.9 (S, s) Models

The existence of fixed costs of adjustment and the investment lumpiness discussed above have given rise to (S, s) type of models.[42] Here is how it works. Considering market size, cost of capital, etc., a firm decides that its optimal capital stock is K^*; in principle, it will invest when $K < K^*$ and disinvest when $K > K^*$. Investment and disinvestment both incur two types of cost. Fixed costs per investment project, whatever its magnitude, imply that the investment projects are infrequent and lumpy. There is a range of inaction $K_U - K_L$, where $K_L < K^* < K_U$, such that if actual capital is in it, i.e. $K_L < K < K_U$, the gain from any investment (to get closer to K^*) is not worth the fixed cost.[43] Now, convex costs imply the opposite: Any project should be small as the costs rise more than proportionately. So, if $K = K_L$, say, it may not be optimal to invest $K^* - K_L$, but only $K_l - K_L$, where $K_L < K_l < K^*$ is a target point; the investment is less than reaching the optimum K^* in order to limit the convex costs. On the right, there is the threshold K_U and target point K_u (with $K^* < K_u < K_U$); but note that the left and right sides need not be symmetric. To summarize, fixed costs are responsible for the inaction ranges (e.g. on the left, $K^* - K_U$)—without such costs, any discrepancy from optimal will be corrected instantaneously; while convex costs are responsible for limiting the action whenever that takes place (i.e. $K_l < K^*$). The situation is depicted in Figure 11.7, adapted from Caballero (1999, fig. 3.3).

---

[42] The best way to understand this model is in relation to a petrol tank: when petrol reaches a low threshold (s—which can be 0), we fill up to a high point (S). This is a one-sided rule (we always fill up, we do not take petrol out); the rule considered in the text is two-sided (possibly asymmetric).

[43] In the petrol tank analogy, the range of inaction is $1 - s$: I will not stop at the petrol station to fill up until petrol drops to s.

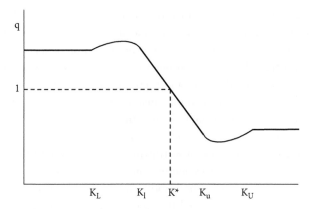

Figure 11.7. Fixed costs, lumpy investment, and marginal q

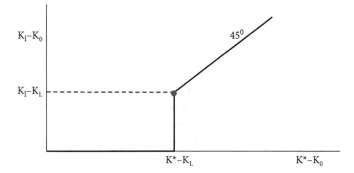

Figure 11.8. Response of investment to 'good news' according to an (S, s) rule

Now, assume the (marginal) q to be the only determinant of investment; the firm invests when $q > 1$ and disinvests when $q < 1$, while equilibrium is $q^* = 1$ which coincides with K^*; q is also depicted in the Figure. To the left of K_L, q is high; the firm is starved of capital and its marginal profitability is high. If it finds itself with $K < K_L$, it will invest to reach a capital stock of K_l (target) as the gain in value justifies all the costs of investing up to that point. In the range $K_l - K_L$, q is even higher but not high enough to motivate the firm to incur the fixed costs; hence, there is no action. On the right side of K^*, q is low as the firm has too much capital and its marginal profitability is low. If $K > K_U$, it will disinvest to K_u, but there will be no action if it happens to be in the range $K_U - K_u$. The key point is that the monotonic relation between investment and q breaks down (see Caballero, 1999): Although q is constant left of K_L, the amount of investment varies (wherever K happens to be, the investment will be $K_l - K$). Additionally, in the range of $K_l - K_L$, q is higher, yet there is no investment.

Now assume an initial situation in which a firm has a capital level, K_0, which is optimal. Consider a rise in the optimal capital from K_0 to $K^* > K_0$; this is prompted by a better outlook in the economy or a reduction in the cost of capital. As the optimal rises, all $K_L < K_l < K_u < K_U$ will move sideways around the new optimal. Figure 11.8 shows the response of investment $(K_l - K_0)$ to the 'favourable development', $K^* - K_0$, measured on the horizontal axis. If initial K_0 is situated in the inaction range, $K_L < K_0 < K^*$ so that

$K^* - K_0 < K^* - K_L$, there will be no investment. If $K_0 < K_L$ so that $K^* - K_0 > K^* - K_L$, there will be an investment of $K_1 - K_0$. So, the inaction range $(K^* - K_L)$ is a critical threshold: if the good news is less than that, nothing will happen; if the good news equal exactly that, there will be less than one-for-one investment (it is easy to check that $K_1 - K_0 < K^* - K_L$; and above this threshold, there will be a one-to-one relationship between the marginal improvement in news and marginal increase in investment: note the 45° line).

What messages do we get out of all this? First, the critical threshold: an improvement in the determinants of investment will not have any effect unless this improvement has a critical mass; fixed costs do not make it worthwhile for a firm to respond to just miniscule improvements in (say) the macroeconomic outlook, the cost of capital or their tax treatment. Second, observe that as the 'good news' $(K^* - K_0)$ rises, there will be more investment projects 'climbing up' the 45° line: the average size of investment projects rises. This insight may explain the finding that the Helfindahl index of concentration of investment projects rises in good times (Doms and Dunne, 1998).

The aggregate implications of the lumpiness of investment at the micro level are still being debated. Doms and Dunne (1998), recently Disney et al. (2020), and many others in-between, generally find aggregate investment is dominated by a few investment episodes (or 'spikes') each year. These findings are increasingly seen as confirming that individual lumpiness does not 'wash out' in the aggregate. Disney et al. (2020) conclude that looking at aggregate data may be misleading; rather, one should more properly look at micro data and from there construct the aggregate picture. Following this approach, they find an empirical role for both scale variables (output, sales) and capital structure (debt, equity). On the other hand, we have analyses such as that of Thomas (2002) who concludes pretty much the opposite, that lumpy investment has negligible aggregate effects and practically does not matter for business cycle dynamics.

11.3.10 Vintages of Capital, Embodied Technical Progress, and Putty-Clay Investment

There is little doubt that existing capital is made up of different 'cohorts' of capital that was installed at different times in the past (much like the fact that cars with different registrations exist at any time; generations of people of different birth; prices that were at set different times; and wine that was bottled at different times in the past—of different 'vintage'). This is the idea of different 'capital vintages'. The models analysed above abstract from this fact. Vintages incorporate the interesting idea that capital does not live for ever, but is scrapped after a period of time; this may depend on (physical) depreciation but also, crucially, on 'economic depreciation', i.e. obsolescence due to newer available technology. The idea that recent technical advancements replace earlier technologies is of course central to the 'Schumpeterian' strand of endogenous growth theory reviewed in Chapter 9, but that literature seems not to have emphasized much the implications for physical capital. The problem with scrapping and economic depreciation is that their timing is endogenous, as the rate at which technological innovations appear is endogenous, depending among other things on the rate at which firms are prepared to replace existing capital and buy the new technology. See Benhabib and Hobijn (2003) and Boucekine et al. (2008) on models emphasizing vintage dynamics.

Economic depreciation is closely related to the idea that newer vintages of capital incorporate better technology, which is therefore 'embodied' (into capital). In fact, buying a new piece of equipment is often the only way of introducing new technology. This is the case e.g. with manufacturing and transport equipment (including cars), communications (think of mobile phones!), and even computers; though software may also be upgraded independently of hardware, and can therefore be 'disembodied'. One would expect this salient feature of the real world to have important implications for investment; e.g. investment must accelerate at the time when new technologies become more quickly available exogenously (e.g. by an accidental technical discovery like the internet). This also has profound implications for growth accounting, as noted.

An interesting paper along these lines is by Abel and Eberly (2012). They consider a model where the technological frontier of capital is shifting all the time because of innovations, but in which the firm can only upgrade its technology at discrete intervals because of the costs of doing so. When however it does do so, the productivity of capital rises abruptly, and so does the optimal level of capital; this results in investment 'gulps' (= big doses) at infrequent intervals. Meanwhile, the firm also keeps adjusting its capital stock at the margin all the time (because of changes in the user cost, etc.). The optimal interval for technology purchases and investment gulps is analysed and related to the (endogenous) value of the firm and the cash flow, i.e. sales revenue net of wages but before investment expenditures. Interestingly (but counter-intuitively), the value of the firm rises as the time of upgrade approaches (probability of upgrade increases), and drops at the moment of installation of new technology; this is because at this point the firm is committed to it, and its options are limited. But, on aggregate, firms' value (measured by Tobin's—average—q) is correlated with the probability of upgrades and investment. In simulation exercises, it is shown that the investment-to-capital ratio is correlated with the cash flow and Tobin's q. The second result 'explains away' empirical findings that Tobin's q matters little (it does, but the coefficient of the effect is low); the former shows that the role of the cash flow is that of a scale variable (as in the accelerator models), and not an indicator of financing constraints (which do not exist in the model).

Finally, a related idea is of 'putty-clay' capital: *ex ante*, before installation, there is a lot of substitutability between capital and labour, as one may choose one of a variety of techniques available for the task at hand. Typically, each of these techniques will entail a different capital-labour ratio, therefore a neoclassical production function is available with a continuum of substitution possibilities between capital and labour to produce a certain amount of output. However, *ex post*, after installation, only the chosen technique and concomitant capital-labour ratio is available. One example may be a haulage firm that needs to buy lorries to move a certain amount of freight about. Each lorry needs one driver, but the firm may buy many small lorries, or a few big ones, thus a variety of capital-labour ratios are available *ex ante*. After the purchase, though, this ratio is nearly fixed. (It may not be entirely fixed if we allow for variable rates of utilization of capital and overtime for labour, e.g. the firm may have some flexibility how many hours to operate the lorries.) Jones (2005) analyses the implications for the production function in general. These features are surely relevant for investment and the value of the firm, more so now than ever with the impending 'fourth-wave' of industrialization based on artificial intelligence (IT, automation, robotics, driverless cars). But detailed analyses along these lines are yet to emerge.

11.3.11 Inventory Investment

Finally, we turn to inventory investment, which is distinct from gross Fixed Capital Formation, but is sometimes included in investment. Inventories are the stocks of goods businesses keep in order to meet demand without delay and to facilitate production. They are quite sizeable. As Blinder and Maccini (1991) report, at the end of 1989, US businesses held over $1 trillion worth of inventories. This is more than 10 per cent of the then US GDP. Ramey and West (1999, T. 3) report inventory levels of the order of 15 per cent of GDP for post-war key OECD economies. In the US (1959–86) data used by Blinder and Maccini (1991), about two-thirds of inventories are held by manufacturing firms and one quarter by traders and retailers, a small percentage (8 per cent) by farms. Of those held by manufacturers, finished products are a small fraction; the majority is materials, supplies, and intermediate goods. Though computerization had not seemed to have much of an effect by the early 1990s (the inventories seemed a stable proportion to sales), it remains to be seen how the advent of the internet, artificial intelligence, and online retailing will affect the inventory holdings; on this more up-to-date work is needed. Whatever their exact nature, inventories are held, the common wisdom suggests, in order for businesses to smooth production in the face of fluctuating sales. As we shall see, however, this is sound reasoning at the micro level, but not correct at the macro level.

Inventory *investment* remains a rather marginal topic of macroeconomics and interest in it fluctuates. Inventory investment remains a very small percentage of GDP (of the order of 0.5 per cent of GDP in economies like the US or the UK) but the change in inventory investment seems to have a disproportionate relationship to output fluctuations; without investigating causality, Blinder and Maccini (1991) show that the change in inventory investment as a percentage of the change in real GNP averages 87 per cent in the post-war US economy (1948–82). Ramey and West (1999, T. 1 and 2) report smaller but still very sizeable figures. This finding in particular would warrant some attention to the topic.

The following seem to be the key stylized facts according to Blinder and Maccini (1991) and Ramey and West (1999):

1. Inventories and sales are co-integrated.
2. Inventories are pro-cyclical and very persistent.
3. Production varies more than sales.

Let us investigate some of these ideas in a simple formal model adapted from Ramey and West (1999); it is based on a 'flexible acceleration for inventories' formulation. Imagine that the firm has a target level of inventories:

$$H_t^* = \alpha D_t + \beta C_t, \quad \alpha > 0, \beta < 0 \tag{11.39}$$

D_t is final demand considered here as exogenous, while C_t captures the costs of production; so we have both the demand and supply sides. Accordingly, the target for inventories increases with final demand and sales (as more stock is needed to facilitate sales) but declines with production costs (as it is costly to produce extra stock). Both D and C fluctuate over time.

It is assumed that there are convex costs to changing inventories due to logistics, storage, etc. The firm aims to keep an inventory stock (H_t) close to optimal (H_t^*) but keeping an eye on the costs of changing inventories as well; it therefore sets the inventory level so as to minimize a weighted average of costs:

$$\text{Min}_{H(t)} \qquad (H_t - H_t^*)^2 + v(H_t - H_{t-1})^2$$

The first term penalizes (quadratically) deviations of the inventory level from the optimal while the second penalizes changes in the level of inventories due to convex adjustment costs, which are parameterized by $v > 0$.

The first-order condition in this simple static minimization exercise is:

$$H_t = NH_{t-1} + \frac{1}{1+v} H_t^*$$

The autoregressive coefficient N, where $0 < N \equiv v/(1+v) < 1$, rises as the costs of adjustment of inventories (v) rise. Solving backwards, we obtain:

$$H_t = \frac{1}{1+v} [H_t^* + NH_{t-1}^* + N^2 H_{t-2}^* + \cdots] \tag{11.40}$$

This is the 'flexible accelerator model' for inventories. The current level of inventories is a weighted average of all past optimal levels, as the firm gradually responded to them. Correspondingly, if we difference (11.40), we get that inventory investment $(H_t - H_{t-1})$ responds to both current and past demand and shocks $(H_t^* - H_{t-1}^*, \text{ etc.})$. So, inventory investment is persistent; the autocorrelation coefficient (N) essentially depends on the prevalence of convex adjustment costs for inventories (v). The greater the costs, the greater the relevance of past targets as inventories move sluggishly towards them, while if costs are zero $(v = N = 0)$, then only current targets matter—we move instantaneously towards them.

Let us now inspect how inventories interact with the wider economy. From national income accounting, without government, capital investment, or external sector, we have:[44]

$$Y_t = D_t + H_t - H_{t-1} \tag{11.41}$$

In other words, inventory investment $(H_t - H_{t-1})$ provides a buffer between output production (Y_t) and sales/final demand (D_t). Combining (11.39–41), we get:

$$Y_t = D_t + \frac{1}{1+v} [H_t^* + (N-1)H_{t-1}^* + (N-1)NH_{t-2}^* + (N-1)N^2 H_{t-3}^* + \cdots] =$$

$$= D_t + \frac{\alpha}{1+v} [D_t + (N-1)D_{t-1} + (N-1)ND_{t-2} + \cdots] + \tag{11.42}$$

$$+ \frac{\beta}{1+v} [C_t + (N-1)C_{t-1} + (N-1)NC_{t-1} + \cdots]$$

For reference, let us observe this equation under no costs of adjustment $(v = N = 0)$:

---

[44] Note that we are temporarily switching to end-of-period formulation, as it is more convenient here.

$$Y_t = D_t + \alpha[D_t - D_{t-1}] + \beta[C_t - C_{t-1}] \tag{11.42'}$$

We see here the main effect of the inventories, namely that they introduce a richer dynamic structure in the output equation. This is evident even in the simple equation with no adjustment costs (11.42') and it is more pronounced with the autoregressive structure when costs do exist (11.42).

Now, let us see whether and how output (Y_t) can have a higher variance than sales (D_t). For simplicity, assume that D_t is made up of purely demand shocks and C_t of pure supply shocks; so that the two are entirely uncorrelated. From (11.42), we have:

$$Var\{Y_t\} = \left[1 + \frac{\alpha}{1+v}\right]^2 Var\{D_t\} + Var\left[\frac{\alpha(N-1)}{1+v}[D_{t-1} + ND_{t-2} + \cdots]\right] +$$
$$+ Var\{cost\ terms\} + 2Cov\left\{\left[1 + \frac{\alpha}{1+v}\right]D_t, \frac{\alpha(N-1)}{1+v}[D_{t-1} + ND_{t-2} + \cdots]\right\}$$

The cost terms are omitted from the covariance as they are unrelated to demand shocks. Thus, $Var\{Y_t\} > Var\{D_t\}$ unless the covariance term is negative and sufficiently strong.

Further, assume that the (de-trended) series are represented by AR processes:

$$D_t = d_t + \delta d_{t-1} + \delta^2 d_{t-2} + \cdots \equiv \Delta(L)d_t$$

and

$$C_t = c_t + \gamma c_{t-1} + \gamma^2 c_{t-2} + \cdots \equiv \Gamma(L)c_t,$$

where d_t and c_t are white-noise error terms and $0 < \delta, \gamma < 1$ (not equal) are persistence parameters; $\Delta(L)d_t$ and $\Gamma(L)c_t$ are lag (L) polynomials of the demand and supply shocks.

Note first that in the benchmark case where the demand shocks are pure white noise $(\delta = 0$ so that $\Delta(L)d_t = d_t)$, the covariance term is zero: The output series will definitely have greater variance than sales. If $\delta > 0$ however, the picture is more complicated. D_t will be correlated with its own lags because of the lag structure in $\Delta(L)d_t$; note also that $N - 1 < 0$, so the covariance term will be negative. Consider the other benchmark case which is to allow general shocks $(\delta > 0)$ but no adjustment costs $(v = N = 0)$; in which case we have:

$$Var\{Y_t\} = [1 + \alpha]^2 Var\{D_t\} + Var\{\alpha D_{t-1}\} +$$
$$+ Var\{\beta C_t\} + 2Cov\{[1 + \alpha]D_t, -\alpha D_{t-1}\} > Var\{D_t\}$$

The inequality follows from $Var\{D_t\} = Var\{D_{t-1}\} > Cov\{D_t, D_{t-1}\}$. Rising adjustment costs$(v, N > 0)$ have a complex effect as they reduce both the variance of the lag structure and the covariance in absolute terms; thus, output is likely to always be more variable than sales, as the empirical evidence quite categorically shows. As mentioned, this theoretical and empirical result refutes the hypothesis that inventories smooth production at the macro level.

Where adjustment costs can be important is in raising the variance of inventory investment in relation to output investment. As stated, both Blinder and Maccini (1991) and Ramey and West (1999) find the fall in inventories to be a sizeable percentage of the fall in GNP during recessions; the former reports a striking average of 87 per cent in the post-war US economy. With reference again to (11.42), we may write:

$$
Var\{H_t - H_{t-1}\} = \left[\frac{\alpha}{1+v}\right]^2 Var\{D_t\} + Var\left\{\left[\frac{\alpha(N-1)}{1+v}[D_{t-1} + ND_{t-2} + \cdots]\right]\right\} +
$$
$$
+ Var\{cost\ terms\} + 2Cov\left\{\left[\frac{\alpha}{1+v}\right]D_t, \quad \frac{\alpha(N-1)}{1+v}[D_{t-1} + ND_{t-2} + \cdots]\right\}
$$

Thus, a greater variance of both the demand and supply shocks raises the variability of inventory investment $(H_t - H_{t-1})$ in relation to output (Y_t). But costs of adjustment do not seem to play a role here, as (following similar reasoning as before) N and v seem to reduce $Var\{H_t - H_{t-1}\}$ in relation to $Var\{Y_t\}$. This is perhaps not surprising after all: adjustment costs make inventories adjust sluggishly and be more stable; it is low costs and rapid adjustment that makes inventory investment more volatile. The interested reader could check all this.

So, what should one make of inventory investment? How important should its study be in the macroeconomics agenda? Given its miniscule percentage in terms of output (inventories are sizeable but their change is small), it is perhaps not item no. 1. All the same, it seems to be an important source of dynamics in the business cycle, so a complete neglect of the subject looks unwise. See Galeotti et al. (2005) for an integration of inventories with business cycles research, particularly the employment aspects of it.

11.4 Housing

11.4.1 Introduction: The Relevance of Housing

Housing is very important in a number of interrelated ways. Here are some key facts:

- Residential (housing) investment is a sizeable sector of GDP; Table 11.1 shows information for 2016 (from the UK Sectoral Accounts 2017, tables 1.1.2 and 1.1.8). UK GDP at current prices was of the order of £2tr in 2016. The items shown in Table 11.9 are partly overlapping. Gross Fixed Capital Formation (in plain English: investment by both public and private sectors) was 17 per cent of GDP, inventory

Table 11.1. The relative importance of housing in 2016 in the UK

Magnitude	GDP	Gross Fixed Capital Formation	Business Investment	Dwellings construction	Other buildings and structures	Inventory investment
Current prices (bn £)	1,963	324	182	73	108	8
% of GDP		17	9	4	6	0.4

Source: UK Sectoral Accounts 2017 (Tables 1.1.2 and 1.1.8)

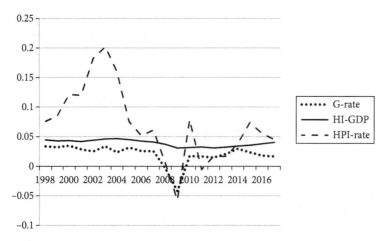

Figure 11.9. GDP growth, housing investment and house price inflation in the UK

Notes: G-rate: Real GDP growth rate; HI-GDP: Housing investment/GDP; HPI-rate: Nominal house price inflation rate.

Source: ONS (Economic accounts, sectoral accounts and house price-to-earnings tables, as available in July 2018) and author's calculations.

investment about 0.4 per cent. Business investment (9 per cent) made up about half of all investment. Residential investment (dwellings construction by both public but mainly private sectors—part of total investment) was about 4 per cent of GDP, while the total construction sector (dwellings and other structures) was about 10 per cent of GDP. In terms of employment, these sectors will have commensurate proportions of the total.

- Housing investment and house prices are generally pro-cyclical; Figure 11.9, with annual data for the UK, 1998–2017, brings this out. That housing investment is pro-cyclical is not a surprise; all components of GDP are. It is more striking that its *share in* GDP is also pro-cyclical (with a correlation coefficient of 0.57 in the data of this graph). In other words, housing investment rises (falls) proportionately more in booms (downturns). This is a consequence of the fact that housebuilding and buying, even maintenance, is a major decision that is undertaken mostly when things are looking up and is severely scaled down when the outlook is gloomier. Nominal house price inflation is also highly pro-cyclical, with a correlation coefficient of 0.66 here.
- In fact, over the last 40 years in the UK and similar economies, house price inflation has often been higher (often much higher) than general inflation, producing an upward long-term trend in the real price of housing; Figure (11.10) shows the real price of houses for France, the UK, and the US. It is an index, where 2010 = 100 for all series.[45] One key observation is that housing is now more expensive in real terms in all countries. This has a number of implications. Housing wealth is higher, which produces wealth effects important for consumption, as discussed below. At the same time, there are distributional effects particularly among different generations. The

---

[45] So, cross-sectional comparisons of the real house price levels are not meaningful. We CANNOT say e.g. that the price of houses in the UK is 25 per cent higher than in the US. What we CAN say is that, from 1970 to 2017, the real house price index has doubled in the US (120/60 = 2, a rise of 100 per cent), has risen by about 150 per cent in France, and nearly quintupled (a rise of nearly 400 per cent) in the UK. Another way of saying the same is that the US-France ratio in 2017 was about 120/100, whereas in 1970 it was 60/40, so that France during that period became *relatively* more expensive. This type of comparison is called 'difference-in-difference'.

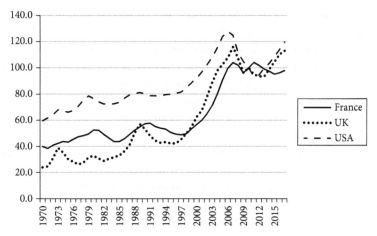

Figure 11.10. Real house prices in selected countries
Source: OECD Statistics

house price-to-income ratio, a key measure of (un)affordability of housing, is now much higher than a generation or two ago. Housing is becoming ever more expensive for those getting on the 'housing ladder' for the first time, i.e. younger generations. We have touched on these issues in Chapter 10 and return to them below.

- At the same time as showing a trend, the series all show persistent, low-frequency swings. For all countries, note the 'roaring' early 2000s, lasting until the financial crisis of 2007–9 which registered large drops. In the UK in particular, the real house price rose fast in the late 1980s—early 1990s; then dropping around 1992–5; then rising fast in the 2000s and again after the 2007–9 crisis. These wild gyrations are bound to be disruptive for the wider economy. Muellbauer and Murphy (1997) present an empirical analysis of UK house price behaviour.
- Formally speaking, for an individual, housing is a private good that enters their utility function; but it is not just 'another consumption good': it is much more important for survival and well-being than most other items of consumption (except food), much more durable than all the others, and a bigger item in any typical household's budget. One effect of its durability is its pro-cyclicality mentioned above.
- For the vast majority of individuals, a house is by far the most valuable piece of wealth they will ever own. Correspondingly, housing wealth is bigger than all other private wealth put together, including the equity value of the firms. From the ONS publication *National Balance Sheet 2017* (table 11), we read that the total housing wealth at the end of 2016 was about £1.5tr; at the same time, equity and investment fund shares were about £0.8tr; and all this to be compared to a total net worth of the UK economy (financial and non-financial) of the order of £10tr. Whichever way we see it, housing wealth is an important part of the total wealth of the economy. As a result, the decision to own a house is not just a consumption decision but also a portfolio (i.e. financial investment) decision; its presence in portfolios, and its fluctuating price, induces powerful wealth effects on other variables such as consumption and labour supply. For example, many households borrow with housing as collateral in order to fund their consumption, a process called 'housing equity withdrawal' or 'equity release' as it reduces the total net worth of the household (which is housing equity

minus the new loans); in the last ten years, this has been of the order of 1–2 per cent of after-tax households income (both are flows).

- The key conclusion of the above is that housing interacts strongly with the rest of the economy. There are estimates that the creation of housing wealth supported the considerable growth in consumption in the 1990s and 2000s (e.g. Case et al., 2005, T1 and 2 show that the coefficient of housing wealth in a regression with consumption per capita as the dependent variable is about 10 and highly significant with international data, somewhat less with US states data; see also Iakoviello, 2005).

- As well as being part of households' net worth, housing also is also the source of big mortgage debts. The origins of the 2007–9 financial crisis lay in the advancement of ultimately unsustainable mortgages to households that could hardly afford them (as in the US 'sub-prime' market). As Chetty et al. (2017) emphasize, the portfolio implications of housing equity and housing debt (i.e. positive and negative equity) are not symmetrical.

It is clear that housing interacts with the wider economy, therefore there is, or should be, a macroeconomics of housing. The topic has attracted considerable attention in the literature with notable contributions, but one gets the feeling that its importance deserves more attention; and the same goes for macro textbooks. This section attempts to fill this gap, without however doing full justice to the subject.

11.4.2 The User Cost of Housing

We shall show here the basic macro model of housing, see e.g. Poterba (1984). The starting point is the individual's optimization problem as set out in (11.16); utility depends on non-durable consumption (C_t) and the stock of housing (H_t—which replaces durables, D_t). The justification is that the housing services we get are proportional to stock.

Before proceeding, we develop the evolution of housing in value terms (pH). The physical stock of housing (H), in beginning-of-period form, evolves according to:

$$H_{t+1} = (1 - \delta)H_t + I_t \tag{11.43}$$

where I_t is now residential investment and $0 < \delta < 1$ is the depreciation rate.[46] First, we would like to value housing by its real price (p_t) so as to show how it enters the wealth constraint. Multiplying (11.43) through by p_t, we get:

$$p_{t+1}H_{t+1} \approx \left(1 - \delta + \frac{p_{t+1} - p_t}{p_t}\right)p_t H_t + p_t I_t \tag{11.43'}$$

This is the case as:

$$(1 - \delta)p_{t+1}H_t = (1 - \delta)(p_{t+1}/p_t)p_t H_t \approx \left(1 - \delta + \frac{p_{t+1} - p_t}{p_t}\right)p_t H_t$$

---

[46] A house's 'half-life' is often considered to be around 40 years. This implies $\delta \approx 0.02$ in annual data.

(11.43') represents the dynamics of housing in which housing stock and investment are both valued by the real price of housing, p_t. The quantity

$$UCH_t \equiv p_t\left(r + \delta - \frac{p_{t+1} - p_t}{p_t}\right) \qquad (11.44)$$

is the 'user cost of housing' (UCH) and plays an important role; we have seen close parallels in connection to both investment and non-durable consumption. This quantity represents the cost of homeownership per unit per period; a kind of quasi-rental if instead of owning a house we decided to lease it period by period. It includes the real interest rate as the opportunity cost of tying funds into housing; depreciation (maintenance) costs; and capital gains (or losses) which effectively reduce the cost of homeownership (or increase it in the case of losses); if taxation applies to housing capital gains, it should be included here, too. It can be seen that over a lifetime, the cost of residential investment would be equal to the accumulated discounted user cost required to lease the same amount of housing. Next, we introduce this into the individual's optimization problem.

11.4.3 Housing in Intertemporal Optimization

The individual's problem is to maximize:

$$U_0 = \sum_{t=0}^{\infty}(1 + \rho)^{-t}u(C_t, H_t) \qquad (11.45)$$

This is subject to an intertemporal budget constraint in which housing expenditure (pI) enters alongside non-durable consumption. (Note that the housing stock does not incur any expenditure as such.) To develop this, assume that real financial assets (A_t) earn the constant real rate of interest (r). Then, we have in every period:

$$C_t + p_t I_t + A_{t+1} - A_t = Y_t^L + rA_t \qquad (11.46)$$

Y_t^L is real labour income. Substituting investment out via (11.43'), we have:

$$C_t + p_{t+1}H_{t+1} - \left(1 - \delta + \frac{p_{t+1} - p_t}{p_t}\right)p_t H_t + A_{t+1} - A_t = Y_t^L + rA_t \qquad (11.46')$$

Consolidating housing and financial assets into a single wealth measure, $W_t \equiv p_t H_t + A_t$, and making use of UCH in (11.44), we can write:

$$C_t + W_{t+1} - W_t + UCH_t H_t = Y_t^L + rW_t \qquad (11.47)$$

The problem now becomes one of maximizing lifetime utility (11.45) with respect to C_t and H_t, subject to the wealth constraint (11.47). We get two first-order conditions. The first is the standard Euler equation for consumption. (Note that the wealth variable W_t above works exactly the same way as A_t in Chapter 5.) Second, we get an analogue to condition (11.18) that regulates the marginal utilities of durables and non-durable consumption, with the addition of capital gains; we now have a proportionality between housing and consumption:

$$\frac{u_H(C_t, H_t)}{u_C(C_t, H_t)} = p_t\left(r + \delta - \frac{p_{t+1} - p_t}{p_t}\right) \tag{11.48}$$

This is the optimal demand for housing for own use: It instructs us to own so many units until the marginal benefit (utility, normalized by the marginal utility of consumption) equals the marginal cost (user cost); alternatively, the marginal rate of substitution between housing and consumption equals the marginal rate of transformation between housing and the general good (the user cost of housing). Taking consumption as given, the marginal benefit is a function of the housing stock. For example, we can assume iso-elastic utility:

$$u(C_t, H_t) = \frac{(C_t^\beta H_t^{1-\beta})^{1-1/\sigma}}{1 - 1/\sigma}, \quad 0 < \beta < 1$$

where $0 < 1 - \beta < 1$ now reflects the importance of housing relative to non-durable consumption. In that case, (11.48) becomes:

$$\frac{u_H(C_t, H_t)}{u_C(C_t, H_t)} = \frac{(1 - \beta)C_t}{\beta H_t} = p_t\left(r + \delta - \frac{p_{t+1} - p_t}{p_t}\right) \tag{11.49}$$

Taking logs (lower-case letters):[47]

$$h_t = B + c_t - \log(UCH_t) \tag{11.49'}$$

Accordingly, the optimal stock of housing is affected positively on the demand side by consumption as an indicator of the state of aggregate economy and the preference-for-housing parameter $B \equiv \log[(1 - \beta)/\beta]$; while on the supply side, housing depends inversely on all the cost elements included in the UCH and positively by capital gains.

11.4.4 A Partial Equilibrium Model of Housing

(11.49') is further linearized as:

$$b_1 H_t = b_0 - p_t(1 + r + \delta) + p_{t+1} \tag{11.49''}$$

$b_0 (\equiv B + c)$ is a demand shifter that captures the state of the economy, as revealed e.g. in general consumption and preference shifts; moreover, though strictly speaking there is a unitary coefficient of housing in (11.49'), we allow for a more general effect on housing via $b_1 > 0$.

---

[47] We assume that UCH > 0 so that logUCH is defined.

Furthermore, after determining the demand for housing via (11.49"), the demand for residential investment (I_t) is derived from the optimal housing stock accumulation equation, $H_{t+1} = (1 - \delta)H_t + I_t$. We now add a supply for residential investment; housebuilders begin constructing new houses when the price of housing rises and they expect greater profits. Ignoring 'time-to-build' considerations, we have a residential investment supply:

$$I_t = i_0 + i_1 p_t \quad i_0, i_1 > 0 \tag{11.50}$$

$i_0 > 0$ is a supply shifter (e.g. due to changes in the prices of inputs to housebuilding such as the price of energy or raw materials)[48] and $i_1 > 0$ is the effect of price on supply. Hence, the accumulation equation (11.43) now becomes:

$$H_{t+1} = (1 - \delta)H_t + i_0 + i_1 p_t \tag{11.50'}$$

The workings of the full housing model can now be illustrated, following Poterba (1984); the model is a partial equilibrium one as it is based on a given wider macroeconomy (output, non-durable consumption, real interest rate, etc.); in other words, it ignores the feedback from housing to the wider economy.

Equations (11.49" and 50') are two dynamic (linear first-order difference) equations in housing, H_t, and its price in real terms, p_t. The system is repeated in matrix form:

$$\begin{bmatrix} p_{t+1} \\ H_{t+1} \end{bmatrix} = D \begin{bmatrix} p_t \\ H_t \end{bmatrix} + \begin{bmatrix} -b_0 \\ i_0 \end{bmatrix} \tag{11.51}$$

Where

$$D \equiv \begin{bmatrix} (1 + r + \delta) & b_1 \\ i_1 & 1 - \delta \end{bmatrix}$$

The long-run effects of permanent exogenous changes in the system are derived when we allow for the variables to reach the steady states ($p_t = p_{t+1} = \cdots$, $H_t = H_{t+1} = \cdots$):

$$b_1 H = b_0 - p(r + \delta) \tag{11.52a}$$

And

$$\delta H = i_0 + i_1 p \tag{11.52b}$$

---

[48] Is the price of land a cost for housebuilding? There has been a long debate on this question, going as far back as David Ricardo. For an individual housebuilder, it surely is a cost, as of course they need land to build on. For the economy as a whole, however, land price is a residual: when house prices are high, so are land prices; the owners of land negotiate higher prices and thereby extract a portion of any monopoly profits enjoyed by housebuilders. This hypothesis receives support from the evidence that land prices are Granger-caused by, rather than causing, house prices (Alyousha and Tsoukis, 1999).

This is a standard demand-supply framework; not surprisingly, shocks (b_0) cause quantity (H) and price (p) to move in the same direction, while supply shocks cause them to move in opposite directions.

Using the methods developed in Appendix 5A, we can also develop the transitional dynamics of the system. In (p, H) space, the steady-state equations (11.52a, b) are down- and up-sloping, marked D and S (remember, they are a D-S system). We also add here the short-run adjustment locus, built as follows. From (11.51), we have:

$$\det D = (1 + r + \delta)(1 - \delta) - b_1 i_1$$

and

$$\text{tr}D = 2 + r > 0$$

The system is saddle-point stable if $\det D < 0$, so the requisite assumption must be made on the parameters to ensure that. Saddle-point stability tallies with the fact that housing is a 'predetermined' variable, adjusting only sluggishly and smoothly; while the house price is a 'jump' variable, adjusting instantaneously and fully flexibly.[49] Under the assumption that $\det D < 0$, we have two roots, either side of unity. Repeating the analysis of Appendix 5A, we find that the stable arm is negatively sloped. It can also be seen that the stable arm is flatter than the D-locus in (p, H) space (11.52a).[50] The situation is depicted in Figure 11.11.

The equilibrium point is E. To unravel the dynamics, it makes sense to think of E as the *new* long-run equilibrium when a certain change has happened. Consider a permanent, unanticipated demand-side boost to the market: The economy starts at E_1 and ends at E: at the end of the process, both the housing quantity and price have increased. Dynamics is read off the stable arm (SA); note that the SA applies to the new equilibrium, not the old

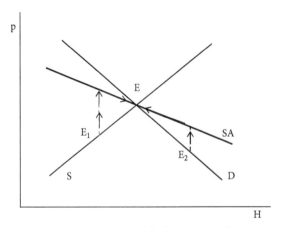

Figure 11.11. Dynamics of the housing market

[49] House prices surely adjust much more flexibly than the housing stock but the assumption is stronger than that: it requires that they are subject to no inertia at all, like a stock price; but there are search costs for both buyers and sellers such that the evolution of house prices is not in reality frictionless.

[50] This is due to the fact that the slope of the D-curve is $-b_1/(r+\delta)$, while that of the stable arm is $-b_1/(1+r+\delta-\lambda)$, where $0 < \lambda < 1$ is the stable eigenvalue.

one. At the time when news about the increased demand first breaks out (e.g. new information is revealed from the statistical offices that the economy is going well), the brunt is taken by the house prices which (are assumed to be able to) adjust instantaneously and discretely. In fact, the house price overshoots its long-run value: after the initial jump, the price level starts declining towards E. Essentially, the UCH is taking on the burden of adjustment: The key is that the housing stock is (plausibly) not allowed to change immediately, so the increase in demand raises only the price; there is an instantaneous prospect of a capital gain, making housing even more attractive. But as the quantity is unable to adjust, the price shoots up. Gradually, the quantity of housing begins to respond through new housebuilding. In the transitional phase, the rise in demand is offset by a rise in UCH that leaves the desired housing stock unaltered or rising slowly in line with supply. The UCH rises through capital losses: the price is falling during the transition. In the steady state (old or new), the price is constant and the capital gains zero.

In contrast, an adverse supply shock (due e.g. to a rise in the price of energy) moves the economy from E_2 to E: the price has risen but quantity has fallen. In this case, there is no overshoooting. So, there is a sharp contrast between the adjustment process following a demand and a supply shock; the former involves overshooting, the latter not. While the precise setup is subject to exact details (e.g. whether the D or SA locus is steeper), the scenario presented here is plausible: House prices are prone to steep rises more in response to a rise in demand than in response to any adverse supply shock. And price overshooting may assume a life of its own, leading on to a disconnect of house prices from fundaments. In Chapter 2, we saw how such a process, called a 'bubble', can form and develop mainly with respect to asset prices (shares, foreign exchange, housing). Such as a process as overshooting and possible bubble may be behind the evolution in real house prices in the UK in the last 30 years mentioned above. See the Guidance for Further Study for more on bubbles.

11.4.5 The Cost of Housing and the Rental Market

Data from the Office of National Statistics (Table: Ratio of house price to workplace-based earnings, April 2018) on the house price-to-earning ratio in England and Wales show the median house price-to-median annual gross earnings (= all wages and salaries including overtime) ratio to have been 7.9 on average across England and Wales, 10.3 in the South East, and 12.4 in London in 2017; these are all up from 7, 8.4, and 7.9 ten years earlier; and 3.6, 4.17, and 4 in 1997. Some important messages can be gleaned from these simple numbers. First, on the runaway course of housing: a typical house once cost maybe four times a typical annual salary and now it costs eight to twelve times, depending on the region. Secondly, the gradual differentiation of London and the South East from the rest of the country; it seems that globalization has brought in a lot more demand for housing there, whether for residential or for investment purposes. London has by now surpassed the rest of the South East in terms of house prices.

But the key message is related to affordability. Mortgage lenders typically do not lend amounts of more than four or five times the household's annual income; 'loan-to-income' ratios of more than 4.5 are rare, considered too risky, and incur higher interest rates. Even loans of that order incur very high interest payments. (For example, if you have a mortgage four times your annual salary and pay an interest rate of 4 per cent on it, 16 per cent of your annual salary goes to interest payments.) So, for the younger generations, getting on the housing ladder is extremely expensive and/or often impossible. As a result, younger people find it harder to get married and have children, as Laeven and Popov (2017) find for the US during the early 2000s (when house prices were rising fast). There are also obvious implications for intergenerational (in)justice (typically, older generations own their houses). This issue remains a challenge for public policy, something that government tries to meet with schemes that provide subsidies for first-time buyers, etc.

As a result of the increasing unaffordability of housing, many households turn towards renting. So, we now look at the analytics of the rental market. Essentially, we now have two sub-markets, the market for stock ownership and the market for rental; the first determines the real house price, the second the rent. The buyer of the stock (owner) is also the seller in the rental market, so the price and the rent will be related. The owner is still subject to the costs involved in the user cost, borrowing costs, depreciation, etc.; against that, they derive a real rent, R_t. So, they will own enough units of housing so as to equate:

$$R_t = (1 + \mu)p_t \left(r + \delta - \frac{p_{t+1} - p_t}{p_t} \right) \tag{11.53a}$$

The real rent should equal the user cost. This allows for landlord monopoly power of $\mu \geq 0$; the competitive case is that of $\mu = 0$; if on the other hand, there is concentration of rental properties in a few hands, then $\mu > 0$. The user (renter), on the other hand, will equate their marginal benefit (utility) and cost (rent, R_t):

$$\frac{u_H(C_t, H_t)}{u_C(C_t, H_t)} = R_t \tag{11.53b}$$

(11.53a, b) are the supply and demand in the rental market and determine the rental, conditional on the real house price. Then, we can determine the demand for ownership as follows. The landlord expects to get R_t for every period t. Note that (11.53a) is a forward-looking relation, determining an asset price (in this case, housing). The stable solution is the forward one, obtained by rewriting (11.53a) as:

$$R_t \approx p_t(1 + (r + \delta)(1 + \mu)) - E_t p_{t+1} \tag{11.53a'}$$

Note that expectations, implicitly assumed so far, are now explicitly introduced. So, solving forward in the usual way, we get:

$$P_t = \sum_{s=0}^{\infty} (1 + (r + \delta)(1 + \mu))^{-s-1} E_t R_{t+s} \tag{11.54}$$

The house price is a discounted sum of all expected future rents to be derived from this property.[51] The discount rate will include borrowing costs (r) and depreciation/maintenance costs (δ), both augmented by monopoly surcharge (μ). Of course, R_t will be an inverse

---

[51] We also impose the transversality condition $\lim_{s \to \infty} (1 + (r + \delta)(1 + \mu))^{-s-1} E_t R_{t+s} = 0$: The growth rate of the rent should be less than $(r + \delta)(1 + \mu)$.

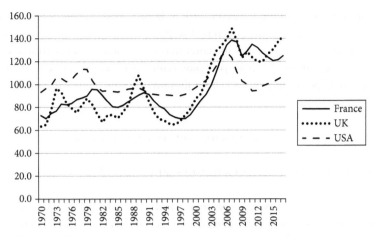

Figure 11.12. Standardized house price-to-rent ratio
Source: OECD

function of the level of housing via the demand of the renters, (11.53b). So, (11.54) becomes the demand for housing stock, to be combined with the supply equation (11.50').

Analytically, we can consolidate (11.53a, b) into:

$$\frac{u_H(C_t, H_t)}{u_C(C_t, H_t)} = R_t = (1 + \mu)p_t\left(r + \delta - \frac{p_{t+1} - p_t}{p_t}\right) \tag{11.55}$$

This is a generalization of (11.49), allowing for landlord monopoly power. If $\mu = 0$, then the rental market does not matter analytically, and we obtain exactly system (11.21). If the landlord monopoly power rises, in terms of Figure 11.12, there will be a tilt inwards of the D-curve left; in the steady state, there will be less housing available, the price will fall but the rental will increase: Interesting implications at a time when the share of the rental market is rising.

As an alternative to homeownership, renting incurs even stronger risks of its own. First, a household spends considerable portions of their income without ever accumulating housing wealth. Secondly, from (11.53a), the rental should be proportional to UCH (allowing for a possible markup); in turn, the UCH should be co-integrated with the real house price level (as the price is the only trending variable while the other elements inside the UCH such as the real interest rate and real capital gains are stationary). The bottom-line: house rental in real terms will be rising in line with house prices. On the whole, this prediction is borne out by the evidence of Figure 11.12 which shows the price-rent ratio to be constant in France, UK, and US, with the exception of a structural break that seems to have happened in the early 2000s.

However, more detailed recent evidence by Joyce et al. (2017) shows that, in real terms, the average (median) private rent paid in the mid-2010s was 53 per cent higher than that in the mid-1990s in London and 29 per cent higher in the rest of Britain. The study also shows that the overall proportion of the population of Great Britain who now live in rented accommodation has risen to 35 per cent, up from 29 per cent in the mid-1990s. This proportion is now comparable to the rental sector that existed until the mid-1980s; but that was in the social sector (council housing), which was more affordable. The rental sector declined considerably from the 1980s onwards as households were allowed to purchase the council houses they lived in. Now, the rental sector is rising again, but this time in the cut-throat private market. This growth in rental housing is heavily concentrated among the young. Just 12 per cent of 25- to 34-year-olds rented privately in the mid-1990s; this has since trebled to 37 per cent. All this is both illuminating and rather unsettling.

11.5 Asset Pricing and the Stock Market

11.5.1 Introduction: 'Financialization' and Stock Market Developments

We finish this chapter with the macroeconomics of the stock market. Stocks (or equity, or shares—these terms are interchangeable, but let us carefully distinguish from inventories) are ownership claims on businesses. Securities are those stocks that are traded in formally organized stock exchanges (or markets); the rest are held and traded privately. There are a number of reasons why one is interested on how the stock market behaves.

1. It is big: The total value of shares listed (market capitalization) in stock markets world-wide was of the order of $75tr in mid-2017, with the US markets accounting for about one third of this value (data from the Stock Market page of Wikipedia).
2. It is increasing: All the activities related to securities-trading and its management are an increasing portion of the wider universe of financial markets. Greenwood and Scharfstein (2013) tell us that the growth of the US securities 'industry' accounts for almost half the overall (3 percentage points) growth of the US financial sector relative to GDP from 1980 to 2007. In particular, the value-added created in the securities industry grew from 0.4 per cent of GDP in 1980 to 1.7 per cent of GDP in 2007, having peaked at 2.0 per cent of GDP in 2001 during the internet boom; it created about $241bn worth of value-added in 2007.
3. Average share prices show an intriguing evolution: Figure 11.13 has data on the stock market index for 1970–2016 for the UK, US, and a composite index of the Euro area (EU-19) backdated to 1987, all data from OECD (all standardized so that 2010 = 100).

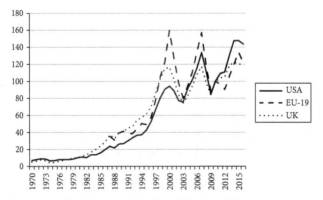

Figure 11.13. Share price indices (2010 = 100)
Source: OECD

We observe a trend-like rise but also large, low-frequency swings of these indices. There is a similarity here with the real house prices of Figure 11.13. A large literature documents and tries to understand these gyrations—see the Guidance for Further Study. They are likely to have serious effects, disrupting business finance, and having large wealth effects that filter through the economy via changes in consumption and the multiplier effects. More 'finance' and a prominent stock market exacerbate the risks associated with such developments. For more, see the Guidance for Further Study section under 'Financialization'.

In a nutshell, the stock market, as well as the wider financial sector, has been growing in importance and interacts strongly with the wider economy. Hence, we take a look at the determinants of the stock market index, without doing justice to the sector which is the subject of a specialized branch of Economics (Financial Economics). We begin with some key models about the pricing of risky assets derived from the theory of consumption.

11.5.2 The Consumption Capital Asset Pricing Model (CCAPM)

The best way to proceed is by recourse to the theory of consumption of Section 11.1, starting particularly from the Euler equation (11.14). In that context, we took the real interest rate as given—exogenous—and asked what that implied for the evolution of consumption, which was the endogenous variable. Now, we turn the tables, so to speak. We take the evolution and dynamics of consumption as given and ask what that would imply if we were to consider the real interest rate as endogenous. The interest rate one has in mind here is the rate of return of a risky asset, like Treasury or corporate bonds—these are financial instruments whose rate of return is uncertain.

We begin with the Euler equation (11.14) in expected terms (cf. also 11.14'):

$$u'(C_t) = \frac{E_t[u'(C_{t+1})(1 + r_{t+1})]}{1 + \rho} \tag{11.56}$$

The main difference from (11.14) is a variable real interest rate in real terms, obtainable by investing in the 'typical' asset. It relates to period $t + 1$—if you abstain from consumption this period, you save by investing in the asset now and the interest accrues next term, so the next period's rate is applicable. So, the expectation is taken over of the product of future marginal utility and the real rate $(1 + r_{t+1})$.

From first principles of statistics, we get:

$$u'(C_t) = \frac{E_t u'(C_{t+1})E_t(1 + r_{t+1}) + Cov[u'(C_{t+1}), r_{t+1}]}{1 + \rho} \tag{11.57}$$

To interpret (11.57), we need to remember that the marginal utility of consumption is inversely related to the level of consumption due to diminishing marginal utility. The first message we get is related to consumption itself, assuming exogenous interest rates. If the covariance of the interest rate with marginal utility is positive ($Cov(.) > 0$ above), that means that the interest rate varies inversely with consumption—it rises in recessions and falls in good times. By providing a high return in bad times, the asset acts as an insurance mechanism, and you would wish to have more of that. Therefore, you save more now, and reduce consumption—hence the marginal utility rises. This is the effect of the positive covariance on the LHS of the above equation.

But our main concern is with the determination of the interest rate assuming an exogenous consumption path. Again, a positive covariance implies that the asset in question acts as insurance, and you want to hold more of this. Demand rises, and since the rate of return is inversely related to the price of a bond (from basics), the rate of return falls—observe that a higher Cov(.) depresses the expected interest rate, given the marginal utilities on either side of (11.57). To put it alternatively, if the asset provides insurance, you will be eager to hold it even if its rate of return were lower.

So, (11.57) provides a bridge between a macro model (the consumption Euler equation) and risky asset pricing (i.e., determination of its rate of return). Its appeal is that it provides a model for asset returns without having to specify fully any portfolio model—the investor need only consider the properties of this asset and its rate of return in relation to consumption. In fact, one may go a step further in spelling out the implications of the model. Imagine that there is an asset which pays a fixed rate of return $\bar{r}$. Applied to this asset, the above formula would give:

$$u'(C_t) = \frac{(1+\bar{r})E_t u'(C_{t+1})}{1+\rho} \tag{11.57'}$$

As this interest rate is known with certainty, its covariance with marginal utility is zero. Dividing (11.57) by (11.57') and rearranging, one obtains the CCAPM, first derived by Breeden (1979):

$$E_t r_{t+1} = \bar{r} - \frac{Cov[u'(C_{t+1}), r_{t+1}]}{E_t u'(C_{t+1})} \tag{11.58}$$

The risky rate of return will be on average (notice the expectation) equal to the riskless rate adjusted by the covariance—the degree to which the risky asset acts as insurance or hedging mechanism. Those assets that do so $(Cov(.) > 0)$ have a lower rate of return than the riskless—sure—rate. As they are in greater demand by risk averse investors—because they provide hedging—their price is driven up and their rate of return down. And what matters for pricing this risky asset is not its own risk—because this can be diversified away and therefore is not rewarded. All that matters is how this asset varies with the whole-market risk (as embodied in the dynamics of consumption) which cannot be diversified away. To the extent that the asset varies together with the market fluctuations $(Cov(.) < 0)$, the asset will be rewarded by an extra rate of return (a 'risk premium'). Intuitive and elegant, the CCAPM has nevertheless been criticized in terms of its empirical performance. The approach is as valid as the Euler equation on which it builds, and we have seen that this is rejected by the data (cf. the rejection of (11.14') by Hansen and Singleton, 1983).

11.5.3 Another Formulation of CCAPM and the 'Equity Premium Puzzle'

Beginning again with (11.56), and assuming iso-elastic utility $(u(C_t) = \frac{C_t^{1-1/\sigma}}{1-1/\sigma})$ with $\sigma > 0$ being the intertemporal elasticity of substitution, we have (cf. 11.14'):

$$1 + \rho = E_t \left\{ \left(\frac{C_{t+1}}{C_t} \right)^{-\frac{1}{\sigma}} (1 + r_{t+1}) \right\} \approx E_t \left\{ (1 + \Delta c_{t+1})^{-\frac{1}{\sigma}} (1 + r_{t+1}) \right\} \tag{11.59}$$

$\Delta c_{t+1} \equiv logC_{t+1} - logC_t$ is the growth rate of consumption between periods t and t + 1 – c is lower-case (log). Using again basic statistics and taking Taylor expansions around a zero expected interest rate and a zero expected consumption growth, we have:

$$E_t \left\{ (1 + \Delta c_{t+1})^{-\frac{1}{\sigma}} (1 + r_{t+1}) \right\} \approx 1 + E_t r_{t+1} - \frac{1}{\sigma} E_t \Delta c_{t+1} + Cov \left\{ r_{t+1}, -\frac{1}{\sigma} \Delta c_{t+1} \right\}$$

Note that we can write, $Cov \left\{ r_{t+1}, -\frac{1}{\sigma} \Delta c_{t+1} \right\} = -\frac{1}{\sigma} Cov \{ r_{t+1}, \Delta c_{t+1} \}$. Therefore, (11.59) yields (approximately):

$$1 + \rho = 1 + E_t r_{t+1} - \frac{1}{\sigma} E_t \Delta c_{t+1} - \frac{1}{\sigma} Cov \{ r_{t+1}, \Delta c_{t+1} \} \tag{11.60}$$

Applying this to the certain asset (with sure rate $\bar{r}$, so Cov(.) = 0), we also have:

$$1 + \rho = 1 + \bar{r} - \frac{1}{\sigma} E_t \Delta c_{t+1} \tag{11.60'}$$

Combining (11.60) with (11.60'), we get:

$$E_t r_{t+1} = \bar{r} + \frac{1}{\sigma} Cov \{ r_{t+1}, \Delta c_{t+1} \} \tag{11.61}$$

This is another version of the CCAPM, the only difference being that we have entered a specific functional form for utility. Again, an asset which provides insurance will have a high interest rate during a time of lower consumption growth (Cov < 0 above), so that its average rate of return will be lower than the certain rate.

Equation (11.61) serves for explaining the 'equity premium puzzle'. σ is the elasticity of intertemporal substitution; as we have discussed, empirical work on this reveals that it is rather low, lower than unity. Let us take equity (company shares) as our uncertain asset here. (The rate of return on this asset is the value of the dividends divided by the price of shares, plus the percentage capital gains on it.) Historically, this rate of return has been much higher (often 5–10 per cent) than the riskless rate of return (interest rate on high street bank deposits). Meanwhile, the covariance of the rate of return on shares with consumption growth has been moderate. But we cannot not verify (11.61) if this information is introduced into it. In other words, the actual average rate of return on this uncertain asset (shares) is much higher than justified by the above formula with historical covariance data and an empirically plausible intertemporal rate of time preference. This is the 'equity premium puzzle', first identified by Mehra and Prescott (1985). A large literature has reaffirmed it since and attempted to explain it. One may readily criticize the special assumptions employed by the model (iso-elastic utility, representative agent, non-durable consumption), but subsequent literature has relaxed many of these (e.g. introducing recursive preferences, Campbell, 1993; consumer heterogeneity, Constantinides and Duffie, 1996). Two lines of attack, in the spirit of behavioural economics, is to invoke more risk aversion than the fully rational models above imply ('loss aversion', Benartzi and Thaler, 1995); and secondly, to introduce 'habits' and 'catching up with the Joneses' effects in consumption (Abel, 1990b; Constantinidis, 1990), that imply a higher risk aversion than given by the intertemporal elasticity of substitution and consumption dynamics that affect the covariance term. But, in the words of Kocherlakota (1996), and in the opinion of many, 'it remains a puzzle'; see Mehra and Prescott (2003) for another review and Azeredo (2014) for a more recent study.

11.5.4 The Capital Asset Pricing Model (CAPM)

Each asset may be thought of as being subject to two independent ('orthogonal') types of risk. One is 'aggregate risk' (also called systematic or undiversifiable risk), common to all firms and assets, like that from the uncertainty of the productivity process (faster or slower growth), energy prices, weather, exogenous (to the private sector) government policies, etc. The other type of risk is 'idiosyncratic', i.e. that related to the individual asset and due, e.g., to the entity that issues it: strengths or weaknesses of management, an individual product falling out of, or into, favour, etc. But the main point is, these idiosyncratic developments and the risk that goes with them 'wash out' on aggregate: one firm's mismanagement will be matched by another's good management, and so on. And the risk that does not 'wash out' on aggregate is by definition aggregate risk.

Now, a clever investor can always defend themselves against all idiosyncratic risk. They can do so by holding a basket of assets (equity, bonds) issued by, as it were, polar opposite firms. For each share they hold of a firm with 'attribute X', they should also hold one from a firm with 'attribute –X'; so that if attribute X proves disastrous, attribute –X will be doing well, and on average they do as well as everybody else. This process is called 'hedging' and the idiosyncratic risk can in this way be 'diversified away'. If so, idiosyncratic risk will not be rewarded at all by financial markets; only aggregate risk will be. This is the message we get from CAPM. This model has a long history in Financial Economics; here, for ease of exposition, we shall derive it from CCAPM, although it was derived independently and predates the CCAPM.

Imagine that there is an asset whose rate of return is perfectly well correlated with the aggregate consumption growth rate. We call this the 'market portfolio'. It is an asset whose risk characteristics are identical to the aggregate of all assets in the economy—the actual market portfolio. The main characteristic of this actual market portfolio and of the miniature asset portfolio that mimics it (the 'market portfolio') is that they are only subject to aggregate risk, and not subject to *any* idiosyncratic risk. Their rate of return is perfectly correlated with the consumption growth rate (in a closed economy): In a good year, the aggregate rate of return is high and so is the increase in resources, resulting in a high growth rate. Call the rate of return of this market portfolio $\hat{r}_t$. We can express the perfect correlation with consumption growth as the linear relation $\hat{r}_t = \gamma \Delta c_t$, $\gamma > 0$. (Though the relationship is not generally one-to-one—the coefficient γ need not generally be unity—the correlation is perfect: a correlation coefficient of unity). Think of $\hat{r}_t$ and Δc_t as being located exactly on a straight line with slope γ. We then have $Cov\{\hat{r}_t, \Delta c_t\} = \gamma Var\{\Delta c_t\} = \frac{1}{\gamma} Var\{\hat{r}_t\}$; the covariance with other assets also can be replaced in the same spirit: $Cov\{r_t, \Delta c_t\} = \gamma Cov\{r_t, \hat{r}_t\}$.

Then, we can apply (11.60) to this asset, so we have three versions of that equation, repeated below:

$$1 + \rho = 1 + E_t r_{t+1} - \frac{1}{\sigma} E_t \Delta c_{t+1} - \frac{1}{\sigma} Cov\{r_{t+1}, \Delta c_{t+1}\} \tag{11.60}$$

$$1 + \rho = 1 + \bar{r} - \frac{1}{\sigma} E_t \Delta c_{t+1} \tag{11.60'}$$

$$1 + \rho = 1 + E_t \hat{r}_{t+1} - \frac{1}{\sigma} E_t \Delta c_{t+1} - \frac{1}{\sigma} Cov\{\hat{r}_{t+1}, \Delta c_{t+1}\} \tag{11.60''}$$

Combining the second with the third, we get:

$$E_t \hat{r}_{t+1} = \bar{r} + \frac{\gamma}{\sigma} Var\{\Delta c_{t+1}\} = \bar{r} + \frac{1}{\gamma\sigma} Var\{\hat{r}_{t+1}\}$$

The last equality simply replaces the variance of consumption with the variance of the market portfolio, repositioning the constants appropriately. Then, first with second:

$$E_t r_{t+1} = \bar{r} + \frac{1}{\sigma} Cov\{r_{t+1}, \Delta c_{t+1}\} = \bar{r} + \frac{1}{\sigma} Cov\{r_{t+1}, \hat{r}_{t+1}\}$$

Combining the last two relations, we finally get the basic equation of the CAPM:

$$E_t r_{t+1} = \bar{r} + \frac{Cov\{r_{t+1}, \hat{r}_{t+1}\}}{Var\{\hat{r}_{t+1}\}} [E_t \hat{r}_{t+1} - \bar{r}] \tag{11.62}$$

This is the Capital Asset Pricing Model, first developed by Sharpe (1964) and Lintner (1965). At its core is the idea that only aggregate risk will be rewarded, since all idiosyncratic risk can be diversified away (hedged). Therefore, the typical uncertain interest rate will offer a premium above the sure asset $(E_t r_{t+1} - \bar{r})$ as compensation of its riskiness only to the extent that it covaries with the market portfolio (as a percentage over the riskiness of the market portfolio); any movement that is out of step (uncorrelated) with the market portfolio will not be rewarded as it can be diversified away. The premium will be scaled up by the premium of the market portfolio over the sure asset [the square brackets], a measure of how well uncertain assets are rewarded on average. You could say that the uncertain premium is the product of the typical asset's 'legitimate' uncertainty times how well each 'unit' of uncertainty is paid.

The ratio of this asset's covariance with the market portfolio over the variance of the market portfolio is called the individual asset's 'beta coefficient':

$$\beta_i \equiv \frac{Cov\{r_{t+1}^i, \hat{r}_{t+1}\}}{Var\{\hat{r}_{t+1}\}} \tag{11.63}$$

where we now specify that we are referring to asset i, so the model is re-expressed as:

$$E_t r^i_{t+1} = \bar{r} + \beta_i[E_t \hat{r}_{t+1} - \bar{r}] \tag{11.62'}$$

If we plot the expected return of any asset $(E_t r^i_{t+1})$ against its beta (β_i), then we obtain the 'security market line' (SML) that is upward-sloping with intercept $\bar{r}$ and slope $[E_t \hat{r}_{t+1} - \bar{r}]$. The SML can help in two ways. First, as a yardstick by which we can evaluate individual asset performances. We can measure the historical risk (beta) and return of any asset and put the measurements on the same graph; any asset that turns out to be above (below) the SML has performed better (worse) than average. Secondly, we can use the SML in order to select asset(s) that suit an investor's preferences. We may think of the SML as a constraint of what is available in terms of risk-return combination (according to the CAPM). An investor will have a utility function over risk and return that will reflect their risk aversion; they will pick up the $(E_t r^I_{t+1}, \beta_I)$ combination (i.e. they will select asset i $= $ I) that represents the point of tangency of their risk-return indifference curves and the SML.

As with its CCAPM cousin, so too has the CAPM been rejected in empirical tests in a large literature; see the review by Fama and French (2004). Perhaps more than all the other assumptions, most restrictive is the fact that there is only one source of risk that is rewarded, namely aggregate risk. Alternative models allow for more than one source of rewarded risk; this then invites the criticism of how to select the most important sources of risk in a systematic way. Among the many contributions, one could take a look at Chen et al. (1986) which investigates risk originating from macroeconomic variables; and Campbell (1996) which incorporates human capital as well as stock market (market) risk as sources of return.

11.5.5 The Term Structure of Interest Rates

Most of this section has been concerned with the stock market and equities (shares); we now briefly turn attention to another financial instrument, namely bonds, in order to briefly examine the relation between short- and long-term interest rates ('the term structure'). Short and long rates refer of course to the interest rates obtainable from bonds of different maturities. Maturity is an almost continuous variable (from a few months all the way to many years), so the distinction is not a binary one; but the short-long sharp division is an instructive one. The term structure is important as the long rates matter for many decisions that have long horizons (such as investment, pensions, mortgages).

Consider two types of bond, one is a one-period, 'zero-coupon' bond. It is worth £1 at expiry (end of time t) and is issued at a price $1/(1 + r)$ one period earlier $(t - 1)$; so, it earns an interest of r_t, payable at t (before expiration). Regarding a long bond, the easiest is to consider a 'consol', a bond that pays a fixed coupon of $c > 0$ for ever; its price in the second-hand market where this bond is traded is p_t. The catch? Such a bond does not exist! But it serves well in illustrating the key issues. The interest rate on this bond is:

$$R_t = \frac{c}{p_{t-1}} \tag{11.64}$$

which is the coupon over the price paid for the bond (end of last period). Now, the effective rate of return obtainable from this instrument for an investor that buys at the end of time $t - 1$ is the cash flow and the resale price next period:

$$1 + \text{rate of return} = \frac{p_t + c}{p_{t-1}}$$

In other words, the rate of return includes interest and capital gains. In equilibrium, the typical investor must be indifferent between the two types of bond (short-long, allowing for risk, which is not considered here); so, we must have:

$$1 + r_t = \frac{p_t + c}{p_{t-1}} \tag{11.65}$$

Solving this relation forward, we can express the current price of the consol (p_t) as the present value of all future coupons (allowing for the variable short interest rate which serves as the discount rate)—this is left as an exercise.

Our main concern is the relation between interest rates. Insert the definition of the long interest rate (11.64) above to get:

$$1 + r_t = \frac{1/R_{t+1} + 1}{1/R_t} = \frac{R_t}{R_{t+1}} + R_t \tag{11.65'}$$

Since

$$\frac{R_{t+1}}{R_t} = 1 + \frac{\Delta R_{t+1}}{R_t},$$

therefore

$$\frac{R_t}{R_{t+1}} = \frac{1}{1 + \frac{\Delta R_{t+1}}{R_t}} \approx 1 - \frac{\Delta R_{t+1}}{R_t}$$

we end up with:

$$r_t = R_t - \frac{\Delta R_{t+1}}{R_t} \tag{11.66}$$

In other words, the short rate should equal the long rate, allowing for the capital gains on the long bond, which are inversely related to the evolution of the rate itself.

In fact, (11.66) is a forward-looking relation. To see this, rewrite it as:

$$R_t r_t + R_{t+1} = R_t(1 + R_t)$$

Linearizing the product terms on both sides using the average real long rate (R), we get:

$$R r_t + R_{t+1} \approx R_t(1 + R) \tag{11.66'}$$

Solving forward iteratively, we get:

$$R_t = \frac{R}{1+R}\sum_{s=0}^{\infty}\frac{r_{t+s}}{(1+R)^s} \tag{11.67}$$

Equation (11.67) is key. It tells us that the long rate is the present value of future short rates, here discounted by R. Note that

$$\frac{R}{1+R}\sum_{s=0}^{\infty}\frac{1}{(1+R)^s} = 1$$

The sum of all the weights (the discount factors times $R/(1+R)$) is unity; each future short rate receives a weight that declines with its distance in the future (s).

In fact, this key idea generalizes to bonds of any maturity. Consider a bond that matures $n \geq 1$ periods after issuance. At the issue date, its interest rate will be given by a formula like:

$$R_t^n = \sum_{s=0}^{n-1} w_s r_{t+s}, \quad w_s > 0 \text{ for all } s \tag{11.67'}$$

Being functions of the interest rate, the weights will be such that they sum to one:

$$\sum_{s=0}^{n-1} w_s = 1.$$

Both the consol rate and the short rate are the polar opposite special cases: the former is the case of an infinite maturity:

$$R_t \equiv R_t^{n\to\infty}$$

the latter of $n = 1$:

$$r_t \equiv R_t^{n=1}$$

If we plot the long rate R_t^n against the maturity, so that r_t will be at one end of the graph and R_t at the other, then we get a graph called the 'yield curve': It expresses current interest rates on bonds of different maturities as a function of their maturity. If the short rates are expected to stay constant, $r_{t+s} = t$ for all s, then we would have: $R_t^n = r$ for all n. In this case, the long rates would be equal to the short one: the yield curve would be horizontal. But in actual data, the yield curve is often upward-sloping. The long rates are higher the longer the maturity. This is because the economy is expected to grow in the future, therefore interest rates may rise to combat inflation. Additionally, the longer bonds involve more risk (although you can always buy and sell, the longer horizon involves more uncertainty), hence the required risk premia are higher. Finally, the 'yield to maturity' is the average of the interest rates *obtainable by the same bond* over its life.

As mentioned, the term structure is quite important. In general, short rates are amenable to monetary policy (the very short-term government bonds are routinely used in the open-market operations of Central Banks), while the long rates are both relevant for long-term decisions but also indicative of structural fundamentals of the economy (long-term prospects, productivity, etc) as their return depends on them. See Campbell (1995) as an introduction to the topic.

Notes on the Literature

We have given a wealth of references already, so we shall be brief here. One could begin with the early but still useful survey paper of Abel (1990a) that explains the basics of both consumption and investment. The surveys by Deaton (1992), Attanasio (1999), and Attanasio and Weber (2010) chart nicely the progression of consumption theory from early aggregative, macro models to more nuanced micro-based studies. Caballero (1999) is a good introduction the modern theory of aggregate investment; Chirinko (1993) is a good survey of early empirical work, including on the accelerator models. See the Spring 2001 issue of the *Oxford Review of Economic Policy* on saving.

Guidance for Further Study

Foreign Direct Investment (FDI)

FDI is investment in a foreign country by nationals or businesses of another that results in an amount of control over the business in which the investment takes place (control of more than 10 per cent of voting rights); in this way, it is distinguished from cross-border portfolio-related capital flows that do not result in any control of any entity. FDI has spiralled since the 1990s as part and parcel of globalization. This fact, and the potential developmental effects it may have, have generated a lot of interest among policy-makers. Economic theorists have generally not focused on FDI much (or almost at all) as they consider it as another form of investment; therefore the analysis of Section 11.3 applies, and it is immaterial whether the provenance is domestic or foreign. Echoing the policy-makers' concerns more, a large empirical literature has attempted to explain the main determinants of FDI and its effects on the growth of the host economy. While there are obvious theoretical priors on both issues, the empirical results are rather inconclusive. (On this, they resemble the results on the determinants of growth in Chapter 9.) The interested reader can look at Chanegriha et al. (2017) as portal into this literature. All this literature is concerned with incoming FDI; an interesting question is how outgoing FDI affects the economy of origin. Might it be related to the de-industrialization that the advanced economies have experienced almost without exception over the last 30 or 40 years? The issue does not seem to have received much attention; but see Feldstein (1995) for an intriguing exception!

Housing as an asset

Another interpretation of the rental-UCH equality (11.53a) is possible if we rewrite it as:

$$\frac{R_t}{P_t(1+\mu)} + \frac{P_{t+1} - P_t}{P_t} - \delta = r$$

The real interest rate available in the 'typical asset' in the economy (r) should be equal to the rate of return from investing in housing, i.e. the rent per pound invested in housing (R/P, adjusted by the requirement to make profit) plus the capital gain minus depreciation/maintenance. Of course, the above should be adjusted by the variances of both the housing and other asset returns: the asset that is riskier should be yielding a higher return in expected terms in order to compensate for its riskiness. For housing in portfolios, see e.g. Flavin and Yamashita (2002) and Chetty et al. (2017).

Now, assuming that relative capital gains (per cent) is a constant, consider how r affects R/p. Furthermore, how can the above shed light on the structural break that seems to have happened in p/R in the 2000s as shown in Figure 11.13? Can you relate this to either the 'secular stagnation' hypothesis or the 'global savings glut' hypothesis (there is a glut of global savings, so that the average real return is low)? Explain.

Gentrification, housing shortfalls, and homelessness

There is much more to housing of course than any model, even the richest one, can convey. Housing is intrinsically linked to social processes such as the evolution of cities, inequality and poverty, and environmental quality, among others, that occupy urban planners, geographers, sociologists, environmentalists, as well as journalists. Among the relevant issues, one may mention gentrification (the process of urban regeneration of run-down neighbourhoods, in which socially mobile, more affluent newcomers displace more working-class traditional residents, who move away and/or see their quality of housing decline; see Foster, 2017). Furthermore, the rise in prices and rents has meant that many households, particularly the young, struggle to get on the ladder, and their quality of housing declines (smaller properties, involving long commuting). At the same time, homelessness also rises. At the root of all this is a shortage of housing; the charity Crisis (2018) estimates that the UK needs 4 million more houses than are currently available; building those, however, would mean encroaching on green areas and environmental degradation. The interested reader is invited to form their own opinion.

The Lucas (1978) pricing model of a risky asset

Consider a risky asset which is traded in the market at price p_t and yields every period a dividend d_t. The investor who buys this at the end of time t and holds it for one period will get a gross return equal to:

$$1 + r_{t+1} = \frac{p_{t+1} + d_{t+1}}{p_t} \tag{11.68}$$

Explain why. This is of course risky; its evolution will be governed by the Euler equation (11.23). Combining, we get the Lucas (1978) formula for the equilibrium price of this asset:

$$p_t = \frac{E_t[u'(C_{t+1})(p_{t+1} + d_{t+1})]}{u'(C_t)(1 + \rho)}$$

The reader is invited to explain this formula intuitively, by recourse to the interpretations of the Euler equation in Chapter 5. Jermann (1998) provides a generalization to an economy with production and an application to asset pricing over the business cycle.

Asset prices, dividends, and earnings

As an illustration, consider again the rate of return available to an asset (11.68). Now, the market participants will compare this to other assets, e.g. the riskless rate, r (assumed constant for simplicity).

Assume also that, in order to hold this asset, the representative investor will require a premium, $\pi > 0$, due to their riskiness. So:

$$1 + E_t r_{t+1} = \frac{E_t(p_{t+1} + d_{t+1})}{p_t} = 1 + r + \pi \tag{11.68'}$$

If the asset is expected to offer a higher (lower) rate than this at time $t+1$, the investors will rush to buy (sell) it at the end of time t, raising (lowering) p_t and reducing (increasing) r_{t+1}. (Note that there is no point in buying (selling) the asset at the end of $t+1$ when the high (low) interest rate r_{t+1} has already been paid.) So, in equilibrium, the equality holds.

We can explore the implications by solving the above forward:

$$p_t = \int_{s=1}^{\infty} E_t d_{t+s}(1 + r + \pi)^{-s} \tag{11.69}$$

The price of the asset is the present value (sum of future stream appropriately discounted) of the currently expected cash flow that the asset gives entitlement to (dividends here, or interest payments in bonds, etc). The riskiness of the asset is considered implicitly by the (constant) risk premium that augments the discount rate (the riskless rate of return, r). Inflation is also taken care of by taking the real riskless rate—everything in the formula above is in real terms.

To see this, assume that the dividend is expected to grow at a constant rate $0 < g < r$ that equals the aggregate economy's real growth rate, from the current level (d_t):

$$p_t = d_t \int_{s=1}^{\infty} (1 + g)^s (1 + r + \pi)^{-s} = d_t \frac{1 + g}{r + \pi - g} \tag{11.69'}$$

This formula makes clear that the real asset price rises with the level of the real dividend and its growth rate (to which it is quite sensitive) and falls with the discount rate and the risk premium. So, the risk premium raises the required return that makes this asset sufficiently attractive; correspondingly, it lowers its price.

An interesting corollary concerns the relation between the return available to an asset and the price-dividend (or price-earnings) ratio, p_t/d_t. From above, noting that, given constant d, r, g, and π, the price level grows at rate g, the return is:

$$1 + r_{t+1} = \frac{p_{t+1} + d_{t+1}}{p_t} = \frac{p_{t+1}}{p_t}\left(1 + \frac{d_{t+1}}{p_{t+1}}\right) = (1 + g)\left(1 + \frac{d_{t+1}}{p_{t+1}}\right)$$

Hence, given the growth rate, the return varies inversely with the price-dividend ratio. Shiller (2005) presents evidence to this effect, particularly when the investment is long term: Investors that buy when the price is high (low) relative to dividends or other earnings make a low (high) return. Hence, a high price-dividend ratio also implies that the subsequent growth of price is negative as the price moves to restore the ratio; a prediction that receives mixed support, see Campbell and Shiller (1998).

Understanding stock market fluctuations

Consider again the asset pricing formula (11.68). Its main message is that asset (share) price will be determined as the present value of future cash flows that this asset gives entitlement to. A large literature has considered whether both the growth and the considerable fluctuations of the stock market indices evident in Figure 11.13 can be explained along these lines (constructing carefully the cash flows as dividends and interest, allowing for risk, incorporated into the risk premium here, a variable riskless rate, etc.). The key question is, are share prices really discounted sums of future dividends/cash flows? As we discuss further below, the answer to this question has a bearing on whether behaviour in financial markets is consistent with Rational Expectations or not.

Among the many contributions, Hall (2001a) attributes a great significance in stock pricing in the rate of return to intangibles, including human capital (on which see Hall, 2001b, as well). In other words, d_t should not be just cash and dividends but also the implicit rate of return to the human capital and the technological expertise of the firm. Hall (2001a) and Barsky and Delong (1993) emphasize the role of a variable growth of dividends. The point is that even modest variations in the expected growth rate can cause large variations in p_t. With these complications in mind, both papers uphold the notion of the share price as the present value of future earnings.

In an interesting twist, Blanchard et al. (1993) consider the role of earnings, such as profits current and future, not on the share price but on investment. Recall that expected cash flow from a marginal product is called the 'marginal q'; this will be a discounted sum such as the $\int_{s=1}^{\infty} E_t d_{t+s} (1 + r + \pi)^{-s}$ above, where d_t is the profits arising from the project. On the other hand, the stock market price (relative to replacement cost) is 'average (or "Tobin"s) q'. Under some fairly stringent conditions, the two coincide; in practice, they differ substantially. Blanchard et al. (1993) show that the 'marginal q' (or more crudely, current profits) is more relevant for investment, while the stock market valuation ('average q') is less so. An interesting corollary, though not emphasized in the paper, is that the 'average q' (stock market valuation) seems to deviate fairly substantially from current profits; e.g. compare fig. Ia with IIIa of Blanchard et al. (1993).

The 'Efficient-Market Hypothesis', stock market fluctuations, and Behavioural Finance

The Efficient-Market Hypothesis (EMH) is a theory in financial economics that states that asset prices fully reflect all available information. There are different versions of the theory depending on exactly what information is taken into account. A direct implication is that there is no possibility of making 'smart money', devising systematic strategies of buying and selling that make profits; at the end of all the trades, the investor should have exactly the same position as at the start (minus transactions costs).

More broadly speaking, the key idea behind the EMH is that all assets accurately reflect all available information on their fundamental determinants (dividend and cash flows, interest rates, and behind them profitability and productivity of firms, the state of the economy, etc.). So, asset prices are firmly anchored on such fundamentals. The EMH is part-and-parcel of Rational Expectations, as mentioned in Chapter 2. Market participants 'coolly' calculate the cash flows they will get from assets (both in terms of expected values and in terms of riskiness) and, in equilibrium, the price they are prepared to pay exactly matches that.

As discussed under 'Understanding stock market fluctuations', the literature has considered whether the share price evolution is compatible with the EMH. The strategy is to consider the asset pricing formula (11.69). Note how this formula embodies the EMH: the rational market participants will consider all available information about the future claims that this asset gives entitlement to and will incorporate this into the price. They will also consider everything else that is relevant, such as the riskiness of the asset (incorporated into the risk premium), the riskless rate, etc. Thus, the price accurately and objectively reflects that information, and there is no possibility of buying cheaply and selling expensively any asset of given characteristics. (But of course you can find a cheap asset to buy if it has such characteristics, e.g. lower riskiness.) The empirical strategy therefore is to ask, are share prices the discounted sums of future cash flows, as the formula stipulates? The null hypothesis is yes, in which case rationality and the EMH are upheld; the alternative is that asset prices reflect subjective judgement and investor sentiment.

Not surprisingly, there are strong views on either side of the debate. We noted that Hall (2001a) and Barsky and Delong (1993), after allowing for real-world extensions, uphold the notion of the share price as the present value of future dividends that underpins the EMH. Critics such as Shiller (1981) argue that the volatility of share prices is incompatible with any reasonable pricing formula such as the above coupled with plausible expectations about future cash flows and the state of the economy more widely. Subjective judgement fuelled by sentiment must be at work; there exist 'fads' (fashion), 'animal spirits' (impulsive behaviour), herding and contagion (the EMH says that each investor evaluates the common information on their own, we do not influence one another), and 'irrational exuberance' (over-reaction to both good and bad news). These are ideas incompatible with strict rationality and the Rational Expectations Hypothesis. They have received a boost after the crisis of 2007–9 which, by revealing the breathtaking complexity and interdependence of many financial instruments, dealt a blow to the notion of accurate pricing of financial assets. In line with Behavioural Economics, Behavioural Finance considers asset pricing in the presence of such behaviour. The interested reader could start with Shiller (2003, 2005) and Shleifer (1999). Many of the models in that area build on the 'Keeping up' and habits extensions to preferences we have reviewed (e.g. Abel, 1990b; Constantinidis, 1990; Gali, 1994; Campbell and Cochrane, 1999).

Bubbles

Bubbles is another instance where asset prices (financial assets, exchange rates, house prices, even the price of Bitcoin) can deviate from fundamentals. The difference from behavioural finance is that, this time, such deviations can be quite rational. Asset prices keep going up not because those assets will yield higher cash flows in the future, but simply everyone expects them to keep going so the profitable strategy is to keep buying—thus fuelling further the price increases. But whether rational or not, bubbles imply a failure of Rational Expectations that postulates that expectations are firmly anchored in an on-average correct (hence, widely shared) model of the economy. In contrast, with bubbles and 'animal spirits' expectations can wander off anywhere.

Popular perception has it that many asset prices (share prices, house prices, sometimes exchange rates) are motivated by bubbles and unconnected to fundamentals. Historically, there have also existed many examples (or, better, episodes that are considered as bubbles). But testing of bubbles is not so straightforward and the results are nuanced and debated. The interested reader can start from the Spring 1990 issue of the *Journal of Economic Perspectives*, which is devoted to bubbles: e.g. Flood and Hodrick (1990) for a formal testing framework, Garber (1990) for historical episodes, and Shiller (2014) for more recent examples.[52] An excellent introduction to the theoretical study of bubbles is Martin and Ventura (2018).

Financialization

The wider financial services sector has been itself growing rapidly over the last 40 years, a process known as 'financialization'. Greenwood and Scharfstein (2013) shows that the US financial services

---

[52] Shiller, who was a co-recipient of the Nobel Prize in Economics in 2013 for his work in empirical asset pricing, is also on the record as saying that the Bitcoin e-currency (or 'cryptocurrency') is driven by 'fads' (shared erroneous beliefs) and is essentially a bubble. At the time of writing (July 2018), there exist several recent interviews by him available online to this effect.

sector contributed 2.8 per cent to GDP in 1950, 4.9 per cent in 1980, and 8.3 per cent in 2006, when it peaked before the financial crisis. From the 'Financialization' lemma of Wikipedia (accessed 11 July 2018), we can glean the following information.

Trading in US equity (stock) markets grew from $136.0 billion (or 13.1 per cent of US GDP) in 1970 to $1.671 trillion (or 28.8 per cent of US GDP) in 1990. In 2000, trading in US equity markets was $14.222 trillion (144.9 per cent of GDP). Note that the value-added of this sector is created by the service charges such as interest, fees, commissions, etc., applicable to this trading turnover; so trading is many times over the valued-added, but the historical evolution of either reveals the growth of the sector. These tendencies of the US stock market are broadly mirrored by various other developed countries (Philippon and Reshef, 2013).

Commensurately, the proportion of household wealth kept in shares has increased: Poterba (2000, T1) shows that the market value of equities in US households' portfolios was about 14 per cent in end-1989 but 32 per cent ten years later (end-1999); compare this with tangible assets (mainly housing) which were 45 per cent in 1989 and 33 per cent in 1999. Poterba (2000, T4) discusses the effects of stock market wealth on consumption (despite its unequal distribution). Greenwood and Scharfstein (2013) show the effects of greater 'finance' (e.g. more access to funds for firms, mainly the small ones and upstarts that do not rely on own funds) but also the perils of more finance. Thus, the bottomline is that the stock market interacts with the macroeconomy in a variety of ways.

An important aspect of equity wealth is its unequal concentration even as proportions of portfolios. Again, Poterba (2000, T2) shows that the top half per cent (0.5 per cent) of US households in 1998 held more than 40 per cent of all equity except those held by pension funds! The 10th decile (top 10 per cent) held about 90 per cent of this stock, the next decile less than 10 per cent and the bottom 80 per cent practically nothing! This is in sharp contrast with other forms of wealth such as bank deposits and housing, which, though still unequally distributed, showed nowhere near the inequality obvious in equity wealth. This suggests some form of costs associated with 'financial literacy' and implies a sharp division of households into 'savers' and 'spenders' (in the terminology of Mankiw, 2000) with obvious implications for the (in)ability of many households to optimize intertemporally in terms of consumption, as discussed. It also has implications for inequality discussed in Chapter 10.

References

Abel, A.B. (1979): *Investment and The Value of Capital*, New York: Garland Publishing.

Abel, A.B. (1990a): Consumption and Investment, in B.M. Friedman and F. Hahn (eds), *Handbook of Monetary Economics*, vol. 2, Amsterdam: Elsevier Science, 725–78.

Abel, A.B. (): Asset Prices under Habit Formation and Catching up with the Jones, *American Economic Review*, 80, 2 (May), 38–42.

Abel, A.B. (1999): The Effects of Irreversibility and Uncertainty on Capital Accumulation, *Journal of Monetary Economics*, 44, 3 (December), 339–77.

Abel, A.B., and J.C. Eberly (1994): A Unified Model of Investment under Uncertainty, *American Economic Review*, 84, 1369–84.

Abel, A.B., and J.C. Eberly (2012): Investment, Valuation, and Growth Options, *Quarterly Journal of Finance*, 2(1), 1–32.

Abel, A.B., A.K. Dixit, J.C. Eberly, and R.S. Pindyck (1996): Options, the Value of Capital, and Investment, *Quarterly Journal of Economics*, 111(3), 753–77.

Alyousha, A., and C. Tsoukis (1999): Implications of Intertemporal Optimisation for House and Land Prices, *Applied Economics*, 31 (December), 1665–71.

Ando, A., and F. Modigliani (1965): The Relative Stability of Monetary Velocity and the Investment Multiplier, *American Economic Review*, 55(4), 693–728.

Angeletos, G.M., D. Laibson, A. Repetto, J. Tobacman, and S. Weinberg (2001): The Hyperbolic Consumption Model: Calibration, Simulation, and Empirical Evaluation, *Journal of Economic Perspectives*, 15(3) (Summer), 47–68.

Attanasio, O.P. (1999): Consumption, in J.B. Taylor and M. Woodford (eds), *Handbook of Macroeconomics*, vol. 1B, Amsterdam: North Holland, 741–812.

Attanasio, O.P. (2000): Consumer Durables and Inertial Behaviour: Estimation and Aggregation of (S, s) Rules for Automobile Purchases, *Review of Economic Studies*, 67(4), 667–96.

Attanasio, O.P., and G. Weber (2010): Consumption and Saving: Models of Intertemporal Allocation and their Implications for Public Policy, *Journal of Economic Literature*, 48(3) (September), 693–751.

Attanasio, O.P., J. Banks, C. Meghir, and G. Weber (1999): Humps and Bumps in Lifetime Consumption, *Journal of Business and Economics Statistics*, 17(1) (January), 22–35.

Attanasio, O.P., P. Koujianou-Goldberg, and E. Kyriazidou (2008): Credit Constraints in the Market for Consumer Durables: Evidence from Micro Data on Car Loans, *International Economic Review*, 49(2), 401–36.

Azeredo, F. (2014): The Equity Premium: A Deeper Puzzle, *Annals of Finance*, 10(3), 347–73.

Barro, R.J. (1999): Ramsey Meets Laibson in the Neoclassical Growth Model, *Quarterly Journal of Economics*, 114(4) (November), 1125–52.

Barsky, R.B., and J.B. De Long (1993): Why does the Stock Market Fluctuate? *Quarterly Journal of Economics*, 108(2) (May), 291–311.

Benartzi, S., and R.H. Thaler (1995): Myopic Loss Aversion and the Equity Premium Puzzle, *Quarterly Journal of Economics*, 110(1), 73–92.

Benhabib, J., and B. Hobijn (2003): Vintage Models, Fluctuations and Growth, in P. Aghion, R. Frydman, J. Stiglitz, and M. Woodford (eds), *Knowledge, Information and Expectations in Macroeconomics: Essays in Honor of Edmund S. Phelps*, Princeton: Princeton University Press, 522–45.

Bernanke, B.B. (1985): Adjustment Costs, Durables, and Aggregate Consumption, *Journal of Monetary Economics*, 15(1) (January), 41–68.

Bernheim, B.D., J. Skinner, and S. Weinberg (2001): What Accounts for the Variation in Retirement Wealth among U.S. Households? *American Economic Review*, 91(4) (September), 832–57.

Blanchard, O.J., C.-Y Rhee, and L. Summers (1993): The Stock Market, Profit and Investment, *Quarterly Journal of Economics*, 108(1), 115–36.

Blinder, A., and L. Maccini (1991): Taking Stock: A Critical Assessment of Recent Research on Inventories, *Journal of Economic Perspectives*, 5(1) (Winter), 73–96.

Breeden, D. (1979): An Intertemporal Asset Pricing Model with Stochastic Consumption and Investment Opportunities, *Journal of Financial Economics*. 7(3) (September), 265–96.

Caballero, R.J. (1999): Aggregate Investment, in J.B. Taylor and M. Woodford (eds), *Handbook of Macroeconomics*, vol. 1B, Amsterdam: Elsevier, 813–62.

Campbell, J.Y. (1987): Does Saving Anticipate Declining Labor Income? An Alternative Test of the Permanent Income Hypothesis, *Econometrica*, 55(6) (November), 1249–73.

Campbell, J.Y. (1995): Some Lessons from the Yield Curve, *Journal of Economic Perspectives*, 9(3) (Summer), 129–52.

Campbell, J.Y. (1996): Understanding Risk and Return, *Journal of Political Economy*, 104(2) (April), 298–345.

Campbell, J., and J. Cochrane (1999): By Force of Habit: A Consumption-Based Explanation of Aggregate Stock Market Behavior, *Journal of Political Economy*, 107(2) (April), 205–51.

Campbell, J.Y., and A. Deaton (1989): Why is Consumption So Smooth? *Review of Economic Studies*, 56, 357–74.

Campbell, J.Y., and R.J Shiller (1998): Valuation Ratios and the Long-Run Stock Market Outlook, *Journal of Portfolio Management*, 24(2), 11–26.

Carrol, C.D. (1992): The Buffer-Stock Theory of Saving: Some Macroeconomic Evidence, *Brookings Papers on Economic Activity*, 2, 61–156.

Carroll, C.D., and M.S. Kimball (1996): On the Concavity of the Consumption Function, *Econometrica*, 64(4) (July), 981–92.

Case, K.E., J.M. Quigley, and R.J. Shiller (2005): Comparing Wealth Effects: The Stock Market versus the Housing Market, *Advances in Macroeconomics (The BE Journals in Macroeconomics)*, 5(1), Article 1.

Chanegriha, M., C. Stewart, and C. Tsoukis (2017): Identifying the Robust Economic, Geographical and Political Determinants of FDI: An Extreme Bounds Analysis, *Empirical Economics*, 52(2) (March), 759–76.

Chen, N.-f., R. Roll, and S.A. Ross (1986): Economic Forces and the Stock Market, *Journal of Business*, 59 (July), 383–403.

Chetty, R., L. Sándor, and A. Szeidl (2017): The Effect of Housing on Portfolio Choice, *Journal of Finance*, 72(3) (June), 1171–21.

Chirinko, R.S. (1993): Business Fixed Investment Spending: Modeling Strategies, Empirical Results, and Policy Implications, *Journal of Economic Literature*, 31(4) (December), 1875–1911.

Clarida, R.H. (1991): Aggregate Stochastic Implications of the Life Cycle Hypothesis, *Quarterly Journal of Economics*, 106(3) (August), 851–67.

Clark, A. E., and C. Senik (2010): Who Compares to Whom? The Anatomy of Income Comparisons in Europe, *Economic Journal*, 120, 573–94.

Clark, A.E., P. Frijters, and M.A. Shields (2008): Relative Income, Happiness, and Utility: An Explanation for the Easterlin Paradox and Other Puzzles, *Journal of Economic Literature*, 46(1) (March), 95–144.

Constantinides, G.M. (1990): Habit Formation: A Resolution of the Equity Premium Puzzle, *Journal of Political Economy*, 98(3) (June), 519–43.

Constantinides, G.M., and D. Duffie (1996): Asset Pricing with Heterogeneous Consumers, *Journal of Political Economy*, 104(2) (Apr.,), 219–40.

Cooper, R.S., and J.C. Haltiwanger (2006): On the Nature of Capital Adjustment Costs, *Review of Economic Studies*, 73(3) (July), 611–33.

Crisis (2018): England Short of Four Million Homes, posted on 18 May; available at: https://www.crisis.org.uk/about-us/latest-news/england-short-of-four-million-homes/

Deaton, A. (1991): Saving and Liquidity Constraints, *Econometrica*, 59(5) (September), 1221–48.

Deaton, A. (1992). *Understanding Consumption*, New York: Oxford University Press.

Disney, R., H. Miller, and T. Pope (2020): Firm-Level Investment Spikes and Aggregate Investment over the Great Recession, *Economica*, 87(345) (January), 217–48.

Doms, M., and T. Dunne (1998): Capital Adjustment Patterns in Manufacturing Plants, *Review of Economic Dynamics*, 1(2), 409–29.

Dynan, K., J. Skinner, and S. Zeldes (2004): Do the Rich Save More? *Journal of Political Economy*, 112(2) (April), 397–444.

Eberly, J.C. (1994): Adjustment of Consumers' Durables Stocks: Evidence from Automobile Purchases, *Journal of Political Economy*, 102(3), 403–36.

Eisner, R., and R.H. Strotz (1963): Determinants of Business Investment, in: Commission on Money and Credit, *Impacts of Monetary Policy*, Englewood Cliffs, NJ: Prentice-Hall, 59–337.

Epstein, L.G., and S.E. Zin (1989): Substitution, Risk Aversion, and the Temporal Behavior of Consumption and Asset Returns: A Theoretical Framework, *Econometrica*, 57(4), 937–69.

Fama, E.F., and K.R. French (2004): The Capital Asset Pricing Model: Theory and Evidence, *Journal of Economic Perspectives*, 18(3) (Summer), 25–46.

Fazzari, S.M., R.G. Hubbard, and B. C. Petersen (1988): Financing Constraints and Corporate Investment, *Brookings Papers on Economic Activity*, 1, 141–95.

Feldstein, M. (1995): The Effects of Outbound Foreign Direct Investment on the Domestic Capital Stock, in M. Feldstein, J. Hines, and R.G. Hubbard (eds), *The Effects of Taxation on Multinational Corporations*, Chicago: University of Chicago Press, 43–66.

Flavin, M. (1981): The Adjustment of Consumption to Changing Expectations about Future Income, *Journal of Political Economy*, 89, 974–1009.

Flavin, M. and T. Yamashita (2002): Owner-Occupied Housing and the Composition of the Household Portfolio, *American Economic Review*, March, 345–62.

Flood, R.P., and R.J. Hodrick (1990): On Testing for Speculative Bubbles, *Journal of Economic Perspectives*, 4(2), 85–101.

Foster, D. (2017): Gentrification isn't a Benign Process: It Forces People from their Homes, *Guardian*, 24 March, https://www.theguardian.com/housing-network/2017/mar/24/gentrification-kings-cross-forces-people-from-housing-crisis

Fraumeni, B.M. (1997): The Measurement of Depreciation in the U.S. National Income and Product Accounts, *Survey of Current Business* (July), 7–23.

Frederick, S., G. Loewenstein and T. O'Donoghue (2002): Time Discounting and Time Preference: A Critical Review, *Journal of Economic Literature*, 40(2), 351–401.

Frey, B.S., and A. Stutzer (2002): What Can Economists Learn from Happiness Research? *Journal of Economic Literature*, 40(2) (June), 402–35.

Friedman, M. (1957): *A Theory of the Consumption Function*, Cambridge, MA: NBER.

Fuhrer, J.C. (2000): Habit Formation in Consumption and its Implications for Monetary-Policy Models, *American Economic Review*, 90(3) (June), 367–90.

Galeotti, M., L. Maccini, and F. Schiantarelli (2005): Inventories, Employment, and Hours, *Journal of Monetary Economics*, 52(3) (April), 575–600.

Galí, J. (1990): Finite Horizons, Life-Cycle Savings, and Time-Series Evidence on Consumption, *Journal of Monetary Economics*, 26(3) (December), 433–52.

Gali, J. (1994): Keeping up with the Joneses: Consumption Externalities, Portfolio Choice, and Asset Prices, *Journal of Money, Credit and Banking*, 26(1) (February), 1–8.

Garber, P.M. (1990): Famous First Bubbles, *Journal of Economic Perspectives*, 4(2) (Spring), 35–54.

Georgarakos, D., M. Haliassos, and G. Pasini (2014): Household Debt and Social Interactions, *Review of Financial Studies*, 27(5) (May), 1404–33.

Goerke, L., and M. Pannenberg (2015): Direct Evidence for Income Comparisons and Subjective Well-Being across Reference Groups, *Economics Letters*, 137(C), 95–101.

Gourinchas, P.-O., and J.A. Parker (2002): Consumption Over the Life Cycle, *Econometrica*, 70(1), 47–89.

Greenwood, R., and D. Scharfstein (2013): The Growth of Finance, *Journal of Economic Perspectives*, 27(2) (Spring), 3–28.

Gross, D.B., and N.S. Souleles (2002): Do Liquidity Constraints and Interest Rates Matter for Consumer Behavior? Evidence from Credit Card Data, *Quarterly Journal of Economics*, 107(1) (February), 149–85.

Hall, R.E. (1978): Stochastic Implications of the Life Cycle-Permanent Income Hypothesis: Theory and Evidence, Journal of Political Economy, 86(6) (December), 971–87.

Hall, R.E. (1988): Intertemporal Substitution in Consumption, *Journal of Political Economy*, 96, 339–57.

Hall, R.E. (2001a): Struggling to Understand the Stock Market, *American Economic Review*, 91(2) (May), 1–11.

Hall, R.E. (2001b): The Stock Market and Capital Accumulation, *American Economic Review*, 91(5) (December), 1185–1202.

Hansen, L.P., and K.J. Singleton (1983): Stochastic Consumption, Risk Aversion, and the Temporal Behavior of Asset Returns, *Journal of Political Economy*, 91, 249–65.

Hassett, K.A., and R.G. Hubbard (1997): Tax Policy and Investment, in A. Auerbach (ed.), *Fiscal Policy: Lessons from Economic Research*, Cambridge, MA: MIT Press, 339–96.

Hayashi, F. (1982): Tobin's Marginal q and Average q: A Neoclassical Interpretation, *Econometrica*, 50, 213–24.

Hayashi, F. (1987): Tests for Liquidity Constraints: A Critical Survey, in T. Bewley (ed.), *Advances in Econometrics, Proceeding of the Fifth World Congress*, New York: Cambridge University Press, 91–120.

Horioka, C.Y. (2010): The (Dis)Saving Behavior of the Aged in Japan, *Japan and the World Economy*, 22(3) (August), 151–8.

Hubbard, R.G. (1994): Investment Under Uncertainty: Keeping one's Options Open, *Journal of Economic Literature*, 32 (December), 1794–1807.

Hurst, E., A. Lusardi, A. Kennickell, and F. Torralba (2010): The Importance of Business Owners in Assessing the Size of Precautionary Savings, *Review of Economics and Statistics*, 92(1) (February), 61–9.

Jappelli, T., and M. Pagano (1994): Saving, Growth, and Liquidity Constraints, *Quarterly Journal of Economics*, 109(1), 83–109.

Jermann U.J. (1998): Asset Pricing in Production Economies, *Journal of Monetary Economics*, 41, 257–75.

Johnson, D.S., J.A. Parker, and N.S. Souleles (2006): Household Expenditure and the Income Tax Rebates of 2001, *American Economic Review*, 96(5), 1589–1610.

Jones, C.I. (2005): The Shape of Production Functions and the Direction of Technical Change, *Quarterly Journal of Economics*, 120(2) (May), 517–49.

Jorgenson, D. (1963): Capital Theory and Investment Behavior, *American Economic Review Papers and Proceedings*, 53(2) (May), 247–59.

Joyce, R., M. Mitchell, and A. Norris Keiller (2017): The Cost of Housing for Low-Income Renters, *IFS Report* (October).

Keynes, J.M. (1936): *The General Theory of Employment, Interest and Money*, London: Macmillan.

Kimball, M. (1990): Precautionary Saving in the Small and in the Large, *Econometrica*, 58(1), 53–73.

Kocherlakota, N.R. (1996): The Equity Premium: It's Still a Puzzle, *Journal of Economic Literature*, 34(1) (March), 42–71.

Kuznets, S. (1955): Economic Growth and Income Inequality, *American Economic Review*, 45, 1–28.

Laeven, L., and A. Popov (2017): Waking up from the American Dream: On the Experience of Young Americans during the Housing Boom of the 2000s, *Journal of Money, Credit and Banking*, 49(5), 861–95.

Laibson, D. (1997): Golden Eggs and Hyperbolic Discounting, *Quarterly Journal of Economics*, 112(2), 443–77.

Laibson, D., A. Repetto, and J. Tobacman (2003): A Debt Puzzle, in P. Aghion, R. Frydman, J. Stiglitz, and M. Woodford (eds), *Knowledge, Information and Expectations in Macroeconomics: Essays in Honor of Edmund S. Phelps*, Princeton: Princeton University Press, 228–66.

Laibson, D., A. Repetto, and J. Tobacman (2007): Estimating Discount Functions with Consumption Choices Over the Lifecycle, NBER Working Paper No. 13314, August.

Lin, X., C. Wang, N. Wang, and J. Yang (2018): Investment, Tobin's q, and Interest Rates, *Journal of Financial Economics*, 130(3) (December), 620–40.

Lintner, J. (1965): The Valuation of Risk Assets and the Selection of Risky Investments in Stock Portfolios and Capital Budgets, *Review of Economics and Statistics*, 47(1), 13–37.

Loayza, N., K. Schmidt-Hebbel, and L. Servén (2000): What Drives Private Saving across the World? *Review of Economics and Statistics*, 82(2), 165–81.

Lucas, R.E. (1978): Asset Prices in an Exchange Economy, *Econometrica*, 46, 1429–45.

Mankiw, N.G. (1982): Hall's Consumption Hypothesis and Durable Goods, *Journal of Monetary Economics*, 10 (November), 417–26.

Martin, A., and J. Ventura (2018): The Macroeconomics of Rational Bubbles: A User's Guide, *Annual Review of Economics*, 10 (August), 505–39.

Mankiw, N.G. (2000): The Savers-Spenders Theory of Fiscal Policy, *American Economic Review*, 90(2) (May), 120–5.

Maurer, J., and A. Meier (2008): Smooth it Like the Joneses? Estimating Peer-Group Effects in Intertemporal Consumption Choice, Economic Journal, 118(527) (March), 454–76.

Meghir, C., and L. Pistaferri (2011): Earnings, Consumption and Lifecycle Choices, in: O. Ashenfelter and D. Card (eds), *Handbook of Labor Economics*, Amsterdam: Elsevier, 773–854.

Mehra, R., and E.C. Prescott (1985): The Equity Premium: A Puzzle, *Journal of Monetary Economics*, 15(2), 145–61.

Mehra, R., and E.C. Prescott (2003): The Equity Premium in Retrospect, in G. M. Constantinides, M. Harris, and R. Stulz (eds), *Handbook of the Economics of Finance*. Amsterdam: North-Holland, 887–936.

Modigliani, F., and R.H. Brumberg (1954): Utility Analysis and the Consumption Function: An Interpretation of Cross-Section Data, in K.K. Kurihara (ed.), *Post-Keynesian Economics*, New Brunswick, NJ: Rutgers University Press, 388–436.

Modigliani, F., and S.L. Cao (2004): The Chinese Saving Puzzle and the Life-Cycle Hypothesis, *Journal of Economic Literature*, 42(1), 145–70.

Muellbauer J. (1983): Surprises in the Consumption Function, *Economic Journal*, 93 (Supplement: Conference Papers), 34–50.

Muellbauer, J., and A. Murphy (1997): Booms and Busts in the UK Housing Market, *Economic Journal*, 107(445) (November), 1701–27.

Nelson, C.R., and C.I. Plosser (1982): Trends and Random Walks in Macroeconomic Time Series: Some Evidence and Implications, *Journal of Monetary Economics*, 10(2),139–62.

Oulton, N., and S. Srinivasan (2003): Capital Stocks, Capital Services, and Depreciation: An Integrated Framework, Bank of England Working Paper No. 192, June.

Philippon, T., and A. Reshef (2013): An International Look at the Growth of Modern Finance, *Journal of Economic Perspectives*, 27(2) (Spring), 73–96.

Poterba, J.M. (1984): Tax Subsidies to Owner-Occupied Housing: An Asset-Market Approach, *Quarterly Journal of Economics*, 99(4) (November), 729–52.

Poterba, J. (2000): Stock Market Wealth and Consuumption, *Journal of Economic Perspectives*, 14(2) (Spring), 99–118.

Prescott, E.C (2004): Why do Americans Work So Much More than Europeans? *FRB Minneapolis—Quarterly Review*, 28(1) (July), 2–14.

Price, S., and C. Schleicher (2005): Returns to Equity, Investment and Q: Evidence from the UK, *Manchester School*, 73(S1) (September), 32–57.

Ramey, V.A., and K.D. West (1999): Inventories, in J.B. Taylor and M. Woodford (eds), Handbook of Macroeconomics, vol. 1B, Amsterdam: North Holland/Elsevier, 863–923.

Sargent, T.J. (1978): Estimation of Dynamic Labor Demand Schedules under Rational Expectations, *Journal of Political Economy*, 86(6), 1009–44.

Sargent, T.J. (1987): *Macroeconomic Theory*, 2nd ed., Bingley, UK: Emerald.

Schiantarelli, F., and G. Georgoutsos (1990): Monopolistic Competition and the Q Theory of Investment, *European Economic Review*, 34(5) (July), 1061–78.

Shapiro, M.D., and J. Slemrod (2003): Consumer Response to Tax Rebates, *American Economic Review*, 93(1) (March), 381–96.

Sharpe, W.F. (1964): Capital Asset Prices: A Theory of Market Equilibrium under Conditions of Risk, *Journal of Finance*, 19(3), 425–42.

Shiller, R.J. (1981): Do Stock Prices Move Too Much to Be Justified by Subsequent Changes in Dividends? *American Economic Review*, 71(3), 421–36.

Shiller, R.J. (2003): From Efficient Markets Theory to Behavioral Finance, *Journal of Economic Perspectives*, 17(1) (Winter), 83–104.

Shiller, R.J. (2005): *Irrational Exuberance*, 2nd ed., Princeton: Princeton University Press

Shiler, R.J. (2014): Speculative Asset Prices, *American Economic Review*, 104(6) (June), 1486–1517.

Shleifer, A (1999): *Inefficient Markets: An Introduction to Behavioral Finance*, New York: Oxford University Press.

Thomas, J. (2002): Is Lumpy Investment Relevant for the Business Cycle? *Journal of Political Economy*, 110(3), 508–34.

Tobin, J. (1969): A General Equilibrium Approach to Monetary Theory, *Journal of Money, Credit and Banking*, 1, 15–29.

Tsoukis, C., and F. Tournemaine (2013): Status in a Canonical Macro Model: Status, Growth, and Inequality, *Manchester School*, 81(S2) (October), 65–92.

Tsoukis, C., F. Tournemaine, and M. Gillman (2017): Hybrid Exponential-Hyperbolic Discounting and Growth without Commitment, *Manchester School*, 85(S2) (December), e45–74.

Ventura, L., and G. Eisenhauer (2005): The Relevance of Precautionary Saving, *German Economic Review*, 6(1), 23–35.

Weil, P. (1990): Non-Expected Utility in Macroeconomics, *Quarterly Journal of Economics*, 105(1) (February), 29–42.

Zeldes, S. (1989): Consumption and Liquidity Constraints: An Empirical Analysis, *Journal of Political Economy*, 97(2) (April), 305–46.

Index

Note: Figures and tables are indicated by an italic "*f*", "*t*" and notes are indicated by "n" following the page numbers.